THE H

WORK

ANALYSIS

METHODS, SYSTEMS, APPLICATIONS AND SCIENCE OF WORK MEASUREMENT IN ORGANIZATIONS

SERIES IN APPLIED PSYCHOLOGY

Jeanette N. Cleveland, Colorado State University
Kevin R. Murphy, Landy Litigation and Colorado State University
Series Editors

Edwin A. Fleishman, Founding series editor (1987–2010)

Jack Kitaeff
Handbook of Police Psychology

Uwe E. Kleinbeck, Hans-Henning Quast, Henk Thierry, and Hartmut Häcker
Work Motivation

Laura L. Koppes
Historical Perspectives in Industrial and Organizational Psychology

Ellen Kossek and Susan Lambert
Work and Life Integration: Organizational, Cultural, and Individual Perspectives

Martin I. Kurke and Ellen M. Scrivner
Police Psychology into the 21st Century

Joel Lefkowitz
Ethics and Values in Industrial and Organizational Psychology

Manuel London
Job Feedback: Giving, Seeking, and Using Feedback for Performance Improvement, Second Edition

Manuel London
How People Evaluate Others in Organizations

Manuel London
Leadership Development: Paths to Self-Insight and Professional Growth

Robert F. Morrison and Jerome Adams
Contemporary Career Development Issues

Michael D. Mumford, Garnett Stokes, and William A. Owens
Patterns of Life History: The Ecology of Human Individuality

Michael D. Mumford
Pathways to Outstanding Leadership: A Comparative Analysis of Charismatic, Ideological, and Pragmatic Leaders

Kevin R. Murphy
Validity Generalization: A Critical Review

Kevin R. Murphy and Frank E. Saal
Psychology in Organizations: Integrating Science and Practice

Kevin Murphy
A Critique of Emotional Intelligence: What Are the Problems and How Can They Be Fixed?

Susan E. Murphy and Ronald E. Riggio
The Future of Leadership Development

Susan E. Murphy and Rebecca J. Reichard
Early Development and Leadership: Building the Next Generation of Leaders

Margaret A. Neal and Leslie Brett Hammer
Working Couples Caring for Children and Aging Parents: Effects on Work and Well-Being

Robert E. Ployhart, Benjamin Schneider, and Neal Schmitt
Staffing Organizations: Contemporary Practice and Theory, Third Edition

THE HANDBOOK OF
WORK
ANALYSIS

METHODS, SYSTEMS, APPLICATIONS AND SCIENCE OF WORK MEASUREMENT IN ORGANIZATIONS

EDITED BY

MARK A. WILSON
NORTH CAROLINA STATE UNIVERSITY

WINSTON BENNETT, JR.
AIR FORCE RESEARCH LABORATORY
WRIGHT-PATTERSON AFB, OHIO

SHANAN G. GIBSON
EAST CAROLINA UNIVERSITY

GEORGE M. ALLIGER
THE GROUP FOR ORGANIZATIONAL EFFECTIVENESS

ASSOCIATE EDITORS

ERICH C. DIERDORFF
DE PAUL UNIVERSITY

SUZANNE TSACOUMIS
HUMAN RESOURCES RESEARCH ORGANIZATION

ROBERT J. HARVEY
VIRGINIA TECH

GREGORY M. HURTZ
CALIFORNIA STATE UNIVERSITY, SACRAMENTO

Routledge
Taylor & Francis Group
New York   London

Endorsements

"When applying some of the new methods described in this book, our research results receive attention from frontline fighter pilots as well as generals, while they at the same time are being accepted in scientific publications. For me, this is strong evidence that the knowledge and insights presented through this book result in top quality research tools. The book is thus an excellent foundation for any work analysis effort."

– Martin Castor, Ph.D.,
Swedish Defense Research Agency (FOI), Sweden

"This handbook addresses a central, indeed arguable 'the'central topic in industrial and organizational psychology and human resource management. Job (or Work) Analysis is the foundation of most human resource procedures and goals, from strategy linked selection and training to goal setting, performance review, feedback and continuous improvement. This handbook intends to give state-of-the-art guidance to practitioners and students about how to conduct reliable and valid job and work analyses to ensure a solid foundation for I/O and HR practice."

– Manuel London,
SUNY Stonybrook, New York

"This comprehensive handbook is destined to become a classic."

– Gavriel Salvendy,
Purdue University and Tsinghua University,China

"Work analysis is at the core of personnel psychology. This volume provides a comprehensive description of job analysis concepts, techniques, and practices that brings to us the leading experts in the field, providing a definitive view of the methods, systems, applications, and research on the topic. This is a great volume that needs to be read by scientists and practitioners interested in job analysis and, more generally, personnel and I/O psychology."

– Walter C. Borman,
Psychology Department, University of South Florida

MIX
Paper from
responsible sources
FSC® C014174
www.fsc.org

Routledge
Taylor & Francis Group
711 Third Avenue
New York, NY 10017

Routledge
Taylor & Francis Group
27 Church Road
Hove, East Sussex BN3 2FA

© 2012 by Taylor & Francis Group, LLC
Routledge is an imprint of Taylor & Francis Group, an Informa business

Printed in the United States of America on acid-free paper
Version Date: 20120208

International Standard Book Number: 978-1-84872-870-7 (Hardback)

Library of Congress Cataloging-in-Publication Data

The handbook of work analysis : methods, systems, applications and science of work measurement in organizations / editors, Mark A. Wilson ... [et al.].
     p. cm. -- (Series in applied psychology)
  Includes bibliographical references and index.
  ISBN 978-1-84872-870-7 (hardcover : alk. paper)
  1. Job analysis. 2. Work measurement. I. Wilson, Mark A. (Mark Alan), 1952-

HF5549.5.J6H356 2012
658.3'06--dc23   2012001512

Visit the Taylor & Francis Web site at
http://www.taylorandfrancis.com

and the Psychology Press Web site at
http://www.psypress.com

Dedication

The Editors would like to dedicate this handbook to two individuals whose contributions to the science and practice of job analysis and work design is beyond question. Not only have both of these individuals excelled at the science and practice in the field, but they have been instrumental in influencing generations of military officers and civilian researchers and helped drive investments and innovations in the field in numerous international agencies. Their collective contributions span more than 135 years. It is with most humble gratitude and respect that we dedicate this new text to Dr. Sidney Gael and Dr. Jimmy L. Mitchell for their lifelong contributions to the field.

Sidney Gael, PhD, began his professional career in 1959 as a civilian research psychologist with the United States Air Force (USAF) at Wright-Patterson AFB, Ohio. There he focused determining personnel requirements and training needs for aircraft and space systems. While employed by the USAF, he participated in a USAF educational program for civil service employees that enabled him to earn his doctorate in industrial psychology. Subsequently, he joined the American Telephone and Telegraph (AT&T) Personnel Research Organization and worked for the Bell System and its affiliated companies for 28 years, after which he entered private practice. While at AT&T, Sidney led the development of the Work Performance Survey System (WPSS), which included structured procedures for constructing and administering task inventory questionnaires, along with a software system for analyzing the resulting data. At this time, there were no commercially available data analysis programs or systems. The WPSS represented one of the first adaptations of the military job-task inventory method to civilian use. The WPSS has been very useful in supporting a variety of human resource functions in areas such as selection, placement, training, and performance evaluation. Based on his experience with the WPSS, Gael authored a book titled *Job Analysis* to serve as a procedural guide for carrying out job-task inventory studies. Subsequently, he took on a huge endeavor to edit the classic, two-volume *Job Analysis Handbook for Business, Industry, and Government*. This handbook has remained the most comprehensive source of information available on a wide variety of job analysis methods and is perhaps the most valuable single contribution to the literature. It is considered by many to be a classic treatise of the field of job analysis. It served as the model for the level of breadth and comprehensiveness we wanted to have in the new handbook. We are grateful to Sidney for his contributions to the field and for giving us such a strong foundation upon which to build this next generation compendium of research and practice.

Jimmy L. Mitchell, PhD, began his Air Force career in 1957 as a psychiatric clinic technician at the United States Air Force Hospital, Wright-Patterson AFB, followed by service as a security police officer with the Strategic Air Command and U.S. Air Forces Europe. He was subsequently assigned to the graduate program at The Ohio State to pursue his master's degree, after which he joined the Civilian Institutions Division of the Air Force Institute of Technology, Wright-Patterson AFB, as an administrator working with civilian university degree programs for Air Force officers and enlisted students. Over the next few years, he served as a military test developer and occupational analyst with the 3700th Occupational Measurement Squadron located at Lackland AFB, Texas; earned a doctorate at Purdue University; and then directed occupational survey studies the USAF Occupational Measurement Center, Randolph AFB, Texas, as the Chief of USAF Airmen Analysis. Jimmy earned his MA at Ohio State in 1966 and his PhD at Purdue in 1978—distinctly having earned his graduate degrees under two major figures in 20th-century job and occupational analysis: Carroll Shartle at Ohio State and Ernest McCormick at Purdue. While at Purdue, his collaboration with Ernest McCormick led to the Professional and Managerial Position Questionnaire. He also authored two chapters in the *Job Analysis Handbook for Business, Industry, and Government* (Gael, 1988) and was considered by almost everyone to be the foremost authority on the history of job analysis in the military. During his last 10 years in the Air Force, Jimmy also served as editor of *Air Force Psychology News*, a quarterly career development newsletter for military behavioral scientists. Jimmy retired from the Air Force in 1984 and he continued his research in job and occupational analysis, first with McDonald Douglas Training Systems and, in 1993, when he founded the Institute for Job and Occupational Analysis (IJOA) in San Antonio, Texas, where he served as Director and Chairman of the Board until his passing. The IJOA was one of Jimmy's dreams—a not-for-profit corporation devoted to the study of the world of work. Jimmy was a superb facilitator and organizer in the field of work analysis and was the founding editor in chief of a new peer-reviewed electronic journal, *Ergometrika*, devoted to the analysis and study of human work. Jimmy was passionate about his profession, had a genuine curiosity for what people did and how they did it, and had a deep devotion to advancing the field of work analysis science and practice. These two characteristics exemplify Jimmy as an innovation leader, a mentor, and as a friend. He was tremendously productive over the course of his career generating ideas and conducting research, which he reported in journals, book chapters, technical reports, and numerous professional conferences. He remained active in the community and in research providing spirited leadership and vision until his untimely passing in December 2000. His legacy lives on in many of us who continue to work in this area and who strive to motivate and encourage the next generation of work analysis researchers and practitioners. In closing, it is important to note that several of the chapters in this volume represent work that he was either directly involved in helping to conduct or that were inspired by his curiosity and his passion. Jimmy was the catalyst for this new handbook and he hosted the workshop that included a number of the chapters in this volume. His legacy is evidenced in many of the pages of this new handbook.

Contents

Series Foreword

EDWIN A. FLEISHMAN

George Mason University and Management Research Institute, Inc.

JEANETTE N. CLEVELAND

Colorado State University

There is a compelling need for innovative approaches to the solution of many pressing problems involving human relationships in today's society. Such approaches are more likely to be successful when they are based on sound research and applications. Our *Series in Applied Psychology* offers books that emphasize state-of-the-art research and its application to important issues of human behavior in a variety of social settings. The objective is to bridge both academic and applied interests.

We are very pleased to have the new *The Handbook of Work Analysis: Methods, Systems, Applications and Science of Work Measurement in Organizations* in this *Series in Applied Psychology*. We feel this is a landmark publication that will, for many years to come, be an important resource for students, researchers, industrial/organizational psychologists, and others concerned with a wide variety of issues relevant to effective human resource management.

The subject of "job analysis" has been part of the field of industrial psychology since its beginnings early in the 20th century. The *Handbook*'s use of the term "work analysis" reflects the broader, more inclusive nature of the issues and problems dealt with in today's world of work.

The *Handbook* greatly extends the monumental contribution brought to this field by Dr. Sidney Gael in his two-volume *Job Analysis Handbook for Business, Industry, and Government*. These volumes were published in 1988 and are now out of print and no longer being printed or distributed by the original publisher. A great deal has happened in this field since the publication of Gael's handbook. While other fine books in this field have been published since 1988, they do not offer the scope of Gael's volumes and cannot reflect the current status of the field.

A few years ago, one of us (Edwin A. Fleishman) met with Sidney Gael, already retired and happy in Los Angeles, and talked about the need for a revised and updated job analysis handbook. He agreed to help in getting whatever transfer of publication rights were needed—but did not want any writing or editorial involvement. We are grateful to Sidney for his immense contributions to this field and hope he is pleased with the book, which includes a dedication to him for his prior work.

We are indebted to our excellent team of editors who supervised this enormous project and carefully reviewed and edited each chapter. The four editors—Mark A. Wilson, Winston Bennett, Jr., Shanan G. Gibson and George M. Alliger—participated in choosing the chapter topics, selecting the authors, and managing this 37-chapter handbook, which is one of the most comprehensive, collaborative publishing efforts in the field.

The editors chose four smart associate editors, with particular expertise in each section of the *Handbook*, to help them review and work with the chapter authors. They are Erich C. Dierdorff, Suzanne Tsacoumis, Robert J. Harvey, and George M. Hurtz.

The *Handbook* has several important features. In shifting the focus from "job analysis" to "work analysis" it acknowledges that the methods and concepts being applied in today's workplaces increasingly extend beyond single jobs and may involve the analysis of larger systems and combinations of different jobs. This is becoming increasingly true, for example, in larger companies and industries, the military, transportation, aviation, and space flight situations. The *Handbook* provides examples of work analysis research and development issues in a wide variety of different workplace situations. In developing the content of the *Handbook*, the panel of editors made special efforts to identify and recruit colleagues who were leaders in the field of work analysis and had made outstanding contributions in research and applications in this field. They were aware of many developments that were not in the published literature and sought out these developers to write chapters about their work.

The *Handbook* attempts to present a balanced presentation of the scientific research basis for many of the work analysis procedures described and to show the linkages to the actual application of this research in defining the procedures to be used in particular work analysis systems. Authors of the various chapters sometimes had strong opinions about the validity and limitations of certain methodologies and approaches and the cautions that must be exercised in the use of these systems for certain work analysis purposes. Many of the developments described have had limited availability before and existed only in technical and contract reports with limited distribution. The *Handbook of Work Analysis* has made these developments available.

The *Handbook* editors, associate editors, and chapter contributors have tried to keep in mind those who teach about work analysis in academic departments that deal with human resource and organizational development issues, but they have also been concerned with the translation of these presentations into actual practice. Consequently, in many chapters, readers will find an outline of the steps to follow in planning or carrying out a particular work analysis method in the workplace.

There are other features of *The Handbook of Work Analysis* that should be pointed out. In terms of historical context, the book features international developments in the use of work analysis and also extends the discussion into the newer important linkages with modern computer technology. The book also provides one of the most extensive bibliographies of research and development in work analysis. The book should be required reading for students and course classes in industrial and organizational psychology and for human resource management.

Acknowledgments

This volume represents a significant and sustained effort on the part of many people around the world. This was indeed a team effort on a monumental scale that resulted in the most comprehensive treatise of work design and job analysis practice and research since the 1980s. With this in mind, we want to make sure we acknowledge the significant support from a variety of key people who helped make this *Handbook* a reality. We would like to start by thanking Dr. Edwin A. Fleischman and Anne Duffy and their team at Taylor & Francis for their unswerving advocacy and support to us throughout the development and completion of the *Handbook*. We would also like to thank our chapter contributors for their work to make the *Handbook* a high-quality resource that will serve the communities if interest for some time to come. We would also like to recognize the central role our numerous reviewers played in working with us and with our contributors on the content for the *Handbook*. We would further like to thank Mr. Randy Agee and Dr. J. W. Cunningham for their insights and their comments on many parts of this text and their superb help on the Dedication contributions. Also, we would like to thank Ms. Antoinette Portrey and Ms. Mary Johnson from L3 Communications at the Air Force Research Laboratory Warfighter Readiness Research Division for their continued efforts managing the web site we used throughout the *Handbook* development process; for their continued support with tracking changes to manuscripts; and for their willingness to take on a variety of logistical and technical activities that were essential to completing the *Handbook*. Finally, we would like to thank all those who have engaged in work analysis research and practice for more than 20 years without an updated work analysis *Handbook*. They kept the fire burning during the long cold night that has finally come to an end.

Editors

Mark A. Wilson, PhD, Associate Professor of Psychology, North Carolina State University, joined the faculty in 1992. He received a BA in psychology from Wartburg College (1975), an MA in experimental psychology from the University of Missouri-Kansas City (1978), and a PhD in industrial/organizational (I/O) psychology from The Ohio State University (1983).

While completing the PhD, he served as project coordinator, technical director, and senior research associate for Organizational Research and Development Inc. on a comprehensive human-resource research project involving human resource planning, job analysis, selection (managerial assessment centers), performance appraisal, and compensation for a market-leading insurance company. The experience drastically altered his view of the field and his research interests. It was while working on the project that he developed his interest in the integration of human resource systems, comprehensive job analysis, his dedication to the scientist-practitioner model and the problems of practitioners, and his love for fieldwork.

Dr. Wilson has always been interested in work measurement issues, models of human job performance in organizations, and research methods. He has consulted and conducted research extensively with numerous large organizations in both the private and public sectors. He has taught graduate and undergraduate management courses as an assistant professor at both Texas Tech (1981–1985) and Iowa State University of Science and Technology (1985–1992). In 1999, he was made an honorary member of the U.S. Army Special Forces. In 2006, he was appointed editor of *Ergometrika*.

Winston "Wink" Bennett, Jr., PhD, is a senior research psychologist and technical advisor for continuous learning and performance assessment research with the Air Force Research Laboratory Human Effectiveness Directorate in Dayton, Ohio. He is a fellow of the Air Force Research Laboratory and is also a fellow of the American Psychological Association. Dr. Bennett and his team conduct and support core collaborative research programs and have garnered more than $100 million in outside funding investment. He and the team are actively involved in research related to performance evaluation, personnel assessment, training requirements identification, and quantifying the impact of organizational interventions, such as interactive high-fidelity immersive simulation environments and job redesign/restructuring and training systems effects on individuals, teams, and organizational learning and effectiveness. He led the development of the Mission Essential Competencies (MECs) methodology. His team's work on MECs was recognized with the 2008 M. Scott Myers Award for Applied Research in the Workplace, presented by SIOP. Dr. Bennett maintains an active presence in the international research community through his work on various professional committees and his contributions in professional journals and forums. He has published more than 90 research articles, textbooks, chapters, and technical reports in the human factors, aviation, and I/O psychology literatures. He serves as a contributing editor and/or as a reviewer for several professional journals. His involvement with the larger psychological research community ensures that communication amongst international military, industry, and academic researchers remains consistent and of the highest quality.

Shanan Gwaltney Gibson, PhD, is an associate professor of management at East Carolina University. Dr. Gibson's research focuses on topics relevant to human resources and organizational development, including work analysis, entrepreneurship, and technology in organizations. She currently serves as a member of the Social Security Administration's Occupational Information Development Advisory Panel. Active in several professional organizations such as the United States Association for Small Business and Entrepreneurship, the Small Business Institute, and the Southeastern Chapter of the Institute for Operations Research and the Management Sciences, Dr. Gibson is also an associate editor of the *Small Business Institute Journal*. She received her PhD in industrial/organizational psychology from Virginia Tech.

George M. Alliger, PhD, is Vice President of Solutions for the Group for Organizational Effectiveness, Inc. He received his PhD in industrial/organizational psychology from the University of Akron and holds a master's degree in clinical psychology from Xavier University. Dr. Alliger has conducted research and published extensively in the area of training, including issues of methods and analysis. His meta-analytic research into training evaluation led to a re-examination of the assumption of convergence among different training measures and won the first annual "Best Research Paper" award from the American Society for Training and Development. He has managed numerous job analyses, training evaluation, test development, and performance certification projects. For more than decade, he taught training, evaluation, and statistics as an assistant and associate professor at the State University of New York at Albany, where he is currently an adjunct faculty member.

Dr. Alliger helped develop the architecture for establishing Mission Essential Competencies that has been widely adopted by the USAF and is now in use by the U.S. Navy. Research from this program won the 2008 M. Scott Myers Award for Applied Research in the Workplace, presented by SIOP.

Associate Editors

Erich C. Dierdorff, PhD, is Associate Professor of Management in the Kellstadt Graduate School of Business at DePaul University in Chicago. He received his PhD in industrial/organizational psychology from North Carolina State University. With regard to teaching, Dr. Dierdorff has received several awards for instructional excellence. His research interests include examining how individuals come to construe the requirements of their work roles, factors that shape this construal process, and the consequences for individual, team, and firm performance. His published research has appeared in the *Academy of Management Journal, Journal of Applied Psychology, Personnel Psychology, Journal of Management,* and *The Leadership Quarterly,* among others. He currently serves on the editorial boards of *Journal of Applied Psychology, Personnel Psychology, Academy of Management Learning & Education,* and *Human Performance.* His human capital consulting has spanned both the private and public sectors for organizations such as Nortel Networks, Siemens Systems, the U.S. Department of Labor (Occupational Information Network [O*NET]), the North Carolina State Bureau of Investigation, and the American Council for the Teaching of Foreign Languages.

Suzanne Tsacoumis, PhD, is vice president of the Workforce and Educational Assessment Division at the Human Resources Research Organization (HumRRO). She has more than 25 years of experience in personnel management research and the implementation of personnel systems. Her work focuses on job analysis, competency modeling, and the development of selection and promotion systems for a broad range of occupations. Much of her work has been in litigious environments or for clients working under a court order or settlement agreement. In addition to her technical work, Dr. Tsacoumis's work as one of HumRRO's vice presidents involves overseeing a multidisciplinary group of psychologists, psychometricians, educational researchers, and database management experts. She has served as an officer on the Executive Board of SIOP, and she earned her PhD from the University of Georgia, specializing in industrial/organizational psychology.

Robert J. Harvey, PhD, has directed both large- and small-scale job analysis projects and has published a number of research articles on both measurement and "process" issues in job analysis. In recent years, he has conducted research dealing with a range of assessment-related topics, including faking in self-report personality inventories, computer-adaptive testing for personality and critical-thinking tests, gender bias in cognitive ability and personality instruments, and the psychometric limitations of the Department of Labor's O*NET occupational analysis system. Currently, he is focusing on developing methods to mitigate faking in personality tests and situational judgement tests and examining the suitability of job-component validation to link the domains of worker traits and general work activities.

Gregory M. Hurtz, PhD, is an associate professor of psychology at California State University, Sacramento (CSUS), where he teaches industrial psychology, statistical methods, and psychological measurement. He is a core faculty member in the I/O master's degree program but contributes equally to the general research and quantitative methods training for both undergraduate and graduate students in the psychology department. His research interests center primarily on applied psychological measurement and statistics, especially as related to the evaluation of tools and procedures for improving work performance in organizations through the selection and training of employees. Prior to joining the faculty at CSUS, he worked full-time for 2 years as a measurement statistician developing and implementing psychometric methods for a battery of more than 40 standardized examinations using both classical test theory and item response theory. He has also worked part-time for nearly 15 years as an independent consultant to public agencies and private organizations and consulting firms on a variety of projects involving work analysis, test development, psychometric analysis, performance measurement, employment and compensation discrimination analysis, and training system development and evaluation. He received his MA in I/O psychology from CSUS in 1997, and in 2002 he earned his PhD in I/O psychology from the University at Albany, State University of New York.

Contributors

Winfred Arthur, Jr., PhD, is a full professor of psychology and management at Texas A&M. He received his PhD in industrial/organizational psychology from the University of Akron in 1988. He is a fellow of the Society for Industrial and Organizational Psychology, the Association of Psychological Science, and the American Psychological Association. He is past associate editor of the *Journal of Applied Psychology* and currently serves on its editorial board along with *Personnel Psychology* and *Industrial and Organizational Psychology: Perspectives on Science and Practice*. His research interests are in human performance; training development, design, implementation, and evaluation; team selection and training; acquisition and retention of complex skills; testing, selection, and validation; models of job performance; personnel psychology; and meta-analysis. He has extensive experience in conceptualizing, developing, and directing projects and research in these areas and has published extensively in these areas. He also consults with a number of clients and consulting firms on the research, development, implementation, and evaluation of personnel and human resource management systems and programs for private, public, municipal, nonprofit, and volunteer organizations.

Stephen G. Atkins, PhD, is a business school research director at Otago Polytechnic of New Zealand. He has previously lectured in Massey University's business psychology program and in the systems management postgraduate program at the Air Force Institute of Technology. Before consulting at the National O*NET Development Center, Dr. Atkins had a lengthy career in space systems engineering and launch-pad safety. Dr. Atkins's research currently focuses on vocational fit and vocational preparation in the humanitarian aid sector.

Rebecca Beard, MS, is a cofounder and executive vice president of The Group for Organizational Effectiveness, Inc., a firm that has provided consulting and research services to many well-known Fortune 1000 companies, mid-sized corporations, and the military. She has more than 25 years consulting experience in the areas of employee, team, and organizational development and has extensive practical experience in learning and development, including diagnostic, research, and implementation efforts and conducting training needs analysis. She was part of the team that developed the Mission Essential Competencies; research from this program won SIOP's M. Scott Myers Award for Applied Research in the Workplace. She received her MS in psychology from Old Dominion University.

Dan A. Biddle, PhD, is the president of the Biddle Consulting Group, Inc., a firm that specializes in human resources and equal employment opportunity consulting and software development. Dr. Biddle has provided expert consulting/witness services in more than 100 cases in the areas of disparate impact, job analysis, and test validation.

Michael L. Brown, BA, is founder and chief executive officer of SkillsNET Corporation. He is an internationally recognized skills and competence framework architect and workforce development futurist with 23 years experience in developing frameworks for large-scale, complex systems to align industry and education readiness programs. He is the inventor of SkillObject job analysis processes and data architecture, co-chairs the International Organization for Standardization Competency working group, and is a contributing scientist to several European Union workforce and labor market alignment research projects.

Michael A. Campion, PhD, is the Herman C. Krannert Chaired Professor of Management at Purdue University, where he has been since 1986. Previous industrial experience (1978–1986) includes 4 years each at IBM and Weyerhaeuser Company. He has an MS and PhD in industrial/ organizational psychology. He has published more than 100 articles in scientific and professional journals and has given more than 200 presentations at professional meetings on topics such as employment testing, interviewing, job analysis, work design, teams, training, turnover, promotion, and motivation. He is among the 10 most published authors in the top journals in his field for the last 3 decades. He is past editor of *Personnel Psychology* (a scientific research journal) and past president of SIOP. In 2009, he was promoted to the Herman C. Krannert Chaired Professorship for contributions and productivity in scientific research. He is also the 2010 winner of the Scientific Contribution Award given by SIOP, which is the lifetime scientific contribution award and most prestigious award given by SIOP. He also manages a small consulting firm (Campion Consulting Services; http://www.campion-services.com).

Jay J. Caughron, PhD, is a graduate of the University of Oklahoma and is presently serving as an assistant professor at Radford University. He studies the management of creativity and innovation, ethical decision making, and sensemaking in ambiguous situations.

Charles M. Colegrove, BS, is a senior military analyst for Alion Science and Technology in the Air Combat Command (ACC) Distributed Mission Operations training program. He has more than 20 years experience in fighter operations and operations training. His main areas of focus for ACC include integrating advanced simulation capabilities into operational training programs and coordinating training research. He also is the command lead for the development and application of Mission Essential Competencies.

Michael D. Coovert, PhD, joined the faculty of the University of South Florida in 1985 and was promoted to associate professor in 1990 and full professor in 1998. He served as associate chair of psychology from 1998 to 2001. Dr. Coovert received his PhD in psychology from The Ohio State University with an emphasis in industrial and organizational psychology. His master's degree is from Illinois State, and his undergraduate degree in computer science and psychology (dual major) is from Chaminade University of Honolulu.

Steven F. Cronshaw, PhD, is a professor in the School of Business at the University of Northern British Columbia. He holds a BA in psychology and a BComm in accounting from the University of Saskatchewan. He completed his graduate work at the University of Akron, where he obtained both an MA and PhD in industrial/organizational psychology. He is a fellow of the Canadian Psychological Association. Dr. Cronshaw is author and co-author of books, book chapters, and journal articles on job analysis, human resources management, and consulting psychology. Much of his research time is now spent in applying process ontology to the study of individual and organizational change.

Joseph W. Cunningham, PhD, studied under Ernest J. McCormick at Purdue University and spent most of his career at North Carolina State University conducting research on quantitative occupational analysis and taxonomy and related career interest and need topics. He coined the term *ergometrics* to describe a quantitative approach to the study of human work and is the founding and senior editor of *Ergometrika*, an online scholarly journal devoted to job analysis research. As part of this research, he and his associates developed the Occupation Analysis Inventory and the General Work Inventory. At a professional conference in 1989 he made the comment that "job analysis is the Rodney Dangerfield of I/O psychology" to point out that greater attention needs to be paid to job analysis research and practice.

Dennis Doverspike, PhD, is a full professor of psychology at the University of Akron, Senior Fellow of the Institute for Life-Span Development and Gerontology, and Director of the Center for Organizational Research. He holds a diplomate in industrial/organizational psychology and in organizational and business consulting from the American Board of Professional Psychology and is a licensed psychologist in Ohio. Dr. Doverspike has more than 30 years of experience working with consulting firms and with public and private sector organizations, including 15 years as executive vice president of Barrett & Associates. Services provided include individual assessments, statistical analysis, development of large-scale assessment systems, job evaluation and job analysis, and expert witness services.

Eric M. Dunleavy, PhD, is a senior consultant at DCI Consulting Group, where he is involved in Office of Federal Contract Compliance Programs audit and litigation consulting. He also serves on staff with the Center for Corporate Equality, which is a national nonprofit employer association based in Washington, DC. Before joining DCI, he was a senior research scientist at the American Institutes for Research, where he worked as an expert witness on class action litigation and was involved in content and criterion-related validity research conducted on behalf of the federal government. He received his doctorate in industrial/organizational psychology with a concentration in data analysis from the University of Houston. He is currently the legal chair of the Personnel Testing Council of Metropolitan Washington, DC and on the editorial board of *The Industrial-Organizational Psychologist* as co-author of the "On the Legal Front" column with Arthur Gutman. He has also published articles in the *International Journal of Selection and Assessment, Journal of Business and Psychology*, and *Industrial and Organizational Psychology: Perspectives on Science and Practice*. He is currently an adjunct faculty member of George Mason University.

Amy M. DuVernet, MS, earned her BA in psychology from the University of North Carolina at Chapel Hill in 2004 and her MS in industrial/organizational psychology from North Carolina State University in 2008. Her thesis work examined the utility of random sampling in meta-analytic research. She is currently working on her dissertation, which investigates sources of inaccuracy in job analysis using meta-analytic techniques. Her predominant research interests center around methodological and statistical issues affecting organizational research.

Edwin A. Fleishman, PhD, is currently Distinguished University Professor Emeritus at George Mason University and is president of Management Research Institute, Inc. He has been a professor at Yale University, director of the American Institutes for Research in Washington, DC; a visiting professor at the University of California, the University of Hong Kong, and the Technion in Israel; and an invited lecturer at many universities around the world. He was elected president of three divisions of the American Psychological Association (APA), including SIOP; Evaluation, Measurement, and Statistics; and Engineering Psychology. He was also elected president of the International Association of Applied Psychology. For 10 years, he served as editor of the *Journal of Applied Psychology*. He is the author of a number of books and more than 300 articles. SIOP presented him twice with its Scott Meyers Award for Applied Research in the Workplace. The APA's Division of Military Psychology awarded him the John Flanagan Award for Lifetime Achievement in Military Psychology. APA's Society of Engineering Psychology awarded him its Franklin Taylor Award for his contributions to military psychology. APA presented him with its Distinguished Scientific Award for the Applications of Psychology and its Award for Distinguished Contributions to the International Advancement of Psychology. He was also the recipient of the James McKeen Cattell Award from the American Psychological Society. The American Psychological Foundation presented him its gold medal for Life Achievement in the Scientific Applications of Psychology.

Peter W. Foltz, PhD, is founder and Vice President for Research at Pearson Knowledge Technologies and a senior research associate at the University of Colorado, Institute of Cognitive Science. He was previously a professor of psychology at New Mexico State University. His research has focused on computational modeling of knowledge, team research, and technologies for automated training assessment. He has published a range of articles on team assessment, information retrieval, natural language processing, training technology, clinical diagnosis, and cognitive modeling. Dr. Foltz has served as principle investigator for research for the U.S. Army, USAF, U.S. Navy, Defense Advanced Research Projects Agency, National Science Foundation, and intelligence agencies.

Jeff Foster, PhD, is Director of Research and Development at Hogan Assessment Systems. He supervises employees responsible for a number of activities associated with assessment development, validation, and maintenance. The group maintains assessments in more than 35 languages and provides technical guidance to assessment distributors in more than 30 countries. Dr. Foster received his PhD in industrial/organizational psychology from the University of Missouri–St. Louis.

Blaine Gaddis, PhD, serves as International Research Manager for Hogan Assessment Systems in Tulsa, Oklahoma. In this role, he is responsible for planning and executing assessment-based selection and development research solutions for domestic and international clients. Dr. Gaddis also manages the adaptation of Hogan products and services to foreign cultures and content maintenance for Hogan's assessment suite. He previously worked for a consulting firm where he conducted complex job analyses to inform job/job family redesign, training improvements, and modifications to selection systems and development initiatives. Dr. Gaddis earned his PhD in industrial and organizational psychology from the University of Oklahoma, where he managed funded research contracts with the U.S. Department of Defense and the National Institutes of Health, among others. He has more than 20 publications and 15 conference presentations to his credit.

Douglas J. Gillan, PhD, is a professor and head of the Department of Psychology at North Carolina State University. He is a fellow of the Human Factors and Ergonomics Society and associate editor of *Human Factors*. His background in psychology ranges from doctoral training in biopsychology and postdoctoral fellowships in animal cognition to work in industry on taste perception (at the General Foods Research Center) and human factors in the space program (at Lockheed Engineering and Sciences Company) to faculty positions in human factors and ergonomics (University of Idaho, New Mexico State University, and North Carolina State University). He has published extensively on the relation between science and practice in human factors.

Thomas R. Gordon, PhD, teaches graduate and undergraduate classes in the psychology department at the University of South Florida in Tampa. He is also Director of Advising and Student Services in the department. His research interests include team process, job analysis, and ethics. Dr. Gordon received a BS from the U.S. Military at West Point in 1961, an MS from Purdue University in industrial relations in 1968, and a PhD in industrial/organizational psychology in 2000.

R. Bruce Gould, PhD, has been an independent I/O psychology consultant for the U.S. Department of Defense and several national and international airlines for 11 years. The consulting concerns development and validation of personnel selection, classification, appraisal, and promotion systems. Dr. Gould is retired from 34 years as an USAF civilian I/O psychology scientist and 26 years as a co-developer and adjunct faculty of the St. Mary's University graduate industrial psychology program. His last position was Chief, Mission Critical Skills Division, Human Effectiveness Directorate, Air Force Research Laboratory. Primary areas of research were development, validation, and defense of enlisted, officer, and civilian personnel systems; task and job analysis systems; prediction of personnel requirements for new weapon systems; and job attitude measurement and design.

Emily Johnson Guder, PhD, is a consultant at Federal Management Partners, Inc., a human capital consulting firm specializing in work with federal agencies. Her consulting experiences include a variety of topics, such as work analysis, leadership development, performance management systems, and survey and scale development.

Nigel Guenole, PhD, is currently the Kenexa High Performance Institute's research manager for the United Kingdom. He is also a lecturer in work psychology and programme director for the M.Sc. Occupational Psychology at Goldsmiths, University of London. His work focuses on applications of modern psychometric approaches, such as structural equation modeling to the study of personality and work attitudes.

Arthur Gutman, PhD, is a professor of psychology at Florida Institute of Technology. He received his PhD in psychology from Syracuse University in 1975. After 2 years as an National Institute of Mental Health Postdoctoral Fellow at the University of Colorado, he joined the faculty at Florida Tech University, where he has been since 1979. He is the author of a leading book on employment law, equal employment opportunity law, and personnel practices and the originator of "On the Legal Front," an editorial department of *The Industrial-Organizational Psychologist.* He has presented several preconference workshops on employment law at annual conferences of SIOP. He has consulted with public and private employers, creating and validating tests, conducting program evaluations, and working on legal issues relating to employment discrimination, including testifying as an expert witness.

Reanna Poncheri Harman, PhD, is a senior consultant at SWA Consulting Inc., where she works on projects related to training evaluation, database design, work analysis, and training needs assessment. Research interests include survey comment response behavior and contextual predictors of job performance.

John Henderson, PhD, is the managing principal of Personnel Science & Solution Architects. The primary focus of his work and research has revolved around assessment and selection system design and validation, alternative job analysis and competency modeling processes, and adverse impact mitigation. He has extensive experience directing and consulting on local and enterprise-wide job analysis projects and in modifying job analytic data collection methods to meet situational demands including the use of virtual and web-based strategies.

Kimberly Hester, BA, is a doctoral student in the Industrial and Organizational Psychology program at the University of Oklahoma. Her research interests include leadership, innovation, and affect.

Joyce Hogan, PhD, specializes in employment test development and validation and human performance. Dr. Hogan is responsible for the development of personality assessment products and directs research projects to validate customized employment testing programs. She received her PhD from the University of Maryland. She taught and was a senior research scientist at The Johns Hopkins University. Dr. Hogan served in many capacities at the University of Tulsa, including chair of the Department of Research and professor in the Department of Psychology. Since her time at the University of Tulsa, Dr. Hogan has dedicated herself to personality assessment development and research for Hogan Assessment Systems, the firm she and Dr. Robert Hogan cofounded in 1987. Dr. Hogan has performed pioneering research on problems in the development of job profiles, job families, and test transportability for various occupations. She is a leading authority on personnel selection and serves as a consultant and expert witness regarding employment discrimination for the U.S. Department of Justice. She is recognized nationally as an expert in human performance and served as editor of *Human Performance* from 1994 to 2000. Dr. Hogan is a fellow of the American Psychological Association. She has authored more than 100 published research articles, chapters, and books. She serves on the editorial boards of *Journal of Applied Psychology, Human Performance, Human Factors,* and *International Journal of Selection and Assessment.*

Scott R. Homan, PhD, is currently an associate professor in technology leadership and innovation at Purdue University. Prior to his appointment to the Purdue faculty, he was a professor of human resource management in the Northwest Nazarene University MBA program in Nampa, Idaho. Dr. Homan earned his PhD in educational human resource development at Texas A&M. He also holds a master's degree in industrial technology and a bachelor's degree in organizational leadership, both from Purdue University. While studying for his doctorate, Dr. Homan participated in cutting-edge research in the field of workforce development. Dr. Homan has also worked for Andersen Consulting (Change Management Services, Chicago World Headquarters Office) and the U.S. Department of Agriculture (New England and Indiana). Currently, Dr. Homan is working with government and private sector business in the area of workforce development and he contributes weekly to the *Wall Street Journal*'s ProfessorJournal.com initiative.

James E. Kuthy, PhD, is a principal consultant at Biddle Consulting Group (BCG), Inc., a firm that specializes in the areas of equal employment opportunity/affirmative action compliance and test development/validation. BCG has a staff of more than 40 employees located in Folsom, California, and maintains several hundred AAP clients and more than 1,000 testing clients in the public and private sectors. Dr. Kuthy specializes in the analysis of jobs and the validation of selection devices for a wide variety of job types. Furthermore, he provides litigation support for clients being audited by government agencies or challenged under Title VII. He is the primary author of *CritiCall Pre-Employment Testing Software* for public safety (911) dispatchers, which is based on a job analysis process that included job experts from more than 45 dispatch agencies from around the United States. Dr. Kuthy holds an MA and PhD in industrial/organizational psychology from the University of Akron.

R. Darrell Laham, PhD, is a scientist, technologist, and entrepreneur who currently runs an alternative energy investment company, Solorado, LLC. He holds a joint PhD in cognitive science and psychology from the University of Colorado at Boulder. In 2005, he retired from Pearson Knowledge Technologies (PKT), a company he cofounded in 1998 as Knowledge Analysis Technologies. For PKT, Dr. Laham served both in technical and business development roles. He was the chief software architect for the company's text analysis software, used primarily in education and intelligence applications. He has managed projects for various government clients, including NASA, the U.S. Department of Defense, and the National Science Foundation.

Charles E. Lance, PhD, is a professor of I/O psychology at the University of Georgia. His work in the areas of performance measurement, assessment center validity, research methods, and structural equation modeling has appeared in such journals as *Psychological Methods, Organizational Research Methods, Journal of Applied Psychology, Organizational Behavior and Human Decision Processes, Journal of Management,* and *Multivariate Behavioral Research.* He is also co-editor of *Performance Measurement: Current Perspectives and Future Challenges* (with Winston "Wink" Bennett and Dave Woehr) and *Statistical and Methodological Myths and Urban Legends: Received Doctrine, Verity, and Fable in Organizational and Social Research* (with Bob Vandenberg). He is a fellow of SIOP and the APA and is a member of the Society for Organizational Behavior. He is currently associate editor of *Organizational Research Methods* and on the editorial board of *Personnel Psychology, Human Performance,* and *Group & Organization Management.*

Elizabeth H. Lazzara, BA, is a doctoral student in the Applied Experimental Human Factors Psychology program at the University of Central Florida and holds a BA in psychology from the University of South Florida. Currently, she is working at the Institute of Simulation and Technology in Orlando, where her primary research as a Multidisciplinary University Research Initiative graduate fellow is the examination of team macrocognition in complex and dynamic environments. She is also involved in other work, including a project funded by the Naval Air Warfare Center linking the relationship between attributes of training games and specific knowledge or skill acquisition.

Edward L. Levine, PhD, is currently a professor in the psychology department at the University of South Florida and served as chair of the department from 1993 to 2001. His research interests include job analysis, personnel selection, control in organizations, and affect at work. He is certified as a diplomate in industrial and organizational psychology by the American Board of Professional Psychology, and he is a fellow of SIOP and the APA. Dr. Levine earned his PhD in industrial/organizational psychology from New York University in 1970.

Jonathan D. Levine, PhD, is an I/O psychologist with more than 16 years experience and has worked for organizations such as APT*Metrics*, Monster.com, and the National Center for O*NET Development. For nearly 10 years, he managed his own consulting firm, Workforce Dynamics, and specialized in occupational classification, job analysis, competency modeling, selection, assessment, and career exploration and development. He currently serves as practice editor of *Ergometrika* and is a member of the Society for Industrial and Organizational Psychology's Electronic Communications Committee. He was a previous recipient of the Jimmy Mitchell Mentor Award for excellence in job analysis. Dr. Levine received his PhD in industrial-organizational-vocational psychology from North Carolina State University.

Rebecca Lyons, BS, is a third-year PhD student in the industrial/organizational psychology program at the University of Central Florida. She is also a graduate research assistant at the Institute for

Simulation and Training, where she is working as a Multi-University Research Initiative Systems for Understanding and Measuring Macrocognition in Teams graduate fellow. She is currently examining macrocognition in teams with a focus on theory development and measurement. She received her BS from Davidson College. Additional research interests include individual and team training, multiteam systems, team performance, and medical simulation. She has co-authored several book chapters related to these areas.

Rosalinda Vasquez Maury, MS, worked for the Department of Manpower, Personnel and Training for Metrica, Inc., headquartered in San Antonio, Texas. She is currently president/CEO of VAnalytic, Inc. She has done many types of research projects for government and private sector clients, including (but not limited to) accession and retention, financial indebtedness, training needs assessment, influence operations, cigarette smoking, and teenage aberrant behavior. In addition, she has extensive experience in survey development, data collection, and data analysis. She received her MS in psychology from the University of Texas at San Antonio in 2003. She also has a BA in psychology from the University of Texas at San Antonio (1999).

Michael A. McDaniel, PhD, is Professor of Management and Research Professor of Psychology at Virginia Commonwealth University. He received his PhD in industrial/organizational psychology from George Washington University in 1986. Dr. McDaniel is nationally recognized for his research and practice in personnel selection system development and validation and for his applications of meta-analysis to the personnel-related research. He has published in several major journals, including *The Academy of Management Journal*, the *Journal of Applied Psychology*, and *Personnel Psychology*. Dr. McDaniel is a member of the Academy of Management and a fellow of SIOP, the APA, and the Association for Psychological Science.

Frederick P. Morgeson, PhD, is currently an associate professor of management at the Eli Broad College of Business at Michigan State University and is a recipient of the 2005 APA Distinguished Scientific Award for Early Career Contribution to Psychology in Applied Psychology. His research involves attempting to understand the nature of work, which includes the design and measurement of work activities, including those assigned to teams. In addition, he studies the effectiveness of different staffing techniques and the role leadership plays in high-risk and team-based environments. Dr. Morgeson received his PhD in industrial/organizational psychology from Purdue University in 1998.

Michael D. Mumford, PhD, is a professor of psychology at the University of Oklahoma, where he is Director of the Center for Applied Social Research. Dr. Mumford is currently working to identify and measure the cognitive processes involved in creative cognition. He also investigates cognitive strategies that can improve ethical decision making when applied while working through ethical problems. Dr. Mumford has also done extensive work on leadership and planning. He is a fellow of the APA and the American Psychological Society.

Peter Musaeus, PhD, is an assistant professor at the University of Aarhus, Department of Psychology. He received his PhD in educational psychology and MS in health psychology from the University of Aarhus. He is a chartered psychologist with the Danish Psychological Association. Dr. Musaeus's primary research areas include workplace and apprenticeship learning. In addition, his research focuses on medical simulation and training. He is currently a visiting professor at the University of Central Florida's Institute for Simulation & Training. He has also served as a visiting scholar at the University of Sussex, UK, and as an Erasmus Student at Universitat de Valencia, Spain.

Robert J. Oberbreckling, MBA, is a founder of Perceptive Research Inc. His interests include applying software systems to problems in cognitive science, natural language processing, machine learning, audio signal processing, and automated human performance measurement, modeling, and assessment. He previously was a senior member of technical staff at Pearson Knowledge Technologies, where he led team communication data collection efforts in the field and created predictive systems for individual and team performance for commercial and military applications.

Frederick L. Oswald, PhD, is an associate professor at Rice University in the industrial-organizational psychology program. His research is concerned with personnel selection and testing issues in organizational, education, and military settings. Specifically, his work deals with defining, modeling, and predicting organizational outcomes (e.g., job performance, turnover, satisfaction) from psychological measures based on cognitive and motivational constructs (e.g., cognitive abilities, personality traits, situational judgment tests, job knowledge and skill, and biographical data). His methodological work in meta-analysis, structural equation modeling, and adverse impact also informs personnel selection issues and psychological testing in the research and legal arenas. In addition to Dr. Oswald's history of publications and large-scale grant-funded projects in these areas, he currently serves as associate editor for two journals, *Journal of Management* and *Journal of Business and Psychology*, and serves on the editorial boards for *Journal of Applied Psychology, Personnel Psychology, Military Psychology, International Journal of Selection and Assessment, Organizational Research Methods, Psychological Methods*, and *Journal of Research in Personality*. Dr. Oswald received his PhD in industrial/organizational psychology in 1999 from the University of Minnesota.

Jeffrey M. Pollack, PhD, is an assistant professor of management in the Robins School of Business at the University of Richmond. He maintains an active research program in entrepreneurship that focuses on the underlying psychological predictors of new venture creation and the determinants of performance both at the firm and individual levels. He has taught courses at the undergraduate and graduate levels on entrepreneurship, business planning, new venture creation, organizational design, industrial/organizational psychology, organizational behavior, and public speaking.

Thomas Powell, PhD, is currently GlaxoSmithKline's Director of Organisational Research. His work supports the company's Global Talent, Leadership, & Organisation Development strategy. At GlaxoSmithKline and other companies, he has lead or supported work analysis efforts for a variety of job families and roles, including sales representatives, production workers, marketing management, and human resources management.

Roni Reiter-Palmon, PhD, is Isaacson Professor of I/O Psychology and the director of the I/O psychology graduate program at the University of Nebraska at Omaha (UNO). She also serves as Director of Research for the Center for Collaboration Science, an interdisciplinary program at UNO. She received her PhD in I/O psychology from George Mason University. Her research focuses on the effect of individual differences, specifically personality and cognitive thought processes; leadership and leader development; creativity and innovation in organizations; team performance and collaboration; and the intersection of leadership, teams, and innovation. Her research has been published in *Journal of Applied Psychology, Creativity Research Journal, The Psychology of Aesthetics, Creativity and the Arts, Human Resources Management Review*, and *Leadership Quarterly*. Her applied experiences include consulting to and grants from Fortune 500 companies as well as the government and military. She is an associate editor for *Journal of Creative Behavior* and serves on the editorial boards of *Journal of Organizational Behavior, The Leadership Quarterly, Journal of Leadership and Organizational Studies, International Journal of Problem Solving and Creativity*, and *The Psychology of Creativity, Aesthetics and the Arts*.

Sylvia G. Roch, PhD, is currently an associate professor of psychology at the University at Albany, State University of New York. Her research interests include performance evaluation, group decision-making, and organizational justice. Dr. Roch received her PhD in industrial/ organizational psychology from Texas A&M in 1997.

Michael A. Rosen, PhD, is an assistant professor in the Department of Anesthesiology and Critical Care Medicine at the Johns Hopkins School of Medicine and a member of the Quality and Safety Research Group. He is a human factors psychologist who focuses on teams, training, performance measurement, decision making, expertise, and simulation. He earned his PhD in applied experimental and human factors psychology from the University of Central Florida in 2010.

Eduardo Salas, PhD, is a university trustee chair and Pegasus Professor of Psychology at the University of Central Florida (UCF), where he also holds an appointment as program director for the Human Systems Integration Research Department at the Institute for Simulation and Training (IST). Previously, he was the director of UCF's Applied Experimental and Human Factors PhD program. Before joining IST, he was a senior research psychologist and head of the Training Technology Development Branch of the Naval Air Warfare Center Training Systems Division for 15 years. Dr. Salas has co-authored over 300 journal articles and book chapters and has co-edited 19 books. His expertise includes assisting organizations in how to foster teamwork, design and implement team training strategies, facilitate training effectiveness, manage decision making under stress, and develop performance measurement tools

Juan I. Sanchez, PhD, is a professor and Knight-Ridder Byron Harless Eminent Chair in the Department of Management and International Business, Florida International University. His areas of expertise are competency modeling and job analysis, performance management, human resource management, and international human resources management. Dr. Sanchez has extensive experience in the development and validation of personnel selection systems; job and task analysis; the design of commercial tests and test batteries; the development of criterion-related validity studies; and the design of training evaluation systems. He has authored numerous papers and articles on industrial/organizational issues and topics, including the consensus of competency ratings, comparison of job analysis methodologies, and the evaluation of work analysis. Dr. Sanchez is a fellow of the APA and SIOP. His editorial positions include serving as associate editor of the *Journal of Occupational and Organizational Psychology*; consulting editor of the *Journal of Applied Psychology*; and editorial board member of *Personnel Psychology, the International Journal of Selection and Assessment,* and *Ergometrika*. Dr. Sanchez received a PhD in industrial/organizational psychology from the University of South Florida.

Darrel L. Sandall, PhD, is the chief executive officer of Integra Management Associates, a management, leadership, and intellectual property consulting organization. Formerly, he was an assistant professor of technology leadership and innovation at Purdue University, and for 10 years he served as the chief skills officer for SkillsNET Corporation. He has extensive experience in workforce optimization, human capital management, and intellectual property management. He has authored numerous peer-refereed research publications and holds a PhD in human resource development from Texas A&M.

Amanda Shipman, BA, is a doctoral student in the industrial/organizational psychology program at the University of Oklahoma. Her research interests include leader cognition, complex problem-solving, and innovation.

Brice M. Stone, PhD, has more than 25 years of research experience in military manpower, personnel, and training issues. Dr. Stone has an established history of applying state-of-the-art statistical techniques to modeling and analysis of personnel issues. He was the principal investigator in the review, evaluation, and analysis of career field training and education for enlisted and officer specialties in the USAF. Dr. Stone joined Metrica, Inc., in October 1990. He received his PhD in economics from Texas A&M.

Eric A. Surface, PhD, is cofounder and president of SWA Consulting Inc., a consulting and applied research firm in Raleigh, NC. He has served as principal investigator on numerous projects related to training, work analysis, validation, and testing and has worked with corporate, military, nonprofit, government, and academic clients. Dr. Surface has expertise in the areas of needs assessment, training evaluation and effectiveness, learning metrics and analytics, survey methodology, rater-based assessments, and validation. He has published in journals such as *Human Performance, Journal of Management, Journal of Applied Psychology, Military Psychology, Organizational Research Methods,* and *Personnel Psychology.* He received his PhD from North Carolina State University, his MA from East Carolina University, and his BA from Wake Forest University. He was a consortium research fellow and postdoctoral fellow with the U.S. Army Research Institute.

David M. Van De Voort, MA, is a partner at Mercer. In a human resources career spanning more than 35 years in corporate, academic, and consulting settings (including 22 years at Mercer), he has advised clients of all industries and sizes on compensation, employee attraction, retention, and performance, manager and leader effectiveness, and organization design. He has taught general management, human resources management, compensation, and applied psychology as an adjunct professor at The Graduate School of Administration-Capital University, Franklin University, The Ohio State University, and the Ohio Peace Officer Academy. He earned his MA in industrial/organizational psychology and statistics at The Ohio State University and his BS in communication and psychology at Illinois State University.

Anton J. Villado, PhD, is an assistant professor of psychology at Rice University. His research interests include individual and team training; the acquisition, retention, and transfer of complex skills; job performance; personnel selection and placement; and quantitative methods (meta-analysis and multilevel modeling). He received his PhD in psychology from Texas A&M in 2008.

Thomas J. Whelan, MS, received his BA in psychology from the University of South Florida in 2002 and his MS in industrial/organizational psychology from North Carolina State University in 2008. His research has been presented at research conferences in the fields of industrial/organizational psychology and management both in the United States and Europe. In addition to conducting research, he has been a consultant for several years in the public and private sectors with organizations such as Lenovo, the U.S. Army Special Forces, and the Marine Special Operations Command.

Deborah L. Whetzel, PhD, is a program manager at the Human Resources Research Organization (HumRRO) and has more than 20 years of experience in personnel selection research and development in both the public and private sectors. Her areas of expertise include job analysis, leadership competency models, performance appraisal systems, and developing and validating assessment processes. She has co-edited two books, *Applied Measurement: Industrial Psychology in Human Resources Management* (Lawrence Erlbaum Associates, 2007) and *Applied Measurement Methods in Industrial Psychology* (Davies-Black Publishing, 1997). Dr. Whetzel has served as an adjunct professor in the graduate program at George Mason University and in the undergraduate program at Virginia Commonwealth University. She earned her PhD at George Washington University, specializing in industrial and organizational psychology.

Kevin J. Williams, PhD, is a professor of psychology and dean of graduate studies at the University at Albany, State University of New York. His current research interests include work motivation and performance, the psychology of blame, and employee assessment and appraisal. He received his PhD in experimental psychology from the University of South Carolina.

Katherine A. Wilson, PhD, is a human factors psychologist at the University of Miami Miller School of Medicine and William Lehman Injury Research Center. She holds a PhD in applied experimental and human factors psychology and an MS in modeling and simulation from the University of Central Florida (UCF). In addition, she holds a BS in aerospace studies from Embry-Riddle Aeronautical University. Dr. Wilson's primary research areas include user interface design and usability testing. In addition, her research focuses on the design, development, implementation, and evaluation of telemedicine and simulation-based training for healthcare personnel. Prior to working at the University of Miami, Dr. Wilson worked as a research assistant at UCF's Institute for Simulation and Training, where her research focused on simulation-based training and teams in complex environments such as healthcare, the military, and aviation.

Mark Woodhouse, PhD, is currently founder and managing partner of the Transitions Partnership, which focuses on developing those factors that contribute to both organizational and individual success. The partnership's foundations are firmly built on the belief that "people really do make a difference" and that success can be built on a platform of inspirational leadership, individual development, and sustained innovation and creativity. Dr. Woodhouse has an MSc in strategic human resource management and a PhD in organizational psychology.

Chris W. Wright, PhD, is an associate professor of psychology at San Francisco State University (SFSU), where he teaches undergraduate and graduate courses on topics related to I/O psychology and applied statistics. His research interests include employee selection and retention, interview techniques, job analysis, and performance measurement. Prior to joining SFSU, he worked extensively as a human resources consultant in the areas of job analysis and test validation for a wide range of public and private sector clients. He earned his PhD in industrial/organizational psychology in 1996 from the University of South Florida.

Part I

WORK ANALYSIS METHODS

Mark A. Wilson
North Carolina State University

Erich C. Dierdorff
DePaul University

Work analysis is often described as foundational to the field. The results of work analysis are often the starting point for nearly any other effort. If work analysis is the foundation of the field, then work analysis methodology is the foundation of work analysis—the place you must start and the decisions you must make as you bring your work analysis to life. There are many methodological decisions to be made in work analysis, and making the wrong decision can have very negative consequences.

The purpose of Part I is to make sure that you make the right methodological decisions when you conduct your work analysis project. Part I features eight chapters that concern methodological issues in work analysis. The authors are a mix of academics and practitioners, and the chapters are written in a way to be useful to both academics and practitioners. Although relevant research is cited where appropriate, there is an emphasis on practical checklists and decision tables. If you master the information provided in Part I on work analysis methodology, you will be well prepared for making methodology-related decisions.

In Chapter 1, the major methodological decisions in work analysis are discussed, with an emphasis on basic conceptual issues and where to go within the handbook for more information on each decision. This chapter also presents a theory of work analysis that is based on role theory and open systems; it argues for the importance of understanding the context in which work analysis is performed.

In Chapter 2, the value of work analysis to organizations is stressed through a case analysis method. Chapter 3 provides a systematic review of the pros and cons of each potential source of work analysis information. This chapter includes a very helpful table to aid in the selection of a source.

Chapter 4 presents a detailed discussion of how to use surveys and interviews to collect work analysis information. This chapter includes several examples and checklists to aid in the data collection process. In Chapter 5, a comprehensive study of where to find work information on the Internet and other less traditional sources of work information is discussed. This chapter also provides an important framework for examining the value of the sources organized by potential application of the information.

In Chapter 6, a number of important questions in the data analysis process are addressed in a step-by-step fashion. This chapter also includes an extensive table for virtually every decision point in the data analysis process and the suggested best practice. Chapter 7 argues that evaluation in work analysis should be focused on the consequences of work analysis efforts. This chapter also suggests future directions for research on the validity of work analysis data.

In the eighth and final chapter of Part I, "Documenting Work Analysis Projects: A Review of Strategy and Legal Defensibility for Personnel Selection," the documentation requirements of work analysis are discussed. This chapter provides useful tables that describe documentation needs for various steps in the work analysis process, as well as a review of relevant laws.

1

Methodological Decisions in Work Analysis
A Theory of Effective Work Analysis in Organizations

Mark A. Wilson

North Carolina State University

It has been a long time since the publication of Gael's (1988) handbook on work analysis, which came along relatively late in the history of the field (Wilson, 2007). Finally, the wait for a new handbook is over. Whether you are looking for initial guidance on how to carry out your first work analysis project, seeking ideas on how you can improve the work analysis that you and your organization already possess, or looking for insight that will lead to your next research project related to work analysis, you have come to the right place.

Because the quality of work analysis documents can vary greatly within and among organizations, you may have asked the following questions:

- Why is there so much variation in the quality, quantity, and currency of the work information that organizations possess?
- Why does one organization really have its act together when it comes to work analysis but another does not?
- Why do some organizations seem so concerned about getting work analysis right, whereas other organizations seem downright hostile to the idea of any work analysis at all?

Work continues to change at a rapid pace (National Research Council, 1999). For this reason and many others, work analysis can be expensive and time consuming. However, it can also pay big dividends to organizations that manage it appropriately. Work analysis may be high quality or low quality; it may be current or out of date. In any case, work analysis (as it exists in most organizations) is the result of a series of decisions that people inside the organizations make, either intentionally or by default. The decision makers are often forced to make important choices without all the necessary facts necessary or an understanding of how their organizational context may be driving the process.

Some work analysis projects are a waste of time and resources because they are not consistent with a number of forces, which may be driving the organization in directions that the work analyst does not anticipate. In work analysis, one size definitely does not fit all. Trying to fit a poorly conceptualized work analysis to the wrong organization can have all kinds of negative consequences for the organization, the person conducting the analysis, and the field of work analysis. This chapter explains the common decisions that are part of every work analysis, defines some commonly used terms, explores the contextual elements that drive work analysis project decisions, and presents a theory about why some work analysis projects fail and some are a success.

WORK ANALYSIS PROCESS DECISIONS

Work analysis is as much about process as it is about outcomes (Harvey, 1991; Morgeson, 2007b; Morgeson & Dierdorff, 2011; Sackett & Laczo, 2003; Sanchez & Levine, 2001). In some contexts, a flawed process will irreversibly damage an otherwise valid work analysis effort. By reviewing the six major decisions in the work analysis process, this chapter provides a conceptual overview of the entire handbook, with special emphasis on work analysis methodology. Although other chapters provide considerably more detail on the specifics of each decision, this discussion highlights the conceptual choices relevant to each decision. Each decision is briefly discussed, key terms are defined, and references to more detailed discussions of the topic in this handbook are provided. In addition, the implications of various choices for each decision on the other decisions are briefly discussed.

In reviewing the decisions, two resources will help you to efficiently use the information provided in the handbook. Figure 1.1 summarizes the main points to be discussed in this section. It is a visual representation of the primary choices available to someone needing to make work analysis decisions. Table 1.1 provides a chapter-by-chapter listing of where you can find more information about each decision discussed in this chapter. For example, if you are struggling with trying to decide what level of detail to use in your work analysis, you can go directly to the chapters in the handbook that provide more information on that decision. In some cases, the chapters listed may have the decision as their primary purpose; in others, the decision may be relevant but more tangential to the primary point of the chapter. Taken together, these resources are your decision support system for work analysis.

How Do You Identify the Need for Work Information Projects?

Work analysis is the first step and the foundation to almost every other activity in industrial and organizational psychology and human resource management. Numerous authors have discussed the various purposes for work analysis (Brannick, Levine, & Morgeson, 2007; Gael, 1983; McCormick, 1979; Prien, Goodstein, Goodstein, & Gamble, 2009). Work analysis information is necessary for everything you do, but different types of work information may not be equally useful for a given purpose. What kind of work analysis information is best suited for the primary purposes for which work information is collected? This question is discussed in more depth here than the following questions because no other chapter is solely devoted to this topic, and misunderstanding the relationship between work analysis information purposes can lead to big problems.

As seen in Figure 1.1, most applications of work analysis information are for decision support, development, or work systems purposes. When you make decisions about work or the worker, you often need to demonstrate that the information used to make the decision is related to the work being performed for both legal reasons (Society for Industrial and Organizational Psychology, 2003) and procedural justice (Blader & Tyler, 2003). If you are reading this chapter with any urgency, it is probably because you are interested in work analysis to support some decision you or your organization has made or wants to make. Work analysis information for decision support is the primary evidence that will be cited when decisions about the worker or the work are challenged. Some examples of relevant decisions include job worth, employee selection, differentiating levels of job performance, and promotion decisions.

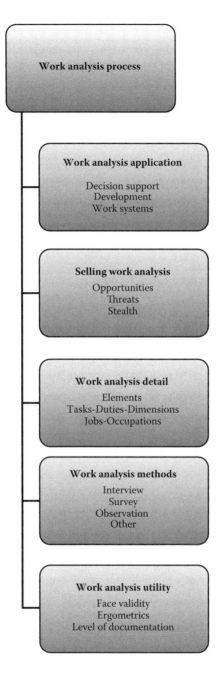

Figure 1.1 Work analysis process.

Because it is evidence used to support the decision, the procedure used to collect the information is as important as the information itself. You should expect that everything about the information and how it was collected will be examined for compliance with known professional standards (e.g., Society for Industrial and Organizational Psychology, 2003). You also should be prepared to document every aspect of the work analysis project (see Chapter 8, this volume). In my experience, the more prepared you are to withstand a challenge, the less likely it is that you will actually have to endure one. To be in this enviable position, you should be able to document how

Table 1.1   Where to Find Information About Methodological Decisions in This Handbook

Important Decisions in Work Analysis						
Need for Work Information	Sales of Work Information	Specificity of Work Information	Source of Work Information	Collecting Work Information	Evaluating Work Information	Presenting Work Information
Summary: Chapter 1	Summary: Chapter 1	Summary: Chapter 1	Summary: Chapter 1	Summary: Chapter 1	Summary: Chapter 1	Summary: Chapter 1
Primary source: Chapter 1	Primary source: Chapter 2	Primary source: Chapter 1	Primary source: Chapter 1	Primary source: Chapter 1	Primary source: Chapter 1	Primary source: Chapter 1

you made each of the decisions discussed in this chapter, as well as how your decisions are consistent with all known professional standards. This handbook is designed to give you the methods, systems, applications, and research that you will need to protect yourself and your organization from potential challenges.

When you collect work information for the purpose of development, you face a different challenge than when you intend to use the information to support a decision. Work analysis for development uses work information collected to assist the worker in some way, such as training needs analysis, basic work orientation and descriptions, and work aids or checklists. The products of these kinds of efforts are procedures for acquiring or using work-related information successfully. The emphasis is on creating a useful tool to drive performance. If the tool has utility for worker development, the specific details of the developmental process are less important. In many cases, the primary factor affecting the utility of work information for developmental purposes is specificity. Work information for developmental purposes is very specific and detailed. The development of these tools involves some trial and error. Much of this information can only be provided by workers who have successfully performed the work. Rather than being used to shield against challenges by providing substantial documentation, this information is used to drive work performance and usability.

Work analysis for the purpose of designing work systems is, to some extent, an integration of these purposes because it shares some of the requirements from both approaches. However, it is also quite distinct because it often grows out of the phrase, "There has got to be a better way." Too often, work systems are developed ad hoc and as an afterthought rather than at the start of the enterprise. Designing work systems is the most creative use of job analysis because organizations can divide the same work into very different categories while still achieving success. It is also the most psychological use. By knowing what demands particular categorizations of work place on a worker, organizations may have the key to long-term and sustainable levels of performance. This process has often been called *strategic work analysis,* which emphasizes the point that work analysis can be used to operationalize organizational goals and objectives (Sanchez, 1994; Shippman, 1999).

The two most common examples of work analysis for work systems are work process improvement and work process development. Like work information for development, specificity is important in collecting work information for work systems. Like work information for decision support, documentation of the process (in this case, procedures and sequence) is also important. A firm understanding of the whole work process—from beginning to end and in considerable detail—is invaluable when considering how to reconfigure components of the process to improve efficiency or increase effectiveness. For a successful work system design, the work analyst should be most concerned with the strategic objectives of the organization. A clear understanding of organizational strategy will drastically reduce the number of viable work system designs that need to be considered.

Purpose affects all the other decisions that you will need to make. You may be reading this hand-book because you already have a problem to solve. You may need work information as the input to support a decision or design a tool or system to help an organization achieve its objectives. A clear understanding of how method and technique relate to the purpose of your work analysis project will be a key factor in the success of any work analysis project. A firm grasp of purpose is the best insurance that your project will be successful, efficient, and justifiable to management.

Before considering other important decisions, first consider the notion of multipurpose work analysis. If you had the necessary time and resources, could you design and conduct the ultimate work analysis project for your organization, which anticipated all of the organization's work infor-mation needs in one comprehensive effort? Earlier in my career, I would have argued that you can (and should) achieve this, but experience and closer examination have convinced me that to try would be a huge mistake for most professionals in most organizations. Rather than anticipating every work information need and having it ready when the need emerges, it is probably best to approach it differently.

The first step in nearly every intervention is to identify and collect the needed work informa-tion for the purpose at hand. In support of this approach, Part III of this handbook describes work analysis for specific applications. Note the number of different methods presented in the various chapters, and then try to imagine providing all of that information in a single project. It would be a daunting task. On the other hand, you could cite Part II of this handbook as evidence in support of multipurpose work analysis systems. It is true that work analyses generated by any of these systems are useful for more than one purpose. However, I am not aware of any case where one system pro-vided all the work information necessary for all the required applications in the typical organiza-tion over any reasonable length of time. This advice may sound inefficient, but the dynamic nature of work and organizations and the need for timely information are likely to subvert your best-laid advance plans. Instead, I suggest using a just-in-time approach to work information needs, as sup-ported by the theory presented later in this chapter.

How Do I Sell the Project to Decision Makers?

Work analysis is not an easy sell, especially if the organization has had any prior experience with it. Work analysis can be very expensive and time consuming; it may disrupt the work environ-ment and force management to confront issues they would rather not address. Therefore, it is important to carefully develop and convey to management why you think a work analysis proj-ect needs to be conducted. Given the risks and complexity involved in selling work analysis, it is advisable to form coalitions with others in the organization who will benefit from the work analysis and spend time conducting information-only discussions before requesting approval of a work analysis project.

As can be seen in Figure 1.1, there are three basic approaches to selling a work analysis. These approaches can be mixed or matched to suit your needs. The *opportunities approach* empha-sizes what the organization will gain by conducting work analysis (e.g., clearer communication of performance standards, better and more effective training, more rational and efficient work processes). With this approach, your natural collaborators may be the line managers who would benefit from the products generated by the work analysis. By getting line management involved in the sale of the project, they are more likely to cooperate with you during data collection if the project is approved.

The *threats approach* to sales places an emphasis on the liabilities an organization may face should some decision be challenged (e.g., hiring, termination, promotion, salary decision). With this approach, your natural collaborators may be the staff managers in human resources and firm lawyers—who see the work analysis as a shield should they be called upon to defend the organization. By getting relevant staff managers and lawyers involved in the sale of the project, they can provide you with considerable skill at crafting successful arguments.

Finally, and because work analysis is often so abstract, a *stealth approach* can be used by creating a small proof of concept with existing resources or inserting a small work analysis effort into another project, which can then be used to demonstrate the potential utility and promise of a larger work analysis project. The advantage of this approach is that you do not need to form coalitions to be successful. The products of this approach can be useful in recruiting collaborators if you move on to one of the other strategies. In addition, with this approach you can test various methods while you are still "under the radar" at much less risk to your credibility.

For additional information and insight on this topic, start with Chapter 2, this volume. This chapter provides a wealth of information and insight on this topic. You also should continue reading the next section of this chapter, in which I discuss the contextual elements in organizations that affect the receptivity of the organization to work analysis. The receptivity section provides a number of ideas to consider before proposing a work analysis project, as well as some predictions as to when work analysis projects are likely to be a success.

What Is the Right Level of Detail?

Just how specific do you need to be when conducting work analysis? As you might guess, increasing specificity of the analysis often leads to greater costs and longer timelines. More specific information also tends to have a shorter shelf life and needs to be refreshed more frequently. One highly attractive feature of very specific work information is that it can always be generalized into fewer and more abstract categories, whereas information that is collected at a more abstract unit of analysis cannot be used for applications in which greater specificity is needed. Thus, you should be only as specific as you need to be to support the purpose of the analysis. Figure 1.2 provides a list of common levels of specificity that are often mentioned (Brannick et al., 2007; Morgeson, 2007a; Prien et al., 2009), ranging from highly specific elements and tasks at the bottom of the pyramid to much more general jobs and occupations at the top of the pyramid. For each potential descriptor, a descriptor name is given along with the likely number of that type of descriptor relevant to one incumbent's activities and an example. The number refers to the frequency of that kind of descriptor in the job (low part of Figure 1.2), the organization (middle part of Figure 1.2), and the labor market as a whole (top part of Figure 1.2).

To make an important point, I have taken the information provided in Figure 1.2 and reorganized and expanded the information into Figures 1.3 and 1.4. It may be easier to understand the specificity question if you keep in mind two very distinct fields of study in work analysis: ergometrics (Cunningham, 1971) and econometrics. These fields use the same data as their primary source of information, but they use the information in very different ways for distinct purposes.

Table 1.2 provides an overview of the distinction I am making between these two fields on a number of different dimensions. If you accept the ideas presented in Table 1.2, then you probably understand why I split Figure 1.2 into an econometric pyramid (Figure 1.3) and an ergometric pyramid (Figure 1.4). Econometrics tries to classify and organize work as a whole into hierarchies, whereas ergometrics tries to describe the specific components of work. Organizations use both pyramids by collecting descriptors of varying levels of detail to identify and describe positions (e.g., the elements, tasks, and duties of a single individual within the organization) and jobs (groups of similar positions). Governments tend to use the econometric pyramid to classify and identify trends about work across organizations.

Regardless of which field is studying work, if the primary purpose is to make comparisons of work across organizations, then the work information must be generalizable and provide the basis for a common metric of work analysis. Figure 1.5 presents the work descriptors from Figure 1.4

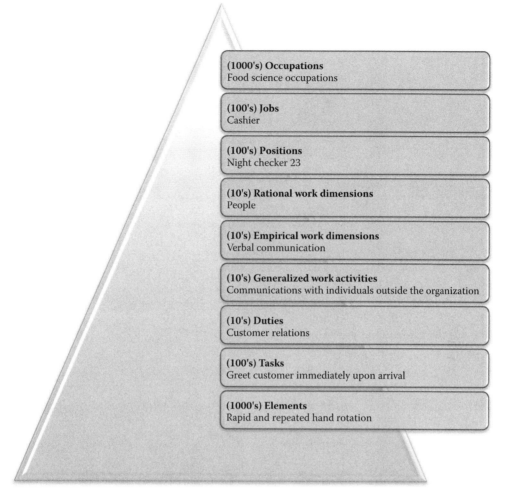

Figure 1.2 Work analysis specificity.

in a two-dimensional space of generality and specificity; it is my view of the generality of various work descriptors. For example, the list of tasks that an individual performs as part of their job in a given organization is highly specific but unlikely to generalize to other organizations. In contrast, rational work dimensions (e.g., data, people, things) are low in specificity but highly generalizable. It is important to understand the information conveyed in Figures 1.3–1.5 and Table 1.2. Decision makers easily confuse the distinctions that they represent.

When evaluating what level of detail to employ in your work analysis, it is important to consider the purpose of the analysis discussed earlier along with the information presented here. Part III of the handbook describes work analysis efforts with specific applications in mind and makes suggestions as to the appropriate level of detail.

Who Will Provide the Information?

When considering the potential sources of work information, the obvious choices are the incumbent, the incumbent's coworkers, and the incumbent's supervisor. These sources are certainly recognized as the subject matter experts. Each source has unique information that the others may not have; in addition, they may have reservations about sharing some or all of what they

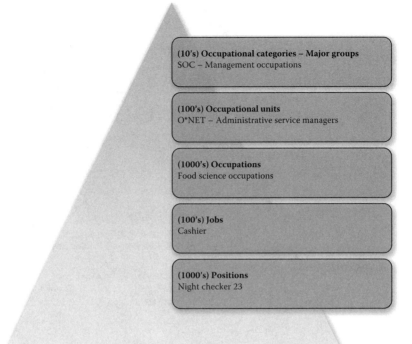

Figure 1.3 Level of specificity of work title systems.

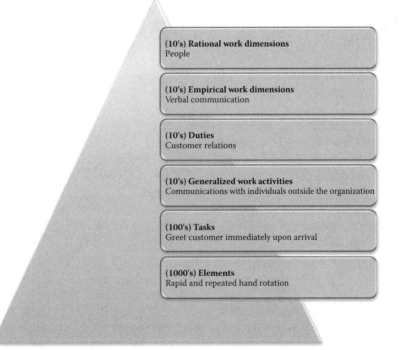

Figure 1.4 Level of specificity of work descriptors.

Table 1.2 Comparison of Ergometric and Econometric Approaches to Work Analysis

Element	Ergometric	Econometric
Definition	Measurement of work as performed by the worker	Measurement of work as a labor market category
Primary scales of measurement	Ordinal, interval and ratio	Nominal
Measurement approach	Decomposed	Holistic
Measurement precision	Moderate to high	Low
Unit of analysis	Position and job	Large aggregations of jobs
Primary purpose/application	Human resources	Policy development
Organizational level	The enterprise	The economy
Primary threats to validity	Internal and statistical conclusion validity	External and construct
Level of legal scrutiny	Moderate to high	Low
Sample systems	Task inventory and position analysis questionnaire	O*NET and standard occupational classification
Primary discipline	Psychology	Economics

know with the organization. Incumbents are certainly aware of what they are doing, but they may see job knowledge as a competitive advantage that is not to be shared without increasing the risk that they will be replaced. Coworkers certainly can provide information on the aspects of an incumbent's work that they witness, but they may have concerns similar to incumbents or may have no knowledge of some aspects of the incumbent's work. Supervisors are unlikely to have the concerns noted above and should have a clear idea of the general work objectives of the incumbent, but they may lack direct experience with the work because of large spans of control and

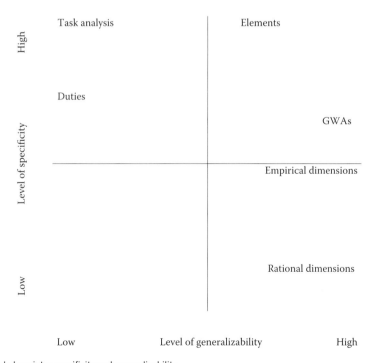

Figure 1.5 Work descriptor specificity and generalizability.

the demands of their own work requirements. Supervisors may intentionally let the incumbent decide how the work is done and instead spend their time identifying important work outcomes. Professional analysts can often help you to sort through these issues, but their presence can also alter the work behavior they are trying to understand. Unfortunately, there is no single source of information, and using multiple sources may cause disagreement in information collected from different sources.

When determining a source, you should also consider how the information you collect will be perceived by sources that were not part of the process. Although it may be possible to exclude particular sources of information from a work analysis effort, making an effort to include them may generate greater acceptance of the results from the standpoint of procedural justice. For a more detailed discussion of sources, see Chapter 3, this volume.

How Will the Information Be Collected?

Observations, interviews, and surveys are the big three of data collection, but alternative methods exist to identify and collect work information (see Chapter 5, this volume). Data collection choices raise a number of procedural and ethical issues that should not be ignored. If you have ever shown up at a work site and said, "I have been sent from headquarters and I am here to analyze your job," then you know this all too well. No matter what method you use, the work process tends to be disturbed. Depending on the level of specificity of the analysis, the size of the disturbance can be substantial.

In general, limited new information about a job will be collected after the third interview or third observation of an incumbent. In addition, interviews and observations generate little new information after 90 minutes. Thus, interviews and observations can be relatively efficient if only a few jobs will be studied. If large numbers of jobs are to be studied at once, standardized or custom-developed surveys may be a better source of information. In addition, they have the advantage of allowing larger numbers of organizational members to be involved in the work analysis effort.

Data collection techniques are such an important topic that two chapters are devoted to the topic: Chapter 4, this volume discusses the traditional methods, whereas Chapter 5, this volume considers promising new methods. As with sources, there is no surefire method of data collection. As a scientist, my view is that more data is better. However, more data also means more resources, greater potential work disruption, and considerably more need to organize, reconcile, and consolidate what you collect. This handbook will help you make the best decision about data collection for your work analysis project.

What Makes Work Information Useful?

I am surprised by how often decision makers are not happy with the results of a work analysis project. Their reaction may result from the way the information is presented, confusion as to how the information supports the purpose, or simply bad presentation of the results. In short, if work information serves the purpose that prompted the work analysis project, then it was a useful effort— although it may not be appreciated. To some extent, work information that is useful in one sense (e.g., documentation of job relatedness) may be less useful in another sense (e.g., reference tool for development).

Because work analysis is presented here as an ongoing process that essentially never ends, it is important to have not only utility but also appreciation and acceptance of the importance and centrality of the effort to the ongoing functioning of the organization. Therefore, you should be very careful about how work-related information is presented to various organizational constituencies. Save the highly detailed procedural and analytic technical reports for your employment attorneys who need all that data should they face discovery to justify some organizational decision. Chapter 8, this volume discusses documentation needs in work analysis projects, with a special emphasis on documentation with legal defensibility in mind.

You should involve various users when designing reports that are based on the work information to be generated so that you have buy-in upfront and to ensure that your project can deliver the information users actually want *before* you collect the information. This recommendation has the added benefit of building a usability analysis into your work analysis projects because the intended users provide suggestions on what they need and how they want to consume the information prior to it being collected. Chapter 7, this volume goes into considerable detail about what really matters in work analysis: the consequences of the effort.

In general, a smaller amount of information presented graphically is more effective than a larger amount of information presented tabularly. Customized reports that deliver the work analysis information in ways to help solve common problems managers face (e.g., 10 tasks that new employees struggle to perform well, key questions concerning work-related knowledge to ask an applicant) are always appreciated.

When designing and customizing reports, it is important to consider the analytical framework that is used to "crunch the numbers." Work analysis data have some interesting analytical challenges that individuals who are otherwise proficient in data analysis may miss based on traditional statistical training. Often, the initial simple descriptive statistics of work information that have been gathered can generate a misleading picture of the true state of affairs. Knowledge of the information provided in Chapter 6, this volume will ensure that you will not fall victim to common errors when you analyze work analysis data.

Important Decisions Summary

This discussion highlights the interrelatedness of these decisions. The decisions are best thought of as different facets of a more integrative question: *What is the appropriate work analysis method for my problem?* The decisions must be considered together rather than sequentially. It is also clear that many questions remain in the field of work analysis. Just note the number of chapters in Part IV of this handbook that concern methodological questions. Perhaps, in addition to successfully completing your work analysis project, you will consider investigating some of the unanswered methodological questions raised throughout the handbook.

A THEORY OF WORK ANALYSIS IN ORGANIZATIONS: AN OPEN SYSTEM

The first part of this chapter presents a number of important decisions in work analysis, but it only hints at the organizational context that helps to shape those decisions. When these contextual variables are ignored, it is perilous for both practical and conceptual work. Disregarding these variables can lead to failed projects. In addition, work context constructs the boundaries for your work analysis projects, whether you realize it or not.

My views have been influenced by open systems theory (Katz & Kahn, 1978; Weick, 1979), role theory (Biddle, 1979, 1986; Dierdorff & Morgeson, 2007; Graen, 1976; Ilgen & Hollenbeck, 1991; Kahn, Wolfe, Quinn, Snoek, & Rosenthal, 1964), and previous authors who have emphasized how context may affect work analysis (Morgeson & Campion, 1997). However, this chapter is only my interpretation of how these ideas fit together in the context of work analysis based on personal experience. It is an initial framework that you should test and modify as needed. Approaching the decisions you have to make about work analysis from the perspective described here may save you from making mistakes that others likely have made. Most importantly, you should use these ideas as a starting point for your own theories that you share with

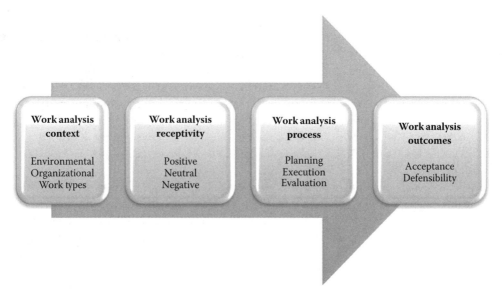

Figure 1.6 Work analysis as an open system.

the field. As others have rightly suggested, there is not enough theory in work analysis research (Morgeson & Dierdorff, 2011).

Figure 1.6 presents an open systems view of work analysis. The outcomes of work analysis are depicted as dependent on a given work analysis process. To the extent that the context in which the activity is performed creates a receptive environment for work analysis, the effort will be a success. Conversely, if the context results in an environment that is not receptive, the same effort may be much less successful or an outright failure. Although the process choices in work analysis remain the same, the context in which they are carried out is potentially unstable. Therefore, the same process may lead to good results at one time in your organization and bad results at another time. You should have a clear and completely honest understanding of your organizational context before beginning a work analysis. That is, you need to conduct a context analysis before conducting a work analysis. The main points of context analysis are briefly discussed here; for more information, see Chapter 17, this volume.

Work Analysis Context

Figure 1.7 provides a list of important work context variables in the categories of environmental characteristics, organizational characteristics, and work types. In the case of environmental and organizational characteristics, the list is not meant to be exhaustive but rather provides exemplars of the kind of information you should be thinking about in each case. Three important elements of the environment of an organization are regulation, competition, and barriers to entry. Organizations that are heavily regulated tend towards higher degrees of documentation and standardization of work and work processes, whereas organizations that face little regulation are not as concerned with documentation and standardization. Organizations that face numerous and competent competitors tend to be concerned with finding efficiencies in work and work processes that can be exploited to gain a competitive advantage, whereas less competition tends to produce organizations with greater slack resources and more discretion in how work is performed. Finally, if the barriers to entry for potential competitors are high and your organization enjoys a relatively competitive position, it is more likely that the organization will be open to experiments and innovation in work

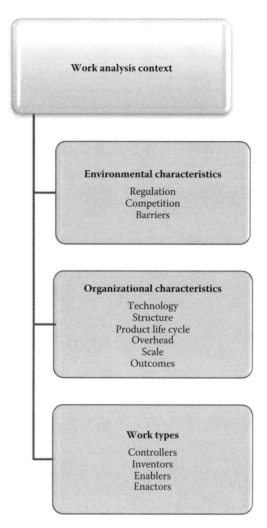

Figure 1.7   Major components of work context.

and work process; this is because the organization will be less concerned about being able to obtain a return on the investment.

You may think of other variables in addition to those discussed here to consider when determining how receptive your organization may be to work analysis. I will use these three variables to illustrate how variation in environment can affect the receptivity of an organization to work analysis efforts.

Space does not permit—indeed, entire books have been written on the subject (Katz & Kahn, 1978; Weick, 1979)—an adequate discussion of the influence of organizational characteristics on work analysis. This chapter provides a few examples of how factors such as technology, structure, and product lifecycle affect the work analysis process. When thinking about organizational characteristics, you should always view them through the dual lens of stability and culture. That is, for a given characteristic, you should consider whether it is in the process of changing (rapidly or slowly) and how central that characteristic is to the culture of the organization (central and definitional, peripheral and opportunistic). Taken together, properties will give you some hint as to the potential impact of a particular characteristic.

Increasingly, organizations are defined and constrained by the technology they use to create and deliver products or services. If this technology is well established and relatively stable, a more favorable climate for work analysis will exist than in an environment with changing and multiple potential technology choices. For example, airlines use relatively stable technology, whereas mobile computing is in a near-constant state of technological change. Similarly, highly functionalized organizations with lots of managerial differentiation create a specialist climate that is more tolerant of work analysis than flat organizations that are full of generalists. For example, the federal government is the ultimate example of a functionalized organization with a high degree of managerial differentiation, whereas nearly any startup small business tends to be a flat organization made up of generalists. Functionalized organizations see work analysis as a means of establishing continuity, whereas flat organizations are in a constant state of flux.

In another example, organizations live and die by the lifecycle of their product or service. When this lifecycle is long and relatively predictable, a work analysis will be seen as an added value. As the cycle shrinks, the organization is too busy planning and managing changeovers to be overly concerned about understanding a particular work process. Commercial construction companies that build office buildings deal in products and services with extended lifecycles. The providers of office equipment have less extended but still stable lifecycles, whereas the providers of information systems for business tend to have relatively short lifecycles. Like environmental characteristics, organizational characteristics provide a complex mix that can impede or propel work analysis projects. Before you launch a work analysis project, you should talk to organizational members with long tenures about the organization's characteristics.

If environmental and organizational characteristics are the more distal variables that place limits on work analysis projects, then the mix of work types in an organization is the more proximal variable that will determine the success of your work analysis. As can be seen in Figures 1.7 and 1.8, all work can be organized into one of four work types. Although an individual incumbent may be doing things that fit in more than one of these categories in a particular organization, all of the work of any organization can be slotted into these four groups. The work type that has the most power in the organization will help to determine the organization's reaction to work analysis efforts.

Enablers and enactors are likely to see work analysis as potentially useful as long as it does not constrain or reduce their flexibility. Because they are responsible for getting things done, work analysis must be a useful tool in the work process rather than an extra task in an already overloaded day. Controllers, as you might expect, tend to love work analysis because it gives them a standard to

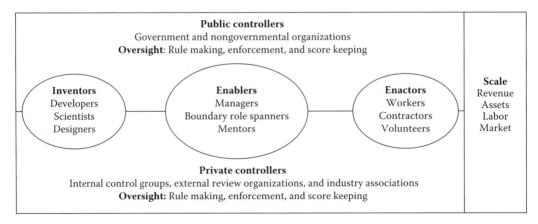

Figure 1.8 A theory of work types.

determine compliance and a means of control by establishing uniform procedures. Finally, inventors see little if any use in work analysis; they would sooner leave than explain anything about their work process to you or anyone else.

The scale variables listed on the right of Figure 1.8 are multipliers. If a particular work type is dominant in an organization, with considerable scale their influence will be even greater because more will be at stake. The person who is perceived to be the source of the gold gets to call the shots, so you should know the source of gold in your organization.

Work Analysis Receptivity

How receptive will your organization be to your work analysis project? You need to answer three questions to have some idea of the likelihood of your success:

1. Does the organization exist in an environment that would be supportive of work analysis?
2. Are the characteristics of the organization itself supportive of work analysis?
3. Is the organization controlled by a work type that will embrace work analysis?

Taken together, these questions represent a context analysis, which should precede your work analysis project. (For more information on context analysis, see Chapter 17, this volume.) There are a number of potential combinations of answers to these questions, so it is important to ask yourself these questions and have a clear, honest answer before beginning your work analysis. To aid in your analysis, Figure 1.9 gives three examples and describes varying levels of work analysis receptivity.

Work Analysis Process

The way work analysis is carried out in an organization is a function of both the purpose of the analysis and the context in which the analysis will take place (see Figure 1.6). The relative importance of the planning, execution, and evaluation of work analysis is not just a function of why the information in being collected (e.g., work information collected to defend a contentious decision must meet the highest psychometric standards and be well documented) but the context where the information is collected and used (e.g., controllers will want more detail than enablers). You may put extra emphasis on the evaluation of the work analysis process in organizations that face highly competitive work environments where efficiency counts. You may need to take much more time carefully planning and selling work analysis in an organization that is predisposed to be less receptive to work analysis. Both purpose and context drive the work analysis process, so you ignore either at your peril. When purpose and context conflict or are not consistent in terms of their procedural implications, you need to present the issue to management for their decision. Use the inconsistency as an opportunity to educate management about the problems the conflict represents rather than trying to make the decision yourself and suffer the consequences. If you are asked to proceed in a context with low receptivity, you have at least predicted the possible problems and may have gained some credibility, if not success.

Work Analysis Outcomes

Just as procedure is affected by the context in which the process occurs, so are the outcomes of work analysis. The relative importance of various work analysis outcomes is also a function of both the purpose of the analysis and the context where the analysis takes place. Figure 1.10 presents work analysis outcomes organized into two general categories: acceptance and defensibility. Work analysis that is not embraced by the organization may still be useful (defensibility), but it is important

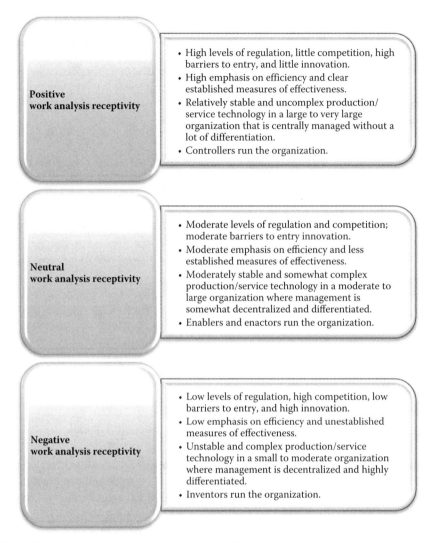

Positive
work analysis receptivity

- High levels of regulation, little competition, high barriers to entry, and little innovation.
- High emphasis on efficiency and clear established measures of effectiveness.
- Relatively stable and uncomplex production/service technology in a large to very large organization that is centrally managed without a lot of differentiation.
- Controllers run the organization.

Neutral
work analysis receptivity

- Moderate levels of regulation and competition; moderate barriers to entry innovation.
- Moderate emphasis on efficiency and less established measures of effectiveness.
- Moderately stable and somewhat complex production/service technology in a moderate to large organization where management is somewhat decentralized and differentiated.
- Enablers and enactors run the organization.

Negative
work analysis receptivity

- Low levels of regulation, high competition, low barriers to entry, and high innovation.
- Low emphasis on efficiency and unestablished measures of effectiveness.
- Unstable and complex production/service technology in a small to moderate organization where management is decentralized and highly differentiated.
- Inventors run the organization.

Figure 1.9 Positive, neutral, and negative work analysis receptivity.

to conduct work analysis in such a way that it is seen as integral and essential to the work or the organization.

For work analysis to be accepted by the organization, the results must be recognizable by the incumbents (face validity and detail-utility-flexibility), and they must be directly involved in the process that produced the results. Senior management must understand why the work analysis needs to be done and should provide the resources and support to carry it out. A work analysis that is properly sold to the organization (see Chapter 2, this volume) is more likely to be accepted.

From the standpoint of outcomes, a defensible work analysis has acceptable psychometrics and is up to date; it is as simple as that. The procedure used to collect the information needs to be well documented, but the essence of what will make the results defendable is the extent to which they are current, reliable, and valid. With modern information systems, there is no reason that work information cannot be constantly updated so that it is always current. However, most organizations tend to update work information in fits and starts, often after the realization that existing

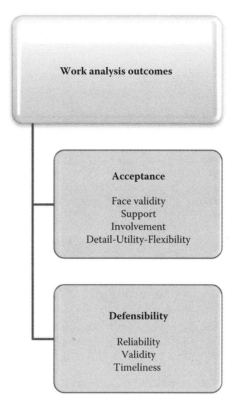

Figure 1.10   Major components of work analysis outcomes.

information is woefully out of date. One way to ensure currency is to integrate work analysis into the organizational change process—although this is often easier said than done. Another option is to monitor performance evaluation documents for work changes. Performance evaluation documents are often a leading indicator that the nature of a job is changing.

More is known about what to expect when examining the reliability of work analysis information (Dierdorff & Wilson, 2003) than about the validity of the same information (Wilson, 1997). Not everyone agrees that the psychometrics of work information is that important of a work analysis outcome (Sanchez & Levine, 2000). It is not easy to talk in terms of specific numbers when considering outcomes. However, if you have enough data to conduct a factor analysis of your work information, you should look for a higher-order solution that resembles data, people, and things. Two large-scale work analysis projects, the O*NET Generalized Work Activities Questionnaire (Jeanneret, Borman, Kubisiak, & Hanson, 1999) and the Common Metric Questionnaire (see Chapter 12, this volume) both reveal this three-factor higher-order structure. These may be the ultimate constructs that are the basis of all work analysis. If you recover them in your data, it is a sign that your efforts have construct validity.

CONCLUSIONS

This handbook represents the very best that the current wizards of work analysis have to offer. However, the theoretical information provided in this chapter is a departure from normal operating procedure for most work analysts. Like all unproven theories, it is a place to start. Theory has not had a large place to date in the history of work analysis, but perhaps it is time for that to change.

I offer my ideas out of a sincere desire to help others avoid mistakes that I have made conducting work analysis. I hope you have gained a better understanding of the decisions you have to make and the context in which you have to make them when doing work analysis.

REFERENCES

Biddle, B. J. (1979). *Role theory: Expectations, identities, and behavior.* New York, NY: Academic Press.

Biddle, B. J. (1986). Recent developments in role theory. *Annual Review of Sociology, 12,* 67–92.

Blader, S. L., & Tyler, T. R. (2003). A four-component model of procedural justice: Defining the meaning of a "fair" process. *Personality and Social Psychology Bulletin, 29*(6), 747–758.

Brannick, M. T., Levine, E. L., & Morgeson, F. P. (2007). *Job and work analysis.* Thousand Oaks, CA: Sage Publications.

Cunningham, J. W. (1971). *"Ergometrics": A systematic approach to some educational Problems.* Raleigh, NC: North Carolina State University, Center for Occupational Education.

Dierdorff, E. C., & Morgeson, F. P. (2007). Consensus in work role requirements: The influence of discrete occupational context on role expectations. *Journal of Applied Psychology, 92*(5), 1228–1241.

Dierdorff, E. C., & Wilson, M. A. (2003). A meta-analysis of job analysis reliability. *Journal of Applied Psychology, 88,* 635–646.

Gael, S. (1983). *Job analysis: A guide to assessing work activities.* San Francisco, CA: Jossey-Bass.

Gael, S. (1988). *The job analysis handbook for business, industry, and government.* New York, NY: John Wiley & Sons.

Graen, G. B. (1976). Role making processes within complex organizations. In M. D. Dunnette (Ed.), *Handbook of industrial and organizational psychology* (pp. 1201–1245). Chicago, IL: Rand McNally.

Harvey, R. J. (1991). Job analysis. In M. D. Dunnette & L. M. Hough (Eds.), *Handbook of industrial and organizational psychology* (2nd ed., pp. 71–164). Palo Alto, CA: Consulting Psychologist Press.

Ilgen, D. R., & Hollenbeck, J. R. (1991). The structure of work: Job design and roles. In M. D. Dunnette & L. M. Hough (Eds.), *Handbook of industrial and organizational psychology* (pp. 165–207). Palo Alto, CA: Consulting Psychologists Press.

Jeanneret, P. R., Borman, W. C., Kubisiak, U. C., & Hanson, M. A. (1999). Generalized work activities. In N. G. Peterson, M. D. Mumford, W. C. Borman, P. R. Jeanneret, & E. A. Fleishman (Eds.), *An occupational information system for the 21st century: The development of O*NET* (pp. 49–69). Washington, DC: American Psychological Association.

Kahn, R., Wolfe, D. M., Quinn, R. P., Snoek, J. D., & Rosenthal, R. A. (1964). *Organizational stress: Studies in role conflict and ambiguity.* New York, NY: John Wiley & Sons.

Katz, D., & Kahn, R. (1978). *The social psychology of organizations* (2nd ed.). New York, NY: John Wiley & Sons.

McCormick, E. J. (1979). *Job analysis: Methods and applications.* New York, NY: AMACOM.

Morgeson, F. P. (2007a). Job analysis. In S. G. Rogelberg (Ed.), *Encyclopedia of industrial/organizational psychology* (Vol. 1, pp. 377–380). Thousand Oaks, CA: Sage Publications.

Morgeson, F. P. (2007b). Job analysis methods. In S. G. Rogelberg (Ed.), *Encyclopedia of industrial/organizational psychology* (Vol. 1, pp. 380–383). Thousand Oaks, CA: Sage Publications.

Morgeson, F. P., & Campion, M. A. (1997). Social and cognitive sources of potential inaccuracy in job analysis. *Journal of Applied Psychology, 82,* 627–655.

Morgeson, F. P., & Dierdorff, E. C. (2011). Work analysis: From technique to theory. In S. Zedeck (Ed.), *APA handbook of industrial and organizational psychology* (Vol. 2, pp. 3–41). Washington, DC: American Psychological Association.

National Research Council. (1999). *The changing nature of work.* Washington, DC: National Academies Press.

Prien, E. P., Goodstein, L. D., Goodstein, J., & Gamble, L. G. (2009). *A practical guide to job analysis.* San Francisco, CA: Pfeiffer.

Sackett, P. R., & Laczo, R. M. (2003). Job and work analysis. In W. C. Borman, D. R. Ilgen, & R. J. Klimoski (Eds.), *Comprehensive handbook of psychology: Industrial and organizational psychology* (Vol. 12, pp. 21–37). New York, NY: Wiley.

Sanchez, J. I. (1994). From documentation to innovation: Reshaping job analysis to meet emerging business needs. *Human Resource Management Review, 4,* 51–74.

Sanchez, J. I., & Levine, E. L. (2000). Accuracy or consequential validity: Which is the better standard for job analysis data? *Journal of Organizational Behavior, 21,* 809–818.

Sanchez, J. I., & Levine, E. L. (2001). The analysis of work in the 20th and 21st centuries. In N. Anderson, D. S. Ones, H. K. Sinangil, & C. Viswesvaran (Eds.), *International handbook of work and organizational psychology* (pp. 71–89). Thousand Oaks, CA: Sage Publications.

Shippman, J. S. (1999). *Strategic job modeling: Working at the core of integrated human resources.* Mahwah, NJ: Lawrence Erlbaum Associates.

Society for Industrial and Organizational Psychology. (2003). Principles for the validation and use of personnel selection procedures (4th ed.). Bowling Green, OH: Author.

Weick, K. E. (1979). *The social psychology of organizing* (2nd ed.). Reading, MA: Addison-Wesley.

Wilson, M. A. (1997). The validity of task coverage ratings by incumbents and supervisors: Bad news. *Journal of Business and Psychology, 12,* 85–95.

Wilson, M. A. (2007). A history of job analysis. In L. L. Koppes (Ed.), *The science and practice of industrial and organizational psychology*. Mahway, NJ: Lawrence Erlbaum Associates.

2

Selling Work Analysis

Thomas Powell

GlaxoSmithKline

Mark Woodhouse

Kenexa

Nigel Guenole

Kenexa

Work analysis is the process of identifying what it is that workers do, the attributes of workers that enable them to do what they do, and the characteristics of the environment in which they do it (Sackett & Laczo, 2003). The work analysis process is fundamental to industrial and organizational (IO) psychology. Nearly every aspect of IO psychologists' work—be it academic or applied—involves either an implicit assumption or demonstrable empirical evidence that they know something about the roles they are selecting people to perform (or in the case of job incumbents, increasing workers' ability to perform the job). In applied settings, however, our experience suggests that businesses often make important work decisions on the basis of inadequate job information.

Although the process of work analysis in applied consulting contexts is often thorough and sophisticated, just as frequently it is informal, haphazard, and poorly documented. The reasons typically given by businesses for not undertaking thorough work analyses range widely. Sometimes, stakeholders without an IO psychology background have a perception that the work analysis process is too time consuming or too costly; they may believe that the output is not useful or is incomprehensible to laypeople. However, it is not just businesses that are reluctant to apply work analysis. To some psychologists, work analysis may be considered esoteric or unnecessary, particularly since the advent of the U.S. Department of Labor's Occupational Information Network (O*NET; Peterson, Mumford, Borman, Jeanneret, & Fleishman, 1998).

This situation is unfortunate and potentially costly to worker productivity and health. Without knowing what it is that workers are supposed to be doing, it is impossible to identify who the best person is for the job, or even to identify who is underperforming and who is performing well. Conducting a thorough job analysis and documenting the process well is also a scientific and objective approach to organizational decision making. These hallmarks of the scientist-practitioner approach to work psychology (Gelade, 2006) will make your personnel-related decisions accurate and defensible.

This chapter shares our consulting experiences and presents what has been effective (and what has not) in our work analysis engagements with business stakeholders. We discuss an approach to work analysis that we feel contributes to an effective work analysis consulting engagement and underscores the value of work analysis outputs to businesses. We hope that our experiences will enable applied psychologists to build a more compelling case for work analyses in their own consulting business and organizations, as work analysis is the platform for almost everything else we do.

We begin from a starting point that assumes the principle question in relation to the analysis of work and jobs—and one that should be answered in every consulting assignment—is not, "Should we do it?" Rather, you should determine what level of rigor is required to provide the basis for effective staffing decisions and organizational development initiatives. In the first section of this chapter, we outline what organizations are trying to achieve by conducting a job analysis. Here we argue that different end-user goals make certain work analysis methods more appropriate than others. We include a discussion of what information different types of customers of work analysis tend to find most compelling. Next, in the context of a case study, we describe how we designed and validated a leadership competency framework (i.e., a worker-oriented job analysis) in a Fortune 500 company. We present the stages we typically go through in a work analysis consulting assignment, how this varies depending on the nature of the role(s) being analyzed, and common mistakes to be avoided. Using the case study as an example, we argue that successfully "selling" work analysis to management requires an understanding, firmly rooted in contextual reality, of their information needs.

THE VALUE OF JOB ANALYSIS TO ORGANIZATIONS

The outputs of work analysis are used by different types of people for different purposes. Learning and organizational development professionals, for example, are often interested in commonalities in the way people go about doing their jobs. As a result, training needs can be addressed by organization-wide training initiatives, such as leadership development initiatives, which are often cost effective and get wide organizational exposure. Business unit managers, on the other hand, often note that their teams have a competitive advantage because of the differences in the exact nature of the work performed across different jobs. For example, in a highly technical role, it is likely that jobs tasks are characterized best by their distinctiveness from other roles in terms of what gets done, rather than their similarity to other jobs. Remuneration specialists are interested in exactly what it is that workers do so that the position can be adequately benchmarked. In these two cases, different approaches to work analysis are warranted.

The first critical task in a work analysis engagement, therefore, is to identify the reason for conducting the work analysis for the job(s) in question. Is the information going to be used in the development of a selection system or to help identify training requirements? There are many different reasons for conducting work analyses, and different purposes require different approaches. This first task will help the client begin to specify how the information about the work in question will be used. Often, management involved in the process has a general notion of the outcomes they are trying to achieve (e.g., "We want to ensure we have the right people for this role"), but they may be less clear about the specific human resource management processes and tools that can help them achieve those outcomes. In some cases, secondary issues may arise at this point, such as whether the work analysis is consistent with organizational objectives or how the work being analyzed is likely to change in the future. The inquiry and discussions resulting from this first critical task will help the client and the consulting team begin to think about the type of work analysis information they will need to meet the client's requirements.

Having established the reason behind the need for work analysis and whether the work analysis is an appropriate step, we usually present the client with two further questions about the type of information they feel would be most useful for their purposes. In personnel selection contexts for which an ideal role profile is required, this information is often a detailed description of the knowledge, skills, and abilities of the worker who can perform the work. On the other hand, when the work analysis output is going to be used to help inform a training needs assessment effort, it is often better to build a

Table 2.1   Common Approaches to Work Analysis

	Specific	Generalized
Task-oriented	Task performance criteria for work sample tests and personnel selection systems	Training needs analysis for job families that require a common skill base
Worker-oriented	Creation of ideal candidate profiles	Competency frameworks to apply across organizations

detailed description of what the worker does. The first approach is considered a worker-oriented analysis, whereas the second is a work-oriented approach. Deciding whether to use an attribute-focused approach or a task-focused approach is the second critical task in a work analysis engagement.

Finally, we ask whether the business is interested in work analytic information for a specific position or whether they intend the results to be applied across many roles in an organization. When highly technical roles are being performed by specialists, it is often necessary to make the work analysis highly specific. When designing competency models that are intended to apply broadly within an organization and across organizational levels, it is necessary to take a broader approach. Deciding on how specific or general the work analysis will be is the third critical task in a work analysis engagement.

By crossing the possible answers to the second and third tasks, we arrive at a two-by-two matrix representing the types of information that emerge from typical work analysis engagements, which sets the direction for the analyses carried out (see Table 2.1). This approach is similar to the model of job performance described by Ones and Viswesvaran (2004), who crossed dimensionality and specificity to arrive at different conceptions of job performance. Here, however, the description of the individual doing the work or the work that gets done is crossed with the degree of specificity to identify work analysis approaches most likely to meet client needs. Even though this matrix is by no means an exhaustive list of job analysis questions and approaches that might be used, based on our experiences it contains the elements of work analysis that end users find useful.

We now briefly consider the types of purposes that are typically served by work analysis engagements that are characteristic of each of the quadrants in Table 2.1. A work analysis engagement that focuses on what the worker does is shown in the upper left; it is intended to be highly specific. A typical reason for a work analysis employing this approach is the creation of work sample tests for job selection in highly technical positions. This analysis approach helps one to identify the likely predictors of performance for the position under scrutiny in an accurate and defensible manner, as well as produce accurate technical skill specifications for role profiles. Work analysis engagements that focus on the workers' knowledge, skills, and abilities are shown in the bottom right; the results are intended to generalize across multiple job families. In these situations, organizations are often interested in competency frameworks that are widely agreed to be worker-oriented work analyses. Large organizations usually have their own set of competencies, which are intended to generalize across jobs within the organization.

A wide variety of important questions dealing with how to go about the work analysis also must be answered, including the following:

- From whom the work information will be obtained (e.g., supervisor, colleague, incumbent)
- How the work information will be obtained (e.g., observation of incumbents, mailed surveys, web-based data collection)
- Whether the information will be gathered in a one-to-one format or by using focus groups
- How the information will be refined and distilled into the format expected by the end user

Each of these questions has different implications for both financial and time-related resources, as well as the quality of the information gained. It is even possible that after completing the critical tasks outlined previously, it will be decided that a resource such as O*net is sufficient and that no further work analysis is required. In our experience, the O*net content model is often appropriate for task-oriented work analyses for specific jobs. However, for worker-oriented analyses that generalize across jobs (e.g., competency models), businesses often want to have widespread consensus on the dimensions; they may feel that is important to embed organizational specific values into descriptions of workers' attributes. For a discussion of the most appropriate approaches and the relative advantages and disadvantages of each, the reader should refer to Chapters 1 and 3, this volume.

CASE STUDY

This case study illustrates the process used in an actual consulting engagement to convince management that work analysis was a required step for the successful design and implementation of a leadership competency model. The case occurred in the context of a broad organizational and leadership development initiative in a global organization with more than 10,000 managers for its approximately 100,000 employees. The leaders and managers of this company worked in several major functional areas including corporate functions, manufacturing and supply, sales and marketing, and research and development. Additionally, the leaders and employees worked in several geographic regions including Europe, Japan/Asia Pacific, Latin America, and North America.

The company grew over several years, mainly as a result of mergers and acquisitions. The combination of growth and a culture of relatively autonomous regional and functional business units resulted in a wide range of behavioral and performance expectations for the company's leaders. Our consultation began following an expressed desire by the leadership and organizational development department in the company to have a single leadership competency model.

At the time of the project initiation, there were many leadership models in place across the company. The models were brought forward from heritage companies (i.e., a leadership model from an acquired company) or put in place for a single major business unit (e.g., a leadership model created for first-line sales leaders in the European business unit). Across the company, the models were used for a variety of purposes, including selection (behaviorally based interviews), performance appraisal, multisource feedback, and leadership development programs.

A challenge that the company faced with the use of multiple models was the complexity and duplication in the design of human resource management tools and processes. For example, at the time of the consulting engagement, there were more than 100 leadership development programs in use across the company. In addition to the obvious cost and complexity of developing and maintaining such a large number of redundant or overlapping programs, there was a hidden cost for the end users. Leaders in the company found it difficult to be clear about their performance expectations and expressed frustration with the challenge of navigating a wide array of leadership development offerings. The result was a strong felt need on the part of the leadership and organizational development community and line leaders for the company to endorse a single leadership model across the company. The challenge for the consulting team was to ensure that the new model was developed using an appropriate work analysis approach.

In the fast-paced and action-oriented environment in the company, there was a risk that once the problem was identified (i.e., too many leadership models) an expedient solution (e.g., choosing the best of the existing models or buying an off-the-shelf leadership competency model) might be a very attractive approach for senior decision makers. Given the importance of leadership effectiveness to overall company performance, it was critical that the resulting competency model be based on a work analysis approach that would appropriately identify the information the organization needed to understand and improve leader performance. To persuade decision makers that a legitimate work analysis approach should form the foundation for the development of the new leadership model, the consultants would need to convince key business stakeholders of the value and practicality of the approach and resulting information.

We began the consulting engagement with pre-entry preparation. Our goal was to identify and understand the key people and political situations that might have a bearing on the work analysis effort. Additionally, we sought to better understand the perspectives, expectations, and other aspects likely to influence the people who would be key to the decision-making process. Because our work was initiated in response to a request from the leadership and organizational development function in the company, the senior leaders of this function, as well as the senior leaders of their customer groups (i.e., business units), were people key to the successful design and implementation of this effort.

Our early conversations with senior leaders of the various business units revealed that they had a vested interest in the quality of their leaders and therefore in the quality of the leader model that would serve as a foundation for future leadership development. Understanding this motivation served us well as the project progressed. Specifically, the business unit leaders had a desire to ensure that the new model was appropriate for their business units. They were concerned that a corporately imposed "generic" competency model would not fit their (perceived) unique business unit. This concern helped us to make an argument for talking with, observing, and generally gathering data about the leadership roles in the various businesses. In essence, we had implicit support for a work analysis approach.

In addition to uncovering the business unit leaders' desire for a leadership model that was robust enough to apply to their specific business units, we discovered that there was widespread belief that the company's leaders were critical to overall company performance. This was reflected across a wide variety of processes and programs aimed at improving individuals' leadership capability and the leadership capability of the company. This view was supported by results from internal employee surveys that showed a strong relationship between leader performance and organizational/workgroup performance. There was also evidence from various assessment programs across the company, as well as from external research, that there were areas of leadership where high-performing leaders typically excelled. Because this was a scientifically oriented organization, we discovered an appetite for a research-based approach to determining the requirements of the leaders' role.

At this point in the process, we now felt we had sufficient support to propose an approach in which we would use a research-based leadership model (Cockerill, 1989) as a starting point, then refine it using a work analysis approach to fit this specific situation and organization. Now that we had sufficient support for doing work analysis, our next line of inquiry was intended to determine what kind of information would be useful for the client and subsequently what work analytic approach would be most appropriate.

We began by seeking additional information relevant to our first critical questions: What is the client's primary goal? Why do they want to identify and understand what leaders across the company do? With the learning and organizational development group functioning as our primary client, we established that the overarching goal was to understand the commonalities in leadership roles across the company. The group believed they could use that understanding to design and implement development initiatives that would improve leadership capability. By understanding the commonalities in leadership roles across the company, the learning and organizational development group would be in a better position to create organization-wide leadership development initiatives and promote consistent performance expectations for leaders. An immediate benefit would be an objective basis for reducing the more than 100 leadership development offerings to a more reasonable and less costly number of programs.

A secondary goal of the effort was to provide a basis for updating other human resource management processes that relied on leadership competencies. A specific example was the process used to provide leaders with multisource feedback for development purposes. As was the case with leadership development offerings, there were many multisource instruments available to leaders, which were based on many different leadership models. It was envisioned that information from the new leadership model would be used to develop a multisource feedback instrument based on common behavioral expectations of leaders, regardless of where they worked in the organization. Although there were many other potential uses for the output of this work analysis effort, it was clear that the primary reason for conducting the work analysis would be to describe the common behaviors and competencies required of leaders across the company.

After establishing the primary purpose for our work analysis, we next inquired into the kind of information that would be most useful for achieving the client's goals. It was clear that there would be very different functionally specific performance expectations across the various leadership roles. For example, one role might be a project leader in research and development, whereas another might be a leader on a packaging line. The kind of information that would be applicable across the majority of leadership positions and therefore useful in human resource management applications across the organization would be general worker-oriented information. This provided further evidence that the client's needs would be well served by information that described the most important competencies and behaviors across the company's leaders. A final area of inquiry, before we developed a proposed approach to conducting the work analysis, involved the level of specificity that would be most interesting and useful to the client. It was obvious from our discussions that key stakeholders intended the results to be applied to many leadership roles across the company. To design a competency model intended to apply broadly within the organization, it would be necessary to be broad in our approach.

The inquiry process described here provided information that set direction for the work analysis project proposed to the client. It also provided a foundation for speaking to key stakeholders about the work using compelling language—that is, language that persuaded them to support and provide funds for work analysis activities in their business units. Specifically, our proposal and subsequent meetings and discussions about the proposed work analysis process used language that clearly showed to the client that the work analysis effort, far from being an esoteric exercise conducted for the benefit of IO psychologists, would provide them with the right information at the right level of specificity for accomplishing their stated goals.

This case describes a situation where work analysis was one of several options available to help the organization achieve a goal of defining a competency model for its leader population. Other options available to the decision makers (e.g., off-the-shelf model, competency model by executive decree) would likely have been initially less expensive and surely faster to put in place. Although our training and experience as IO psychologists convinces us that work analysis is foundational to any application that requires an accurate understanding of a job or role, the same cannot be said of many senior decision makers. For a number of reasons, senior leaders often make important personnel decisions, such as who to put in roles or how to develop people for a role, on the basis of inadequate job information. For example, in the company where this case took place, one of the primary leadership models in use throughout the company had been created in a short workshop exercise with senior executives. The details of the model (i.e., specific leader behaviors and expectations) were refined or filled in later by human resources professionals. Although the process was engaging and interactive for the senior executives involved, it was not a work analysis process with sufficient rigor to support the many processes to which it was later applied (e.g., selection, performance appraisal, multisource assessment).

SUMMARY

To guide senior leaders' decisions in the case study presented in this chapter, we created a compelling argument that had key stakeholder needs as its starting point. The success of the approach we used to convince key stakeholders and decision makers to conduct a work analysis was based less on our expert opinion of the inherent value of work analysis and more on our efforts to understand the goals and requirements of key stakeholders. By developing an understanding of the contextual realities in which the request came to us and by seeking to clarify the client's explicit and implicit needs using the three critical tasks presented in this chapter, we were able to create a proposal and a way of talking about work analysis that fit the client's language and needs. In doing so, we shaped the discussion and the subsequent decision-making process so that it was focused on business requirements and operational plans to meet those requirements.[1]

REFERENCES

Cockerill, T. (1989). *Managerial competence as a determinant of organizational performance.* Unpublished doctoral dissertation. London Business School, London, England.

Gelade, G. A. (2006). But what does it mean in practice? The Journal of Occupational and Organizational Psychology from a practitioner perspective. *Journal of Occupational and Organizational Psychology, 79,* 153–160.

Peterson, N. G., Mumford, M. D., Borman, W. C., Jeanneret, P. R., & Fleishman, E. A. (1998). *The Occupational Information Network (O*NET).* Washington, DC: American Psychological Association.

Sackett, P. R., & Laczo, R. M. (2003). Job and work analysis. In W. C. Borman, D. R. Ilgen, & R. J. Klimoski (Eds.), *Comprehensive handbook of psychology, Vol. 12: Industrial and organizational psychology* (pp. 21–38). New York, NY: John Wiley & Sons.

Viswesvaran, C., & Ones, D. S. (2004). Perspectives on models of job performance. *International Journal of Selection and Assessment, 8,* 216–226.

---

[1] The views expressed herein are the authors' and do not necessarily reflect the views of any other person or organization.

3

Identifying Appropriate Sources of Work Information

Emily Johnson Guder

Federal Management Partners

Just as there is no one best method for analyzing work (Society for Industrial and Organizational Psychology, 2003), there is no single best source of work information. Rather, the appropriateness of any one source is largely determined by the nature of the work to be analyzed and the purpose of the analysis. Across situations, however, it is likely that more sources will mean more perspectives and, as a result, a more complete picture of the work. This chapter is designed to highlight important considerations that surround what has been deemed one of the most critical decisions in the process of analyzing work (Harvey, 1991): the identification of sources of work information. The following sections discuss the traditional sources of work information (e.g., job incumbents, supervisors, work analysts), as well some sources that have only recently begun to receive attention in the work analysis literature (e.g., other organizational members, customers). Table 3.1 summarizes the key points of this discussion.

JOB INCUMBENTS

Job incumbents are probably the most frequently used sources of work information—and with good reason. Because incumbents are directly involved with the work on a day-to-day basis, they can provide a description of the job tasks and activities as they are currently performed. Of the sources discussed in this chapter, incumbents would be expected to have the most direct and personal relationship with the work. Compared with some other (nonincumbent) sources who are able to share unique perspectives and opinions regarding what or how work *should* be done, incumbents' direct relationship with the work means they will often possess the most accurate and complete knowledge of the work itself, as it is *actually* performed. This is especially true when work is unobservable, as in the case of knowledge work. In these cases, nonincumbent observers, such as job analysts or external clients, may have a difficult time understanding and making judgments about work tasks or activities.

Sanchez (2000) asserted that there are some situations for which incumbent and nonincumbent sources will provide very similar work information, such as when jobs are not data complex, when the work analysis is designed to collect high-level (rather than specific) information, and when other knowledgeable sources (e.g., trained analysts) are available. In these cases, there may be little appreciable benefit to including incumbents as sources, at least in terms of the quality of information collected. However, even in these cases, soliciting information from incumbent sources may still be worthwhile. When incumbents believe that they had a voice in

Table 3.1 Summary of Sources of Work Information

Source	Types of Information	When to Use	Other Considerations
Incumbents	Information about work tasks and activities, as they are currently performed	Whenever available, especially when the following are true: • Work is complex, knowledge-based, or otherwise difficult to observe. • Other qualified sources are not available. • When there may be user-acceptance issues associated with not involving incumbents.	When selecting participants: 1. Include incumbents with varied experience levels (although minimum tenure requirements may be appropriate). 2. Opt for use of sampling procedures rather than supervisor nominations. 3. Do not focus exclusively on the top performers or most satisfied employees. Incumbents may overstate the abilities or competencies required to perform the work, especially when there is a perception that doing so will be personally beneficial.
Supervisors	KSAO information Perspectives on how work *should* be performed	When supervisors directly observe the work When incumbent sources are not feasible (e.g., due to low verbal ability or high turnover) When there may be user-acceptance issues associated with not involving supervisors	Although less of a concern than with incumbents, supervisors may be motivated to inflate ratings.
Trained work analysts	KSAO information, including trainability Work context information	When more abstract judgments are needed When other sources may be motivated to provide inaccurate information When other sources' time is at a premium	Work analysts must familiarize themselves with the work, which often requires extensive observations and interviews and can be costly.
Other organizational members	Information about the interactions with other units required to perform the work Information about how the work fits into larger work processes	When interactions with other units is an important facet of work performance When other units come in direct contact with some aspect or product of the work When units work interdependently	
External customers or clients	Perspectives on how or what work *should* be performed	When work is customer-focused When customers come in contact with some aspect or product of the work	

KSAO = knowledge, skills, abilities, and other characteristics.

the work analysis process, they may be more likely to accept subsequent changes that occur as a result of the analysis.

Assuming that nearly every job analysis will require at least some consultation with the individuals who currently perform the job, the question quickly becomes, "Which incumbents should be consulted?" In jobs for which the total number of incumbents is very small, including all incumbents may be appropriate. On the other hand, it will often be the case that including every incumbent is impractical and unnecessary. In these cases, some sort of sampling procedure will be required.

One solution might be to allow supervisors to nominate incumbents for participation in work analysis, although research indicates that this may be unwise. Such a procedure will probably not produce a sample that is representative of the entire incumbent population. By excluding subsets of the population from the analysis, the information generated may be incomplete or otherwise inaccurate. Some researchers have pointed out that samples selected by supervisors may include disproportionate numbers of individuals who have especially positive beliefs or feelings about the work (Conte, Dean, Ringenbach, Moran, & Landy, 2005; Sanchez, Zamora, & Viswesvaran, 1997). This is problematic because work attitudes have the potential to influence work analysis information (Landy, 2003). For example, incumbents who are satisfied with their jobs may be more likely than those who are dissatisfied to view (and therefore rate) their job as being important (Morgeson & Campion, 1997). In a study conducted by Conte et al. (2005), incumbent's satisfaction, commitment, and job involvement were all found to be positively related to ratings of task importance and the frequency with which the tasks were performed. It seems that there is good reason to suspect that when supervisors are allowed to hand-pick incumbents for participation, the resulting work information will be substantially different than what would have been generated from a randomly selected incumbent sample.

Another potential pitfall involved in identifying incumbent sources of information involves focusing exclusively on those workers who have considerable experience with the work in question. Although the logic that people who have done the job the longest will also know the job the best is certainly intuitively appealing, the reality is often more complicated. To illustrate, Landy and Vasey (1991) found that the activities that experienced police officers reported spending the majority of their time performing were not the same activities that less experienced officers reported spending time on. More experienced officers tended to focus more on noncriminal interventions, court-related activities, and first aid, whereas less experienced officers reported being more involved in basic criminal interventions, sweeps and raids, and traffic activities. In some jobs, it may be that workers with more experience are afforded more discretion regarding what tasks they choose focus on, whereas less experienced workers are left to do the less desirable tasks. In fact, Landy and Vasey suggested that this seniority effect is a likely cause of the observed differences in information provided by the police officers in their study. It is also possible to imagine cases where different expectations exist for employees with different levels of experience or where different activities are required to be successful. As an example, Borman, Dorsy, and Ackerman (1992) pointed out that it is reasonable to expect that a less experienced salesperson's time is best spent building a client base, whereas a more experienced salesperson might devote considerable time to maintaining existing relationships. In other cases, it may be that certain aspects of the work require skills or knowledge that are developed through experience and, as such, these tasks are more likely to be performed by the more experienced workers.

The bottom line is that when information about the job comes only from highly experienced incumbents, the result will be a description of the work activities performed by those incumbents. Are their activities the same as those of less experienced workers? In some cases, the answer will be yes; in others, they probably are not the same. In any particular situation, the only way to know for certain would be to involve incumbents with varying levels of ability in the sample, using the range of tenure in the entire incumbent population as a guide.

One caveat regarding incumbent experience is that, in many situations, it is probably a good idea to set some minimum tenure requirement for participation. The idea here is that all participants should have at least enough time on the job that they can be expected to be familiar with all the various tasks and requirements involved in the work. A minimum of 6 months of experience has been suggested as a general rule (Gatewood & Feild, 1994; Harvey, Anderson, Baranowski, & Morath, 2007), although this will certainly vary from job to job. If the organization specifies a probationary period for newly hired employees, this period might be used as a guide for setting the tenure requirement. There may also be situations in which it would be advisable to set a maximum tenure requirement, particularly if the work analysis is geared towards assessing the activities of newer employees and there is reason to expect that the most senior employees will not be able to provide this information (Gatewood & Feild, 1994).

Another common mistake related to selecting incumbents to provide input is the decision to involve only those incumbents who have earned the highest performance appraisal ratings. Although it is not unreasonable to expect the top performing incumbents possess the most complete knowledge of the work, Sanchez (2000) cautioned that procedural knowledge and declarative knowledge are two separate constructs. Just because an individual can perform a job exceptionally well does not mean he or she will be able to describe the work with the same level of expertise. In addition, when the intention of the work analysis is to determine what is required of the worker for adequate performance, collecting information solely from top performers risks overstating the requirements of a job which would, in turn, affect human resource practices based on the results of the analysis (e.g., Conte et al., 2005; Morgeson & Campion, 1997). Moreover, if the work analysis information that the performance appraisal tool is based on is not up to date, using performance ratings to select incumbent information sources might be a bit like putting the cart before the horse.

In most work analysis studies, the ideal sampling strategy will be some form of stratified random sampling in which incumbents are classified according to important variables and then sampled randomly from within those classifications. Among the variables that should be considered are tenure (as discussed previously), gender, and ethnicity (Gatewood & Feild, 1994), as well as potential differences among the incumbent population with regard to geography, work shift, technology, and equipment (Peterson & Jeanneret, 2007). When females or ethnic minorities make up only a small portion of the total incumbent population, it may be necessary to overrepresent them in the sample, which ensures that their views are adequately reflected in the information collected (Gatewood & Feild; Goldstein, Zedeck, & Schneider, 1993).

Although incumbents' direct experience with the day-to-day work makes them excellent sources of task information, the same may not be true when it comes to information about worker requirements (i.e., the knowledge, skills, abilities, and other characteristics [KSAOs] required to perform the work). Providing information about the human attributes needed to perform work successfully, in comparison to describing the tasks or activities that one performs at work, requires one to make more abstract inferences and judgments (Harvey, 1991; Morgeson & Campion, 2000). When these judgments are made by incumbents, there is reason to believe worker requirements might be overestimated. One theory is that incumbents asked to rate the ability requirements of their jobs may instead rate themselves, and these self-ratings can be influenced by a desire to paint oneself in a positive light (Morgeson, Delaney-Klinger, Mayfield, Ferrara, & Campion, 2004). Self-presentation, or impression management, occurs in the work context when individuals are motivated to present information (truthful or otherwise) about themselves in order to further their own personal goals. These goals include protecting oneself against being fired or receiving a pay cut, increasing one's salary, and advancing one's career (Baumeister, 1989). Because information about ability requirements cannot be verified in the same way that work task information can be (e.g., through direct observation), it is thought to be more vulnerable to inflation due to self-presentation motives (Morgeson & Campion, 1997).

A study conducted by Morgeson et al. (2004) offers some initial support for the hypothesis that incumbents' ratings of abilities are more vulnerable to inflation than are task statements. The authors found that, although not true of task ratings, incumbents tended to identify abilities that were actually nonessential to their jobs, perhaps because abilities can often be read as socially desirable qualities, whereas statements about tasks tend to be more socially neutral. Employees wishing to present themselves in a positive light may be able to do so by reporting that their work requires a wide range of abilities. On the other hand, endorsing tasks or activities that are not relevant may be judged as doing very little to further this goal and, in fact, could be deemed counterproductive if the employee believes that this information can be verified. The results of the Morgeson study are especially noteworthy because the incumbents in that sample believed they were providing work analysis information as part of a human resources initiative that would not impact them directly; thus, self-presentation would do little to further their personal goals.

Ability ratings are likely to be most inflated when the incumbent perceives some benefit to making a good impression, such as when information is being collected to determine compensation or when there is a perceived threat of downsizing (Morgeson & Campion, 1997). In these situations, the inflation effect may be considerably more pronounced than what was observed in the study. When considering whether incumbents might be an appropriate source of ability ratings or similar information, careful consideration should be given to organizational culture and other factors that might influence these ratings.

SUPERVISORS

Another traditional source of work information is the incumbent's immediate supervisor. Supervisors may be preferred to incumbents as information sources in situations for which incumbents might lack the verbal ability required to accurately describe their work or the rate of incumbent turnover is very high. Supervisors who directly observe the work being analyzed can be a valuable source of information about the KSAOs required for the incumbent to perform the work successfully (Gatewood & Feild, 1994; Goldstein, Zedeck, & Schneider, 1993). Because supervisors typically have observed a number of individuals performing the work, they may have insight regarding the KSAOs that enable some incumbents to perform the work effectively, whereas others are less successful. Compared to KSAO information generated by incumbents, information provided by supervisors should be less likely to be affected by self-presentation processes than information provided by incumbents (Morgeson & Campion, 1997; Morgeson et al., 2004). Of course, because supervisors, like incumbents, stand to be affected by the results of the work analysis, they may provide inaccurate information when they perceive there to be a personally beneficial reason to do so. In most cases, however, supervisors would not be expected to have the same motivation to inflate ratings that incumbents might have and therefore can be a very useful source of work information.

Unfortunately, collecting work information from supervisors may be a considerable burden for the organization because supervisors' time may come at considerable cost. As a result, supervisors are often involved in the work analysis process after information has been collected from incumbents and other sources, serving primarily to verify the completeness and relevance of the information. When work is not complex and when incumbents and supervisors work very closely together, there is some evidence that the two sources will provide largely redundant information;

therefore, it may not be necessary to include supervisors in the analysis (Manson, Levine, & Brannick, 2000). Even in these cases, however, there may be value in including both sources. For instance, the inclusion of both groups may bolster the face validity and acceptance of the work analysis products.

Like incumbents, supervisors who are very new to the organization will probably not be able to provide much useful information. A minimum tenure requirement, generally 6 months on the job, may be useful (Gatewood & Feild, 1994; Harvey et al., 2007). Of course, even experienced supervisors may not be able to accurately judge all aspects of the incumbent's work. A supervisor should only be asked to provide information about aspects of the work for which he or she could be expected to be reasonably familiar. Among the situations in which one would want to be especially careful collecting information from supervisors are those in which spans of control are very large, the work is very complex, the majority of work activities are unobservable, or considerable change is taking place. In addition, supervisors who have no direct experience with the work may be able to provide very limited information.

Finally, some scholars have pointed out that a supervisor's perspective regarding the work of incumbents may be more be more characteristic of how the work should be performed, rather the tasks and activities that incumbents actually do perform (e.g., Gatewood & Feild, 1994). Therefore, information collected from supervisors tends to be most useful when it is collected to supplement information from other sources, rather than as an exclusive source of work information.

TRAINED WORK ANALYSTS

Of the sources discussed so far, trained work analysts are well suited to provide objective and valid work information through their education, experience, and outsider status. Trained analysts are typically familiar with the language of work analysis instruments and the process of rating various aspects of work, both of which may be entirely foreign to other sources. Particularly when it comes to judging the KSAOs required to perform tasks (Baranowski & Anderson, 2005), the difficulty of learning those KSAOs (Jones et al., 2001), and other judgments of more abstract items, trained analysts' familiarity and experience with these types of tasks can be a significant advantage over incumbent or supervisor sources.

Another situation in which it is useful to enlist trained analysts is when information about the context in which work is performed is to be included in the analysis. Organizational members often become used to their work environment over time or may lack the experience in other environments against which to compare their current situation. Professional analysts, on the other hand, will typically be familiar with a wide range of working conditions and can likely draw much more accurate conclusions about the demands of a particular work context. For example, Sanchez and Levine (1999) recounted the story of an analyst who asked incumbents about the level of noise they typically experienced when working in the engine room of a cruise ship. The incumbents reported that the noise was not loud, but the analyst's visit to the work location produced an entirely different conclusion. Although the noise may not have seemed excessive to incumbents who had grown accustomed to it, either through their experiences on that ship or through their experiences in similar work environments, the work analyst could compare the engine room environment to a much wider array of workplace environments and determine that the working conditions in the engine room were indeed extreme.

Although incumbents and some supervisors may be motivated to provide inflated ratings on items pertaining to socially desirable tasks or KSAOs, work analysts are highly unlikely to be affected by this source of inaccuracy (Morgeson & Campion, 1997). For example, Smith and Hakel

(1979) found that incumbents' and supervisors' ratings were significantly higher than analysts' ratings of socially desirable items on a structured job analysis questionnaire (i.e., the Positional Analysis Questionnaire; McCormick, Jeanneret, & Meacham, 1972).

Because providing accurate work information is a central aspect of the analysts' job, they should be more motivated to take the task seriously than other sources, who are asked to take time away from their primary assignment to participate in the analysis. By hiring trained analysts, an organization is "purchasing the services of skilled individuals to perform their jobs" (Gatewood & Feild, 1994, p. 311). This can be especially advantageous when instruments that are extremely long or tedious are being used, as well as in other situations for which alternate sources might lack sufficient motivation to give the work analysis procedures their full attention. The use of trained analysts in lieu of incumbents or supervisors to complete some of the more time-consuming work analysis tasks can also help ensure that the production losses associated with taking organizational members away from their work is minimal.

Although trained analysts have the beneficial qualities of being familiar with work analysis methods and instruments and they are less vulnerable to various biases that might affect organizational members, their outsider status means that their initial knowledge of the work will be severely limited. As a result, for analysts to be effective as a source of work information, they must first familiarize themselves with the work to be the analyzed. In most cases, this will mean considerable time spent conducting interviews and observations and, as a result, considerable cost and burden for the organization. However, prevailing research suggests that these costs are worthy ones. Analysts' familiarity with the work seems to be related to the accuracy of work information provided (Harvey & Lozada-Larsen, 1988). If an analyst has insufficient information about the work, he or she may be prone to making inaccurate ratings based on stereotypes or irrelevant information, perhaps influenced by past analyses of seemingly similar work (Harvey, 1991; Morgeson & Campion, 1997).

OTHER ORGANIZATIONAL MEMBERS

In many organizations, work is becoming increasingly boundaryless (Ashkenas, Ulrich, Jick, & Kerr, 1995), with increasing crossfunctional coordination of activities. Although the majority of an employee's work activities might have once been performed in relative isolation, many assignments now blur the boundaries between different employees' jobs, requiring substantial interaction and cooperation with members of other teams or divisions (Sanchez & Levine, 1999). In these cases, the work activities of one unit have direct impact on the activities of other organizational units. To ensure that information about work processes is not deficient, members of these units should certainly be involved in the analysis. Moreover, it may be the case that these interactions themselves constitute essential work activities with their own requisite KSAOs.

Although organizational members beyond incumbents and supervisors have yet to receive considerable attention as sources of work information, this is likely to change in the future. Sanchez and Levine (1999) made the point that the traditional use of incumbents and supervisors as the only sources of work information comes from organizational structures where incumbents were accountable only to their supervisor and had limited interaction with other parties. As approaches to work analysis adapt to reflect changes in the nature of work (e.g., increased employee empowerment and accountability to parties other than one's immediate supervisor), information sources will increasingly include individuals from throughout the organization. Brannick and Levine (2002) similarly noted that, in organizations where work is highly interconnected, members of other units provide valuable information about how the work being analyzed fits into the larger organizational context.

One approach to ensuring that all relevant sources of information are included is what Sanchez and Levine (2001) referred to as a *360-degree approach*. In this approach, once all major job functions have been identified, the recipients of those functions are identified as additional sources of work information. These recipients may include not only individuals within the organization, but also external customers or clients, who are discussed in the following section.

CUSTOMERS

Like other organizational members, customers represent another source of work information that has received relatively little attention but will likely be seeing much more in the future. As the ones ultimately impacted by the work, customers should be able to provide unique perspective on how work should be done, which aspects are critical, which are not, and the like. Moreover, because they stand to directly benefit from any improvements resulting from the analysis, they may be especially motivated to provide accurate and useful information. Particularly when the goals of the work analysis include establishing standards for performance or identifying tasks that should be performed by the worker but are not, end users may provide valuable insight (Brannick & Levine, 2002).

The unique perspective sometimes held by customers is illustrated by a study in which information about the work involved in writing police reports was collected from two sources: police personnel, who are responsible for report writing, and district attorneys, who are the end users of police reports. The researchers found that although police reported that both grammar and content are important aspects of report writing, district attorneys rated the importance of grammar to be much lower (Truxillo, Paronto, Collins, & Sulzer, 2004). In a situation such as this one, ignoring the end-user perspective could result in training or performance interventions centered around aspects of the work that have very little impact on those who ultimately use the work products. Supplementing information collected from other sources with client or customer perspectives may provide a clearer picture of the essential and nonessential aspects of the work.

In the retail and service industries, mystery shoppers may be employed to provide information on the activities and behaviors of employees. The use of focus groups may also be a practical way to solicit customer input. Although Sanchez and Levine (1999) aptly noted that focus groups can be problematic because group dynamics may sometimes produce inaccurate information, focus groups may be a useful way to involve sources who may not have been involved otherwise. For instance, community groups have been used to inform the analysis of police work (Brannick & Levine, 2002).

Of course, the customer perspective is a limited one. Customers will only be able to speak to the aspects of the work that directly affect them. For example, a client might be able to identify the characteristics of the work product that ensure its utility, but may be less clear as to how such a product is created. Thus, customers and clients should only be asked to provide information regarding aspects of the work about which they would have sufficient knowledge.

CONCLUSIONS

In recent decades, a shift has occurred in the way work is organized, from the jobs and rigidly defined collections of responsibilities to constantly changing assignments that blur boundaries between jobs and organizational units (Sanchez & Levine, 1999, 2001). These changes mean that, more than ever before, gathering work information from many unique perspectives is critical to developing a complete understanding the work. This chapter is intended to serve as a starting point for determining which sources are relevant for a given work situation, as well as the considerations that come along with the various sources.

REFERENCES

Ashkenas, R., Ulrich, D., Jick, T., & Kerr, S. (1995). *The boundaryless organization: Breaking the chains of organizational structure.* San Francisco, CA: Jossey-Bass.

Baranowski, L. E., & Anderson, L. E. (2005). Examining rating source variation in work behavior to KSA linkages. *Personnel Psychology, 58,* 1041–1054.

Baumeister, R. F. (1989). Motives and costs of self-presentation in organizations. In R. A. Giacalone & P. Rosenfeld (Eds.), *Impression management in the organization* (pp. 57–70). Hillsdale, NJ: Lawrence Erlbaum Associates.

Borman, W. C., Dorsy, D., & Ackerman, L. (1992). Time-spent responses as time allocation strategies: Relations with sales performance in a stockbroker sample. *Personnel Psychology, 45,* 763–777.

Brannick, M. T., & Levine, E. L. (2002). *Job analysis: Methods, research, and applications for human resource management in the new millennium.* Thousand Oaks, CA: Sage Publications.

Conte, J. M., Dean, M. A., Ringenbach, K. L., Moran, S. K., & Landy, F. J. (2005). The relationship between work attitudes and job analysis ratings: Do rating scale type and task discretion matter? *Human Performance, 18,* 1–21.

Gatewood, R. D., & Feild, H. S. (1994). *Human resource selection* (3rd ed.). Fort Worth, TX: Dryden Press.

Goldstein, I. L., Zedeck, S., & Schneider, B. (1993). An exploration of the job analysis-content validity process. In N. Schmitt & W. C. Borman (Eds.), *Personnel selection in organizations* (pp. 3–34). San Francisco, CA: Jossey-Bass.

Harvey, J. L., Anderson, L. E., Baranowski, L. E., & Morath, R. A. (2007). Job analysis: Gathering job-specific information. In D. L. Whetzel & G. R. Wheaton (Eds.), *Applied measurement: Industrial psychology in human resources management* (pp. 57–95). Mahwah, NJ: Lawrence Erlbaum Associates.

Harvey, R. J. (1991). Job analysis. In M. D. Dunnette & L. M. Hough (Eds.), *Handbook of industrial and organizational psychology* (2nd ed., Vol. 2, pp. 71–163). Palo Alto, CA: Consulting Psychologists Press.

Harvey, R. J., & Lozada-Larsen, S. R. (1988). Influence of amount of job descriptive information on job analysis rating accuracy. *Journal of Applied Psychology, 73,* 457–461.

Jones, R. G., Sanchez, J. I., Parameswaran, G., Phelps, J., Shoptaugh, C., Williams, M., & White, S. (2001). Selection or training? A two-fold test of the validity of job-analytic ratings of trainability. *Journal of Business and Psychology, 15,* 363–389.

Landy, F. J. (2003). Job analysis and job evaluation: The respondent's perspective. In H. Schuler, J. L. Farr, & M. Smith (Eds.), *Personnel selection and assessment: Individual and organizational perspectives* (pp. 75–90). Hillsdale, NJ: Lawrence Erlbaum Associates.

Landy, F. J., & Vasey, J. (1991). Job analysis: The composition of SME samples. *Personnel Psychology, 44,* 27–50.

Manson, T. M., Levine, E. L., & Brannick, M. T. (2000). The construct validity of task inventory ratings: A multitrait-multimethod analysis. *Human Performance, 13,* 1–22.

McCormick, E. J., Jeanneret, P. R., & Meacham, R. C. (1972). A study of job dimensions based on the Position Analysis Questionnaire. *Journal of Applied Psychology, 79,* 347–368.

Morgeson, F. P., & Campion, M. A. (1997). Social and cognitive sources of potential inaccuracy in job analysis. *Journal of Applied Psychology, 82,* 627–655.

Morgeson, F. P., & Campion, M. A. (2000). Accuracy in job analysis: Toward an inference-based model. *Journal of Organizational Behavior, 21,* 819–827.

Morgeson, F. P., Delaney-Klinger, K., Mayfield, M. S., Ferrara, P., & Campion, M. A. (2004). Self-presentation processes in job analysis: A field experiment investigating inflation in abilities, tasks, competencies. *Journal of Applied Psychology, 89,* 674–686.

Peterson, N. G., & Jeanneret, P. R. (2007). Job analysis: Overview and description of deductive methods. In D. L. Whetzel & G. R. Wheaton (Eds.), *Applied measurement: Industrial psychology in human resources management* (pp. 13–56). Mahwah, NJ: Lawrence Erlbaum Associates.

Sanchez, J. I. (2000). Adapting work analysis to a fast-paced and electronic business world. *International Journal of Selection and Assessment, 8,* 207–215.

Sanchez, J. I., & Levine, E. L. (1999). Is job analysis dead, misunderstood, or both? New forms of work analysis and design. In A. I. Kraut & A. K. Korman (Eds.), *Evolving practices in human resource management* (pp. 43–68). San Francisco, CA: Jossey-Bass.

Sanchez, J. I., & Levine, E. L. (2001). The analysis of work in the 20th and 21st centuries. In N. Anderson, D. Ones, H. Sinangil, & C. Viswesvaran (Eds.), *Handbook of industrial, work, and organizational psychology* (pp. 71–89). Thousand Oaks, CA: Sage Publications.

Sanchez, J. I., Zamora, A., & Viswesvaran, C. (1997). Moderators of agreement between incumbent and non-incumbent ratings of job characteristics. *Journal of Occupational and Organizational Psychology, 70,* 209–218.

Smith, J. E., & Hakel, M. D. (1979). Convergence among data sources, response bias, and reliability and validity of a structured job analysis questionnaire. *Personnel Psychology, 32,* 677–692.

Society for Industrial and Organizational Psychology. (2003). Principles for the validation and use of personnel selection procedures. Retrieved September 17, 2011, from http://www.siop.org/_Principles/principlesdefault.aspx

Truxillo, D. M., Paronto, M. E., Collins, M., & Sulzer, J. L. (2004). Effects of subject matter expert viewpoint on job analysis results. *Public Personnel Management, 33,* 33–46.

4

Work Analysis Questionnaires and App Interviews

David M. Van De Voort

Mercer

Thomas J. Whelan

North Carolina State University

Perhaps the most common work analysis scenario is a job incumbent (or supervisor) updating an existing job description or completing a work analysis questionnaire, followed by an interview to confirm and validate the responses. This approach implies that documenting a job is a task no more sophisticated than inventorying widgets. In fact, a job is not an object that is subject to the laws of physics and physical measurement. Rather, a job is a complex social-psychological construct, and work analysis is a measurement task more akin to an attitude survey than to a counting task (see Figure 4.1). Effective work analysis via interviews and questionnaires undoubtedly requires careful planning and a pragmatic assessment of the complexity of the work analysis effort. This chapter defines work analysis interviews and questionnaires, provides recommendations for their use, and discusses many of the issues likely to be encountered in the course of collecting data.

WHAT IS A JOB?

According to *The Handbook for Analyzing Jobs* (U.S. Department of Labor, 1972), a *job* is a group of positions which are identical with respect to their major or significant tasks and sufficiently alike to justify their being covered by a single analysis. There may be one or many persons employed in the same job. In turn, a *position* is a collection of tasks constituting the total work assignment of a single worker. There are as many positions as there are workers. At the risk of tedious reductionism, a *task* is one of the distinct activities that constitute logical or necessary steps in the performance of work by the worker. A task is created whenever human effort, physical or mental, is exerted to accomplish a specific purpose.

Campbell, Dunnette, Lawler, and Weick (1970) called out the inadequacy of this static definition of a job. They described three dynamic characteristics of a job, which must be considered when performing work analysis:

1. Time-based changes, such as retail management jobs during the holiday season versus February
2. Employee-based changes, such as a recently promoted chief financial officer versus a 20-year seasoned veteran

Figure 4.1   What is a job?

3. Situation-based changes, such as public relations jobs in the aftermath of an accounting scandal

The static definition of a job, as previously stated, fails to capture job features, characteristics, and components that may be critical to a particular work analyst's purpose. Like the blind men and the elephant, the nature of a job depends upon what part of the job the analyst touches:

- The compensation analyst attends to job responsibilities.
- The incentive plan designer looks for job results.
- The curriculum developer seeks job-required knowledge and skill requirements.
- The safety engineer discerns repetitive motion behaviors.

Note that a job analysis is not a job. Perhaps the most repeated phrase in this handbook is "depending upon the *purpose* of the job analysis."

The use of questionnaires and interviews to measure the job features that are relevant to a particular work analysis purpose is a significant undertaking. With proper planning at the outset of a work analysis effort, a higher quality of data can be collected. The adage of "garbage in, garbage out" certainly applies in work analysis, and the importance of the collection of data to the overall effectiveness of the work analysis effort cannot be underestimated.

WORK ANALYSIS INTERVIEWS AND QUESTIONNAIRES DEFINED

Interviews

A work analysis interview is a meeting between two or more people for the purpose of exchanging information about a job or series of jobs. More than one interviewer or interviewee may participate in the interview, such as when the interviewer requires technical backup or other support. For example, if the interviewer is external to the organization, it may be helpful to have another knowledgeable member of the organization support the interviewer and provide contextual information about the nature of the work environment and the organization's goals and processes. Interviewers must develop the skills that enable them to ask appropriate questions about the target job of job incumbents, immediate supervisors, and other job knowledgeable individuals. Then the interviewer should record the information so that it can be recaptured after the interview is completed.

Lastly, the interview results need to be presented in a most meaningful form, such as in an integrated report about the target job that summarizes the data gathered from all pertinent interviews.

An interview may be highly structured or unstructured. Usually work analysis interviews are highly structured and are conducted in a quiet room away from the work site, particularly when safety is a factor. Alternately, the interviews may be conducted at the work site where performance of job activities can be observed and discussed. In a group interview, two or more job-knowledgeable individuals are questioned about the same job at the same time. A group interview is sometimes referred to as a subject matter expert conference. Typically, information obtained through interviewing is combined with job information obtained through other job analytic techniques. Interviews alone, however, may be sufficient to provide all of the job information needed when only relatively few incumbents hold the job of interest and they all work at the same or nearby locations.

Questionnaires

The work analysis questionnaire can be conceptualized as a self-administered interview that is very carefully constructed. As is the case with other methods, questionnaires may be administered to individuals or to groups of respondents (incumbents, supervisors, or other job-knowledgeable employees) in a face-to-face situation or through the Internet or mail.

Generally, work analysis questionnaires are structured and can be purchased or customized. If the questionnaire is unstructured or open ended, respondents usually are asked to list job activities and describe them in their own words. An unstructured questionnaire is easy to develop but can be problematic to analyze reliably. For instance, unstructured questionnaires may be subject to affective bias, in which an individual's attitude about the job potentially skews his or her responses to a work analysis instrument (e.g., Schnake & Dumler, 1985). Moreover, unstructured questionnaires require the development of scoring rubrics or other means of organizing and/or quantifying the resulting data. The creation of such scoring means and the process of applying them to returned questionnaires can be labor intensive. As such, the most effective work analysis questionnaires are highly structured and designed to capture the same basic information across a range of jobs.

Questionnaires are most efficient—in fact, they are almost indispensable—when a large sample of incumbents working at numerous locations is to be surveyed about the work they perform. For this same reason, a purchased questionnaire may not necessarily capture pertinent aspects of the job across locations. Therefore, some customization is often desired to maximize the collection of useful job information.

THE ROLE OF WORK ANALYSIS QUESTIONNAIRES AND INTERVIEWS IN REGULATORY COMPLIANCE

The need and specifics of compliance with federal, state and local legislation such as the Equal Pay Act of 1963, equal employment opportunity and affirmative action, pay equity legislation in Canada, the Americans with Disabilities Act of 1990 are described in detail elsewhere in this handbook. *Job relatedness* and *essential job functions* are concepts at the heart of almost all of these regulations.

Completed work analysis questionnaires and work analysis interview notes—including the demographic details about by whom, from whom, and under what circumstances the questionnaires or interviews were completed—are the source documents and first link in an evidentiary chain that is critical to defending an employer against allegations of disparate treatment. Even though the work analysis data and information elicited via questionnaire or interviews may be subject to sophisticated and elaborate data reduction, description, inference, and analysis protocols, the original completed questionnaires and interview notes should be filed and preserved according to the sponsoring organization's document preservation policy and in consultation with legal counsel.

As such, interviews and questionnaires provide different means through which to provide a solid foundation for ensuring regulatory compliance; one method may be more appropriate or efficient depending on the circumstances. To the extent that interviews permit dynamic questions to be asked, they are more time consuming to administer than questionnaires. Further, interviews are able to provide greater detail as to the job context, so they are best to employ when the number of incumbents or other possible sources of work analysis information is low, being that there are fewer sources from which to obtain data.

Questionnaires often necessitate more standardization, so they may not provide depth of detail about a job. However, their efficiency facilitates the realistic collection of data from large numbers of incumbents with far greater efficiency than interviews, so they are best to employ when there are many sources of work analysis information available. In this way, the decision to use interviews or surveys (or some combination of both) when collecting data can be seen as a cost-benefit evaluation of the amount of time expended to interview the necessary individuals versus the efficiency with which they could be administered a questionnaire, with the intended goal of gathering sufficient information for compliance with existing legislation.

ACCESS, ACCEPTANCE, AND ACCURACY OF WORK ANALYSIS QUESTIONNAIRES AND INTERVIEWS

Work analysis is intrusive. The primary appeal of questionnaire-based work analysis is that it is less intrusive than almost any other work analysis method. However, this may also make it more likely that the work analysis data is not captured because it is easier for an incumbent or supervisor to neglect to return the questionnaire. For this reason, questionnaires are less appropriate when there are few incumbents from whom data is to be collected, as failing to capture work analysis data is less likely when interviews are employed. Nevertheless, management permission for access to job incumbents and their supervisors, as well as winning acceptance from management and subject matter experts, are *sine qua non* for obtaining accurate job data and information.

Executives and Managers

Managers perceive work analysis as the ultimate human resources "busy work." Particularly in the case of questionnaires, executives and managers may be less likely to respond to the work analysis effort compared to employees (Cycyota & Harrison, 2006). Educating managers about legal requirements and liabilities under the Equal Pay Act, equal employment opportunity, the Fair Labor Standards Act (FLSA) of 1938, and other regulations can help win acceptance. There is no greater asset to a work analysis effort than testimony from an executive who has personally experienced a U.S. Department of Labor investigation under FLSA or an employee lawsuit.

It is important that all participants appreciate that a work analysis questionnaire or interview is not merely a compliance exercise but rather a necessary and critical input to ensuring the following:

- Positions are appropriately classified as exempt or nonexempt under FLSA.
- Hiring and performance standards reflect realistic job requirements.
- Job title, grade level, and pay align with job responsibilities.
- Training programs build upon relevant skills and knowledge.

Employees and Supervisors

Obstacles to obtaining accurate questionnaire and interview responses will occur, even with full management support. When employee trust in management is low, a work analysis effort can raise employee fears of downsizing and/or scrutiny of personal performance. Even when trust is not an issue, differing perspectives may make work analysis a contest between commonality and consolidation versus elaboration and specificity. Incumbents and immediate supervisors tend to maximize the uniqueness and complexity of their work; at the same time, the objective of the human resources function is to find commonalities that simplify program design and general people management processes. The ultimate balance in work analysis is to accurately document similarities and differences among and between jobs so that the employer may act on critical similarities and differences while correctly identifying trivial differences and ignoring trivial similarities.

Whether differences and similarities are trivial or critical between jobs, the accuracy of work analysis data should not go without investigation. If the quality of data is ignored, the analyst will not be able to assess the accuracy of data within the same job. For instance, although incumbents are likely to be the most familiar with aspects of the job(s) being analyzed, they may not necessarily be the most reliable source of information. Compared to supervisors or analysts, incumbents may inflate the importance of parts of the job, leading to a potentially skewed work analysis (e.g., Morgeson, Delaney-Klinger, Mayfield, Ferrara, & Campion, 2004). In addition, the reliability of the data gathered from multiple sources may not be consistent (Dierdorff & Wilson, 2003). It is imperative that data gathered from interviews and/or questionnaires for each job is scrutinized to assess the accuracy of the information.

Positive communication to explain the purposes and potential employee benefits of the work analysis project is key. Transparency is preferred because employees tend to fill in information gaps with assumptions that are more negative than the truth (unless the purpose of the work analysis project truly *is* nefarious). Employees should be told that they are critical to the success of the project, are the ultimate best source of information about their job, and will be best served by accurately and completely completing the questionnaire or interview. Promising and then following through to provide employees who give information/input with the opportunity to see the output/products of the analysis helps win employee cooperation.

Unions

Because work analysis questionnaires and interviews go direct to the worker, they may be objectionable to union leaders who prefer to act as a go-between and minimize direct management contact with their members. The potential for driving reductions in force, changing work rules, or supporting negotiations makes work analysis a particular concern for unions.

Of course, management has the right to collect information about work, jobs, and employees, with or without union support. Nevertheless, the accuracy of the output benefits from union collaboration. Union acceptance can by maximized by the following:

- Emphasizing that the goal of the analysis is an objective and accurate understanding of jobs and work
- Adopting a collaborative and transparent posture
- Inviting union leadership participation in project planning

CONDUCTING THE WORK ANALYSIS INTERVIEW

The interview is an important work analysis tool for gathering detailed job facts and is a focal step in many work analysis designs. Job analysts, therefore, should learn to conduct interviews so that they obtain job information that is as accurate and complete as possible. Before scheduling work analysis interviews, it is essential that the interviewer be well prepared to conduct the interview.

Planning for the Interview

The interviewer should have a clear plan for the interview. Some planning considerations include

1. Interview objectives should be explicit (e.g., identify tasks performed by job incumbents).
2. The class of interviewee should be identified (e.g., immediate supervisors, job incumbents with 6 or more months in the job title, or both).
3. The general approach that will be used to accomplish the interview should be specified and reviewed (e.g., degree of structure, one or more interviewees and interviewers).
4. The general procedure that will be used to accomplish the interview should be specified and reviewed (e.g., onsite logistics, amount of technological mediation, interview scheduling, interview length).
5. Materials and equipment that will be needed to carry out the interview should be available (e.g., special forms or equipment to record information and job documents, videoconferencing capability if needed).

The site where the interviews will take place is an especially important consideration. Interviews should be held in a quiet room that affords privacy and where the interview process will not be disturbed. The room should be conveniently located for the interviewees and contain sufficient facilities—chairs, a table to spread out job-related materials, electrical outlets, and presentation technologies as needed. An exception, of course, is when an interview is combined with observation of the work being performed at the work site.

Type of Interview

A series of three types of interviews—referred to as initial, verification, and follow-up interviews—has proven to be useful for compiling accurate and complete lists of job activities prior to developing a job task inventory questionnaire. The interviews are used to obtain and refine information abut tasks performed by incumbents in the target jobs.

The initial interview is the first interview at a work location. The initial interview provides a large part of the job information from which task statements will be prepared, especially when job documentation is scarce. The interviewer should use task statements extracted from other sources as a guide for conducting the initial interview.

The verification interviews are conducted at each work location subsequent to the initial interview. Verification interviews serve to check and modify job information obtained from all sources and to obtain additional information that may have been overlooked previously. In a sense, all interviews conducted to support the development of a job task inventory are verification interviews.

The follow-up interviews are conducted with a small group of incumbents and supervisors to review, modify if necessary, and edit each task statement included in a draft of the final task lists. The idea is to make certain that the task statements are expressed in the language that is used on the job and familiar to employees, are technically correct and unambiguous, and accurately reflect the job tasks.

Initial and verification interviews should be carried out in at least two work locations (when applicable) to determine if variations occur in the way a job is performed at different locations. The idea, of course, is to reduce the chance of biasing the questionnaire with task statements that are peculiar to a particular location. A criterion, for instance, of 10% new tasks at the second location should be established to determine whether interviews should be conducted at multiple locations. If 10% or more new tasks are added to the task list, it may be necessary to conduct interviews at another location. The significance of the additional task statements should be taken into account. It is also advisable to check with incumbents at the first location to determine whether an area of work was inadvertently omitted. If that turns out to be the case, the interview process can be safely terminated. Marked variation found in target job tasks obtained at a third location would indicate the need to consult with a job expert.

After a draft task list is prepared, interviewers can initiate follow-up interviews. Optimally, interview sites should be selected where the target jobs are being performed in accordance with general company practices. The extent to which the task statement list is modified as a result of a follow-up interview should indicate when to conclude the follow-up interview process.

Who to Interview

Interviewees should be experienced job incumbents and supervisors who have current knowledge of the target job. Interviews with supervisors usually yield about the same information as interviews with jobholders, but supervisors may generally feel less threatened, have a better perspective regarding job responsibilities, and know how the job should be performed (e.g., the criterion domain). There is some evidence that incumbents and supervisors may tend to agree on critical tasks, but discrepancies may arise in which tasks are most important (e.g., Mueller & Belcher, 2000). The interviewer should use his or her judgment to balance these sources of information after seeking as much clarification as possible. If the opportunity to observe the job being performed is available, incorporate that information into ordering tasks by importance. It should be noted, however, that supervisors often are consumers of the outcomes of subordinates' tasks, and therefore they might have a different viewpoint and provide responses that diverge from those of incumbent employees (Truxillo, Paronto, Collins, & Sulzer, 2004). Although differences between supervisors' and incumbents' views of the work should be identified and addressed, care must be exercised so that neither the supervisors nor incumbents feel that the veracity of the information they provided is being challenged. Verification questions can be phrased as "Did I get this right?" or "I wonder if this is correct?"

The quantity and quality of information obtained during interviews often depend to some extent on how well interviewees are informed about the upcoming interview. Supervisors should inform the interviewee in advance about the reason for the interview, its location, scheduled time, expected length, and the work-related materials that should be brought to the interview, such as forms and records received and/or dispatched, as well as documents such as blueprints, sketches, major references, job practices, and performance aids. Supervisors should also permit the interviewee sufficient time to organize these materials in preparation for the interview. The materials brought to the interview can serve to generate discussion of items that initiate work activities and of accomplishments.

Interviewing Techniques

Interviews rarely progress neatly within specified boundaries. Occasionally, interviewees discuss details when general information about the job is desired. They also tend to revert to sequences of work already discussed. It is not unusual for an interviewee to vacillate between specific details and general information; it is up to the interviewer to cope with the information presented. It is important that the interviewer not be sidetracked. Interviewers should always keep the objective of the interview in mind: to obtain information about a job from which a complete and accurate picture of the job can be formed. The use of a few basic interviewing techniques and principles, as noted in the next sections, should help establish an interview pattern, put interviewees in an appropriate frame of mind, and aid in obtaining the desired job information rapidly and efficiently.

Communicating

Interviewees will not know whether the information they provide is the kind of information sought unless the interviewer communicates with them. The interviewer can communicate either with verbal responses such as "yes" and "I understand" or nonverbally with head nodding. Being an interview, the interviewer and interviewee are engaged in social interaction; such communication can facilitate an interviewee giving valid information. The interviewer's behavior can reinforce the kinds of responses being made by the interviewee, thereby increasing the likelihood that similar kinds of responses will continue to be forthcoming. The primary function of this kind of communication is to let the interviewees know that they are on the right track.

Prompting

A very important skill for interviewers to possess is to be able to prompt for pertinent job information during the interview. This maintains a cadence of conversation between the interviewer and interviewee to encourage a flow of information. Should interviewees not understand what is wanted, be unable to verbalize, or simply be reluctant to talk about their work, they should be encouraged with prompts, such as the following:

> One activity you might perform is reviewing work logs. Do you do this? [If the answer is affirmative, the interviewer should continue.] I'll write that one down. Now, tell me some of the other things you do. Let's take a look at some of the examples of the work materials you brought with you. What do you do with this form?

Probing

Interviewers undoubtedly will have to make use of probes. A probe is a question that asks an interviewee to clarify a point. Probes become necessary during an interview when the information being presented is too general or vague or if the interviewer has a question about the information. The probe should be an open-ended question that allows for a free-ranging response rather than a simple "yes" or "no." Probing is a skill that can be mastered with some practice.

In one probing technique, the interview asks short questions that begin with *how, what, who, when, where,* and *which*. For example, after the interviewee's statement of "I provide information to the marketing department," a series of clarification questions could be asked, such as the following:

- What kind of information do you provide?
- How do you provide it?
- When do you provide it?

The interviewer can also use echo words that are aimed at obtaining specific information. After the statement "I work with service orders," the interviewer could attempt to obtain more specific information by echoing, "Work with?" The interviewee will probably elaborate with an explanation such as, "Yes, I check and file them. And I remove old ones from the files." Once again, an echo probe (e.g., "Check them?") might encourage further elaboration.

The interviewer can also expand points that are inconsistent with previous information. Inconsistencies may be due to the interviewer's unfamiliarity with job details or inability to distinguish between similar situations. Interviewers can explain that they are unfamiliar with job details: "I don't understand that last sequence. I thought the outputs were mailed to comptrollers. I guess I had it wrong. Could you please go over those activities again?"

Interviewers should always convey the idea that the interviewee is the job expert. Interviewers should never argue with the interviewee. If inconsistencies remain an issue after a brief review, the questionable information should be flagged for later re-examination and cross-comparison.

The following kinds of questions and behavior should be avoided when probing:

1. *Closed-end questions or those that can be answered simply "yes" or "no."* For instance, questions that being with "Do you…?" should not be used.
2. *Questions that begin with "why."* These questions tend to sound judgmental and interviewees may feel that they are being asked to justify their activities. *Why* questions usually place interviewees on the defensive, and they can easily become uncooperative.
3. *Questions and behavior that inadvertently bias responses and diminish the accuracy of the information obtained.* Leading questions (e.g., "You process service orders, don't you?") can create the impression that the activity is expected to be performed and interviewees may respond accordingly, even though the work is not part of their job.

Similarly, facial expressions that communicate approval and disapproval of information should be controlled because interviewees may respond accordingly; they may provide additional information that they have been led to believe is desired, or they may stop responding altogether. Finally, a sudden change in note-taking consistency is important, and interviewees should be informed if a change is planned.

Control

Interviewers should concentrate on the main issues while maintaining a relaxed businesslike atmosphere. Indications of overcontrol include very brief responses, lack of interest on the part of the interviewee, and excessive talking by the interviewer. Control can be relaxed by refraining from interrupting the interviewee, returning to a subject with which the interviewee was comfortable, and changing one's facial expression and posture. However, interviews can also be undercontrolled. Generally, indications of undercontrol are overly long answers or frequent talking about extraneous subjects by the interviewee, too many interviewee questions, and a very lengthy interview. Control can be regained by summarizing relevant points and redirecting the interviewee to a topic of interest. At times, it may be best to be direct and say, "For the sake of time, we'll have to move on to another topic."

Silence

There are bound to be periods of silence during an interview. Silence should be expected and used to advantage. An interviewee may just need time to think or to make associations that might not surface if every gap in conversion was filled with comments or rapid-fire questions. At key points, silence can encourage the interviewee to talk. When an interviewee is responding appropriately and then stops talking, resist the tendency to jump in with a question. The interviewee will probably resume talking about the topic at hand. If a period of silence is creating a discomfort for the interviewee, the interviewer should ask a question about a previous item or bring up a new topic. Too much silence can be embarrassing and interfere with the continued conduct of the interview.

Interview Aids

A number of aids are available that can be useful in carrying out an interview. In a case in which the interview goal is to identify tasks performed by job incumbents, the interviewer can formulate a list of task statements on the basis of preliminary study of the job and use the list during the interview as an interview guide. Interviewees would be asked to review each task statement on the list, correct errors, refine general work activity statements, and add tasks not included on the list. The interviewer simply would guide the interviewee through the task list.

A fresh copy of the task list should be used for each interview, but the task list may be modified to reflect information obtained in previous interviews. The task list should look like a working draft to encourage interviewees to consider it critically, and there should be sufficient opportunity for the interviewee to offer alternate wording, additional tasks, and other information. The task list can be organized by functions, with tasks listed alphabetically or sequentially under function headings, to make it easier to review the task list.

Interviews to identify tasks can be conducted without the aid of a preliminary task list, but the interview will take longer and there is a greater chance that the interviewee will not be understood. In the unlikely case that job documentation is unavailable, the job does not lend itself to observation, or the time available is too short, the interviewer should at least discuss the job with job experts to get an idea for the functions and terminology involved before initiating the interview. A useful approach is to back up the interviewer with a job expert, who sits in on the interview as an observer and, if necessary, can clarify a description or otherwise fill in gaps. The procedure combines the benefits of having a trained interviewer to obtain information in a useful form as well as a job expert to contribute to completeness and clarity.

WORK ANALYSIS INTERVIEW CHECKLIST

The following is a checklist for interviewers. The checklists for Phases 2 and 3 should be reviewed prior to each interview and completed after the interview has concluded.

Phase 1: *Prepare for the Interview*
❐ Gather information from secondary sources (e.g., organizational charts, existing job documentation).
❐ Schedule enough time (at least 1 hour).
❐ Structure the interview to ensure that the desired data pertinent to the work analysis project will be collected.
❐ Explain the purpose of the interview to the interviewee when scheduling.

Phase 2: *Conduct the Interview*
❐ Introduce yourself and describe purpose and procedures.
❐ Ask interviewee for identifying information.
❐ Create a relaxing environment without allowing for indefinite "chit-chat."
❐ Ask broad/general questions in the beginning; use more conversational techniques later in the interview.
❐ Ask questions in a logical sequence with follow-up questions where necessary to capture the needed data.
❐ Give the incumbent time to think about his or her answers to interview questions.
❐ Take detailed notes and listen.
❐ Ask for more information that may contextualize the data already captured.
❐ Maintain control of the interview but avoid dominating the exchange.

Phase 3: *Close the Interview*

❐ Explain the next steps of the work analysis project.

❐ Close the interview with courtesy.

❐ Summarize your notes immediately after the interview.

WHAT KIND OF INFORMATION IS NEEDED FROM A WORK ANALYSIS INTERVIEW?

The goal of gathering all of the above types of information is to ensure that enough information is collected to provide a foundation of high job relevance for all the products of work analysis, such as selection tools and training design (see Figure 4.2). Although a single purpose for work analysis, such as identifying hiring requirements, may drive the focus of an interview, it is important to be as thorough as possible. The value of work analysis data is in its comprehensiveness, particularly when that information will be used by an organization in the future.

Figure 4.3 provides a sample work analysis interview guide that illustrates examples of how to obtain multiple types of needed information from an interviewee.

JOB DESCRIPTION TEMPLATE AS A WORK ANALYSIS QUESTIONNAIRE

The most elementary form of a work analysis questionnaire is to simply provide the incumbent, supervisor (or other subject matter expert) with a blank job description template to complete. Figure 4.4 depicts a universal template for this purpose.

DESIGNING AND ADMINISTERING WORK ANALYSIS QUESTIONNAIRES

Questionnaire Format and Organization

Questionnaires may be prepared in booklet form or as a web page, preferably with the following sections:

1. Cover page or initial salutation
2. Introduction to the survey
3. Personal information
4. Directions for responding to the first question about each task
5. Task or behavior list with response format
6. Directions for responding to additional questions about tasks
7. Space for additional comments
8. Conclusion

A professional-looking questionnaire will elicit greater respect and more careful attention than one with a haphazard appearance, regardless of whether the questionnaire is administered on paper or online. The cover page or initial salutation should make it clear that the organization endorses the survey, should contain the title of the survey, identify the target jobs, and include the name of the sponsoring organizations. The introduction should explain the purpose of the survey and how accurate responses to the questionnaire can help the work analysis effort, describe the questionnaire briefly, and assure the respondents that their answers will be treated as confidential. Directions for returning (if on paper) or submitting (if online) completed questionnaires should also be included in the introduction.

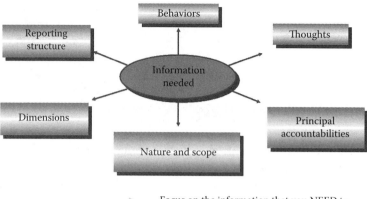

Focus on the information that you NEED to obtain from the interview to make most efficient use of the time alloted.

Figure 4.2 Information needed from job analysis interviews.

Introduction

As you know, [company name] is embarking on a major effort to document our jobs. We will need about one hour today to discuss your job's major responsibilities, knowledge and skill requirements, key challenges, and competencies. Once we complete the interview, we will prepare a draft description in the coming weeks that you will have an opportunity to review for accuracy and completeness. We will then forward the description on to your immediate manager for his/her review. Thank you for taking the time to meet with us.

Identifying Information

Let's start by confirming your job title, who you report to in [company name], including their title, and the individual's name.

Questions

1. *Please provide an overview of your role in the organization. How would you characterize the primary purpose of your job? What is the key end result that you are trying to accomplish? What would the "headline" be for your job?*
2. *Walk us through the 3–5 major areas that you are accountable for at [company name]. We want to focus on the major activities that fall under your direction. Help us to understand how the work gets done in your area and the key priorities. We will want to spend some time on each of these major areas so that we fully understand the nature and scope of what your job does as well as the associated key end results.*
3. *What are some of the most difficult and complex challenges that you face in your job?*
4. *What types of decisions are you able to make on your own? Which decisions do you refer to others in the organization?*
5. *Which jobs do you primarily interact with at [company name]? Who are your primary external contacts? What is the nature of these internal and external interactions?*
6. *Which jobs report to you organizationally? How many FTE (full-time equivalent) employees report to each of your direct reports?*
7. *What dollar dimensions are associated with your job? How large are the typical projects that you are involved with at [company name]?*
8. *We need to document the knowledge and skill requirements for your job. What are the minimum requirements for your position? What are the desired requirements? Note: We are not looking for your personal resume here or your particular background. Rather, think in terms of if [company name] had to fill your job tomorrow—what would the Company look for in the areas of knowledge and skill requirements?*
9. *Are there particular competencies (key behaviors and qualities) that are required in your job for outstanding performance? Please list those that you see as being most critical.*
10. *Are there any special physical requirements and/or working conditions related to this job?*
11. *What other aspects of your job haven't we covered that you feel are important for us to know about?*

Figure 4.3 A sample work analysis interview guide.

ORGANIZATION XYZ	
JOB TITLE:	**REPORTS TO:**
UNIT/DEPARTMENT:	**JOB/FAMILY:**
JOB PURPOSE:	

Key Accountabilities	Key Activities

Required Qualifications

Technical/professional skills, expertise, and qualifications

Performance Metrics

Financial (limits/mandates, etc.)	*Nonfinancial (customers/staff, etc.)*

Main Contacts (External and Internal)

Contact group	*Purpose*	*Frequency*

Working Conditions

Describe below any working conditions that pose risks to self or others

Physical Abilities

Describe physical abilities required to perform the job, such as "ability to repeatedly lift weights as much as 50 pounds up to 20 times per hour"; describe physical abilities required, including but not limited to hearing, seeing, climbing, balancing, lifting, and manipulating/controlling materials, and equipment

Figure 4.4   Universal job description template.

Personal information should be obtained in the questionnaire because it will be used in data analyses. Data can be analyzed for subsets of the total sample that align with personal information items, such as location, job title, job tenure level, experience level, and so on. Identification information can also be used to contact respondents for further elaboration should the need arise. Personal information sheets should allow sufficient space for responses, and simple and clear options should be available where there is a choice. For example, when requesting a respondent's job title, a list of job titles might be provided to choose from. The respondent simply can check the appropriate job title or record a code associated with the job title in the appropriate space on the personal information sheet. By contrast, the questions "How many previous jobs have you held in the organization?" does not require a code because it can be answered with an actual numerical response.

Each section of the questionnaire should contain directions designed to help respondents complete the questionnaire correctly and return it successfully. Effective directions for responding to questions about task statements, for example, should contain a few completed examples and a few examples that respondents can work through. In addition, it is vital to provide clear instructions for the desired format of responses if a rating scale is not provided. For instance, if a questionnaire asks a respondent to estimate how much time per week or per month is spent on a specific task, there should be unambiguous directions about whether the response should be in hours (e.g., 4.5 hours per week) or in days (e.g., 2.25 days per month).

Task statements should be listed in a questionnaire in accordance with guidelines as follows:

- List task statements alphabetically under a broader work activity heading in bold print, such as a function or duty.
- Number the task statements consecutively. The number can serve as task identification and is especially useful for data analysis.
- List task statements on the left side of the page and place associated response choices on the right side.
- Leave sufficient space between task statements so that respondents can easily match task statements with associated answer spaces.

The questionnaire should allow respondents to write tasks that they perform that are not included in the questionnaire and to comment on the questionnaire in general. Commonly, however, open-ended requests for information are not likely to produce useful information without investing time to classify responses and assess the importance of including data from open-ended requests if not all respondents provided an answer.

The questionnaire should conclude by thanking respondents and reminding them of how to return the completed questionnaire (if administered on paper) or provide a confirmation that responses have been successfully submitted (if administered via the Internet).

Data Reduction Considerations

Questionnaire responses generally are entered into a computer or submitted directly into a database by the respondent, and therefore the design of the questionnaire is important to the data process. Ideally, responses should be entered exactly as they appear on the questionnaire, which is easy to accomplish if the questionnaire is online and data entry is automated. If responses require transcription into a database, however, data entry clerks will likely have to search for some data or translate a few responses to accurately assign data codes. As such, data entry clerks should be given comprehensive instructions, usually in the form of a data record layout that specifies what data should be entered where, to promote accurate data entry.

Because of the additional expense of time to transcribe paper questionnaires into any computerized database, the costs of labor to do so should be weighed against the logistical and technical likelihood of creating a web-based questionnaire tool. If there are not a large number of questionnaires that require data entry, it may be easier to administer a questionnaire on paper than to put it online. Paper questionnaires are also vital when the incumbents or other job information sources do not have Internet access to complete a questionnaire. When there is a large number of questionnaires to be administered, designing a web-based work analysis questionnaire may significantly cut down on the administrative work needed to reduce data to a usable form, as well as reduce the possibility of errors due to transcription.

Although the design of a questionnaire should encourage the completion and return of the instrument by an incumbent or supervisor, there are also considerations of design that can facilitate the timeliness of the work analysis process. A few data entry solutions, listed by economic priority, include the following:

1. Have an editor review the questionnaire for quality multiple times while it is being revised to ensure the data makes intuitive sense in the layout of the way it will be recorded. In addition, pilot the questionnaire process from beginning to end to identify and remedy any points of failure in recapturing the work analysis information.
2. When applicable, an editor should create a methodology of coding responses on the questionnaire so that data entry can be accomplished directly from the questionnaire.
3. When applicable, provide data entry clerks with response-associated codes so that they can use the questionnaires as the media but perform table lookups as needed to standardize or code some responses.
4. Have the questionnaire data organized such that data entry (by either the respondent or a clerk) and data organization facilitates later analysis.

The main goal is to use questionnaires as the data entry media to the fullest extent and minimize the number of responses that require an editor or data entry clerk to perform table lookups or translations.

Pilot Testing and Producing the Questionnaire

Before a questionnaire is printed and distributed, it should be pilot tested with a few representative respondents. Even if a questionnaire was constructed and reviewed carefully in accordance with guidelines and best practices, respondents still may experience problems with some parts of the questionnaire. Therefore, the temptation to rush into distributing a questionnaire as soon as the preliminary draft becomes available should be resisted.

A pilot questionnaire should be administered by a work analysis team member who can observe respondents as they complete the questionnaire and identify problems that they encounter, regardless of whether paper or Internet administration is employed. Respondents should complete the questionnaire in accordance with directions, with the exception that they be encouraged to ask questions or discuss problems with the questionnaire as they arise. Problems raised or questions asked should be recorded for further study. Comments should be elicited from respondents when they complete the pilot questionnaire about difficulties that they may have experienced in understanding the directions or providing responses. Pilot respondents should also be questioned about the completeness of the questionnaire. The pilot questionnaire should be examined for errors, omissions, and indications of other problems. Wording, item-keying direction (e.g., positively or negatively worded questions), response format, and so forth should be reviewed and revised based on the results of pilot administration.

If it is not feasible to directly observe a pilot group, questionnaires should be sent to a small group of job incumbents who are representative of prospective respondents. Such a procedure may provide information about distribution and collection methods, as well as about questionnaire content and format. An evaluation sheet should be included with each questionnaire as a way of compensating for the lack of direct observation. Pilot respondents can be asked to list any problems that they encountered with directions, responses, and so on. They might also be asked to list any items that they feel have been omitted but would round out the questionnaire. Returned pilot questionnaires should be screened carefully for evidence of confusion or difficulty in answering questions. If a problem is evident but the reason for it is unclear, respondents may be contacted for clarification. Generally, though, the root cause of problems will likely be obvious. Again, the questionnaire should be reviewed and revised based on the results of pilot administration.

When the pilot test is completed and the questionnaire has been modified accordingly, it is ready to be used in a work analysis. The final text copy should be checked and double checked for errors to ensure the quality of the final survey. If it is being printed, the final version should also be checked with respect to the margins, position of the copy, page numbers, and so forth. The printing order should be large enough to cover contingencies and the quality of the paper ordered should be checked, as well as the information about printed return envelopes for the questionnaire. If administering online, the final version should be checked with respect to browser rendering, display of the copy on different screen resolutions, navigation troubleshooting, and so on.

Distributing and Collecting Questionnaires

Effective distribution and return of work analysis questionnaires is dependent on detailed and careful planning. After the locations of the participating organizations have been identified, the strategy for the data collection process can proceed. In a large organization, the steps for reaching the appropriate respondents and collecting the desired data are as follows:

- Field coordinators are identified.
- Field coordinators are informed of survey requirements. They help to determine the number of respondents and survey sites.
- Project manager sends questionnaires and detailed distribution instructions to the field coordinators.
- Field coordinators distribute questionnaires directly to target job incumbents or to supervisors, who can complete the questionnaire if they are the desired information source or distribute the questionnaires to the appropriate incumbents.
- If administered on paper, incumbents will complete the questionnaires, seal them in the envelopes provided, and either mail them directly to the data processing center or return them to their supervisors, who will forward the envelopes to the data processing center and notify the responsible coordinator. If administered online, completed questionnaires can be processed immediately and receipt confirmation relayed back to the incumbent or field coordinator.
- Coordinators track survey progress and report weekly to the project manager.

The data processing center may be an outside firm hired to log and examine questionnaires, code certain responses, and forward the questionnaires to the organization where the data will be processed and readied for analysis, or it may also be a company organization. In the small organizations, some of the above steps will not be necessary, but a work analysis project manager should be able to get the gist of what has to be done to distribute the questionnaires to the appropriate respondents.

Details that must be attended to when planning the distribution of survey materials include the following:

- Determine the total sample size requirements and expected number of respondents per survey site.

- Prepare instructions for field coordinators and supervisors.
- Specify respondent job titles so that they will be easily recognized by supervisors.
- Compile a current list of e-mail and/or physical mailing addresses for field coordinators.
- Include addressed return envelopes in each package, if applicable.

When field coordinators are designated, they should be called to inform them of the role that they are expected to play in the project. Items that should be discussed with field coordinators include the following:

- The purpose of the survey
- The survey method
- The date materials will be provided and the completion date objective
- Sample size and survey site requirements
- Respondent characteristics
- Questionnaire administration procedures
- Questionnaire return information
- The work analysis team member to contact for guidance and problem resolution

The call to field coordinators should be followed by correspondence that clearly spells out the specific instructions. Correspondence containing instructions also is needed for field managers, supervisors, and respondents. Instructions for each of the groups will differ depending on the role that the individual will play in the work analysis effort.

Instructions to the field coordinator should emphasize that it is the mainstream work performed by target jobholders that is of primary concern, not work performed by a few employees who may have target job titles but are performing special project work. In other words, respondents should represent typical jobholders, not special or temporary subgroups. Coordinators should be given sample size instructions so that they have some leeway in specifying the number of respondents per survey site. Often, operational and other circumstances enter into the picture and the coordinator is the best one to determine specific numbers of respondents. For instance, if the requirement for a particular location is six respondents but the supervisor's group contains seven target job incumbents, the coordinator should have the discretion to elect to survey all incumbents in the supervisory group rather than exclude one. The instructions should also mention that it may not be necessary to obtain data from every location where a target job is performed. In fact, for some purposes, two or three locations may be sufficient.

Field supervisors and managers should be notified of the cooperation expected in the forthcoming survey before they receive any questionnaire materials. Otherwise, the survey will come as a complete surprise, and questionnaire administration may not be afforded appropriate attention and care. The work analysis team should provide field coordinators with copies of all instructions that are meant to be forwarded to field managers and supervisors. Generally, these instructions should contain a brief statement about the purpose of the survey and the need for cooperation in obtaining the desired job information. The major emphasis should be on getting the questionnaire to appropriate jobholders and on returning completed questionnaires. Supervisors should also be informed of the amount of time that each respondent will likely devote to completing the questionnaire. Finally, they should be told whether the questionnaire may be completed by jobholders individually at their workstations or in small groups and that the information supplied by each respondent will be treated confidentially (if, of course, that is the case).

Sampling

The sample size may affect the accuracy of the outcome values that would have been obtained if all target jobholders responded to the questionnaire. If information about all possible variations of the way work is performed is required, then every target job incumbent should complete a work analysis questionnaire. From a practical standpoint, appropriate statistics can be used to describe work on the basis of questionnaire data obtained from a sample, and inferences can be made about the work performed by the job incumbent population from knowledge of work performed by the sample; that is, it is advisable to generalize from the sample to the population. Sample data are of use only insofar as they allow reasonable accurate inferences about the population. Sampling can keep costs down; it reduces questionnaire completion time and the amount of data collected and processed. In addition, sampling makes it possible to avoid the practical problems associated with administering questionnaires to hundreds or even thousands of job incumbents.

Hard-and-fast rules regarding minimum and maximum sample sizes for administering questionnaires in work analysis projects do not exist. In work with job inventory questionnaires, stable information can be obtained with much smaller samples than customarily have been sought, as the requirements of description do not demand the same rigor as prediction (e.g., selection purposes). The idea is to sample job incumbents and yet obtain essentially the same results as would be obtained by surveying all target job incumbents. If the job incumbent population is relatively small, it probably will require very little additional expenditure to acquire a larger percentage of the total, perhaps even 100%.

To some extent, sample size should be determined by the number of factors that will be studied to determine their effect on the way work is perceived and performed. For instance, to investigate task difficulty for male and female employees by educational level and by location would require comparisons of task difficulty indices calculated separately for males and females at different locations and varying education levels. As the number of variables to be compared increases, so will the need for larger samples to enable those comparisons. Conversely, this complexity also introduces more opportunity for bias in the results of a work analysis to the extent that members of a subgroup differ both within that subgroup and across subgroups in a way that does not represent all jobholders or pertinent sources of job information. In other words, sample size is a concern if there is reason to believe that the sample may not represent the population, which can be the case even when small samples omit only a few individuals.

Two important sample size values to consider are as follows:

1. The number (percentage) of all job incumbents desired for the survey sample
2. The number of respondents sought per work group in each participating organization

The number of job incumbents per organization, of course, will be needed. Organization census data, if available, are very useful for specifying preliminary numbers of respondents. If organization census data are unavailable, field coordinators will have to provide that information. The work analysis project manager can then use the information to determine the number of respondents that should be surveyed in each organization. The project manager should bear in mind that, in general, questionnaires in work contexts tend to yield a response rate of approximately 50% (Anseel, Lievens, Schollaert, & Choragwicka, 2010). Further, the possibility of nonresponse biasing the work analysis data must be taken into account to prevent erroneous applications of the data to selection, promotion, and compensation practices (Stetz, Beaubien, Keeney, & Lyons, 2008).

Coordinators can be requested to select survey sites randomly if there are no special location requirements. A random sample of survey sites within a company/organization can be obtained simply by listing the locations alphabetically and selecting among them according to a prede-termined percentage. If, for example, a 25% sample of locations is desired and a list of potential sites contains 20 locations, then every fourth location on the list could be selected as a survey site. Another way to select survey sites is to use a random numbers table to determine which locations will be used. As is the case when sampling respondents, a smaller percentage of locations should be drawn when the location list is long than when it is short. For example, if there are 50 potential survey sites, 10 randomly drawn sites probably may cover the preponderance of major variations in work. If there are only 10 locations, 4 or 5 survey sites should suffice, assuming that there are enough target job incumbents at the locations selected to meet the sample quota. If not, sample sites should be drawn until the sample quota can be met at the sites selected.

Distributing Questionnaires

The number of questionnaires administered should exceed the desired sample size by at least 20% to allow for various contingencies. Field coordinators' contact details are needed for distribution purposes because it is coordinators who will circulate questionnaires within their organizations. Paper surveys should be packed and mailed in sufficient numbers to each coordinator, and remain-ing questionnaires should be sent to and stored by the work analysis project manager.

Paper and web-based questionnaires should be provided to coordinators on an agreed-upon date; if for some reason the schedule cannot be kept, the coordinators should be notified. In addi-tion to a sufficient number of questionnaires or means of online distribution, each coordinator should receive the following:

- A review of instructions for coordinators
- Cover letters
- Instructions for managers and supervisors who will distribute questionnaires to their subordinates
- Special answer sheets (if needed)

Paper questionnaire returns can be handled in several ways. Respondents can mail question-naires directly to the data center in the addressed envelopes provided, or they can seal them in envelopes and return them to their supervisors, who will package them and send them either to the field coordinator or to the data center. If completed questionnaires are not funneled through coordinators en route to the data center, supervisors should be requested to notify coordinators how many questionnaires were distributed, completed, and returned. A third alternative is to have respondents return completed questionnaires to their supervisors, who will quickly review them for completeness and then package and send them to the data center or field coordinator. The third alternative, however, should not be employed if at all possible because it obviates confidentiality; some analysts feel that respondents will be biased by the knowledge that supervisors will examine the questionnaires. So, at the risk of receiving some incomplete or erroneously completed question-naires, it would be wise to avoid the third alternative whenever possible.

Completed questionnaires may require some review and coding before data reduction can begin. If need be, an outside firm can handle the clerical work, especially if the survey is a large one (the clerical firm's address can be used as a return address for the questionnaires). The clerical work to be accomplished is to log returned questionnaires, compare the number of completed question-naires returned to the number distributed per organization, check questionnaire data for omissions or illegible/irrelevant responses, code responses as needed (e.g., grouping questionnaires by loca-tion), and inform the project manager about delayed returns and missing responses. If illegible or omitted responses need to be corrected (e.g., if an item is being used to subgroup questionnaires has been omitted), respondents can be contacted through the field coordinator and/or immediate supervisor so that the information can be obtained.

Both the work analysis project manager and field coordinators should track survey progress. Generally, the project manager is interested in the number of questionnaires mailed to each coordinator or returned online and how each participating organization is progressing towards its survey objective. A tracking system and communication protocol should be set up so that it is easy to determine the status of the survey in each participating organization, regardless of whether the questionnaire format is on paper or web-based. When organizations have completed their part of the survey, correspondence should be sent to the field coordinators thanking them for their participation and cooperation, with copies sent to their managers. Contact with other survey participants to express appreciation and thanks should be left to the field coordinators.

Uses for Questionnaire Results

The quality of the data collected with work analysis questionnaires and the kinds of results generated are important, but equally important is the way the results are applied. After all, the reason that jobs are analyzed is to provide information to support human resource administration and management programs.

Analyses of questionnaire results can be very useful, for example, for identifying task statements that should be included in further analyses. Decision criteria, however, are needed to identify those task statements that should be included in additional applications and those that will be set aside. Task importance information can be crucial for establishing accurate training requirements. First, however, it is necessary to distinguish the important tasks from tasks that are less critical to organizational outcomes of interest. The point selected to make the distinction should be toward the high end of an importance rating scale continuum. One way to proceed is to single out tasks that attained reasonably high averages—for example, an average of at least 5 on a 7-point importance scale—and then concentrate on only those tasks performed by at least 50% of the job incumbents surveyed.

Task statements selected on the basis of statistical analysis of questionnaire data can be used directly in a number of ways. Computerized reports of task inventories, for instance, are highly detailed job descriptions and can serve as such. The format of the generated reports can be rearranged somewhat on the basis of statistical results (e.g., tasks can be rank ordered within functions and form the major part of a job description). The questionnaire results can certainly play a role in the preparation of more conventional narrative job descriptions.

Significant or important tasks can be the starting point for establishing formal training requirements and for developing training materials and courses. Although task statements by themselves are sufficient for identifying topics that should be covered by training, further division of tasks into subtask work activities is necessary to use the information for specifying the training materials that have to be developed. If job training is already available, training materials can be reviewed in conjunction with job inventory questionnaire results to determine whether or not all significant tasks are covered by the training. Should there be significant tasks that are not covered, new training can be developed to cover those tasks. Less significant tasks can also be examined in light of existing training to make certain that the training covers critical job aspects. Should formal training be concerned with the less significant tasks? The critical tasks identified by the work analysis survey may be incorporated in formal training when appropriate, although some may be related to on-the-job training.

Significant tasks identified in the analysis of questionnaire data can also be used to develop rating forms on which job performances can be evaluated based on the identified job tasks. Significant tasks can be selected to represent the various functions performed by employees, and performance effectiveness in those significant tasks can be rated by supervisors. Overall performance effectiveness can be gauged by combining task ratings. The results can be used to deliver performance feedback or developmental counseling to employees about tasks that they perform very well and tasks that need some improvement.

Another use for questionnaire results is to compare job information obtained from different sources. Job content information obtained from a questionnaire survey can be compared with work methods documented in company practices, specifications, standards, and training to determine whether work is being accomplished in accordance with the way jobs and training were initially designed. Reasons for differences between standards and actual practice can be investigated to determine whether the jobs should be brought into line with the standards or whether the standards should be modified to accord with the way the jobs are being performed.

Survey results can also be used to compare tasks performed by incumbents in the same job working at different locations. Observed differences, especially in task occurrence, might indicate that the job is not being performed the same way at each location. Another comparison that can be made with survey results is between tasks performed by employees working in different but related jobs to identify overlap. Yet another comparison that can be made is to contrast supervisors' views of the tasks that should be performed with the tasks that incumbents report they actually perform.

WORK ANALYSIS QUESTIONNAIRE CHECKLIST

The following is a checklist for work analysis questionnaires. The checklists for Phases 2 and 3 should be reviewed prior to each interview and completed after the interview has concluded.

Phase 1: *Develop/Review Questionnaire*
❐ Gather information from secondary sources (e.g., organization charts, existing job documentation).
❐ Develop/revise task and/or ability statements with clear, concise instructions on what the item is asking and how respondents are expected to answer.
❐ Review questionnaire content to ensure that the desired data pertinent to the work analysis project will be collected.
❐ Review and remove redundancies from questions for clarity.
❐ Devise strategy for questionnaire administration and return, determine target sample size, and identify field coordinators as applicable.
❐ Develop/design questionnaire salutation, introductory instructions, questionnaire layout and presentation, and directions for return.

Phase 2: *Pilot Testing*
❐ Pilot questionnaire (preferably with two or more persons not involved in Phase 1) to make sure all questions are understandable and clear and the administration process functions as expected.
❐ Revise questionnaire content as necessary based on feedback/observations from pilot respondents.
❐ Revise administration process as necessary based on feedback/observations from pilot respondents.
❐ Revise layout/instructions as necessary based on feedback/observations from pilot respondents.
❐ If needed, develop guidelines for data entry of questions/comments.
❐ Contact field coordinators to prepare for questionnaire distribution.

Phase 3: *Distribution and Collection of Questionnaires*

❐ Quality control entire questionnaire prior to distribution to ensure all revisions from pilot testing are included and coherent.

❐ Begin distribution of questionnaires appropriate to format (send paper copies or Internet links to field coordinators).

❐ Track questionnaire return and review completed questionnaires for content to determine if follow-up with a respondent is needed.

❐ Notify field coordinators when target sample goal has been achieved and thank them for their cooperation.

COMPUTER DATABASES AND WORK ANALYSIS DATA

Even the most ardent job analyst would confess that work analysis is a labor-intensive and potentially mind-numbing transfer of information from source to record to file and from file to transformation/analysis to application to report. Because recording, moving, manipulating, and tracking data and information is what computers do best, it is no surprise that effectively designed and scrupulously maintained databases of work analysis information are ultimately the most efficient and powerful work analysis tools. Computer databases are necessary to efficiently analyze a geographically dispersed workforce, as well as track and document rapidly changing job content. For large organizations, databases can justify the considerable investment in development and infrastructure costs (Cascio, 1998).

Computers have supported work analysis for almost as long as computers have been around, from the Comprehensive Occupational Data Analysis Program developed by the U.S. military to the mainframe-based early incarnations of the Position Analysis Questionnaire (McCormick, Jenneret, & Mecham, 1972), to software like Mercer's JobMaster software. One challenge for computer-supported work analysis is the sheer amount of information that can be generated by a work analysis project. The JobScope work analysis system developed by Nationwide Insurance in the early 1980s (Page & Van De Voort, 1989) to perform multimethod/multidimensional work analysis on 14,000 employees performing about 1,300 jobs taxed the limits of computing capacity of the most powerful desktop computers of the era. Although computers are significantly more powerful now and therefore are able to process a much greater amount of data points, the added complexity of work analysis data often demands careful consideration of how data is to be organized and stored in such a way that data is neither lost nor misappropriated due to poorly designed archiving of information. To this extent, the structure of a database of work analysis information cannot be overlooked.

Computerized Questionnaires: Mercer Operations Scanner

Mercer's Operations Scanner is an example of a contemporary, web-based work analysis questionnaire (Figure 4.5). In today's environment, web-based applications and cloud computing provide unprecedented computing power and fast, inexpensive, and user-friendly questionnaire development and administration platforms. With advances in computer power and convenience, computerized work analysis systems are much more than automated questionnaires.

THE COMPETENCY PARADOX

This chapter only indirectly addresses the issue of competencies. The competency paradigm has dominated human resource management for almost 20 years. Job descriptions are almost as likely to include competencies as tasks, duties, and responsibilities. Yet it is exceedingly rare that the term

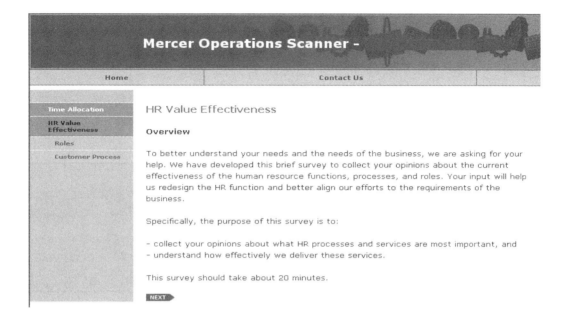

Figure 4.5   Operations Scanner screenshots.

competency is applied as intended by either the management strategists or human resource management thought leaders who championed the concept.

The Management Strategist Perspective

Hamel and Prahalad (1994) defined core competence as "the collective learning in the organization, especially how to coordinate diverse production skills and integrate multiple streams of technologies" (Hamel & Prahalad, 1994, p. 82). Numerous management theorists (e.g., Campbell & Sommers Luchs, 1997; Mitrani, Dalziel, & Fitt, 1992; Nadler & Tushman, 1999) defined *core competence* as a key organizational resource that could be exploited to gain competitive advantage.

	Column 1	Instructions	Column 2
		1. Read the numbered statement. In Column 1, use the pull-down menu to select the response that best describes the significance of the statement to your current position, the work you most frequently and most typically perform	
		2. In Column 2, use the pull-down menu to select the response that best describes how demanding or difficult the statement is compared to the work you most typically or most frequently perform. If your job includes work similar to the Statement, but at a higher capability level or with more demanding requirements, respond **Much More Demanding**, or **More Demanding**. If you perform similar work, but at a lower capacity level or less demanding requirements, respond **Less Demanding**, or **Much Less Demanding**. If the Statement closely describes the work you typically or frequently perform, respond **About the Same**. Even if your response in Column 1 was **Not Part of My Job** or **Not Important**, you should still respond in Column 2, based upon your evaluation of how demanding each statement is relative to the work that you DO most typically or most frequently perform.	
	1. How significant to your job is the capability or credential in each statement?	**Examples**	*2. Compared to this statement, my job is:*
	Not part of my job	**E1. Carries golf bags around golf course for players, handing clubs to players as requested**	**More Demanding**
	Very important	**E2. Manages all aspects of projects throughout the project lifecycle including project scope, schedule, resources, quality, costs and change**	**About The Same**
	Not important	**E.3. Optimizes the performance of enterprise business intelligence tools by defining data to filter and index that add value to the user**	**Less Demanding**
	1. How significant to your job is the capability or credential in each statement?		*2. Compared to this statement, my job is:*
A.		**Project Management**	
1	Not part of my job	Establishes and maintains quality and performance standards and measurements	Much Less Demanding
2	Not part of my job	Develops detailed schedules, estimates, resource plans, and status reports	About the same
3	Not part of my job	Establishes and achieves goals which have significant business impact	About the same
4	Essential	Approves planned expenditures	About the same
5	Somewhat important	Fields client concerns, escalating issues and changes	Much Less Demanding
6	Essential	Defines tasks; creates schedule, team work plans and other project documents	About the same

Figure 4.6   A questionnaire format for competency development.

7	Essential	Manage largest, most complex, most strategically important projects	About the same
8	Not part of my job	Leads multiple large unrelated projects or one very large project	Much Less Demanding
9	Essential	Identifies issues affecting work progress and recommends solutions	Much Less Demanding
10	Essential	Integrates tracking on multiple projects to provide overall program status	Less Demanding
11	Essential	Develops methods to measure customer satisfaction	Much Less Demanding
12	Essential	Facilitates team meetings to ensure effective business decisions are reached	Much Less Demanding
13	Essential	Enforces standards, frameworks, or methodologies	Much Less Demanding
14	Essential	Supports project activities as instructed	Much Less Demanding
15	Essential	Identifies opportunities for cross-discipline participation & engages personnel	Much Less Demanding

Figure 4.6   Continued.

The Human Resource Perspective

White (1959) introduced the term *competence* to describe personality characteristics associated with superior performance and high motivation. McClelland (1973, 1976) described characteristics underlying superior performance as *competency,* introducing the approach to the consulting firm that became Hay McBer. Rigorous adherents to the McBer paradigm define competency as underlying characteristics of people that are causally related to effective or superior performance in a job, generalizing across situations, and enduring for a reasonably long period of time (Boyatzis, 1982; Spencer & Spencer, 1993).

Both management strategists and human resources thought leaders describe competencies as distinctive, either to the firm as in core competencies or as behaviors that differentiate excellent performers from all others. Despite the concepts of specificity and uniqueness inherent in both organizational and behavioral competencies, few organizations have been willing to invest the considerable effort required to identify their distinctive competencies. Too many organizations proclaim their competency models after a few hours spent in a conference room wordsmithing one of the many proprietary competency frameworks now promoted by various consultants. Such "conference room competency models" are unlikely to deliver any competitive business advantage or differentiate excellent performance. In addition, functions such as hiring, firing, advancement, pay, or other human resource decisions based upon competencies that are not demonstrably job-related or essential pose substantial compliance risk relative to the regulatory forces described previously in this chapter.

Competency Questionnaires

The McBer method for developing competencies, the Behavioral Event Interviews, is a variation of the tried and true Critical Incident Technique (Flanagan, 1954). Readers interested in the Critical Incident Technique are referred to Chapter 11, this volume. It would be very difficult to capture in a questionnaire the rich job performance information generated by the Critical Incident Technique or Behavioral Event Interviews. However, Figure 4.6 depicts a work analysis questionnaire format that provides quantitative measures of two important features of the job elements (whether one chooses to see them as behaviors or tasks), which are *essentiality to the job* and *relative difficulty.* The essentiality rating speaks for itself; the relative difficulty rating provides the basis for competency-like scaling of job elements.

APPENDIX: A COMPENDIUM OF BATTLE-TESTED QUANTITATIVE REQUIREMENTS SCALES

BASIC JOB REQUIREMENTS: Reading in English

- ❐ 1. Requires reading to understand simple instructions (e.g., lists, notes, labels).
- ❐ 2. More than Level 1 but less than Level 3.
- ❐ 3. Requires reading to verify accuracy (e.g., check spelling, proofread documents).
- ❐ 4. More than Level 3 but less than Level 5.
- ❐ 5. Requires reading to understand common business English (e.g., instruction manuals, work procedures).
- ❐ 6. More than Level 5 but less than Level 7.
- ❐ 7. Requires reading to understand complex material (e.g., technical reports, equipment specifications, financial agreements, government regulations, contracts, income statements/balance sheets, research papers, journal articles).
- ❐ 8. More than Level 7 but less than Level 9.
- ❐ 9. Requires reading of the most complex types of written material and translating the meaning and implications of that material for others to use (e.g., consent decrees, tender offers, government requests for proposal, proposed legislation, scientific articles, engineering studies).
- ❐ 10. Reading is more demanding than described in Level 9.

For Jobs That Require Reading MULTIPLE Languages

What languages in addition to English must be read, and at what reading level? (Not your personal capabilities should they be greater than what is required by the job.)

Additional Languages	**Reading Level** (1 to 10, from above)
_____	_____
_____	_____
_____	_____
_____	_____

BASIC JOB REQUIREMENTS: Writing in English

- ❐ 1. No writing required for this job.
- ❐ 2. More than Level 1 but less than Level 3.
- ❐ 3. Requires writing to record basic information (e.g., completing forms, taking messages).
- ❐ 4. More than Level 3 but less than Level 5.
- ❐ 5. Requires writing to provide information (e.g., form letters, short memorandums).
- ❐ 6. More than Level 5 but less than Level 7.
- ❐ 7. Requires writing to creatively explain or describe moderately complex or creative information (e.g., instruction manuals, internal company newsletters).
- ❐ 8. More than Level 7 but less than Level 9.
- ❐ 9. Requires writing with precise language to creatively communicate complex information (e.g., formal business reports, articles for periodicals or non-refereed professional journals, contracts, product brochures, press releases).
- ❐ 10. Reading is more demanding than described in Level 9 but less than Level 11.

❏ 11. Requires writing to communicate highly complex, abstract, and/or sensitive information (e.g., scientific articles for refereed journals, responses to lawsuits, securities/government tax negotiations, merger/acquisition due diligence).

❏ 12. Reading is more demanding than described in Level 11 but less than Level 13.

❏ 13. Creates original messages to promote specific company interests and agendas for delivery to both large and highly specialized audiences using diverse media (e.g., speeches for top executives to stock market analysts; original works, such as novels and screenplays).

❏ 14. Writing requirement is typically higher than Level 13.

For Jobs That Require Writing in MULTIPLE Languages

What languages in addition to English must be written, and at what level? (Not your personal capabilities should they be greater than what is required by the job.)

Additional Languages   **Writing Rating** (1 to 14, from above)

....

....

BASIC JOB REQUIREMENTS: Mathematics/Numerical Skills

❏ 1. Less than Level 2.

❏ 2. Basic arithmetic (addition, subtraction, multiplication, and division of whole numbers).

❏ 3. More than Level 2 but less than Level 4.

❏ 4. Add, subtract, multiply, and divide fractions and decimals.

❏ 5. More than Level 4 but less than Level 6.

❏ 6. Compute ratios, rates, percentages, discount, interest, profit/loss, commission, markup and/or selling price. Draw and interpret bar/pie graphs. *(Or comparable skills)*

❏ 7. More than Level 6 but less than Level 8.

❏ 8. Calculate time-value of money or cash flow discounts. Perform break-even analysis. Use geometry and trigonometry in practical applications ("shop math"). Calculate single-line queuing (wait-line) analysis. Compute reorder points. *(Or comparable skills)*

❏ 9. More than Level 8 but less than Level 10.

❏ 10. Use calculus, correlation/regression, linear programming, complex (multiline) queuing analysis. Compute Black-Scholes formula or capital asset pricing model (CAPM) for stock options. Calculate economic order quantity. *(Or comparable skills)*

❏ 11. More than Level 10 but less than Level 12.

❏ 12. Use multiple regression, factor analysis, time-series analysis, etc. Use advanced financial techniques to hedge risk via options, futures, and forwards contracts. Compute actuarial projections. Perform long-term asset-to-liability modeling. *(Or comparable skills)*

❏ 13. Typical math/numerical skills required on this job are greater than described in Level 12.

BASIC JOB REQUIREMENTS: Computer Skills

❏ 0. Computer skills are not needed for this job.

❏ 1. Use a computer, following clear instructions and procedures (e.g., electronic mail, basic data entry, listing database information).

❏ 2. More than Level 1 but less than Level 3.

❐   3. Use applications to produce basic/standard output (e.g., word processing, graphics, spreadsheets).

❐   4. More than Level 3 but less than Level 5.

❐   5. Use applications to produce complex output (e.g., advanced spreadsheet macros, highly complex graphics and tables, database reports, HTML coding). Define user specifications and functionality as input to analyst-programmers based on knowledge of work processes.

❐   6. More than Level 5 but less than Level 7.

❐   7. Program in COBOL, Assembler, JAVA, UNIX, or 2GL language. Provide software or hardware support for PC/desktop/microcomputer systems based on practical experience and knowledge of software and hardware. Create and administer production databases.

❐   8. More than Level 7 but less than Level 9.

❐   9. Provide technical problem diagnosis and resolution using knowledge of mainframe or server system architecture (hardware, software, and database interaction). Create logic database designs. Use data systems analysis and programming. Use ETL in creation of data warehouses. Use data modeling.

❐   10. More than Level 9 but less than Level 11.

❐   11. Create mainframe or server systems programming specifications (not just user functionality requirements); document systems, programs, and databases. Perform data warehouse administration, advanced data systems development, and advanced data modeling.

❐   12. More than Level 11 but less than Level 13.

❐   13. Design/develop operating system software, multiplatform system architecture, mainframe/host system performance and capacity modeling. Design integrated hardware/software/database solutions for business problems. Perform data warehouse/enterprise storage management design. Lead CMMI, ITIL, or comparable process implementation.

❐   14. More than Level 13 but less than Level 15.

❐   15. Design and implement enterprise information technology strategy.

❐   16. More than Level 15.

BASIC JOB REQUIREMENTS: Manual Skills

> Indicate whether each type of manual activity is:
>   4 = Critical part of this job
>   3 = Major part of this job
>   2 = Part of this job
>   1 = Minor part of this job
>   0 = NOT or very infrequent part of this job

FOR EXAMPLE

1. Tending

Placing materials in or removing them from machines. Starting, stopping, and observing the functioning of machines or equipment. Adjusting materials or controls of machine such as changing guides, setting timers, clearing jams, and adjusting switches to maintain performance.

Replace toner cartridges. Fill bins or supply conveyors. Un-jam a photocopier.

☐ **2. Manipulating/Driving/Steering**

Use tools or special devices to work, guide, or move objects or materials. Starting, stopping, and controlling the actions of machines or equipment for which a course must be steered or guided in order to fabricate, process, or move things or people.

> *Operate a telephone switchboard. Drive an automobile. Operate a lift truck.*

☐ **3. Controlling**

Starting, stopping, controlling, and adjusting the progress of a machine or equipment as work is in progress. Involves observing gauges, dials, or other controls and continuously regulating the operation of the equipment and materials to attain a work standard.

> *Operate a personal computer, video camera, or packaging machine.*

☐ **4. Precision Work**

Select appropriate tools, objects, or materials and adjust and use tools to attain demanding standards of results in variable work situations.

> *Prepare scale drawings. Paste-up print copy. Interior painting. Finish carpentry.*

BASIC JOB REQUIREMENTS: Formal Education

Indicate the level of education *minimally required* to perform this job. This may be higher or lower than the education level of current incumbents in the job.

- ❏ 1. Less than Level 2.
- ❏ 2. *United States:* 8th grade. *Other countries:* secondary education (e.g., *graduado escolar,* middle school, *scoola media*).
- ❏ 3. More than Level 2 but less than Level 3.
- ❏ 4. *United States:* high school diploma. *Other countries:* completed senior secondary or vocational school (e.g., diploma, FE college, gymnasium, high school, *lycee,* FPII y/o BUP).
- ❏ 5. More than Level 4 but less than Level 6.
- ❏ 6. Studies more advanced than secondary or vocational school but not at a university (e.g., junior college, postgymnasium).
- ❏ 7. More than Level 6 but less than Level 8.
- ❏ 8. Earned bachelor's degree (e.g., *diplomatura, laurea breve,* license).
- ❏ 9. More than Level 8 but less than Level 10
- ❏ 10. Earned master's degree (e.g., MA, MS, MPA, MFA, MBA, laurea).
- ❏ 11. More than Level 10 but less than Level 12.
- ❏ 12. Earned doctoral degree (e.g., PhD, EdD, MD, DO, JD, LLB, DPharm).
- ❏ 13. More than Level 12.

If you checked Level 10 or above, please write in below the discipline(s) in which the required master's or doctoral degrees should be earned:

BASIC JOB REQUIREMENTS: Continuing Education

Mark (✓) only one box that describes the effort needed to keep skills and knowledge at levels to *meet the requirements of the job.* Use the small box between two levels if the skill level required for this job falls between two descriptions.

- ❒   1. Skill and knowledge requirements are stable.
- ❒   2. More than Level 1 but less than Level 3.
- ❒   3. Skill and knowledge requirements change slowly over time. Time and effort needed to keep current is limited and generally during scheduled, paid work hours.
- ❒   4. More than Level 3 but less than Level 5.
- ❒   5. Skill and knowledge requirements change frequently. Keeping current requires some unpaid time and effort outside of usual work hours.
- ❒   6. More than Level 5 but less than Level 7.
- ❒   7. Skill and knowledge requirements change continuously and require significant unpaid effort outside of usual working hours to maintain.
- ❒   8. More than Level 7.

Licensing or Certification (e.g., driver's license, CPA, CEBS, PE, CNE)

❒$_0$ Licenses/certifications are not required for this job (go to next question).
❒$_1$ License/certificates **desirable** but not required. Please specify:

_____

❒$_2$ License/certificates **required.** Please specify:

_____

BASIC JOB REQUIREMENTS: Experience

Mark (✓) only one box indicating the *minimum amount of directly related work experience* required to do this job. To be successful on this job requires completion of …

A 2-year associate's degree PLUS on-the-job experience of:
- ❒ 1 day or less
- ❒ 1 week or less
- ❒ 1 month or less
- ❒ 1 year or less
- ❒ 1–3 years
- ❒ 3–6 years
- ❒ 6–10 years
- ❒ More than 10 years
- ❒ This job could not be performed by a person whose formal education was limited to a 2-year associate's degree, no matter how much on-the-job experience they obtained.

A 4-year baccalaureate degree PLUS on-the-job experience of:
- ❒ 1 day or less
- ❒ 1 week or less
- ❒ 1 month or less
- ❒ 1 year or less
- ❒ 1–3 years
- ❒ 3–6 years

❒ 6–10 years
❒ More than 10 years
❒ This job could not be performed by a person whose formal education was limited to a 4-year baccalaureate degree no matter how much on-the-job experience they obtained.

A master's degree PLUS on-the-job experience and continuing professional education of:
❒ 1 day or less
❒ 1 week or less
❒ 1 month or less
❒ 1 year or less
❒ 1–3 years
❒ 3–6 years
❒ 6–10 years
❒ More than 10 years
❒ This job could not be performed by a person whose formal education was limited to a master's degree no matter how much on-the-job experience they obtained.

An earned doctorate PLUS on-the-job experience and continuing professional education (include postdoctoral studies/internships as on-the job experience) of:
❒ 1 day or less
❒ 1 week or less
❒ 1 month or less
❒ 1 year or less
❒ 1–3 years
❒ 3–6 years
❒ 6–10 years
❒ More than 10 years

BASIC JOB EXPERIENCE: Professional Know-How

❒ **Qualified but Inexperienced**
Has completed the prescribed academic degree, professional instruction, supervised practice, and certification/licensure examinations
- Has mastered the core/essential knowledge base
- Knows analytical rules that guide applied action
- Able to perform basic/standard procedures and protocols
- Relies on buddy system/coach to demonstrate applied skills and to guide decisions

❒ Job requires knowledge of professional principles and concepts *beyond* that of a qualified but inexperienced professional but *less than* an independent practitioner

❒ **Independent, Proficient Professional Practitioner**
Proficiently applies established professional knowledge, standards, and systems of practice to:
- Deal with clients/customers
- Establish an effective course of professional action/intervention
- Deal with emergency or crisis situations with the professionally prescribed standard response
- Intuitively grasp familiar, stable professional situations; In unfamiliar, dynamic, or crisis situations, applies analytical rules to arrive at prescribed decisions and actions

- Recognizes changes in conditions and reacts appropriately to improve condition, seeking validation of actions in advance as appropriate
- Effective in relationships with clients/customers, professional peers, and other members of the professional/service team
- Coaches less experienced professional practitioners

❐ Job requires concept knowledge of professional principles and concepts *beyond* that of an independent, proficient practitioner but *less than* expert

❐ **Expert Practitioner**
- Intuitive, holistic understanding of complex and dynamic or crisis situations based on broad and deep applied professional experience
- Recognizes early, subtle changes in conditions and intervenes flexibly or creatively to avert degradation or initiate improvement of situation
- Skilled in conflict management and effectively managing the most challenging relationships with and among clients/customers, professional peers, and other members of the professional/service team
- Mentors peers to acquire fine points of professional practice

❐ Job requires knowledge of professional principles and concepts *beyond* that of an expert practitioner

BASIC JOB REQUIREMENTS: Problem-Solving Complexity

Mark (✓) only one box that best describes the kind of problems this job solves independently. Consider only the typical problems with which it deals. Typical problems are those encountered frequently. Use the box between two levels if the skill level required for this job falls between two descriptions.

❐ 1.
❐ 2. Carries out one- or two-step tasks (e.g., transport, stack, weigh). The problems that occur are expected (e.g., misplaced or mispackaged materials). There are standard solutions.
❐ 3.
❐ 4. Carries out tasks which require a sequence of steps usually performed in a particular order (e.g., process forms, type letters). The problems may be frequent but easy to recognize.
❐ 5.
❐ 6. Solves problems in situations where most problems have occurred before. Solutions are familiar. The solutions are based on past practices.
❐ 7.
❐ 8. Work is diversified and involved, resulting in some unique problems. Judgment is required to adapt standard practices and principles to meet new conditions.
❐ 9.
❐ 10. Deals with situations for which there are no precedents. Work is governed by broad directions, objectives, and policies. Because conditions change frequently, this job must use creativity and judgment. There is considerable latitude in the decisions that are made.
❐ 11.

JOB CHARACTERISTIC: Breadth of Impact

Mark (✓) only one box indicating the organizational level typically affected by decisions made in this job. Use a box between two levels if the job requirement falls between two descriptions.

- ❐   1.
- ❐   2.   Decisions typically affect only this job
- ❐   3.
- ❐   4.   Decisions typically affect this job or its immediate work group
- ❐   5.
- ❐   6.   Decisions typically affect multiple work groups/coworkers
- ❐   7.
- ❐   8.   Decisions typically affect a single function or a single operating department (e.g., credit, operations, accounting, payroll)
- ❐   9.
- ❐   10.   Decisions typically affect multiple staff functions and/or multiple operating departments (e.g., human resources and finance)
- ❐   11.
- ❐   12.   Decisions typically impact the entire organization
- ❐   13.

JOB CHARACTERISTIC: Consequence of Errors

This question deals with the consequence of errors made by an incumbent in this job. Assume in answering that all normal care and judgment are exercised, and that normal work guidelines and rules are followed.

Please mark (✓) only one box indicating the typical consequences of errors in this job. Use a box between two levels if your answer falls between two descriptions.

- ❐   1.
- ❐   2.   Errors cause delays, inefficiencies, or unnecessary expense specific to this job.
- ❐   3.
- ❐   4.   Errors cause delays, inefficiencies, or unnecessary expense and affect the work of others in this job's immediate work group, team, or department.
- ❐   5.
- ❐   6.   Errors cause delays, inefficiencies, or unnecessary expense or loss of revenue. The error would have a measurable short-term (less than 1 year) financial impact. [Describe below.]
- ❐   7.
- ❐   8.   Errors decrease revenue or profits sufficient to create an identifiable reduction in profit that shows up on the corporate annual profit and loss statement. [Describe below.]
- ❐   9.
- ❐   10.   Errors have a critical negative impact on operations or services that measurably decrease long-term company performance and shareholder value. [Describe below.]
- ❐   11.

Provide brief examples of errors that have *actually* occurred, the cost, and the circumstances in which the illustrative error happened:

JOB REQUIREMENT: Organizing Scope

This question deals with this job's responsibility for organizing work. Please mark (✓) only one box indicating the level most typical in this job. Use a box between two levels if the job requirement falls between two descriptions.

❐ 1.
❐ 2. Performs activities planned by others.
❐ 3.
❐ 4. Plans day to day activities of *this job only.*
❐ 5.
❐ 6. Assists in developing plans by creating/compiling forecasts, program/product recommendations, and other financial or policy data.
❐ 7.
❐ 8. Organizes priorities, allocation of resources, etc., to meet operational objectives of a department or function and/or to implement a project, program, or product.
❐ 9.

JOB REQUIREMENT: Internal Relationship Management

Mark (✓) only one box indicating the typical internal customer contacts needed to do this job.

❐ 1. Job duties do not require contacts outside the immediate work group.
❐ 2.
❐ 3. Work occasionally requires internal contacts outside the work group to exchange work-related information.
❐ 4.
❐ 5. Work requires occasional internal contacts outside the work group to reach agreement on different points of view. Interactions can impact continued working relations with internal customers.
❐ 6.
❐ 7. Work requires internal contacts outside the work group to resolve mutual problems and/or to collaborate on work procedures, including team projects.
❐ 8.
❐ 9. Work requires internal contacts outside the work group to persuade or gain cooperation and acceptance of ideas. Job requires tact and diplomacy to avoid conflict.
❐ 10.
❐ 11. Work routinely requires internal contacts outside the work group in situations requiring persuasion and resolution of conflict.
❐ 12.
❐ 13. Work routinely requires internal contacts outside of work group to resolve controversial positions and to negotiate sensitive issues.

JOB REQUIREMENT: External Relationship Management

Check only one box indicating the *typical* external contacts needed to do this job.

❐ 0. Job duties do not require contacts external to the organization.
❐ 1.
❐ 2. External contact involves furnishing or obtaining factual information over the telephone, in writing, or in person. Requires normal courtesy and professionalism in dealing with others.

❏   3.
❏   4. External contact is over the telephone, in writing, or in person for ongoing service, handling regular transactions, and providing detailed information about a specific set of products, services, capabilities, issues, or questions.
❏   5.
❏   6. External contact over the telephone, in writing or in person to resolve complaints, make adjustments, or correct mistakes about a specific set of products, services, capabilities, issues, or questions.
❏   7.
❏   8. External contact is in person or over the telephone for direct selling or representing a variety of products, programs, services, or capabilities.
❏   9.
❏   10. External contact to resolve serious complaints, manage key relationships, make significant adjustments, handle high-profile meetings, or deal with very sensitive issues or relationships.
❏   11.
❏   12. Primary responsibility for creating or expanding relationships with major customers, key individuals, or critical external organizations.

JOB REQUIREMENT: Responsibility for Others

Please mark (✓) the first box on the left if an item **does not apply**. Otherwise, mark (✓) box 2 or 3 as defined in the scale below to indicate this job's highest level of responsibility for the activities listed. You should mark (✓) only one box for each item in the list.

Level of Responsibility: Mark (✓) the appropriate box

None = No responsibility for activity

Contributory = Provides input or makes recommendations

Primary = The most directly responsible decision maker (even though superiors may approve and human resources may require documentation or policy compliance)

None	Contrib.	Primary	
$\square_0$	$\square_1$	$\square_2$	1. Training and/or coaching other associates
$\square_0$	$\square_1$	$\square_2$	2. Scheduling, providing daily work direction to other associates
$\square_0$	$\square_1$	$\square_2$	3. Scheduling overtime for other associates
$\square_0$	$\square_1$	$\square_2$	4. Scheduling vacation for other associates
$\square_0$	$\square_1$	$\square_2$	5. Performance evaluation for other associates
$\square_0$	$\square_1$	$\square_2$	6. Hiring
$\square_0$	$\square_1$	$\square_2$	7. Disciplinary action
$\square_0$	$\square_1$	$\square_2$	8. Terminating
$\square_0$	$\square_1$	$\square_2$	9. Salary administration (determining and adjusting salaries)

Describe below any other type of "people" responsibility not included above:

_____

_____

_____

JOB CHARACTERISTIC: General Financial Responsibility

1. What is the amount of annual expense and/or revenue (i.e., budget) for which this job is responsible?
   $_____ , _____ , _____ , _____ . 0 0
   millions, 100 thousands, thousands, hundreds

2. What is the largest expenditure an incumbent in this job can make **without** review and approval by the immediate supervisor? (i.e., "signature authority"):
   $_____ , _____ , _____ , _____ . 0 0
   millions, 100 thousands, thousands, hundreds

   Briefly explain the kinds of financial decisions, responsibility, and impact of this job.

JOB CHARACTERISTIC: Budget Responsibility

Mark (✓) only one box indicating the type of budget responsibility most typical in this job. Use a box between two levels if the job requirement falls between two descriptions.

- ❒ 1. No responsibility for developing or monitoring an operating budget.
- ❒ 2. More than Level 1 but less than Level 3.
- ❒ 3. Assists in developing a budget by providing data or recommendations.
- ❒ 4. More than Level 3 but less than Level 5.
- ❒ 5. Shares accountability for the performance against a budget or manages a portion of a departmental budget.
- ❒ 6. More than Level 5 but less than Level 7.
- ❒ 7. Develops and manages a single operating budget; accountable for performance against that budget.
- ❒ 8. More than Level 7 but less than Level 9.
- ❒ 9. Manages subordinates who prepare budgets; accountable for the combined performance to these budgets.
- ❒ 10. More than Level 9 but less than Level 11.
- ❒ 11. Shares accountability for the performance of a single P&L.
- ❒ 12. More than Level 11 but less than Level 3.
- ❒ 13. Primary accountability for the performance of a single P&L.
- ❒ 14. More than Level 13 but less than Level 15.

❐   15. Shares accountability for the performance of multiple P&Ls.
❐   16. More than Level 15 but less than Level 17.
❐   17. Primary accountability for the performance of multiple P&Ls.
❐   18. More than Level 17.

JOB CHARACTERISTIC: Overall Financial Impact

Jobs do not need to directly manage revenue or expense budgets in order to have financial impact. For example:
- Facilities jobs require decisions about leases, service contracts, etc.
- Finance jobs require judgments about taxes, allocations, and depreciation.
- Distribution center jobs require actions to safeguard inventory.
- Management information systems jobs require decisions about use of staff time and software/hardware purchases.

1. Financial Impact of Input or Recommendations
Mark (✓) one box that indicates the annual dollar impact (in US$) of this job in terms of responsibilities, decisions, judgments, or actions for which this job *provides input* or *makes recommendations*.

❐$_1$ **Less than $1,000**   ❐$_5$ **At least $500,000**

❐$_2$ **At least $1,000**   ❐$_6$ **At least $5 million**

❐$_3$ **At least $5,000**   ❐$_7$ **At least $50 million**

❐$_4$ **At least $50,000**   ❐$_8$ **At least $100 million**

                                    ❐$_9$ **More than $1 billion**

2. Formal Financial Accountability
What is the dollar impact (in US$) of this job in terms of responsibilities, decisions, judgments, or actions for which this job has *the primary formal accountability or authority,* perhaps subject to review for compliance with budgets or accounting procedures or financial policy?

❐$_1$ **Less than $1,000**   ❐$_5$ **At least $500,000**

❐$_2$ **At least $1,000**   ❐$_6$ **At least $5 million**

❐$_3$ **At least $5,000**   ❐$_7$ **At least $50 million**

❐$_4$ **At least $50,000**   ❐$_8$ **At least $100 million**

                                    ❐$_9$ **More than $1 billion**

JOB CHARACTERISTIC: Working Conditions

Note: It is important in these questions that you respond based on what is needed to do this job under *typical* conditions.

Please mark (✓) the first box on the left if an item does not apply. Otherwise, mark (✓) box 2, 3, or 4 as defined in the scale below to indicate how often the activity is needed. You should also mark (✓) only one box for each item in the list.

How Often **Scale**

> **Occasionally** = **1% to 20%** of the time
> **Frequently** = From **21% to 50%** of the time
> **Constantly** = At least **51%** of the time

<u>Never</u>	<u>Occasionally</u>	<u>Frequently</u>	<u>Constantly</u>	
$\square_0$	$\square_1$	$\square_2$	$\square_3$	1. Controls information which, if communicated beyond its intended audience, would have an immediate, measurable, negative impact on the organization's financial performance, shareholder value, or ability to do business in the future
$\square_0$	$\square_1$	$\square_2$	$\square_3$	2. Traveling, excluding overnight stays
$\square_0$	$\square_1$	$\square_2$	$\square_3$	3. Traveling, including overnight stays
$\square_0$	$\square_1$	$\square_2$	$\square_3$	4. Traveling, regular business trips of 4 or more days at one time
$\square_0$	$\square_1$	$\square_2$	$\square_3$	5. Working under tight time constraints, with no choice as to work to be performed *today* due to inflexible deadline
$\square_0$	$\square_1$	$\square_2$	$\square_3$	6. Work or work product is continuously and systematically measured against precise, inflexible, quantitative standards of quantity, quality, and accuracy

<u>JOB REQUIREMENT: Physical Job Requirements: Lifting Strength</u>

Please mark (✓) the box that best describes the physical work typically performed on this job.

- ❐   1. **Very Light Work** – Lifting 5 kg (10 pounds) maximum and occasionally lifting and/or carrying small items. This level applies to the majority of office work.
- ❐   2. **Light Work** – Lifting 10 kg (20 pounds) maximum with frequent lifting and or carrying objects weighing up to 5 kg (10 pounds).
- ❐   3. **Medium Work** – Lifting 20 kg (50 pounds) maximum with frequent lifting and or carrying of objects weighing up to 10 kg (25 pounds).
- ❐   4. **Heavy Work** – Lifting 45 kg (100 pounds) maximum with frequent lifting and or carrying of objects weighing up to 20 kg (50 pounds).
- ❐   5. **Very Heavy Work** – Lifting objects in excess of 45 kg (100 pounds) with frequent lifting and or carrying of objects weighing 20 kg (50 pounds) or more.

Physical Job Requirements: Agility (Climbing and Balancing)

Indicate on the lines below the frequency of climbing and balancing in this job.

    0 = Not present

    1 = Occasionally = up to 33% of the time on the job

    2 = Frequently = from 33% to 66% of the time on the job

    3 = Constantly = more than 66% of the time on the job

_____ **1. Climbing** – Ascending or descending ladders, stairs, scaffolding, ramps, poles, using feet, and legs and or hands/arms

_____ **2. Balancing** – Avoid falling when walking on narrow, slippery, moving surfaces

REFERENCES

Anseel, F., Lievens, F., Schollaert, E., & Choragwicka, B. (2010). Response rates in organizational science, 1995–2008: A meta-analytic review and guidelines for survey researchers. *Journal of Business and Psychology, 25,* 335–349.

Boyatzis, R. E. (1982). *The competent manager: A model for effective performance.* New York, NY: John Wiley & Sons.

Campbell, A., & Sommers Luchs, K. S. (1997). *Core competency-based strategy.* London, UK: Thomson Publishing.

Campbell, J. P., Dunnette, M. D., Lawler, E. E., III, & Weick, K. E., Jr. (1970). Managerial behavior, performance, and effectiveness. New York, NY: McGraw-Hill.

Cascio, W. F. (1998). *Applied psychology in human resource management* (5th ed.). New York: Prentice-Hall.

Cycyota, C. S., & Harrison, D. A. (2006). What (not) to expect when surveying executives: A meta-analysis of top manager response rates and techniques over time. *Organizational Research Methods, 9,* 133–160.

Dierdorff, E. C., & Wilson, M. A. (2003). A meta-analysis of job analysis reliability. *Journal of Applied Psychology, 88,* 635–646.

Flanagan, J. C. (1954). The critical incident technique. *Psychological Bulletin, 51,* 327–358.

Hamel, G., & Prahalad, C. K. (1994). *Competing for the future.* Cambridge, MA: Harvard Business School Press.

McClelland, D. (1973). Testing for competence rather than for 'intelligence.' *American Psychologist, 28*(1), 1–14.

McClelland, D. (1976). *A guide to job competency assessment.* Boston, MA: McBer.

McCormick, E. J., Jeanneret, P. R., & Mecham, R. C. (1972). A study of job characteristics and job dimensions as based on the Position Analysis Questionnaire (PAQ). *Journal of Applied Psychology, 56,* 347–368.

Mitrani, A., Dalziel, M., & Fitt, D. (1992). *Competency based human resource management.* London, UK: Kogan Page.

Morgeson, F. P., Delaney-Klinger, K., Mayfield, M .S., Ferrara, P., & Campion, M. A. (2004). Self-presentation processes in job analysis: A field experiment investigating inflation in abilities, tasks, and competencies. *Journal of Applied Psychology, 89,* 674–686.

Mueller, M., & Belcher, G. (2000). Observed divergence in the attitudes of incumbents and supervisors as subject matter experts in job analysis: A study of the fire captain rank. *Public Personnel Management, 29,* 529–555.

Nadler, D. A., & Tushman, M. (1999). The organisation of the future: Strategic imperatives and core competencies for the 21st century. *Organisational Dynamics, 27*(1), 45–58.

Page, R. C., & Van De Voort, D. M. (1989). Job analysis and HR planning. In W. F. Cascio (Ed.), *Human resource planning, employment, and placement* (pp. 2.34–2.72). Washington, DC: Bureau of National Affairs.

Schnake, M. E., & Dumler, M. P. (1985). Affective response bias in the measurement of perceived task characteristics. *Journal of Occupational Psychology, 58,* 169–166.

Spencer, L., & Spencer, S. (1993). *Competence at work: A model for superior performance.* New York, NY: John Wiley & Sons.

Stetz, T. A., Beaubien, J. M., Keeney, M. J., & Lyons, B. D. (2008). Nonrandom response and rater variance in job analysis surveys: A cause for concern? *Public Personnel Management, 37,* 223–242.

Truxillo, D. M., Paronto, M. E., Collins, M., & Sulzer, J. L. (2004). Effects of subject matter expert viewpoint on job analysis results. *Public Personnel Management, 33,* 33–46.

U.S. Department of Labor. (1972). *Handbook for analyzing jobs.* Washington, DC: U.S. Government Printing Office.

White, R.W. (1959). Motivation reconsidered: The concept of competence. *Psychological Bulletin, 66,* 297–333.

5

Using Secondary Sources of Work Information to Improve Work Analysis

Erich C. Dierdorff

DePaul University

Today's practitioners of work analysis face a host of challenges that must be met in order to build effective high-performance human resource systems. Similar to many human resource activities, these challenges frequently stem from a lack of stakeholder acceptance regarding the critical nature of work analysis efforts. Although outlining the ways to address all of these challenges is beyond the scope of the present chapter, there is an underlying theme that pervades such criticisms—namely, the *overall efficiency* with which thorough work analysis efforts can be undertaken.

One potential tactic to increase the efficiency of work analysis is to incorporate secondary sources of work information. Indeed, work analysis can be a very labor-intensive process and practitioners may frequently lack adequate resources with which to undertake work analysis projects. Thus, the extent to which other sources of work information can be used to facilitate local work analysis efforts holds the promise of increased efficiency and cost reduction. Toward this end, the overall goal of this chapter is to describe a systematic process for using secondary sources of work information for work analysis. To accomplish this goal, this chapter first defines what comprises a secondary source of work information. Next, some secondary sources are described, and their role in the conventional work analysis process is defined. Third, several best practices regarding how to incorporate secondary sources into work analysis efforts are discussed and illustrative examples are provided. Finally, the chapter concludes with a discussion of using secondary sources in different situations commonly encountered by work analysis practitioners.

WHAT EXACTLY IS A SECONDARY SOURCE?

Put simply, secondary sources are reputable external sources that provide some type of world of work information to supplement or augment local work analysis efforts. Several aspects of this definition are worthy of particular attention. First, to be of value, secondary sources of work information must be *reputable*. The data that are presented should have been gathered using a systematic approach or, if this is indiscernible, come from a source where one can make a reasonable assumption that a systematic process was followed. In other words, Uncle Bob's list of critical competencies posted on his blog would generally not be considered very reputable. (Unless Uncle Bob is an experienced work analyst, of course!) Secondary sources will themselves vary in terms of reputability, which also has several practical implications. This latter point is addressed in more detail later in the chapter.

Second, as the label implies, secondary sources are *external* to the organization. That is, these sources exist outside the firm to encompass various repositories or locations of relevant reference material. Although such reference material is available in print form (e.g., technical reports, training manuals, job advertisements), the vast majority will be accessible via the Internet. Relying on web-based sources has the added benefit of allowing a practitioner to more efficiently locate electronically available work analysis information through the use of search engines such as Google or Bing. With this in mind, the primary emphasis in this chapter is on using Internet-based secondary sources of work information. However, the processes described are equally applicable to hardcopy secondary sources as well.

Third, the definition denotes that secondary sources provide different *types* of information about the world of work. Secondary sources will provide work information that spans different domains important to conducting work analysis, such as work requirements (e.g., task and responsibilities), worker requirements (e.g., knowledge, skills, and abilities [KSAs]; traits), and work context features (e.g., work design characteristics). Further, work information from secondary sources will vary in terms of the level of data that are provided. For example, some sources may offer rather specific information focused on a particular position or job, whereas others describe details at the occupation- or profession-level. Still others may be situated at a very molar level with information about industry-level trends.

The last component of the definition is that secondary sources *supplement* or *augment* local work analysis efforts. Although it may be a subtle definitional property at first glance, this aspect is absolutely essential for effective use of secondary sources. Put bluntly, work information from secondary sources should not replace local data collection or verification. Rather, the most judicious uses of data from secondary sources are to guide, facilitate, bolster, and/or enhance local work analyses undertaken by practitioners at their particular organizations on the particular work roles or jobs that are of interest. In this sense, secondary sources can provide for better, more focused use of actual hands-on analysis time by priming the analyst with information about what remains to be collected during local work analysis efforts.

WHERE DO SECONDARY SOURCES FIT INTO THE WORK ANALYSIS PROCESS?

The typical work analysis process begins with determining the intended purpose (or purposes) of the information to be collected, followed by researching the target work role (or roles), identifying potential respondents, choosing data collection methods, and finally analyzing and summarizing the collected data (Brannick, Levine, & Morgeson, 2007). Secondary sources of work information are most relevant after the intended purpose is designated and the target role becomes the focus of research. If thoroughly completed, this important step in the work analysis process holds two potentially beneficial ramifications. First, existing information on the target work role allows the practitioner to build a conceptual foundation on which to proceed with the work analysis effort. That is, researching the target role can produce information that enables a more effective work analysis project. Second, the more data that are located and determined to be relevant, the greater the efficiency and speed with which a practitioner can complete the work analysis project. For example, if existing in-house information (e.g., previous work analysis results) or secondary source information is abundant, one might only need to conduct very focused local verifications of these findings (e.g., convene a subject matter expert panel review of the information).

The specific intended purposes or uses of work analysis results are wide ranging and have significant downstream implications for how the work analysis project is ultimately conducted (see Chapter 1, this volume). These consequences similarly hold for how secondary sources might supplement work analysis efforts. For example, if the intended purpose of a work analysis is to produce information for designing training programs, secondary source information related to critical tasks and skills at the job level would likely be most salient. Because the intended purposes of work analysis results are addressed elsewhere and have similar consequences for using secondary sources, a more general focus on the different situations in which a work analysis practitioner may find him or herself will better highlight the potential value of using secondary sources of work information.

Broadly speaking, there are at least three different situations where locating and incorporating secondary sources of work information into local work analysis efforts would be highly desirable. One situation is when a practitioner is beginning a completely new work analysis project to examine either a work role that is new to the organization or one that has not been the focus of previous work analysis. Another situation is when a practitioner is faced with old or "stale" data from a work analysis conducted several years prior and there is a pressing need to update or refresh these past findings. In both of these situations, the more secondary source information that can be accumulated about a target work role, the more local efforts can subsequently focus on data collection methods seeking to review and verify secondary source findings instead of methods for generating new data from scratch. A final situation for which secondary sources hold significant practical value is when a practitioner must forecast future organizational needs, such as when work analysis information is used for human resource planning or strategy (Cronshaw, 1989; Schneider & Konz, 1989). Using secondary source information in each of these situations will be discussed in more detail later in this chapter.

EXAMPLES OF SECONDARY SOURCES

Although the specific types of secondary sources that are available to practitioners are quite numerous, such sources typically fall into four general categories. These categories are summarized in Table 5.1. It is important to note that the categories are not necessarily exhaustive but are broad enough to encompass the vast majority of secondary sources that may come into play during work analysis projects. Categorizing secondary sources also helps to better depict the different types of work information they provide, as well as their relative strengths and weaknesses. These categories are discussed in the following sections.

Occupational and Career Information Systems (Category 1 Sources)

Secondary sources within this category are typically the most expansive repositories of work information. These sources tend to provide a wide range of work information, spanning work and worker requirements and work context data. They also tend to be very reputable in that the data they provide are generally based upon systematic and thorough data collection procedures. The work information provided is at the job level or occupation level, but primarily the latter. Most

Table 5.1   Categories of Secondary Sources

Category	Primary Sources
1. Occupation and career information systems	Federal or state governments
2. Employment advertisements	Job or position boards and professional associations
3. Certification and training resources	Professional associations and universities or community colleges
4. Research and technical reports	Industry groups, "think tanks," and university research centers

of these available sources will be sponsored or maintained by governmental agencies. Specific examples include the following:

- The U.S. Department of Labor's Occupational Information Network (O*NET) – http://www.online.onetcenter.org
- New Zealand's Kiwi Careers or Career Services – http://www.careers.govt.nz
- Canada's National Occupational Classification – http://www5.hrsdc.gc.ca/NOC/English/NOC/2006/Welcome.aspx
- Australia's Job Guide – http://www.jobguide.thegoodguides.com.au

To further illustrate the nature of these secondary sources, it is helpful to describe one of these systems in a little more detail. O*NET is arguably the single most expansive and rich secondary source of work information currently available to practitioners (Morgeson & Dierdorff, 2010). In fact, O*NET will often provide enough information to be the only secondary source needed for many local work analysis projects. As an occupational system, O*NET provides data exclusively focused on occupations. However, the online database is easily searchable with job- or position-level titles, and such titles are also displayed in the system as reported job titles. The work information provided by the O*NET system comprises six major areas: worker characteristics, worker requirements, experience requirements, occupation requirements, workforce characteristics, and occupation-specific information (Mumford & Peterson, 1999; Peterson et al., 2001). Table 5.2 shows specific examples of the descriptors in each of these areas of O*NET.

Using occupational and career information systems as secondary sources of work information has several strengths. First, relative to the other three categories of secondary sources, these systems generally have the largest and most diverse amount of work data. These characteristics mean that such systems will often be beneficial to a wide range of specific purposes of work analysis projects (e.g., training, selection, performance management). Second, the data provided by these

Table 5.2   Secondary Source Information in O*NET

Domain	Descriptor Types	Select Examples
Occupation requirements	Generalized work activities	Getting information; performing administrative activities
	Detailed work activities	Administer medications or treatments; analyze psychological testing data
	Work context	Structured/unstructured work; freedom to make decisions
Worker requirements	Basic skills	Speaking; critical thinking
	Cross-functional skills	Negotiation; social perceptiveness; time management
	Knowledge	Economics and accounting; biology
	Education	Required level of education; instructional program required
Worker characteristics	Abilities	Perceptual speed; stamina; finger dexterity
	Work styles	Initiative; attention to detail
	Occupational interests	Realistic; investigative; artistic
	Occupational values	Achievement; recognition; independence
Occupation-specific information	Tasks	Record patients' medical information and vital signs; review blueprints to determine work details and procedures
	Tools and technology	Theodolites; project management software; power saws
Workforce characteristics	Labor market information	Wages; employment statistics
	Occupational outlook	Employment projections (e.g., growth, shrinkage)
Experience requirements	Experience and training	Related work experience and on-the-job training

sources are trustworthy in that they have been collected using rigorous scientific procedures to ensure the quality of the responses from incumbents and professional analysts, the sources that tend to populate these systems. Third, the data provided in occupational and career information systems are representative of the labor force at large, which enhances the generalizability of these secondary sources. Fourth, many of these secondary sources (e.g., O*NET) allow direct access to source databases as well as survey instruments to collect further local work analysis data. Finally, the data in these systems are standardized and organized in taxonomies of titles, as opposed to the self-reported titles that appear in other secondary source categories (e.g., employment advertisements).

However, occupational and career information systems are not without some weaknesses as well. First, the information in these systems may be too general to be directly used (verbatim) in local work analysis efforts. For instance, most data are captured at the occupational level (e.g., retail salespersons), whereas a practitioner may need more specific information that pertains to the requirements of a particular position or job (e.g., home appliance salesperson). Second, by design the information contained in occupational and career information systems is generic in nature. This means that the information will not be in the "language of the firm" and thus may not reflect proprietary processes, technology, or software that are important to performance. Interestingly, a final weakness actually stems from the strengths of these systems. Because secondary sources in this category provide such expansive and representative data maintained by respected governmental entities, these characteristics might lull practitioners into falsely believing that work analysis efforts needed to locally verify secondary source information are unnecessary.

Employment Advertisements (Category 2 Sources)

This category of secondary sources encompasses the variety of job or position postings available online. Such postings can be found on various types of web sites including full-service providers (e.g., Monster and CareerBuilder), services focused on a particular states or regions (e.g., CalJobs), job boards maintained by professional associations (e.g., Society for Industrial and Organizational Psychology, the American Bar Association), and external job advertisements listed by specific organizations. These sources tend to vary widely in the precise type of work information that is provided. For example, some postings include job descriptions and specifications that list in detail important tasks and KSA requirements. Still other postings may merely list a very general description of one or two major role responsibilities. As expected, the level at which the data are focused in these postings is the position or job level. The reputability of these sources also substantially varies, primarily because the procedures by which the work information was acquired are frequently indiscernible. However, sometimes the amount of information contained in a given posting provides a glimpse into the thoroughness of research. For instance, it is reasonable to assume that a fairly rigorous process was followed if a posting is able to provide a detailed description spanning duties, KSAs, work experience, and work context.

Using employment advertisements as secondary sources of work information has several strengths. First, the sheer number of possible postings available to practitioners is likely to be substantial. However, the number of available references is also contingent upon the particular role that is being researched. Factors such as industry-level changes or a growing/shrinking economy are likely to impact the number of advertisements available. Another strength of using these secondary sources is that when multiple references are located (which is typically the case), a practitioner can easily cross-reference the information from different postings. This triangulation approach may help to overcome issues associated with a given source's reputability. A third strength stems from the level of information specificity of secondary sources in this category. Because the work information is provided at the position or job level, one can always aggregate the information into broader job groupings or occupations, unlike Category 1 sources for which disaggregation (i.e., going directly from general to specific) is not feasible without additional data collection.

Employment advertisements also have some weaknesses that are important to note. First, as touched upon previously, the availability of job postings is typically ample but can vary widely depending on the job that is being researched. Thus, unlike the first category of secondary sources for which the systems are designed to encompass all major occupations in a given labor force, employment advertisements may only offer work information on a portion of such work roles (i.e., those jobs that are in demand). Second, using employment advertisements as secondary sources is a bit more labor intensive because practitioners need to establish a consensus across different references in order to ensure thoroughness and veracity. That is, the lack of information about how data were collected to create the postings necessitates additional research to verify completeness (e.g., checking for consistency across different advertisements). A final weakness is that many employment advertisements have a strong tendency to use firm-specific and/or occupation-specific jargon. For example, acronyms for various technology or software are frequently found in job postings without further explanation as to what they actually represent. This probably becomes more problematic for firm-specific jargon for which it is more difficult to figure out the precise meaning of such verbiage. In addition, if a practitioner is in the situation where the focal job is new to the organization or is wholly unfamiliar with the job, the jargon in employment advertisements can be rather confusing.

Certification and Training Resources (Category 3 Sources)

Secondary sources in this category comprise published competency models, educational curricula, training programs, and certification and licensure requirements. Similar to employment advertisements, professional associations are a key location to find this type of secondary source. Other fruitful providers include university or community college curricula and union training programs germane to the target role of the work analysis. The kinds of work information frequently found in these secondary sources are worker requirements, such as knowledge and skills, although major work activities are often mentioned or can be inferred from the training content (e.g., a course on graphic design software implies "designing"). The level of the information in certification and training resources is typically occupation level.

One advantage of using certification and training resources is that the information is generally offered by reputable sources that have a significant stake in a thorough understanding of the target work role. For example, professional associations exist to serve their constituent members who are of particular professions (i.e., occupations). In addition, substantial effort is required to develop curricula for training programs, which helps to bolster the confidence a practitioner can have in the information provided. Finally, these secondary sources are frequently quite detailed and, because they are focused on teaching or vetting successful performance, will provide comprehensive coverage of the most important requirements of a given role.

There are some weaknesses associated with using certification and training resources as well. First, there are availability issues that coincide with these secondary sources of information. In short, not all occupations have certification or licensure requirements or formal training programs. Second, even when these secondary sources do exist for a target role, some references may restrict access to only members of the professional association or to participating students and trainees. Third, although these sources can provide detailed work information, practitioners will often be required to make inferences about the activity requirements of the target role (e.g., tasks or duties). Such inferences are frequently necessary because worker requirements (e.g., key knowledge or skill domains) and tools or technology usage (e.g., machines or software) are commonly the primary emphasis in these secondary sources.

Technical and Research Reports (Category 4 Sources)

This final category of secondary sources includes governmental technical reports, industry white papers, and research briefs. Professional associations, industry associations, governmental entities, private policy institutes, and university research centers generally author these materials. The type of work information found in these secondary sources is most often about the broad context in which work is performed. For example, the purpose of many reports in this category is to delineate important industry trends, new technology, or shifts in the profession. Technical and research reports will sometimes provide direct references to work and worker requirements as well, although less frequently than the other three categories. The level of information in these secondary sources varies widely, with some reports focused on very specific jobs, whereas others discuss an entire industry domain. As an example of the latter, a large number of research reports are aimed at describing the current and future impact of the "green economy" on jobs and workers (Dierdorff et al., 2009).

One benefit of using this category of secondary sources is that most reports are evidence based and derived from systematic research conducted by experts in a given area. Another strength is that these secondary sources can help work analysis practitioners to keep abreast of important changes in the world of work. This is especially salient for work analysis efforts that are used for human resource planning purposes for which emphasis is placed on forecasting future human capital needs. Finally, technical and research reports commonly provide broader information than what is usually found under the purview of work analysis. For example, reference topics often encompass descriptions of broader contextual factors, such as industry trends and changing meta-technology (e.g., biotechnology). These molar forces, although not typically an emphasis of work analysis efforts, are influential nonetheless because they shape the way work is performed.

One major weakness of this category is that these sources are probably the least available in comparison to the other three categories. Therefore, locating these sources is likely to be more search intensive, even when they do exist. Another weakness is some reports are too broadly oriented to be of direct use in local work analysis projects. That is, the information provided is so far removed from work and worker requirements it becomes infeasible to translate the information to meet the current work analysis project's goals. Similarly, some reports may be too hypothetical in nature, such as those that offer predictions of where an industry is headed or what might be the next best technological innovation. Finally, even when these reports do provide information relevant to work and worker requirements, they seldom provide lists of specific tasks or KSAs. Therefore, practitioners must make extensive inferences to derive work and worker requirements from the information given by these secondary sources. As an example, numerous healthcare industry and government reports discuss the major shift in medical recordkeeping from paper-based filing to electronic medical records (EMR) using specialized database software (EMR software platforms). Yet, precisely how this impacts the requirements of roles associated with medical recordkeeping is rarely discussed beyond general comments about using EMR software.

HOW TO USE SECONDARY SOURCES

Although the amount and intended use of secondary source data will vary from work analysis project to project, there is a general process that can be followed to maximize the value of secondary source information. This process entails seven sequential steps, which are briefly described below. Also discussed are several key factors that enhance the effectiveness of this process. Finally, illustrations of using the process for each of three situations discussed earlier (i.e., new work analysis project, updating a previous work analysis, and work analysis for forecasting) are presented.

The first step in the process of using secondary sources is contingent on the initial step of any work analysis—namely, determining the intended purpose of the work analysis results. From this initial step, a practitioner can determine the types of work information that are desired (tasks, responsibilities, KSAs, context variables) and the target work role (or roles) to be analyzed. Once these decisions are made, this first step to using secondary sources also requires a practitioner to identify the broad industry areas in which target roles reside. Identifying the relevant industry helps to guide more focused searching to locate useful secondary sources. Table 5.3 shows the expected value of work information from the four secondary source categories relative to the major purposes of work analysis (described in Part III, this volume).

The second step is to directly search secondary sources that fall into the occupational and career information system category. The most fruitful source with which to begin is the O*NET online system because of its expansive coverage of different occupations and types of work information. Here, the practitioner would search O*NET for the target role to find the work and worker requirements most germane to work analysis at hand. Also, it is useful to search the related occupations that are provided by the O*NET system, which can often lend additional insight into the target role. In addition, O*NET displays lists of reported job titles for each occupation. These should be recorded for use in subsequent steps that require broader keyword searching of Internet-based sources. If secondary information obtained from this step is deemed sufficient, a practitioner can skip ahead to the fifth step.

The third step involves more general searching techniques to locate potentially useful secondary sources from the other three secondary source categories. Practitioners can use search engines such as Google or Bing to accomplish this step. Critical to this step is the choice and use of keyword searching. Typically, simply searching on the target job title will produce the most hits. However, more focused searching can result from including additional terms, such as the type of secondary source (e.g., "civil engineer" and "certification" or "licensure" or "training"), the type of work information (e.g., "civil engineer" and "skills" or "knowledge"), or the industry in which the work role is usually found (e.g., "transportation" or "construction"). From a practical standpoint, keyword searching is most efficient when it begins with the most focused attempts (very specific and numerous keywords) and then expands to increasingly more general attempts until new information is no longer found or sufficient information is obtained.

The fourth step is to establish consensus across the multiple references found in the third step. Even for the most reputable of sources, it is sound practice to confirm the work information from a given reference with other references. One rule of thumb to follow is that the less likely a reference's information seems to have been based on systematic research, the more confirming

Table 5.3 Value Contribution of Secondary Sources by Work Analysis Purpose

	Category 1	Category 2	Category 3	Category 4
Work design/redesign	Moderate	Low	Low	Low
Work descriptions and recruitment	High	High	Moderate	Low
Test development	Moderate	Low	High	Low
Work simulations	Low	Low	Moderate	Low
Performance evaluation	Moderate	Low	Moderate	Low
Training needs	Low	Low	High	Moderate
Compensation	Moderate	Moderate	Low	Moderate
Career planning	High	High	High	Moderate

Category 1 = occupation and career information systems; Category 2 = employment advertisements; Category 3 = certification and training resources; Category 4 = research and technical reports.

evidence is needed to establish consensus. For example, if a practitioner comes across only a single job advertisement that provides what appears to be the perfect list of duties and KSAs for his or her target role, the next step would still be to find other references that provide consistent information.

The fifth and sixth steps entail recording the secondary sources that have been referenced and summarizing the findings. Recording the secondary sources that were consulted is important not only for purposes of documentation, but also for building a database of useful secondary sources for future work analysis projects. Procedures to summarize the results of searching secondary sources of work information are similar to those used for work analysis in general (see Chapters 6 and 8, this volume).

Finally, the seventh step is to conduct additional in-house data collection as part of a local work analysis project. The main purpose of this last step is twofold: to verify the secondary source information with primary sources (i.e., the firm's members) and to capture additional work information that was not found in secondary sources but is needed to meet the goals of the work analysis project.

Some Critical Success Factors

There are three factors in particular that are essential for making work analysis more efficient through the use of secondary sources. The first factor is a thorough understanding and appreciation for the inferences that are required when trying to use secondary sources for work analysis. Few secondary sources provide the direct results of a work analysis (with the exception of some sources in the first two categories). In this sense, practitioners should expect the available work information to be frequently indirect. Thus, it is incumbent upon the practitioner to extrapolate meaning from secondary sources to apply to his or her current work analysis. It is important to note that some of these inferences are more complex and perhaps more tenuous (Dierdorff & Morgeson, 2009). For example, inferring the type of required knowledge or skills from a secondary source listing of equipment or software is markedly more straightforward than inferring the impact of industry-level changes on specific work activities. The major implication here is that the more complex or indirect the inference, the more the practitioner needs to rely on his or her own work analysis expertise. Further, such expertise should be honed through a deeper understanding of the target role and the context in which it is performed. Fortunately, a thorough review of secondary sources can contribute to a more comprehensive understanding.

A second factor that is critical for successful use of secondary sources is corroborating evidence. This factor probably cannot be overstated. Establishing consensus across different secondary sources is one of the few ways to ensure that the information obtained is reliable and generalizable. The unchecked nature of many Internet-based sources all but necessitates corroboration of secondary source information. In addition, as mentioned previously, using references from some categories of secondary sources (e.g., employment advertisements) will typically require more corroboration than references in other categories (e.g., occupational and career information systems).

A final contributing factor to successful use of secondary sources is the local verification of the collected work information. It would be extremely poor practice to treat secondary source information as the primary source of work analysis information (not to mention the potential legal complications of this choice). As discussed at the outset of this chapter, using secondary sources is the second phase in a work analysis project where researching the target role(s) a priori is the task at hand. Recall as well that one of the benefits of using secondary sources is the enhanced expediency of local work analysis projects because not all data must be locally derived. However, sound work analysis practice dictates that all data, whether from secondary sources or from local efforts, should be checked for quality and thoroughness (see Chapters 7 and 8, this volume).

Using Secondary Sources in Different Work Analysis Situations

Earlier in this chapter, three general situations in which work analysis practitioners may find secondary sources particular value were described: when a practitioner is beginning a completely new work analysis project, faced with old data from a work analysis conducted several years prior, or forecasting future organizational needs as part of human resource planning. In each of these situations, all four categories of secondary sources will be relevant to work analysis projects. However, some secondary source categories will be more (or less) pertinent in some situations.

When the focus of a work analysis is to examine a work role that is new to the organization or one that has not been the focus of previous work analysis, secondary sources from all four of the categories will be useful. Following the steps outlined above, Category 1 secondary sources would be particularly salient because the more data that can be located and collected, the less need for lengthy and labor-intensive local efforts to generate new work information. Once the practitioner obtains a solid base of work information using Category 1 sources, the emphasis shifts to secondary sources in Categories 2 and 3. Here, the practitioner's general goal is to locate secondary sources that are relevant to the target work role in order to produce additional work information that fills in any gaps due to moving from occupation-level data to job-level data, gives more job- or industry-specific details (e.g., certain technology or equipment use, typical work processes), and corroborates Category 1 information. When it is time to turn to local verification, the practitioner will have several options. For example, designated managers of the target role could simply review the secondary source information (if it does not yet exist in the firm), or incumbents, managers, or subject matter experts could directly rate and review the information (if the role already exists). In the latter option, additional cost savings could be realized if respondents were randomly selected to either provide direct ratings or to review/revise the secondary source information.

Often practitioners are faced with a situation in which there is a pressing need to update or refresh past work analysis findings. The emphasis here is on quickly finding holes in the pre-existing work analysis data and then revising these data with more recent information. Thus, there is a premium on identifying what may have changed in terms of how the target work role is performed (e.g., new technology, new standards or work practices, new credentials). These needs make secondary sources from Categories 2 and 3 likely to be most salient to practitioners. In terms of the steps discussed earlier, most effort would be placed on locating, corroborating, and summarizing secondary source information. Local verification remains important; however, it is probably sufficient to restrict such efforts to summary reviews by key stakeholders (e.g., panel reviews by managers and/or senior incumbents).

When using work analysis to support human resource planning, practitioners need secondary sources to provide information that allows decision makers to forecast future human capital needs. These needs include the acquisition of new human capital, such as when a firm's strategy takes it into a new product or service market, as well as investing in current human capital, such as when extensive retraining or cross-training efforts are undertaken. In this scenario, secondary sources from Category 4 are most salient because they tend to describe broader shifts in industry practices, technology, and employment growth (or shrinkage). Further, the main aim of many Category 4 secondary sources is to predict what particular industries or markets will look like in the future. Also, relevant in this scenario are Category 3 secondary sources that outline the key tasks, skills, and knowledge that are requisite to the target role(s) of the work analysis. These secondary sources are particularly useful if the goal of the work analysis is to support the design of retraining programs. Because of the proactive, future-oriented focus of this situation, local verification of secondary source information is minimally needed. Here, practitioners would likely need to thoroughly document the secondary source findings and present them to an organization's senior leadership engaged in the planning effort. Individuals involved in training and development, as well as recruitment and selection, may also need to review the secondary source information because of the direct implications for their particular roles (e.g., designing a recruitment strategy to locate and attract people for the expected new positions).

PARTING THOUGHTS

This chapter sought to describe a systematic process for using secondary sources of work information for work analysis. In doing so, secondary sources were defined and placed within the process for conducting work analysis in general. The relative strengths and weaknesses of different kinds of secondary sources were discussed, as well as the steps practitioners should follow when using these sources. As portrayed in this chapter, there are a variety of available secondary sources that practitioners can bring to bear in their own work analysis projects. The extent to which practitioners can leverage these sources holds the promise of substantially increasing the overall efficiency of work analysis.

Interestingly, secondary sources of work information have long been recognized and used in work analysis projects. For instance, the *Dictionary of Occupational Titles* (U.S. Department of Labor, Employment and Training Administration, 1977) has a rich history of informing countless local work analysis efforts—a history that the developers of O*NET seek to continue. Yet, it is important to note that the low cost and easy availability of secondary sources is a relatively recent state of affairs. These benefits have been primarily realized through the impact of information technology, specifically the widespread accessibility of Internet-based sources of work information. This accessibility now makes secondary sources viable mechanisms through which to improve work analysis. However, the newness of a heavier reliance on secondary sources to augment work analysis projects also creates a strong need for research in this area. Case studies of organizations effectively using secondary sources as well as focused empirical studies seeking to assess the consequences for the quality of work analysis data when using secondary sources (e.g., reliability, utility, acceptance, validity) are prime examples of the types of evidence sorely needed. Hopefully, this chapter's depiction of the practical value of using secondary source of work information will not only increase their applications in practice but will also act as a catalyst for future research efforts as well.

REFERENCES

Brannick, M. T., Levine, E. L., & Morgeson, F. P. (2007). *Job analysis: Methods, research, and applications for human resource management* (2nd ed.). Thousand Oaks, CA: Sage Publications.

Cronshaw S. (1989). Job analysis: Changing nature of work. *Canadian Psychology, 39,* 5–13.

Dierdorff, E. C., & Morgeson, F. P. (2009). Effects of descriptor specificity and observability on incumbent work analysis ratings. *Personnel Psychology, 62,* 601–628.

Dierdorff, E. C., Norton, J. J., Drewes, D. W., Kroustalis, C. M., Rivkin, D., & Lewis, P. (2009). *Greening of the world of work: Implications for O*NET-SOC and new and emerging occupations.* Retrieved September 18, 2011, from http://www.onetcenter.org/reports/Green.html

Morgeson, F. P., & Dierdorff, E. C. (2010). Job and work analysis: From technique to theory. In S. Zedeck (Ed.), *APA handbook of industrial and organizational psychology* (Vol. 2, pp. 3–41). Washington, DC: American Psychological Association.

Mumford, M. D., & Peterson, N. G. (1999). The O*NET content model: Structural considerations in designing jobs. In N. G. Peterson, M. D. Mumford, W. C. Borman, P. R. Jeanneret, & E. A. Fleishman (Eds.), *An occupational information system for the 21st century: The development of O*NET* (pp. 21–30). Washington, DC: American Psychological Association.

Peterson, N. G., Mumford, M. D., Borman, W. C., Jeanneret, P. R., Fleishman, E. A., Campion, M. A., … Dye, D. M. (2001). Understanding work using the occupational information network (O*NET): Implications for practice and research. *Personnel Psychology, 54,* 451–492.

Schneider, B., & Konz, A. M. (1989). Strategic job analysis. *Human Resource Management, 28,* 51–63.

U.S. Department of Labor, Employment and Training Administration. (1977). *Dictionary of occupational titles* (4th ed.). Washington, DC: Government Printing Office.

6

Analyzing Work Analysis Data

ROBERT J. HARVEY

Virginia Tech

This chapter focuses on methods for analyzing work analysis data, a task that nominally occupies one of the later steps in a work analysis project. By obvious necessity, data analysis only occurs after the project has been planned, after the sources and methods of data collection have been determined, and after data have been collected. However, in the course of describing the major decision points and questions that must be addressed when analyzing work analysis data, I will make frequent reference to decisions that were made (or perhaps were *not* made) during earlier stages of the project (a situation that is especially common when using archival work analysis data).

Rather than detailing step-by-step procedures for analyzing work analysis data to address every imaginable human resources function, I chose to identify a common core of frequently encountered questions, issues, and choice points that face practitioners who use work analysis data to solve human resources problems (see Table 6.1). For each, I offer my suggestions regarding what I find to represent best practices that should be encouraged, as well as potential pitfalls that should be avoided.

Of course, significant disagreement may exist regarding what represents a best practice (or pitfall) in a given applied human resources situation. For example, sharp differences exist regarding the question of how (or if) practitioners should attempt to document the accuracy and quality of work analysis ratings (e.g., Harvey & Wilson, 2000; Sanchez & Levine, 2000). Likewise, for reasons described in more detail in this chapter, I find all attempts to use single-item rating scales to directly quantify abstract, hypothetical work-activity or worker-trait constructs to be ill advised. However, advocates of this holistic rating strategy can easily be found (e.g., Peterson, Mumford, Borman, Jeanneret, & Fleishman, 1999), and single-item holistic ratings form the foundation of the Occupational Information Network (O*NET) database collected by the U.S. Department of Labor to replace the venerable *Dictionary of Occupational Titles* (DOT; U.S. Department of Labor, 1991).

In cases where sharp disagreement exists, I attempt to identify the reasons why my best-practices recommendations diverge, but readers may make their own decisions as to which approach should be taken. Clearly, the specifics of your project and organization (particularly, the degree to which the legal defensibility and job-relatedness of the work analysis results must be documented) should guide your choice of data collection methods and data analytic strategies.

Sid Gale elicited much laughter from the audience of researchers and practitioners who attended a work analysis symposium (Harvey, 1985) when he noted that "there's nothing funny about job analysis." Bill Cunningham (1989, p. 7) made a similar point—to less amusement—when he made the following observation:

> When I first started back in the [1960s], job analysis was a very lonely area to work in. Over the years, it has not been very popular relative to some of the more glamorous activities in [industrial and

Table 6.1 Major Decision Points and Suggested Best Practices in Analyzing Work Analysis Data

Phase of Project/Type of Decision	Decision Point	Decision Issues/Best Practices Recommendations
I. Questions you wish had been addressed earlier in the project	A. Do you have enough raters?	1. It's difficult to have too much data! Try to sample 100% of eligible raters and achieve a 100% return rate even if it adds to the timeline. Without a 100% sample you won't have the data to examine/revise the job title taxonomy (II.E below) to reduce true within-title variability if needed (as so often is the case). 2. Always check to determine whether differential response rates exist for different types of raters (e.g., demographic, performance level, geographic). If you failed to collect adequate demographic data on the raters, go back and collect it now. 3. Be sure you have enough data profiles to justify your planned uses of the data (especially ones that involve deriving prediction equations), and continue or restart data collection until you do.
	B. Did you use the right raters?	1. Raters with questionable motivation, inadequate job familiarity, and/or instrument familiarity or comprehension tend to produce poor quality ratings. 2. The quality of the work analysis ratings you collect tends to be directly proportional to the amount of accountability that raters perceive. Accountability is enhanced by including a formal review process (see #5), and it is effectively absent when data are collected from anonymous raters. 3. Collecting ratings using trained, objective job analysts is consistently superior to using job incumbents and supervisors in terms of data quality and accuracy (given the highly questionable motivation seen among many incumbents and supervisors), especially if the work analysis data are being collected for high-stakes human resources applications. 4. Using job analysts to collect data does suffer from potential concerns regarding overreliance on title-based stereotypes. Be sure analysts have adequate firsthand experience with the position/job being rated in the organization in question to reduce the temptation to rely on stereotypes or prototypes evoked by the title itself that may or may not be accurate in describing how the job is performed in this setting. 5. Always try to include an independent review to ensure ratings accuracy, especially when using incumbents or supervisors as raters. When using analysts, this can be accomplished by using multiple analysts to rate each entity and assessing cross-analyst convergence when rating a common target. 6. Even very large samples do not compensate for the use of questionable raters. If the raters suffer from significant concerns regarding motivation, job familiarity, or quality, consider redoing the data collection with better rating sources. In terms of defensibility, the Achilles heel of most human resources projects centers on the credibility of the raters who provided the work analysis data and the conditions under which it was collected. If you are worried about defending your human resources system against an equal employment opportunity (EEO) challenge, do not skimp on rater quality.

C. Have you collected the right data?

1. The qualitative content and behavioral specificity of the data collected must be consistent with the human resources purpose you intend to address. If it is not consistent, then it is time to revisit the data collection stage and collect ratings that match your purpose. This is particularly an issue when archival work analysis data are being considered for use in a new human resources application.

2. Many human resources functions require you to be able to make meaningful, level-based comparisons between organizational entities (collecting data using a nonrelativistic rating scale). To be able to do so, each rated entity (position, job, occupation) must be rated on a *common metric* of content (i.e., the same profile of work descriptors, described using the same rating scales).

D. Have you rated at the appropriate level of analysis?

1. Do not start the rating process by rating abstract characteristics of jobs. You can always "aggregate up" if needed later, but it's impossible to disaggregate work analysis ratings to add additional behavioral detail or specificity after the fact.

2. The higher the behavioral abstraction of the rated work elements, the more difficult it becomes to rate them accurately, and to later defend the quality of those ratings if challenged.

3. Using single-item scales to directly rate highly abstract constructs (i.e., the holistic rating strategy used in the O*NET and F-JAS) is not recommended because of both the poor psychometric properties of such ratings and the total absence of data that could be used to defend the accuracy or validity of the holistic inferences.

4. Even in the unlikely event that high interrater agreement is seen using holistic rating methods (see II.A below), such findings *do not* provide convincing evidence regarding the quality or accuracy of holistic ratings. This is due to the fact that they attempt to directly rate hypothetical, unobservable, latent constructs. For example, although it may be interesting to note that 99% of a sample of experts agreed that a total of 5,299 angels can dance on the head of a given pin, even perfect cross-rater agreement proves nothing when the things being rated are hypothetical and not amenable to direct observation or verification.

5. The work analysis rating process should be as descriptive as possible; this is not the time to be asking raters to make large inferential leaps. To the degree that you require raters to use as little inference or abstraction as possible, you will greatly facilitate both ratings quality and your ability to verify and later defend the work analysis database if needed.

6. If you are tasked with addressing a human resources issue with a work analysis database that has not been rated at an appropriate level of analysis/behavioral specificity, strongly consider going back and collecting the appropriate type of data.

continued

Table 6.1 Major Decision Points and Suggested Best Practices in Analyzing Work Analysis Data (Continued)

Phase of Project/Type of Decision	Decision Point	Decision Issues/Best Practices Recommendations
	E. Did anything funny happen when collecting the data?	1. Even if you are in good shape on the above design/decision points, always check to see if unexpected things or events occurred during the data collection process that might make you reconsider your situation. This is particularly the case if the data collection process is conducted by others or archival data are used.
		2. If events occurred during the data collection process that raise significant questions, especially regarding rater motivation or accountability (e.g., a major labor-management dispute occurred while collecting data from incumbents; the individuals in charge of collecting the data decided to allow anonymous ratings; important items were left out of the survey), you should carefully consider how important the issues of data verifiability and ratings quality issues are for the project. Redoing the data collection may be the best solution if the work analysis ratings are being used to drive a high-stakes human resources function.
	F. Do you have adequate backups and version control?	1. The work analysis data collection and analysis process is usually an iterative one, especially if ratings are deleted or changed due to quality concerns, the job title taxonomy needs to be revised to deal with within-title heterogeneity, ratings are revised as a result of a review/verification process, or if derived scores need to be formed from the basic work analysis ratings.
		2. Maintaining adequate backups and version control (to track changes to the data that occur over time) is essential for both documentation purposes and to help minimize the risk of data analysis errors (see III.G). The content versioning system (CVS) tools that are used in software development or document management are equally useful when managing an evolving work analysis database.
II. Getting the data ready	A. What quality are the data in terms of rater agreement?	1. If multiple analysts rate a common position, job, occupation, or if multiple incumbents rate a given job, it is essential to closely examine the degree of cross-rater agreement.
		2. If the rated work elements have sufficient behavioral specificity and objectivity, demonstrating strong agreement between properly motivated raters who are rating a common target offers solid evidence in support of an inference of data quality and accuracy.
		3. Conversely, even perfect cross-rater agreement has little or no probative value regarding an inference of data quality or accuracy when abstract, not-directly-observable, or hypothetical elements are rated.
		4. However, the lack of strong cross-rater agreement offers compelling evidence against an inference of data quality or accuracy. That is, if the same target is rated, a lack of agreement unavoidably implies that at least some of the raters are erroneous.
		5. If you lack confidence that a common target is being rated (e.g., when multiple incumbents rate a common job title, or several analysts rate a common occupational title), a lack of strong cross-rater agreement may simply reflect the fact that true differences exist between the target being judged by each rater. Lack of agreement is an indicator that the job-title taxonomy should be examined and revised if necessary to form sufficiently homogeneous clusters (see II.E).

6. Profile-similarity correlations should not be viewed as interrater reliability estimates in a classical test theory (CTT) sense (e.g., Crocker & Algina, 1986).

7. Reliability estimates computed for individual rated items (e.g., the intraclass correlation [ICC]) should use appropriate choices of error terms and not simply the version (e.g., the ICC case 3 formula) that tends to produce the highest numerical value. Even when using the most appropriate choice of an error term for the given situation, you should closely consider the numerous assumptions (many of which may be completely untenable) that underlie the practice of interpreting such agreement indices as "reliability" estimates (particularly ones that assume independence of errors across raters, items, or targets).

8. If level-sensitive rating scales are used (which is strongly recommended; see I.C), it is critical that cross-rater agreement be quantified using indices that are sensitive to *absolute* rating deviations (e.g., Euclidean distances) and not simply to relative similarity of profile shape (e.g., cross-rater profile correlations). In work analysis, the level of the rating is usually highly critical information, and if some judges consistently rate too high or low, such disagreement should not be ignored (as it is when profile-correlation indices are used).

9. Whether or not one chooses to view rater-agreement indices as estimates of reliability, it is critical not to set too low of a standard for what constitutes acceptable agreement. The widely used rule of thumb that an agreement index value above .70 represents acceptable agreement has been shown to be far too lenient. Indeed, it is not difficult to generate random responses that show cross-profile rs and r_{wg} agreement levels in the .70s (and in many cases, far higher, especially when, as with work analysis data, the population distributions of the ratings tend to be highly skewed).

10. If using the r_{wg} agreement index, it is highly recommended that you compute your own locally meaningful error-term estimate (i.e., the amount of cross-rater item variance that would define a highly unacceptable lack of agreement). Many researchers and practitioners use the maximum variance error estimate, which can be far larger than the variance one would see if totally random ratings were made. The practical effect of such a choice is to substantially inflate the cross-rater agreement levels and potentially lead to the misleading conclusion that adequate agreement is present even when very low true agreement exists. As Harvey and Hollander (2002) demonstrated, r_{wg} agreement values in the .80s and .90s can easily be produced when *random* ratings are sampled from the types of skewed population distributions that are commonplace in work analysis ratings.

11. The amount of cross-rater disagreement than can be deemed acceptable is not a constant, but varies considerably as a function of many factors, including the degree to which the human resources function being addressed is mission critical or litigious, the number of items in the rating profile, and especially, the number of rated items that can be identified as does-not-apply (DNA), especially by people with little job knowledge or with only minimal information. As DNA rates increase, the level of agreement deemed adequate must be increased. If any DNA agreements on obviously irrelevant items are likely, cross-rater agreement targets should be set far higher than the .70 rule-of-thumb commonly applied.

continued

Table 6.1 Major Decision Points and Suggested Best Practices in Analyzing Work Analysis Data (Continued)

Phase of Project/Type of Decision	Decision Point	Decision Issues/Best Practices Recommendations
		12. Depending on the human resources purpose being served, even relatively small cross-rater disagreements may be highly significant in practice. This is especially the case when disagreements are eliminated prior to performing the real data analyses by forming mean profiles across multiple raters for each job (see II.C). If raters disagree, it is critical to determine why they disagree; if it is due to error, the erroneous ratings must be corrected.
		13. If disagreement is due to true within–title differences (see II.E), you must determine whether the level of disagreement will affect the applied decisions that will be based on the work analysis results. Depending on the application, even relatively small true differences can produce substantial bottom–line differences in a consequential validity sense. However, in other applications, even larger differences may not be practically significant (e.g., when the purpose of the study is primarily to determine *which* activities apply, versus which are DNA).
		14. When assessing ratings agreement, it is critical that agreement indices be computed at the level of analysis at which the ratings were actually made. Never attempt to estimate either the reliability or validity of work analysis ratings (or a work analysis data collection instrument or process) by correlating profiles of mean ratings produced from separate groups of raters who judge a common target (e.g., a group of 20 incumbents versus 20 supervisors). Due to the exaggerating effects of aggregation bias (see II.C), even in relatively small groups of raters cross-group mean profile correlations in the .70s, .80s, and higher can be produced even when totally random ratings are made. Cross-group mean profile correlations grossly exaggerate the true degree of rater agreement that is present at the level at which ratings are actually made.
B. What additional quality indices should you examine?		1. The cross-rater agreement indices discussed above provide at best a limited measure of data quality, especially as the intrinsic verifiability and observability of the rated work elements decrease. Indices that get more directly at the question of ratings quality should also be examined when possible.
		2. When a common target is rated by multiple judges, a very useful index of rater performance can be computed from the number of items in the rated profile that are given DNA ratings, and/or rated at a very low level. Raters who are careless or lack motivation can often be spotted by virtue of their making far fewer non-DNA ratings in comparison to more diligent raters.
		3. Conversely, raters who are a little too motivated (e.g., to make the job appear more important or demanding) may be detected by virtue of their rating appreciably more items as non-DNA than others rating the same target. In both cases, a final determination regarding ratings quality can only be made by a review of the ratings in question by a suitably motivated subject matter expert (SME).

4. Including a number of items in the rating profile that you know for a fact are *not* relevant to the jobs being rated (and then counting the number of these that receive non-DNA ratings) provides a useful index of rater motivation or oversensitivity (e.g., Stutzman, 1983). Whether endorsed due to carelessness, lack of comprehension, or a desire to exaggerate, ratings provided by such judges are candidates for deletion from the database (see II.F).

5. Conversely, you can compute an undersensitivity index based on the number of DNA ratings that are given to items that you know are part of the jobs in question. Whether omitted due to inattention, lack of language skills, or a desire to minimize less glamorous aspects of the job, raters who score high on this type of undersensitivity index are candidates for deletion.

6. If abstract work dimension scales are formed and estimated using item response theory (IRT), a range of appropriateness indices (AIs) or person-fit indices (PFIs) can be computed to provide an index of the overall consistency or plausibility of an item response profile. Although such indices cannot detect dissimulation or incorrect responding when it occurs in a highly consistent fashion, they are effective in spotting smaller numbers of aberrant responses. As with all such indices, their primary value is in identifying possible aberrant response profiles; an in-depth examination of the ratings by a suitable SME must then follow to determine whether corrections to the ratings are needed.

C. Are there aggregation bias issues?

1. The distortions caused by *aggregation bias* (e.g., James, 1982) are widespread and potentially very severe. Aggregation bias reflects the fact that as cross-rater disagreement increases, the mean profile computed from heterogeneous ratings provides an increasingly inaccurate and misleading view of how work is actually performed on the entities (e.g., positions, jobs) that were rated. In extreme cases, the mean profile may not accurately describe *any* of the raters' ratings from which it is computed.

2. Given that nontrivial within-title variability is commonplace, unless the data analyses being planned will be performed using the disaggregated rated profiles (as opposed to the aggregated mean profiles), you must carefully assess the degree to which appreciable variability exists around the average profile.

3. If you have followed the above best-practice recommendation and conducted a thorough, item-level review and verification of the work analysis ratings, any remaining within-title variability arguably reflects *true* differences between entities. If you deem the amount of remaining heterogeneity to be large enough to risk aggregation-bias problems, revising the title taxonomy to form more homogeneous titles is indicated (see II.E).

4. Consistent with the points made in II.A, it is impossible in the abstract to set a fixed rule of thumb as to how much within-title heterogeneity is acceptable. For some human resources functions, it may be safe to simply eliminate the disagreement by forming a mean profile; for other functions, doing so may invite disaster (e.g., when attempting to defend the quality and accuracy of the work analysis ratings in an EEO challenge to a selection system).

continued

Table 6.1 Major Decision Points and Suggested Best Practices in Analyzing Work Analysis Data (Continued)

Phase of Project/Type of Decision	Decision Point	Decision Issues/Best Practices Recommendations
		5. One potential way to evaluate the amount of bottom-line impact of aggregation bias is to use simulation studies to perform a type of sensitivity analysis. For example, if the work analysis data are being used as input to a regression equation to predict worker-trait requirements in a JCV study (see III.F) or to predict pay rates in a compensation study, comparisons can be made between the predicted values obtained from the group-mean aggregate profile versus those obtained using individual rating profiles as predictors. If the differences are within a range deemed tolerable, this would support the argument that the aggregation process is appropriate. If sufficiently divergent predictions are obtained between different profiles holding the same title, however, questions regarding the appropriateness of the aggregation would result.
	D. Is agreement an artifact of DNAs?	1. As was noted in II.A, interpreting cross-rater profile agreement indices in the absence of an explicit consideration of DNA rates is highly inadvisable. Even with very substantial disagreement among raters, the presence of a handful of DNA agreements can be sufficient to produce the false *appearance* of adequate cross-rater agreement.
		2. When preparing to analyze work analysis data, you must determine the degree to which agreement on items that are *not performed* on the job in question represents valuable information, and what its relative importance is *vis-à-vis* cross-rater agreement on items that are relevant to the job.
		3. Depending on the type of work analysis data collection survey being used, substantial numbers of items are likely to be DNA for any given job (this is particularly the case for both task-inventory surveys designed to be given to a range of highly heterogeneous job titles, and for so-called worker-oriented surveys like the CMQ and PAQ). In the latter cases, the percentage of items that are irrelevant and rated DNA may approach 50% or more of the items.
		4. In such cases, one might well conclude that although interesting, DNA agreements on obviously irrelevant items are not particularly meaningful, and that cross-rater agreement indices should be computed *after* removing irrelevant DNA agreements. This would particularly be indicated in cases in which ratings of only the non-DNA items will represent the primary focus of subsequent data analyses, and when there is not a significant need to make meaningful cross-title comparisons between task-dissimilar titles.
		5. In other cases, precisely the opposite conclusion might be reached by arguing that it is essential that raters be able to agree on both what does apply and what does not. This is particularly the case when a common-metric approach to work analysis is taken (i.e., all raters judge the same items, using the same rating scales), and it is important to be able to make meaningful comparisons between dissimilar titles. In such cases, in which the primary comparisons of interest may be made at the more abstract work-dimension level of analysis (see II.H), agreement levels for both DNA and non-DNA items are critical because the work-dimensions scores are computed using the full profile of item responses (including DNAs).

E. Do you need to revise the job title system?

1. In my experience, it is exceedingly common (to the point of being universal) that the existing job-title system in place in an organization suffers from serious shortcomings. The above-mentioned issues of nontrivial true within-title heterogeneity are often present, and if serious enough, the only effective solution is to revise the title taxonomy in a fashion that splits overly heterogeneous titles into more homogeneous clusters (see Harvey, 1986, for more detail on the quantitative analyses involved in empirically deriving title taxonomies).

2. A second problem is often present as well. Here, the trouble is the opposite situation of having too many titles, drawing distinctions where no meaningful differences exists, and awarding different titles to positions that perform effectively the same work. One common cause of this is the practice of giving job title promotions to workers in lieu of a pay raise (as well as the illegal practice of creating separate titles for male versus female-dominated jobs that perform similar work, but receive different pay).

3. Regardless of the cause, the solution for this second type of taxonomic flaw is the opposite of the solution to the overly-heterogeneous title problem. Here, quantitative methods are used to combine currently-distinct titles.

4. Few organizations undertake a work analysis project with the explicit goal of revising their job title taxonomy. However, in many cases it becomes clear after collecting the work analysis data (and taking a close look at cross-rater, within-title variability) that the inadequacies of the current title taxonomy are so serious that it must be revised prior to performing the analyses that were the original focus of the project.

F. Should you discard questionable data?

1. Many of the best-practice recommendations made above lead to the present question: Are the questions regarding data quality of a given rater or data source so significant that you should discard their data?

2. Especially in cases in which you cannot follow the best-practice recommendation (see I.B.5) to provide a detailed quality review/editing of all work analysis ratings, discarding profiles that appear aberrant in terms of the various quality indices described above may be the most effective course of action available.

3. Best-practice recommendation I.A.1 (i.e., sample 100% of positions in each title) is highly beneficial here. When only small samples of respondents are sampled from each target title, the impact of deleting a questionable profile becomes more significant.

G. Do you need to renorm, transform, or rescale?

1. It is often the case that the original work analysis ratings must be transformed in some fashion before the real data analyses of interest can be performed. One of the most common reasons for doing so occurs when common-metric, standardized surveys are used, and the primary data-analytic interest lies in the more abstract work-dimension scores that are estimated by the survey. Here, factor-scoring or other methods (e.g., IRT) can be used to estimate the more abstract work-dimension constructs from the observed item responses.

continued

Table 6.1　Major Decision Points and Suggested Best Practices in Analyzing Work Analysis Data　(Continued)

Phase of Project/Type of Decision	Decision Point	Decision Issues/Best Practices Recommendations
		2. After computing the work-dimension scores, additional transformed scores may also be computed (e.g., percentiles giving the rank of the score in a normative population of interest). Given that many work analysis items and scales tend to follow a decidedly nonnormal distribution, providing percentiles in addition to factor analytic or IRT-based z-scores can aid considerably in the interpretation and use of the work-dimension scales.
		3. Transformations of the item responses themselves may also be performed, including ones that are of an ipsative nature (which normally should be avoided). For example, to counter the tendency for some raters to consistently rate higher or lower than others, practitioners may self-norm each rater's profile to attempt to equate them for different overall levels (e.g., by subtracting each rater's grand mean from each item rating). Although doing so compromises the level-based cross-job comparability of the ratings, it may be helpful if one's primary focus is on a single job title, and the objective of the study is to identify the activities that tend to be the most frequent or important, etc., *within* that title.
H. Do you need to estimate more abstract work characteristics?		1. Although it is necessary to rate relatively detailed and objective aspects of work in order to reduce ratings subjectivity and allow for independent verification (see I.D), many human resources functions are best addressed when a more abstract view of work is taken. This is particularly the case when meaningful comparisons must be made between task-dissimilar titles.
		2. Computing the abstract job- or work-dimension scores noted above offers a best-practices solution to the conflict between needing more-abstract data to drive human resources decisions, but requiring judges to rate more-specific work elements to enhance data quality and verifiability. That is, a clear paper trail exists between the higher-specificity original job ratings and the more-abstract work-dimensions scores derived from them. If the original item ratings are verifiable (and were indeed verified) and if the scoring system itself exhibits adequate psychometric properties, subsequent uses of the abstract work-dimension scores can be defended by showing the existence of this direct, well-documented linkage back to the original item ratings.
		3. Some have argued (see I.D) that it is far quicker and cheaper to simply make direct, holistic ratings of abstract work-dimension constructs (effectively skipping the need to collect ratings of more detailed, verifiable work characteristics). For example, this approach has been taken by the O*NET (e.g., Peterson et al., 2001) and the F-JAS (e.g., Fleishman & Mumford, 1991). At least with respect to the question of speed and data-collection cost, there is no doubt that simple holistic ratings are quicker and cheaper to collect than the time and cost associated with developing and administering a longer, more detailed inventory.

4. However, such procedures cannot be advanced as a best-practice recommendation; indeed, my best-practices recommendation is to avoid holistic ratings in all cases. Ample research has demonstrated that holistic ratings of abstract, hypothetical traits exhibit poor psychometric properties (especially interrater agreement), and often very poor convergence with ratings of the same traits obtained via traditional "decomposed judgment" measurement processes (e.g., Butler & Harvey, 1994; DeNisi, Harvey, & Shaw, 1977; Gibson, Harvey, & Harris, 2007; Harvey & Hollander, 2002; Harvey, Wilson, & Blunt, 1994). There is no basis for any practitioner to assume that the very consistent findings of poor psychometric properties and poor convergence with traditional defensible estimates will not also occur in his or her own project.

5. The total absence of a paper trail that leads directly back to ratings of observable, verifiable, objective aspects of work (which could be cited to defend the accuracy and job-relatedness of the work analysis database should it be challenged) further argues against the practice of direct holistic rating of abstract work constructs. Simply put, if your human resources function demands that jobs be rated in terms of abstract work-dimension constructs, derive such ratings from more specific, verifiable work analysis ratings; do not rate them directly. There is no free lunch when it comes to collecting defensible, accurate work analysis data.

III. Analytic strategies and methods

A. What basic descriptive analyses are needed?

1. Nicely enough, in many if not most work analysis projects, the actual data analytic procedures are quite simple in nature (e.g., computation of means, standard deviations, ranges; sorting of rated elements by average time-spent, importance). Even for more complex applications, a common core of such basic descriptive data analyses is typically performed.

2. The *Uniform Guidelines* (1978) offer a number of essential best-practices regarding work analysis information in the context of test validation, including reporting basic descriptive information on ratings relevant to criticality, importance, and consequence of error of individual rated elements.

3. In addition, whenever multiple rated profiles are collected for a given organizational target, the results of all of the above-mentioned analyses regarding documenting cross–rater agreement and rating quality should be presented using both the original sample, and the final sample (if questionable profiles were removed).

B. Is there a good way to document content-coverage adequacy?

1. Particularly in projects that are focused on identifying selection tests or laying the groundwork for a content-validity argument, the question of trying to empirically document the content-coverage adequacy of one's work analysis survey often arises.

2. One approach to this problem that is often seen (but which will not receive a best-practice recommendation here) involves including questions in the work analysis survey (which typically is a task-inventory style instrument custom-developed for the project) that ask the rater to judge (e.g., on a 0–100% scale) what percentage of the major activities of the job were covered by the survey. If the average coverage rating given for each job is sufficiently high, the practitioner cites such evidence as an indication of the content-coverage adequacy of the instrument.

continued

Table 6.1 Major Decision Points and Suggested Best Practices in Analyzing Work Analysis Data (Continued)

Phase of Project/Type of Decision	Decision Point	Decision Issues/Best Practices Recommendations
		3. Unfortunately, both the extensive literature on judgment heuristics (e.g., Tversky & Kahneman, 1974) and the limited research literature in the work analysis domain (e.g., Wilson, 1997) strongly question the degree to which raters are capable of providing high-quality judgments of this type. Specifically, Wilson (1997) showed that even after making dramatic reductions in the known-applicable content in a work analysis survey, raters still gave relatively high ratings regarding the content-coverage percentages.
	C. Do you need to link job-side data to person-side requirements?	1. The data analytic process becomes more complicated when the work analysis data are being collected to drive human resources functions dealing with employee selection, disability determination, rehabilitation, and other uses that require us to bridge the "two worlds of work"—that is, job-side work activities versus person-side worker traits that are predictive of job performance—described by Dunnette (1976).
		2. Three basic strategies for making this linkage can be identified in practice: (a) deriving *empirical* linkages between the job-side work analysis database and the levels of the person-side traits needed for successful job performance; (b) deriving *rational* linkages between the work analysis results and the person–trait requirements; and (c) skipping the job-side work analysis process entirely, and instead directly rating the person-side trait requirements (typically, using single-item holistic rating scales, as in the O*NET *Abilities* survey, and the F-JAS questionnaire).
		3. In terms of best-practice recommendations, Approach (a) comes closest to satisfying the goals of minimizing subjectivity, and providing a demonstrable paper trail that leads back to a defensible, verifiable work analysis database. Option (b), although widely used and at times successfully defended in court, does not get a best-practices recommendation due to its inherently high level of subjectivity (which becomes extreme when job incumbents or supervisors comprise the members of the SME panels that perform the rational linking). Option (c) employs the holistic-rating approach, which was dismissed earlier due to extreme subjectivity, the lack of any paper trail linking the person-side trait requirements directly back to the ratings in a defensible work analysis database, and its well-documented poor psychometric properties and lack of convergence with the results of empirical linking methods.
		4. Several methods exist for implementing the approach in (a), most notably the traditional criterion-related validation (CRV) study preferred by the *Uniform Guidelines*, as well as the job-component validity (JCV) method (see below).

D. If so, how must the linkage be documented?

1. Considerable variability exists within the field regarding the question of what constitutes adequate and appropriate evidence to support the validity of a given person-side worker selection requirement. This ranges from the relatively strict position taken in the *Uniform Guidelines* to the more flexible recommendations offered in the APA *Standards* and the SIOP *Principles*.

2. In terms of best-practice recommendations, this question can only be answered on a case-by-case basis, after carefully considering your position regarding the tradeoff that exists between the cost of performing the upfront work needed to collect empirical validity evidence, versus the downstream costs that might occur if the selection procedures face EEO challenge.

3. In the wake of the *Ricci v. DeStefano* (2009) Supreme Court decision, an argument can be made that a safe strategy would be to always conduct an empirical validation study to provide the organization with the strongest possible defense in the event that an EEO challenge occurs. Although formerly it seemed safe to recommend that an organization might not need to perform an extensive work analysis and empirical validation study if its procedures somehow managed to avoid producing adverse impact, that advice seems far less persuasive in this post-*Ricci* period.

4. Of the two main empirical methods for providing validity evidence, the JCV method offers the most direct linkage between the person-side trait specifications and the job-side work analysis database. That is, although a traditional CRV study directly links the person-side traits to *job performance*, it offers little or nothing in the way of empirical evidence to show how the job-side database of work activity ratings is directly linked to the *person-side tests* being considered for use as selection requirements.

5. However, JCV has received far less scrutiny in EEO cases than the traditional CRV study recommended by the *Uniform Guidelines*. Additionally, because JCV empirically links the job-side work dimensions to the person-side worker traits (rather than linking the person-side traits to measures of job performance), the task of converting JCV's predicted person-trait scores into operational hiring procedures (e.g., setting minimum cutoff scores on each person-side trait) is less clear than in a criterion-related validity study. That is, although JCV may provide a very accurate estimate of the mean level of a person-side trait seen among proficient employees, in many situations the size of the *range* of trait scores around that mean that is seen among proficient employees is quite substantial. This is particularly a concern when minimum-acceptable levels for the person-side traits are sought.

6. Accordingly, a conservative best-practice recommendation would be that practitioners should establish the linkage of the work analysis database to the person-side requirements using JCV methods, then follow with some type of empirical CRV study to document the linkage between the person-side requirements and measures of job performance, and provide a firmer foundation for identifying cutoff scores or target score ranges.

continued

Table 6.1 Major Decision Points and Suggested Best Practices in Analyzing Work Analysis Data (Continued)

Phase of Project/Type of Decision Decision Point	Decision Issues/Best Practices Recommendations
E. Should you look for interaction effects or nonlinear effects?	1. For both the CRV and JCV methods of collecting validation evidence, practitioners have long assumed that they only need to look for *linear* relations (either when predicting person–side traits from work dimensions, or when predicting job performance from person–side traits). That is, is there a significant (linear) correlation between the predictor(s) and criterion? 2. An argument can be made that you should also be looking for nonlinear effects, either ones involving nonlinear relations between individual predictors and the criterion (e.g., as in polynomial regression, using squared, cubed, etc., predictors), or ones involving interaction effects (i.e., where the nature of the relation between a predictor and the criterion varies as a function of the values of one or more other predictors). Of course, estimating more complex prediction models underscores the need to collect large samples (see I.A). 3. In terms of best-practice recommendations, in my view practitioners should at a minimum look for the existence of sizable nonlinear effects when deriving either CRV or JCV equations if the sample size allows it. Obviously, some researchers and practitioners who believe that predictor–criterion relationships are always quite simple and straightforward—for example, the more radical advocates of validity generalization (VG) methods—will disagree. However, simply put, if it takes a more complex equation to accurately model the *true* relations that exist in reality between predictors and criteria, the resulting increase in complexity is arguably more than offset by the increased accuracy and fidelity of the model. 4. It is especially important to search for nonlinear prediction relations in cases in which compensatory types of relations may be present (e.g., in disability or rehabilitation applications, where you are interested in determining whether a disability-induced lower degree of skill in one domain can be compensated for by a higher score in a different domain). Clearly, when multiple traits are relevant to success, there is ample reason to believe that more than one "success profile" can exist (e.g., harder effort or increased service-orientation compensating for lower cognitive ability), and that compensatory or interactive relations may exist among the predictors.
F. If predicting external variables, how big an R^2 do you need?	1. The question as to how large a correlation must be before you consider a predictive relationship to be practically significant or useful has long been debated, and it is impossible to offer best-practice recommendations that would apply to all applications. Clearly, as the Taylor-Russel and subsequent utility models have demonstrated, in the right circumstances (e.g., low selection ratio and base rate) even a numerically small correlation can produce appreciably utility. 2. Regarding the converse, there appears to be a tendency (particularly when using JCV models to link work analysis results to person–side trait requirements) to view the very strong correlations that are often seen (e.g., LaPolice, Carter, & Johnson, 2008, reported *R*s in the .80s predicting ability requirements from work dimension scores) as *prima facie* evidence of the "consequential validity" or practical significance of the JCV prediction model.

3. However, my best-practices recommendation is that practitioners should determine the usefulness of a given prediction model in the situation in which it will be applied. Rather than focusing on the size of the correlations with external variables, you should instead focus on assessing the amount of *prediction error* that is seen when the equation is applied, especially the amount that exists in the range of the criterion scale that is of primary interest.

4. For example, a JCV model with an impressive-looking $R = .70$ explains less than half of the variance in the criterion. Even when evaluating predicted values in the middle range of the criterion scale, sizable errors of prediction may result. However, for situations in which the practitioner focuses on ranges of scores outside the middle (e.g., when predicting the overall strength demands of a job for rehabilitation or disability applications, work analysis often focuses on the lowest levels of the scale, where "sedentary" work is distinguished from jobs with higher physical demands), the size of the errors of prediction may increase substantially.

5. In such cases, it has been demonstrated (Harvey, 2009) that even JCV models with Rs in the mid .80s may produce unacceptably large errors of prediction, a finding that strongly questions the practical utility or consequential validity of such models for applications such as the one described above. However, when used in a different setting or for a different purpose, the same JCV model might be found to offer acceptable utility and precision.

G. Should you check for analytic mistakes?

1. My final best-practices recommendations when analyzing work analysis data focus on the question of data-analysis errors; specifically, should practitioners spend nontrivial effort auditing their own analyses and searching for potential mistakes? I strongly recommend that when analyzing and reporting data in work analysis projects, you should assume that mistakes are present everywhere and spend significant time double-checking for errors in the preparation and collection of the data, as well as in the subsequent analyses.

2. Although it is difficult to estimate the percentage of cases in which the results of work analysis projects (or published research articles) reflect data-analytic errors, it is likely to be a nontrivial number that is much higher than many would imagine or prefer. Advancements in computer technology that allow researchers and practitioners to highly automate the data collection and analysis processes have exacerbated this process, further removing the closeness of contact between the data and the data analyst.

3. One strategy for increasing your odds of discovering mistakes or anomalous situations in the data is to graphically examine as much of the data as possible. Do not just compute a regression or correlation analysis; also graphically plot the bivariate relationships, the values predicted by the equations, examine the residuals for patterns, etc. Likewise, it is always a good idea to examine univariate frequency distributions of all items or derived scores that are used as a means for identifying odd findings that may reflect a more serious problem.

4. Finally, a relatively easy to implement best-practice recommendation is for practitioners to include in their reports copies of all raw data, as well as all program code and/or analytic output used to assemble the database that is analyzed, to perform all transformations or manipulations of the database, and to perform the actual analyses of interest. This serves a valuable documentation function in general, and one that will be especially welcome if you must revisit the project in the future (e.g., in an EEO challenge).

organizational] psychology. Job analytic research and development is expensive, time-consuming, and laborious. It is sometimes difficult to publish, and it does not seem to hold a strong attraction for students. In short, job analysis might be characterized as the Rodney Dangerfield of [industrial and organizational] psychology: it doesn't get a lot of respect.

Despite the passage of time, one can easily conclude that these observations are equally applicable today. They are especially apt with respect to characterizing the main question addressed in this chapter: What is the best way to analyze my work analysis data? Simply put, there's nothing funny or popularity-enhancing about the task of trying to make sense of a potentially very large mass of empirical data describing what workers do on their jobs, and the situation becomes even more challenging if one seeks to link such work analysis data to person-side constructs to develop worker-trait specifications for selection or placement purposes.

Cunningham's observation that the area of work analysis is underrepresented in published research remains true decades later. Indeed, the relative lack of published work analysis research studies that are relevant to practitioners is arguably even more pronounced today. These articles tend to focus on theory-driven issues that offer limited guidance for those who actually conduct job analyses. This unfortunate situation makes my task of offering sound, empirically based recommendations to practitioners especially challenging.

The lack of empirical research notwithstanding, it is still not difficult to identify a list of important questions that must be addressed and/or decisions that must be made when analyzing work analysis data. Table 6.1 provides descriptions of each decision point and best-practice recommendation. The following sections highlight important aspects of each and provide practical examples from actual work analysis studies to further illustrate each point.

QUESTIONS YOU WISH HAD BEEN ADDRESSED EARLIER

This section considers several questions that, in an ideal world, should be resolved satisfactorily when a project is first designed. However, based on my experience, it is hardly unusual to encounter questions that should have been resolved before the data were collected but that surface during the data analysis phase. This is especially the case when archival work analysis data are used to drive a new human resources function.

Do You Have Enough Raters?

One issue that should have been addressed well before the data analysis phase concerns the question of whether you have collected data from a large enough sample of raters (or other sources of job information) to meet your needs. At one level, the answer to this question obviously depends on the specific bottom-line human resources needs you are attempting to address in you project (a topic that is beyond the scope of this chapter).

However, the question is still worth considering, even at this late date in your project. On more than one occasion, I have had to recommend to a client that they should collect more data, especially in cases in which survey-based data collection methods involving incumbents or other first-hand subject matter experts (SMEs) were used. People do not participate in work analysis studies for the amusement value that results from doing so, and SMEs often view the task as an imposition or a low priority. Consequently, concerns regarding sample size often arise for practitioners due to inadequate response rates that occur during data collection.

Before proceeding with the real data analyses, response rate data should be examined in as much detail as possible. In particular, you should determine the degree to which certain subgroups of SMEs may have responded at appreciably higher or lower rates than others. It is often the case that the overall response rate in survey-based projects conducted using job incumbents leaves much room for improvement and that the SMEs who consider themselves to be the busiest and/or most accomplished tend to participate at the lowest rates. In either case, if higher-performing incumbents are indeed systematically underrepresented in the final sample that will be analyzed (or if the sample is otherwise biased, such as in terms of respondent demographics), the potential for subsequent data analyses to provide a similarly biased view of the job cannot be dismissed.

Of course, to conduct such analyses at this point, you must have had the foresight to collect as much information on each respondent as possible in order to calculate subgroup breakdowns in response rates. Fortunately, unless you have committed the cardinal mistake of collecting work analysis data anonymously (which should be avoided at all costs from a data-quality perspective), you still have the ability to collect supplemental background or demographic information needed after the fact.

In any event, when your study involves collecting data from multiple raters who hold or rate a common job, taking whatever efforts are needed to achieve a response rate that approaches 100% will help satisfy a number of concerns later in the process. Postponing the data analysis process until additional nonrespondents can be induced to participate should be considered. Particularly when the defensibility of the human resources decisions based on the work analysis is a significant concern, achieving as high a response rate as possible makes the practitioner's task of later defending the representativeness and comprehensiveness of the sample much easier. With a sufficiently high response rate, the inevitable question of whether the nonrespondents differ significantly from the responsive SMEs can be sidestepped.

Did You Use the Right Raters?

Along similar lines, the question of whether the right raters were sampled when your work analysis database was collected is critical. Again, although it would have been preferable to deal with this issue before collecting your data, it is nevertheless a question that should be answered satisfactorily before proceeding with the analyses of substantive interest.

Unfortunately, if it is determined that the sources of information from whom the work analysis ratings were collected are problematic, the remedy is not as simple as prompting nonrespondents to participate. This situation is especially likely to occur in situations in which the work analysis practitioner was brought into an ongoing project or when the project uses archival data collected to drive a different human resources purpose.

Although it may not increase your popularity with the client if you now question whether the raters who provided your data represent appropriate sources for the purposes of the present project, deciding that you need alternative sources and/or additional data collection may represent the most effective response. This is particularly the case when the work analysis project is being conducted to provide data that will drive sensitive human resources processes and decisions (e.g., employee selection, minimum competency standards, compensation). Obviously, work analysis studies are as sensitive to the "garbage in, garbage out" phenomenon as any other. For all but the most trivial applied purposes, it is far better to determine that the database in hand is insufficient to answer the questions being posed (and to then collect data that are) than it is to simply hope for the best and press on.

What makes a source of information "right" for a given project? The answer varies depending on the purpose to be served, but the key questions to be asked concern whether the raters are adequately familiar with the work to be rated, whether they can effectively understand and complete the data collection process (e.g., for survey-based methods, such issues as adequate reading level, language proficiency), and perhaps the most troubling practical issue, whether they possess the proper motivation to provide accurate and comprehensive information.

Although collecting data from incumbents who have adequate job tenure ensures that raters will have direct familiarity with the target job, in many cases significant questions may arise regarding the capacity of incumbents to comprehend the rating task and provide unbiased ratings. If you are confronted with the prospect of having to use an existing database collected from unproctored incumbents (especially one collected for a high-stakes purpose or collected under conditions of low rater accountability), careful consideration should be given to whether it would be best to collect additional data, using appropriate procedures to ensure ratings quality and rater accountability.

Although some may regard my take on this issue to be unduly cynical, based on over 30 years of experience collecting data from all types of sources under all types of conditions, I have formed the deeply held belief that unless trained, unquestionably objective, professional job analysts are used to collect your work analysis ratings, practitioners should always include a formal process for reviewing and independently verifying the work analysis ratings. In the absence of a formal review process, the degree to which incumbents and supervisors may provide blatantly incorrect and invalid responses never ceases to amaze. This is especially the case when ratings are provided anonymously, as I discovered when the person responsible for overseeing the onsite data collection for a large work analysis project in which I was involved informed me that, on her own, she had decided that it would be best to tell the raters to not identify themselves. Even without the ability to go back and audit individual rating profiles, a cursory examination of the ratings made it quite clear that under conditions of low accountability, raters can (and do) provide some highly questionable responses to standardized work analysis surveys.

Have You Collected the Right Data?

Even with a sufficiently large sample that relied on SMEs who are appropriately knowledgeable and motivated, you must further ensure that you have actually described the right content when collecting your work analysis database. This general issue was the focus of Chapter 1, and it gets at the question of whether the purpose driving your work analysis study (e.g., developing an employee selection system, revising the job title taxonomy) can be served effectively by the available data.

Beyond the obvious issue of whether you have described qualitatively appropriate and comprehensive work content in your data collection instrument, the most compelling question concerns the degree to which you need to draw meaningful comparisons (either between various rated organizational entities or between multiple raters describing a common target), and the degree to which those comparisons must be level-sensitive in nature. That is, for human resources applications that focus on only a single organizational entity at a time (e.g., collecting data to develop a content-valid job knowledge test for a single job), one may conclude that no pressing need exists to draw meaningful comparisons (level-sensitive or otherwise) between the job in question and other jobs in the organization or within the job itself (i.e., between the multiple positions that perform it).

However, even in such cases, there may still be a need to be able to draw meaningful level-sensitive comparisons between the various tasks or work activity elements that are rated (e.g., to determine which are performed the most frequently or are the most critical). Other than for the presumably unusual case in which only a single rater is used to provide data, adequate assessment of cross-rater agreement requires the ability to make level-sensitive comparisons between raters.

In general, work analysis practitioners typically have a need to be able to draw meaningful, level-sensitive comparisons within each title (e.g., to determine whether the multiple raters judging each title rate a given activity at the same level), between different titles (e.g., to rank each job based on its standing on a given compensable factor when developing a compensation system), and also within individual ratings profiles (e.g., to see which activities are most important or frequent). The key to being able to make such comparisons in a sound fashion is to use an appropriate, nonrelativistic rating scale (Harvey & Wilson, 2000).

Simply put, you must rate each job characteristic on a rating scale, or metric, that maintains a constant meaning across raters, items, and jobs (e.g., how frequently the activity is performed, whether incumbents are required to be proficient at time of hire, consequences of error). Relativistic rating scales, such as relative time spent (RTS) or relative importance (RI) are widely used to collect work analysis data. However, by definition, they fail to provide a constant level-sensitive rating-scale metric across situations (or even across items within a given survey).

In effect, such ratings are *ipsative,* meaning that each rater's scores are effectively self-normed by virtue of being made relative to some property that varies across positions, jobs, or raters. For example, in an RTS scale, the rater is asked to determine whether the amount of time spent on the activity in question is higher or lower than a standard reference point (e.g., the amount of time spent on the average task performed on the job). Because different raters may use very different reference activities for making this judgment, making any level-based comparisons across raters using such scores is highly problematic.

The use of ipsative rating procedures offers the apparently desirable effect of maximizing the amount of rating variance (across items) for each rater; that is, because ratings are made relative to an average reference activity, all raters should produce nontrivial numbers of above- and below-average ratings. However, obvious problems arise in relativistic rating tasks due to the fact that each rating point does not, in an absolute sense, refer to the same amount of the characteristic being rated. For example, when rating RI, even if two raters judge a given activity to be more important than their average activity, the absolute level of importance of the benchmark used to define each rater's average activity may vary dramatically. An example of this is when a first-line supervisor of laborers and the CEO of a major corporation both rate negotiating as having higher-than-average importance. Even if both jobs are rated as a *4* on a 5-point RTS or RI scale, the *4* value does not connote the same amount of the trait (e.g., importance, time) and offers substantial potential for leading to erroneous conclusions when ratings are compared across different raters, positions, jobs, or organizations.

If you have already collected a database composed of relativistic RTS- or RI-type judgments and are now ready to analyze your data (or you have been asked to perform additional analyses on an archival database), the limitations of ipsative data do not necessarily mean that there is nothing useful that can be done. Indeed, before belatedly coming to realize their significant limitations, I collected literally millions of task-analysis ratings using RTS and RI scales. However, as is discussed in more detail in Harvey and Wilson (2000), the choice to use relativistic scales to collect job data clearly limits what analyses can (or should) be performed and the types of conclusions that can be drawn. In many cases, the only fully unambiguous information that can be gained from relativistic or otherwise ipsative work analysis ratings results from dichotomizing the multipoint RTS or RI ratings to form a binary applicable/not-applicable rating for each activity, given that such scales typically use a meaningful *does not apply* (DNA) option as their lowest rating point.

Have You Rated at the Appropriate Level of Analysis?

This question focuses primarily on identifying the correct level of behavioral abstraction at which to describe job characteristics or activities. Based on the results of empirical studies conducted in a wide range of rating situations, as well as classic studies documenting the limits of human information capability (e.g., Butler & Harvey, 1988; Cornelius & Lyness, 1980; DeNisi & Shaw, 1977; Gibson, Harvey, & Harris, 2007; Gratias, 1999; Harvey & Hollander, 2002; Harvey, Wilson,

& Blunt, 1994; Miller, 1956; Tversky & Kahneman, 1974), in my assessment it is abundantly clear that as the level of abstraction of the rated work activity (or worker-trait requirement) increases, the psychometric quality and accuracy/validity of direct holistic ratings of such characteristics decreases.

For example, Butler and Harvey (1988) found that when the abstract *work dimension* scores produced by factor-scoring the more behaviorally specific items rated in the Position Analysis Questionnaire (PAQ; McCormick, Jeanneret, & Mecham, 1972)—that is, the traditional *decomposed-judgment* rating strategy—were compared to direct holistic ratings of the identical work dimensions, the correlations of the holistic versus decomposed ratings of each abstract work dimension approached zero. Likewise, DeNisi and Shaw (1977) demonstrated that direct holistic self-ratings of worker-ability trait requirements exhibited very low convergent validity correlations with scores on the same ability traits measured via standardized, multi-item tests. Similarly, Gibson et al. (2007) demonstrated that ratings of general work activity constructs made using the single-item holistic scales used by the O*NET exhibited very poor convergent correlations with abstract work dimension scores produced using the decomposed-judgment strategy from ratings collected using the Common-Metric Questionnaire (CMQ; Harvey, 1991b). Harvey and Hollander (2002) demonstrated that the level of cross-rater agreement seen among the actual raters who initially populated the national O*NET database was disturbingly low (in many cases, lower than the levels that would be expected from random ratings).

Despite the fact that it is not difficult to find highly visible examples (e.g., O*NET) in which direct, single-item holistic ratings are made of highly abstract work-activity and worker-trait constructs, work analysis practitioners should avoid holistic ratings in all situations (especially for mission-critical human resources applications for which the ability to document the psychometric quality and accuracy of the work analysis ratings is essential). The only real advantage that can be claimed for the holistic rating approach is that it may be quicker and cheaper than using traditional work analysis methods to describe observable, verifiable work activities and characteristics.

However, if the consequence of this potential reduction in data collection effort and cost is that the resulting work analysis ratings will likely exhibit poor interrater agreement and lack any meaningful capacity for independent review in order to document their accuracy/validity, one must strongly question whether the resulting cost-benefit tradeoff is worth it. Fortunately, practitioners need not rely on direct holistic rating of abstract job characteristics in order to describe abstract aspects of work.

Since the 1960s, job analysts have used decomposed-judgment rating methods to statistically combine ratings of more specific, defensible, verifiable work activities to form scales to describe abstract work dimensions using the common-metric, standardized work analysis tools pioneered by the PAQ and its predecessors (e.g., Palmer & McCormick, 1961). More recently, additional common-metric work analysis surveys (e.g., the CMQ, and the managerially targeted executive checklist [EXCEL] instrument developed by Lozada-Larsen, 1988) were developed to rate more behaviorally specific items than earlier instruments, further enhancing the potential for documenting the quality and accuracy of the work analysis item ratings upon which subsequent human resources decisions may be based, and in using defensible, decomposed-judgment strategies to estimate abstract work-activity constructs.

Did Anything Funny Happen When Collecting the Data?

Best efforts and planning notwithstanding, unplanned events may occur during work analysis data collection that have the potential to impact the quality of the results. In addition to the surprise noted earlier (i.e., finding out after the ratings were collected that the surveys had been administered anonymously), a variety of other unplanned events have occurred that caused me to question whether I should proceed with data analysis or collect supplemental ratings (including labor-management disputes, employee layoffs and cutbacks, corporate reorganizations, and the bankruptcy of the parent corporation).

In short, the work analysis practitioner should expend the effort necessary to determine whether any unanticipated events may have inadvertently turned his or her work analysis study into an interrupted-time-series quasi-experiment. If you are unfortunate enough to find yourself in such a position and the decision is made to proceed with the analyses, the importance of conducting thorough quality-control checks on the data becomes even more important than it usually is.

Do You Have Adequate Backups and Version Control?

Advances in computer-based survey administration and data analysis have dramatically reduced the time and effort required to conduct a large-scale work analysis project relative to the paper-and-pencil based technologies that were the state of the art when I began working in the work analysis area. However, the downside to this increased power is the fact that it is now quite easy to become overwhelmed by the magnitude of information that can be collected, as well as by the challenge of maintaining adequate version control over revisions and edits that are made to the database to determine what the most correct and current version actually is.

To deal with this situation, work analysis practitioners should invest in content versioning system software and use it to allow the many changes and edits that may occur over time (especially if you always conduct an independent review and verification of all work analysis ratings obtained from any source other than trained, professional, suitably motivated job analysts). In many cases, your ability to later produce the evidence needed to document the job-relatedness and validity of human resources practices based on the work analysis data may depend heavily on being able to document a clear paper-trail back to the original item ratings collected during the work analysis project. Clearly, having adequate version control (and adequate physical backups of the database) makes this task much easier should the need later arise.

GETTING THE DATA READY

Numerous choice points and tradeoffs should be addressed during the process of assembling the work analysis data and laying the groundwork for the real data analyses. Unfortunately, many practitioners often cut corners at this point, which can lead to potentially significant problems down the road (especially for projects conducted for the purpose of producing data that will be used to drive employee selection or placement decisions).

What Quality Are the Data in Terms of Rater Agreement?

Assume that you have a large enough sample of data, have sampled rating sources adequately, and collected job ratings from suitably knowledgeable and motivated raters. If so, you must next consider the question of how to assess and document the quality of the ratings on which you are going to base your work analysis conclusions.

At minimum, when multiple sources of information describe a common target (e.g., multiple position incumbents rating the same job, multiple occupational analysts describing the same occupation), the practitioner should be able to offer evidence that sufficiently high cross-rater agreement is present. If significant questions can be raised regarding low levels of cross-rater agreement—especially if the observed levels of agreement do not appreciably exceed the level of agreement that would be achieved when considering random ratings collected under the same conditions (e.g., Harvey & Hayes, 1986; Harvey & Hollander, 2002)—the practitioner should seriously consider whether proceeding with the data analysis process is appropriate.

For example, Harvey and Hollander (2002) examined the degree of cross-rater agreement that was present among the occupational analysts who collected the initial database for the O*NET. Unfortunately, an examination of cross-rater profile agreement indices showed that on average O*NET raters agreed at levels that were comparable to those that would be expected from random ratings of the same surveys; in a nontrivial number of cases, negative correlations were actually present between individual rater profiles. Although many continue to maintain that systems based on the holistic O*NET-type rating scales provide an adequate empirical foundation on which important human resources decisions can be based (e.g., Fleishman & Mumford, 1991; Hubbard et al., 2000; Jeanneret & Strong, 2003; LaPolice, Carter, & Johnson, 2008; Peterson et al., 1999, 2001), I find it difficult to imagine any situation in which I could confidently use work analysis data from raters who agreed at the levels seen in random data.

In cases in which apparent quality-based issues arise based on the presence of poor cross-rater agreement levels (e.g., when multiple raters judge the same target), practitioners have two basic choices:

1. Figure out why the disagreement is present and attempt to remediate it, such as by discarding questionable rating profiles, changing incorrect ratings, or revising the job title system.
2. Ignore or eliminate it, such as by forming a mean profile for each job that eliminates cross-rater variability.

I strongly recommend the first strategy, given the significant distortions that can be caused by aggregation bias (discussed later).

In terms of the type of agreement index that should be used, a number of issues that should be considered are presented in Table 6.1. Of particular note is the question of whether profile similarity indices are sensitive to level-based disagreement between raters (e.g., Euclidean distances, absolute-value discrepancies) or only the general shape of the profiles (e.g., cross-rater profile correlations). As a practical matter, I recommend that work analysis practitioners always report level-sensitive indices unless you are in the highly undesirable situation of having collected relativistic or ipsative data that do not allow meaningful level-sensitive comparisons to be made in the first place.

A common practice that should be avoided is reporting apparently acceptable-looking cross-rater correlations that conceal unacceptable levels of disagreement in terms of the actual level of the ratings. For example, Figure 6.1 shows the overall scores on the Data, People, and Things factors that underlie the O*NET general work activity (GWA) survey's scales for six analysts who rated one occupation. If you ignore Rater 3's score on the third factor, you see strong similarity in the general shapes of their profiles; however, in a level-sensitive sense, actual cross-rater agreement is quite poor (e.g., Rater 1 consistently rates fully two standard deviations below Rater 5, and only Rater 6 falls consistently close to the overall group-mean profile). If only the average cross-rater profile correlation had been reported, a misleading conclusion would be reached.

What Additional Quality Indices Should You Examine?

One of the few work analysis topics relevant to practitioners that has received attention in the research literature concerns the performance of various practical tools for quantifying work analysis rating quality (i.e., going beyond demonstrations that raters show acceptable-appearing levels of agreement). These range from relatively simple techniques to ones that involve advanced psychometric methods.

On the simpler end of the scale, a number of methods based on classical test theory (e.g., Cortina, 1993; Crocker & Algina, 1986) have been used in job analytic studies to quantify the apparently quality of the ratings. For example, although few practitioners have the capacity or inclination to

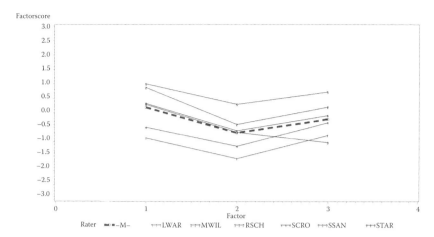

Figure 6.1   Rating profiles for 6 O*NET raters rating OU 58008, computed using factor scores on the three overall latent dimensions. The group mean profile is represented by the dashed line.

use the full test-retest approach to assessing ratings reliability (i.e., by requiring each SME to complete each work analysis survey twice), if several rated items are repeated in a long work analysis rating questionnaire, it is possible to compute a quality index based on the degree to which each SME answers the repeated items consistently. Results using this method (e.g., Wilson, Harvey, & Macy, 1990) indicate that an often surprising number of SMEs respond in an inconsistent fashion, a finding that raises questions regarding the quality of their ratings of the nonrepeated items.

On the other end of the complexity continuum, a number of studies (e.g., Harvey, 2004, 2005) have shown that item response theory (IRT) person-fit or appropriateness indices (AIs) offer promise with respect to being able to detect aberrant work analysis response profiles. Essentially computed as a byproduct of the process of using IRT to estimate abstract work dimension scores from an array of related item responses, these AIs are sensitive to the presence of item responses that are not logically consistent with other responses in the profile. Although such indices are not useful when a completely consistent (but false) rating profile is made, they may be quite effective in spotting cases in which, for whatever reason, questionable ratings are present.

Are There Aggregation Bias Issues?

One of the biggest practical challenges that arises in a large number of work analysis projects concerns the adequacy of the organization's existing job title system (i.e., the way in which positions are clustered to form jobs). Almost invariably, the practitioner finds that there are some jobs that have high levels of true within-title heterogeneity in work activities and demands, as well as the converse situation of job title proliferation in which several different job titles seem to perform essentially the same activities.

The former case is the issue of concern with respect to aggregation bias (e.g., James, 1982). The essential problem of aggregation bias is that when sufficiently large true within-title heterogeneity is present, the mean profile that may be computed to describe the job (i.e., by averaging the ratings obtained from its multiple positions) may not do a very good job of accurately describing the activities performed by the individual positions holding that job title. As true within-title heterogeneity increases, the job-mean profile provides an increasingly inaccurate and misleading summary of what the job actually involves.

Figure 6.2 graphically illustrates the potentially significant distortions that can result from relying on the mean profile from heterogeneous raters to make applied decisions; this figure

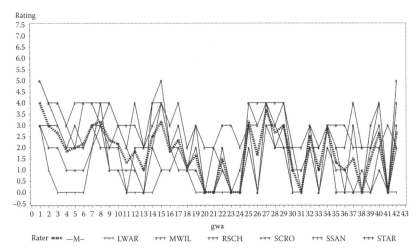

Figure 6.2   Item-level response profiles from the same six actual O*NET occupational analysts used in Figure 6.1, in this case holistically rating the 42 O*NET general work activity constructs. The dashed line represents the group aggregate profile.

shows the ratings profiles for the same raters and occupation in Figure 6.1, except at the item level. On the O*NET rating scale, ratings of 0 (actual DNA) and 1 (an extremely low level) are shown below the horizontal line; items receiving these ratings can be deemed effectively irrelevant to the job. Although this scale has a maximum rating of 7, due to the nature of the rating anchors the highest 2–3 rating points define extraordinarily high levels that are seldom seen in practice (e.g., hover a helicopter in strong wind, gain cooperation from a culturally diverse group of executives hostile to your company). Consequently, for most of the rated GWA items, the levels of disagreement seen in Figure 6.2 are massive, covering most of the effective range of the scale.

For example, for this clerical occupation, ratings of GWA 3 (*Monitoring processes, materials, or surroundings*) range from totally irrelevant (i.e., lower than 1, which is anchored as "check to see if baking bread is done") through 4 ("test electrical circuits"), with an average of 2.75. For GWA 5 (*Estimating the quantifiable characteristics of products, events, or information*), ratings range from totally irrelevant through 4 ("estimate the time required to evacuate a city in the event of a major disaster"), with a mean of 2 ("estimate the size of household furnishings to be crated").

The results in Figure 6.2 further illustrate the concerns raised previously regarding attempts to holistically rate highly abstract constructs using imprecise scales. In my assessment, a practitioner would likely experience considerable difficulty if challenged as part of an equal employment opportunity lawsuit to document and defend the accuracy of such ratings, especially given that the O*NET rating scale points are anchored using activities (e.g., baking bread, testing electronic circuits, evacuating cities, hovering helicopters) that are obviously completely irrelevant to the specific job being analyzed.

Whatever the cause, as a practical matter these O*NET raters clearly experienced difficulties in agreeing. That is, even if you largely ignore level-based differences and focus on cross-rater profile correlations to index agreement, the fact that such values range from $r = .40$ to a high of only .73 (mean = .55) should raise red flags regarding their performance and the meaningfulness of the group-mean profile. Unfortunately, as Harvey and Hollander (2002) demonstrated, the mean cross-rater agreement seen in this job is hardly unusual in the O*NET database; indeed, the average cross-rater agreement seen across all O*NET occupations was only approximately .55. The fact that such values overestimate the true interrater agreement that would be seen if fully level-sensitive indices were used underscores the points made previously regarding the need to ensure that adequate agreement is present before proceeding to the data analyses of substantive interest.

Is Agreement an Artifact of DNAs?

Although you can use measures of interrater agreement as an index of work analysis ratings quality, this begs the question of how high the agreement levels should be before you deem them to be adequate. As is described in more detail in Table 6.1, the .70 rule of thumb that is commonly seen in practice for agreement indices such as r_{wg} and cross-rater correlations is arguably far too low and lenient, especially if raters are able to easily identify obviously irrelevant items as being DNA (see Harvey & Hayes, 1986; Harvey & Hollander, 2002). Although I cannot state an absolute cutoff that should be used in such cases, the studies noted previously demonstrated that interrater agreement levels in the .80s and even low .90s can easily be achieved by combining a relatively small number of DNA agreements with totally random ratings of the remaining items.

For example, Figure 6.3 shows the GWA item ratings from the O*NET analysts who rated the occupation of treasurers, controllers, and chief financial officers. As in Figure 6.2, very significant disagreement exists on a number of rated items; for example, on the clearly relevant GWA 7 (*Evaluating information to determine compliance with standards*), ratings range from 2 (unanchored, but one point above "review forms for completeness") through 6 ("make a ruling in court on a complicated motion"), with an average of 4.5 (slightly above "evaluate a complicated insurance claim for compliance with policy terms"). However, despite considerable disagreement on applicable GWA items, several cases of reasonably good agreement on DNA items are present (e.g., GWA 20, *Operating vehicles, mechanized devices, or equipment* and GWA 21, *Drafting, laying out, and specifying technical devices, parts, and equipment*).

Indeed, when these DNA rating "agreements" are included, the full-profile correlations for this occupation range from $r = .58-.88$, with mean $r = .75$ and median $r = .79$ (values that lie well above the .70 rule-of-thumb many practitioners consider adequate). Obviously, such results considerably overstate the level of agreement seen on the applicable GWAs.

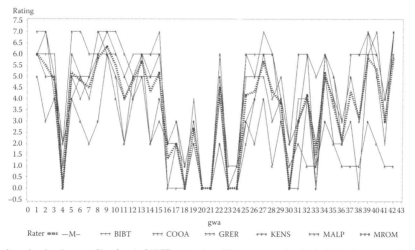

Figure 6.3   Item-level ratings profiles for six O*NET raters describing an upper-level administrative occupation on the GWA survey. The dashed line indicates the group aggregate profile.

Should the Job Title System Be Revised?

In cases in which the level of within-title heterogeneity is sufficiently high to raise concerns regarding aggregation bias, the practical solution is straightforward (at least in theory): revise the job title taxonomy by splitting too-abstract titles to form more homogeneous ones (e.g., Harvey, 1986). Aggregation bias can lead to many significant problems (e.g., Harvey, 2009a), and the likelihood that you may encounter it in practice provides a strong argument for seeking to achieve 100% sampling of incumbents in each job title of interest to the work analysis project. That is, if only subsets of incumbents are sampled, the full extent of any true within-title heterogeneity problems cannot be determined. In such cases, your practical remedies with respect to revising the position-to-job linkages in the organization's title taxonomy are significantly limited by your inability to determine where the positions that were not sampled should be slotted in the revised job title system.

Should You Discard Questionable Data?

An alternative means to avoid aggregation-bias issues when the within-title heterogeneity occurs across raters (as opposed to positions, as was illustrated in Figures 6.1–6.3) consists of discarding rating profiles that are deemed erroneous. Although the task of identifying aberrant ratings can be aided via the kinds of quantitative indices discussed previously, it must be stressed that such information should only be used as a means to help identify profiles that should be subjected to a more in-depth, item-by-item review for accuracy. That is, although it would be tempting when looking at the data in Figure 6.1 to simply discard Rater 3 because of the lack of match to the profiles produced by the other raters, it is entirely possible that Rater 3's aberrant score on the third element in that profile may be the most accurate one of the group.

As an example, once when I was conducting a review of work analysis ratings on a work analysis project that used the CMQ, I encountered a case in which an incumbent in the *streets laborer* job reported that he was required to use firearms. Suspecting this was a clear case of an invalid rating, I was quite surprised to find out that the worker did indeed use shotguns (loaded with blanks) to scare away flocks of birds that were nesting in trees and causing a nuisance. Therefore, unless you rate job activities that are objective enough to allow for independent verification—*and* you rate them on nonrelativistic scales that have an unambiguous meaning—it is impossible to determine the veracity of work analysis data.

Do You Need to Renorm, Transform, or Rescale?

As described in Table 6.1, work analysis practitioners often must rescale or otherwise transform the raw item ratings prior to performing the substantive analyses of interest. One common reason for doing so may be to try to salvage something useful when problematic methods have been used to collect the work analysis data (e.g., the ipsative or relativistic rating scale problem noted earlier).

One issue involving transformations that is surprisingly complicated concerns the use of percentiles. Normally, standard best-practice recommendations for presenting psychological test results suggest the following:

1. In addition to reporting scale scores for derived work dimensions (e.g., *z*-scores), practitioners should also report the percentile rank of each score to aid in interpretation.
2. Because they technically represent ordinal data (i.e., ranks), practitioners should avoid performing any quantitative or statistical analyses on percentiles (i.e., any operation that assumes at least an interval level of measurement).

However, it is typically the case that when using standardized, common-metric work analysis instruments that the work dimension scores produced by factor-analytic, IRT, or other scoring methods exhibit striking nonnormal distributions that typically have a strong positive skew, with most scores falling toward the low end of each dimension. In addition to the usual problems that result when such data are used (e.g., determining a useful index of such simple things as central tendency and variability), if such scores are standardized to lie on a z-score metric in a larger reference population, some very strange-appearing z-scores can result that fall far outside the usual −3 to +3 range one expects to see for standardized variables (especially on the high end).

Beyond their odd-appearing values (with double-digit values being common on some CMQ work dimensions at the high end), a potentially serious practical problem may arise, such that different jobs that score very similarly with respect to the percentile rank of a given dimension score might have wildly different z-score values on the dimension. For example, on one CMQ work dimension, a z-score of 4.6 lies at the 99th percentile, a score of 3.4 lies at the 98th percentile, and a z-score of 0.74 defines the 90th percentile. However, the difference between the z-scores defining the 59th versus 50th percentiles is only −0.198 versus −0.140, a far smaller range on the z-score metric.

In such cases, the argument can be made that analyses of the percentile ranks (rather than the z-scores) might represent the most meaningful approach. At some ranges of the scale, very large z-score differences may translate into very small differences in terms of where such a score would locate one in the larger normative distribution of scores on the dimension. However, doing so may invoke the wrath of purists who adhere to Stevens's taxonomy of scale types (e.g., see Crocker & Algina, 1986).

Do You Need to Estimate Abstract Work Characteristics?

As noted previously, I take an adamant position regarding the total inadvisability of using single-item holistic rating scales to directly measure abstract work-activity constructs. For example, O*NET's GWA survey uses single-item scales to rate nebulous and multidimensional constructs including getting information, processing information, analyzing data or information, making decisions and solving problems, performing general physical activities, handling and moving objects, performing administrative activities, and communicating with people outside the organization. Not surprisingly, research studies have consistently shown that such holistic ratings exhibit highly questionable psychometric properties, and they are by definition extremely difficult to independently assess with respect to their accuracy. The reason I take such a hard line regarding this practice is that far superior methods are available to deal with cases in which the human resources purpose at hand requires work analysis practitioners to measure and analyze highly abstract constructs, such as when deriving equations using the job-component validation (JCV) method to use work dimensions to predict ability or personality trait requirements of jobs.

Far more precise (and defensible) estimates of abstract work-activity constructs can be produced by statistically combining ratings of a larger number of more-specific work activities using decomposed-judgment methods (e.g., factor-analytic, IRT, unweighted linear composite scoring) than could ever be produced using the 5- or 7-point Likert scales in the O*NET, which are primitive by comparison. For example, in the case of the O*NET dimension *Communicating with People Outside the Organization*, one could identify and rate literally dozens of different types of people outside the organization that the worker must contact (e.g., executives, regulators, laborers, sales representatives, technical/professional specialists, the public, customers), and describing a wide range of potential interactions that may be performed with each type of contact (e.g., supervising, taking information, mentoring, delegating, exchanging information, formally negotiating).

If you as a practitioner found yourself in an equal employment opportunity challenge trying to defend the accuracy of a job's score on a dimension such as *Communicating with People Outside* *the Organization,* there is absolutely no question that your task would be dramatically easier if you relied on traditional decomposed-judgment methods (which provide a clear paper trail back to ratings of verifiable, detailed work activity) versus a single-item rating of the job on the O*NET's Likert scale, which anchors only three of the seven possible rating points (i.e., *1* = "have little contact with people outside the organization," *4* = "make standard presentations about available services," and *6* = "prepare or deliver press releases"). This would especially be the case if, for example, the required external contacts involved coordinating the activities of a group of high-level executives and regulators, and did not involve either making standard presentations or delivering press releases.

Of course, if you are not using an existing common-metric instrument as the basis for estimating abstract work dimension scores, you must perform your own scale-development activities. The most popular methods for doing involve first performing some type of factor analysis—either exploratory (in the case that you do not feel sufficiently confident regarding both the nature and number of the underlying work-activity constructs, as well as the linkages of individual rated items to constructs) or confirmatory. You then should follow up with traditional psychometric analyses (e.g., internal consistency reliability estimates for each scale, item-total correlations) to verify that you have indeed succeeded at forming composites that measure a common underlying characteristic.

Based on my experience, it is clearly safest to begin by using exploratory factor analytic methods to identify the effective dimensionality of a larger item pool and to not assume that your a priori ideas regarding the number of latent constructs—or the ways in which individual items link to them—are necessarily correct. For example, in the case of the CMQ, the factor structure seen in the data (e.g., Fine, Harvey, & Cronshaw, 2004; Harvey, 2004a) clearly diverged from the a priori views of the latent structure of work seen in the ways in which the instrument's sections are organized.

Likewise, in another example of the severe limitations of holistic rating strategies in work analysis, Figure 6.4 shows the scree plot of eigenvalues obtained in an exploratory factor analysis of the 42 Likert scales in the O*NET GWA survey. It is critical to stress that each of these single-item scales is supposed to measure a separate underlying construct that is empirically distinct from the remaining single-item scales (e.g., *Selling or Influencing Others* versus *Controlling Machines and Processes*). If the GWA survey had performed as it should have, the scree plot should show a relatively flat line, reflecting the fact that each single-item scale indeed measures distinct content.

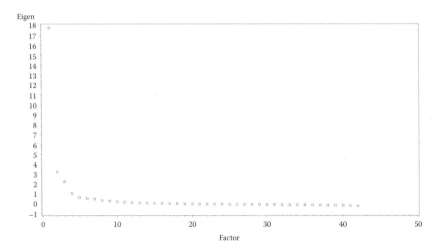

Figure 6.4   Scree plot of eigenvalues from factor analysis of 42-item O*NET GWA survey.

Unfortunately, as is clearly evident in Figure 6.4, the effective dimensionality of these rated elements is far lower than its developers intended, with a three-factor solution explaining over 90% of the common variance at the rater level of analysis (the Data, People, and Things factors produced by this solutions are the ones shown in Figure 6.1). Such findings underscore both the unsuitability of the holistic rating strategy in work analysis, as well as the need for practitioners to conduct and report such analyses to provide evidence of the construct validity of the work analysis measures being used.

ANALYTIC STRATEGIES AND METHODS

Once you have ensured that you have an adequate sample, have asked the right questions, have data of adequate quality, and have transformed it appropriately for the purpose at hand, you can finally consider the actual data-analytic issues that are likely to arise in a work analysis study.

What Basic Descriptive Analyses Are Needed?

I cannot overemphasize the need to become highly familiar with the work analysis database at a descriptive level. One way to accomplish this is by always computing and closely examining the types of analyses presented in Figures 6.1–6.3 with respect to within-title agreement, as well as in Figure 6.4 with respect to the construct validity of the rated items.

Although computing numerical indices of within-title variability and cross-rater agreement is important, there is no substitute for graphically examining the work analysis database to put such numbers into context. Similar examinations of univariate frequency distributions (of both rated items and derived scale scores) should be conducted as well. For example, as shown in Figure 6.5, they can determine the severity of the positive skew that is commonly seen in work analysis ratings. In this case, the scores represent the factor score estimates of the Data factor produced by factoring the O*NET GWA ratings.

Is There a Good Way to Document Content-Coverage Adequacy?

In many work analysis projects, one of the goals is to demonstrate that the work analysis has comprehensively spanned the content domain of work activities required by the job in question (e.g., when the work analysis results are used to develop a job-knowledge test or licensing exam). This of course begs the question of how one can derive numerical indices to support such a claim of content-coverage adequacy.

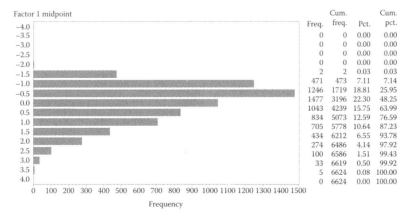

Figure 6.5 Frequency distribution of factor score estimates for Factor 1 (FJA's Data) underlying the O*NET GWA survey.

As is described in more detail in Table 6.1, this represents an area in which it is difficult to identify a best-practices recommendation. Although some methods for doing so have achieved widespread use (e.g., asking incumbents to provide a direct rating of the percentage of their work activities that the work analysis survey covers), the limited research available (e.g., Wilson, 1997) suggests that such indices do not provide a satisfactory solution to the problem.

Do You Need to Link Job-Side Data to Person-Side Requirements?

Clearly one of the most contentious questions facing work analysis researchers and practitioners (e.g., Harvey, 2009a) concerns the issue of how you should go about using work analysis information to make inferences regarding the personal traits and characteristics of workers that are required for successful job performance (i.e., job or worker specifications). I have considered this issue in detail elsewhere (e.g., Harvey, 1991a; Harvey & Wilson, 2000). Of the several approaches described in Table 6.1, I will simply stress here that there is no easy answer to the problem.

In particular, the oft-repeated point will again be made: The use of single-item holistic ratings to directly infer the levels of various person-side traits and constructs needed to perform a job represents a totally unsatisfactory solution and is a clear pitfall that should be avoided. Simply put, all of the problems noted above with respect to using holistic judgment to describe abstract job-side constructs (e.g., *Making Decisions and Solving Problems*) apply with equal force and severity when used on the person-side to infer the required level of constructs such as *Originality, Deductive Reasoning, Mathematical Reasoning, Spatial Orientation, Selective Attention, Reaction Time,* or *Trunk Strength,* which are directly rated in the O*NET Abilities survey and the highly similar Fleishman F-JAS instrument (e.g., Fleishman, 1992; Fleishman & Mumford, 1991; Fleishman & Reilly, 1992; Fleishman, Wetrogan, Uhlman, & Marshall-Mies, 1995).

Indeed, in addition to the standard limitations of holistic judgments, one can also add the very difficult problem of identifying the minimum required levels when one grants that a compensatory model for linking abilities to job performance may be present. That is, if it is possible that people with different ability profiles may be equally successful on the job and that higher scores on some job-relevant traits may compensate for lower scores on other traits, the concept of the minimum required level of a given trait becomes essentially meaningless. The minimum required for one trait may vary as function of the worker's scores on other traits that may compensate for it.

If So, How Well Must the Linkage Be Documented?

The short answer to this question is, it depends on how concerned you as a work analysis practitioner are with respect to the possibility that you may be required in the future (perhaps in an adversarial legal context) to defend the utility, validity, and job relatedness of the worker-selection criteria developed using the results of the work analysis project. Assuming you are concerned to at least some degree, Table 6.1 summarizes a range of possible strategies, along with their advantages and disadvantages. The overall view I would add here is simply that, short of the "gold standard" local criterion-related validation study recommended by the *Uniform Guidelines* (1978), all of the other available methods suffer from potentially significant limitations.

In particular, although the JCV technique has proven to be capable of achieving strong levels of prediction when empirically using job-side activity profiles to predict the levels of person-side trait constructs seen among proficient incumbents (e.g., Jeanneret & Strong, 2003; LaPolice et al., 2008; Wagner & Harvey, 2005), JCV is potentially open to criticism with respect to the question of how one can convincingly demonstrate that in addition to predicting the level of the trait you would expect for a given job, you can also prove that the trait in question is required in order to perform the job successfully.

Although earlier PAQ-based studies (e.g., McCormick et al., 1972) made use of a somewhat convoluted method in which they also attempted to predict the validity coefficient that would be expected when using a given person-side trait to predict job performance (as well as the expected mean level of the trait in successful incumbents), I have never viewed these predicted validity coefficients as being capable of providing particularly convincing evidence.

Should You Look for Interaction or Nonlinear Effects?

The above concerns regarding the degree to which JCV-based predictions of worker-trait requirements can withstand close scrutiny in an adversarial legal context when appreciable adverse-impact is present are amplified considerably if one allows for the possibility that interactive effects are present with respect to the ways in which person-side ability traits predict job performance. One example of the way such effects may occur was previously described with respect to the compensatory selection model.

Although hardcore proponents of validity generalization methods (e.g., Schmidt, Hunter, & Pearlman, 1981) become apoplectic at the mere suggestion that moderator effects may occur, in my assessment the possibility that the minimum-required level of Ability Trait A might vary depending on a worker's profile of scores across Ability Traits B–F that are also predictive of performance is hardly farfetched. This represents an area of critical potential importance to practitioners that has received very little attention in the research literature.

A similar point may be raised regarding the need to model nonlinear relationships between person-side constructs and job performance (in a criterion-related validation sense) and between job-side predictors and person-side trait scores (in a JCV sense). For example, a linear increase in the level of overall decision-making complexity in a job may be associated with a corresponding linear increase in the level of cognitive ability seen among job incumbents at the lower levels of the scale, but at the higher end of the scale the same rate of increase may be associated with a much sharper rise in the level of cognitive ability seen among incumbents in a JCV study.

The overall takeaway points are straightforward: In mission-critical or litigious applications, practitioners are strongly advised to collect as much empirical data as possible to justify any inferred linkages between work analysis job-side results and person-side worker specifications. Additionally, to the extent that it is reasonable to suspect that compensatory or moderator effects are present with respect to how person-side constructs lead to successful job performance (whether it be optimal, average, or minimally-acceptable performance as the criterion), the entire concept of setting minimum cutoffs on predictor traits becomes highly problematic. In short, if you cannot state what the required minimum level of a given trait should be without simultaneously considering the worker's scores on a range of other traits that interact with it to produce job performance, the concept of the minimum-required value becomes essentially meaningless.

If Predicting External Variables, How Big an R^2 Do You Need?

Another potential concern with the use of methods such as JCV to link the person- and job-side domains of Dunnette's (1976) two worlds of work was described in Harvey (2009b). Simply put, although the studies deriving JCV models have reported what appear to be very impressive levels of prediction by applied psychology standards, with multiple R values in some cases reaching the .80s (e.g., LaPolice et al., 2008), I demonstrated that on a case-by-case basis the magnitude of the errors of prediction can still be unacceptably large in practice (Harvey, 2009b).

This is especially the case when work analysts seek to make predictions that fall toward either the high or low ends of the criterion scale. This was illustrated in Harvey (2009b) by deriving a JCV model predicting the overall *Dictionary of Occupational Titles* strength level seen in an occupation from a profile of work dimension scores. Although R values in the .80s could easily be achieved when deriving the JCV model, when actually applying it to predict the strength level that would be expected for individual occupations in the lower ranges of the scale that are critical for disability and rehabilitation applications, clearly unacceptable levels of prediction errors were seen.

Such findings would presumably be difficult to explain if the selection procedures based on such methods were challenged in court. When combined with the fact that many JCV studies produced R values that fall far below these levels (e.g., Jeanneret & Strong, 2003), it becomes clear that although it may prove useful in the overall process of linking person- and job-side domains, JCV is far from the "magic bullet" that will allow us to solve this critical problem.

Should You Check for Analytic Mistakes?

Although it perhaps should go without saying, I will nevertheless conclude by stating that work analysis practitioners should rigorously check their procedures and results to determine if mistakes may have occurred at some point during the work analysis process. Although the increased use of automation and computers to collect and analyze work analysis data has clearly made the process quicker and easier, it has also made it much easier to commit mistakes that may be difficult to detect without concerted effort.

REFERENCES

Butler, S. K., & Harvey, R. J. (1988). A comparison of holistic versus decomposed rating of Position Analysis Questionnaire work dimensions. *Personnel Psychology, 41,* 761–771.

Cornelius, E. T., & Lyness, K. S. (1980). A comparison of holistic and decomposed judgment strategies in job analyses by job incumbents. *Journal of Applied Psychology, 65,* 155–163.

Cortina, J. M. (1993). What is coefficient alpha? An examination of theory and applications. *Journal of Applied Psychology, 78,* 98–104.

Cunningham, J. W. (1989, August). Discussion. In R. J. Harvey (Ed.), *Applied measurement issues in job analysis.* Symposium conducted at the American Psychological Association convention, New Orleans, LA.

Crocker, L., & Algina, J. (1986). *Classical and modern test theory.* New York, NY: Holt, Rinehart, & Winston.

DeNisi, A., & Shaw, B. (1977). Investigation of the uses of self-reports of abilities. *Journal of Applied Psychology, 62,* 641–644.

Dunnette, M. (1976). Aptitudes, abilities, and skill. In M. D. Dunnette (Ed.), *Handbook of industrial and organizational psychology.* Chicago, IL: Rand McNally.

Fine, S. A., Harvey, R. J., & Cronshaw, S. F. (2004, April). *FJA strategies for addressing O*NET limitations in a post-DOT environment.* In E. A. Fleishman (Chair), *Things, data, and people: Fifty years of a seminal theory.* Symposium conducted at the Annual Conference of the Society for Industrial and Organizational Psychology, Chicago, IL.

Fleishman, E. A. (1992). *Rating scale booklet: F-JAS: Fleishman job analysis survey.* Palo Alto, CA: Consulting Psychologists Press.

Fleishman, E. A., & Mumford, M. (1991). Evaluating classifications of job behavior: A construct validation of the ability requirement scales. *Personnel Psychology, 44,* 253–575.

Fleishman, E. A., & Reilly, M. E. (1992). *Administrator's guide: F-JAS: Fleishman job analysis survey.* Palo Alto, CA: Consulting Psychologists Press.

Fleishman, E. A., Wetrogan, L. I., Uhlman, C. E., & Marshall-Mies, J. C. (1995). *Abilities.* In *Development of prototype occupational analysis network (O*NET) content model: Volume I: Report.* Salt Lake City, UT: Utah Department of Employment Security.

Gibson, S. G., Harvey, R. J., & Harris, M. L. (2007). Holistic versus decomposed ratings of general dimensions of work activity. *Management Research News, 30,* 724–734.

Gratias, M. E. (1999). *Scaling behavioral anchors on The Occupational Information Network.* Paper presented at the Society for Industrial and Organizational Psychology, Atlanta, GA.

Harvey, R. J. (1985, August). A comparison of data analysis techniques in job analysis. In E. T. Cornelius (Chair), *Comparative job analysis research.* Symposium presented at the American Psychological Association Convention, Los Angeles, CA.

Harvey, R. J. (1986). Quantitative approaches to job classification: A review and critique. *Personnel Psychology, 39,* 345–357.

Harvey, R. J. (1991a). *Job analysis.* In M. Dunnette & L. Hough (Eds.), *Handbook of industrial and organizational psychology* (2nd ed.). Palo Alto, CA: Consulting Psychologists Press.

Harvey, R. J. (1991b). *The common-metric questionnaire.* San Antonio, TX: The Psychological Corporation.

Harvey, R. J. (2004, April). *Empirical foundations for the Things-Data-People taxonomy of work.* In E. A. Fleishman (Chair), *Things, data, and people: Fifty years of a seminal theory.* Symposium conducted at the Annual Conference of the Society for Industrial and Organizational Psychology, Chicago, IL.

Harvey, R. J. (2005, April). *IRT strategies for identifying rater quality in job analysis ratings.* In C. VanIddekinge (Chair), *Group differences in job analysis ratings.* Symposium conducted at the Annual Conference of the Society for Industrial and Organizational Psychology, Los Angeles, CA.

Harvey, R. J. (2009a). *The O*NET: Do too-abstract titles + unverifiable holistic ratings + questionable raters + low agreement + inadequate sampling + aggregation bias = (a) validity, (b) reliability, (c) utility, or (d) none of the above?* Paper presented at the 2009 meeting of the Review of the Occupational Information Network (O*NET) Panel conducted by the National Academies of Science, Washington, DC.

Harvey, R. J. (2009b). *Job-component validation (JCV) Rs > .80 do not ensure consequential validity.* Paper presented at the 2009 meeting of the Review of the Occupational Information Network (O*NET) Panel conducted by the National Academies of Science, Washington, DC.

Harvey, R. J., & Hayes, T. L. (1986). Monte Carlo baselines for interrater reliability correlations using the Position Analysis Questionnaire. *Personnel Psychology, 39,* 345–357.

Harvey, R. J., & Hollander, E. (2002, April). Assessing interrater agreement in the O*NET. In M. A. Wilson (Chair), The O*NET: Mend it, or end it? Symposium conducted at the Annual Conference of the Society for Industrial and Organizational Psychology, Toronto, ON.

Harvey, R. J., & Wilson, M. A. (2000). Yes Virginia, there is an objective reality in job analysis. *Journal of Organizational Behavior, 21,* 829–854.

Harvey, R. J., Wilson, M. A., & Blunt, J. H. (1994, April). *A comparison of rational/holistic versus empirical/decomposed methods of identifying and rating general work behaviors.* Paper presented at the Annual Conference of the Society for Industrial and Organizational Psychology, Nashville, TN.

Hubbard, M., McCloy, R., Campbell, J., Nottingham, J., Lewis, P., Rivkin, D., & Levine, J. (2000). *Revision of O*NET Data Collection Instruments.* Raleigh, NC: National Center for O*NET Development.

James, L. R. (1982). Aggregation bias in estimates of perceptual agreement. *Journal of Applied Psychology, 67,* 219–229.

Jeanneret, P. R., & Strong, M. H. (2003). Linking O*NET job analysis information to job require predictors: An O*NET application. *Personnel Psychology, 56,* 465–492.

LaPolice, C. C., Carter, G. W., & Johnson, J. W. (2008). Linking O*NET descriptors to occupational literacy requirements using job component validation. *Personnel Psychology, 61,* 405–441.

Lozada-Larsen, S. R. (1988). Going beyond criticism: Management work theory and research. (Unpublished doctoral dissertation). Rice University, Houston, TX.

McCormick, E. J., Jeanneret, P. R., & Mecham, R. C. (1972). A study of job characteristics & job dimensions as based on the Position Analysis Questionnaire (PAQ). *Journal of Applied Psychology, 56,* 347–368.

Miller, G. A. (1956). The magical number seven, plus or minus two: Some limits on our capacity for processing information. *Psychological Review, 63,* 81–97.

Palmer, G. J., & McCormick, E. J. (1961). A factor analysis of job activities. *Journal of Applied Psychology, 45,* 289–294.

Peterson, N. G., Mumford, M. D., Borman, W. C., Jeanneret, P. R., Fleishman, E. A., & Levin, K. Y. (1997). *O*Net final technical report.* Salt Lake City, UT: Utah Department of Workforce Services.

Peterson, N. G., Mumford, M. D., Borman, W. C., Jeanneret, P. R., & Fleishman, E. A.(1999). *An occupational information system for the 21st Century: The development of O*NET.* Washington, DC: APA Books.

Peterson, N. G., Mumford, M. D., Borman, W. C., Jeanneret, P. R., Fleishman, E. A., Levin, K. Y., … Dye, D. M. (2001). Understanding work using the Occupational Information Network (O*NET): Implications for practice and research. *Personnel Psychology, 54,* 451–492.

Ricci v. DeStefano, U.S. 07-1428 (2009).

Sanchez, J. I., & Levine, E. L. (2000). Accuracy or consequential validity: Which is the better standard for job analysis data? *Journal of Organizational Behavior, 21,* 809–818.

Schmidt, F. L., Hunter, J., & Pearlman, K. (1981). Task differences as moderators of aptitude test validity in selection: A red herring. *Journal of Applied Psychology, 66,* 166–185.

Stutzman, T. M. (1983). Within classification job differences. *Personnel Psychology, 36,* 503–516.

Tversky, A., & Kahneman, D. (1974). Judgment under uncertainty: Heuristics and biases. *Science, 185,* 1124–1131.

Uniform Guidelines on Employee Selection Procedures. (1978). *Federal Register, 43,* 38290–38315.

U.S. Department of Labor. (1991). *Dictionary of occupational titles (DOT): Revised fourth edition.* Washington: Author.

Wagner, T. A., & Harvey, R. J. (2005, April). *JCV predicting DOT worker-trait requirements from CMQ job analysis ratings.* Paper presented at the Annual Conference of the Society for Industrial and Organizational Psychology, Los Angeles, CA.

Wilson, M. A. (1997). The validity of task coverage ratings by incumbents and supervisors: Bad news. *Journal of Business and Psychology, 12,* 85–95.

Wilson, M. A., Harvey, R. J., & Macy, B. A. (1990). Repeating items to estimate the test-retest reliability of task inventory ratings. *Journal of Applied Psychology, 75,* 158–163.

7

Evaluating Work Analysis in the 21st Century

EDWARD L. LEVINE
University of South Florida

JUAN I. SANCHEZ
Florida International University

The analysis of work—that is, the decomposing of tasks, bundles of tasks, or activities that constitute positions, jobs, occupations, and even entire systems—has been of great usefulness in education, ergonomics, industrial engineering, organizational development, and human resource management (Gael, Cornelius, Levine, & Salvendy, 1988). The methods of analysis traditionally captured under the rubric of job analysis have deep and well-established historic roots (Mitchell, 1988; Primoff & Fine, 1988). Despite the longstanding tradition and the demonstrated pragmatic benefits, job analysis has come under fire (Harvey, 1991; Morgeson & Campion, 1997; Sanchez & Levine, 1999b). The nature of these attacks is twofold. First, some have argued that job analysis is an obstacle to organizational innovation because it creates artificial boundaries that interfere with the successful adoption of innovative management practices (Olian & Rynes, 1991). Sanchez (1994) and Sanchez and Levine (1999a) argued that this line of criticism is off target, in part because such criticisms are directed at obsolescent uses of job analysis information, not at the analysis of work per se. To deal with these criticisms, they advocated the use of the term *work analysis* instead of the traditional term *job analysis*. The former term obviates the negative connotations associated with antiquated aspects of scientific management and smokestack industry, and it conveys more accurately the full range of the applications or purposes that such analyses may serve.

A second stream of criticisms has argued that the quality of job analysis information is suspect and that the information is inaccurate due to a variety of biases and cognitive limitations, such as flaws in the judgments made by subject matter experts (see Morgeson & Campion, 1997, for a review). The term *accuracy* demands a consensually agreed-upon gold standard, which a fuzzy, socially constructed concept like the job does not permit. Sanchez and Levine (2000) maintained that this line of thinking is also unlikely to advance the practice of work analysis because it conceives the analysis of work as a measurement instrument intended to capture a questionable "true" score. Instead, they viewed work analysis as a set of tools intended to facilitate the inferences regarding the important work activities and work specifications that should be the basis for selection, training, compensation, and other human resource management practices. On the one hand, we fully support studies that are aimed at improving the quality (reliability and validity) of work analysis data, as opposed to so-called accuracy, such as the meta-analysis on the reliability of job analysis data by Dierdorff and Wilson (2003). On the other hand, evaluation of work analysis data should scrutinize not only the psychometric quality of the data but also more importantly the consequences of work analysis in terms of human resource management programs and practices. This argument derives incremental strength from the notion that organizations in today's global and hypercompetitive economy must justify costs and demonstrate the value added by programs such as work analysis. Only research directed toward consequential outcomes can provide the crucial information needed to meet these objectives.

Evaluations that examine the consequences of work analysis, however, face an important shortcoming: The fact that the procedures and criteria used to turn work-analytic information into meaningful human resource management practices have themselves been limited. One purpose of this chapter is to explore the criteria and procedures used to evaluate work analysis methods and information. A key theme is the notion that validity, including consequential validity, as defined by neoclassical psychometric theory rather than so-called accuracy is the touchstone of such evaluations (Sanchez & Levine, 1999b). Messick (1995) maintained that consequential validity includes the impact on respondents of how their scores are used. Furthermore, the standards for educational and psychological tests (American Educational Research Association, 1999) note that consequential evidence is one of the key elements under girding validity judgments. This notion is pivotal in work analysis because the resulting descriptions of work are not directly used to make decisions about employees, but rather to inform the design of the practices and programs that will facilitate such decisions. For instance, job descriptions are not directly used to select employees, but instead to inform the selection procedures.

Therefore, the consequences of work analysis are not immediately seen by employees. They are instead mediated by a series of transformation rules through which work-analytic data inform the practices and programs that follow from work analysis. This places a premium on the manner in which consequences of work analysis programs may be assessed. Thus, our second purpose is to offer suggestions for needed research on the validity of work analysis. This chapter begins with a discussion of an expanded notion of validity in the context of work analysis. Following this, illustrative changes in the work world are described, and how work analysis methods must evolve to maintain their validity for these purposes is depicted. Finally, suggestions are offered for future investigations of the validity of work analysis methods and information, with special attention to how the military may contribute.

VALIDITY OF WORK ANALYSIS

Surprisingly little attention has been paid to the meaning of validity in the context of work analysis (Manson, Levine, & Brannick, 2000). Harvey (1991), in an extensive treatment of job analysis, defined validity in terms of the operations used by some to assess a loosely defined notion of validity. He mentions such approaches as lie scales (in which items not in the job are included in questionnaires), comparisons of reported time spent against more objectively measured amounts of time spent on tasks, and task coverage judgments by subject matter experts of the extent to which the reported data from a work analysis capture the full extent of a job's contents. The validity of subject matter experts' task coverage ratings, however, has been challenged elsewhere (Wilson, 1997). Morgeson and Campion (1997) speak to the absence of bias as an indicant of validity. Others have looked at inter rater agreement as a surrogate for validity, which is better conceptualized as an assessment of reliability rather than validity (Manson et al., 2000). Levine, Ash, Hall, and Sistrunk (1983), in a study comparing work analysis methods, finessed the issue by defining validity as the comprehensiveness and quality of information yielded by a work analysis as judged by job analysis experts.

How then should you approach the notion of validity in a work-analytic context? First, you must divorce the notion of validity from accuracy. The latter term is only applicable when there is an acceptance of the existence of an objective reality that represents the work under study and when you have established a standardized representation of that reality. Although this view is not shared by others (Harvey & Wilson, 2000), we argue that work analysis deals with a social construction of work, and from a philosophical perspective the notion of an underlying objective reality independent of observers or judges is not tenable (Connell & Nord, 1996).

To better understand the notion of a job, one needs to examine its historical antecedents. In fact, the conceptualization of the job title as a separate entity from the individual or incumbent holding such a job title can be traced to the industrialization era, which led to the transformation of an economy organized around farmers and artisans to one organized around laborers. The levels of mass production that characterized the industrial era created a need for division of labor, vertical integration, and economies of scale. Under such circumstances, it made sense to conceptualize jobs as separate from individuals because economies of scale dictated the need for large numbers of individuals performing the exact same functions. In fact, multiple individuals are said to hold the same job title when they have similar responsibilities. Although it has been argued that the stable and long-lasting jobs of the past will no longer be available in a rapidly changing business world (Bridges, 1994), the analysis of work remains pivotal for human resource management.

What is established via work analysis is a consensually shared percept or construction of what the work consists of, the environmental conditions under which the work occurs, and the attributes needed by the worker or by the elements of the working system. Asking whether or not this shared construction is accurate, therefore, is futile. That is, the shared perception probably reflects the aggregate of behaviors displayed by job incumbents over time, but there is quite a bit of "legitimate" variability in those perceptions, and the aggregate is just a compromise intended to represent the manner in which an "average" job incumbent performs the duties of the job.

Second, given the conception of an intangible construct or bundle of constructs as the product of a work analysis, the notion of construct validity drawn from neo-classical psychometric theory is germane. Modern conceptions of validity are unitarian in nature and allow for several types of evidence that provide insight into the extent of validity, the search for consequences of a construct's impact being one such strategy (Society for Industrial and Organizational Psychology, 2003).

Third, validity is not a quality intrinsic to a psychological construct but instead must have relevance to some purpose (Guion, 1965; Society for Industrial and Organizational Psychology, 2003). This dictum applies as well to a percept labeled a task, a function, or a job. The validity of a work analysis resides in its capacity to serve one or more purposes (Levine, Thomas, & Sistrunk, 1988).

Based on these considerations, we assert that the validity of a work analysis is most convincingly established when it is shown to be instrumental in accomplishing the objectives that gave rise to the analyses in the first place. Obviously, the analysis should successfully capture the job's underlying constructs that are critical in such areas as selecting, compensating, training, or evaluating the performance of employees, but a successful analysis does not automatically guarantee that the programs developed as a result of the analysis will be successful. Indeed, a successful analysis should be accompanied by a series of transformation guidelines that facilitate its impact on the various human resource programs that it intends to inform. Thus, validity of a work analysis for a particular purpose is the extent to which the work analysis adds incrementally to the effectiveness or efficiency of individual- or system-level interventions that are derived from it.

Where does that leave you in regard to studies that deal with the quality of the information, even including the construct validity of scales used to document and quantify judgments of work components? As we have suggested, these are legitimate precursors and necessary to the establishment of the validity of a work analysis. Such research may be compared to the strategy of using evidence based on test content where the quality of the test, the care in its construction, its reliability, and the comprehensiveness of its sampling of a domain of interest all create a presumption of validity. However, because work analysis deals with a set of psychological constructs (i.e., constructs related to the work being accomplished), you must necessarily proceed to some estimation of the extent to which the constructs articulate with the purpose or purposes at hand. Again, to make an analogy to the valid use of a test, the notion that a test validly measures a construct such as anxiety must be buttressed by the judgment, based on data and theory, that the construct is a key contributor to performance or work attendance. Where work analysis is at issue, often such judgments are not based on empirical data but on the reasoned degree of fit between the work analysis data and the purpose at hand. This judged degree of fit would be strengthened greatly by demonstrations that successful human resource programs have been derived from rigorous work analyses. Thus the validity of work analyses rests on not only whether work requirements are adequately identified, but also on a demonstration of the fact that work analyses accomplish the purposes they are intended to serve.

In this chapter, as we contemplate a selected set of the changes taking place in the world of work, we rely on judgmental assessments of the extent to which work analyses articulate with the changes. However, our suggestions for future research offered in the last section focus directly on the need to establish a strong, empirically based track record under girding the validity of work analysis in terms of the (presumably beneficial) consequences of its use.

Sanchez and Levine (1999a) outlined a select set of the changes taking place in many of today's organizations. The potentially dramatic changes in military work brought about by revolutionary technology (e.g., night-vision equipment, mobile communication devices) clearly illustrate some of these changes. The evolving role of the military in the current era adds to the technological change: smaller and faster deployments, peacekeeping operations, and military support of drug trafficking control are examples of the new demands faced by the military.

Using the notion of building blocks for job analysis methods provided by Levine (1983), we suggest alternatives needed for work analysis descriptors and methods to maintain validity for the various purposes they must serve. First, we briefly summarize the changes noted in that paper that have altered traditional patterns of work. Then we outline the manner in which work analysis may articulate with these changes, relying upon the more current treatment of Brannick, Levine, and Morgeson (2007). Of course, when jobs retain their traditional form, standard techniques of work analysis already developed will still be applicable.

Modern Patterns of Work

Increasingly more often, employees are called upon to assume broadened responsibilities. Boundaries between jobs are becoming less and less distinct. In an era where self-directed work teams are widely used (e.g., Nygren & Levine, 1996), the ambiguity extends to the distinction between labor and management. Work is more dynamic and the pace of change in responsibilities seems to have accelerated. Networks of people and machines organized into work systems have gained in importance, which places a premium on interaction rather than individual performance. Often these interactions must take place across long distances and across national boundaries. The notion of accountability to customers and the building of customer loyalty have jointly become a *sine qua non* of organizational success. The military is not exempt from this concern with customer satisfaction. In an all-volunteer military, customer (i.e., recruit) satisfaction is a critical concern.

The flattening of organizational hierarchies has also led to limited opportunities to build careers within organizations, and turbulent global economic forces have mitigated in favor of short-term rather than long-term employment. Several of these factors have altered the nature and level of compensation provided to employees and the manner in which compensation is set. In the face of the increasing diversity of the workplace, cultural sensitivity and the management of conflict take on critical importance. Emotions and personality are now much more a center of attention, as are values and attitudes—all of which are manifested behaviorally partly in the form of so-called contextual performance or citizenship (Borman & Motowidlo, 1993). Finally, cost containment within a mercilessly competitive environment has driven many staff functions out of organizations often to outside providers. Activities including but not limited to work analysis, which are not considered part of the core elements of an organization's competitive advantage, are among such functions.

Necessary Responses in Work Analysis Methods

How must work analysis methods respond to maintain validity? We organize our suggestions into the five building blocks of such methods (Brannick et al., 2007):

1. Types of data
2. Sources of data
3. Methods of collecting data
4. Levels/units of analysis
5. Management of information that includes dissemination, storage, and retrieval of information

Types of Data

The emergence of teams and networks or systems of people and machines strongly mitigates in favor of team- or system-level descriptors in addition to descriptors applicable to individual performers. Clearly, an interdisciplinary focus involving such disciplines as industrial engineering, ergonomics, and industrial and organizational psychology is mandated. Mission and function analysis at the macro level, such as allocation of functions to elements within a network (including robots), are called for in the service of such purposes as system design, job design, training, and selection (Harris, 1988; Levine & Baker, 1991; Nof, 1988; Price & Pulliam, 1988). Workflow analysis is likewise necessary (e.g., Hupp, Polak, & Westgaard, 1995), and the dimension of time may be necessary for such purposes as workload assessment (Busby & Hutsell, 1988).

Broader and more organizationally relevant descriptors of personal attributes—sometimes referred to as competencies—are likely to be helpful. Sanchez and Levine (1999a) cited the example of customer service in a health setting. Attributes associated with activities that are described in traditional terms, such as taking vital signs and administering prescribed medications, speak to specific knowledge and skill components. However, the manner in which the services are provided to the consumer layers on top of these a required emotional display and value orientation that would otherwise be lost in relying solely on the skeletal aspects of the tasks. Thus, even if you continue to rely on work activities as a descriptor type, you should insure that the statements of activities reflect these added aspects. The set of attributes or competencies derived from the activities will then be more complete. However, the validity of these broader descriptors often referred to as competencies should not be taken for granted. The process of identifying competencies requires a sizeable inferential leap because competency modeling often fails to account for the specific tasks performed at work (Schippmann et al., 2000). Lievens, Sanchez, and De Corte (2004) recently demonstrated that the validity of broadly scripted competencies can be enhanced when applying sound work analysis procedures, such as providing subject matter experts with an opportunity to study task inventories.

Work taking place in the context of teams—and more generally, the increasingly interactive workplace—raises the issue of all attributes associated with being a team player. The lexicon to be used in work analysis must be more fully developed to accommodate these facets of work.

Broader definitions of human attributes are likely also to be more serviceable in the face of dynamic changes in work, and the likelihood that an employee may be assigned to a variety of units within an organization.

At the opposite end of the spectrum, fine-grained task analysis of complex tasks within complex environments may be necessary for training (Van Cott & Paramore, 1988) or cognitive modeling (Olson & Olson, 2003). Mental operations can be the subject of scrutiny, even in team settings in which shared mental models may facilitate team performance (Salas & Cannon-Bowers, 1997). They are critical for the understanding of team structure and function (Ilgen, Hollenbeck, Johnson, & Jundt, 2005).

In terms of scales to be used in quantifying judgments in a work analysis, there will be a need to do more customizing. For example, instead of the traditional scales as time spent, organizations may need information on the extent to which functions are core or may be outsourced. Ratings of the impact of error on customer service should also prove useful.

You also should not neglect the environment or the stressors and hazards it presents to the worker. Once again, an interdisciplinary perspective is called for and could involve molecular analyses of physiological demands on the worker imposed by extreme work environments or mental workload assessment (Casali & Wierwille, 1988; Kamon, 1988; Sulsky & Smith, 2005). On the other end of the spectrum, identification of environmental conditions that represent threats to worker health and safety will continue to be a concern in light of the fast pace of work and the rate of change in responsibilities (Siegel, 1988). The salutary effects of worker control suggest that work analysis may be profitably directed toward increasing control while moderating unwarranted demands (Spector, 2006).

Sources of Data

Where job holders have typically been the source of choice for work analysts and immediate supervisors the checkpoint for an alternate perspective, new patterns of work demand great care in selecting sources of data and the types of data or judgments they are called upon to provide. Job incumbency is neither a necessary nor a sufficient condition for subject matter experts in work analysis (Sanchez, 2000). Targets or beneficiaries of work processes, including customers, recent military recruits, and clients, may be enrolled in focus groups to aid in the design of work processes. Future assignments not yet designed should benefit from the input of diverse representatives drawn from different functional areas that would eventually interface with the new workers. Computer simulations can be employed to model future work and provide indications of human attribute needs (Polito & Pritsker, 1988).

The nature of the data or judgments should likewise enter into the selection of sources. Incumbents, for example, often are unable to make judgments about constructs with which they may be unfamiliar or have an inappropriate frame of reference. Asking many types of incumbents to judge tolerance for ambiguity required in their setting is likely to be puzzling, as incumbents may lack an adequate standard of comparison regarding "normal" levels of ambiguity in other jobs. Another example is asking incumbents about noise levels to which they have adapted over time. We can remember asking workers about noise levels in power plants or a ship's engine room—where the noise was deafening—only to be informed that they did not find the noise levels out of the ordinary.

Estimates of difficulty of learning are often more informative when coming from trainers than incumbents. However, current knowledge of the trainability of human attributes is limited and often times plagued by stereotypical conceptions and value judgments concerning the extent to which human nature is amenable to change. The consequential validity approach may shed light on the validity of trainability judgments when such judgments are contrasted against learning criteria such as the extent to which trainees improve their pretraining and posttraining performance (Jones et al., 2001).

Cross-domain investigations, such as linkages between work activities and the human attributes required to perform such activities, are still in their infancy. The identification of the human attributes or skill sets that underlie a task or a set of tasks calls for controlled experiments of the kind pioneered by Fleishman and his colleagues (Hogan & Fleishman, 1979) and also for field studies (Sanchez & Fraser, 1994). However, researchers should approach the study of work activity-human attribute links with caution because these modules of work-analytic knowledge are likely to change depending on the manner in which work activities are combined. For instance, coordination and integration skills do not only follow from specific tasks, but from the number and manner in which tasks are combined and performed. In this respect, estimates of the human attributes required by bundles of tasks are not necessarily equal to the sum of the attributes required by each individual task, just as the whole is seldom equal to the sum of its parts.

Methods of Data Collection

As technology evolves, the possibilities for greater efficiencies in data collection grow. Electronic performance monitoring offers a rich source of data. Reviews of phone calls recorded automatically for customer service representatives or telemarketers can be an alternate source of critical incidents, which in our experience have been difficult for incumbents in many lines of work to generate. Surveys and interviews, the hallmark of traditional job analysis, can now be administered online or by telecommunication.

On the other hand, the bandwidth limitations make this technology far from completely foolproof, as we recently discovered when conducting televideo interviews of professional employees. In too high a proportion of cases, picture quality was borderline, connections continually were broken or never made, and we had to resort to speakerphone interviews. These problems should subside as technology improves and becomes more user-friendly. Groupware will likewise facilitate the involvement of teams in an analysis either in real time or in nominal groups, such as those used with the Delphi technique (Olson & Olson, 2003).

When deciding between sources of data involving human judgment (i.e., subjective) or those involving more objective data, such as electronic records of activity counters and activity time, work analysts should remain mindful of the importance of collecting information about the incumbent's subjective experience of work. Such data come by necessity from individual accounts that describe not only work, but also the emotions that surround it. Thus, open-ended formats such as interviews and surveys continue to be a useful tool in work analysis.

When cost is an issue, research has shown that work analysis collected in face-to-face groups using carefully selected subject matter experts offers an acceptable alternative to large-scale surveys of incumbents. Levine, Maye, Ulm, and Gordon (1997) reported that judgmental data drawn from such groups exhibited good reliability and resulted in outcomes in the context of developing minimum qualifications across 14 diverse jobs. Sanchez and Levine (1998) analyzed this database further and found that group-level characteristics, such as group size, did not affect the quality of data as reflected in such criteria as interrater reliability. Ash, Levine, Higbee, and Sistrunk (1982) compared survey data from incumbents with data derived from panels of subject matter experts and found close correspondence.

The use of extant databases such as that offered by the Occupational Information Network (O*NET), which provides broad information about the nature of work, may serve as a stepping stone to a more rigorous and specific work analysis process. Indeed, the content model used to organize the database is quite rich and includes, as described in some detail by Brannick et al. (2007), worker requirements (such as knowledge), experience requirements (such as vocational training or amount of experience), worker characteristics (such as vision), occupational requirements (such as making decisions), occupation-specific requirements (such as tasks), and occupation characteristics (which are represented by links to other databases containing information on wages for example). While O*NET's content model is quite comprehensive, problems have been noted in such areas as the scales used to assess aspects of the data, currency of the data, and the lack of rigorously established evidence of validity (e.g., Brannick et al., 2007; Harvey & Wilson, 2010). O*NET and other extant databases may perhaps be most usefully employed as first steps in a work analysis process that will target a job, occupation, or work process with a greater degree of focus and specificity.

Where future jobs and work are contemplated, expert systems embedded in computer models can provide useful inputs to an analysis (Coovert, Craiger, & Cannon-Bowers, 1996). Less technology-based approaches may also be useful. Brainstorming and the creation of scenarios attempting to capture what a future work assignment and its environment will look like should be employed, especially where an emerging technology that has not been used before is involved.

Levels/Units of Analysis

Given the increasing complexity of work and its context, valid work analysis is more likely to be multilevel in nature. As Levine and Baker (1991) showed in testing a method for analyzing the work of teams, activities, or tasks and personal attributes at the level of the individual team member, as well as team level, work flow and analysis of work sequencing must both be present when the target of analysis is a network, team, or system. The use of theoretically derived dictionaries of descriptors for various aspects of the analysis will both streamline and render more valid the information yielded by an analysis. Raymark, Schmit, and Guion (1997) offered an example in the personality domain.

Management of Information

Information and database management can be critical to the success of work analysis (Brannick & Levine, 2002). Speed is often of the essence in modern organizations. Dissemination may be facilitated by means of current technology, although care must be exercised to ensure that information and data are circulated only to proper sources (i.e., those with a need to know). Storage requires failsafe systems and suitable backup, and there might well be a function where the keepers of the information are notified automatically about the possible need to update the data. Retrieval, as is exemplified by the O*NET, should be feasible at any of multiple levels commensurate with the needs of those who may make inquiries of the database. In addition, user-friendly linkages across databases should also be built in, so that such purposes as transitions of people from military to civilian occupations is facilitated.

SUGGESTIONS FOR FUTURE INVESTIGATIONS OF THE VALIDITY OF WORK ANALYSIS

There has been a proliferation of studies dealing with the internal quality of work analysis information (e.g., Dierdorff & Wilson, 2003). Generally, it has been a matter of faith that once the quality of the data has been ensured, good outcomes will follow. On the other hand, the use of work analysis could be accused of being overhead on top of the overhead costs usually associated with staff functions such as training. Absent compelling evidence, some may view work analysis as a mere adjunct feeding the security needs of those working in human resources or related disciplines—or worse, as the organizational scientists' answer to snake oil, a presumed cure-all with no real value.

Recognizing the dangers of using distal outcome data in evaluating the validity of work analysis, we proffered several suggestions for research that speaks to consequential validity (Sanchez & Levine, 1999b). As a starting point, we identified four kinds of inferences supported by work analysis, derived and modified from a set suggested by Gatewood and Feild (1994). These are further modified here and include the following:

1. Derivation of worker or team member attributes, such as knowledge, skills, abilities, and other characteristics (KSAOs), from work activities or system/equipment specifications
2. Derivation of organizational interventions based on work activities or human attributes, such as job or system design, selection programs, or training programs
3. Work performance indicators at the level of individuals, teams, or systems inferred from work activities, sequences, or measures of workload
4. The effectiveness of organizational interventions inferred from comparisons with work performance indicators

Perhaps the acid test of the validity of work analysis comes from the fourth member of the set, despite the possibility that intervening circumstances and variables could confound one's ability to draw conclusions. Following Huselid (1995), we quantify the extent to which formal work analysis, together with work-analytic procedures (including the transformation guidelines through which analyses impact human resource programs), are involved in an organization's operations and correlate this with indexes of organizational effectiveness.

Using a more microscopic approach, Levine, Ash, and Bennett (1980) conducted a study in the context of selection that falls within the second alternative. They analyzed four jobs using four different job analysis methods, and had human resource specialists develop examination plans from the resulting reports. These examination plans were then evaluated by a separate group of experts. Results suggested that the critical incidents technique resulted in somewhat more favorable examination plans. Had they been able to validate the examinations flowing from the examination plans against the performance measures derived from the same analyses, the study would have attained the standard set in the fourth listed member of the list.

In the context of training, three training programs might be established: one derived from a work analysis using fairly broad descriptors, one derived from general reviews of how to achieve performance results in a select set of dimensions, and one derived from an even more detailed task analysis. Performance measures derived from an integration of the broad and the fine-grained work analysis would serve as the criteria against which to validate the training programs. An alternate approach similar to the study by Levine et al. (1980) might have training contents judged by trainers and subject matter experts who were ignorant of whether work analysis played a role in their development of the training or the level of detail of the work analysis data.

Manson (2004) pioneered this new consequential validity model by examining the consequences of varying the amount of work-analytic information across four conditions based on the amount and specificity of information. Human resource professionals with personnel selection experience developed selection plans, and a separate panel of selection experts rated the quality of such plans. The results supported the collection of moderate and high-comprehensive information and the collection of specific rather than broad information. The use of complete task and KSAO inventories, however, did not lead to better selection plans than top-10 task and KSAO inventories. Therefore, the payoff from detailed work analyses appears to plateau after reaching an optimal break-even or equilibrium point balancing practicality and selection plan quality.

Another critical research approach might analyze different ways to make the inferential leaps from work analysis data to applications. For example, you could make empirical comparisons of validity between assessment batteries devised by close adherence to detailed work analysis data versus loose coupling of test types to the data. Alternatively, you might conduct a cognitive task analysis to see how experts use work analysis information to formulate training programs as compared to novices, assuming that the training programs devised by experts are judged superior. These kinds of studies would enable the formulation of sorely needed guidelines for transforming work analysis data into applications.

Studies like these (if done systematically) could help establish work analysis standards in addition to providing data about the value of work analysis. For example, if broad descriptors worked equally well or better than the more labor-intensive and fine-grained units, work analyses could end at the broader level. Concerns such as cost and time to completion are paramount in today's competitive environment. Similarly, such studies could determine whether the painstakingly crafted linkages between work activities and worker attributes add value (e.g., Goldstein & Ford, 2002). Clearly, the lack of clear standards, rules, or tested theories in such aspects as how to make such inferences as are called for in work analysis weakens the case for fine-grained detail in the work-analytic process.

The nature of the research called for is likely to be expensive and time consuming, so the question emerges as to the auspices under which such research might be meaningfully conducted. Mitchell (1988) has documented well the critical role played by the military in developing, improving, and applying work analysis methods. Its leadership would benefit from conducting the kinds of studies suggested here. The diversity of work types, available sample sizes, and the wide range of interventions practiced in the services would add immeasurably to the rigor of the studies. It is our hope that the military will see fit to exercise the same level of commitment and leadership it has historically assumed in definitive studies of the role and validity of work analysis.[1]

REFERENCES

American Educational Research Association. (1999). *Standards for educational and psychological testing.* Washington, DC: Author.

Ash, R. A., Levine, E. L., Higbee, R. H., & Sistrunk, F. (1982, March). *Comparisons of task ratings from subject matter experts versus job incumbents.* Paper presented at the annual meeting of the Southeastern Psychological Association, New Orleans, LA.

Borman, W. C., & Motowidlo, S. J. (1993). Expanding the criterion domain to include elements of contextual performance. In N. Schmitt & W. C. Borman (Eds.), *Personnel selection in organizations* (pp. 71–98). San Francisco, CA: Jossey-Bass.

Brannick, M. T., Levine, E. L., & Morgeson, F. P. (2007). *Job and work analysis: Methods, research, and applications for human resource management* (2nd ed.). Thousand Oaks, CA: Sage.

Bridges, W. (1994, September). The end of the job. *Fortune,* 62–74.

Busby, R. E., & Hutsell, W. R. (1988). Workload analysis and personnel scheduling. In S. Gael (Ed.), *The job analysis handbook for business, industry, and government* (pp. 536–553). New York, NY: John Wiley & Sons.

Casali, J. G., & Wierwille, W. W. (1988). Mental workload assessment. In S. Gael (Ed.), *The job analysis handbook for business, industry, and government* (pp. 687–714). New York, NY: John Wiley & Sons.

Connell, A. F., & Nord, W. R. (1996). The bloodless coup: The infiltration of organization science by uncertainty and values. *Journal of Applied Behavioral Science, 32,* 407–427.

Coovert, M. D., Craiger, J. P., & Cannon-Bowers, J. A. (1996). Innovations in modeling and simulating team performance: Implications for decision making. In R. A. Guzzo & E. Salas (Eds.), *Team effectiveness and decision making in organizations* (pp. 291–332). San Francisco, CA: Jossey-Bass.

Dierdorff, E. C., & Wilson, M. A. (2003). A meta-analysis of job analysis reliability. *Journal of Applied Psychology, 88,* 635–646.

Gael, S., Cornelius, E. T., III, Levine, E. L., & Salvendy, G. (Eds.). (1988). *The job analysis handbook for business, industry and government.* New York, NY: Wiley.

Gatewood, R. D., & Feild, H. S. (1994). *Human resource selection* (3rd ed.). Orlando, FL: Dryden Press.

Goldstein, I. L., & Ford, J. K. (2002). *Training in organizations* (4th ed.). Belmont, CA: Wadsworth.

Guion, R. M. (1965). *Personnel testing.* New York, NY: McGraw-Hill.

---

[1] An abbreviated version of this chapter was presented at the Job Analysis Workshop preceding the 14th International Occupational Analyst Workshop, San Antonio, TX, on April 4, 2005.

Harris, D. H. (1988). Network analysis. In S. Gael (Ed.), *The job analysis handbook for business, industry, and government* (pp. 672–682). New York, NY: John Wiley & Sons.

Harvey, R. J. (1991). Job analysis. In M. D. Dunnette & L. M. Hough (Eds.). *Handbook of industrial and organizational psychology* (2nd ed., Vol. 2, pp. 71–163). Palo Alto, CA: Consulting Psychologists Press.

Harvey, R. J., & Wilson, M. A. (2000). Yes Virginia, there is an objective reality in job analysis. *Journal of Organizational Behavior, 21*(7), 829–854.

Harvey, R. J., & Wilson, M. A. (2010, April). *Discriminant validity concerns with the O*NET holistic rating scales.* Paper presented at the Annual Conference of the Society for Industrial and Organizational Psychology, Atlanta, GA.

Hogan, J. R., & Fleishman, E. A. (1979). An index of the physical effort required in human task performance. *Journal of Applied Psychology, 64,* 197–204.

Hupp, T., Polak, C., & Westgaard, O. (1995). *Designing work groups, jobs, and workflow.* San Francisco, CA: Jossey-Bass.

Huselid, M. A. (1995). The impact of human resource management practices on turnover, productivity, and corporate financial performance. *Academy of Management Journal, 38,* 635–672.

Ilgen, D. R., Hollenbeck, J. R., Johnson, M., & Jundt, D. (2005). Teams in organizations: From input-process-output models to IMOI models. In S. T. Fiske, A. E. Kazdin, & D. L. Schacter (Eds.), *Annual Review of Psychology* (Vol. 56, pp. 517–544). Palo Alto, CA: Annual Reviews Inc.

Jones, R. G., Sanchez, J. I., Parameswaran, G., Phelps, J., Shoptaugh, C., Williams, M., et al. (2001). Selection or training? A two-fold test of the validity of job-analytic ratings of trainability. *Journal of Business and Psychology, 15,* 363–389.

Kamon, E. (1988). Physiological basis for the design of work and rest. In S. Gael (Ed.), *The job analysis handbook for business, industry, and government* (pp. 715–730). New York, NY: John Wiley & Sons.

Levine, E. L. (1983). *Everything you always wanted to know about job analysis.* Tampa, FL: Mariner.

Levine, E. L., Ash, R. A., & Bennett, N. (1980). Exploratory comparative study of four job analysis methods. *Journal of Applied Psychology, 65,* 524–535.

Levine, E. L., Ash, R. A., Hall, H. L., & Sistrunk, F. (1983). Evaluation of job analysis methods by experienced job analysts. *Academy of Management Journal, 26,* 339–348.

Levine, E. L., & Baker, C. V. (1991, April). *Team task analysis: A procedural guide and test of the methodology.* Paper presented at the 6th Annual Conference of the Society for Industrial and Organizational Psychology, St. Louis, MO.

Levine, E. L., Maye, D. M., Ulm, R. A., & Gordon, T. R. (1997). A methodology for developing and validating minimum qualifications (MQs). *Personnel Psychology, 50,* 1009–1924.

Levine, E. L., Thomas, J. N., & Sistrunk, F. (1988). Selecting a job analysis approach. In S. Gael (Ed.), *The job analysis handbook for business, industry, and government* (pp. 339–352). New York, NY: John Wiley & Sons.

Lievens, F., Sanchez, J. I., & De Corte, W. (2004). Easing the inferential leap in competency modeling: The effects of task-related information and subject matter expertise. *Personnel Psychology, 57,* 881–904.

Manson, T. M. (2004). *Cursory versus comprehensive job analysis for personnel selection: A consequential validity analysis.* Doctoral dissertation, University of South Florida, Tampa.

Manson, T. M., Levine, E. L., & Brannick, M. T. (2000). The construct validity of task inventory ratings: A multitrait-multimethod analysis. *Human Performance, 13*(1), 1–22.

Messick, S. (1995). Validity of psychological assessment: Validation of inferences from person's responses and performances as scientific inquiry into score meaning. *American Psychologist, 50,* 741–749.

Mitchell, J. L. (1988). History of job analysis in the military. In S. Gael (Ed.), *The job analysis handbook for business, industry, and government* (pp. 30–37). New York, NY: John Wiley & Sons.

Morgeson, R. P., & Campion, M. A. (1997). Social and cognitive sources of potential inaccuracy in job analysis. *Journal of Applied Psychology, 82,* 627–656.

Nof, S. Y. (1988). Job analysis for robots. In S. Gael (Ed.), *The job analysis handbook for business, industry, and government* (pp. 587–613). New York: John Wiley & Sons.

Nygren, R., & Levine, E. L. (1996). Leadership of work teams: Factors influencing team outcomes. In M. Beyerlein & D. Johnson (Eds.), *Advances in interdisciplinary studies of work teams: Team leadership* (pp. 67–105). Greenwich, CT: JAI Press.

Olian, J. D, & Rynes, S. L. (1991). Making total quality work: Aligning organizational processes, performance measures, and stakeholders. *Human Resource Management, 30,* 303–333.

Olson, G. M., & Olson, J. S. (2003). Human computer interaction: Psychological aspects of the human use of computing. In S. T. Fiske, D. L. Schacter, & C. Zahn-Waxler (Eds.), *Annual Review of Psychology* (Vol. 54, pp. 491–516). Palo Alto, CA: Annual Reviews Inc.

Peterson, N. G., Mumford, M. D., Borman, W. C., Jeanneret, P. R., & Fleishman, E. A. (Eds.). (1998). *The occupational information network (O*NET)*. Washington, DC: American Psychological Association.

Polito, J., & Pritsker, A. A. B. (1988). Computer simulation and job analysis. In S. Gael (Ed.), *The job analysis handbook for business, industry, and government* (pp. 570–586). New York, NY: John Wiley & Sons.

Price, H. E., & Pulliam, R. (1988). Functional analysis and allocation of functions. In S. Gael (Ed.), *The job analysis handbook for business, industry, and government* (pp. 639–650). New York, NY: John Wiley & Sons.

Primoff, E. S., & Fine, S. A. (1988). A history of job analysis. In S. Gael (Ed.), *The job analysis handbook for business, industry, and government* (pp. 14–29). New York, NY: John Wiley & Sons.

Raymark, P. H., Schmit, M. J., & Guion, R. M. (1997). Identifying potentially useful personality constructs for personnel selection. *Personnel Psychology, 50,* 723–736.

Salas, E., & Cannon-Bowers, J. A. (1997). Methods, tools, and strategies for team training. In M. A. Quiñones & A. Ehrenstein (Eds.), *Training for a rapidly changing workplace* (pp. 249–280). Washington, DC: American Psychological Association.

Sanchez, J. I. (1994). From documentation to innovation: Reshaping job analysis to meet emerging business needs. *Human Resource Management Review, 4,* 51–74.

Sanchez, J. I. (2000). Adapting work analysis to a fast-paced and electronic business world. *International Journal of Selection and Assessment, 8*(4), 207–215.

Sanchez, J. I., & Fraser, S. L. (1994). An empirical approach to identify job duty-ksa linkages in managerial jobs: A case example. *Journal of Business and Psychology, 8*(3), 309–325.

Sanchez, J. I., & Levine, E. L. (1998, April). *Sources of inaccuracy in job analysis and suggestions for remediation.* Paper presented at the 13th Annual Conference of the Society for Industrial and Organizational Psychology, Dallas, TX.

Sanchez, J. I., & Levine, E. L. (1999a). Is job analysis dead, misunderstood, or both? New forms of work analysis and design. In A. I. Kraut & A. K. Korman (Eds.), *Evolving practices in human resource management* (pp. 43–68). San Francisco, CA: Jossey-Bass.

Sanchez, J. I., & Levine, E. L. (1999b, April). *Inaccuracy in job analysis data: How does one know?* Paper presented at the 14th Annual Conference of the Society for Industrial and Organizational Psychology, Atlanta, GA.

Sanchez, J, I., & Levine, E. L. (2000). Accuracy or consequential validity: Which is the better standard for job analysis data? *Journal of Organizational Behavior, 21,* 809–818.

Schippmann, J. S., Ash, R. A., Battista, M., Carr, L., Eyde, L. E., Hesketh, B., … Sanchez, J. I. (2000). The practice of competency modeling. *Personnel Psychology, 53,* 703–740.

Siegel, A. I. (1988). Identification of potential hazards and job stress. In S. Gael (Ed.), *The job analysis handbook for business, industry, and government* (pp. 796–803). New York, NY: John Wiley & Sons.

Society for Industrial and Organizational Psychology. (2003). *Principles for the validation and use of personnel selection procedures* (4th ed.). College Park, MD: Author.

Spector, P. E. (2006). *Industrial and organizational psychology: Research and practice.* Hoboken, NJ: John Wiley & Sons.

Sulsky, L., & Smith, C. (2005). *Work stress.* Belmont, CA: Thomson Wadsworth.

Van Cott, H. P., & Paramore, B. (1988). Task analysis. In S. Gael (Ed.), *The job analysis handbook for business, industry, and government* (pp. 651–671). New York, NY: John Wiley & Sons.

Wilson, M. A. (1997). The validity of task coverage ratings by incumbents and supervisors. *Journal of Business and Psychology, 12,* 85–95.

8

Documenting Work Analysis Projects

A Review of Strategy and Legal Defensibility for Personnel Selection

ARTHUR GUTMAN

Florida Institute of Technology

ERIC M. DUNLEAVY

DCI Consulting Group

This chapter reviews strategies for documenting work analysis data. These data are used in the development of personnel selection procedures (i.e., any tool used to make an employment decision, such as hiring, promotion, termination, and pay raises). The documentation of work analysis data is critical for both organizational strategy and legal defensibility. Because work analysis is a tool for making decisions, documenting what those decisions are based on seems intuitive. Work analysis is not a static process, and there are many ways and tools for conducting and using a work analysis. For work analysis data to be useful to the organization, they must be presented in a way that is interpretable. Of course, in some situations work analyses may be summarized in ways that are unintelligible to the layperson responsible for making high-level organizational decisions.

For example, many practitioners have been faced with situations early in their careers when a client or manager asked for a translation of work analysis reports into nontechnical terms, "take-home" messages, and action items. However, work analysis documentation should be stringent enough to meet legal defensibility requirements stemming from potential equal employment opportunity (EEO) court challenges. Thus, the work analyst is challenged with balancing two competing goals: (a) presenting work analysis results in a manner that can be understood by the layperson and is usable to the organization, and (b) ensuring that the details of the work analysis are sufficient to survive legal scrutiny.

Understanding the take-home messages and potential implications of a work analysis effort can offer organizations a competitive advantage in developing personnel selection procedures. Specifically, well-documented work analysis data should provide the organization with a conceptual connection between work requirements and the worker characteristics (e.g., knowledge, skills, abilities, competencies) necessary to perform those requirements. This conceptual link can be used as the foundation for developing appropriate measures of work performance (e.g., work samples, performance appraisals), as well as for measures of constructs used in hiring, promotion, termination, and other employment decisions that affect applicants and/or employees. These data may also be used in a number of smaller scale efforts, including job description development, realistic job previews, career progression plans, training need identification, curriculum development, job evaluations, and compensation worth analyses.

When work analysis data are used to develop personnel selection procedures, the legal defensibility of those procedures may be challenged legally. For example, a challenge to a personnel selection procedure may reduce to whether the challenged procedure is related to the job in question and/or whether data suggest that less discriminatory yet equally appropriate alternative procedures were available. For example, a personnel selection decision may be challenged because White applicants were hired at a substantially higher rate than minority applicants. In this situation, documentation of a work analysis (as the foundation of a content validity study) may be the focal point in determining whether the selection procedure used to make hiring decisions is job related, and therefore whether it will survive a legal challenge. If that documentation is unavailable or inadequate, the employer may be found guilty of unintentionally discriminating against a particular group of applicants or employees.

Both the Equal Employment Opportunity Commission (EEOC) and Office of Federal Contract Compliance Programs (OFCCP) enforce antidiscrimination law, and both agencies have exerted substantial enforcement effort related to personnel decision systems that may affect a large class of potential victims of discrimination (Dunleavy & Gutman, 2007). Personnel selection tools involved in hiring, promotion, termination, and compensation exemplify systems that affect a large group of potential victims of discrimination. Thus, the current EEO enforcement landscape only increases the need for adequate work analysis documentation.

This chapter presents work analysis documentation considerations from the perspectives of organizational strategy and legal defensibility. These topics are presented in a number of ways. First, a case study is described illustrating development and validation of a selection procedure using work analysis documentation as the general foundation for content-oriented validity evidence. Second, a framework for the common phases of a work analysis project is presented, as are some documentation considerations for each phase. This section also links documentation considerations to the case study for exemplary purposes. Third, a set of legal defensibility considerations are presented, with particular emphasis on using work analysis data to support the use of personnel selection tools. This section reviews both case law and technical authorities. Fourth, a review of common mistakes in documenting work analysis data and a treatment of some more recent legal defensibility challenges that may relate to work analysis is presented. Finally, the chapter closes with some general recommendations regarding work analysis given the changing nature of work in the 21st century, as well as additional resource recommendations.

A CASE STUDY DEMONSTRATING WORK ANALYSIS DOCUMENTATION IN SUPPORT OF A PERSONNEL SELECTION PROCEDURE

The following is a reenactment of actual events surrounding the development and validation of a test battery commissioned by a large engineering firm. The purpose of the test battery was to hire entry-level technicians that maintain and repair equipment used to manufacture wafers and assemble chips. Names are changed to protect the confidentiality of the firm and the participants, and there are some alterations for the purposes of exposition. However, the actual procedures used and results obtained are faithfully represented. The case study includes both a content validity and a criterion validity component. Portions of both studies were done contemporaneously. They are reported as separate components for the purposes of exposition.

An industrial and organizational (IO) psychologist, Dr. Good, was hired to address the following problem. Previously, the firm hired entry-level technicians based on minimum qualifications gleaned from resumes and background checks focusing primarily on prior education, training, and work history. Applicants deemed to possess the requisite minimum qualifications were interviewed by managers, who were all engineers. Those passing the interview were hired for a two-month probationary period. There were two problems with this method of selection. First, on average, only 8 of 10 interviewees were found acceptable for probationary hiring. Second, 50% of those found acceptable for were terminated during or after probationary period for poor performance and/or inability to learn new processes. The firm hired Dr. Good to improve upon both percentages.

Preliminary Steps

Dr. Good met with the director of human resources, Mr. Deeds and two engineers, Mr. Pouba and Ms. Brane. After reading written material describing the entry-level technician job, Dr. Good outlined the general steps Deeds would have to take to ensure that all participants, including engineers and incumbent entry-level technicians, understood the mission and were on board. Dr. Good arranged a meeting with Pouba and Brane, during which he outlined nine major duty areas for the entry-level technician job based on his reading material. Pouba and Brane suggested that two of these areas were essentially the same (troubleshooting and equipment repair), and the following eight major duty areas were established:

1. Repetitive tasks
2. Training new technicians
3. Use of test equipment
4. Working with engineering personnel
5. Troubleshooting and repairing equipment
6. Record keeping
7. Ordering spare parts/equipment
8. Safety

Dr. Good then arranged a 3-hour job observation in which Pouba and Brane demonstrated critical job tasks within each of these eight duty areas.

Work Analysis

Deeds gathered two subject matter expert (SME) groups, each with six members. No engineers were used in the work analysis phase. Both groups (SME1 and SME2) were representative of race, gender, and seniority of entry-level technicians. There were two phases in the work analysis study, a job task phase and a knowledge, skill, and ability (KSA) phase.

In the job task phase, SME1 was presented with the major duty areas and asked to compose critical job task statements within each duty area in a focus group format. Each job task statement was structured to represent an activity, with or without equipment, to fulfill a purpose. Examples were provided (e.g., inspection of equipment, with meter, to determine proper functioning). Each job task was then independently rated by SME1 members on a 5-point scale for task complexity and consequences of error. These ratings were then multiplied for each SME1 member, and means were computed. A mean multiplicative value of 10 was used as benchmark to operationally define critical tasks. SME2 examined and rated the tasks generated by SME1 in a shortened version of the SME1 procedure, and a final list of critical tasks was generated.

In the KSA phase, SME1, operating as a focus group, generated KSAs associated with the critical tasks. The KSAs were then graded by individual members on the basis of four questions:

1. Is the KSA necessary for new workers? *(Answer yes or no.)*
2. Is it practical to expect a new hire to have the KSA? *(Answer yes or no.)*

3. Is trouble likely if the KSA is ignored? *(Rate 1–5.)*
4. Does the KSA distinguish average and superior performers? *(Rate 1–5.)*

As in the job task phase, SME2 verified the answers provided by SME1. A total of 62 KSAs were generated; 18 for knowledge, 10 for skills (with equipment), 29 for general abilities (without equipment), and 5 personal characteristics.

A *yes* answer to Question 1 was required to qualify for the final group of KSAs. A *yes* answer to Questions 1 and 2 meant a KSA would require training prior to employment. Among KSAs with *yes* answers to Question 1, mean multiplicative ratings of 10 or higher on Questions 3 and 4 were used as the benchmark, and KSAs above benchmark were examined to determine suitability for testing versus other methods of assessment (e.g., resumes, background checks). The following knowledge areas and abilities were deemed suitable for testing:

Knowledge		Abilities	
K1	Units of measurement	A1	Problem solving
K2	Electrical systems	A2	Deductive reasoning
K3	Basic math	A3	Reading comprehension
K4	Basic electronics	A4	Following directions
K5	Basic mechanics	A5	Written instructions

Content Validity Strategy

Dr. Good presented the work analysis results to Deeds, Pouba, and Brane, and proposed a test battery consisting of three component tests. Test 1 was a prior in-house test previously developed by Good for the firm's wafer technicians and assemblers. The in-house test assessed basic abilities in math, reading comprehension, and following directions. Test 2 consisted of three subtests in the commercially available Differentially Aptitude Test (DAT), including abstract reasoning, mechanical reasoning, and spatial relations. Test 3 was an electronics knowledge test to be developed internally because there was no in-house or commercially available electronics knowledge test suitable for the firm.

Dr. Good explained that a content valid test or test battery adequately samples the job domain, as well as the KSAs required to perform critical job tasks (i.e., criterion relevance). It also avoids assessment of irrelevant or marginal job tasks or KSAs (i.e., criterion contamination). The grid below was presented to demonstrate how the proposed test battery fulfilled both criteria:

	In-House Test	Abstract Reasoning DAT	Mechanical Reasoning DAT	Spatial Relations DAT	Electronics Knowledge Test
Units of measurement					X
Electrical systems					X
Basic math	X				X
Basic electronics					X
Basic mechanics			X		
Problem solving		X		X	X
Deductive reasoning		X		X	X
Reading comprehension	X				
Following directions	X				
Written instructions	X				

Test Development Phase

The electronics knowledge test was developed using a single group of SMEs, all engineers, including Pouba and Brane. There were two sessions. In Session 1, the SMEs identified five major electronic knowledge components, including the following:

1. *Ohm's law calculations*: Calculation of voltage, current, and/or resistance based on circuit diagrams
2. *Rectification, regulation, and induction*: Circuit diagrams to examine knowledge of the function of rectifiers, transformers, and capacitors with respect to both inputs and outputs
3. *Component identification*: Recognition of component parts, including capacitors, electrolytic capacitors, crystals, transistors, Zener diodes, inverters, gates, mosfets, and buffer amps
4. *Component knowledge*: How the component's parts are used
5. *Troubleshooting*: Troubleshooting (or problem-solving) questions, including items based on oscilloscope diagrams, nonelectrical tracing circuits, and circuits taken directly from manuals covering the firm's actual equipment

In Session 2, SME1 generated between 10 and 15 items for each knowledge area for a total of 60 items. Subsequently, the SMEs individually rated each item on a 5-point scale, where *1* = low value, *3* = average value, and *5* = high value. These ratings were averaged and filed for subsequent use.

Preliminary Selection Tool Data

Deeds arranged for administration of the in-house test, DAT subtests, and electronics knowledge to 80 incumbent entry-level technicians, which included all entry-level technicians with at least 1 year of experience with the firm. The entry-level technicians were informed that the testing was for research purposes only and that the test results would be known only to Dr. Good and his associates. The purpose of the study was explained, questions were fielded, and the test was subsequently administered in single 3-hour sessions to 20 entry-level technicians at a time.

Preliminary Demographic Data

Descriptive statistics were computed for four demographic variables, including frequencies and percentages for race, gender, and job level (i.e., Levels I and II), as well as means and standard deviations for age. There was an insufficient number of minorities and women among the 80 entry-level technicians for subsequent adverse impact statistics. Differences related to age were nonthreatening, as older entry-level technicians outperformed younger entry-level technicians on measures related to knowledge (but not initiative). This was attributable to superior performance by higher level entry-level technicians, a factor positively correlated with age. Job level was used as a covariate in all subsequent analyses.

Reliability of the EKT Test

Individual test items were examined using correlations between each item and total score, percentage correct per item, and the aforementioned SME item ratings. Five items were eliminated on this basis, yielding a final electronics knowledge test with 60 items. Internal consistency reliability for the final 60 items was assessed using Cohen's alpha, which was acceptable at .90. The alphas for the five components of the test were also acceptable, ranging from .85 to .92.

Work Analysis Report

After these pilot results, the organization was content with initial evidence supporting the use of a test for personnel selection. The final work analysis report was divided into four components.

Component 1 was a five-page executive summary outlining the results of the work analysis study and the evidence for content validity. This summary used bullet points to illustrate the major work requirements, worker characteristics, and test content. A few figures were used to demonstrate summary content validity evidence (e.g., mean frequency, importance).

Component 2 was a full report detailing each of the aforementioned procedures and results. This included a review of rating scales, with particular emphasis on frequency, importance, and criticality ratings. Rater agreement was also presented. Component 3 was an appendix that documented the SME processes, including names, dates, and procedures, and other statistics not included in the main body of the report. Finally, Component 4 was a two-page job description including the major duty areas, the critical job tasks within each duty area, the KSAs associated with critical job tasks, working conditions, and prerequisite educational and work history minimum qualifications.

The executive summary served the needs of interested stakeholders with short attention spans. The main body and appendix served the needs of interested stakeholders who want complete detail, including federal agencies that administer EEO laws. Lastly, the job description was used for recruitment purposes.

Criterion-Related Validity Strategy

For the criterion validity study, the firm's internal performance appraisals evaluated entry-level technicians on a 4-point scale on four dimensions and a global rating as follows:

1. Quality orientation/attention to detail
2. Problem solving/judgment
3. Initiative
4. Technical knowledge
5. Global rating

These dimensions were consistent with the job requirements documented in the work analysis study. However, the actual (or operational) performance ratings were restricted in range to values of 3 and 4. This was an anticipated outcome. To solve the problem, an experimental performance appraisal study was conducted.

Appraisers (all engineers) were gathered by Deeds for a 3-hour training session conducted by Dr. Good. Dr. Good explained that the experimental ratings were for research purposes only, would be held in confidence by Dr. Good, and would therefore not affect the status of any of the entry-level technicians appraised. Dr. Good then explained the statistical problems associated with restriction in range and rater biases (e.g., halo effects, leniency, stringency, central tendency). Primary and secondary ratings were obtained. Primary ratings were for entry-level technicians under direct supervision and included ratings on a 9-point scale for both the four dimensions and the global rating. Secondary ratings were for entry-level technicians supervised by others, and included only the global ratings.

Raw scores for the in-house test, DAT subtests, and electronics knowledge test were converted to z-scores, and t-scores were computed by adding 10 to each individual Z score. Thus, by definition, mean performance was 10.0 for the in-house test, each subtest of the DAT, and the electronics knowledge test.

Preliminary descriptive statistics (means and standard deviations) were then computed for each of the predictors. They were comparable across the in-house test, each of the three DAT subtests, and the electronics knowledge test for the sample as a whole. However, Level II entry-level technicians scored significantly higher on the electronics knowledge test (but not the in-house test or DAT). Critically, the correlation between primary and secondary global ratings resulted in an acceptable reliability coefficient ($r = .73$).

With regard to criterion measures, means and standard deviations were computed for the performance appraisals for the sample as a whole and for job level. Means were comparable within and across job levels for two of the dimensions (attention to detail and initiative), but were significantly higher for the Level II entry-level technicians on the other two dimensions (problem solving and technical knowledge) and the global rating. Correlations among the four dimensions and global rating were high, ranging from .63 (between technical knowledge and initiative) to .91 (between global rating and attention to detail). For purposes of exposition, the global scores will be used to illustrate criterion validity below.

There was strong evidence of criterion validity for the individual tests, incremental validity for the test battery as a whole, and utility for the electronics knowledge test and a composite of the in-house test and DAT subtests. The individual correlations (i.e., validity coefficients) were moderated by job level. The validity coefficients for Level I entry-level technicians were .59 for the in-house test, .53 for the DAT, and .35 for the electronics knowledge test. The validity coefficients for Level II entry-level technicians were .31 for the in-house test, .27 for the DAT, and .51 for the electronics knowledge test. All validity coefficients were corrected for unreliability, and both the raw and corrected validity coefficients were reported. A multiple regression analysis showed incremental validity. That is, there were significantly higher multiple R values for the test battery as a whole as compared to individual validity coefficients for the whole sample and for Level I and Level II entry-level technicians.

Utility was estimated by using global performance appraisal ratings of 5 or 6 (out of 9) as an estimate of average performance and global ratings of 7 or higher as an estimate of superior performance. The percentages of the entry-level technicians showing average and superior global ratings were 69.7% and 21.1%, respectively, for the whole sample. In comparison, these percentages were 78.9% and 39.5% for the top one-third performers on the electronics knowledge test, and 76.3% and 31.6% for the top one-third performers on a composite of the in-house test and DAT subtests.

Critical Decisions

Dr. Good met again with Deeds, Pouba, and Brane to explain two critical decisions: cutoff scores and the combination of the component tests. It was agreed that test results would serve as the first step of a multiple hurdle in which applicants were screened for subsequent interviews by engineers. The cutoff score for the electronics knowledge test was set at one half a standard deviation below, and the cutoff score for the composite of the in-house test and DAT was set at one standard deviation below the total sample means. Failure to reach either cutoff was grounds for exclusion, with exceptions made for applicants that scored one half a standard deviation or higher above the incumbent sample on the electronics knowledge test.

Final Report

A similar strategy was used to communicate results of the criterion study as was used for the work analysis report. A two-page executive summary outlined criterion results of the work analysis study and the evidence for content and criterion validity. Component 2 was a full report detailing each of the aforementioned procedures and results. Component 3 was an appendix that documented all of the specific statistical analyses.

What Does This Case Study Demonstrate?

This case study identifies a number of important issues regarding the documentation of work analysis. For example, note the following:

- The purpose of the project was clearly identified, as were specific strategies intended to meet various goals.

- Initial job information was reviewed and a baseline set of major duties were documented.
- Information about the number, adequacy, and representation of SMEs used in focus groups was documented.
- Data collection procedures were described.
- Work behavior and worker characteristic information were included.
- Other summary data were presented (e.g., descriptive statistics, rater agreement indices).
- Relevant decisions made based on SME evaluation were clearly documented.
- Summary statistics were described, as were psychometric analyses of the quality of the work analysis data.
- Content validity linkage data were included.
- Additional context (e.g., pilot testing, how work analysis data were used for criterion development in the criterion study) was documented, although some of this information was presented separate from the work analysis report.
- The work analysis was clearly used at various stages of multiple validation strategies.

DOCUMENTING VARIOUS PHASES OF A WORK ANALYSIS PROJECT

As the case study demonstrates, work analysis data are critical for both proximal and distal personnel selection work. That is to say, work analysis data may be used immediately after being collected for a content or criterion validity study, or may be used years later to conduct a job worth analysis, or to determine if the advent of a new technology has substantially changed a job and the worker characteristics necessary to perform that job. In most instances, the role of work analysis data in the short term is well understood and documentation strategies can be catered toward that end. However, it is difficult to predict how work analysis data may be used in the future, and as such the work analyst should consider best practice documentation strategies for the long term.

Figure 8.1 displays a chronology of work analysis phases, and this framework may be used in considering documentation strategies in each phase. Both short-term and long-term organizational goals should be considered, as should the employment decisions made from procedures developed from work analysis data and corresponding legal defensibility considerations. As the figure shows, the process may be cyclical in nature, such that the conclusions based on one completed work analysis could be used for planning another work analysis or for developing a different validation strategy. This notion is consistent with the dynamic nature of human resource management. Phases include initial planning, instrument development, data collection, summarizing results and creating a deliverable, making decisions based on the results, and evaluating the deliverable and considering next steps.

Phase 1: Initial Job Planning

During the initial planning phases of a work analysis project, a number of considerations should be evaluated and documented, and the specific documentation strategies depend on relevant context. From a strategy perspective, it is often useful to document the expected steps in the work analysis project up front, with a description of each phase and expectations of the deliverable at that phase. It is also useful to consider the legal defensibility of the envisioned process.

Generally, the work analyst should document any available baseline information about the jobs of interest. For example, perhaps training materials, an older work analysis, and/or job descriptions can be leveraged for initial information, and initial work behavior and worker characteristic lists are available. Even if no work analysis has been conducted before, there may be already existing taxonomies available to document and summarize work relevant data, leading to what

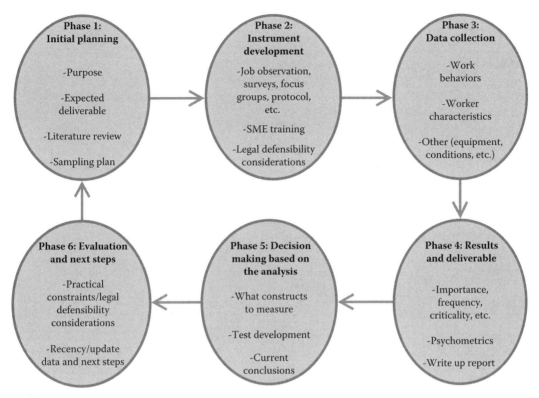

Figure 8.1   A framework for documenting phases in a work analysis.

is often called a deductive analysis. For example, the Position Analysis Questionnaire offers a variety of already existing taxonomies (see http://www.paq.com). Additionally, the Occupational Information Network (O*NET) is a federally-funded database system that provides work behavior, worker characteristics, and linkage documentation systems (Peterson & Jeanneret, 1997). Both of these may offer reasoning starting points.

On the other hand, some work analysis projects start with no previously existing information. In other words, the work analyst is responsible for collecting baseline data and developing documentation and summary systems for such items as work behaviors, worker characteristics, equipment, work conditions, and recent changes (Williams & Crafts, 1997). This situation generally requires more consideration upfront simply because information taxonomies must be developed. For example, the work analysts should develop a sampling plan to ensure that an adequate number of SMEs are available for the research and that this group generalizes well to the population of workers of interest. The work analyst would also want to consider some initial models for how data should be collected. Table 8.1 presents a general set of steps in the work analysis that one might expect to see at the beginning of a work analysis report. This table is simply intended to provide a general overview of the process.

Phase 2: Instrument Development

With regard to specific information about the work and relevant worker characteristics to perform that work, the work analyst should document how initial lists were developed. This may include source material from already existing taxonomies or work analysis reports, and/or the processes used to generate initial lists (usually focus groups, interviews, and job observations). This phase may also include the classification of other information, including tools, equipment, work conditions

Table 8.1   Example Process for a Work Analysis Project

Work Analysis Phase	Purpose of Phase
Starting point	Identify baseline job information. Consider steps, timeline, and deliverable.
Job observation (20 hours) and interviews ($n = 10$)	Verify/revise baseline info or develop initial work behavior and worker characteristic lists. Collect contextual info on the job, equipment, work conditions, changes, etc.
Work survey ($n = 40$)	Identify critical work behaviors.
Worker characteristic survey ($n = 40$)	Identify critical worker characteristics.
Linkage exercises ($n = 20$)	Prioritize worker characteristics as they relate to the job.
Summary analyses	Summarize previous steps via descriptive statistics and agreement indices (e.g., intraclass correlations).
Assessment development	Develop assessment items that capture appropriate worker characteristics.
SME review of assessment ($n = 10$)	Verify that test content links to worker characteristics.
Pilot test ($n = 100$)	Collect data and assess psychometrics.
Assessment evaluation and next steps	Assess adverse impact, make revisions, and consider the adequacy of accumulated evidence and legal defensibility.
Deliverable	A content validity study and recommended next steps for validation research.

(e.g., weather issues, volume variability, deadlines), and whether or not any core aspects of the job have changed. Generally, the work analyst may go through multiple iterations of instruments to be used for data collection; these instruments may be administrative in nature (e.g., sign in sheets, schedules, assignments) or more directly related to data collection (e.g., SME training documents, focus group protocols, interview scripts).

Phase 3: Data Collection

Regardless of the work analysis phase, from a legal defensibility perspective, it is critical to document the actual methods and processes used to collect and summarize data. This includes any job observation, interview, focus group, or survey conducted as part of the work analysis. From a legal defensibility perspective, the work analyst may benefit from treating method and process documentation like they would a methods section in a research report for a scholarly journal. Issues related to the methods themselves and the SMEs who participated in those methods should both be recorded, although this information may fit better in an appendix as opposed to the text of a report.

One of the more common criticisms of work analysis data used in content-oriented validation research is that the SMEs used in the analysis do not represent the general workforce. This misrepresentation may exist along various dimensions, including gender, race, age, tenure, job title, and quality of work. If this criticism is true, it is a damaging one because the job information collected may not accurately depict the work as it exists in reality. For this reason, it is important to develop and document a sampling plan that generalizes to the workforce. We recommend that summary information such sample size and sample characteristics be documented. Additionally, it is also useful to keep a running table of SMEs who participate in various processes, as seen in Table 8.2. It is also generally a good idea to include the actual work analysis tools (e.g., job observation form, interview script, survey) in an appendix to the work analysis report. Alternatively, the work analyst could present actual instruments in the text, as Table 8.3 exemplifies.

With regard to the actual processes, keeping track of each individual data collection allows for easy data summary. For example, something like Table 8.4 could be used to document job observations, and maintenance of this worksheet would allow for easy summary of job observation efforts and evaluation of whether the observations represent the workforce as a whole. Other data that are

Table 8.2   Example of Subject Matter Expert Table

Subject Matter Expert	Race	Sex	Age	Job Title	Tenure (years)	Previous Job	Supervise Job in Question?	Comments
1	B	M	30–39	Adm	4	None	Y	
2	W	M	20–29	Whse	6	Whse	Y	
3	B	M	40–49	Adm	7	None	Y	
4	B	F	50–59	Oper	1	Whse	Y	
5	H	M	50–59	Adm	1	None	Y	Left workforce for 20 years
6	W	M	40–49	Adm	3	Adm	Y	
7	W	M	30–39	Oper	9	None	Y	
8	W	F	60–69	Whse	11	Adm	Y	New team leader
9	H	M	20–29	Adm	2	None	Y	

Adm = administrative; Oper = operator; Whse = warehouse.

Table 8.3   Example Work Requirement Survey Sheet

Survey Item	Scale
Do employees in this job perform this behavior?	1. Yes 2. No
How often is this behavior performed on this job?	1. Never 2. Yearly 3. Monthly 4. Daily 5. Multiple times a day
How important is this work behavior to successful job performance?	1. Not important at all 2. Somewhat important 3. Important 4. Extremely important
Is this work behavior necessary to perform on the first day of the job?	1. Yes 2. No

Note that a worker characteristic survey sheet would include similar scales measuring things such as:

- How frequently is this worker characteristic seen on the job?
- How important is worker characteristic to performing the job?
- Does this worker characteristic differentiate adequate workers from inadequate workers?

Table 8.4   An Example Job Observation Worksheet

Date	Location	Number of Subject Matter Experts	Time Spent (hours)	General Description
1/1/2008	Washington, DC	10	4	Observed warehouse workers on the job
2/1/2008	New York City (1)	7	3	Observed supervisors oversee warehouse production
2/1/2008	New York City (2)	5	6	Observed administrative workers on the job
4/1/2008	Miami	11	7	Observed administrative workers on the job
4/15/2008	Pittsburgh	13	10	Observed operator jobs

often measured in survey format include data about tools, equipment, contextual differences in job duties (e.g., location differences in work). Again, it is also a good idea to keep documentation of the actual surveys that are used.

Phase 4: Results and Deliverables

Summary data should also be included in the work analysis report; this should be intuitive because it is this summary data that will likely be used to make a series of important decisions. With regard to SME ratings, these data are often represented via descriptive statistic tables like Table 8.5, which presents summary linkage data. Bar or line graphs may also offer illustrative methods of demonstrating these data. General agreement and/or reliability indices also fit into this category. Oftentimes these data are fairly simple and can be presented in the text. In other situations, it may be more appropriate to present these data in some form of a matrix.

Phase 5: Decision-Making Based on the Analysis

It is also important to document decisions made based on a work analysis, as would be appropriate in a content-oriented validity strategy. Recall the example in the case study of a linkage matrix of worker characteristics and jobs for which those characteristics are important. In this example, perhaps inclusion criteria were empirical rules using importance, the extent to which a characteristic differentiates successful from unsuccessful performance, and a more subjective expert opinion of practical constraints such as measurement difficulties and budgetary constraints. In a stand-alone content validity report, this section would include decisions related to pilot testing and initial test evaluation.

In any technical report, an obvious challenge is to describe conclusions from complex data in ways that audience members without technical expertise can understand. For example, general communication style issues can differentiate a useable report from one that seems insurmountable to the nontechnical manager who is responsible for making decisions based on a work analysis. Some general communication strategies for presenting key points and implications from work analysis data include the following:

- Create a short executive summary written in nontechnical style that summarizes the major conclusions/deliverables from the work analysis.
- Use bullet points when feasible, particularly in the executive summary.
- When appropriate, summarize data via graphs or figures. These are often more engaging and less complex than tables and can be used break up the text of the document.

Table 8.5 Example of Summary Linkage Data (Based on 56 Subject Matter Experts)

KSA	Importance	Frequency	Criticality	Necessary on Day 1?	Can Be Trained Easily on the Job?	Distinguishes Successful from Unsuccessful?
A	4.1	4.5	4.2	Y (88%)	N (63%)	Y (100%)
B	4.6	4.2	4.5	Y (80%)	N (61%)	Y (75%)
C	3.8	3.6	3.7	N (56%)	Y (67%)	Y (68%)
D	2.9	4.0	3.3	Y (91%)	N (52%)	N (63%)
E	3.1	3.0	3.1	N (62%)	N (38%)	N (60%)
F	3.4	2.1	3.0	N (38%)	N (12%)	N (40%)
G	4.7	3.8	4.4	Y (67%)	N (20%)	Y (88%)
H	3.4	3.4	3.4	N (10%)	N (28%)	N (50%)
I	4.0	4.8	4.3	Y (91%)	N (0%)	Y (89%)

- Consider placing a potentially large portion of technical information in a series of appendices in a stand-alone document. This may allow both the technical expert and the layperson to read the text of the report; the layperson can ignore the appendices, while the technical expert can thumb through the text and appendices simultaneously.
- Include a "Next Steps" section to conclude the work analysis report; this section ensures that the audience can understand the temporal nature of the project.

Phase 6: Evaluation and Next Steps

This concluding phase in the work analysis process is general in scope and may or may not link to additional work analysis or other validation research. Additionally, this step may be on hold for an extended amount of time as more information about the selection procedure or job is collected. This section could include a review of practical constraints on the current work analysis that may spur more research, additional legal defensibility concerns, and any issues related to whether the jobs of interest may have changed. Any job changes may require additional research. Because these job changes could occur years after a work analysis has been conducted, it is often difficult to determine whether this phase has concluded because it is impossible to predict the future. Table 8.6 summarizes these phases and details more specific documentation considerations.

OVERVIEW OF EEO LAWS FOR WHICH WORK ANALYSIS MAY PLAY A ROLE

The work analytic documentation strategies described previously are particularly important when a selection procedure based on a work analysis comes under legal defensibility scrutiny. This section describes a number of EEO laws that collectively offer protections against workplace discrimination based on race, color, religion, sex, national origin, age, and disability. Title VII of the Civil Rights Act of 1964 is the most comprehensive law, protecting five of these classes: race, color, religion, sex, and national origin. Age is covered in the Age Discrimination in Employment Act of 1967; disability is covered in the Americans with Disabilities Act of 1990 (ADA) and its precursor, the Rehabilitation Act of 1973.

Other important laws include Executive Order 11246, the 5th, 13th, and 14th Amendments to the U.S. Constitution, and the Equal Pay Act of 1963. Unlike Title VII, which protects all members of each protected class, Executive Order 11246 generally applies to underutilization of minorities and women. The 5th and 14th Amendments provide equal protection in federal and state/local entities, respectively, and the 13th Amendment has overlapping coverage with Title VII based on race, color, religion, and national origin, but not sex. The Equal Pay Act is a surgical statute covering equal pay for equal work based on sex. Equal pay for equal work is also covered in Title VII based on race, color, religion, sex, and national origin.

A final point to note is that virtually all of these laws have been amended. The most noteworthy amendments are the EEO Act of 1972, which extended Title VII coverage to federal, state, and local governments, the Civil Rights Act of 1991, which added compensatory and punitive damages and jury trials to Title VII, and also affected several of the other laws cited above, and the ADA Amendments Act of 2008, which authorized important changes in how we define being disabled within the meaning of the ADA. At the time this chapter was written, the Ledbetter Fair Pay Act had recently been signed into law and President Obama had created a multi-agency task force on pay equity. These political initiatives may substantially change the landscape of compensation discrimination enforcement.

There are several areas in which work analysis has been featured in case law. For present purposes, we focus on three of them: (a) adverse impact of tests and other selection criteria, (b) the definition of essential job functions in disability cases, and (c) compensation discrimination under the Equal Pay Act.

Table 8.6   A Matrix of Work Analysis Phases, Typical Tasks, and Documentation Considerations

Phases	Phase I: Initial Planning	Phase II: Instrument Development	Phase III: Data Collection	Phase IV: Results and Deliverable	Phase V: Decision Making	Phase VI: Evaluation and Next Steps
Typical tasks	• Identify purpose • Envision deliverable • Set up timeline • Conduct literature review • Develop sampling plan	Develop job observation, surveys, focus groups, etc. SME training Pilot measures Revise measures Legal defensibility considerations	Schedule collections Strategize data maintenance Collect data on work behaviors, worker characteristics, other (equipment, conditions, etc.) Evaluate whether sampling plan was met	Summarize results with descriptive, tables, figures, etc. Interpret results Assess psychometric properties of data collection instruments Write up results in an executive summary Prepare full report with appendices Request feedback and revise deliverable Submit deliverable	Consider what constructs to measure Make decisions Test development Pilot test Revise test Conduct other research Make recommendations based on available information	Consider practical constraints/legal defensibility considerations Review recency of data Supplement data as necessary Plan next research steps
Documentation considerations	• Write up a summary of the literature review • Record the sampling plan and possible difficulties • Create spreadsheets with assignments, timelines, etc.	Create a list of materials reviewed Document the instrument development process Capture any SME and expert reviews of the instruments Start an appendix with all instruments Keep pilot statistics Conduct an initial audit using UGESP as a model	Create and update an SME list Document a list of final instruments Create a summary of where data were collected	Develop a psychometric appendix with relevant supporting data Summarize all descriptive data Write an executive summary of results	Write down construct inclusion criteria and the decision process Write a reasonable alternatives section for the report Write a content validity report with linkage of selection procedure to work analysis data Write a pilot test section	Conduct a "final" audit using UGESP as a model Document recency studies Refine longer-term validation plan

Adverse Impact

Adverse (or disparate) impact occurs when an otherwise facially neutral test or other selection criterion disproportionately excludes a higher percentage of one group as opposed to another. For example, in *Griggs v. Duke Power* (1971), Duke Power required a high school diploma and passing scores on two cognitive tests (the Bennett and Wonderlic tests) for entry in or promotion to higher-level jobs. The cognitive tests excluded 94% of black applicants compared to 42% of white applicants. The high school graduation rate in North Carolina at the time was 34% for whites, but only 12% for blacks. A unanimous Supreme Court struck down both requirements, ruling that if an employment practice produces adverse impact, there must be a "manifest relationship" between the challenged practice and the "employment in question."

Then, in *Albemarle v. Moody* (1975), Albemarle used the high school diploma, Wonderlic, and Revised Beta Exam for hiring. Aware of the *Griggs* ruling, Albemarle hired an expert to correlate test scores with job performance ratings. However, it was a hasty effort conducted shortly before trial. Indeed, the expert was not even on site when the study was conducted. One of the more glaring errors was absence of work analysis data. Thus, as noted by the Fourth Circuit in *Moody v. Albemarle* (1973):

> In developing criteria of job performance by which to ascertain the validity of its tests, Albemarle failed to engage in any job analysis. Instead, test results were compared with possibly subjective ratings of supervisors who were given a vague standard by which to judge job performance. Other courts have expressed skepticism about the value of such ill-defined supervisor appraisals.

Albemarle lost, and the *Griggs* and *Albemarle* rulings formed the basis for the *Uniform Guidelines on Employee Selection Procedures* (UGESP; U.S. Equal Employment Opportunity Commission et al. 1978). After *Griggs* and *Albemarle*, adverse impact rulings with work analysis implications occurred primarily in the lower courts. The most important early rulings were in *Guardians v. Civil Service* (1980) and *Gillespie v. Wisconsin* (1985), which established precedents for content validity, cutoff scores, and rank ordering. The most important recent ruling is *Lanning v. SEPTA* (1999), which on the surface contradicts precedents established in *Guardians*, *Gillespie* and most other relevant rulings.

Guardians addressed a portion of the UGESP implying that content validity is insufficient to support tests of mental processes. Accordingly:

> A selection procedure based on inferences about *mental processes* cannot be supported solely or primarily on the basis of content validity. Thus, a content strategy is not appropriate for demonstrating the validity of selection procedures which purport to measure traits or constructs such as intelligence, aptitude, personality, common sense, judgment, leadership and spatial ability.

The Second Circuit Court struck down this guidance in *Guardians*, and established the following five steps to support content validity regardless of the construct measured:

1. Suitable work analysis
2. Reasonable competence in test construction
3. Test content related to job content
4. Test content representative of job content
5. Scoring systems selecting applicants that are better job performers

The five steps have been supported in several subsequent cases, most notably, *Gillespie v. Wisconsin* (1985) and *Police Officers v. Columbus, Ohio* (1990), and most recently, in *Gulino v. NY State* (2006).

It is now commonly accepted in the courts that content validity is sufficient to prove that a test is job-related, as long as the work analysis is properly conducted, the test is properly created and scored, and the test is broadly representative of critical KSAs. For example, in *Green v. Washington State* (1997), virtually all of the steps established in *Guardians* were violated, resulting in the rejection of a job element exam. Five failures were cited, including: test items that are not representative of critical KSAs, measurement of abstract concepts, failure to measure intended KSAs, items with no clear-cut answers, and measurement of KSAs learned on the job.

Precedent for cutoff scores and rank ordering were also established in *Guardians* and *Gillespie*. The UGESP are vague with respect to cutoff scores, stating only that they "should normally be set as to be reasonable and consistent with normal expectations of acceptable proficiency within the work force." However, in *Guardians*, the Second Circuit ruled:

> An employer may establish a justifiable reason for a cut-off score by, for example, using a professional estimate of the requisite ability levels, or, at the very least by analyzing the test results to locate a logical break-point in the distribution of scores.

Additionally, in a series of questions and answers relating to the UGESP, the EEOC gave the following answer to Question 62:

> Use of a selection procedure on a ranking basis may be supported by content validity if there is evidence from job analysis or other empirical data that what is measured by the selection procedure is associated with differences in levels of job performance.

Question 62 was subsequently cited *Gillespie* to support both strict rank ordering and cutoff scores.

The *Lanning* case featured an aerobic capacity test for the hiring of transit authority police officers that adversely impacted female applicants. There were two Third Circuit rulings. In *Lanning I* (*Lanning v. SEPTA*, 1999), the Third Circuit adopted new rules for cutoff scores, ruling that cutoff scores must measure "the minimum qualifications necessary for successful performance of the job in question." In *Lanning II* (*Lanning v. SEPTA*, 2002), the Third Circuit supported the challenged cutoff score under these new rules.

In its original ruling, the district court favored SEPTA (*Lanning v. SEPTA, 1998*). The court was particularly impressed with work analysis data showing the importance of aerobic capacity to officer and public safety, and multiple regression data showing the relationship between aerobic capacity and successful criminal arrests and commendations for field work. On remand after *Lanning I*, the district court cited the following passage from the Society for Industrial and Organizational Psychology (SIOP, 2003):

> Judgment is necessary in setting any critical or cutoff score. A fully defensible empirical basis for setting a critical score is seldom, if ever, available. The only justification that can be demanded is that critical scores be determined on the basis of a rationale which may include such factors as estimated cost-benefit ratio, number of openings and selection ratio, success ratio, social policies of the organization, or judgments as to require knowledge, skill or ability on the job. If critical scores are used as a basis for rejecting applicants, their rational or justification should be made known to the users. (p. 47)

The district court then reiterated its earlier ruling, and the Third Circuit affirmed the district court in *Lanning II*.

The *Lanning I* ruling was criticized by members of the IO community (e.g., DeNisi, 1999; Sharf, 1999). In our opinion, these criticisms are valid. Nevertheless, in view of *Lanning II*, it is not clear that *Lanning I* is as threatening as first thought. For example, several of the major features of the case study are consistent with the reasoning used in *Lanning II*, including use of the work analysis to establish critical KSAs, test creation based solely on these KSAs, and establishment of a cutoff score based on the average performance of existing incumbents.

Essential Job Functions and the ADA

The ADA defines a qualified individual with a disability as one who can perform all essential job functions with or without reasonable accommodation. The EEOC Interpretive Guidelines supports this definition with the following two steps for determining qualification:

> The *first step* is to determine if the individual satisfies the prerequisites for the position, such as possessing the appropriate educational background, employment experience, skill, licenses, etc. The *second step* is to determine whether or not the individual can perform the essential functions of the position held or desired with or without reasonable accommodation.

In other words, Step 1 means having prerequisite KSAs for essential job functions and Step 2 means performing those essential job functions either with or without reasonable accommodation. For present purposes, our focus is on Step 1.

The following analogy by the Seventh Circuit in *Miller v Illinois* (1996) illustrates the distinction between essential and marginal job duties. Accordingly:

> If it is reasonable for a farmer to require each of his farmhands to be able to drive a tractor, clean out the stables, bale the hay, and watch the sheep, a farmhand incapable of performing any of these tasks except the lightest one (watching the sheep) is not able to perform the essential duties of his position.

In this hypothetical example, it would be a reasonable accommodation to eliminate marginal duties, such as watching sheep, but not essential duties, such as driving tractors, cleaning stables, or baling hay.

More realistic examples of essential versus marginal duties are illustrated in *Borrowski v Valley Central* (1995) and *Stone v. Mt. Vernon* (1997). In *Borrowski*, a school librarian with memory and concentration deficits was able to perform the essential duties of actual librarian work, but could not control her students during class. Borrowski requested a teacher's aide, but the school refused. The Second Circuit ruled that her request is reasonable as long the duty in question is not essential, an issue that was remanded back to the district court for a jury to decide.

In *Stone*, a fire chief denied a paraplegic former firefighter a bureau job involving deskwork. The chief claimed that all bureau personnel must fight fires in emergencies, which obviously, Stone could not do. However, two long-term bureau employees testified such emergencies had never occurred, and fighting fires was deemed nonessential for the job in question.

More recently, in *PGA v. Martin* (2001), Casey Martin, a professional golfer, challenged a PGA rule requiring competitors to walk the golf course during PGA events. Martin suffered from a circulatory disease that restricted blood flow in his right leg and made it difficult for him to walk on a golf course without pain. He requested use of a golf cart as a reasonable accommodation, which the PGA denied on grounds that it would "fundamentally alter" its tour events. The Supreme Court disagreed, ruling:

> The use of carts is not inconsistent with the character of golf, the essence of which has always been shot-making. The walking rule ... is neither an essential attribute of the game itself nor an indispensable feature of tournament golf.

The implications of these rulings are clear. Employers cannot put themselves outside the reach of the ADA by arbitrarily defining what is fundamental or essential to a job. Rather, what is essential versus marginal must stand up to a work analysis in order to survive a court challenge. Additionally, employers that use tests requiring nonessential skills to take, or which assess marginal skills, are also vulnerable.

Compensation and the Equal Pay Act

The Equal Pay Act requires equal pay for equal work based on sex, with exceptions for seniority and merit, and any other factor other than sex (e.g., educational background). Other statutes also use Equal Pay Act rules, including Title VII, the Age Discrimination in Employment Act of 1967, and the ADA. Equal work means that jobs are substantially equal with respect to skill, effort, responsibility and working conditions. Jobs differing on any one of these dimensions are not equal. Work analysis is featured in two ways: (a) as a basis for job evaluations that establish compensation for different jobs, and (b) in distinguishing between essential job duties that make given job titles "substantially equal."

The connection to job evaluation is illustrated in *American Federation of State, County and Municipal Employers (AFSCME) v. State of Washington* (1985), where the State of Washington compared pay scales based on internal versus external worth. For internal worth, 600 points were assigned to jobs based on skill (280), mental effort (140), accountability (160), and working conditions (20). For external worth, other employers were surveyed to determine prevailing market rates. The state found that jobs with 70% or more females were underpaid relative to job evaluation rates, but were paid at or near prevailing market rates. The state chose to use market forces and AFSCME filed a Title VII suit, claiming that market forces adversely impact females. However, borrowing from a parallel case in *Spaulding v. Wa*shington (1984), the Ninth Circuit ruled that adverse impact claims require a specific employment practice and that market forces do not constitute an employment practice.

The connection to "substantially equal" jobs is illustrated in several early Equal Pay Act cases. Many of these cases occurred in an era in which it was common to segregate men and women in different areas of a workplace and/or to classify women into lower paying job titles even though the lower and higher paying jobs were substantially equal. Examples of job titles deemed substantially equal include male orderlies and female nurses (*Hodgson v. Brookhaven*, 1970) and male tailors and female seamstresses (*Brennan v. City Stores*, 1973). Additionally, in two cases that combined EPA and Title VII charges, female bindery workers were found to perform work essentially equal to male bookbinders (*Thompson v. Sawyer,* 1982), as were female stewardesses in relation to male pursers (*Laffey v. Northwest Airlines*, 1984).

There were several cases in which employers attempted to justify pay differentials on grounds that were deemed to be artificial. For example, in *Shultz v. Wheaton* (1970), the employer argued that male selector-packers were paid more than their female counterpart because males were expected to be more flexible and perform the work of "snap up boys," and they were required to left heavy objects. The Third Circuit viewed this as an example of artificially generated job classifications because the snap-up work paid the same hourly rate as selector-packer, and females were prohibited from lifting heavy objects because of union rules.

Similar rulings were rendered in *Hodgson v. Brookhaven* (1970) and *Hodgson v. Daisy* (1971). In *Brookhaven*, the Fifth Circuit ruled that additional marginal duties performed by male orderlies were insufficient to justify higher pay as compared to female nurses, and in *Daisy*, the Eighth Circuit ruled that light-duty tasks with greater mental effort performed by females were substantially equal to heavy-duty tasks with greater physical effort performed by males.

Lastly, in *Corning v. Brennan* (1975), Corning attempted to justify higher pay for males and females that had the same job titles on ground than males working the night shift worked under more hazardous conditions than females working the day shift. The Supreme Court ruled that the surroundings and hazards were not different across these shifts.

In short, the moral for substantially equal work in the Equal Pay Act (and related statutes) parallels the moral for essential job functions in the ADA. That is, marginal extra duties do not make otherwise equal jobs unequal.

LEGAL/PROFESSIONAL AUTHORITIES AND WORK ANALYSIS

The work analyst may refer to a number of technical authorities that, in part, identify what makes a work analysis adequate or inadequate. These authorities may be used in assessing the legal defensibility of a selection procedure as described above. However, the scope and purpose of these authorities differ (Jeanneret, 2005; Stelly & Goldstein, 2007). For example, the UGESP were written by a joint committee representing the EEOC, the U.S. Department of Labor, the U.S. Department of Justice, and the Civil Service Commission, and as such were developed explicitly for enforcement considerations. These guidelines are enforced as law by the OFCCP and are the most referred authority in EEOC-related litigation (Jeanneret, 2005). As stated in the UGESP:

> These guidelines incorporate a single set of principles which are designed to assist employers, labor organizations, employment agencies, and licensing and certification boards to comply with requirements of Federal law prohibiting employment practices which discriminate on grounds of race, color, religion, sex, and national origin. They are designed to provide a framework for determining the proper use of tests and other selection procedures.

The UGESP contain a number of sections relevant to work analysis. For example, on the expertise necessary to conduct adequate work analysis research, the U.S. Equal Employment Opportunity Commission et al. (1978) stated:

> Professional supervision of selection activities is encouraged but is not a substitute for documented evidence of validity. The enforcement agencies will take into account the fact that a thorough job analysis was conducted and that careful development and use of a selection procedure in accordance with professional standards enhance the probability that the selection procedure is valid for the job. (Section 9B)

On the role of work analysis in all validation strategies, the U.S. Equal Employment Opportunity Commission et al. (1978) stated:

> Any validity study should be based upon a review of information about the job for which the selection procedure is to be used. The review should include a job analysis except as provided in section 14B(3) of this section with respect to criterion-related validity. Any method of job analysis may be used if it provides the information required for the specific validation strategy used. (Section 14-A)

On the role of work analysis in supporting the use of criteria in a criterion-related validity strategy, the U.S. Equal Employment Opportunity Commission et al. (1978) stated:

> There should be a review of job information to determine measures of work behavior(s) or performance that are relevant to the job or group of jobs in question. These measures or criteria are relevant to the extent that they represent critical or important job duties, work behaviors or work outcomes as developed from the review of job information. (Section 14-B(2))

On the use of criteria that are not supported by a work analysis, the U.S. Equal Employment Opportunity Commission et al. (1978) stated:

> Certain criteria may be used without a full job analysis if the user can show the importance of the criteria to the particular employment context. These criteria include but are not limited to production rate, error rate, tardiness, absenteeism, and length of service. (Section 14-B-3)

On the role of work analysis in content-oriented research, the U.S. Equal Employment Opportunity Commission et al. (1978) stated:

> There should be a job analysis which includes an analysis of the important work behavior(s) required for successful performance and their relative importance and, if the behavior results in work product(s), an analysis of the work product(s). (Section 14C(2))

On the role of work analysis in construct validity research, the U.S. Equal Opportunity Employment Commission (1978) stated:

> There should be a job analysis. This job analysis should show the work behavior(s) required for successful performance of the job, or the groups of jobs being studied, the critical or important work behavior(s) in the job or group of jobs being studied, and an identification of the construct(s) believed to underlie successful performance of these critical or important work behaviors in the job or jobs in question. Each construct should be named and defined, so as to distinguish it from other constructs. (Section 14 D(3))

It is important to note that the UGESP have been featured in a growing number of controversies in recent years, stemming primarily from a perceived disconnect between the science of personnel selection and the law. Much of this disconnect relates to the fact that the UGESP were written decades ago but still serve as the most dominant authority in adverse impact case law. Clearly, the science of personnel selection has advanced considerably since 1978.

For example, the UGESP were written before the "Unitarian" concept of validity was developed and accepted by the scientific community. Landy (1986) was among the first to decry "Trinitarian" distinctions in the UGESP between content, criterion, and construct validity. The Trinitarian view, advocated in the UGESP, treats criterion validity as the preferred method for proving job relatedness. In contrast, the Unitarian view holds that any evidence of what a test measures adds to our understanding of job relatedness, regardless of how it is collected. Thus, as noted in the prior section, the UGESP dictum that "inferences based on mental processes cannot be supported solely or primarily on the basis of content validity" contradicts the more modern Unitarian view.

As discussed elsewhere (Gutman, 2005; Landy, Gutman, & Outtz, 2010; Stelly & Goldstein, 2007), the UGESP dictum on content validity has caused quite a bit of confusion in understanding whether content-oriented research is appropriate for supporting the use of measures of constructs such as cognitive abilities and personality traits. Given the advent of the Unitarian perspective of validity, it seems reasonable that a rational linkage of critical work behaviors to the worker characteristics necessary to perform those behaviors and a linkage between procedures and those worker characteristics would meet UGESP requirements, regardless of what constructs are being measured. For example, these requirements are illustrated in *Guardians* (1980) and its progeny, as well as in our featured case study. Fortunately for practitioners, acceptance of well-performed content validity studies is now accepted in case law.

Nevertheless, despite the general acceptance of *Guardians* and its progeny, the reader should be mindful that a literal interpretation of this UGESP dictum may still be used by enforcement agencies, particularly the OFCCP, and state and local civil rights agencies. Therefore, it is recommended that other evidence (e.g., criterion-related validity) be gathered when it is technically feasible. For example, in the featured case study, a criterion validity study was technically feasible. However, there may be other situations, most notably when municipalities face large-scale hiring or promotion of police or firefighters, that criterion validity studies are less feasible because of contextual factors (e.g., impracticality of administering an examination more than once because applicants are likely to memorize questions and pass them on).

There are other important disconnects. For example, the UGESP define test fairness in an ambiguous fashion. From a scientific perspective, the requirement of a fairness study (without formally defining fairness) is not consistent with research findings that tests are generally fair from a moderated multiple regression perspective.

Guion (1998) provided a very interesting perspective on UGESP, its development, and inconsistencies between UGESP and the current science of selection. For example, he wrote that "the document is not static. Judicial and administrative decisions have modified some interpretations.... the guidelines provisions on content validity (and construct validity) are confused and confusing." With regard to work analysis, Guion pointed out the following:

> Even the most careful job analysis is subjective. Job analysis is not science, even when it is used in scientific research or guided by scientific thought. It is an information gathering tool to help managers or researchers what to do next. (p. 93)

In spite of these disconnects, there are reasonable arguments supporting the belief that the UGESP still meet its intended EEO purpose (e.g., Biddle, 2008). Additionally, our conversations with practitioners in the field suggest that many have adapted to the requirements of the UGESP, as written and modified by case law, and it would be a burden to adapt to new updated rules. A final point to note is that the U.S. Equal Employment Opportunity Commission et al. (1978) recognized the UGESP would someday become outdated, stating "new strategies for showing the validity of selection procedures will be evaluated as they become accepted by the psychological profession." Many of the new strategies are discussed in the most recent edition of the *Principles for the Validation and Use of Personnel Selection Procedures* (SIOP, 2003) and the *Standards for Educational and Psychological Tests* (American Educational Research Association [AERA], American Psychological Association, & National Council on Measurement in Education, 1999), and it is to these authorities we turn to next.

The *Principles for the Validation and Use of Personnel Selection Procedures* (SIOP, 2003) were written by a division within the American Psychological Association (APA). This document provides scientific guidance specifically for those involved in the development and implementation of employment selection systems. The purpose is stated as the following:

> To specify established scientific findings and generally accepted professional practice in the field of personnel selection psychology in the choice, development, evaluation, and use of personnel selection procedures designed to measure constructs related to work behavior with a focus on the accuracy of the inferences that underlie employment decisions. (SIOP, 2003, p. 1)

Toward that end, guidance is framed toward those making employment decisions with selection procedures, and as such focuses on research, application, operational use, and the evaluation of selection procedures.

As expected, the principles include information directly related to work analysis. In fact, the principles take a Unitarian perspective on validation research and present the analysis of work as a precursor to all selection procedure support. Note that these principles were most recently updated in 2003, and as such they include more recent scientific advances as compared to UGESP.

In fact, some in the field of personnel selection advocate the use of the principles in the enforcement context, although the principles themselves state that they are not intended to be a technical translation of existing or future regulations. Specific guidance on work analysis is provided in the following extracts.

On the definition of work or work analysis, SIOP (2003) stated:

When they are intended to support the underlying validity or use of a selection procedure, these Principles apply. The term "analysis of work" is used throughout this document and subsumes information that traditionally has been collected through job analysis methods as well as other information about the work, worker, organization, and work environment. (p. 10)

On the general purposes of work analysis work, SIOP (2003) stated:

There are two major purposes for conducting an analysis of work. One purpose is to develop selection procedures. Part of this process is an analysis of work that identifies worker requirements including a description of the general level of ability, skill, knowledge, or other characteristics needed. Such an analysis of work would determine the characteristics workers need to be successful in a specific work setting, or the degree to which the work requirements are similar to requirements for work performed elsewhere. The other purpose is to develop or identify criterion measures by assembling the information needed to understand the work performed. (p. 10)

On the appropriateness of particular work analysis strategies, SIOP (2003) stated:

There is no single approach that is the preferred method for the analysis of work. The analyses used in a specific study of work are a function of the nature of work, current information about the work, the organizational setting, the workers themselves, and the purpose of the study. Understanding the organization's requirements or objectives is important when selecting an appropriate method for conducting an analysis of work. (p. 11)

On the level of detail required of a work analysis, SIOP (2003) stated:

The level of detail required of an analysis of work is directly related to its intended use and the availability of information about the work. A less detailed analysis may be sufficient when there is already information descriptive of the work.... situations that require a more detailed analysis of work may include those in which there is little existing work information available and the organization intends to develop predictors of specific job knowledge. (p. 11)

Regarding initial considerations in content-oriented strategies, SIOP (2003) stated:

The content-based validation study specifically demonstrates that the content of the selection procedure represents an adequate sample of the important work behaviors, activities, and/or worker KSAOs defined by the analysis of work. This involves choosing subject matter experts, defining the content to be included in the selection procedure, developing the selection procedure, establishing the guidelines for administration and scoring, and evaluating the effectiveness of the validation effort. (p. 22)

On the evaluation of content validity evidence, SIOP (2003) stated:

The documented methods used in developing the selection procedure constitute the primary evidence for the inference that scores from the selection procedure can be generalized to the work behaviors and can be interpreted in terms of predicted work performance. The sufficiency of the match between selection procedure and work domain is a matter of professional judgment based on evidence collected in the validation effort (Goldstein, Zedeck, & Schneider, 1993). (p. 25)

The *Standards for Educational and Psychological Testing* (AERA et al., 1999, p. 2) were generally written for the "professional and for the educated layperson and addresses professional and technical issues of test development and use in education, psychology, and employment." Because this purpose is broader than other authorities, the standards cover a much wider range of topics. For example, the standards spend more time on test-taker rights than the other technical authorities.

Generally, the standards and the principles are in agreement on most topics, primarily because both technical authorities are affiliated with the APA and were written at a similar period of time. Although the standards do not go into as much detail on work analysis topics as the principles, specific information is offered.

On the use of work analysis for transportability of criterion support to a new job, AERA et al. (1999) stated:

> Evidence of predictor-criterion relationships in a current local situation should not be inferred from a single previous validation study unless the previous study was done under favorable conditions….and if the current situation corresponds closely to the previous situation….comment: close correspondence means that the job requirements or underlying psychological constructs are substantially the same (as deemed by a job analysis). (Standard 14.7)

On content-oriented validity, AERA et al. (1999) stated:

> Evidence of validity based on test content requires a thorough and explicit definition of the content domain of interest. For selection, classification, and promotion, the characterization of the domain should be based on the job analysis. (Standard 14.8)

On generalizing content-oriented validity to a new job, AERA et al. (1999) stated:

> If evidence based on test content is a primary source of validity evidence supporting the use of a test for selection into a particular job, a similar inference should be made about the test in a new situation only if the critical job content factors are substantially the same (as is determined by a work analysis). (Standard 14.11)

In summary, the work analyst has the opportunity to use any of the three technical authorities discussed above to evaluate the professional and legal defensibility of a selection procedure where a work analysis provides the crux of supporting evidence. Given the purpose of each authority, it may be most appropriate to use the UGESP, as updated by the principles. Although the UGESP do not capture recent advances in the science of selection, they are most likely to be used in enforcement context (Biddle, 2005), are backed by the U.S. government, and are the most often cited authority in case law (Jeanneret, 2005). As such, using UGESP as a legal defensibility template may most closely mirror the perspective of an enforcement agency or an opposing expert witness whose intention is to point out flaws in work analytic research. The UGESP include technical standards and documentation requirements for content-oriented, criterion, and construct validity studies. Table 8.7 shows how some of the technical standards from section 14C of the UGESP can be used to evaluate the legal defensibility of a selection system supported via a content validity study built upon a work analysis. Section 15-3-C of the UGESP describes the documentation requirements of a content validity study.

As Table 8.7 shows, a number of considerations are related to the legal defensibility of a selection procedure based on a content validity study that leverages a work analysis. These considerations span the different phases of a work analysis project. Additionally, these technical standards demonstrate the longitudinal nature of supporting the use of a selection procedure and highlight the use of a work analysis as a starting point for this supporting evidence. As described by Landy (2007),

Table 8.7   Using UGESP as a Template for Assessing Legal Defensibility

Technical Standard from the UGESP	Consideration
Appropriateness of content validity study	What types of constructs are being assessed?
Analysis of the job	Are observable work behaviors identified?
	Sample size?
	Demographic/job/job level representation?
	Appropriate data collection and analysis methods?
Development of selection procedures	Link between procedure and job analysis data (e.g., observable work behavior)?
Standards for studies	Representation of content domain?
Reliability according to the guidelines	Reliability analyses of the selection procedure?
	Reliability of SME ratings in a job analysis?
Operational use	Is the cut score reasonable?
	Are the most important aspects of the job incorporated in operationalization?
Ranking according to the guidelines	Is the construct linearly related to performance?
	Does the procedure measure aspects of performance that differentiate among levels of job performance?

content-oriented approaches are more on the abstract end of the continuum of validity evidence, but all of the technical authorities are in agreement on the importance of understanding work behaviors before developing selection procedures intended to predict those behaviors.

RECENT LEGAL DEFENSIBILITY TRENDS

Given the case law and technical authorities presented earlier in this chapter, we conclude with some common and more recent legal defensibility issues related to the use of a work analysis project as a foundation for supporting the use of a selection procedure. Certainly there are a number of common mistakes in documenting work analysis data, and many of these have been made before and after the UGESP were written. Other issues are more recent in nature and demonstrate strategic enforcement initiatives and potential loopholes in technical authorities and/or case law. Note that many of these issues could be unavoidable practical constraints; if job analysts document these limitations in the technical report, they could alleviate these limitations in future research.

Some of the more common and long-standing mistakes in documenting work analysis include the following:

- Conducting a work analysis on too small of a sample of SMEs. Although no rule of thumb exists with regard to an adequate sample size, work analysis can usually be done with 5–10 SMEs, although this number depends on a variety of contextual factors.
- Having an SME group that is not representative of the general job population of interest along various dimensions, including but not limited to demographics, performance, and experience.
- Conducting work analysis without linking an assessment to the actual KSAs it is purported to measure. In other words, a work analysis is a necessary but not sufficient phase in a content validity study, and it is possible to conduct a work analysis without supporting the use of a selection procedure (Seberhagen, 2004).
- Not documenting SME agreement given particular measurement designs (e.g., intraclass correlations, corrected Pearson correlations, G-theory estimates; Putka, Le, McCloy, & Diaz, 2008).

One more recent legal defensibility issue concerns the requirement of considering and documenting reasonable alternatives in the adverse impact scenario. Recall that even if an employer demonstrates the job-relatedness of a selection procedure, the enforcement agency/plaintiff can still demonstrate that said procedure is discriminatory if there existed an equally valid and less adverse alternative that the employer knew or should have know about but still did not use. Unfortunately, this issue has become a legal defensibility grey area in the sense that little specific guidance is available via technical authorities, and the enforcement agency/plaintiff burden of demonstrating an equally valid alternative is just beginning to emerge in case law (e.g., *Hayden v. Nassau County,* 1999; *Johnson v. City of Memphis,* 2006; *Bradley v. City of Lynn,* 2006; *Ricci v. Destefano,* 2006).

Despite the greyness of this issue, there are some alternatives open to rational speculation. For example, an alternative could in theory be a measure of a different construct (e.g., an integrity test instead of a cognitive ability test), a different measure of the same construct (e.g., using an interview method instead of a paper-and-pencil test), or a different scoring parameter of the same construct (e.g., lowering the cut score and/or combining multiple predictors). However, what is "equally valid"? Could this be established via correlations in an already existing criterion study or in SME ratings in a work analysis? In the already existing work analysis case, could the equal validity criterion simply be construct rank-ordering based on frequency, importance, or critically ratings?

Likewise, what is "less adverse"? Is it simply anything producing a lower adverse impact ratio, or is it any procedure that does not produce a statistically significant difference in pass rates (assuming that the selection procedure that was implemented had a significant disparity)? The enforcement agency/plaintiff burden to demonstrate a reasonable alternative is also unclear; is the burden simply to articulate a reasonable alternative based on the literature, previous work conducted by the test vendor, or speculation? Or does the plaintiff burden match the employer burden in phase two of an adverse impact scenario, where the test user must demonstrate job-relatedness via research? These issues appear to consider both scientific and socially derived value judgments.

When content validity research is used, this issue often focuses on the worker characteristic identification and/or linkage phase of the work analysis. For example, already available and well-designed work analysis documentation may provide a list of alternatives in the form of other KSA lists that were rated by SMEs but eventually not chosen to be measured and used for selection. In this situation, existing work analysis reports may provide enforcement agencies and plaintiff experts with alternatives in the form of other constructs that were not measured. In some situations, this available work analysis data may actually provide useful alternatives to consider. This assumes that the constructs of interest would likely produce less adverse impact and would be a reasonable predictor of job performance for the jobs of interest. Of course, this alternative does not shed light on the specific reasonable alternative burden required of enforcement agencies/plaintiffs.

Of course, there is a potentially infinite universe of KSAs that could be measured for the purpose of selection. In fact, it is impossible for the selection procedure developer to analyze and document the entire job domain. Perhaps SIOP (2003) stated it best:

> The domain need not include everything that is done on the job. The researcher should indicate what important work behaviors, activities, and worker KSAOs are included in the domain, describe how the content of the work domain is linked to the selection procedure, and explain why certain parts of the domain were or were not included in the selection procedure. (p. 22)

Guion (1998) also spoke to this general issue, stating that, with regard to work analysis,

> Clarity counts more than detail. Lawyers and courts want more detail than is useful. Too much detail can muddle matters; what is needed is a clear enough understanding of the job to move on to the next step, the development of one or more predictive hypotheses…information needed is not necessarily the information desired. (p. 59)

Regardless of the arguments against arbitrary identification of alternatives based on previous work analysis information, it is generally a useful strategy to include in a content validity technical report a short section that explicitly documents the consideration of alternatives constructs and methods. Any inclusion criteria for selecting a construct to measure could be included in this section, as well as why particular construct(s) were chosen for measurement and others that were not.

Note that there are no hard-and-fast rules for inclusion criteria for measurement, although job relatedness and adverse impact should obviously be considered. Practical considerations like administration time, development time, and budgetary constraints could also be included in this section. Additionally, a review of cut score decisions and methods of measurement could also be included in this section. This section could also present a plan related to the longitudinal consideration of reasonable alternatives (e.g., proactive adverse impact analyses, an analysis of alternative cut scores when predictor-criterion relationships are available). Of course, it is impossible to take expert judgment out of the equation in determining which constructs should be assessed and which should not; as such, the work analyst should make a reasonable argument for measuring specific constructs given the available data that support that decision.

Another issue of recent legal defensibility focus is on the currency or recency of work analytic data. This issue has become an important issue as the nature of work has changed from a product-based environment to a service-based environment (Cascio, 1995). In this new world of work, innovations in technology, automation, and the advent of cross-functional work teams have essentially moved many traditional jobs into a continual state of flux. In this situation, previous work analytic information may no longer be relevant, even in situations where these data are only a few years old. In situations where the job has changed, any selection procedure based on an outdated work analysis may no longer be appropriate, and as such the work analysis should be updated. In recent years, enforcement agencies have taken a fairly liberal stance on this issue, essentially criticizing any work analysis conducted in the recent past as outdated and inaccurate without supporting evidence. There are no hard-and-fast rules related to this issue, although enforcement agencies have generally suggested that the shelf life of a content validity study is about 5–7 years. According to SIOP (2003):

> There should be a periodic audit of the use of the selection procedures. Departures from established procedures often occur over time and new findings in psychological or psychometric theory may be relevant to one or more of the assessment procedures in use.

Bobko, Roth, and Buster (2008) published research on assessing the currency of work analysis data. This research was conducted under a consent decree stemming from employment discrimination litigation and was accepted by a court of law. They developed a multiphase system that evaluates the currency of already existing work analysis. Generally, this process includes the following steps:

1. Obtain an understanding of the job and the prior work analysis results.
2. Invite subject matter experts to a two-part meeting.
3. Conduct an SME discussion of what tasks and/or KSAs might have changed in recent years; focus on reasons for any major changes.

4. Use the same work behavior and worker characteristic scales and criteria for inclusion as in the previous work analysis questionnaire to ask SMEs to individually rate any work behaviors or worker characteristics that were suggested as possible changes (e.g., additions or deletions).

At the end of the process, the selection procedure user can determine whether the available work analysis is still current. If these data are outdated, small- or large-scale changes may be required. In some situations, small changes should be documented and the selection procedure can still be supported as job related. In the worst case scenario, the current selection procedure is no longer appropriate and should be revised or even replaced; these changes may require a new content validity study or other strategy.

CONCLUDING THOUGHTS

This chapter reviewed strategies for documenting work analysis data from both organizational strategy and legal defensibility perspectives. As the chapter suggests, the work analyst can use a variety of strategies in documenting work analytic data, and the case study work analysis framework provides one way of considering what to document and how. As the legal defensibility and technical authority sections show, documenting the appropriate information in professionally sound fashion can play an important role in the defensibility of a selection procedure that is supported by the use of a work analysis. Regardless of the strategies used, there are four major points we feel are worth emphasizing.

First, jobs change over time. This places a premium not only on periodic updates of work analysis data, but also on periodic evaluation of the selection procedures to ensure that they are as connected to the changes in work as they were to the original work. This proactive strategy should be documented appropriately each step of the way.

Second, the law changes over time. Thus, what seems like a best practice or even a legal practice at one point in time is only one major Supreme Court ruling away from being outdated. In the absence of major Supreme Court rulings, the forceful rulings are at the circuit court level, and what is the law in one circuit may not be the law in another circuit.

Third, and closely connected to the previous point, regulations change along with critical court decisions. It is a good rule of thumb to believe that every time the Supreme Court makes a major ruling, or a lower court makes a controversial ruling, the EEOC will have something to say about it. A good way to keep up with regulatory changes is to periodically visit the EEOC web site (http://www.eeoc.gov).

Fourth, the science of personnel selection continues to evolve, and with it, so does the research basis for supporting the use of a test or test battery and the technical authorities. For example, the last two revisions of SIOP principles have featured new material on topics such as validity generalization. Additionally, in between revisions of technical authorities, there is always relevant research in the field that, for example, compares traditional paper-and-pencil tests to other tests (e.g., situational judgment tests and assessment centers), reviews inaccuracies in work analysis rating, and considers the appropriateness of psychometric techniques when humans make ratings.

In closing, we reiterate that work analysis is not a static process. There are many ways and tools for conducting a work analysis, and there are many ways to use a work analysis. The main recommendations we have focused on in this chapter are to (a) document the work you do so that professional and lay audiences alike can understand what was done, and (b) assume that there will be a legal challenge for any work you do, so documentation must include important information that enforcement agencies and courts will want to see.

FURTHER READING

Brannick, M. T., & Levine, E. L. (2002). *Job analysis: Methods, research and applications for human resource management in the new millennium.* Thousand Oaks, CA: Sage Publications.

Gibson, W. M., & Caplinger, J. A. (2008). Transportation of validation results. In S. M. McPhail (Ed.), *Alternative validation strategies: Developing new and leveraging existing validity evidence.* San Francisco, CA: Jossey Bass.

Gutman, A. (2000). *EEO law and personnel practices* (2nd ed.). Thousand Oaks, CA: Sage Publications.

Harvey, R. (1990). Job analysis. In M. Dunnette & L. Hough (Eds.), *Handbook of industrial and organizational psychology* (2nd ed., Vol. 1, pp. 71–163). Palo Alto, CA: Consulting Psychologists Press.

Kleiman, L. S., & Faley, R. H. Assessing content validity: Standards set by the court. *Personnel Psychology, 31,* 701–713.

Malos, S. (2005). The importance of valid selection and performance appraisal: Do management practices figure in case law? In F. J. Landy (Ed.), *Employment discrimination litigation: Behavioral, quantitative, and legal perspectives.* San Francisco, CA: Jossey Bass.

Outtz, J. L., & Landy, F. J. (2005). Concluding Thoughts. In F. J. Landy (Ed.), *Employment discrimination litigation: Behavioral, quantitative, and legal perspectives.* San Francisco, CA: Jossey Bass.

Thompson, D., & Thompson, T. (1982). Court standards for job analysis in test validation. *Personnel Psychology, 35,* 865–874.

Viswesvaran, C. (2003). Introduction to special issue: Role of technology in shaping the future of staffing and assessment. *International Journal of Selection & Assessment, 11,* 107–112.

REFERENCES

Albermarle Paper Co. v. Moody, 422 U.S. 405 (1975).

American Educational Research Association [AERA], American Psychological Association, & National Council on Measurement in Education. (1999). *Standards for educational and psychological testing.* Washington, DC: American Psychological Association.

American Federation etc. (AFSCME) v State of Washington (CA9 1985) 770 F.2d 1401.

Banks, C., & Cohen, L. (2005). Wage and hour litigation: I-O Psychology's new frontier. In F. J. Landy (Ed.), *Employment discrimination litigation: Behavioral, quantitative, and legal perspectives.* San Francisco, CA: Jossey Bass.

Biddle, D. (2005). *Adverse impact and test validation: A practitioners guide to valid and defensible employment testing.* Burlington, VT: Gower.

Biddle, D. A. (2008). Are the uniform guidelines outdated? Federal guidelines, professional standards, and validity generalization. *The Industrial-Organizational Psychologist, 45,* 17–23.

Bobko, P., Roth, P. L., & Buster, M. A. (2008). A systematic approach for assessing the currency ("up-to-dateness") of job-analytic information. *Public Personnel Management, 37,* 261–277.

Borrowski v. Calley Central School District, 63 F.3d 131 (Ca. 2 1995).

Bradley v. City of Lynn, 443 F. Supp. 2d. 145 (D. Mass 2006).

Brennan v. City Stores, Inc., 479 F.2d 235 (Ca. 5 1973).

Cascio, W. F. (1995). Whither industrial and organizational psychology in a changing nature of work? *American Psychologist, 50,* 928–939.

Corning Glass Works v. Brennan, 417 U.S. 188 (1974).

DeNisi, A. (1999). A message from your president. *The Industrial-Organizational Psychologist, 37,* 2.

Dunleavy, E., & Gutman, A. (2007). EEO enforcement activity in 2007: A sign of things to come? *The Industrial-Organizational Psychologist, 46,* 77–83.

Gillespie v. State of Wisconsin, 771 F.2d 1035 (Ca. 7 1985).

Goldstein, I., Zedeck, S., & Schneider, B. (1993). An exploration of the job analysis-content validity process. In N. Schmitt & W. Borman (Eds.), *Personnel selection in organizations.* San Francisco, CA: Jossey-Bass

Green v. Washington State, WL 17802 (1997).

Griggs v. Duke Power Co., 401 U.S. 424 (1971).

Guardians of NY v. Civil Service Commission, 630 F.2d 79 (Ca. 2 1980).

Guion, R. M. (1998). *Assessment, measurement, and prediction for personnel decisions.* Mahwah, NJ: Lawrence Erlbaum Associates.

Gulino v. State Education Department, 461 F.3d 134 (Ca. 2 2006).

Gutman, A. (2005). Adverse impact: Judicial, regulatory, and statutory authority. In F. J. Landy (Ed.), *Employment discrimination litigation: Behavioral, quantitative, and legal perspectives.* San Francisco, CA: Jossey Bass.

Hayden v. Nassau County, 180 F.3d 42 (Ca. 2 1999).

Hodgson v. Brookhaven General Hospital, 470 F.2d 729 (Ca. 5 1970).

Hodgson v. Daisy Mfg. Co., 445 F.2d 823 (Ca. 8 1971).

Jeanneret, R. (2005). Professional and technical authorities and guidelines. In F. J. Landy (Ed.), *Employment discrimination litigation: Behavioral, quantitative, and legal perspectives*. San Francisco, CA: Jossey Bass.

Johnson v. City of Memphis, 355 F. Supp. 2d 911 (W. D. Tenn. 2006).

Laffey v. Northwest Airlines, 740 F.2d 1071 (Ca. DC 1984).

Landy, F. J. (1986). Stamp collecting versus science: Validation as hypothesis testing. *American Psychologist, 41,* 1183–1192.

Landy, F. J. (2007). The validation of personnel decisions in the twenty-first century: Back to the future. In S. M. McPhail (Ed.), *Alternative validation strategies: Developing new and leveraging existing validity evidence*. San Francisco, CA: Jossey Bass.

Landy F. J., Gutman, A., & Outtz, J. (2010). Legal issues related to employment discrimination: Major principles and exemplar case law. In J. L. Farr & N. T. Tippens (Eds.), *The handbook of employee selection* (pp. 627–648). Hillsdale, NJ: Lawrence Erlbaum Associates.

Lanning v. SEPTA, No. 97-1161 (E. D. Pa. 1998).

Lanning v. SEPTA, 181 F.3d 478 (Lanning I) (Ca. 3 1999).

Lanning v. SEPTA, 308 F.3d 286 (Lanning II) (Ca. 3 2002).

Miller v. Illinois, 107 F.3d 483 (Ca. 7 1996).

Moody v. Albemarle, 474 F.2d 134 (Ca. 4 1973).

Peterson, N. G., & Jeanneret, P. R. (1997). Job analysis: Overview and description of deductive methods. In D. L. Whetzel & G. R. Wheaton (Eds.), *Applied measurement methods in industrial psychology*. Palo Alto, CA: Davies-Black.

PGA Tour v. Martin, 532 U.S. 661 (2001).

Police Officers for Equal Rights v. City of Columbus, 916 F.2d 1092 (Ca. 6 1990).

Putka, D. J., Le, H., McCloy, R. A., & Diaz, T. (2008). Ill-structured measurement designs in organizational research: Implications for estimating interrater reliability. *Journal of Applied Psychology, 93,* 959–981.

Ricci v. Destefano, 30 F.3d. 88 (Ca. 2 2008).

Schultz v. Wheaton Glass Co., 421 F.2d 259 (Ca. 3 1970).

Seberhagen, L. (2004, August). A job analysis is not a validation study. *Personnel Testing Council of Metropolitan Washington D.C. Newsletter, 26,* 8.

Sharf, J. (1999). Third Circuit's Lanning v. SEPTA decision: Business necessity requires setting minimum standards. *The Industrial-Organizational Psychologist, 37,* 2.

Society for Industrial and Organizational Psychology. (2003). *Principles for the validation and use of personnel selection procedures* (4th ed.). Bowling Green, OH: Author.

Spaulding v. University of Washington, 740 F.2d 686 (Ca. 9 1984).

Stelly, D. J., & Goldstein, H. J. (2007). Application of content validation methods to broader constructs. In S. M. McPhail (Ed.), *Alternative validation strategies: Developing new and leveraging existing validity evidence*. San Francisco, CA: Jossey Bass.

Stone v. City of Mount Vernon, 118 F.3d 92 (Ca. 2 1997).

Thompson v. Sawyer, 678 F.2d 257 (Ca. DC 1982).

U.S. Equal Employment Opportunity Commission, U.S. Civil Service Commission, U.S. Department of Labor, U.S. Department of Justice. (1978). Uniform Guidelines on employee selection procedures. *Federal Register, 43,* 38295–38309.

Williams, K. M., & Crafts, J. L. (1997). Inductive job analysis: The job/task inventory method. In D. L. Whetzel & G. R. Wheaton (Eds.), *Applied measurement methods in industrial psychology*. Palo Alto, CA: Davies-Black.

Part II

WORK ANALYSIS SYSTEMS

SHANAN GWALTNEY GIBSON
East Carolina University

If honesty is the best policy, then I have a confession to make. As a graduate student in industrial-organizational psychology, I did not choose job analysis as my dissertation topic for any of the typical reasons. I did not think it was the means by which I would make the world a better place; it was not a "hot" topic in the field; it was not even something I found immensely intriguing. But I have a practical streak and perhaps a soft spot for what I saw as an underdog in the field. Hence job analysis presented itself as an area that was appropriate and changing (O*NET was just coming online), as well as something everyone on my committee would approve! Perhaps it was not an auspicious beginning, but little did I know how things would change in the coming decade.

With job analysis, there is no record of industrial psychologists coming to blows over a highly controversial topic—not just because they are a pretty easygoing group of scientist-practitioners, but because job analysis simply is not seen as an area of contentious debate in most regards. The one and only exception to this might be the issue of what is the right way to conduct a job analysis. What is the appropriate construct for analysis? How exactly should one describe the world of work? Should work be described as a series of tasks? What about the abilities or personality one must possess in order to perform work? Does work context matter? The not-so-simple answer is that all of these are important and potentially correct, but the real question is this: For what purpose are you conducting your job analysis? Given the myriad potential answers to this question, each of these approaches, plus others, deserve consideration. Part II of this volume examines the dominant schools of thought in this arena of job analysis.

In Chapter 10, the various approaches to analyzing and documenting the knowledge and cognitive processes associated with performing work are examined. As the world is arguably moving into a knowledge economy, the ability to document the cognitive aspects of work, in addition to the more traditional tasks or behaviors required by work, is of great importance to those involved in many human resources functions including selection and training.

Chapter 11 covers what is considered by many to be the fundamental job analytic technique. Perceived by many as the only right was to approach job analysis, task analysis is actually extremely flexible and broadly applicable to both research and organizational needs.

Generalized work dimension analysis is the topic of Chapter 12. This moderate-specificity technique is appealing to many because it presents the potential for making cross-job comparisons and uncovering underlying similarities of requirements in different jobs that may be obscured by more traditional task analytic approaches. In addition to examining work dimension analysis in the general sense, this chapter also reviews several commercially available, empirically developed generalized work dimension analysis instruments.

Chapter 13 focuses in on the development, validation, and many applications of the Fleishman Job Analysis Survey (F-JAS). Similar to techniques that analyze the cognitive basis of work, the F-JAS focuses on another less visible aspect of work—abilities. Furthermore, just as with generalized work dimensional analysis, the F-JAS focuses on using a discrete set of descriptors that are applicable across many jobs, thus enabling cross job comparisons.

A second method of analyzing jobs that focuses on the worker's attributes instead of the demands of the job is considered in Chapter 14. Personality-based job analysis shifts the description of jobs from the more tangible tasks and behaviors to the personal characteristics associated with performance. In addition to detailing the technique, this chapter also provides an overview of a personality-based job analytic instrument, the Performance Improvement Characteristics.

Chapter 15 details the rich history of functional job analysis (FJA). As a task-based job analytic technique, FJA identifies the task-based processes inherent to the worker, work, and work organization. FJA is conducted using a highly structured approach that is dependent on highly trained analysts and recognizes things, data, and people as the underlying dimensions of all work.

The U.S. Department of Labor's Occupational Information Network (O*NET) is the topic of Chapter 16. This chapter examines the history of the O*NET, its current applications in career exploration and research, and areas of potential examination in the future. As the replacement for the *Dictionary of Occupational Titles*, the O*NET represents a significant vocational guidance tool that has potential for use in numerous areas.

Chapter 17, the final chapter in Part II, looks at the environments in which work occurs. As a method of analyzing work, context can have important implications for understanding such things as occupational hazards and working conditions, worker productivity, and even the social environments and communication relationships of an organization. Although frequently addressed as an afterthought in job analysis, context should not be dismissed as it is an important piece of the work description process.

Although each of the aforementioned chapters takes a different approach to what is measured in relation to the world of work, there are similarities that that should be noted. A primary commonality is the need to give careful consideration to how one actually conducts the job analysis. Regardless of what you choose to measure (e.g., tasks, behaviors, abilities, context), identifying the purpose for your analysis, choosing the subject matter experts to be sources of your data, determining proper scales or measurements to be used, and deciding how the data is to be analyzed are all issues that must be addressed. Furthermore, each of these decisions has significant implications for both the psychometric soundness and the usefulness of your analysis.

As a job analyst, there are many options to be considered and decisions to be made in order to fulfill your job analytic purpose. Remember, although there is not necessarily a right answer to the question of what job analytic method is best, distinctions do exist among them. It is hoped that Part II provides you with both insight and guidance when choosing your job analysis method.

9

Important Contributors to Job Analysis in the 20th and Early 21st Centuries

MARK A. WILSON

North Carolina State University

JOSEPH W. CUNNINGHAM

North Carolina State University

This chapter provides brief descriptions of the careers of the important contributors to job analysis in the 20th and early 21st centuries. In the first section, the careers of 24 contributors to job analysis research and practice are briefly described. Although more could be (and has been) written about many of these individuals and their contributions, we chose a single-paragraph approach to make the chapter more approachable. These brief career descriptions are followed by three vignettes that are meant to bring to life the contributions of important contributors to the field of job analysis. Additional narrative histories of job analysis are available for interested readers (Cunningham, 2000; Mitchell, 1988; Mitchell & Driskill, 1996; Primoff & Fine, 1988; Uhrbrock, 1922; Wilson, 2006).

In the final section, several distinctive commonalities are identified that exist among the remarkably varied individuals who comprise the important contributors to job analysis. This chapter is not meant to replace previous histories but to provide more detail about the individuals who helped make the history.

IMPORTANT JOB ANALYSIS CONTRIBUTORS

Frederick W. Taylor, while working at the Midvale Steel and Bethlehem Steel companies, developed a method for analyzing tasks in terms of more basic elemental motions, each of which he timed by stopwatch. Tasks were redesigned based on their elemental motions, and standard task performance times were estimated by combining the individual times of the rearranged elements (Barnes, 1940). Well before the formal introduction of modern goal-setting theory and expectancy theory, Taylor emphasized the importance of setting specific work goals for employees and providing them with regular feedback of results, training them to work effectively, and promoting their expectation that effort will be rewarded (Wren & Greenwood, 1998). Known as the father of scientific management and a pioneer in time study, Taylor described his approach in the books *The Principles of Scientific Management* (1911a) and *Common Sense Applied to Motion and Time Study* (1911b).

    Frank B. Gilbreth and **Lillian E. Gilbreth**, two other prominent figures in the scientific management movement, combined his engineering background with her training in psychology in developing some of the early methods of motion study (McCormick, 1979). Frank began his career in the construction industry, later leaving the trade to become a full-time consultant in collaboration with Lillian. Lillian completed her doctorate at Brown University, continued consulting after Frank's death, and held faculty appointments at Purdue University, the Newark College of Engineering, and the University of Wisconsin (Gilbreth, 1998; Wren & Greenwood, 1998). Part of the Gilbreth's approach involved formulation of a set of generic activities or elements, called *therbligs,* which are applicable to the analysis of any physical task. Task efficiency was improved through elimination of unnecessary elements and rearrangement of the remaining ones. This may have been the first worker-oriented approach to job analysis (Gilbreth, 1911; Gilbreth & Gilbreth, 1916, 1917).

Hugo Munsterberg, one of the founders of applied psychology in the United States, immigrated from Germany, where he had earned his doctorate in experimental psychology under Wilhelm Wundt, to join the faculty at Harvard University. The most publicly acclaimed psychologist of his time, Munsterberg wrote many popular magazine articles and books on the application of psychology to a wide range of problems (Schultz & Schultz, 1996). Inspired by Frederick Taylor's work, Munsterberg embarked on consulting activities in industry related to such problems as employee selection and workplace design (Schultz & Schultz, 1996; Wren & Greenwood, 1998). Among his many contributions was his pioneering application of systematic methods in estimating job requirements for personnel selection purposes. His book, *Psychology and Industrial Efficiency* (1913), served as a model for the emerging field of industrial psychology, and he is considered by many to be the father of the field, along with Walter Dill Scott (Berry, 1998; Blum & Naylor, 1968).

Walter Van Dyke Bingham founded the Department of Applied Psychology at the Carnegie Institute of Technology in 1915. Bingham, as well as Munsterberg, was an early proponent of job analysis as an essential step in the development of personnel selection and performance appraisal systems (Bingham, 1939; Bingham & Moore, 1941; Ghiselli & Brown, 1955). While at the Carnegie Institute and while serving with the U.S. Department of War during World Wars I and II, he influenced the development of several large-scale job-analysis efforts, conducted by such organizations as the Division of Cooperative Research at the Carnegie Institute, the American Council of Education, the Occupational Research Program of the U.S. Employment Service, and the Committee on Classification of Personnel for the U.S. Army (Ferguson, 1952; Thurstone, 1952).

Walter Dill Scott, although best known for his work in the field of advertising, also made significant contributions to the advancement of systematic work analysis, serving during World War I with Walter Bingham as co-director of the Committee on the Classification of Personnel in the U.S. Army. Before the war, Scott had been involved in establishing trait requirements for sales occupations. Carrying some of that work over to the U.S. Army's classification committee, he oversaw the development of job specifications for officer and enlisted specialties. After World War I, Scott and his associates founded the first psychological consulting firm, the Scott Company of Philadelphia, through which they applied the U.S. Army's job analysis procedures to problems in the private sector. Their procedures were described in the book *Personnel Management* (Scott, Clothier, & Spriegel, 1954).

Morris S. Viteles, working through the National Research Council, developed a questionnaire containing the descriptions of 32 trait requirements on which jobs were rated. The resultant ratings for each job were displayed in a graphic profile called a *job psychograph* (Viteles, 1923). Perhaps the first of the structured job-analysis questionnaires, Viteles' psychograph was the prototype for the U.S. Employment Service (USES; 1944) Worker Characteristics Form and the forerunner to later generations of attribute-requirement inventories, including the USES's subsequently expanded worker trait requirements (Droege, 1988; Trattner, Fine, & Kubis, 1955; U.S. Department of Labor, 1956, 1991) as well as some of the instruments in the U.S. Department of Labor's Occupational Information Network (O*NET; Peterson, Mumford, Borman, Jeanneret, & Fleishman, 1999). Viteles (1932) authored one of the early books on industrial psychology.

Carroll L. Shartle became Chief of the Worker Analysis Section of the U.S. Department of Labor's newly formed Occupational Research Program in 1935, which later became the Occupational Analysis Section of the USES. While in that position, he oversaw the development of the Worker Characteristics Form and publication of the first edition of the *Dictionary of Occupational Titles* (U.S. Department of Labor, Employment and Training Administration, 1977). Following World War II, Shartle joined the faculty at the Ohio State University where he developed the Work Analysis Forms in collaboration with Ralph M. Stogdill (Shartle & Stogdill, 1957) and authored *Occupational Information* (Shartle, 1952), which saw three editions from 1944 to 1959 and was the first book devoted exclusively to job and occupational analysis. This book established occupational analysis as a field of study and introduced a number of useful methods, concepts, and definitions, such as the now generally accepted distinctions between the terms *position, job,* and *occupation.*

John C. Flanagan began his career in 1935 at the Cooperative Test Service, later joining the U.S. Army Air Corps at the beginning of World War II (Koppes, 1999). While serving as director of the Army Aviation Psychology Program, he developed the critical incident technique (CIT), which involved the recording of job incumbent behaviors that were particularly effective or ineffective in producing successful outcomes (Flanagan, 1949, 1954). Although designed primarily to support the pilot selection program, the CIT was also used in training program development, the diagnosis of flight failures, and the development of criteria for combat leadership (Bownas & Bernardin, 1988). After the war, Flanagan joined the faculty at the University of Pittsburgh and became founding president of the American Institutes for Research where he continued to develop and apply the CIT, which has found widespread use in both the private and public sectors. In addition to the aforementioned applications, the CIT has been used in job design and in the development of performance appraisal systems (Bownas & Bernardin). Flanagan made other significant methodological contributions in the areas of selection, test development, and educational measurement.

Ernest J. McCormick, after working for 2 years with the Cotton Garment Code Authority in New York City, joined the USES in 1935 where he served as Chief of the Planning Unit (Koppes, 1999). After subsequent stints with the Bureau of the Census, the Selective Service System, and the Bureau of Naval Personnel, he joined the faculty at Purdue University. At Purdue, he pioneered the development of structured job analysis methodology based on generic worker-oriented descriptors, from which he derived general job dimensions or "components" with applications in such areas as ability-requirement estimation, job evaluation and classification, performance evaluation, and person-job matching (McCormick, 1959; McCormick & Jeanneret, 1988). This line of research culminated in the development of the Position Analysis Questionnaire (PAQ; McCormick, Jeanneret, & Mecham, 1972), the best known and most researched instrument of its genre and the precursor to several subsequent general job analysis questionnaires (Cornelius, Hakel, & Sackett, 1979; Cunningham, Boese, Neeb, & Pass, 1983; Cunningham, Wimpee, & Ballentine, 1990; Harvey, 1991a, 1991b). The PAQ and some of its progeny contributed to the recent development of the generalized work activities in the Department of Labor's O*NET system (Jeanneret, Borman, Kubisiak, & Hanson, 1999). McCormick authored the books *Job Analysis* (McCormick, 1979), *Industrial Psychology* (McCormick & Tiffin, 1974), and *Human Engineering* (McCormick, 1957), one of the early works in that field.

Sidney A. Fine joined the USES in 1940 (working initially under Carroll Shartle) where he was instrumental in forming the Functional Occupational Classification Project (FOCP). An approach known as Functional Job Analysis (FJA) emerged from the FOCP research findings as organized under a conceptual framework developed by Fine (1955). The FJA approach involves a structured procedure for writing task statements, which are then rated in terms of (a) the worker's level of involvement with the three functional hierarchies of things, data, and people and (b) the levels of reasoning, math, and language required. The functional hierarchies were incorporated into the third and fourth editions of the *Dictionary of Occupational Titles* and subsequently into the *Canadian Classification and Dictionary of Occupations* (Fine & Getakate, 1995). After 20 years of service with the USES, Fine continued the development of FJA at the Upjohn Institute for Employment Research, the Advanced Research Resources Organization, and through private consulting (Fleishman, 1999). The FJA approach has been applied in such areas as test development, job design, performance appraisal, training, and job evaluation. In collaboration with others, Fine has authored two recent books on FJA (Fine & Cronshaw, 1999; Fine & Getkate, 1995).

Ernest S. Primoff, along with Sidney Fine, joined the USES in 1940, later transferring to the U.S. Civil Service Commission (now the Office of Personnel Management) where he remained for a substantial part of his career. While serving with the Civil Service Commission, Primoff developed the Job Element Method (JEM) for systematically determining job requirements (Primoff & Eyde, 1988). He carried out pioneering work in the application of the JEM to develop job-specific personnel selection tests and to synthetically validate standardized tests for selection purposes. His synthetic validation procedure involved the estimation of (a) a job's requirements for a specified set of job elements representing different worker behaviors and attributes and (b) the weights of standardized tests on the job elements. These values were then combined to derive "J-coefficients" representing estimated test validities (Primoff, 1957, 1959). The JEM has also been applied in the development of training programs, performance rating systems, and experience and training accrediting plans.

John L. Holland began his career in the field of vocational counseling at Western Reserve University and with the Veterans Administration, later joining the faculty at Johns Hopkins University (Holland, 1999). In a 1959 journal article, he introduced his theory of personality types and work environments (Holland, 1959), which he elaborated in his subsequent book, *Making Vocational Choices* (Holland, 1973, 1985a, 1997). The heuristic value and empirical support of Holland's theory is unsurpassed in the field of vocational psychology (Gottfredson, 1999; Gottfredson & Richards, 1999). The theory's constructs have been operationalized in two self-report questionnaires, the Vocational Preference Inventory (Holland, 1967, 1985b) and the Self-Directed Search (Holland, 1970; Holland, Fritzsche, & Powell, 1994), and have been applied more recently to the description and classification of jobs and occupations through the *Dictionary of Holland Occupational Codes* (Gottfredson & Holland, 1996; Gottsfredson, Holland, & Ogawa, 1982) and the Position Classification Inventory (Gottsfredson & Holland, 1991). In combination, these instruments are designed to promote compatible relationships between people and their work environments. The Holland model has been incorporated recently into the Department of Labor's O*NET system (Rounds, Smith, Hubert, Lewis, & Rivkin, 1999; Sager, 1999).

Edwin A. Fleishman has made a number of important pioneering contributions in identifying abilities and other requirements of work and providing concepts and methods for measuring them. At the Personnel Research Board at the Ohio State University, he identified dimensions for describing leadership behavior and developed the Supervisory Behavior Description Questionnaire (Fleishman, 1953) to analyze managerial job requirements. At the Air Force Skills Component Research Laboratory and subsequently as a professor at Yale University, he combined experimental and factor analytic methods to identify and measure the fundamental psychomotor abilities required in complex task performances (Fleishman, 1958, 1964, 1972; Fleishman & Hempel, 1956). While director of the American Institutes for Research in Washington, he established a taxonomy project under support of the U.S. Department of Defense (Fleishman, 1975, 1982). This effort culminated in the book *Taxonomies of Human Performance* (Fleishman & Quaintance, 1984), which established the centrality of task constructs in describing human behavior and provided criteria for developing and evaluating task classifications. Another outgrowth of this work was the development of the Fleishman Job Analysis Survey (F-JAS) based on his taxonomy of cognitive, psychomotor, physical, and sensory-motor abilities (Fleishman, 1992). While president of the Advanced Research Resources Organization and later as professor at George Mason University, Fleishman directed numerous applications of the F-JSAS in a wide variety of work settings and published the *Handbook of Human Abilities* (Fleishman & Reilly, 1992), which provides definitions of the abilities in his taxonomy along with examples of jobs and tasks that require them and tests that measure them. Fleishman's taxonomy and measurement system has been incorporated recently into the U.S. Department of Labor's O*NET system (Costanza, Fleishman, & Marshall-Mies, 1999; Fleishman, Costanza, & Marshall-Meiss, 1999).

In 1952, **Raymond E. Christal** joined the Air Force Human Resources Laboratory (AFHRL) in San Antonio, Texas, where he worked for most of his professional career. In collaboration with colleagues at the AFHRL (now the Human Resources Directorate of the Armstrong Laboratory), Christal developed the job-task inventory method, a structured job-analysis procedure that has seen widespread use in the military, public, and private sectors (Christal, 1974; Christal & Weissmuller, 1988; Morsh, Madden, & Christal, 1961). Under this approach, incumbents or subject matter experts are presented with a comprehensive list of task statements with instructions to check the tasks that are performed in the job and then rate those tasks on a relative time-spent scale (and occasionally on a relative learning-difficulty scale). Combined with a powerful software package, the Comprehensive Occupational Data Analysis Programs (CODAP; Christal & Weissmuller, 1988; Phalen & Mitchell, 1993), the job-task inventory technique has proved to be a very useful tool in the development of training programs. It has also been used in determining personnel qualification requirements, identifying job types, and developing performance appraisal and job evaluation systems. In addition to his significant role in disseminating the job-task inventory technique throughout the military services and government, Christal helped introduce the method to education, business, and industry (Christal, 1970; Gael, 1983).

Donald G. Paterson, Rene V. Dawis, and **Lloyd H. Lofquist,** along with others at the University of Minnesota, carried out a long line of research on occupational trait requirements. In the 1920s, Paterson initiated a program in counseling services at Minnesota that provided a model for programs at other institutions and a training ground for many leaders in the field, including, among others, Lloyd Lofquist and Rene Dawis (Super & Bohn, 1970). Within that setting, Paterson and his associates developed the Minnesota Occupational Rating Scales and an accompanying counseling profile providing ability-requirement estimates for 432 occupations (Crites, 1969; Paterson, Gerken, & Hahn, 1941, 1953; Shartle, 1952). After earning their doctorates at Minnesota, Dawis and Lofquist joined the faculty there, where in collaboration with their associates (George W. England, David J. Weiss, and others) they initiated the Work Adjustment Project, a long-range research and development effort oriented toward vocational counseling. An important product of that effort was the Theory of Work Adjustment, the project's overarching conceptual framework, which relates the characteristics of the individual to those of the work environment (Dawis, English, & Lofquist, 1964; Dawis, Lofquist, & Weiss, 1968). This theory served as the framework for the development of three assessment tools: the Minnesota Importance Questionnaire, a self-report need inventory, and the Minnesota Job Description and Satisfaction Questionnaires, two companion devices for describing the reinforcement characteristics of the job and the individual's satisfaction with them. These instruments are described in two books, *Adjustment to Work* (Lofquist & Dawis, 1969) and *A Psychological Theory of Work Adjustment* (Dawis & Lofquist, 1983), as well as in various reports published under the *Minnesota Studies in Vocational Rehabilitation*. The Minnesota Job Description Questionnaires and Minnesota Importance Questionnaire, the two most researched instruments of their kind, have been adapted for use in the Department of Labor's O*NET system (McCloy et al., 1999; Sager, 1999).

Sidney Gael began his professional career in 1959 as a research psychologist with the U.S. Air Force at Wright-Patterson Air Force Base, where he focused on the determination of personnel requirements and training needs for aircraft and space systems. While employed by the Air Force, he participated in a U.S. Air Force educational program for civil service employees that enabled him to earn his doctorate in industrial psychology. Subsequently, he joined the American Telegraph and Telephone (AT&T) Personnel Research Organization and worked for the Bell System and its affiliated companies for 28 years, after which he entered private practice. At AT&T, Gael initiated and directed the development of the Work Performance Survey System (WPSS), which included structured procedures for constructing and administering task inventory questionnaires, along with a software system for analyzing the resultant data. One of the first adaptations of the military job-task inventory method to civilian use, the WPSS has proved useful in supporting a variety of human resource functions in such areas as employment and placement, training, and performance evaluation (Gael, 1977). Based on his experience with the WPSS, Gael authored a book, *Job Analysis* (Gael, 1983), to serve as a procedural guide for carrying out job-task inventory studies. Subsequently, he undertook the monumental task of editing the two-volume *Job Analysis Handbook for Business, Industry, and Government* (Gael, 1988). The *Handbook* is the most comprehensive source of information available on a wide variety of job analysis methods and is perhaps the most valuable single contribution to the literature in this field to date.

Eric Prien began his career in 1959 at Standard Oil of Ohio but he spent the bulk of his career in academia at Memphis State University. His job analysis research was often focused on important issues for job analysis practitioners, and he wrote an influential review of the job analysis literature (Prien & Ronan, 1971). He has founded Performance Management Associates and has maintained an extensive consulting practice.

P. Richard Jeanneret began his career as an aviation psychologist with the U.S. Navy but has spent the bulk of his career as a consultant to management. He studied under Ernest J. McCormick at Purdue University. Part of his doctoral dissertation involved the development of the Position Analysis Questionnaire (McCormick, Jeanneret, & Mecham, 1972). He has played a leading role in O*Net project (Jeanneret et al., 1999). Widely published in job analysis and having established one of the most successful consulting practices involving job analysis issues, he and his associates have played the leading role in getting the private sector to adopt a generic approach to job analysis.

Edward L. Levine began his career in 1972 as chief of Arizona's Selection Resource Center. He joined the faculty of University of South Florida in 1977, where he has carried out a prolific academic and consulting career focusing on job analysis issues. Although he is perhaps best known for his work in comparative job analysis research (Ash & Levine, 1980; Levine, Ash, & Bennett, 1980; Levine, Ash, Hall, & Sistrunk, 1983), he has also been a popularizer of job analysis for practitioners (Levine, 1983) and is the coauthor of what has become one of the standard references in job analysis (Brannick & Levine, 2002).

Juan I. Sanchez began his career in 1981 working as a job analyst for CAMPSA, a Spanish petroleum company. He studied under Ed Levine at the University of South Florida. Although he had extensive experience in international business, he has spent the bulk of his career as a faculty member in both the Department of Psychology followed by the Department of Management and International Business at Florida International University. As a practitioner of job analysis, he led the movement to bring job analysis methods into the 21st century (Sanchez, 1994). He has written extensively on a number of issues related to job analysis but is perhaps best known for his work on the psychometric properties and evaluation of job analysis (Sanchez & Levine, 2000; Sanchez, Prager, Wilson, & Visweswaran, 1998).

Michael A. Campion studied under Paul Thayer at North Carolina State University. He was a successful practitioner for almost a decade at Weyerhaeuser Company followed by IBM beginning in 1978. Known to many industrial and organizational psychologists as the former president of the Society of Industrial and Organizational Psychology and editor of *Personnel Psychology,* he has made important contributions to job analysis research. Perhaps best known in job analysis for his work on job design (e.g., Campion & McClelland, 1991), he has also played an important role in the discussion of potential moderators of job analysis results (Morgeson & Campion, 1997). He has collaborated with Fredrick P. Morgeson on a number of his job analysis research contributions. Morgeson will most certainly be a listed among the important contributors to job analysis research in future histories.

Robert J. Harvey began his career at Rice University in 1982 but has spent the bulk of his professional life at Virginia Tech. He started the first computer LISTSERV devoted to job analysis in the early 1990s, along with one of the original web sites devoted to job analysis. Harvey authored the Common Metric Questionnaire as an incumbent accessible generic job analysis instrument (Harvey, 1991a). He has led a movement to systematically examine the psychometric properties of job analysis data (along with the first author of this chapter; see Wilson, 2006). As a relentless critic of the psychometric qualities of job analysis data, he has often been critical of other job analysis research. He is perhaps best known for his job analysis chapter in the 1991 edition of the *Handbook of Industrial and Organizational Psychology* (Harvey, 1991b).

Jimmy L. Mitchell began his career in the U.S. Air Force in 1957 as a psychiatric clinic technician. He spent 27 years in the Air Force where he spent the majority of his time on occupational analysis issues and achieved the rank of Lt. Colonel. He studied under both Carroll Shartle at the Ohio State University and Ernest McCormick at Purdue University, where he earned his masters and PhD degrees, respectively. He founded the Institute for Job and Occupational Analysis in 1993 after retiring from McDonnell Douglas Astronautics Company. He developed the Professional and Managerial Position Questionnaire with Ernest McCormick. He wrote two influential histories of military job analysis (Mitchell, 1988; Mitchell & Driskill, 1996) and was a tireless promoter of the best in job analysis research and practice. Shortly before his untimely death in 2000, he founded and was editor-in-chief of *Ergometrika*, a new peer-reviewed electronic journal devoted to the field of job analysis research. For a more detailed account of Jimmy Mitchell's life and accomplishments, see Cunningham (2001).

Joseph W. Cunningham studied under Ernest J. McCormick at Purdue University and spent the majority of his career at North Carolina State University conducting research on quantitative occupational analysis and taxonomy and related career interest and need topics. He coined the term *ergometrics* to describe a quantitative approach to the study of human work (Cunningham, 1971) and is the founding and senior editor of *Ergometrika*, online scholarly journal devoted to job analysis research (Cunningham, 2000). As part of this research, he and his associates developed the Occupation Analysis Inventory (Cunningham, Boese, Neeb, & Pass, 1983) and the General Work Inventory (Cunningham, Wimpee, & Ballentine, 1990). At a professional conference in 1989, he made the comment that "job analysis is the Rodney Dangerfield of [industrial and organizational] psychology" (Cunningham, 1989) to point out that greater attention needs to be paid to job analysis research and practice.

JOB ANALYSIS CAREER VIGNETTES

Raymond Christal

Raymond Christal put the final version of the technical report back in the file and gave it to his assistant. He was happy with the results, and he did not really care if he saw it again. The results had been briefed up the line, and most importantly it had led to changes in how the U.S. Air Force designed and implemented training for airmen. He was always looking for ways to improve the life and survivability of airmen. This report had fared much better with the officials than his famous *How to Select a Harem* technical report, which was an excellent description of how to use multiple regression for policy capturing (Christal, 1968). That technical report won a Golden Fleece Award as evidence of wasteful government spending from a senator who had obviously not bothered to read the report. Although Christal relished the opportunity to go hunting and was deeply religious, the real love of his life was the search for the truth through empirical research. He was very impressed with how Flanagan (1949) had used the study of a few critical job tasks (i.e., critical incidents) of pilots to dramatically improve pilot training and safety.

On this day, Ray had a big idea he was interested in discussing with his next appointment. If a few critical tasks could make such a difference in safety training of pilots, what would a complete understanding of *all* the tasks necessary for each of the numerous Air Force military occupation specialties (MOS) mean for the training and safety of airmen? From this particular big idea came the CODAP with hundreds of task inventories for broad swaths of Air Force MOSs. The CODAP was made possible by access to computing resources that were unavailable to the typical private employer at the time. The task inventory approach to job analysis drastically reduced training costs and increased the effectiveness of training in the Air Force.

Along with Flanagan before him and Sid Gael (1983) who popularized task analysis in the private sector, Raymond Christal demonstrated the practical benefits of task analysis on a massive scale and earned his place among the greats of job analysis. By today's hypothesis-driven, theoretical standards, research in Ray's lab was decidedly atheoretical. "Christal's Caldron" was the nickname for the numerous analyses that were performed in search of patterns in the data. After several false retirements, Christal was at the AFHRL when he decided to break for lunch one day, but he never returned. He died in his car while pursing another big idea; he was an unabashed practitioner and dust bowl empiricist of the best kind.

Earnest McCormick

It was an important time in Earnest McCormick's career. He was finally making real progress on an entirely new approach to job analysis—one that held the promise of reducing much of the burden and costs associated with the task-analytic approach. His students often found him at his desk when they arrived in the morning and still there when they took their leave at night. When one particular graduate student arrived to discuss his research, Mac reached for the manuscript he had put in his desk drawer the previous day. To the absolute horror of the student, a bat flew out of the drawer and began a menacing flight around the office. Mac continued the conversation as he swatted at the bat with the papers and slowly moved to open the office window. After the bat exited the office through the now open window, Mac closed the window and sat down as if nothing was particularly unusual about the whole incident. He was much more interested in discussing the research on the Worker Activity Profile, which would eventually evolve into the PAQ, the first truly generalized approach to job analysis. No single academic has contributed more to the field of job analysis research than Ernest McCormick. The PAQ was important not only for the development of empirically derived work dimensions but also for the enormous effort needed to norm the results of the instrument based on all known work as defined by the 1970 U.S. Census.

Sidney Fine

Sidney Fine walked into the conference room carrying one of those inflatable donuts, which he placed in the chair before he sat down. Although Sid was by no means tall, the device was not being used to raise his stature but to reduce his obvious discomfort. He had been asked to the meeting as one of the luminaries in the field of job analysis by a consulting firm that was retained by the U.S. Department of Labor to revise the *Dictionary of Occupational Titles* and the underlying job analytic system on which it was based. As the founder of functional job analysis, he had a direct hand in the creation of the *Dictionary of Occupational Titles* during his long career in government service. He listened patiently as the new content model of what would eventually form the heart of what was to be called O*Net was explained to the distinguished panel. Other panel members made a number of admiring statements about the model and expressed optimism about the project to the consultants and the U.S. Department of Labor officials present. When Sid's turn, came he launched into a withering critique of the model, pointedly telling everyone that it would be an inadequate replacement for the *Dictionary of Occupational Titles*. (Of course, nothing in the telling of this story is meant as a criticism of the O*Net project. This story occurred early in the development of O*Net and the project and content model have changed substantially since that time. Rather, this story is meant to represent Sid as the tireless and vigorous defender of the FJA approach to job analysis that O*Net was meant to replace.)

A few years later, Sid was one of two discussants on a panel concerning cognitive task analysis at the annual meeting of the Society for Industrial and Organizational Psychology. Usually discussants have at least a few kind comments about each paper, but Sid did not like anything about cognitive task analysis and said so in highly specific and no uncertain terms. The next discussant was R. J. Harvey, himself no stranger to giving highly detailed critiques of other job analysts' research, brought the house down simply by observing that he rarely got to play the role of "good cop, warm and fuzzy reviewer." Both stories, one told to the first author and the other personally witnessed, are classic Sidney Fine. He has spent a lifetime developing functional job analysis, conducting job analysis research, and writing books. He is the only living member of a group of three individuals who have played the largest role in the field of job analysis.

CONCLUSIONS

We have had the honor of getting to personally meet many of the individuals featured in this chapter during our careers. A few similarities among the contributors featured here are worth mentioning. First and most importantly, all are ardent followers of the scientist-practitioner model that is so central to industrial and organizational psychology. Many of the important scientific contributions discussed here began as practical problems approached in new and creative ways. A second similarity is a common entrepreneurial streak that led many into instrument development and consulting. More often than not, many of these individuals took their ideas to the marketplace with considerable success. Finally, many would be described as very down-to-earth individuals who went about their work in an unassuming manner. At the end of the day, these are people you could look forward to drinking a beer with and the importance of their scientific contributions would never come up in the conversation.[1]

REFERENCES

Ash, R. A., & Levine, E. L. (1980). A framework for evaluating job analysis methods. *Personnel, 57*(6), 53–59.

Barnes, R. M. (1940). *Motion and time study* (2nd ed.). New York, NY: John Wiley & Sons.

Berry, L. M. (1998). *Psychology at work: An introduction to industrial and organizational psychology* (2nd ed.). Boston, MA: McGraw-Hill.

Bingham, W. V. (1939). Halo, invalid and valid. *Journal of Applied Psychology, 23,* 221–228.

Bingham, W. V., & Moore, B. V. (1941). *How to interview.* New York, NY: Harper.

Blum, M. L., & Naylor, J. C. (1968). *Industrial psychology: Its theoretical and social Foundations* (Rev. ed.). New York, NY: Harper & Row.

Bownas, D. A., & Bernardin, H. J. (1988). Critical incident technique. In S. Gael (Ed.), *The job analysis handbook for business, industry, and government* (pp. 1120–1137). New York, NY: John Wiley & Sons.

---

[1] Part of this chapter was previously published in Cunningham, J. W. (2000). Introduction to a new journal. *Ergometrika, 1,* 1–23.

Brannick, M. T., & Levine, E. L. (2002). *Job analysis: Methods, research, and applications for human resource management in the new millennium.* Thousand Oaks, CA: Sage Publications.

Campion, M. A., & McClelland, C. L. (1991). Interdisciplinary examination of the costs and benefits of enlarged jobs: A job design quasi-experiment. *Journal of Applied Psychology, 76,* 186–198.

Christal, R. E. (1968). Selecting a harem and other applications of the policy-capturing model. *Journal of Experimental Education, 36,* 35–41.

Christal, R. E. (1970). Implications of Air Force occupational research for curriculum design. In B. B. Smith & J. Moss, Jr. (Eds.), *Report of a seminar: Process and techniques of vocational curriculum development.* Minneapolis: Minnesota Research Coordinating Unit for Vocational Education, University of Minnesota.

Christal, R. E. (1974). *The United States Air Force occupational research project* (Report No. AFHRL-TR-73-75). Lackland AFB, TX: Occupational Research Division.

Christal, R. E., & Weissmuller, J. J. (1988). Job-task inventory analysis. In S. Gael (Ed.), *The job analysis handbook for business, industry, and government* (pp. 1036–1050). New York, NY: John Wiley & Sons.

Cornelius, E. T., Hakel, M. D., & Sackett, P. R. (1979). A methodological approach to job classification for performance appraisal purposes. *Personnel Psychology, 32,* 283–297.

Costanza, D. P., Fleishman, E. A., & Marshall-Mies, J. (1999). Knowledges. In N. G. Peterson, M. D. Mumford, W. C. Borman, P. R. Jeanneret, & E. A. Fleishman (Eds.), *An occupational information system for the 21st century: The development of O*NET* (pp. 71–90). Washington, DC: American Psychological Association.

Crites, J. O. (1969). *Vocational psychology: The study of vocational behavior and development.* New York, NY: McGraw-Hill.

Cunningham, J. W. (1971). *"Ergometrics": A systematic approach to some educational Problems.* Raleigh, NC: North Carolina State University, Center for Occupational Education.

Cunningham, J. W. (1989, August). *Discussion.* In R. J. Harvey (Chair), *Applied measurement issues in job analysis.* Symposium conducted at the annual meeting of the American Psychological Association, New Orleans, LA.

Cunningham, J. W. (2000). Introduction to a new journal. *Ergometrika, 1,* 1–23.

Cunningham, J. W. (2001). Jimmy L. Mitchell, PhD *The Industrial-Organizational Psychologist, 38*(4), 185–187.

Cunningham, J. W., Boese, R. R., Neeb, R. W., & Pass, J. J. (1983). Systematically derived work dimensions: Factor analyses of the Occupation Analysis Inventory. *Journal of Applied Psychology, 68,* 232–252.

Cunningham, J. W., Wimpee, W. E., & Ballentine, R. D. (1990). Some general dimensions of work among U.S. Air Force enlisted occupations. *Military Psychology, 2,* 33–45.

Dawis, R. V., England, G. W., & Lofquist, L. H. (1964). *A theory of work adjustment.* Minneapolis, MN: Industrial Relations Center, University of Minnesota.

Dawis, R. V., & Lofquist, L. H. (1983). *A psychological theory of work adjustment.* Minneapolis, MN: University of Minnesota Press.

Dawis, R. V., Lofquist, L. H., & Weiss, D. J. (1968). *A theory of work adjustment: A revision.* Minneapolis, MN: Industrial Relations Center, University of Minnesota.

Droege, R. C. (1988). Department of Labor job analysis methodology. In S. Gael (Ed.), *The job analysis handbook for business, industry, and government* (pp. 993–1018). New York, NY: John Wiley & Sons.

Ferguson, L. (1952). A look across the years, 1920–1950. In L. L. Thurstone (Ed.), *Applications of psychology: Essays to honor Walter V. Bingham* (pp. 1–17). New York, NY: Harper.

Fine, S. A. (1955). A structure of worker functions. *Personnel and Guidance Journal, 34,* 66–73.

Fine, S. A., & Cronshaw, S. F. (1999). *Functional job analysis: A foundation for human resources management.* Mahwah, NJ: Lawrence Erlbaum.

Fine, S. A., & Getkate, M. (1995). *Benchmark tasks for job analysis: A guide for functional job analysis (FJA) scales.* Mahwah, NJ: Lawrence Erlbaum.

Flanagan, J. C. (1949). Critical requirements: A new approach to employee evaluation. *Personnel Psychology, 2,* 419–425.

Flanagan, J. C. (1954). The critical incident technique. *Psychological Bulletin, 51,* 327–358.

Fleishman, E. A. (1953). The description of supervisory behavior. *Journal of Applied Psychology, 37,* 1–6.

Fleishman, E. A. (1958). Dimensional analysis of movement reactions. *Journal of Experimental Psychology, 55,* 438–453.

Fleishman, E. A. (1964). *The structure and measurement of physical fitness.* Englewood Cliffs, NJ: Prentice-Hall.

Fleishman, E. A. (1972). Structure and measurement of psychomotor abilities. In R. N. Singer (Ed.), *The psychomotor domain: Movement behavior.* Philadelphia, PA: Lea & Febinger.

Fleishman, E. A. (1975). Toward a taxonomy of human performance. *American Psychologist, 30,* 1127–1149.

Fleishman, E. A. (1982). Systems for describing human tasks. *American Psychologist, 37,* 821–834.

Fleishman, E. A. (1992). *Fleishman Job Analysis Survey* (F-JAS). Potomac, MD: Management Research Institute.

Fleishman, E. A. (1999). Series forward. In S. A. Fine & S. F. Cronshaw (Eds.), *Functional job analysis* (pp. ix–xi). Mahwah, NJ: Lawrence Erlbaum.

Fleishman, E. A., Costanza, D. P., & Marshall-Mies, J. (1999). Abilities. In N. G. Peterson, M. D. Mumford, W. C. Borman, P. R. Jeaneret, & E. A. Fleishman (Eds.), *An occupational information system for the 21st century: The development of O*NET* (pp. 175–196). Washington, DC: American Psychological Association.

Fleishman, E. A., & Hempel, W. E., Jr. (1956). Factorial analysis of complex psychomotor performance and related skills. *Journal of Applied Psychology, 40,* 96–104.

Fleishman, E. A., & Quaintance, M. K. (1984). *Taxonomies of human performance: The description of human tasks.* Potomac, MD: Management Research Institute.

Fleishman, E. A., & Reilly, M. E. (1992). *Handbook of human abilities: Definitions, measurements, and job task requirements.* Potomac, MD: Management Research Institute.

Gael, S. (1977). Development of job task inventories and their use in job analysis research. *JSAS Catalog of Selected Documents in Psychology, 7,* 25.

Gael, S. (1983). *Job analysis: A guide to assessing work activities.* San Francisco, CA: Jossey-Bass.

Gael, S. (Ed.). (1988). *The job analysis handbook for business, industry, and government.* New York, NY: John Wiley & Sons.

Ghiselli, E. E., & Brown, C. W. (1955). *Personnel and industrial psychology.* New York, NY: McGraw-Hill.

Gilbreth, F. B. (1911). *Motion study.* New York, NY: Van Nostrand.

Gilbreth, F. B., & Gilbreth, L. M. (1916). *Fatigue study.* New York, NY: Sturgis & Walton.

Gilbreth, F. B., & Gilbreth, L. M. (1917). *Applied motion study: A collection of papers on the efficient method to industrial preparedness.* New York, NY: MacMillan.

Gilbreth, L. M. (1998). *As I remember: An autobiography.* Norcross, GA: Engineering & Management Press.

Gottfredson, G. D. (1999). John L. Holland's contributions to vocational psychology: A Review and evaluation. *Journal of Vocational Behavior, 55,* 15–40.

Gottfredson, G. D., & Holland, J. L. (1991). *The Position Classification Inventory: Professional manual.* Odessa, FL: Psychological Assessment Resources.

Gottfredson, G. D., & Holland, J. L. (1996). *Dictionary of Holland occupational codes* (3rd ed.). Odessa, FL: Psychological Assessment Resources.

Gottsfredson, G. D., Holland, J. L., & Ogawa, D. K. (1982). *Dictionary of Holland occupational codes.* Palo Alto, CA: Consulting Psychologists Press.

Gottsfredson, L. S., & Richards, J. M., Jr. (1999). The meaning and measurement of environments in Holland's theory. *Journal of Vocational Psychology, 55,* 57–73.

Harvey, R. J. (1991a). *The Common Metric Questionnaire (CMQ): A job analysis system.* San Antonio, TX: Psychological Corporation.

Harvey, R. J. (1991b). Job analysis. In M. D. Dunnette & L. M. Hough (Eds.), *Handbook of industrial and organizational psychology* (2nd ed., Vol. 2, pp. 71–164). Palo Alto, CA: Consulting Psychologists Press.

Holland, J. L. (1959). A theory of vocational choice. *Journal of Counseling Psychology, 6,* 35–45.

Holland, J. L. (1967). *Manual for the Vocational Preference Inventory* (6th rev.). Palo Alto, CA: Consulting Psychologists Press.

Holland, J. L. (1970). *The self-directed search for career planning.* Palo Alto, CA: Consulting Psychologists Press.

Holland, J. L. (1973). *Making vocational choices: A theory of careers.* Englewood Cliffs, NJ: Prentice-Hall.

Holland, J. L. (1985a). *Making vocational choices: A theory of vocational personalities and work environments* (2nd ed.). Englewood Cliffs, NJ: Prentice-Hall.

Holland, J. L (1985b). *Manual for the Vocational Preference Inventory* (Rev. ed.). Odessa, FL: Psychological Assessment Resources.

Holland, J. L. (1997). *Making vocational choices: A theory of vocational personalities and work environments* (3rd ed.). Englewood Cliffs, NJ: Prentice-Hall.

Holland, J. L. (1999). Resume. *Journal of Vocational Behavior, 55,* 5–14.

Holland, J. L., Fritzsche, B. A., & Powell, A. B. (1994). *The Self-Directed Search technical manual.* Odessa, FL: Psychological Assessment Resources.

Jeanneret, P. R., Borman, W. C., Kubisiak, U. C., & Hanson, M. A. (1999). Generalized work activities. In N. G. Peterson, M. D. Mumford, W. C. Borman, P. R. Jeanneret, & E. A. Fleishman (Eds.), *An occupational information system for the 21st century: The development of O*NET* (pp. 105–126). Washington, DC: American Psychological Association.

Koppes, L. L. (1999). Ideal of science: Persons behind the SIOP awards. *The Industrial Psychologist, 36,* 75–86.

Levine, E. L. (1983). *Everything you always wanted to know about job analysis.* Tampa, FL: Mariner Typographers.

Levine, E. L., Ash, R. A., & Bennett, N. (1980). Exploratory comparative study of four job analysis methods. *Journal of Applied Psychology, 65,* 524–535.

Levine, E. L., Ash, R. A., Hall, H. L., & Sistrunk, F. (1983). Evaluation of job analysis methods by experienced job analysts. *Academy of Management Journal, 26,* 339–348.

Lofquist, L. H., & Dawis, R. V. (1969). *Adjustment to work.* New York, NY: Appleton-Century-Crofts.

McCloy, R. A., Waugh, G., Medsker, G., Wall, J., Rivkin, D., & Lewis, P. (1999). *Determining the occupational reinforcer patterns for O*NET occupational units: Volumes I (Report) and II (Appendix).* Raleigh, NC: National Center for O*NET Development, Employment Security Commission of North Carolina.

McCormick, E. J. (1957). *Human engineering.* New York, NY: McGraw-Hill.

McCormick, E. J. (1959). The development of processes for indirect or synthetic validity: III. Application of job analysis to indirect validity (A symposium). *Personnel Psychology, 12,* 402–413.

McCormick, E. J. (1979). *Job analysis: Methods and applications.* New York, NY: AMACOM.

McCormick, E. J., & Jeanneret, P. R. (1988). Position Analysis Questionnaire. In S. Gael (Ed.), *The job analysis handbook for business, industry, and government* (pp. 825–842). New York, NY: John Wiley & Sons.

McCormick, E. J., Jeanneret, P. R., & Mecham, R. C. (1972). A study of job characteristics and job dimensions as based on the Position Analysis Questionnaire (PAQ). *Journal of Applied Psychology, 56,* 347–368.

McCormick, E. J., & Tiffin, J. (1974). *Industrial Psychology* (6th ed.). Englewood Cliffs, NJ: Prentice-Hall.

Mitchell, J. L. (1988). History of job analysis in military organizations. In S. Gael (Ed.), *The job analysis handbook for business, industry, and government* (pp. 30–36). New York, NY: John Wiley & Sons.

Mitchell, J. L., & Driskill, W. E. (1996). Military job analysis: A historical perspective. *Military Psychology, 8,* 119–142.

Morgeson, F. P., & Campion, M. A. (1997). Social and cognitive sources of potential inaccuracy in job analysis. *Journal of Applied Psychology, 82,* 627–655.

Morsh, J. E., Madden, J. M., & Christal, R. E. (1961). *Job analysis in the United States Air Force* (Report No. WADD-TR-61-113). Lackland Air Force Base, TX: Personnel Laboratory, Wright Air Development Division.

Munsterberg, H. (1913). *Psychology and industrial efficiency.* Boston, MA: Houghton Mifflin.

Paterson, D. G., Gerken, C. D'A., & Hahn, M. E. (1941). *The Minnesota Occupational Rating Scales and Counseling Profile.* Chicago, IL: Science Research Associates.

Paterson, D. G., Gerken, C. D'A., & Hahn, M. E. (1953). *Revised Minnesota Occupational Rating Scales.* Minneapolis, MN: University of Minnesota.

Peterson, N. G., Mumford, M. D., Borman, W. C., Jeanneret, P. R., & Fleishman, E. A. (Eds.). (1999). *An occupational information system for the 21st Century: The development of O*NET.* Washington, DC: American Psychological Association.

Phalen, W. J., & Mitchell, J. L. (1993). Innovations in occupational measurement technology for the U.S. military. In *Proceedings of the Eight International Occupational Analysts Workshop* (pp. 12–16). San Antonio, TX: U.S. Air Force Occupational Measurement Squadron.

Prien, E. P., & Ronan, W. W. (1971). Job analysis: Review of research findings. *Personnel Psychology, 24,* 371–396.

Primoff, E. S. (1957). The J-coefficient approach to jobs and tests. *Personnel Administration, 20,* 34–40.

Primoff, E. S. (1959). The development of processes for indirect or synthetic validity: IV. Empirical validations of the J-coefficient. *Personnel Psychology, 12,* 413–418.

Primoff, E. S., & Eyde, L. D. (1988). Job element analysis. In S. Gael (Ed.), *The job analysis handbook for business, industry, and government* (pp. 807–824). New York, NY: John Wiley & Sons.

Primoff, E. S., & Fine, S. A. (1988). A history of job analysis. In S. Gael (Ed.), *The job analysis handbook for business, industry, and government* (pp. 14–29). New York, NY: John Wiley & Sons.

Rounds, J. B., Jr., Smith, T., Hubert, L., Lewis, P., & Rivkin, D. (1999). *Development of occupational interest profiles for the O*NET: Volumes I (Report) and II (Appendices).* Raleigh, NC: National Center for O*NET Development, Employment Security Commission of North Carolina.

Sager, C. E. (1999). Occupational interests and values. In N. G. Peterson, M. D. Mumford, W. C. Borman, P. R. Jeanneret, & E. A. Fleishman (Eds.), *An occupational information system for the 21st century: The development of O*NET* (pp. 197–212). Washington, DC: American Psychological Association.

Sanchez, J. I. (1994). From documentation to innovation: Reshaping job analysis to meet emerging business needs. *Human Resource Management Review, 4,* 51–74.

Sanchez, J. I., & Levine, E. L. (2000). Accuracy or consequential validity: which is the better standard for job analysis data? *Journal of Organizational Behavior, 21,* 809–818.

Sanchez, J. I., Prager, I., Wilson, A., & Viswesvaran, C. (1998). Understanding within-job title variance in job-analytic ratings. *Journal of Business and Psychology, 12,* 407–420.

Schultz, D. P., & Schultz, S. E. (1996). *A history of modern psychology* (6th ed.). Fort Worth, TX: Hartcourt Brace.

Scott, W. D., Clothier, R. C., & Spriegel, W. R. (1954). *Personnel management* (5th ed.). New York, NY: McGraw-Hill.

Shartle, C. L. (1952). *Occupational information* (2nd ed.). New York, NY: Prentice-Hall.

Shartle, C. L., & Stogdill, R. M. (1957). *Work analysis forms*. Columbus, OH: Bureau of Business Research, The Ohio State University.

Super, D. E., & Bohn, M. J. (1970). *Occupational psychology*. Belmont, CA: Wadsworth.

Taylor, F. W. (1911a). *The principles of scientific management*. New York, NY: Harper.

Taylor, F. W. (1911b). *Common sense applied to motion and time study*. New York, NY: Harper.

Thurstone, L. L. (1952). Preface. In L. L. Thurstone (Ed.), *Applications of psychology: Essays to honor Walter V. Bingham* (pp. i–ix). New York, NY: Harper.

Trattner, M. H., Fine, S. A., & Kubis, J. F. (1955). A comparison of worker requirement ratings made by reading job descriptions and by direct observation. *Personnel Psychology, 8,* 183–194.

U.S. Department of Labor. (1956). *Estimates of worker trait requirements for 4000 jobs*. Washington, DC: U.S. Government Printing Office.

U.S. Department of Labor, Employment and Training Administration. (1977). *Dictionary of occupational titles* (4th ed.). Washington, DC: Government Printing Office.

U.S. Department of Labor, Employment and Training Administration. (1991). *The revised handbook for analyzing jobs*. Washington, DC: U.S. Government Printing Office.

U.S. Employment Service. (1944). *Training and reference manual for job analysis*. Washington, DC: Superintendent of Documents.

Uhrbrock, R. S. (1922). The history of job analysis. *Administration, 3,* 164–168.

Viteles, M. S. (1923). Job specifications and diagnostic tests of job competency designed for the auditing division of a street railway company. *Psychological Clinic, 14,* 83–105.

Viteles, M. S. (1932). *Industrial psychology*. New York, NY: W.W. Norton.

Wilson, M. A. (2006). Chapter 9: A history of job analysis. In L. L. Koppes (Ed.), *The science and practice of industrial and organizational psychology*. Mahway, NJ: Lawrence Erlbaum Associates.

Wren, D. A., & Greenwood, R. G. (1998). *Management innovators: The people and ideas that have shaped modern business*. New York, NY: Oxford University Press.

10

Cognitive Task Analysis
Methods for Capturing and Leveraging Expertise in the Workplace

Michael A. Rosen
University of Central Florida

Eduardo Salas
University of Central Florida

Elizabeth H. Lazzara
University of Central Florida

Rebecca Lyons
University of Central Florida

Whether the issue is capturing the expertise held in individuals exiting the workplace, designing training programs to develop more experts at a faster pace, or building technologies that support expert performance in attempts to raise the ceiling of performance, there is an increasingly salient need for robust and reliable methods for capturing cognition in the workplace. Cognitive task analysis (CTA) is a broad set of tools, techniques and approaches for eliciting, analyzing, and representing the knowledge and cognitive processes involved in task performance. This chapter outlines the purpose and utility of CTA, reviews what a general CTA process comprises, reviews the general categories of CTA methods and highlights their relative strengths and weaknesses, and discusses some critical needs for the further development of CTA.

THE PURPOSE OF COGNITIVE TASK ANALYSIS

In general, the purpose of CTA is to understand a specific aspect of human cognition related to a task (e.g., goal generation, decision making, judgments, or cognitive skills underlying a physical task) in a way that can be combined with behavioral task analysis to gain a complete understanding of task performance. This understanding can then be used in the application of CTA to workplace needs. One manner of conceptualizing the purpose of CTA is to look at the criteria by which the success of CTA is measured. These criteria include the following (Klein & Militello, 2001):

1. Making a significant discovery about the performance, judgments, and decisions of experts in a task domain

2. Communicating and representing that discovery effectively so that practitioners can develop an understanding of the findings and put them to use
3. Making a meaningful impact so that the findings of the project afford the development of interventions (e.g., displays, training) that fulfill the stated goals of the project

Historically, CTA is applied to meet these objectives in several different research traditions or threads (Hoffman & Woods, 2000), including the following:

1. The development of training programs, especially the design of scenarios for simulation-based training (Chipman, Schraagen, & Shalin, 2000; Militello & Hutton, 1998; Schaafstal & Schraagen, 2000)
2. Assessment and selection tools (DuBois & Shalin, 1995; Hunt & Joslyn, 2000)
3. Interface design to support expert performance (Byrne, 2003; Kieras & Meyer, 2000; Seamster, Redding, & Kaempf, 1997)
4. The development of performance aids (DuBois & Shalin, 2000)
5. Developing an understanding of work cultures, specifically in relation to change
6. Replacing ineffective normative models of decision making in the workplace

THE GENERALIZED COGNITIVE TASK ANALYSIS PROCESS

Best practices in CTA have and continue to evolve. The development of CTA processes and methods has been driven by both top-down theoretical perspectives on human cognition and expertise (Ericsson & Smith, 1991), as well as bottom-up pragmatic concerns such as the return on investment of the time and effort on the part of the elicitor/analyst (Hoffman, 1987, 2002). The overview of the CTA process presented in this section is a synthesis of several prescriptions of how a CTA should be conducted (Chipman et al., 2000; Crandall, Klein, & Hoffman, 2006). We describe CTA in terms of five core phases:

1. Exploring and defining what to analyze
2. The selection of knowledge elicitation strategies
3. The knowledge elicitation activities
4. Data analysis
5. Knowledge representation

The first two phases of CTA frame the CTA efforts and give direction and focus to the core CTA processes of knowledge elicitation, data analysis, and knowledge representation. An overview of these phases is provided in Table 10.1.

Exploring and Defining What to Analyze

Activities in the preliminary phase of a CTA—exploring and defining what to analyze—are crucial to its success. Mistakes made during this phase can cascade through the lifecycle of the project and ultimately limit the effectiveness of the end products. Key issues to address at the beginning of a CTA include defining a vision for the CTA, determining which aspects of the tasks to focus on, identifying and gaining the support of experts, and bootstrapping.

Clearly defining a vision for the CTA provides guidance for the many decisions to be made throughout the remainder of the process. This vision should be developed collaboratively between the analysts and the sponsors and include the scope and purpose of the project, as well as a set of specific goals. Crandall et al. (2006) recommend developing a kernel statement for the effort, which

Table 10.1   Overview of Phases, Activities, and Outcomes in the Cognitive Task Analysis (CTA) Process

CTA Phase	Representative Activities	Output of Phase
Preliminary phase (exploring and defining what to analyze)	Define the scope and purpose of the CTA • Clearly articulate the question the CTA must answer for sponsoring the organization(s) Determine which tasks warrant a CTA • Use standard methods (e.g., informal interviews, questionnaires) to determine the importance and complexity of tasks Identify experts (proficiency scaling) Gain commitments of time and effort from identified experts Bootstrapping (bringing the analyst up to speed on the task domain) • Analysis of existing task-related documentation (if available), including traditional task analyses, training materials, and standard operating procedures • Informal interviews with experts	A set of deliverables, the ultimate products of the CTA A statement of purpose for the CTA A basic understanding of the tasks and the target domain Access to subject matter experts Focus for the CTA effort • A set of tasks where CTA can make the biggest impact
Identifying knowledge representation	Determine the abstract nature of knowledge involved in the task Choose the CTA methods and techniques that are most likely to be effective. • Match methods to (a) characteristics of the work domain, (b) purpose of the CTA, (c) cognitive style of the expert, and (d) pragmatics (e.g., access, time constraints)	The CTA strategy • Set of knowledge elicitation, analysis, and representation techniques to be used
Knowledge elicitation	Data collection (asking questions and making observations) • Interviews • Field observations • Process tracing techniques • Simulations • Automated data capture • Questionnaires	Raw data • Transcriptions of interviews • Video/audio recordings and notes from observations • Self-report data
Data analysis	Decomposing data • Reducing quantity, but maintaining content, of large amounts of protocol data • Extracting process (or cognitive trace) information from data • Making inferences about knowledge and processes not directly represented in data Creating a big picture • Look for themes and trends between large units of analysis (e.g., multiple experts, tasks)	An explanation of how complex cognitive work is accomplished • Models of the domain of work • Models of the experts' knowledge in the domain • Models of expert processes and reasoning • Chronologies • Process diagrams
Putting knowledge representations to use	Communicate findings effectively to sponsors and system and training designers Create impact and provide representations that can be used to meet the overall goals of the CTA	Input to: • Training development • Sociotechnical system design • Interface and display design Knowledge preservation

is a concise statement that describes the key questions the CTA must answer. This statement will inform decisions about the types of situations to investigate, what types of people will be of interest, what aspects of expertise are most relevant, and the form of the CTA end products (Annett, 2000; Crandall et al., 2006).

An important step in the CTA process is identifying where to focus the effort of the project, essentially finding the tasks where CTA can have the greatest impact (Militello & Hutton, 1998; Shepherd & Stammers, 2005). CTA is most appropriate for complex tasks that are ill-structured, difficult to learn, take place in dynamic environments, have an inherently high degree of uncertainty, and require real-time decision making and multitasking (Gordon & Gill, 1997). The cognitive complexity of a task can be assessed by considering the amount of knowledge necessary for task performance, the number, complexity and variety of goal/action sequences and their dependence on environmental cues, and properties of the perceptual patterns that must be recognized during the task (DeVries & Gordon, 1994; Gordon & Gill, 1997). Hutton, Millter, and Thordsen (2003) have employed a process called *cognimeter* to perform initial analyses of prospective tasks. This process involves first considering the criticality and procedural characteristics of a task. If a task is both highly critical and nonprocedural, it is considered a good candidate task and is given further cursory examination (not a full CTA) to assess its associated cognitive challenges (e.g., the processes that are used, such as decision making and coordination).

The ability to identify experts within organizations is an obvious necessity. Unfortunately, this has proven to be a difficult task in practice, as the indicators most commonly associated with expertise (e.g., certifications, years of experience, identification by peers) have been found to be weakly related to levels of performance in many contexts (Camerer & Johnson, 1991; Shanteau, 1992). There are several methods (collectively known as proficiency scaling) available that can be used to determine the levels of proficiency within a specific domain and organization (Hoffman & Lintern, 2006). For example, objective measures of performance on representative tasks for the domain are generally considered the "gold standard" for determining levels of expertise (e.g., Ericsson & Lehmann, 1996). However, these are often difficult to obtain in organizations and domains with dynamic environments and ill-defined tasks (Shanteau, 1992).

Interviews can be used to gather information about career and educational experience and to estimate hours of experience within a domain, a classic and commonly used indicator of expertise. Network analysis and multidimensional scaling techniques can be useful for determining who in the organization is perceived to be an expert (Stein, 1992, 1997). Additionally, metrics for determining relative levels of expertise based on the reliability and consistency of discrimination judgments of stimuli from a domain of expertise have been developed and validated (Shanteau, Friel, Thomas, & Raacke, 2005; Shanteau, Weiss, Thomas, & Pounds, 2003; Weiss & Shanteau, 2003).

A successful CTA relies on an effective analyst/elicitor. The effectiveness of the analyst/elicitor in turn depends in large part on the ability of that analyst to rapidly develop proficiency within a domain. The analyst must acquire the fundamental knowledge involved in the task as well as the specialized vocabulary. This process is known as bootstrapping (Hoffman, Shadbolt, Burton, & Klein, 1995) and table top analysis (Flach, 2000). It is essential in facilitating accurate and efficient communication between the elicitor and the experts. Bootstrapping is often achieved via a review of existing documentation (e.g., training materials, existing traditional task analyses, documented standard operating procedures) and informal interviews with subject matter experts (Crandall et al., 2006). Structured interview protocols and questionnaires can maximize efficiency in the bootstrapping process. That is, analysts who have not gone through an extensive development of proficiency within a domain can be effective knowledge elicitors if they have tools (i.e., structured and formalized knowledge elicitation protocols) developed by analysts who have developed proficiency in the domain. The expertise necessary for conducting a CTA can be transferred to a degree from the analyst to the tools (e.g., protocols) used by the analyst.

Identifying Knowledge Representations

After a clear vision for the CTA project has been set, specific CTA methodologies can be chosen. There are a wide variety of methods available, and the choice of which one(s) to employ should be driven by the nature of the task (Klein & Millitelo, 2001). By identifying, in general terms, the type of knowledge being used by experts during performance on the tasks of interest, the analyst can better choose the methods to be employed (Chipman et al., 2000; Hoffman & Lintern, 2006). A contentious issue in the earliest days of CTA was the idea of differential access (e.g., Evans, Jentsch, Hitt, Bowers, & Salas, 2001); that is, it was proposed that different knowledge elicitation techniques tap into different types of knowledge (i.e., declarative and procedural). This idea, however, has given way in large part to what Hoffman and Lintern (2006) described as differential utility—the idea that the usefulness of specific techniques varies depending on such things as characteristics of the work domain, cognitive style of the expert, and the purposes of the analysis. A second factor driving the selection of knowledge elicitation methods is the ultimate purpose of the CTA. For example, end products of concept mapping activities are very useful for developing computer interfaces. Concept maps capture the structure of an expert's domain knowledge and therefore provide good guidance on how to organize features of the software tools used by experts. However, concept maps may not be well suited for developing training content.

Knowledge Elicitation

This stage of the CTA process is where the analyst collects data from the expert that will be used to make inferences about knowledge and cognitive processes. Knowledge elicitation techniques are reviewed in a later section of this chapter. One often-raised objection to the use of knowledge elicitation to extract information about expert performance is rooted in the nature of expertise. Most accounts of expertise highlight the tacit, nonconscious, and automatic nature of expert performance (Dreyfus & Dreyfus, 1986). On the surface, this would imply that an expert would be unable to verbalize their performance processes. However, although automaticity and nonconscious processes play a large role in expert performance (Salas, Rosen, & DiazGranados, 2010), experts are capable of monitoring their automatic processes. This is considered essential to the continuous improvements in performance exhibited by experts (Ericsson, Krampe, & Tesch-Romer, 1993). Additionally, Hoffman and Lintern (2006) argued that there is no empirical proof that there is such a thing as knowledge that cannot be verbalized and that the core issue is really that the knowledge elicitation technique must provide appropriate scaffolding—support for experts in articulating what they know. This scaffolding arises from both the characteristics of knowledge elicitation tool (e.g., probe questions) and the abilities of the elicitor.

Data Analysis

A CTA effort should result in an *analysis* of the cognitive work (as opposed to a *description*) done in a specific domain. Klein and Militello (2001) described a range of CTA outcomes from lists of cognitive functions involved in a particular task, itemizations of the cues and corresponding subprocesses involved in performance, and robust explanations of how the cognitive work of a task is accomplished. A task description is the result of information collected on a task without a specific future purpose in mind. As a result, practitioners simply describe any information that they believe may be of interest to individuals in the future. In contrast, a task analysis must be guided by specific research questions. Data is collected in order to answer the proposed questions and not just provide voluminous descriptive information with nebulous practical utility (Annett, 2000).

Knowledge elicitation and data analysis are more closely bound for some methods than others. For example, in the development of concept maps the knowledge elicitation and analysis stages are often concurrent and highly iterative (Crandall et al., 2006; Olson & Bilossi, 1991). Other methods, such as protocol analysis, involve a cleaner break between knowledge elicitation (e.g., the collection and storage of "raw" protocol data) and the analysis of the data. Data can be collected for verbal protocols and analyzed at a later date and in multiple ways (Bainbridge & Sanderson, 2005).

Putting Knowledge Representations to Use

After the data have been collected and analyzed according to the methodologies selected in accordance with the goals and vision of the CTA effort, what is next? How are these representations of knowledge and cognitive processes translated into products beyond the CTA? The end product of the CTA can be viewed in terms of the output of the analysis phase (e.g., varieties of knowledge representations). However, the effectiveness of these products can only be gauged in terms of the value they add to the stated goals of the project (e.g., developing training, displays). This final stage is perhaps the weakest link in the CTA process (Chipman et al., 2000). However, methods of cognitive systems engineering provide an excellent bridge between the knowledge requirements generated from a CTA and practical solutions to problems of system design. There are a variety of approaches to cognitive system engineering (Vicente, 1999; Woods & Hollnagel, 2005), but all of these techniques involve translating an understanding of the cognitive demands of work (achieved via some type of CTA) into tools that support this work. The task of incorporating expert knowledge representation into any type of end product is one of the most challenging aspects of CTA.

KEY CTA KNOWLEDGE ELICITATION METHODOLOGIES

The number of options available for assessing the knowledge and cognitive processes involved in expert task performance continues to grow. The number and variety of these techniques makes a comprehensive review impractical. Therefore, this section examines some general categories of CTA methodologies, providing descriptions of the general category and example methods as well as information about the relative strengths and weaknesses of these methods. Several categorization schemes for CTA methods exist (e.g., Crandall et al., 2006; Hoffman et al., 1995; Militello, 2001; Shadbolt, 2005), but we adopt Cooke's (1994) organization based on the mechanics of the technique and the type of knowledge elicited (Militello, 2001). As summarized in Table 10.2, there are four categories of knowledge elicitation techniques: process tracing, interview and observation, indirect/conceptual methods, and simulation and contrived tasks.

Process Tracing Techniques

Process tracing techniques involve the capture of task performance processes in a way that allows inferences to made about the cognitive processes or knowledge involved in performance (Ford, Schmitt, Schechtman, Hults, & Doherty, 1989). In general, process tracing techniques are used for "externalizing internal processes or producing external signs that support inferences about internal workings" (Woods, 1993, p. 233). Data such as eye movements, verbal reports, computer usage patterns (e.g., keystrokes), and other observable actions are recorded concurrently with performance (in some cases, process tracing is done retrospectively) on specific tasks of interest (Cooke, 1994). Process tracing techniques generally provide a large amount of detailed information and, as discussed in the overview of the CTA process, determining which task to focus these types of techniques on is an important issue. Process tracing techniques include verbal and nonverbal reports

Table 10.2 Overview of Cognitive Task Analysis (CTA) Methods

Category of Methods	Examples	General Strengths	General Weaknesses
Process tracing techniques	Protocol analysis Decision analysis Information sampling Verbal reports Nonverbal reports	Rich quantity and quality of information Readily applicable to real-world settings Methods are process-oriented; they focus on sequences of activity	Data collection and analysis can be time consuming for many of the methods Some methods used concurrently with task performance may alter performance processes (e.g., verbalizing aspects of performance not generally verbalized)
Interview and observation	Critical decision method Critical incident technique Structured/semistructured/unstructured interviews Field observations	Rich data Techniques have face validity to experts; they are familiar with them Techniques are highly flexible and applicable in most contexts Focusing on critical incidents is highly efficient Gives real-world perspective on work processes Identifies individual differences in performance	Time consuming to analyze Retrospective techniques produce data with uncertain reliability due to memory degradation Gaining access to field observations can be difficult Access to time with experts is generally limited Observation can be reactive
Indirect/conceptual methods	Concept maps Pairwise relatedness ratings Abstraction hierarchies Repertory grid technique Sorting techniques Multidimensional scaling, network scaling, cluster analysis	Can be very efficient (especially when combined with interview techniques) Helps experts make tacit knowledge explicit Knowledge elicitation and analysis are combined for concept mapping	Methods do not have high face validity for most domain experts
Simulations and contrived tasks	Simulated task environment (ranging from high to low fidelity) Tasks that deviate from real world task (hypotheticals)	Allows for merger of experimental control and real-world task complexity Allows for observation of performance for tasks that occur at a low frequency on the job Allows for observation of performance during events that would be unsafe in the real world	Risk of collecting data that is not valid in real context of performance Construction and validation of simulation takes time, effort, and money

(both concurrent with task performance and retrospective), information monitoring, protocol analysis, and decision analysis. Protocol analysis is the most common process tracing technique and is discussed in more detail in the following section.

Protocol Analysis

Protocol analysis is a method designed to use verbal reports as indicators of cognition, as a means to draw valid inferences about the cognitive underpinnings of complex behaviors (Ericsson & Simon, 1993; Weber, 1990). Primarily, it is a data reduction tool that enables an analyst to maintain the content of verbal reports while reducing the usually unmanageably large size of these reports in a theoretically valid manner (Walker, 2005). Introspection and interviews are some of the oldest and simplest techniques for gaining insight into the workings of the mind (Ericsson, 2006). Similarly, introspection and various types of verbal reports of thought processes have been found to be highly reactive; they change the nature of what they intended to capture (see Ericsson & Crutcher, 1991). However, protocol analysis is a set of conditions that specify the types of verbal reports that can be elicited about thought processes that do not alter those processes. In general, protocol analysis elicits the most valid and complete records of thought processes by having the expert perform controlled tasks that are representative of the target tasks in the real world and collecting the verbalizations of the expert during this process (Ericsson & Simon, 1993). The expert externalizes the internal dialogue; they are not asked to analyze their thoughts or to provide descriptions or explanations of how or why they are doing some aspect of the task. These types of demands are sources of reactivity. Experts are asked to stay focused on the task at hand and only provide vocalizations to the thoughts that become active in attention during task performance. In this way, a trace that supports the analysis of the sequence and content of cognitive processes is captured. For reviews of evidence supporting the validity (and nonreactivity) of protocol analysis techniques, see Ericsson and Simon (1993, 1998).

Eliciting verbal reports in protocol analysis is a process of asking (and training) the expert to think aloud during task performance. This is done either concurrently or retrospectively (Shadbolt, 2005). For retrospective think-alouds, experts are asked to vocalize their thoughts while observing a video or audio recording of their performance. This is generally only done when the task prohibits concurrent verbalization (e.g., the task itself requires a high degree of verbalization). Additionally, the cognitive walkthrough is a variant of protocol analysis commonly used in research for interface design. This involves the expert engaging in a type of mental simulation in which they provide verbalizations of thoughts while imagining they are performing a task without actually performing it (Bainbridge & Sanderson, 2005). These verbalizations must then be coded according to a previously established set of criteria. The coding criteria is categorized according to goals, observations, hypotheses, and decisions (Crandall et al., 2006). Various methodologies for conducting a protocol analysis have been devised (Walker, 2005; Bainbridge & Sanderson, 2005); however, the appropriate method depends upon the goals of the analysis and the particular domain of the task. There is no one procedure for conducting a protocol analysis. However, protocol analysis generally involves three stages (Bainbridge & Sanderson, 2005). First, the think-aloud data are recorded and transcribed. It is inevitable that ambiguities will arise when later analyzing the data, so it is important to capture as much of the task context as possible (e.g., what was happening when the expert had a specific verbalization). Second, the researcher prepares the data for analysis by identifying a general structure in the protocol by grouping the utterances into hierarchical sections of activity. The analyst then searches and identifies meaningful units in the data that can be inferred to represent discrete mental processes. Once these units have been identified, various tools such as formal descriptive languages can be used to assist in abstractions from the protocol data and inferences about cognitive processes that are not explicitly represented in the data. Third, techniques such as content analysis, sequential analysis, and modeling are applied.

Interview and Observation

There is no substitute for observing actual work practices in their naturalistic setting. The practical wisdom of cognitive task analysts is that if the opportunity arises to observe real world performance, take it (e.g., Crandall et al., 2006). This is the best way to assess the full social and physical environment of work, to see how procedures and performance are adapted to fit the work context (Stanton, Baber, & Young, 2005). Field observations provide information not possible using other methods; however, it is often not feasible to conduct field observations for logistic or safety reasons (e.g., target tasks are low frequency). Additionally, the observers must be highly skilled. Ethnomethodology is an approach to observing work practices that is concerned with uncovering the socially situated nature of expertise and expert performance (Clancey, 2006). These ethnomethodological tools are commonly used in a variety of disciplines including cognitive anthropology (Hutchins, 1995; D'Andrade, 1995), an important contributor to present-day CTA. Most importantly, ethnomethodology contributes an understanding of the broader social context of work practices. This information is crucial to understanding the influences and constraints on expert performance such as cultural characteristics of the workplace, information that cannot be gained through other methods.

Interviews are a classic technique at gaining insight about a particular topic. An interviewer attempts to elicit knowledge from a subject matter expert either using a structured, semistructured, or unstructured interviewing technique (Shadbolt, 2005). A structured interview follows strict guidelines consisting of standardized and typically closed-ended questions that are established prior to conducting the interview; an unstructured interview is more informal, lacks standardization, and flows naturally. All interviewing techniques are useful for extracting missing knowledge and providing an alternative solution to the many logistical complications surrounding observations. However, this technique does have some disadvantages (e.g., difficulty accessing experts, availability of a well-trained interviewer). Also, interviewees may give an inaccurate account of events and be reluctant to disclose information. In the following sections, we describe two related approaches to interviews.

Critical Incident Technique

The critical incident technique (CIT) is a "set of procedures for collecting direct observations of human behavior in such a way as to facilitate their potential usefulness in solving practical problems" (Flanagan, 1954, p. 327). CIT is a flexible and adaptive approach that involves having individuals recount events that occur prior to, during, and after critical incidents. An incident is any activity that allows for inferences and predictions regarding the person conducting the activity. Five critical steps to conducting CIT have been identified by Flanagan (1954). First, the general aims or objectives of the overall task must be specified. Typically, there are multiple objectives, and they are determined by those who possess complete authority over the task (e.g., stakeholder, employers, employees). Second, the plans and specifications for conducting the CIT must be set. This includes identifying individuals who will be observed and who will perform the observations (e.g., internal employee, external consultant) and obtaining records of previous critical incidents including the place, people involved, and events that were involved. The critical incidents selected should be both relevant and important to the general aim of the CIT. The final steps of a CIT include collecting the data (i.e., gathering and recording observations), analyzing the data (i.e. summarizing, explaining, and applying observations), and making interpretations based on the data collected.

Critical Decision Method

Critical decision method (CDM; Crandall et al., 2006; Hoffman, Crandall, & Shadbolt, 1998; Klein, Calderwood, & MacGreggor, 1989) is a more modern approach to CIT, and in many ways it is a type of hybrid between CIT and retrospective protocol analysis. CDM is a semistructured interview of experts to elicit knowledge in a specific domain. Because this method generally focuses on unusual incidents that do not ordinarily occur, it affords for the analysis of aspects of expertise that would not appear in ordinary situations. Due to the atypicality of the events, it is advantageous to generate a timeline surrounding the incident that will be used to describe the expert's decision-making process. The expert is instructed to use retrospection and recall past events and elaborate on particular events uninterrupted to avoid interjecting biases from the interviewer. The benefit of using retrospection is that it is less disruptive. The interviewer should use precise questions as opposed to generic questions. Because the questions are standardized, the data generated is more reliable than in unstructured interviews. Asking questions about specific details produce more information than asking about general ideas. The questions should require the decision maker to evaluate their decision making strategies.

Like CIT, CDM is not a strict set of procedures, but an approach designed to be flexible for adaptation to different contexts. The structure of the CDM does not lie in the protocols or probe questions used, but in the set of phases or "sweeps" that increasingly examine an incident at great levels of specificity (Crandall et al., 2006). There are four general sweeps to a CTA (Klein & Armstrong, 2005):

1. An incident is identified that holds promise for generating discoveries about underlying cognitive processes and knowledge involved in task performance.
2. The analyst and participant construct a detailed timeline of the incident, showing the sequence of events as they unfolded.
3. The points within the timeline are deepened by eliciting information about the knowledge and processes used at each decision point.
4. Hypothetical "what-if" questions are posed to the participant to further enrich the understanding of the decision process and highlight differences between how novices and experts would approach the task.

There are several advantages to using the CDM. It is applicable to naturalistic settings; therefore, it can be useful in training exercises. Additionally, the CDM does not require the use of labor-intensive artificial simulations to recreate events or the time-consuming observations necessary for low-frequency events. The incidents have already happened. The main drawback to CDM and CIT is that they rely on an individual's memories of past events. These memories may be inaccurate and misrepresent the decision-making processes that actually occurred. Therefore, finding external support for the timeline of events and other verifiable pieces of the CDM is a critical step in establishing the validity of information gathered through CDM and CIT.

Indirect/Conceptual Methods

The third category of knowledge elicitation techniques is the indirect or conceptual methods. This category includes methods generally targeted at assessing the structure of an expert's knowledge (Cooke, 1994). A robust finding in the expertise literature involves the differences in knowledge structure between experts and novices (Bordage & Zacks, 1984; Chi, Feltovich, & Glaser, 1981; Chi & Ohlsson, 2005; Feltovich, Johnson, Moller, & Swanson, 1984). Techniques for capturing the structural characteristics of knowledge generally involve three steps. First, the concepts or knowledge elements must be elicited by some means, often through interview techniques. Second, the manner in which the expert organizes these concepts is captured, often through sorting techniques or pairwise comparison ratings. Third, this relational data is analyzed, often through network scaling, multidimensional scaling, or graph construction. The next section provides more detail about the concept mapping class of conceptual knowledge elicitation techniques.

Concept Mapping

Concept mapping is a technique used to generate meaningful diagrams that represent knowledge (Hoffman & Lintern, 2006; Shadbolt, 2005). Crandall et al. (2006) provide a six-step overview of a generalized concept mapping process. First, the bounds of the domain must be drawn and the questions of interest must be defined in order to provide focus to the effort. Additionally, focus questions can be used to generate the original set of concepts. For example, a set of 5 or 10 high level concepts that the expert deems most important to the question can serve as the starting point for the mapping. Second, these concepts are placed in an initial arrangement. The most inclusive concepts should be located toward the top and the most specific concepts should be arranged towards the bottom. Third, linkages are drawn between the concepts using words that define the connection between the concepts. This creates sets of propositions in the form of a node (i.e., concept) → relation → node. The relationships can be unidirectional or bidirectional; many-to-one and one-to-many relationships are all possible. Relationships can be of various types, such as causal, classification, nominal, explanatory, or procedural (Weick & Bougon, 1986). Fourth, once the connections have been established, the map should be refined by adjusting the concepts and changing the linking labels. A quality concept map of a complex domain must go through several iterations of refinement to clarify the concepts and relationships. Fifth, the possibility of new relationships in the concept map is explored. This is done as needed, as new knowledge is brought to bear on the concept map. The concept mapping process often requires that experts make explicit what is often left tacit. Therefore, revision and refinement of the concept map can be an ongoing process. Finally, once a concept map has been created, a knowledge model can be constructed—a set of hyperlinked concept maps.

Automated Knowledge Elicitation

As should be clear by this point, conducting a cognitive task analysis can be extremely time consuming, labor intensive, and require the participation of many individuals. Consequently, automating some aspects of this procedure is an attractive proposition. There have been several success stories in the development of automated knowledge elicitation procedures, especially of the concept mapping variety. For example, Shute, Torreano, and Willis (2000, p. 72) reported on DNA (i.e., "**d**ecompose a domain into its constituent elements, **n**etwork the elements into an inheritance hierarchy, and **a**ssess the ensuing knowledge structure for validity and reliability"), a CTA tool designed to support instructional design. The software tool asks the participants questions during the interviewing phase. The questions vary depending upon the domain and type knowledge being elicited. The network aspect of the model synthesizes the knowledge into a structure. It allows the participant to rearrange and organize the information. The assessment aspect of the model examines the validity and reliability of the obtained information. It validates the knowledge by analyzing comparable data obtained from different experts on the same subject matter. DNA reduces the amount of time and labor required to perform a CTA by automating the majority of the interviewing process.

Simulations and Contrived Tasks

Simulation provides a means to bring the real world in to the laboratory; that is, the benefits of experimental control can be combined with rich, complex, and realistic tasks that are representative of on the job performance (Ward, Williams, & Hancock, 2006). Using simulation to capture expert performance has three main advantages over field observations:

1. Simulation facilitates the observation of low-frequency events.
2. Data capture and collection is simplified due to increased control. (All types of data, from keystroke level data and eye tracking information to voice communications and performance outcomes, are most often easily collected in and stored in simulators.)
3. The creation deviates from reality (i.e., the real-world task).

This third advantage is similar to the reason what-if questions are asked in the CDM—to further investigate the nature of an expert's understanding of a task. However, there is debate over exactly what types and degrees of deviations from reality are useful (Crandall et al., 2006). Simulation has drawbacks in that it can be expensive and time consuming to construct and validate a simulation of a task environment.

The most effective method of cognitive task analysis depends upon the objective of the task and the context of the situation. Using multiple methods is often the most efficient approach because each method possesses both benefits and drawbacks (Crandall et al., 2006). The amount of time necessary to implement the technique, the amount of training required for qualified observers/elicitors, and the cost-effectiveness of the technique are all necessary issues to take into consideration when determining which method(s) will produce the best CTA results. Table 10.3 provides a set of guidelines for conducting a CTA. These guidelines are a summary of the information reviewed

Table 10.3 Guidelines for Conducting Cognitive Task Analysis (CTA)

Guideline 1: Develop a strong vision for the CTA.	Clearly define the purpose of the CTA. Make sure the sponsoring agency is in agreement with the vision of the CTA. Articulate the specific questions the CTA seeks to answer.
Guideline 2: Create ownership and buy-in from experts.	CTA requires commitment from experts—make sure they are on board. Ensure access to experts for observations, interviews, and other.
Guideline 3: Understand as much of the domain as possible.	A knowledge elicitor/analyst must develop a basic understanding of the work domain—and quickly. Review all available documentation and training materials.
Guideline 4: Develop a protocol.	Ensure structure and consistency across observations and interviews with different experts. Structured protocols can focus your knowledge elicitation activities on the critical questions of the CTA and help you avoid getting lost in the richness of the domain.
Guideline 5: Choose knowledge elicitation methods based on goals and constraints.	Base your choice on the nature of the task, time and monetary constraints, the ultimate purpose of the CTA.
Guideline 6: Collect question-focused data.	Focus data collection on answering the specific questions articulated in the CTA vision.
Guideline 7: Look for the big picture.	CTAs can produce vast amounts of data. Attend to themes across experts and tasks.
Guideline 8: Communicate and translate the CTA findings to ensure they are put to use.	Make sure the output of the CTA is not esoteric. Someone will need to understand it and use it. Frame the CTA products in terms of the overall purpose of the efforts (e.g., training development, display design).

thus far in this chapter and are offered as a set of minimum requirements needed for conducting a CTA. Specifically, these guidelines will help novice cognitive task analysts guide their work.

A LOOK TOWARD THE FUTURE: CRITICAL COGNITIVE TASK ANALYSIS RESEARCH NEEDS

The CTA tradition has contributed to the growth of the general task analysis field by making great strides in analysts' abilities to deal with the complexities of covert cognitive aspects of performance. There are, however, several critical needs to address. First, CTA practitioners must remove the magic from the process. That is, a set of systematic, robust, and readily accessible procedures and principles must be articulated in a manner that allows for widespread use. Efforts have been made to streamline the CTA process (e.g., Crandall et al., 2006; Militello & Hutton, 1998). However, expertise in CTA remains a scarce resource. Second, there is a great need for CTA methods capable of capturing cognitively intensive tasks performed by teams. The term *macrocognition* has been used in reference to this knowledge and cognitively intensive team problem-solving activities; it has been defined as "the internalized and externalized high-level mental processes employed by teams to create new knowledge during complex, one-of-a-kind, collaborative problem solving" (Letsky, Warner, Fiore, Rosen, & Salas, 2007, p. 2). Beginning steps towards capturing, analyzing, and representing this type of work have been taken, but better methods are needed. Third, as has been previously noted, translating the products of CTA into interventions to support and improve individual, team, and organizational performance is the weakest link the CTA process. It is critical to develop methods for transitioning CTA products into organizational interventions and guidance. CTA is an expensive process. Advances in some of the areas discussed in this chapter can reduce this cost, but ultimately the cost effectiveness of CTA will be judged on its ability to make an impact in terms of organizational effectiveness.

KEY RESOURCES

The key sources for each of the methods are cited in this chapter with their descriptions. However, several general sources for information on CTA are available. Crandall et al. (2006) provided a comprehensive and practical guide. Hoffman and Militello (2008) provided an extensive review of CTA methods and concepts from a cross-disciplinary perspective. Schraagen, Chipman, and Shalin (2000) provided a variety of methods and examples of applications of CTA. Vicente (1999) focused on application of cognitive work analysis to interface design. Ericsson and Simon (1993) provided a definitive guide on verbal protocol analysis.

CONCLUDING REMARKS

Knowledge based economies rely on human cognitive work to create value. CTA offers a means to capture the existing expertise within an organization. This expertise can then be leveraged through training, selection, assessment, and system design to yield a net benefit for the organization. In this chapter, we provided a general overview of the processes, methods, and tools available for eliciting, analyzing, and representing the knowledge of experts. The need for such methods is increasingly salient, as is the need for further developing CTA methods to improve accessibility.[1]

---

[1] This chapter was partially supported by the Office of Naval Research Collaboration and Knowledge Interoperability Program and Office of Naval Research MURI Grant #N000140610446. The views expressed are those of the authors and do not necessarily reflect their organizations or sponsoring agencies.

REFERENCES

Annett, J. (2000). Theoretical and prgamatic influences on task analysis methods. In J. M. Schraagen, S. F. Chipman, & V. L. Shalin (Eds.), *Cognitive task analysis* (pp. 25–37). Mahwah, NJ: Lawrence Erlbaum Associates.

Bainbridge, L., & Sanderson, P. (2005). Verbal protocol analysis. In J. R. Wilson & E. N. Corlett, (Eds.), *Evaluation of human work: A practical ergonomics methodology* (3rd ed., pp. 159–184). Boca Raton, FL: Taylor & Francis.

Bordage, G., & Zacks, R. (1984). The structure of medical knowledge in the memories of medical students and general practitioners: Categories and prototypes. *Medical Education, 18,* 406–416.

Byrne, M. D. (2003). Cognitive architecture. In J. A. Jacko & A. Sears (Ed.), *The human-computer interaction handbook: Fundamentals and emerging applications* (pp. 97–117). Mahwah, NJ: Lawrence Erlbaum Associates.

Camerer, C. F., & Johnson, E. J. (1991). The process–performance paradox in expert judgement: How can experts know so much and predict so badly? In K. A. Ericsson & J. Smith (Eds.), *Toward a general theory of expertise: Prospects and limits* (pp. 195–217). Cambridge, UK: Cambridge University Press.

Chi, M., Feltovich, P., & Glaser, R. (1981). Categorization and representation of physics problems by experts and novices. *Cognitive Science, 5,* 121–152.

Chi, M. T. H., & Ohlsson, S. (2005). Complex declarative learning. In K. J. Holyoak & R. G. Morrison (Eds.), *The Cambridge handbook of thinking and reasoning* (pp. 371–399). New York, NY: Cambridge University Press.

Chipman, S. F., Schraagen, J. M., & Shalin, V. L. (2000). Introduction to cognitive task analysis. In J. M. Schraagen, S. F. Chipman, & V. L. Shalin (Eds.), *Cognitive task analysis* (pp. 3–23). Mahwah, NJ: Lawrence Erlbaum Associates.

Clancey, W. J. (2006). Observation of work practices in natural settings. In K. A. Ericsson, N. Charness, P. J. Feltovich, & R. R. Hoffman (Eds.), *The Cambridge handbook of expertise and expert performance* (pp. 127–145). Cambridge, UK: Cambridge University Press.

Cooke, N. J. (1994). Varieties of knowledge elicitation techniques. *International Journal of Human-Computer Studies, 41*(6), 801–849.

Crandall, B., Klein, G., & Hoffman, R. R. (2006). *Working minds: A practitioner's guide to cognitive task analysis.* Cambridge, MA: The MIT Press.

D'Andrade, R. G. (1995). *The development of cognitive anthropology.* Cambridge, UK: Cambridge University Press.

DeVries, M. J., & Gordon, S. E. (1994). *Estimating cognitive complexity and the need for cognitive task analysis.* Paper presented at the Human Factors and Ergonomics Society 38th Annual Meeting, Santa Monica, CA.

Dreyfus, H. L., & Dreyfus, S. (1986). *Mind over machine: The powers of human intuition and expertise in the era of the computer.* New York, NY: The Free Press.

DuBois, D., & Shalin, V. L. (1995). Adapting cognitive methods to real world objectives: An application to job knowledge testing. In P. Nichols, S. Chipman, & R. Brennan (Eds.), *Cognitively diagnostic assessment* (pp. 189–220). Hillsdale, NJ: Lawrence Erlbaum Associates.

DuBois, D., & Shalin, V. L. (2000). Describing job expertise using cognitively oriented task analyses (COTA). In J. M. Schraagen, S. F. Chipman, & V. L. Shalin (Eds.), *Cognitive task analysis* (pp. 41–55). Mahwah, NJ: Lawrence Erlbaum Associates.

Ericsson, K. A. (2006). Protocol analysis and expert thought: Concurrent verbalizations of thinking during experts' performance on representative tasks. In K. A. Ericsson, N. Charness, P. J. Feltovich, & R. R. Hoffman (Eds.), *The Cambridge handbook of expertise and expert performance* (pp. 223–241). Cambridge, UK: Cambridge University Press.

Ericsson, K. A., & Crutcher, R. J. (1991). Introspection and verbal reports on cognitive processes—two approaches to the study of thought processes. *New Ideas in Psychology, 9,* 57–71.

Ericsson, K. A., Krampe, R. T., & Tesch-Romer, C. (1993). The role of deliberate practice in the acquisition of expert performance. *Psychological Review, 100*(3), 363–406.

Ericsson, K. A., & Simon, H. A. (1993). *Protocol analysis: Verbal reports as data.* Cambridge, MA: The MIT Press.

Ericsson, K. A., & Lehmann, A. C. (1996). Expert and exceptional performance: Evidence of maximal adaptation to task. *Annual Review of Psychology, 47,* 273–305.

Ericsson, K. A., & Simon, H. A. (1998). How to study thinking in everyday life: Contrasting think-aloud protocols with descriptions and explanations of thinking. *Mind, Culture, and Activity, 5*(3), 178–186.

Ericsson, K. A., & Smith, J. (Eds.). (1991). *Toward a general theory of expertise: Prospects and limits.* Cambridge, UK: Cambridge University Press.

Evans, A. W., Jentsch, F., Hitt, J. M., II, Bowers, C., & Salas, E. (2001). Mental model assessments: Is there convergence among different methods? *Proceedings of the 45th Annual Meeting of the Human Factors and Ergonomics Society*. Santa Monica, CA: Human Factors and Ergonomics Society.

Feltovich, P. J., Johnson, P. E., Moller, J. H., & Swanson, L. C. S. (1984). The role and development of medical knowledge in diagnostic expertise. In W. J. Clancey & E. H. Shortliffe (Eds.), *Readings in medical artificial intelligence*. Reading, MA: Addison-Wesley.

Flach, J. M. (2000). Discovering situated meaning: An ecological approach to task analysis. In J. M. Schraagen, S. F. Chipman, & V. L. Shalin (Eds.), *Cognitive task analysis* (pp. 87–100). Mahwah, NJ: Lawrence Erlbaum Associates.

Flanagan, J. C. (1954). The critical incident technique. *Psychological Bulletin, 51,* 327–358.

Ford, J. K., Schmitt, N., Schechtman, S. L., Hults, B. M., & Doherty, M. L. (1989). Process tracing methods: Contributions, problems, and neglected research questions. *Organizational Behavior and Human Decision Processes, 43*(1), 75.

Gordon, S. E., & Gill, R. T. (1997). Cognitive task analysis. In C. E. Zsambok & G. Klein (Eds.), *Naturalistic Decision Making* (pp. 131–140). Mahwah, NJ: Lawrence Erlbaum Associates.

Hoffman, R. R. (1987). The problem of extracting the knowledge of experts from the perspective of experimental psychology. *The AI Magazine, 8,* 53–66.

Hoffman, R. R. (2002). *An empirical comparison of methods for eliciting and modeling expert knowledge.* Paper presented at the Proceedings of the 46th Meeting of the Human Factors and Ergonomics Society, Santa Monica, CA.

Hoffman, R. R., Crandall, B., & Shadbolt, N. R. (1998). Use of the critical decision method to elicit expert knowledge: A case study in the methodology of cognitive task analysis. *Human Factors, 40,* 254–276.

Hoffman, R. R., & Lintern, G. (2006). Eliciting and representing the knowledge of experts. In K. A. Ericsson, N. Charness, P. J. Feltovich, & R. R. Hoffman (Eds.), *The Cambridge handbook of expertise and expert performance* (pp. 203–222). Cambridge, UK: Cambridge University Press.

Hoffman, R. R., & Militello, L. G. (2008). *Perspectives on cognitive task analysis: Historical origins and modern communities of practice.* New York, NY: Psychology Press.

Hoffman, R. R., Shadbolt, N. R., Burton, A. M., & Klein, G. (1995). Eliciting knowledge from experts: A methodological analysis. *Organizational Behavior and Human Decision Processes, 32*(2), 129–158.

Hoffman, R. R., & Woods, D. D. (2000). Studying cognitive systems in context: Preface to the Special Section. *Human Factors, 42*(1), 1–7.

Hunt, E., & Joslyn, S. (2000). A functional task analysis of time-pressured decision making. In J. M. Schraagen, S. F. Chipman, & V. L. Shalin (Eds.), *Cognitive task analysis* (pp. 119–132). Mahwah, NJ: Lawrence Erlbaum Associates.

Hutchins, E. (1995). *Cognition in the wild*. Cambridge, MA: The MIT Press.

Hutton, R., Millter, T., & Thordsen, M. (2003). Decision-centered design: Leveraging cognitive task analysis in design. In E. Hollnagel (Ed.), *Handbook of cognitive task design* (pp. 323–416). Mahwah, NJ: Lawrence Erlbaum Associates.

Kieras, D. E., & Meyer, D. E. (2000). The role of cognitive task analysis in the application of predictive models of human performance. In J. M. Schraagen, S. F. Chipman, & V. L. Shalin (Eds.), *Cognitive task analysis* (pp. 237–260). Mahwah, NJ: Lawrence Erlbaum Associates.

Klein, G., & Armstrong, A. A. (2005). Critical decision method. In N. Stanton, A. Hedge, K. Brookhuis, E. Salas, & H. Hendrick (Eds.), *Handbook of Human Factors and Ergonomics Methods* (pp. 35–38). Boca Raton, FL: CRC Press.

Klein, G. A., Calderwood, R., & MacGregor, D. (1989). Critical decision method for eliciting knowledge. *IEEE Transactions on Systems, Man, and Cybernetics, 19*(3), 462–472.

Klein, G., & Militello, L. (2001). Some guidelines for conducting a cognitive task analysis. In E. Salas (Ed.), *Advances in Human Performance and Cognitive Engineering Research* (Vol. 1, pp. 163–199). Oxford, UK: Elsevier.

Letsky, M., Warner, N., Fiore, S. M., Rosen, M. A., & Salas, E. (2007). *Macrocognition in Complex Team Problem Solving.* Paper presented at the 11th International Command and Control Research and Technology Symposium, Cambridge, UK.

Militello, L. G. (2001). Representing expertise. In E. Salas & G. Klein (Eds.), *Linking expertise and naturalistic decision making* (pp. 247–264). Mahwah, NJ: Lawrence Erlbaum Associates.

Militello, L. G., & Hutton, R. J. B. (1998). Applied cognitive task analysis (ACTA): A practitioner's toolkit for understanding cognitive task demands. *Ergonomics, 41*(11), 1618–1641.

Olson, J. R., & Biolsi, K. J. (1991). Techniques for representing expert knowledge. In K. A. Ericsson & J. Smith (Eds.), *Toward a general theory of expertise: Prospects and limits* (pp. 240–285). Cambridge, UK: Cambridge University Press.

Salas, E., Rosen, M. A., & DiazGranados, D. (2010). Expertise-based intuition and decision making in organizations. *Journal of Management, 36*, 941–973.

Schaafstal, A., & Schraagen, J. M. (2000). Training of troubleshooting: A structured, task analytical approach. In J. M. Schraagen, S. F. Chipman, & V. L. Shalin (Eds.), *Cognitive task analysis* (pp. 57–70). Mahwah, NJ: Lawrence Erlbaum Associates.

Schraagen, J. M., Chipman, S. F., & Shalin, V. L. (Eds.). (2000). *Cognitive task analysis*. Mahwah, NJ: Lawrence Erlbaum Associates.

Seamster, T. L., Redding, R. E., & Kaempf, G. L. (1997). *Applied cognitive task analysis in aviation*. Brookfield, VT: Avebury Aviation.

Shadbolt, N. (2005). Eliciting expertise. In J. R. Wilson & E. N. Corlett (Eds.), *Evaluation of human work* (pp. 185–218). Boca Raton, FL: Taylor & Francis.

Shanteau, J. (1992). Competence in experts: The role of task characteristics. *Organizational Behavior and Human Decision Processes, 53*, 252–266.

Shanteau, J., Friel, B. M., Thomas, R. P., & Raacke, J. (2005). Development of expertise in a dynamic decision-making environment. In T. Betsch & S. Haberstroh (Eds.), *The routines of decision making* (pp. 251–270). Mahwah, NJ: Lawrence Erlbaum Associates.

Shanteau, J., Weiss, D. J., Thomas, R. P., & Pounds, J. (2003). How can you tell if someone is an expert? Empirical assessment of expertise. In S. L. Schneider & J. Shanteau (Eds.), *Emerging perspectives on judgement and decision research* (pp. 620–639). Cambridge, UK: Cambridge University Press.

Shepherd, A., & Stammers, R. B. (2005). Task analysis. In J. R. Wilson & N. Corlett (Eds.), *Evaluation of human work* (3rd ed., pp. 129–157). Boca Raton, FL: CRC Press.

Shute, V. J., Torreano, L. A., & Willis, R. E. (2000). DNA: Providing the blueprint for instruction. In J. M. Schraagen, S. F. Chipman, & V. L. Shalin (Eds.), *Cognitive task analysis* (pp. 71–86). Mahwah, NJ: Lawrence Erlbaum Associates.

Stanton, N., Baber, C., & Young, M. S. (2005). Observation. In N. Stanton, A. Hedge, K. Brookhuis, E. Salas, & H. Hendrick (Eds.), *Handbook of human factors and ergonomics methods* (pp. 21–27). Boca Raton, FL: CRC Press.

Stein, E. W. (1992). A method to identify candidates for knowledge acquisition. *Journal of management information systems, 9*, 161–178.

Stein, E. W. (1997). A look at expertise from a social perspective. In P. J. Feltovich, K. M. Ford, & R. R. Hoffman (Eds.), *Expertise in context* (pp. 181–194). Menlo Park, CA: The MIT Press.

Vicente, K. J. (1999). *Cognitive work analysis: Toward safe, productive, and healthy computer-based work*. Mahwah, NJ: Lawrence Erlbaum Associates.

Walker, G. (2005). Verbal protocol analysis. In N. Stanton, A. Hedge, K. Brookhuis, E. Salas, & H. Hendrick (Eds.), *Handbook of human factors and ergonomics methods* (pp. 31–39). Boca Raton, FL: CRC Press.

Ward, P., Williams, A. M., & Hancock, P. A. (2006). Simulation for performance and training. In K. A. Ericsson, N. Charness, P. J. Feltovich, & R. R. Hoffman (Eds.), *The Cambridge handbook of expertise and expert performance* (pp. 243–262). Cambridge, UK: Cambridge University Press.

Weber, R. P. (1990). *Basic content analysis*. London, UK: Sage Publications.

Weick, K. E., & Bougon, M. G. (1986). Organizations as cognitive maps: Charting ways to success and failure. In H. P. Sims & D. A. Gioia (Eds.), *The thinking organization: Dynamics of organizational social cognition* (pp. 102–135). San Francisco, CA: Jossey Bass.

Weiss, D. J., & Shanteau, J. (2003). Empirical assessment of expertise. *Human factors, 45*(1), 104–114.

Woods, D. D. (1993). Process-tracing methods for the study of cognition outside of the experimental psychology laboratory. In G. Klein, J. Orasanu, R. Calderwood, & C. E. Zsambok (Eds.), *Decision making in action: Models and methods* (pp. 228–251). Norwood, NJ: Ablex.

Woods, D. D., & Hollnagel, E. (2005). *Joint cognitive systems*. Boca Raton, FL: CRC Press.

11

Five Questions Concerning Task Analysis

Douglas J. Gillan

North Carolina State University

Every good story needs to address a number of questions. The story of task analysis that I relate in this chapter discusses five questions: what, why, when, how, and whither. In other words, this chapter provides a broad overview that takes the reader back to the past of task analysis and forward to its future. The story tells the reader why one might analyze a task, as well as how to conduct such an analysis. Implicit in the story are questions of who should do task analyses and where to conduct the analysis. In addressing these questions, I do not propose that I have given definitive answers, just some ideas and approaches.

Table 11.1 provides a summary of the steps in a task analysis presented in this chapter. In a sense, Table 11.1 provides a task description of task analysis. In considering this table, keep in mind that the analyst has great flexibility in performing these steps.

QUESTION 1: WHAT IS TASK ANALYSIS?

Before you can begin to consider task analysis, you need to define what is meant by a task. Dictionary definitions focus on a task as a piece of work. The term "task" comes from the Latin *taxare*, meaning to evaluate, estimate, or assess (also the Latin root for the English word "tax"). *Taxare* became the Middle English *taske*, which meant tax or imposed work. Over the years, the sense of imposition has been lost. Relatedly, the word "job" comes from the Middle English *jobbe*, or piece (as in a piece of work), which may be an alteration of *gobbe*, or a small bit (as in *gob*).

Table 11.2 shows a number of work-related terms that vary as a function of the time scale for the work. Task and job are in the middle of the scale. Job, however, can mean a small piece of work (e.g., "My job is to make the sandwiches"), but it can also mean one's employment in a profession at a particular company. A task is more typically a piece of work rather than long-term employment. In my experience, when people meet and are discussing their occupations, they are much more likely to ask "What is your job?" than "What is your task?" Likewise, when your boss says, "I have a new task for you," you are more likely to think that he has a piece of work for you, not a new major position within the organization.

Tasks tend to be oriented around the accomplishment of a single major goal. Meeting that goal often requires that it be decomposed into a set of subgoals. Accomplishing the subgoals is done by completing steps in the task where the steps involve the application of operators. For example, suppose you have a goal of writing a paper on task analysis. That goal breaks down into subgoals of writing the a number of sections about the topic. To write the first section, you have to open a Microsoft Word file and then write the first sentence, which involves perceptual, cognitive, and motor operators related to both writing and typing. If you are a skilled writer, you may have a set

Table 11.1   Summary of the Steps in a Task Analysis

Step	Description
Step 1	Collect task-relevant data
	• Based on archival data
	• Based on observation of task
	• Naturalistic observation
	• Structured observation
Step 2	Develop task lexicon and taxonomy
Step 3	Produce a task description
	• Narrative description
	• Flowchart
Step 4	Apply analytical method(s)
	• Hierarchical task analysis
	• Goals, operators, methods, and selection rules model
	• Modular analysis
	Recomposition approaches
	• PRONET
	• Multidimensional scaling

of steps that you always apply together in the same order, which is called a *method* (Card, Moran, & Newell, 1983).

As this example suggests, tasks often involve an interaction with a technological system. The system can be advanced and complex technology (e.g., a computer, car, airplane) or simple technology (e.g., pencil and paper, graph, set of instructions, shovel). In addition, performing the task—especially using technology—often requires special training. Both the design of technology and the design of training systems can be aided by a thorough task analysis.

The example of writing a paper also highlights an important point: People do tasks for a reason. In disciplines such as human-computer interaction and human factors, researchers sometimes forget that the purpose of using technology is to perform a task and the purpose of performing a task is to accomplish a goal.

The term *analysis* comes from the Greek *analuein*, meaning to undo or dissolve. This original use relates to the current meaning of analysis as breaking an object or event into its elements. Task analyses can dissolve a task into a number of different elements, depending on the level of the analysis—task steps, operators, or processes. In addition to simply identifying the elements of an

Table 11.2   The Context of a Task Within Work Terms

Work	Time Scale
Profession	Decades
Career	Years
Job	
Task	Days, hours, minutes
Goals	Minutes, seconds
Methods	
Task steps	
Operators	Seconds, milliseconds
Perceptual/cognitive/motor processes	

object or event, analyses often describe the relationships among the elements: temporal, spatial, physical, causal, and/or semantic. Task analyses are most likely to describe the temporal and spatial relationships among task elements.

In recent years, much of the attention on task analyses has been directed towards cognitive task analysis (CTA; see Chapter 10, this volume; see also Crandall, Klein, & Hoffman, 2006; Hollnagel, 2003). This chapter focuses on the more traditional form of task analysis.

QUESTION 2: WHY DO TASK ANALYSIS?

Task analysis is one of the most important tools in applied cognitive and perceptual psychology. It is a useful tool for designing interfaces to computer systems and telerobotic devices, designing training programs, developing cognitive models, and developing research hypotheses. Task analysis is flexible and broadly applicable across tasks and different end products.

Jonassen, Tessmer, and Hannum (1999) proposed that the reasons that instructional designers conduct task analysis include the following:

- Defining the learner's goals and objectives
- Describing the learner's tasks and subtasks
- Specifying the type of knowledge in a task (e.g., declarative, structural, procedural)
- Selecting appropriate learning outcomes
- Identifying instructional activities that result in learning
- Constructing performance assessments and evaluation

The reasons for doing a task analysis for user interface design overlap with the ones identified by Jonassen et al. (1999) in defining the user's goals, describing the user's tasks, and constructing evaluations. In addition, interface designers benefit from task analyses in developing interface concepts and interface prototypes.

QUESTION 3: WHEN MIGHT YOU DO TASK ANALYSIS?

A task analysis is typically done early in the design process. In interface design, designers often want to have a substantial amount of information about the user, the tasks that the user will try to do on the system, and the system characteristics. Likewise, for the design of an instructional system, the designers want to know about the learner's tasks and required knowledge for those tasks early in the design process. Accordingly, a task analysis is often one of the first tasks that a design team may complete.

Although the task analysis is most often done early in the design process, it may also provide useful information later in the process. So, if the design team has completed a task analysis, they may find that as they learn more during the design they will want to modify the task analysis. Or, even if the design team did not conduct a task analysis and the design is nearly complete, they may want to conduct an analysis then. Given that task analysis data can be useful in developing system evaluations, a designer might find that the data from the analysis would still be useful during the test and evaluation phase late in the design process.

QUESTION 4: HOW DO YOU CONDUCT A TASK ANALYSIS?

Many different approaches to task analysis exist (Diaper & Stanton, 2004a). In fact, there may be as many approaches to task analysis as there are people conducting task analyses. No single best method for every user and every circumstance exists. The measure of the goodness of a task analytic method is whether it provides the user with the necessary information.

This section describes some of the steps that nearly all task analysis methods use and will provide detailed information about several specific methods. The goal of this chapter is to be descriptive of multiple approaches to task analysis rather than being prescriptive of the way that task analysis must be done. Along the route of the description of task analysis, I will point out points at which the analyst may want to give careful consideration of the mapping between the task analysis that is being designed and the information that is needed.

Data Collection

Task analysis almost always begins with collection of data about the task. The data collection may be from archival data, such as instruction manuals or other sets of directions. Typically, the instructions will be most useful if they have been written by the designer(s) of the task or by other task experts. In many cases, the task analyst will not have such detailed information about the task and will have to collect data via observation of the task. If the task is one that occurs frequently and in observable circumstances, then the analyst may simply be able to freely observe the task, either by direct observation or by videotaping the task. An alternative to free observation is structured observation, which is observation of the task in a controlled environment. Examples of a controlled environment would include one in which the person performing the task would follow a scenario and/or would use a specific technological system, often a computer, to perform the task. The scenario and system would provide the structure. Sometimes, observation of the task is not possible, but task experts are available. In those cases, an interview with the expert can provide sufficient raw data for the subsequent analysis.

Consider an example that I will use throughout this section of the chapter: buying a beverage from a vending machine. A task analyst might observe such a transaction between human and system either directly or by means of a video camera that would record the task. Alternatively or in addition, the analyst might interview the purchaser to get a retrospective account of the actions involved in purchasing the beverage. This example is followed in a series of figures throughout this section of the chapter.

Task Lexicon and Taxonomy

Once the analyst has the data from the task, what can be done with the data? Sometimes, a simple description of the task provides the analyst with all of the information that is needed. For example, the description may reveal hidden steps in the task of which the analyst was previously unaware. A task description can be greatly aided by the use of two related tools: a task lexicon and a task taxonomy. The task lexicon lists and defines all of the major terms (i.e., the task components) that the analyst will use in describing the task. The definition should be precise and operational, whenever possible, and should relate to the common definition of the term in the most typical fields of practice. For example, in an analysis of the task of a novice using a word processor to type a letter (Cooke & Gillan, 1999), task terms included Pause and Nav-Lttr (navigating through the letter), among others. Defining a pause required specifying the minimum amount of time that a user might not be actively engaged in any other task components in order to qualify as a true pause. For example, an analyst would want to be sure that a novice user's search for the correct key during continuous typing would not be counted as a pause. Because Cooke and Gillan chose to define task components in terms of functions rather than specific behaviors, Nav-Lttr defined several different behaviors, such as using arrow keys, scrolling, and using page-up/page-down keys to move through a document, under the term Nav-Lttr.

The task taxonomy is most useful for tasks with many different terms used in the description. A task analyst might use a taxonomy to categorize or group terms that are semantically similar, that are similar in complexity, or that occur at similar parts of the task. For example, Lee, Plaisant, Parr, Fekete, and Henry (2006) developed a taxonomy of graph visualization terms based in part on the complexity of the task component. Under low-level components, they included retrieve value, compute derived value, scan, and correlate. Rather than simply categorizing task terms, a task taxonomy might be used to structure the relations between and among task terms, such as by developing a semantic network.

The task lexicon and taxonomy serve the valuable purposes of (a) allowing other analysts to replicate a task analysis, and (b) permitting the same analyst to return to reanalyze the task or enhance an existing analysis. In the absence of well-defined task analysis terms and components and a clear set of relationships among the terms, even the same analyst might select different terms or use a given term in a different way at a later date.

When creating a task-relevant language for task description, the analyst needs to decide the level of analysis. Should you describe the task at a motor performance level, a behavioral level, a functional level, or in terms of goals? The answer to that question depends on the purpose of the task analysis. If the goal in conducting a task analysis is to design input devices, then the motor performance level or the behavioral level may be most appropriate. However, if the purpose is to develop a training system, then the functional level may be better if it allows the system designer to identify what knowledge needs to be acquired and how that knowledge can be delivered.

The task terms for buying a beverage from a vending machine could be very detailed, such as reaching in the pocket or purse, identifying quarters, putting a quarter in the change slot, and pushing the button. However, for this example, it will be more useful to keep the terms at the functional or goal-oriented level: find, search, and select. Figure 11.1 shows the terms and an example task lexicon.

Task Description

After developing the task lexicon and taxonomy, the analyst will be ready to provide a task description. One format for the task description is a narrative (e.g., Jonassen et al., 1999). The narrative flow of the description is based on the temporal sequence of the task steps, moving from the overarching goal of the task to each step in sequence to accomplish that goal. An alternative to a narrative format is a flowchart, in which each task step is contained in a box with arrows leading

Perception-oriented task components

Find	Navigate through space seeking vending machine target
Identify	Match target image with actual vending machine
Search	Scan soda vending machine (SVM) display of sodas
Examine	Visually compare items with target image

Motor-oriented task components

Get	Move from inside to outside
Insert	Place money in SVM's money slot
Select	Input to SVM interface to indicate desired soda
Put	Move from outside to inside

Motivation-oriented task components

Enjoy	Positive emotional response

Figure 11.1   Examples of task lexicon and task taxonomy for the task of buying a beverage from a vending machine.

from box to box to indicate the temporal sequence of the task (Stanton, 2004). The flowchart format can also vary in complexity, with additional types of containers (e.g., circles to indicate the start or end of a task, rectangles to show an action, and diamonds to indicate a decision) and connectors (e.g., labeled arrows). If the additional complexity of the flowchart provides the analyst with benefits in understanding the task, developing an end product, or communicating about the task with other analysts or other stakeholders, then the additional effort would be worthwhile. However, if the analyst does not gain from the complexity, then the lost time and increased effort alone makes it counterproductive; the complexity may make the flowchart harder to understand and communicate.

After completing a useful task description that provides the initial level of task decomposition, the analyst probably should decide whether there is enough information to move from analysis to the next stage of the effort, whether that is the design of an interface or a training system or the redesign of a task. If unsure, the analyst might try to move to the next stage in design and see if there is enough information about the task to begin to create initial design concepts. The analyst can always return to the task analysis if additional information is needed.

Figure 11.2 shows an example of a description of the task of buying a beverage. The description is simple for purposes of illustration and provides a step-by-step decomposition of the task. Also, the task format is neither a fully integrated narrative nor a flowchart, but it is shown in a step-by-step format that could be easily converted to either format.

Analytical Methods

Moving on from the task description takes the analyst into additional methods, which take the descriptive information and elaborate on it. Perhaps the most popular such method is hierarchical task analysis (HTA; Annett, 2004; Stanton, 2006). The original basis of HTA was the test-operate-test-exit (TOTE) model of task performance (Miller, Galanter, & Pribram, 1960). HTA provides a representation of the decomposition of the task from a goal into subgoals and task components. In addition, the HTA frequently provides additional information related to the problems or errors that can arise at each step of the task, as well as recommended solutions to those problems. Because of its

---

Step 1: **Find** vending machine room
Step 2: **Identify** soda vending machines (SVMs) in vending machine room
Step 3: **Search** SVM 1 for desired soda brand (X)
Step 4: **Search** SVM 2 for desired soda brand (X)
Step 5: **Search** SVM 3 for desired soda brand (X)
Step 6: **Search** SVM 3 for cost of Brand X
Step 7: **Search** SVM 3 for money slot
        Does it accept quarters only?
        Does it accept dollars and quarters?
Step 8: **Find** change in pocket
Step 9: **Get** change from pocket
Step 10: **Examine** change for quarters
Step 11: **Get** wallet from pocket
Step 12: **Examine** bills in wallet for $1.00 bills
Step 13: **Get** one $1.00 bill from wallet
Step 14: **Put** wallet in pocket
Step 15: **Put** unneeded change in pocket
Step 16: **Insert** money into SVM 3
Step 17: **Select** Brand X on SVM 3 button array
Step 18: **Get** soda
Step 19: **Enjoy** a refreshing beverage

Figure 11.2 Example of a task description for the task of buying a beverage from a vending machine.

hierarchical information, the format of the HTA is often a flowchart—either simple or complex—or a task analysis table in which the task steps are in the left most column, with additional information (e.g., potential errors, consequences of the error, likelihood of an error, solutions to the errors) in columns to the right. The tabular format allows the analyst to read across from the task to the elaborative information. Both the flowchart and the table have a vertical structure that is based, in part, on the temporal sequence of the task. However, both formats can depart from the temporal flow to show alternative task steps, such as when errors occur.

Figure 11.3 shows how the HTA method might be used to analyze the example task of buying a soda. The example uses the tabular format for HTA and adds information to the task steps related to potential errors.

Task step	Error probability	Error consequence	Criticality of error
1: **Find** closest vending machine room	Low	No soda or delay in getting soda plus extra effort	High
2: **Identify** soda vending machines (SVMs) in vending machine room	Low	No soda or delay in getting soda plus extra effort	High
3: **Search** SVM 1 for desired soda brand (X)	Low	Miss soda on SVM 1	Low
4: **Search** SVM 2 for desired soda brand (X)	Low	Miss soda on SVM 2	Low
5: **Search** SVM 3 for desired soda brand (X)	Low	Miss soda on SVM 3	Low
6: **Search** SVM 3 for cost of Brand X	Low	Possibility of insufficient funds	High
7: **Search** SVM 3 for money slot • Quarters only? • Dollars and quarters?		Possibility of insufficient funds	High
8: **Find** change in pocket	Low	Possibility of insufficient funds	High
9: **Get** change from pocket	Medium	1. Repeat step 9 2. Pick up change from floor	Medium
10: **Examine** change for quarters	Low	Possibility of insufficient funds	High
11: **Get** wallet from pocket	Low	1. Repeat step 11 2. Pick up wallet from floor	Medium
12: **Examine** bills in wallet for $1.00 bills	Medium	1. Repeat step 12 2. No soda	Medium
13: **Get** one $1.00 bill from wallet	Low	1. Repeat step 13 2. Pick up $1.00 bill from floor	Medium
14: **Put** wallet in pocket	Low	1. Repeat step 11 2. Pick up wallet from floor	Medium
15: **Put** unneeded change in pocket	Medium	1. Repeat step 15 2. Pick up change from floor	Medium
16: **Insert** money into SVM 3	Medium	1. Repeat step 16 2. Pick up change and/or $1.00 bill from floor	Medium
17: **Select** Brand X on SVM 3 button array	Medium	Wrong soda	High
18: **Get** soda	Low	1. Repeat step 18 2. Pick up soda from floor	Medium
19: **Enjoy** a refreshing beverage	Low	Clean soda off front of shorts	High

Figure 11.3 Example of hierarchical task analysis for the task of buying a beverage from a vending machine.

Another popular approach to task analysis at this point is based on goals, operators, methods, and selection rules (GOMS) modeling (Card et al., 1983). The GOMS approach was based on Newell and Simon's (1972) general problem solver (GPS), in which problem solving was conceived of as a series of goals, subgoals, and operators. In both the GPS and GOMS, operators are the simple actions that the user performs to accomplish a subgoal. These actions can be either overt behaviors or cognitive acts; accordingly, GOMS is often considered under CTA methods. Methods are sequences of operators that commonly occur in order, and selection rules are the rules by which the person performing the task can choose one method over another. Following completion of a task description, a task analyst who wanted to perform a GOMS analysis would take each step of the task and identify the goal (which is a subgoal to the overarching goal for the task), a selection rule (if there were multiple methods), a method (if a common sequence of operators were typically performed), and the operator. GOMS analyses can be developed at several different levels from the functional level down to the keystroke (motor task) level. Additional information that can be gleaned from a GOMS model includes estimates of the time to perform a task, the optimal sequence of task steps, and a relative evaluation of two system concepts (e.g., Gray, John, & Atwood, 1993). Examples of GOMS analyses using the GOMS Language can be found in Kieras (2004).

A third method that takes the decomposed task and adds information involves the development of modules for each task step. The modules consist of the subgoal that the step is designed to accomplish, the action performed during the step to meet the subgoal, the information needed to perform the action, and the consequence of the action. This method has been useful in developing standards for use interface design and models of interaction with technology (e.g., Gillan & Lewis, 1994). The information that is added to the task description can be useful in many different ways. For example, the design team might decide whether the information needed to complete the step would be in the world or in the head (Norman, 1988). If the information needed to be in the world, then the designers would have an initial idea of the design of information display for that step in a task. In contrast, if the information should be in the head, the designers would have identified necessary training for the user. In addition, identifying the consequence of the action also provides ideas concerning the presentation of information to the user. If the consequence of an action were not immediately evident, then the system would need to make the consequence perceptible. Also, the consequence should be related to the subgoal so that the user is aware that the subgoal has been met (or not) and can move on to the next task step (or repeat the present step or try a different action). This approach helps to identify potential errors based on the assumption that they would occur due to the lack of information to perform the action and/or the lack of appropriate information about the consequence of the action. Figure 11.4 shows a selection of the steps of a modular task analysis of buying a soda.

The three approaches to task analysis described in this section might be called decomposition-plus because each adds information to the decomposed description of the task. An alternative approach might be called recomposition because it creates a task structure from the decomposed description. An example of this approach is PRONET (e.g., Cooke & Gillan, 1999; Cooke, Neville, & Rowe, 1996; Gillan & Cooke, 1998, 2001), a method derived from the Pathfinder network analysis of relatedness data (e.g., Schvaneveldt, 1991). Rather than using relatedness ratings, the most common source of data for Pathfinder networks, PRONET begins with a task description. The task description is then used to produce a task step transition frequency matrix. This matrix lists the number of times one type of task step follows another type of task step. For example, in a word processing task, the step of saving the document will be followed by quitting the application with a fairly high frequency. A task step transition frequency matrix can be developed for any lag between steps; the one-step lag (i.e., adjacent task steps) is probably the most useful. So, the matrix lists task

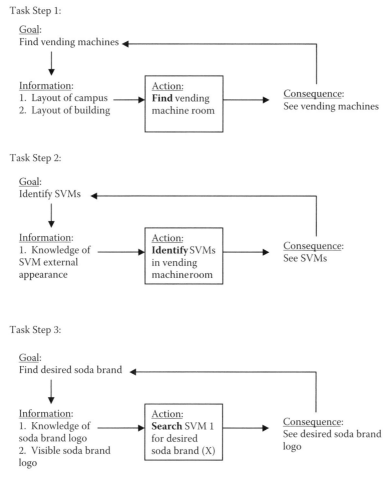

Figure 11.4   Example of modular task analysis for the task of buying a beverage from a vending machine.

components across the leftmost vertical column and top horizontal row of the matrix, with each cell containing the frequency with which the component listed in the horizontal row is followed by the component in the vertical column.

For PRONET, the transition frequency data are used to derive transition probabilities—the frequency of a given transition out of all transitions for that task component. So, if saving a document is followed by quitting the application 10 times and saving is followed by other task components 40 times, the transition probability for save-quit is .20. The transition probability data are structured in a table just like that used for the transition frequency data. Typically, a criterion level is used to eliminate low probability transitions (i.e., to set them to zero), with the decision about what constitutes a low probability left up to the analyst.

Once the transition matrix has been developed and the criterion applied, the Pathfinder algorithm is applied to the data. Pathfinder creates a network, based on certain assumptions (which are represented as parameters in the algorithm) that determine the complexity of the network—that is, the number of links among the nodes. In a PRONET network, the task components are the nodes and the transition probabilities determine the links, with link weight a function of the transition probability. When one task component never or rarely follows another, the Pathfinder algorithm eliminates the link between them. Likewise, it will eliminate a link that has a nonzero value (that is, a nonzero transition probability) if a more efficient multilink path is available (with efficiency being one of the assumptions that is defined by setting a parameter). This is comparable to a driver opting to avoid a direct route between points *A* and *X* if it is faster to travel indirectly on routes from *A* to *B* and *B* to *X*.

The PRONET network can be visualized, with task components (nodes) linked to one another. This visual representation of the task can provide added value to the analyst in several ways. First, links with high weightings indicate two task components that tend to co-occur with high probability. For an instructional system, the designer might want to train these components at the same time; for interface design, the interface should place the display and control elements related to these task components close together in space. Second, task components that are not linked to any other components may indicate underused parts of a task (such as a menu item that is rarely used or is randomly accessed and bears no temporal or causal relationship to other items). Third, the structure of the network can be informative. For example, networks may consist of a set of highly interconnected nodes with limited connections to nodes outside of that set—a structure that could be considered a subnetwork. Such a structure would indicate that the task components tend to co-occur and should be trained together or have interface elements grouped together spatially. A second structure that is diagnostic is a node that has many connections to other nodes (i.e., a central node). A central node might indicate a critical task component that should be highly trained in an instructional system or be readily available on an interface.

Figure 11.5 takes the data from the task description and shows the PRONET analysis. The network shows two subnets: the one at the top of the figure from the early perceptually-oriented task steps and the one at the bottom from the later motor-oriented task steps. *Get* serves as a central node, with the *Find–Get* link connecting the two subnets. The link weights (the numbers next to the lines connecting the nodes) are based on the task transition probabilities.

Tullis, Sperling, and Steinberg (1986) applied multidimensional scaling (MDS) to a functional task analysis in much the same way as PRONET has been used with Pathfinder. They created a task transition probability matrix based on a task description of Space Station crew activities, then analyzed the data using MDS to produce one-, two-, and three-dimensional solutions. A MDS solution

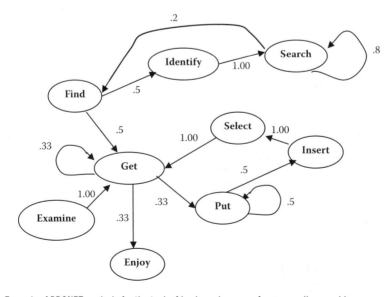

Figure 11.5 Example of PRONET analysis for the task of buying a beverage from a vending machine.

indicated that the functional task components (e.g., eating, training, dressing and undressing, sleep) could be organized around a group versus individual dimension and a private versus public dimension. In addition to revealing the dimensions underlying the activities, the MDS solution could be used to help design the architectural layout of the Space Station crew modules by identifying the need for private crew quarters, a work space for individual astronauts, and a work space for teams of astronauts.

A task analyst is likely to consider the choice among these various methods of analysis that can be applied to the task description data to be another proof-of-pudding point. Because of time and money constraints, it probably is one. However, the task description could be analyzed with one or more than one of these methods. Each method provides unique information, so that the use of more than one approach would provide a fuller picture of the task.

QUESTION 5: WHITHER TASK ANALYSIS?

What might the future hold for task analysis? Diaper and Stanton (2004b) have speculated on the future of task analysis. I suspect that task analysis—both CTA and traditional task analysis—will continue to be used in many different forms for as long as task analysis provides useful information for designers. And, given the number of design disciplines—from usability to education to science—that currently find task analysis methods useful, I anticipate that these methods will be in use far into the future.

Key questions about task analysis can be addressed by imagining what task analysis will be like in the future. In 50 years, task analysis methods will likely still be in use, but they will probably be markedly different methods from those being used today.

One critical concern is that task analysis is labor and time intensive. Automated data collection will make task analysis easier and more efficient to conduct. Currently, keystroke capture programs can be used to identify many of the tasks that humans do on computers. Future data capture programs may possibly involve computer-based identification of tasks from video. Researchers have had success in automated analysis of the behavior of simple animals (Hicks, Socorro, & Levin, 2006). In addition, military and homeland security researchers are working towards automated analysis of human behavior. All of this research will ultimately serve to benefit the analysis of human task-related behavior by reducing the time and effort required to collect the data for task analysis.

Second, the analytical methods that described for description-plus and for recomposition often seem to be disconnected from modern theories of human performance. Can these analytical approaches be integrated with theories that make principled predictions about human performance? In the future, the programs that simulate human performance, such as SOAR (Newell, 1990) and ACT-R/PM (Anderson & Lebiere, 1998; Byrne & Anderson, 1998) may be merged with task analytic methods to produce tools that make precise quantitative predictions about human performance with new versions of systems and about learning with instructional systems. As a part of the research program that results in the merger of simulation programs and task analysis methods, a substantial amount of research can be done to validate various approaches to task analysis—specifically to discover which approaches are most valuable in subsequent technological and instructional design.

Third, both psychology and human factors have been influenced strongly in the recent past by developments in the ability to measure neural activity, especially brain activity imaging and the measurement of electrical activity. How might this trend affect task analysis methods? As methods like measuring electroencephalograms and event-related potentials become more mobile, they may become part of the toolkit of the task analyst. The analysis of observable behavior during a task may then be supplemented by observation of concurrent brain activity. This could lead to insights about the perceptual, decision, and motor processes underlying task-oriented behavior.

IMPORTANT REFERENCE MATERIALS

The literature is replete with many books, chapters, and articles that discuss task analysis, many of which are valuable because they describe the basics of the method. I have selected five books, three of which are of historical importance and two of which provide useful, comprehensive summaries. Historically, formal task analysis may be thought to have begun with the time studies of Frederick Taylor, who developed early methods to examine tasks as objects that can be decomposed into meaningful units. Taylor's 1911 book, *The Principles of Scientific Management,* can be read as a historical artifact, but it also provides an interesting argument against a holistic view of work and in favor of an analytical approach. Another historically important book is *Plans and the Structure of Behavior* (Miller, Galanter, & Pribram, 1960). This book is one of the seminal books for the development of cognitive psychology; it could be seen as a precursor of cognitive task analysis, as well as a key text for task analysis. This book presented the TOTE model described in this chapter, which was developed to provide a more cognitive alternative to the reflex arc as the basic unit of behavior. As with Taylor's approach, the TOTE model is important because it provides an analytical approach to problem solving behavior.

A third book that has both historical and more current interest is *The Psychology of Human-Computer Interaction* (Card, Moran, & Newell, 1983). This book helped to define the discipline of human-computer interaction and to identify how perceptual, cognitive, and motor psychology could be applied to address issues in the use of computers. For task analysis, the key feature of this book is the GOMS model, which provides a systematic and structured approach to describing tasks in terms of the goals and operators used to meet those goals (with methods as collections of goals and methods as techniques to select among competing methods), and a variety of analytical tools that can be applied to that description.

Finally, two summaries provide different approaches to describing task analysis, as befits its place as an academic artifact and a useful practical tool. Diaper and Stanton (2004a) edited *The Handbook of Task Analysis for Human-Computer Interaction,* a volume that serves as a broad reference for methods of task analysis, especially as applied to the use of computers. However, the discussion of the methods can be easily applied to almost any technology or even to education. The book describes in great detail many of the task description and analytical methods that I have briefly discussed in this chapter. In *User and Task Analysis for Interface Design,* Hackos and Redish (1998) took a more practical approach to task analysis than the Diaper and Stanton book. It provides much good advice for considering users and their tasks, but also for the nuts and bolts of actually conducting a task analysis, including all of the activities necessary to prepare for and conduct a site visit in order to conduct the task analysis.

REFERENCES

Anderson, J. R., & Lebiere, C. (1998). *The atomic components of thought.* Hillsdale, NJ: Lawrence Erlbaum Associates.

Annett, N. A. (2004). Hierarchical task analysis. In D. Diaper & N. S. Stanton (Eds.), *The handbook of task analysis for human-computer interaction* (pp. 67–82). Mahwah, NJ: Lawrence Erlbaum Associates.

Byrne, M. D., & Anderson, J. R. (1998). Perception and action. In J. R. Anderson & C. Lebiere (Eds.), *The atomic components of thought* (pp. 167–200). Hillsdale, NJ: Lawrence Erlbaum Associates.

Card, S. K., Moran, T. P., & Newell, A. (1983) *The psychology of human-computer interaction.* Hillsdale, NJ: Lawrence Erlbaum Associates.

Cooke, N. J., & Gillan, D. J. (1999). Representing human behavior in human-computer interaction. In *Encyclopedia of computer science and technology* (Vol. 40, Suppl. 25, pp. 283–308). New York, NY: Marcel Dekker.

Cooke, N. J., Neville, K. J., & Rowe, A. L. (1996) Procedural network representations of sequential data. *Human-Computer Interaction, 11,* 29–68.

Crandall, B., Klein, G., & Hoffman, R. R. (2006). *Working minds: A practitioner's guide to cognitive task analysis.* Cambridge, MA: The MIT Press.

Diaper, D., & Stanton, N. S. (2004a). *The handbook of task analysis for human-computer interaction.* Mahwah, NJ: Lawrence Erlbaum Associates.

Diaper, D., & Stanton, N. S. (2004b). Wishing on a star: The future of task analysis. In D. Diaper & N. A. Stanton (Eds.), *The handbook of task analysis for human-computer interaction* (pp. 603–619). Mahwah, NJ: Lawrence Erlbaum Associates.

Gillan, D. J., & Cooke, N. J. (1998). Making usability data more usable. *Proceedings of Human Factors and Ergonomics Society 42nd Annual Meeting* (pp. 300–304). Santa Monica, CA: HFES.

Gillan, D. J., & Cooke, N. J. (2001). Using Pathfinder networks to analyze procedural knowledge in interactions with advanced technology. In E. Salas (Ed.), *Human-technology interaction in complex systems* (Vol. 10, pp. 125–161). Greenwich, CT: JAI Press.

Gillan D. J., & Lewis, R. (1994). A componential model of human interaction with graphs: I. Linear regression modelling. *Human Factors, 36,* 419–440.

Gray, W. D., John, B. E., & Atwood, M. E. (1993). Project Ernestine: Validating a GOMS analysis for predicting and explaining real-world performance. *Human-Computer Interaction, 8,* 237–309.

Hackos, J. T., & Redish, J. C. (1998). *User and task analysis for interface design.* New York, NY: John Wiley & Sons.

Hicks, C., Sorocco, D., & Levin, M. (2006). Automated analysis of behavior: a computer-controlled system for drug screening and the investigation of learning. *Journal of Neurobiology, 66,* 977–990.

Hollnagel, E. (2003). Prolegomenon to cognitive task design. In E. Hollnagel (Ed.), *Handbook of cognitive task design* (pp. 3–15). Mahwah, NJ: Lawrence Erlbaum Associates.

Jonassen, D. H., Tessmer, M., & Hannum, W. H. (1999). *Task analysis methods for instructional design.* Mahwah, NJ: Lawrence Erlbaum Associates.

Kieras, D. (2004). GOMS model for task analysis. In D. Diaper & N. S. Stanton (Eds.), *The handbook of task analysis for human-computer interaction* (pp. 83–116). Mahwah, NJ: Lawrence Erlbaum Associates.

Lee, B., Plaisant, C., Parr, C. S., Fekete, J.-D., & Henry, N. (2006). Task taxonomy for graph visualization. In *BELIV '06: Proceedings of the 2006 conference on beyond time and errors* (pp. 1–5). New York, NY: ACM Press.

Miller, G. A., Galanter, E., & Pribram, K. (1960). *Plans and the structure of behavior.* New York, NY: Holt.

Newell, A. (1990). *Unified theories of cognition.* Cambridge, MA: Harvard University Press.

Newell, A., & Simon, H. (1972). *Human problem solving.* Englewood Cliffs, NJ: Prentice-Hall.

Norman, D. (1988). *The psychology of everyday things.* New York, NY: Basic Books.

Schvaneveldt, R. W. (1991). *Pathfinder associative networks: Studies in knowledge organization.* Norwood, NJ: Ablex.

Stanton, N. A. (2004). Psychology of task analysis today. In D. Diaper & N. S. Stanton (Eds.), *The handbook of task analysis for human-computer interaction* (pp. 569–584). Mahwah, NJ: Lawrence Erlbaum Associates.

Stanton, N. A. (2006). Hierarchical task analysis: Developments, applications, and extensions, Applied Ergonomics, 37, 55–79.

Taylor, F. W. (1911). *The principles of scientific management.* New York, NY: Harper.

Tullis, T. S., Sperling, B. B., & Steinberg, A. L. (1986). The use of multidimensional scaling for facilities layout: An application to the design of the space station. In Proceedings of the Human Factors Society 30th Annual Meeting (pp. 38–42). Santa Monica, CA: Human Factors and Ergonomics Society.

12

Generalized Work Dimension Analysis

SHANAN GWALTNEY GIBSON

East Carolina University

Imagine that you are a business owner who has recently invested thousands of dollars (in both capital and labor) to conduct a series of job analyses that an industrial psychologist convinced you would provide utility and legal protection. Now imagine your frustration when you want to create a pay-grade structure using your new job analyses but are told by the same psychologist that your data actually do not allow for this. Imagine you want to validate a physical ability test for several of your production and warehouse jobs, but you cannot do that either because your jobs are not described using a common language that promotes cross-job comparisons. No wonder the very phrase *job analysis* carries such negative connotations for those in organizations.

Although you may find it occasionally desirable to have extremely detailed, job-specific data about a single job within your organization, the uses for this type of data can be limited. It is more frequently desirable to have job information that allows you to make comparisons across different job titles. Identifying similarities can allow you to develop selection tools, classify jobs for compensation purposes, or identify common training needs. The ability to compare the nature of work across varying job titles or occupational categories is the hallmark of generalized work dimension analysis. Standardized job analysis questionnaires that are applicable to numerous positions are now readily available, and movement toward instruments that provide cross-job relative ratings and allow comparison of task-dissimilar positions has occurred. This chapter examines generalized work dimension analysis—what it is, its overall purpose, its history, best practices in conducting, and examples of efforts that have used a generalized work dimension analysis approach to job analysis. The chapter concludes with areas for future research and additional resources for the reader.

WHAT IS GENERALIZED WORK DIMENSION ANALYSIS
AND WHAT PURPOSE DOES IT SERVE?

Examine several chapters on job analysis and you will find several different ways of classifying the various types of job analysis methodologies that exist (e.g., Brannick & Levine, 2002; Harvey, 1991; Wilson, 2007). Most frequently, generalized work dimension analysis is classified in a manner that focuses on its moderate specificity and its worker-orientation as opposed to those job analytic techniques that use a task-based metric and adopt a job-oriented philosophy.

Although rich in detailed information, task- or job-oriented job analysis techniques are often considered lacking in many respects. Because the emphasis is necessarily on the job, the relativistic ratings that are typically made with most task-oriented instruments are not suitable for the purpose of comparing task-dissimilar positions that may have other underlying similarities or requirements. Generalized work dimension analysis (sometimes referred to as *worker-oriented*) philosophies of job analysis have been proposed as a means of addressing these limitations and facilitating cross-job comparisons. According to McCormick, Jeanneret, and Mecham (1972), the basic premise of work dimension analysis is that there exists a relatively small set of general work behaviors that apply to all jobs and that one can describe all jobs in terms of how much of each of these general work behaviors are involved. Generalized work dimension philosophies of job analysis seek to describe jobs on a common set of descriptors that are more behaviorally and technologically abstract than are tasks (McCormick, 1976).

As pointed out by Harvey (1991), the distinction between what is a generalized work dimension and what is a task-oriented statement is not always readily apparent. Theoretically, for each worker-oriented statement in an inventory, one should be able to identify several discrete tasks that demonstrate the performance of the worker-oriented item. However, some worker-oriented items are considerably more specific than others and might be equally well considered task-oriented items.

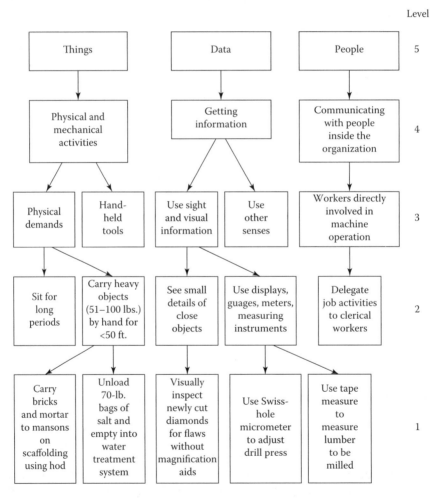

"Does the job require you to..."

Figure 12.1 Depiction of various levels of job-analytic data that might be collected. Level 4 is consistent with what is referred to as a dimension. However, job analytic instruments typically include items that are more characteristic of Level 2 and/or Level 3, which are then statistically aggregated.

Unfortunately, no standard exists against which one may use to decide if the statements are too broad or holistic to be rated accurately.

Figure 12.1 depicts the various types of job analytic information that might be collected as part of a job analysis. Level 1 is characteristic of tasks that are associated with job-oriented/task-based job analysis methodologies, whereas Levels 3 and 4 are more characteristic of what is typically considered a generalized work dimension. However, dimensions are not typically rated at this level and more decomposed ratings are typically given of items that are written at Level 2 and aggregated as appropriate. This particular figure was developed as part of the ongoing efforts of the U.S. Social Security Administration (2009) to replace the *Dictionary of Occupational Titles,* as discussed later in this chapter.

In sum, generalized work dimension analysis is characterized by its use of moderate specificity items that describe a job in terms of the worker activities and allow for cross-job comparisons. Although not always easily differentiated from their more "micro" task-based peers based on simple wording, their ability to facilitate comparisons of different jobs is their hallmark.

HISTORY OF GENERALIZED WORK DIMENSION ANALYSIS

Wilson (2007, p. 229) categorized methods of job analysis by "schools of thought." He described generalized work dimension analysis as developing from a desire to create a common metric that could be applied to all jobs and would address the high costs and inefficiencies associated with existing task-based methodologies. This generalist approach aimed to provide a language for describing all jobs, revealing commonalities typically obscured by using the functional language of the worker.

Ernest J. McCormick and his students created the first generalized work dimension job analysis instrument. Building upon their Worker Activity Profile (McCormick, Cunningham, & Gordon, 1967), the Position Analysis Questionnaire (PAQ; McCormick, Jeanneret, & Mecham, 1972) sought to characterize work situations and human behaviors in terms of a group of "common denominators" (McCormick et al., 1967; p. 417) that represented the underlying structure of all work.

In the years since the PAQ was introduced, several other taxonomies of generalized work dimensions have been developed for job analytic purposes and currently several worker-oriented instruments exist for you to choose among. As each has its proponents and detractors, what follows next is simply an overview of many popular generalized work dimension instruments. Although some may argue that I have included instruments that focus on dimensions that are not strictly worker-oriented in the sense of job activities, each of these instruments was designed with the intent of being cross-job relative.

GENERALIZED WORK DIMENSION ANALYSIS INSTRUMENTS

The Position Analysis Questionnaire

One of the most widely used and researched worker-oriented instruments is the PAQ (McCormick et al., 1972). The PAQ consists of 194 items or job elements that fall into the following categories:

1. Information input (i.e., where and how workers get the information they use for the job)
2. Mental processes (i.e., the reasoning, planning, and decision making involved in the job)
3. Work output (i.e., the physical activities the worker performs and the tools or devises used)
4. Relationships with other persons
5. Job context (i.e., physical and social environment in which the work is performed)

The individual items provide for checking an item if it applies or for rating it on an appropriate rating scale, such as importance, time, or difficulty.

Although the average item reliability of the PAQ has been found to be .80, it has been noted that the questionnaire has some faults. The first issue centers on the domain of jobs appropriately covered; the PAQ appears most suited for use with blue-collar or manufacturing jobs, as opposed to professional, managerial, or some technical jobs (Cornelius, Schmidt, & Carron, 1984; DeNisi, Cornelius, & Blencoe, 1987). Secondly, because the PAQ does not describe specific work activities, behavioral similarities in the jobs may mask genuine task differences between them. For example, a police officer's profile is quite similar to a housewife's (according to Arvey & Begalla, 1975) because of the troubleshooting and emergency-handling orientation required by both positions.

Additionally, readability is an issue with the PAQ; it requires a college-graduate reading level in order to comprehend the items (Ash & Edgell, 1975). Hence, the PAQ should not be given to job incumbents or supervisors unless their jobs require educational levels substantially higher than 10–12 years. Finally, the PAQ has been criticized on the basis of the potential for it to be used in such a matter that cross-job comparisons are untenable due to the potential for raters making within-job-relative ratings (Harvey, 1991). Instructions for making ratings may encourage respondents to rate importance only with respect to the job's other applicable tasks and not in relationship to other jobs.

The Job Element Inventory

In an effort to make a worker-oriented instrument more widely applicable, the Job Element Inventory (JEI; Cornelius & Hakel, 1978) was developed. By editing the PAQ, a 153-item questionnaire using only one rating scale (relative time spent) was developed. This new questionnaire had a much lower reading level than the PAQ (10th grade), and factor analytic studies indicated that the JEI shared a very similar factor structure with the PAQ (Harvey & Lozada-Larsen, 1988). Although an obvious improvement in regard to reading level, the other criticisms of the PAQ still stand for the JEI.

The Fleishman Job Analysis Survey

Focusing largely on the theory that the best way to analyze a job is in terms of the personal characteristics and traits required of the incumbents, the Fleishman Job Analysis Survey was developed (F-JAS; Fleishman, 1975, 1992; Fleishman & Reilly, 1992). Its objective is to describe jobs in terms of the abilities required to perform the jobs. The abilities-requirements taxonomy is intended to reflect the fewest independent ability categories that describe performance in the widest variety of tasks.

Areas covered by the F-JAS taxonomy include 21 cognitive abilities (e.g., problem sensitivity, flexibility of closure, spatial organization, selective attention); 10 psychomotor abilities (e.g., arm-hand steadiness, multilimb coordination, response orientation); 9 physical abilities (e.g., dynamic flexibility gross body equilibrium, explosive strength); and 12 sensory abilities (e.g., glare sensitivity, auditory attention, sound localization; Fleishman, Costanza, & Marshall-Mies, 1999). Because the items to be rated are quite broad and holistic in nature, rating scales that define each ability, distinguish it from related abilities, and provide examples of tasks that require different levels of the ability are used to facilitate understanding and reliable ratings among the respondents as well as provide a framework allowing comparisons across different jobs.

Evidence of the F-JAS's comprehensiveness has been reported in several studies. Hogan, Ogden, and Fleishman (1979) found that 80% of the tasks performed by warehouse workers could be assigned to one or more of the ability categories. Similar findings have been reported in regard to U.S. Army officers (Mumford, Yarkin-Levin, Korotkin, Wallis, & Marshall-Mies, 1985), Federal Bureau of Investigation special agents (Cooper, Schemmer, Jennings, & Korotkin, 1983), and New York City police officers (Landy, 1988). Reports of reliabilities for the instrument vary across the positions and types of respondents used, from .66 (Romashko, Hahn, & Brumbach, 1976) to in excess of .90 when using 15 or more judges for several different jobs (Hogan, Ogden, & Fleishman, 1978).

Despite the large amount of research that has been conducted on the F-JAS, it has its critics. Some industrial-organizational psychologists that believe that inferred human characteristics are not the correct unit of measurement for job analysis because they are not directly observed and require broad inferences. In fact, some might argue that the F-JAS is not a job analysis instrument at all; however, I have chosen to include it here because it is unequivocally a worker-oriented instrument that would allow comparisons across jobs.

The Occupation Analysis Inventory

Aimed at developing a taxonomy of job dimensions that were relevant to occupational education and guidance with an emphasis on career exploration, the Occupation Analysis Inventory (OAI; Cunningham, Boese, Neeb, & Pass, 1983) was built based upon the methodology of McCormick et al. (1972). However, unlike the PAQ, the OAI specifically included items that fell into both the worker-oriented and the job-oriented domains. In addition, the OAI's emphasis on occupational decision making resulted in a significantly larger taxonomy of job dimensions that were typically more specific than those found in the previously mentioned PAQ.

According to Cunningham et al. (1983), the development of the OAI represented the first effort to statistically derive a set of job dimensions that included both functional/technological content and general work activities and was still generally applicable across job titles. Despite this, the overall length and literacy requirements of the OAI hampered its potential use in projects involving diverse respondents and/or large job samples.

The General Work Inventory

The General Work Inventory (GWI; Ballentine & Cunningham, 1981; Cunningham & Ballentine, 1982) was based upon selected factors from the OAI but is significantly shorter, written at a less technical level, and is intended for use by any literate individual with an appropriate degree of job familiarity. As with the OAI, the GWI includes a combination of worker- and work-oriented dimensions and seeks to provide a reliable and valid job analytic method that is both cross-job relative and able to provide the more detailed information typically associated with task-based analyses.

In research using enlisted members of the U.S. Air Force, the GWI taxonomy of work dimensions was found to be both reliable and valid; however, the portions of the instrument based upon more worker-oriented dimensions performed stronger than those sections containing mostly job-oriented dimensions (Cunningham, Wimpee, & Ballentine, 1990). The GWI is believed to have potential for not only describing jobs, but also classifying them, providing training requirements, and aiding the person-job matching efforts of organizations such as the military.

The Common Metric Questionnaire

A relatively new job analysis instrument that seeks to address the dilemmas faced by some of the other worker-oriented instruments, while still enabling the comparison of task dissimilar jobs with a broad worker-oriented philosophy, is the Common Metric Questionnaire (CMQ; Harvey, 1990). CMQ ratings are made on absolute scales that describe how much of a work activity is present such that meaningful cross-job comparisons are possible.

The CMQ was written using an eighth-grade reading level and includes items that are equally appropriate to executive, professional, and managerial positions as to nonmanagerial, manufacturing, or blue-collar jobs (Harvey, 1993). Consistent with Harvey's (1991) prescription that job analysis be concerned with the measurement of observables, the CMQ was designed such that it includes items that are more behaviorally abstract than some tasks but less behaviorally abstract than some of the other, more holistic instruments that include unobservable job and person characteristics.

The CMQ collects over 2,000 item-level ratings that can be combined to describe jobs in terms of 80 work dimensions (a holistic component), or when greater specificity is required, the decomposed item-level data can be used (Harvey, 1993). Despite the numerous ratings composing each of the 80 work dimensions, median coefficient alpha for the scales is .86 (Harvey, 1993).

O*NET

Perhaps the most ambitious addition to the spectrum of worker-oriented job analysis instruments is the U.S. Department of Labor's Occupational Information Network (O*NET). This instrument is currently being used by the U.S. government for the purpose of collecting data on thousands of positions as part of an ongoing research endeavor aimed at replacing the *Dictionary of Occupational Titles* (DOT; U.S. Department of Labor, 1991).

Because of the highly specific, task-level data collected and presented in the DOT, it was determined that the DOT was unsuitable for current needs. Namely, it could not be used for rapid assessment of the skills, knowledge, and other characteristics required by a job family or for showing how skill levels in one job may relate to those of other jobs (Dunnette, 1999). It was decided that the new occupational information system, the O*NET, would need to possess occupational information allowing for cross-job comparisons, information that includes the tasks and behaviors involved in the work and the conditions under which the work is performed, the requirements imposed on incumbents, and attributes arising from experience (e.g., skills and expertise) as well as the more basic individual attributes (including abilities, interests, and personality characteristics). The General Work Activities scale of the O*NET is most akin to a general work dimensions job analysis instrument; however, its items are written at a significantly more abstract level than are the other instruments presented here and its holistic nature has been criticized by researchers (Gibson, Harvey, & Harris, 2007; Harvey, 2009). Chapter 16, this volume provides detailed information about O*NET.

CONDUCTING A GENERALIZED WORK DIMENSION JOB ANALYSIS

The steps involved in conducting a generalized work dimension are, quite frankly, the same steps that should be followed in any job analytic endeavor (Brannick & Levine, 2002). What follows is a summary of the steps in this process along with areas for consideration and best practices associated with each step as they relate to using a generalized work dimension approach.

Step 1: Identify the Purpose of Your Job Analysis

With all due respect to Lewis Carroll, if you do not know where you are going with your job analysis, any road will *not* get you there! The information an organization requires dictates the appropriate job analysis methodology. Although multipurpose job analyses do exist, most job analyses are conducted for a single purpose (Wilson, 2007). If your needs include highly detailed task information, within-job relative data, generalized work dimension analysis will not meet your needs.

Step 2: Match Your Purpose to the Appropriate Job Analysis Methodology

As stated above, generalized work dimension analysis may not be the appropriate choice for all personnel management activities. However, for activities that are based on identifying work activity commonalities among jobs, a moderate-specificity tool may be ideal. Selection, job evaluation, and job classification have all been successfully addressed via this approach to job analysis (Brannick & Levine, 2002).

Step 3: Select Your General Work Dimension Analysis Tool

In some instances, an inductive approach to job analysis is perfectly appropriate; however, because the purposes that are associated with generalized work dimension analysis are typically oriented toward identifying commonalities, inductive approaches are not frequently seen. As described earlier, there are several empirically derived (deductive) worker-oriented instruments from which you can choose. However, within these options, all are not comparably useful depending on your purpose. For example, a major criticism of the PAQ and several of its derivatives is a reliance on within-job relative rating scales. As noted by Harvey (1991), even if one begins with cross-job relative dimensions, rating these on a metric that is within-job relative will result in a situation where meaningful comparisons cannot be made. For example, while the work dimension decision making may very likely occur across many jobs, asking someone to rate its occurrence on a relative time spent (RTS) scale would yield ratings that could not be compared across jobs; however, if one used an absolute frequency scale (e.g., yearly, monthly, daily), a common metric would be obtained that allowed for comparisons across diverse occupations. Hence, an important consideration in choosing your job analytic tool is not only its level of specificity, but also its rating scale metric.

A second consideration in choosing one's job analysis instrument is the content domain covered. For example, the Professional and Managerial Position Questionnaire (PMPQ; Mitchell & McCormick, 1979) and the Management Position Description Questionnaire (MPDQ; Tornow & Pinto, 1976) are both directed toward groups of upper-level occupations. Similarly, Lozada-Larsen (1988) created a moderate-specificity instrument that uses a cross-job relative rating scale; her Executive Checklist would be entirely appropriate if one were interested in jobs of this nature. However, if you require information on jobs found across numerous organizational levels, you should consider instruments that are appropriate to all manner of jobs and are written at reading levels that allow for diverse individuals to provide job-related ratings.

Step 4: Choose Your Subject Matter Experts

This is an area where you also have several options; subject matter experts frequently include expert job analysts, job incumbents, and job supervisors. Unfortunately, not all subject matter experts appear to provide comparable job data. Because impression management behaviors are aimed at having others view us in a particular light (Schlenker, 1980), completing job analysis instruments provides an opportunity for incumbents and supervisors to provide information that may cause others to view them as highly competent, industrious, and perhaps even deserving of a raise. Unlike incumbents and supervisors, job analysis experts have nothing to gain by engaging in self-presentation strategies that will distort job ratings; their "outsider" status protects them from social pressures toward rating conformity and they typically have been specifically trained in the job analysis process. However, expert analysts may be quite expensive; it is a time-intensive endeavor for them to fully familiarize themselves with a given job, much less several jobs within an organization.

Several studies have provided support for the contention that expert job analysts are the preferred source of job data. For example, Jeanneret, Borman, Kubisiak, and Hanson (1999) reported a disturbing tendency for incumbents to produce higher mean ratings than job analysts on the O*NET's Generalized Work Activity scales (at times by a full point on the 0–7 scale), noting that "essentially, incumbents are reporting that their job is more complex than is seen by the analysts" and that "significant, and in some cases substantial, differences in means are evident between the two sources" (p. 125). Similarly Gibson, Harvey, and Harris (2007) replicated the disturbing findings of Jeanneret et al. regarding the tendency of incumbents to overrate their jobs and raised further questions based on the troubling levels of disagreement seen among raters of the O*NET's Generalized Work Activities scale.

In general, although it may be tempting to use job-naïve raters or rely exclusively on job incumbents in your process, this simply is not advised. In all instances, the courts have indicated that job analysts should be individuals who have sufficient experience with a job to be well familiarized with all of the tasks and duties associated with it (Thompson & Thompson, 1982). Consistent with Harvey (1991), it is recommended that a job analysis use as many well-informed sources as possible.

Step 5: Conduct Your Job Analysis

There are several different ways a subject matter expert may gain job-relevant information; direct observation, interviews, and completion of questionnaires are most common. If an expert job analyst is involved and must become familiarized with the job via contact with incumbents, it is important that an open environment of trust is created. By explaining the purpose of the analysis, what types of information are sought, assuring confidentiality of responses, and answering any questions incumbents may have, you hope to create a nonthreatening and participative situation (Brannick & Levine, 2002). If you have chosen an existing deductive job analytic tool, subject matter experts should complete the associated questionnaires (either in paper-and-pencil format or in a computerized version), providing answers to questions such as whether or not specific worker behaviors are part of the job in question, how frequently the activity occurs, and the criticality of errors.

In many ways, if you have done due diligence in delineating your purpose, carefully choosing your instrument, and identifying your subject matter experts, actually conducting the job analysis is the easy part. The instruments described earlier are all structured, provide specific instructions, and have prescribed scoring mechanisms.

Step 6: Utilization and Evaluation

Utilization of your job analysis should flow directly from your planned purpose for it. However, one of the appealing attributes of a general work dimensions analysis is that the data collected is a series of generic work descriptors that can be used in multiple arenas based upon the analysis conducted. Differing types of analysis or levels of aggregation may allow an organization to group similar jobs together for purposes of job evaluation, classification, development of selection tools, or common training requirements.

Unfortunately, as with many personnel management tools, the rush to use the outputs of a major project frequently overshadows the need to examine the quality of the data collected. However, the importance of considering the reliability and validity of job analysis data cannot be overstated because legal requirements for it have been mandated (Uniform Guidelines for Employee Selection Procedures, 1978). At a minimum, consideration of interrater reliability, interrater agreement, and completeness of information are all warranted (Dierdorff & Wilson, 2003; Harvey & Wilson, 2000; Morgeson & Campion, 2000).

GENERALIZED WORK DIMENSION ANALYSIS IN ACTION

Because of the popularity of several generalized work dimension instruments, numerous examples of their use in organizations exist. This section reviews distinctive uses of two existing instruments (the classic PAQ and the newer CMQ) and provides an overview of an ongoing project within the U.S. Social Security Administration that, while not making use of any single generalized work dimension instrument, is oriented toward a generalized work dimension analysis model.

For many organizations, a major issue is the validation of selection tests, and if possible, the generalization of said validity to similar jobs within the organization. Unfortunately, one roadblock in this process has been the historical reliance on task-based job analytic techniques that conceal legitimate job similarities and therefore preclude test transportability. Hoffman (1999) reports on a project that developed a test transportability procedure using the PAQ to validate a physical abilities test that had previously been validated for the American Gas Association using a job-oriented task analysis. Unfortunately, the earlier validation yielded very narrow test transportability as there was very limited task overlap among the positions. However, the true question of interest was not how much task overlap existed between jobs, but rather how similar were the job's physical requirements. Hoffman used PAQ dimensions as the basis for creating job families and evaluating job similarity. Selected PAQ attributes were used to estimate the physical demands requirements of jobs and job families. In his discussion of findings, Hoffman concludes that the PAQ can assist with construct-related validation through both its job attribute scores and the Job Component Validity model embedded within the PAQ.

Although a relative newcomer compared with the PAQ, the CMQ has been used extensively for both classification, selection, and job evaluation purposes. As an example of its usefulness, Harvey (1993) reported its ability to not only effectively predict compensation levels, but also to create a job pay grade structure. This was accomplished via a policy capturing point factor approach whereby job related data was actually regressed on external pay data obtained from the Occupational Employment Statistics provided by the U.S. Department of Labor. Because the CMQ maintains a large computerized database of completed job analyses, it was possible to sample a large group of jobs (208 titles), classify them based upon their similarities on general work dimension profiles, and then use this information to develop the pay-predicting equation, which was benchmarked for external equity. Additionally, it was possible for Harvey to group said job titles into a nine-level pay grade system based upon empirically derived factors; pay systems such as this are likely to exhibit large degrees of both defensibility and utility. For further details on this particular use of the CMQ, see Chapter 25, this volume.

In 2008, the U.S. Social Security Administration created the Occupational Information Development Advisory Panel under the Federal Advisory Committee Act. The panel's purpose is to assist the Social Security Administration in its efforts to replace the *Dictionary of Occupational Titles* with a new occupational information system (OIS) as part of its disability determination processes. Although preliminary in its activities, the panel published its content model and classification recommendation for the Social Security Administration Occupational Information System (U.S. Social Security Administration, 2009). The panel's activities and recommendations clearly represent efforts to identify an appropriate generalized work dimension analysis instrument for Social Security Administration uses, and in the absence of one, create a taxonomy of generalized work dimensions to serve as the basis of the Social Security Administration's new occupational information system.

Given that any OIS adopted or created by Social Security Administration must comprehensively cover all work in the economy as it is done by workers, initial efforts focused on examining existing empirically developed generalized work dimension analysis instruments. Eleven work taxonomies were identified and considered by the Work Taxonomy and Classification Subcommittee; however, it was determined that no single taxonomy provided the breadth of coverage that would be required by the U.S. Social Security Administration (2009). In response to this shortcoming, a rather novel approach was undertaken by the subcommittee whereby all of the general work dimensions from all of the identified taxonomies were combined, duplicates removed, and a single taxonomy including worker-oriented, contextual, and some work-oriented dimensions was ultimately recommended as the starting point from which item writing and pilot testing should proceed. The work dimensions are identified not only by their source(s) but also by whether or not they would likely fall into data, people, things, or other contextual factors. Table 12.1 provides the generalized work dimension list resulting from this effort. Readers may note that dimensions are present that represent all of the instruments reviewed earlier in this chapter.

The outcomes of the U.S. Social Security Administration job analytic project are still unknown. If, however, they do proceed with the development of a new generalized work dimension analysis instrument that encompasses the vast majority of job dimensions already empirically established as part of other instruments, the outcome would be nothing short of historic. No other entity outside of the federal government likely has the resources to create an instrument that is applicable to the entire world of work, includes metrics that are cross-job relative, and measures work at a level of specificity that is useful for numerous decision-making arenas. Readers are encouraged to follow the Social Security Administration's progress as it proceeds with its endeavor to create an occupational information system that effectively replaces the *Dictionary of Occupational Titles* for purposes of disability adjudication.

UNANSWERED QUESTION IN GENERALIZED WORK DIMENSION ANALYSIS

As befits any area of scientific practice, there is still much to debate in the arena of generalized work dimension analysis. One issue which has recently seen a significant consideration within the field is the question of quality in job analysis (Dierdorff & Wilson, 2003; Harvey & Wilson, 2000; Morgeson & Campion, 2000). Because differences exist with regard to the reliability seen in instruments of differing specificity (with most generalized work dimensions being considered moderately specific) and among different types of raters, further research is needed to identify contextual and/or individual factors that may be at work.

Consistent with this, the need for additional research related to job analysis validity is also required. Dierdorff and Wilson (2003, p. 644) noted that "There are at least two explanations for the lack of validity studies for job analysis data. One is that they have not been done and hence cannot be reported. The other is that they have been done and the results are not good so they reside in a file drawer, unreported in the hope that it is an artifact." Neither of these are desirable states of being and underscore the need for investigations of both reliability and validity as they apply to job analysis in general and the accuracy of generalized work dimension analysis in particular.

A final issue for future research focuses on the absence of a single, widely accepted taxonomy of generalized work dimensions that applies to all work in the economy. As the work by the U.S. Social Security Administration's Work Taxonomy and Classification Subcommittee made evident, although there is significant overlap among the various popular instruments, only a few efforts have been made to comprehensively cover all aspects of work, using a moderate-specificity instrument, including cross-job relative rating scales, written at a reading level that enables subject matter experts of all types to successfully complete, with adequate reliability and accuracy for an organization's purposes. It is a tall order, but one that is worth pursuing.

Table 12.1   Recommended Work Taxonomy Dimensions for the U.S. Social Security Administration

Taxonomic Source	D/O/P/T	Consolidation of Dimensions Sorted by D/O/P/T
CMQ	D	Managerial decision making: acquire/start/sell businesses
CMQ	D	Managerial decision making: financial
CMQ	D	Managerial decision making: prods/services, higher impact
CMQ	D	Managerial decision making: products/services, lower impact
CMQ	D	Managerial decision making: strategic planning, entire organization
CMQ	D	Take info, orders, interview
CMQ*	D	Info/decide/resolve: high level
CMQ*	D	Info/decide/resolve: lower level
CMQ*	D	Info/decide/resolve: mid level
CMQ*	D	Info/decide/resolve: professional/technical
CMQ*, O*NET*, SOC*	D	Computer language use/programming
CMQ, O*NET*, SOC*	D	Technical/scientific/computers-machines
GWI	D	Stockkeeping/bookkeeping
O*NET	D	Estimating the quantifiable characteristics of products, events, or information
O*NET	D	Evaluating information to determine compliance with standards
O*NET	D	Judging the qualities of objects, services, or people
O*NET, SOC*	D	Scheduling work and activities
O*NET	D	Updating and using relevant knowledge
OAI	D	Biological testing/inspection activities
OAI	D	Environmental planning and maintenance
OAI	D	Technical planning and drawing
OAI, GWI, O*NET, SOC*	D	Utilization and processing of numerical data
OAI, WAP*, SOC*	D	Routine clerical and administrative activities
PAQ	D	Attentive/discriminating work demands
PCTAQ*	D	Individual/job-related decision making
PCTAQ*, O*NET*	D	Individual/job-related planning
CMQ	O	Language use/foreign
CMQ, SOC*	O	Safety/damage to others
PAQ	O	Variable vs. regular work schedule
PMPQ	O	Relevant experience
PMPQ	O	Special training
PMPQ*	O	Educational requirements
WAP	O	Hourly pay vs. salary
WAP	O	Job-related/required apparel
GWI, OAP	O-Cognitive	Spatial/object perception and tracking
GWI, PAQ	O-Cognitive	Perceptual interpretation

continued

Table 12.1 Recommended Work Taxonomy Dimensions for the U.S. Social Security Administration (Continued)

Taxonomic Source	D/O/P/T	Consolidation of Dimensions Sorted by D/O/P/T
O*NET	O-Cognitive	Thinking creatively
PAQ, OAI	O-Cognitive	Environmental awareness
PCTAQ	O-Cognitive	General cognitive information processing
PCTAQ*	O-Cognitive	Cognitive attention, focus
CMQ, SOC*	O-Context	Enforcement/demanding conditions
CMQ, PAQ	O-Context	Hazardous/unpleasant work environment
GWI	O-Context	Regulated/standardized work
MPDQ	O-Context	Autonomy of action
MPDQ	O-Context	Complexity and stress
WAP	O-Context	Job security vs. performance-dependent income
WAP	O-Context	Outdoor work
PMPQ, PCTAQ*	O-Interpersonal	Interpersonal activities
OAI	O-Physical	Activities related to coordination
OAI	O-Physical	Activities related to balance
OTHER	O-Physical	Activities related to hand function
OTHER	O-Physical	Activities related to manual materials handling
OTHER	O-Physical	Activities related to position tolerance
WAP	O-Physical	Activities related to mobility/movement
OTHER	O-Sensory	Activities requiring olfactory senses
OTHER	O-Sensory	Activities requiring tactile senses
PAQ	O-Sensory	Visual input from devices/materials
PAQ	O-Sensory	Visual input from distal sources
PCTAQ	O-Sensory	Audio attention
CMQ	P	Entertain
CMQ	P	Managerial decision making: POM/HR higher level
CMQ	P	Managerial decision making: POM/HR, lower level
CMQ	P	MDM: implementing
CMQ ,SOC*	P	Treatment/therapy
CMQ*	P	Communication: press/media
CMQ*	P	Communication: public/customers/clients
CMQ*	P	Communication: regulators, government
CMQ*, SOC*	P	Communication: students/children/civic
CMQ*, SOC*	P	delegating
CMQ*, SOC*	P	Resolving conflicts
CMQ*	P	supervision: sales/service
CMQ*, OAI*, WAP*, PAQ*, MDPQ*	P	Supervision: lower level

continued

Table 12.1   Recommended Work Taxonomy Dimensions for the U.S. Social Security Administration   (Continued)

Taxonomic Source	D/O/P/T	Consolidation of Dimensions Sorted by D/O/P/T
CMQ*, OAI*, WAP*, PAQ*, MDPQ*, SOC*	P	Supervision: middle level
CMQ*, WAP*, PAQ*, PMPQ*, SOC*	P	Communication: mid-level exchange information
CMQ, O*NET*, SOC*	P	Negotiation
CMQ, WAP*, O*NET*, SOC*	P	Persuade/sell
MDQ, SOC*	P	Advanced consulting
O*NET	P	Developing and building teams
OAI	P	Communication: verbal
OAI,SOC*	P	Improving/monitoring the physical performance, capability and adjustment of others
OAI, PMPQ, SOC*	P	Instructing
OTHER	P	Communication: written
OTHER	P	Project management
CMQ, SOC*	T	Operating office equipment
CMQ, SOC*	T	Operating powered tools/equipment
CMQ, OAI*, O*NET*	T	Operating heavy/offroad vehicles
CMQ, OAP*, WAP*, PAQ*,SOC*	T	Operating processing/moving machines
CMQ, OAP*, WAP*, PAQ*	T	Operating stationary machines
GWI, SOC*	T	Activities related to performing arts
O*NET, SOC*	T	Activities related to inspecting equipment, structures, or materials
OAI, SOC*	T	Activities related to assembly/fabrication
OAI, SOC*	T	Activities related to food preparation/processing
OAI, SOC*	T	Activities related to physical science and technology
OAI, GWI, SOC*	T	Activities related to visual aesthetics
OAI, GWI, O*NET	T	Activities related to electrical/electronic repair, maintenance
OAI, GWI, O*NET, SOC*	T	Activities related to mechanical repair, maintenance
OAI, GWI, OAP, SOC*	T	Activities related to botany/plants
OAI, GWI, OAP, SOC*	T	Activities related to building/repairing structures
OAI, GWI, WAP, SOC*	T	Activities related to working with animals
PAQ	T	Activities related to handling/manipulating and use of finger-controlled devices
SOC	T	Activities related to personal care and service occupations

Dimensions were sorted according to whether they best fell into the category of data, other, people, or things (D/O/P/T).

ADDITIONAL RESOURCES

As a relatively new development within the job analytic field, generalized work dimension analysis has made great strides in a rather short time. In a chapter directed toward end users and practitioners, I obviously could not have done justice to the large field of research that has established these instruments and tested their usefulness within both the empirical and organizational realms. As such, readers are encouraged to consider several other sources of information when considering a generalized work activity job analysis.

To truly understand what is meant by generalized work dimension analysis, one should read the seminal works in the field. The work of Ernest J. McCormick and his students not only established this methodology but also created the framework for its appropriate use. Job analyses characterized by Wilson (2007) as belonging to the functionalist, generalist, and taxonomist schools of thought are also frequently associated with worker-oriented instruments. In particular, works by Edward L. Levine, P. Richard Jeannerette, Joseph W. Cunningham, and Robert J. Harvey have all either resulted in a generalized work dimension instrument or popularized an existing one.

The Internet provides interested parties with access to much information related to generalized work dimension analysis and job analysis in general. In particular, web sites for the various worker-oriented instruments provide a wealth of information, including research monographs and white papers. Web sites that provide overviews of job analysis instruments and a journal devoted to the measurement of work are all resources that readers may find helpful:

- The PAQ: http://www.paq.com
- The CMQ: http://www.pstc.com
- The O*NET: http://online.onetcenter.org
- The Job Analysis Network: http://www.job-analysis.net/G012.htm
- *Ergometrika*: http://www.ergometrika.org

REFERENCES

Arvey, R. D., & Begalla, M. E. (1975). Analyzing the homemaker job using the Position Analysis Questionnaire (PAQ). *Journal of Applied Psychology, 60,* 513–517.

Ash, R. A., & Edgell, S. L. (1975). A note on the readability of the Position Analysis Questionnaire (PAQ). *Journal of Applied Psychology, 60,* 765–766.

Ballentine, R. D., & Cunningham, J. W. (1981, October). Development of the General Work Inventory. In *Proceedings of the 23rd Annual Conference of the Military Testing Association* (pp. 125–133). Arlington, VA.

Brannick, M. T., & Levine, E. L. (2002). *Job analysis: Methods, research and applications for human resource management in the new millennium.* Thousand Oaks, CA: Sage Publications.

Cooper, M. A., Schemmer, F. M., Jennings, M., & Korotkin, A. L. (1983). *Developing selection standards for Federal Bureau of Investigation special agents.* Bethesda, MD: Advanced Research Resources Organization.

Cornelius, E. T., & Hakel, M. D. (1978). *A study to develop an improved enlisted performance evaluation system for the U.S. Coast Guard.* Washington, DC: Department of Transportation, United States Coast Guard.

Cornelius, E. T., Schmidt, F. L., & Carron, T. J. (1984). Job classification approaches and the implementation of validity generalization results. *Personnel Psychology, 37,* 247–226.

Cunningham, J. W., & Ballentine, R. D. (1982). *The general work inventory.* Raleigh, NC: Authors.

Cunningham, J. W., Boese, R. R., Neeb, R. W., & Pass, J. J. (1983). Systematically derived work dimensions: Factor analyses of the Occupation Analysis Inventory. *Journal of Applied Psychology, 68*(2), 232–251.

Cunningham, J. W., Wimpee, W. E., & Ballentine, R. D. (1990). Some general dimensions of work among U.S. Air Force enlisted occupations. *Military Psychology, 2*(1), 33–45.

DeNisi, A. S., Cornelius, E. T., III, & Blencoe, A. G. (1987). Further investigation of common knowledge effects on job analysis ratings. *Journal of Applied Psychology, 72,* 262–268.

Dierdorff, E., & Wilson, M. (2003). A meta-analysis of job analysis reliability. *Journal of Applied Psychology, 88*(4), 635–646.

Dunnette, M. D. (1999). Introduction. In N. G. Peterson, M. D. Mumford, W. C. Borman, P. R. Jeanneret, & E. A. Fleishman (Eds.), *An occupational information system for the 21st century: The development of O*NET.* Washington, DC: American Psychological Association.

Fleishman, E. A. (1975). Toward a taxonomy of human performance. *American Psychologist, 30,* 1127–1149.

Fleishman, E. A. (1992). *Rating scale booklet: F-JAS.* Palo Alto, CA: Consulting Psychologists Press.

Fleishman, E. A., & Reilly, M. E. (1992). *Administrator's guide: F-JAS.* Palo Alto, CA: Consulting Psychologists Press.

Fleishman, E. A., Costanza, D. P., & Marshall-Mies, J. (1999). Abilities. In N. G. Peterson, M. D. Mumford, W. C. Borman, P. R. Jeanneret, & E. A. Fleishman (Eds.), *An occupational information system for the 21st century: The development of the O*Net* (pp. 175–198). Washington, DC: American Psychological Association.

Gibson, S., Harvey, R., & Harris, M. (2007). Holistic versus decomposed ratings of general dimensions of work activity. *Management Research News, 10*(30), 724–734.

Harvey, R. J. (1990). *The common-metric job questionnaire for the analysis and evaluation of jobs (field test version 1.12).* San Antonio, TX: The Psychological Corporation.

Harvey, R. J. (1991). Job analysis. In M. D. Dunnette & L. M. Hough (Eds.), *Handbook of industrial and organizational psychology* (2nd ed., Vol. 2, pp. 71–163). Palo Alto, CA: Consulting Psychologists Press.

Harvey, R. J. (1993). *Research monograph: Development of the Common-Metric Questionnaire (CMQ).* Blacksburg, VA: Personnel Systems and Technologies Corporation & Virginia Polytechnic Institute & State University.

Harvey, R. J. (2009, April 17). *The O*NET: Do too abstract titles + unverifiable holistic ratings + questionable raters + low agreement + inadequate sampling + aggregation bias = (a) validity, (b) reliability, (c) utility, or (d) none of the above?* Background paper prepared for the meeting of the Review of the Occupational Information Network (O*NET) panel conducted by the National Academies of Science, Washington, DC.

Harvey, R. J., & Lozada-Larsen, S. R. (1988). Influence of amount of job descriptive information on job analysis rating accuracy. *Journal of Applied Psychology, 73,* 457–461.

Harvey, R. J., & Wilson, M. (2000). Yes Virginia, there is an objective reality in job analysis. *Journal of Organizational Behavior, 21*(7), 829–854.

Hoffman, C. (1999). Generalizing physical ability test validity: A case study using test transportability, validity generalization, and construct-related validation evidence. *Personnel Psychology, 52*(4), 1019–1041.

Hogan, J. C., Ogden, G. D., & Fleishman, E. A. (1978). *Assessing the physical requirements in selected benchmark jobs (Final Rep. 3012).* Bethesda, MD: Advanced Research Resources Organization.

Hogan, J. C., Ogden, G. D., & Fleishman, E. A. (1979). *The development and validation of tests for the order selector job at Certified Grocers of California, Ltd.* Bethesda, MD: Advanced Research Resources Organization.

Jeanneret, P. R., Borman, W. J., Kubisiak, U. C., & Hanson, M. A. (1999). Generalized work activities. In N. G. Peterson, M. D. Mumford, W. C. Borman, P. R. Jeanneret, & E. A. Fleishman (Eds.), *An occupational information system for the 21st century: The development of the O*Net* (pp. 105–125). Washington, DC: American Psychological Association.

Landy, F. J. (1988). Selection procedure development and usage. In S. Gael (Ed.), *The job analysis handbook for business, government, and industry* (pp. 271–287). New York, NY: John Wiley & Sons.

Lozada-Larsen, S. R. (1988). *Going beyond criticism: Management work theory and research.* Unpublished doctoral dissertation, Rice University.

McCormick, E. J. (1976). Job and task analysis. In M. D. Dunnette (Ed.), *Handbook of industrial and organizational psychology.* Washington, DC: APA Books.

McCormick, E. J., Cunningham, J. W., & Godon, G. (1967). Job dimensions based on factorial analyses of worker-oriented job variables. *Personnel Psychology, 20,* 417–430.

McCormick, E. J., Jeanneret, P. R., & Mecham, R. C. (1972). A Study of job characteristics and job dimensions as based on the Position Analysis Questionnaire (PAQ). *Journal of Applied Psychology Monograph, 56*(4), 347–368.

Mitchell, J. L., & McCormick, E. J. (1979). *Development of the PMPQ. A structured job analysis questionnaire for the study of professional and managerial positions. PMPQ Report No.1.* Lafayette, IN: Occupational Research Center, Department of Psychological Studies, Purdue University.

Morgeson, F., & Campion, M. (2000). Accuracy in job analysis: Toward an inference-based model. *Journal of Organizational Behavior, 21*(7), 819–827.

Mumford, M. D., Yarkin-Levin, K., Korotkin, A. C., Wallis, M. R., & Marshall-Mies, J. (1985). *Characteristics relevant to performance as an Army leader: Knowledge, skills, abilities, and other characteristics, and general skills.* Alexandria, VA: U.S. Army Research Institute for the Behavioral and Social Sciences.

Romashko, T., Hahn, C. P., & Brumbach, G. B. (1976). *The prototype development of a job-related physical testing for Philadelphia policeman selection.* Washington, DC: American Institutes for Research.

Schlenker, B. R. (1980). *Impression management: The self-concept, social identity, and interpersonal relations.* Monterey, CA: Brooks/Cole.

Thompson, D. E., & Thompson, T. A. (1982). Court standards for job analysis in test validation. *Personnel Psychology, 35,* 865–874.

Tornow, W. W., & Pinto, P. R. (1976). The development of a managerial job taxonomy: A system for describing, classifying, and evaluating executive positions. *Journal of Applied Psychology, 61*(4), 410–418.

Uniform guidelines on employee selection procedures. (1978). *Federal Register, 43,* 38290–38315.

U.S. Department of Labor. (1991). *Dictionary of occupational titles (4th ed., rev.).* Washington, DC: U.S. Government Printing Office.

U.S. Social Security Administration. (2009). *Content model and classification recommendations for the Social Security Administration Occupational Information System.* Retrieved from http://www.ssa.gov/oidap/Documents/Occupational Information Development Advisory Panel.pdf

Wilson, M. (2007). A history of job analysis. In L. L. Koppes (Ed.), *Historical perspectives in industrial and organizational psychology* (pp. 219–241). Mahway, NJ: Lawrence Erlbaum Associates.

13

The Fleishman Job Analysis Survey
Development, Validation, and Applications

JAY J. CAUGHRON
Radford University

MICHAEL D. MUMFORD
The University of Oklahoma

EDWIN A. FLEISHMAN
Management Research Institute

Job analysis serves many purposes for researchers and organizations, including selection and assessment of personnel, comparing jobs, setting salaries, job redesign, and advancing understanding of the knowledge, skills, abilities, and other attributes that are associated with job performance and other work-related outcomes. Jobs are typically described as an assortment of tasks that must be performed in order to successfully fulfill the duties and functions assigned to a given position in an organization (Cascio & Aguinis, 2005; Gael, 1983). Individuals who perform the same tasks and duties to fulfill similar functions are said to hold the same job which can be described by a single job analysis (Gael, 1983; McCormick, 1979). Because jobs vary from organization to organization with regard to the exact tasks that are performed by job incumbents and because some jobs can involve a wide variety of tasks, it becomes difficult for job analysts to provide a comprehensive, yet concise, description of jobs based on task statements that transfers across locations, organizations, and time (Fleishman & Mumford, 1988).

The Fleishman Job Analysis Survey (F-JAS) is a deductive technique that focuses primarily on the description of the abilities a worker needs to successfully complete job relevant tasks. F-JAS was designed to provide a descriptive taxonomy of human abilities for as many tasks as possible with the fewest possible descriptors (Fleishman, 1967; Fleishman & Quaintance, 1984). Stated another way, the purpose of F-JAS was to provide a highly generalizable technique that would enable job analysts to describe the ability requirements workers would need to meet in order to perform a given job.

Job analysis data can be collected and described at the level of jobs, tasks, behaviors, or abilities. The purpose for which the job analysis is being conducted should be the predominant factor a job analyst considers when deciding which level is the most appropriate. The F-JAS sets human abilities required for task performance as the level of analysis, given that abilities are defined as relatively enduring traits of an individual (Fleishman & Mumford, 1988). This is called the *ability requirements approach* (Fleishman & Quaintance, 1984). The logic of this approach is that the abilities required for the performance of a given job actually vary little compared with the specific tasks required for job performance. Tasks vary in the degree to which they require a given set of human abilities for successful completion. Thus, having information linking the human abilities necessary for adequate task performance will provide organizations and job analysts with important information for subsequent decision making, measure development, and a host of other human resource functions such as comparing jobs or setting performance standards (Fleishman & Mumford, 1988).

The F-JAS is a job analysis system that consists of three primary parts. The first part is Fleishman's ability taxonomy. This taxonomy defines a wide variety of human abilities that have been derived from an extensive set of studies regarding human performance on a wide variety of work-related tasks (Fleishman & Mumford, 1988, 1991; Fleishman & Quaintance, 1984). The second part consists of the scales used to link jobs and tasks to the human abilities required to perform them. These scales consist of 7-point rating scales with task anchored markers. They were developed and refined in a line of research conducted by Fleishman and colleagues (Fleishman & Mumford, 1988; Fleishman & Quaintance, 1984; Theologus & Fleishman, 1973; Theologus, Romashko, & Fleishman, 1973) such that good reliability can be obtained by individuals who are familiar with the jobs they are rating but who do not need expert knowledge of Fleishman's ability taxonomy. As with other job analysis procedures, the individuals who use the task anchored rating scales to rate jobs are referred to as subject matter experts (SMEs). Subject matter experts are individuals who have knowledge about the job, usually because they currently perform the job (incumbents) or because they supervise or train others who perform the job. Third, and finally, is the rating procedure used when actually gathering data at a given organization.

This procedure, developed by Fleishman and colleagues, has proven useful in a wide variety of real-world settings (Cooper, Schemmer, Gebhardt, Marshall-Mies, & Fleishman, 1982; Inn, Schulman, Ogden, & Sample, 1982; Jones & Prien, 1978; Myers, Gebhardt, Price, & Fleishman, 1981; Myers, Jennings, & Fleishman, 1981; Romashko, Brumback, Fleishman, & Hahn, 1974; Romashko, Hahn, & Brumback, 1976; Zedeck, 1975). In the following sections of this chapter, we discuss how the F-JAS was developed, the evidence currently available that demonstrates the validity of the F-JAS, and some practical issues involved in using the F-JAS system.

DEVELOPMENT

Originally called the Manual for the Ability Requirement Scales, the F-JAS has a long history of research and application in a wide variety of settings (Fleishman, 1975). Cunningham et al. (1996) and Landy (1988) called the F-JAS the most rigorously developed and widely used of the ability requirement inventories and brought attention to the multiyear research programs that proceeded it. Wilson (2007) pointed out that Fleishman's taxonomy of human attributes, developed through programmatic experimental–correlational studies over many years, is the only generally accepted common language to describe human attributes and represents a significant advance in the understanding of the demands that work places on workers.

Work on the F-JAS began with the development of a comprehensive taxonomy by which human abilities could be defined and categorized. Fleishman and colleagues have produced an extensive line of research developing the abilities taxonomy, with the goal of maintaining parsimony while providing for the widest range of flexibility regarding the description of task performance (e.g., Cooper et al., 1982; Fleishman, 1975, 1982; Fleishman & Hogan, 1978; Fleishman & Mumford, 1988; Fleishman & Quaintance, 1984; Theologus & Fleishman, 1973; Theologus et al., 1973). The result of this effort is a set of 52 cognitive, psychomotor, physical, and sensory-perceptual abilities. Further research has led to the addition of 21 social/interpersonal abilities (Fleishman, 2000).

SCALES

The original list of 52 human abilities was developed over a multiyear program of research, involving an extensive review of factor analytic studies of human abilities, as well as experimental examination of abilities required for performance on specific tasks (e.g., Fleishman, 1964, 1972b, 1975; Fleishman & Mumford, 1991; Fleishman & Quaintance, 1984; Theologus & Fleishman, 1973; Theologus et al., 1973). Generally speaking, this line of research consisted of subjects performing a series of tasks designed to tap a certain aspect of human ability. Correlations between performance on these tasks was examined, and an ability category was hypothesized to underlie the performance of tasks that were significantly correlated with each other. Factor analytic studies were then used to confirm that items' testing performance on a hypothesized ability were grouped together. Once an ability category was suggested by these factor analytic studies, further hypotheses were generated in order to refine the definition and boundaries of that particular ability category (Fleishman & Quaintance, 1984). This iterative process of examining literature to identify abilities, factor analytic studies to identify and explore abilities, and further specification of ability definitions by experimental research is the same basic pattern that has been followed for the majority of empirically derived ability categories in the F-JAS (Fleishman & Quaintance, 1984).

To be more specific, the starting point for developing a list of cognitive and perceptual abilities, and their definitions, was the work of Guilford, Carroll, and French (Carroll, 1976; Guilford, 1967; French, 1951; French, Ekstrom, & Price, 1963). The psychomotor and physical abilities lists were developed from early factor analytic studies by Fleishman and colleagues (Fleishman, 1954, 1958, 1962, 1964, 1972b; Fleishman & Quaintance, 1984). In this line of research, factor analysis was used to identify discrete abilities. Following this step, experimental studies were conducted in which specific tasks were selected to test hypotheses about how these abilities were related to each other and to fine tune the ability definitions (Fleishman, 1978; Fleishman & Quaintance). The end result of this extensive line of research was a set of 52 cognitive sensory-perceptual, psychomotor, and physical abilities.

Recent additions to the F-JAS include 21 task-anchored rating scales spanning the social/interpersonal requirements of jobs. These scales were developed and evaluated following procedures used in the development of such scales for other domains of human abilities (Gilbert & Fleishman, 1992a). Examples of jobs that may have special requirements for social/interpersonal abilities include jobs emphasizing team work, sales, interfacing with the public, or working with supervisory/management personnel. Specific examples of jobs requiring social/interpersonal abilities include flight attendant, counselor, and retail salesclerks. However, the particular social ability required depends on the particular job tasks performed in the different jobs. This brought the total number of abilities covered by the F-JAS taxonomy to 73. Table 13.1 presents selected examples of these abilities and their definitions.

Interrater reliabilities and standard deviations for the social/interpersonal abilities from multiple raters have been found to be in the ranges of those found for cognitive, physical, psychomotor, and other ability domains (e.g., Fleishman, Cobb, & Spendolini, 1976; Friedman, Fleishman, & Fletcher, 1992; Gilbert & Fleishman, 1992b). *The Handbook of Human Abilities* (Fleishman & Reilly, 1992), which provides expanded definitions of each ability in the taxonomy and more detailed descriptions of jobs, was revised and enlarged to include parallel treatment for the social/interpersonal domain. These volumes include descriptions of the kinds of assessments and specific assessment instruments (and their publishers) that can be used to assess the various social/interpersonal abilities in this domain of human performance (Fleishman, Reiter-Palmon, & Reilly, 2011).

Table 13.1   Example of the Abilities and Their Definitions Selected From Among 73 Abilities Measured by the Fleishman Job Analysis Survey

Abilities	Examples
Cognitive Abilities	
Verbal abilities	
Written comprehension	The ability to read and understand information and ideas presented in writing.
Idea generation and reasoning	
Fluency of ideas	This is the ability to come up with a number of ideas about a given topic. It concerns the number of ideas produced rather than the quality, correctness, or creativity of the ideas.
Quantitative abilities	
Mathematical reasoning	The ability to understand and organize a problem and then to select a mathematical method or formula to solve the problem.
Memory	
Memorization	The ability to remember information such as words, numbers, pictures, and procedures.
Perceptual abilities	
Speed of closure	This is the ability to quickly make sense of information that at first seems to be without meaning or organization. It involves the degree to which different pieces of information can be combined and organized into one meaningful pattern quickly. The material may be visual or auditory.
Spatial abilities	
Spatial orientation	This is the ability to tell where you are in relation to the location of some object, or to tell where the object is in relation to you. This ability allows you to keep oriented in a vehicle as it changes location and direction. It helps keep you from getting disoriented or lost as you move about in a new environment.
Attentiveness	
Selective attention	This is the ability to concentrate on a task without getting distracted. When distraction is present, it is not part of the task being done. This ability also involves concentrating while performing a boring task.
Psychomotor Abilities	
Fine manipulative abilities	
Arm-hand steadiness	The ability to keep the hand and arm steady while making an arm movement or while holding the arm and hand in one position.
Control movement abilities	
Multilimb coordination	The ability to coordinate movements of two or more limbs together while sitting, standing, or lying down. It does not involve performing the activities while the body is in motion.
Reaction time and speed abilities	
Reaction time	This is the ability to give *one* fast response to one signal (e.g., sound, light, picture) when it appears. This ability is concerned with the *speed* with which the movement can be *started* with the hand, foot, or other parts of the body.
Physical Abilities	
Physical strength abilities	
Static strength	The ability to exert maximum muscle force to lift, push, pull, or carry objects.
Endurance	
Stamina	This is the ability to exert one's self physically over a period of time without getting winded or out of breath.

Table 13.1   Example of the Abilities and Their Definitions Selected From Among 73 Abilities Measured by the Fleishman Job Analysis Survey (Continued)

Abilities	Examples
Flexibility, balance, and coordination	
Extent flexibility	This is the ability to bend, stretch, twist, or reach out with the body, arms, and/or legs.
Sensory Abilities	
Visual abilities	
Visual color discrimination	This is the capacity to match or discriminate between colors. This capacity also included detecting differences in color purity (saturation) and brightness (brilliance).
Auditory and speech abilities	
Speech recognition	This is the ability to hear and understand the speech of another person. It is an ability that requires some thought to accomplish.
Social Abilities	
Dependability	This is the ability to be reliable and responsible to others. This ability involves being disciplined, conscientious, and trustworthy in fulfilling obligations and tasks expected by others.
Assertiveness	This is the ability to express one's beliefs and opinions boldly and actively. This ability involves speaking up and taking initiative when working with others.

Source: Adapted from Fleishman, E. A., *Fleishman Job Analysis Survey*, Management Research Institute, Potomac, MD, 1992; Fleishman, E. A., *Fleishman Job Analysis Survey (F-JAS-2): Social-Interpersonal Scales*, Management Research Institute, Potomac, MD, 1996. With permission.

The next major phase in the development of F-JAS was the generation of specific task examples to provide anchors of low, medium, and high levels for each of the 73 ability rating scales. This involved two phases. The first was the generation, by different subject groups, of large numbers of task examples of low, medium, and high levels for each separate ability. Large groups of subjects were assembled and presented, in turn, with a blank 7-point rating scales containing only the ability definition and some distinctions from other abilities with which it might be confused. Subjects were instructed to generate familiar tasks that they felt would fall at the low, medium, and high levels for each ability described. Thousands of such examples were generated. After editing and elimination of duplications, reduced sets of these tasks were administered to other groups of raters, who were asked to assign scale values from 1 to 7 to each task.

Data analyses were conducted to determine the means and standard deviations of these values as a basis for selecting and placing task anchors on each ability requirements rating scale. For each of the 73 ability rating scales, it was possible to select three tasks (one at the high end, one in the medium range, and one at the low end of the scale) with low standard deviations (indicating high agreement and reliability between raters on task placement) for each of the 73 abilities in the F-JAS. Another criterion for selection of task anchors was that they be generally familiar ones.

APPLICATIONS

Whether the job is to be analyzed at the job, behavior, or task level, a description appropriate to the desired level of analysis must be obtained. Ideally, there will be pre-existing job description materials available. However, if appropriate descriptive information is not available, all is not lost. The job analyst can generate these materials and supply them to the raters. Alternatively, it has been found that subject matter experts with extensive expertise regarding the job of interest can still achieve acceptable levels of interrater reliability without these descriptive materials. The steps for using the F-JAS are summarized in Figure 13.1.

```
┌─────────────────────────────────────────┐
│ Step 1: Review job description materials and │
│        the F-JAS Administrator's Guide.   │
└─────────────────────────────────────────┘

┌─────────────────────────────────────────┐
│ Step 2: Select incumbents, supervisors, or │
│              trainers (SMEs).             │
└─────────────────────────────────────────┘

┌─────────────────────────────────────────┐
│ Step 3: Have the SMEs rate jobs (or tasks) │
│      using the F-JAS ability rating scales. │
└─────────────────────────────────────────┘

┌─────────────────────────────────────────┐
│ Step 4: Determine mean ability scores     │
│      obtained from the SMEs for each job. │
└─────────────────────────────────────────┘
```

Figure 13.1   Action steps for using the Fleishman Job Analysis Survey.

Step 1: Review Job Description Materials and the F-JAS Administrators' Guide

It is important that the descriptive materials to be used by the raters be reviewed before being used. If the analysis is to be done at the task level, these materials should be in the form of a task listing from a thorough job analysis of the job to be rated (Fleishman & Mumford, 1988). It is recommended that a panel of 5–10 incumbents and their supervisors are asked to specifically note any tasks that are missing from the list. Along with suggesting new tasks to be added to the list, these reviewers are also asked to clarify any ambiguous task statements in order to enhance clarity. This is usually an iterative process terminated once the SMEs agree that 90% of the tasks for a given job are listed in a clear, unambiguous fashion (Fleishman & Mumford, 1988).

The F-JAS is often used at the job level of analysis as well. When it is being used in this way, descriptive materials should describe the job at the job level. Alternatively, SMEs with extensive expertise regarding the job of interest should be chosen and asked to make judgments at the job level rather than the task level. SMEs with extensive experience in dealing with a given job usually do not have difficulty making job level ratings and demonstrate high levels of interrater agreement, even in the absence of job description materials.

Step 2: Select Incumbents, Supervisors, and/or Trainers (SMEs)

After obtaining the appropriate descriptive information, the next step in using the F-JAS can begin. The job analyst must select a number of subject matter experts to serve as raters. Some debate exists about the qualities that an SME should possess, with most researchers arguing that SMEs with the highest level of expertise should be chosen (Landy & Vasey, 1991).

It is also important to consider the number of SMEs that should be selected for an F-JAS job analysis. Research on the reliability that can be expected from using the F-JAS technique for describing jobs and tasks suggests that 20 SMEs be used as raters. However, a minimum of 10–15 may be used to still obtain interrater reliabilities in the .70–.80 range for most scales (Fleishman & Mumford, 1991; Fleishman & Quaintance, 1984). It should be noted that sufficient levels of interrater reliability can be obtained with smaller numbers of SMEs, provided that they have a high level of expertise regarding the job of interest. However, using too few raters can result in a lack of stability and reliability in ratings.

Step 3: Have the SMEs Rate Jobs (or Tasks) Using the F-JAS Ability Rating Scales

Once a comprehensive task listing is developed and SMEs have been selected to serve as raters, they can begin the process of rating each task. The raters should be given instructions for how to make their ratings using the 7-point ability scales in the F-JAS booklet. The raters are then asked to rate each job (or task) for each ability, first making a judgment as to whether a given ability is required at all for a given job and secondly, if it is required, to what extent the ability is required for job/task performance (Fleishman & Mumford, 1988; Fleishman & Quaintance, 1984).

As can be seen in Figure 13.2, the rating scales provide the definition of each ability and compare the ability to other similar abilities. This comparison is made so that SMEs can make sure to accurately isolate and rate the ability of interest rather than a closely related ability. Additionally, specific examples of tasks are used as anchors on the 7-point rating scale to help the SMEs calibrate their ratings and help ensure adequate levels of interrater reliability. Some training regarding the use of the F-JAS ability rating scales may be needed. However, given the straightforward nature and simplicity of this technique and the F-JAS materials, any training requirements for using the rating scales are normally quite low.

Step 4: Determine Mean Ability Scores Obtained From the SMEs for Each Job

Once the ratings have been collected from the raters, the job analyst should determine whether or not suitable levels of reliability between raters have been obtained. Typically, this is performed after checking interrater reliability to ensure that the findings from the ability ratings are stable and reliable. If some items have low reliability coefficients, a consensus meeting may need to be convened in order to reach suitable levels of agreement or determine why the reliability is low. It is often the case that differences at various job sites can account for a lack of interrater reliability (e.g., shelf height at one location is higher than at another location). It may also be necessary to drop certain raters if they are frequently in disagreement with the other raters.

Application Summary

In summary, an F-JAS job analysis consists of four steps. First, a review of appropriate and thorough job description materials must be undertaken. If no such materials exist, job analysts can offset this limitation by using SMEs with high levels of expertise regarding the job. Second, the job analysts must select the SMEs for the project. It is important to consider the limitations of a given job analysis effort when choosing SMEs (e.g., the number of SMEs available and the quality of existing job descriptive materials). Third, SMEs should use the F-JAS ability rating scales to rate jobs (or tasks) according to the required level of each ability required for acceptable levels of performance. Fourth, and finally, the mean ability scores for each job should be calculated. Any items demonstrating low levels of interrater reliability must be addressed before calculating the mean rating for each ability in each job.

USES OF THE F-JAS

Information gathered from using the F-JAS can be used for many purposes typically served by job analysis. Selection of employees based on the degree to which their abilities match those required by a given job is one such use. Although the use of job samples is likely to be more predictive of performance for specific jobs, developing selection procedures based on abilities has some advantages. In some instances, applicants could experience an injury performing a job sample if they do not possess the requisite level of strength, flexibility, or other attributes required for performance (Fleishman & Mumford, 1988). Additionally, using ability requirement assessments are likely to prove less expensive than the development and assessment of a job sample. It is also likely that a generic assessment system, such as an ability requirement evaluation, would prove more useful than job specific techniques in some situations. For example, when a large volume of applicants are being assessed for multiple different job openings a generic ability assessment is likely to be highly efficient for matching applicants to positions.

Written comprehension: This is the ability to read and understand written sentences and paragraphs.

How written comprehension is different from other abilities		
Written comprehension: Involves reading and understanding written words and sentences	vs.	*Oral comprehension:* Involves listening to and understanding words and sentences spoken by others
		Oral expression and written expression: Involves speaking or writing words and sentences so others will understand

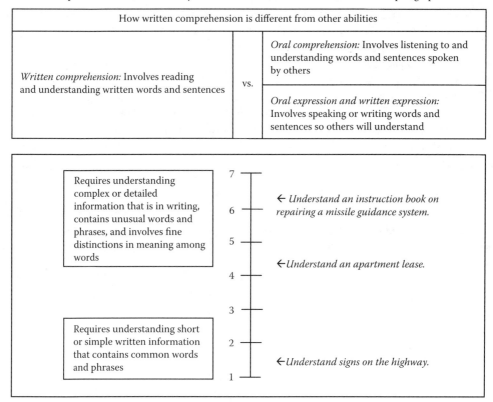

Dependability: This is the ability to be reliable and responsible to others. This ability involves being disciplined, conscientious, and trustworthy in fulfilling obligations and tasks expected by others.

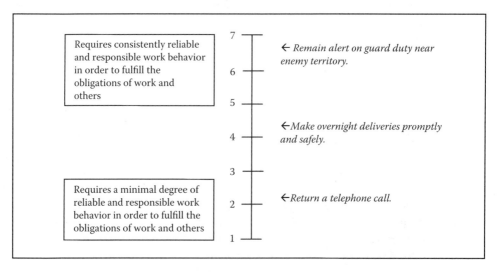

Figure 13.2 Example F-JAS rating scales. (Adapted from Fleishman, E. A., *Fleishman Job Analysis Survey*, Management Research Institute, Potomac, MD, 1992; Fleishman, E. A., *Fleishman Job Analysis Survey (F-JAS-2): Social-Interpersonal Scales*, Management Research Institute, Potomac, MD, 1996. With permission.)

F-JAS has been used successfully for a wide variety of job analysis and test development projects regarding several different job types in both the public and private sectors (Fleishman & Mumford, 1988). Examples in the private sector include jobs in manufacturing, communication, electric power, research and development, supermarkets, warehouse operations, oil refineries, timber and paper manufacturing, and pipeline companies. Public agencies include many city, county, and, state governments, as well as those in the federal government. Examples of using the F-JAS on the local level include defining the ability requirements for law enforcement officers, correctional officers, and firefighters. On a larger scale, the U.S. government has used the F-JAS on projects for the Army Research Institute, the Navy Medical Research Institute, Aberdeen Proving Ground, Logistics Management Research Institute, Navy Research and Development Center, National Aeronautics and Space Administration, the Air Force Personnel Laboratory, Nuclear Regulatory Agency, and Marine Corps.

The assessment of ability requirements using Fleishman's ability taxonomy has been used to develop several ability tests with acceptable if not high levels of criterion-related validity (Cooper, Schemmer, Gebhardt, Marshall-Mies, & Fleishman, 1982; Hogan, Ogden, & Fleishman, 1979; Myers, Gebhardt, Price, & Fleishman, 1981). Additionally, this technique is particularly well suited for developing job-related measures in which job relevance can be easily justified given the procedure for linking abilities to critical job tasks (Fleishman & Mumford, 1988).

Performance standards can also be set using this ability profiling technique. Typically this is done by evaluating tasks for a variety of jobs. Performance standards can then be set by selecting those tasks that are rated highest for a given ability scale across a wide variety of jobs. These tasks can then be used to assess the extent to which an individual possesses a given ability. Should an individual be able to successfully complete the task, it can be assumed that they are also able to perform tasks that require lower levels of the same ability. This can be a cost-effective, objective approach to assessing whether or not an individual possesses the requisite level of ability to perform a given set of job tasks (Fleishman & Mumford, 1988; Myers, Gebhardt, & Fleishman, 1979).

Another use of ability requirements, as measured by F-JAS, has been to assist in setting medical standards, where various disease symptomologies and their severity have been linked to the different ability requirements of jobs, particularly their physical ability requirements. Occupational medical specialists were able to link disqualifying symptomologies in relation to different levels of job requirements. These linkages, together with appropriate diagnostic measures, have been combined into physician's manuals for guidance in setting medical standards for job assignment, remediation, or disqualification, using these methods for jobs with varying levels of ability requirements (Gebhardt & Schemmer, 1985; Hogan, Ogden, & Fleishman, 1979). This kind of information is valuable in assessing whether workers can return to their jobs or can do other jobs (Fleishman, 2003). A summary of these developments was presented as part of a Social Security Administration report (Fleishman, 1999).

Using ability requirements in the F-JAS also presents professionals and researchers with a common metric whereby jobs can be classified, categorized, and compared (Fleishman & Mumford, 1988). As such, F-JAS was used as one method for describing and classifying jobs for the U.S. Department of Labor's Occupational Information Network (O*NET; Fleishman, Costanza, & Marshall-Mies, 1999). Situations calling for the classification of a wide variety of jobs can use ability requirements as a means of clustering jobs together that have similar requirements (Fleishman & Mumford, 1988; Fleishman & Quaintance, 1984; Hogan, Ogden, & Fleishman, 1978).

Given that large databases linking jobs to their requisite abilities, such as O*NET, are now being created and maintained, individuals can be matched to jobs based on their abilities (Converse, Oswald, Gillespie, Field, & Bizot, 2004). This has the potential to benefit many job seekers, especially those seeking employment for the first time. Being able to match individuals to jobs that they find challenging but also have the ability to perform has the potential to not only increase worker satisfaction, but also to reduce the cost of finding qualified individuals and replacing those who do not have the abilities needed to successfully perform a job.

The F-JAS has been used in the context of defining ability requirements of jobs and for use in personnel decisions about selection, job transfers, promotions, and assignment to training. It has also been used to examine a variety of different issues, including the relationship of the ability requirements and factors affecting human performance. One such study showed that objectively determined error rates, made while performing job tasks in nuclear power plants, were significantly related to the numbers, types, and levels of the different human abilities required, as measured by F-JAS. These findings, which were replicated in U.S. Army job tasks, have important implications for job redesign as well as for personnel assignment and training (Buffardi, Fleishman, Morath, & McCarthy, 2000).

Another recent innovation in the use of F-JAS includes its use for projecting future abilities to perform jobs not yet in existence. One example of this is the use of F-JAS in the selection of air traffic control personnel for a new system currently under development in Germany. By administering the F-JAS to SMEs knowledgeable about the operational, functional, and equipment changes unfolding with the development of the new air traffic control system, the investigators were able to compare the future and current job ability requirements. This enabled them to make recommendations about personnel selection and assignments taking into account changing ability requirements (Eissfeldt, 2002). A similar project in Europe also made use of the F-JAS in a project to help phase in the use of a new army tank. There was a need to examine the extent to which the ability requirements of tank personnel would or would not change when the shift was made to the new tank. Using information gathered from experts knowledgeable about the two types of tanks, the F-JAS was used to make a determination about tank personnel ability requirements and to provide guidance in designing a simulator that would better match the abilities required by personnel assigned to the new tanks.

VALIDATION

The use of the F-JAS has resulted in the development of several lines of validity evidence. Various conceptualizations of validity have been suggested by social science researchers. Here we will employ Messick's (1995) taxonomy of validity because it provides a comprehensive, well-organized way in which to discuss the available evidence for the validity of the F-JAS system.

Content Validity

Evidence for a measure's content validity provides information bearing on a measure's content relevance, representativeness, and technical quality (Lennon, 1956; Messick, 1989). One aspect of content validity is a measure's comprehensiveness. Evidence bearing on this point can be garnered by examining the systematic manner in which F-JAS was developed (as described previously). However, empirical studies have also provided evidence for the comprehensiveness of F-JAS (Fleishman & Mumford, 1991). For example, Hogan et al. (1979) conducted a series of panel discussions regarding jobs performed by warehouse workers. This discussion found that 80% of the tasks warehouse workers perform can be categorized into one or more of the ability categories provided by the F-JAS. Similarly, Landy (1988) found that 81.1% of job activities performed by New York City police officers could be assigned to one of the F-JAS ability categories.

Another important aspect of content validity is parsimony. A measure that obtains a high level of comprehensiveness, but does so merely by including a large and unwieldy number of dimensions, is far less useful than one that obtains the same level of coverage with fewer dimensions. However, the hallmark of a parsimonious measurement system is not that it has few categories, but rather that it has just the right number of categories to sufficiently describe the domain at hand. In this case, it is important to determine if the 73 ability categories of the F-JAS can be used to adequately and accurately describe what people do for a wide variety of jobs. Empirical evidence seems to suggest that it does. The F-JAS has been used to study professional jobs (e.g., attorneys, accountants, industrial managers), manual labor jobs (e.g., mechanics, equipment operators), and military jobs (e.g., pilots, cryptographers, maintenance personnel; Cooper et al., 1987; Fleishman & Friedman, 1990; Hogan, Ogden, & Fleishman, 1978). In each case, SMEs used a minimum of 80% of the F-JAS ability categories when describing the abilities required for successful job performance (as indicated by receiving at least 4 points on a 7-point scale).

Structural Validity

Data providing evidence for the fact that the scoring of a measure is consistent with the structure of the construct domain is structural validity. In the case of the F-JAS, this involves providing evidence for the fact that the ability rating scales have been organized into distinct, mutually exclusive categories, and that those categories are an accurate reflection of what is known about human abilities (Fleishman & Mumford, 1991).

One source of validity evidence bearing on structural validity is the reliability with which raters are able to classify tasks according to the abilities required to perform the task. If independent raters agree that a certain set of abilities are required for the performance of a task, it suggests that their classification of tasks using an ability requirement taxonomy, such as that provided by the F-JAS, is not random. This is one line of evidence suggesting that the structure of the domain is accurately reflected in the measurement tool used to assess the domain. Several studies have been conducted examining the use of ability requirements scales in describing tasks. Data compiled by Fleishman and Mumford (1988, 1991) indicate that interclass reliability coefficients range from .77 to .97 with an average reliability of .87.

Another line of research providing evidence of structural validity are studies demonstrating that the assignments made within categories result in a coherent, meaningful, and interpretable set of relationships between tasks. Studies by Hogan, Ogden, and Fleishman (1978) of grocery warehouse workers and Cooper et al. (1987) of military personnel demonstrated that raters using F-JAS requirement scales did group tasks into coherent, meaningful, and interpretable categories. The study of grocery warehouse workers, for example, raters grouped tasks such as "steer a tug close to merchandise to be selected" and "drive a tug slowly around corners" together under the control precision ability. Similarly, in the study by Cooper et al. (1987) of military personnel, tasks such as "troubleshooting" and "component alignment" were grouped together under the information ordering ability. Similar findings were found for a wide variety of U.S. Navy and Marine Corps jobs, ranging from cryptographers to pilots.

External Validity

Convergent and divergent validity evidence composes what Messick (1995) called *external validity,* which includes evidence indicating that a measure is correlated appropriately with other measures of related constructs. External validity also includes evidence that performance on the items presented on a measure accurately assesses an individual's ability to perform on a broader range of items that may be encountered in the real world. One line of evidence that addresses the internal and external validity issue stems from work done comparing the relationships between jobs categorized using the F-JAS. Studies regarding the classification of a wide variety of jobs using the F-JAS ability ratings for those jobs showed that jobs such as firefighters, police officers, and emergency medical technicians tend to have very similar patterns of ability ratings. These same jobs also show a very different pattern of ratings from teachers, attorneys, and clerks (Fleishman & Hogan, 1978; Hogan, Jennings, Ogden, & Fleishman, 1978; Weldon, 1983).

Further convergent and divergent validity evidence can be obtained by comparing F-JAS to other ability taxonomies. Alternative ability taxonomies include those developed by Drauden (1988), Lopez (1988), and Primoff and Eyde (1988). These taxonomies emphasize many of the same abilities as the F-JAS ability requirements scales, such as stamina, physical strength, visual acuity, hearing, memory, oral expression, written expression, numerical ability, and perceptual speed (Fleishman & Mumford, 1991). Given that these taxonomies were developed for different purposes than F-JAS and using different theoretical starting points, the fact that there is a high degree of overlap between them provides additional convergent validity evidence for the ability requirements taxonomy proposed for the F-JAS (Fleishman, 1972a, 1975, 1982; Fleishman & Mumford, 1988; Fleishman & Quaintance, 1984).

Substantive Validity

Substantive validity is evidence demonstrating that a measure is consistent with theoretical rationales for task performance, including evidence demonstrating that the measure can detect the psychological processes involved in task performance. Given that substantive validity evidence speaks to the nature of the relationship between a measurement tool and theoretically driven understanding of the domain in question, it is important to revisit the conceptual basis F-JAS was built upon.

In essence, the most fundamental assumption underlying the development of F-JAS requirement scales, as well as the job analysis system associated with it, is twofold: (a) the specific abilities required to perform the tasks associated with a job vary, and (b) the ability level an individual needs to successfully complete job tasks varies from task to task (Fleishman & Mumford, 1991). Further, the primary assumption with regard to measurement of abilities is that if performance on a cluster of tasks is highly correlated, then there is a common ability that drives performance of those tasks. Alternatively, when the performance of a group of tasks show little or no correlation, it is assumed that a collection of different abilities drive performance of those tasks rather than one common ability (Fleishman & Quaintance, 1984).

Given that Fleishman's ability taxonomy is being continually updated and revised, not all areas have received equal scrutiny. However, researchers have noted the systematic and exhaustive nature of work that has been put forth in the development of the taxonomy (Landy & Trumbo, 1980). In light of the strong theoretical and empirical research used in developing and refining the F-JAS, there is ample reason to conclude that the ability requirements approach to job analysis developed by Fleishman and colleagues demonstrates substantial levels of validity with regard to its theoretical underpinnings.

Generalizability

Generalizability evidence includes indicators that a measure's properties and interpretations hold across populations and settings. Evidence suggesting that Fleishman's ability requirements taxonomy is valid across different locations can be seen in studies by Zedeck (1975) and Hogan, Ogden, and Fleishman (1978). In Zedeck's study, installer-repairman tasks were rated for the cognitive and physical abilities required to perform them in various sites in Southern California. Cross-site agreement was found to be high in this study ($r = .68$). Similarly, Hogan et al. examined the cognitive, psychomotor, and physical abilities required for performance of warehouse worker tasks in three different cities. When the researchers compared the mean ratings from incumbents in each of the three cities, only one significant difference was found ($p < .05$). After further investigation, it was found that this difference could be accounted for by a difference in particular task demands at one of the locations. Specifically, the shelves at one location were higher, which required a greater level of extent flexibility (Fleishman & Mumford, 1988).

Consequential Validity

This is perhaps the most controversial form of validity evidence suggested by Messick (1995). However, given that job analysis results are often used to make real world decisions, it is relevant to consider the positive and negative outcomes likely to result from using the F-JAS. One important outcome that would be expected for the F-JAS is the prediction of future performance based on ability requirement ratings. Studies examining the relationship between judges' ratings of ability requirements and subsequent performance have been conducted (Fleishman, 1954; Fleishman & Quaintance, 1984; Theologus & Fleishman, 1973). In one study conducted by Fleishman (1954), mean ability ratings were used as predictors and task performance as the criterion in a multiple regression analysis using 27 tasks performed by 400 individuals. The results demonstrated that across multiple ability scales, highly significant relationships with performance were obtained (Fleishman & Quaintance, 1984).

AVAILABILITY OF F-JAS MATERIALS AND RESOURCES

If you decide to use the F-JAS for a job analysis project, there are several resources available to assist you. Definitions and behaviorally anchored scales for the currently up-to-date list of 73 abilities can be found in the *Administrator's Guide to the Fleishman Job Analysis Survey* (Fleishman & Reilly, 1995). Fleishman and Reilly (1992) also described measures that can be used to assess each of the 73 abilities in the *Handbook of Human Abilities: Definitions, Measurements, and Job Task Requirements*.

F-JAS materials, including the *Administrator's Guide to the Fleishman Job Analysis Survey* (Fleishman & Reilly, 1995), rating scale booklets, answer sheets, tally materials, and the *Handbook of Human Abilities: Definitions, Measurements, and Job Task Requirements* (Fleishman & Reilly, 1992), can be obtained from the Management Research Institute (11304 Spur Wheel Lane, Potomac, MD 20854; http://www.managementresearchinstitute.com). These materials have now been translated from English into several other languages (including French, German, Spanish, Romanian, and Danish versions) and distributed by publishers in their respective countries. The English version of the F-JAS has also become available for online administration for data collection, instant scoring, summarization, and reporting of results across rater groups through the Performance Assessment Network (http://www.pan.com).

FUTURE DIRECTIONS

A number of opportunities exist for future research regarding the ability requirements approach to job analysis. First and foremost, the development of new human abilities needs to be systematically examined as they are uncovered. Should the abilities have relevance for work-related issues, a definition and rating scale should be developed for each. Similarly, as new uses for the F-JAS ability scales arise, modifications will need to be made such that the extensive body of research findings with regard to human abilities can be brought to bear.

Advances in technology consistently prompt the development and refinement of existing tools; this is likely to be the case with F-JAS as well. As data gathering for job analysis is shaped by advances in technology, it is likely that F-JAS will need some updating and modification. It is difficult to predict the changes that can occur, but as organizations spread out geographically, it may become necessary for the F-JAS to be translated into multiple languages.

Similarly, as job analysts are required to gather data across multiple locations, sometimes across national and cultural boundaries, the procedures for using F-JAS to conduct a job analysis may change. It is also likely that as employers seek to hire employees from countries that lack well-developed educational systems, using abilities to select employees for training will become increasingly useful.

SUMMARY

In this chapter, we have examined a body of work that has culminated in the development and use of the F-JAS. The system, which is based on an extensive multiyear experimental and factor analytic research program, was concerned with the development and evaluation of a comprehensive taxonomy of human abilities. The chapter described the taxonomy and the measurement system that was developed to evaluate the extent to which the particular abilities were required for performance in a wide range of different jobs and work settings. Many practical applications of the F-JAS were described. Examples of extensive validation studies, using the F-JAS for different purposes in the workplace, were presented. Also described were a number of different types of applications of the F-JAS in a variety of work settings for a diverse set of jobs.

Additional sources of information and references to the work of many individuals, agencies, and companies that have used the F-JAS or carried out research related to its development were presented. The international aspects of F-JAS usage were mentioned, such as translations of the F-JAS into a number of different languages, including French, German, Romanian, Danish, and Spanish. The availability and the source of F-JAS in an online administration version were cited. These recent developments are important in the light of the increasing internationalization of U.S. companies and agencies.

ACKNOWLEDGEMENTS

The authors acknowledge the diligence and valuable assistance provided by Amanda Shipman and Kimberly Hester throughout the preparation of this chapter.

REFERENCES

Buffardi, L. C., Fleishman, E. A., Morath, R. A., & McCarthy, P. M. (2000). Relationships between ability requirements and human errors in job tasks. *Journal of Applied Psychology, 85,* 551–564.

Carroll, J. B. (1976). Psychometric tests as cognitive tasks: A new "structure of intellect." In L. Resnick (Ed.), *The nature of intelligence.* Hillsdale, NJ: Lawrence Erlbaum.

Cascio, W. F., & Aguinis, H. (2005). *Applied psychology in human resource management* (6th ed.). New York, NY: Prentice-Hall.

Converse, P. D., Oswald, F. L., Gillespie, M. A., Field, K. A., & Bizot, E. G. (2004). Matching individuals to occupations using abilities and the O*NET: Issues and an application in career guidance. *Personnel Psychology, 57,* 451–487.

Cooper, M. A., Schemmer, F. M., Fleishman, E. A., Yarkin-Levin, K., Harding, F. D., & McNelis, J. (1987). *Task analysis of Navy and Marine Corps occupations: Taxonomic basis for evaluating CW antidote/pretreatment drugs.* Bethesda, MD: Advanced Research Resources Organization.

Cooper, M. A., Schemmer, F. M., Gebhardt, D. L., Marshall-Mies, J., & Fleishman, E. A. (1982). *Development and validation of physical ability tests for jobs in the electric power industry.* Bethesda, MD: Advanced Research Resources Organization.

Cunningham, J. W., Powell, T. W., Wimpee, W. E., Wilson, M. A., & Ballentine, R. D. (1996). Ability-requirement factors for general job elements. *Military Psychology, 8,* 219–234.

Drauden, G. (1988). Task inventory analysis in industry and the public sector. In S. Gael (Ed.), *The job analysis handbook for business, industry, and government* (Vol. 2, pp. 1051–1071). New York, NY: Wiley.

Eissfeldt, H. (2002). Ability requirements for DFS controllers—Current and Future. In H. Eissfeldt, M. C. Heil, & D. Broach (Eds.), *Staffing the ATM system: The selection of air traffic controllers*. Burlington, VT: Ashgate Publishing Company.

Fleishman, E. A. (1954). Dimensional analysis of psychomotor abilities. *Journal of Experimental Psychology, 48,* 437–454.

Fleishman, E. A. (1958). Dimensional analysis of movement reactions. *Journal of Experimental Psychology, 55,* 438–453.

Fleishman, E. A. (1962). The description and prediction of perceptual-motor skill learning. In R. Glaser (Ed.), *Training research and education*. Pittsburgh, PA: University of Pittsburgh Press.

Fleishman, E. A. (1964). *The structure and measurement of physical fitness*. Englewood Cliffs, NJ: Prentice Hall.

Fleishman, E. A. (1967). Development of a behavior taxonomy for describing human tasks: A correlational-experimental approach. *Journal of Applied Psychology, 51,* 1–10.

Fleishman, E. A. (1972a). On the relation between abilities, learning, and human performance. *American Psychologist, 27,* 1017–1032.

Fleishman, E. A. (1972b). Structure and measurement of psychomotor abilities. In R. N. Singer (Ed.), *The psychomotor domain*. Philadelphia, PA: Lea & Febinger.

Fleishman, E. A. (1975). *Manual for the ability requirements scales*. Bethesda, MD: Management Research Institute.

Fleishman, E. A. (1978). Relating individual differences to the dimensions of human tasks. *Ergonomics, 21,* 1007–1019.

Fleishman, E. A. (1982). Systems for describing human tasks. *American Psychologist, 37,* 821–834.

Fleishman, E. A. (1992). *Fleishman Job Analysis Survey*. Potomac, MD: Management Research Institute.

Fleishman, E. A. (1996). *Fleishman Job analysis Survey (F-JAS-2): Social-interpersonal scales*. Potomac, MD: Management Research Institute.

Fleishman, E. A. (1999). Linking components of functional capacity domains with work requirements. In G. S. Wunderlick (Ed.), *Measuring functional capacity and work requirements: Summary of a workshop*. Washington, DC: Institute of Medicine, National Research Council.

Fleishman, E. A. (2003). Physical abilities in work settings. In R. Fernandis-Ballestaras (Ed.), *Encyclopedia of psychological assessment*. London, UK: Sage Publications.

Fleishman, E. A., Cobb, A. T., & Spendolini, M. J. (1976). *Development of ability requirement scales of Yellow Page jobs in the Bell System*. Potomac, MD: Management Research Institute.

Fleishman, E. A., Costanza, D. P., & Marshall-Mies, J. (1999). Abilities. In N. Peterson, M. Mumford, W. Borman, P. Jeanneret, & E. Fleishman (Eds.), *An occupational information system for the 21st century: The development of O*NET* (pp. 175–195). Washington, DC: American Psychological Association.

Fleishman, E. A., & Friedman, L. (1990). *Cognitive competencies related to management performance requirements in R&D organizations*. Fairfax, VA: George Mason University, Center for Behavioral and Cognitive Studies.

Fleishman, E. A., & Hogan, J. C. (1978). *Taxonomic method for assessing the physical requirements of jobs: the physical abilities analysis approach*. Bethesda, MD: Advances Research Resources Organization.

Fleishman, E. A., & Mumford, M. D. (1988). Ability requirement scales. In S. Gael (Ed.), *The Job Analysis Handbook for Business, Industry, and Government* (pp. 917–935). New York, NY: John Wiley & Sons.

Fleishman, E. A., & Mumford, M. D. (1991). Evaluating classifications of job behavior: A construct validation of the ability requirement scales. *Personnel Psychology, 44,* 733–575.

Fleishman, E. A., & Quaintance, M. K. (1984). *Taxonomies of human performance: The description of human tasks*. Potomac, MD: Management Research Institute.

Fleishman, E. A., & Reilly, M. E. (1992). *Handbook of human abilities: Definitions, measurements, and job task requirements*. Potomac, MD: Management Research Institute.

Fleishman, E. A., & Reilly, M. E. (1995). *Administrator's guide to the Fleishman Job Analysis Survey (F-JAS)*. Potomac, MD: Management Research Institute.

Fleishman, E. A., Reiter-Palmon, R., & Reilly, M. E. (2011). *Handbook of human abilities: Definitions, measurements, and job task requirements*. Potomac, MD: Management Research Institute.

French, J. W. (1951). *The description of aptitude and achievement tests in terms of rotated factors*. Chicago, IL: University of Chicago Press.

French, J. W., Ekstrom, R. B., & Price, L. A. (1963). *Kit of reference tests for cognitive factors*. Princeton, NJ: Educational Testing Service.

Friedman, L., Fleishman, E. A., & Fletcher, J. (1992). Cognitive and interpersonal abilities related to the primary activities of R&D managers. *Journal of Engineering and Technology Management, 4,* 211–242.

Gael, S. (1983). *Job analysis: A guide to assessing work activities.* San Francisco, CA: Jossey-Bass.

Gebhardt, D. L., & Schemmer, F. M. (1985). *Development of physical performance selection tests for paramedics in the city of Los Angeles.* Bethesda, MD: Advanced Research Resources Organization.

Gilbert, J., & Fleishman, E. A. (1992a). *Interpersonal dimensions of work: A taxonomy and preliminary scale development.* Fairfax, VA: Center for Behavioral and Cognitive Studies, George Mason University.

Gilbert, J., & Fleishman, E. A. (1992b). *Fleishman's job analysis survey: Social and interpersonal abilities.* Potomac, MD: Management Research Institute.

Guilford, J. P. (1967). *The nature of human intelligence.* New York, NY: McGraw-Hill.

Hogan, J. C., Jennings, M. C., Ogden, G. D., & Fleishman, E. A. (1978). *Determining the physical ability requirements of Exxon apprentice jobs.* Bethesda, MD: Advanced Research Resources Organization.

Hogan, J. C., Ogden, G. D., & Fleishman, E. A. (1978). *Assessing the physical requirements in selected benchmark jobs.* Bethesda, MD: Advanced Research Resources Organization.

Hogan, J. C., Ogden, G. D., & Fleishman, E. A. (1979). *The development and validation of tests for the order selector job at Certified Grocers of California, Ltd.* Bethesda, MD: Advanced Research Resources Organization.

Inn, A., Schulman, D. R., Ogden, G. D., & Sample, R. A. (1982). *Physical ability requirements of Bell System jobs.* Bethesda, MD: Advanced Research Resources Organization.

Jones, M. A., & Prien, E. P. (1978). A valid procedure for testing the physical abilities of job applicants. *Personnel Administrator, 23,* 33–38.

Landy, F. J. (1988). Selection procedure development and usage. In S. Gael (Ed.), *The job analysis handbook for business, government, and industry.* New York, NY: John Wiley & Sons.

Landy, F. J., & Trumbo, P. A. (1980). *Psychology of work behavior.* Homewood, IL: Dorsey.

Landy, F. J., & Vasey, J. (1991). Job analysis: The composition of SME samples. *Personnel Psychology, 44,* 27–50.

Lennon, R. T. (1956). Assumptions underlying the use of content validity. *Educational and Psychological Measurement, 16,* 294–304.

Lopez, F. M. (1988). Threshold trait analysis system. In S. Gael (Ed.), *The job analysis handbook for business, industry, and government* (vol. 2, pp. 880–901). New York: John Wiley & Sons.

McCormick, E. J. (1979). *Job analysis: Methods and applications.* New York: AMACOM.

Messick, S. (1989). Meaning and values in test validation: the science and ethics of assessment. *Educational Researcher, 18,* 5–11.

Messick, S. (1995). Validity of psychological assessment: Validation of inferences from persons' responses and performances as scientific inquiry into score meaning. *American Psychologist, 50,* 741–749.

Myers, D. C., Gebhardt, D. L., & Fleishman, E. A. (1979). *Development of physical performance standards for Army jobs.* Washington, DC: Advanced Research Resources Organization.

Myers, D. C., Gebhardt, D. L., Price, S. J., & Fleishman, E. A. (1981). *Development of physical performance standards for Army jobs: Validation of the Physical Abilities Analysis methodology.* Bethesda, MD: Advanced Research Resources Organization.

Myers, D. C., Jennings, M. C., & Fleishman, E. A. (1981). *Development of job-related medical standards and physical tests for court security officer jobs.* Bethesda, MD: Advanced Research Resources Organization.

Primoff, E. S., & Eyde, S. D. (1988). Job element analysis. In S. Gael (Ed.), *The job analysis handbook for business, industry, and government* (vol. 2, pp. 807–824). New York, NY: John Wiley & Sons.

Romashko, T., Brumbach, G. B., Fleishman, E. A., & Hahn, C. P. (1974). *Development of a procedure to validate physical tests.* Washington, DC: American Institutes for Research.

Romashko, T., Hahn, C. P., & Brumback, G. B. (1976). *The prototype development of job-related physical testing for Philadelphia policeman selection.* Washington, DC: American Institutes for Research.

Theologus, G. C., & Fleishman, E. A. (1973). Development of a taxonomy of human performance: Validation of the ability scales for classifying human tasks. *JSAS Catalog of Selected Documents in Psychology, 3,* 26–27.

Theologus, G. C., Romashko, T., & Fleishman, E. A. (1973). Development of a taxonomy of human performance: A feasibility study of ability dimensions for classifying human tasks. *JSAS Catalog of Selected Documents in Psychology, 3,* 25–26.

Weldon, L. (1983). *Recommendations for physical ability testing and medical guidelines for the city of Pittsburgh.* Bethesda, MD: Advanced Research Resources Organization.

Wilson, M. A. (2007). A history of job analysis. In L. L. Koppes (Ed.), *Historical perspectives in Industrial and Organizational Psychology* (pp. 219–241). Mahwah, NJ: Lawrence Erlbaum Associates.

Zedeck, S. (1975). *Validation of physical abilities tests for AT&T craft positions: Program report with special emphasis on detailed job analyses.* New York, NY: American Telephone and Telegraph Co.

14

Personality-Based Job Analysis

JEFF FOSTER

Hogan Assessment Systems

BLAINE GADDIS

Hogan Assessment Systems

JOYCE HOGAN

Hogan Assessment Systems

When the prevailing professional belief is that personality has little relevance for the study of work performance, there is no need for personality-based job evaluations. This conventional wisdom persisted for at least two decades, from the 1960s through the 1980s. The tide of research evidence suggesting that personality variables are systematically related to job performance began to rise in the early 1990s. Hough and Oswald (2008) summarize personality-prediction research findings over the past 15 years. They conclude that personality variables predict job performance (Hogan & Holland, 2003), counterproductive work behavior (Berry, Ones, & Sackett, 2007), team performance (Peeters, Van Tuijl, Rutte, & Reymem, 2006), job satisfaction (Judge, Heller, & Mount, 2002), and major life outcomes (Roberts, Kuncel, Shiner, Caspi, & Goldberg, 2007).

In the domain of job performance, personality measures predict overall job performance, task performance, training performance, objective indices of productivity, managerial effectiveness, and organizational promotion. Also predicted are criteria associated with integrity, innovation, goal setting, and cultural adaptation (Hough & Oswald, 2008). In short, the empirical links between personality variables and meaningful multidimensional job criteria require a reconsideration of ways to evaluate jobs for personality-based requirements that facilitate job performance.

Despite the increased use of personality measures in the workplace, most structured job analysis procedures do not capture personality requirements (Guion, 1992). Although incumbents and supervisors typically describe effective and ineffective job performance in terms of personality characteristics, job analysts previously ignored such information, focusing heavily on "job-oriented" as opposed to "worker-oriented" job requirements. Nevertheless, when work analysts record job information provided by incumbents and supervisors, invariably it contains information about personal characteristics associated with job performance. In this chapter, we review the current status of *personality-based job analysis* (a term we use interchangeably with work analysis) and provide directions for future research. We also outline appropriate methods for conducting personality-based job analysis by providing an illustrative example using the Performance Improvement Characteristics (PIC; Hogan & Rybicki, 1998). The PIC is a structured job analysis instrument developed to assess personality-based, worker-oriented requirements. Table 14.1 outlines steps for administering, scoring, and interpreting the PIC.

Table 14.1   Job Analysis Process for the Performance Improvement Characteristics

Step	Description
1. Review job information	Begin job analysis by reviewing all available information (e.g., job descriptions, performance metrics) for the target job.
2. Identify and train SMEs	Identify at least 8–10 SMEs (incumbents, supervisors, other job experts) to complete the PIC.
3. Data collection	Administer PIC and collect additional job analysis data if applicable (e.g., interviews, observation, SME focus groups).
4. Data analysis	Examine reliability of SME responses and identify which personality-based scales are most related to performance in the target job(s).
5. Incorporate with other data	Review PIC results along with other information (e.g., other job analysis data, validity information).
6. Reporting results	Deliver PIC results, providing appropriate interpretive information based on the intended use of the HPI (e.g., selection or development).

HPI = Hogan Personality Inventory; PIC = Performance Improvement Characteristics; SME = subject matter expert.

JOB ANALYSIS TECHNIQUES

The classic job analysis methods, such as time and motion studies, sought to identify tasks and instruct those who perform them (e.g., Gilbreth, 1911; Taylor, 1923). Proponents of these approaches soon realized that individual differences in worker behaviors affected task performance (Primoff & Fine, 1988). Subsequent efforts led to job analysis methods for identifying the behaviors required to complete tasks and worker-oriented approaches designed to specify knowledge, skills, abilities, and other characteristics (KSAOs).

Sparks (1988) was careful to point out that statutory law does not prescribe job analysis as a condition necessary for compliance. However, one of the most influential documents guiding personnel decisions, the *Uniform Guidelines on Employee Selection Procedures* (Equal Opportunity Employment Commission, 1978), expressed a clear preference for basing assessments on job analyses that identify "work behavior" associated with tasks. These guidelines specify that KSAOs should be defined in terms of "observable behaviors and outcomes" (p. 228), or those that are "able to be seen, heard, or otherwise perceived by a person other than the person performing the action" (p. 232). Specifying job analytic information in terms of concrete and observable behaviors reduces inaccuracies resulting from management of self-presentation and impression by individuals providing the information (Morgeson & Campion, 1997). These efforts underscore the importance of describing jobs using clear, observable, and verifiable terminology.

Job-Oriented Approaches

Job-oriented approaches describe work in technical and behaviorally explicit terms. Using these methods, analysts identify work *elements*, or "the smallest unit into which work can be divided without analyzing separate motions, movements, and mental processes" (Cascio, 1987 p. 185). These elements represent behavioral building blocks of *tasks*, which (a) involve an action or series of actions performed closely in time, (b) have clear starting and stopping points, (c) result in performance of a meaningful objective, and (d) belong to a specific job. Moreover, tasks should be observable and as behaviorally explicit as possible (Harvey, 1994).

Professionals may use several techniques to execute a job-oriented job analysis. For example, Gael (1990) and Gatewood and Feild (1998) suggested that interviews with subject matter experts (SMEs) represent an effective method for compiling task information. Using the functional job analysis, analysts not only interview SMEs, they review job-related reference materials and conduct on-site observations (Veres, Locklear, Sims, & Prewett, 1996). In the mid-1960s, the Air Force Human Resources Laboratory developed Comprehensive Occupational Data Analysis Programs, which used information from multiple jobs to automatically process, organize, and report occupational data (Jansen, 1985; Phalen, 1975). Finally, some analysts use the critical incident technique to identify behaviors associated with particularly effective or ineffective task performance (Flanagan, 1954). Unlike other work-oriented methods, this approach focuses on critical *behaviors* as much as tasks and allows professionals to use behavioral critical incidents as scale anchors to illustrate effective and ineffective task performance (Gael, 1988).

Worker-Oriented Approaches

Worker-oriented job analysis aims to describe the human characteristics involved in performing task-related behaviors rather than describe tasks (McCormick, 1976; Veres et al., 1996). By focusing on individual characteristics, worker-oriented methods identify broad similarities between dissimilar jobs and may, therefore, be used "off the shelf" for many different jobs (Gatewood & Feild, 1998; Harvey, 1994). Common examples of worker-oriented job analysis instruments include the Position Analysis Questionnaire (McCormick & Jeanneret, 1988), the Occupational Analysis Inventory (Cunningham, Boese, Neeb, & Pass, 1983), the Ability Requirement Scales (Fleishman & Mumford, 1988), and the Threshold Traits Analysis System (Lopez, 1988).

Perhaps the best known of these instruments is the Position Analysis Questionnaire, which describes general work behaviors in terms of information input, mental processes, work output, relationships with other people, job context, and other job characteristics. The Position Analysis Questionnaire uses rating scales and a standardized deductive method for collecting worker-oriented data (Gatewood & Feild, 1998; Peterson & Jeanneret, 1997). Considering potential problems caused by the reading difficulty of the Position Analysis Questionnaire, Harvey, Friedman, Hakel, and Cornelius (1988) created the Job Element Inventory. The Job Element Inventory uses the same item format and underlying content as the Position Analysis Questionnaire but considers only relative time spent on each item.

A similar structural relationship exists between the Occupational Analysis Inventory and the General Work Inventory (Ballentine & Cunningham, 1981). Research using the Occupational Analysis Inventory (Boese & Cunningham, 1975) describes five categories underlying its items: information received, mental activities, work behavior, work goals, and work context. The General Work Inventory is a shorter and less technical alternative to the Occupational Analysis Inventory developed for large-scale data collection using "any literate respondent who is familiar with the job" (Cunningham, Wimpee, & Ballentine, 1990, p. 34).

The Ability Requirement Scale provides a taxonomic system for describing and measuring job activities. This method evaluates human abilities needed to perform job tasks and identifies potential measures for predicting these abilities. As a follow-up to the Ability Requirement Scale, Fleishman and Mumford (1991) developed the Fleishman Job Analysis Survey to examine personal attributes required across jobs. The taxonomy of abilities included with this technique contains 52 cognitive, physical, psychomotor, and sensory abilities.

Finally, the Threshold Traits Analysis System is a trait-oriented job analysis technique designed to identify the personal characteristics required for a job. Traits, which represent the vital link between job demands and worker performance, are divided into five major categories: physical, mental, learned, motivational, and social. Physical, mental, and learned traits represent *ability* or "can do" factors, whereas motivational and social traits reflect *attitudinal* or "will do" factors (Lopez, Kesselman, & Lopez, 1981). The Threshold Traits Analysis System foreshadowed later personality-based job analysis tools by including personality-related constructs (e.g., adaptability, dependability, perseverance) among its 33 dimensions. The U.S. Department of Labor's

Occupational Information Network (O*NET) and other taxonomic systems borrowed from both the content and structure of the Threshold Traits Analysis System.

Hybrid Approaches

Some methods combine job- and worker-oriented approaches (Sanchez & Levine, 1999). Designed as a replacement for the U.S. Department of Labor's *Dictionary of Occupational Titles*, O*NET uses multiple descriptors to provide job- and worker-oriented "windows" into specific jobs, a common language for describing different jobs, and a hierarchical taxonomy for classifying occupational descriptors. Job-oriented information may be referenced as occupational requirements (e.g., generalized work activities, work context, organizational context), occupation-specific requirements (e.g., occupational skills, knowledge, tasks, duties, machines and equipment), and occupation characteristics (e.g., labor market information, occupational outlook, wages). Worker-oriented information appears as experience requirements (e.g., training, experience, licensures), worker requirements (e.g., basic and cross-functional skills, knowledge, education), and worker characteristics (e.g., abilities, occupational values and interests, work styles; Peterson et al., 2001).

The Work Profiling System (Saville & Holdsworth, 1995) consists of three job analysis questionnaires for managerial and professional jobs, service and administrative jobs, and manual and technical jobs. Questionnaires include a job content section to identify tasks and a job context section to establish physical environment, responsibility for resources, compensation, and other contextual aspects of the job. Analysts can use this information to determine methods for matching candidates to the job's key requirements.

Personality-Based Job Analysis

Despite efforts to incorporate worker characteristics into job analysis, industrial-organizational psychologists have largely ignored specific personality characteristics required for successful job performance. Raymark, Schmit, and Guion (1997, p. 724) observed that "if the job analysis method emphasizes only cognitive or psychomotor aspects of jobs, it is likely that only cognitive or psychomotor predictors will be hypothesized." Job analysts often lack vocabulary and methods for describing personal characteristics. Therefore, they rarely look for personality-related characteristics despite research demonstrating that personality-based job analysis ratings predict the criterion-related validity of personality scores (Cucina, Vasilopoulos, & Sehgal, 2005).

Employers actively seek information about personality when hiring new employees. For example, Brinkmeyer (1995) analyzed more than 6,000 job postings from nine U.S. national newspapers to determine what employers require from applicants. She reported that employers emphasized five general qualities: previous job experience (53%), specific educational requirements (50%), interpersonal skills (49%), technical skills (48%), and salary level (12%). Brinkmeyer categorized interpersonal skills into six dimensions: communication skills, sensitivity to others, sociability, collaborative problem solving, organization, and responsibility. These results demonstrate that employers recruit for interpersonal skills about as often as job experience, educational requirements, and technical skills, and they value individual characteristics that are difficult to capture with traditional job analysis methods.

To fill this gap, Hogan and Hogan (1995) developed a taxonomy of personality-related job analysis ability statements for use in job analysis. They analyzed critical job tasks and abilities through a linkage process specified by Goldstein, Zedeck, and Schneider (1993). Across jobs, results indicated that raters frequently rate personality-based ability statements as critical for job performance, providing useful information for test and criterion specification.

Other job analysts have developed customized instruments for capturing personality-based job requirements. For example, a joint-service military classification effort identified personality-based descriptions as a job analysis method required for successful job performance (Knapp, Russell, & Campbell, 1995). Building on this research, Sumer, Sumer, Demirutku, and Cifci (2001) created a personality-based job analysis for identifying critical characteristics in prospective military officers. Finally, the Personality-Related Position Requirements Form (PPRF) evaluates 12 personality-related dimensions. Research shows that the PPRF reliably differentiates jobs in terms of characteristics required for success (Raymark et al., 1997). The 107 items comprising the PPRF require SMEs to respond to the item stem, "Effective performance in this position requires the person to…," indicating the extent to which each behavior is associated with job performance on a three-point rating scale ranging from 0 (*not required*) to 2 (*essential*).

The emergence of these instruments signals a shift from job-specific tasks to direct assessment of personal characteristics related to performance. To illustrate how job analysis can identify the personality-based requirements for a job, we present an example using the PIC (Hogan & Rybicki, 1998). Hogan Assessment Systems (hereafter "Hogan") developed the PIC for use in selection and development applications. It represents one of the most robust personality-based job analysis instruments based on the Five-Factor Model (FFM) of personality.

THE PERFORMANCE IMPROVEMENT CHARACTERISTICS JOB ANALYSIS

The PIC identifies the personal characteristics needed for a job and the degree to which they enhance performance. It contains 48 items that align with the FFM (Digman, 1990) of personality and the seven primary scales on the Hogan Personality Inventory (HPI; Hogan & Hogan, 2007). Hogan developed the PIC using a three-step process: (a) generating observable and verifiable behavioral statements reflecting each personality dimension, (b) ensuring relevance of FFM items across the spectrum of occupational work, and (c) building a survey mechanism for SMEs to indicate the extent to which each characteristic would improve performance in a given job. Table 14.2 presents the PIC's seven scales and their definitions. Figure 14.1 displays a copy of the PIC with its complete item content.

Development

The FFM provides a systematic method for classifying individual differences in social and work behavior. These five dimensions, which are based on observers' descriptions of others, capture the content of virtually any personality assessment (Wiggins & Pincus, 1992). As a result, the FFM represents the paradigm for modern personality research and is particularly relevant for job analysis because it provides a taxonomy of observer ratings. Applications of the FFM for job analysis tell us about the reputation of individuals who exhibit behaviors associated with successful

Table 14.2 Performance Improvement Characteristics Scale Definitions

Scale Name	Definition
	Would performance be improved if the incumbent…
Adjustment	Is calm and self-accepting
Ambition	Takes initiative and displays self confidence
Sociability	Needs or enjoys social interaction
Interpersonal sensitivity	Is perceptive, tactful, and sensitive
Prudence	Is conscientious and conforming
Inquisitive	Shows creativity and an interest in solving problems
Learning approach	Remains up-to-date with job-related knowledge

PERFORMANCE IMPROVEMENT CHARACTERISTICS JOB ANALYSIS

HOGAN

NAME: _____   ID: _____

Instructions

Personal characteristics affect job performance as a _____ . Below is a list of characteristics used to describe behavior. Please provide a rating of the extent to which each characteristic improves performance as a _____ . Use the scale below to mark your responses in the blanks provided.

Does **Not** Improve Performance	**Minimally** Improves Performance	**Moderately** Improves Performance	**Substantially** Improves Performance
0	1	2	3

Would job performance improve if the incumbent _____?

1. Is steady under pressure _____
2. Is not easily irritated by others _____
3. Is relaxed and easy-going _____
4. Doesn't worry about his/her past mistakes _____
5. Stays calm in a crisis _____
6. Rarely loses temper _____
7. Doesn't complain about health problems _____
8. Trusts others -- is not suspicious _____
9. Gets along well with supervisors and authority figures _____
10. Takes initiative -- solves problems on his/her own _____
11. Is competitive _____
12. Is self-confident _____
13. Is positive _____
14. Takes charge of situations _____
15. Has clear career goals _____
16. Enjoys speaking in front of groups _____
17. Seems to enjoy social interaction _____
18. Likes social gatherings _____
19. Likes meeting strangers _____
20. Needs variety at work _____
21. Wants to be the center of attention _____
22. Is witty and entertaining _____
23. Is warm and friendly _____
24. Is tolerant (not critical or judgmental) _____

25. Is kind and considerate _____
26. Understands others' moods _____
27. Likes being around other people _____
28. Is good-natured, not hostile _____
29. Is self-controlled and conscientious _____
30. Supports the organization's values _____
31. Is hard-working _____
32. Does as good a job as possible _____
33. Pays attention to feedback _____
34. Likes predictability at work _____
35. Rarely deviates from standard procedures _____
36. Respects authority _____
37. Is imaginative and open-minded _____
38. Is interested in science _____
39. Is curious about how things work _____
40. Likes excitement _____
41. Enjoys solving problems and puzzles _____
42. Generates good ideas and solutions to problems _____
43. Likes cultural activities _____
44. Keeps up on advances in the profession _____
45. Likes to learn new things, enjoys education & training _____
46. Is good with numbers _____
47. Remembers details _____
48. Reads in order to stay informed _____

RESEARCH INFORMATION ONLY -- OPTIONAL

1. Indicate **all** your years of experience with the **job** you just described as a (name of job described): _____
_____ Supervisor   _____ Incumbent   _____ Trainer   _____ Other: _____

2. Gender: ____ Male   ____ Female

Figure 14.1   The Performance Improvement Characteristics (Hogan & Rybicki, 1998). (Copyright © 1998 by Hagan Assessment Systems. All rights reserved.)

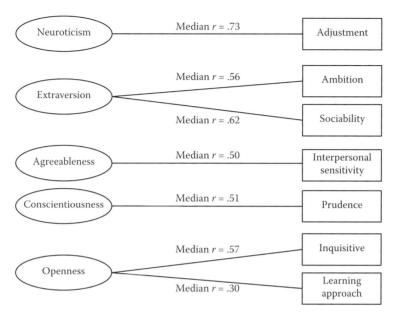

Figure 14.2 Relationships between the Hogan Personality Inventory (HPI) and Other Five-Factor Model inventories. Median correlation coefficients summarize HPI relationships with the NEO PI-R (Goldberg, 2000), Goldberg's (1992) Big-Five Markers (Hogan & Hogan, 2007), Personal Characteristics Inventory (Mount & Barrick, 2001), and the *Inventario de Personalidad de Cinco Factores* (Salgado & Moscoso, 1999). The ranges of correlates are as follows: adjustment/emotional stability/neuroticism (.66 to .81); ambition/extraversion/surgency (.39 to .60); sociability/extraversion/surgency (.44 to .64); interpersonal sensitivity/agreeableness (.22 to .61); prudence/conscientiousness (.36 to .59); inquisitive/openness/intellect (.33 to .69); learning approach/openness/intellect (.05 to .35).

job performance. The five dimensions are surgency, agreeableness, conscientiousness, emotional stability, and intellect/openness to experience.

The HPI is the first measure of personality developed specifically to assess the FFM in occupational settings within a normal population. It contains seven primary scales aligned with the FFM, as shown in Figure 14.2. Although Hogan developed the PIC for use with the HPI, job analysts can use PIC results to hypothesize predictor-criterion relationships across any number of FFM measures.

The development of the PIC was based on research using the FFM structure with adjective checklist item content to indicate worker requirements (Hogan & Arneson, 1987). SMEs used this checklist to describe the characteristics of an ideal employee in a specific job. This method yielded positive results and suggested that a similar approach could identify important worker characteristics required for a range of jobs. For example, researchers found that the checklist reliably differentiated between jobs, both supervisors and high-performing incumbents agreed on the profile of the ideal workers, and the profile of the ideal *worker* differed from that of the ideal *person* (Hogan & Rybicki, 1998). Based on these findings, professionals can use the PIC, in conjunction with test validation research for personnel selection and development, for any job where people interact with others.

PIC Characteristics and Procedures

When completing the PIC (see Figure 14.1), SMEs rate jobs using 48 items on a 4-point rating scale with responses corresponding to 0 (does not improve performance), 1 (minimally improves performance), 2 (moderately improves performance), and 3 (substantially improves performance).

Hogan scores PIC results by aggregating SME ratings to form a seven-dimension profile that reflects the personality characteristics most relevant to successful job performance. After data collection, Hogan computes normative scores derived from a PIC archive containing data from more than 1000 jobs. Analysts plot these results on a graph that represents the optimal personality profile for predicting successful job performance. Each scale is comprised of five to nine items, with no item overlap between the seven scales. Across items, the PIC has an average phrase length of 4.5 words, an average word length of 5.5 letters, and an average of 1.6 syllables per word. Based upon these results, Flesch-Kincaid analyses indicate that the PIC is consistent with a seventh grade reading level.

Internal consistency reliability estimates for PIC scales range between .76 (adjustment) and .87 (interpersonal sensitivity), with an average of .83. One-month interval test-retest reliability estimates range between .60 (learning approach) and .84 (Inquisitive), with an average of .71. Also, the PIC demonstrates convergent and discriminant validity with the PPRF (Hogan & Rybicki, 1998).

Research indicates that the PIC effectively differentiates between jobs, and scores on PIC scales correspond to HPI scales that predict successful job performance. Hogan and Rybicki (1998) evaluated the discriminating power of the PIC by comparing results from 11 jobs spanning the six major occupational types in Holland's (1985, 1997) Realistic, Investigative, Artistic, Social, Enterprising, Conventional (RIASEC) vocational theory and a range of occupational classifications from the *Dictionary of Occupational Titles* (U.S. Department of Labor, 1991). Their results demonstrated that various personality characteristics are differentially important across different jobs. For example, SMEs indicated that sociability is more important for sales jobs than management jobs. Also, SMEs indicated that ambition is more important for management, sales, and research jobs than secretarial or material handling jobs. Finally, although SME ratings for adjustment varied between jobs, these ratings all fell within one standard deviation of the mean of the normative sample, indicating that being calm and resilient to stress represents an important personal characteristic across jobs.

Meyer and Foster (2007) evaluated relationships between PIC results and HPI criterion-related validity across jobs. Specifically, they examined the utility of three different approaches (partial weighting, full weighting, and profile similarity) to validate the PIC. They weighted HPI data from seven archival studies using each method according to PIC profiles for the same and different jobs and correlated these results with performance. By weighting the HPI results for a given job by the PIC profile for that job, the HPI predicted supervisory ratings of job performance. Moreover, results showed that the HPI was most predictive of job performance when weighted according to its corresponding PIC profile.

When PIC data are gathered for a job, Hogan classifies the job into one of seven job families: managers and executives, professionals, technicians and specialists, operations and trades, sales and customer support, administrative and clerical, and service and support. Hogan derived these job families from the nine job classifications used by the Equal Employment Opportunity Commission. Using archival data, results from one-way analyses of variance reveal that scores for all seven PIC scales vary significantly by job family ($p < .01$). Table 14.3 presents the average PIC scores by job family. Figure 14.3 displays average normative PIC profiles for each of the seven job families.

These results are generally consistent with those found by Hogan and Rybicki (1998). For example, SME ratings indicate that adjustment and sociability are most important for managerial and sales jobs. Inquisitive is most important for managers. Service and support jobs require the highest levels of interpersonal sensitivity. Ratings on adjustment vary by job family, but all fall approximately within one standard deviation of one another. The same is true for prudence and learning approach.

Table 14.3   Performance Improvement Characteristics Results by Job Family

Job family	N	Adjustment		Ambition		Sociability		Interpersonal Sensitivity		Prudence		Inquisitive		Learning Approach	
		M	SD	M	SD	M	SD	M	SD	M	SD	M	SD	M	SD
Managers and executives	185	19.95	2.39	17.48	1.88	9.73	2.91	13.67	2.22	18.23	1.94	13.77	2.52	11.83	1.57
Professionals	98	19.05	2.40	15.76	2.32	7.85	2.45	12.47	2.66	18.48	2.12	12.64	2.55	11.97	1.54
Technicians and specialists	38	18.17	3.00	14.72	2.06	6.39	2.43	11.61	2.14	18.27	2.20	12.26	2.55	11.60	1.50
Operations and trades	42	19.49	1.94	14.88	2.09	6.28	2.91	12.03	2.55	19.62	1.42	11.38	2.82	10.98	1.81
Sales and customer support	40	18.91	1.75	17.31	1.32	10.05	2.22	13.55	1.87	18.10	1.43	12.69	1.30	11.50	.99
Administrative and clerical	27	19.48	1.35	15.69	1.94	7.07	2.07	12.55	1.84	18.71	1.45	10.87	1.69	11.58	1.06
Service and support	14	20.03	1.83	16.24	1.53	9.30	1.58	14.63	1.35	19.31	1.46	11.30	1.73	10.89	1.29

M = mean; N = number of jobs; SD = standard deviation.

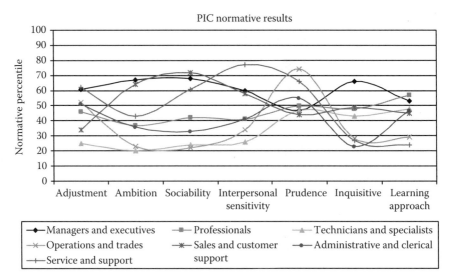

Figure 14.3   Normative performance improvement characteristics results by job family.

In summary, although personality contributes to job performance across contexts, many traditional job analysis techniques fail to investigate personality. As a result, these techniques conclude that cognitive and psychomotor predictors represent critical worker characteristics, with personality playing a minor or even trivial role. However, during the last decade, personality-based job analysis instruments such as the PPRF and the PIC demonstrate that personality-based job analysis results differentiate between jobs and identify characteristics required for successful performance. Results from personality-based job analyses can serve a number of purposes, such as developing hypotheses about personality scales most predictive of job performance, specifying training needs, and identifying behaviors associated with successful performance to construct performance rating forms for criterion validation.

ILLUSTRATIVE APPLICATIONS

To illustrate the steps for conducting a personality-based job analysis, we present PIC results for three jobs: a chief executive officer (CEO) in a regional real-estate company, sales representatives in a national telecommunications company, and drivers in a southeast transportation company. Hogan collected PIC data for all three jobs as part of test validation efforts designed to establish selection profiles for high-potential job applicants. The process used for these job analyses followed the procedures outlined in Table 14.1.

Step 1: Review of Existing Job Analysis Information

Personality-based job analysis should begin with a review of existing job analysis information. During this step, analysts should collect and review available job information using existing job descriptions, job postings, structured job interviews, focus groups, observations, and existing performance metrics. This information provides the foundation for comparing and interpreting personality-based job analysis results.

In addition to collecting PIC data, Hogan reviewed job descriptions and conducted job analysis interviews for all three sample jobs. Hogan also conducted focus groups to collect additional job content for the CEO job. For all three jobs, analysts used this information to provide job-specific context in which to interpret PIC results.

Step 2: Identify and Train SMEs

Step 2 involves identifying SMEs for collecting job analysis data. SMEs should be familiar with job requirements and behaviors associated with successful performance. Although supervisors and high-performing job incumbents typically serve as SMEs, others with knowledge of the job may also serve as raters, including coworkers and peers, clients/customers, human resource representatives, or former job incumbents.

SME training helps ensure that job analysis results are consistent across raters and serve as a valid indicator of job requirements. Individual training provides an opportunity to clarify the purpose of the job analysis and its instructions, helps establish a common frame of reference for SMEs to complete ratings, and gives SMEs an opportunity to ask questions about the survey or the process used for collecting and using data.

Hogan collects data from 8–10 SMEs for each job. Both supervisors and high-performing job incumbents served as SMEs for the three sample jobs. For the CEO job, coworkers and peers highly familiar with the target job also served as SMEs. For all three jobs, SMEs received instructions on the purpose and procedures for completing the PIC prior to data collection. Hogan analysts provide PIC training by telephone, web-based seminars, or in-person meetings.

Step 3: Data Collection

The next step is the collection of job performance data. Structured job analysis instruments are often available online and in paper-and-pencil formats. We recommend storing data until results require updating. Like validation results, analysts should update job analysis results when there are significant changes to a job or a sufficient amount of time has passed. Following recommendations provided by most professionals regarding the currency of validation results (Schmit, Lundquist, & Beckman, 2008), we recommend that analysts update job analysis results every 5 years.

For online administrations, SMEs complete the PIC on a web site accessed using Hogan-generated user identifications and passwords. For paper-and-pencil administrations, Hogan mails materials to SMEs, who complete the forms and fax completed answer sheets back to analysts. SMEs completed PICs for the sample jobs using the online format for the CEO ($n = 8$) and sales representative ($n = 23$) jobs and the paper-and-pencil format for the driver job ($n = 18$).

Step 4: Data Analysis

After data collection, analysts should review the reliability of their results. Hogan used intraclass correlations (Shrout & Fleiss, 1979) to assess the reliability of PIC results. Specifically, Hogan uses a two-way random effects model to test for absolute agreement among ratings. Two-way random effects models are appropriate when drawing raters from a larger population of potential SMEs. Absolute agreement takes the magnitude of rating differences into account when computing reliability.

Hogan requires a reliability coefficient of .80 before proceeding with further analyses. When reliabilities fall below this level, analysts correlate individual item-level responses to identify potential outliers, which are removed from further analyses. If no outliers exist, data from additional raters may be required to achieve adequate reliability ratings.

Figure 14.4 presents normative PIC profiles for the three sample jobs. Intraclass correlation estimates were .84, .94, and .89 for the CEO, sales representative, and driver jobs, respectively. As seen, PIC results indicate that successful CEOs deal well with stress (high adjustment), are driven to succeed (high ambition), enjoy interacting with others (high sociability), and seek out new methods for approaching work and work processes (high inquisitiveness). Successful sales representatives are also characterized by high ambition and sociability, but not adjustment or inquisitiveness.

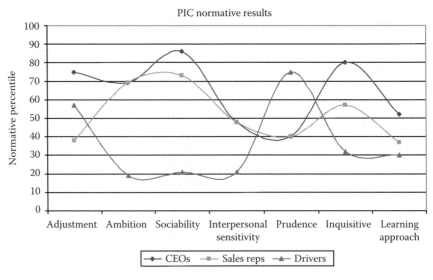

Figure 14.4 Normative performance improvement characteristics results for chief executive officer, sales representative, and driver jobs.

In contrast, other than requiring moderate levels of adjustment, successful drivers are primarily characterized by an ability to follow rules and adhere to regular practices and job structure (high prudence). As these results demonstrate, although commonalities exist across jobs, job type can moderate the relationship between personality scales and job performance.

Step 5: Incorporating Job Analysis Results With Validity Data

Next, analysts should compare results to additional information about the job during Step 1 and information about the predictive validity of personality measures. Examining similarities and differences across data collected through multiple methods helps ensure that results are valid and will generalize to future job applicants and incumbents. Differences can be important indicators of recent or impending job changes, a failure to collect or interpret data accurately, or a lack of consensus about the job's requirements among SMEs.

Hogan compares PIC results to other job information, archival PIC information for similar jobs, and results from an additional job analysis survey: the Competency Evaluation Tool (CET;

Table 14.4 Highest Rated Competencies for Chief Executive Officer, Sales Representative, and Driver Jobs

	Chief Executive Officer	Sales Representative	Driver
1	Judgment	Integrity	Dependability
2	Industry knowledge	Achievement orientation	Safety
3	Trustworthiness	Trustworthiness	Trustworthiness
4	Leadership	Dependability	Work attitude
5	Achievement orientation	Oral communication	Job knowledge
6	Decision making	Planning/organizing	Integrity
7	Building partnerships	Sales ability	Detail orientation
8	Organizational commitment	Consultative sales	Verbal direction
9	Conflict resolution	Flexibility	Organizational commitment
10	Stress tolerance	Stress tolerance	Stress tolerance

Hogan Assessment Systems, 2006). The CET asks SMEs to indicate the degree to which each of 56 listed competencies relates to successful performance in the target job. A brief definition accompanies each listed competency to align raters' frames of reference. Raters evaluate each competency using a five-point scale ranging from 0 (*not associated with job performance*) to 4 (*critical to job performance*).

After SMEs complete the CET, Hogan computes mean criticality ratings for each competency across raters and a mean criticality rating across competencies. Analysts define critical competencies as those with mean scores one standard deviation above the average. Typically, eight to twelve competencies meet this requirement. Table 14.4 presents the critical competencies from the CET for CEO, sales representative, and driver jobs.

After identifying critical competencies, Hogan examines relationships between scores on each HPI scale and supervisory ratings of competency related behaviors. These data come from the Hogan research archive, which contains criterion-related validity evidence from more than 250 jobs. Relationships are derived from meta-analysis results examining the empirical validity of each HPI scale for predicting conceptually aligned job behaviors. As demonstrated by Hogan and Holland (2003), individual personality scales are more predictive of job performance measures when conceptually aligned with specific work outcome measures. Researchers often underestimate the predictive validity of personality assessments when they only use procedures that focus on the relationships of individual personality scales to overall job performance.

Furthermore, very few applied personality inventories produce only one scale intended to represent an accurate and valid representation of personality. Instead, the majority of personality instruments produce multiple scales intended for simultaneous examination and interpretation. Therefore, Hogan identifies PIC scales most related to job performance, determines the mechanisms by which specific PIC scales contribute to job performance through conceptually aligned job-critical competencies, and leverages these results to predict successful performance in the target job.

Step 6: Reporting and Communicating Results

A critical component of any job analysis involves effectively documenting and communicating results to key stakeholders. Documentation should include detailed information about the job analysis setting, process, and results. The interpretation and communication of results may differ based on the intended use of job analysis data (e.g., selection, development, job comparison).

If the purpose of the job analysis is to incorporate personality assessment into personnel selection, Hogan uses PIC results to create a profile to distinguish between high-, moderate-, and low-potential job applicants. In such a selection context, Hogan provides additional information, such as estimated pass rates and adverse impact analyses based upon archival assessment data for similar jobs.

Alternatively, when the purpose of the job analysis is to facilitate incumbent development, Hogan uses PIC and CET results to provide incumbents with information about the personality characteristics and competencies most closely associated with successful job performance. Specifically, PIC results provide insights into behavioral attributes required for success in the job, whereas CET results reflect how those behaviors translate into successful performance. For example, the HPI adjustment scale is significantly related to multiple CET dimensions, including stress tolerance, work attitude, teamwork, customer service, and dependability. Developmental plans for individuals with low scores on Adjustment may focus on these areas if CET results indicate they are essential for successful job performance.

Organizations also collect job analysis data for other purposes, such as comparing the personality-based requirements of two jobs. For example, when employers use PIC and CET results to compare jobs, analysts graph PIC results and compare CET ratings to determine the degree of between-job similarity. Specifically, Hogan constructs 95% confidence intervals for each PIC scale by adding and subtracting 1.96 (SE_{msmt}) to and from each raw score scale mean. Overlap between CET ratings provides additional evidence of between-job similarity. To conduct these analyses, Hogan computes Tilton's (1937) overlap statistic, dividing the number of CET dimensions rated as important or unimportant in both jobs (N_s) by the sum of N_s and the number of CET dimensions rated differently across the jobs (N_d). This calculation allows analysts to determine the percent of job-critical competencies that the two jobs share. Job similarity comparisons provide a useful means of determining how effective one profile may be for multiple jobs or if criterion-related evidence can be transported from one job to another (Hogan, Davies, & Hogan, 2007).

Summary

Both job context and the purpose of the job analysis play critical roles in determining how to approach these steps. For example, job type and level may affect the selection of SMEs. For higher-level jobs, multiple supervisors or incumbents may not be available. As with our CEO example, peers and coworkers often serve as SMEs for senior executive jobs. In addition, very little existing information, such as job descriptions or performance metrics, may exist for new jobs. In such cases, job analysis results can serve as important indicators of how well key stakeholders, or those designing the job, agree on the objectives and personal characteristics required for success.

Furthermore, analyses, interpretation, and implementation of job analysis results may differ based upon the purpose of the job analysis. For selection, comparing job analysis results with information establishing the validity of the personality constructs under examination is critical for establishing predictive profiles. In contrast, comparing results across multiple profiles is critical for establishing job similarity. Analysts must first define the purpose of the job analysis before they can examine, communicate, and implement results.

DISCUSSION

Despite the increased use of personality measures in the workplace (Hough & Oswald, 2008), relatively few methods for analyzing jobs using personality-related terminology exist. Although some worker-oriented job analysis methods do take personality-related constructs into account, few job analysis instruments are designed to assess personality characteristics. In this chapter, we have described steps for developing and applying personality-based job analysis instruments.

Similar to other worker-oriented methods, there are several advantages to using structured, personality-based job analysis instruments such as the PIC. First, they allow professionals to draw cross-job comparisons because all jobs are measured using the same dimensions and rating scales. This also provides information about the appropriateness of transporting validity information from one job to another, as specified by the *Principles for the Validation and Use of Personnel Selection Procedures* (Society for Industrial and Organizational Psychology, 2003). However, unlike other worker-oriented methods, the PIC aligns with one personality instrument, the HPI, which predicts a wide range of important individual behaviors across jobs and organizations. Nevertheless, because the PIC is sufficiently representative of the FFM, it can be used to align with any FFM personality-based inventory. Finally, by measuring broad personality-related constructs instead of narrowly defined job tasks, the PIC offers a more robust approach to job analysis than job-oriented methods, which cannot adapt to contexts in which tasks are ambiguous or change over time.

No one job analysis method can capture *all* of the individual characteristics essential for successful job performance. Instead, analysts should use information provided by instruments like the

PIC in conjunction with additional job analysis information to gain a comprehensive understanding of job requirements. Such information may include educational or certification requirements, job descriptions, existing performance metrics, data gathered during interviews or focus groups, or validity evidence gathered for other jobs with similar personality requirements.

Analysts should conduct personality-based job analysis when their organization considers including personality measures in human resource interventions. Once analysts identify the personality characteristics associated with successful job performance, they can use the results to create profiles to identify high-potential job applicants, pinpoint developmental opportunities with current job incumbents, and structure training programs around the behaviors associated with these characteristics. Applications are most effective when they rely on accurate and reliable information gained through job analysis.

Although job-oriented approaches provide valuable information concerning the tasks that are critical for performance, jobs cannot be clearly or completely defined using only a list of specific tasks. Failure to consider personality in job analysis efforts results in failure to capture individual characteristics that are essential for success across jobs. Furthermore, when jobs change, it is critical that organizations identify the individual characteristics that facilitate incumbents' accommodation to a new role. Similarly, when new jobs evolve that require total workforce staffing, an *a priori* job analysis of the "unborn" job is essential for developing selection tools used to populate a new workforce.

Personality-based job analysis provides an effective method for comparing jobs to one another and assessing individual potential across multiple jobs. Just as individual personality characteristics predict multiple outcomes, individuals possessing certain characteristics may be successful across multiple jobs. For example, the HPI Ambition scale is the most predictive scale across managerial and sales jobs. However, this should come as no surprise because this scale measures the degree to which a person is self-confident, goal oriented, and driven (Hogan & Hogan, 2007). The PIC is designed to create a profile of the "ideal" employee for a specific job. Just as PIC profiles can be compared to one another, individual HPI scores can be compared to multiple PIC profiles to assess candidate fit.

The paucity of research on personality-based job analysis instruments creates opportunities for future research in this area. First, researchers should explore different item and response formats. For example, items assessing deficiencies within organizations may prove more effective for identifying training needs than items written to identify ideal employee profiles. Second, researchers should explore alternative methods for assessing individual fit to an ideal profile. Because personality constructs differentially predict performance in different jobs, researchers should examine methods for weighting personality variables when creating ideal profiles and comparing individual scores to these profiles. Along those lines, alternatives for comparing ideal profiles to one another also warrant investigation. For example, researchers have yet to examine the potential benefits of excluding scales unrelated to job performance when comparing ideal profiles. Finally, job analysis methods require continuous refinement to enhance their predictive accuracy for forecasting the job requirements employers need to acquire and develop workforce talent.

Readers interested in obtaining additional information on personality-based job analysis should consult Cucina et al. (2005) for a detailed account of the predictive validity of such methods. Raymark et al. (1997) present support for the utility of these techniques in differentiating between jobs in terms of the personal attributes required for successful performance. Finally, for more information about the PIC and its development, readers can consult two resources: Hogan and Arneson (1987) summarized research of the development of personality-based adjective checklist items that preceded the development of the PIC, and Hogan and Rybicki (1998) provided a detailed account of the development and validation of the PI.

REFERENCES

Ballentine, R. D., & Cunningham, J. W. (1981). Development of the General Work Inventory. *Proceedings of the 23rd Annual Conference of the Military Testing Association* (pp. 125–133). Arlington, VA: Military Testing Association.

Berry, C. M., Ones, D. S., & Sackett, P. R. (2007). Interpersonal deviance, organizational deviance, and their common correlates: A review and meta-analysis. *Journal of Applied Psychology, 92,* 410–424.

Boese, R. R., & Cunningham, J. W. (1975). Clusters of occupations based on systematically derived work dimensions: An exploratory study. *Catalog of Selected Documents in Psychology, 53,* 52.

Brinkmeyer, K. R. (1995). *Employers' requirements for interpersonal skills of workers.* Paper presented at the 10th annual conference of the Society of Industrial and Organizational Psychology, Orlando, FL.

Cascio, W. F. (1987). *Applied psychology in personnel management* (3rd ed.). Englewood Cliffs, NJ: Prentice-Hall.

Cucina, J. M., Vasilopoulos, N. L., & Sehgal, K. G. (2005). Personality-based job analysis and the self-serving bias. *Journal of Business and Psychology, 20,* 275–290.

Cunningham, J. W., Boese, R. R., Neeb, R. W., & Pass, J. J. (1983). Systematically derived work dimensions: Factor analyses of the Occupational Analysis Inventory. *Journal of Applied Psychology, 68,* 232–252.

Cunningham, J. W., Wimpee, W. E., & Ballentine, R. D. (1990). Some general dimensions of work among U.S. Air Force enlisted occupations. *Military Psychology, 2,* 33–45.

Digman, J. M. (1990). Personality structure: Emergence of the five-factor model. *Annual Review of Psychology, 41,* 417–440.

Equal Employment Opportunity Commission, Civil Service Commission, Department of Labor, & Department of Justice. (1978). Uniform guidelines on employee selection procedures. *Federal Register, 43,* 38290–38315.

Flanagan, J. C. (1954). The critical incident technique. *Psychological Bulletin, 54,* 327–358.

Fleishman, E. A., & Mumford, M. D. (1988). Ability requirements scales. In S. Gael (Ed.), *The job analysis handbook for business, industry, and government* (Vol. 2, pp. 917–935). New York, NY: John Wiley & Sons.

Fleishman, E. A., & Mumford, M. D. (1991). Evaluating classifications of job behavior: A construct validation of the ability requirement scales. *Personnel Psychology, 44,* 523–575.

Gael, S. J. (Ed.). (1988). *The job analysis handbook for business, industry, and government.* White Plains, NY: John Wiley & Sons.

Gael, S. J. (1990). *Job analysis: A guide to assessing work activities.* San Francisco, CA: Jossey-Bass.

Gatewood, R. D., & Feild, H. S. (1998). *Human resource selection* (4th ed., pp. 245–369). Fort Worth, TX: Dryden Press.

Gilbreth, F. B. (1911). *Motion study.* Princeton, NJ: Van Nostrand.

Goldberg, L. R. (1992). The development of markers for the Big Five factor structure. *Psychological Assessment, 4,* 26–42.

Goldberg, L. R. (2000). Hogan Personality Inventory and the NEO-PI-R correlation coefficients. Unpublished data based on the International Personality Item Pool (IPIP) project.

Goldstein, I. L., Zedeck, S., & Schneider, B. (1993). An exploration of the job analysis-content validity process. In N. Schmitt, W. Borman, & Associates (Eds.), *Personal selection in organizations* (pp. 3–34). San Francisco, CA: Jossey-Bass.

Guion, R. M. (1992). *Matching position requirements and personality traits.* Paper presented at the 7th annual coference of the Society of Industrial and Organizational Psychology, Montreal, Canada.

Harvey, R. J. (1994). Job analysis. In M. D. Dunnette & L. M. Hough (Eds.), *Handbook of industrial and organizational psychology* (2nd ed., Vol. 2, pp. 71–163). Palo Alto, CA: Consulting Psychologists Press.

Harvey, R. J., Friedman, L., Hakel, M. D., & Cornelius, E. T. (1988). Dimensionality of the Job Element Inventory, a simplified worker-oriented job analysis questionnaire. *Journal of Applied Psychology, 73,* 639–646.

Hogan Assessment Systems. (2006). *Competency Evaluation Tool manual.* Tulsa, OK: Author.

Hogan, J., & Arneson, S. (1987). *Using the "Big Five" personality dimensions in job analysis.* Paper presented at the 2nd annual conference of the Society for Industrial-Organizational Psychology, Atlanta, GA.

Hogan, J., Davies, S., & Hogan, R. (2007). Generalizing personality-based validity evidence. In S. M. McPhail (Ed.), *Alternative validation strategies: Developing new and leveraging existing validity evidence* (pp. 181–229). San Francisco, CA: Jossey-Bass.

Hogan, J., & Holland, B. (2003). Using theory to evaluate personality and job-performance relations: A socio-analytic perspective. *Journal of Applied Psychology, 88,* 100–112.

Hogan, J., & Rybicki, S. (1998). *Performance Improvement Characteristics job analysis manual.* Tulsa, OK: Hogan Assessment Systems.

Hogan, R., & Hogan, J. (1995). *Hogan Personality Inventory manual.* (2nd ed.). Tulsa, OK: Hogan Assessment Systems.

Hogan, R., & Hogan, J. (2007). *Hogan Personality Inventory manual.* (3rd ed.). Tulsa, OK: Hogan Assessment Systems.

Holland, J. L. (1985). *Manual for the self directed search.* Odessa, FL: Psychological Assessment Resources.

Holland, J. L. (1997). *Making vocational choices: A theory of vocational personalities and work environments* (3rd ed.). Odessa, FL: Psychological Assessment Resources.

Hough, L. M., & Oswald, F. L. (2008). Personality testing and industrial-organizational psychology: Reflections, progress, and prospects. *Industrial and Organizational Psychology: Perspectives on Science and Practice, 1,* 272–290.

Jansen, H. P. (1985). Training emphasis task factor data: Methods of analysis. *U.S. Air Force Human Resources Laboratory (AFHRL) Technical Report*, May, 1985; TR-84-50 [AL/HRPP].

Judge, T. A., Heller, D., & Mount, M. K. (2002). Five-factor model of personality and job satisfaction: A meta-analysis. *Journal of Applied Psychology, 87,* 530–541.

Knapp, D., Russell, T., & Campbell, J. (1995). Building a joint-service classification research roadmap: Job analysis methodologies. *U.S. AMRL Technical Report,* January, 1995; AL/HR-TP-1994-0027.

Lopez, F. M., Kesselman, G. A., & Lopez, F. E. (1981). An empirical test of a trait-oriented job analysis technique. *Personnel Psychology, 34,* 479–502.

Lopez, F. M. (1988). Threshold Traits Analysis system. In S. Gael (Ed.), *The job analysis handbook for business, industry, and government* (Vol. 2, pp. 880–901). New York, NY: John Wiley & Sons.

McCormick, E. J. (1976). Job and task analysis. In M. D. Dunnette (Ed.), *Handbook of industrial and organizational psychology* (pp. 651–696). Chicago, IL: Rand McNally.

McCormick, E. J., & Jeanneret, P. R. (1988). Position Analysis Questionnaire (PAQ). In S. Gael (Ed.), *The job analysis handbook for business, industry, and government* (Vol. 2, pp. 825–842). New York, NY: John Wiley & Sons.

Meyer, K. D., & Foster, J. L. (2007). *Exploring the utility of three approaches to validating a job analysis tool.* Paper presented at the 22nd annual conference of the Society for Industrial-Organizational Psychology, New York, NY.

Morgeson, F. P., & Campion, M. A. (1997). Social and cognitive sources of potential inaccuracy in job analysis. *Journal of Applied Psychology, 82,* 627–655.

Mount, M. K., & Barrick, M. R. (2001). *Personal Characteristics Inventory manual.* Libertyville, IL: Wonderlic.

Peeters, M. A. G., Van Tuijl, H. F. J. M., Rutte, C. G., & Reymen, I. M. M. J. (2006). Personality and team performance: A meta-analysis. *European Journal of Personality, 20,* 377–396.

Peterson, N. G. & Jeanneret, P. R. (1997). Job analysis: Overview and description of deductive methods. In D. L. Whetzel & G. R. Wheaton (Eds.). *Applied measurement methods in industrial psychology* (pp. 13–50). Palo Alto, CA: Davies-Black.

Peterson, N. G., Mumford, M. D., Borman, W. C., Jeanneret, P. R., Fleishman, E. A., Levin, K. Y., … Dye, D. M. (2001). Understanding work using the occupational information network (O*NET): Implications for practice and research. *Personnel Psychology, 54,* 451–492.

Phalen, W. J. (1975). Comprehensive occupational data analysis programs (CODAP): Ordering of hierarchically grouped case data (KPATH) and print KPATH (PRKPTH) programs. *U.S. Air Force Human Resources Laboratory (AFHRL) Technical Report,* August, 1975; TR-75-32 [AL/HRPP].

Primoff, E. S., & Fine, S. A. (1988). A history of job analysis. In S. Gael (Ed.), *The job analysis handbook for business, industry, and government* (Vol. 1, pp. 14–36). New York, NY: John Wiley & Sons.

Raymark, P. H., Schmit, M. J., & Guion, R. M. (1997). Identifying potentially useful personality constructs for employee selection. *Personnel Psychology, 50,* 723–736.

Roberts, B. W., Kuncel, N. R., Shiner, R., Caspi, A., & Goldberg, L. R. (2007). The power of personality: The comparative validity of personality traits, socio-economic status, and cognitive ability for predicting important life outcomes. *Perspectives on Psychological Science, 2,* 313–345.

Salgado, J. F., & Moscoso, S. (1999, May). *Construct validity of two personality inventories based upon the Five-Factor Model (FFM).* Paper presented at the 14th annual conference of the Society for Industrial-Organizational Psychology, Atlanta, GA.

Sanchez, J. I., & Levine, E. L. (1999). Is job analysis dead, misunderstood, or both? New forms of work analysis and design. In A. I. Kraut & A. K. Korman (Eds.), *Evolving practices in human resources management: Responses to a changing world of work* (pp. 43–68). San Francisco, CA: Jossey-Bass.

Saville & Holdsworth, Ltd. (1995). *Work Profiling System* (WPS, updated version). London, UK: Author.

Schmit, M. J., Lundquist, K. K., & Beckham, S. K. (2008). *Expert opinions on the "shelflife" of a validation study.* Poster session presented at the 23rd Annual Conference of the Society for Industrial Organizational Psychology, San Francisco, CA.

Shrout, P. E., & Fleiss, J. L. (1979). Intraclass correlations: Uses in assessing reliability. *Psychological Bulletin, 86,* 420–428.

Society for Industrial and Organizational Psychology. (2003). *Principles for the validation and use of personnel selection procedures* (4th ed.). Bowling Green, OH: Author.

Sparks, C. P. (1988). Legal basis for job analysis. In S. Gael (Ed.), *The job analysis handbook for business, industry, and government* (Vol. 1, pp. 37–47). New York, NY: John Wiley & Sons.

Sumer, H. C., Sumer, N., Demirutku, K., & Cifci, O. (2001). Using a personality-oriented job analysis to identify attributes to be assessed in officer selection. *Military Psychology, 13,* 129–146.

Taylor, F. W. (1923). *Principles of scientific management.* New York, NY: Harper.

Tilton, J. W. (1937). The measurement of overlapping. *Journal of Educational Psychology, 28,* 656–662.

U.S. Department of Labor. (1991). *Dictionary of occupational titles.* Washington, DC: U.S. Government Printing Office.

Veres, J. G. III, Locklear, T. S., Sims, R. R., & Prewett, A. J. (1996). Job analysis in human resource management practice. In G. R. Ferris & M. R. Buckley (Eds.), *Human resources management: Perspectives, context, functions, and outcomes* (3rd ed., pp. 122–154). Englewood Cliffs, NJ: Prentice-Hall.

Wiggins, J. S. & Pincus, A. L. (1992). Personality: Structure and assessment. *Annual Review of Psychology, 43,* 473–504.

15

Functional Job Analysis

Steven F. Cronshaw

University of Northern British Columbia

This chapter describes the history, theory, methodology, and application of functional job analysis (FJA). The late Dr. Sidney A. Fine developed and refined FJA during several decades beginning in the late 1940s. FJA relies on the controlled and disciplined use of job language as the primary medium to describe task-based work. Widely referenced in the literature of human resources management (HRM) and industrial/organizational (I/O) Psychology, FJA is based on a comprehensive theory of the work-doing system and has seen extensive use in many organizations as an informational platform to support a broad range of HRM applications, including recruitment, selection, training, and performance appraisal. In the current chapter, six key FJA principles are discussed along with the job analysis methodology and applications that derive from them. An extended FJA example from the firefighter occupation is used throughout the chapter to illustrate the seamless interconnections between FJA theory, methodology, and application. The chapter concludes with a list of commonly asked questions about FJA and responses to them, along with recommended readings.

STEPS IN FUNCTIONAL JOB ANALYSIS

FJA identifies the task-based processes inherent to the worker, work, and work organization by utilizing an in-depth theory and methodology refined and perfected by Sidney Fine over his several decades of FJA development. The complex and interrelated processes of the work-doing system are discovered through the organic processes emergent within the FJA focus group, and these processes can be elicited and managed only by an expert facilitator. Put another way, a high-quality job analysis process is necessary to yield a high-quality job analysis outcome.

Figure 15.1 presents the typical activities that take place in the course of an FJA project. These activities take place across five interconnected phases, each of which consists of one or more steps. As Figure 15.1 shows, these phases and the steps within them comprise a sequential and logical flow of mutually reinforcing activities. FJA has checks and balances built into it whereby feedback loops contained within the Figure 15.1 schematic provide the information needed to enhance and improve the FJA process, either within the individual project (e.g., use of ratings to help in editing the task bank) or for future projects (e.g., use of participant evaluations from Phase 2 to inform subsequent training of analysts in Phase 1).

Phase 1: Preparation

The FJA process begins with a carefully selected, well-trained facilitator. Only those individuals with a respectful and appreciative attitude toward workers and their contributions should be

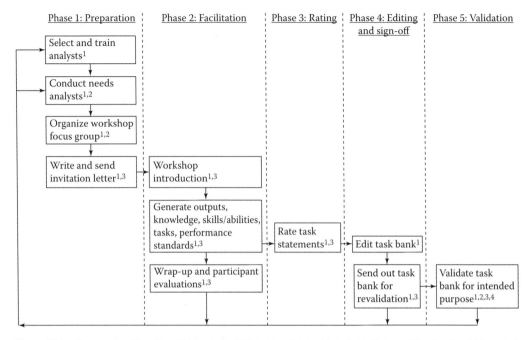

Figure 15.1 The process of functional job analysis. Stakeholders involved in individual steps of the functional job analysis process are (1) the functional job analyst(s), (2) organization management, (3) focus group participants, and (4) other job incumbents outside the FJA focus group.

selected and trained as functional job analysts. Those selected for the facilitator role must receive extensive classroom training in FJA theory, principles, and application supplemented with role playing in process facilitation of FJA focus groups, writing FJA task statements, and rating those task statements using the FJA rating scales. Those individuals showing sufficient skill and promise in FJA facilitation after the classroom training is complete should observe the facilitation of at least one FJA focus group and then successfully conduct one or more FJA focus groups under supervision before being certified as a functional job analyst. The functional job analyst, duly prepared for his or her duties, is then ready to facilitate focus groups through which FJA task banks are generated.

There must be a legitimate and pressing need for FJA or the final outcome will disappoint both the analyst and the management sponsor. A needs analysis is strongly advised before FJA is considered for use as an HRM tool. The needs analysis should be conducted with the organization lead or sponsor who has expressed an interest in FJA as well as other management decision makers who may have interest in, or be impacted by, the outcomes of an FJA project. At this time the sponsor is educated about FJA, its purpose, its fundamental principles and potential applications, and its strengths and limitations as an HRM tool. The first and most important needs analysis question that should be directed toward management is the following: What organizational issue, problem, or concern do you wish to resolve through the use of FJA? Most often, managers respond with general statements ("We need to improve our training for front-line personnel" or "There are too many errors and accidents on the production floor"), and some incisive probing of the responses to this initial question will be needed to clarify and pinpoint the underlying issue, problem, or concern. The second question is, How do you think FJA can help? In most cases, the manager will not be clear on this point: He or she has heard about FJA from a colleague or has seen FJA referenced in a trade publication. It will be up to the consultant or analyst to help the manager

(a) make the relevant connections between FJA and the organization need, and (b) decide *in an informed and knowledgeable way* whether and how FJA is right for their organization. If FJA does not provide a clear path to resolving management's issue, problem, or concern, then the consultant or analyst should feel comfortable proposing a non-FJA means that does or referring the client to another consultant. Above all, the organization sponsor must understand that FJA is the means to informing the resolution of the organization issue, problem, or concern; it is not an end in itself. The sponsor must be clear that enough time and resources must be invested beyond the delivery of the FJA task bank to develop and deliver the applications that address the underlying organization concern. The mutual understanding of the client's needs and the role of FJA in meeting these needs should be documented in writing and approved by both client and analyst before work proceeds.

After mutual agreement on the need for FJA, one or more FJA focus groups are organized to analyze the job(s) concerned. The organization sponsor usually provides or rents facilities for the FJA workshop(s); often a room in the organization's training facility suffices for this purpose. Equipment and supplies needed for the workshop(s) are usually provided by the client organization and include a flipchart easel with paper, masking tape, and marking pens. The recruiting of workshop participants, normally six, is an important matter that requires careful attention. The organization sponsor, with assistance of other client managers involved in the FJA project, are asked to identify six highly experienced job incumbents who are especially knowledgeable about the job. For purpose of ecologic validation, it is a good idea to ask the sponsor to nominate incumbents who are reasonably representative of the facilities or units within which the job is performed. In addition, proactive efforts should be taken to ensure diversity among the workshop participants: Management should nominate individuals of both sexes and from relevant minority groups to participate in the FJA workshop. Given that the typical FJA workshop has only six individuals recruited as subject mater experts, it can be a challenge to get a diverse makeup of workshop participants, but perseverance on this matter pays dividends in greater legal defensibility of the job analysis results and a more productive workshop process.

The FJA consultant should write an invitation letter, which is sent to each nominee. The letter invites the nominee to participate in the FJA workshop and provides an overview of what the individual can expect if he or she agrees to participate. It is important to state in the letter the use to which the FJA results will be put and to emphasize that FJA is not an assessment of worker performance but rather provides a description of job duties and work performed. It is the right of a nominee not to participate in the FJA workshop, and both management and consultant should make it clear that participation is strictly voluntary. If management provides an initial list of 8–10 suitable participants, there will be little delay in starting the workshop if a nominee decides to turn down the workshop invitation or a supervisor cannot release the employee for the time needed because of scheduling difficulties or unusual production demands.

Phase 2: Facilitation

The typical FJA workshop takes two full days to complete. The facilitator starts the first morning by outlining the two-day workshop schedule and presenting the major points of FJA, especially the generic structure of task statements. Participants often question the reasons that management is conducting the workshop and the analyst must answer these questions directly and forthrightly (failure to do so will destroy the trust that is essential to a productive and mutually satisfactory FJA workshop). The facilitator then asks the question, What do you get paid for? With further probing, this question will elicit the outputs listed on the flipchart. Care must be taken to ensure that the outputs are not overly specific—in which case they are tasks that are best elicited later in the workshop. For example, outputs for the job of firefighter would include "fighting structural fires," "attending training," and "performing ancillary duties (in the fire hall)." Five to ten outputs typically are listed, depending on the job; more than 10 outputs suggest that the analyst and group participants are getting bogged down in too much detail for this phase of the analysis (note that the outputs later serve as a general framework to guide generation of the more detailed task statements). The participants may miss one or more outputs at this juncture of the workshop, but these can be picked up and written into the output list at any time during the two-day workshop. It should not take more than 30–45 minutes to write up the output list.

After the flipchart sheet for the outputs is posted on the wall for further reference, the analyst poses two additional questions: What do you need to know to do what you get paid for? (to elicit a list of knowledge), and What skills/abilities do you need to apply your knowledge? (to elicit a list of skills and abilities). Both lists are written up and posted for further reference. The knowledge list for the firefighter job would include such items as "knowledge of departmental standard operating procedure (SOP)" and "knowledge of cardiopulmonary resuscitation"; the skills and abilities list would include "driving fire engines/rescue vehicles" and "emotional control in stressful situations." The two lists should be completed and posted by the end of the first morning; again, more items are added to the lists as they are identified later in the workshop.

The bulk of the time is spent eliciting and documenting the tasks that the workers perform (i.e., "What do you do to get the work done?"). The facilitator asks the group participants to choose an output and the tasks under that output are generated and written down on the flipchart before moving on to the next output. The technical procedures for writing the task statements, as well as the illustrative task statement for the job of firefighter, are given under the FJA principles later in this chapter. The analyst must keep the generic task statement structure and the things/data/people (TDP) functional hierarchies in mind as each task is generated, mentally reviewing the content of all task statements for completeness, adherence to the FJA conventions governing control over job language, and ability to rate the task statement within the TDP functional hierarchy. When the analyst finds weakness in the organization or wording of the task statement written on the flipchart, the group must be consulted to help correct these deficiencies before moving on to the next task. Sometimes groups become quite adept at reviewing their task statements and may correct the analyst when a bad call is made, such as when the analyst confuses a result with an action. In this event, the workshop participants have, through osmosis, acquired a deep understanding of the FJA process and can be counted on to produce a very high-quality task bank by the end of the workshop.

The collection and recording of the task statements normally takes the group into the middle of the second afternoon. Many FJA projects require the identification of performance standards, such as for performance appraisal or training purposes. If so, the remainder of the second day is taken up with answering the following question: What standards do you work toward—yours or your organization's? The participants will have mentioned many of these standards earlier in the workshop in connection with specific tasks, and it is a good idea to make note of them at that time. These previously mentioned standards can be presented to the group as a starting point and then augmented as the group raises and discusses additional standards. The performance standards are written down on the flipchart and posted with the rest of the FJA information from the two-day session. The two-day focus group should end with a brief wrap-up (10–15 minutes), during which the next steps in the FJA project are reviewed with the group, and then the participants individually complete a short survey measuring their satisfaction with aspects of workshop quality, facilitator skill, and the physical layout of the facilities.

It may be useful to have a second analyst present who enters the flipchart information into an onsite computer throughout the workshop. This information can be printed and given to the participants at the end of the first day so they can have personal copies of the evolving FJA task bank to read and review. Furthermore, the immediate availability of a typed task bank at the conclusion of the workshop considerably shortens the time needed to edit the task bank.

Phase 3: Rating

It is often useful to rate the task statements on the FJA scales listed in Table 15.1. The ratings serve two purposes: (a) They confirm that the task statements are consistently written in conformance with FJA theory and methodology, and (b) they are used as supplemental data in user applications such as selection, training, and job design. Ratings most often are done by the analyst and compared with those of a second analyst. When the two analysts disagree, the difference in ratings is discussed until consensus is reached on a final rating. Sometimes the workshop participants are asked to rate their task bank, although this requires scheduling a third day for the workshop.

Phase 4: Editing and Sign-Off

The analyst reads the task bank as soon as possible after completion of the workshop and makes nonsubstantive grammatical improvements and corrections of wording, spelling, and punctuation. The edited task bank is then sent back to the workshop participants who (a) check off whether or not they perform each task, and (b) add tasks or other information they believe to be missing from the task bank (it is rare for participants to suggest additional tasks at this point). To revalidate the task bank, the participants are then asked to sign off and return a statement that the task bank "covers at least 95% of the work I do."

Phase 5: Validation

Cronshaw et al. (2007) presented a five-component model for the validation of FJA task data and applied it to a large scale job redesign project in Veterans Affairs hospitals. As might be expected, FJA validation takes a fundamentally different direction than other job and work analysis methods. The first two FJA validation strategies, linguistic and experiential validation, assess the adequacy of linguistic and process inferences that are at the core of FJA theory and methodology. The third ecological, validation strategy, uses Brunswikian concepts of representative design (Brunswik, 1956) to assess the relevance and applicability of FJA task statements across different settings, such as units or departments in the organization. The fourth strategy, hypothetical-criterial validation, assesses the extent to which the FJA data is generative of scientific hypotheses concerning the structure and dynamics of work processes and provides empirical support for the predictions deriving from those hypotheses. The fifth strategy, social-organizational validation, is taken from models originally developed in the field of applied behavior analysis (Wolf, 1978) and evaluates the extent to which the FJA task bank has found acceptance in the user community. The mix of validation strategies used in a project will vary according to the specific inferences that need to be validated. It is important to note that the legal and professional defensibility of FJA projects is enhanced by the inclusion of a validation component.

HISTORY OF FUNCTIONAL JOB ANALYSIS

Functional job analysis was developed by the late Dr. Sidney A. Fine and emerged as a byproduct of the work he initiated in 1948 and conducted under the Functional Occupational Classification Project funded by the U.S. Department of the Air Force. Over the second half of the 20th century and into the 21st century, Dr. Fine devoted an extraordinary degree of focus and commitment to refining his FJA system and applying it to a wide range of human resource (HR) problems and applications. He achieved signal success in his work, with FJA now recognized as a staple in job and work analysis in virtually all textbooks dealing with this topic as well as in many reference works in HRM and I/O Psychology. FJA is described by Ryan and Sackett (1992) as one of the job analysis methods most used by practitioners. A study by Levine, Ash, Hall, and Sistrunk (1983) found that experienced job analysts gave high effectiveness ratings to FJA across 11 organizational purposes, including job description, and performance appraisal. More recently, Mitchell, Alliger, and Morfopoulos (1997) suggested that FJA is the most appropriate job analysis method (out of the five that they reviewed) when compliance with the provisions of Americans with Disabilities Act of 1990 is at issue.

FJA THEORY AND PRINCIPLES

Schmitt and Chan (1998) credit FJA as one of the few methods of job and work analysis that is grounded in a theory of organization. The truth of the matter goes even further: FJA is based on deep epistemological and ontological assumptions about work process and dynamics. The task statement, which is the FJA centerpiece, embodies work process in its description of the actions that workers take to achieve results within a broader set of organizational activities, and it also describes the enablers that make these worker instrumentalities possible. FJA relies on linguistic means—that is, the careful and controlled use of job language to achieve its purpose of capturing and representing work processes. FJA combines the advantages of its grounding in process and linguistics into a unique formulation that captures the essentials of task-based work as well as workers' contributions; at the same time, FJA maximizes the informativeness and relevance of job analysis information within a compact and standardized format.

The processes described by FJA are part of the larger work-doing system, which consists of three interacting components: worker, work, and work organization. The ultimate goal of the human resources practitioner is to help management and workers engage these three components and bring them into alignment to increase organizational efficiency; effectiveness; productivity; and worker safety, wellness, and growth. FJA views management and worker goals in a well-run and productive organization as being complementary. For example, improvements in worker safety through the provision of safety training and job redesign contributes to achieving management's goals of efficiency, effectiveness, and productivity through fewer workdays lost and lower workers' compensation payments. The same HRM interventions benefit the workers by reducing number of accidents, injury rates, and work-related stress. With this in mind, the FJA information (i.e., the FJA task bank) is best used with a full and balanced understanding of its place within the larger work-doing system from the perspectives of both managers and workers.

Given its roots in process and linguistics, FJA espouses a set of principles that determine its conduct and use as well as validation of the inferences made from FJA data. A description of six key FJA principles is now given, along with an explanation of each principle.

FJA Principle: The Task Is Recognized as the Basic Unit of Work

The Russian chemist Dmitri Mendeleev made a major advancement in our understanding of the physical universe when he arranged the elements in order of their atomic number in the periodic table. He thereby demonstrated that the Greek philosopher Democritus was correct: The seemingly endless variety of substances in the universe, everything from interstellar matter to tennis balls, is reducible to a small number of basic building blocks (i.e., atoms) that can be combined and rearranged into all the material substances of everyday experience. In a similar manner, the task is the basic building block of the work-doing system, and the very large number of often highly complex work arrangements apparent to managers and workers are explicable in terms of (re)arrangements of a relatively small number of basic tasks.

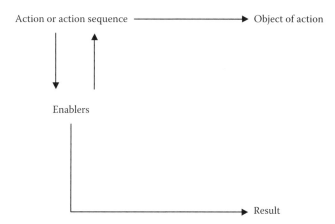

Figure 15.2 Generic structure of the functional job analysis task statement.

FJA operationalizes the work task in terms of a written task statement defined as an action or action sequence grouped through time, designed to contribute a specified end result to the accomplishment of an objective, and for which functional levels and orientation can be reliably assigned (Fine & Cronshaw, 1999). The task statement contains certain linguistic components, always in the order shown in Figure 15.2.

The action or action sequence (what the worker does) and the result (what gets done) contained in the task statement are further described under the next FJA principle. The enablers in Figure 15.1 are of three types:

1. Prefaced by the phrase "drawing on" are the informational and people resources that enable the action(s) to achieve the result, including knowledge of technical schemes (know-how) or operational procedures (how-to), SOPs, training content and materials, supervisory instructions, and information from coworkers.
2. Prefaced by "using" are the physical resources that enable the action(s), including tools, machinery, equipment, and work aids.
3. Prefaced by "relying on" are the worker adaptations developed, refined, and internalized through a series of previous job experiences (e.g., safety awareness, attention to detail, initiative).

A task statement for the job of firefighter now illustrates all of the task components in the required order:

Holds hose nozzle, turns nozzle collar to adjust intensity of water discharge, drags/repositions hose within the fire scene with assistance of other firefighters, judges fire characteristics and situational factors (e.g., type of combustibles, size of fire, wind direction and force), and listens to/speaks into emergency radio, drawing on firefighter training, departmental SOP, knowledge of radio communication procedures, instructions from incident commander, and verbal/nonverbal communication with other firefighters (e.g., hand signals), using personal protective equipment (breathing apparatus mask and air tank, turn-out gear) and emergency radio, and relying on safety and situational awareness, self-control, and teamwork skills in order to direct water stream onto burning structure.

All tasks in the world of work have things, data, and people (TDP) involvements; this is easily seen in the above example, in which the firefighter handles a hose (things), evaluates his or her portion of the fire scene (data), and communicates by radio with the incident commander (people).

Table 15.1   Scale Ratings for the Firefighter Task

FJA Scale	Level	Orientation
Things function	1A (Handling)	Things, 45%
Data function	4 (Analyzing)	Data, 40%
People function	2 (Exchanging information)	People, 15%
Worker instructions	2	
Reasoning development	4	
Mathematical development	1	
Language development	2	
Work technology[a]	2 (Flexible application)	
Work interaction[a]	3 (Bilateral assistance)	

[a]   These sociotechnical demand scales are found in Cronshaw and Alfieri (2003). The remainder of the scales are found in Fine and Getkate (1995) or Fine and Cronshaw (1999).

The functional skill (TDP) complexity of this task and the relative involvements of the worker in TDP can be quantified using the FJA scales (see Fine & Getkate, 1995). Scales assessing the level of worker instructions and general educational development required for this task are also found in Fine and Getkate. Cronshaw and Alfieri (2003) develop and present scales for assessing the sociotechnical demands of the task to augment the FJA scales. The ratings on all the above scales for the firefighter task are given in Table 15.1. The reliability of these FJA scales has been demonstrated to be adequate for most purposes when designing HR interventions; specifically, research studies have shown interrater reliabilities of the FJA scales to range from very good to excellent (Cronshaw, Chung-Yan, & Schat, 2006; Schmitt & Fine, 1983).

FJA Principle: FJA Makes a Fundamental Distinction Between What Workers Do and What Gets Done

Workers are hired and paid and are an essential part of the productive process because they make a unique contribution over and above the other elements in the work-doing system (e.g., machines, equipment, physical plant, organizational structures). Serious mistakes in managing people are made if this basic fact is not clearly recognized and represented in job analysis. Consequently, the FJA statement begins with one or more action verbs—each of which is directed to an object—that clearly and unambiguously describe what the worker does as a direct contribution to task accomplishment. The result of task performance—what gets done—is written at the end of the task statement, after the connective phrase *in order to,* in recognition that it consists of both the self-motivated and self-directed contributions of the worker (what he or she does) and the contribution of the task enablers, many of which are provided by management. The firefighter task above illustrates the distinction between actions and results. The action verb-object phrases "holds nozzle," "turns nozzle collar," "drags hose," "judges fire characteristics and situational factors," and "listens to/speaks into emergency radio" fall within the decisional discretion of the worker and are the gist of what workers do to hold up their side of the employment relationship. The result, "to direct water stream onto burning structure," represents the partial achievement of the larger system objective, which in this case is to put out the fire. The difference between "what the worker does" and "what gets done" is a function of changing perspective from that of the worker on one hand to that of the larger work-doing system on the other.

The most frequent mistake in FJA is to substitute task results for worker actions. The perceptual field of workers (as FJA focus group participants) is directed primarily to the results they achieve on the job rather than the particulars of the actions in which they engage to get those results. As

Polanyi (1983) would put it, the meaning of the work performed is habitually displaced away from the self toward the entities in the environment in which the worker is acting. As a consequence, when the workshop participants suggest a result in place of an action, the analyst must be careful to further probe the putative result to uncover the underlying and preceding action(s). As the FJA workshop progresses, the participants typically widen their perspective, using action verbs more frequently and results less frequently when describing their work. If participants offer verbs with vague and generalized meanings in place of specific action verbs, the facilitator should probe further. For example, statements such as "I run the department" or "I make widgets" have no value for FJA purposes until they are narrowed down to unambiguous statements of the specific actions performed and the results achieved.

FJA Principle: Job Language Must Rigorously Differentiate Between Description and Evaluation

In FJA, work processes can be worded in two ways: (a) as factual descriptions of workers doing X and Y getting done, worded largely in verb-noun phrases, that is, task statements, and (b) as the same factual material modified and qualified by adjectives and adverbs, that is, performance standards. An example will serve to illustrate the linguistic shift from the descriptive stance (a) to the evaluative one (b). The following two performance standards are derived from the firefighter task statement:

1. Carefully and continuously adjusts water discharge to extinguish combustibles in the involved area (this descriptive standard specifies the level of performance expected of the worker while performing one aspect of the task).
2. Fire spreads to other areas of the structure 0% of the time (this quantifiable standard specifies the desired systems outcome achieved by performing the task).

These performance standards seem, at face value, to derive logically from their corresponding task statement; however, not all stakeholders to the FJA work will see it this way. There nearly always are differences in stakeholder opinion, for example, between managers and workers, on three aspects of performance measurement: (a) which performance standards apply to a given task; (b) whether and how the performance standards proposed for the task by other stakeholders are relevant, appropriate, or sufficient; and (c) the extent to which personal and situational causes contribute to achievement of the standard. Taking the second aspect above as an example, it is a fact that firefighters drive emergency vehicles (e.g., pumper trucks) and that they do so for an agreed-upon purpose (e.g., to convey personnel, equipment, and other resources to the fire scene). Therefore, it usually is a routine matter to bring all stakeholders in the job analysis project to an agreement that the job-descriptive language contained in the FJA task statement is a fair and accurate representation of what the workers do and what gets done. However, when it comes to proposing the definitions and measurements of worker performance—that is, performance standards—which are derived from that task, stakeholder consensus evaporates. Although all parties would agree that the firefighter should drive the truck carefully and safely to the fire scene, a city politician or insurance adjuster is likely to insist that, "to be safe" (and so to reduce accident risk and legal liability), the firefighter must never exceed the posted speed limits or violate traffic laws, whereas the department fire fighters will argue that speed limits can sometimes be "safely" exceeded and traffic laws must be contravened, albeit in a "safe manner," to get to the fire scene more quickly. Much confusion and a Gordian knot of application results if the job analyst conflates the descriptive language of the task statement with the evaluative language of the performance standards. This is why FJA requires their strict separation.

FJA Principle: Things, Data, and People Are Explicitly Recognized as the Ontological Primitives Underlying All Work

As Sidney Fine (n.d., p. 16) eloquently stated:

> The "organism" [i.e., the worker] is an organic unity of three inseparable parts: physical potential (thingness), information potential (mindness), and interpersonal potential (peopleness). These three potentials in various levels and combinations are demanded by jobs of the worker. They account for the ways in which he functions and can function in relation to what jobs expect of him.

Sidney Fine operationalized thingness, mindness, and peopleness in terms of the functional hierarchies of TDP, given in Figure 15.3. The levels within the three hierarchies represent the complexity of the respective worker functions. Every task (as well as every job and occupation) in the world of work can be classified on all three scales of TDP.

FJA Principle: All Work Requires Three Types of Worker Skills

Functional skills enable people to appropriately process TDP on simple to complex levels, drawing on their physical, mental, and interpersonal resources (Fine & Cronshaw, 1999). They are expressed as gerunds and the three hierarchical structures of functional skill are presented in Figure 15.3. Again, the TDP functional and orientation ratings for the firefighter task are given in Table 15.1. *Specific content skills* enable people to perform a specific job to predetermined standards using specific equipment, technology, and procedures and relying on functional skills (Fine & Cronshaw, 1999). They are expressed as gerunds; in the case of the firefighter task they are found in the enablers section of the task statement. *Adaptive skills* enable people to manage themselves in relation to the demands of conformity and/or change in particular situations (Fine & Cronshaw, 1999). They are worded as nouns or noun phrases (e.g., impulse control, safety

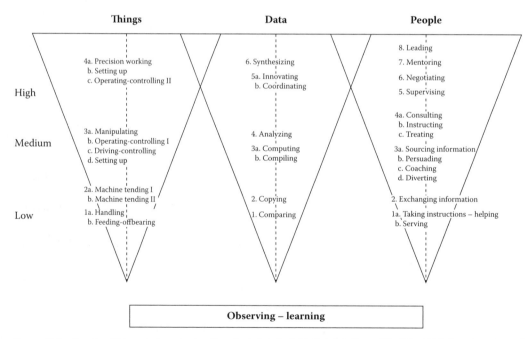

Figure 15.3 Functional job analysis worker function chart. Note that detailed definitions of the things/data/people scales and levels are given in Fine and Getkate (1995) and Fine and Cronshaw (1999).

awareness in the firefighter task) and are found after "relying on" at the end of the enablers section of the task statement.

Whenever one type of skill is used, the other two are also engaged. The three types of skills develop over different time horizons and from different sets of antecedent experiences. Adaptive skills are acquired throughout the course of life experience, beginning in early childhood on a practically subconscious level. They determine the willingness of the person to enter into and engage with a given work context. For example, a person who has developed a personal value and style of risk aversion is not predisposed to pursue a career as a firefighter and is not willing to enter a fire scene because of a deep apprehension of the hazards inherent to firefighting situations. Adaptive skills are crucial in activating functional and specific content skills. Functional skills develop as the developing child comes into increasing contact with TDP at home, during play, and in school. They allow the person to realize agency and relation from their transactions with the physical, informational, and interpersonal particulars present in the environment. Specific content skills are learned on the job in connection with specific tasks, for example, in formal training or through supervisor demonstrations, or are acquired through self-study, (sometimes off-the-job) as a means of achieving specific work objectives. They begin to develop much later than adaptive and functional skills (i.e., after the person has taken employment). The three types of skills are mutually reinforcing and interdependent in resourcing worker performance on the job.

FJA Principle: The Analyst Is an Active Participant in the Job Analysis Process

The Analyst Is An Active Participant in the Job Analysis Process Questionnaire-based job analysis methods, such as the Position Analysis Questionnaire (McCormick & Jeanneret, 1988) and the Common-Metric Questionnaire (Harvey, 1991), train interviewers to draw out sufficient information from job incumbents to make reliable ratings one-by-one on the many molecular items comprising a questionnaire instrument. The compilation and organization of these ratings into a meaningful structure of work is left to a computer program, which provides printouts of summary results to the end user. By comparison, FJA extensively and intensively involves the job analyst throughout the job analysis process. The analyst is responsible for eliciting job information from job incumbents (usually and ideally in six-person focus groups), expertly facilitating the group process and helping the participants to sort and organize the information into the *a priori* categories made explicit by FJA theory. As Fine (n.d.) noted, the analyst is responsible for defining the perceptual field of the job for herself and the group participants. FJA also makes the extensive use of generative grammar by linguistically standardizing the writing of task statements in terms of constructions with multiple branches, thus maximizing the understandability of the job analysis results (Chomsky, 1965). FJA produces job analysis results that validate well and support useful applications (Levine et al., 1983), but it makes considerable demands on the training and skills of the analyst and requires him or her to make an insistent and continuous contribution to the job analysis process.

FJA APPLICATIONS

FJA supports a number of applications in HRM and I/O psychology. Fine and Cronshaw (1999) described in detail applications of FJA to recruitment, selection (both testing and interviewing), training, performance appraisal, career development and coaching, pay, job design, and equal employment opportunity/disability issues. The FJA example given in this chapter for the job of firefighter is transparent in its support for a range of HRM applications (of which two—training and selection—are discussed here). The task statement, along with its performance standards and scale ratings, provides the beginning of a task bank well suited for development of firefighter train-ing programs in the classroom and in the field. Two of the three categories of enablers in that task ("drawing on" and "using") identify the training content that is required if the firefighter is to per-form the task to the following applicable performance standards:

1. Knowledge of departmental SOP regarding deployment/use of hoses, radio communica-tion procedures on the fire ground, and the purpose and function of the incident com-mand structure
2. Specific content skills in *communicating* with other firefighters by voice and through hand signals during hose deployments (procedure), and *wearing/carrying* personal protective equipment including self-contained breathing apparatus (equipment)

Specific content skills for firefighters are best acquired through realistic training simulations such as live fire burns closely supervised by training and line officers. In particular, trainees will require repeated training simulations before they become confident, comfortable, and adept at working within the constricted vision and mobility imposed by the personal protective equipment. Depending on training program objectives, FJA performance standards are identified for either minimum levels of training proficiency or training mastery that firefighters must achieve before deployment on firefighting assignments.

The selection of firefighters requires assessment of job applicants' functional and adap-tive skills. It should be stressed that in most circumstances neither selection on the basis of specific content skills nor training aimed *directly* at developing functional or adaptive skills is productive or useful. The trainee, however, must draw heavily on a complete repertoire of pre-existing functional and adaptive skills when acquiring specific content skills during training; rigorous selection and placement are the only means of ensuring that the necessary functional and adaptive skills are in place when the training program begins. In the firefighter case, functional skills are referenced directly by the action verbs in the previously presented task statement along with the TDP scale ratings in Table 15.1; to wit, the firefighter (a) handles and adjusts hoses and fittings (Things Level 1: handling); (b) evaluates fire conditions and situational factors (Data Level 4: evaluation); and (c) communicates with the incident com-mander by radio and other firefighters in person (People Level 2: exchanging information). Selection tools suited to assessing these functional skills are standardized tests, situational tests, or work samples. The adaptive skills required for the firefighter task are given under the third category of enablers ("relying on"). These skills, safety and situational awareness, self-control, and teamwork, are best assessed by the FJA-based structured interview as described in Fine and Cronshaw (1999). As can be seen, FJA theory and methodology plays a practical and important role in pinpointing the types of skills that are implicated in different types of HRM interventions as well as suggesting means through which these skills can be assessed and taught.

A number of other theory-driven interventions can be derived from the firefighter illustra-tion given in this chapter but cannot be developed further here because of space limitations. The reader is invited to consult the book by Fine and Cronshaw (1999) and further explore those possibilities.

OTHER QUESTIONS AND ISSUES

Next are some questions about FJA and responses to them meant to correct some misunderstand-ings in the academic and trade literatures.

Is FJA a Quantitative Technique?

The typical quantitative approach to job and work analysis requires large groups of subject matter experts to rate isolated fragments of job description on scales of criticality, importance, time spent, or the like, after which researchers attempt to rebuild an underlying structure of work dimensionality through application of quantitative methods such as factor or cluster analyses. As shown in this chapter, FJA eschews these reductionistic and mechanistic methods, preferring to rely on a holistic systems model, verbally based job description, and disciplined control of job language; therefore, FJA is definitely *not* a quantitative method of job analyses. The misconception that FJA is a quantitative technique probably results from cursory reviews that mistakenly equate it with the rating scales used in a secondary and supportive capacity within the FJA system.

Are FJA Task Statements Too Long and Wordy?

An FJA task statement should contain only as many words as needed to validly describe the essentials of the systems module. Complete sentences in the form of written task statements are needed if FJA is to keep intact the natural Gestalt of the work-doing system contained within the systems module along with its complex process interdependencies. However, task statements can become too long and wordy if strict and disciplined control over job language is lost, that is, if the FJA method is not used properly. This problem is overcome by the proper training and supervision of job analysts.

Are Tasks Outmoded As a Means for Describing Work?

As described under the FJA principles, the task is the basic unit of analysis for the work-doing system and is so for a good reason. Without a detailed and in-depth understanding of the tasks that workers perform, job and work analysis runs the risk of dealing in idealized abstractions bearing only a tenuous and indirect relationship to the everyday realities of the work experience. For this reason, task-based analysis will continue as a mainstay for the job and work description.

Have Systems Such as the O*NET Shown That FJA Is Outdated?

A job or work analysis method should be evaluated on its merits, such as those described in this chapter, rather than being dismissed *in toto* by uninformed, pejorative, and sometimes self-serving statements of this type. The FJA is grounded in a very different set of assumptions than are O*NET and its cognates; consequently, the O*NET or the quantitative methods from which it is derived, their successes or popularity, or for that matter their deficiencies and limitations, are properly seen as irrelevant to the value and future prospects of FJA.

Some questions that practitioners and organization sponsors often ask and want addressed before continuing with an FJA-based project include the following.

Is FJA Too Involved and Expensive for Our Purpose?

This question often reveals that management has doubts about the usefulness of job or work analysis in general. They may want the HR manager or I/O consultant to provide an immediate solution to their concerns at the lowest possible cost, and job analysis as a preparatory step is viewed as an unnecessary and wasteful luxury that will delay and add cost to the quick and expedient solution they are demanding. An answer to the question of whether FJA or any other job/work analysis project is too involved or expensive requires a careful consideration of long-term costs and benefits (an analysis that managers also may believe is unnecessary and wasteful). As shown in this chapter, FJA is an in-depth method that requires highly skilled analysts combined with a high degree of commitment and support from management and sponsors. If the sponsoring organization has the vision and the desire to use the FJA information to its maximum potential as the primary job descriptive database across a number of interrelated HR activities (including recruitment, selection, training, performance appraisal, and career development/coaching), then it will find an investment in FJA very worthwhile.

Should I Tell the Union About the FJA Project or Get Them Involved in the Project?

FJA is meant to be a cooperative effort between workers and management. The union has a legitimate role as the sole and legally certified representative protecting the interests and rights of the employee group(s) involved in the FJA. If the union has reservations about how the job analysis data will be used or believes that the union membership might be disadvantaged by their participation in an FJA project, these concerns need to be discussed and resolved honestly and forthrightly between management and the union representatives before an FJA is conducted. Involvement of the union in a steering committee overseeing the FJA project(s) is highly desirable. Management will find that FJA provides more positive and productive outcomes if the union, where it exists, takes an active role in the job analysis effort.

Can I Perform an FJA With Fewer Than Six Workshop Participants?

The author has conducted a number of FJAs with single job incumbents. Whereas the typical six-person FJA workshop allows active group participants to compensate for one or two passive individuals, the single-person interview is only successful if the job incumbent is highly verbal, has the motivation to participate, and possesses sufficient experience in that position. FJA workshops can be held with two or three incumbents, but with similar provisos. The analyst will have to assess the willingness and ability of the workshop participants on a case-by-case basis when three or fewer job incumbents are available to participate in the workshop, proceeding only if there is a good prospect of success. As a practical matter, the author has encountered few cases where these smaller workshops and individual interviews could not go ahead.

Should the Participants' Managers Be Present During or Participate in the Workshop?

A manager's presence will cause anxiety and defensiveness among the workshop participants and sideline their crucial contributions to the FJA process.

Future research on FJA should focus on the language-based factors that largely determine its efficacy and usefulness as a job analysis tool. Detailed syntactic analysis (Chomsky, 1965) of FJA task statements would help to explain the reasons for their high levels of clarity and acceptability for final users (Cronshaw et al., 2007). Such studies could provide prescriptions for improving and enhancing the use of job language for other work and job analysis methods as well. Although quantitative analysis and stringent statistic control over numerically based measurement of job analysis content are common today, there is very little work exploring the *linguistic* structures and elements required for maximally informative job analysis results. FJA-based research into these questions could prompt important advancements in work and job analysis (see Fine, Harvey, & Cronshaw, 2004, pp. 6–7).

REFERENCE MATERIALS

The two definitive FJA references are the books *Functional Job Analysis: A Foundation for Human Resources Management* by Sidney A. Fine and Steven F. Cronshaw (1999) and *Benchmark Tasks for Job Analysis: A Guide to Functional Job Analysis (FJA) Scales* by Sidney A. Fine and Maury Getkate (1995). The first book covers in depth the theory, methodology, and applications of FJA; the second provides many examples of FJA tasks referenced to specific levels across all the FJA scales that can be used for training and practice in the use of the scales. These two books are highly recommended as basic references for anyone considering the use of FJA. Other sources that further explore FJA theory and applications are Cronshaw and Fine (2003) for job redesign; Fine and Cronshaw (1994) for development and validation of biodata items; and Olson, Fine, Myers, and Jennings (1981) for development of performance standards.

REFERENCES

Brunswik, E. (1956). *Perception and the representative design of psychological experiments.* Berkeley, CA: University of California Press.

Chomsky, N. (1965). *Aspects of the theory of syntax.* Cambridge, MA: The MIT Press.

Cronshaw, S. F., & Alfieri, A. J. (2003). The impact of sociotechnical demands on use of worker discretion and functional skill. *Human Relations, 56,* 1107–1130.

Cronshaw, S. F., Best, R., Zugec, L., Warner, M. A., Hysong, S. J., & Pugh, J. A. (2007). A five-component validation model for functional job analysis as used in job redesign. *Ergometrika, 4,* 12–31.

Cronshaw, S. F., Chung-Yan, G. A., & Schat, A. C. H. (2006). *Comparative reliabilities of functional job analysis scale ratings obtained through independent rating and consensus discussion.* Unpublished manuscript.

Cronshaw, S. F., & Fine, S. A. (2003). The evaluation of job redesign processes. In J. E. Edwards, J. C. Scott, & N. S. Raju (Eds.), *The human resources program evaluation handbook* (pp. 301–321). Newbury Park, CA: Sage Publications.

Fine, S. A. (n.d.). *Functional job analysis: A field theoretical and perceptual approach.* Unpublished manuscript.

Fine, S. A., & Cronshaw, S. F. (1999). *Functional Job Analysis: A foundation for human resources management.* Mahwah, NJ: Lawrence Erlbaum Associates.

Fine, S. A., & Cronshaw, S. F. (1994). The role of job analysis in establishing the validity of biodata. In S. S. Stokes, M. D. Mumford, & W. A. Owens (Eds.), *The biodata handbook: Theory, research, and applications.* Palo Alto, CA: Consulting Psychologists Press.

Fine, S. A., & Getkate, M. (1995). *Benchmark tasks for job analysis: A guide to functional job analysis (FJA) scales.* Mahwah, NJ: Lawrence Erlbaum Associates.

Fine, S. A., Harvey, R. J., & Cronshaw, S. F. (2004, April). *FJA strategies for addressing O*NET limitations in a post-DOT environment.* In E. A. Fleishman (Chair), *Things, Data, and People: Fifty years of a seminal theory.* Symposium presented at the annual conference of the Society for Industrial and Organizational Psychology, Chicago, IL. Retrieved from http://harvey.psyc.vt.edu/Documents/SIOP2004.Fine.Harvey. Cronshaw.in.Fine.symposium.pdf

Harvey, R. J. (1991). *The Common-Metric Questionnaire (CMQ): A job analysis system.* San Antonio, TX: The Psychological Corporation.

Levine, E. L., Ash, R. A., Hall, H., & Sistrunk, F. (1983). Evaluation of job analysis methods by experienced job analysts. *Academy of Management Journal, 26,* 339–348.

McCormick, E. J., & Jeanneret, P. R. (1988). Position Analysis Questionnaire (PAQ). In S. Gael (Ed.), *The job analysis handbook for business, industry, and government* (Vol. 2, pp. 825–842). New York, NY: John Wiley & Sons.

Mitchell, K. E., Alliger, G. M., & Morfopoulos, R. (1997). Toward an ADA-appropriate job analysis. *Human Resource Management Review, 7,* 5–26.

Olson, H. C., Fine, S. A., Myers, D. C., & Jennings, M. C. (1981). The use of functional job analysis in establishing performance standards for heavy equipment operators. *Personnel Psychology, 34,* 351–364.

Polanyi, M. (1983). *The tacit dimension.* Gloucester, MA: Peter Smith.

Ryan, A. M., & Sackett, P. R. (1992). Relationships between graduate training, professional affiliation, and individual psychological assessment practices for personnel decisions. *Personnel Psychology, 45,* 363–387.

Schmitt, N., & Chan, D. (1998). *Personnel selection: A theoretical approach.* Thousand Oaks, CA: Sage Publications.

Schmitt, N., & Fine, S. A. (1983). Inter-rater reliability of judgments of functional levels and skill requirements of jobs based on written task statements. *Journal of Occupational Psychology, 56,* 121–127.

Wolf, M. M. (1978). Social validity: The case for subjective measurement or how applied behavior analysis is finding its heart. *Journal of Applied Behavior Analysis, 11,* 203–214.

16

O*NET
The Occupational Information Network

JONATHAN D. LEVINE

Workforce Dynamics

FREDERICK L. OSWALD

Rice University

Serving as the federal source of occupational information in the United States since 1998, the Occupational Information Network (O*NET) was established by the U.S. Department of Labor, Employment, and Training Administration and is still going strong. Not only does the O*NET collect and provide data on more than 800 occupations, it is a valuable resource for a wide array of stakeholders such as researchers, practitioners, job seekers, career explorers, vocational counselors, businesses, and state, federal, and local government agencies. The O*NET has proved to be much more than a data collection program or a static and simple listing of occupations and descriptions; it is a vast, dynamic, and useful system of information, services, tools, and applications.

As we will discuss in greater detail, the O*NET is a hierarchical classification scheme consisting of a logically ordered series of occupational codes and titles that spans most of the world of work. Via occupational analyses, the O*NET maintains and updates detailed occupational profiles consisting of knowledge, skills, abilities, work activities, work styles, background, education and training requirements, and work context. The O*NET's web-based application, O*NET OnLine, allows easy and flexible access to its information and data. The O*NET also provides a series of crosswalks that allows someone to link to other occupational classification systems. The O*NET is a robust vocational guidance tool, consisting of several career-oriented assessments that are tied to its occupations, allowing users to explore occupations and potential career choices. The O*NET Academy provides online courses, step-by-step tutorials, and training sessions, all geared toward keeping one's knowledge of O*NET current. Finally, the O*NET web site provides a wealth of resources, including databases and files, research documents, job analysis questionnaires, pertinent hyperlinks, a toolkit for businesses, testing and assessment guides, human resource applications, and more, all free of charge.

This chapter takes the reader on a tour of the O*NET's past, present, and future. A brief history is described that includes its predecessor, the *Dictionary of Occupational Titles*, the origins of the O*NET Content Model, and the evolution of its classification structure. Next is a discussion of the National Data Collection Program, through which the O*NET gathers, updates, and maintains information on its many occupations. Following that, a summary of O*NET's tools and resources, examples of research and human resource applications, and a description of how O*NET may be used in a work analysis are provided. The chapter concludes with implications and thoughts regarding the future of the O*NET.

HISTORY

First conceptualized in the 1990s, the O*NET was initially developed as a replacement for the U.S. Department of Labor's outmoded *Dictionary of Occupational Titles* (DOT). The DOT, last revised in 1991, was a massive effort, resulting in an encyclopedic book containing detailed information on more than 12,000 occupations. To reduce what was a very expensive, time-consuming, and labor-intensive effort, the DOT's information was condensed and then computerized, and the O*NET was born.

The Dictionary of Occupational Titles

Beginning in 1934, approximately 54,000 job analyses were carried out, and the information gathered was incorporated into the first edition of the DOT, published in 1939. The fifth and final edition was published in 1991 and included information on more than 12,000 occupations (U.S. Department of Labor, 1991). The detailed job-specific information contained in the DOT served many purposes, such as informing job analyses, aiding in the development of job descriptions, and providing a coding and classification system that was used regularly by state government agencies.

The DOT was not without shortcomings, however. For example, Dye and Silver (1999) mentioned that it provided a very mechanistic view of jobs and was not equipped to describe important relationships between occupations, skills transferability, and the incorporation of new technology, changes in critical skills, and new workplaces. In their view, the DOT had become outmoded. In a similar vein, after his brief overview of the DOT's limitations, Dunnette (1999) suggested that "the current DOT cannot be used for rapid assessment of the skills, knowledge, and other characteristics required by a job family or for showing how skill levels in one job may relate to those of other jobs" (p. 5). Although the DOT represented a monumental effort reflecting the collection, analysis, and updating of detailed job-specific information, the information and technology was not flexible enough to configure jobs differently according to different job requirements and/or job characteristics, nor could it be quick enough to adapt to the changing nature of today's world of work. Subsequent to this criticism, it was determined that an approach to occupational information management was needed that was focused on collecting the types of data that allowed for improved cross-job comparisons and ideally would result in a computerized database that was more user friendly, flexible, and could gracefully merge with other federal databases.

More specifically, the Advisory Panel for the DOT (APDOT), commissioned by the Secretary of Labor, recommended the creation of a new occupational information system. The APDOT set forth that a new system should

> promote the effective education, training, counseling, and employment of the American work force. The DOT should be restructured to accomplish its purpose by providing a database system that identifies, defines, classifies, and describes occupations in the economy in an accessible and flexible manner. Moreover, the DOT should serve as a national benchmark that provides a common language for all users of occupational information. (U.S. Department of Labor, 1993, p. 6)

In other words, the panel voiced the need for a standardized, automated occupational system that could serve as a common language across a variety of stakeholders. To this end, the APDOT developed an initial framework that organized variables describing both work and worker characteristics (U.S. Department of Labor, 1993), which is in line with traditional person-based and task-based approaches to job analysis.

The O*NET Content Model

A more comprehensive structural model based on a "multiple windows" approach was developed, which suggests that jobs may be usefully described and comprehended from various viewpoints (Mumford & Peterson, 1999). In early 1995, the new name was introduced—O*NET, the Occupational Information Network—and, accordingly, the model became known as the O*NET Content Model (see Figure 16.1). According to Dye and Silver (1999), the new name served to "discard the baggage associated with the old DOT name and help people envision the forward-thinking, high-tech nature of the project" (p. 18).

The O*NET Content Model consists of six domains that contain both job- and worker-oriented variables that cut across occupations (see Figure 16.1). The Content Model provides a common framework for answering "a host of questions about jobs that otherwise would prove difficult to answer" (Mumford & Peterson, 1999, p. 30).

The six primary domains, or "windows," in the Content Model are worker characteristics, worker requirements, experience requirements, occupational requirements, workforce characteristics, and occupation-specific information. Some pertinent subdomains are knowledge, skills, abilities, generalized work activities, work styles, work context, background, education and training, and tasks. Questionnaires based on these subdomains, or descriptor variables, have been used to collect occupational data in the National O*NET Data Collection Program. These domains and the Data Collection Program will be discussed in greater detail later in this chapter.

O*NET 98: The First Electronic, Public Release

In 1996, a large-scale data collection effort was carried out that concluded almost two years later. The culmination of this and other related efforts led to the release of the O*NET 98, the first O*NET database and computer-based tool. At the time of this initial release, the O*NET 98 Viewer, a computer-based application, could be used to search and access the data and information about its 1,122 broad occupations, then called Occupational Units.

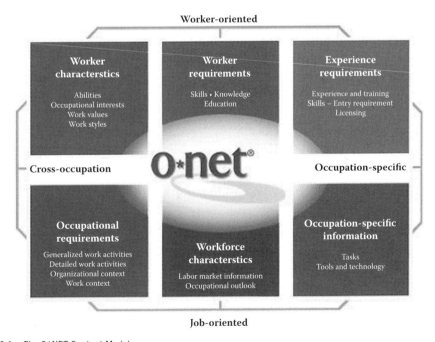

Figure 16.1   The O*NET Content Model.

All of the O*NET 98 occupational data were collected on the six Content Model domains using rating scales that reflected a combination of level, importance, frequency, and other characteristics. Using a procedure recommended by Fleishman and Mumford (1988), level ratings were obtained using seven-point behaviorally anchored scales. The anchors, placed at low, middle, and high points along the seven-point scale, contained specific behavioral examples at a given level and were developed using a judgmental scaling approach (Childs & Whetzel, 1995; Peterson, Mumford, Borman, Jeanneret, & Fleishman, 1995). Importance ratings were collected using a five-point scale. For the Generalized Work Activity domain only, in addition to level and importance, frequency data were obtained using a seven-point scale. Job analysts and graduate students in industrial-organizational psychology were trained on these various instruments and served as raters. After psychometric analyses (e.g., interrater reliability, agreement, descriptive statistics), the data were compiled, averaged, and normalized, and shortly thereafter the O*NET 98 database was finalized and released for public use.

The O*NET 98 data was not without shortcomings and critics. First, factor analyses suggested that the 52 variables pertaining to the domains of Abilities, Skills, Knowledge, and Generalized Work Activities are not entirely distinct from one another. Although even highly correlated variables have the potential to demonstrate useful amounts of discriminant validity across different criteria (Stanley & Wang, 1969), factor analysis indicated useful ways to reduce or collapse the O*NET measures into a smaller number. It is not surprising that there is content overlap, given that experts had been working separately within each domain. Rather than relying heavily or solely on factor analysis, we would suggest a comprehensive review of the content of the O*NET measures to ensure that overlap is minimized across Content Model domains. Variables could then be cross-listed in multiple domains.

Second, because of the overly broad nature of the O*NET and its lack of specific physical descriptors, the Economic Research Institute (ERI; see http://www.erieri.com or http://www.paq.com) argued that "what the designers of the O*NET failed to appreciate was that their new database would not fulfill the needs of the disability determination process" (PAQ Services, Economic Research Institute, 2011, p. 2). In this vein, the Social Security Administration (SSA, 2004) released a *Request for Information* (RFI) that stated:

> [The US] DOL has not formally updated the DOT since 1991 and has no plans to do so. Instead, DOL is developing an entirely new system, the *Occupational Information Network* (O*NET). SSA has determined through contracted and other research that [they] cannot use O*NET, or occupational information derived in part from O*NET, in SSA's disability evaluation process. (p. 1)

Because of this shortcoming, the SSA's release of their RFI, and their belief that the U.S. Department of Labor should not have dispensed with the DOT, the ERI automated the 1991 version of the DOT and embarked on a commercial project that updated and enhanced it; the resulting product is called the Occupational Assessor & Survey or eDOT (ERI, 2004) and is maintained and regularly updated by PAQ Services.

Despite these specific criticisms, the National Center for O*NET Development continued to forge ahead and has put forth several updates and expansions to the database over the ensuing years. The O*NET Center (see http://www.onetcenter.org/dataPublication.html) provides the data publication schedule, beginning April 2003, in Table 16.1. The table includes the database version, the date released, and the number of occupations with comprehensive revisions that were updated. Prior to April 2003 and subsequent to the O*NET 98 release, there were three updates. O*NET 3.0 and 3.1, released in August 2000 and June 2001, respectively, were updates that reflected changes made because of the O*NET's conversion to the Standard Occupational Classification (SOC)

Table 16.1   The O*NET Database Release Schedule

O*NET Database Version	Release Date	Occupations Updated (n)
5.0	April 2003	54
6.0	July 2004	126
7.0	December 2004	100
8.0	June 2005	100
9.0	December 2005	100
10.0	June 2006	100
11.0	December 2006	101
12.0	June 2007	100
13.0	June 2008	108
14.0	June 2009	117
15.0	June 2010	120
15.1	February 2011	0
16.0	July 2011	107

system. O*NET 4.0 was released in June 2002 and was the last database containing the original job analyst and graduate-student data.

The O*NET Occupational Classification

Occupations contained in the O*NET were organized in a standardized manner that would promote the ease of use by various government agencies collecting, disseminating, and using occupational data on a continuous basis. The original schema for organizing occupations and data contained in the O*NET 98 release was the coding and classifications in the SOC system used by the Bureau of Labor Statistics in their Occupational Employment Statistics program. Just two years after the release of O*NET 98, the SOC was revised; then, the Office of Management and Budget mandated that all Federal reporting agencies adopt the SOC. Adhering to this mandate, O*NET became one of the first agencies to transition its data to a SOC-compliant occupational system (Levine, Nottingham, Paige, & Lewis, 2000). This second version and release of O*NET was called O*NET-SOC 2000, which contained 1,094 or 974 data-level occupations, in which *data-level* refers to those occupations for which data are collected in the O*NET Data Collection Program.

Since that time there have been major updates to the O*NET-SOC taxonomy; one in 2006, another in 2009, and one most recently in 2010. The 2010 O*NET-SOC taxonomy revision was necessary in order to incorporate the recently updated 2010 SOC structure (National Center for O*NET Development, 2010). In each subsequent release, the number of occupations contained in the O*NET-SOC changed. For example, in the very first release (O*NET 98), there were 1,122 occupations; in O*NET-SOC 2000 there were 1,094 occupations; in O*NET-SOC 2006 there were 949 (812 data-level) occupations (National Center for O*NET Development, 2006); and in O*NET-SOC 2009, there were 1,102 (965 data-level) occupations. The current O*NET-SOC 2010 taxonomy contains 1,110 (974 data-level) occupations. The number of occupations between 2006 and 2010 increased mainly because the National Center for O*NET Development embarked on an initiative that would identify and add new and emerging occupations (National Center for O*NET Development, 2009a). Data are continually being collected on the descriptive occupational variables contained in the O*NET-SOC taxonomy. Clearly, the O*NET is in a process of continuous updating, akin to the world of work itself.

THE O*NET DATA COLLECTION PROGRAM

The U.S. government has committed itself to a long-term investment in the O*NET, not only in terms of the effort and resources required to collect information across a wide spectrum of occupations, but also in keeping the O*NET database updated as the nature of occupational requirements and employee skills change over time in response to the powerful forces of globalization, technology, and consumer demand. Regarding quality of the data collection process, the U.S. Department of Labor and the National Center for O*NET Development conducted a pretest in June 2001 to determine how survey characteristics affect resulting response rates from job incumbents to create surveys that minimize burden and maximize the chances for complete and reliable data. For each occupation, one can obtain descriptive information about the latest available data, including the Content Model domains with available data, the year of data collection, and the source of the data (i.e., incumbent or analyst). At the point of writing this chapter, O*NET data collection efforts will be funded by the U.S. Office of Management and Budget through May 2012.

There are a number of issues pertaining to data collection on such a large scale. The first issue is that of a sampling plan; the O*NET attempts to implement an appropriate and scientifically sound sampling plan. However, any researchers sampling across a large set of occupations and businesses will face many challenges and decision points. The number of occupations within a higher-level occupational title differs; the heterogeneity (or homogeneity) implied by a given occupational title differs; some occupations change more rapidly than others; the percentage of individuals who work within any individual occupation differs; the number of organizations accessible for data collection differs; and the reasons underlying differing response rates likely differ. These are but a few important considerations when deciding how to sample, weight, and aggregate occupational data. The O*NET conducts two-level, stratified, random sampling, where businesses are sampled according to their representativeness within the North American Industry Classification System's framework; then, incumbents within these businesses are randomly selected to complete the standardized O*NET questionnaires. To reduce the burden of survey response, the O*NET variables are divided across four questionnaires, and incumbents are randomly assigned to complete one of the four questionnaires, along with providing demographic information. Incumbents provide much of the current O*NET data, although job analysts are the ones who complete information in the Ability domain.

The second issue is the question of whether job analysts, experienced job incumbents, or both should be rating worker characteristics and work requirements for a given occupation. Job analysts are raters who have specific training in making ratings across occupations; thus, they have a broad perspective of the world of work and arguably can provide ratings that make appropriate comparisons across jobs. However, analysts lack the deep experience for any given job that may lend itself to more reliable and valid ratings for specific job information. Conversely, experienced job incumbents have this experience but may lack the perspective to provide ratings that are calibrated with the broader context of the world of work (e.g., welders may indicate that their job has a lot of demands for writing because they have to complete paperwork every day; however, those demands for writing are nothing like the heavy writing demands of a playwright). Given these tradeoffs between analyst and incumbent ratings, it is worth comparing their reliability and validity.

Research generally indicates that individual ratings by analysts tend to be more reliable than those by incumbents, and analysts also tend to provide lower mean ratings, consistent with the notion that they are keeping the broader context of the world of work in mind when making ratings (Tsacoumis & Van Iddekinge, 2006). Regarding job analyst ratings, research shows they do tend to be more reliable for more observable and specific characteristics and less reliable otherwise (Dierdorff & Morgeson, 2009). Keeping these findings in mind, there is evidence that aggregate ratings by both analysts and incumbents are reliable and that their ratings show reliable patterns of convergent and discriminant validity on the O*NET characteristics.

Critics of reliability coefficients for occupational ratings are of the opinion that the reliability of an aggregated rating may be questionable because aggregates may hide important sources of error and specific variance that have substantive meaning (Harvey, 2000). This is true for any source of error variance in classical test theory, and therefore the same can be applied to most any aggregate (e.g., a scale score that averages across items, a 360-degree performance rating that averages across peers). The critical question that follows, then, is that aggregate scores may be reliable, but what are they reliable for? This question pertains to our third issue in large-scale data collection: the question of validity.

The O*NET data have yet to be implemented widely in organizational research, where validity evidence is often obtained. However, initial research involving the O*NET is promising. The O*NET descriptors have a substantively interpretable factor structure that makes empirical distinctions across the major domains of the Content Model (e.g., Hadden, Kravets, & Mutaner, 2004; Hanson, Borman, Kubisiak, & Sager, 1999; Scott & Mantegna, 2009). The O*NET descriptors, in tandem with a theory of human cognitive ability, have been used in a career exploration process that matches individuals to occupations (Converse, Oswald, Gillespie, Field, & Bizot, 2004). The O*NET descriptors also have been found to be valid predictors of independent survey data on adult literacy requirements of occupations (LaPolice, Carter, & Johnson, 2008) as well as occupational health risk behaviors and outcomes (Alterman et al., 2008). Future organizational research could incorporate data on O*NET variables as a moderator of criterion-related validities within a larger synthetic validity database. The data could also be used for synthetic validity, namely to help estimate validities for new occupations that contain the job components of other existing jobs for which O*NET and validity data are available (Steel, Huffcutt, & Kammeyer-Mueller, 2006).

TOOLS AND RESOURCES OF THE O*NET

The O*NET has come a long way since the initial 1998 release. It has improved, been updated numerous times, overcome criticisms, and grown far beyond its origins as solely a database of occupational information. The O*NET is now a vast system of tools and resources that has been employed far and wide, useful for many different applications and in many different settings. This section provides a summary of many of the tools and resources that comprise what is currently considered a comprehensive and state-of-the-art occupational analysis, classification, and career exploration system.

O*NET OnLine

O*NET OnLine (see http://online.onetcenter.org) is a user-friendly, web-based application that allows users to search and access occupational data. The O*NET OnLine application typically utilizes the most recent data currently available and is updated when necessary to reflect taxonomy changes, more current occupational information, and the addition of new and emerging occupations. As described by the National Center for O*NET Development, O*NET OnLine allows users to explore occupations; search for occupations based on one's skills; view occupational summary information, including work and worker requirements; and access detailed occupational data and information, such as skills, knowledge, abilities, and work activities.

Users also can match occupations from other systems to O*NET-SOC occupations, and they can hyperlink to many other related career-information and labor-market web sites (see http://www. onetcenter.org/online.html). The list below provides some specifics about many of the features available in the application.

1. Search options
   - *Find occupations* – Users can search by keyword, code, industry or career cluster, job zone, job family, and science, technology, engineering, and math discipline.
   - *Occupations quick search* – Available on all site pages, keywords or codes are used to locate occupations.
   - *Crosswalk search* – Codes or titles from other federal agency classification systems can be entered to find corresponding O*NET-SOC occupations.
   - *Skills search* – Users specify their own skills or skills of interest to locate occupations with similar skills profiles.
   - *Tools and technology search* – Specific machines, tools, equipment, and software terms can be entered to find high-demand occupations.
2. Results screens
   - *Summary report* – Provides a snapshot of the occupations' descriptive information, which includes a brief description, tasks, knowledge, skills, abilities, work activities, work context, interests, job zone, work styles and values, related occupations, and wages and employment trends. (Wage and employment trend data is sourced from the Bureau of Labor Statistics [see http://www.bls.gov], specifically 2010 wage data and projected occupation growth from 2008 to 2018.)
   - *Detailed report* – For all descriptor domains, more comprehensive data than what is contained in the summary report is presented. Additional information, including tools and technology, educational requirements from the Bureau of Labor Statistics, and normalized data for the various *occupational* descriptor domains, is provided.
   - *Custom report* – This allows the user to specify which occupational information is displayed.

O*NET also provides a robust "Help" section (see http://online.onetcenter.org/help) that does a thorough job of listing its various features. Information about all its web site and content areas, such as custom reports, scales, ratings, and standardized scores, job zones, and specific vocational preparation, is described in detail. Finally, instructions and resources are available for those who are interested in building applications or linking from an external web site to one or more areas of the O*NET web site.

O*NET Questionnaires

The O*NET Questionnaires are the occupational analysis instruments used in the ongoing National Data Collection Program. All questionnaires, except for Abilities, are available in both English and Spanish and are downloadable from the O*NET web site. The specific questionnaires are as follows: Knowledge, Skills, Abilities, General Work Activities, Work Context, Background, Education and Training, and Work Styles. Task questionnaires are also available, and data are collected on tasks for all O*NET-SOC occupations.

The questionnaires have been revised since their initial development and use during occupational analyst-oriented data collection efforts through April 2004. Because data are now collected from actual job incumbents randomly selected from various businesses across the country, questionnaires were automated and had to be reworded to improve readability and interpretability, and they were shortened to reduce the burden of responding. The reader is referred to the report titled *Revisions to O*NET Data Collection Instruments*, which provides a comprehensive narrative about the revisions made to the questionnaires (Hubbard et al., 2000).

Examples of some of the items and scales from the different questionnaires are presented in Figure 16.2.

(a) **Ability item**

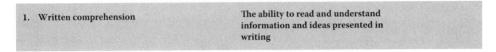

A. How <u>important</u> is WRITTEN COMPREHENSION to the performance of *your current job?*

* If you marked Not Important, skip LEVEL below and go on to the next activity.

B. What <u>level</u> of WRITTEN COMPREHENSION is needed to perform *your current job?*

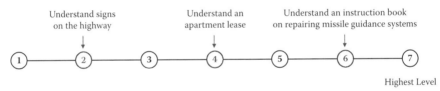

(b) **Skill item**

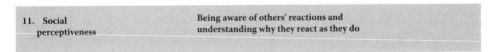

A. How <u>important</u> is SOCIAL PERCEPTIVENESS to the performance of *your current job?*

* If you marked Not Important, skip LEVEL below and go on to the next skill.

B. What <u>level</u> of SOCIAL PERCEPTIVENESS is needed to perform *your current job?*

Figure 16.2   O*NET questionnaires: Item and scale examples.

(c) Knowledge item

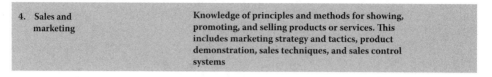

A. How <u>important</u> is SALES AND MARKETING knowledge to the performance of *your current job*?

* If you marked Not Important, skip LEVEL below and go on to the next knowledge area.

B. What <u>level</u> of SALES AND MARKETING knowledge is needed to perform *your current job*?

(d) Generalized work activity item

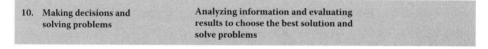

A. How <u>important</u> is MAKING DECISIONS AND SOLVING PROBLEMS to the performance of *your current job*?

* If you marked Not Important, skip LEVEL below and go on to the next activity.

B. What <u>level</u> of MAKING DECISIONS AND SOLVING PROBLEMS is needed to perform *your current job*?

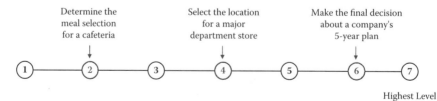

Figure 16.2 Continued

O*NET 16.0 Production Database

The O*NET 16.0 database is a relational database consisting of a host of files organized by more than 1,000 O*NET-SOC codes. File layouts, core data files, and supporting documentation (e.g., data dictionary, technical documentation) are downloadable from the "Developer's Corner" area of the O*NET web site. All of this information is provided to support development efforts carried out

(e) Work context items

2. How frequently does your current job require <u>public speaking</u> (one speaker with an audience)?

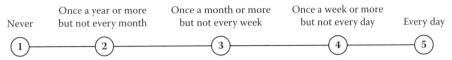

17. How often does your current job require you to work <u>outdoors, exposed to all weather conditions</u>?

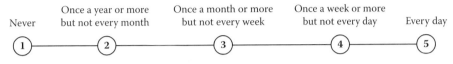

(f) Work styles item

4. Leadership   Job requires a willingness to lead, take charge, and offer opinions and direction

How <u>important</u> is LEADERSHIP to the performance of *your current job*?

Figure 16.2 Continued

not only by government and quasigovernment agencies, but also private businesses and individuals developing new and innovative applications.

According to the National Center for O*NET Development's web site, "[The] twelfth, [most recent] major update from the O*NET Data Collection Program brings the number of comprehensively updated occupations to 857" (O*NET Resource Center, n.d.). Some highlights of this most recent update include (a) the update of tasks and task statement ratings, (b) the update of abilities, work activities, knowledge, work context, work styles, and job zone data, (c) the update of training and work experience, and education data, and (d) the addition of green occupations and green task statements. The next major O*NET database update and estimated release is currently scheduled for July 2012.

For those considering embarking on developing projects or products that incorporate the O*NET Database, it is important to mention that there are certain guidelines to which developers must attend and adhere. The National Center for O*NET Development provides would-be developers with the following special notice (see http://www.onetcenter.org/database.html):

> Individuals may use O*NET database products freely for their own personal use. If use includes developing other products, software, or system applications using O*NET, users are subject to the terms and conditions described in the O*NET Database Products User Agreement. Users intending to develop other products, software, or systems applications using O*NET database products should register their use by completing the Certification Form—O*NET Database Products.

Supplemental Data Files

In addition to a downloadable database, several supplemental files are available that can be used to create tools and applications. Examples of these files are provided below. Other supplemental data files not listed here can be found by accessing http://www.onetcenter.org/supplemental.html.

Detailed Work Activities

Originally developed as part of a U.S. Department of Labor Employment and Training initiative called the Labor Exchange Skills Project, the Detailed Work Activities (DWAs) are a set of cross-occupational, skill-oriented, and work content statements. They are "intermediate" occupational descriptors because they are more specific than the Generalized Work Activities yet more general than the occupation-specific task statements at the level of detail found in the former DOT. Because of the DWA's cross-occupational nature, occupational comparisons and matching are possible.

> The more general nature of the [DWAs] in contrast to O*NET task elements facilitates cross-occupational correspondence and helps displaced workers identify new areas of work that match their capabilities. In addition, educators, job seekers, researchers, and employers can use the DWAs to perform analysis of transferable skills and skill gaps. (National Center for O*NET Development, 2003, p. 3)

Lay Titles

Lay titles are alternate job titles associated with the O*NET-SOC occupations. The database contains more than 40,000 of these titles that are linked to many of the O*NET-SOC codes. These titles can be used to develop keyword search, job matching, and occupational classification applications. By culling data from various sources, such as job incumbents, occupational experts, and other classification systems, the lay title database is continually being enhanced and updated.

Emerging Tasks

Emerging tasks are those tasks identified by job incumbents or occupational experts during the Data Collection Program that they believed were not represented by the current O*NET task lists for their respective occupation. The tasks are "written in" by respondents in the task portion of the survey, and they are subsequently analyzed; if approved, they are incorporated into the O*NET as new, emerging tasks (Van Iddekinge, Tsacoumis, & Donsbach, 2003). The current Emerging Tasks file (as of June 2009) contains more than 500 new task statements.

Tools and Technology

Organized into the United Nations Standard Products and Service coding structure, this file contains detailed information about machines, equipment, tools, and software that may be required to perform the various O*NET occupations. "Emphasis is placed on cutting edge technologies and workplace practices" (see http://www.onetcenter.org/supplemental.html#tools_tech).

Career Exploration Tools

The O*NET system offers three self-assessment, career exploration tools to provide users with vocational guidance. First is the Ability Profiler, an aptitude-oriented self-assessment that provides information about nine occupationally relevant aptitude domains: verbal ability, arithmetic reasoning, computation, special ability, form perception, clerical perception, motor coordination, finger dexterity, and manual dexterity. Second, the Interest Profiler, developed from Holland's Realistic, Investigative, Artistic, Social, Enterprising, and Conventional model of vocational interests (see Holland, 1985), allows the user to identify occupations based on his or her interests. Finally, the Work Importance Profiler is an instrument that helps individuals explore occupations based on an assessment of six work-oriented values: achievement, independence, recognition, relationships, support, and working conditions. Most measures are available in both paper-pencil and computerized formats.

All career assessment results link to a host of O*NET-SOC occupations and associated information that the user may wish to explore. In addition, for each of these instruments, user guides, score reports, master occupation lists, and other materials are available for perusal by individuals, businesses, and developers.

O*NET Toolkit for Businesses

The O*NET Toolkit for Businesses is a resource that provides comprehensive information about its various features. Employers, human resource professionals, vocational specialists, and career counselors may use the Toolkit to learn about developing job descriptions, human resource planning, job design, organizational design and development, training needs analysis, career development, succession planning, and workforce development. The Toolkit provides examples of how to get started on some of the above-mentioned objectives. Specifically, the Toolkit includes (a) a quick reference guide, (b) a guided tour of O*NET OnLine, (c) O*NET at Work (two case studies: developing job descriptions and employee re-skilling and retention), and (d) the O*NET Content Model and all occupational analysis questionnaires (see http://www.onetcenter.org/toolkit.html).

The O*NET Academy

The O*NET Academy (see http://www.onetacademy.com) provides ongoing online training that includes self-paced courses, tutorials, and live webinars to the wide array of stakeholders that O*NET serves. Online courses cover a range of topics such as "using O*NET for demand-driven service delivery" and "how to administer the O*NET Ability Profiler." Various 15-minute overviews about the value of O*NET are also provided. Examples of these are titled "Value of O*NET for Employers" and "Value of O*NET for Job Seekers." Posted webinars offer trainees and other interested individuals information about skills transferability, "tomorrow's" jobs, new and emerging occupations, tools for those transitioning out of the military, and older workers in transition.

The O*NET-SOC Taxonomy

The O*NET-SOC taxonomy is a hierarchical classification structure based on the SOC (Bureau of Labor Statistics, n.d.). The SOC schema consists of six-digit codes and occupational titles, with the code sequence reflecting an occupational hierarchy, the initial segment of the code reflecting the broadest tier, and the end of the code reflecting the most narrow tier. There are five different levels; the broadest level consists of 23 major groups, which divide into 96 minor groups, which in turn subdivide into 449 broad occupations that then narrow into 820 detailed occupations. The O*NET-SOC has a fifth level of occupational detail beyond that provided by the SOC. As such, the 820 detailed occupations refine themselves even further into 1,102. Figure 16.3 shows a sample section of the classification structure.

17-0000 Architecture and Engineering (Major Group)
17-1000 Architects, Surveyors, and Cartographers (Minor Group)
17-1010 Architects, Except Naval (Broad Occupation)
17-1011 Architects, Except Landscape and Naval (Detailed Occupation)
17-1012 Landscape Architects (Detailed Occupation)
17-1020 Surveyors, Cartographers, and Photogrammetrists (Broad Occupation)
17-1021 Cartographers and Photogrammetrists (Detailed Occupation)
17-1022 Surveyors (Detailed Occupation)
17-1022.01 Geodetic Surveyors (O*NET Level 5 Occupation)

Figure 16.3   Sample section of the Standard Occupational Classification structure with added O*NET detail.

APPLICATIONS OF THE O*NET

The O*NET's tools, resources, and data have been applied in many different settings. This section presents a handful of examples of some of these applications, both in research and in practice. For a more comprehensive listing of applications and programs that have incorporated O*NET products, the reader is referred to the document *O*NET Products in Action* (National Center for O*NET Development, 2009b), which can be accessed via the O*NET web site, http://www.onetcenter.org/paw.html.

O*NET in Research

The O*NET descriptors, questionnaires, and occupational data have been used in a wide array of research. To provide but a few examples, Zhang and Snizek (2003) explored occupations, job characteristics, and the use of alcohol and drugs. They combined O*NET 98 analyst data with drug and alcohol use data collected by the 1997 Substance Abuse and Mental Health Services Administration survey and examined the relationships between eight job dimensions and workers' prior and current drug and alcohol use. Results showed a negative correlation between steady employment and job security with use of alcohol and drugs. In addition, a negative correlation was found between job variety and cocaine use. Specifically, when a job offered a greater variety of tasks and activities, workers' likelihood of using cocaine was 64% less (of course, this finding is merely correlational, not causal).

Converse et al. (2004) examined person-occupation matching for career guidance purposes using the O*NET and an ability-based matching application. In their article, the authors presented practical issues that were faced when using O*NET during this process and how the issues were addressed. These issues included (a) ensuring the jobs and individuals were measured on acceptable metrics, (b) incorporating the information about both the required level of a variable and its importance, (c) computing appropriate profile similarity indices that operationalize person-occupation fit in the intended manner, and (d) dealing with the breadth of occupations suggested by person-job fit statistics.

Rotundo and Sackett (2004) studied which skills would be most valuable and thus demand higher pay. The job evaluation literature and labor-market wage theorists hypothesize about skill-wage relationships and often differ in their theoretical interpretations. The researchers linked the skill and ability data from O*NET and other sources to wage data and then conducted a job-level evaluation to determine which skills/abilities had the strongest relationships with wages. Results showed that most of the variance in wage was accounted for by a general cognitive ability factor.

In another vein, Liu, Spector, and Jex (2005) examined job control and job strain, comparing multiple data sources. In their study, they included job-stress data from the O*NET and found that the O*NET stressor variable was related to physical and behavioral strains. They further conclude that "[there] is something in the objective environment that plays a role in employees' physical well-being and behavior" (p. 325).

More recently, Forstmeier and Maercker (2008) developed the concept of motivational reserve and examined the relationship between lifetime motivational abilities and current cognitive status, mild mental impairment, and psychological well-being in individuals' elder years. Using the O*NET they developed a procedure to estimate participants' motivational and cognitive abilities based on their jobs. Though they concluded that "O*NET-estimated motivational abilities predicted cognitive status, psychological well-being, and odds of mild cognitive impairment" (p. 886), correlations were not statistically significant.

LaPolice et al. (2008) used job component validation and linked O*NET descriptors to occupational literacy requirements. They related the O*NET Knowledge, Skill, Ability, and Generalized

Work Activity data from 902 occupations in the O*NET 5.1 database to literacy test scores that they obtained from the National Center for Education Statistics' national adult literacy survey. Correlations ranged from .79 to .81, and results demonstrated that at the broad occupational level, the O*NET descriptors were good predictors of three different applied adult literacy types (prose, document, and quantitative literacy).

Finally, Taylor, Li, Shi, and Borman (2008) explored the transportability of job information across countries using three O*NET questionnaires: Generalized Work Activities, Skills, and Work Styles. More than 1,000 employees in more than 350 businesses in New Zealand, China, and Hong Kong responded to the questionnaires. The authors found mean differences in item ratings between participants from each country. When compared with archival data from job incumbents in the United States, the authors concluded that, for many applications, O*NET job information was likely to transport well across countries.

O*NET in Practice

Classification System Development

In early 2001, one of the leading online job boards, Monster.com, decided to develop and incorporate an occupational classification system into its database as a way to organize its resume submission and matching system more effectively. After extensive research both domestically and abroad, the O*NET-SOC was chosen to be the framework for a system that would organize, by job title, more than approximately 60 million resumes. The O*NET-SOC was not entirely sufficient to classify all resumes, so tailoring it became essential. For example, the O*NET-SOC had limited detail for occupational areas such as computers, information technology, and finance. With the help of occupational classification experts and trained job analysts, these and other areas were expanded to meet specific business needs while at the same time maintaining the O*NET-SOC-based coding structure. Initially, the new, enhanced system was named the O*NET-SOC+, but because it was continually tailored, it was renamed the Monster Occupational Classification. To this day, O*NET-SOC serves as the Monster Occupational Classification's underlying structure.

Assessment and Development

Jeanneret, D'Egidio, and Hanson (2004) devoted an entire chapter to assessment and development opportunities using the O*NET. Specifically, the chapter "links O*NET to assessment and development in the workplace and [examines] possible workplace assessment and development applications…" (p. 192). Jeanneret et al. point out the O*NET's database can inform job analysis and, more specifically, can be used to create job families, establish job similarity, and develop worker safety and health guidelines. The O*NET also may be used as a helpful starting point for developing a job-relevant selection process. The O*NET system's occupational characteristics information, specifically labor market and wage data, could be used as the foundation for compensation system development. Finally, O*NET descriptor domains, such as Abilities, Generalized Work Activities, Knowledge, and Skills, together may be leveraged to create a "comprehensive performance management system" (p. 196). In the development area, the O*NET can help match individuals to occupations and career choices and inform training and related program development, such as educational and licensure programs.

Dislocated Workers Reemployment

Dislocated workers are those who have been laid off from industries and/or occupations with limited reemployment potential in their self-selected local labor market. They are at risk for far higher durations of unemployment as well as severely diminished wages in their next job. They often have family responsibilities and other fiscal constraints to pursuing further training that would add to their store of human capital that they can market to land a wage-appropriate position. In response to the dislocated worker problem, a Vermont-based technology company, Hoover & Johnson, developed the *Job Coach*, a suite of reemployment applications based on the O*NET-SOC and using the O*NET DWAs. Because skills are transferable among occupations, DWAs allow a person with prior occupational experience to amass a "skills bank" that can be compared to every O*NET occupation present in their self-selected labor market. The goal of this application is to move a person from a declining industry or occupation to industries or occupations with either growth potential or networking opportunities for the individual. A person with a DWA profile that has been transferred from other occupations has ammunition to pursue new jobs and negotiate a higher starting wage based on past, skill-oriented experience.

Career Information Systems

According to the National Center for O*NET Development (2009b), a wide range of organizations—state workforce agencies, educational institutions, the military, and private companies—have employed O*NET products for purposes of assessment and career exploration. For example, the Occupation and Skill Computer-Assisted Researcher, a product developed by the Texas Workforce Commission/Career Development Resources, uses the O*NET's Work Importance Locator to help displaced workers find employment. The Fairbanks (Alaska) Job Center incorporates the O*NET Interest Profiler and Work Importance Locator into its career workshops. The Mid-Valley Special Education Cooperative employs O*NET Skills, Work Styles, Knowledge, and Ability statements to assist students with resume development. Careerway (see http://www.careerway.com), a career guidance web site developed by Bigby, Havis & Associates, used O*NET descriptor data and questionnaire items to profile users for skills gap analysis and job matching purposes. Finally, the web site http://www.careeronestop.com utilizes O*NET data in several applications, such as *mySkills myFuture, Veterans ReEmployment,* and *My Next Move,* all intended to help people explore careers and find a job.

Adaptive Test Development

A private company, Adaptiqs (http://www.adaptiqs.com), used the O*NET questionnaires to create a successful neural network-based adaptive testing tool. The patent-pending technology can be used to deliver web-based tests and assessments. This platform uses artificial intelligence to "optimize the process" and has been shown to reduce the time and cost of administration compared with traditional testing (Bublitz, 2007).

USING O*NET IN WORK ANALYSIS

Work analysis is a process of examining work by breaking it down into smaller, more manageable components, such as tasks, activities, worker requirements, and work context, for the purposes of informing and improving human resource functions; job analysis and occupational analysis, for example, are two types of work analysis. A good work analysis can be expensive and time consuming, particularly if it begins with little or no readily available information. Because the O*NET system has detailed information about hundreds of occupations and easily obtainable and deployable questionnaires, it can be leveraged as a starting point in just about any work analysis effort. Furthermore, using O*NET can help streamline a work analysis, reduce the associated time and cost, and possibly enhance the quality of information gathered. Steps in a work analysis that involves O*NET are described below (these steps and examples have been adapted from Levine & Cunningham, 1999).

Table 16.2   Matrix of O*NET Content Model Domains and Human Resource Purposes

	Worker Requirements	Worker Characteristics	Experience Requirements	Occupation Requirements	Occupation Characteristics	Occupation-Specific
HR Planning						
Work/workforce	HD	D	HD	HD	HD	HD
Mobility	HD	D	HD	D	HD	HD
HR development						
Training	U	U	D	HD	U	HD
Staffing	HD	HD	HD	HD	D	HD
Performance	D	D	D	D	U	HD
HR utilization						
Job description	D	HD	HD	HD	U	HD
Job design	U	U	U	HD	U	HD
Efficiency/safety	D	U	U	HD	U	HD
Job class/comp	HD	D	HD	HD	HD	HD

D = desirable; HD = highly desirable; HR = human resource; U = unnecessary.

Steps in a Work Analysis

Designing the Project

This first step involves determining the project's specific purpose. The O*NET Content Model provides information that can help in this regard. Table 16.2 highlights several potential purposes in human resources practice crossed with the O*NET Content Model domains. Should the information presented not be detailed enough, the O*NET is hierarchically structured, so more specific levels of the hierarchy may be explored. For example, project planning may be as fine-grained as the questionnaire-item level. Note that although the O*NET may provide much information required to perform a work analysis, there will often be occasions where information must be supplemented or tailored to the situation at hand.

Data Collection

Why reinvent the wheel when descriptive occupational data may be culled directly from the O*NET database? The O*NET codes link to other federal databases containing job data that can be put to good use. Oftentimes the information in the O*NET database alone will suffice, but other times the data will need to be customized or appended. Another data collection approach may involve administering the O*NET questionnaires to supervisors and incumbents or subject matter experts and trained work analysts. There will be times, however, when O*NET instruments are too general and must either be customized, supplemented, or replaced by more job-specific information.

Analyzing Data

Data should be analyzed at different levels of analysis, depending on the purpose. For development of job specifications, which are typically short summaries, O*NET data could be analyzed at a higher, more general level. For more detailed, lengthy job reports, data can be analyzed at a finer level of specificity, possibly at the questionnaire-item level. Examples of other human resource applications where O*NET item-level (knowledge, skills, general work activity) data can be informative are in job classification and training.

Presenting Information

To quote prior work, "The presentation of data to end-users can be organized via the O*NET Content Model. Each of the broad domains (experience requirements, occupation requirements, worker requirements, etc.) and/or their narrower subdivisions can serve as the headings for a report of the work analysis project. Alternatively, these can provide headings for appendices that contain the full details of information more broadly summarized in the body of a report" (Levine & Cunningham, 1999, p. 22).

Legal Considerations

A work analysis should reflect up-to-date job information and be based on scientifically sound measures, and O*NET can help in this regard. First, because the O*NET involves the electronic collection and storage of data, it provides a basis for tracking occupational changes across the U.S. workforce. Second, the General Work Activities domain can serve as a template for collecting and presenting data on job-specific tasks and activities. Third, O*NET offers tested scales with potentially useful anchors that can be used to collect important data about job-specific activities. Finally, it is important to note that the systematic manner in which the O*NET measures and data were developed does not by itself guarantee the defensibility of a work analysis that uses these measures and data. For instance, one would also want to know about the specific motivation, purpose, and context of the work analysis, the process by which the work analysis was carried out, and the qualifications of the people involved in the work analysis.

IMPLICATIONS AND DIRECTIONS

The O*NET has come a long way since its inception in 1998. It has grown by leaps and bounds and is now a comprehensive occupational classification and analysis and career exploration system with a large number of diverse users. As evidenced by the aforementioned discussion, the O*NET system has become a vast suite of useful tools and resources, a far cry from its more simplistic beginnings as a database of analyst-based occupational information. Shortly after O*NET's release, Peterson, Borman, Hanson, and Kubisiak (1999) speculated as to some future implications and directions. Specifically, they highlighted that the O*NET could be used in areas such as educational policy and skills standards development, school-to-work transition, dislocated workers, and high-performance workplaces. Further, they state, "Although more data are needed before this potential can be fully realized, results to date suggest that O*NET will substantially benefit all of these initiatives" (p. 294). They were right on the mark because many of these areas have come to fruition, such as the development of school-to-work and dislocated worker applications.

Nearly a decade later, our review of the general trends of development, research, and application for the O*NET database and related materials indicates that the O*NET has clearly gained in its breadth, usefulness, and prominence as a flexible and functional tool for a wide array of stakeholders involved in employment- and career-related activities. In this concluding section, we outline a few possible avenues for future developments of the O*NET, although we are certain that there are many others that are either already underway or in the planning stages.

First, the O*NET was developed from the Content Model as a "top-down" approach that identified relevant domains of worker and work characteristics. We believe that the O*NET could be further refined or extended in a "bottom-up" approach as well, namely by examining the current host of applications to which the O*NET is put, asking those who use these applications how the O*NET could be improved to serve their needs more effectively. This may lead to changes in both the content of the O*NET (e.g., developing application-specific measures) as well as its format (e.g., using feedback about O*NET applications to improve the user experiences when responding to questionnaires and/or interpreting and using O*NET information). The "bottom-up" approach can also help determine whether the O*NET variables that seem redundant from a psychometric stand-point (e.g., high correlations or factor loadings) end up distinguishing themselves across different applications (e.g., show differential validity).

Second, the O*NET data may be usefully implemented in meta-analyses relevant to organizations. Often, characteristics that serve as moderators in a meta-analysis are gleaned from the individual contributing studies themselves. However, the O*NET can provide a rich supply of additional data on the occupations represented in each study by matching the occupations represented in each sample to the O*NET database, using the SOC as a crosswalk. When used in this way, the O*NET has the potential to unlock a large number of undiscovered moderator effects that lie within large meta-analysis data sets that contain samples from a diverse array of occupations.

Third, there are parts of the O*NET system that are long overdue for updates. For example, it has been nearly 10 years since the first major revision of the O*NET questionnaires. Because of potential problems with behavioral anchors; abstract wording of some of the items' definitions; and significant advances in data collection methodologies, modalities, and technologies, it would be worthwhile to revisit the possibility of updates on several different fronts to provide a better respondent experience, reduce response burden, tap new areas of job requirements information, and improve data quality. A second example is the DWAs, which were last updated in 2003. The DWAs are a set of cross-occupational, skill-oriented statements that have tremendous potential in job-matching, career placement, and skills-gap analysis, and they have been used successfully in military-to-civilian and dislocated worker applications. Updating and maintaining the DWA data going forward would be beneficial to many stakeholders.

Finally, it behooves the US Department of Labor and National Center for O*NET Development to promote and extend innovative research and development efforts. For example, targeted validation studies of the O*NET questionnaires, behavioral anchors, and the data itself could be carried out. New and more specific data could be gathered, such as occupational minimum qualifications and job-specific skills. Online reporting applications could be developed that would supply valuable information, in real-time, to employers and researchers during data collection. Adaptive technology or artificial intelligence could be incorporated into the O*NET survey instruments, providing faster, more streamlined user experiences and leading to more accurate data. Web-based, interactive, or video game-based career exploration applications could be developed that would provide a fun, informative, and engaging experience for job seekers, students, veterans, career counselors, and the like. Peterson et al. (1999) stated that "a tremendous degree of technical and practical progress has been made… [And] much good work has been done, but much remains to be done" (p. 295). The same holds true today of the O*NET. Thus, it will be exciting and important for stakeholders in areas such as work analysis, vocational guidance, and career development to follow and contribute to the O*NET's progress in years to come.

WEB SITE RESOURCES

Adaptiqs – http://www.adaptiqs.com
U.S. Bureau of Labor Statistics – http://www.bls.gov
CareerOneStop – http://www.careeronestop.com
CareerWay – http://www.careerway.com
Economic Research Institute – http://www.erieri.com
Monster – http://www.monster.com
O*NET Academy – http://www.onetacademy.com
O*NET Resource Center – http://www.onetcenter.org
O*NET Resource Center production database – http://www.onetcenter.org/database.html

O*NET Resource Center data publication schedule – http://www.onetcenter.org/dataPublication.html
O*NET OnLine – http://www.onetcenter.org/online.html
O*NET Products at Work – http://www.onetcenter.org/paw.html
O*NET supplemental data files – http://www.onetcenter.org/supplemental.html
O*NET tools and technology file – http://www.onetcenter.org/supplemental.html#tools_tech
O*NET OnLine Help – http://online.onetcenter.org/help
PAQ Services – http://www.paq.com
PAQ Services eDOT – http://www.paq.com/pdf/e-dot-methodology.pdf

REFERENCES

Alterman, T., Grosch, J., Chen, X., Chrislip, D., Petersen, M., Krieg, E., … Muntaner, C. (2008). Examining associations between job characteristics and health: Linking data from the occupational information network (O*NET) to two US national health surveys. *Journal of Occupational and Environmental Medicine, 50,* 1401–1413.

Bublitz, S. T. (2007, April). *Using O*NET for adaptive career assessments.* Paper presented at the annual meeting of the Society for Industrial and Organizational Psychology, New York.

Bureau of Labor Statistics. (n.d.) *Standard occupational classification.* Retrieved from http://www.bls.gov/soc/

Childs, R. A., & Whetzel, D. L. (1995). Scaling studies. In *Technical memorandum: Tryout of O*NET questionnaires and anchor scaling.* Washington, DC: American Institutes for Research.

Converse, P. D., Oswald, F. L., Gillespie, M. A., Field, K. A., & Bizot, E. (2004). Matching individuals to occupations using abilities and the O*NET: Issues and an application in career guidance. *Personnel Psychology, 57,* 451–487.

Dierdorff, E. C., & Morgeson, F. P. (2009). Effects of descriptor specificity and observability on incumbent work analysis ratings. *Personnel Psychology, 62,* 601–628.

Dunnette, M. D. (1999). Introduction. In N. G. Peterson, M. D. Mumford, W. C. Borman, P. R. Jeanneret, & E. A. Fleishman (Eds.), *An occupational information system for the 21st century: The development of O*NET* (pp. 3–7). Washington, DC: American Psychological Association.

Dye, D. & Silver, M. (1999). The origins of O*NET. In N. G. Peterson, M. D. Mumford, W. C. Borman, P. R. Jeanneret, & E. A. Fleishman (Eds.), *An occupational information system for the 21st century: The development of O*NET* (pp. 9–19). Washington, DC: American Psychological Association.

Economic Research Institute. (2004). *Methodology/disclaimer: Occupational assessor & survey—eDot software and databases.* Retrieved from http://www.paq.com/pdf/e-dot-methodology.pdf

Economic Research Institute. (2011). *Salary & costs comparisons.* Retrieved from http://www.erieri.com

Executive Office of the President/Office of Management and Budget. (2000). *Standard occupational classification manual.* Lanham, MD: Bernan Associates.

Fleishman, E. A., & Mumford, M. D. (1988). The ability requirements scales. In S. Gael (Ed.), *The job analysis handbook for business, industry, and government* (pp. 917–935). New York, NY: John Wiley & Sons.

Forstmeier, S., & Maercker, A. (2008). Motivational reserve: Lifetime motivational abilities contribute to cognitive and emotional health in old age. *Psychology and Aging, 23(4),* 886–899.

Hadden, W., Kravets, N., & Muntaner, C. (2004). Descriptive dimensions of US occupations with data from the O*NET. *Social Science Research, 33,* 64–78.

Hanson, M. A., Borman, W. C., Kubisiak, U. C., & Sager, C. E. (1999). *Cross-domain analyses.* In N. G. Peterson, M. D. Mumford, W. C. Borman, P. R. Jeanneret, & E. A. Fleishman (Eds.), *An occupational information system for the 21st century: The development of O*NET* (pp. 247–258). Washington, DC: APA.

Harvey, R. J. (2000). Yes, Virginia, there *is* an objective reality in job analysis. *Journal of Organizational Behavior, 21,* 829–854.

Holland, J. L. (1985). *Self-directed search professional manual.* Odessa, FL: Psychological Assessment Resources.

Hubbard, M., McCloy, R. A., Campbell, J. P., Nottingham, J., Lewis, P., Rivkin, D., & Levine, J. D. (2000). *Revision of O*NET data collection instruments.* Raleigh, NC: National Center for O*NET Development.

Jeanneret, P. R., D'Egidio, E. L., & Hanson, M. A. (2004). Assessment and development opportunities using the Occupational Information Network (O*NET). In M. Hersen & J. C. Thomas (Eds.), *The handbook of psychological assessment, Volume 4: Industrial/organizational assessment* (pp. 192–202). New York, NY: Wiley.

LaPolice, C. C., Carter, G. W., & Johnson, J. W. (2008). Linking O*NET descriptors to adult literacy requirements using job component validation. *Personnel Psychology, 61*, 405–441.

Levine, E. L., & Cunningham, J. W. (1999). *How O*NET can cut the work in your work analysis (and make it better, too!).* Unpublished work.

Levine, J. D., Nottingham, J., Paige, B., & Lewis, P. (2000). *Transitioning O*NET to the standard occupational classification.* Raleigh, NC: National Center for O*NET Development.

Liu, C., Spector, P. E., & Jex, S. M. (2006). The relation of job control with job strains: A comparison of multiple data sources. *Journal of Occupational and Organizational Psychology, 78*, 325–336.

Mumford, M. D., & Peterson, N. G. (1999). The O*NET content model. In N. G. Peterson, M. D. Mumford, W. C. Borman, P. R. Jeanneret, & E. A. Fleishman (Eds.), *An occupational information system for the 21st century: The development of O*NET* (pp. 21–30). Washington, DC: APA.

National Center for O*NET Development. (2003). *Summary report: Updating the detailed work activities.* Raleigh, NC: National Center for O*NET Development.

National Center for O*NET Development. (2006). *Updating the O*NET-SOC taxonomy.* Raleigh, NC: National Center for O*NET Development.

National Center for O*NET Development. (2009a). *New and emerging occupations of the 21st century: Updating the O*NET-SOC taxonomy.* Raleigh, NC: National Center for O*NET Development.

National Center for O*NET Development. (2009b). *O*NET products at work.* Raleigh, NC: National Center for O*NET Development.

National Center for O*NET Development. (2010). *Updating the O*NET-SOC taxonomy: Incorporating the 2010 SOC structure, summary and implementation.* Raleigh, NC: National Center for O*NET Development.

O*NET Resource Center. (n.d.). *Highlights of the O*NET 16.0 database.* Retrieved from http://www.onetcenter.org/database.html.

PAQ Services, Economic Research Institute. (2011). *Methodology/disclaimer. Occupational assessor & survey (OA/OA+)—eDOT software and databases* (professional & consultant editions). Retrieved from http://www.paq.com/pdf/e-dot-methodology.pdf

Peterson, N. G., Borman, W. C., Hanson, M. A., & Kubisiak, U. C. (1999). Summary of results, implications for O*NET applications, and future directions. In N. G. Peterson, M. D. Mumford, W. C. Borman, P. R. Jeanneret, & E. A. Fleishman (Eds.), *An occupational information system for the 21st century: The development of O*NET* (pp. 289–295). Washington, DC: American Psychological Association.

Peterson, N. G., Mumford, M. D., Borman, W. C., Jeanneret, P. R., & Fleishman, E. A. (1995). *Development of prototype Occupational Information Network (O*NET) content model* (Vols. I and II). Salt Lake City, UT: Utah Department of Workforce Services.

Rotundo, M. & Sackett, P. R. (2004). Specific versus general skills and abilities: A job level examination of relationships with wage. *Journal of Occupational and Organizational Psychology, 77*, 127–148.

Scott, A. J., & Mantegna, A. (2009). Human capital assets and structures of work in the US metropolitan hierarchy (an analysis based on the O*NET information system). *International Regional Science Review, 32*, 173–194.

Social Security Administration. (2004). *Request for information*, Posted June 24, 2004, Solicitation Number: OSD-03-0002.

Stanley, J. C., & Wang, M. D. (1969). Restrictions on the possible values of r_{12}, given r_{13} and r_{23}. *Educational and Psychological Measurement, 29*, 579–581.

Steel, P., Huffcutt, A. I., & Kammeyer-Mueller, J. (2006). From the work one knows the worker: A systematic review of the challenges, solutions, and steps towards creating synthetic validity. *International Journal of Selection and Assessment, 14*, 16–36.

Taylor, P. J., Li, W. D., Shi, K., & Borman, W. C. (2008). The transportability of job information across countries. *Personnel Psychology, 61*, 69–111.

Tsacoumis, S., & Van Iddekinge, C. H. (2006, April). *A comparison of incumbent and analyst ratings of O*NET skills* (Report No. FR05-66). Alexandria, VA: Human Resources Research Organization.

U.S. Department of Labor. (1993). *The new DOT: A database of occupational titles for the 21st century.* Washington, DC: U.S. Government Printing Office.

U.S. Department of Labor. (1991). *Dictionary of occupational titles.* (5th Ed. Rev.). Washington, DC: U.S. Government Printing Office.

Van Iddekinge, C., Tsacoumis, S., & Donsbach, J. (2003). *A preliminary analysis of occupational task statements from the O*NET data collection program* (Technical Report No. FR-02-52). Raleigh, NC: National Center for O*NET Development.

Zhang, Z. & Snizek, W. E. (2003). Occupation, job characteristics, and the use of alcohol and other drugs. *Social Behavior and Personality, 31*(4), 395–412.

17

Context Analysis

Reanna Poncheri Harman

SWA Consulting Inc.

It is a hot summer day. You are reclined in your lounge chair with a tropical drink in hand, reading the *Handbook of Work Analysis*, when suddenly you hear a piercing whistle from the lifeguard stand. You look up as the lifeguard climbs down from the stand and runs to the water to make a rescue. Luckily the lifeguard is well trained and the rescue is a success.

As you imagined this scenario, where did you picture yourself? Were you sitting on a crowded East Coast beach with 20 swimmers in the water? Were you sitting on a mostly deserted beach in a tropical paradise with only three swimmers in the water? Were you at the outdoor community pool in your local neighborhood on a busy Saturday afternoon? Or perhaps you were at an indoor swimming facility on the rooftop of a luxury hotel?

In each of these scenarios, the same job title (lifeguard) is used to identify the individual who was making the rescue. The key difference among these scenarios is the work context. For example, in the first three scenarios the lifeguard works primarily outdoors, whereas in the last scenario the lifeguard works indoors. There are many other potential contextual differences (e.g., number of swimmers in the water, age of swimmers, presence of other lifeguards) between these scenarios that can impact the lifeguard's job tasks and the knowledge, skills, and abilities that are required. This example illustrates an often overlooked, yet important, component of work analysis—the work context.

Psychologists have recognized that work context plays a central role in understanding human behavior (e.g., Lewin, 1936). Despite the widespread acknowledgement that context plays a critical role in advancing our science, industrial/organizational (I/O) psychologists have struggled to incorporate a consideration of context into many domains (Cappelli & Sherer, 1991; Johns, 2006), including our foundational practice of work analysis (Dierdorff, Rubin, & Morgeson, 2009). Recent calls for a more serious consideration of context in work analysis reveals that context analysis has not been effectively incorporated into either work analysis research or practice (Dierdorff et al., 2009). This chapter will review research and practice related to context analysis, highlighting definitions and operationalizations of work context that have been explored. In addition, the chapter will discuss methods for conducting context analysis, identify important choice points and best practices, review unanswered questions, and describe relevant reference materials.

Examining the definition of "analysis of work" offered in the *Principles for the Validation and Use of Personnel Selection Procedures* (Society of Industrial and Organizational Psychology, 2003) reveals context's centrality to this practice: "any method used to gain an understanding of the work behaviors and activities required, or the worker requirements (e.g., knowledge, skills, abilities, and other characteristics), and the context or environment in which an organization and individual may operate" (p. 66). Unfortunately, in both work analysis practice and research, examining context often is secondary to examining work behaviors and worker requirements (Dierdorff et al., 2009).

This treatment of context is not unique to work analysis; it is ubiquitous in our field. Despite years of acknowledging context's importance (e.g., Cappelli & Sherer, 1991; Funder, 2009; Peters & O'Connor, 1980), I/O psychologists are still struggling to incorporate consistent and effective analysis of context in both research and practice. There have been many potential explanations for this oversight (e.g., emphasis on the individual resulting from the cognitive revolution; see Cappelli & Sherer, 1991), but regardless of the reasons, it is clear that our field would benefit from a more explicit and consistent consideration of context. This is especially true for work analysis because examining context is part of its core purpose.

There are many uses for information gleaned from context analysis. Strong, Jeanneret, McPhail, Blakley, and D'Egidio (1999) argued that context analysis plays an important role in work analysis. As these researchers pointed out, context analysis can be used to assess occupational hazards and working conditions that can compromise employee health in order to improve worker safety and well-being. Information gleaned from this practice can also be used to enhance design of selection and compensation systems and can improve realistic job previews by providing more complete information to job applicants (Strong et al., 1999). Other researchers have suggested the need for context analysis in understanding work role requirements (Dierdorff et al., 2009) and for work design (Morgeson & Humphrey, 2006).

Several recent empirical studies have highlighted the important role that context plays in understanding a variety of workplace phenomena. For example, Dierdorff and Surface (2007) demonstrated that context explains significant variance in peer job performance ratings. In this study, the researchers examined peer ratings of five performance dimensions (teamwork, physical proficiency, social interaction, tactical proficiency, and leadership) across three different training situations. Related to context, they found that "the proportion of variance associated with systematic contextual effects accounted for the largest proportion of variance in all peer rating variables regardless of dimension" (Dierdorff & Surface, 2007, p. 115). The finding that context accounted for a larger percentage of variance than actual ratee performance in this study certainly supports studying context in ratings research and in other areas.

Additional studies have highlighted the value of context analysis in particular. Lindell, Clause, Brandt, and Landis (1998) explored time spent on task and task importance ratings from job incumbents working for local emergency planning committees. According to the authors, most states have a local emergency planning committee in every county. Like the lifeguard example that opened the chapter, this study focuses on a job (information coordinator) that can vary considerably with regard to contextual features from one location to another. Some examples provided by Lindell et al. are "community resources, community support, and vulnerability to chemical hazards" (p. 770). Consistent with their hypotheses, the researchers found that organizational context correlated significantly with time spent on task ratings, but not with task importance ratings. In particular, organizational size and amount of boundary spanning were the two contextual variables that correlated most highly with time spent on task ratings. This study reveals the central role context plays when collecting any type of job analytic ratings from incumbents. The tasks and knowledge, skills, abilities, and other characteristics (KSAOs) required may differ based on the work context.

Dierdorff et al. (2009) investigated contextual influences on managerial work role requirements and found that occupation accounted for 4–39% of variance in the importance of managerial work role requirements. Furthermore, the researchers linked different aspects of discrete context (i.e., task context, social context, and physical context) to relevant managerial work role requirements. For example, consistent with the authors' hypothesis, social context (operationalized as interdependence and interpersonal conflict) accounted for more variance in importance of inter-personal managerial role requirements than conceptual and technical/administrative require-ments. The authors make a direct connection between their findings and implications for work analysis practice: "Most important, the present results demonstrate that it is critical to explore context as part of a thorough work analysis" (Dierdorff et al., 2009, p. 984).

Both theoretical rationale and empirical support can leave no doubt that context matters. Although its importance is widely acknowledged, the empirical exploration of context in I/O psychology is just beginning to mature. Context received much attention in the 1970s when the interactionist perspective reigned supreme in psychology (Magnusson, 1981; Terborg, 1981), but the cognitive revolution that followed directed attention back toward the individual (Cappelli & Sherer, 1991). There is currently a resurgence of interest in context but much foundational work is still needed.

WHAT IS CONTEXT?

Before reviewing context analysis research and practice, it is important to dedicate a few para-graphs to a definitional discussion. The term "context" is often used synonymously with other terms, such as "situation" or "environment." Several researchers have offered definitions of work context. For example, Cappelli and Sherer (1991) define context as "the surroundings associated with phenomena which help to illuminate that [sic] phenomena, typically factors associated with units of analysis above those expressly under investigation" (p. 56). Similarly, Mowday and Sutton (1993) defined context as "stimuli and phenomena that surround and thus exist in the environment external to the individual, most often at a different level of analysis" (p. 198). Johns (2006) provided a comprehensive discussion of context that offered the following definition of context: "situational opportunities and constraints that affect the occurrence and meaning of organizational behavior as well as functional relationships between variables" (p. 386).

In all of these definitions, context is described very broadly. Cappelli and Sherer (1991) and Mowday and Sutton (1993) described context as behavioral surroundings, whereas Johns (2006) was slightly more specific, distinguishing between situational opportunities and constraints. That these definitions are broad is not inappropriate; context is a huge domain. Lewin's famous equa-tion, $B = f(P,E)$, is in essence tackling both the "E" in the equation and the comma (person-situation interactions) when studying context (Terborg, 1981). Many researchers have provided definitions, organizing frameworks, taxonomies, and typologies of context, and this topic is worthy of a hand-book itself. Though there is agreement as to what broadly defines context, there is much less agree-ment when it comes to the specifics.

Johns's (2006) article provided a framework for conceptualizing context that incorporates much previous work that has been done as far as defining and conceptualizing context. He made a distinction between omnibus context (broad) and discrete context (particular). He likened good research to a good story and likens omnibus context to the literary questions of *who, what, when, where*, and *why*. Johns's fundamental argument is that I/O psychologists need to do a better job of contextualizing their research. I would argue that, similarly, I/O psychologists need to do a bet-ter job of contextualizing work analysis. Analyzing the omnibus context as a component of work analysis involves gathering information to answer these five questions about the work analysis proj-ect being conducted. Johns defined discrete context as "specific situational variables that influence behavior directly or moderate relationships between variables" (p. 393). He further described dis-crete context as encompassing the physical, social, and task environments, which is consistent with frameworks proposed by other researchers (Hattrup & Jackson, 1996; Mowday & Sutton, 1993). Most instruments used in job analysis that measure context investigate variables that can be placed into one of these three categories. The next section reviews some job analysis systems that examine context to demonstrate the current state of context analysis.

CONTEXT ANALYSIS: STATE OF RESEARCH AND PRACTICE

In practice, examining context is not typically a central focus of work analysis. Strong et al. (1999) provided a succinct yet accurate summary of the current state of context analysis:

> The study of these constructs has often been only a supplemental component of job analysis procedures that focus mainly on work tasks and behaviors. Almost all job analysis instruments assess some aspect of the work environment (Gael, 1988; Ghorpade, 1988), but investigation of these variables has been very fragmented. (p. 128)

Algera and Greuter (1998) provided a similar assessment and argue that examining context is one systematic deficiency of job analysis methods: "Most job analysis methods only touch very briefly upon the context of the job" (p. 143). Peterson and Jeanneret's (2007) overview of deductive job analysis techniques (defined as methods that use already developed knowledge, taxonomies, or instruments) provided additional evidence supporting these observations. Some, but not all, deductive job analysis instruments they review (see Peterson & Jeanneret, 2007, Table 2.1) reference work/job context, work setting, or working conditions. Furthermore, there are no known deductive approaches that exclusively focus on collecting information about the work context in the absence of other job analytic information.

Brannick, Levine, and Morgeson (2007) classified job analytic approaches as work-oriented (focus is on work itself), worker-oriented (focus is on the worker characteristics needed to do the job), and hybrid approaches (focus on both the work and worker characteristics). Conceptually, context analysis fits most appropriately with the work-oriented approaches, "methods that concentrate primarily on what the worker does, including tasks, tools, machines, and work context" (Brannick et al., 2007, p. 23). However, measurement of context can be found in worker-oriented approaches as well (i.e., the Position Analysis Questionnaire [PAQ]). The interaction between context and the worker is emphasized in these approaches. It is possible either to change the context to fit the worker or to select workers who will succeed in a particular context. I will briefly review examples of approaches and instruments that measure context and will borrow from Brannick et al.'s (2007) classification of job analytic methods as an organizing framework for this review.

Work-Oriented Approaches

One work-oriented approach is the U.S. Department of Labor (1972) functional job analysis (DOL FJA). The part of the DOL FJA that measures context focuses exclusively on the physical work environment. As described by Brannick et al. (2007, p. 45):

> Environmental conditions concern the relative amounts of time spent inside and outside; extreme cold and heat; wet and/or humid conditions; noise; vibration; various hazards such as mechanical, electrical, or explosives; and atmospheric conditions such as fumes, dust, gases, and poor ventilation.

The primary source of information in this approach is a trained job analyst who consults both existing information and collects new information by observing and interviewing job incumbents.

Ghorpade (1988) described two systems in addition to the DOL FJA that include measurement of work context: the Versatile Job Analysis System (Bemis, Belenky, & Soder, 1983) and the Factor Evaluation System (U.S. Civil Service Commission, 1977). Both systems were designed to be used for job evaluation. The Factor Evaluation System focuses primarily on the physical work environment and includes items that assess risk, discomfort, and safety hazards in a work environment for job evaluation and determination of compensation. The Versatile Job Analysis System includes an assessment of the physical environment, but it also defines additional elements of context: type of supervision received, guidelines (manuals, policies, forms) available, research/analysis/reports, accountability/consequences of error, personal contacts, supervision exercised, physical demands, work hazards, and personal demands/stress.

Another work-oriented approach that differs from the others described in this section is the critical incident technique (CIT; Flanagan, 1954). CIT is considered an inductive job analytic technique because it involves the collection of new information that is not intended to fit into an established framework. Brannick et al. (2007) and Harvey, Anderson, Baranowski, and Morath (2007) identified the three main pieces of information that are deemed essential for CIT: statement of context, employee behavior, and consequences of behavior. Although this technique focuses on worker behavior, collecting work context information is essential to this process. This technique will be discussed in more detail later in this chapter.

Worker-Oriented Approaches

Although it may seem counterintuitive, there are some systems that primarily focus on worker attributes but also include an emphasis on context. For example, the PAQ is a primarily worker-oriented approach that includes items that measure the physical and social work environment. Brannick et al. (2007) justified examining context even in approaches where worker attributes are the primary focus in the following statement: "a person needs to have whatever is needed to cope with the job. For example, a person may need the ability to work alone or in noisy or dusty environments" (p. 61). This view emphasizes the interaction between the worker and the work environment and the importance of collecting information about context in conjunction with information related to worker behavior and worker attributes.

Hybrid Approaches

Hybrid approaches focus on both the work and worker and describe working conditions or work context broadly. For example, the Common Metric Questionnaire (CMQ; Harvey, 1993) includes 47 questions to assess work context according to the following taxonomy: demanding work situations, working conditions, risks and hazards, work autonomy, tasks and skill variety, feedback, self-development, working apparel, work schedule, reward system, licensing or certification, and training, education, and experience.

The Occupational Information Network (O*NET) is another hybrid approach. The O*NET content model includes an emphasis on work context, and researchers at O*NET have developed a work context taxonomy (Strong et al., 1999). Using previous taxonomic development across disciplines and relevant theoretical models, the researchers developed the O*NET work context taxonomy. The O*NET work context taxonomy includes three higher-order dimensions: interpersonal relationships, physical work conditions, and structural job characteristics. Each higher-order dimension is divided into second-order dimensions (i.e., interpersonal relationships: communication, responsibility for others, type of role relationships, conflictual contact with others; physical work conditions: work setting, job demands, environmental conditions; structural job characteristics: competition, criticality of position, pace and scheduling, routine vs. challenging work), which are then further divided into item-level constructs.

Several important points can be made based on this brief review. First, it is evident after reviewing these systems that there as many definitions and operationalizations of context as there are approaches that incorporate them. Some systems focus exclusively on the physical work environment (e.g., DOL FJA), whereas others define context more broadly, incorporating the social environment and other job characteristics (e.g., PAQ, O*NET). The second point is that work context appears in approaches with very diverse purposes (i.e., work vs. worker-oriented). This shows that regardless of purpose, there is a general acknowledgement that context is important for accomplishing work analysis goals. Finally, it is clear that work context does not play a central role in these approaches to work analysis, as several researchers have noted (Algera & Greuter, 1998; Strong et al., 1999). The next section will review areas for improvement when studying work context.

AREAS FOR IMPROVEMENT

Context analysis traditionally has been recognized, at least by definition, as central to work analysis. In addition, the measurement of context has been incorporated into many work analysis systems; however, both context analysis theory and practice would benefit from more serious attention. This section will review several areas for improvement context analysis, but most (if not all) can be applied more broadly to studying context in psychology.

Emphasis

Context analysis has not taken a primary role in work analysis, despite its acknowledged importance (Strong et al., 1999). This is not surprising when considering context's treatment in the broader psychology literature. For decades, countless researchers have identified context as essential to understanding human behavior (e.g., Cappelli & Sherer, 1991; Johns, 2006; Lewin, 1936), and although context has not been completely ignored, psychological research and practice have been slow to fully embrace calls to examine context. Johns (2006) addresses the claim that psychologists *do* currently study context with the following response: "The point being made here is not that context is never studied. Rather, it is that *its influence if often unrecognized or underappreciated*" (p. 389, emphasis in original). This observation applies well to the context's treatment in work analysis. Context is examined, but there is a need for increased emphasis and integration with other information collected as part of a comprehensive work analysis.

Conceptualization and Definitions of Context

The work analysis systems that incorporate context (e.g., O*NET, PAQ, CMQ) use different organizational frameworks, and many of these frameworks define context very narrowly, focusing exclusively on the physical work environment. The key challenge is one faced by the entire psychological community: to define and develop and organizational framework for context.

Many researchers have asserted that the lack of an organizing framework limits our ability to understand fully the role that context plays in predicting workplace behavior (e.g., Frederiksen, 1972; Funder, 2009; Hattrup & Jackson, 1996; Johns, 2006; Page, Wilson, Meyer, & Inkson, 2003; Schneider, 1978). Over the past several decades, researchers have offered definitions and frameworks for context, but there are no widely accepted frameworks for studying context like there are for many person-centered constructs (e.g., the Five Factor Model of Personality; McCrae & Costa, 1987).

Finally, context is often treated in isolation when examined in existing deductive job analytic approaches. Existing systems provide a mechanism for collecting information about context, but they do not show how context relates to other collected information or how context may interact with worker characteristics to impact workplace behavior. It is essential to adopt a framework that integrates contextual information with other information collected in work analysis.

Context Measurement

There are several areas where the measurement of contextual variables can be improved. I will focus on deductive approaches, such as those reviewed in the previous section, when reviewing areas for improved measurement. With the exception of some inductive approaches, such as CIT, many existing context measures focus exclusively on quantitative measurement. Although there are many advantages to an exclusively quantitative approach (i.e., faster data processing), there is some information that is more appropriately captured using a qualitative approach.

Brannick et al. (2007) stated that there is a trend toward more quantitative measurement in work analysis, although "qualitative descriptions still have their place in such documents as job descriptions" (p. 18). I would argue that qualitative information should not be restricted to job descriptions and should play a larger role in work analysis. Johns (2006) encouraged researchers to collect qualitative data to gain a more complete understanding of context effects in psychological research. Similarly, collecting and analyzing qualitative information for context analysis will accomplish a similar goal. Zickar and Carter (2010) noted that there has been a resurgence of interest in qualitative methods in I/O psychology. In their article, which called for increased attention toward ethnographic research, Zickar and Carter (pp. 315–316) acknowledged the role that qualitative methods plays in job analysis: "The spirit of ethnography is already part of the recommendations for job analysts who are recommended to observe workers even if they are administering objective job analysis instruments." Qualitative methods not only would enhance the information collected in individual job analysis projects, they will aid in theory development for the practice of context analysis in organizations.

Incorporating qualitative data collection and analysis is one area where measurement can be enhanced, but there are also many ways to improve existing quantitative measurement. Most existing, quantitative deductive measures (i.e., PAQ, O*NET) use many single items with different rating scales (i.e., level, frequency, importance, etc.) to measure facets of context as opposed to taking a construct approach to measurement. When developing the O*NET taxonomy, the researchers developed item-level constructs and associated technical definitions for each second-order factor. Though many of the second-order factors are associated with multiple item-level constructs, many of the item-level constructs are measured by a single item, and many of these use different rating scales.

The researchers justify this approach by arguing that using multiple items per construct would lead to excessive item burden for raters and that, because of the objective nature of most items, single-item measurement can lead to reliable results (Strong et al., 1999). However, the results of this taxonomic development reveal that interrater agreement is a concern. Most of the single-item measures of context contain rating scales with eight scale anchors, making high interrater agreement a challenging standard to achieve.

The final measurement concern is that current approaches tend to treat context as static and unchanging as opposed to dynamic. Many existing instruments assess the current organizational context without thinking about anticipated changes in work context. This observation is related to strategic job analysis (Sanchez, 1994; Siddique, 2004; Singh, 2008). As work analysis becomes more strategic in focus, context analysis will need to do the same.

CONTEXT ANALYSIS: STEP-BY-STEP

Few would argue that it is important to study and understand work context; however, as mentioned, this is often not translated into practice. There is currently no single, widely accepted method for conducting a context analysis, and this chapter does not endorse a single approach. Instead, this section broadly defines a procedure for conducting context analysis in conjunction with a larger work analysis project and highlights the key decision points in the process. The broad steps outlined (Figure 17.1) are the same as the main steps that would be taken in any job or work analysis study (see Chapter 9 in Brannick et al., 2007), but for each step I will emphasize ways to focus on measuring and documenting work context.

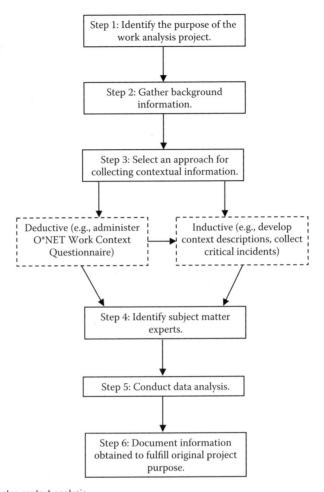

Figure 17.1 Step-by-step context analysis.

Step 1: Identify the Purpose of the Work Analysis Project

Work analysis should be conducted with a purpose in mind. As Wilson (2007) argued, "Purpose drives all the subsequent decisions that need to made in conducting a job analysis" (p. 235). Brannick et al. (2007) identified several major uses for work analysis information. Examining and documenting context plays an important role in accomplishing these goals (see Table 17.1 for examples linking context analysis goals to typical work analysis goals). Contextual information serves many purposes, which highlights the importance of context analysis in any work analysis project.

It is important to be clear about work analysis project goals so that necessary information can be gathered about the work context. For example, if the work analysis project goal is to improve job safety by identifying environmental hazards in the workplace, the context analysis should focus on the physical environment and working conditions that may be hazardous or compromise worker safety. If, on the other hand, the purpose is to develop job descriptions to enhance realistic job previews for new employees, the context analysis may focus on the social environment and relationships with peers and supervisors. Many variables can be measured when studying work context, and it may be unnecessary or impractical to measure the entire domain of work context. Defining the project's purpose will help to narrow the focus of context analysis on information that is relevant.

Table 17.1 Purpose of the Project and Role of Context Analysis

Purpose[a]	Role of Context Analysis[b]
Job description	Job descriptions can provide important information to job applicants about the contextual demands of the job. Brannick et al. (2007) note that "statements about hazards, shift work, etc., are sometimes included in job descriptions" (p. 179).
Job classification	Job classification involves grouping jobs with similar characteristics. It is possible to classify jobs on the basis of contextual job features, such as classifying dangerous jobs.
Job evaluation	The goal of job evaluation is to determine the worth of jobs to employers. It is important to analyze contextual features of jobs to determine if there are any elements of the environment that would impact the value of the work to the employer (i.e., working in hazardous conditions).
Job, team, and system design and redesign	When jobs, teams, or systems are redesigned, an understanding of context is necessary. Most often, the goal of redesign is increased efficiency, which may be accomplished through changes to the context.
Human resource requirements and specifications	This refers to the KSAOs needed to perform the job. Context can moderate the relationship between employee characteristics and job performance. Solutions may include altering the context to fit workers or selecting workers who will succeed in particular contexts.
Performance appraisal	The context may prevent or enable a person to perform well in a particular job. It is important to understand and document elements of context that may influence performance and take those into consideration when doing performance appraisal.
Training	When determining training needs, it is important to consider the work context. In addition, understanding context can enhance transfer of training to the extent that the training context is consistent with work context in key areas.
Worker mobility	Much work analytic information is used for vocational or career counseling. Information about context is highly important when making career decisions.
Workforce planning	When organizations plan jobs for the future, understanding context will enhance recruitment and selection efforts to ensure good fit.
Efficiency	Making a job more efficient often involves altering the work context.
Safety	There may be elements of the work environment that compromise worker safety, and analyzing context can highlight those areas.
Legal and quasilegal requirements	Examining context may provide options for making reasonable accommodations for workers.

KSAOs = knowledge, skills, abilities, and other characteristics.

[a] The list of purposes is from Brannick et al. (2007).

[b] The roles of context analysis described in this table are not intended to be exhaustive. There are other potential uses for contextual information for each of these purposes, and this table is meant to provide examples.

Best Practices

- Define the scope of the work analysis project by identifying the relevant domain of contextual information needed to accomplish the project's purpose.
- When conducting any work analysis project, consider the work context. Research has shown that context does matter and impacts important organizational outcomes.
- Link collection of contextual information to the overall project purpose.

Step 2: Gather Background Information

This initial information gathering provides the foundation for the remaining steps in the work analysis project. When gathering background information, it is important to seek resources that provide insights about the physical, social, and task environments. For example, organizational charts will help provide information about the relationships between job roles in the organization that may shed light on the social work environment.

At this stage in the process, it is helpful for an analyst to think about the work context broadly; he or she should note any important or obvious contextual features in the work environment that may impact tasks or work behaviors performed on the job or influence KSAOs needed to perform the job. For example, if you were conducting a work analysis project to examine a lifeguard job, it would be helpful to gather information about the different work environments in the organization. Are all lifeguards hired by the organization contracted to work at community swimming pools or are there other types of facilities (e.g., water parks) or environments (e.g., beaches, lakes) where lifeguards will work? Awareness and observation of work environment at this early stage in the process is critical for future steps.

Best Practices

- Identify all possible background information sources that can provide insight about work context.
- Ask specific questions to uncover possible variations in work context for the job being analyzed.
- Review work context taxonomies or typologies before gathering background information. Use the taxonomy or typology as a checklist to ensure that information has been gathered about relevant aspects of context.

Step 3: Select an Approach for Collecting Contextual Information

The analyst must make an important choice at this point: whether to use information available from deductive job analysis methods, collect new data using an inductive approach, or combine both approaches. The context analyst must make this decision by carefully considering the work analysis project's purpose and the resources available. Peterson and Jeanneret (2007) made the following recommendation:

> Deductive analyses are generally more appropriate when a large-scale employee selection or promotion system is to be developed for a variety of jobs, and the inductive system is generally more appropriate when a single job or a small set of highly similar jobs is the focus. (p. 53)

The next section discusses some resources and key points to consider for both deductive and inductive approaches.

Deductive Approaches

Peterson and Jeanneret (2007) provided a list of available deductive job analysis instruments. Of those listed, the following instruments measure some aspect of the work environment or context: CMQ, General Work Inventory, Job Analysis Guide, Minnesota Job Description Questionnaire, O*NET, PAQ, and Transition to Work Inventory. Excluding the Job Analysis Guide and the Transition to Work Inventory, databases are available for many of these instruments. The interested reader is encouraged to refer to Peterson and Jeanneret (2007) for additional information about these instruments.

An analyst may choose to use information about context already available, such as that provided in a database associated with a deductive approach described above. If the occupation under investigation is available in the database and the work context information is sufficient, there may be no need to collect additional information. However, this information may not be sufficient for the project purpose. O*NET OnLine (http://online.onetcenter.org) provides one example of this information.

Recall the example that opened this chapter of the lifeguard who successfully rescues a swimmer in distress. If you were interested in understanding the work context for this job, you may go to O*NET online and type "lifeguard" into the search engine. Doing this would yield one "hit": a job description for "Lifeguard, Ski Patrol, and Other Recreational Protective Service Workers." This job description includes information related to work context. The highest-rated aspect of work context is "contact with others," followed by "responsible for others' health and safety." Regardless of the scenario that you envisioned at the beginning of the chapter (i.e., a lifeguard at the local pool or on a crowded beach), these aspects of context are important. However, some other highly rated aspects of work context are "work with work group or team" and "coordinate or lead others." These may, in fact, be important aspects of work context in some situations (e.g., multi-lifeguard facilities, in emergency response situations) but not for others (e.g., single-lifeguard facilities).

It is important to note that these O*NET descriptions of work context were gathered via ratings across many different organizations and contexts and, therefore, represent the average or typical context for this job. The purpose of the O*NET work context taxonomy is to distinguish between jobs. In reference to the O*NET work context taxonomy, Strong et al. (1999) noted that,

> Our taxonomy is not an exhaustive listing of variables that could be classified as part of the work context; rather the taxonomy consists of those variables in the work environment that are likely to affect workers and that will provide information about the differences and similarities between jobs. (p. 130)

If a deductive approach is deemed insufficient, an analyst may use a questionnaire developed under an existing deductive approach but collect new data from subject matter experts (SMEs). For example, the O*NET Work Context Questionnaire is freely available on the O*NET web site for organizations to use. However, it is important for the analyst to recognize that using an existing measure or information gathered from an existing measure involves accepting the contextual taxonomy or typology adopted by the instrument's developers. If the underlying contextual dimensions are insufficient or if the information from existing measures does not meet the project purpose, a more tailored, inductive approach to context analysis will be necessary.

Inductive Approaches

In many cases, it will be necessary to collect new, job-specific information about the work context. In a chapter that complements Peterson and Jeanneret's (2007) discussion of deductive job analysis, Harvey et al. (2007) provided a discussion of inductive job analytic techniques. In their chapter, Harvey et al. described a seven-step process that is based on job-task analysis and the critical incident technique (Flanagan, 1954). Although there are many other data collection methodologies that can be used when taking an inductive approach, this process will be used to highlight ways to incorporate context analysis in a typical work analysis project.

Contextualizing Task Statements

One key step in work-oriented approaches to job analysis, including the task inventory approach (Gael, 1983), is the developing of task statements. Task statements are often developed after observing workers on the job or interviewing job incumbents and follow a highly structured format: verb, object, and qualifier (Gael, 1983). The qualifier is the element of the task statement that adds information about work context (i.e., how, when, where, or why tasks are performed; Gael, 1983; Harvey et al., 2007).

From the analyst's perspective, the qualifier is essential to the task statement. However, the qualifier is often treated as supplementary information. In their chapter, Harvey et al. (2007) stated that "the

Qualifier is needed only when this information is critical to understanding the job, and cannot be implied from the verb and the object" (p. 63). Although adding qualifiers to every task statement could become redundant, this approach is appealing because it not only documents work context, it also makes explicit connections between the tasks performed and the context in which they are performed.

Researchers who study context must confront the challenge of identifying which contextual elements are important to measure. When writing tasks statements, the analyst focuses on the job tasks and investigates only those elements of context that directly relate to tasks performed. To make sure the critical aspects of context are documented, it is essential for the analyst to pay particular attention to the work context when observing job incumbents and to ask specific questions about the context in which tasks are performed when interviewing incumbents. It also may be helpful for the analyst to review work context taxonomies/frameworks prior to conducting interviews or observations to increase awareness of possible contextual influences on performance.

Developing Context Descriptions

In addition to contextualizing task statements, it may be important to develop separate context descriptions to provide a means for evaluating the context independent of the tasks performed on the job. Just like work behavior, task, and KSAO statements, context descriptions can be initially written by work analysts and then revised and finalized through interviews, observations, and workshops with SMEs.

The analyst should begin by selecting a framework for work context to be used in the project; he or she can then develop descriptions for relevant work context dimensions. This approach mirrors that used in the development of O*NET's work taxonomy (Strong et al., 1999). However, keep in mind that the O*NET approach is very broad and seeks to differentiate jobs, whereas a tailored, inductive approach has a more defined purpose. Therefore, the context descriptions can be more limited in scope and can focus only on environmental elements that are important to the job(s) in question. These context descriptions can be used in job descriptions or can serve as the basis for developing a questionnaire to collect additional ratings about the work context.

Context Analysis Questionnaires

In the job-task analysis approach described by Harvey et al. (2007), a Job Analysis Questionnaire is developed after work behavior, task, and KSAO statements are finalized. Context descriptions can be either included on a Job Analysis Questionnaire if context analysis is part of a larger work analysis project or included in a separate questionnaire dedicated specifically to rating work context (CAQ). These context statements can then be rated by SMEs.

On the O*NET Work Context Questionnaire, context descriptions are evaluated on many different scales. Strong et al. (1999) provided details about the rating scales used on this questionnaire, which include frequency, importance, and many others that relate to the construct being measured. For example, when measuring the level of automation involved in a particular job, the scale used ranges from 1 (low automation) to 7 (high automation). An analyst must carefully consider what aspects of context are important to measure and develop appropriate scales. Thinking carefully about the main purpose and intended outcome of the work analysis project will also provide insights about the scale that should be used. For example, if an analyst is working on a project and there is a concern with improving efficiency, incumbents can be asked to rate the extent to which contextual elements enhance or interfere with their ability to successfully perform their job.

Critical Incident Technique

The critical incident technique (CIT) developed by Flanagan (1954) is another inductive method that can be used to collect information about the work context. There are three components to a critical incident: (a) "the situation, including the context or events leading up to the behavior," (b) "the individual's behavioral response to the situation," and (c) "the outcome of the behavioral response" (Harvey et al., 2007, p. 73). As Harvey et al. noted, CIT "has the capacity to provide much more explicit situation-oriented information concerning the job than behavior- or worker-oriented approaches" (p. 73). Although CIT is already widely used in work analysis projects, it is very likely that the contextual information gathered using this approach is often overlooked.

The key to eliciting critical incidents with useful contextual information is training SMEs to provide high-quality examples of work behaviors and the events and setting surrounding the behaviors. It is important for analysts to encourage SMEs to provide examples that represent variations in work context. In addition, SMEs should be encouraged to provide sufficient details about the setting and situation leading up to events in the workplace. Explicit questions that probe information about who, what, when, where, and why should be used.

Best Practices

- Select an approach for gathering contextual information that is aligned with project purpose. Consider existing deductive approaches and inductive approaches and select the approach(es) that best meet the project goals.
- Although this section focused on a few methods for collecting context information, collecting contextual data can be integrated into any work analysis approach.

Step 4: Identify Subject Matter Experts

As with any work analysis project, SMEs who will be involved in providing information about work context should be selected carefully. When developing the O*NET work context taxonomy, ratings were collected from job incumbents as well as trained analysts. Strong et al. (1999) found different results when comparing job incumbent context ratings to job analyst context ratings. They noted that many context dimensions could not be rated by analysts who had only read job descriptions. The researchers note that actually performing the job, or at the very least observing the job, may be necessary for rating some context dimensions (Strong et al., 1999). Therefore, analysts who may only read task lists or brief job descriptions may be unable to evaluate work context accurately. This suggests that either job incumbents should be used to gather work context ratings or analysts who will make ratings must observe/perform the job prior to providing ratings.

The analyst should identify job incumbents from diverse contexts who are sufficiently familiar with the job (e.g., have been in the position at least 6 months; Harvey et al., 2007). Including job incumbents who work in diverse physical environments (e.g., different buildings), social environments (e.g., different work groups), or task environments (e.g., different departments within the organization) will increase understanding of contextual variations within the same job.

Best Practices

- If trained analysts are used to provide ratings or information about work context, ensure that the analysts either observe or perform the job.
- When selecting SMEs, identify job incumbents who work in diverse physical, social, and task environments.

Step 5: Conduct Data Analysis

Once the project purpose, the work context domain, and the approach (i.e., deductive, inductive, or both) are determined, it is possible to collect and document information about the context. If a deductive approach is chosen and existing information will be used, then extensive data analysis may not be necessary. However, it is likely that at least some new information will need to be collected from job incumbents or those who are familiar with the specific job in question.

Traditionally, job analysis data has been collected by observing, interviewing, and surveying incumbents; reviewing company records; and, in some cases, doing the work itself (Brannick & Levine, 2002). The same methods for data collection can be applied to context analysis. However, there are some additional data collection methods that may enhance information quality.

The contextualized task statements or contextual descriptions can be analyzed by examining the ratings provided by SMEs. When examining task, KSAO, and work behavior ratings, it is typical to look for consistency or agreement between raters so that ratings can be aggregated (Harvey et al., 2007). However, disagreement between raters may reveal contextual differences within the same job. These disagreements should be investigated further to determine if there are any important differences in the work environment that may impact the way tasks are performed or the worker characteristics that are needed to perform the job.

In addition to examining the variability in ratings, the ratings should be examined to determine which contextual elements have the most influence on job performance. This is accomplished by examining the quantitative ratings, but it should also be based on qualitative information collected during interviews or observations or when gathering critical incidents.

Although many work analysis projects primarily focus on gathering and analyzing quantitative data, qualitative analysis plays an important role when analyzing contextual information. Qualitative information is gathered at many different points in a typical work analysis project and includes information obtained from individual and group interviews and observations and when collecting critical incidents. There are two potential approaches for analyzing the qualitative contextual information, such as the information that would be obtained when collecting critical incidents: (a) using an existing work context taxonomy or typology to content analyze elements of the situation, or (b) developing a work context taxonomy or typology that is specific to the project based on analyzing qualitative data. There are several excellent resources on qualitative methodology and content analysis that can be used when planning and conducting qualitative analysis (e.g., Krippendorff, 2003; Neuendorf, 2001; Saldana, 2009).

Best Practices

- Match the analysis to the approach selected.
- For quantitative analysis, examine variability in ratings to determine if there is contextual variation across work contexts in the organization.
- Use qualitative analysis when appropriate.
- Consider developing a work context taxonomy specific to the project if appropriate.

Step 6: Document Information Obtained to Fulfill Original Project Purpose

Once the data have been collected and analyzed, it is important to provide appropriate documentation to fulfill the original project purpose. For a project that involves analyzing work context, it is necessary to indicate the framework for exploring context that was used in the study. In addition, it is very important to document where data were obtained and note the contextual variation that may have existed between groups. If a company is interested in developing job descriptions for lifeguards, but there is considerable diversity in work context from one location to another within a company (i.e., indoor vs. outdoor locations and how that impacts exposure to the elements), this would be important to note in project documentation. Contextual variation may also point to areas where reasonable accommodations can be made. For example, there may be a medical reason why an applicant for a lifeguard job may be unable to work outdoors. The hiring organization may be able to accommodate this medical situation by placing the applicant at an indoor facility if they are available in the organization.

Although information obtained from work analysis traditionally has been documented in text (i.e., written job descriptions or evaluations), there are some other options for documenting information that may be particularly relevant when documenting work context. Using still image, video, or audio can provide rich, contextual information that other methods do not. Videotaping the worker on the job can provide information about how the context impacts task performance and how that context may vary within an organization across the same job. Although this information is traditionally obtained through observation, the video-based documentation enhances the information quality, creating a permanent record of what was observed. This also enhances communication of information to the intended audience. Video-based job descriptions may enhance recruitment and selection efforts in an organization by providing more realistic job previews to applicants. This technique also has been used to document hazardous situations in the workplace (e.g., Paquet, Mathiassen, & Dempsey, 2006) and has many other potential uses when documenting work context.

Best Practices

- Ensure that the documentation corresponds to the original project purpose.
- Make sure that the project documentation includes information about the work context taxonomy or typology used in the project.
- Make sure any contextual variation observed is documented.
- Use documentation appropriate for the contextual information being measured. Consider using still image-, audio-, or video-based documentation.

UNANSWERED QUESTIONS

There are many unanswered questions related to context analysis because the work context is often overlooked in work analysis research and practice. One fundamental question, unfortunately, lacks a straightforward answer: What elements of context should be measured in a work analysis project? This question essentially asks for a contextual taxonomy or framework for measuring work context. Although several researchers have developed taxonomies specific to work context (e.g., Harvey, 1993; Strong et al., 1999), there has been very little published empirical work to validate these taxonomies aside from that conducted by the instruments' creators during initial development.

For example, Ford, Wiggins, and Griepentrog (2009) explored the factor structure for the generalized work activity, work context, and skill taxonomies in the O*NET content model. The researchers point out two important limitations related to the initial development of the O*NET work context taxonomy: (a) The taxonomy was based on a small number of occupations (37 occupations) in the O*NET database, and (b) very little empirical work was initially conducted to validate this taxonomy. Ford et al. addressed these limitations by conducting a confirmatory factor analysis on the work context taxonomy for 801 occupations. Ford et al.'s final recommendation was for a seven-factor solution (responsibility for others, work conditions/job hazards, physical activity, decision making, routine vs. challenging work, level of competition, and time pressure), even though several fit indices for this model were borderline (comparative fit index = .91, square root mean residual = .08) and one did not satisfy recommendations for good fit (root mean square error of approximation = .14). Note that Vandenberg and Lance (2000) and Millsap (2002) recommended that the root mean square error of approximation and square root mean residual be below .08, whereas Hu and Bentler (1999) recommended that the comparative fit index be above .90, but values closer to 1 are better. Many items from the work context model were removed because of conceptual overlap with other O*NET dimensions, poor factor loadings, or the item only described a small number of jobs.

This study provides an important advancement in terms of refining the work context taxonomy in the O*NET content model and highlights an important research need in context analysis. Because context is not often central to many work analysis efforts, much foundational work is still needed. Work analysts should continue to measure context and conduct analyses to evaluate the psychometric properties of those measures.

IMPORTANT REFERENCE MATERIALS

There are several excellent resources available that can assist analysts who conduct context analysis. There are both theoretical and empirical articles related to developing contextual frameworks or taxonomies that should be consulted (e.g., Johns, 2006; Hattrup & Jackson, 1996; Strong et al., 1999). Strong et al.'s (1999) chapter describes the development of the O*NET work context taxonomy and is one of the best resources available for exploring context in work analysis. Even if the O*NET framework or Work Context Questionnaire are not used in a particular project, analysts can consult this chapter for ideas on how to develop a customized measure of work context. In addition to these sources, Peterson and Jeanneret's (2007) chapter from *Applied Measurement: Industrial Psychology in Human Resources Management* provides a table (see Table 2.1 in their chapter) that lists deductive job analysis methods and indicates the type of information included (i.e., whether work context elements are included). This can be useful when identifying the approach to be used in conducting context analysis.

This chapter highlighted current research and practice as it relates to context analysis and outlined a process for conducting context analysis. In many ways, context analysis is uncharted territory in work analysis. When conducting research for this chapter, it was challenging to find resources that focused on the work context. As many researchers have pointed out, work analysis more often focuses on tasks and KSAOs, and context is often treated secondarily or, worse yet, not at all. However, this trend is changing. Researchers are continuing to discover the importance of work context (e.g., Barrett, Mesquita, & Smith, 2010; Dierdorff et al., 2009), and there is general acknowledgement of the need to enhance our understanding in this area. That this chapter is included in this handbook is evidence that context analysis is an important component of work analysis and that it deserves more explicit attention. For this momentum to continue, I/O researchers and practitioners must continue to explore and study context in a variety of domains, especially in work analysis.

REFERENCES

Algera, J. A., & Greuter, M. A. M. (1998). Job analysis. In P. J. D. Drenth, H. Thierry, & C. J. de Wolff (Eds.), *Handbook of work and organizational psychology* (Vol. 3, 2nd ed., pp. 141–164). East Sussex, UK: Psychology Press.

Barrett, L. F., Mesquita, B., & Smith, E. R. (2010). The context principle. In B. Mesquita, L. F. Barrett, & E. R. Smith (Eds.), *The Mind in Context* (pp. 1–22). New York, NY: The Guilford Press.

Bemis, S. E., Belenky, A. H., & Soder, D. A. (1983). *Job analysis: An effective management tool*. Washington, DC: The Bureau of National Affairs.

Brannick, M. T., & Levine, E. L. (2002). *Job analysis: Methods, research, and applications for human resource management in the new millennium*. Thousand Oaks, CA: Sage.

Brannick, M. T., Levine, E. L., & Morgeson, F. P. (2007). *Job and work analysis: Methods, research, and applications for human resource management* (2nd ed.). Los Angeles, CA: Sage.

Cappelli, P., & Sherer, P. (1991). The missing role of context in OB: The need for a meso-level approach. In L. L. Cummings & B. M. Staw (Eds.), *Research in organizational behavior* (Vol. 13, pp. 55–110). Greenwich, CT: JAI Press, Inc.

Dierdorff, E. C., Rubin, R. S., & Morgeson, F. P. (2009). The milieu of managerial work: An integrative frame-work linking work context to role requirements. *Journal of Applied Psychology, 94,* 972–988.

Dierdorff, E. C., & Surface, E. A. (2007). Placing peer ratings in context: Systematic influences beyond rate per-formance. *Personnel Psychology, 60,* 93–126.

Flanagan, J. C. (1954). The critical incident technique. *Psychological Bulletin, 51,* 35–42.

Ford, M. T., Wiggins, B., & Griepentrog, B. K. (2009, April). *Confirmatory factor analyses of O*NET ratings.* Paper presented at the 24th annual meeting of the Society for Industrial and Organizational Psychology, New Orleans, LA.

Frederiksen, N. (1972). Toward a taxonomy of situations. *American Psychologist, 27,* 114–123.

Funder, D. C. (2009). Naïve and obvious questions. *Perspectives on Psychological Science, 4,* 340–344.

Gael, S. (1983). *Job analysis: A guide to assessing work activities.* San Francisco, CA: Jossey-Bass.

Gael, S. (1988). Job descriptions. In S. Gael (Ed.), *The job analysis handbook for business, industry, and govern-ment* (Vol. I, pp. 71–89). New York, NY: Wiley.

Ghorpade, J. V. (1988). *Job analysis: A handbook for the human resource director.* Englewood Cliffs, NJ: Prentice Hall.

Harvey, R. J. (1993). *Research monograph: The development of the CMQ.* San Antonio, TX: The Psychological Corporation.

Harvey, J. L., Anderson, L. E., Baranwoski, L. E., & Morath, R. A. (2007). Job analysis: Gathering job-specific information. In D. L. Whetzel & G. R. Wheaton (Eds.), *Applied measurement: Industrial psychology in human resources management.* Mahwah, NJ: Erlbaum.

Hattrup, K. & Jackson, S. E. (1996). Learning about individual differences by taking situations seriously. In K. R. Murphy (Ed.), *Individual differences and behavior in organizations* (pp. 507–547). San Francisco, CA: Jossey-Bass.

Hu, L., & Bentler, P. M. (1999). Cutoff criteria for fit indexes in covariance structure analysis: Conventional criteria versus new alternatives. *Structural Equations Modeling, 6,* 1–55.

Johns, G. (2006). The essential impact of context on organizational behavior. *Academy of Management Review, 31,* 386–408.

Krippendorff, K. (2003). *Content analysis: An introduction to its methodology.* (2nd ed.). Thousand Oaks, CA: Sage.

Lewin, K. (1936). *Principles of topological psychology.* New York, NY: McGraw-Hill.

Lindell, M. K., Clause, C. S., Brandt, C. J., & Landis, R. S. (1998). Relationship between organizational context and job analysis task ratings. *Journal of Applied Psychology, 83,* 769–776.

Magnusson, D. (Ed.). (1981). *Toward a psychology of situations: An interactional perspective.* Hillsdale, NJ: Lawrence Erlbaum Associates, Inc.

McCrae, R. R., & Costa, P. T., Jr. (1987). Validation of the five-factor model of personality across instruments and observers. *Journal of Personality and Social Psychology, 52,* 81–90.

Millsap, R. E. (2002). Structural equation modeling: A user's guide. In F. Drasgow & N. Schmitt (Eds.), *Measuring and analyzing behavior in organizations: Advances in measurement and data analysis* (pp. 257–301). San Francisco, CA: Jossey-Bass.

Morgeson, F. P., & Humphrey, S. E. (2006). The work design questionnaire (WDQ): Developing and validating a comprehensive measure for assessing job design and the nature of work. *Journal of Applied Psychology, 91,* 1321–1339.

Mowday, R. T., & Sutton, R. I. (1993). Organizational behavior: Linking individuals and groups to organiza-tional contexts. *Annual Review of Psychology, 44,* 195–229.

Neuendorf, K. A. (2001). *The content analysis guidebook.* Thousand Oaks, CA: Sage.

Page, C., Wilson, M., Meyer, D., & Inkson, K. (2003). "It's the situation I'm in": The importance of managerial context to effectiveness. *Journal of Management and Development, 22,* 841–862.

Paquet, V. L., Mathiassen, S. E., & Dempsey, P. G. (2006). Video-based: Ergonomic job analysis. *Professional Safety, 51,* 27–35.

Peters, L. H., & O'Connor, E. J. (1980). Situational constraints and work outcomes: The influences of a frequently overlooked construct. *The Academy of Management Review, 5,* 391–397.

Peterson, N. G., & Jeanneret, P. R. (2007). Job analysis: Overview and description of deductive methods. In D. L. Whetzel & G. R. Wheaton (Eds.), *Applied measurement: Industrial psychology in human resources manage-ment.* Mahwah, NJ: Erlbaum.

Saldana, J. (2009). *The coding manual for qualitative researchers.* Thousand Oaks, CA: Sage.

Sanchez, J. (1994). From documentation to innovation: Reshaping job analysis to meet emerging business needs. *Human Resource Management Review, 4,* 51–74.

Schneider, B. (1978). Person-situation selection: A review of some ability-situation interaction research. *Personnel Psychology, 31,* 281–297.

Siddique, C. M. (2004). Job analysis: A strategic human resource management practice. *International Journal of Human Resource Management, 15,* 219–244.

Singh, P. (2008). Job analysis for a changing workplace. *Human Resource Management Review, 18,* 87–99.

Society of Industrial and Organizational Psychology, Inc. (2003). *Principles for the validation and use of personnel selection procedures* (4th ed.). Bowling Green, OH: Author.

Strong, M. H., Jeanneret, P. R., McPhail, S. M., Blakley, B. R., & D'Egidio, E. L. (1999). Work context: Taxonomy and measurement of the work environment. In N. G. Peterson, M. D. Mumford, W. C. Borman, P. R. Jeanneret, & E. A. Fleishman (Eds.), *An occupational information system for the 21st century: The development of O*NET* (pp. 127–146). Washington, DC: American Psychological Association.

Terborg, J. R. (1981). Interactional psychology and research on human behavior in organizations. *Academy of Management Review, 6,* 569–576.

U.S. Civil Service Commission. (1977). *Instructions for the Factor Evaluation System.* Washington, DC: U.S. Government Printing Office.

U.S. Department of Labor. (1972). *Handbook for analyzing jobs.* Washington, DC: U.S. Government Printing Office.

Vandenberg, R. J., & Lance, C. E. (2000). A review and synthesis of the measurement invariance literature: Suggestions, practices, and recommendations for organizational research. *Organizational Research Methods, 3,* 4–69.

Wilson, M. A. (2007). A history of job analysis. In L. L. Koppes (Ed.), *Historical perspectives in industrial and organizational psychology* (pp. 219–241). Mahwah, NJ: Erlbaum.

Zickar, M. J., & Carter, N. T. (2010). Reconnecting with the spirit of workplace ethnography: A historical review. *Organizational Research Methods, 13,* 304–319.

Part III

WORK ANALYSIS APPLICATIONS

GEORGE M. ALLIGER
The Group for Organizational Effectiveness

GREGORY M. HURTZ
California State University, Sacramento

For many reasons that corresponded to other similar developments at that time, around the turn of the 20th century there was an increasing desire to be able to describe work in an objective or "scientific" way. Industrial-organizational psychologists often want to describe jobs separately from the particular characteristics and uniqueness of any one job holder. For this reason, job analysis involves obtaining the views, opinions, and attitudes from many job holders of a given job, for any one job incumbent's views will be idiosyncratic. Job analysis is thus largely inductive in nature. It draws general conclusions by building up a picture of a job from a myriad of observations by or about job incumbents.

This process of distilling the objective from the subjective can be so much fun—although some might argue that the words *fun* and *work analysis* should not be used in close proximity. However, consider the process. First, the work analyst listens to and questions job holders about their work. The work analysts hears the job holders' perspectives on what they have to do, how they work their equipment, and how they interact with colleagues, customers, and managers—in short, how they accomplish their work in the midst of every challenge and difficulty. Then, the work analyst reduces and collates the resultant data into a useful form. In my experience, that process has been fun. Often, it has felt like a privilege to see how seriously people think and how deeply they feel about their work. Hopefully this has been—or will be—your experience too.

Once a work analysis is completed, its outcomes (i.e., description of the job and/or description of required worker characteristics) almost invariably serve as input for one or more other interesting processes: a selection test, work redesign, job simulation, and so forth. Part III powerfully illustrates this fundamental role of work analysis; it underpins a large portion of what work psychologists do.

Each chapter in Part III presents a clear exposition of how the outcomes of work analysis can be successfully applied to various organizational needs and requirements. The chapters are intentionally short and to the point. Tables, figures, and step-by-step processes are used to provide easy-to-assimilate content. Practitioners should find these chapters helpful and practical. However, each chapter also reflects state-of-the-art scholarship and can be profitably read by students and professors as well.

In Chapter 18, Amy M. DuVernet tackles the important process of altering the requirements for a job or jobs to address any of a number of organizational needs. Naturally, you have to understand a job in order to think about redesigning it, so job analysis is a critical step. Like the other authors in Part III, DuVernet places work analysis within a clearly delineated process relevant to her topic, from identifying objectives to evaluation.

As DuVernet clearly points out, job redesign raises any number of interesting questions for the practitioner. Should a work analysis be done only on the focal job or also on others on that the focal job impinges (e.g., other jobs that affect and are affected by the focal job through input/output, communication, or control dependencies)? At what level (e.g., task, task cluster, duty) should the work analysis be completed? Should a questionnaire be used or should the job analysis be more "blank slate"? Should the (fascinating) construct of Growth Need Strength (Hackman & Lawler, 1971) be assessed prior to any job redesign to examine the likelihood that the redesign will have its desired effects? When reading this chapter, you will begin to appreciate both the promise and the challenge of job design and redesign as well as the central role of job analysis.

Chapter 19 by Gregory M. Hurtz (my invaluable associate editor for Part III) and Chris W. Wright covers one of the most immediate and important outcomes from a job analysis. Work descriptions indeed are the most public face of work analysis. They are the first impression of job seekers everywhere regarding a potential job, helping them make what may be one of the most important decisions of their lives.

Hurtz and Wright first provide a very useful definition of a job description, which includes the work, the tools, the environment, and characteristics of the worker. However, they augment this core definition, or first layer, with other layers: databasing of descriptions and their electronic dissemination, user interactivity, and multimedia. The implications of these layers are carefully elaborated by the authors within the context of Barber's (1998) model of employee recruitment (attracting applicants, maintaining their interest, and persuading them to accept an offer). Clearly, this is a new era of technology-enabled recruitment, so Hurtz and Wright review some of the questions raised by technology, as well as the obvious benefits.

In Chapter 20, Dan A. Biddle and James E. Kuthy discuss how work analysis supports the development of legally defensible work initiatives. In particular, they review legal developments in the United States, including and following the Civil Rights Act of 1964, and how the work analyst should understand and can respond to these developments when making decisions in hiring, training, identifying essential functions, and so forth.

Biddle and Kuthy offer a clearly delineated process, or template, for carrying out a job analysis that will easily support validation efforts and adhere to guidance such as the Uniform Guidelines (Equal Employment Opportunity Commission [EEOC], 1978). Even if the job analysis approach you are adopting is different from the one advocated in this chapter, a careful study of the steps in the presented process can provide real guidance to the practitioner.

Dennis Doverspike and Winfred Arthur, Jr. address work analysis and tests in Chapter 21. The authors address both how work analysis can help you choose an appropriate off-the-shelf test, as well as how it can be the basis for constructing a custom test. The reader should note the careful emphasis on relating latent constructs to measures, which is the most fundamental principle for test development—and one with which, if you hold to it, you cannot go far wrong. Together with

Biddle and Kuther's previous chapter on EEOC compliance, you are provided with a solid basis for understanding why and how to create valid, reliable measures that will meet the objectives you have for them (e.g., selection) and stand up to close scrutiny (even when that scrutiny is unfriendly, as in the case of litigation).

Doverspike and Arthur provide a chapter that is a model of clarity and utility, with its step-by-step processes, checklists, and illustrative figures. Their chapter is very thorough and should be extremely useful to the practitioner. Wondering about how to link tasks to knowledge, skills, abilities, and other characteristics (KSAOs)? How many test items to write in order to have a sufficient number once the poorer items are culled? How to differentially weight test items? You will find the answers in Chapter 21.

Chapter 22 on work simulations was written by Deborah L. Whetzel, Michael A. McDaniel, and Jeffrey M. Pollack. Simulations have both similarities and some striking differences to a standard test of knowledge. One critical benefit of simulations is positive applications reactions to them; face validity can be very important (Shotland, Alliger, & Sales, 1998). As the authors are careful to point out, when developing a simulation, you will still need to ensure the traditional aspects of reliability and validity.

Whetzel et al. describe how to build both high- and low-fidelity simulations. In high-fidelity simulations, the applicants actually complete a task; in the lower fidelity simulations, they describe how they would respond in various situations. It is useful to be reminded that low-fidelity simulations are an option and that building a simulation need not be a budget-busting affair. Regardless, with the advent of greater virtual reality technologies, there are great opportunities for new, imaginative work simulations. However, the need for basic, solid development practices will not disappear, and this chapter should benefit anyone considering the development of a work simulation.

In Chapter 23, Sylvia G. Roch and Kevin J. Williams address the important and thorny topic of building effective performance appraisals from a work analysis. They first consider the state of performance appraisal (malaise and dissatisfaction), but cogently argue that it can and should perform a useful role within an organization. For this to happen, however, performance appraisal needs to be part of an overall performance management system, which itself is part of an integrated human resources system that also includes training, compensation, talent management, and so forth. All of this taken together supports employee competence and motivation.

Of course, central to a good performance evaluation system is its design, and here work analysis is foundational. One job analysis method favored by Roch and Williams is the critical incidents method (Flanagan, 1954), which should provide some awareness of a fundamental continuity and even stability in work psychology to go along with all the change and new developments. It is from work analysis that job performance dimensions as well as measurable behaviors are obtained. These measureable behaviors are, it seems, the *sine qua non* of any performance appraisal. Without them, it would neither valid nor accepted by managers or employees. However, Roch and Williams stress that one has to build carefully on the work analysis foundation, not only in instrument development, but in training and communications.

No handbook section on work analysis applications would be complete without a chapter on training needs analysis. In Chapter 24, Eric A. Surface addresses this topic. Identification of work tasks and/or KSAOs within the context of a training needs analysis is very common, so once again the fundamental nature of work analysis is revealed. Surface thus provides a complete and grounded view of training needs analysis. The reader may be surprised to see all the needed parts and pieces of a training needs analysis, as well as how all of these parts fit together.

Surface is careful to place training needs analysis within the larger organizational context. The chapter conveys clearly to the reader the need for good problem diagnosis throughout the training needs analysis process. It may be that the so-called training need is not a need at all. The chapter has several tables that will guide the practitioner in carrying out this diagnosis—and indeed the entire training needs analysis process.

If job analysis is defined as a broad body of techniques that developed to describe jobs objectively (i.e., independent of any job holder), then what is termed *job evaluation* is a kind of job analysis as well as an application of it. In Chapter 25, Robert J. Harvey covers the role of work analysis in determining pay via job evaluation. To many, the compensation differences among jobs can seem arbitrary. Arbitrariness is exactly what should be avoided. Unless one is arguing for a complete flattening of the compensation landscape so that everyone earns the same, then you need a method to evaluate the contributions of jobs to an organization and society.

Harvey examines job evaluation methods, reviewing the strengths and weaknesses of each; you will find here a lucid exposition, for example, of whole-job and compensable factor methods. Harvey persuasively argues for the approach he calls the Policy Capturing Point Factor method as a way to minimize subjectivity. The last section of the chapter is an intriguing and useful illustration of this method, using a large sample of over 200 occupations.

Chapter 26 about career planning was written by Stephen G. Atkins. Like work design in Chapter 18, career planning entails that useful idea of worker-occupation or worker-job fit. If a worker has preferences for certain aspects of work and they are absent from his or her job, the worker likely will be dissatisfied with that job. Conversely, if there is a match between preferences and job characteristics, satisfaction is much more likely. Therefore, methods are needed to assess worker preferences, jobs, and the degree of match between them.

Atkins provides an example study that measures job fit, then analyzes and interprets the results. Be prepared to think about the squared Euclidean distance metric versus that of Minkowski when assessing fit—but do not be scared off by either. Throughout, Atkins provides useful clear advice and guidance to those interested in career planning, including readers with the unique job of career development managers.

In Chapter 27, Brice M. Stone and Rosalinda Vasquez Maury describe the development of the Training Impact Decision Support System (TIDES) for the U.S. Air Force. The goal of TIDES is to manage the training careers of Air Force personnel; among other things, it allows the estimation of the dollar benefits of various training program decisions over entire careers. As you can imagine, building a modeling system as capable as TIDES requires detailed information on jobs. Stone and Vasquez Maury describe how those data are collected and used. They provide several examples of the system, including how TIDES results can help career managers understand the impact of decisions on consolidating training or otherwise restructuring career fields.

Chapter 28, which focuses on a web-based approach to job analysis, was written by Darrel L. Sandall, John Henderson, Roni Reiter-Palmon, Michael Brown, and Scott R. Homan. The authors argue forcefully that job analysis needs to take advantage of newer technology to become more time efficient, cost effective, and easily updatable. Specifically, they present a sophisticated approach that uses a web-based system to data collection from subject matter experts (SMEs), using both SME identification of work-relevant existing information (e.g., generalized work activities) and SME generation of new information (e.g., labels for groups of tasks). Interestingly, they point out that this system can be fully distributed, proctored, or some combination of these. This balance should be carefully assessed here and throughout the domain of work psychology as work is increasingly automated. Analyzing work via distributed means can only be more common and important, and this chapter is a welcome addition to this handbook.

As I reviewed each chapter in Part III, I marveled at the breadth of topics covered, the competence of the authors, and the exciting current state of the applications of work analysis. I trust that you, the reader, will appreciate the work here as much as I did.

REFERENCES

Barber, A. E. (1998). *Recruiting employees: Individual and organizational perspectives.* Thousand Oaks, CA: Sage Publications.

Civil Rights Act of 1964, 42 U.S.C. § 2000e et seq. (1964).

Equal Employment Opportunity Commission. (1978). *Uniform guidelines.* Washington, DC: Author.

Flanagan, J.C. (1954). The critical incident technique. *Psychological Bulletin, 51,* 327–358.

Hackman, J. R., & Lawler, E. E. (1971). Employee reactions to job characteristics [Monograph]. *Journal of Applied Psychology, 55,* 259–286.

Shotland, A., Alliger, G. M., & Sales, T. (1998). Face validity in the context of personnel selection: A multi-media approach. *International Journal of Selection and Assessment, 6,* 124–130.

18

Using Job Analytic Information to (Re)Design Jobs
Best Practices and Methods

Amy M. DuVernet

North Carolina State University

Work design can be defined as the way that jobs are structured. It includes the types, duration, sequences, and methods of tasks that workers are asked to perform; the available technology for completing such tasks; and the social and physical contexts surrounding them. Although work/job design has been associated with a variety of labels (e.g., job design, lean production, quality of life, job engineering; Garg & Rastogi, 2005; Morgeson & Campion, 2003), a recent trend in the literature uses the term *work* design rather than *job* design as a way of acknowledging the idea that jobs cannot be designed in isolation and instead must be designed with consideration of the broader organizational context (Humphrey, Nahrgang, & Morgeson, 2007). Within this chapter, the terms *work design* and *job design* are used interchangeably; however, it should be noted that organizational context is greatly important to the design of work.

Work design has stimulated a great deal of research within the fields of industrial and organizational psychology, ergonomics, medical sciences, human factors, and industrial engineering (Campion, Mumford, Morgeson, & Nahrgang, 2005). Researchers have studied how the design of work relates to a variety of outcomes, including job satisfaction, work motivation, job performance, withdrawal behaviors, and employee physical and mental well-being. Indeed, much research has confirmed the important role that work design plays in determining worker attitudes and behaviors (Humphrey et al., 2007). In their recent meta-analysis, Humphrey et al. found that 14 work characteristics explained one third of the variance in job performance and more than half of the variance in job satisfaction. It is clear that the design of work can have a significant impact on both employees and organizations.

This chapter begins with background information about the various approaches that have been used to design work, followed by a description of a typical work design process; it concludes with suggestions for future research. Throughout these sections, the role of work analysis in the process of work design is highlighted.

PERSPECTIVES ON JOB DESIGN

Jobs can take a variety of forms, and the methods used to design them are as numerous. Before delving into the steps involved in work design, a discussion of various job design approaches is warranted. These vary in the types of job characteristics that are manipulated, as well as the types of outcomes that are anticipated to result. The following information is organized around Campion's interdisciplinary framework of work design; based on a review of the job design literature, Campion delineated four distinct work design approaches: mechanistic, motivational, biomechanical, and perceptual-motor (Campion, 1988; Campion & Thayer, 1985).

Campion's Interdisciplinary Framework

Mechanistic Approach

Some of the earliest systematic work design endeavors in the United States can be found in the principles of scientific management proposed by Taylor (1911) and in the time and motion studies conducted by Gilbreth (1911). Both scientific management and the time and motion studies stressed task specialization and simplification as methods of increasing productivity through efficient work processes. More specifically, both analyzed the physical movements required to complete job tasks in an effort to determine the most appropriate sequence and duration of motion; these were then used to design work around the most efficient movements. These approaches forged the way for later work design and job analytic efforts by establishing systematic methods of analyzing jobs.

Similar to these early endeavors, the mechanistic approach to job design aims to increase worker productivity and efficiency as well as reduce costs related to training, selection, and compensation by emphasizing task specialization and simplification principles. In addition, this model proposes that simplifying jobs will decrease burnout through reduced effort requirements, thus allowing workers a better chance of satisfactory performance and performance efficacy (Hsieh & Chao, 2004). Although this approach has proved largely successful in achieving the goal of productivity, critics argue that jobs based on this approach are often repetitive and dissatisfying to job incumbents (Morgeson & Campion, 2003).

Motivational Approach

Later work adopted a motivational approach in an attempt to address these criticisms by intentionally focusing on designing satisfying jobs, and in this way, motivating employees to exert their best efforts towards job performance. The goals of this approach include increased job satisfaction, intrinsic motivation, and reduced organizational costs related to turnover. The motivational model has received the greatest attention within the research literature, perhaps because of its perceived success in achieving its intended outcomes (Morgeson & Campion, 2003).

An example of the motivational approach can be found in the Job Characteristics Model proposed by Hackman and Oldham (1976), which asserts that five job characteristics must be present for employees to feel motivated to exert effort within their jobs: task significance (the extent to which a job has a significant effect on others), skill variety (the extent to which a job requires numerous and various skills), task identity (the extent to which a job enables the completion of an entire portion of work), feedback (the extent to which a job provides feedback about performance), and autonomy (the extent to which a job provides an individual worker with the discretion to schedule and carry out work as he or she sees fit). Research on these characteristics has shown that they positively influence both satisfaction and intrinsic motivation (Humphrey et al., 2007).

Structuring work around teams of individual employees through the formation of semiautonomous and autonomous teams can also be motivating; jobs based on this type of design are organized around self-directed teams that are given responsibility for determining the most appropriate sequences and procedures for completing work tasks. Research has indicated that autonomous team designs increase communication and problem-solving skills (Morgeson et al., 2006), autonomy (Maupin, 1990; Wall & Martin, 1987), task significance, task identity, feedback, and skill variety (Maupin, 1990). Unfortunately, team designs also can have negative effects; reduced productivity may result because of group polarization, which occurs when teams make decisions that are more extreme than their individual members would have made, and social loafing, which occurs when individual team members do not exert as much effort toward team performance as they would in individual tasks (Morgeson et al., 2006).

Perceptual-Motor Approach

The perceptual motor approach arose as a response to increased reliance on technology within organizations, which shifted the tasks of employees from that of manual operations to more mentally challenging work. Work designs of this type attempt to limit the information processing requirements placed on employees to reduce their mental workload, thus minimizing the probability of errors and accidents related to mental fatigue. For example, a perceptual-motor redesign effort could entail allocating quality monitoring tasks to technology systems to minimize the attention requirements of the job incumbent. Unfortunately, like the mechanistic approach, work designs that emphasize perceptual-motor features can result in jobs that are monotonous because of the reduction of cognitive and skill requirements on the job (Campion, 1988; Morgeson & Campion, 2003).

Biological Approach

Finally, the biological approach designs jobs to reduce the stress, strain, and fatigue related to physical performance requirements. Similar to the mechanistic and perceptual-motor approaches, this approach can increase costs because it may require the modification of existing equipment (Campion, 1988). For example, Lin, Wang, and Drury (2007) investigated the soles of employees' boots; they found that the elasticity and shock absorption of the boots significantly affected work outcomes, including employee fatigue. Recommendations from this study included equipping employees with specific kinds of boots.

Other Approaches to Job Design

In addition to the approaches laid out in Campion's (1988) interdisciplinary model, several other job design methods have been proposed, including the Social Information Processing approach and the Sociotechnical Systems Theory approach. The Social Information Processing perspective asserts that perceived job characteristics are not always based on objective work characteristics; instead, research has shown that social cues influence perceptions of the job (Griffin, Bateman, Wayne, & Head, 1987; Salancik & Pfeffer, 1978). Social cues can direct individuals' attention to certain parts of the job, making them more salient than others. For example, an employee may become dissatisfied with his or her salary, if his or her coworkers are constantly asserting that they are not fairly compensated for their work. For this reason, this type of job design focuses on manipulating the content and timing of social cues as a method of influencing employees' perceived job characteristics (Morgeson & Campion, 2003). An example of this approach can be found in Grant's (2008) study, in which he manipulated task significance by providing employees' stories that depicted the important influence of their job on others; these stories positively impacted both performance and employee attitudes.

Another interdisciplinary model of job design can be found in the principles proposed by Trist and Bamford's (1951) sociotechnical systems theory. This theory attempts to design work systems in a way that optimizes both the technical (machine and technology) and social (people and societal) systems of the organization. For example, in a manufacturing environment that requires flexibility, a sociotechnical design approach might utilize the social system to encourage employees to seek and develop multiple skills. In this way, the social system would be complimentary to the complexity of the technical system (Liu, Shah, & Schroeder, 2006). Critics of this model assert that its principles have not been clearly articulated or tested (Morgeson & Campion, 2003). On the contrary, Cherns (1976, 1987) has proposed nine principles of sociotechnical systems theory work design (see Table 18.1); recently, Liu et al. (2006) attempted to match these principles to specific work

Table 18.1 Nine Principles of Sociotechnical Systems Theory

Principle	Definition
Compatibility	Design should be compatible with the long-term goals of the organization.
Minimal critical specifications	Jobs should be flexible, with as few task requirements as possible.
Variance control	Unexpected deviation from standard procedures should be controlled as closely as possible to their source.
Information flow	Employees should have timely access to feedback information.
Boundary location	Information should flow freely; boundaries should be designed in a way that they do not hinder information flow.
Multifunctionality	Employees should possess the skills and opportunities to perform a diverse range of jobs.
Support congruence	Social support should be designed to reinforce desirable behaviors.
Human values	The needs and health of employees should be an important value for the organization.
Incompletion	Design is a continuous process that should be constantly evaluated and revised.

The principles presented here are from the sociotechnical systems theory as proposed in Cherns (1976, 1987).

design practices. Their work suggests that many of these work design practices are similar to those proposed by the Job Characteristics Model. For example, they suggest employee empowerment as a work design practice that matches the Sociotechnical Systems Theory principles of compatibility and minimal critical specification. By involving employees in the work design effort and allowing them the opportunity to shape their job tasks (i.e., increasing employee autonomy), the job should be more flexible and the goals of compatibility and minimal critical specification will be achieved.

WORK DESIGN PHASES: A STEP-BY-STEP GUIDE

There is no single best way to go about designing jobs. Nonetheless, it is possible to specify steps that should be followed to maximize the chance of success in any work design effort. All work design efforts should be grounded firmly in a well-conducted job analysis. Additional necessary steps include conducting a needs assessment, generating and evaluating different configurations of the job in question, implementing the best of these configurations, evaluating the work design implementation, and revising the design when necessary. These phases of work design should be thought of as a general guide that can be tailored to the specific purposes of each unique job design (see Figure 18.1). In addition, a specific example of a work redesign endeavor is described at the end of this section in Figure 18.2.

Phase 1: Needs Assessment and Job Analysis

The first phase in this multiphase process is needs assessment (Goldstein & Ford, 2002). Jobs are frequently designed without a proper initial needs assessment (Minors, Nicholson, & Koscielniak, 1999), and without this crucial step, work design efforts risk implementing changes that are not targeted to organizational needs and work design objectives. The ultimate purpose of a needs assessment is to correctly specify the goal(s) of a job design effort and to gather job analytic information that can be used to design the job. For example, a particular effort may include a goal of increased productivity and decreased turnover. Alternatively, the goal may be to increase job satisfaction and decrease absenteeism. It is important to determine these needs at the beginning of a job design effort so that subsequent phases can be guided by specific organizationally relevant objectives.

Brannick, Levine, and Morgeson (2007) have asserted that there are three broad organizational needs that job designs can address: production systems needs, socio-organizational needs, and individual needs. Production systems needs embody the goals of efficiency and maximum

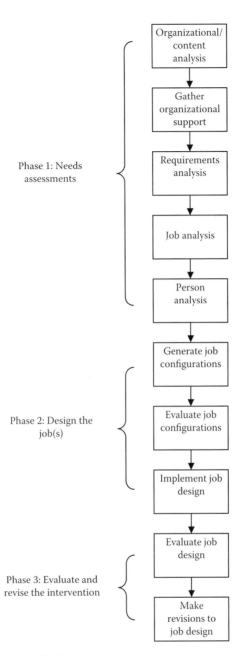

Figure 18.1   Steps involved in the work (re)design process.

productivity. Socio-organizational needs deal with the social aspects of work. Finally, individual needs encompass attitudinal issues, such as job satisfaction and motivation, as well as issues with the physical environment of work, such as safety and comfort (Brannick et al., 2007). These broad organizational needs can be broken down into specific outcome variables. Table 18.2 presents a list of outcome variables that were reviewed in a recent meta-analysis of the work design literature organized by the broad need that each addresses (Humphrey et al., 2007). Although not intended to provide an exhaustive list of all possible objectives or work characteristics, Table 18.2 provides the reader with an idea of the varied types of positive outcomes that may result from proper attention

Table 18.2   Relationships Between Organizational Needs, Common Job Design Objectives, and Characteristics of the Job

Organizational Need	Objective	Job Characteristic	Direction
Production/ socio-organizational	Absenteeism	Task identity, feedback from the job, autonomy, social support	−
Production	Objective performance	Autonomy, skill variety, task significance, task identity, feedback from the job, autonomy, interdependence, social support	+
	Subjective performance	Task significance, task identity, feedback from the job, autonomy, task variety, interdependence, feedback from others, social support	+
Individual/production	Burnout/exhaustion	Skill variety, task significance, task identity, autonomy, feedback from others, social support	−
	Overload	Social support	−
	Overload	Task variety, job complexity	+
Individual	Anxiety	Feedback from the job, autonomy, social support	−
	Compensation satisfaction	Skill variety, task significance, task identity, feedback from the job, autonomy, task variety	+
	Growth satisfaction	Skill variety, task significance, task identity, feedback from the job, autonomy, interdependence, social support	+
	Internal work motivation	Skill variety, task significance, task identity, feedback from the job, autonomy, interdependence, feedback from others, social support	+
	Job involvement	Skill variety, task significance, task identity, feedback from the job, autonomy, job complexity, interdependence, feedback from others	+
	Job satisfaction	Physical demands	−
	Job satisfaction	Skill variety, task significance, task identity, feedback from the job, autonomy, work methods autonomy, task variety, job complexity, interdependence, feedback from others, social support, interaction outside the organization, work conditions, information processing	+
	Promotion satisfaction	Skill variety, task significance, task identity, feedback from the job, autonomy, task variety	+
	Role ambiguity	Feedback from the job, autonomy, social support	−
	Role conflict	Feedback from the job, autonomy, social support	−
	Stress	Task identity, feedback from the job, autonomy, interdependence, feedback from others, social support, work conditions	−
	Turnover intentions	Interdependence, feedback from others, social support	−
Individual/ socio-organizational	Supervisor satisfaction	Skill variety, task significance, task identity, feedback from the job, autonomy, task variety	+
	Organizational commitment	Skill variety	+

These relationships are based on meta-analytic results from Humphrey et al. (2007). Positive (+) signs indicate positive relationships; negative (−) signs indicate negative relationships.

to work design. In addition, this table can be used to target specific work characteristics for redesign. For example, if a work design endeavor aims to reduce role ambiguity, Table 18.2 can be used to determine whether the redesigned job should include higher levels of feedback, autonomy, or social support.

Organizations may also choose to design or redesign jobs because of downsizing or growth. When organizations face economic challenges, downsizing could provide a feasible option for meeting those challenges. In this case, a job analysis should be used to identify obsolete tasks that can be eliminated as well as necessary tasks that should be retained in the redesigned job. When economic growth requires an organization to create new jobs, job design or redesign could lead to the reallocation and creation of job tasks (Campion et al., 2005). In this scenario, a job analysis can be used to gather information from subject matter experts about the types of job outcomes and tasks required by the new job.

Finally, the accommodation of individuals with disabilities also can be a goal of job design. The information collected during job analysis can be used to determine if changes in the job can reasonably be made to accommodate employees with disabilities (Mitchell, Alliger, & Morfopoulous, 1997). This is important because the Americans with Disabilities Act of 1990 states that organizations must make reasonable accommodations to allow individuals with disabilities to successfully complete the job (Brannick et al., 2007).

Needs assessments are composed of a number of individual steps, including organizational and contextual analysis, the gathering of organizational support, requirements and job analyses, and person analysis (Goldstein & Ford, 2002). These steps are discussed below.

Needs Assessment Phase – Step 1: Organizational and Context Analysis

The first step of needs analysis is organizational analysis. Briefly, organizational analyses gather information about organizational goals and values as well as organizational context. During this step, it is important to gather information about the structural characteristics, physical environment, and social contexts that surround the job because each of these can influence whether or not a job (re)design effort is successful (Carayon, Alvarado, & Hundt, 2007; Cordery, 1997; Wall & Martin, 1987). Evidence for the importance of such variables can be found in Humphrey et al.'s (2007) meta-analysis, which found that both social and work context characteristics (e.g., temperature, noise, social support) explained additional variance in a number of organizationally relevant outcomes (e.g., subjective performance, job satisfaction, withdrawal behaviors, and organizational commitment) above those explained by characteristics specific to the job.

Needs Assessment Phase – Step 2: Organizational Support

The next step is to gather organizational support. Work design influences a number of individuals, and their cooperation can be pivotal for successful implementation. One way to ensure organizational support is to involve the affected parties in the design process, which can be accomplished through the formation of a liaison team (Carayon et al., 2007; Korunka & Vitouch, 1999). This has the added benefit of capitalizing on the fact that these individuals are valuable sources of information about the job (Goldstein & Ford, 2002).

Needs Assessment Phase – Step 3: Requirements and Job Analysis

Having gathered organizational support, the next step is to conduct a requirements analysis to identify the type of job analytic information that should be collected as well as to create a plan of action for gathering this information. There is no single most appropriate type of job analytic information necessary for a work design effort; instead, the type of information collected should be informed by the goals of the job design (Brannick et al., 2007). As should be clear from Part II of this volume, there are many ways to conduct job analyses, so a careful examination of the advantages and disadvantages of each type of analysis is important (Goldstein & Ford, 2002).

One consideration that must be addressed is the determination of whether information should be gathered for one job or for a number of jobs. It is advisable to gather information about *at least* two positions: the focal job and that of its supervisor. In many cases, the redesign of subordinate jobs will necessitate a redesign of the supervisor's job, especially when subordinates are given more responsibility and control over their tasks (Cordery & Wall, 1985). Job redesign efforts should include a job analysis of all jobs that could be affected. Although time and resources will act as restraints, it should be noted that the focal job likely impacts a number of different positions within the organization, and each of the positions should be subjected to job analysis. Finally, if the goals of the design project are to redistribute work across a number of job positions, it will be important to collect information about all of those jobs.

Another important consideration is the determination of the appropriate unit of information to collect during the analysis. Information could be gathered at a number of different levels of specificity; Morgeson and Campion (2002) have recommended the use of the task cluster, which consists of a group of relatively interdependent tasks and activities that are performed by one person and generally make up a whole portion of work. This level of analysis has advantages over the other options; some options, such as tasks, can produce an unmanageable amount of information, whereas others, such as duties, may be too broad to allow for significant design options because most jobs are composed of only a few duties (Campion et al., 2005). In contrast, task clusters offer the advantage of being relatively small in number (most jobs will consist of 10–15 clusters), which allows for units composed of enough information for job reconfiguration while also minimizing the information processing requirements of the work design agent(s) (Campion et al., 2005).

A decision must also be made about the type of data to be collected. In many cases, subjective data (collected from job incumbents, supervisors, etc.) can provide valuable information about the job; however, more objective sources of information such as the *Dictionary of Occupational Titles* and/or the Occupational Information Network could also prove useful. Because these are discussed in Chapter 16, this volume, they will not be fully explicated here; however, a good example of the use of these databases in job design can be found in Morgeson and Humphrey's (2006) study. They used these databases to examine the extent to which subjectively measured aspects of jobs converged with objective sources of data. This is an important consideration because subjective perceptions may not accurately reflect the objective properties of the job (Morgeson & Humphrey, 2006; Salancik & Pfeffer, 1978).

The requirements analysis also should consider the use of multiple job analysis techniques. For example, process analyses, functional job analyses, and ability requirements analyses can be useful. A process analysis is used to determine the sequence of and processes involved in each task cluster as well as in the overall job. This can be used to create a diagram depicting the flow of tasks involved in the job, which should provide valuable and easily accessible visual information about the job for later use (Brannick et al., 2007; Carayon et al., 2007). This information could be used to determine which processes will be affected during job design. A functional job analysis could prove useful in the job design effort because it provides information about the required level of interaction with data, people, and things within the job (Fine, 1955). Morgeson and Campion (2003) surveyed and summarized the job design literature into three common topics of investigation: job complexity, social environment, and physical demands. Interestingly, they noted that these correspond with the three dimensions of work (data, people, and things, respectively) measured by functional job analysis, which provides support for the utility of this type of analysis for job design. Finally, analyses of the ability requirements necessary for each task cluster can identify tasks that could be moved down the hierarchical chain to less skilled members of the organization or that could be moved horizontally to other jobs. For example, Molleman and Van Knippenberg (1995) used this type of information to determine that certain responsibilities could be shifted from head nurses to their subordinate nurses to free up the head nurses for other tasks.

Many job analysis questionnaires have been designed specifically for the purpose of job design. Table 18.3 summarizes the most commonly used measures and provides information about the strengths and weakness of each. These vary in terms of the job design approaches that they use to measure job characteristics. Information gathered from these questionnaires can be used to identify job characteristics for work design intervention. For example, an organization dealing with high absenteeism might choose to administer the Work Design Questionnaire (Morgeson & Humphrey, 2006) because of its ability to measure job characteristics across the various job design approaches. If the Work Design Questionnaire results indicate that the job involves relatively low levels of social support and skill variety, low job satisfaction could be the reason for high absenteeism. In this case, the organization should consider redesigning the job to include more of these characteristics. If instead the Work Design Questionnaire indicates high physical demands associated with the job, the high levels of absenteeism could be the result of employee fatigue. In this case, redesigning the job to require lower levels of physical demands could be warranted.

Once decisions are made about each of the aforementioned points, a job analysis can be conducted to gather information about the job. Information gathered during this analysis will be used in the next phase of the job design process.

Needs Assessment Phase – Step 4: Person Analysis

After collecting job analysis information, another useful step is to conduct a person analysis, which focuses on job incumbents and collects information about their levels of knowledge, skills, abilities, and other characteristics (Goldstein & Ford, 2002). This step provides information about individual differences that could potentially moderate the relationships between job characteristics and outcome variables. In addition, it provides information about job incumbents' skill and ability levels, which can be used in evaluating their ability to complete other kinds of tasks that may be added to their jobs.

Much research has centered on the role of individual differences in determining the outcomes of work design. Humphrey et al. (2007) found that Growth Needs Strength, or an individual's need for challenging and stimulating work, is a moderator of the relationship between motivational work design approaches and job satisfaction. Additional individual differences that have been shown to moderate the relationship between job characteristics and job design outcomes include psychological flexibility (Bond, Flaxman, & Bunce, 2008), proactive personality (Fuller, Marler, & Hester, 2006), and self-efficacy (Williams & Lillibridge, 1992).

Although researchers have identified individual difference moderators (Bond et al., 2008; Humphrey et al., 2007), in general, the direction of the relationships between work design features and outcome variables is the same across varying levels of those individual differences. For example, Bond et al. found that job control was more highly negatively related to absenteeism for individuals with high psychological flexibility; however, the relationship between job control and absenteeism was still negative for those with low psychological flexibility. When designing jobs for a large number of people, it often is more important to consider the average level of these variables within the population of employees rather than their full range (Campion et al., 2005; Morgeson & Campion, 2003). For this reason, information should be collected to determine the average knowledge, skills, abilities, and other characteristics within the incumbent workforce to ensure that they are not extreme enough to interfere with job design outcomes; for example, if an incumbent workforce exhibits a low average in terms of Growth Needs Strength, motivational job design approaches may not have their intended effect.

Table 18.3 Available Surveys for Gathering Job Analysis Information in the Job Design Process

Survey	Source	Description	Advantages	Disadvantages
Job Diagnostic Survey	Hackman & Oldham (1975)	• Based on the Job Characteristics Model • Measures the level of task significance, task identity, task variety, autonomy, and feedback provided by the job • 15 items • Variable response format	• Extensively studied and used (Morgeson & Campion, 2003) • Large amount of criterion-related validity evidence • Relatively short	• Limited to characteristics of the JCM • Mixed support for its proposed factor structure (e.g., Pierce & Dunham, 1978) • Complex format and items require high level of ability in respondents (Morgeson & Campion, 2003)
Job Characteristics Inventory	Sims, Szilagyi, & Keller (1976)	• Based on the Job Characteristics Model • Measures the level of variety, autonomy, feedback, dealing with others, task identity, and friendship contained within the job • 30 items • Five-point Likert-scale response format	• Evidence for its reliability and proposed factor structure (Pierce & Dunham, 1978) • Simple language and ratings scale (Morgeson & Campion, 2003)	• Limited to motivational properties of the job • Larger number of items (compared with the JDS)
Multimethod Job Design Questionnaire	Campion & Thayer (1985); Campion (1988)	• Based on Campion & Thayer's (1985) interdisciplinary framework for job design approaches • Measures elements related to four approaches to job design including the motivational approach, the mechanistic approach, the perceptual-motor approach, and the biological approach	• Is not limited to a specific approach to job design • Evidence for its reliability and validity (Campion, 1988; Edwards, Scully & Brtek, 2000)	• Mixed results for its proposed factor structure (Edwards et al., 2000) • May not cover all of the dimensions of each job design approach (Edwards et al., 2000)
Work Design Questionnaire	Morgeson & Humphrey (2006)	• Measures elements of the work (e.g., ergonomics and physical demands); motivational (e.g., job complexity, task variety, and information processing requirements); and social contexts (e.g., social support and interdependence)	• Is not limited to a specific approach to job design • Allows for the collection of contextual information related to the physical and social environment of the job	• Relatively new and untested • Limited evidence for its proposed factor structure, reliability, and validity (Morgeson & Humphrey, 2006)

JCM = Job Characteristics Model; JDS = Job Diagnostic Survey.

Phase 2: Examine, Compare, and Evaluate Different Configurations of the Job(s)

During the next phase of work design, different job configurations are examined to determine if they adequately meet job design objectives. This phase is composed of a generation step, a comparison and evaluation step, and an implementation step.

Job Design Phase – Step 1: Generation of Different Job Configurations

The first step of the second phase involves examining the ways in which tasks can be reconfigured. Much like brainstorming, this step aims to identify possibilities in a creative fashion, without evaluation (Morgeson & Campion, 2002). These reconfigurations should start with the core elements or tasks identified during job analysis that are central to the way that the job is defined. Different configurations can then be built around this core (Morgeson & Campion, 2002). For example, core components of a teacher's job may include student interaction and lesson planning; other tasks, such as planning field trips, may be more peripheral to the job. The two core tasks should likely remain teacher responsibilities whereas peripheral tasks may be reallocated to other positions (e.g., the school administrative assistant could be reassigned the responsibility of planning field trips). The results of this phase should provide information about the scope of each configuration, the directions in which each configuration of tasks will flow, and the roles that the individuals will play within these configurations (Nadin, Waterson, & Parker, 2001).

Job Design Phase – Step 2: Compare and Evaluate Different Configurations of the Job(s)

After a sufficient number of possible job configurations have been proposed, the next step is to evaluate them using a set of criteria to assess their ability to meet the work design objectives (Morgeson & Campion, 2002; Nadin et al., 2001). These criteria should address the anticipated benefits, costs, and implications of each configuration (Nadin et al., 2001). Possible benefits may include increased job satisfaction and motivation, whereas costs could result from reduced productivity or communication. Finally, implications of the job design refer to all the systems that may need to change or that may be affected by the design effort. For example, employees may need additional training to transition into their new roles (Carayon et al., 2007; Korunka & Vitouch, 1999). In addition, employees who are further up in the hierarchy may be affected because certain types of redesigns in a subordinate position could necessitate changes to the job of the supervisor (Brewer, 2000; Cordery & Wall, 1985).

To establish the criteria for evaluating each job configuration, the relationships between the desired outcomes and various job characteristics should be considered. Job characteristics that are likely to lead to desired outcomes should be evaluated and given priority within each job configuration. For example, Nadin et al. (2001) describe a job redesign in which 12 criteria (autonomy, skill variety, training, communication, physical security, etc.) were identified as important job design objectives and used to evaluate various job configuration possibilities.

It is also important to consider the mediators or mechanisms by which job characteristics will influence the desired outcomes. This step may illuminate relationships between job characteristics and outcomes that could have gone unnoticed. For example, Burr and Cordery (2001) found that the relationship between employees' ability to utilize a full range of skills and job satisfaction was mediated by their self-management efficacy. Table 18.4 presents a list of a number of mediators that have been investigated throughout the job design literature; this list can be used as a starting point for determining the influences of various job characteristics on work design outcomes.

As the newly configured jobs are evaluated, it may become apparent that certain types of job designs increase some desired outcomes while decreasing others. Unfortunately, recent research has identified tensions between the various approaches to job design that can lead to tradeoffs between each (Campion et al., 2005; Morgeson & Campion, 2002). For example, it has been observed that when satisfaction improves through the use of the motivational approach, efficiency

Table 18.4   Mediational Relationships

Job Characteristic	Mediator	Outcome	Source
Five JCM characteristics (autonomy, feedback, task variety, task identity, and task significance)	Empowerment	Job satisfaction and organizational commitment	Liden, Wayne, & Sparrowe (2000)
Skill variety/task significance/task identity	Experienced meaningfulness	Internal motivation and job satisfaction	Humphrey et al. (2007)
Autonomy	Experienced responsibility for work outcomes	Internal motivation and job satisfaction	Humphrey et al. (2007)
Autonomy	Learning of new information/skills	Job performance	Parker, Wall, & Jackson (1997)
Autonomy	Skill utilization	Job satisfaction	Morrison, Cordery, Girardi, & Payne (2005)
Autonomy	Quick response to and anticipation of problems	Job performance	Wall, Jackson, & Davids (1992)
Task significance	Perceived social impact	Job dedication	Grant (2008)
Task significance	Perceived social worth	Citizenship behavior	Grant (2008)
Biomechanical workload	Perceived job demands	Burnout	Cullen, Silverstein, & Foley (2008)
Work method control	Self-management efficacy	Task motivation	Burr & Cordery (2001)

JCM = Job Characteristics Model.

tends to decrease (Campion & McClelland, 1991). This could be because of the higher training costs and compensation requirements associated with the changes required by motivational designs. In contrast, mechanistic designs can increase efficiency while simultaneously decreasing job satisfaction (Morgeson & Campion, 2003). Though this may seem bleak, Campion et al. (2005) suggest a number of techniques that can be used to balance competing objectives (see Table 18.5). Morgeson

Table 18.5   Techniques for Minimizing Job Design Approach Tradeoffs

Technique	Definition
Compromise	Weigh potential costs of each approach and choose best fit; this technique makes clear the potential costs of various approaches and allows interested parties a choice of which outcomes are most valued.
Level separation	Implement one design technique at the job level and another at the organizational level; this technique allows the organization to promote certain design goals during job design and others during organizational design.
Sequential	Apply one approach and subsequently apply another; this technique places a necessary order of implementation on job design approaches to capitalize on the key features of both approaches.
Synthesis	Implement specific components from a variety of competing perspectives; this technique identifies desirable design features from multiple approaches and attempts to implement them simultaneously in a noncompetitive fashion.
Hybrid	Adopt an interdisciplinary approach, such as STS; this technique uses an already established synthesis type design approach that is intended to capture key features from a variety of competing job design approaches.

Adapted from Campion, M. A., Mumford, T. V., Morgeson, F. P., and Nahrgang, J. D., *Human Resource Management*, 44, 4, 367–390. STS = sociotechnical systems theory.

and Campion (2002) recently implemented the synthesis technique and discovered that when specialization was increased without increasing work simplicity, job satisfaction levels increased and training requirements remained the same.

Lastly, when trying to determine the value of each configuration, it is often difficult to predict how they will relate to outcomes. The evaluation step is, of course, subjective and not error free. The best option for organizational decision makers is to use past research to make informed hypotheses about the anticipated outcomes of work design features. Remember, this is an iterative process; if initial attempts to structure the job are not entirely successful, revisions will need to be made (Campion et al., 2005).

Job Design Phase – Step 3: Implement the Job Design/Redesign

Implementing the work design configuration anticipated to result in the most benefits and least costs is the next step. There are a couple of practices that can be useful to gain employee acceptance during this step. First, when the organization is up front about the goals, time frame, and implications of the work design, there is a greater likelihood that the implementation will go smoothly. Clear communication is key to acceptance of these changes (Carayon et al., 2007). Second, leaders can play a valuable role during this step. Supervisors are significant agents in job design because they can help with the transition and provide support to subordinates (Cordery & Wall, 1985; Drach-Zahavy, 2004). It is important to ensure that they are aware of and accept their essential role in the work design implementation phase.

Phase 3: Evaluate the Work Design and Make Necessary Revisions

The last phase of work design is to evaluate the job based on design objectives and to determine whether those objectives have been met. If they have not been accomplished, or if unanticipated and undesirable consequences of the job design become apparent, revisions to the newly designed job configuration should be made.

Evaluation and Revision Phase – Step 1: Evaluate the Work Design

The first step of the last phase is to measure the extent to which the work design was successful in achieving the design objectives using the same measures employed in the needs assessment phase. In this way, the levels of specific outcomes and job characteristics after job design can be compared with levels before job design to determine if the job design resulted in its intended effect.

Evaluative data should be collected at multiple times because initial benefits may decrease when employees become accustomed to their newly configured jobs, and some benefits may not be realized until the employees have adjusted to their jobs. In addition, costs associated with the design may be large initially but decrease over time (Campion et al., 2005). For example, Griffin (1991) found that initial increases in attitudinal variables following a work redesign intervention were not maintained over a four-year period. In contrast, they discovered that although performance did not change after a six-month period, it did increase after two years and maintained this increased level after four years.

Evaluation and Revision Phase – Step 2: Rinse and Repeat

The previous step may identify areas of the job that still need improvement. When this occurs, the job should be examined to determine if other aspects can be modified to improve outcomes. Molleman and Van Knippenberg (1995) report a job redesign that reduced the task specialization of nurses within four hospital settings by allocating patients rather than tasks to nurses (i.e., the nurses were responsible for all tasks that a specific patient required). The redesign achieved its goal of increasing nurse autonomy; however, it also resulted in the unintended effect of lowering the nurses' performance ratings. Investigations into this effect indicated that the lower performance

Description of the work design endeavor:

The introduction of a new billing system has streamlined tasks such that two positions can now apparently be combined into one. Originally, a customer service representative interacted with new customers in order to determine their service needs. Next, this representative reported those needs to a billing specialist who set up a monthly invoice for the customer. The new billing system has simplified this process such that the customer service representative can handle setting up the monthly invoice on his or her own, thus eliminating the need for the billing specialist.

Phase 1: Needs assessment

1. Organizational/contextual analysis: Gather information about the physical, structural, and social characteristics of both jobs, including information about the compensation systems for both jobs. Identify the organizational values and goals to which the newly configured job must adhere.
2. Gathering support: Form a liaisons team composed of individuals from each job as well as their supervisors. Use this team to learn more about the two jobs and to make decisions about the job analysis plan.
3. Requirements analysis and job analysis: Determine the most appropriate job analytic technique(s); gather information about task requirements in each job. Determine the essential/core tasks within each job; in this case, determining the best services for a specific customer is essential to the customer service job, and ensuring that the proper state taxes are applied to customer bills is essential to the billing specialist. Additionally, close attention should be paid to the way that the new billing system and the incumbent will interact; the billing system may require changes to the way tasks are currently preformed.
4. Person analysis: Determine the KSAOs of current job incumbents in both jobs. Be sure to gauge KSAOs necessary for interacting with the new billing system.

Phase 2: Evaluate configurations of the job

1. Generate job configurations: Brainstorm ways that job tasks from each position can be combined. This should start with the core tasks of each job (e.g., determining the best services for a specific customer and ensuring the proper taxes are applied to bills). Other tasks assigned to this job should revolve around the core tasks.
2. Evaluate job configurations: Determine the ability of current job incumbents to complete the tasks required by each job configuration. For example, customer service skills may not have been necessary for the billing specialists before the jobs were combined; it is likely that these will be important to the newly designed job. Determine the costs and feasibility of each job configuration; the new configuration may require training to develop KSAOs or revisions of the current compensation systems.
3. Implement the new design: Disseminate information about the changes. Utilize the liaisons team to gather support for this change.

Phase 3: Evaluate and revise the work design

1. Evaluate changes: Gather information about the success of the new position. This information should include data related to the performance of job incumbents as well as their levels of satisfaction.
2. Revise the work design: If unintended consequences of the newly combined job are discovered, revisions should be made to ensure that this job is designed to properly meet organizational needs. For example, low customer satisfaction may be discovered; changes should be made to ensure that customer service representatives can balance demands related to customer service and billing. One solution could be to decrease the number of customers that each representative interacts with daily, thus emphasizing quality over quantity.

Figure 18.2 Work design in practice.

ratings were caused by complications with doctors finding the specific nurse in charge of a given patient; because this problem was identified, the organization was able to address the issue by providing the nurses with communication devices that allowed them to be quickly located.

FUTURE RESEARCH

Although a vast amount of research has been conducted on the role of work design in organizational functioning, interest in this field has declined over the past 20–30 years (Humphrey et al.,

2007; Morgeson & Campion, 2003). However, there are still many unanswered questions that need to be addressed. These include questions about designing work to best meet challenges related to new technology and globalization, the role of time and career level in the design process, the extent to which subjective measures of work properties match objective measures, and the possibility of nonlinear relationships between job characteristics and outcomes. These areas for future research are discussed below.

As organizations have evolved and adjusted to changing environmental conditions such as new technologies and globalization, jobs have also changed their form. Telework, or work that can be performed from varying locations, is becoming more and more prevalent as telecommuting and virtual organizations continue to gain popularity. Flextime and compressed work schedules that allow employees flexibility in their work hours also have become more common (Brewer, 2000). Jobs of this type tend to be less defined, and individuals within them are typically required to be highly flexible in the roles that they fill. Because these jobs present conditions of less certainty and more cognitive, social, and emotional demands, the role of job characteristics may vary in these situations (Burr & Cordery, 2001). For example, Barnett, Gordon, Gareis, and Morgan (2004) found that employees involved in flextime arrangements reacted more negatively to psychological contract violations than employees with more traditional work schedules. In addition, Ehrhart and Chung-Herrera (2008) have proposed that telework provides even more opportunities for job enlargement and enrichment than are provided by traditional jobs. Future research will need to investigate the relationships between work design features and outcomes within this new generation of jobs.

Certain research weaknesses have been lamented within the job design literature for decades (Morgeson & Campion, 2003; Wall & Martin, 1987); it is clear that future research should address these. First, most job design research has been cross-sectional in nature and therefore cannot take the role of time into account (Morgeson & Campion, 2003). However, the effects of work design efforts may vary over time. Fried, Grant, Levi, Hadani, and Slowik (2007) have proposed a model of the way that time influences individual interpretations and reactions to job characteristics. This model suggests that individuals in the early stages of their careers may be more willing to accept jobs that are low in motivational qualities. Zeffane (1994) provides evidence for the possibility that individuals in different career stages focus on different job characteristics; his study showed that task variety was the most important determinant of nonmangerial staffs' satisfaction, whereas formalization and participation were the most important determinants of managerial staff satisfaction. It is clear that more research is needed to investigate the role of time and career level in job design.

Another research design weakness that has permeated the job design literature is the use of common methods for data collection. Unfortunately, when common methods are used to collect data, alternative explanations can be made for any observed relationships (Morgeson & Campion, 2002). For example, job incumbents may be motivated to respond to surveys in a socially desirable manner. If a work design effort collects information about task significance and job satisfaction through job incumbent surveys, it will be difficult to determine whether the observed relationship between the two variables is due to socially desirable responding or the true nature of the relationship. Future research should include more varied methods of data collection.

The use of self-report techniques also introduces the possibility that objective job characteristics differ from incumbent perceptions of those characteristics, as is proposed by social information processing theory (Salancik & Pfeffer, 1978). It is clear that future research should incorporate more objective types of data to investigate variables that may influence differences between objective and subjective measures. One interesting intersection of the role of time and subjective measures in job design efforts can be found in research conducted by Vance and Biddle (1985). The authors found that as job incumbents gained more experience in their jobs, the influence of social cues on perceived job characteristics decreased.

Finally, research about job design generally has assumed that the relationships between job characteristics and outcome variables are linear (Humphrey et al., 2007; Warr, 1987). This assumption, however, needs to undergo more testing. Several researchers have hypothesized that there are optimal levels of job characteristics; once these job characteristics surpass that optimal level, the benefits that result from them decrease. Indeed, Warr's vitamin model proposes that the role of job characteristics in employee outcomes is analogous to the effects of vitamins on health outcomes. Taking vitamins is beneficial to health to a certain extent, beyond which the benefits either plateau or begin to have detrimental effects on health with more vitamin consumption. Similarly, many job characteristics could potentially demonstrate this type of nonlinear relationship. Research into this topic has been mixed. Xie and Johns (1995) found that employee exhaustion was highest when levels of job complexity were both high and low; in contrast, employee exhaustion was lowest when job complexity levels were moderate. Jeurisson and Nyklíček (2001) found that a linear regression better described the relationship between both job demands and mental well being and job autonomy and well being. Future research is needed to determine which, if any, of the relationships that have been studied within the work design literature are nonlinear in nature.

CONCLUSION

The process of work design is complicated and must be tailored to the specific organization and job in question. This chapter has attempted to provide the reader with relevant information about the process. Space constraints, however, have limited the amount of information contained within the chapter; therefore, the reference list includes a number of suggestions for further reading. Among these are sources that contain information about downsizing (Campion et al., 2005; Mishra & Spreader, 1998), provide comprehensive models of job design (Garg & Rastogi, 2005; Humphrey et al., 2007; Morgeson & Campion, 2003; Parker, Wall, & Cordery, 2001), summarize research and theory related to telework (Brewer, 2000; Fried et al., 2007), discuss the historic origins of job design (Parker, 2002), and provide case examples of organizational design efforts (Carayon et al., 2007; Nash, Grant, & Bartolucci, 2000).

FURTHER READING

Campion, M. A., Mumford, T. V., Morgeson, F. P., & Nahrgang, J. D. (2005). Work redesign: Eight obstacles and opportunities. *Human Resource Management, 44*(4), 367–390.

Fried, Y., Grant, A. M., Levi, A. S., Hadani, M., & Slowik, L. H. (2007). Job design in temporal context: A career dynamics perspective. *Journal of Organizational Behavior, 28*(7), 911–927.

Garg, P., & Rastogi, R. (2005). New model of job design: Motivating employees' performance. *Journal of Management Development, 25*(6), 572–587.

Humphrey, S. E., Nahrgang, J. D., & Morgeson, F. P. (2007). Integrating motivational, social, and contextual work design features: A meta-analytic summary and theoretical extension of the work design literature. *Journal of Applied Psychology, 92*(5), 1332–1356.

Mishra, A. K., & Spreader, G. M. (1998). Explaining how survivors respond to downsizing: The roles of trust, empowerment, justice, and work redesign. *Academy of Management Review, 23*(3), 567–588.

Morgeson, F. P., & Campion, M. A. (2003). Work design. In W. C. Borman, D. R. Ilgen, R. J. Klimoski, W. C. Borman, D. R. Ilgen, & R. J. Klimoski (Eds.), *Handbook of psychology: Industrial and organizational psychology* (Vol. 12, pp. 423–452). Hoboken, NJ: John Wiley & Sons, Inc.

Nash, M. G., Grant, J. S., & Bartolucci, A. A. (2000). Clinical and operational outcomes of a work redesign model. *National Academies of Practice Forum: Issues in Interdisciplinary Care, 2*(3), 203–210.

Parker, S. K. (2002). Designing jobs to enhance well-being and performance. In P. Warr & P. Warr (Eds.), *Psychology at work* (5th ed, pp. 276–299). New York, NY: Penguin Press.

Parker, S. K., Wall, T. D., & Cordery, J. L. (2001). Future work design research and practice: Towards an elaborated model of work design. *Journal of Occupational and Organizational Psychology, 74*(4), 413–440.

REFERENCES

Barnett, R. C., Gordon, J. R., Gareis, K. C., & Morgan, C. (2004). Unintended consequences of job redesign. *Community, Work, & Family, 7,* 227–246.

Bond, F. W., Flaxman, P. E., & Bunce, D. (2008). The influence of psychological flexibility on work redesign: Mediated moderation of a work reorganization intervention. *Journal of Applied Psychology, 93*(3), 645–654.

Brannick, M. T., Levine, E. L., & Morgeson, F. P. (2007). *Job and work analysis: methods, research, and applications for human resource management* (2nd ed.). Thousand Oaks, CA: Sage Publications.

Brewer, A. M. (2000). Work design for flexible work scheduling: Barriers and gender implications. *Gender, Work and Organization, 7,* 33–44.

Burr, R., & Cordery, J. L. (2001). Self-management efficacy as a mediator of the relation between job design and employee motivation. *Human Performance, 14*(1), 27–44.

Campion, M. A. (1988). Interdisciplinary approaches to job design: A constructive replication with extensions. *Journal of Applied Psychology, 73,* 467–481.

Campion, M. A., & McClelland, C. L. (1991). Interdisciplinary examination of the costs and benefits of enlarged jobs: A quasi-experiment. *Journal of Applied Psychology, 76,* 186–198.

Campion, M. A., Mumford, T. V., Morgeson, F. P., & Nahrgang, J. D. (2005). Work redesign: Eight obstacles and opportunities. *Human Resource Management, 44*(4), 367–390.

Campion, M. A., & Thayer, P. W. (1985). Development and field evaluation of an interdisciplinary measure of job design. *Journal of Applied Psychology, 70,* 29–43.

Carayon, P., Alvarado, C. J., & Hundt, A. S. (2007). Work design and patient safety. *Theoretical Issues in Ergonomics Science, 8*(5), 395–428.

Cherns, A. (1976). The principles of sociotechnical design. *Human Relations, 29,* 783–792.

Cherns, A. (1987). Principles of sociotechnical design revisited. *Human Relations, 40,* 153–161.

Cordery, J. (1997). Reinventing work design theory and practice. *Australian Psychologist, 32*(3), 185–189.

Cordery, J. L., & Wall, T. D. (1985). Work design and supervisory practice: A model. *Human Relations, 38*(5), 425–440.

Cullen, J. C., Silverstein, B. A., & Foley, M. P. (2008). Linking biomechanical workload and organizational practices to burnout and satisfaction. *Journal of Business and Psychology, 23*(1), 63–71.

Drach-Zahavy, A. (2004). The proficiency trap: How to balance enriched job designs and the team's need for support. *Journal of Organizational Behavior, 25*(8), 979–996.

Edwards, J. R., Scully, J. A., & Brtek, M. D. (2000). The nature and outcomes of work: A replication and extension of interdisciplinary work-design research. *Journal of Applied Psychology, 85*(6), 860–868.

Ehrhart, K. H., & Chung-Herrera, B. G. (2008). HRM at your service: Developing effective HRM systems in the context of E-service. *Organizational Dynamics, 37*(1), 75–85.

Fine, S. A. (1955). A structure of worker functions. *Personnel and Guidance Journal, 34,* 66–73.

Fried, Y., Grant, A. M., Levi, A. S., Hadani, M., & Slowik, L. H. (2007). Job design in temporal context: A career dynamics perspective. *Journal of Organizational Behavior, 28*(7), 911–927.

Fuller, J. B., Marler, L. E., & Hester, K. (2006). Promoting felt responsibility for constructive change and proactive behavior: Exploring aspects of an elaborated model of work design. *Journal of Organizational Behavior, 27*(8), 1089–1120.

Garg, P., & Rastogi, R. (2005). New model of job design: Motivating employees' performance. *Journal of Management Development, 25*(6), 572–587.

Gilbreth, F. B. (1911). *Motion study.* London: Constable and Company.

Goldstein, I. L, & Ford, J. K. (2002). *Training in organizations* (4th ed.). Belmont, CA: Wadsworth.

Grant, A. M. (2008). The significance of task significance: Job performance effects, relational mechanisms, and boundary conditions. *Journal of Applied Psychology, 93*(1), 108–124.

Griffin, R. W. (1991). Effects of work redesign on employee perceptions, attitudes, and behaviors: A long-term investigation. *Academy of Management Journal, 34*(2), 425–435.

Griffin, R. W., Bateman, T. S., Wayne, S. J., & Head, T. C. (1987). Objective and social factors as determinants of task perceptions and responses: An integrated perspective and empirical investigation. *Academy of Management Journal, 30,* 501–523.

Hackman, J. R., & Oldham, G. R. (1975). Development of the job diagnostic survey. *Journal of Applied Psychology, 60,* 159–170.

Hackman, J. R., & Oldham, G. R. (1976). Motivation through the design of work: Test of a theory. *Organizational Behavior and Human Performance, 16,* 250–279.

Hsieh, A., & Chao, H. (2004). A reassessment of the relationship between job specialization, job rotation and job burnout: Example of Taiwan's high-technology industry. *International Journal of Human Resource Management, 15,* 1108–1123.

Humphrey, S. E., Nahrgang, J. D., & Morgeson, F. P. (2007). Integrating motivational, social, and contextual work design features: A meta-analytic summary and theoretical extension of the work design literature. *Journal of Applied Psychology, 92*(5), 1332–1356.

Jeurisson, T., & Nyklíček, I. (2001). Testing the Vitamin Model of job stress in Dutch health care workers. *Work & Stress, 15*(3), 254–264.

Korunka, C., & Vitouch, O. (1999). Effects of implementation of information technology on employees' strain and job satisfaction: A context-dependent approach. *Work & Stress, 13*(4), 341–363.

Liden, R. C., Wayne, S. J., & Sparrowe, R. T. (2000). An examination of the mediating role of psychological empowerment on the relations between the job, interpersonal relationships, and work outcomes. *Journal of Applied Psychology, 85*(3), 407–416.

Lin, C., Wang, M. J., & Drury, C. G. (2007). Biomechanical, physiological and psychophysical evaluations of clean room boots. *Erognomics, 50,* 481–496.

Liu, G., Shah, R., & Schroeder, R. G. (2006). Linking work design to mass customization: A sociotechnical systems perspective. *Decision Sciences, 37*(4), 519–545.

Maupin, R. J. (1990). Redesigning management consulting practices. *Leadership & Organization Development Journal, 11*(4), 3–9.

Minors, P., Nicholson, T., & Koscielniak, J. M. (1999). Job redesign in health care: Making old look new again. In M. A. Rahim, R. T. Golembiewski, K. D. Mackenzie, M. A. Rahim, R. T. Golembiewski, & K. D. Mackenzie (Eds.), *Current topics in management* (Vol. 4, pp. 213–224). Philadelphia, PA: Elsevier Science.

Mishra, A. K., & Spreader, G. M. (1998). Explaining how survivors respond to downsizing: The roles of trust, empowerment, justice, and work redesign. *Academy of Management Review, 23*(3), 567–588.

Mitchell, K. E., Alliger, G. M., & Morfopoulous, R. (1997). Toward an ADA-appropriate job analysis. *Human Resource Management Review, 7,* 5–26.

Molleman, E., & Van Knippenberg, A. (1995). Work redesign and the balance of control within a nursing context. *Human Relations, 48*(7), 795–814.

Morgeson, F. P., & Campion, M. A. (2002). Minimizing tradeoffs when redesigning work: Evidence from a longitudinal quasi-experiment. *Personnel Psychology, 55*(3), 589–612.

Morgeson, F. P., & Campion, M. A. (2003). Work design. In W. C. Borman, D. R. Ilgen, R. J. Klimoski, W. C. Borman, D. R. Ilgen, & R. J. Klimoski (Eds.), *Handbook of psychology: Industrial and organizational psychology* (Vol. 12, pp. 423–452). Hoboken, NJ: John Wiley & Sons, Inc.

Morgeson, F. P., & Humphrey, S. E. (2006). The work design questionnaire (WDQ): Developing and validating a comprehensive measure for assessing job design and the nature of work. *Journal of Applied Psychology, 91*(6), 1321–1339.

Morgeson, F. P., Johnson, M. D., Campion, M. A., Medsker, G. J., & Mumford, T. V. (2006). Understanding reactions to job redesign: A quasi-experimental investigation of the moderating effects of organizational context on perceptions of performance behavior. *Personnel Psychology, 59*(2), 333–363.

Morrison, D., Cordery, J., Girardi, A., & Payne, R. (2005). Job design, opportunities for skill utilization, and intrinsic job satisfaction. *European Journal of Work and Organizational Psychology, 14*(1), 59–79.

Nadin, S. J., Waterson, P. E., & Parker, S. K. (2001). Participation in job redesign: An evaluation of the use of a sociotechnical tool and its impact. *Human Factors and Ergonomics in Manufacturing, 11*(1), 53–69.

Nash, M. G., Grant, J. S., & Bartolucci, A. A. (2000). Clinical and operational outcomes of a work redesign model. *National Academies of Practice Forum: Issues in Interdisciplinary Care, 2*(3), 203–210.

Parker, S. K. (2002). Designing jobs to enhance well-being and performance. In P. Warr & P. Warr (Eds.), *Psychology at work* (5th ed, pp. 276–299). New York, NY: Penguin Press.

Parker, S. K., Wall, T. D., & Cordery, J. L. (2001). Future work design research and practice: Towards an elaborated model of work design. *Journal of Occupational and Organizational Psychology, 74*(4), 413–440.

Parker, S. K., Wall, T. D., & Jackson, P. R. (1997). "That's not my job": Developing flexible employee work orientations. *Academy of Management Journal, 40*(4), 899–929.

Pierce, J. L., & Dunham, R. B. (1978). Research notes. *Academy of Management Journal, 21,* 123–128.

Salancik, G R., & Pfeffer J. (1978). A social information processing approach to job attitudes and task design. *Administrative Science Quarterly, 22,* 427–456.

Sims, H. P., Szilagyi, A. D., & Keller, R. T. (1976). The measurement of job characteristics. *Academy of Management Journal, 19,* 195–212.

Taylor, F. W. (1911). *The principles of scientific management.* New York, NY: W. W. Norton.

Trist, E. L., & Bamford, K. W. (1951). Some social and psychological consequences of the Longwall method of coal-getting. *Human Relations, 4,* 3–38.

Vance, R. J., & Biddle, T. F. (1985). Task experience and social cues: Interactive effects on attitudinal reactions. *Organizational Behavior and Human Decision Processing, 35*(2), 252–265.

Wall, T. D., Jackson, P. R., & Davids, K. (1992). Operator work design and robotics system performance: A serendipitous field study. *Journal of Applied Psychology, 77*(3), 353–362.

Wall, T. D., & Martin, R. (1987). Job and work design. In C. L. Cooper & I. T. Robertson (Eds.), *International review of industrial and organizational psychology 1987* (pp. 61–91). Oxford, England: John Wiley & Sons.

Warr, P. (1987). *Work, Unemployment, and Mental Health.* Oxford, England: Clarendon Press.

Williams, K. J., & Lillibridge, J. R. (1992). Perceived self competence and organizational behavior. In K. Kelley (Ed.), *Issues, theory, and research in industrial/organizational psychology* (pp. 155–184). Holland, The Netherlands: Elsevier Science.

Xie, J. L., & Johns, G. (1995). Job scope and stress: Can job scope be too high? *Academy of Management Journal, 38,* 1288–1309.

Zeffane, R. M. (1994). Correlates of job satisfaction and their implications for work redesign: A focus on the Australian telecommunications industry. *Public Personnel Management, 23*(1), 61–76.

19

Designing Work Descriptions to Maximize the Utility of Employee Recruitment Efforts

Gregory M. Hurtz

California State University, Sacramento

Chris W. Wright

San Francisco State University

Work descriptions are used for many purposes internal to organizations, but their most transparent use outside the organization's human resource department is in the realm of employee recruitment. It goes something like this: There is a vacant position that must be filled; the work description is updated and used to advertise the open position internally to other organization members and/or externally to potentially interested job seekers. The job title and work description are the "meat" of the advertisement and will either catch a job seeker's eye or not.

An effective and attractive work description can contribute greatly to the utility, or payoff, of recruitment and selection efforts by attracting high-quality applicants and keeping them interested in the job and the organization to the extent that they are likely to accept employment if an offer is made. A large part of this contribution is avoidance of the potentially costly effects of an ineffective work description that is dull, unattractive, and either leaves a position vacant for an extended period or attracts subpar applicants so that the position must be filled with less than ideal employees.

This chapter has several interrelated goals. First, it provides a working definition of a work description and outlines its desired components both in terms of structure and content. Next, the chapter frames this "core" definition of a work description as a usable document and as the foundation on which several layers of multimedia technology features can be added to disseminate and market the description in an effective manner for employee recruitment purposes. Finally, the discussion of work descriptions is placed into a model of employee recruitment phases and the chapter argues that both the "meat" of the core description and the attractiveness of the extra layers of technology-enhanced features can increase the overall utility of all phases of recruitment efforts in terms of attracting high-quality applicants who are likely to remain with the organization.

WORK DESCRIPTIONS

Definition

Job descriptions are typically defined simply as brief summaries of a job. This insufficient definition is perhaps why job descriptions are often so short that they lack functionality. The term "work

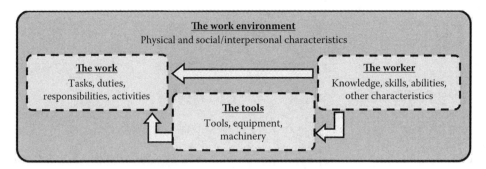

Figure 19.1   Schematic representation of the focal points of a work description.

description" adopted here implies a broader focus commensurate with the broadening of the term "job analysis" to "work analysis," which extends the practice to "other information about the work, worker, organization, and work environment" (Society for Industrial and Organizational Psychology, 2003, p. 10). Based on an amalgamation and extension of "job description" definitions from multiple sources (e.g., Aamodt, 2004; Brannick, Levene, & Morgeson, 2007; Cascio, 1998; Society for Industrial and Organizational Psychology, 2003), we provide a working definition of a "work description" as follows:

> A relatively brief, written summary of the work analysis results that includes information about (a) the **work** in terms of the tasks, duties, responsibilities, behaviors, and activities; (b) the **tools** that are used to carry out this work; (c) the physical and social **environments** in which this work is performed; and (d) the **worker** in terms of the requisite knowledge, skills, abilities, and other personal characteristics that are needed to carry out the work effectively.

The focal points of this definition of work description are displayed in Figure 19.1. As depicted in this figure, the work (tasks, duties, etc.) is carried out within a physical and social work environment by workers with particular characteristics who often use particular tools and equipment in the process. A good work description should describe all of these elements, keeping in mind that one of the primary goals is to communicate essential information about the work in a way that is comprehensible to the "job novice" rather than the "job expert" (Brannick et al., 2007). To echo Brannick et al.'s warning, "because the point of the [work] description is to communicate the essence of the [work] to someone who is not familiar with it, it is very easy to write a bad [work] description but surprisingly hard to write a good one" (p. 178).

Components and Format of a Basic Work Description

The work description is much like an abstract of a scientific paper or an executive summary of a business report. It gives a relatively brief snapshot, often in two to five pages (Aamodt, 2004)[1], outlining the results of the more comprehensive work analysis report. Although there is no established formula for the content and structure of a work description document, Brannick et al. (2007) identified four typical sections of a work description based on their own collective experience and on past literature such as Gael's (1988) *Job Analysis Handbook for Business, Industry, and Government*. These sections of the work description are (a) identifiers such as job title, classification, and any organization-specific codes for the job; (b) a summary statement that gives a brief synopsis of the

---

[1] Aamodt (2004) notes that business professionals often resist lengthy work descriptions (often keeping them to one page), whereas industrial/organizational psychologists often prefer them to be longer. We concur with Aamodt's assessment that descriptions that are too brief are not likely to contain enough information to be of value for the various purposes such a description serves.

mission, objectives, or "essence" of the work that is performed; (c) an organized listing of critical duties and tasks involved in the work, which expands on the summary statement (and is taken directly from the work analysis); and (d) other information about the work such as supervision, minimum education or experience requirements, working conditions, or any other specifics that an applicant would need to know or be assessed on when determining their fitness for the job. Other frequently included factors that would fall under this "other information" listing are materials and tools or machinery used, the social environment, and conditions of employment (Cascio, 1998).

These same general guidelines are followed here in terms of the critical information we believe should comprise the foundation of a work analysis in its most basic form, although in keeping with Figure 19.1 and our definition of work descriptions, the fourth section is separated into components that explicitly call for describing (a) the worker, (b) the tools and equipment, and (c) the work environment. Recommended elements of a work description are displayed and briefly described in Figure 19.2, with some expanded discussion below. Although the chapter gives a relatively brief overview of what should be included in each section, the information to include cannot be prescribed exactly; the work analyst will need to employ some professional judgment in how to best describe a particular job or position using this framework within the purpose and context of the organization for which the work description is being written. In addition, though much of the core information used for this description comes from the work analysis, a standardized survey instrument such as Morgeson and Humphrey's (2006) Work Design Questionnaire might prove to be a useful source of supplemental information.

Identifiers

In this section, identifying information such as job title, classification, and any organization-specific codes for the job is included. This information identifies the job and the position in the hierarchy of the organization in a way that follows the classification scheme established by the human resources department. The classification relates to the pay scale and job level, and it perhaps provides a reference to external job classification systems such as those indexed in the O*NET. We recommend using identifiers that allow one to draw connections to the O*NET, which provides additional information about the job families and occupations to which the work relates.

Summary of Work

This summary gives a brief synopsis of the mission, objectives, or "essence" of the work that is performed. This is often given in narrative form, such as a paragraph that a non-job expert can read relatively quickly to get a good general understanding of the work.

Description of Work Performed

Here, a listing of critical tasks involved in the work is provided. It expands on the summary statement using additional details from the work analysis. This task listing is typically organized logically into duty areas, or clusters of related tasks, which are presented in their order of importance or criticality as determined by subject matter expert ratings. Usually only those tasks that exceed some threshold of importance or criticality are listed. Depending on the job and whether the work description is for a specific job in an organization versus a broad job family, classification, or occupation, these descriptors may occur at different levels of specificity. We recommend using language and descriptors that aid in the process of relating the work activities to a broad-ranging taxonomy such as that indexed in the O*NET system (see Jeanneret, Borman, Kubisiak, & Hanson, 1999) or the Common Metric Questionnaire (see Harvey, 1993). This encourages the establishment of a common language for work description across jobs and organizations and avoids unnecessary time spent deriving labels that end up being largely synonymous with those already in existing

---

Work Description

(1) **Identifiers:** (Insert job title, classification, and any organization-specific codes or information that identifies or classifies the job.)

(2) **Summary of work:** (Insert a summary statement that gives a brief synopsis of the mission, objectives, or "essence" of the work that is performed.)

---

(3) **Description of work performed:** (Insert an organized listing of critical duties, tasks, and activities involved in the work that expands on the summary statement with relevant detail; optionally, an established taxonomy of work activities such as the O*NET or CMQ will provide structure to this listing and provide a common language for cross-job comparisons.)

(4) **Description of tools and equipment:** (Insert information regarding tools, equipment, and machinery used when carrying out the work.)

(5) **Description of the work environment:** (Insert information regarding the physical environment and working conditions in which the work is carried out, and the social/interpersonal environment and supervisory structure of the work; again, an established taxonomy of work environments such as that used in the O*NET or CMQ should ideally be utilized.)

(6) **Description of the worker requirements:** (Insert information regarding minimum education, training, certification, and/or experience requirements and other essential, and helpful, personal characteristics; established taxonomies of knowledge, skills, abilities, and work styles will help provide structure and common language for cross-job comparisons.)

Figure 19.2   Recommended elements of a work description.

taxonomies. It also may help organizations to streamline the development of selection and training techniques through strategies such as synthetic validation (Scherbaum, 2005).

Description of Tools and Equipment

Here, any tools, equipment, or machinery used on the job should be stated. Much of this information often is incorporated into the task statements of the previous section or in the listing of knowledge and skills for a later section below; however, it is informative to list this information clearly in its own section as well.

Description of the Work Environment

Here the physical/environmental setting of the work (e.g., privacy, proximity to others, exposure to extreme environmental conditions, hazards, or potential for injury) is described as well as the social/interpersonal aspects of the work environment (e.g., communication methods and norms, types of work role relationships, team/group work, and degree of responsibility for others). This serves to provide accurate information about the conditions of the environment in which the work is conducted. It is especially crucial to note here any extreme conditions such as working outdoors in hot or cold environments and exposure to potentially hazardous substances or dangerous situations. Also noteworthy, however, are the more moderate demands of an indoor office environment and the physical surroundings of the workspace, as well as potential stressors such as work pace, job demands, and pressure to meet deadlines. The description should identify whether the work is carried out primarily in social isolation, in collaborative work teams, or independently but near other people. A clear statement of the degree of direct and/or indirect supervision of the work should also be included, in addition to a statement of whether the work involves the responsibility of supervising others (and how many individuals are supervised). Here again the use of an established taxonomy of work environments such as that used in the O*NET system (see Strong, Jeanneret, McPhail, Blakley, & D'Egidio, 1999) or Common Metric Questionnaire is recommended.

Description of the Worker Requirements

This section describes the required knowledge, skills, abilities, and other personal characteristics (KSAOs) determined through the work analysis to be necessary for effective job performance, especially in light of those factors described prior to this point in the work description. These worker requirements should generally be grouped and organized into a logical order and presented in such a way that job seekers can easily ascertain whether they possess those requirements and/or how they may acquire them (e.g., training and experience requirements). If the job requires minimum qualifications, such as specific education, licensure/certification, training, or experience, these should be stated clearly in this section. Once again, established taxonomies of knowledge, skills, abilities, and work styles (e.g., see Borman, Kubisiak, & Schneider, 1999; Costanza, Fleishman, & Marshall-Mies, 1999; Fleishman, Costanza, & Marshall-Mies, 1999; and Mumford, Peterson, & Childs, 1999) could be adopted here at least as an overarching framework to aid in cross-job comparisons.

THE ROLE OF WORK DESCRIPTIONS IN EMPLOYEE RECRUITMENT

The goal of any organizational selection and placement program is to fill job openings with high-quality applicants. Industrial/organizational psychologists have devoted a great deal of attention to the design and validation of techniques used to assess applicants' capabilities once they enter the hiring pipeline, and it is well established among industrial/organizational psychologists (even if not recognized as much by human resource professionals; Ryan & Tippins, 2004) that the use of professionally developed selection tools play a crucial role in hiring from the standpoint of both organizational utility and legal defensibility. The importance of the recruitment function in the applicant flow model, however, is often overlooked or given insufficient attention (Ryan & Tippins, 2004).

According to Gatewood, Feild, and Barrick (2007), the three goals of recruitment are to (a) enlarge the size of the applicant pool in a cost-efficient manner, (b) ensure compliance with legal and social workforce demographic targets, and (c) improve the utility of the selection process by maximizing the ratio of qualified versus unqualified applicants. Too often, though, the recruitment process is designed primarily to meet the first two objectives (Wanous, 1992). The result is a large pool of applicants introduced into the selection process without proper regard for their fitness for the job. To be maximally effective and produce high-quality hires whose expertise and interests match job openings, the hiring system needs high-quality recruits. This section describes how work descriptions can be used to build recruitment tools that are grounded in job-relevant information and designed to attract and retain the best applicants.

A discussion of the various recruitment techniques and their usefulness for specific situations is beyond the scope of this chapter. Instead, we will focus on the recruitment process more broadly and show how work descriptions can be used to maximize recruitment effectiveness. We start by considering how work descriptions can be expanded upon to serve their crucial role in the recruitment process.

Expanding the Core Work Description via Information and Communication Technology

Figure 19.2 provides a template for writing a work description that will be useful for a variety of human resource purposes. The information in that description is the core description of the job and the work activities performed—the "meat," as described earlier. However, increasing attention has been given to how this core description is presented, especially when the purpose is to recruit and attract job applicants. Since 2000, a body of research has emerged about both the positive and negative effects of practices such as "e-recruiting" and embedding work descriptions within corporate web sites (see, e.g., Allen, Mahto, & Otondo, 2007; Allen, Van Scotter, & Otondo, 2004; Braddy, Meade, & Kroustalis, 2006; Cober, Brown, Keeping, & Levy, 2004; Cober, Brown, Levy,

Cober, & Keeping, 2003; Dineen, Ash, & Noe, 2002; Feldman & Klaas, 2002; Maurer & Liu, 2007; Pfieffelmann, Wagner, & Libkuman, 2010; Sylva & Mol, 2009). The purpose here is not to provide an exhaustive review of this literature, however both recruitment and job search activities are more frequently being done online and the qualities of an organization's recruitment web site can go a long way toward keeping applicants interested or losing them quickly. This body of research literature suggests that factors such as perceptions of organizational culture and person-organization fit, organizational attraction, and intentions to pursue and join the organization can be affected by perceptions of the recruitment web site.

Of particular importance for building a heuristic model to guide expansion of work descriptions is the distinction between the *content* of a recruitment web site (e.g., the details of the work description and other organizational information) and the *style* in which that content is portrayed (e.g., aesthetics, usability, and interactivity; Cober et al., 2003; Cober, Brown, & Levy, 2004). The research of Cober et al. has demonstrated that both content and style influence applicant perceptions of the organization during recruitment. Closely aligned to this distinction, the comprehensive work description (described earlier) gives a solid foundation for the content factor when it comes to recruitment, but stylistic considerations must be given equally thorough attention when the goal is to enhance recruitment utility by attracting employees and maintaining their interest.

To this end, outlined here are four "layers" of work description, depicted in Figure 19.3, as a guiding framework for the use of work analysis in employee recruitment. Layer 1 is the traditional printed (or printable) work description as defined earlier, which provides the core content drawn from an analysis of work. This layer is the foundation on which the remaining layers build. Layer 2 does not add content to this foundational core, nor really any stylistic modifications, but adds an electronic system for organizing and disseminating the work descriptions, possibly with targeted dissemination to particularly qualified and/or underrepresented groups of potential applicants. This second layer essentially involves placing the information from the first layer into an electronic database where work descriptions are organized and indexed and then made widely available for searching and viewing or downloading, usually via the Internet. This has become standard practice with mainstream use of the Internet for job seeking. Individual organizations often have their own searchable web sites for work descriptions of open positions, and many third-party web sites exist

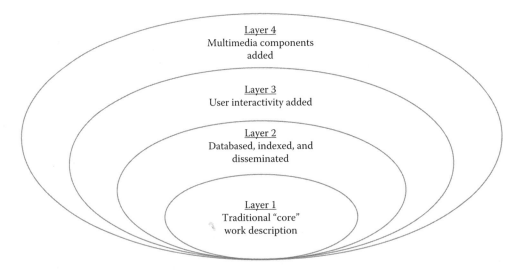

Figure 19.3   Layers of increasingly sophisticated technology-enhanced work descriptions.

to help job-seekers find work descriptions for open positions across many organizations based on key words related to the job titles, type of organization, education/experience requirements, geographic location, and other search fields.

Layer 2 has undoubtedly become common in the practice of posting jobs and recruiting applicants, and when the practice emerged, it represented a significant step ahead from the purely paper-based and locally available work descriptions that were not as easily searched, found, and distributed. However, Layer 2 only provides the core job content; it stops short of more fully utilizing the technology media to better inform and attract job applicants. Layer 3 begins to add stylistic features of aesthetics, vividness, and interactivity (Cober et al., 2003; Maurer & Liu, 2007). Here the work description begins to have added elements of color and graphics, as well as interactivity such as the capability for individuals to request additional information (most likely through hyperlinks or menus within the work description itself) about key components of the work description as they research a job or position. This section includes more utilization of basic Internet browser technology, beyond the simple delivery of an electronic image of what is essentially a paper work description.

We define Layer 3 as using only "basic" components of browser technology to emphasize an important point when considering potential subgroup differences in access to computing technology among the applicant population. As noted by Ployhart, Schneider, and Schmitt (2006), recruitment web sites that require advanced "cutting edge" browser features available only in the newest software versions may inadvertently exclude individuals without access to the newest technology. To the extent that this lack of access may occur more often among some protected classes under civil rights law, this may produce adverse impact issues and run counter to affirmative action efforts in recruitment. In addition, web site features that are not accessible to job applicants with disabilities (see http://www.section508.gov and http://www.access-board.gov/sec508/standards.htm) can also exclude a class of potential applicants protected under the Americans with Disabilities Act. Even very old browser software, however, will properly display hyperlinks, menus, and other features programmed with basic HTML code. The typical level of access to up-to-date computing technology in the target applicant population for a particular type of job must therefore be considered when planning a recruitment web site.

Although Layer 3 adds basic user interactivity in the search for additional job information, it is conceptualized here as a largely static information system where additional text is provided at the user's request or external links are available to other Internet locations. This can be very useful, but Layer 4 adds another element that often would involve more cutting-edge software technology for proper viewing: increased use of graphics, audio, video, and two-way communication technologies. Photos of the job site or relevant equipment may be provided either one at a time or in slideshows with audio accompaniment. Work flow diagrams or other work-related illustrations may be presented with animation or with audio clips. Video clips of work, equipment, personal testimonials, virtual tours of work sites, or any other aspect of the work that would be more effectively described through a multimedia presentation could be embedded within the work description for display through a web browser where users can start, stop, rewind, and replay the information at will to become familiar with the job and nature of the work. In addition, two-way communication tools such as message boards, instant messaging or on-line chat tools, and video conferencing or video calling using webcam technology could be linked into the web-based work description.

Utilizing these multimedia types as modes of communicating work- and organization-related information, building on the largely text-based information already provided in Layers 1 through 3, is likely to influence job seekers' perceptions of message credibility and satisfaction with the communication process; it potentially could result in more positive attitudes toward the organization that may lead to a greater likelihood of joining the organization (Allen et al., 2004). Again,

Table 19.1   Some Potential Links Between the Layers of Work Description and the Phases of Employee Recruitment and Selection

Layer of Work	Layer of Work Description	Phase of Recruitment and Selection		
		Phase 1: Attracting Applicants	**Phase 2: Maintaining Applicant Interest**	**Phase 3: Persuading Applicants to Accept Offers**
1	The traditional printed work description	Provides the core information for describing and marketing the job		
2	The electronically indexed and disseminated work description	Disseminates the work description so job seekers may find it and become aware of the job opening		
3	The electronic work description with user interactivity	Provides additional work information; links to company information, general descriptions of organizational missions, values, and culture, prescreening questionnaires or self-tests, and application blanks	Provides further details about the organizational culture to help applicants judge person/organizational fit; provides additional information about the advertised position, the work context, realistic job preview information, contact information for recruiters or other designated employees (perhaps all protected by a log-in screen); this information remains available at the applicants' fingertips through the Internet	
4	The multimedia work description	Adds photo slideshows, audio/video clips of employee testimonials, etc., to add more realistic and "personal" information to attract applicants to the organization	Additional photos, audio/video clips, employee testimonials, etc., that are more directly tied to the specific work unit and position; provides deeper information that job seekers are looking for at this stage; provides a live or near-live communication tool with recruiters or other key organizational members, such as instant messaging, chat, or video conferencing	

To enhance recruitment utility, and regardless of the medium used to transmit the recruitment message (e.g., print, electronic, web, audio/video), Phase 1 efforts should endeavor to convey specific, detailed, and accurate information about the most important aspects of the job as defined through the work description. Research has shown that more specific information tends to increase applicant interest in pursuing a job interview, whereas organizations providing less information in their job postings tend to be seen as less attractive by job seekers (Allen et al., 2004; Allen et al., 2007; Barber & Roehling, 1993; Feldman, Bearden, & Hardesty, 2006; Roberson, Collins, & Oreg, 2005). Further, recruitment advertisements with less information, or with only general information, may yield larger numbers of unqualified applicants who are not suitable for hire (Feldman et al., 2006; Mason & Belt, 1986). Perhaps the unqualified applicants do not have enough information to know they are unqualified, or perhaps the lack of specificity is seen as an open invitation to take a "long shot." At the same time, the lack of specific information may dissuade the best applicants who are thorough in their job search activities and seek out more detailed information. Dissuading the best applicants while at the same time failing to dissuade unqualified applicants is obviously not an optimal method of attracting a strong applicant pool.

So, what type of information should be included in Phase 1 recruitment efforts? At a minimum, materials should contain the job title and/or job type; the minimum qualifications, including any education, credentials, or work experience needed; a brief listing of the critical job duties and KSAOs needed to perform those duties; the work location and/or environment; a short description of the organization; and an indication of whether the work is part or full time. When considering what additional information to include, particular emphasis should be placed on job information that may influence applicants' decisions to apply (or not apply) for the job, such as work shifts, travel requirements, and salary and benefits. Most or all of this information is included in the work description outline described earlier. In addition, Reeve and Schultz (2004) recently demonstrated that applicants seek and use information about the steps in the selection process when deciding whether or not to apply, so the selection process should be described early on. For many jobs, Layer 3 or 4 of a technology-enhanced work description would be an ideal vehicle for conveying much of this supplementary detail early in the process in a way that is both informative and appealing to qualified job applicants.

As a case in point for demonstrating the potential gain in utility of providing pivotal information for job seekers' decision-making early in the recruitment process, one of the authors was asked by a major metropolitan transit agency to review an interview process for selecting bus operators. Agency representatives were concerned about the poor quality of their applicant pool as well as attrition from the selection process. The interview was the final step in a lengthy process that included an application screen, a paper-and-pencil minimum skills test, and two video-based situational judgment tests. In the course of reviewing the interview, it became apparent that several interview questions, which had been included late in the selection process, were designed to gather (and provide) information that would have been more effective in Phase 1 of the recruitment process and written into the work description itself. Examples included questions that asked whether applicants were willing to work required night and weekend shifts and whether they had experience driving oversized vehicles. Answers to these questions were crucial in determining one's ability or willingness to meet critical job requirements; had this information about work shifts and experience requirements been provided earlier, the unqualified or uninterested job seekers could have self-selected out of the application process early, which would have saved the organization valuable time and resources, leaving only more able and willing applicants to continue through the lengthy application process. Given the increased costs involved for these applicants with little to no potential for gain, recruitment utility was hindered.

An even clearer case in point for managing Phase 1 recruitment efforts to maximize utility comes from the job of entry-level firefighter. In most jurisdictions, the minimum qualifications needed to apply for such a job are few but the starting salaries are competitive, so applicant pools are large, particularly in major metropolitan areas. Large applicant pools are generally viewed as positive in the evaluation of recruitment efforts because the organization can then be more selective in deciding who to hire. However, the selection process for firefighters typically involves multiple hurdles, many of which are cost prohibitive (e.g., physical ability tests, interviews) and are followed by several months of a training academy that they must complete successfully before starting probationary duty. The accumulation of costs in the recruitment and selection of firefighters is considerable, making it crucial that these expenses are only paid for applicants with true potential to help the organization realize gains from the recruitment and selection process. With such high costs, there is a clear tradeoff between increasing the number of applicants and the payoff of being more selective (Carlson et al., 2002).

In this particular context, the tradeoff is very likely to be realized because the minimum qualifications to apply for the job are not restrictive, and many applicants become interested in this job through exposure to archetypical representations of firefighters in popular culture and are often unaware of the actual day-to-day job duties and experiences of firefighters. For example, a significant proportion of their time at work may actually be spent housekeeping, cooking, and participating in physical and technical training. Further, most calls for emergency services involve medical matters, not firefighting. In addition, applicants need to be made aware that firefighters work at heights and in extreme conditions, that they maintain an unorthodox schedule that requires them to live in the firehouse for 24-hour periods, that they are required to work on holidays, and that they must accept the fact that the fire department is a paramilitary organization in which orders from superiors must be followed without question. Finally, they should be informed that the selection process for the job is rigorous and lengthy from the time of application to the time of hire.

Following the notion of the realistic job preview (RJP), which involves presenting both the positive and negative aspects of the job during the recruitment and selection process (Breaugh, 2008; Wanous, 1992), an accurate depiction of these realities of the firefighter job and the selection process for the job can be accomplished in Layers 3 or 4 of a technology-enhanced work description. This can be carried out by translating critical tasks and duties into still-frame or motion-picture visual depictions and/or audio clips for use in job advertisements and web portals, perhaps depicting a "week in the life" of a firefighter. Tasks that represent the physical KSAOs that are needed at entry, such as the ability to operate heavy tools and equipment, drag victims from fire and accident scenes, lift patients onto stretchers, and climb ladders and stairs while wearing heavy protective gear, could be included. In addition, lists of duties such as first-responder medical intervention, firefighting, ventilation, postincident salvage and overhaul, training, and community outreach can be arranged in order of frequency or displayed in a hyperlinked graphic so applicants clearly see what percentage of their time they would spend fighting fires versus engaging in other less "exciting" activities. The result would be a comprehensive, accurate depiction of the job that would allow potential applicants to make an informed decision early on about whether to proceed through the application process. If the reality check serves to turn a subset of unserious applicants off to the notion of pursuing this profession, unnecessary costs can be avoided. At the same time, if they serve to further reinforce and motivate the more serious and well-informed applicants, then gains may be more likely. It is important to recall our previous warning, however, that the use of technology-enhanced work descriptions may result in adverse impact to the extent that protected subgroups differ in access to the required technology to interact fully with the RJP information. In light of potential legal challenges, employers should track applicant statistics and offer lower fidelity alternatives to track and/or reduce potential adverse impact.

An example of the effective use of Layer 3 work description information for an RJP is the recruitment process for emergency communication specialists (911 operators) by a city in central Florida. The main web page provides work descriptive information in text and photographs. A hyperlink at the bottom of the page directs prospective applicants to an RJP form that they must complete and sign. The RJP form asks them to indicate their willingness to perform tasks and comply with work requirements by responding to a "yes/no" checklist. Examples of items to which they are asked to respond include their willingness to work all major holidays, work the night shift, interact with adults and children in extreme distress, and make decisions with life or death consequences. Applicants are informed that they will not be considered for employment unless they endorse all of the statements. In addition, they must sign the form and bring it to their civil service test session. This ensures that applicants have not only reviewed a description of the nature of the work, but that they have also carefully considered it before applying.

If Phase 1 efforts are successful, the pool of potential applicants will be composed of individuals who are interested in the job and have an understanding of the minimum qualifications, work requirements, and selection process. However, because Phase 1 efforts are typically designed to reach large numbers of applicants, they are usually presented somewhat impersonally through advertisements, brochures, and web sites. In Phase 2, recruiters and other members of the organization interact with applicants more directly to present more detailed information about the job and the organization. As in Phase 1, the effective use of work description information can make a significant impact on the outcome of the recruitment process.

Phase 2: Maintaining Applicant Interest

In the second phase of the recruitment process, a pool of applicants has been generated and the focus shifts toward maintaining the applicants' interest in the organization. This phase can be characterized as a two-way communication process where the organization is evaluating the applicants while the applicants are simultaneously evaluating the job and organization. The Layer 1 and 2 work description at this stage has virtually exhausted its functionality as the applicants seek additional information—information that could be communicated effectively at Layers 3 or 4. Though the importance of simpler personal contact via face-to-face, telephone, or e-mail communication should not be overlooked, information available 24/7 via a web portal should prove beneficial to inform applicants and maintain their interest through interactivity and even "playfulness" (Cober et al., 2004). In addition, web content or automated communication tools could be configured to provide up-to-date information, such as the number of remaining job openings and other time-sensitive updates.

Although the role of the recruiter is to build on Phase 1 efforts and maintain applicant interest in the job, research indicates that recruiters do not always do an effective job of conveying the most useful information to applicants. Breaugh and Starke (2000) report that applicants are frequently dissatisfied with the amount of job-relevant information they receive from recruiters. Maurer, Howe, and Lee (1992) surveyed engineering students entering the job market and found that recruiters often did not provide information about basic job characteristics such as wages or benefits. In addition, there was a significant positive relationship between the level of satisfaction with the amount of information received and the expressed likelihood of accepting a job offer.

Although withholding some information, such as salary, may be intentional, it is sometimes the case that recruiters simply do not possess the knowledge of the job necessary for them to perform their role adequately and attract quality applicants. In one of the author's own experience upon finishing a doctorate degree, he was surprised to find that a major consulting firm in the industrial/organizational psychology field sent what appeared to be two lower-level assistants with virtually no job knowledge to conduct a structured recruitment screening interview at a job placement fair at a major industrial/organizational research conference. Though the use of a structured interview showed good intentions for a careful selection process, the inability of the recruiting staff to answer questions and their somewhat juvenile behavior at times (e.g., giggling, admitting they did not really understand the questions nor the answers) did not maintain the interest of serious job seekers at the conference. This experience is corroborated by research that shows that most organizations do not provide any training to their recruiters, and the small percentage of organizations that do offer training give, on average, less than 15 hours of training (Barnard, 2003; Rynes & Boudreau, 1986). To adequately train recruiters to communicate the information that is most valuable for applicants, organizations should use the work description as the primary reference point.

Another example of the use of work descriptions to train recruiters comes from one of the author's work with a regulatory organization. The primary technical classification in this organization was a regulatory analyst. The regulatory analyst was a very broad classification with primary job responsibilities encompassing policy research and consulting on a wide variety of issues related to public utilities and transportation regulation. At the entry level, the minimum qualification was a bachelor's degree in economics, finance, public policy, or a related field. The nature of the position and the starting salary dictated that the primary applicant pool was new or recent college graduates, most of whom presumably knew very little about the job and had not considered it as a career option. Therefore, the recruitment challenge was to inform potential applicants from different academic disciplines about the job in a way that would encourage them to pursue it.

The majority of the recruitment took place on college campuses, either by classroom visits or through career center sponsored events. For classroom visits, recruiters were selected to match the setting based on their academic discipline. If the class was macroeconomics, for example, the recruiter would be a regulatory analyst with academic training in economics who could articulate the nature of their work and how it incorporated issues such as productivity, marginal cost, and price determination in revenue and customer forecasting. At career fairs, which tended to attract students from a variety of disciplines, multiple recruiters attended to match recruits with a current employee who had similar academic training.

Prior to attending recruitment events, recruiters were trained to focus on the actual work performed by regulatory analysts. Because the organization employed regulatory analysts in many different departments and roles, recruiters reviewed work descriptions and job analysis results so they were able to speak generally about the essential functions and important KSAOs for new employees. They also reviewed a list of questions applicants frequently asked. Topics included salary and benefits, opportunities for advancement, and organizational culture. Finally, recruiters were urged to portray the job in realistic terms in a way that highlighted both its positive and potentially unattractive aspects. The positive work descriptors included challenging, analytical work with significant impact on public policy. Conversely, delivering testimony during legislative proceedings was highlighted as a potential negative work task. Throughout, the process was designed to introduce the organization to applicants with objective data about the organizational mission, how the work tasks of regulatory analysts supported the mission, and the career opportunities that were available within the classification.

Using the work description to inform the recruitment strategy enhances the organization's ability to target the intended applicant pool. It can also be valuable in situations where the job title does not communicate the full scope of the job duties. The organization discussed above, for example, also employed mechanical, civil, and electrical engineers. However, many of the engineers employed by the agency did not perform traditional engineering work and instead conducted studies of capital costs, financial structure, inventories, and depreciation. Recruiters were trained to describe these duties to applicants to establish realistic expectations and reduce attrition among those hired.

In a similar situation, one of the authors had a consulting engagement with a research hospital that employed switchboard operators who worked one of three shifts: morning, day, or night. All operators were required to rotate between shifts during their tenure. The work description was standard for the profession, with the exception of the night shift. In this organization, night shift switchboard operators were required to process admissions for patients who checked into the hospital after hours. Admissions processing included a number of tasks that were not associated with typical switchboard operator work, such as completing paperwork, verifying insurance coverage, and securing bed space for patients. Because career switchboard operators from other organizations comprised the primary applicant pool, most would not expect the additional duties to be included in the work description. Therefore, it would be critical for recruiters to relate this information to applicants before they progressed too far into the selection process. Ideally, higher-level work descriptions, especially with 24/7 access during the two-way communication process between applicants and the organization, would be used to reinforce the recruiter's message and to highlight the unorthodox duties.

Using the work description as the informational benchmark for recruiters not only makes practical sense, but there is research to support the use of job relevant information in this stage of the process. In a survey of 50 organizations, Carless (2007) found that the use of job analysis and the accuracy of recruitment information were both predictors of recruitment effectiveness. Similar results were found among potential recruits for a sales representative job. Applicants rated the organization as more attractive when they received more realistic information about the time pressures of the job and the types of interactions with others that the job required, compared with those who received only positive information about those job attributes (Thorsteinson, Palmer, Wulff, & Anderson, 2004). Thus, the RJPs discussed in the context of Phase 1 should be a continued practice through Phase 2.

Taylor and Bergmann (1987) surveyed applicants at several stages of a single recruitment process, from campus interview to job offer. Later in the process, at three stages (site visit, job offer, and job acceptance) that correspond to Phases 2 and 3 of Barber's (1998) model, work descriptive information had a significant impact on applicants. Information about the level of responsibility, opportunity for advancement, and whether they perceived the work as interesting were the best predictors of applicant ratings of company attractiveness, probability of offer acceptance, job offer decision, and intent to stay with the company. Though Taylor and Bergmann concluded that "the major practical implication seems to be that the recruitment message predominates over its media" (p. 282), Cober et al. (1993; Cober et al., 2004) more recently found that both the message (content) and media (style) were important in bringing about positive recruitment outcomes. In the context of the current chapter, these conclusions serve as reminders that Layer 1 of the work description possesses the crucial information, but the additional layers are likely to be important as well.

Phase 3: Persuading Applicants to Accept Offers

In the first two phases, the majority of the recruitment effort is directed toward identifying the best applicants and encouraging them to apply and remain interested. If this process is successful it will yield a group of qualified applicants, many of whom may have numerous job offers to consider. In the final phase, the focus of the recruitment process shifts toward persuading those applicants to accept job offers. Issues of person-job fit and person-organization match are paramount. Conventional wisdom geared toward "closing the deal" may be that this is the point at which the positive aspects of the job should be overemphasized or that the strategy should be to "sell" the organization to make the job seem more attractive. However, research indicates that the best practice involves maintaining realism and providing accurate information that highlights the most important aspects of the work and to match applicant characteristics and preferences with those aspects to ensure the best possible person-organization fit. Again, the work description is the foundation of this approach.

Recent research about the factors that influence organizational attractiveness suggest that applicants' level of familiarity with the organization, perceptions of the job and the organization, and trait inferences about the organization may be important predictors (Lievens, Van Hoye, & Schreurs, 2005). In a study of potential applicants to a military organization, for example, participants were more attracted to the organization if they were more familiar with it as an employer, if they were aware that the job offered team-oriented work activities and a diversity of work tasks, and if they felt the organization was an exciting and prestigious place to work (Lievens et al., 2005). The authors suggested that the organization could benefit by promoting these attributes in their recruitment messages, and much of the information needed to frame these messages could be gleaned from work descriptions and promoted in a Layer 4 description.

Consider a retail organization that operates in a marketplace with numerous competitors that offer similar products. The organization has distinguished itself from its competitors, and in turn boosted profits and market share, by emphasizing superior customer service. To maintain this image and level of success, the organization needs to recruit and hire applicants who have strong customer service competencies and who are comfortable working in a culture that sets high service expectations for its employees. In this situation, it is reasonable to assume that many prospective applicants, even those with previous retail customer service experience, may be unaware of the organization's mission and how it impacts the work environment.

Throughout the recruitment process, the organization could use advertisements, Layers 3 or 4 of a work description, RJPs, and recruiters to communicate the link between organizational brand and the job duties in an attempt to attract the highest quality applicants. At the job offer stage, hiring managers could reiterate the importance of customer service and discuss the aspects of the organization and the job that make it an ideal match for someone with outstanding customer service potential. This message could be reinforced with tangible situational examples that illustrate the connection between the employee and the organizational mission. These could be framed around tasks and KSAOs from the work description and presented in a variety of ways. Recruits could watch a video that shows sales associates following up with customers after purchases to verify product satisfaction or contacting other retail outlets, including competitors, to locate desired merchandise. Meetings or online chats could be arranged with current employees to discuss the links between customer service performance and job satisfaction, pay, and promotional opportunities. Managers could conduct store walkthroughs to give recruits the opportunity to observe the job and experience typical customer service interaction. At the end of the process, managers can be confident that the best applicants have received sufficient information about the job, from the point of application to job offer, to allow them to make an informed choice about whether the organization is the best fit for them.

Conclusion

The goal of this section has been to illustrate the importance of incorporating specific information that can be gleaned directly from the work description into all phases of the recruitment cycle. Our rationale, which is supported by research evidence, is that more focused, work-centered recruitment will yield higher-quality applicants who are a better match for both the job and the organization (Chapman, Uggrslev, Carroll, Piasentin, & Jones, 2005). Our hope is that practitioners will be proactive in using work description information as the foundation for their recruitment efforts. We also advocate the full utilization of available technology to create Layers 3 and 4 for work descriptions that, in our opinion, can result in a substantial return on investment for the recruitment process because they can go a long way toward satisfying the best applicants' desires to acquire and have access to increasingly detailed information. In any particular situation, however, we encourage practitioners to think in terms of utility as projected gains minus costs, and perhaps implement Carlson et al.'s (2002) methods for estimating the potential return on investment of new recruitment efforts. In addition, it is important to consider the warnings regarding the potential for excluding members of the applicant pool who do not have sufficient access to the requisite technology.

SUMMARY AND FUTURE DIRECTIONS

In this chapter, we provided a definition of a work description along with a recommended structure for the components of information to include in this description. We advocated for the use of established taxonomies, such as those incorporated into the O*NET or Common Metric Questionnaire systems, when defining the information within the work description to foster in our field a common language for describing work. We also looked ahead to the future of work description, where more of what our information and communication technologies have to offer can be adopted to describe the nature of work with more substance and fidelity beyond static text. We suggested that this practice has the potential to be an invaluable asset throughout the stages of employee recruitment and to help enhance the utility of recruitment and selection efforts. We provided a number of examples based on experience and past research where organizations' recruitment efforts at the stages of attracting applicants, maintaining their interest, and persuading them to accept a job offer were, or could have been, greatly improved by more effective use of work description information. We encourage practitioners and researchers to explore the use of what we define as Layers 3 and 4 for work descriptions and evaluate their impact on the utility of the recruitment efforts following Carlson et al.'s (2002) methods. Even without the use of information technology, however, any recruitment efforts should be closely tied to the core work description.

REFERENCES

Aamodt, M. G. (2004). *Applied industrial/organizational psychology* (4th ed). Belmont, CA: Wadsworth.

Allen, D. G., Mahto, R. V., & Otondo, R. F. (2007). Web-based recruitment: Effects of information, organizational brand, and attitudes toward a web site on applicant attraction. *Journal of Applied Psychology, 92,* 1696–1708.

Allen, D. G., Van Scotter, J. R., & Otondo, R. F. (2004). Recruitment communication media: Impact on prehire outcomes. *Personnel Psychology, 57,* 143–171.

Barber, A. E. (1998). *Recruiting employees: Individual and organizational perspectives.* Thousand Oaks, CA: Sage.

Barber, A. E., & Roehling, M. V. (1993). Job postings and decision to interview: A verbal protocol analysis. *Journal of Applied Psychology, 78,* 845–856.

Barnard, J. K. (2003). *Toward a unifying framework of recruiter performance and organizational effectiveness.* Paper presented at the Mid-West Research-to-Practice Conference in Adult, Continuing, and Community Education, Columbus, OH.

Borman, W. C., Kubisiak, U. C., & Schneider, R. J. (1999). Work styles. In N. G. Peterson, M. D. Mumford, W. C. Borman, P. R. Jeanneret, & E. A. Fleishman (Eds.), *An occupational information system for the 21st century: The development of the O*NET* (pp. 213–226). Washington, DC: American Psychological Association.

Braddy, P. W., Meade, A. W., & Kroustalis, C. M. (2006). Organizational recruitment website effects on viewers' perceptions of organizational culture. *Journal of Business and Psychology, 20,* 525–543.

Brannick, M. T., Levine, E. L., & Morgeson, F. P. (2002). *Job and work analysis: Methods, research, and applications for human resource management* (2nd ed). Thousand Oaks, CA: Sage.

Breaugh, J. A. (2008). Employee recruitment: Current knowledge and important areas for future research. *Human Resource Management Review, 18,* 103–118.

Breaugh, J. A., & Starke, M. (2000). Research on employee recruitment: So many studies, so many remaining questions. *Journal of Management, 26,* 405–434.

Carless, S. A. (2007). Graduate recruitment and selection in Australia. *International Journal of Selection and Assessment, 15,* 153–166.

Carlson, K. D., Connerley, K. L., & Mecham, R. L. (2002). Recruitment evaluation: The case for assessing the quality of applicants attracted. *Personnel Psychology, 55,* 461–490.

Cascio, W. F. (1998). *Applied Psychology in Human Resource Management* (5th ed). Upper Saddle River, NJ: Prentice-Hall.

Chapman, D. S., Uggrslev, K. L., Carroll, S. A., Piasentin, K. A., & Jones, D. A. (2005). Applicant attraction to organizations and job choice: A meta-analytic review of recruiting outcomes. *Journal of Applied Psychology, 90,* 928–944.

Cober, R. T., Brown, D. J., Keeping, L. M., & Levy, P. E. (2004). Recruitment on the net: How do organizational web site characteristics influence applicant attraction? *Journal of Management, 30,* 623–646.

Cober, R. T., Brown, D. J., & Levy, P. E. (2004). Form, content, and function: An evaluative methodology for corporate employment web sites. *Human Resource Management, 43,* 201–218.

Cober, R. T., Brown, D. J., Levy, P. E., Cober, A. B., & Keeping, L. M. (2003). Organizational web sites: Web site content and style as determinants of organizational attraction. *International Journal of Selection and Assessment, 11,* 158–169.

Costanza, D. P., Fleishman, E. A., & Marshall-Mies, J. (1999). Knowledges. In N. G. Peterson, M. D. Mumford, W. C. Borman, P. R. Jeanneret, & E. A. Fleishman (Eds.), *An occupational information system for the 21st century: The development of the O*NET* (pp. 71–90). Washington, DC: American Psychological Association.

Dineen, B. R., Ash, S. R., & Noe, R. A. (2002). A web of applicant attraction: Person–organization fit in the context of web-based recruitment. *Journal of Applied Psychology, 87,* 723–734.

Feldman, D. C., Bearden, W. O., & Hardesty, D. M. (2006). Varying the content of job advertisements: The effects of message specificity. *Journal of Advertising, 35,* 123–141.

Feldman, D. C., & Klaas, B. S. (2002). Internet job hunting: A field study of applicant experiences with on-line recruiting. *Human Resources Management, 41,* 175–192.

Fleishman, E. A., Costanza, D. P., & Marshall-Mies, J. (1999). Abilities. In N. G. Peterson, M. D. Mumford, W. C. Borman, P. R. Jeanneret, & E. A. Fleishman (Eds.), *An occupational information system for the 21st century: The development of the O*NET* (pp. 175–195). Washington, DC: American Psychological Association.

Gael, S. (1988). *The job Analysis Handbook for Business, Industry and Government.* New York, NY: John Wiley & Sons.

Gatewood, R., Feild, H. S., & Barrick, M. (2007). *Human resource selection* (6th ed.). Mason, OH: South-Western.

Harvey, R. J. (1993). *Research monograph: Development of the Common-Metric Questionnaire (CMQ).* Personnel Systems & Technologies Corporation. Retrieved from http://harvey.psyc.vt.edu/Documents/monograph.pdf

Jeanneret, P. R., Borman, W. C., Kubisiak, U. C., & Hanson, M. A. (1999). Generalized work activities. In N. G. Peterson, M. D. Mumford, W. C. Borman, P. R. Jeanneret, & E. A. Fleishman (Eds.), *An occupational information system for the 21st century: The development of the O*NET* (pp. 105–125). Washington, DC: American Psychological Association.

Lievens, F., Van Hoye, G., & Schreurs, B. (2005). Examining the relationship between employer knowledge dimensions and organizational attractiveness: An application in a military context. *Journal of Occupational and Organizational Psychology, 78,* 553–572.

Mason, N. A. & Belt, J. A. (1986). Effectiveness of recruiting specificity in recruitment advertising. *Journal of Management, 12,* 425–432.

Maurer, S. D., Howe, V., & Lee, T. W. (1992). Organizational recruiting as marketing management: An interdisciplinary study of engineering graduates. *Personnel Psychology, 45,* 807–833.

Maurer, S. D., & Liu, Y. (2007). Developing effective e-recruiting websites: Insights for managers from marketers. *Business Horizons, 50,* 305–314.

Morgeson, F. P., & Humphrey, S. E. (2006). The Work Design Questionnaire (WDQ): Developing and validating a comprehensive measure for assessing job design and the nature of work. *Journal of Applied Psychology, 91,* 1321–1339.

Mumford, M. D., Peterson, N. G., & Childs, R. A. (1999). Basic and cross-functional skills. In N. G. Peterson, M. D. Mumford, W. C. Borman, P. R. Jeanneret, & E. A. Fleishman (Eds.), *An occupational information system for the 21st century: The development of the O*NET* (pp. 49–69). Washington, DC: American Psychological Association.

Pfieffelmann, B., Wagner, S. H., & Libkuman, T. (2010). Recruiting on corporate web sites: Perceptions of fit and attraction. *International Journal of Selection and Assessment, 18,* 40–47.

Ployhart, R. E., Schneider, B., & Schmitt, N. (2006). *Staffing organizations: Contemporary practice and theory* (3rd ed). Mahwah, NJ: Lawrence Erlbaum.

Reeve, C. L., & Schultz, L. (2004). Job-seeker reactions to selection process information in job ads. *International Journal of Selection and Assessment, 12,* 343–355.

Roberson, Q. M., Collins, C. J., & Oreg, S. (2005). The effects of recruitment message specificity on applicant attraction to organizations. *Journal of Business and Psychology, 19,* 319–339.

Ryan, A. M., & Tippins, N. T. (2004). Attracting and selecting: What psychological research tells us. *Human Resource Management, 43,* 305–318.

Rynes, S. L. & Boudreau, J. W. (1986). College recruiting in large organizations: Practice, evaluation and research implications. *Personnel Psychology, 39,* 729–757.

Scherbaum, C. A. (2005). Synthetic validity: Past, present, and future. *Personnel Psychology, 58,* 481–515.

Society for Industrial and Organizational Psychology, Inc. (2003). *Principles for the Validation and Use of Personnel Selection Procedures* (4th ed.). Bowling Green, OH: Author.

Strong, M. H., Jeanneret, P. R., McPhail, S. M., Blakley, B. R., & D'Egidio, E. L. (1999). Work context: Taxonomy and measurement of the work environment. In N. G. Peterson, M. D. Mumford, W. C. Borman, P. R. Jeanneret, & E. A. Fleishman (Eds.), *An occupational information system for the 21st century: The development of the O*NET* (pp. 127–145). Washington, DC: American Psychological Association.

Sylva, H., & Mol, S. T. (2009). E-recruitment: A study into applicant perceptions of an online application system. *International Journal of Selection and Assessment, 17,* 311–323.

Taylor, M. S., & Bergmann, T. J. (1987). Organizational recruitment activities and applicants' reactions at different stages of the recruitment process. *Personnel Psychology, 40,* 261–285.

Thorsteinson, T. J., Palmer, E. M., Wulff, C., & Anderson, A. (2004). Too good to be true? Using realism to enhance applicant attraction. *Journal of Business and Psychology, 19,* 125–137.

Wanous, J. P. (1992). *Organizational entry.* Reading, MA: Addison-Wesley.

20

Using Job Analysis as the Foundation for Creating Equal Employment Opportunity in the Workplace

DAN A. BIDDLE

Biddle Consulting Group, Inc.

JAMES E. KUTHY

Biddle Consulting Group, Inc.

Employers make important decisions about job candidates or current employees every day. Who will be hired? Who will get a promotion and/or a pay raise? Who will be offered professional development opportunities? In an increasingly diverse U.S. workforce, and in light of increasing protections for workers from historically underutilized or oppressed societal groups, the past several decades have seen expanded attention given to the achievement of an ideal state of equal employment opportunity (EEO) for all. EEO is achieved when practices, procedures, and/or tests (PPTs) that are used for making personnel decisions offer everyone who is qualified a chance to succeed. A thorough analysis of work provides crucial data for ensuring that EEO objectives are being met.

Although civil rights laws dating back to the 1800s were designed to offer some degree of federal protection from discrimination, many scholars trace the beginning of the more recent advances in EEO in the workplace to the Civil Rights Act of 1964 (CRA 1964). One section of the act, referred to as Title VII, prohibits employment discrimination based on race, sex, color, religion, and national origin. Furthermore, the CRA 1964 took the bold step of creating the Equal Employment Opportunity Commission (EEOC), which was directed to eliminate unlawful employment discrimination.

Since 1964, the federal government has adopted a number of other laws that address a relatively wide range of EEO issues, all of which are enforced by the EEOC. This includes the Civil Rights Act of 1991 (CRA 1991), which provides monetary damages in cases of intentional employment discrimination and prohibits the adjustment of test scores on the basis of race/ethnicity; and the Age Discrimination in Employment Act of 1967, which is designed to protect the employment rights of individuals who are 40 years of age or older. Along similar lines, the EEOC also enforces the Americans with Disabilities Act of 1990 (ADA 1990; including the 2008 amendments), which prohibits discrimination on the basis of disability.

In addition to the laws listed above, there are executive orders that have been specifically designed to address the selection activities of federal contractors. There are also numerous state and local regulations that prohibit many types of discrimination, including some that are not protected under federal law. At the heart of enforcing all of these legal regulations is the analysis of work that informs and underlies the human resource practices that lead to decisions about employees.

JOB ANALYSIS

Whenever decisions are made about current or potential employees, it is important that they are based on a thorough and accurate understanding of the job in question, which can help make certain that all qualified candidates are given an equal opportunity to succeed. That is, a position with incorrectly understood requirements may not permit qualified candidates a fair opportunity to be selected. The best way that a job can be understood is through a thorough analysis of the work-related behaviors of those who hold the job, which is commonly referred to as a *job analysis*.

This chapter will examine some of the requirements and standards for conducting job analyses that can lay the foundation for addressing EEO objectives while also providing examples of business-related reasons why job analyses provide a solid foundation for many types of work-related decisions. As seen in other chapters of this handbook, these decisions include, but are not limited to, informed hiring and promotional decisions, the development or improvement of employee training, strategic planning, establishing salary and wage ranges, and the development of effective performance evaluation systems. Table 20.1 provides examples of some of the many uses and benefits of a job analysis, with particular emphasis on the relevance to legal and EEO issues.

One of the most critical uses of a job analysis is to help address legal requirements when making employment-related decisions. Legal actions related to these requirements are most commonly triggered when the PPTs used by employers result in *adverse impact* against a subgroup of job candidates or employees. Adverse impact is defined by the federal *Uniform Guidelines on Employee Selection Procedures* (Equal Opportunity Employment Commission, 1978, 1979) as "A substantially different rate of selection in hiring, promotion, or other employment decision which works to the disadvantage of members of a race, sex, or ethnic group" (Section 16). Adverse impact is sometimes referred to as "disparate impact" (Section 16B). PPTs used by an employer that result in adverse impact against a subgroup can only be justified if the employer *makes a demonstration* that it is "job related for the position in question and consistent with business necessity" (to address the requirements of the CRA 1991, Section 703[k][1][A][i]).

In litigation settings, this standard is usually met by demonstrating how the PPT follows the federal *Uniform Guidelines* (EEOC, 1978) as well as professional standards such as the *Standards for Educational and Psychological Testing* (American Educational Research Association, 1991) and the *Principles for the Validation and Use of Personnel Selection Procedures* (Society for Industrial and Organizational Psychology, 2003). In some instances, they must also conform to precedents of parallel or lower courts that have applied unique criteria to certain testing circumstances or types of PPTs.

The requirements of the *Uniform Guidelines* (EEOC, 1978) apply to PPTs that are used as a basis for any employment decision. This includes, but is not limited to, employment decisions such as hiring, promotion, demotion, nominations for training or development; referrals by employment agencies or others; and reductions in force. Though the *Uniform Guidelines* do not formally constitute a set of legal requirements, they have consistently been awarded "great deference" starting as early as the *Griggs v. Duke Power Company* (1971) case. They have also been unilaterally adopted verbatim as a legal standard in several court cases, for example, *Brown v. the City of Chicago* (1996, 1998).

Interestingly, some courts have ruled that some types of procedures used to make selection decisions, such as job performance appraisals, do not require a full *Uniform Guidelines*-style job analysis to be valid (Barrett & Kernan, 1987). Instead, the level of evidence of nondiscriminatory action (i.e., validity) is generally dictated by the type of personnel action that is taken (Miller, Kaspin, & Schuster, 1990). Even so, Barrett and Kernan indicated that basing a performance appraisal process on an analysis of the job is likely to help employers minimize potential liability when evaluating employees. Furthermore, as will be discussed later, essential functions for ADA compliance are

Table 20.1   Uses for a Job Analysis in Establishing Equal Employment Opportunity Compliance of Human Resource Functions

Uses of the Job Analysis	Benefits
Validating selection procedures	Provides evidence of job relatedness and fairness of selection procedures, which is useful in the event of a legal challenge or government audit. Required under the *Uniform Guidelines* (EEOC, 1978) for some types of validation.
Creating or choosing selection procedures	Provides information that is helpful when selection procedures are being developed or when employers are shopping for previously-developed procedures to ensure they have direct links to relevant components of work.
Developing job descriptions	Identifies tasks performed by employees who hold a particular job title, along with the overall job responsibilities. Also useful for identifying the minimum qualifications required to successfully perform the job, creating job announcements, and providing a realistic preview of a job. This all may be particularly relevant to federal contractors for achieving workforce diversity through affirmative action plans. Includes, but is not limited to, identifying training, experience, or education that qualified job candidates should possess as specified by the U.S. Department of Labor's (2005) "Internet applicant" rule.
Indentifying essential functions of and reasonable accommodations for the job under the ADA 1990 for qualified individuals	The term *qualified individual with a disability* means an individual with a disability who, with or without reasonable accommodation, can perform the essential functions of the employment position. A job analysis can be used to identify those essential functions. Moreover, the ADA requires employers to make "reasonable accommodation" for workers; some job analyses provide information that can assist in identifying such accommodations.
Identifying pay or wage ranges	Identifies similarities and differences between jobs or job groupings for compensation purposes to ensure equitable pay decisions.
Creating effective performance evaluations	Aids in the creation of effective performance-evaluation procedures by providing a common frame of reference for evaluating employees by identifying job-related performance standards, along with objectives and goals that successful employees should meet. Helps organizations achieve uniform standards for evaluating their diverse workforce members.
Developing effective training	Provides a needs assessment that identifies what training content should be offered and to whom, along with indentifying the depth and breadth of the training. Helps to ensure that training is linked to work-related outcomes. When tied to unbiased performance evaluations, training opportunities are more likely to be equally available to all employees who need them.

ADA = Americans with Disabilities Act; EEOC = Equal Opportunity Employment Commission.

not necessarily extracted directly from a job analysis, but a job description is one piece of critical information that helps to make this determination. Relying on a job analysis would seem to make good business sense when making any type of employment decision, no matter whether the courts require such an analysis or not.

It is important to notice that the legal requirement cited above (and by association, the federal *Uniform Guidelines*) uses a verbal phrase (i.e., making a *demonstration*) when defining the employer's burden for proving job relatedness for their PPT that is exhibiting adverse impact in a hiring or promotional setting. Making such a "demonstration" typically involves framing an *empirical connection* between the researched job requirements and the at-issue PPT through a job analysis process. In practice, an employer must identify important or critical knowledge, skills, or abilities (KSAs) and/or work behaviors or work outcomes (based on the type of validity evidence being asserted, as required by Sections 14B3 and 14C2 of the *Uniform Guidelines*) before a PPT can be shown to be job related and thus be justifiable when exhibiting adverse impact. Because of these requirements, it is reasonable to state that the topic of job analysis is foundational to the process of establishing validity in Title VII situations.

Employers should be aware that the *Uniform Guidelines* state that it is the "user's responsibility to determine that the validity evidence is adequate to meet the Guidelines" and that "employers should not use selection procedures which are likely to have a disparate impact without reviewing the evidence of validity to make sure that the standards of the Guidelines are met" (EEOC, 1979, p. 12001). In other words, it is the employer, not the test publisher or developer, that is liable if a PPT does not address the applicable validity standards.

There are two U.S. Supreme Court cases that are frequently cited as indicating that an analysis of the job is required when determining the validity of any PPT. The first is *Griggs v. Duke Power Company* (1971). In this case, the Supreme Court indicated that a PPT that lacked a meaningful study of its relationship to job performance and that resulted in adverse impact against a protected class of test takers was not valid. More specifically, the court indicated that "what Congress has commanded is that any tests used must measure the person for the job and not the person in the abstract" (401 U.S. 424, 436).

The second case is *Albemarle Paper Company v. Moody* (1975) where the Supreme Court reinforced the importance of an analysis of the job when it stated:

> A test may be used in jobs other than those for which it has been professionally validated only if there are "no significant differences" between the studied and unstudied jobs. The study in this case involved no analysis of the attributes of, or the particular skills needed in, the studied job groups. [Therefore] there is accordingly no basis for concluding that "no significant differences" exist among the lines of progression [referring to advancement within the organization], or among distinct job groupings within the studied lines of progression. (422 U.S. 405, 432)

In other words, without an analysis of the job, a PPT will typically not be accepted as being valid.

More recently, the federal government has passed regulations that seem to be designed to encourage employers that are federal contractors to conduct job analyses, even if there is no adverse impact present. This is in regards to the basic qualification regulations that have been adopted by the U.S. Department of Labor's Office of Federal Contract Compliance Programs for the acceptance of Internet job applications (OFCCP, 2005; 41 CFR Part 60-1). *Basic qualifications* in this context refers to qualifications that a federal contractor advertises to potential job applicants or criteria that a contractor has established in advance for the selection of job applicants. According to the U.S. Department of Labor's guidelines, the qualifications must be:

1. Noncomparative features of a job seeker (e.g., 3 years of experience in a particular position rather than comparative requirements such as being one of the top five among the candidates in years of experience)
2. Objective (e.g., a bachelor's degree in accounting rather than the more subjective "a technical degree from a good school")
3. Relevant to performance of the particular position

It is the third prong of the requirements for federal contactors accepting Internet applications that is most directly related to the job analysis process. Although the requirements do not specifically require a job analysis, it seems likely that the Department of Labor would follow the guidance of the U.S. Supreme Court in the *Albemarle Paper Company v. Moody* (1975) case, which indicated that, "Job relatedness cannot be proved through vague and unsubstantiated hearsay" (422 U.S. at

428 n. 23, 95 S. Ct. 2362). Instead, it seems likely that the Department of Labor would require some sort of analysis of the job for an employer that acts as a federal contractor to be able to demonstrate that the basic requirements are relevant to the job.

It is important to note that this "third prong" for federal contractors who are accepting Internet applications preemptively requires "job relevancy" before adverse impact occurs. However, if an employer's basic qualifications exhibit adverse impact after they have been placed online, the higher "validation requirement" of CRA 1991 (described above) applies.

In addition to the job analysis requirements under CRA 1991 that are triggered after the employer's PPT has demonstrated adverse impact, the ADA 1990 also is relevant for job analysis. The ADA 1990 requires that employers carefully research the job duties that are represented as *job requirements* (the current term of art is *essential functions*) throughout the selection process and requires that job seekers represent they can perform such essential functions with or without reasonable accommodations that do not create an undue hardship on employers. The research methods by which job duties can be classified as essential functions are covered within this chapter.

VALIDITY EVIDENCE AS A DEFENSE FOR POLICIES, PRACTICES, AND TESTS IN THE FACE OF ADVERSE IMPACT

Another factor that affects the level of detail that a job analysis must address when validating employment-related PPTs is the type of validation strategy that will be used to show that the PPT is job related. There are two primary methods used for validating tests that have adverse impact against a protected group of job candidates: content validity and criterion validity. (There is also a third validation methodology mentioned in the *Uniform Guidelines*—construct validity—but that method is seldom used in actual practice, so we will not address it here). The following is a description of the content- and criterion-related approaches to validation.

Content-Related Validity

A content validity study links the essential outcomes of a job analysis (the job duties and/or KSAs) to the PPT. Thus, content validity is formed by creating a nexus between the job and the PPT. It relies on a process that requires job experts to provide judgments (usually by providing ratings on surveys) regarding if and how well the PPT represents and measures the important parts of the job. That is, content validity is simply the rational demonstration that the content of a selection, training, promotion, or other important job decision tool reflects the content of the job itself.

For example, a word processing test that measures skills in using word processing software to edit and format business correspondence would likely be content valid for an administrative professional's job. Likewise, for example, an entry-level physical ability test measuring physical performance at a fire scene, such as deploying a charged hose line or carrying a ladder, uses a content validity approach for the position of firefighter.

In *Kirkland v. New York State Department of Correctional Services* (1975), the U.S. Supreme Court indicated that the cornerstone in the construction of a content valid examination is the job analysis. When using a content-related approach for validity, it is important that the analysis shows that both the content and context of the PPT are similar to work behaviors or work samples or to a sample of a work product. As specified in Section 14C4 of the *Uniform Guidelines*, "to be content valid, a selection procedure measuring a *skill or ability* should either closely approximate an observable work behavior, or its product should closely approximate an observable work product. If a test purports to sample a *work behavior* or to provide a sample of a work product, the *manner* and *setting* of the selection procedure and its *level and complexity* should closely approximate the work situation" (p. 38302, emphasis added).

This delineation between "skill and ability" and "work sample" tests is important when using a content validity strategy because different requirements pertain to each. The key distinction is that skill and ability tests have a relaxed requirement when it comes to mirroring the job, and work sample tests should resemble the manner, setting, and level of complexity of the job.

For example, a retail customer service position may require reading comprehension skills at about the 12th-grade level to read and understand training materials, directions for store operations, and various instructions required for performing the job. A police officer may also require reading comprehension skills at about the 12th-grade level to read and understand summaries of laws and regulations and department policies and procedures. A 12th-grade-level reading comprehension test could be used for both of these positions, even if the test included content that was irrelevant to each.

A work sample test, on the other hand, needs to closely resemble the manner, setting, and level of complexity of the target position. Such tests typically present a job simulation exercise to the applicant that closely reflects the content and context of the job and measures whether the applicant can adequately perform the simulation, which should be setup in a way that measures the applicant's ability to complete the test without prior job-related training (see Section 14C1 of the *Uniform Guidelines*). With work sample tests, there is less of a requirement to specify the precise skills and abilities that are measured by the test because the test so closely represents the job. The *Uniform Guidelines Questions and Answers* (EEOC, 1979) provides additional clarification regarding this skill/ability versus work sample test distinction:

> *Question 73:* Must a selection procedure supported by content validity be an actual "on the job" sample of work behaviors?
> *Answer:* No. The Guidelines emphasize the importance of a close approximation between the content of the selection procedure and the observable behaviors or products of the job, so as to minimize the inferential leap between performance on the selection procedure and job performance. However, the Guidelines also permit justification on the basis of content validity of selection procedures measuring knowledge, skills, or abilities which are not necessarily samples of work behaviors if: (1) The knowledge, skill, or ability being measured is operationally defined in accord with Section 14C(4); and (2) that knowledge, skill, or ability is a prerequisite for critical or important work behaviors. (p. 12006)

EEOC v. The Dial Corporation (2005) provides an example of a work sample test that did not sufficiently resemble the manner, setting, and level of complexity of the position. In this case, the district court ruled that a physical ability test that had adverse impact against women was not justified based on content validity. This ruling was unanimously upheld in 2006 by the U.S. Court of Appeals for the Eighth Circuit. The appeals court also upheld the approximately $3.3 million award to 52 female job applicants who had been rejected for the job based on their performance on the work-sample test. The appeals court indicated that "an employer using the business necessity defense must prove that the practice was related to the specific job and the required skills and physical requirements of the position," (*EEOC v. The Dial Corporation*, 2006, p. 7) as previously indicated by the courts in the *Belk v. Southwestern Bell Telephone Co.* (1999) case.

In the at-issue position in this case, employees repetitively lifted and carried a 35-pound rod of sausages a distance of approximately 10 feet, placed them on a rack, and then returned 10 feet to the starting position to lift and carry the next rod of sausages. However, during the test, job applicants were required to lift and carry simulated rods of sausages in both directions. The employer argued that the test was very representative of the actions performed on the job. However, the court ruled that the test was more difficult than the actual work performed on the job because employees on the job only carry the sausages in one direction, thereby having a brief respite while they walk back to lift and carry the next batch. Thus, although the content of the test seemed similar to the content of the job, the fashion in which the work-sample task was performed during the test was sufficiently different from how the task was performed on the job, invalidating its use.

When using a content validity strategy, testing professionals have long been familiar with the requirements for the content of the test to be related to the contents of the job, but some have been less aware of the requirement that the context must also be similar for work sample tests. The *Uniform Guidelines Questions and Answers* (EEOC, 1979) state, "Where the content and context of the selection procedure are unlike those of the job, as, for example, in many paper-and-pencil job knowledge tests, it is difficult to infer an association between levels of performance on the procedure and on the job" (p. 12005). For example, though a paper-and-pencil test of some dimension of job knowledge (e.g., equipment safety procedures) might be appropriate for a job that requires the ability to read, it is likely to not be an appropriate testing method for jobs that do not require the ability to read. Thus, the content of the job may affect the context in which testing takes place. This would be determined by linking the results of the job analysis to the PPT. This does not rule out the use of, for example, knowledge testing for selection, but it requires that the reading level of any test not be higher than that required by the job itself.

Criterion-Related Validity

Section 14B(2) of the federal *Uniform Guidelines* (EEOC, 1978) requires an analysis of the job if a criterion-related approach to validity is used. Criterion-related validity is based on the finding of statistically significant similarity (i.e., with a probability value less than .05) between a PPT and a criterion that represents important or critical work behaviors or work outcomes. One interesting benefit of this type of validity is that the employer is not pressed to define exactly what the PPT is measuring. Although it is typically a good idea to know and describe to applicants the KSAs that are measured by the PPT to potentially increase the applicants' perception of the fairness of that PPT, it is not a legal requirement to do so because the PPT is statistically related to job performance. By contrast, content validity has specific requirements for the employer to show and describe the KSAs that are being measured by the PPT and how they are related to the job (see 15C4–5 of the *Uniform Guidelines*). Interestingly, the U.S. Department of Labor (2000) indicates that test takers view tests that show a high degree of job relatedness as being fairer than other types of tests (p. 4-2). This is further supported by evidence that giving job applicants information about the job related-ness of a selection test significantly enhances both their immediate reactions to the test and their later reactions when test results are provided (Truxillo, Bauer, Campion, & Paronto, 2002).

Beyond evaluating just statistical significance, some courts have ruled that the strength of the relationship (i.e., the size of the correlation) could affect whether a PPT is valid or not. For example, in *Clady v. County of Los Angeles* (1985), the court stated: "In conclusion, the County's valida-tion studies demonstrate legally sufficient correlation to success at the Academy and performance on the job. Courts generally accept correlation coefficients above +.30 as reliable. … As a general principle, the greater the test's adverse impact, the higher the correlation which will be required" (para. 88). Furthermore, the U.S. Department of Labor's guidelines for interpreting validity coef-ficients indicate that a correlation coefficient value less than 0.11 is unlikely to be useful, implying that criterion-related coefficients of less than 0.11 would not be useful for demonstrating validity even if the relationship was statistically significant.

As mentioned above, the *Uniform Guidelines* (EEOC, 1978) require an analysis of the job if a criterion validity approach is being used. However, the job analysis requirement in this instance seems to be much less stringent than when content validation is used. When criterion-related valid-ity is used the user must merely review "job information to determine measures of work behavior(s) or performance that are relevant to the job or group of jobs in question" p. 38300. This section goes on to say, "These measures or criteria are relevant to the extent that they represent critical or important job duties, work behaviors or work outcomes as developed from the review of job information" (p. 38300).

Furthermore, the *Uniform Guidelines* (EEOC, 1978) indicate there are some criteria that can be used without a full job analysis if the user can show the importance of the criteria to the particular employment context. These are criteria that include, but are not limited to, production rate, error rate, absenteeism, tardiness, and tenure (i.e., length of service).

Interestingly, criteria used for validation can also include performance during training if the relevance of the training can be shown either (a) by comparing the content of the training program with important or critical work behaviors or (b) by demonstrating a relationship between measure of job performance and measures of training performance. This issue of using success in training as a criterion for successful job performance when validating a test initially came to the forefront with the ruling by the U.S. Supreme Court in *Washington v. Davis* (1976). The Supreme Court ruled that employment practices must "have a demonstrable and rational relationship to important job-related performance objectives identified by management" and that "success in training" (para. 426) is one example of a possible objective. The court further stated, "The job-relatedness of an entrance examination may be demonstrated by proof that scores on the examination predict properly measured success in job-relevant training (regardless of whether they predict success on the job itself)" (para. 426).

It is interesting to note that Section 14B(3) of the *Uniform Guidelines* (EEOC, 1978) requires that when training is used as a criterion, "success in training should be properly measured and the relevance of the training should be shown either through a comparison of the content of the training program with the critical or important work behavior(s) of the job(s), or through a demonstration of the relationship between measures of performance in training and measures of job performance" (p. 38301). Once again, it seems that a study of the work behaviors should be performed.

Criterion-related validity can be achieved by correlating PPT scores to several different types of job performance measures, including both subjective and objective measures. The most typical subjective performance measures include supervisor ratings and/or peer ratings of work products (quality and/or quantity) or job performance and performance review scores. It is important to note that Section 15B of the *Uniform Guidelines* (EEOC, 1978) require that criterion measures consist of *actual job performance* and not ratings of the overall KSAs believed to be held by the incumbents (unless they are defined in terms of observable aspects of job behavior). Objective measures can include quantifiable work output measures (e.g., number of widgets produced per hour); quality-related measures (e.g., number of widgets returned because of defects); absenteeism; turnover; disciplinary actions; safety incidents; and other aspects of performance that are gathered and recorded in a uniform and consistent manner.

A job analysis can also be beneficial when a user wishes to transport a finding of validity based on a criterion-related study at one job to another job. Section 7B(2) of the federal *Uniform Guidelines* (EEOC, 1978) indicates that the findings of a criterion-related validity study conducted by one user can be acceptable to another user if, among other requirements, an appropriate job analysis shows that the major work behaviors performed by those holding the original job and those performed by the new user's job are "substantially the same."

Maximizing EEO Compliance at Key Steps in a Job Analysis Study

Various methods and systems of work analysis are covered in other sections of this handbook, each of which has varying degrees of relevance to particular applications and uses of the job analysis information. Developing a thorough and accurate job analysis is the most important step in providing evidence of content validity (it is also important for criterion-related validity, but less so). In addition, validity provides the foundation for the claim that a PPT fosters EEO.

however, these gains must be weighed against potential costs in terms of excluding subgroups of applicants without sufficient access to the required technology (e.g., high-speed internet access, current browser versions, compact disc or digital video disc drive if information is available in this format). In some professions, such as those in the technology industry, this may not be an issue, but in other industries it very well may be a legitimate limiting factor in terms of access to or proper display of job-related information.

Caveats and Challenges

As with any new venture in the application of technology, potential drawbacks must be considered alongside the potential benefits. Would all the time, effort, and cost involved in developing extra text, audio, and video content and then programming the web sites have sufficient payoff? What would be the standards for developing this content? Whose responsibility would it be (e.g., the job analyst)? How much information is too much, so that the job seekers become overwhelmed and lose sight of the crucial content? Would the enhanced use of technology, especially in the case of real-time, two-way communication tools, require a level of ongoing monitoring and support that is beyond the capabilities of the organization to maintain (which could lead to frustration and counteract any positive benefits)? Would real-time, two-way communication with organization members, rather than prescreened and edited messages and information, raise any public relations risks or, worse yet, any legal risks for the organization? Does the use of technology put some job seekers, who do not have access to sufficient computing power, at a disadvantage in their job search and ultimately their career opportunities? Do organizations want to provide *that* much inside information on the Internet for all to see, including their competitors? These are important questions for organizations to consider if they contemplate the use of multimedia-enhanced work descriptions. If such issues are surmountable, we believe the payoff would be worthwhile, especially in terms of recruitment utility.

Using Work Descriptions to Maximize Recruitment Utility

As a guiding framework for considering the importance of the work description for recruitment, Table 19.1 provides an overview of Barber's (1998) three-phase depiction of the employee recruitment and selection process and a discussion of the role of work descriptions in each phase. To paraphrase Barber's model, recruitment and selection involves (a) attracting applicants, (b) maintaining their interest, and (c) persuading them to accept job offers. Citing this model, Carlson, Connerley, and Mecham (2002) argued that models of employee selection utility also should be applied to the antecedent recruitment efforts to quantify the return on investment of adopting particular recruitment practices, for example, in terms of the number of qualified applicants a practice attracts and the likelihood they will stay interested and accept an offer of employment. In addition to these potential "gains" in applicant quality, Maurer and Liu (2007) cite anecdotal evidence that recruiting over the Internet comes with significant cost and time savings. Consistent with these suggestions, as summarized in Table 19.1, we argue that effective use of expanded work descriptions (Layers 3 and 4) should usually do more to increase recruitment utility than the traditional Layer 1 or 2 work description alone.

Phase 1: Attracting Applicants

According to this model, the first phase of the recruitment process is designed to persuade individuals to apply for the job. This involves both a thorough and informative core work description (Layer 1) and a means for that work description to be disseminated and found by potential job applicants (Layer 2). We propose as well that additional features at Layers 3 and perhaps 4 can help to draw applicants in at this early stage and increase their interest in pursuing the job.

There are numerous ways to complete a solid job analysis. Although there is no single right way, the steps below, adopted from the Guidelines Oriented Job Analysis (Biddle Consulting Group, 2008) process, are provided as a template for developing a job analysis designed to provide a foundation for validation. The Guidelines Oriented Job Analysis has been supported in numerous EEO cases (e.g., *Forsberg v. Pacific Northwest Bell Telephone Co*, 1988; *Gilbert v. East Bay Municipal Utility District*, 1979; *Martinez v. City of Salinas*, 1978; *Parks v. City of Long Beach*, 1984; *Sanchez v. City of Santa Ana*, 1979; *Simmons v. City of Kansas City*, 1988; and *United States v. City of Torrance*, 1993) and has been reviewed in several textbooks and articles (e.g., Buford, 1985, 1991; Bemis, Belenky, & Soder, 1984; Campbell, 1982; Sturm, 1979). We note that the Guidelines Oriented Job Analysis method follows task and KSA analysis methods similar to those covered earlier in this handbook as its foundation, but it is tailored specifically to achieving *Uniform Guidelines* and EEO compliance. Guidelines Oriented Job Analysis consists of an eight-step process, each of which are described briefly below.

Step 1: Assemble and Train a Panel of Qualified Job Experts

Job experts are qualified job incumbents who perform or supervise the target position. They generally should represent the demographics of the employee population, be experienced and active in the position they represent, represent functional areas and/or shifts of the position, and consist of between 10% and 20% of supervisors for the target position. Some courts have relied on as few as seven to ten job experts for providing judgments and ratings about job and PPT characteristics (e.g., *Contreras v. City of Los Angeles*, 1981; *United States v. South Carolina*, 1978). Guidance regarding the number of job experts necessary to obtain a statistically reliable and accurate estimate regarding job information has been described by Biddle (2006).

Experts participating in a job analysis should be trained on the overall process and be informed that their responses should be both independent and confidential (i.e., not disclosed to anyone outside the job expert panel).

Step 2: Job Experts Write Job Duties

In this step, job experts independently write job duties performed in the target position without regard to how important those duties are or how frequently they are performed. Having each job expert independently record duties her or she performs—without a group or paired discussion— helps to ensure that the final combined list of duties is as complete as possible.

Before the job duties are compiled into a master list (which is the next step, described below), it is generally a good idea to insure that each job duty includes a description of the outcome or work product that is a result of performing the duty. Mitchell, Alliger, and Morfoopoulos (1997) indicate that outcome-oriented (not method-oriented) job analyses that include work products are more likely to aid job experts in determining whether a job function is essential, as defined by the ADA 1990. They further point out that including outcomes and work products can allow for "identification of a degree of job flexibility" and can also be useful for "identifying potential reasonable accommodations" (p. 3).

Step 3: Consolidate Duties Into a Master Duty List

A 70% consensus rule (e.g., agreement by seven of 10 job experts on which duties are performed by those who hold the target job) is suggested for duties to be placed on the consolidated master list. A lower ratio may be used if the master list of job duties will be sent in survey form to a larger job expert sample to obtain their feedback.

Step 4: Job Experts Write KSAs (and Physical Requirements)

Have the job experts repeat the process described in Step 2, but now for the KSAs, including physical requirements. The following definitions can be helpful for this step:

- *Knowledge*: A body of information applied directly to the performance of a duty; for example, knowledge of medical standards, codes, laws, and regulations
- *Skill*: A present, observable competence to perform a learned physical duty; for example, skill in build wood furniture following written design specifications
- *Ability*: A present competence to perform an observable duty or to perform a non-observable duty that results in a product; for example, ability to present complex technical information to students in a classroom setting
- *Physical requirements*: Either skills or abilities that are physically related (e.g., color vision, sitting, standing, lifting, carrying, etc.)

Some job analyses also identify personal characteristics that employees need to successfully perform a target job. These are characteristics that are not as concrete as individual KSAs. Examples include dependability, conscientiousness, or stress tolerance. Section 14C of the *Uniform Guidelines* (EEOC, 1978) does not permit measuring abstract traits in content-validated selection process unless they are clearly operationally defined in terms of observable aspects of job behavior. For example, the characteristic dependability, if left undefined, is too abstract to directly measure in a selection process. If it can be defined as "promptness and regularity of attendance," which is an observable work behavior, it can be measured. If one desires to include personal characteristics in the selection process, they must be turned from abstract ideas to concrete, observable skills and abilities.

Step 5: Consolidate KSAs

For this step, the job experts repeat the process described in Step 3, but for the KSAs (including physical requirements).

Step 6: Have Job Experts Provide Ratings for Duties and KSAs

The job experts and supervisors can provide ratings now that a final list of duties and KSAs has been compiled. For job duties, job experts can provide the following ratings:

- *Frequency of performance*: This is not a requirement under the *Uniform Guidelines* for content validity, but it is useful for several practical reasons (note, however, that it is required for criterion-related validity studies). One of the useful purposes for this rating is for determining which job duties constitute essential functions under the ADA 1990 (Section 1630.2[n][3][iii]).
- *Importance*: The importance rating is perhaps one of the most critical ratings that job experts provide. Section 14C2 of the *Uniform Guidelines* states that the duties selected for a PPT (e.g., a work sample test) "should be critical work behavior(s) and/or important work behavior(s) constituting most of the job" (p. 38302). Thus, the *Uniform Guidelines* are clear that when using content validity for a work sample test, the PPT can be linked to a single critical duty (critical is later defined by the *Uniform Guidelines* as "necessary") or several important duties that constitute most of the job.

For KSAs, job experts can rate:

- *Links of KSAs to duties*: This step can be key for establishing content validity evidence. By linking the duties to the KSAs, a nexus is created showing where, for example, actual job skills are applied on the job. Completing this step addresses Section 14C4 of the *Uniform Guidelines*.

- *Frequency*: Though it is a good idea to obtain a direct rating of KSAs' frequencies from job experts, this question can also be answered by determining the job duty with the highest frequency rating to which the KSA is linked.
- *Importance*: This is perhaps the most important rating in a content validity study because the *Uniform Guidelines* require that a PPT measuring a KSA should be shown to be a "necessary prerequisite" of "critical or important work behaviors" and shown to be "used in the performance of those duties" (Sections 14C4 and 15C5). Because the *Uniform Guidelines* make this clear distinction between only *important* versus *critical or necessary*, the importance rating scale should take this into consideration by making a clear demarcation in the progression of importance levels between important and critical. A PPT measuring KSAs should be linked to critical and/or important work duties, and should be rated as critical or necessary by job experts.

After all ratings are collected, they should be reviewed for accuracy and completeness, and then averages for each job duty and KSA rating should be calculated. This should be performed before proceeding further because supervisors will consider the rating averages in subsequent steps.

Obtaining the opinions of additional job experts can be achieved using a job analysis survey. A job analysis survey can be prepared by providing the duties and KSAs in survey form to additional job experts and having those job experts rate the content of each, in addition to the other ratings described above. It is suggested to provide extra space on the job analysis survey where the additional job experts can record and rate additional duties or KSAs that had not been previously identified while completing the job analysis survey.

Step 7: Have Two (or More) Supervisors Review the Completed Job Analysis and Assign Supervisor Ratings

After the final job duty and KSAs have been rated by the job experts and the ratings have been averaged, convene two or more supervisors (these supervisors may have participated in the first six steps of the process) to assign additional job analysis ratings. The ratings that supervisors should provide for job duties include:

- *Percentage of time*: Evaluating the percentage of time that incumbents spend on a particular duty is one of several factors that should be considered when making essential function determinations under the ADA 1990 (Section 1630.2[n][3][iii]). Although helpful, it is not absolutely required for content validation studies.
- *Best worker*: What job duties distinguish the minimal worker from the best worker? Job duties that are rated high on the best worker rating are those that, when performed above the bare minimum, distinguish the best performers from the minimal. For example, helping guests with luggage and occasionally lifting boxes may be necessary for a hotel receptionist position. However, performing these job duties at a level above the minimum will not likely make any difference in a person's overall job performance. It would likely be other job duties such as greeting hotel guests and completing check-in/check-out procedures in a timely and friendly fashion that would distinguish between the minimal and the best workers for this job. The average rating on this scale can provide guidance for using a work sample type of content validity PPTs on a pass/fail, ranking, or banding basis (see Section 14C9 of the *Uniform Guidelines* [EEOC, 1978]). It is not necessary to obtain this rating for job duties unless the employer desires to validate a work sample type of PPT (i.e., a PPT that relies on linkages to job duties and not necessarily KSAs). We note that some practitioners refer to the best worker scale as a "more is better" scale.

- *Fundamental*: Fundamental job duties are duties that constitute "essential functions" under the ADA 1990 (Section 1630.2[n]). This rating is helpful but not necessary for validating PPTs. Under the ADA 1990, a job duty may be considered fundamental to the job in any of the following ways:
  - The duty is frequently performed (check the frequency rating) and/or the proportion of work time spent on it is significant (check the average percentage of time rating).
  - The consequence to the purpose of the job is severe if the job duty is not performed or if it is performed poorly (check the average Importance rating).
  - Removing the job duty would fundamentally change the job. In other words, the duty is fundamental because the reason the job exists is to perform the duty.
  - There are a limited number of employees available among whom the performance of this job duty can be distributed.
  - The duty is so highly specialized that the incumbent was placed in the job because of his/her expertise or ability to perform this particular job duty.
- *Assignable (to others)*: Can this job duty be readily assigned to another incumbent without changing the fundamental nature of the position? In such instances, the job duty should not be considered as an essential function under the ADA 1990 unless all employees must perform this duty at some point during their tenure. For example, a job duty can be determined to be fundamental (using the fundamental duty rating) and hence essential under the ADA 1990; however, if such job duty can be readily assigned to another employee without changing the fundamental nature of the job, the job duty can be re-designated as not essential. Job duties that are frequently performed or take up a large proportion of work time and that are important or critical probably are not easily assigned to others. Duties that occur infrequently and/or require a small percentage of work time can sometimes be assumed by others, regardless of how important or unimportant they are.

For KSAs, supervisors can rate:

- *Minimum versus helpful qualifications*: This rating can help determine which KSAs should be included in a selection process. Minimum qualifications are those that the applicant or candidate must have prior to entry into the position; helpful qualifications can still be included in the selection process (if they meet the other requirements discussed herein), but are not absolute necessities prior to entry.
- *Best worker*: Which KSAs distinguish the minimal from the best worker? KSAs that are rated high on the best worker rating are those that distinguish the best performers from the minimal performers. For example, possessing superior levels of interpersonal skills, rather than superior physical abilities, will likely make a difference in a person's overall job performance as a hotel receptionist. Therefore, when a selection process is assembled for this position, interpersonal skills should be measured using a ranked or banded test, whereas physical abilities should be measured using a pass/fail test (see Section 14C9 of the *Uniform Guidelines* [EEOC, 1978]).
- *Level needed for success (for job knowledge only)*: This rating identifies the level of job knowledge that is required on the first day on the job. For example, some job knowledge domains are needed only at a level of general familiarity, whereas other job knowledge domains need to be learned at a mastery level. The data from these ratings are useful for choosing the job knowledge that should be included in a written job knowledge test (see Section 14C4 of the *Uniform Guidelines* for specific requirements for measuring job knowledge in a selection process).

- *Level needed upon entry*: This rating identifies how much of a KSA is required the first day on the job. For example, will some on-the-job training be provided, or will candidates be required to bring all of the KSAs with them on the first day of the job, with no additional levels attained after hire? This rating, which provides direction on which KSAs to screen in a selection process, is a requirement of the *Uniform Guidelines* (Section 14C1).

Step 8: Prepare Final Job Analysis Document, Including Descriptive Statistics for Ratings

After compiling the job expert and supervisor rating data, a report should be compiled that provides descriptive statistics (e.g., means and standard deviations) for each rated item. The final list of job duties and KSAs can be entered directly into the job analysis document, along with the means and standard deviations that accompany each, to compile a final job analysis for a position.

BENEFITS OF CONDUCTING A SOLID JOB ANALYSIS

Job analysis can be an expensive and time-consuming process. Why should employers consider conducting a job analysis to validate a PPT that may not have adverse impact if it is not required of them?

There are two major benefits for the employer when an appropriate job analysis is conducted. First, it helps to ensure that the selection process is measuring key, relevant job requirements in a reliable and consistent manner. This, of course, helps screen better workers into the workforce. Even if the validation process increases the effectiveness of a selection process only slightly, the results over years and hundreds of applicants can sometimes be astounding.

Second, a well-constructed job analysis generates evidence (for use in litigation) that the PPTs are "job related for the position in question and consistent with business necessity" (to address the requirements of CRA 1991, Section 703[k][1][A][i]). Furthermore, Section 9B of the *Uniform Guidelines* (EEOC, 1978) specifies that enforcement agencies will take into account whether a thorough job analysis was conducted when determining whether a PPT is valid for a particular job.

Related to this benefit, a solid job analysis that supports a validated PPT can also dissuade potential plaintiffs from even beginning the lawsuit process if the relationship between the PPT and the job is self-evident (called *face validity*). Applicants are much less likely to challenge a PPT if it looks and feels like the actual job. Likewise, plaintiffs' attorneys will be discouraged from gambling with the time and money necessary to wage a validation war if the employer has conducted good-faith validation studies.

SUMMARY

Job analyses serve many useful purposes, including employment selection, training development, and pay-range development. Formal guidance as to what the results of a job analysis conducted for employee-selection purposes should contain come mostly from the federal *Uniform Guidelines* (EEOC, 1978), the ADA 1990, and court precedence. There is much less hard and fast guidance available for job analyses conducted for other purposes. Users are cautioned to consult with their legal counsel if the actions they take based on the job analysis may have a potentially different impact or outcome for members of different protected subgroups.

The *Uniform Guidelines* (EEOC, 1978) require employers to conduct a job analysis (or provide sufficient job analysis data) in virtually all situations when adverse impact occurs against a certain group of impacted persons. The results of a job analysis provide the foundation for a validation study that can be used as evidence of non-discrimination in the event of a legal challenge. Furthermore, the ADA 1990 specifies that employees be required to perform essential functions of a job with or without reasonable accommodation, so the work behaviors associated with those functions must be appropriately identified. Furthermore, the U.S. Department of Labor has recently enacted a regulation that requires federal contractors to be able to show that basic qualifications that are used when accepting Internet applications are related to the job. Finally, even if there were no regulations or legal requirements surrounding job analysis, it would be in the employer's best interest to conduct a solid analysis of work to identify the key KSAs and their related work behaviors to increase the utility (i.e., payoff) of the PPTs they use. All of these factors should lead employers to strongly consider using job analyses to help insure the validity and fairness of the PPTs they use.

REFERENCES

Age Discrimination in Employment Act of 1967. Public Law 90-202 (1967).

Albemarle Paper Company v. Moody, 422 U.S. 405 (1975).

Americans with Disabilities Act of 1990 (ADA). Public Law 101-336 (1990).

American Educational Research Association, American Psychological Association, & National Council on Measurement in Education. (1999). *Standards for educational and psychological testing.* Washington, DC: American Psychological Association.

Barrett, G. V., & Kernan, M. C. (1987). Performance appraisal and terminations: A review of court decisions since Brito v. Zia with implications for personnel practices. *Personnel Psychology, 40,* 489–503.

Belk v. Southwestern Bell Telephone Co., 194 F.3d 946, 951 (8th Cir. 1999).

Bemis, S. E., Belenky, A. H., & Soder, D. A. (1984). *Job analysis: an effective management tool.* Washington, DC: Bureau of National Affairs.

Biddle, D. A. (2006). *Adverse impact and test validation: a practitioner's guide to valid and defensible employment testing* (2nd ed.). Burlington, VT: Ashgate Publishing Company.

Biddle Consulting Group, Inc. (2008). *Guidelines Oriented Job Analysis (GOJA).* Folsom, CA: Author.

Brown v. City of Chicago, 917 F. Supp. 577 (N.D. Ill. 1996).

Brown v. City of Chicago, 8 F. Supp. 2d 1095 (ND. Ill. 1998).

Buford, J. A. (1985). *Recruiting and selection: concepts and techniques for local government.* Auburn, AL: Alabama Cooperative Extension Service, Auburn University.

Buford, J. A. (1991). *Personnel management and human resources in local government.* Auburn, AL: Center for Governmental Services, Auburn University.

Campbell, T. (1982). Entry-level exam examined in court. *The Western Fire Journal, 34* (7), 28–32.

Civil Rights Act of 1964. (1964). Public Law 88-352, 78 Statute at Large 241.

Civil Rights Act of 1991. (1991). Public Law 102-166.

Clady v. County of Los Angeles, 770 F.2d 1421 (9th Cir. 1985).

Contreras v. City of Los Angeles, 656 F.2d 1267 (9th Cir. 1981).

EEOC v. The Dial Corporation, 3-02-CV-10109 S.D. Iowa (2005).

EEOC v. The Dial Corporation, 469 F.3d 735 (8th Cir. 2006).

Equal Employment Opportunity Commission, Civil Service Commission, Department of Labor, and Department of Justice. (1978). Adoption of Four Agencies of Uniform Guidelines on Employee Selection Procedures. *Federal Register, 43*(38), 290–38,315.

Equal Employment Opportunity Commission, Civil Service Commission, Department of Labor, and Department of Justice. (1979). Adoption of Questions and answers to clarify and provide a common interpretation of the Uniform Guidelines on employee selection procedures. *Federal Register 11*(44), 996–12,009.

Forsberg v. Pacific Northwest Bell Telephone Co., 840 F.2d 1409 (9th Cir. 1988).

Gilbert v. East Bay Municipal Utility District, DC CA, 19 EPD 9061 (1979).

Griggs v. Duke Power Company, 401 U.S. 424 (1971).

Kirkland v. New York State Department of Correctional Services, 520 F.2d 420 (1975).

Martinez v. City of Salinas, DC CA, No. C-78-2608 SW (S.J.) (1978).

Miller, C. S., Kaspin, J. A., & Schuster, M. H. (1990). The impact of performance appraisal methods on Age Discrimination in Employment Act cases. *Personnel Psychology, 43,* 555–578.

Mitchell, K. E., Alliger, G. M., & Morfopoluos, R. (1997). Toward and ADA-appropriate job analysis. *Human Resource Management Review, 7*(1), 5–16.

Office of Federal Contract Compliance Programs (OFCCP) (2005). *Internet applicant final rule* (Issued on October 7, 2005). 41 C.F.R § 60-1.

Parks v. City of Long Beach, DC CA, No. 84-1611 DWW (Px) (1984).

Sanchez v. City of Santa Ana, DC CA, No. CV-79-1818 KN (1979).

Simmons v. City of Kansas City, DC KS, No. 88-2603-0 (1988).

Society for Industrial and Organizational Psychology, Inc. (2003). *Principles for the validation and use of personnel selection procedures* (4th ed.). Bowling Green, OH: Author.

Sturm, R. D. (1979). Mass validation: The key to effectively analyzing an employer's job classifications. *Public Personnel Management, 8*(5), 277–281.

Truxillo, D., Bauer, T., Campion, M., & Paronto, M. (2002). Selection fairness information and applicant reactions: A longitudinal field study. *Journal of Applied Psychology, 87*(6), 1020–1031.

U.S. Department of Labor. (2000). *Testing and assessment: An employer's guide to good practices.* Washington, D.C.: Author.

U.S. Department of Labor. (2005). *Definitions.* 41 CFR 60-1.3. Washington, D.C.: Author.

United States v. City of Torrance, DC CA, No. 93-4142-MRP (RMCx) (1993).

United States v. South Carolina, 434 US 1026 (1978).

Washington v. Davis, 426 U.S. 229 (1976).

21

The Role of Job Analysis in Test Selection and Development

DENNIS DOVERSPIKE

The University of Akron

WINFRED ARTHUR, JR.

Texas A&M University

Industrial/organizational (I/O) psychologists and assessment consultants commonly construct selection test batteries that are used to staff jobs. A selection test battery can consist of a number of selection methods, including paper-and-pencil tests, structured interviews, work samples, simulations, reference checks, and background investigations. Each of these methods can, in turn, be designed to assess a variety of knowledge, skills, abilities, and other characteristics and competencies (Arthur & Villado, 2008). Furthermore, for each construct-method combination, the consultant can choose to (a) use an off-the-shelf, previously developed, standardized instrument, or (b) develop tailored or customized instruments (e.g., locally developed tests either for personnel selection or licensure and certification purposes) based on local information. Regardless of the choice or approach, the starting point for the process will be a job analysis study. That is, in the selection test battery development process, job analysis is the first step. Consequently, in terms of a process model, job analysis is the input, test selection or development is the throughput, and the final selection test battery, ready for administration, is the output.

The objective of this chapter is to discuss the use of job analysis in the development of selection test batteries. In doing so, two related approaches are identified and discussed. The first entails the use of job analysis information as the basis for construct identification and the subsequent choice or selection of a specified test. This approach is germane in situations where the assessment consultant is interested in using an existing (off-the-shelf) instrument. The second approach focuses on the use of job analysis as the foundation for test development, specifically item writing and subsequent test construction. This is pertinent in situations where the consultant is interested in creating and validating a new, locally developed instrument.

Because specific job analysis methods and techniques are reviewed in other chapters in this handbook, our discussion is limited to the unique aspects of job analysis as they pertain to developing a selection test battery from the viewpoint of a practitioner, consultant, or assessment professional. We hope that the information presented here will serve as a guide and blueprint to both the personnel psychology researcher and test developer and as an information and knowledge resource for I/O psychology and human resource management graduate students.

JOB ANALYSIS OVERVIEW

Job analysis is recognized as the first critical step in any personnel-related test development and validation effort, and it allows for an examination of the characteristics that make an optimal person-job match possible (Binning & Barrett, 1989). Legal guidelines and sound professional practice recommend the use of a thorough and up-to-date job analysis. According to Section 14A of the *Uniform Guidelines* (Equal Employment Opportunity Commission [EEOC], 1978), "Any validity study should be based upon a review of information about the job for which the selection procedure is to be used. The review should include a job analysis . . ." (p. 38300). Although the *Uniform Guidelines* and case law do not specify any particular approach to job analysis, most methods rely on some combination of interviews, observation, and questionnaires. In recent years, federal agencies have shown a preference for job analysis methods that involve comprehensive and detailed questionnaires; however, there is no scientific literature that suggests this method leads to more accurate results than other methods.

In the selection context, a product of the job analysis process is a narrative description, which provides information on the following:

- The major work behaviors (MWBs; or duties) and tasks (behavioral components)
- The knowledge, skills, abilities, and other characteristics (KSAOs, where other characteristics include personality dimensions and competencies), which often cluster into psychological constructs such as cognitive ability or job knowledge
- The minimum qualifications (including education and experience)
- Linkages between the MWB, tasks, KSAOs, minimum qualifications, test constructs, methods, items, and weights

JOB ANALYSIS FOR SELECTION OF TEST CONSTRUCTS AND METHODS

A job analysis has often been the critical step in defending the validity of selection devices regardless of the type of test, construct assessed, or validation strategy. Job analysis is a pivotal process in test development because it allows for the identification of the minimum qualifications and specific KSAOs required to perform the job. These KSAOs are then used in later steps to facilitate the development of appropriate examinations. Especially in content-related validation, it is through these steps that linkages are established between test content, KSAOs, and the tasks and MWBs that comprise the job. The sequence of general job analysis steps (along with the test development and test selection process) is schematically illustrated in Figure 21.1.

To develop a selection test battery, the test developer must make a series of decisions based on the results of the job analysis. These decisions include the following:

- What psychological constructs should be measured by the battery?
- What methods should be used to assess the constructs?
- How should each test in the battery be used?

Our intent in this section is not to review all of the possible approaches to and methods for developing a selection battery. Instead, we identify and discuss a series of steps that can be used to arrive at professionally sound and defensible decisions concerning the content and format of a test battery. These steps are summarized in Table 21.1 and illustrated in Figure 21.1. Regardless of the specific approach used to complete each step, the goal is one of developing a

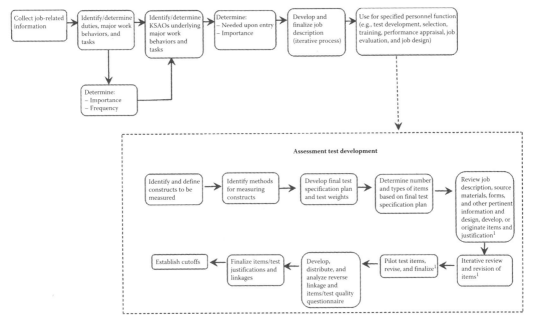

Figure 21.1   Sequence of general job analysis steps.[1] Item writing steps only.

comprehensive description of the job, which can then be used to link behaviors on the job to potential test content.

Review Existing Information

In most cases, there will be existing information about the job in question, although, in some instances, the analysis may be one of a future, currently nonexisting job. The job analyst should begin by reviewing the professional and scientific literature for existing job and competency descriptions. This includes resources such as the *Dictionary of Occupational Titles* (DOT) and the O*NET. After considering widely available materials, the analyst should review previous job descriptions, International Organization for Standardization 9000 materials, and training manuals obtained from the organization.

Table 21.1   Steps for Using Job Analysis to Identify Tests Included in a Selection Battery

1. Review existing information.
2. Create and distribute first draft of the job description to subject matter experts.
3. Conduct first set of job analysis interviews; create and distribute second draft.
4. Create job analysis and task-knowledge, skills, abilities, and other characteristics linkage questionnaire.
5. Distribute and analyze questionnaire; summarize data and create final draft.
6. Identify and define constructs to be measured.
7. Identify methods for measuring constructs.
8. Develop reverse linkage questionnaires.
9. Distribute and analyze reverse linkage questionnaires.
10. Develop final test specification plan.
11. Make decisions regarding cutoffs and weights.

Create and Distribute First Draft of the Job Description to SMEs

Based on the initial review, the analyst can complete an initial draft of the job analysis narrative. We use the term job description here to include a listing of the following:

- Major responsibilities
- Major duties and tasks
- KSAOs
- Minimum qualifications

Once the first draft is created, it can be distributed to subject matter experts (SMEs) for review and comment. At this point, the SMEs will probably be higher level managers or highly experienced supervisors. The draft can be sent out by mail or handed to the SMEs during an in-person interview. In either case, the SMEs should make appropriate comments and return the job description to the analyst.

Conduct First Set of Job Analysis Interviews and Then Create and Distribute the Second Draft

At this point, the analyst is ready to schedule job analysis interviews. The structure of the interviews may fall anywhere on the completely structured to completely unstructured open-ended continuum. We recommend a semistructured interview that introduces some basic level of standardization but also permits some flexibility, which we have found to be essential. Regardless of the degree of structure, the purpose of the interview is to review, develop, and refine duty, task, and KSAO statements, including minimum qualifications.

It is important for the analyst to keep in mind the intended product, which is a functional selection battery. That is, at the end of this process, the analyst should be able to identify the constructs to be measured and the methods for measuring said constructs. If during the early stages of the job analysis interview process sufficient relevant information is not being obtained to allow for an initial identification of the selection test battery components, then the interview format should be modified accordingly. Of course, the interviews should also be coupled with onsite visits and observations. So, after completing the interviews (and onsite visits and observations), a second draft of the job description narrative should be written and distributed to SMEs for a second round of reviews.

Establishing trust and rapport with SMEs can be a challenge because SMEs often erroneously suspect and are concerned that the interviews are a precursor to a reorganization or downsizing, or that the information will be used for some purpose other than that which has been presented to them. However, most SMEs seem to appreciate the idea of being involved in developing tests for use in the selection of future employees. Therefore, it is imperative that the job analyst make all SMEs aware of—and if necessary, try to convince them of—the specific purpose of the job analysis. This can be done through initial conversations in the process of setting up the interviews but also during the first few minutes of the interview.

Create Job Analysis and Task–KSAO Linkage Questionnaire

Once the second draft has been reviewed and feedback obtained from the SMEs, the analyst or consultant can begin the process of drafting a job analysis and task-KSAO linkage questionnaire. Following up the interviews with a questionnaire allows one to canvas a much larger number of incumbents or potential raters than would be the case with the interview alone. The questionnaire design will consist of several parts, as illustrated in Figure 21.2. First, there will be ratings of tasks. This will follow the classic structure of a job analysis questionnaire where ratings of a variety of task characteristics are collected. The most common of these are ratings of importance and time spent (or frequency).

IMPORTANCE How important is this task for successfully performing your job ?	FREQUENCY How often do you perform this task?
Rate each task using the following scale:	Rate each task using the following scale:
0 = Not part of my job	0 = No time spent on this task
1 = Of little importance	1 = A few times per year or less
2 = Of some importance	2 = Once a month
3 = Moderately important	3 = Once a week
4 = Very important	4 = Once a day
5 = Extremely important	5 = More than once a day

MWB Band TASKS	Importance	Frequency
A. Operates production machines	⓪ ① ② ③ ④ ⑤	⓪ ① ② ③ ④ ⑤
A1. Sets up machines	⓪ ① ② ③ ④ ⑤	⓪ ① ② ③ ④ ⑤
A2. Monitors while running	⓪ ① ② ③ ④ ⑤	⓪ ① ② ③ ④ ⑤
B. Handles materials and product	⓪ ① ② ③ ④ ⑤	⓪ ① ② ③ ④ ⑤
B1. Ensures there is sufficient stock	⓪ ① ② ③ ④ ⑤	⓪ ① ② ③ ④ ⑤
B2. Palletizes product	⓪ ① ② ③ ④ ⑤	⓪ ① ② ③ ④ ⑤

Figure 21.2   Sample job analysis questionnaire.

A second component of the questionnaire involves generating ratings of task-KSAO linkages. This may be done in any one of several ways. The SME may be asked to identify KSAOs corresponding to specific tasks or tasks corresponding to specified KSAOs, or a task by KSAO matrix may be created (see Figure 21.3). Regardless of the specific format, the SME is asked to make some type of rating to link a task to a KSAO. Needed-upon-entry ratings are also obtained at this point (see Figure 21.3).

Distribute and Analyze Questionnaire, Summarize Data, and Create Final Draft

Once the questionnaire is created, it can be distributed to SMEs. Depending on the availability of computers and access to online resources, the questionnaire could be disseminated electronically, including web-based administration, or in a paper-and-pencil format.

At this point a number of decisions must be made. One is whether everyone (i.e., all job incumbents) should be surveyed or whether some sampling plan to obtain a subset of eligible responders should be used. Unless the sample sizes are so large as to make it cost prohibitive, we favor distributing the questionnaire to all incumbents. This has the advantage of giving every employee a voice and fostering a sense of participation. In addition, it is a good idea to oversample underrepresented sex and ethnic groups. Such oversampling can also target specific groups of interest such as various work shifts, newer employees, and specific technical areas.

A second issue is whether supervisors should be surveyed along with incumbents. To obtain complete coverage and permit triangulation to assess the degree of inflationary biases, if any, we strongly recommend surveying both groups.

A third and related issue is anonymity. If possible, it is preferable to identify the source of job analysis information. This allows for a matching up of supervisors and incumbents. However, organizational politics or practical realities may require anonymity.

When the questionnaires are returned, they are analyzed using the appropriate statistical techniques. The quantitative data are then used to create a final version of the job description narrative.

NEEDED UPON ENTRY **Is the KSAO needed on the first day on the job?**	**IMPORTANCE** **How important is the KSAO for performing the MWB indicated?**
Rate each KSAO using the following scale:	Rate each KSAO using the following scale:
No = KSAO can be acquired after entry into the job and is NOT needed on the first day on the job. Yes = KSAO is needed at entry (i.e., on the first day on the job).	0 = Not part of my job 1 = Of little importance 2 = Of some importance 3 = Moderately important 4 = Very important 5 = Extremely important

TASKS	Needed upon entry?		Importance
A. Operates production machines			
1. Knowledge of how to use computer to check orders and stock	N	Y	⓪ ① ② ③ ④ ⑤
2. Ability to read instructions and orders	N	Y	⓪ ① ② ③ ④ ⑤
3. Ability to perform simple math	N	Y	⓪ ① ② ③ ④ ⑤
4. Ability to use graphing calculator	N	Y	⓪ ① ② ③ ④ ⑤
5. Skill in using palletizing machine	N	Y	⓪ ① ② ③ ④ ⑤
B. Handles materials and product			
1. Knowledge of how to use computer to check orders and stock	N	Y	⓪ ① ② ③ ④ ⑤
2. Ability to read instructions and orders	N	Y	⓪ ① ② ③ ④ ⑤
3. Ability to perform simple math	N	Y	⓪ ① ② ③ ④ ⑤
4. Ability to use graphing calculator	N	Y	⓪ ① ② ③ ④ ⑤
5. Skill in using palletizing machine	N	Y	⓪ ① ② ③ ④ ⑤

Figure 21.3   Sample questionnaire for collecting knowledge, skills, abilities, and other characteristics-task linkage information.

Any differences between the results from the questionnaire and the draft job description should be reconciled. This may include dropping tasks with ratings that indicate that they may be outside the sphere of the job domain. In terms of cutoffs for dropping tasks, there is no general rule of thumb that can be applied in all situations. The development of decision rules should be based on the exact response scales used to obtain ratings as well as the overall distribution of responses. It is also customary to structure and format the job description such that the major work behaviors are listed in order of descending importance.

Identify and Define Constructs to Be Measured

At this point, the decision-making phase, in terms of translating the job analysis information and results into a selection test battery, begins. The analyst or consultant moves beyond the traditional job analysis by adding additional steps that convert the job analysis information into an operational selection test battery.

The initial identification of constructs will be based on the literature review and the drafts of the job description. Although it is possible to use the generated KSAO statements, the statements themselves are usually too specific and detailed to be of much use from the perspective of an off-the-shelf test or selection methods; however, they are crucial in constructing locally validated instruments.

Therefore, to allow statements to serve both purposes, the KSAOs are usually combined into higher level constructs or competencies. This pooling can be accomplished using either rational sorts and judgments or statistical procedures such as cluster or factor analysis. Our experience has been that more parsimonious and usable results are obtained through rational analyses that rely on subjective, expert judgment. Needless to say, this requires a certain level of expertise, which is usually acquired through experience with multiple job analysis and selection projects.

The development of classification schemes for aptitudes in psychology has been a frustrating enterprise. Nevertheless, certain taxonomies have achieved relatively widespread acceptance, especially in the area of personality (as reflected, for example, in the five-factor model of personality). However, no simple scheme seems to exist for the organization of specific job knowledges, which is one of the most critical areas for selection test development. Thus, the analyst must often again rely on expert judgment based on extended experience with the jobs in question.

The identification of a given construct as falling into the designation of a specific KSAO is also a source of much frustration and confusion. Unfortunately, there is no easy or simple solution. The *Uniform Guidelines* (EEOC, 1978) definitions of the knowledge, skills, and abilities components do not provide much guidance, nor do most selection textbooks. From a practical perspective, it is often difficult to separate a skill from its corresponding ability and knowledge; this would seem to be one of the reasons for the increasing preference to refer to KSAO clusters as "competencies"—a more general term. Nevertheless, Table 21.2 presents examples of some commonly used constructs in personnel selection. We do not present these as a definitive, all encompassing list but instead as illustrative examples.

Table 21.2   Examples of Some Commonly Used Constructs and Methods in Personnel Selection

Constructs		Methods
Knowledge	**Ability**	Multiple-choice, paper-and-pencil tests
Job knowledge	General mental	Constructed-response paper-and-pencil tests
Education/training	Verbal	Computer-administered tests
Experience/work history	Quantitative/numerical	Unproctored Internet-based tests
	Psychomotor	Video tests
	Perceptual	Interviews
Skill	Spatial	Simulations, role plays, work samples, and performance tests
Communication	Mechanical	Assessment centers
Reading	Speed of information	Oral exams
Writing	processing	Individual assessment
Listening	Memory	Situational judgment tests
Speaking	Attention	
Critical thinking	Physical	
Social perceptiveness		
Organizing and planning		**Multiple construct methods**
Time management	**Attitudinal**	Biodata or biographical information blanks
Interpersonal	Values	Person-organization fit
Leadership	Drive/motivation	Background and credit checks
Persuasion/negotiation	Vocational interests	References and letters of recommendation
	Hobbies/other interests	Minimum qualifications
Personality		
Conscientiousness		
Agreeableness		
Emotional stability		
Openness		
Extraversion		
Locus of control		
Integrity		

Identify Methods for Measuring Constructs

Once the KSAOs are clustered into constructs, the next step is to decide on the best methods for measuring the specified constructs. It is worth noting that although the test developer may have limited control over what the final constructs may be—they are determined, after all, by the results of the job analysis—she or he has a lot more leeway in determining the methods of assessment. Consequently, in deciding which method to use to measure a specified construct, issues such as reliability, validity, usability, cost, practicality, and likely subgroup differences should be taken into account.

Methods for measuring constructs can be found in any testing or selection textbook. A short list of some commonly used methods in personnel selection is presented in Table 21.2. Once the methods of measurement have been identified—the test developer may decide to use more than one method—the assessment consultant then has two choices in terms of how to proceed. As previously noted, the first is to use an existing or "off-the-shelf" instrument, and the second entails the development of a locally validated assessment tool. This section of the chapter focuses on the assessment professional using an off-the-shelf approach; in the next section we will discuss locally developed assessments.

In addition to determining the methods, the weights to be assigned to each method are also determined in this step. As discussed in some detail later in the chapter, test weights can be mechanically derived, sometimes using fairly complicated quantitative schemes. However, weights also may be determined via human judgment based on the job analysis process.

Develop Reverse Linkage Questionnaires

To facilitate the presentation of this step, some clarification of terms is necessary. To show that a test represents important KSAOs or task statements, we must identify and confirm the linkages between the test and the job analysis information. This can be done in a forward manner or working backward from the test construct. With a forward-linkage approach, the KSAO (or task statement) leads to the identification of test content, whereas with reverse linkage we work backward from the specific test content to the identification of associated KSAOs (or task statements). Thus, by *reverse linkage* we are referring to a rating of the extent to which a test item, and subsequently the test, captures a specific KSAO or task statement. Although it is difficult to find mention of it in the *Uniform Guidelines* (EEOC, 1978) or in traditional job analysis practice, the ability to provide documentation of the reverse linkage between the test and the KSAO or task strengthens confidence regarding the validity of the inferences that can be made on the basis of the test's scores. So, although the development of reverse linkages should probably be considered as a recommended but not required step, it provides additional documentation and supporting evidence for the efficacy of the judgments made in developing the test. Figure 21.4 presents a sample questionnaire for capturing reverse linkages between tests and tasks. This questionnaire could be revised to provide for linkages between tests and KSAOs as well.

Distribute and Analyze Reverse Linkage Questionnaires

If ratings are needed, the reverse linkage questionnaire (see Figure 21.4) can be distributed to a sample of SMEs. Because this questionnaire may include clues to the test content, important security issues may arise from the distribution of this questionnaire. In several instances, it is not uncommon to require SMEs to sign some sort of nondisclosure agreement. However, we are unaware of any research that speaks to the effectiveness of such agreements. After the questionnaires are returned, the data can be entered into an appropriate database and relevant statistical analyses carried out.

After reviewing a copy of the test listed in the **first column**, please use the rating scale below to rate the extent to which what it is measuring is relevant to the performance of the listed task.

1 = Not at all relevant
2 = A little relevant
3 = Moderately relevant
4 = Very relevant
5 = Extremely relevant

TEST CONSTRUCT	TASKS			
	A. Operates production machines	B. Handles material and product	C. Performs set up and changeovers	D. Participates in quality improvement programs
Computer-administered test of ability to read instructions and orders	① ② ③ ④ ⑤	① ② ③ ④ ⑤	① ② ③ ④ ⑤	① ② ③ ④ ⑤
Work sample test of ability to use computer to check orders and stock	① ② ③ ④ ⑤	① ② ③ ④ ⑤	① ② ③ ④ ⑤	① ② ③ ④ ⑤
Computer-administered test of ability to perform simple math	① ② ③ ④ ⑤	① ② ③ ④ ⑤	① ② ③ ④ ⑤	① ② ③ ④ ⑤

Figure 21.4   Sample questionnaire for reverse linkage of tests to tasks.

Develop Final Test Specification Plan

At this point, using the expert judgment of the test constructor or job analyst, a final test specification plan can be developed from all available or collected information. The final plan serves the purpose of linking the tests to the tasks and/or KSAOs. Again, the level of specificity may vary depending on the consultant's objectives. The linkages, whether forward, reverse, or both, will be especially critical in evaluating the content of the tests. A review of individual test items is likely to occur when working with locally developed tests. This topic is covered in the second half of this chapter.

Make Decisions Regarding Cutoffs and Weights

The final step, and perhaps the most difficult, is to make final decisions regarding the appropriate cutoffs and weights for each test. Cutoffs refer to points on the test or the test battery that define categorization into groups for differential treatment. An example of a decision that might be reached is to fail someone on the test or battery based on their having received a score of less than 70%, which would prevent the individual from acquiring the job. There can be cutoffs on individual tests or corresponding to a total score from a weighted combination of instruments.

Other than the use of cognitive ability tests, no topic generates as much controversy as the setting of cutoffs. The establishment of appropriate cutoffs is likely to add another step or questionnaire to the job analysis. Although it is possible to set cutoffs based on statistical methods, in many cases the appropriate cutoff score is arrived at using a judgmental method (Cizek & Bunch, 2007), the most common being the Angoff method. (See Woehr, Arthur, & Fehrmann [1991] for one review of cutoff score methods.)

Judgmental methods to setting cutoffs require an additional questionnaire, which is usually completed by the SMEs. It may be possible to combine this questionnaire with the reverse linkage questionnaire to save time.

To combine the scores from individual tests into an overall, total, or combined score, rules must be developed for determining the relative weight of the tests in the battery. Weighting is a controversial topic in spite of a great deal of research indicating that unit weights are typically just as effective (if not more so) than other methods for setting (differential) weights (Bobko, Roth, & Buster, 2007). However, if one chooses not to use unit weights, then it is worth noting that the questionnaire approach that we have discussed produces quantitative data that can be used to weight the tests. For example, KSAOs or the associated test constructs can be assigned a weight based on their relative importance compared with all the other test constructs. This procedure is still judgmental in nature and would require a much longer discussion than is possible in this chapter. That being said, Arthur, Doverspike, and Barrett (1996) present a job analysis-based method for developing test weights where ratings derived from the job analysis process are used to arrive at weights for individual tests.

A form for documenting the process of linking constructs to methods is presented in Figure 21.5. First, the weight to be assigned to a test construct is determined, either through human judgment or complicated quantitative formulas that can be applied to the data from the job analysis. Once the construct weights are established, the weight value can be distributed among the various methods or assessment devices that have been identified. For example, as illustrated in Figure 21.5 for the construct of *Motivation*, the test developer has decided to use more than one method to measure Motivation. Motivation has a weight of .20 in the battery. The test developer has decided to assign half of this weight value (.10) to the paper-and-pencil inventory and has assigned less value to the interview (.05) and the work sample (.05). This distribution of weights was based on the judgment of the job analyst, informed by the results of the quantitative data from the job analysis.

Summary

Up to this point, we have discussed the use of job analysis in making decisions concerning the constructs to be measured in a selection test battery. Once the constructs are identified, methods for assessing them must be chosen. Although it is possible to use off-the-shelf tests, another option is to develop a test locally. To do so, the consultant must construct an instrument by writing items and by collecting psychometric data. In the second half of this chapter, we discuss the use of job analysis for item writing purposes.

JOB ANALYSIS FOR TEST ITEM WRITING PURPOSES

This second major section of the chapter presents a series of steps for using the results of a job analysis to design and develop a test tailored to a specific situation or client, building on the job analysis performed using the steps already presented above (see also Table 21.1). We assume that the assessment professional has already completed the steps in the process for the selection of test constructs and methods but has decided to develop the assessment tools instead of simply using existing instruments.

The issues discussed and addressed in this section are also germane for researchers and practitioners in the licensure and certification test development practice. Although most of our examples may be in the context of selection tests, the underlying issues are equally applicable to licensure and certification settings.

Test Constructs	Final Weight	Test Methods					
		Work Sample	Interview	Computer-Administered Knowledge and Ability Test	Situational Judgment Test	Training and Experience	Paper-and-Pencil Personality Inventory
Ability to perform simple math	.50			Y (.50)			
Ability to read instructions and orders	.20	Y(.10)		Y (.10)			
Knowledge of how to use computer to check orders and stock	.10	Y (.05)				Y (.05)	
Motivation	.20	Y (.05)	Y (.05)				Y (.10)

Figure 21.5   Final test battery specification plan.

Our intent in this section is not to review all of the methods that have been proposed for development of a local instrument, but to describe steps that can be used to arrive at professionally sound and defensible decisions concerning the content of a test. These steps are applicable to any test regardless of the construct being measured or the method of assessment. Thus, with appropriate modifications based on the method and construct, the steps would be equally applicable to a paper-and-pencil multiple-choice test of verbal ability, a computerized measure of conscientiousness, or a work sample that encompasses the repair of a car engine. To facilitate presentation and make it less abstract, we use tests for production employees as an example.

The steps that compose the use of job analysis for item writing purposes are summarized in Table 21.3 and illustrated in Figure 21.1. Regardless of the specific approach used to complete each step, the goal is one of developing a test with sound psychometric properties, where the individual items can be linked back to job behaviors and KSAOs. Again, the steps presented in Table 21.3 assume that the consultant has completed the steps outlined in Table 21.1.

Table 21.3   Steps in Using Job Analysis for Item Writing Purposes

1. Review job description, source materials, forms, and other pertinent information.
2. Determine the number and types of items based on final test specification plan.
3. Design, develop, and originate items and justification.
4. Iterative review, revisions, and finalizing prepilot items.
5. Pilot test items.
6. Revise items based on pilot data.
7. Develop, distribute, and analyze reverse linkage and item quality questionnaires.
8. Finalize items, justifications, and linkages.

Steps in this table, beginning with Step 1, assume that the steps described in Table 21.1, Step 1 through at least Step 7, have been completed.

Review Job Description, Source Materials, Forms, and Other Pertinent Information

The first step calls for a review of the materials, including the job analysis, used to identify the constructs underlying the tests that one wishes to develop. For example, for a production worker, we have identified four potential tests. The first one is a reading ability test, the second a shop math test, the third a work sample test of simple computer use, and the fourth a personality-based measure of motivation. Each test is intended to be a locally developed and validated test. But from where will our content come?

One approach is to rely on source materials actually used to learn or perform the job. During the job analysis interview, the incumbents and supervisors can be asked where and how different information underlying the KSAOs was learned or acquired. So, for our example, incumbents and supervisors may have indicated that they learned how to operate the various machines by taking a community college or some other technical school training course before applying for the job. They read and studied manuals that described how to operate different machines. This provided information regarding reading levels, type of content, and the degree of comprehension required. All of this information will be useful for designing a locally developed reading test.

As part of these courses, they also used a factory shop measurement book to learn the types of measuring devices they need to know on the job. This book requires that the reader have a certain level of mathematical sophistication to understand the content and complete the exercises. This information allows us to identify the measurement textbook as an important source for writing test items for our shop math test. Of course, we need to be careful to tap levels of reading and math needed for successful *entry* into the course because we do not want to test for knowledge gained after entry into the job.

Determine the Number and Types of Items Based on Final Test Specification Plan

At this point, the constructs and methods have been identified, along with weights for the associated constructs and methods. The weights for the constructs and methods can be turned into the exact number of items that will appear in the final test. A simple mathematical conversion is often possible. In Figure 21.6, we have an overall weight for the math test of .50; the overall weight was determined, or derived, from the job analysis. In addition, five specific KSAOs have been identified along with the associated weights for each KSAO. The weights can now be used to determine the number of items for each specific KSAO.

For example, consider a situation where we decide to have a 50-item math test to match the 50% weight of the math test in the complete selection battery. We find that our first associated ability element, *working with angles, measuring angles, adding angles*, has an associated weight of .10. This would suggest that 10 items on the final test (out of 50 items) should be on the topic of working with angles. Similarly, 5 items would be written for reading statistical tables, 5 for micrometers and gauges, 20 for adding and subtracting production numbers, and 10 for understanding decimal numbers.

It should be noted that an alternative approach is to simply assign weights to subsections of the test based on the relative weights of the ability elements. Thus, if we only had five items about angles, we could simply double the weight or award two points for correct answers to the section dealing with working with angles.

Design, Development, and Originate Items and Justification

We are now ready to start the item writing process. Fortunately, there is a substantial amount of published information about writing items as well as item writing rules and practices (e.g., see Haladyna, 2004). Item writers should be trained in proper item construction and documentation.

A decision must be made as to the number of items that will be generated given the *final* number of items desired for the test. Although psychometric texts often recommend writing two to five

Ability Elements	Weight	Number of Items to be Written for Pilot Testing	Number of Items on Final Test
Ability to perform simple math	.50	100	50
– Work with angles; measuring, addition	.10	20	10
– Reading statistical tables	.05	10	5
– Using micrometers and gauges	.05	10	5
– Adding and subtracting production numbers	.20	40	20
– Understanding decimal numbers up to five decimal places	.10	20	10

Figure 21.6   Sample form for determining and specifying the number of test items.

times the number of items needed for the final test, this is unrealistic for most practical purposes. For personality tests, the analyst might write twice as many items as needed. For knowledge or ability tests, it may be sufficient to write a smaller set of additional items because the cost of writing items tends to be greater. For example, for a 50-item test, it may be sufficient to write 10 additional items for try-out during the piloting process. In the example provided in Figure 21.5, there will be two items written for piloting for each item required in the final test. However, item writing can be expensive, often requiring an hour or more of professional time per item. In addition, for some KSAOs, even very important ones, it may be difficult if not impossible to write appropriate items or to generate a sufficient number of items. As a result, compromises may have to be made concerning the number of items to be written for pilot testing.

Iterative Review, Revisions, and Finalizing Prepilot Item

Once the items are written, they need to be reviewed and revised. It is often a good idea to develop a formal checklist for this process. Figure 21.7 presents a checklist that can be used for item review purposes. This checklist includes ratings of job-relatedness for each item as well as item quality. In addition, the last column represents an Angoff-type rating that can be used in setting an overall cutoff on the test as discussed previously. The bottom section of Figure 21.7 presents a list of additional metrics or indicators on which items could be rated. However, whereas job-relatedness, item quality, and Angoff ratings could be and are typically obtained from SMEs (e.g., supervisors and expert incumbents), usually after extensive training (Fehrmann, Woehr, & Arthur, 1991; Hurtz & Auerbach, 2003), the ratings of the additional metrics (e.g., meets professional standards, sensitivity, bias) are expected to be obtained from professional experts. Such highly experienced item writers and testing experts are trained in the rules of item construction as well as in the review of tests for cultural sensitivity.

Pilot Test Items

The items can now be piloted. Obviously, test subjects are needed to pilot test the items. The participants in this process can be students, temporary hires, or incumbents, although incumbents introduce serious security issues. The items may be piloted with or without source materials. Items tested with source materials made available to the participants is basically analogous to an open-book exam, and the objective here is primarily to confirm that the test content *can* be located in the source materials.

Regardless of the specific approach taken, test security is a concern in piloting, especially when the test subjects are incumbents. The leakage of information about the items on the test may jeopardize the security of the test. For high-stakes testing, such as public safety positions, the use of incumbents may represent such a significant risk that their use would not be recommended.

After data collection, the next step is to calculate basic item statistics such as item difficulty, item discrimination, number of omits, response count, and response discrimination. The analyses should

ITEM NO.	ITEM	JOB-RELATEDNESS: Is KSAO measured by item **essential** (3), **useful but not essential** (2), or **not necessary** (1) to the performance of the job?	ITEM QUALITY: 0 = unacceptable 1 = acceptable If unacceptable. why? 1 = Biased 4 = Too easy 2 = Ambiguous 5 = Too difficult 3 = Inaccurate REASON		PROBABILITY A MINIMALLY COMPETENT CANDIDATE WILL ANSWER CORRECTLY (0 TO 100)
1	[Addition problem]	① ② ③	⓪ ①	① ② ③ ④ ⑤	
2	[Subtraction problem]	① ② ③	⓪ ①	① ② ③ ④ ⑤	
3	[Multiplication problem]	① ② ③	⓪ ①	① ② ③ ④ ⑤	
4	[Addition problem]	① ② ③	⓪ ①	① ② ③ ④ ⑤	
5	[Division problem]	① ② ③	⓪ ①	① ② ③ ④ ⑤	

ADDITIONAL METRICS ON WHICH ITEMS COULD BE RATED BY A PROFESSIONAL ITEM WRITER OR TESTING EXPERT:
- Is the linkage to the task clear?
- Is the linkage to the KSAO clear?
- Is the keyed answer clearly the best or correct one?
- Is there sufficient justification for the best answer?
- Does the item meet professional item writing standards?
- Could the item be considered biased as a function of sex?
- Could the item be considered biased as a function of race?
- Could the item be considered biased as a function of age?
- Is the reading level appropriate?

Figure 21.7   Sample item rating form.

also include comparisons of various protected class groupings. Carrying out even basic procedures for the analysis of test items does require some level of expertise in statistical analysis and psychometrics. A description of such processes is beyond the scope of this chapter but can be found in most psychometric texts (see Table 21.4). In addition, specialized computer programs are available for item analysis (e.g., Iteman, Assessment Systems Corporation, St. Paul, MN) as well as more general statistical programs such as SAS and SPSS.

Revise Items Based on Pilot Data

Based on the pilot data, the items on the test can be revised. This may include rewriting items (e.g., altering item stems or alternatives to clarify the correct answer or to adjust item difficulty), writing new items, and deleting others.

Develop, Distribute, and Analyze Reverse Linkage and Item Quality Questionnaires

Once the items have been revised and the selection of items completed, a reverse linkage process, such as that illustrated in Figure 21.8, should be undertaken. This process ensures that the

Table 21.4   Selected Job Analysis Test Development Resources

Books	Topic
Brannick, M. T., Levine, E. L., & Morgenson, F. P. (2007). *Job and work analysis* (2nd ed.). Thousand Oaks, CA: Sage.	Job analysis
Cascio, W. F., & Aguinis, H. (2011). *Applied psychology in human resource management* (7th ed.). Upper Saddle River, NJ: Prentice Hall.	General selection and testing
Crocker, L. M., & Algina, J. (1986). *Introduction to classical and modern test theory.* New York: Holt, Rinehart, & Winston.	Testing and psychometrics
Gatewood, R. D., Field, H. S., & Barrick, M. (2010). *Human resource selection* (7th ed.). Mason, OH: South-Western.	General selection and testing
Guion, R. (2011). *Assessment, measurement, and prediction for personnel decisions* (2nd ed.). New York, NY: Routledge.	General selection and testing
Haladyna, T. M. (2004). *Developing and validating multiple-choice test items* (3rd ed.). Mahwah, NJ: LEA.	Testing and psychometrics; item construction
Web sites	
http://www.assess.com/xcart/product.php?productid=500&cat=0&page=1&featured	Angoff method
http://www.hr-guide.com	HR topics, including job analysis
http://harvey.psyc.vt.edu	Job analysis
http://www.job-analysis.net/018.htm	Job analysis
http://www.siop.org/_Principles/principlesdefault.aspx	Selection principles
http://www.assess.com/xcart/product.php?productid=541	Statistical software (Iteman)
http://www.sas.com	Statistical software (SAS)
www.ibmcom/software/analytics/spss	Statistical software (SPSS)
http://www.uniformguidelines.com	Uniform guidelines

relevance of each item can be linked backed to the job through the KSAO it measures, the link between that KSAO and a specified MWB, and the presence of the MWB in job description. In addition, an item-quality questionnaire, similar to that presented in Figure 21.7, can be used to obtain additional critical information about items and, subsequently, the test. Analysis of these data serves as a critical basis for selecting the final pool of items.

Finalize Items, Justifications, and Linkages

At this point, the assessment consultant can make final decisions concerning the items to be included in each test. For each item, the linkages should be identified, including the linkages between tasks and KSAOs (see Figures 21.3, 21.4, and 21.8). The final test can then be constructed and subsequently added to the other locally developed tests to create a battery.

Summary

Building on the steps presented in the first section, in this second section we discuss the use of job analysis to construct a locally developed instrument for inclusion in a selection test battery. Regardless of the format chosen, this involved identifying appropriate content, which can be used

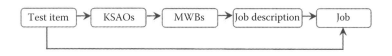

Figure 21.8   Conceptual linkage of test item to the job.

in the development of stimuli, items, and rating scales. Job analysis plays a critical role in that it allows for the documentation of linkages between the content of the test, KSAOs, and tasks.

ALTERNATIVES TO JOB ANALYSIS

The present chapter has focused on job analysis as the foundational basis for identifying test constructs, methods, and specific item content. However, there are both academics and practitioners who would argue that job analysis is not needed in the development of test batteries. Consequently, in the next section we briefly review posited alternatives to job analysis-focused test development.

General Reputation

An organization may simply base its testing decisions on the assessments used by other organizations or suggested by a testing company salesperson. This is a simple but unscientific approach. More critically, it does not meet any guidelines for validation or standards as suggested by the American Educational Research Association, American Psychological Association, and the National Council on Measurement in Education's *Standards for Educational and Psychological Testing* (1999), the Society for Industrial and Organizational Psychology's *Principles for the Validation and Use of Personnel Selection Procedures* (2003), or the EEOC's (1978, 1979, 1980) *Uniform Guidelines*. However, even where it may be appropriate to adopt a test based on some rudimentary consideration of the possibility of transfer or transportability, it should be recognized that job analysis may serve as the basis for determining whether the positions in question belong to the same family or class.

General Attributes

A second alternative approach is to make selection decisions based on general attributes that seem to apply to all jobs. This approach is supported by some academics within the meta-analysis and validity generalization tradition. That is, one could argue that certain tests or specific constructs have been found to be valid for all or almost all jobs (Schmidt & Hunter, 1998). This would include the use of cognitive ability and personality assessments of conscientiousness. But, as discussed below, even in this case, job analysis—either directly or indirectly—plays an important role via its relevance in issues such as job classification and synthetic validity and transportability, which are germane in the use of general attributes.

Dustbowl Empiricism or Purely Empirical Approach

Another approach is the purely empirical. In this type of study, an instrument is administered and performance data are collected. Those tests or constructs having the highest correlations with performance are identified for inclusion in the selection battery. The risks and problems with this approach were identified by Nunnally and Bernstein (1994). Although construct identification and test development can be conducted from such a purely empirical perspective, there has been a trend toward the identification of constructs based on rational approaches, including identification of KSAOs through job analysis as the initial step or foundational basis for even criterion-related approaches.

Worker-Oriented Questionnaires

Instead of the identification of tasks and KSAOs, one could move directly to the ratings of global worker characteristics. This is the central idea behind worker-oriented questionnaire approaches. The best known worker-oriented approaches are associated with the Position Analysis Questionnaire (McCormick & Jeanneret, 1988). The use of the Position Analysis Questionnaire or other worker-oriented approaches would probably still be best seen as a modified job analysis approach or as a supplement to task-based job analysis.

Worker-oriented approaches such as the Position Analysis Questionnaire have also been used in the context of synthetic validity. This approach involves combining validity information across similar jobs or job families, where the similarities are based on common KSAOs or worker characteristics. Synthetic validity is especially useful in situations where there are relatively few incumbents in targeted job families. The *Uniform Guidelines* (EEOC, 1978) also provide provisions for transportability or transfer studies in situations where primary validity studies would otherwise not be possible.

Summary

Although test development approaches have been proposed that bypass or downplay job analysis, we would argue that even these alternative approaches can be strengthened by the collection of traditional job analysis information, specifically data about tasks and KSAOs.

COMMON MISTAKES IN JOB ANALYSIS FOR TEST DEVELOPMENT

The most common mistake—one that is probably encountered regardless of the purpose of the job analysis—is analyzing the person rather than the job. This mistake occurs when the identification of characteristics to be tested is based on the individual in the job rather than the job itself. This is a common outcome or problem associated with an overreliance on information from incumbents. It can also occur when supervisors attempt to oversell the characteristics required for jobs under their supervision. The chances of making this mistake can be minimized by performing a thorough and detailed job analysis.

A second mistake is one that pertains to too little detail being obtained from a job analysis. Test development cannot be based upon a one-page job description. Nor can it be based on task information or KSAO information alone. To adequately document test development efforts, it is necessary to collect and document detailed information on tasks *and* KSAOs. This is true because both are necessary for a complete understanding of the job; in addition, it could be argued that both sources of information are necessary for purposes of meeting specified legal requirements and professional standards.

An issue that arises in the use of job analysis for test purposes is security. We have already addressed this issue, but we repeat it here because a failure to maintain the security of information related to testing has been a major factor in undermining the best-intentioned selection processes. This is especially true in public sector testing. Consistent messages must be sent concerning the purpose of job analysis and testing. Appropriate procedures must be put into place to protect the confidentiality of individual information, test content, and test procedures because when incumbents and SMEs are used to provide information on jobs, review tests, or pilot test items, security concerns arise. Although some public jurisdictions and municipalities use nondisclosure agreements in an effort to address these concerns, it is unclear as to whether such agreements are effective.

OTHER RESOURCES

This volume contains several other resources about job analysis, most of which would be useful in the context of conducting a job analysis specifically for testing purposes. In addition to these sources, a list of some books and web resources that would be helpful in the context of using job analysis to develop a selection battery is presented in Table 21.4.

CONCLUSION

This chapter discusses the use of job analysis in the development of a selection test battery. Legal guidelines and sound professional practice recommend the use of a thorough and up-to-date job analysis, but to meet the demands of selection battery development, the associated job analysis must be designed to generate detailed information relevant to the linkage of tasks and KSAOs to constructs and test content. The use of job analysis is discussed in two situations: (a) use of off-the-shelf, previously developed, standardized instruments, and (b) locally developed tests.

As mentioned earlier, although there is no research or case law to support the use of questionnaire approaches over other approaches, and although there is research that would argue that humans lack the information processing abilities for many of the required tasks (e.g., making fine distinctions regarding the importance or criticality of KSAOs or detailed task statements), federal agencies nonetheless now seem to prefer questionnaire-based job analysis because of the availability of data and documentation. Thus, in our discussion, we have relied heavily on the use of questionnaire methods, although we still recognize the validity and acceptability of alternative methods such as interviews and observation. Indeed, we not only frequently use these latter methods in our own work, but we have been and continue to be successful in defending their use when our assessment tools have been legally challenged.

As with many other areas of job analysis, it is critical that the analyst keep the final product in mind. In this case, of course, the final product will be a practical selection battery. An efficient job analyst can obtain a great deal of relevant information in relatively little time; on the other hand, an inexperienced analyst, or one who ignores the product goal, can waste a great deal of time and resources without obtaining the detail needed to construct and defend the test battery. As with any professional field, the difference is often one of experience with both testing and jobs. This supports the importance of supervised internships for test assessment professionals, which involve experience with job analysis techniques and test development and construction.

REFERENCES

American Educational Research Association, American Psychological Association, & National Council on Measurement in Education. (1999). *The standards for educational and psychological testing.* Washington, DC: American Educational Research Association.

Arthur, W. Jr., Doverspike, D., & Barrett, G. V. (1996). Development of a job analysis-based procedure for weighting and combining content-related tests into a single test battery score. *Personnel Psychology, 49,* 971–985.

Arthur, W. Jr., & Villado, A. J. (2008). The importance of distinguishing between constructs and methods when comparing predictors in personnel selection research and practice. *Journal of Applied Psychology, 93,* 435–442.

Binning, J. F., & Barrett, G. V. (1989). Validity of personnel decisions: A conceptual analysis of the inferential and evidential bases. *Journal of Applied Psychology, 74,* 478–494.

Bobko, P., Roth, P. L., & Buster, M. A. (2007). The usefulness of unit weights in creating composite scores: A literature review, application of content validity, and meta-analysis. *Organizational Research Methods, 10,* 689–709.

Cizek, G. J., & Bunch, M. B. (2007). *Standard setting: A guide to establishing and evaluating performance standards on tests.* Thousand Oaks, CA: Sage.

Equal Employment Opportunity Commission, Civil Service Commission, Department of Labor, & Department of Justice. (1978). Uniform guidelines on employee selection procedures. *Federal Register, 43,* 38290–38309.

Equal Employment Opportunity Commission, Office of Personnel Management, Department of Justice, Department of Labor, & Department of the Treasury. (1979). Adoption of questions and answers to clarify and provide a common interpretation of the Uniform Guidelines on Employee Selection Procedure. *Federal Register, 44,* 11996–12009.

Equal Employment Opportunity Commission, Office of Personnel Management, Department of Justice, Department of Labor, & Department of the Treasury. (1980). Adoption of additional questions and answers to clarify and provide a common interpretation of the Uniform Guidelines on Employee Selection Procedure. *Federal Register, 45,* 29529–29531.

Fehrmann, M. L., Woehr, D. J., & Arthur, W. Jr. (1991). The Angoff cutoff score method: The impact of frame-of-reference training. *Educational and Psychological Measurement, 51,* 857–872.

Haladyna, T. M. (2004). *Developing and validating multiple-choice test items* (3rd ed.). Mahwah, NJ: Lawrence Erlbaum Associates.

Hurtz, G. M., & Auerbach, M. A. (2003). A meta-analysis of the effects of modifications to the Angoff Method on cutoff scores and judgment consensus. *Educational and Psychological Measurement, 63,* 584–601.

McCormick, E. J., & Jeanneret, P. R. (1988). Position Analysis Questionnaire (PAQ). In S. Gael (Ed.), *The job analysis handbook for business, industry, and government* (Vol. 2, pp. 825–842). New York, NY: Wiley.

Nunnally, J. C., & Bernstein, I. H. (1994) *Psychometric theory* (3rd ed.). New York, NY: McGraw-Hill.

Schmidt, F. L., & Hunter, J. E. (1998). The validity and utility of selection methods in personnel psychology: Practical and theoretical implications of 85 years of research findings. *Psychological Bulletin, 124,* 262–274.

Society for Industrial and Organizational Psychology (2003). *Principles for the validation and use of personnel selection procedures* (4th ed.). College Park, MD: Author.

Woehr, D. J., Arthur, W., Jr., & Fehrmann, M. (1991). An empirical comparison of cutoff score methods for content-related and criterion-related validity settings. *Educational and Psychological Measurement, 51,* 1029–1039.

22

Work Simulations

Deborah L. Whetzel
Human Resources Research Organization

Michael A. McDaniel
Virginia Commonwealth University

Jeffrey M. Pollack
University of Richmond

Imagine that you are applying for a job as an administrative assistant. The employer might interview you or administer tests of job knowledge or personality. The employer might also have you participate in a simulated work day. You are escorted to a desk with a phone and a computer and are told the simulation has begun. Soon, holographic images of your supervisor and coworkers appear, much like a science-fiction movie, and you begin your simulated day interacting with your computer-generated colleagues. The simulation is being scored to determine how well you handle the job requirements. Good luck; your evaluation has started.

Increasingly, employers are turning to work simulations for both selection and training purposes. Although advanced technology is not needed to create and administer simulations for most jobs, technological advances are making sophisticated work simulations more common and economical to develop. Multiple options already exist to select and train employees using advanced technologies (ICT Results, 2008). Employers currently use various in-house options or commercial vendors that offer such services (Employment Technologies Corporation, 2008; Furst Person, 2004; Houran, 2007).[1]

In this chapter, we discuss (a) what work simulations are, (b) the role of work analysis in work simulations, (c) their advantages and limitations, (d) their psychometric properties (e.g., validity, reliability, and subgroup differences), (e) how to create simulations (e.g., development and scoring methods), and (f) future potential developments. Included in our discussion are common concerns, references to useful resources, and integrative examples indicative of main principles.

WHAT ARE WORK SIMULATIONS?

Work simulations are methods of evaluating examinees' performance on tasks that are psychologically or physically similar to what they would do on the job (Callinan & Robertson, 2000; Ployhart, Schneider, & Schmitt, 2006). Depending on one's perspective, this definition applies to a wide

---

[1] The authors have no relationship with these vendors and neither lobby for nor against using the companies and/or products listed. The authors only use the companies and products as examples.

range of procedures including assessment centers, work sample tests, performance tests, competency tests, and situational judgment tests (McDaniel, Hartman, Whetzel, & Grubb, 2007; Truxillo, Donahue, & Kuang, 2004), and it is consistent with definitions used in the literature (Bobko, Roth, & Buster, 2005; Felker, Curtin, & Rose, 2007; Roth, Bobko, & McFarland, 2005; Truxillo et al., 2004).

Work simulations can be categorized by various characteristics, as described by Callinan and Robertson (2000). Fidelity refers to the extent to which the simulation is similar to the job. Some authors have distinguished between psychological fidelity and physical fidelity (Binning & Barrett, 1989; Goldstein, Zedeck, & Schneider, 1993). Psychological fidelity exists to the extent that the test samples the job-related knowledge, skills, and abilities required for essential job duties. Physical fidelity is the extent to which the test simulates the actual job tasks. Callinan and Robertson argued that work simulations can be classified according to the extent that they involve hands-on performance and are performed in a real-world setting. Palmer, Boyles, Veres, and Hill (1992) described work simulations for clerical jobs that involved proofreading and filing. These work simulations were clearly hands-on and the tasks performed were very close to a real-world setting and thus could be considered to have high fidelity. At the other extreme, situational judgment tests (Weekley & Ployhart, 2006) present job-related problem scenarios and ask respondents about various actions that might be taken in response to the scenario. Motowidlo, Dunnette, and Carter (1990) called these tests *low-fidelity simulations*. These work simulations do not require hands-on performance and, rather than experience a real-world problem, examinees read a paragraph or view a video about a hypothetical scenario. A common assessment center simulation, the *in-basket*, falls in the mid-range of fidelity. In an in-basket simulation, the respondent is told to assume a manager's role in an organization and is asked to respond to e-mails, requests, and problem situations (e.g., personnel issues). Although the job might require an incumbent to process material in an in-basket, the material to be processed is unlikely to be identical to the information found on the job, and the time limits and other constraints of the in-basket simulations reduce the fidelity of the simulation.

Bandwidth concerns the breadth of the work simulation. The Palmer et al. (1992) proofreading and filing work simulations covered important aspects of the job but did not cover all of the job. Clerical employees engage in various forms of communication (e.g., face to face and e-mail) and maintain interpersonal relationships. Felker et al. (2007) noted that, ideally, all job tasks under all important working conditions would be incorporated into a simulation, but there are several factors that prevent this. First, there are feasibility issues. Simulating all tasks in a job would usually result in a simulation that is too long and too expensive to build and administer. Also, a work simulation should not include tasks that might result in damage to expensive equipment or that might result in injury. Second, job tasks vary widely in their duration, frequency, difficulty, and importance. Although clerical employees may sharpen pencils, it is probably not a task that one would want to include in a work simulation because of its trivial nature. Later in the chapter, we discuss approaches to selecting the content of a work simulation.

Work simulations can be distinguished by whether they assess work *processes* or work *products* (Felker et al., 2007). When a work product is important but is not how one arrives at the end result, the work simulation and its scoring should focus on the output of the task. For example, a simulation for a clerical employee might be preparing a statistical table. The preparation of such a table can be approached in different ways. The work process is less important than producing an accurate and presentable table. On the other hand, the focus of the work simulation may be on the process when the performance of particular steps is important. For example, a clerical employee who needs to respond to an angry customer needs to communicate politely, correctly receive and convey information, and diffuse the customer's anger. In such a simulation, the process by which the employee handles the interaction is important. As another example, consider a work simulation test for a plumber fixing a clogged sink drain. There are multiple ways to score such a simulation, two of which are a checklist and an outcome-based measure. When a plumber unclogs a drain, there are multiple steps to accomplish the task. If an evaluator had a checklist and watched the applicant go through these steps, the evaluator could check off the items as a way to score the process. Alternatively, imagine the same situation, but instead of completing a checklist, the evaluator leaves and comes back in fifteen minutes and simply checks to see if the drain is unclogged—a simple outcome-based scoring method where the end result is either achieved or not.

Testing format is another way in which work samples may vary. Often, process steps may be scored "go/no go" (i.e., either the person performed the step or not). On the other hand, situational judgment tests are often scored by determining how many optimal responses examinees selected when they were provided a set of response options and they could indicate the most and/or least likely action they would take in a given situation. Simulations with higher fidelity (e.g., those assessing aircraft maneuvers) involve machine scoring so that variables such as reaction time can be assessed. Assessment centers often require raters to judge performance using behaviorally based rating scales.

This chapter will focus on work simulations and the use of work analysis in developing such measures. Work simulations are useful for personnel selection, criterion development in employment test validation studies, job training, licensure examinations, training certifications, and in various education applications (Ferrari, Taylor, & VanLehn, 1999).

THE ROLE OF WORK ANALYSIS IN WORK SIMULATIONS

Work analysis provides the foundation for developing work simulations. To develop a realistic work simulation, one must understand the nature of the work being simulated via a work analysis. This section describes issues in the conduct of work analysis that may be considered when developing work simulations. Later in this chapter, we describe methods for using work analysis information to create work simulations.

The first issue to consider is the level of specificity of the work analysis. There is a continuum of specificity ranging from the description of high-level job attributes to the description of minute details of a job. At one end of the continuum, competency modeling involves the use of broad descriptors of human attributes (e.g., problem solving) that make "an effort to understand the organization's mission, values, strategy, and broad goals" (Sanchez & Levine, 2001, p. 84). This level of analysis may be too general for the purpose of creating work simulations. On the other hand, the study of individual movements, characteristic of time and motion studies (Taylor, 1911), may be too specific. Between these two extremes, using traditional job analysis, one identifies duties, tasks, and the knowledge, skills, abilities and other characteristics (KSAOs) needed to perform the tasks. This is probably most useful for work simulations because the tasks often form the basis for the simulation to be created. Using the linkages between tasks and KSAOs, one can identify specific KSAOs measured by the work simulation.

A related issue to consider is the source of work analysis data. Peterson and Jeanneret (2007) made a distinction between inductive and deductive job analysis. Deductive methods are those "that emphasize the use of existing knowledge or taxonomies of job information during analysis of the focal job" (Peterson & Jeanneret, 2007, p. 13). Examples include the Position Analysis Questionnaire and the Occupational Information Network (O*NET). Inductive methods, on the other hand, involve collecting new, detailed information, usually from subject matter experts (SMEs). Inductive approaches are typically most useful as input for work simulations because the level of detail provided by SMEs is useful for creating simulation exercises.

Once a work analysis has been conducted, one must consider the purpose and context in which work simulations are developed. The purpose for creating a work simulation will inform many decisions made during its development. The advantages and disadvantages of work simulation are described below.

Advantages and Limitations of Work Simulations

Work simulations are used increasingly because of their many advantages compared with traditional methods of gauging future job performance quality (Ames & Bailey, 2005; Felker et al., 2007). These advantages include practicality, useful levels of criterion-related validity, perceptions of less adverse impact than other selection procedures, and positive applicant reactions (Callinan & Robertson, 2000; Schmidt & Hunter, 1998; Truxillo et al., 2004). Some employers turn to work samples because they perceive that the tests are less likely to be challenged as part of legal discrimination cases.

However, work simulations have several disadvantages (Callinan & Robertson, 2000; Felker et al., 2007; Truxillo et al., 2004). Work simulations can be expensive to build and maintain. The development process typically involves substantial input from individuals who are knowledgeable about the job. Also, test development expertise is required to assess the job content to be simulated and to determine how performance will be scored reliably. Some work simulations may require expensive equipment to be built or adapted. Because work samples are targeted to a job, an employer with many types of jobs may need many work simulations. Also, as jobs change, the work simulation may become outdated and require revision. Work simulations can be costly to administer. Often, they need to be administered individually or with a small number of applicants, and test administrators need to be trained. Finally, some work simulations require that respondents have substantial knowledge of the job. Such work simulations may not be appropriate for entry-level selection if the respondents are to receive extensive training after being hired. For example, because new police cadets are taught how to fire a gun after they are hired (during academy training), a work simulation used to screen police officer applicants may not involve firing weapons.

PSYCHOMETRIC CHARACTERISTICS OF WORK SIMULATIONS

In the field of industrial/organizational psychology, there is some controversy over the use of simulations for selection. For selection, several low-fidelity simulations (e.g., situational judgment tests and situational interviews) measure several different constructs simultaneously, and it is difficult to assess internal consistency, reliability, and construct validity. Therefore, these kinds of measures are considered methods of measurement rather than measures of a single construct. Below, we discuss the reliability of high-fidelity work samples.

Reliability

Work simulations in military settings have reported very high interrater agreement (Felker et al., 2007; Knapp & Campbell, 1993). For example, Carey (1990) and Felker et al. (1988) reported agreements exceeding 90% between test scorers and "shadow" scorers for a variety of Marine Corps job sample tests. Further, Hedge, Lipscomb, and Teachout (1988) reported agreements across pairs, ranging from approximately 75% to 90% across teams of test administrators for three Air Force occupations. Felker et al. (2007) noted that a plausible explanation for these high reliabilities is the care with which the work sample tests were developed. During the Joint Performance Measurement project, the military services devoted substantial effort and resources to the design and administration of work samples (Campbell et al., 1990; Green & Wigdor, 1991). As such, these simulations were subject to extensive pilot testing and were revised as needed to achieve high reliability.

One might assume that work samples developed as either predictors or as criterion instruments in the published literature reflect the high end of care taken to develop such measures. Often, work simulations in applied settings may be developed with far fewer resources and may yield much lower reliability. Work simulations can be expected to have lower reliability when the measures are developed quickly and are not pilot tested; when the scoring requires subjectivity, lacks standardization in administration, and has too few scorable tasks; and when scorers are untrained.

Validity

Much research suggests that work simulations are highly valid predictors of job performance (Hunter & Hunter, 1984; Reilly & Warech, 1993; Schmitt, Gooding, Noe, & Kirsch, 1984). For example, Hunter and Hunter (1984) obtained a mean corrected validity coefficient of .54 across studies assessing the validity of work simulations, and Schmitt et al. (1984) found an observed validity of .32 (albeit on a fairly small sample).

More recently, Roth et al. (2005) provided a comprehensive summary of the criterion-related validity of work simulations. They found that previous meta-analyses were flawed in their lack of data or there were methodological problems (e.g., range enhancement of validities by including only those who scored at the top and bottom thirds of the distribution). Their results show that work simulations had a mean observed validity of .26 ($k = 54$, $n = 10,469$), which increased to .33 when measures of job performance (supervisor ratings) were corrected for attenuation. As previously mentioned, it is important to remember that the general category of work simulations encompasses the measurement of multiple constructs (as opposed to measures that assess a single construct, such as general mental ability). The validity of a work sample will likely vary with the constructs assessed.

There are several constructs that potentially moderate the validity of work samples, such as the status of the participant (applicant vs. incumbent), measure of job performance (subjective vs. objective), criterion versus predictor conceptualization, type of sample (military vs. nonmilitary), and job complexity (Roth et al., 2005). Their results were inconclusive regarding sample differences (applicant vs. incumbent) because of insufficient data for applicants ($k = 1$, $n = 24$). The use of objective versus subjective measures did not have a strong influence on sample validity (.27 vs. .26, respectively). Whether the work simulation was used as a predictor or as a criterion also was not a meaningful moderator, as the correlations were .29 and .25, respectively. The use of military versus nonmilitary samples did not seem to moderate the validity (.25 vs. .28, respectively), nor did job complexity (correlations ranged from .25 to .28 for each of three levels of job complexity). Roth et al.'s (2005) results suggest that work sample measures may not be as valid as previously believed and that meaningful moderators have yet to be discovered.

The criterion-related validity of low-fidelity work simulations, in the form of situational judgment tests, has been evaluated in many primary studies (Chan & Schmitt, 1997; Hanson & Borman, 1989; Motowidlo et al., 1990; Smith & McDaniel, 1998). Two meta-analyses have examined the criterion-related validity of situational judgment tests (McDaniel, Morgeson, Finnegan, Campion, & Braverman, 2001; McDaniel et al., 2007). In the second and more recent meta-analysis, the overall validity of situational judgment tests across 118 coefficients was .26 ($n = 24,756$), regardless of instruction type. These validity results are almost entirely based on concurrent validity studies (e.g., research typically conducted using job incumbents, rather than applicants, as subjects). Their results showed that response instructions influenced the constructs measured by the tests, such that tests with knowledge instructions had higher correlations with cognitive ability and tests with behavioral tendency instructions showed higher correlations with personality constructs. Results also showed that response instructions had little moderating effect on criterion-related validity.

Regarding the validity of assessment centers, there is substantial agreement that these measures can yield scores that predict job performance (Dean, Roth, & Bobko, 2008), and meta-analyses have provided corrected validities of .28 (Hardison & Sackett, 2004) to .36 (Gaugler, Rosenthal,

Thornton, & Bentson, 1987). In fact, some researchers have stated that the "predictive validity of assessment centers is now largely assumed" (Borman, Hanson, & Hedge, 1997, p. 313).

In the educational arena, research and thought have been devoted to considerations of aspects of validity that guide the development of work simulations. Miller and Linn (2000) outline six aspects of construct validity of performance-based assessments. These include content, substantive, structural, generalizability, external, and consequential. The content aspect of validity focuses on the relevance and representativeness of the assessment's content. The substantive aspect focuses on processes used by examinees when they respond and on the similarity of the processes with the construct the assessment is designed to measure. The structural aspect addresses the adequacy and appropriateness of scoring and scaling. The generalizability aspect focuses on replicability of results across various levels and facets of the assessment procedure (e.g., across raters and tasks). The external aspect concerns convergent and discriminant evidence showing a relationship (or non-relationship) between the assessment and other performance measures. The consequential aspect focuses on the degree to which assessments have the intended positive effects and plausible unintended negative effects. These aspects of validity are important to consider during the development of work simulations.

Subgroup Differences

Much of the literature surrounding subgroup differences and work simulations suggest that these tests are associated with lower levels of adverse impact than traditional measures of cognitive ability (Cascio, 2003; Gatewood & Field, 2001; Reilly & Warech, 1993; Salgado, Viswesvaran, & Ones, 2001; Schmitt, Clause, & Pulakos, 1996). Bobko et al. (2005) point out that much of that literature has used incumbent samples rather than applicant samples and, as a result, the estimates are subject to range restriction from prior selection. Thus, these estimates would likely underestimate the magnitude of subgroup differences.

Concerning subgroup differences on assessment centers, Dean et al. (2008) conducted a meta-analysis and found a mean d for Black–White differences of .52 ($k = 17$, $n = 8,210$). When examinee type (applicant vs. incumbent) was examined, d values were .56 for applicants ($k = 10$, $n = 3,682$) and .32 ($k = 6$, $n = 1,689$) for incumbents. In addition, they found an overall male-female mean d of -0.19, showing that women, on average, obtained slightly higher scores than men.

Bobko et al. (2005) conducted a primary study in which they analyzed two data sets from public sector jobs and showed that the adverse impact of work sample tests may be more extensive than previously thought. Two different assessment centers were used, one for each job. The first assessment center included a technical exercise, an in basket, a counseling exercise, and a set of oral responses to incidents (interruptions to other work). The exercises were scored for content (what was said or written) and for process (oral or written communication skills). The Black–White d values ranged from -0.06 for the content of the counseling exercise to 0.80 for the technical score (the d on the overall score was 0.73). Positive values indicate White subjects, on average, scored higher than Black subjects. Bobko et al. noted that the process dimensions were associated with smaller Black–White d values than other components. The second assessment center included three exercises: a map reading test, a technical exercise, and a role-play exercise. The Black–White d values ranged from 0.12 for the human relations ability score on the role play to 0.80 for the map-reading score (the d on the overall score was 0.73). The three dimensions measured by the role-play exercise were associated with the smallest Black–White differences. Note that, in both cases, the numbers of Blacks tested were small ($n = 31$ and 33, respectively), but the results were consistent. The authors note that the values of d for both work sample exams are close to the value of d (0.72) associated with the Wonderlic test of general mental ability when selecting applicants for medium complexity jobs (Roth, Bevier, Bobko, Switzer, & Tyler 2001). For both data sets, to the extent that the exercises were *g*-loaded (e.g., technical exercise and map reading), the *d* values are higher than exercises loaded with more personality-related constructs.

Regarding subgroups differences on situational judgment tests, Whetzel, McDaniel, and Nguyen (2008) conducted a meta-analysis of mean race and sex differences in situational judgment test performance. On average, White subjects performed better on situational judgment tests than Black, Hispanic, and Asian subjects ($d = 0.38$, $k = 62$, $n = 42,178$; $d = 0.24$, $k = 43$, $n = 14,195$; $d = 0.29$, $k = 25$, $n = 16,515$, respectively). Women performed slightly better than men ($d = -0.11$, $k = 63$, $n = 37,829$). They investigated two moderators of these differences: (a) loading of *g* or personality, and (b) response instructions. Mean race differences between Black, Hispanic, Asian, and White examinees in situational judgment test performance were largely explained by the cognitive loading of the situational judgment test such that the larger the cognitive load, the larger the mean racial differences. The effect of personality loading on race differences (Black–White and Asian–White) were smaller to the extent that situational judgment tests are correlated with emotional stability. Hispanic–White differences were smaller to the extent that situational judgment tests were correlated with conscientiousness and agreeableness. Cognitive loading had minimal effect on male-female score differences; however, score differences were larger, favoring women, when situational judgment tests were correlated with conscientiousness and agreeableness. Knowledge response instructions showed greater race differences than behavioral tendency instructions. The mean correlations show that these differences are largely due to the greater *g*-loading of knowledge instructions.

In summary, work simulation measures, whether assessment center exercises or situational judgment tests, exhibit nontrivial performance differences based on race, such that, on average, White subjects perform better than Black subjects on these measures. For both assessment centers and situational judgment tests, this is more likely if the tests are *g* loaded rather than personality (noncognitively) loaded. In both assessment centers and situational judgment tests, women, on average, performed slightly better than men, perhaps because of the interpersonal nature of both kinds of assessments.

As a result of these findings, one might consider developing video-based situational judgment tests to reduce the *g*-loading of such assessments. For assessment centers, rather than have people write their answers to exercises (e.g., the in-basket), they might describe their answers verbally to scorers. Assessment centers also might focus more on role playing rather than exercises that require a high degree of analytical thinking. However, given the useful validities of *g*-loaded measures, one may achieve lower group differences at the cost of reduced validity (Ployhart & Holtz, 2008).

HOW TO CREATE WORK SIMULATION MEASURES

Although it is possible to purchase work simulations off the shelf, for most purposes it is more common to develop them for a specific job or organization because there often are job knowledge requirements embedded in the simulation. In this section, we describe methods for developing these tests. Because performance tests come in a variety of types and formats (e.g., assessment centers, situational judgment tests, hands-on performance tests), we provide a generic approach based on what these measure have in common. Although the approach described is generic, we use examples that focus on one or another specific kind of test. When needed, we discuss the development of high- and low-fidelity simulations separately. For readers interested in additional guidance, we recommend Gatewood and Field (2001), Guion (1998), and Felker et al. (2007). This part of the chapter will follow an outline similar to that used by Felker et al. (2007) and Truxillo et al. (2004).

How to Select Test Content

When constructing a work simulation measure, the first decision concerns the part(s) of the job domain to be tested. Ideally, all tasks would be tested under all important working conditions;

however, for safety and other practical reasons, this is usually not feasible. Similar to the development of other types of tests, the challenge is to select a small number of tasks that represent the larger pool of job tasks so that test performance can be generalized to the job. This is typically conducted in two steps: (a) specify the total performance domain for the job, and (b) devise a valid and defensible sampling strategy for selecting tasks from that domain.

The job performance domain can be described in a number of ways, either through a complete job analysis describing tasks and KSAOs that compose a job, a critical incident approach in which SMEs describe examples of performance at various levels of proficiency, or a competency-based approach in which SMEs describe, in broad strokes, what attributes are needed to perform a job. Competency-based approaches often do not provide sufficient detail for creating work simulations, and they will not be described further here. For more description of competency-based approaches, see Shippman et al. (2000) and Ulrich, Brockbank, Yueng, and Lake (1995).

The use of a particular job analysis method depends on the type of simulation to be developed. Job and task analyses are frequently used to develop higher-fidelity simulations (e.g., hands-on measures of performance and assessment centers), whereas critical incidents are often used to develop lower-fidelity simulations (e.g., situational judgment tests) because task information provides detailed data useful for developing assessment center exercises; critical incidents provide big picture situations that are useful for creating scenarios for situational judgment tests. Strategies for sampling from the domain vary based on whether high- or low-fidelity simulations are developed, and they are described separately below.

High-Fidelity Performance Tests

In addition to a complete list of tasks, when higher-fidelity tests are being constructed the results of a job and task analysis should focus on contextual or environmental conditions of task performance, chronological dependences of task performance (which tasks require performance before other tasks), and interaction requirements (when the performance of tasks requires interaction with others).

Felker et al. (2007) described two methods of task selection commonly used by the U.S. military: (a) the four- and eight-factor models and (b) the Difficulty, Importance, and Frequency model. In the first method, test developers rate each task in the domain on up to eight of the following descriptors:

1. Percentage of the workforce performing the task
2. Task delay tolerance (degree of flexibility before task must be performed)
3. Consequences of inadequate task performance
4. Task learning difficulty
5. Percentage of time spent performing task
6. Probability of deficient task performance
7. Immediacy of task performance (urgency)
8. Frequency of task performance

The first four of these descriptors comprise the four-factor model and the entire set make up the eight-factor model. Job analysts/SMEs rate each task in the domain on each of the four or eight descriptors, and cutoffs are set for defining the relevance of each factor. Examples of cutoffs are the percentage of the workforce performing the task (cutoff is 40% or more) and consequences of inadequate performance (1 = minor, 7 = major; cutoff is 5). Tasks that meet or exceed a selected set of cutoffs are selected for testing.

The Difficulty, Importance, and Frequency model also requires that SMEs provide task ratings. Using this method, job analysts/SMEs rate each task on the following:

1. *Difficulty*: Learning difficulty, probability of deficient performance, or both
2. *Importance*: Consequence of inadequate performance, task delay tolerance, and time spent performing the task
3. *Frequency*: How often the task is performed and the percentage of people performing the task

As with the four- and eight-factor models, SMEs provide ratings on each of the Difficulty, Importance, and Frequency dimensions, and decisions are made about whether the tasks should be included for testing.

Gatewood and Field (2001) described other important criteria to be used in selecting tasks for testing, including the following:

1. Tasks in which the total time required for completion is reasonable
2. Tasks that are representative of the job in terms of difficulty or complexity, as tasks that are too easy or too difficult will not help to distinguish among examinees in terms of proficiency
3. Tasks that require less expensive materials, equipment, or facilities
4. Tasks that have standardized operations or products or have easily defined verbal or inter-action components, as it is easier to develop and score situations based on such tasks

Once tasks are generated, most job analysis processes involve the specification of KSAOs for performing those tasks. As indicated by Harvey, Anderson, Baranowski, and Morath (2007), knowledge refers to specific types of information that people must know to perform a job (Williams & Crafts, 1997); skills can be thought of as the capabilities needed to perform a task, which can be developed over time and with exposure to multiple situations; and abilities are an individual's relatively enduring capabilities for performing a particular range of different tasks (Fleishman, Costanza, & Marshall-Mies, 1997). Other characteristics include occupational values and interests and work styles (Peterson, Mumford, Borman, Jeanneret, & Fleishman, 1997); personal preferences and interests (Holland, 1973); and individual difference variables (Jackson, 1967) that facilitate the performance of a job.

This discussion so far has focused primarily on hands-on performance tests; however, the processes described above are useful for developing assessment centers as well. As Tsacoumis (2007) noted, the first step in developing an assessment center is to review current job analysis data. Specifically, the exercise developer needs to review the task-KSAO linkages (which KSAOs are needed to perform which tasks) to generate ideas about possible exercises that simulate job tasks.

Regardless of which kind of high-fidelity simulation is being developed, there are a variety of issues to consider during task selection. Not only should characteristics of the tasks themselves be considered (e.g., importance, difficulty, and linkage to KSAOs), but the practical issues surrounding the testing of those tasks (e.g., equipment availability) are of paramount importance.

Lower-Fidelity Performance Tests

As mentioned previously, lower-fidelity performance tests (e.g., situational judgment tests and oral interviews) present applicants with problem situations that may be encountered on the job and ask them to describe, verbally or in writing, how they would respond.

Domain sampling strategies for these kinds of tests typically involve having SMEs generate critical incidents. Critical incidents (Flanagan, 1954) include descriptions of a situation encountered by an employee, what the employee did in response to the situation, and the result of the employee's actions. A form for collecting critical incidents is shown in Figure 22.1. To create a situational judgment test, hundreds of such incidents are collected, typically as part of a series of workshops; they are then sorted by job analysts or SMEs into dimensions according to behavioral similarity. Once performance dimensions are identified, a second group of SMEs engages in a retranslation process in which they sort incidents into the given dimensions. Once agreement is reached about which incidents describe each dimension, the test development process can be started.

How to Develop Work Simulations

The test development process for both higher- and lower-fidelity work simulations entails generating test situations that represent each of the tasks or performance dimensions identified above. For higher-fidelity simulations, in which the respondent actually performs a task or part of a task, the goal is to generate a number of task situations. For lower-fidelity simulations, in which respondents are asked to describe what they would do or effective actions in a situation, the goal is to generate a

Critical incident form					Participant # _____
1. What was the situation leading up to the event? [Describe the context.]					
2. What did the employee do?					
3. What was the outcome or result of the employee's action?					
4. Circle the number below that best reflects the level of performance that this event exemplifies.					
1	2	3	4	5	6	7
Highly ineffective			Moderately effective			Highly effective

Figure 22.1 Sample critical incident form.

number of problem situations. In this section, we describe general approaches for developing and scoring high- and low-fidelity simulations. We then discuss procedures for setting passing scores.

High-Fidelity Work Simulation Development

Once the tasks are selected, there are many other issues to consider when developing a work sample. High-fidelity performance tests require examinees to perform a task, or an essential part of a task, under conditions similar to how the task is performed on the job. As with all kinds of tests, work samples must be administered in the same way and under the same conditions so that all examinees have the same opportunity to demonstrate their ability. Thus, instructions for administering work sample tests are critical for standardizing how the tests are administered and scored.

Because high-fidelity performance tests represent abstractions of the actual work performed on the job, decisions need to be made regarding which compromises in psychological fidelity are necessary to accommodate the practical constraints of the test environment (Felker et al., 2007). Physical fidelity often must be sacrificed when it is impossible to duplicate exact working conditions or when doing so is costly. Instead, these conditions are simulated in such a way as to elicit the same knowledge and skills needed to perform the task, thus ensuring the test's psychological fidelity. For example, it is generally not feasible to test all truck drivers on all possible driving conditions in a standardized way. However, requiring examinees to drive around portable obstacles at certain speeds and brake at different speeds (as determined by the job analysis) may adequately simulate skills needed in many driving conditions, such as wet roads and heavy traffic (Felker et al., 2007).

When administering work simulation tests, some authenticity may be lost because of practical considerations. For example, tasks may be tested only in part because they are too long or too trivial to be tested in their entirety. In such cases, examinees might be given the information necessary to perform the task or they might be asked to walk through a particular step rather than demonstrate it when actually testing the step is infeasible (Hedge & Teachout, 1992).

The next step in developing high-fidelity performance tests is to devise procedures for scoring performance. Because scoring high-fidelity simulations is often done in real time as the task is performed, scoring requires familiarity with the task. Felker et al. (2007) make several recommendations for ensuring that the performance of steps of a task are accurately and reliably scored. First, performance steps need to be observable. Thus, if a checklist is used, similar to that in Figure 22.2, action verbs should be used (e.g., set the X switch, install the thingamajig). Steps that call for "checking," "inspecting," "reading," or "observing" are not observable in that the scorer does not know if the examinee is really "checking" or "reading," and if they are, one does not necessarily know what they are "checking." Second, standards for performance should be objective. For example, "drives an 18-wheel vehicle around a set of obstacles adequately" is not particularly useful because there is no observable method for assessing adequacy. "Drives an 18-wheel vehicle around a set of obstacles at 35 mph without knocking down any cones" specifies the standard to be met by the examinee. Another important recommendation is to use job aids in the tests, especially when the tasks are lengthy or complicated or when job incumbents are not expected to memorize specific procedures. Having them look something up in a manual can be incorporated into the test and still be scorable. Training test administrators is an important feature of work sample tests. Training approaches should focus on scorers' ability to observe behavior and to make judgments based on their observations (Hedge & Kavanagh, 1988). In addition, having scorers practice performing, observing, and rating the tasks they will be scoring is an important training component. Using two or more independent raters is helpful to identify possible scoring differences and to assess interrater reliability.

For scoring product tests, one can develop a score sheet that documents what the end-product should look like. It also is helpful to develop a sample of the work product so that scorers can compare the examinee's product to the correct work product.

<table>
<tr><td colspan="3" align="center">Unclogging a sink drain</td></tr>
</table>

Test date: _____	Examinee: _____	
Scorer: _____	Examinee ID: _____	

Say: This sink is clogged and you need to enable water to run through it smoothly. You are to use the materials provided. Do you have any questions? Begin.

Performance steps:	Go	No-Go
1. Remove the basket strainer.	——	——
2. Run hot water until it reaches two inches deep.	——	——
3. Try a suction plunger.	——	——
4. Put a pail under the sink.	——	——
5. Remove the cleanout plug and washer.	——	——
6. Try to unclog with screwdriver.	——	——
7. Use an auger.	——	——
8. Run hot water to clear residue when unclogged.	——	——

Figure 22.2   Example of a score sheet for a plumber task. (Adapted from http://www.atexinspects.com/Plumbing-Clogs.html.)

Assessment center tasks (e.g., in baskets, analysis exercises, and role plays) are high-fidelity simulations often used for supervisory or managerial positions (Tsacoumis, 2007). As described above, for other high-fidelity simulations, one defines the job content using a job/task analysis and identifies the KSAOs or competencies to be assessed. Then, working with SMEs (who are approximately one level above the target position), the developers generate ideas for different job simulations. One simulation might be a role play in which the examinee, in the role of a supervisor, meets with an employee (the scorer) to discuss a project. Another simulation might be an in-basket task during which examinees review materials typically found on a supervisor's desk (e.g., incorrectly completed time sheets, scheduling conflicts, and employee requests), and the examinee indicates the action he or she would take for each item. An analysis exercise might include some technical feature of the job that a supervisor might need to assess and present to employees. Then, rating scales are developed that provide scorers with observable behaviors at various levels of proficiency against which to compare examinee behavior. An example of such a rating scale is provided in Figure 22.3. Specific details about the development of each kind of assessment center exercise are beyond the scope of this chapter. For a description of how to develop and score such exercises, see Tsacoumis (2007).

Low-Fidelity Work Simulation Development

As mentioned previously, low-fidelity performance tests present examinees with problem situations that might be encountered on the job and ask them to provide information about a set of possible responses. Critical incidents, as described above, are useful for this purpose. Once incidents are generated and sorted into dimensions, scenarios are created that form the question in a situational judgment test. When the questions are developed, the response options are generated. One approach for generating response options is to ask the group of SMEs who generated the critical incidents to describe how outstanding, average, and poor job incumbents would deal with each situation. Another approach is to ask job incumbents with low levels of experience how they would deal with each problem (Motowidlo, Hanson & Crafts, 1997).

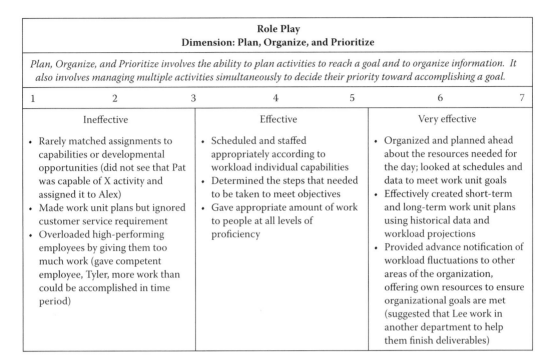

Role Play Dimension: Plan, Organize, and Prioritize						
Plan, Organize, and Prioritize involves the ability to plan activities to reach a goal and to organize information. It also involves managing multiple activities simultaneously to decide their priority toward accomplishing a goal.						
1	2	3	4	5	6	7
	Ineffective		Effective		Very effective	
	• Rarely matched assignments to capabilities or developmental opportunities (did not see that Pat was capable of X activity and assigned it to Alex) • Made work unit plans but ignored customer service requirement • Overloaded high-performing employees by giving them too much work (gave competent employee, Tyler, more work than could be accomplished in time period)		• Scheduled and staffed appropriately according to workload individual capabilities • Determined the steps that needed to be taken to meet objectives • Gave appropriate amount of work to people at all levels of proficiency		• Organized and planned ahead about the resources needed for the day; looked at schedules and data to meet work unit goals • Effectively created short-term and long-term work unit plans using historical data and workload projections • Provided advance notification of workload fluctuations to other areas of the organization, offering own resources to ensure organizational goals are met (suggested that Lee work in another department to help them finish deliverables)	

Figure 22.3   Sample assessment center rating scale.

The scoring algorithm is developed by having SMEs rate the responses for effectiveness. The mean of their ratings and agreement indices are then used to scale the response options. When asking examinees to rate the effectiveness of each option, their responses are scored against the SMEs' ratings, and higher scores are achieved to the extent that they are in agreement. When asking examinees to select what they would most or least likely do, the SMEs' ratings would be used to identify the most or least effective response, and applicants correctly choosing each alternative would receive a score of 1 for the item; otherwise they would receive a 0. Other scoring methods are described by McDaniel and Whetzel (2007) and Motowidlo et al. (1990). An example of a situational judgment test item is shown in Figure 22.4.

Setting Passing Scores

Many researchers (e.g., Schmidt, Mack, & Hunter, 1984) have shown that top-down approaches to selection enhance the utility of a selection procedure for organizations, and the *Principles for the Validation and Use of Personnel Selection Procedures* (Society of Industrial and Organizational Psychology, 2003) noted that, with valid predictors, a top-down approach is best for organizations. However, because this practice maximizes adverse impact (especially when tests are *g*-loaded), users of tests often have used cutoff scores such that everyone above a certain score is equally likely to be selected. Consequently, the process used for setting defensible cutoff scores is of great importance, especially if the tests are used for high-stakes decisions. If it is necessary to set a passing score for a work simulation, particularly one that reflects minimum job performance, a commonly used method, based on expert judgment, is the Angoff method (Angoff, 1971). The Angoff method is typically used for content validated tests, and it has been used to set passing scores for work samples (e.g., Truxillo, Donahue, & Sulzer, 1996) and certification tests (e.g., Busch & Jaeger, 1990). Despite its subjectivity, the Angoff method has withstood legal challenge (e.g., Biddle, 1993).

You are working on a project with a coworker. This project has a very tight time frame and your boss is very interested in having it completed on time. Your coworker is not pulling his/her share of the workload.

a. Confront your coworker with his/her nonperformance.
b. Leave the coworker alone hoping that the problem will correct itself when he/she sees how much work you are doing.
c. Talk to your boss about the situation so that he will intervene.
d. Talk to another coworker about this problem to see if this has happened before.
e. Ask your boss for a time extension on the project.
f. Ask your coworker if he/she is having family problems that could be affecting his/her work.

Figure 22.4 Example of a situational judgment test item.

Using the Angoff method, judges are asked to review test items and to estimate the percentage of minimally competent persons who could answer the item correctly or the likelihood that a minimally competent person would answer the item correctly. The cutoff is based on the average estimate across items and judges. Detailed recommendations regarding the implementation of this method are given in several reviews (e.g., Biddle, 1993; Truxillo et al., 1996). These involve using a fairly large number of judges (7–10) who represent demographic and geographic diversity and various organizational units so that the resulting cutoffs will seem fair to stakeholders.

Extensions of the Angoff approach include having panelists estimate the typical score that an examinee will earn on a question (Hambleton, Jaeger, Plake, & Mills, 2000), having panelists not only estimate the minimum number of score points for borderline examinees, but also estimate the distribution of scores of borderline examinees at basic, proficient, and advanced proficiency levels (Reckase, 2000).

FUTURE POTENTIAL DEVELOPMENTS

Since the mid-2000s, technological advances have greatly changed the field of testing, and the implications for simulation testing are profound. These changes involve how simulations are both administered and scored. There are also advances in job analysis, although at a less dramatic pace. As the processes associated with both job analysis and testing evolve, the use of work simulations will continue to advance in terms of delivery and frequency of use.

Concerning the delivery of work simulations, virtual reality is becoming more of an option. The use of avatars (i.e., computer-based personalities that individuals create and manage in an online environment) is prevalent in many areas of life. Even at grocery stores, one can follow the movements of an avatar in self-serve checkout lines. One can imagine the flexibility in using avatars instead of video-based tests for situational judgment tests.

Work simulations may also be used more frequently in on-the-job training. In a variety of work tasks, particularly those involving computer applications, one can be taught how to complete certain tasks using simulations. For example, computer security applications involving fingerprint scanners are often accompanied by tutorials that teach the user how to scan the fingerprint device. Such software can involve practice trials that assess the adequacy of the user's mastery of the presented materials. Work simulations developed in virtual worlds, such as Second Life, have been used to simulate operating rooms (Gerald & Antonacci, 2009). Second Life also has been used to simulate Air Force bases, using the program MyBase, which allows the public to access information about the Air Force using virtual characters who chat by voice and text. Another virtual continent called SciLands is devoted to science and technology education. Although these examples represent high-fidelity simulations built with many bells and whistles, there is some evidence that low-fidelity simulation can achieve high levels of transfer of training without the costs associated with the use of high-fidelity simulators (Thomas, 2009).

Use of the Internet for testing has been a hotly debated topic. Tippins (2009) summarized several issues with using unproctored Internet testing (e.g., test security and cheating). Because of the low cost of administering tests through the Internet (no travel for examinees, no test administrators at various locations), many companies are using unproctored testing, especially for noncognitive tests. Much attention has been devoted to statistical detection of cheating as well as prevention of cheating (e.g., requiring some form of identification) prior to taking the test. Solutions to these issues include the development of a large item bank of simulations so that all examinees do not receive the same stimulus.

FURTHER READING

The references that follow present additional reading and resources concerning work simulations. Our recommended reading includes major reviews of work simulations with emphasis on applicant screening, work samples (narrowly defined), and situational judgment tests. Referring readers to Internet resources is a tricky business because web site addresses may change. We list sites that are likely to have some permanence. Readers may wish to conduct their own web searches. We also did not provide any references to technology sources (e.g., software) because it is outside of our expertise; the field is evolving rapidly and anything we could offer would likely be out of date by the time this book is published.

Bobko, P., Roth, P. L., & Buster, M. A. (2005). Work sample selection tests and expected reduction in adverse impact: A cautionary note. *International Journal of Selection and Assessment, 13*(1), 1–10.

Callinan, M., & Robertson, I. T. (2000). Work sample testing. *International Journal of Selection and Assessment, 8*, 248–260.

Felker, D. B., Curtin, P. J., & Rose, A. M. (2007). Tests of job performance. In D. L. Whetzel & G. R. Wheaton (Eds.), *Applied measurement: Industrial psychology in human resources management* (pp. 319–348). Mahwah, NJ: Lawrence Erlbaum.

McDaniel, M. A., & Whetzel, D. L. (2007). Situational judgment tests. In D. L. Whetzel & G. R. Wheaton (Eds.), *Applied measurement: Industrial psychology in human resources management* (pp. 235–258). Mahwah, NJ: Lawrence Erlbaum.

Ployhart, R., & Weekley, J. (Eds.). (2006). *Situational judgment tests: Theory, measurement, and application.* San Francisco, CA: Jossey-Bass.

Roth, P. L., Bobko, P., & McFarland, L. A. (2005). A meta-analysis of work sample test validity: Updating and integrating some classic literature. *Personnel Psychology, 58,* 1009–1037.

Society for Industrial and Organizational Psychology, Inc. (2011). *Work samples and simulations.* Retrieved from http://www.siop.org/workplace/employment%20testing/samplesandsimulations.aspx
This web site provides a brief overview and a link to other employment testing information.

Tsacoumis, S. (2007). Assessment centers. In D. L. Whetzel & G. R. Wheaton (Eds.), *Applied measurement: Industrial psychology in human resources management* (pp. 259–292). Mahwah, NJ: Lawrence Erlbaum.

Truxillo, D. M., Donahue, L.M., & Kuang, D. (2004). Work samples, performance tests, and competency testing. In J. C. Thomas & M. Hersen (Eds.), *Comprehensive handbook of psychological assessment* (4th ed, pp. 345–367). Hoboken, NJ: John Wiley and Sons.

Stanford School of Medicine, Center for Immersive and Simulation-Based Learning. (2011). *Real training from simulated experiences.* Retrieved from http://cisl.stanford.edu[2]

National Training and Simulation Association (homepage). Retrieved from http://www.trainingsystems.org[3]

---

[2] This organization develops work simulations to aid in the training of medical professionals.

[3] This organization is a professional organization of companies that provides simulations used for training, primarily for the U.S. Military.

REFERENCES

Ames, B., & Bailey, B. (2005, June). *Pennsylvania's computer-administered work simulation assessments.* Paper presented at the 29th annual meetings of the IPMAAC, Orlando, FL.

Angoff, W. H. (1971). Scales, norms, and equivalent scores. In R. L. Thorndike (Ed.), *Educational measurement* (2nd ed., pp. 121–208). Washington, DC: American Council on Education.

Biddle, R. E. (1993). How to set cutoff scores for knowledge tests used in promotion training, certification, and licensing. *Public Personnel Management, 22,* 63–79.

Binning, J. F., & Barrett, G. V. (1989). Validity of personnel decisions: A conceptual analysis of the inferential and evidential bases. *Journal of Applied Psychology, 25,* 499–513.

Bobko, P., Roth, P. L., & Buster, M. A. (2005). Work sample selection tests and expected reduction in adverse impact: A cautionary note. *International Journal of Selection and Assessment, 13,* 1–10.

Borman, W. C., Hanson, M. A., & Hedge, J. W. (1997). Personnel selection. *Annual Review of Psychology, 48,* 299–337.

Busch, J. C., & Jaeger, R. M. (1990). Influence of type of judge, normative information, and discussion on standards recommended for the National Teacher Examinations. *Journal of Educational Measurement, 27,* 145–163.

Callinan, M., & Robertson, I. T. (2000). Work sample testing. *International Journal of Selection and Assessment, 8,* 248–260.

Campbell, C. H., Ford, P., Rumsey, M. G., Pulakos, E.D., Borman, W.C., Felker D.B., ... Riegelhaupt, B. J. (1990). Development of multiple job performance measures in a representative sample of jobs. *Personnel Psychology, 43,* 277–300.

Carey, N. B. (1990). *An assessment of surrogates for hands-on tests: Selection standards and training needs (CRM 90-47).* Alexandra, VA: Center for Naval Analyses.

Cascio, W. (2003). *Managing human resources: Productivity, quality of work life, and profits* (6th ed.). Boston, MA: McGraw-Hill.

Chan, D., & Schmitt, N. (1997). Video-based versus paper-and-pencil method of assessment in SJTs: Subgroup differences in test performance and face validity perceptions. *Journal of Applied Psychology, 82,* 143–159.

Dean, M. A., Roth, P. L., & Bobko, P. (2008). Ethnic and gender subgroup differences in assessment center ratings: A meta-analysis. *Journal of Applied Psychology, 93,* 685–691.

Employment Technologies Corporation. (2008). Easy Simulation Teller Vision. Retrieved from http://www.etc-easy.com/_products/tellervision/index.htm

Felker, D. B., Crafts, J. L., Rose, A. M., Harnest, C. W., Edwards, D. S., Bowler, E. C., ... McHenry, J. J. (1988). *Developing job performance tests for the United States Marine Corps infantry occupational field* (AIR-47500-9/88-FR). Washington, DC: American Institutes for Research.

Felker, D. B., Curtin, P. J., & Rose, A. M. (2007). Test of job performance. In D. L. Whetzel & G. R. Wheaton (Eds.), *Applied measurement: Industrial psychology in human resources management* (pp. 319–348). Mahwah, NJ: Lawrence Erlbaum.

Ferrari, M., Taylor, R., & VanLehn, K. (1999). Adapting work simulations for schools. *Journal of Educational Computing Research, 21,* 25–53.

Flanagan, J. C. (1954). The critical incident technique. *Psychological Bulletin, 41,* 237–358.

Fleishman, E. A., Costanza, D. C., & Marshall-Mies, J. C. (1997). Abilities. In N. G. Peterson, M. D. Mumford, W. C. Borman, P. R. Jeanneret, & E. A. Fleishman (Eds.), *O*NET: An occupational information network* (pp. 175–195). Washington, DC: American Psychological Association.

Furst Person. (2004). *How will that job candidate manage your calls? Find our before you hire them.* Retrieved from http://www.furstperson.com/furstperson-tools/interactive-simulations/service-brick-mortar/

Gatewood, R., & Field, H. (2001). *Human resource selection* (5th ed.). Fort Worth, TX: Harcourt College Publishers.

Gaugler, B. B., Rosenthal, D. B., Thornton, G. C. III, & Bentson, C. (1987). Meta-analysis of assessment center validity. *Journal of Applied Psychology, 72,* 493–511.

Gerald, S., & Antonacci, D. M. (2009). Virtual world learning spaces: Developing a Second Life operating room simulation. *EDUCAUSE Quarterly Magazine, 32.* Retrieved from http://www.educause.edu/EDUCAUSE+Quarterly/EDUCAUSEQuarterlyMagazineVolum/VirtualWorldLearningSpacesDeve/163851

Goldstein, I. L., Zedeck, S., & Schneider, B. (1993). An exploration of the job analysis-content validity process. In N. Schmitt, W. C. Borman, & Associates (Eds.), *Personnel selection in organizations* (pp. 3–34). San Francisco, CA: Jossey-Bass.

Green, B. F. Jr., & Wigdor, A. K. (1991). Measuring job competency. In A. K. Wigdor & B. F. Green (Eds.), *Performance assessment for the workplace* (pp. 53–74). Washington, DC: National Academies Press.

Guion, R. M. (1998). *Assessment, measurement, and prediction for personnel decisions.* Mahwah, NJ: Lawrence Erlbaum.

Hambleton, R. K., Jaeger, R. M., Plake, C. M., & Mills, C. (2000). Setting performance standards on complex educational assessment. *Applied Psychological Measurement, 24,* 355–366.

Hanson, M. A., & Borman, W. C. (1989, April). *Development and construct validation of a situational judgment test of supervisory effectiveness for first-line supervisors in the U.S. Army.* Paper presented at the 4th annual conference of the Society for Industrial and Organizational Psychology, Atlanta, GA.

Hardison, C. M., & Sackett, P. R. (2004, April). *Assessment center criterion-related validity: A meta-analytic update.* Paper presented at the 2004 meeting of the Society for Industrial and Organizational Psychology, Chicago, IL.

Harvey, J. L., Anderson, L. E., Baranowski, L. E., & Morath, R. A. (2007). Job analysis: Gathering job-specific information. In D. L. Whetzel & G. R. Wheaton (Eds.), *Applied measurement: Industrial psychology in human resources management* (pp. 57–95). Mahwah, NJ: Lawrence Erlbaum.

Hedge, J. W., & Kavanagh, M. J. (1988). Improving the accuracy of performance evaluations: Comparisons of three methods of performance appraiser training. *Journal of Applied Psychology, 73,* 68–73.

Hedge, J. W., Lipscomb, M. S., & Teachout, M. S. (1988). Work sample testing in the Air Force job performance measurement project. In M. S. Lipscomb & J. W. Hedge (Eds.), *Job performance measurement: Topics in the performance measurement of Air Force enlisted personnel* (AFHRL-RP-87-58). Brooks Air Force Base, TX: Air Force Human Resources Laboratory.

Hedge, J. W., & Teachout, M. S. (1992). An interview approach to work sample criterion measurement. *Journal of Applied Psychology, 77,* 453–461.

Holland, J. L. (1973). *Making vocational choices: A theory of careers.* Englewood Cliffs, NJ: Prentice Hall.

Houran, J. (2007, November). *Employee screening with job-simulation videos.* Retrieved from http://www.hvs.com/Jump/?aid=3023

Hunter, J. E., & Hunter, R. F. (1984). Validity and utility of alternative predictors of job performance. *Psychological Bulletin, 96,* 72–98.

ICT Results (2008, June). *Holodeck 1.0? Star Trek-style displays make their debut.* Retrieved from http://www.sciencedaily.com/releases/2008/06/080604195058.htm

Jackson, D. N. (1967). *Personality research form manual.* Goshen, NY: Research Psychologists Press.

Knapp D. J., & Campbell, J. P. (1993). *Building a joint service classification research roadmap: Criterion related issues* (AL/HR-TP-1993-0028). Brooks Air Force Base, TX: Armstrong Laboratory, Manpower and Personnel Research Division.

McDaniel, M. A., Hartman, N. S., Whetzel, D. L., & Grubb, W. L. (2007). Situational judgment tests, response instructions and validity: A meta-analysis. *Personnel Psychology, 60,* 63–91.

McDaniel, M. A., Morgeson, F. P., Finnegan E. B., Campion, M. A., & Braverman, E. P. (2001). Predicting job performance using Situational Judgment Tests: A clarification of the literature. *Journal of Applied Psychology, 86,* 730–740.

McDaniel, M. A., & Whetzel, D. L. (2007). Situational judgment tests. In D. L. Whetzel & G. R. Wheaton (Eds.), *Applied measurement: Industrial psychology in human resources management* (pp. 235–258). Mahwah, NJ: Lawrence Erlbaum.

Miller, M. D., & Linn, R. L. (2000). Validation of performance-based assessments. *Applied Psychological Measurement, 24,* 367–378.

Motowidlo, S. J., Dunnette, M. D., & Carter, G. W. (1990). An alternate selection procedure: The low fidelity simulation. *Journal of Applied Psychology, 75,* 640–647.

Motowidlo, S. J., Hanson, M. A., & Crafts, J. L. (1997). In D. L. Whetzel & G. R. Wheaton (Eds.), *Applied measurement methods in industrial psychology* (pp. 241–260). Palo Alto, CA: Davies-Black Publishing.

Palmer, C. I., Boyles, W. R., Veres, J. G., & Hill, J. B. (1992). Validation of a clerical test using work samples. *Journal of Business and Psychology, 7,* 239–257.

Peterson, N. G., & Jeanneret, P. R. (2007). Job analysis: Overview and description of deductive methods. In D. L. Whetzel & G. R. Wheaton (Eds.), *Applied measurement: Industrial psychology in human resources management* (pp. 13–56). Mahwah, NJ: Lawrence Erlbaum.

Peterson, N. G., Mumford, M. D., Borman, W. C., Jeanneret, P. R., & Fleishman, E. A. (Eds.). (1997). *O*NET: An occupational information network.* Washington, DC: American Psychological Association.

Ployhart, R. E. & Holtz, B. C. (2008). The diversity–validity dilemma: Strategies for reducing racioethnic and sex subgroup differences and adverse impact in selection. *Personnel Psychology, 61,* 153–172.

Ployhart, R. E., Schneider, B., & Schmitt, N. (2006). *Staffing organizations: contemporary practice and theory* (3rd ed.). Mahwah, NJ: Lawrence Erlbaum.

Reckase, M. D. (2000). *The evolution of the NAEP achievement levels setting process: A summary of the research and development efforts conducted by ACT.* Iowa City, IA: ACT.

Reilly, R., & Warech, M. (1993). The validity and fairness of alternatives to cognitive tests. In L. Wing & B. Gifford (Eds.), *Policy issues in employment testing* (pp. 131–224). Boston, MA: Kluwer.

Roth, P. L., Bevier, C. A., Bobko, P., Switzer, F. S., & Tyler, P. (2001). Ethnic group differences in cognitive ability in employment and educational settings: A meta-analysis. *Personnel Psychology, 54,* 297–330.

Roth, P. L., Bobko, P., & McFarland, L. A. (2005). A meta-analysis of work sample test validity: Updating and integrating some classic literature. *Personnel Psychology, 58,* 1009–1037.

Salgado, J., Viswesvaran, C., & Ones, D. (2001). Predictors used for personnel selection: An overview of constructs, methods, and techniques. In N. Anderson, D. Ones, H. Sinangil, & C. Viswesvaran (Eds.), *Handbook of industrial, work, & organizational psychology* (pp. 165–199). London, UK: Sage.

Sanchez, J. I., & Levine, E. L. (2001). The analysis of work in the 20th and 21st centuries. In N. Anderson, D. Ones, H. Sinangil, & C. Viswesvaran (Eds.), *Handbook of industrial, work, & organizational psychology* (pp. 71–89). London, UK: Sage.

Schmidt, F. L., & Hunter, J. E. (1998). The validity and utility of selection methods in personnel psychology: Practical and theoretical implications of 85 years of research findings. *Psychological Bulletin, 124,* 262–274.

Schmidt, F. L., Mack, M. J., & Hunter, J. E. (1984). Selection utility in the occupation of U.S. park ranger for three modes of test use. *Journal of Applied Psychology, 69,* 490–497.

Schmitt, N., Clause, C., & Pulakos, E. D. (1996). Subgroup differences associated with different measures of some common job relevant constructs. In C. Cooper & I. Robertson (Eds.), *International review of industrial and organizational psychology* (Vol. 11, pp. 115–139). New York, NY: John Wiley.

Schmitt, N., Gooding, R. Z., Noe, R. A., & Kirsch, M. (1984). Meta-analysis of validity studies published between 1964 and 1983 and the investigation of study characteristics. *Personnel Psychology, 37,* 407–422.

Shippman, J. S., Ash, R. A., Battista, M., Carr, L., Eyde, L. D., Hesketh, B., … Sanchez, J. I. (2000). The practice of competency modeling. *Personnel Psychology, 53,* 703–740.

Smith, K. C., & McDaniel, M. A. (1998, April). *Criterion and construct validity evidence for a situational judgment measure.* Paper presented at the 13th annual conference of the Society for Industrial and Organizational Psychology, Inc., Dallas, TX.

Society of Industrial and Organizational Psychology, Inc. (2003). *Principles for the validation and use of personnel selection procedures* (4th ed.). College Park, MD: Author.

Taylor, F. W. (1911). *The principles of scientific management.* New York, NY: Harper and Brothers.

Thomas, M. (2009). Integrating low-fidelity desktop scenarios into the high fidelity simulation curriculum in medicine and aviation. Retrieved from http://www.unisanet.unisa.edu.au/staff/MatthewThomas/Paper/Thomas_DesktopScenarios.pdf

Tippins, N. (2009). Internet alternatives to traditional proctored testing: Where are we now? *Industrial and Organizational Psychology: Perspectives on Science and Practice, 2*(1), 2–10.

Truxillo, D. M., Donahue, L. M., & Kuang, D. (2004). Work samples, performance tests, and competency testing. In J. C. Thomas, & M. Hersen (Eds.), *Comprehensive handbook of psychological assessment* (4th ed., pp. 345–367). Hoboken, NJ: John Wiley and Sons.

Truxillo, D. M., Donahue, L. M., & Sulzer, J. L. (1996). Setting cutoff scores for personnel selection tests: Issues, illustrations, and recommendations. *Human Performance, 9,* 275–295.

Tsacoumis, S. (2007). Assessment centers. In D. L. Whetzel & G. R. Wheaton (Eds.), *Applied measurement: Industrial psychology in human resources management* (pp. 259–292). Mahwah, NJ: Lawrence Erlbaum.

Ulrich, D., Brockbank, W., Yueng, A. K., & Lake, D. G. (1995). Human resource competencies: An empirical assessment. *Human Resource Management, 34,* 473–495.

Weekley, J. A., & Ployhart, R. E. (2006). An introduction to situational judgment testing. In J. A. Weekley & R. E. Ployhart (Eds.), *Situational judgment tests* (pp. 1–10). Mahwah, NJ: Lawrence Erlbaum Associates.

Whetzel, D. L., McDaniel, M. A., & Nguyen, N. T. (2008). Subgroup differences in situational judgment test performance: A meta-analysis. *Human Performance, 21,* 291–309.

Williams, K. M., & Crafts, J. L. (1997). Inductive job analysis: The job/task inventory method. In D. L. Whetzel & G. R. Wheaton (Eds.), *Applied measurement methods in industrial psychology* (pp. 51–87). Palo Alto, CA: Consulting Psychologists Press, Inc.

23

Building Effective Performance Appraisals From an Analysis of Work

Sylvia G. Roch
University at Albany, State University of New York

Kevin J. Williams
University at Albany, State University of New York

This chapter examines the use of performance appraisals (PAs) in organizations; specific attention is paid to the role of work analysis in building effective appraisal systems. Organizations use PAs for many different purposes, ranging from salary administration, employee feedback, and termination decisions to serving as a criterion for organizational research and selection test validation research. When used properly, PA is a valuable human resource management tool, helping organizations staff positions, identify training needs, and reward employees. Performance appraisal is also essential for effective coaching and development of personnel.

Despite their prevalence, many PA systems are fraught with problems. Ratings are widely viewed as inaccurate and biased. In many organizations, ratings are highly inflated. Supervisors do not like appraising subordinates because of discomfort stemming from evaluation apprehension and concern over maintaining productive work relations. Workers do not view the appraisal process as fair and do not act on the feedback provided by appraisals. In fact, employee performance is just as likely to decrease as it is to increase after receiving appraisal feedback (Latham, Almost, Mann, & Moore, 2005).

In this chapter, we discuss the potential and problems of PA and identify common pitfalls. We describe effective PA systems and emphasize the role that work analysis plays in avoiding the common pitfalls. Successful performance appraisal requires a solid understanding of the performance domain, the critical tasks and work behaviors that reflect an individual's contributions to an organization. We discuss how work analysis information is used to make several critical decisions, such as deciding which behaviors to assess, designing instruments to dependably measure these behaviors, and identifying sources that can provide detailed information about incumbent behavior. A general theme that runs through the chapter is that PA should not be seen as an isolated task, for example, as something that is done once or twice a year to satisfy organizational requirements. Rather, it should be seen as an integral part of an ongoing performance management system designed to motivate employees to improve performance. Performance appraisal also should not be seen as an isolated human resource function but part of an integrated human resource system that includes selection, training, compensation, and any other human resource practice.

THE STATE OF PRACTICE: MALAISE AND DISSATISFACTION WITH APPRAISALS

Organizations seem to have a love-hate relationship with PA. Although PAs are widely used and serve many different human resource functions, they are also widely disliked because of problems associated with their use. Survey results indicate that relatively few employees believe that their organization's PA system helps them improve performance (DeNisi & Pritchard, 2006).

Table 23.1 lists four categories of problems commonly associated with PAs. Perhaps the most frequently mentioned problems concern both the rater and the rating instrument. For example, raters are too lenient, raters fail to differentiate workers to any meaningful degree, and the most critical behaviors are not being rated. In addition, PAs routinely send mixed messages (Murphy & Cleveland, 1995). For example, the organization may promote the message that PA is important, but managers who do a good job evaluating performance are rarely rewarded for it. Furthermore, rating dimensions may not capture important aspects of the job, and PA ratings are often not linked to organizational decisions, such as whom to promote, terminate, or train. Performance appraisals also force raters to make distinctions among employees, which can demoralize employees. Similarly, PAs routinely disappoint employees who expect better ratings. Many managers are also uncomfortable being in the position of both a rater and counselor. Thus, it is not surprising that the typical PA has been characterized as "given by someone who does not want to give it to someone who does not want to get it" (Bowman, 1999, p. 557).

Although there is no denying that there are many problems associated with PAs, if proper attention and consideration is given to how PA systems are constructed, appraisals can be a useful and valued resource for organizations. One explanation for the current state of affairs is that PA research has not been successful at addressing the pressing concerns that organizations have surrounding the assessment of job performance. Until around 1990, PA research was dominated by two themes: a search for the ideal rating instrument and an understanding of the cognitive processes that underlie rater judgments. With regard to the first theme, no rating format emerged that would dramatically improve accuracy (Landy & Farr, 1980), even though this research led to an understanding of how to build good instruments. On the second theme, the cognitive research provided an understanding of the processes by which raters reach appraisal decisions (see DeNisi & Williams, 1988, for a review) and suggested ways in which raters could be accurate. However, as

Table 23.1   Common Problems With Performance Appraisal Systems

Problem Category	Specific Example Problems
1. The process	• A single appraisal is used for multiple purposes. • The appraisal process is not seen as fair. • Lack of a consistent frame of reference for performance.
2. The instrument	• Ratings make spurious differentiations (e.g., via forced distribution systems). • The rating instrument is poorly constructed. • Critical job behaviors are not clearly defined.
3. The rater	• Highly inflated ratings; raters tend to be lenient in their ratings. • Raters fail to differentiate between workers and thus fail to provide organizations with useful information. • Raters receive insufficient rewards for accurate appraisals. • Raters are uncomfortable providing appraisal feedback to subordinates. • Raters are not motivated to be accurate. • Raters do not trust other raters to be accurate. • Raters are politically motivated.
4. The ratee	• Ratees do not feel that the most important behaviors are being rated. • Ratees do not accept the ratings.

Longenecker, Sims, and Gioia (1987) showed in their seminal article, managers are not concerned with accuracy when assigning ratings but are concerned with managing their employees.

Thus, PA researchers realized that their focus should not be on rating accuracy; instead, the key to PA in organizations is understanding rater motivation and both rater and ratee reactions. As Levy and Williams (2004) stated in their review, "Perhaps no area within the PA literature has seen such a dramatic increase in research attention since 1990 as ratee reactions to PA processes" (p. 889). The Levy and Williams review of the social context of PA also explores a host of factors that influence PA practice, ranging from organizational culture and climate to supervisor and subordinate relationships. Thus, we now understand not only why PA is such a disliked process and the many social factors that can influence it, but why this research has not yet resulted in many improvements to the practice of PA.

Another possible reason for the limited impact of appraisal research is that PA is often treated as a discrete task by organizations and is not tied into larger issues of performance management. Performance management is a broad set of coordinated organizational activities aimed at improving worker performance (DeNisi & Pritchard, 2006). Whereas PA has often been seen as an end in itself, placed in the broader context of performance management it can be a tool for improving performance. The performance management movement emphasizes continuous improvement, and thus PA becomes something that is done frequently rather than once or twice a year. Table 23.2 lists important questions that should be asked and issues for consideration when evaluating the quality of a PA system from a performance management perspective. An effective PA system is more than having a psychometrically sound rating instrument. It involves creating a climate in which

Table 23.2   Important Questions and Considerations for an Effective Performance Appraisal System

Questions	Issues and Considerations
Is the PA system legally defensible?	Review legal requirements. Establish linkages to work analysis. Provide documentation (paper trail).
Are the purpose and goals of the PA clearly articulated?	Align PA goals with organizational goals. One system or multiple systems?
Is there a precise definition of performance?	Consider all dimensions of job performance, including task and contextual performance.
Are the rating instruments work-related and behavior-based?	Establish link between work analysis data and the appraisal instrument. Decide on absolute versus relative formats. Ensure that raters have opportunity to observe performance. Identify raters (supervisors, peers, clients, or self).
Are the raters willing and able to rate accurately?	Rater training for quality of ratings *and* feedback. Build "buy in." Reward raters for quality appraisals. Emphasize rater accountability. Build trust between raters. Remove politics from rating process.
Do ratees accept the PA system?	Train ratees for PA procedures and for receiving feedback. Build "buy in". Promote procedural justice. Provide grievance channels.
Is the appraisal ongoing with continuous communication and coaching?	Establish regular review periods (decide on appropriate frequency). Decide what gets communicated (task behaviors, performance level, relative performance, strengths and weaknesses, etc.). Incorporate goal setting.

all parties believe that appraisals are being given by someone who wants to give them to someone who wants to receive them.

THE ROLE OF ANALYSIS OF WORK

Basing the performance appraisal system on a sound analysis of work can reduce a number of the concerns discussed in all four categories of Table 23.1. A rigorous analysis of work provides an empirical basis for developing standards of performance and for determining what is good and what is poor performance. It also ensures that the behaviors that are observed and assessed are critical to successful job performance. A sound work analysis may also result in a PA system that is acceptable to both the rater and the ratee because it captures the key behaviors needed to perform the job. It is important to realize that PA is not just the sheet or screen that managers use to insert ratings, but includes an entire system: rating instrument, rater and ratee training programs, feedback sessions, grievance channels, etc.

As shown in Figure 23.1, work analysis plays two general roles in the design of an effective PA system. First, it is used to define the dimensions of performance on which employees will be assessed. Second, work analysis is used to identify important and measurable behaviors that form the basis of PA instruments and rater training. As we discuss below, different work analysis methods may be called upon to provide information relevant to these two roles. Although the process may seem burdensome, the value gained by having a comprehensive understanding of both the performance dimensions that define a job and the behaviors that differentiate effective from ineffective behavior is immense.

For example, it is more likely that both rater training and the rating instrument will capture important aspects of the job if the work analysis was competently conducted and thus does a good job of both defining performance in terms of relevant job dimensions and defining behaviors associated with these job dimensions. Overall, it is more likely that PA ratings are linked to promotion

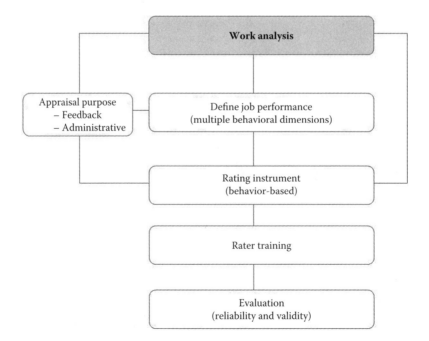

Figure 23.1   Critical steps in constructing a performance appraisal system.

decisions, training, etc., if all of the human resource functions are based on a common foundation: a sound work analysis. Just as the rating instrument should be part of a PA system, the PA system should be part of the larger human resource system, which includes selection, PA, training, and compensation. All human resource functions should be aligned by a common, comprehensive work analysis.

ORGANIZATIONAL ANALYSIS

It is important to keep in mind that PA systems are embedded in organizational contexts. Understanding the current nature of an organization and its culture, climate, and practices will facilitate the development and implementation of an effective PA system. Thus, before conducting an analysis of work for PA purposes, it is a good idea to conduct at least an informal organizational analysis. This recommendation is consistent with the longstanding practice in personnel training to conduct a three-stage needs analysis: an organizational analysis, a task analysis (a type of work analysis), and a person analysis (which uses PA information; see Goldstein & Ford, 2002, for a detailed description of training needs analysis).

The organizational analysis should include an assessment of the current organizational situation, including the existing PA system, human resource practices, organizational culture, and organizational and job design. When examining the existing PA system, it is useful to note both the successful and less successful components of the system. For example, the rating instrument may be viewed as easy to use but it may also be perceived as missing the relevant parts of the job. It may be that the instrument does include the relevant dimensions but different raters have different ideas of what constitutes a good rating on any given dimension. By examining the existing PA system, one may gain valuable insights into what does and what does not work in the particular organization.

Aside from investigating the strengths and weaknesses of the current system, it may also be a good idea to gauge the amount and type of support in the organization for changing or updating the PA system. As seen in Table 23.3, some good questions to ask include, Who wants the change? Does this organization need a new PA system or just more training? Are ratings influenced by political concerns, that is, do raters consider their own personal goals or the goals of their units when evaluating employees? *Rating climate* should also be assessed. Rating climate refers to shared perceptions regarding the usefulness and integrity of performance ratings in the organization. Understanding the rating climate will help to determine such things as whether rater motivation will be a problem.

Table 23.3 Questions to Ask During an Organizational Analysis

1. Who wants to change the performance appraisal system (or implement a new one)?
2. Does this organization need a new performance appraisal system or is it possible that problems stem from other human resource practices such as selection or training?
3. Are performance ratings very political? That is, do raters use performance ratings to accomplish personal goals or gain advantages for their units?
4. How do the employees perceive the performance appraisal system? Does it differ by organizational level?
5. For what purposes are performance ratings used in this organization?
6. What are the goals of the performance appraisal system?
7. Is there an existing organizational competency model? If so, what is the role of this competency model in human resource practices (including performance appraisal)?
8. What aspects of the current performance appraisal system are successful?
9. What aspects of the current performance appraisal system are not successful?
10. Is there an existing work analysis?

Also, at this stage, it is a good idea to establish the PA's purpose, objectives, and goals. It is important to discern the PA goals for all stakeholders and to decide whether one PA system can achieve all their goals or whether some goals are incompatible. Murphy and Cleveland (1995) provide a good overview of the influence of goals on PA. For example, if the employee's goal is to receive feedback, this goal may be incompatible with an organization's goal to compare employees. Thus, it is important that the goals of the PA system are clear and agreed upon by the relevant parties before a PA system is created or updated. Last, but perhaps most importantly, it is important to determine whether the organization has an existing competency model that is expected to drive all human resource functions.

DEFINING JOB PERFORMANCE

Assuming the organizational analysis points toward further evaluation and possible redevelopment of the PA system, the first step will be to clearly define what is meant by "job performance." At a generic level, job performance is the degree to which a worker helps the organization to reach its goals (Campbell, 1989). Thus, the first task is to define the dimensions of performance. Traditionally, many organizational scholars have adopted a one-dimensional view of job performance in which employee contributions are aggregated into a global summary judgment of performance. For example, an organization may combine ratings of production quantity, quality, and efficiency into a general or composite measure of employee performance. This judgment tends to focus solely on performance of tasks most central to the job role.

Since the early 1990s, researchers have expanded their view of performance and have embraced a multidimensional perspective. Borman and Motowidlo (1997) distinguished between task and contextual performance. Task performance refers to behaviors that transform inputs and raw materials into the goods and services that represent the organization's products. These are tasks and activities that relate directly to the core functional and technical aspects of an organization, things that are likely to be delineated in a standard job description. Contextual performance, by contrast, refers to behaviors that support and maintain task performance. These behaviors are not central to one's main tasks, but they support the social and psychological environment in which tasks are performed. Contextual performance includes the cooperative, altruistic, and civic-minded behaviors that define organizational citizenship (Organ, 1988).

Contextual performance is seen as important for most jobs because most jobs are embedded in social structures (Motowidlo & Schmit, 1999), and it thus becomes the glue that holds the organization together. In fact, raters have difficulty disentangling contextual and task performance in their ratings. Researchers have shown that contextual performance influences performance ratings, even when the rating dimensions only assess task performance (e.g., Rotundo & Sackett, 2002; Whiting, Podsakoff, & Pierce, 2008). Although such conflation of contextual and task performance may reflect an employee's overall contribution to the organization, it would be preferable to have a PA system that separates them as much as possible. The results of a work analysis could be used to construct an instrument that specifies both job-specific task behaviors and more generic contextual behaviors related to job success. Thus, the first task in devising a PA system is to define the performance domain for a job and its associated performance dimensions. Both the definition of performance and the dimensions should be based on a work analysis.

Once the performance dimensions have been identified, the next step is to operationalize the dimensions. A debated topic in the PA literature is whether performance should be defined in terms of behaviors or outcomes (the results of behavior). Advocates of the behavioral approach define the job in terms of behaviors that individuals should and should not do. Note that there is an implicit evaluative component to viewing performance in behavioral terms; that is, behaviors can be evaluated as positive or negative in regards to organizational goals (Motowidlo, Borman, & Schmit, 1997). Advocates of the outcome approach describe the job in terms of outcomes achieved. Job outcomes are typically assessed with objective measures, or those requiring few judgments on the part of appraisers (e.g., sales generated, production counts).

There are pros and cons to each approach. An individual can perform all of the desired behaviors but still not arrive at a positive outcome, perhaps because of circumstances beyond her control. Alternatively, the desired outcome may be reached in different ways and sometimes despite incorrect behaviors. This may leave workers unsure of how they arrived at the desired end state and unsure of their ability to replicate success. Also, many white collar jobs do not have objective measures that can be directly linked to an employee, or the available objective measures may only capture a small portion of an employee's performance. For example, the number of reports turned in on time does not provide any information regarding the quality of the reports and other important job tasks, such as working effectively in teams.

An unfortunate result of this situation is that the aspects of a job not captured by objective measures are likely to be ignored by workers. The use of objective measures results in holding workers accountable for results but not for how they achieve the results. Not only does this make it difficult to identify the reasons for success or failure, it also promotes a "results at all cost" mentality, which may increase chances of unethical behavior (Latham & Wexley, 1994). Our view, which is consistent with that of many experts (e.g., Motowidlo & Schmit, 1999; Murphy & Cleveland, 1995), is to concentrate on behaviors. Managers need to be able to tell workers what they must do to improve or perform effectively, not just that they failed to meet established standards. In addition, outcomes are often influenced by factors outside the control of the individual, and various constraints operate differently on different individuals, making it difficult to evaluate the importance of the constraints. This makes it difficult to determine workers' unique contributions to an organization. When evaluating someone, it is best to focus on the things that he or she can control, and behaviors are more under direct control than results. For these and other reasons, subjective ratings are often used and will be the focus of the discussion that follows.

In summary, our view of job performance is one that is behavioral and multidimensional. The implication of this view is that the PA system should provide judgments about multiple dimensions of job performance. This view of job performance has important implications for how work analysis is conducted. Specifically, the work analysis should be designed to capture the behavioral and multidimensional nature of job performance.

How Should Performance Dimensions Be Defined?

Traditional work analysis techniques such as task inventories (Brannick, Levine, & Morgeson, 2007) can be used to delineate the primary tasks that encompass a job. These tasks can then be grouped into dimensions of work activities, from which performance dimensions are derived. Conversely, worker-oriented methods of work analysis (e.g., the Position Analysis Questionnaire) can be used to identify the major work activities and behaviors that encompass a job. Performance dimensions can be created based on this information, but because most PA instruments are intended for local use, task-oriented methods such as task inventories are typically preferred.

It may, however, be worthwhile to expand beyond traditional work analysis techniques when defining performance. As mentioned earlier, contextual performance may also be of importance to an organization. Or, an organization may have an organizational-level competency model and require that this competency model drive all human resource practices. If this is the case, one should take this competency model into account when determining performance dimensions.

Incorporating contextual performance and organization-wide competencies into a PA instrument presents many challenges. Competencies and contextual performance are broad dimensions of performance that may not apply equally across jobs within an organization. Performance dimensions such as "accountability" and "cooperation" are difficult to operationalize and may lack face validity from the perspective of employees. However, organization-wide performance management systems and competency-based models require some common rating metrics that can be applied across jobs. One solution would be to create a PA system that acknowledges explicitly the distinctions between job-specific dimensions, general competencies, and contextual performance. For example, raters could be required to rate employees on job-specific tasks, organizationally relevant competencies, and contextual performance dimensions. The job-specific dimensions would focus on the specific duties and responsibilities outlined in the employee's job description. The competencies would be general dimensions applicable across jobs within an organization (e.g., oral communication, dependability, customer focus), most often part of an organization's competency model. Finally, the contextual dimensions would be factors that support success in all jobs (e.g., cooperative behavior).

An important point that we wish to stress is that there are tradeoffs involved between including contextual performance and competencies versus using a traditional work analysis approach when determining performance dimensions. Job-tailored PA instruments provide the specificity that increases the capability for giving detailed feedback and thus potentially improving employee performance. Also, as nicely illustrated by Shippmann et al. (2000), in their article discussing the differences between competency modeling and traditional work analysis, traditional work analysis focusing on tasks is more likely to withstand legal challenges. Nonetheless, it may be a good idea (and even a necessity) to take an existing organizational-level competency model into consideration. The competency model is often closely linked to organizational strategy and goals; thus, by including these competencies in the PA system, the PA system can be more closely aligned with the other human resource systems in helping the organization to achieve its goals. It may be possible to blend the competency models into a work analysis, given some creativity. However, as discussed in-depth in the Society for Industrial & Organizational Psychology's (2003) *Principles for the Validation and Use of Personnel Selection Procedures*, it is very important that one documents every step taken to identify performance and the rationale behind these steps in anticipation of potential lawsuits.

What Behaviors Should Be Rated?

Once the dimensions of performance have been identified by a work analysis, regardless of whether they are based on traditional methods or a blended approach of work analysis and competency modeling, the specific behaviors that define effective and ineffective performance for each dimension must be identified. This often involves the use of additional work analysis techniques. This is an important step because the method chosen influences how performance is operationalized. It determines standards of performance and determines what is seen as important and what is not. There are plenty of methods discussed elsewhere in this book, each with a slightly different focus and utility. For PA purposes, it is critical to have reliable and valid information regarding effective performance. That is, useful appraisal instruments need to distinguish between effective and ineffective workers (Latham & Wexley, 1994).

Many experts advocate using the critical incident technique (CIT; Brannick et al., 2007; Latham & Wexley, 1994) for developing PA instruments because it highlights the difference between effective and ineffective behavior. The CIT was developed by Flanagan (1954) and is a systematic method for collecting, analyzing content, and classifying observations of work behaviors. How to conduct a critical incidents analysis is described Chapter 6 of this volume, and thus we will not describe it in depth, other than to say that it is an excellent way of gathering examples of good and poor behaviors that may be useful in creating the appraisal instruments. As pointed out by Brannick et al. (2007), the CIT focuses on the context of the situation, what the person did in the situation, and what happened as a result, thereby focusing attention on behaviors under the control of the employee and on the specific job behaviors that result in good or poor performance. By focusing on behaviors that result in poor or good performance, the CIT helps to focus work analysis information by ignoring "typical or ordinary" behaviors that are not diagnostic of good or poor performance.

Figure 23.2 presents an example of a CIT applied to the job of field officer for a state government's alcohol and substance abuse agency. Experienced field officers were asked to list critical incidents that reflected three levels of proficiency: (a) highly effective behaviors, indicative of superior performance, (b) adequate or competent behavior that met minimal standards of acceptability but could still be improved, and (c) behaviors that did not reach minimal standards of acceptability and are an indication that training is needed.

The behaviors were collected, content analyzed, and rated for relevance by a separate group of subject matter experts. Finally, the behaviors were classified into job requirements. Figure 23.3 presents the final cataloging of behaviors for one aspect of the substance abuse field officer job.

Another advantage of CIT is that it increases the likelihood that PAs are accepted by employees. Research suggests that employee acceptance of PA ratings increases when there is agreement between raters and ratees regarding what constitutes good and poor performance (e.g., Murphy & Cleveland, 1995). By focusing specifically on explicit performance examples, CIT is a good method for identifying content-valid exemplars of good and poor performance.

Critical Incident Interview
Alcohol and Substance Abuse Field Officer

We would like your help in identifying the behaviors that distinguish effective from ineffective performance by field officers. By effective performance, we mean behavior that when it occurs or when you see it happen, you recognize it as superb and wish all officers would do the same thing under similar work circumstances. By ineffective performance, we mean behavior that when it occurs or when you see it happen, you recognize it as inadequate and would make you question the ability of the officer to do the job. We are asking for your help because you are very familiar with the goals and objectives of the field officer's job, you frequently observe field officers performing their jobs, and are able to tell the difference between good, average, and poor performance.

1. Please recall at least three job situations that you have experienced or observed that were handled in a highly effectively manner by a field officer. Describe each situation below and indicate what exactly the officer did that was effective.

---

2. Please recall at least three job situations that you have experienced or observed that were handled in an average manner by a field officer. That is, the officer performed in an adequate or competent manner that met minimal standards for acceptable performance, but could still be improved. Describe each situation below and indicate what exactly the officer did that was effective.

---

3. Please recall at least three job situations that you have experienced or observed that were handled in a poor manner. That is, the officer performed in a way that did not reach minimal standards of acceptability and are an indication that training is needed. Describe each situation below and indicate what exactly the officer did that was effective.

Figure 23.2   Critical incident interview form used for alcohol and substance abuse field officer job. (Adapted from Latham, G. P. and Wexley, K. N., *Increasing Productivity Through Performance Appraisal* (2nd ed.), Addison-Wesley, Reading, MA, 1994.)

(a)
- Analyzed all data available to develop a thorough knowledge base for a program.
- Made effective decision based on data available to her at the time.
- Used all resources available to gather information and data.
- Reviewed available data but did not "analyze."
- Provided results but did not explain data or provide documentation or suggest corrective actions.
- Unwilling or unable to analyze data.
- Unwilling to address sources of poor performance.
- Maintained active frequent oversight of program data reporting.
- Communicated with provider effectively to improve performance and address performance problems.
- Was not able to access or comprehend data in the agency database.
- Showed no interest in accessing performance data.
- Did not know how interpret data for improved performance.
- Was aware of available systems that monitor performance and is able to interpret data.
- Educated himself to become aware of technology improvements to analyze data.
- Was able to communicate and interpret data effectively.
- Failed to intervene in a timely manner; did not stay in touch with program until crisis occurred
- Was not aware of what system the agency has in place that monitors performance.

(b)
Work task: *Analyzing data and applying results to improve program performance.*

Highly effective:
- Develops action plan to improve performance based on thorough analysis of data
- Maintains active and frequent oversight of program data reporting.
- Explores and is aware of technology improvements to analyze data.

Average in effectiveness:
- Provides results but does not suggest corrective action.
- Reviews available data but does not analyze.
- Sporadically monitors program data reporting.

Highly ineffective:
- Unwilling or unable to analyze data.
- Is not aware of what system the agency has in place for monitoring performance.
- Does not know how to interpret data for improved performance.

Figure 23.3 Sample critical incidents generated by subject matter experts (a) and final categorized behaviors (b) for one performance dimension for the job of alcohol and substance abuse field officer.

The critical incidents analysis is not the only work analysis technique that could be used in the context of PA. Task inventories and functional job analysis (see Part 2 of this volume) may be helpful because both can provide information regarding the specific tasks that workers are expected to perform (Brannick et al., 2007). Other techniques may also be adapted to meet the needs of PA. It is critical that whatever method is used, it identifies the important job dimensions and provides behavioral examples.

It should be stressed that the work analysis should focus on behaviors and not worker characteristics (Brannick et al., 2007). Though understanding worker characteristics is important for personnel selection, for PA purposes, understanding how well someone has performed on the job is of importance. For example, when selecting an employee, one may be interested in whether this employee is conscientious. However, when appraising performance, one is interested in whether the employee arrived on time for work and meetings, completed assignments on time, and followed all the appropriate steps when completing tasks, that is, whether the employee in fact exhibits conscientious behaviors.

As Brannick et al. (2007), Murphy and Cleveland (1995), and many other PA experts advocate, it is vital that only behaviors under the control of the employee be appraised. An employee may not be able to control whether UPS delivers needed documents on time but can control whether he or she ordered goods and materials, taking into account that they may not be delivered on time. To improve performance, employees can only change their own behaviors; they have limited control over the behaviors of others. It is most useful, especially for developmental purposes, if the PA system focuses on behaviors under the control of the individual.

As specified in Kluger and DeNisi's (1996) feedback intervention theory, it is also more useful to give specific behavioral- and task-focused feedback rather than feedback directed at personal qualities (Kluger & DeNisi, 1996). For example, telling an employee that he or she needs to be at work on time more often and needs to be more careful to follow the proscribed steps when completing tasks will be more productive than telling an employee that he or she has low conscientiousness. Telling a person that he or she is deficient in conscientiousness or any other personal trait most likely will lead to a defensive reaction on the part of the employee and provides no clear guidance regarding how to improve performance. Giving employees specific behavioral feedback, on the other hand, provides them with clear guidelines for how to increase their performance. Thus, regardless of the work analysis method used, it should be a method that focuses on tasks, not personal or worker-oriented characteristics, and it should be a method that provides behavioral information regarding what are effective and ineffective behaviors.

WORK ANALYSIS AND THE SPECIFIC PROBLEMS ASSOCIATED WITH PERFORMANCE APPRAISAL

Even though basing the PA instrument on a sound work analysis can help to reduce problems in all four categories identified in Table 23.1, there are also specific decisions and design features associated with the four general categories—the system, the instrument, the rater, and the ratee—that should not be overlooked. Work analysis in general is helpful in reducing the specific problems in these four categories.

The Performance Appraisal Process

One of the major problems associated with PA is that often it is used for several purposes. It can be a mistake to try to use the same appraisal for multiple purposes because the goals of the appraisals may not be aligned. An appraisal used for developmental purposes may focus on a broader set of behaviors, use a different instrument, and rely on different rating sources (e.g., peers, subordinates) than an appraisal used for determining pay raises or promotion (Cleveland, Murphy, & Williams, 1989; Murphy & Cleveland, 1995).

For example, using the same PA for both administrative and feedback purposes puts the rater in a difficult position because he or she now has competing motivations when completing the ratings. The type of goal held by the rater, such as whether to motivate employees or decide whom to promote, influences the ratings given (Murphy, Cleveland, Skattebo & Kinney, 2004). The rater most likely will feel a push to provide higher ratings for administrative purposes to ensure that his or her subordinates are more likely to receive the pay raise, promotion, or bonus, and thus be happy. However, if the rater wants the performance of his or her subordinates to increase, accurate performance feedback is important to achieve this goal (Murphy & Cleveland, 1995). Furthermore, using appraisals for incompatible purposes may also be seen as less fair by both the raters and ratees.

Thus, collecting information regarding the eventual use of the PA system should be part of the work analysis, specifically the organizational analysis. Careful considerations should be given not to design a PA system for incompatible purposes. Clarifying the purposes of the appraisal may also help to establish a common frame of reference. It is important that everyone has a common conceptualization of both the purpose of the appraisal and the relevant behaviors for each performance dimensions, which will be discussed in more depth below in the context of training.

The Appraisal Instrument

The next category of problems in Table 23.1 is associated with the appraisal instrument. Many problems associated with the instrument can be avoided not only by basing the instrument on the work analysis to ensure job relevance, as discussed earlier, but also by carefully considering what type of instrument, or what rating format, is to be used to evaluate individuals. Many different appraisal instruments have been proposed since the 1960s, ranging from graphic scales to behaviorally anchored scales to relative percentile scales.

During this time, there has been a shift from trait-based to behavior-based instruments. Trait-based instruments assess personality variables such as conscientiousness, creativity, and achievement drive. These characteristics are defined in general and sometimes ambiguous terms and thus are particularly susceptible to rater biases.

Behaviorally based scales assess performance in terms of specific behaviors critical to the job rather than in terms of general traits. Importantly, they incorporate behavioral exemplars that reflect various degrees of performance effectiveness and are capable of providing specific and direct feedback to employees about their performance. Several different behavior-based instruments exist, each of which incorporates behavioral statements generated by work analysis techniques such as the CIT.

For example, behaviorally anchored rating scales, which result from an in-depth process involving many organizational members, use behavioral exemplars identified by the CIT as anchors of the rating scale. Subject matter experts are used to create scale values for examples of highly effective, average, and highly ineffective behaviors, and then these behaviors are placed as anchors on the scale according to their established scale value. Behavior observation scales require raters to evaluate the frequency with which employees perform specific behaviors. The CIT is used to generate behaviors that reflect varying degrees of performance effectiveness, and raters indicate the frequency of occurrence for each behavior on a numeric scale (e.g., ranging from 1 = never to 6 = always). An example of a behavior observation scale for the substance abuse field officer position is displayed in Figure 23.4.

1. Maintains active and frequent oversight of program data reporting					
1	2	3	4	5	6
Never	Seldom	Occasionally	Sometimes	Often	Always

2. Proposes corrective action within meaningful time frames					
1	2	3	4	5	6
Never	Seldom	Occasionally	Sometimes	Often	Always

3. Develops action plan to improve performance based on thorough analysis of data					
1	2	3	4	5	6
Never	Seldom	Occasionally	Sometimes	Often	Always

4. Explores and is aware of advances in techniques to analyze data					
1	2	3	4	5	6
Never	Seldom	Occasionally	Sometimes	Often	Always

5. Unwilling or unable to analyze data					
1	2	3	4	5	6
Never	Seldom	Occasionally	Sometimes	Often	Always

Figure 23.4 Example items from a behavioral observation scale for the job of alcohol and substance abuse field officer.

Another example of a behavioral-based format is the mixed standard scale. The mixed standard scale consists of sets of conceptually compatible behavior statements that describe high, medium, and low levels of performance within a particular job dimension. The judgment required of the rater is more straightforward than with other methods: the rater is simply asked to indicate how accurate the statement is of a ratee. An example of a mixed standard scale for the substance abuse field officer job is presented in Figure 23.5. For a more detailed description of how to construct these and other rating scales, see Latham and Wexley (1994) and Bernardin and Beatty (1984).

Several reviews of the rating instrument literature already exist (see Bernardin & Beatty, 1984; Landy & Farr, 1980; and Tziner & Kopelman, 2002), so we will not conduct a separate review but rather summarize their conclusions. First, no specific rating instrument is universally superior to all others. Human error can appear in any appraisal context regardless of the instrument, and raters can intentionally distort responses on any instrument. Second, behaviorally based instruments are superior to trait instruments with respect to fostering employee development and improvement. There seems to be growing consensus among researchers and practitioners that the appraisal method should be based on critical behaviors that distinguish effective from ineffective performance. As Newman, Kinney, and Farr (2004) stated, "the specific format of the final rating

Performance dimension: Analyzing data and applying results to improve program performance

1.	Reviews data but does not "analyze"	☐ Not at all accurate	☐ Somewhat accurate	☐ Highly accurate
2.	Maintains active/frequent oversight of program data reporting	☐ Not at all accurate	☐ Somewhat accurate	☐ Highly accurate
3.	Is not aware of what system the agency has in place for monitoring performance	☐ Not at all accurate	☐ Somewhat accurate	☐ Highly accurate
4.	Provides results but does not provide documentation or suggested corrective action	☐ Not at all accurate	☐ Somewhat accurate	☐ Highly accurate
5.	Sporadically monitors program data reporting	☐ Not at all accurate	☐ Somewhat accurate	☐ Highly accurate
6.	Does not know how to interpret data for imporved performance	☐ Not at all accurate	☐ Somewhat accurate	☐ Highly accurate
7.	Analyzes all data available to develop a thorough knowledge base for a program	☐ Not at all accurate	☐ Somewhat accurate	☐ Highly accurate
8.	Explores and is aware of technology imporvements to analyze data	☐ Not at all accurate	☐ Somewhat accurate	☐ Highly accurate
9.	Unwilling or unable to analyze data	☐ Not at all accurate	☐ Somewhat accurate	☐ Highly accurate

Figure 23.5 Mixed standard scale for the job of alcohol and substance abuse field officer.

instrument does not generally have a major impact on the quality of the ratings that are obtained, given that the behavioral dimensions and scale anchors are developed from a careful analysis of the job and its content" (p. 375).

One criticism of the appraisal instruments discussed so far is that they focus on the average performance of individuals and fail to take into account the considerable intraindividual variation that exists in performance (Fisher & Noble, 2004). That is, individuals' performance may vary considerably from day to day, and this variability may represent important input into the appraisal process. The performance distribution assessment method (Kane, 1986) attempts to capture within-person variability by asking raters to report the percentage of time that ratees display each of five levels of performance (ordered from very poor to very good). Woehr and Miller (1997) showed that a distributional rating instrument is a viable alternative. Approaches such as this may be particularly valuable for performance management programs that emphasize continuous improvement.

The Raters

Carefully considering who should provide the ratings and what kind of training the raters should receive can minimize many of the problems associated with raters listed in Table 23.1. The work analysis, especially the organizational analysis, is useful in helping to make these decisions. Several sources of ratings exist in organizations: supervisors, peers, subordinates, self, and customers (both internal and external).

Supervisory ratings are the most common source of performance information but are not without limitations. Supervisors often have limited opportunity, or fail to allot sufficient time, to observe employee behavior. As a result, the quality of ratings suffers, and ratees tend to view the appraisal process as unfair. Also, supervisors are knowledgeable about the job being rated but may not be familiar with the specific rating instrument.

Peers should have more access to performance information than supervisors because they interact with each other much more than do supervisors. The major drawback to using peers as raters is pressure stemming from conflicts of interests. Peers may perceive an advantage for themselves if they rate others poorly or may feel compelled to provide high ratings to peers with whom they interact on a daily basis. Thus, peer ratings are most useful when used for feedback or developmental purposes.

Subordinate ratings may also be effective when used as feedback for supervisors. Anonymous feedback from subordinates has been found to produce positive change in leaders' behaviors (e.g., Walker & Smither, 1999). However, subordinates may lack understanding or knowledge of all the requirements of a supervisor's job and thus subordinate ratings are often not useful for administrative purposes.

Workers have more information about themselves than do other rating sources, so one might argue that self-ratings should be of higher quality than supervisor, peer, or subordinate ratings. That may be true if ratings were kept to oneself (although the self-perception literature shows that lack of self-insight occurs quite often), but the research evidence suggests that self-ratings have limited utility in organizational settings. Self-ratings show little agreement with peer and supervisor ratings (e.g., Harris, & Schaubroeck, 1988; Conway & Huffcutt, 1997), and self-appraisals are poor predictors of future performance (Latham & Mann, 2006).

Thus, each source has its strengths and weakness and different sources may be preferred for different purposes. Peer and subordinate ratings may be appropriate for feedback and employee development purposes. Supervisor ratings are most appropriate for administrative purposes. As noted earlier, the organizational analysis should include collecting information regarding the purpose of the appraisal. When designing an appraisal system, one should ascertain that the type of raters to be used is aligned with the purposes of the appraisal system.

However, not only is it important to choose the type of raters best aligned with the purpose of the PA system, it is also important to train the raters. If raters do not know how to use the appraisal instrument correctly or are not motivated to do so, the validity and utility of PA is diminished. Considerable research in the 1980s and 1990s concentrated on identification and elimination of common rater errors. Table 23.4 summarizes the common rater errors and biases.

Several different training methods have been proposed to improve rater accuracy but have yielded inconsistent results. The type of rater training that tends to be most effective is frame-of-reference training according to Woehr and Huffcutt's (1994) meta-analysis. This is also the type of rater training most closely tied to the contents of the rating instrument, and thus the work analysis. Conceptually, frame-of-reference training can improve rating accuracy through two processes: (a) by helping raters understand what behaviors constitute specific levels of performance in specific dimensions, and (b) by establishing performance prototypes that allow raters to counteract normal information loss (i.e., forgetting) by categorizing ratee performance based on the performance prototypes presented during the training (e.g., Woehr & Huffcutt, 1994).

On a concrete level, frame-of-reference training consists of first allowing the raters to become familiar with the rating instrument, giving them an understanding of the dimensions, the types of behaviors that fall into each dimension, and which behaviors are associated with what rating level. All of this information should be derived from an analysis of work. Practice and feedback are also vital to frame-of-reference training. Raters often practice placing example written behaviors into performance dimensions and assigning ratings to the behaviors, followed by rating videotaped examples of job-related behavior. Raters receive feedback regarding how closely their ratings match the ratings of expert raters for both the written behaviors and the videotaped performances. Any discrepancies between the raters and the expert raters are discussed in depth.

The Woehr and Huffcutt (1994) meta-analysis also identified other types of successful training methods, such as behavioral observation training and rater error training. Both of these training methods are more generic and are not tied to a specific work analysis. In their original formulation of behavioral observation training, Thornton and Zorich (1980) distinguished between observation and judgment processes in PA, with behavioral observation training focusing on the observation process. Topics discussed in behavioral observation training include how to observe carefully, how to watch for specific behaviors, and how to avoid several systematic errors of observation. Rater error training includes a discussion of common rater errors, such as those shown in Table 23.4. This type of training provides an explanation of these types of rater error and a warning to not commit these errors.

As highlighted by the Woehr and Huffcutt (1994) meta-analysis, if conducted correctly, rater error training can increase rating accuracy; however, if conducted incorrectly, rater error training can decrease accuracy. What distinguished rater error training conducted correctly from that conducted incorrectly is whether the training forces raters to avoid any rating distributions that seem to show leniency, severity, middle tendency, etc. The issue is that a rater may have all excellent (or poor) employees, and thus a rating distribution that shows mostly high (or low) ratings may not represent rater error but may accurately represent employee performance. Thus, the correct type of

Table 23.4   Common Rating Errors

Rating Error	Definition
Leniency	Habitually assigning ratings that are too high or too positive
Severity	Habitually assigning ratings that are too low or too negative
Halo	Artificially high intercorrelations among dimension ratings; perceptions of positive or negative qualities in general or of one dimension of rating influence ratings on other dimensions
Central tendency	Habitually assigning ratings that cluster around a central or mid-point of a rating scale
Restricted range	Habitually assigning ratings that show low variance across dimensions

rater error training makes raters aware of the possible rater errors but does not force them to assign ratings that fall into a prescribed distribution.

The Ratees

The last category of problems listed in Table 23.1 revolves around the ratee. However, it is often difficult to disentangle methods that address problems associated with the ratee from those associated with the rater. This is the case for both ratee training and user reactions (both rater and ratee); thus, both of these issues will be discussed from the perspective of both the ratee and the rater.

Training for the employees who will be rated is often neglected. Explaining the appraisal procedures to the employees and discussing the benefits of feedback may enhance ratee buy-in and feedback acceptance. Raters may be more willing to provide accurate feedback to ratees if they know that the ratees buy in to the importance of the feedback and view it as valuable. Feedback is more likely to lead to performance improvements if it is accepted by the person receiving the feedback (e.g., Kluger & DeNisi, 1996).

It also may be a good idea to show employees the rating instrument that will be used to appraise their performance. If the dimensions are well defined, that is, based on a sound analysis of work, knowing what dimensions are on the rating instrument may allow employees to focus their efforts on the aspects of the job that have been identified as important. However, this may be a double-edged sword. If the instrument does not include important aspects of the job, the employee may ignore those aspects of the job not covered by the PA instrument and focus only on those aspects that will be rated.

Last, having a sound instrument and both raters and ratees who understand the PA system will not ensure that the system will be successful. Raters must be motivated to use the instrument to rate employees accurately, and ratees must accept and be motivated to act on feedback stemming from the appraisal. Thus, it is not surprising that rater and ratee reactions and motivation have received much research attention since 1990 (Levy & Williams, 2004). Since the late 1980s, we have learned much regarding both rater and ratee reactions to PA. Practices associated with PA such as frequency of evaluation, supervisor's knowledge of the ratee, opportunity for participation, previous performance ratings, opportunity to voice concerns, and due process influence the overall perceived fairness of PAs (e.g., Greenberg, 1986; Levy & Williams, 2004). The type of rating instrument also influences both ratee and rater perceptions, such as perceived accuracy, satisfaction, confidence, fairness, and ease of use (e.g., Hedge & Teachout, 2000; Kingstrom & Bass, 1981). Thus, a well designed rating instrument can help to promote positive reactions to the PA system.

LEGAL CONCERNS

As with any human resource function, avoiding lawsuits regarding PAs and, if lawsuits cannot be avoided, winning lawsuits are a concern for organizations. From what we know, it seems that the courts are more interested in whether the process of conducting a PA is fair than the outcome of the PA. Whether a sound analysis of work has been conducted and used to develop the PA system is part of the process that seems to interest the courts.

Werner and Bolino (1997) examined 295 U.S. Circuit Court decisions between 1980 and 1995 and found that whether a work analysis was used to develop the PA instrument correlated significantly (.40) with the court's decision. Other characteristics of the PA system that seem to play a significant role in the court's decisions include written instructions to raters, review of the appraisal results with employees, rater triangulation (i.e., rater agreement), rater training, and validation. It should be noted that validity was only mentioned in nine lawsuits, but the existence of validation evidence and judicial verdict were perfectly correlated, with the organization winning the case only if it had validity evidence. However, it should be noted that these findings are almost 15 years old.

Malos (1998) does an excellent job of discussing the many laws and legal principles that have implications for PA. Malos concludes that it is best from a legal standpoint that PA systems are "objective rather than subjective; should be job-related or based on job analysis; should be based on behaviors rather than traits; should be within the control of the ratee; should relate to specific functions, not global assessments; and should be communicated to the employee" (p. 80); Malos also provides some excellent procedural recommendations.

CONCLUSION

The analysis of work plays a foundational role in developing a sound appraisal system that is in line with all of an organization's human resource functions. As discussed, a sound work analysis can do much to mitigate the problems listed in Table 23.1 and employees' negative impressions of PA. However, even the most soundly developed PA system, one based on a well-done work analysis, cannot address all of the problems associated with PA. Unfortunately, employee perceptions of the PA system may be influenced as much by how it is used as by the quality of the system. Even a well-designed system could be used in a highly political or ineffective manner. Thus, for the PA system to be effective at achieving its goals, it is as important that the organization clearly communicates the value of the PA system to achieve buy-in from employees, both raters and ratees, as it is to develop a sound PA system based on a work analysis. However, organizations need to make organizational decisions (e.g., promotion) and employees need developmental feedback, regardless of whether there is a good PA system in place. Given these needs, it is better—for all the reasons mentioned in this chapter—to make organizational decisions and provide feedback based on a PA system that is founded on a well-done work analysis than to make decisions or provide feedback more haphazardly.

REFERENCES

Bernardin, H. J., & Beatty, R. W. (1984). *Performance appraisal: Assessing human behavior at work.* Boston, MA: Kent-Wadsworth.

Borman, W. C., & Motowidlo, S. J. (1997). Task performance and contextual performance: The meaning for personnel research. *Human Performance, 10,* 99–109.

Bowman, J. S. (1999). Performance appraisal: Verisimilitude trumps veracity. *Public Personnel Management, 28,* 557–576.

Brannick, M. T., Levine, E. L., & Morgeson, F. P. (2007). *Job and work analysis: Methods, research, and applications for human resource management.* Thousand Oaks, CA: Sage Publications.

Campbell, J. P. (1989). The definition and measurement of performance in the new age. In D. R. Ilgen & E. D. Pulakos (Eds.), *The changing nature of performance: Implications for staffing, motivation, and development* (pp. 399–429). San Francisco, CA: Jossey-Bass.

Cleveland, J. N., Murphy, K. R., & Williams, R. E. (1989). Multiple uses of performance appraisal: Prevalence and correlates. *Journal of Applied Psychology, 74,* 130–135.

Conway, J., & Huffcutt, A. I. (1997). Psychometric properties of multisource ratings: A meta-analysis of subordinate, supervisor, peer, and self-ratings. *Human Performance, 10,* 331–360.

DeNisi, A. S., & Pritchard, R. D. (2006). Performance appraisal, performance management and improving individual performance: A motivational framework. *Management and Organization Review, 2,* 253–277.

DeNisi, A. S., & Williams, K. J. (1988). Cognitive approaches to performance appraisal. *Research in Personnel and Human Resources Management, 6,* 109–155.

Fisher, C. D., & Noble, C. S. (2004). A within-person examination of correlates of performance and emotions while working. *Human Performance, 17,* 145–168.

Flanagan, J. C. (1954). The critical incident technique. *Psychological Bulletin, 51,* 327–358.

Greenberg, J. (1986). Determinants of perceived fairness of performance appraisal. *Journal of Applied Psychology, 71,* 340–342.

Goldstein, I. L., & Ford, K. J. (2002). *Training in organizations: Needs assessment, development, & evaluation* (4th ed.). Belmont, CA: Wadsworth.

Harris, M. M., & Schaubroeck, J. (1988). A meta-analysis of self-supervisor, self-peer, and peer-supervisor ratings. *Personnel Psychology, 41,* 43–62.

Hedge, J. W., & Teachout, M. S. (2000). Exploring the concept of acceptability as a criterion for evaluation performance measures. *Group and Organization Management, 25,* 22–44.

Kane, J. S. (1986). Performance distribution assessment. In R. A. Berk (Ed.), *Performance assessment: Methods and applications* (pp. 237–273). Baltimore, MD: John Hopkins University Press.

Kingstrom, P. O., & Bass, A. R. (1981). A critical analysis of studies comparing behaviorally anchored ratings scales (BARS) and other rating formats. *Personnel Psychology, 34,* 263–289.

Kluger, A. N., & DeNisi, A. S. (1996). The effects of feedback interventions on performance: Historical review, meta-analysis, and a preliminary feedback inventory. *Psychological Bulletin, 119,* 254–284.

Landy, F. J., & Farr, J. L. (1980). Performance rating. *Psychological Bulletin, 87,* 72–107.

Latham, G. P., Almost, J., Mann, S., & Moore, C. (2005). New developments in performance management. *Organizational Dynamics, 34,* 77–87.

Latham, G. P., & Mann, S. (2006). Advances in the science of performance appraisal: Implications for practice. *International Review of Industrial and Organizational Psychology, 21,* 295–337.

Latham, G. P., & Wexley, K. N. (1994). *Increasing productivity through performance appraisal* (2nd ed.). Reading, MA: Addison-Wesley.

Levy, P. E., & Williams, J. R. (2004). The social context of performance appraisal: A review and framework for the future. *Journal of Management, 30,* 881–905.

Longenecker, C. O., Sims, H. P., & Gioia, D. A. (1987). Behind the mask: The politics of employee appraisal. *The Academy of Management Executive, 1,* 183–193.

Malos, S. B. (1998). Current legal issues in performance appraisal. In J. W. Smither (Ed.), *Performance appraisal: State of the art in practice* (pp. 49–94). San Francisco, CA: Jossey-Bass.

Motowidlo, S. J., Borman, W. C., & Schmit, M. J. (1997). A theory of individual differences in task and contextual performance. *Human Performance, 10,* 71–83.

Motowidlo, S. J., & Schmit, M. J. (1999). Performance assessment in unique jobs. In D. R. Ilgen & E. D. Pulakos (Eds.), *The changing nature of performance: Implications for staffing, motivation, and development* (pp. 56–86). San Francisco, CA: Jossey-Bass.

Murphy, K. R., & Cleveland, J. N. (1995). *Understanding performance appraisal: Social, organizational, and goal-based perspectives.* Thousand Oaks, CA: Sage Publications.

Murphy, K. R., Cleveland, J. N., Skattebo, A. L., & Kinney, T. B. (2004). Raters who pursue different goals give different ratings. *Journal of Applied Psychology, 89,* 158–164.

Newman, D. A., Kinney, T., & Farr, J. L. (2004). Job performance ratings. In J. C. Thomas (Ed.), *Comprehensive handbook of psychological assessment* (Vol. 4, pp. 373–388). New York, NY: Wiley and Sons.

Organ, D. W. (1988). *Organizational citizenship behavior: The good soldier syndrome.* Lexington, MA: D.C. Heath.

Rotundo, M., & Sackett, P. R. (2002). The relative importance of task, citizenship, and counterproductive performance on global ratings of job performance: A policy capturing approach. *Journal of Applied Psychology, 87,* 66–80.

Shippmann, J. S., Ash, R. A., Battista, M., Carr, L., Eyde, L. D., Hesketh, B., … Sanchez, J. I. (2000). The practice of competency modeling. *Personnel Psychology, 53,* 703–739.

Society for Industrial and Organizational Psychology, Inc. (2003). *Principles for the validation and use of personnel selection procedures* (4th ed.). Bowling Green, OH: Author.

Thornton, G. C., & Zorich, S. (1980). Training to improve observer accuracy. *Journal of Applied Psychology, 65,* 351–354.

Tziner, A., & Kopelman, A. (2002). Is there a preferred performance rating format? A non-psychometric approach. *Applied Psychology: An International Review, 51,* 479–503.

Walker, A. G., & Smither, J. W. (1999). A five-year study of upward feedback: What managers do with their results matters. *Personnel Psychology, 52,* 393–423.

Werner, J. M., & Bolino, M. C. (1997). Explaining U.S. Courts of Appeals decisions involving performance appraisal: Accuracy, fairness, and validation. *Personnel Psychology, 50,* 1–25.

Whiting, S. W., Podsakoff, P. M., & Pierce, J. R. (2008). Effects of task performance, helping, voice, and organizational loyalty on performance appraisal ratings. *Journal of Applied Psychology, 90,* 125–139.

Woehr, D. J., & Huffcutt, A. I. (1994). Rater training for performance appraisal: A quantitative review. *Journal of Organizational and Occupational Psychology, 67,* 189–205.

Woehr, D. J., & Miller, M. M. (1997). Distributional ratings of performance: More evidence for a new rating format. *Journal of Management, 23,* 705–720.

24

Training Needs Assessment
Aligning Learning and Capability With Performance Requirements and Organizational Objectives

ERIC A. SURFACE

SWA Consulting Inc.

This chapter focuses on a critical aspect of the training process: training needs assessment (TNA). Although many terms are used to describe this process—such as training needs analysis, gap analysis, or front-end analysis—Rossett (1987) designated TNA as an umbrella term. Rossett's approach has been adopted in this chapter; however, *analysis* is used when *assessment* threatens to be overused. TNA is a systematic process that applies work analysis techniques and procedures to identify and specify training requirements that have been linked to deficiencies in individual, team, or organization performance to develop learning objectives to address the identified deficiencies. These evidence-based objectives in turn guide design, delivery, and evaluation of training to close the gaps in underlying knowledge, skills, abilities, or other characteristics (KSAOs) or competencies that are related to the identified performance deficiencies. Although there is no strong consensus on specific TNA procedures (Rossett, 1987) and there are many TNA resources offering slightly different approaches, most processes include the same basic steps, starting with an initiating or triggering event that requires a TNA to be considered and using work analysis techniques to determine training requirements.

Table 24.1 presents a customizable TNA process consisting of four phases, which will be discussed and elaborated upon in this chapter. The first two phases are about determining if there is an issue and whether or not it is related to training. Once an issue related to deficiencies in work-related KSAOs has been identified, the third phase is conducting the actual TNA, and the fourth is evaluating the results of the TNA. Although the implementation of the process is often adapted to the specific context by the needs analyst, the generic process is a good starting point when planning a TNA. As will be discussed, an abbreviated process can be used under many circumstances, such as when an organization has invested in a well-specified competency model and only wants to identify the training needs of individuals within the scope of that model (see the Empower TNA Within the Organization's Competency Model section later in this chapter). The objective of this chapter is to present the TNA process and some of the factors that can potentially impact it to help human resources and training professionals make decisions about implementing the TNA process in their organizations.

Table 24.1 Steps Within Each Phase of the Generic TNA Process

Phase	Step	Description
Needs identification	1	Identify an event, issue, or opportunity that may require a TNA.
	2	Clarify and evaluate the event, issue, or opportunity with the available information to verify a potential need exists (preliminary gap analysis).
	3	Determine the potential value to the organization associated with addressing the need identified by the event, issue, or opportunity and the potential risk of not addressing it.
	4	Decide if the identified need and its perceived value warrant committing resources to a TNA and seek stakeholder approval for next phase of the TNA, if required.
Needs specification	5	Create an initial definition of the need space identified in the need identification phase.
	6	Conduct a more thorough gap analysis refining the need space.
	7	Analyze the nature of the gap and related need within context to identify key drivers and potential solutions.
	8	Specify potential solutions within the constraints of the context, refining the need space.
	9	Evaluate potential solutions and determine if training is a viable component.
	10	If training is determined to be part of the solution, then seek TNA phase approval.
TNA	11	Design and plan a customized TNA process with stakeholders.
	12	Conduct the TNA implementation within the constraints of the context.
	13	Analyze the data and report the results at the appropriate level of detail for decisions.
	14	Make decisions and take action based on TNA results.
TNA evaluation	15	Monitor and evaluate action based on the TNA and determine if need was addressed.
	16	Recommend modifications or iterative improvements as appropriate.

POTENTIAL SCOPE OF TNA IMPACT

Organizations invest in training and development opportunities to enhance the capability of their workforces to achieve desired outcomes and objectives. The American Society of Training and Development estimates U.S. organizations spent $134.39[1] billion on employee learning and development in 2007 and $134.07 billion in 2008; companies in the American Society of Training and Development Benchmarking Forum spending an average of $1608.88 per employee in terms of direct training expenditures in 2007 and $1587.73 per employee in 2008 (Paradise, 2008; Paradise & Patel, 2009). Although the effectiveness of learning expenditures must be measured on a case-by-case basis throughout evaluation, the likelihood of learning activities achieving the desired results increases when training objectives, design, delivery, and evaluation are linked to work performance requirements and organizational objectives and outcomes.

TNA provides a mechanism for aligning organizational objectives and organizational capability through specifying focused, relevant training requirements and objectives that drive training design and measurement (Goldstein, 1993; Salas & Cannon-Bowers, 2001). In essence, TNA facilitates the transfer of appropriate learning to the work environment, increasing organizational capability to address performance requirements at the focal level(s) (individual, team, business unit, or organizational) and to achieve organizational objectives (Alvarez, Salas, & Garofano, 2004). The more alignment between learning, capability, performance, and context created throughout

---

[1] All values in U.S. dollars. Total learning and development expenditures by U.S. organizations include internal and external sources of learning and development. For example, in 2007, $134.39 billion was composed of $83.62 billion for internal sources and $50.77 billion for external sources of learning and development (Paradise, 2008).

the system, the more likely individual, team, and organizational outcomes will be achieved. For example, a recent study found a strong link between TNA comprehensiveness and organizational effectiveness (van Eerde, Tang, & Talbot, 2008). This ability to impact desired outcomes positively through alignment makes needs assessment a critical first step in the learning and performance process (Goldstein, 1993; Salas & Cannon-Bowers, 2001). Given the amount of money spent annually on training by organizations in the United States and throughout the world, the impact and return on investment for TNA is potentially great, making it a value-adding activity.

PREVALENCE OF TNA

Despite the importance of TNA for the effective alignment of training, transfer, and performance with organizational objectives and the potential return on investment of TNA activities, no comprehensive data on the frequency and thoroughness of needs assessment activities exist. Therefore, the state of current practice is unclear. According to the American Society of Training and Development's 2008 *State of the Industry Report*[2] (Paradise, 2008) and 2009 *State of the Industry Report* (Paradise & Patel, 2009), most American Society of Training and Development BEST award winning companies (40 winners in 2007; 39 in 2008) reported having defined processes for aligning learning initiatives and priorities with individual and organizational performance goals. Some sort of needs assessment or analysis was likely involved in the processes reported to the American Society of Training and Development by the BEST companies, such as the use of personal development plans, performance management systems, competency matrices, and tracking of employee learning history (Paradise & Patel, 2009). However, no statistics of actual TNA activities were reported, and no data were presented on the prevalence of these activities for the other companies who provided data to the American Society of Training and Development in 2007 (316 companies including BEST winners participated; Paradise, 2008) or in 2008 (301 companies including BEST winners participated; Paradise & Patel, 2009). Although whether these examples provide evidence of TNA activities in organizations could be debated, it is not useful because this is the best information about TNA that we have from practice.

The research literature does little to help clarify the situation. Although there are exceptions (e.g., Dierdorff & Surface, 2008; van Eerde et al., 2008), a dearth of TNA research, corresponding to the lack of data on TNA practice, exists (Aguinis & Kraiger, 2009; Kraiger, 2003; Salas & Cannon-Bowers, 2001). If a recent meta-analysis on training effectiveness (Arthur, Bennett, Edens, & Bell, 2003) is to be taken as representative, then the outlook is bleak for TNA in organizational practice. Arthur et al. reported that only 6% of studies (22 of 397) included in the meta-analysis reported a needs assessment had been conducted. It is unclear whether needs assessments were conducted and not reported or just not conducted. Therefore, given the current information on TNA, the actual prevalence of TNA activities in organizations is unknown but the available data suggest that the technique is underused given its potential value.

CHAPTER OVERVIEW

If (a) maximizing the effectiveness of learning expenditures by increasing the alignment between employee learning, capability, and performance of work activities is critical for achieving individual and organizational objectives and outcomes, and (b) TNA is the primary mechanism for creating and ensuring this alignment, then the current state of affairs is problematic. There seems to be a discrepancy between the desired state (maximizing the potential benefit of learning and

---

[2] The ASTD *State of the Industry Report* is based on the previous year's data (e.g., 2008 report is based on 2007 data).

creating value through the alignment of training and performance created by effective TNA) and the current state (the lack of evidence that TNA activities are being used by organizations). This gap between recommended best practice and actual practice related to TNA suggests there is a need to be addressed and presents an opportunity for this chapter.

The question to ask is, Is the lack of knowledge about TNA process and its implementation one of the causes underlying the identified gap? If it is, then this chapter can help prepare practitioners by providing knowledge and insights into conducting TNA implementations. Thus, the main objectives of the chapter are as follows:

- Provide and elaborate on a TNA process
- Review some of the issues/factors that impact the TNA process
- Identify and discuss trends in the workplace impacting TNA
- Provide ideas to improve the practice of the TNA process
- Make a case for the importance of engaging in the TNA process
- Provide a list of additional readings and resources

IS A TNA NECESSARY?

Many practitioners struggle with the decisions of whether or not to conduct a TNA, and if yes, how elaborate a TNA to conduct. There is no decision that is correct all the time. The necessity and scope of a TNA really does depend on the specifics of the situation. The standard recommendation is often to conduct a full TNA with a task and KSAO analysis every time. This is not practical or feasible for all situations, and there are many cases in which a full task and KSAO analysis is not necessary or the TNA process can be narrowed dramatically. TNA is not one-size-fits-all when it comes to the details of implementation.

Sometimes a TNA is not needed. For example, the issue may be clearly unrelated to training; or, the training requirements may be well-defined but evaluation data show the real issue is that training is poorly designed and/or delivered, and this is why it fails to achieve the identified training objectives (i.e., the *training* needs to be redeveloped, not the learning objectives). Other times a narrow or abbreviated TNA is appropriate (see Gupta, 2005, for an example of a "mini needs assessment" process.). For example, to comply with federal regulation, an organization with well-defined training requirements and an effective training program may periodically identify individuals who need refresher training through individual-focused TNA (i.e., person analysis; McGehee & Thayer, 1961). Using the TNA process to select the best solution for a specific organization and its objectives should be the focus, not one particular approach. TNA can vary in terms of purpose, focus, scope, depth, sources of information, time, technology, cost, and output. Some of these are specified or constrained from the outset and others vary. The effective needs analyst creates a TNA that works within his or her situational constraints using the process in Table 24.1 as a guide.

Initiating or Triggering Events

Typically, the TNA process is initiated when a deficiency is suspected and communicated, resulting in further analysis to determine if a need exists. A need is basically a gap between what is desired and what is currently available. This actual or perceived deficiency is often communicated as a red flag from some other source of information, such as an employee survey, or triggered by an event, such as the implementation of a new manufacturing process. Table 24.2 presents sources or events that can indicate the need for a TNA. This list should not be viewed as exhaustive, nor should all the sources of information or events be considered to apply to all organizational contexts. Although a TNA may not be required every time, these sources of information or events offer an excellent

Table 24.2 Sources and Events That Can Indicate the Need to Initiate the TNA Process

1. Training and program evaluation findings
2. Input from supervisors, managers, and leaders
3. Input from personnel, teams, or work groups
4. Input from customers, clients, and partners
5. Results from organizational surveys and studies
6. Results from individual development planning, 360° feedback, and performance appraisal/management systems
7. New training requirements
8. Work analysis data (collected for other purposes)
9. Institutional process for determining training requirements
10. Changes in business strategy, doctrine, or mission
11. Changes in law or regulation
12. Changes in organizational structure or operating environment
13. Business or mission results
14. Implementation of new technology, systems, equipment, processes, or procedures
15. Organizational metrics such as attrition, error rates, accidents, customer complaints, etc.

Content adapted and supplemented to include business context from the "Battle Command Training Program" (TRADOC publication no. 350-70) by the U.S. Army Training and Doctrine Command (1999) (http://www.tradoc.army.mil/tpubs/regs/r350-70/index.html). Information is not presented in any order of importance and is not an exhaustive list.

starting point for engaging the process in Table 24.1 and should trigger an organization to decide whether or not to initiate a TNA intervention.

For example, an organizational survey identified dissatisfaction with supervision as an issue. Is this an opportunity for a TNA? Is there a gap between current and desired states? Are there implications of this dissatisfaction? What if the same survey indicates that employees who are dissatisfied with supervision are significantly more likely to indicate intentions to leave the organization? Is turnover a concern for your organization? What is the value to the organization of addressing the issue versus the risk of not addressing it? Does this provide sufficient justification to continue the TNA process? This perceived supervision issue may or may not be related to a training issue (e.g., lack of knowledge or skill). It may or may not be important to the organization. The organization may or may not implement a TNA. The point is that engaging in the TNA process can help the organization decide whether or not to move forward with the process and how to move forward. The questions in the above example roughly correspond to the needs identification phase of the TNA process in Table 24.1.

Some of the events presented in Table 24.2 require training and, therefore, the TNA process should be initiated. In these cases, the first two phases in Table 24.1 are largely decided for the organization. However, the resulting TNA implementations may vary greatly. For example, changes to public law or regulations require training to communicate the changes and to ensure compliance behaviors. The audience, the gap, and the KSAOs to close the gap are identified by the regulatory agency's actions; the mandated training and/or the specific modifications or additions to the law or regulation will drive training content, standards, and participants. Because the *who* and *what* of the training are identified, the TNA needs to focus on specifying *what* is to be trained in sufficient detail so the best *how* can be devised for the *who* within the organization. This situation requires the specification of learning objectives from the regulation content and of learning methods and techniques for the potential trainees within the organization to inform the training design.

Another example is purchasing new manufacturing equipment. The equipment vendor may provide training for operating the new equipment, but a narrow TNA may be required because the vendor's training likely does not cover how the equipment fits into your company's specific manufacturing process (unless your company is replacing the entire process) or may not take into account the unique aspects of your company's physical work environment. Of course, some events, such as changing core business strategy, can have such a pervasive impact on all aspects of the organization that a needs assessment is definitely required. Depending on the extent of the change, the resulting needs assessment may uncover many opportunities for learning as well as other interventions, such as changes to compensation, to ensure successful execution of the new strategy.

Judgment Is Required

A TNA is not always necessary, nor are all TNA implementations the same. Judgment is required on the part of the organization's learning and performance experts throughout the process. It is always up to the organization to decide on engaging the process, regardless of the trigger event, issue, or opportunity. Table 24.2 provides some sources of information and events that can indicate the need for a TNA. The TNA process in Table 24.1 offers the steps (1–4) in the needs identification phase to determine the need for a TNA implementation based on the information or events such as the ones in Table 24.2. Steps (5–10) in the needs specification phase suggest a method for determining whether or not the identified need can be addressed by training. Some events trigger an unquestioned need for training (e.g., changes in federal regulation) and, therefore, address many of the steps in the first two phases of the TNA process. However, in many circumstances, there is no unquestioned requirement, and these decisions are up to the organization and the judgment of its experts. Once the decision is made to move forward, the practitioner should design the most effective TNA implementation for his or her situation. However, many decisions must be made along the way. The next section elaborates on the process and the questions that should be asked and answered.

TNA PROCESS: ASKING AND ANSWERING QUESTIONS

Table 24.1 presents a customizable TNA process to guide specific needs assessment interventions. Though one might question whether needs assessment is an intervention, it is described as such here because implementing one can have impact beyond its information collecting function. Collecting TNA data in an organization signals the importance of an issue for the organization and its leadership and focuses attention on the issue. The impact can be as simple as creating awareness that previously did not exist. My firm recently conducted a domain-focused needs assessment within an organization. It was sponsored by the element of the organization tasked with oversight and resourcing for this specific performance domain. One of the questions asked of the respondents was whether they were aware of this element and its services. Sixty-two percent of leaders in the organization who responded to the survey had not heard of the element. They have now. What if these newly informed leaders start requesting resources and support, resulting in a spike in requests that the sponsor is not prepared to deal with all at once? Just asking the question could potentially have an impact on resources and workload. Therefore, the needs assessment process should be entered into, planned, and executed with care and the potential consequences understood. Following the TNA process to guide decisions limits risk and helps to ensure success.

The TNA process is really about asking and answering appropriate questions at each phase and step of the process to achieve the needs assessment objectives (Arthur et al., 2003). This chapter conceptualizes the TNA process in the four phases depicted in Table 24.1. The first phase, the needs identification phase, was introduced in the previous section and focuses on determining whether or not a TNA should be conducted. The first phase relies heavily on events or available sources of information (see Table 24.2) to indicate a TNA is needed and provides a gate to implementation of the second phase, the needs specification phase. The needs identification phase includes a preliminary gap analysis—an assessment of the difference between current and desired states—to determine if a gap and need exists. This preliminary analysis helps an organization to assess if a TNA is needed with less up-front investment. If no need is found, the resources of conducting a full gap analysis are saved.

Once a need is identified and the decision is made to move forward, the second phase focuses on defining and specifying the need space and determining whether or not learning can address the need. The *need space* refers to the initiating or triggering event (the initiator); the identified gap between current and desired states; and the related need, its drivers, its context, and its potential solutions. Basically, understanding the need space requires taking a systems perspective on the triggering event, issue, or opportunity within the organization to determine the best solution(s) to the identified need. Some authors, such as Franklin (2005), would call the combination of the needs identification phase and needs specification phase by the term front-end analysis, consisting of gap and root cause analyses.

If the needs specification phase determines that training is at least a partial solution, then the training needs assessment phase can be designed and implemented. This third phase corresponds to what might be thought of as the traditional TNA process, which includes organizational, work (task and KSAO), and person levels of analysis. It should be noted that many authors would incorporate the first and second phases into the organizational level of TNA. The advantage of the multiphase structure presented here is it allows stakeholders to focus on the critical decisions at the appropriate time and limits the impulse to delve directly into a full task and KSAO analysis. The fourth and final phase, the TNA evaluation phase, focuses on assessing the impact of the decisions that resulted from the TNA process on the identified need—i.e., did the training or other interventions from the TNA close the identified KSAO gap? It offers an opportunity for TNA process improvement and indicates whether the need still exists to be addressed. The remainder of this section elaborates on the four phases and associated steps of the TNA process (Table 24.1) and provides examples of questions that should be asked and answered (Table 24.3).

Needs Identification Phase

As described in the Initiating or Triggering Events section, once an initiating event, issue, or opportunity is identified (Table 24.1, Step 1), the initial phase of the TNA process has begun. Table 24.2 presents a list of example initiating events, issues, and opportunities (or initiators). The need analyst must determine whether or not the initiator represents an underlying need (Table 24.1, Step 2). This is done by conducting a preliminary gap analysis to determine if there is sufficient evidence of a need to proceed. The gap and associated need may not be completely defined or validated by this preliminary analysis, or, if the gap and associated need are straightforward, no additional gap analysis beyond the preliminary may be needed in the second phase. Regardless, there should be sufficient evidence from the initiator to suggest whether a gap does exist and enough information to assess the value of closing the gap to the organization.

Is the initiator clearly described and understood? What leads stakeholders to believe a need exists? What evidence (broadly defined) is available for the initiator? What is the source and quality of this evidence? Is additional evidence from other sources easily available? What are the current and desired states for the initiator? Is there a potential need (or gap between the current and desired states) for this initiator? In Step 2, the initiating event, issue, or opportunity is clarified and evaluated to determine if the process moves forward to determine the value of the potential need to the organization (Table 24.1, Step 3).

Step 2 revolves around determining if the event, issue, or opportunity warrants pursuit. If the organization decides the initiator does not provide sufficient evidence of an underlying need, then the process stops at Step 2. In addition, the initiator may be found to be flawed (i.e., no evidence or

Table 24.3   Examples of Questions Throughout the TNA Process

Phase	Step	Example Questions
Needs identification	1	What is the initiating event, issue, or opportunity? Is the initiator clearly described?
	2	What evidence is available for the initiator? What is the source and quality of the evidence? What are the current and desired states for this initiator? Is there a potential need for this initiator?
	3	Is addressing the potential need (closing the gap) of value to the organization? What are the risks of not investigating the potential need? What are the potential costs and benefits of pursuing or not pursuing the TNA process associated with this need? Is the value sufficient to recommend continuing the TNA?
	4	Is the recommendation approved? Do we move to the needs specification phase?
Needs specification	5	What is the definition of the need space? Do we have enough detail on the current and desired states? Is a more thorough gap analysis needed?
	6	What information about the need space is lacking? What sources of information are available to complete the gap analysis? What metrics and standards will be used to calculate the gap?
	7	Why does the gap exist? What are the potential drivers or root causes of the gap? What contextual and systemic factors are impacting the gap? What potential solutions are suggested?
	8	What are the detailed descriptions of the potential solutions? How are the potential solutions linked to the gap? What is their projected impact on the gap and associated need?
	9	Which solutions are feasible? Which solutions will have the desired impact on the gap? What option(s) is/are the most viable? Is training a viable component of the solution? Is a TNA needed?
	10	Is the TNA approved? If no training solution is required, have the other solutions been presented and approved or forwarded to the appropriate stakeholders?
TNA	11	What are the factors to consider in designing this TNA? What are the most appropriate approaches and techniques to accomplish the TNA in this context? Is a full task and KSAO analysis required?
	12	What are the key success factors for executing the planned TNA? Has the TNA been marketed? Are senior leaders communicating support? Is the participation rate sufficient? Is more marketing required?
	13	How should the data be analyzed? What is the appropriate level for presenting the results? What is the product of the TNA? What are the recommendations for training selection or design and delivery?
	14	What decisions about the training solution are approved and implemented? How are they to be evaluated?

Table 24.3   Examples of Questions Throughout the TNA Process (Continued)

Phase	Step	Description
TNA evaluation	15	Did the training or learning intervention result in the development of needed KSAOs? Did the KSAOs translate into capability and performance that closed the identified gap and addressed the need?
	16	What lessons learned can be applied to future TNAs or the iterative cycles of this TNA?

KSAO = knowledge, skills, abilities, and other characteristic. Not an exhaustive list of questions.

invalid evidence that a gap exists). For example, a division manager calls saying that the annual climate survey indicates there is a supervision problem and that all first-line supervisors need training. This initiates the first and second steps of this phase of the TNA process. Upon completing a preliminary gap analysis in Step 2, it is discovered that the manager had seized on a few very vivid, negative comments from the employee survey, and otherwise the survey data indicate no issue with supervision. A quick review of relevant available data—such as employee complaints against supervisors, employee absenteeism, employee transfers, accidents, error rates in production, supervisor performance data, and disciplinary actions against supervisors—suggests no major issues with first-line supervisors exist. Therefore, the process should stop at Step 2. In this situation, the needs analyst indicates she has done due diligence and builds a solid case with the evidence to support the decision not to move forward with the request for training. Dismissing the initiator in Step 1 or 2 and *not* engaging in Step 2 or 3 is not advisable unless the available evidence provides a compelling case, as in the example above, or the organization is in extreme circumstances with no resources to pursue TNA. However, if sufficient evidence of a potential need exists, the process should continue to Step 3.

Step 3 is all about determining if the potential need has enough value to recommend continuing the TNA to the needs specification phase. Is addressing the potential need (closing the gap) of value to the organization? If so, how much value? What are the risks of not continuing the process? If this need exists and is not addressed, what is the potential cost to the organization? What is the likely cost of the TNA in the second phase? Is the value sufficient to recommend continuing the TNA? Based on the best available information, a value proposition must be created for continuing the process: What are the potential costs and benefits of pursuing or not pursuing the TNA process for this need? In addition, the value proposition depends on factors external to the need itself, such as resource constraints and competing priorities.

During Step 3, the need analyst must ask questions about the value of the potential need; competing priorities; available resources such as money, expertise, and time; and other constraints and issues; the answers to these questions should be incorporated into the value analysis process to generate the recommendation. The goal of Step 3 is to formulate a defensible and persuasive argument for continuing the process or not, yielding a recommendation either way. Then, the argument and recommendation must be presented and a decision made (Table 24.1, Step 4). If the need analyst is also the decision maker, then Steps 3 and 4 are combined. A defensible argument based on the available evidence is still needed to inform and justify the decision. If other stakeholders will make the decision and not the need analyst, then structuring the TNA pitch is important.

Making the case and decision for initiating events is often relatively straightforward. For example, if there is a new regulation, manufacturing process, or tool that will impact how work is done and standardized training is required, then no questions need to be answered. Many events, such as regulatory changes, dictate the first phase of the TNA process—there is a trigger, the underlying need exists, and there are consequences and/or value to the organization. The second phase of the TNA process may be dictated as well. The case for and decision about an issue or opportunity is not always as clear cut. Focusing on uncovering as much relevant, easily accessible evidence to inform the decision is a key success factor for dealing with initiating issues and opportunities. Ask lots of questions. The questions and examples presented above and in the previous Initiating or Triggering Events section can serve as a basic guide to this stage of the process. Table 24.3 provides sample questions across all four phases for the steps in the TNA process in one convenient location.

Needs Specification Phase

Once a need is determined to exist and to be of sufficient value to address, the organization can decide to continue the TNA process to the needs specification phase. The purpose of this phase is to fully understand the need space—the initiating event, the identified gap between current and desired states, and the related need, its drivers, its context, and its potential solutions—and to determine and evaluate potential solutions to address the need. This phase culminates in the determination of whether or not training or some other learning intervention, such as mentoring, is part of the solution to close the gap and address the need. If the need is related to a deficiency in KSAOs, then a TNA must be conducted to determine the training requirements and objectives to inform successful selection or design of training content and delivery of that content. If no KSAO deficiency is involved, then a TNA need not be conducted and the other nontraining solutions should be planned and implemented as appropriate.

The first step in this phase is creating an initial definition of the need space identified by the triggering event, issue, or opportunity (Table 24.1, Step 5). Using all available evidence from the preliminary gap analysis and the value analysis conducted in the needs identification phase, this definition is created to inform the specification process. What is the current definition of the need space? What information is known and unknown about the gap and need? Do we have thorough enough detail about the current and desired states? Use the current definition and what it is lacking to develop the exact process to assess and specify the need space: What information is missing? This process can be customized to the specific case. For example, as mentioned in the previous section, some initiators and gaps are very straightforward and no additional gap analysis is required beyond the preliminary one, such as in the case of implementing a new work process. The gap is between the current state—knowledge, comprehension, and application of the current process, if one exists, and no knowledge, comprehension, and application of the new one—and the desired state—knowledge, comprehension, and application of the new process. In this situation, a more thorough gap analysis is not needed (Table 24.1, Step 6), and the answers to questions in the other steps in the needs specification phase are straightforward because the difference between the current and desired states revolves around KSAO deficiencies that must be addressed, which requires a TNA.

When required, the next step in the needs specification phase is conducting a more thorough gap analysis to refine the need space (Table 24.1, Step 6). This is often combined with the following step of analyzing the nature of the gap and associated need to identify key drivers (also called root causes; Franklin, 2005) and potential solutions (Table 24.1, Step 7). Defining the current and desired states is fairly straightforward and requires talking to stakeholders and seeking out all sources of information associated with the gap, such as policy documents, individual performance data, individual training histories, sales numbers, absenteeism, compensation data, and organizational survey data. It may involve original data collection in some cases, such as a survey of incumbents and/or supervisors. Quantitative and qualitative data are both useful but the source should always be considered. See the Further Reading section for readings that discuss needs assessment data, such as Altschuld (2010).

The idea is to define the current and desired states with sufficient detail to calculate the gap and analyze why the gap exists and, therefore, generate a list of potential solutions. Two components of the need space, the appropriate metrics and associated standards, are needed for this gap calculation and the linkage of the need (gap) to business objectives and goals. For example, if manufacturing team leaders are believed to be ineffective and are preventing their teams from meeting their production goals, then metrics and standards that allow a comparison between current and desired states are necessary. What metrics would indicate the quality of team leaders? What metrics would indicate the team leaders' impact on production? What are the standards on these metrics for effective and ineffective team leaders (which will be important for person analysis)? What data are readily available? For example, production numbers are readily available. How do these differ across teams? How much of a difference can be related to team leaders? What level indicates an effective team leader and under what conditions? These questions identify the types of metrics and evidence required for the gap analysis and how we analyze and evaluate them. In the case above, the data might be sufficient for conducting a multilevel statistical analysis to determine if team leaders have a significant impact on team production across teams. If feasible, this would provide a metric and a standard for describing and discussing the gap. Team leader characteristics could be included in the model, which could indicate potential drives or causes of the gap.

There are many organizational systems that can impact the gap analysis and that can be potential drivers, or root causes, of the gap. A deficiency in worker capabilities—KSAOs requiring training—is just one potential key driver of the gap. Steps 6 and 7 require an in-depth analysis of the gap and its context with the organizational system. Organizations are collections of interacting systems and subsystems that can impact individuals, teams, and their behavior. Although it is beyond the scope of this chapter, systemic and contextual factors can be described by any number of models or categories. For example, recommended by Franklin (2005), Gilbert (1978) provides six categories that cover the majority of contextual factors: information and feedback, environment and resources, consequences and incentives, motivation and expectations, knowledge and skills, and capability. Figure 24.1 presents a fairly straightforward model of TNA and how it fits in

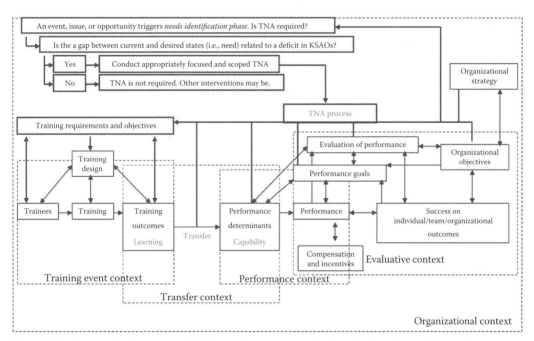

Figure 24.1   Conceptual and process model of how needs assessment aligns learning, transfer, capability, performance, and outcomes with an organization's context. Boxes with broken lines represent the influence of numerous contextual factors that might impact an organization or an organizational process. The training needs assessment process is represented by the solid lines and boxes. Some relationships have been excluded to simplify the model.

Table 24.4   Environmental Factors to Consider When Analyzing the Need Space and Specifying Solutions

1.	Unclear expectations
2.	Poor communications
3.	Unclear policies
4.	Unclear or inconsistent performance standards
5.	Poor feedback or performance management
6.	Lack of resources
7.	Lack of opportunity to perform
8.	Insufficient time to perform
9.	Lack of peer support
10.	Lack of supervisor or management support
11.	Disruptive work environment
12.	Insufficient or inaccessible information or data
13.	Unsupportive or ineffective policies, processes, and procedures
14.	Inadequate equipment, tools, or technology
15.	Counterproductive consequences for performance
16.	Lack of career prospects or career development
17.	Lack of on-the-job performance support
18.	Frequent work stoppages or disruptions due to external factors
19.	Inadequate job requirements or selection procedures
20.	Insufficient or ineffective compensation systems or incentives

Adapted from Stolovitch, H. D. and Keeps, E. J., in *American Society for Training & Development Handbook for Workplace Learning Professionals*, American Society for Training & Development, Alexandria, VA, 2008.

the organizational system, and Table 24.4 presents some environmental factors that might inhibit successful interventions (Stolovitch & Keeps, 2008). Although a discussion of the model and environmental factors are beyond the scope of this chapter, models and frameworks should guide your analysis. For example, Figure 24.1 suggests alternative drivers and solutions to gaps, such as compensation and performance management, which should be investigated as part of the analysis. The point is to consider all relevant systemic and contextual factors that might impact the gap. This will help with generating a list of potential solutions as the last component of the step and evaluating them in the next step.

Once the analysis in Step 7 is complete, all potentially viable solutions should be specified in sufficient detail to allow for evaluation, planning, and implementation if accepted (Table 24.1, Step 8). The key components of the specification are (a) the detailed description of the solution, (b) the linkage between the solution and the gap, and (c) the projected impact of implementing the solution on the gap and the initiating event, issue, or opportunity. These specifications should be written in a clear and consistent way across all solutions being considered. If only one solution emerges, the task is straightforward. Because a single need space can involve different criteria (e.g., job performance), standards across those criteria and different business objectives, it is important that the potential solutions are specified using the same or similar metrics to allow for effective evaluation of options in Step 9. At this point, training may or may not be a viable solution. If the need is not related to a deficiency in KSAOs, then training would not be a solution for specification.

From the TNA perspective, the evaluation of potential solutions (Table 24.1, Step 9) serves two purposes: evaluating all the potential solutions for impact and feasibility and determining whether or not training is one of the viable solutions. What are the evaluation criteria for the potential solutions? As part of the initial planning for the needs specification phase, these evaluation criteria should be determined by the organization. Is the cost of implementation an important feasibility criterion for your organization? For training, one important feasibility criterion is transfer climate. Will the application of learned KSAOs be supported and facilitated in the work environment? If the work or organizational environment will not support training, it is not a viable solution for the need. Other solutions might be more feasible and, therefore, more effective.

Another legitimate concern is the impact on closing the gap and addressing the need. Will the solution fully or partially address the need? What standard of impact is acceptable for a solution? For example, your company is starting a new product line and needs workers with a specific skill set. One potential solution would be to train workers from other product lines to work on the new line. Is this an effective solution? It would depend on whether the organization was scaling back the other lines and had sufficient workers who could learn the new KSAOs to the cover the need. What if it would take three years to staff the new line with this solution? Is this a complete or partial solution? It depends on the evaluation criteria and standard of impact for closing the gap. The evaluation and determination of whether training is a viable part of the solution is up to each needs analyst. The point is to have a set of criteria established a priori to guide the decision, including standards for evaluating the impact of the solution on the gap.

If training is determined to be part or all of the solution to the identified need, then seek approval from the appropriate stakeholders to start the training needs assessment phase (Table 24.1, Step 10). At this point, it might be necessary to make the case for the TNA, so one must be prepared to present the case developed in the first and second phases of the process. The scale of TNA interventions can vary from simple (a very narrow focus) to complex (all jobs and units in a multinational corporation), with obvious resource implications. Usually, the planning should take place with the stakeholders after initial approval is provided. For the more complex (costly) TNA interventions, doing some initial planning and cost analysis prior to seeking approval can help win support for the initiative by defining required resource commitments and the expected return for those commitments as well as the timeline. Again, the process can be adapted to each situation.

Training Needs Assessment Phase

At this point, there is a verified need that has a deficiency in knowledge and/or skill as its root cause, requiring training as at least a partial solution. TNA is necessary to determine *what* needs to be trained, *how* it needs to be trained, and *who* needs to be trained to best close the gap. The data gathered during the training needs assessment phase will inform training content, design, delivery, and evaluation. These data are crafted into specific learning objectives that are used to select or to develop training interventions. The success of the training in addressing the need—closing the identified knowledge and/or skill gap—rests on the effectiveness of the TNA, the translation of TNA data into learning objectives, and the training design. TNA and the subsequent specification of learning objectives create alignment throughout the entire system. An effective TNA ensures linkage and alignment between needed knowledge and skill capabilities, performance, outcomes, and business objectives. If the TNA is poorly executed and the learning objectives are not properly specified, then the training, even if well designed, will not address the need. The first two phases of the process in Table 24.1 are about ensuring there is a verifiable need related to knowledge and/or skill deficiencies that can be feasibly addressed with a training intervention. This phase is about analyzing the need space and identifying and specifying the knowledge and/or skill in sufficient detail to create effective training.

Needs analysts can arrive at this point through different paths. In some cases, an event in Step 1, such as a change in government regulation, dictates training. A triggering event, issue, or opportunity initiates a rigorous application of the needs identification phase and then the needs specification phase, resulting in training being identified as a viable solution. An abbreviated needs assessment is conducted within an established competency model to identify KSAOs to be trained and individuals who need to be trained, and the process starts here. A required, well-specified training program exists and the organization periodically conducts person analysis to determine who needs refresher training. A strategic needs assessment identifies a future need for knowledge and skills that does not currently exist. Regardless of how the needs analyst finds herself here, the training needs assessment phase is all about collecting the most appropriate data from the most appropriate people using the most appropriate techniques within the constraints of the organization. As with the other phases, this phase is all about asking and answering questions. What knowledge and skills need to be trained? How are these best trained? Who needs to be trained? What factors need to be considered to optimize transfer? Is full task and KSAO analysis required? What is the appropriate level of data to collect? Who should be asked to participate? What is the best data collection technique? How should the data be analyzed? Who will be responsible for developing learning objectives from the data? Who will design and deliver the training?

Although these questions can seem overwhelming, there are many books and articles that address TNA planning, data collection and analysis, and reporting. Some of these are listed in the Further Reading section at the end of the chapter. There are chapters in Parts II and III, this volume, that cover specific work analysis methods and systems that can be used to collect appropriate task and KSAO data. A detailed presentation of the process, techniques, and issues is beyond the scope of this chapter. This is the beginning of the development process for a novice needs analyst. The approach adopted here is to provide a macrolevel process and to review the traditional TNA framework—organizational, task and KSAO, and person analyses (Goldstein, 1993)—to help needs analysts understand the holistic nature of TNA and become effective consumers of the more detailed process information in the other resources.

The macrolevel process is very straightforward. The TNA must be designed and the implementation planned (Table 24.1, Step 11). For any TNA process to be effective, it must (a) consider the objective and need space; (b) involve stakeholders in planning; (c) address the constraints of the situation; (d) address the correct questions to yield the required data; (e) use appropriate techniques for data collection and analysis; (f) ask the correct individuals to participate; (g) have sufficient resources for implementation; and (h) have support from leaders at all levels. Once the process is designed and the implementation planned, the TNA is conducted within the constraints of the context (Table 24.1, Step 12). Depending on the objectives, the data collection could focus on tasks and KSAOs, only knowledge and/or skill, identifying organizational constraints to the training, identifying individuals who require training, or all of the above. Regardless, the execution never goes as smoothly as one would hope. The key is to monitor the implementation and make adjustments.

Once the collection is complete, the data must be processed, verified, and analyzed to produce the promised deliverables (Table 24.1, Step 13). The data analysis should be specified in the design (Step 11). It should be focused on achieving the objectives and deliverables of the TNA. Considering the data and analysis to achieve objectives must be done a priori. It is too late once data have been collected from an incorrect level of specificity for the required analysis, for example. The deliverables should be spelled out in Step 11 and agreed upon by all stakeholders. This will inform the data collected and how it is analyzed and reported. Is the deliverable the task and KSAO data only? Is it learning objectives? Is it recommendations about training design features and transfer strategies? Having a clear end point during planning is a key success factor.

Finally, there may be any number of decisions to be made and actions taken based on the TNA results and deliverables (Table 24.1, Step 14). Will the training be purchased off the shelf or custom built? Who will design and develop the training if it is to be custom built? Who will deliver the training? When will the training be conducted? Will training be required? For whom will it be required? What actions need to be taken to prepare individuals for the training? Does the training need to be marketed? What actions are needed to facilitate transfer? Is a companion training program needed for supervisors? Remember, the TNA is just the beginning of the training odyssey. The effectiveness of the training at addressing the gap depends on how well TNA data is translated into training by the decisions and actions taken in Step 14. Before moving on to the TNA evaluation phase, a brief overview of the traditional TNA framework—organizational, task and KSAO, and person analyses—is provided.

Organizational analysis is about determining whether or not the capability exists where it is needed and how best it can be developed or acquired. A thorough organizational analysis determines the goals and objectives of the TNA and provides the linkage between training objectives and organizational objectives, outcomes, resources, and constraints. This includes identifying and specifying all the organizational and contextual factors (or potential constraints) that might influence the design, delivery, and outcomes of the learning intervention (Goldstein, 1993; Salas & Cannon-Bowers, 2001). Factors or potential constraints that will influence transfer must be considered as well because it is the mechanism through which learning becomes the capability needed to support performance. There are many potential constraints to be investigated. Does the climate support conducting the training? Is the tempo of operations or business so high that training will be viewed negatively as distraction? Are the resources available? Sufficient computer access may not exist to support computer-based training, which limits delivery options. What organizational policies will impact training and transfer? A skill-based pay system that provides incentives for some skills but not for others will impact what training employees might select to attend. Organizational support, learning orientation, and training reputation can also foster positive attitudes toward training, which can increase employee participation (Hurtz & Williams, 2009).

Task or task and KSAO analysis (e.g., Arthur et al., 2003; Goldstein, 1993) is about identifying what must be learned so the organization has the underlying capability for the performance needed to support organizational objectives and outcomes. The key questions are as follows:

- What capability is required for desired performance?
- What must be trained or learned to ensure the desired performance?

The resulting analysis should identify and specify the learning objectives and content that will guide design, delivery, and measurement. The resulting work analysis should be at the appropriate level for its goals, context, and work content. For example, if you determine that training on a new manufacturing process is required for successful performance, then a task-level analysis is required because the procedure must be specified exactly. Also, the analysis could be focused on the mental processing and requirements for performance as well, requiring a cognitive task analysis component to complement traditional methods (Salas & Cannon-Bowers, 2001). This analysis should also include an analysis of the conditions under which the work will be performed and the KSAOs necessary to perform the work. What conditions in the work environment will impact performance and, therefore, training? What KSAs are necessary to perform the work or learn the skills necessary to perform the work? Creating effective learning objectives requires complete information about the work, the conditions under which it is performed, and the underlying KSAOs required. The TNA should also identify the cues and cognitions that enable the learner to apply the learned knowledge and skills, which can be incorporated into the training and transfer design (Salas & Cannon-Bowers, 2001). The goal of this task and KSAO analysis is to identify what must be learned to ensure the learning transfers to the desired capability and performance.

Traditionally, person-level analysis (Goldstein, 1993; McGehee & Thayer, 1961) focuses on which individuals need what training. However, the focus of the "person" analysis could easily be a standing or impromptu team, department, or unit. Team-level analyses are becoming more common, especially as teams are being created to pursue high-stakes projects, such as product development, which might take years. The main objective is to determine who needs to be trained on what KSAOs or competencies, regardless of the who. Person analysis falls into two categories: event driven and ongoing. Event-driven person analysis results from a deficiency or need being identified and, therefore, a needs assessment being conducted. Ongoing person analysis provides organizations with a systematic process for identifying individual development needs. Because these ongoing person analyses are tied directly or indirectly to performance requirements and organizational objectives, the resulting individual learning objectives and interventions develop capability that should transfer to performance and achieving organizational outcomes. Regardless of whether it is event-driven or ongoing, the individuals and teams who require training to develop the capability to perform must be identified effectively; otherwise, an organization's learning outcomes are not maximized and its learning dollars are not well spent.

TNA Evaluation Phase

Context impacts individual and group behavior and related processes in organizations. Figure 24.1 provides an illustration of contexts within the organizational system. Taking an ongoing, continuous improvement approach to identifying and addressing capability needs is important for success. The TNA evaluation phase asks questions about whether the identified KSAO gaps were closed by the training intervention or other learning interventions (e.g., mentoring) that followed from the training needs assessment phase. Ultimately, the concern is about whether the issue, opportunity, or event that triggered the TNA process was addressed (Table 24.1, Step 15). This information could be used to modify the intervention, to suggest a new intervention if the underlying reason for the TNA still persists, or to indicate the intervention is no longer needed if the underlying reason for the TNA has been resolved. Some TNA processes may continue indefinitely because of legal requirements or the need for ongoing person analysis. Evaluation also provides an opportunity to learn about the effectiveness of the TNA process and to make evidence-based process improvements (Table 24.1, Step 16).

The evaluation phase has two foci: Did the training or learning intervention result in the development of needed KSAOs, and did the KSAOs translate into capability and performance that addressed the triggering issue, opportunity, or event? The first is training evaluation, specifically summative evaluation, of proximal outcomes. The trained KSAOs can be measured and certified by assessments after training. Measurement before and after training is required if judgments about the effectiveness of the training are required for process improvement. The second is training evaluation of more distal outcomes, such as transfer and performance, and their impact on the underlying reason for the TNA intervention. Data should be collected related to the use of the trained KSAOs on the job, the job or team performance, and outcomes. These data provide an indication of whether or not the learned KSAOs actually translated to performance and addressed the triggering event, issue, or opportunity. The specific evaluation design, measurement, and data will vary based on the specifics the situation. A full treatment of evaluation is not possible here, but many resources about training and program evaluation exist that can guide practitioners.

Saliently including the TNA evaluation phase in the process communicates that TNA is related to training design, delivery, and evaluation and should not be viewed in isolation. The goal of TNA is to identify and specify a gap and a solution to address that gap, which is related to the underlying event, issue, or opportunity. The diagram in Figure 24.1 demonstrates the interrelationships among all the components of the process. Learning, transfer, performance, and the context in which these occur are important factors in the system and, therefore, must be considered in the TNA design and implementation and subsequent design, delivery, and evaluation of training (or other intervention). The TNA process does not exist in a vacuum and data are required throughout the system for effective TNA.

Issues Affecting TNA Implementation

There are a number of contextual factors and design choices that can influence the effectiveness of the TNA process. Although full treatment is beyond the scope of this chapter, Table 24.5 presents six potential issues that should be considered when planning a TNA implementation. This consideration allows the practitioner to determine if these factors are points of concern and to plan the process to mitigate these factors if they are concerns. These issues can range from technology availability to participation. For example, technology can streamline the TNA process, making it more efficient and effective, but many manufacturing and service organizations do not provide computer access on the job for their employees, making web-based TNA impractical. Participation is important to data representativeness and can be improved by leaders and managers communicating support and asking for participation. Many of the issues that impact TNA quality have to do with data collection and analysis methodology choices and execution. There are numerous books about TNA methods (see the Further Reading section at the end of the chapter). Another issue is the availability of data on key components, such as transfer and performance, which might not be collected by the organization. The point of this section is not to provide an exhaustive list of contextual and design issues impacting TNA implementation and effectiveness but to create awareness that these

Table 24.5   Six Issues Affecting TNA Implementation

Technology availability	Technology can make conducting the TNA process more efficient and effective. However, for example, many workers do not have consistent access to computers for web-based surveys. Plan according to your technology context. Paper surveys still collect data.
Premature diagnosis	Jumping straight from "I need training" to collecting task and KSAO data and developing and delivering training has set back many organizations. Follow the process. It will keep you on the right path.
Lack of leadership support	Without leadership support, it will be difficult to gain sufficient resources and participation for a successful TNA. Market TNA and gain leader support early (see the Making the Case for TNA section).
Who is asked?	Consider the impact of who is asked to participate. Are the relevant individuals—the most knowledgeable about the event, issue, or opportunity—being invited to participate? Is the group representative of the target population? Are there group differences in terms of opportunity to perform? Are there existing KSAO differences that might impact the responses? For example, Dierdorff and Surface (2008) found that skill levels affected TNA ratings. Consider this as part of your data collection or sampling plan.
Participation	Nonresponse can have dramatic impacts on TNA results. Leadership support and effective marketing of and communication about the TNA are critical to participation. If your organization has unions, union support is also critical. Create a participation plan as part of the upfront planning.
Poor data collection methodology	Collecting data is not as simple as typing a few items into an online survey engine (although it can be for narrow-domain TNA). Data collection—whether it is surveys, focus groups, interviews, observations, documentation reviews, or a combination—can have a very negative impact on TNA if flawed. Data collection and analysis take expertise. Do not be afraid to hire an expert to do this if it is not your area of expertise.

This is not meant to be an exhaustive list. KSAO = knowledge, skill, ability, or other characteristic.

issues exist and should be thought through as the TNA is planned and executed. These issues operate at the microlevel to impact TNA. The next section introduces societal and organizational trends at the macrolevel that could impact TNA.

FACTORS/TRENDS AFFECTING TNA

Instead of focusing on TNA solely from a traditional perspective, one goal of this chapter is to look into the future and determine trends in the workplace that might impact TNA practice. This is not to say that traditional approaches to TNA are not valuable and will not continue to be used. For example, in process-oriented jobs such as manufacturing, food service, and auditing, task and KSAO analysis of the work to determine the tasks and the relevant knowledge and skill requirements to guide training will continue to be important. However, this will not be the case in other contexts. To be prepared, organizations need to be aware of relevant workplace trends and determine their impact on TNA and other human resource processes. Examining the writings of workplace futurists is a useful place to start. Table 24.6 presents 10 current trends that will impact the 2020 workplace (Meister & Willyerd, 2010). Meister and Willyerd also make a number of predictions about the future workplace, such as, "Your mobile device will become your office, your classroom and your concierge" (p. 215); "The corporate curriculum will use video games, simulations and alternative reality games as key delivery modes" (p. 221); and "Corporate social networks will flourish and grow inside companies [being used for informal learning]" (p. 223), and provide many current examples and suggest more widespread adoption by 2020. Nine of their 20 predictions have implications for TNA.

Most of these trends and predictions suggest the same impact on TNA. Here are some thoughts based on Meister and Willyerd (2010). The workplace of the future will require, and future workers will demand, immediate identification, specification, and resourcing of their learning needs because learning will be focused on meeting the immediate demands of their jobs in their context. Their learning solutions will be customized, increasingly socially constructed, participatory, often informal, and will need to be delivered on demand. Cutting-edge knowledge and skills will be seen even more as a provider of individual and organizational advantage, and lifelong learning will be a business requirement and a highly desired attribute among workers. Technology will play a large role in learning needs identification and resourcing, with mobile devices and social

Table 24.6 Trends Currently Affecting or That Will Affect the 2020 Workplace

1. Shifting workforce demographics
2. The knowledge economy
3. Globalization
4. The digital workplace
5. The ubiquity of mobile technology
6. A culture of connectivity
7. The participation society
8. Social learning
9. Corporate social responsibility
10. Millennials in the workplace

Adapted from Meister, J. C. and Willyerd, K., *The 2020 Workplace: How Innovative Companies Attract, Develop, and Keep Tomorrow's Employees Today*, HarperCollins, New York, 2010.

technologies such as multiplayer videogames playing increasing roles. Granted, these are a few examples of trends that will likely impact some organizations and industries more than others. However, organizations should be aware of the potential impact of these trends on TNA in their organizational contexts. Basically, if you think stakeholders complain about the time a TNA takes now, just wait until 2020. The speed and flexibility of need identification, specification, and resourcing will have to increase. It will be a business necessity. In the fast-paced competitive environment, which authors such as Meister and Willyerd predict, organizations will live and die based on their ability to meet changing performance requirements.

Besides the work of futurists, important trends can be identified by listening to what training professionals are discussing at conferences and meetings. Table 24.7 presents a brief sidebar of two examples of these trends: the increase of informal learning and the focus on "scrap learning" as opposed to "transfer." Trends can be identified from the research community as well. Kraiger (2008a) discussed the three generations of instructional models—first, second, and third—and the implications for training; in his response article (Kraiger, 2008b), he lamented that none of the commentaries had addressed the implications for needs assessment. The choice of instructional model definitely has implications for needs identification and specification and how work analysis methods are implemented. Table 24.8 presents a brief discussion.

IDEAS TO IMPROVE TNA PRACTICE

Of course, basing a TNA intervention on sound work analysis methods and systems is the best way to improve TNA practice. Some examples of other potential ideas to improve TNA practice

Table 24.7   Two Current Trends in Training with Implications for TNA Practice

Trend	Description and Implication for TNA
Informal learning[a]	Informal learning, such as Google searches and peer-to-peer learning, is on the rise (Paradise, 2008; Paradise & Patel, 2009). Informal learning is appealing—it is under the control of the individual, timely, context relevant, and related to current performance requirements. The challenge is facilitating (a) individual identification of training needs that are appropriately addressed by on-the-job informal learning, (b) identification of informal learning options, and (c) the match between them in real time. Organizations will have to provide tools to facilitate informal learning and related TNA. Many organizations have knowledge-sharing portals or databases on their corporate networks where employees are encouraged to share knowledge and ask for help with problems, such as customer support issues. Informal learning options can enhance customer support (a business objective) while providing learning opportunities that transfer, such as reduced call time when the same customer service issue is encountered. Peer-to-peer matching sites are another example.
Scrap learning	Scrap learning, or wasted learning from training, has been a recent addition to our lexicon. It is basically the inverse of transfer. However, the trend for learning professionals is to talk more about scrap learning than about transfer. Although the goal of transfer of learning (and reduction of scrap) has always been implicit to the TNA, the concept of scrap learning is more intuitive for most laypeople. How we sell TNA and talk about the process and findings may be assisted by the term *scrap learning*. Concerns about scrap learning provide an emphasis for ensuring that TNA processes include steps for identifying contextual factors that are barriers to the application of learned knowledge and skill. Factors related to scrap learning, such as lack of supervisor support, should be explicitly evaluated.

[a] Paradise (2008) describes a study conducted by the American Society of Training and Development and the Institute for Corporate Productivity that defines informal learning as "A learning activity that is not easily recognizable as formal training and performance support. Generally speaking, it takes place without a conventional instructor and is employee-controlled in terms of breadth, depth, and timing. It tends to be individualized, limited in scope, and utilized in small chunks" (Paradise, 2008, p. 25).

Table 24.8 Three Generations of Instructional Models and TNA

Instructional Model[a]	How TNA Fits With the Model
First generation	The organization identifies the need, the content, and design of the training; for whom training is required; and how and when training will be delivered. The organization has all the decision power and assumes all the responsibility for the TNA process and effectiveness. Individuals provide information in TNA and participate in training. The first-generation model is appropriate in many contexts, especially where there are high-stakes (e.g., safety) or a standard work process (e.g., complex manufacturing) and training must be standardized.
Second generation	The shift is to learner-centered instruction, including more learner control and learner-constructed content (Kraiger, 2008a). Organizations identify training requirements or facilitate individuals in doing so and provide formal training opportunities, but the learner is more of an active participant in TNA and training. The role of the organization is to provide authentic training experiences and facilitate learner exploration and learning. The organization identifies needs and priorities and provides resources, but the responsibility is shared with the individual. Individuals may be given responsibility to identify their needs and construct their own training experience from the available corporate training resources or within a training program or event. Technology has made this possible. Learning can now be customized to each individual learner within the confines of the learning content and design. Organizations are facilitators and have a responsibility to ensure TNA leads to the purchase or design of training tools or platforms that allow for learner choice and customization. However, the individual learner has a much greater responsibility for his or her learning experience.
Third generation	The organization allows work teams or groups to identify, define, and address their learning needs. Learning is socially constructed. Individual training needs can be socially constructed because understanding of skill and knowledge requirements of the job in the individual's context and related deficiencies (needs for training) are influenced by peers and their understandings. The shift in responsibility is complete. Individuals and their teams or work groups have the lion's share of the process. The organization's role is that of facilitator on both ends of the process. Meister and Willyerd (2010) identified social learning as one of their workplace 2020 trends. In second- and third-generation models, organizations still have the responsibility for directing learning activities to be aligned to strategy and business needs.

[a] This should not be construed as an endorsement of any one of the models over the others. The goal is for organizations to think about the TNA responsibilities under each model. All three instructional models have their relevance to learning in organizations.

are presented in Table 24.9. The examples selected attempt to address some of the issues, factors, and trends that impact or will potentially impact TNA, as discussed in previous sections. These examples are meant to be representative of the range of potential solutions, not exhaustive. Some of the ideas are quite simple and result in abbreviated TNA interventions, such as the use of existing data to streamline the TNA intervention (Noe, 2009). Others, such as web-enabling the entire TNA process, are quite involved. Others leverage trends in society, such as the increasing prevalence of social media use (Meister & Willyerd, 2010). Others address the supply side of the equation (i.e., availability of training resources), which is necessary to facilitate a real-time match of individual needs with formal and informal learning resources. The remainder of this section focuses on four of the ideas covering the range of potential improvements to the TNA process: (a) Empower TNA within the organization's competency model; (b) use pulse surveys for TNA; (c) use social media and technologies for TNA; and (d) embed TNA in technology-delivered training options.

Empower TNA Within the Organization's Competency Model

A well-developed competency model can be used to streamline the TNA process (Noe, 2009). Linked to strategic objectives and to organizational and performance outcomes, a competency

Table 24.9   Ideas for Improving TNA Practice

1.	Make use of existing data to streamline the TNA intervention.
2.	Web-enable the entire TNA process.
3.	Use technology to reduce costs and improve TNA timeliness.
4.	Develop a streamlined TNA process for your organization.
5.	Focus on performance enhancement.
6.	Empower TNA within the organization's competency model.
7.	Embed TNA in technology-delivered training options.
8.	Use pulse surveys for TNA.
9.	Use smart phones for TNA.
10.	Use social media for TNA.
11.	Use social media to match needs with informal learning opportunities (e.g., mentoring).
12.	Create a training portfolio of formal and informal resources for your organization.
13.	Use technology to conduct periodic training resources audits.
14.	Use technology to match identified needs to organizational resources in real time.

model narrows the domain of focus and priority for needs identification and specification and resourcing to address training needs. This allows the organization to provide thorough resources in these competency domains, including tools to help individuals and teams identify learning needs and match needs to existing formal and informal resources. Because competencies are typically designed to be valid across an organization (Green, 1999; Noe, 2009), they can be used to generalize TNA processes, such as person analysis, across jobs and teams. Because the need space is limited to the competency model, tools can be developed and implemented to allow for real-time need identification and resource matching and delivery. Employees and teams or work groups are empowered within a limited need space to take control of their learning. Using competency models as the basis for learning needs assessment and fulfillment is a way for organizations to provide an efficient and effective solution that covers the most relevant KSAOs. There will always be the need for TNA and training outside the domains of the competency model, and this approach will not work for some organizations and contexts. However, this is a viable solution that can be used to improve an organization's capability related to its performance and business objectives and retain control of the learning process while empowering individuals and teams to take responsibility for their own learning.

Use of Pulse Surveys for TNA

Pulse surveys are short, focused surveys that can be sent out periodically to the entire population or a sample of the organization. The idea is to "take the pulse" of the organization on a particular issue. These surveys are easy options to identify and specify training needs within a focused domain, such as a competency model, or to provide a periodic vehicle for individuals to bring potential needs to the attention of the organization. Pulse surveys can be delivered via a web site, e-mail, or smart phone. Table 24.10 describes a pulse survey implementation. This particular survey is being used to identify potential needs within a competency model and is designed for a smart phone and has no more than one or two questions per screen. It can also be used to identify general needs periodically or to conduct a task and KSAO analysis in a very narrow domain. The pulse survey is effective for identifying areas where the organization needs to develop training resources. An extension would be to use the pulse survey for person-level analysis, specify the nature of the training within each competency, and recommend training options to the individual.

Table 24.10   Example of a Pulse Survey Used for TNA

1. Respondent has previously signed up to participate in pulse TNA surveys via his or her smart phone.
2. Respondent receives an e-mail or text with a customized link (allowing for fewer items).
3. Respondent clicks on the link.
4. Respondent receives introduction screen about pulse TNA survey related to core competencies, which asks, "Are your training needs being met?" (branches to end if yes)
5. If no, respondent is asked, "Indicate in which of XYZ Company's three core competencies you have training needs (select all that apply)."
6. For each selected competency, the participant is asked, "Please describe in a tweet-sized statement (140 characters or less) what you need specifically," and "Can we contact you to follow up?"
7. Respondent is asked about participant in current training.
8. Respondent is thanked.

Use Social Media for TNA

As Meister and Willyerd (2010) pointed out, there are a number of trends, such as a culture of connectivity, millennials in the workplace, and the participation society, aligning to push the use and adoption of social media in organizations. For example, one of their predictions for the 2020 workplace is that organizations will require social media skills of employees. Will future work analyses bear this out as an employee requirement? Social media can be adopted now to improve both sides of the TNA process: identifying needs and resources to meet those needs. Using social media can be as simple as creating an online, interactive community via the company web site or using social media tools, such as Twitter. Having a company web site listing and providing learning resources or a web site where employees can discuss their jobs and share knowledge are not new ideas. But, these sites could be turned into "learning mash ups" that bring everything learning together for the organization. These could be leveraged for TNA across organization, work, and person levels. These sites could include TNA tools that identify individual training requirements within a narrow domain, such as the corporate competency model, and recommend existing training tools for the individual.

Using social media to match individual needs with informal learning opportunities, such as peer-to-peer learning, is a fairly straightforward use. Now, individuals are tapping their social networks for information, job leads, and mentors. Why not for learning opportunities or training recommendations as well? Real-time chats, instant messaging, and video conferencing could be used by teams or groups to develop learning requirements. Of course, the data from board postings, Twitter messages, and chats could be mined to identify training requirements so the company can more quickly provide formal training resources for prevalent and important deficiencies. A team of researchers at Carnegie Mellon University found fairly high correlations between consumer confidence and public opinion polls and the sentiment word frequencies in Twitter messages of the same period (O'Connor, Balasubramanyan, Routledge, & Smith, 2009). If this technique could be applied to TNA surveys, then it could be used for the needs identification and needs specification phases of the TNA process.

Embed TNA in Technology-Delivered Training Options

Second-generation instructional models revolve around learner-centered instruction and more learner control over the learning content and process (Kraiger, 2008a). Well-designed, technology-delivered training offers the promise of learner control. However, many learners do not know how to optimize their own learning or to diagnose their learning needs. Given the increased reliance on technology-delivered training and the push for more effective use of training resources, organizations should purchase or create technology-delivered training that provides an individual-level needs assessment (person analysis) and uses it to help the learner guide learning. By using the organization's competency model to narrow training offerings to domains linked to organizational strategy and objectives, the organization can focus on purchasing or developing computer-based training, simulations, virtual worlds, videogames, and smart phone applications that include a person analysis linked to these organizationally valued competencies. This has the benefit of using existing information to eliminate the majority of the TNA process and of being linked to organizational objectives. Embedded person analysis and dynamic creation of individualized training guidance within technology-delivered training should become standard.

Although not an exhaustive list of potential ideas or solutions to improve TNA, the goal of this section was to provide a few examples to show the range of what can be done now. TNA will only increase in importance, and trends now being developed in the workplace indicate the need to use technology more effectively to identify training needs using work analysis techniques and linking them to resources to meet the demands of the future workforce and competitive marketplace.

MAKING THE CASE FOR TNA

If learning objectives are not adequately known or are improperly specified prior to design (or purchase) and implementation of training initiatives, the likelihood that employee learning will be aligned with capability requirements, performance, or organizational objectives is not very high (Goldstein, 1993). Lack of alignment between training objectives and the capability requirements underlying performance and organizational objectives yields ineffective training; it does not address the identified gap between desired and actual states. If the ineffective training does address the need, it will be by accident. We know TNA is a mechanism for aligning training with capability and performance requirements and outcomes in organizations; therefore, it optimizes the likelihood training will successfully address the identified need. Given the importance of learning for organizational competitiveness and the prevalence and expense of learning initiatives, the TNA process should be used extensively. However, the current evidence suggests TNA is not prevalent. A gap between current and desired states of practice exists. How do we make the case for TNA?

To sell TNA, the training practitioner needs to understand why TNA is not conducted more frequently, both in general and within their organization specifically. Although there are likely additional reasons that are idiosyncratic to any specific case, Table 24.11 presents seven common, interrelated reasons why TNA is not used.

Keep in mind that some of these can be valid reasons for not conducting a TNA, but they can be excuses as well. For example, cost and the perceived value can be legitimate issues for an organization. If the identified need (gap in capability) is not a high priority for or of value to the organization, then cost and potential return on investment are important initial decision factors for implementing the TNA process, and the decision may be not to implement in the case of no or limited value or priority. However, if the organization uses cost to justify jumping straight from a potential gap to a training solution without conducting a TNA, then cost is being used as an excuse to not follow a beneficial practice that will likely optimize the value of the training investment and save money.

Table 24.11   Seven Common Reasons Why TNA Is Not Conducted

1. Time	TNA takes too long, and the solution is needed now.
2. Expertise	The organization does not have in-house TNA expertise.
3. Lack of leadership support	The key stakeholders do not support it.
4. Cost	The TNA process is too expensive and will add too much cost to the training.
5. Lack of perceived value	There is no immediately tangible benefit or return on investment.
6. Leadership certainty	"I know what the problem is and I know training is the solution. There is no need to waste time and money on a TNA."
7. Lack of TNA awareness	In many organizations, training decisions are made by nontraining experts who just do not know or understand the training process.

This is not an exhaustive list, and each situation will likely have idiosyncratic factors that affect the use of TNA.

If viewed from a sales perspective, the items in Table 24.11 are "customer objections" to be overcome or opportunities to educate the customers about the product (TNA). In each case, one should be prepared to overcome the most likely objections and to educate the stakeholder. As an internal consultant or practitioner, there is an advantage of knowing the culture, the stakeholders, and the most likely issues. What is important in the culture? What have been the stakeholders' reasons for not doing TNA in the past? Every organization has values, a shared history, and even a mythology. Stakeholders have their own values and histories. Use this information. For external consultants, who may not have such insights, the best option is to provide salient examples of the value of TNA and the risk of not conducting a TNA. Presenting a business or mission case for TNA is important. These cases work for internal practitioners as well.

Practitioners need to make a case for TNA. This case is related to but different from the case for learning. The result of the TNA might be a nontraining solution, so selling learning as a solution comes at the end of the needs specification phase, when it is clear the gap is related to a KSAO deficiency and the TNA phase is required. Although every situation is different and the specific organization and stakeholders will influence the argument presented, Table 24.12 presents information that could be highlighted when crafting a logical and relevant argument for TNA.

Arguing from data or projections can be effective if the stakeholders are data-based decision makers. Often, the most effective tool is to use an example related to the organization's core business or mission. For example, many consumer products companies spend millions of dollars

Table 24.12   Potential Information to Make the Case for TNA

1. High-level overview of TNA and the TNA process
2. Specific benefits of TNA and the increased alignment with business objective and performance requirement created by TNA
3. Conducting the TNA process in phases optimizes the effectiveness of resource expenditures
4. Initial quick identification and specification of the potential issue and solutions optimizes the effectiveness of resource expenditures
5. Options to reduce the time and cost associated with TNA; abbreviated TNA using existing data or with an existing competency model
6. Why TNA should be conducted in this case
7. Expected value or return on investment achieved by conducting TNA in this case
8. Potential risks or costs associated with not conducting TNA in this case
9. Cost and benefit data or projections to make your point
10. Examples from corporate history or culture to support the use of TNA

This is not meant to imply an order of importance or to be an exhaustive list.

identifying and specifying customer needs and developing and testing associated products. These companies would never develop a product without sufficient market research. TNA is basically the same process. There are many examples of failed products and services for which the need was incorrectly identified or specified. Your organization may even have an example that is part of its mythology. This works for mission-based organizations as well. In the military, planning a mission without a clear objective and accurate intelligence would not be endorsed by many, if any, leaders. Some nonprofit organizations use software to identify potential donors and specify (customize) their pitch for donations. Examples abound for most organizations.

Each case is different. The point is to make a well-formed, relevant argument for conducting a TNA. Use your knowledge of the organization and the stakeholders to help shape the argument. Not every argument will be successful, but do not be discouraged. The potential benefits of TNA—increased effectiveness of training, increased alignment of capability with performance requirements, and increased organizational effectiveness—are worth the continued effort. TNA will never be conducted unless someone advocates for it.

As a final note, with this text being *The Handbook of Work Analysis*, it is important to mention that TNA is not possible without work analysis methods such as task analysis, task and KSAO analysis, and cognitive task analysis. Hopefully, this chapter helps the reader to understand and better engage in the TNA process. When planning TNA interventions, readers should integrate the contents of this chapter with other chapters in this volume to develop an effective solution.

FURTHER READING

TNA cannot be thoroughly addressed in a single chapter and probably not a single book. To offer the reader more resources, we have provided a list of TNA-relevant references below. Because this chapter focuses more on TNA decisions, most of these refererences are focused on the nuts and bolts of the TNA process, such as data collection. Many of the chapters in this volume provide excellent references when planning the work analysis components of the TNA process.

Altschuld, J. W. (Ed.). (2010). *The needs assessment kit* (Vols. 1–5). Thousand Oaks, CA: Sage.

Altschuld, J. W., & Witkin, B. R. (2000). *From needs assessment to action*. Thousand Oaks, CA: Sage.

Austin, M. (1998). *Needs assessment by focus group* (Infoline issue 9401). Alexandria, VA: American Society for Training & Development.

Burner, K. J. (2010). From performance analysis to training needs assessment. In K. H. Sibler & W. R. Foshay (Eds.), *Handbook of improving performance in the workplace: Vol. 1. Instructional design and training delivery* (pp. 144–183). San Francisco, CA: Pfeiffer.

Elliott, P. H. (2008). Identifying performance and learning gaps. In E. Biech (Ed.), *American Society for training & development handbook for workplace learning professionals* (pp. 107–125). Alexandria, VA: American Society for Training & Development.

Franklin, M. (2005). *Performance gap analysis* (Infoline issue 0603). Alexandria, VA: American Society for Training & Development.

Gupta, K. (2005). *Conducting a mini needs assessment* (Infoline issue 9611). Alexandria, VA: American Society for Training & Development.

Gupta, K., Sleezer, C. M., & Russ-Eft, D. F. (2007). *A practical guide to needs assessment* (2nd ed.). San Francisco, CA: Pfeiffer.

Sparhawk, S. (2002). *Strategic needs analysis* (Infoline issue 9408). Alexandria, VA: American Society for Training & Development.

Stone, R. D. (2009). *Aligning training for results: A process and tools that link training to business*. San Francisco, CA: Pfeiffer.

Tobey, D. D. (2007). *Data collection for needs assessment* (Infoline issue 0704). Alexandria, VA: American Society for Training & Development.

Waagen, A. K. (1998). *Task analysis* (Infoline issue 9808). Alexandria, VA: American Society for Training & Development.

REFERENCES

Aguinis, H., & Kraiger, K. (2009). Benefits of training and development for individuals and teams, organizations, and society. *Annual Review of Psychology, 60,* 451–474.

Altschuld, J. W. (Ed.). (2010). *The needs assessment kit* (Vols. 1–5). Thousand Oaks, CA: Sage.

Alvarez, K., Salas, E., & Garofano, C. M. (2004). An integrated model of training evaluation and effectiveness. *Human Resource Development Review, 3,* 385–416.

Arthur, W. Jr., Bennett, W. Jr., Edens, P. S., & Bell, S. T. (2003). Effectiveness of training in organizations: A meta-analysis of design and evaluation features. *Journal of Applied Psychology, 88,* 234–245.

Dierdorff, E. C., & Surface, E. A. (2008). Assessing training needs: Does work experience and capability matter? *Human Performance, 21,* 28–48.

Franklin, M. (2005). *Performance gap analysis* (Infoline issue 0603). Alexandria, VA: American Society for Training & Development.

Gilbert, T. F. (1978). *Human competence: Engineering worthy performance.* New York, NY: McGraw-Hill.

Goldstein, I. L. (1993). *Training in organizations: Needs assessment, development, and evaluation* (3rd ed.). Pacific Grove, CA: Brooks/Cole.

Green, P. C. (1999). *Building robust competencies: Linking human resource systems to organizational strategies.* San Francisco, CA: Jossey-Bass.

Gupta, K. (2005). *Conducting a mini needs assessment* (Infoline issue 9611). Alexandria, VA: American Society for Training & Development.

Hurtz, G. M, & Williams, K. J. (2009). Attitudinal and motivational antecedents of participation in voluntary employee development activities. *Journal of Applied Psychology, 94,* 635–653.

Kraiger, K. (2003). Perspectives on training. In W. C. Borman, D. R. Ilgen, & R. J. Klimoski (Eds.), *Comprehensive handbook of psychology: Vol. 12. Industrial and organizational psychology* (pp. 171–192). Hoboken, NJ: Wiley & Sons.

Kraiger, K. (2008a). Transforming our models of learning and development: Web-based instruction as enabler of third-generation instruction. *Industrial and Organizational Psychology, 1,* 454–467.

Kraiger, K. (2008b). Third-generation instructional models: More about guiding development and design than selecting training methods. *Industrial and Organizational Psychology, 1,* 501–507.

McGehee, W., & Thayer, P. W. (1961). *Training in business and industry.* New York, NY: Wiley & Sons.

Meister, J. C., & Willyerd, K. (2010). *The 2020 workplace: How innovative companies attract, develop, and keep tomorrow's employees today.* New York, NY: HarperCollins.

Noe, R. A. (2009). *Learning system design: A guide to creating effective learning initiatives.* Alexandria, VA: SHRM Foundation.

O'Connor, B., Balasubramanyan, R., Routledge, B. R., & Smith, N. A. (2009, May). *From tweets to polls: Linking text sentiment to public opinion time series.* Paper presented at the 4th International Association for the Advancement of Artificial Intelligence Conference on Weblogs and Social Media, Washington, D. C.

Paradise, A. (2008). *2008 state of the industry.* Alexandria, VA: American Society for Training & Development.

Paradise, A., & Patel, L. (2009). *2009 state of the industry.* Alexandria, VA: American Society for Training & Development.

Rossett, A. (1987). *Training needs assessment.* Englewood Cliffs, NJ: Educational Technology.

Salas, E., & Cannon-Bowers, J. A. (2001). The science of training: A decade of progress. *Annual Review of Psychology, 52,* 471–499.

Stolovitch, H. D., & Keeps, E. J. (2008). Selecting solutions to improve workplace performance. In E. Biech (Ed.), *American Society for Training & Development handbook for workplace learning professionals* (pp. 107–125). Alexandria, VA: American Society for Training & Development.

van Eerde, W., Tang, K. C. S., & Talbot, G. (2008). The mediating role of training utility on the relationship between training needs assessment and organisational effectiveness. *International Journal of Human Resource Management, 19,* 63–73.

25

Compensation

ROBERT J. HARVEY

Virginia Tech

This chapter examines ways in which job analysis data may be used when setting job compensation rates, a process often termed *job evaluation*. Many strategies for setting pay rates exist (Caruth & Handlogten, 2001; Henderson, 2005); however, most make relatively little use of detailed, objective job analysis data—especially those approaches that address strategic compensation issues (Balkin & Gomez-Mejia, 1984; Devers, Cannella, Reilly, & Yoder, 2007; Murthy, 1977). This chapter focuses on job evaluation techniques that are based on direct linkages to verifiable job analysis data, paying particular attention to a variant of the point factor method that uses policy capturing to predict market compensation rates from the *work dimensions* measured by standardized job analysis questionnaires. This technique has received comparatively little attention, despite the fact that it embodies far less subjectivity than methods that rely on holistic judgments to measure compensable factors. Its use is illustrated using work dimension scores produced by the Common-Metric Questionnaire (CMQ; Harvey, 1991a) to predict market wage-survey compensation rates.

WHOLE-JOB METHODS

A number of different taxonomies have been proposed for categorizing the various methods that are available to practitioners for developing employee compensation systems (e.g., Devers et al., 2007; Henderson, 2005). At their core, however, all such methods can be reduced to one of two basic approaches:

1. Methods that make compensation decisions by considering each job as a holistic, undifferentiated entity (i.e., whole-job methods)
2. Methods that rely on some form of decomposed-judgment strategy (Chapter 29, this volume) that involves first quantifying jobs in terms of a profile of characteristics deemed relevant to compensation (i.e., compensable factors), and then combining or comparing the compensable factor scores in order to reach an overall decision regarding each job's value to the organization

Whole-job methods will not be examined in detail here because they are outside the focus of this handbook (i.e., identifying job analysis best practices). Most whole-job methods require levels of subjective judgment that are so high that I cannot recommend them as best practices. However, one method that I classify as a whole-job strategy—market wage surveys—does play a key role in providing the criterion data used in the policy capturing point factor (PCPF) method that is examined in detail in this chapter. Additionally, several of the concepts used in the whole-job methods, which are summarized in the following sections, are relevant to the more detailed compensable factor methods discussed in this chapter.

Ranking

Whole-job compensation methods are all quite straightforward and arguably the simplest version is the ranking method. As the name suggests, this technique involves simply ranking the jobs in question (typically, using a compensation committee composed of individuals familiar with the jobs) in terms of their overall perceived value or worth to the organization. Ranking is consistent with the common practice of developing compensation structures that classify each job into one of a number of ordered categories (termed *pay grades*). Once the jobs are arranged into relative rank order, the practitioner simply identifies the points at which to draw the dividing lines that determine each pay grade's upper and lower boundaries. If multiple compensation structures are desired (e.g., for managerial versus nonmanagerial titles), the process is repeated for the sets of job titles contained in each pay structure.

Advantages of the ranking method center on its relative simplicity and bottom-line focus. However, its potential disadvantages are numerous, including the following:

1. Its simplicity decreases in inverse proportion to the number of titles that must be ranked. With large numbers of titles, it can become quite cumbersome.
2. It may be difficult to achieve high levels of agreement across judges with respect to the relative ranking of similar jobs. Often, the final ranks are determined via consensus judgment of the compensation committee.
3. Because they are effectively ordinal data, the distances between jobs in terms of their rank orderings cannot be interpreted as quantitatively meaningful information—a fact that complicates the task of identifying the dividing points that form the pay grades.
4. The method relies on a holistic judgment strategy, whereby jobs are treated as undifferentiated entities when ranked. This raises fundamental questions regarding subjectivity and the inability to produce independent, verifiable job analysis data to justify the overall ranking decisions (see Chapter 29, this volume, for further discussion of the undesirable properties of the holistic judgment strategies in the job analysis process).

A variant of the ranking method involves making paired comparisons between all possible combinations of jobs in the pay structure (i.e., taken two at a time). Although this may simplify the rating task somewhat (in the sense that raters need only determine which job in each pair is more valuable to the organization, rather than having to rank all of the job titles at once in terms of their overall value), the number of paired comparisons required increases dramatically as the number of titles in the system increases.

Some researchers have reached positive conclusions regarding the paired-comparison approach to clustering jobs (Sackett, Cornelius, & Carron, 1981), claiming that this relatively simple procedure can—at least in very small samples of jobs—produce results that are similar to those that would be obtained when more detailed job analysis methods are used to determine job similarity. However, the unavoidable fact remains that single-item holistic judgments of overall job similarity (a) are by definition highly subjective; (b) offer no demonstrable "paper trail" linking bottom-line compensation and job-similarity decisions back to defensible, verifiable ratings of objective work activities; and (c) exhibit poor psychometric properties (e.g., low reliability) and often near-zero levels of convergence with results obtained using traditional job analytic methods (Butler & Harvey, 1988; Gibson, Harvey, & Harris, 2007; Chapter 29, this volume).

Job Classification

A variant of the ranking procedure is termed *classification* or *job classification*. Job classification is distinct from the use of the same term to denote the process of empirically forming job title taxonomies via statistical analysis of detailed job analysis ratings (Harvey, 1986). This method also relies on overall holistic judgments of each job's worth to the organization. However, rather than ranking all jobs to be included in the pay system, in the classification method the compensation committee first determines the number of pay grades (or classes) to be contained in the compensation system (and the corresponding ranges of pay for each) and then asks raters to make simple categorical judgments to sort each job into one of the classes.

Advantages and disadvantages are effectively the same as for the ranking method. Advantages center on simplicity, whereas disadvantages focus on the near total lack of demonstrable job-relatedness. Neither method necessarily requires that any detailed job analysis data be collected on the jobs to be slotted into pay grades. In many cases, the only job analysis information that is involved in the process consists of short (typically narrative) job descriptions of each title. To the extent that the organization or practitioner developing the pay system is concerned with being able to later explain why a given job was sorted into a given pay grade (and to defend that decision using detailed, verifiable, empirical data describing each job's required work activities and context), both the ranking and classification methods have little to offer.

Wage Surveys

A final whole-job approach for determining compensation rates involves conducting surveys of other employers of interest (either in the local labor market, or more broadly defined) and asking each to state the level of compensation given to each job on the list being surveyed. Often, as an inducement to participate, each organization is provided with summary results of the wage survey when it is completed (e.g., listing averages and ranges of compensation for each job).

The titles being surveyed could span the full set contained in the compensation system in question. However, more typically, they represent only a subset of key or benchmark jobs that are found in most or all of the organizations participating in the wage survey. In the former case in which all jobs in the pay structure are included in the survey, the task of converting such information into a pay decision is relatively straightforward, with the primary decision being one of determining the organization's policy with respect to the market (i.e., paying above-market average rates to reward current employees and encourage applicants, paralleling the market averages, or paying below-market rates to reduce overall system costs).

Advantages of this approach center on its bottom-line, market-driven focus when setting compensation rates, as well as the clear empirical evidence (in a dollar-denominated metric) that the organization can cite if it needs to be able to explain why a certain job received its given level of pay. However, in cases in which the survey collects data on only the subset of key jobs, an obvious disadvantage can be seen with respect to the question of what should be done regarding the nonkey jobs. Although some combination of the techniques used in the other whole-job methods (e.g., classification) can be used to slot the nonkey jobs into the pay grade structure defined by the key jobs, all of the above-noted disadvantages associated with such methods would then apply.

As with any survey-based procedure, concerns may arise regarding the degree to which an appropriate comparison population of organizations has been selected, as well as whether the organizations that are sampled respond in adequate numbers and in a representative fashion. Indeed, questions can be raised regarding the underlying value of seeking to quantify a "market wage" in the first place (Rynes & Milkovich, 1986). As Rynes and Milkovich noted, "both the construct and the measurement of the market wage have not been sufficiently examined by either academics or the courts" (p. 71). They concluded by criticizing researchers and practitioners for a collective "failure to recognize that the estimation of market wages requires a measurement process based on a series of subjective judgments" (p. 88). That is, although the bottom-line, dollar-denominated nature of the data collected as part of the market wage survey process may appear to be highly objective and methodologically rigorous, the process by which such data are collected offers numerous opportunities for subjective judgments to be introduced. For example, the person in each surveyed organization who is responsible for reporting back the wage data for the surveyed titles must make a qualitative judgment as to whether each key job is indeed present in that organization. This task may be considerably complicated by the fact that different organizations use different titles to describe similar jobs and/or use the same titles to describe jobs that perform appreciably different work.

Equity Issues

For all methods of developing compensation structures, three general types of equity issues should be considered when describing the properties of a given pay system (Henderson, 2005). That is, regardless of the specific method that is used to set pay rates, concerns may arise regarding the following:

1. *Internal equity,* or the degree to which the jobs in an organization's pay system are correctly scaled in terms of their value to the organization
2. *External equity,* or the degree to which each job in the system is paid correctly in comparison to how other employers of interest pay workers who hold the same job title
3. *Individual equity,* or the degree to which the pay given to the individuals who hold a common job title reflects their relative contributions or value to the organization

The latter issue is relevant primarily to the performance appraisal/reward/incentive procedures used by an organization (Lawler, 1987), and hence it is not directly of concern here. In contrast, both internal and external equity represent potentially critical concerns when developing or evaluating a compensation system. Unfortunately, it is often the case that taking steps to enhance one will tend to raise concerns regarding the other; this is especially the case with respect to the whole-job methods.

For example, the wage survey strategy will tend to produce pay systems that excel in terms of external equity because the internal rates are derived directly from consideration of the rates paid in the external market for each job. However, they may or may not exhibit strong internal equity, especially if the relative scarcity of qualified employees in some jobs tends to inflate their market value and an abundance of qualified applicants in other titles tends to depress their wages. Conversely, the ranking and classification methods may excel regarding internal equity, at least with respect to the equity perceptions that are held by the compensation committee. They nonetheless show significant limitations regarding external equity, especially if the organization tends to value some jobs more or less highly than is the case in the external labor market chosen for comparison.

In sum, although there is no single best answer with respect to how practitioners can achieve the optimum balance between internal versus external equity when developing a compensation system, it is nevertheless an issue that should receive active consideration when using job analysis results to drive compensation functions. In contrast to the limited flexibility regarding this issue that is seen for the whole-job methods, which tend to be strongly biased toward one alternative or the other, at least some of the compensable factor methods considered next provide the practitioner with a range of options for balancing internal versus external equity concerns.

COMPENSABLE FACTOR METHODS

Despite the fact that whole-job methods offer clear advantages in terms of simplicity and a bottom-line focus (and, in the case of wage surveys, in providing a means for ensuring external equity), they suffer from significant concerns with respect to the degree to which they provide organizations with the data needed to defend the accuracy, fairness, or job-relatedness of their compensation systems and decisions if challenged. The process of setting compensation rates arguably falls somewhat below the high level of concern and complexity regarding legal defensibility associated with employee selection practices. In addition to numerous federal laws (e.g., Equal Pay Act of 1963, Age Discrimination in Employment Act of 1967, Americans with Disabilities Act of 1990, Title VII of the Civil Rights Act of 1964) and court decisions (e.g., *Ledbetter v. Goodyear Tire & Rubber Co,* 2007), practitioners may also need to comply with a host of state and/or local regulations regarding what constitutes fair pay practices. In some cases, this can also include dealing with the controversial issue of comparable worth (Rynes & Milkovich, 1986).

To the extent that legal defensibility concerns are important with respect to your organization's compensation systems, the whole-job methods summarized above do not receive best practices recommendations. Although one might counter that a system based on a well-conducted wage survey allows an organization to objectively value its jobs based on the external labor market, one could easily counter that many aspects of the process of conducting wage surveys are potentially problematic and/or subjective (Rynes & Milkovich, 1986).

In particular, when conducting a market wage survey, one must effectively assume that for each job in question, functionally identical work activities are performed across all of the different organizations that participate in the survey (i.e., that differences in pay rates that may exist across organizations for a given job reflect differences in each organization's pay policies, not systematic differences in required work activities or working conditions). Given that significant levels of within-title heterogeneity in work activity are often seen both within and between organizations and between different sources (e.g., incumbents versus supervisors verus job analysts) for providing job ratings (Green & Stutzman, 1986; Hazel, Madden, & Christal, 1964; Meyer, 1959; Sanchez & Levine, 2000; Smith & Hakel, 1979; Stutzman, 1983), the validity of that assumption can easily be called into question. Likewise, to the extent that past pay practices in the market may have had discriminatory overtones (e.g., of the type where jobs dominated by male employees received higher pay than those dominated by female employees, even when performing similar work—a formerly widespread situation that gave rise to the Equal Pay Act of 1963), relying on the results from market wage surveys may effectively perpetuate such practices.

The compensable factor-based methods considered in this section were developed to deal with the types of limitations noted above regarding whole-job methods. Although many of these methods suffer from potential concerns of their own (especially regarding subjectivity and content coverage), the fact that they explicitly acknowledge that jobs must be described in terms of their scores across a range of compensable factors—not judged as an undifferentiated, holistic entity—offers many potential advantages over whole-job methods. This is especially the case with respect to their capacity to provide a documentary paper trail that traces the way in which verifiable job analysis item ratings were ultimately linked to the overall compensation rates given to jobs.

Traditional Point Factor

Kilgour (2008, p. 37) considered the point factor approach to represent "the oldest and most commonly used formal approach to job evaluation." However, he also noted that a number of concerns may exist:

The point factor method of job evaluation consists of a large number of discretionary decisions that result in something that appears to be entirely objective and, even, scientific.... If the pay system is designed and implemented in good faith, errors made along the way should cancel out and result in an outcome that is acceptable. However, human resources and compensation professionals should be aware and somewhat humbled by the discretionary decisions underlying the apparent objectivity.

With respect to the question of subjectivity, concerns do not typically arise due to the fact that this method (at least nominally) relies on a decomposed-judgment process (Butler & Harvey, 1988). That is, compensable factor methods score each job in the compensation system in terms of an array of compensable factors, and then combine the compensable factor scores to form an overall point value for ordering jobs and defining their overall value to the organization.

Rather, concerns with these methods typically focus on what the compensable factors are and how they are rated. That is, popular implementations of the point factor method typically describe jobs in terms of only a handful of abstract compensable factors, often the identical criteria specified by the Equal Pay Act in order to determine whether jobs perform equivalent work (i.e., skill, effort, responsibility, and working conditions). The fact that the point factor method analyzes jobs in terms of multiple dimensions of work activity (instead of holistically considering them as undifferentiated entities) is in one sense a positive characteristic. However, the fact that such nebulous compensable factors are rated in traditional applications of the point factor method raises the usual set of concerns that arise when attempts are made to holistically rate unobservable, hypothetical constructs (Butler & Harvey, 1988; Gibson, Harvey, & Harris, 2007; Chapter 29, this volume).

Even if more detailed, traditional decomposed-judgment methods of job analysis are used to describe each job, concerns regarding the accuracy of ratings collected for compensation purposes are always present. Harvey (Chapter 6, this volume) discussed the methods for attempting to detect rating problems, including the appropriateness indices examined in Harvey (2005) and the lower-technology approaches described in Green and Stutzman (1986) and Wilson, Harvey, and Macy (1990). As Kilgour (2008, p. 39) observed,

A word of caution is in order. Incumbents may "fluff up" the job either in the honest belief that it requires more or is of greater importance than it is or on the logical assumption that it is in their self-interest to do so. Similarly, it may be in the supervisor's interest to inflate the job's worth. He or she has to work with the incumbent(s) and, in addition to the social pressures involved, is to some extent their representative. There may also be some self-interest involved.

Beyond criticizing the point factor approach with respect to the way it often relies on psychometrically questionable methods to assign scores (termed *degrees*) for jobs on each compensable factor, questions may also be raised regarding the methods used to combine the factor scores to form the overall point value for the job. In many cases, the relative weighting given to each compensable factor is simply derived rationally (e.g., by having compensation committee members allocate 100 points across the factors to reflect their relative importance). Although such rational methods for weighting factors may prove useful with respect to increasing perceptions of the internal equity of the system, they clearly beg the question of whether the overall point values will exhibit good external equity with respect to prevailing wage rates in the labor market(s) of concern.

There is no a priori reason to believe that the perceptions of the compensation committee on the relative value of each compensable factor will parallel the ways in which those same factors tend to be valued by the external labor market (i.e., in a policy capturing sense). For example, a compensation committee may choose to assign a positive value and/or sizable weight to a factor that reflects working in demanding or unpleasant environmental conditions. However, as an empirical matter, if a policy capturing study is conducted to predict market wage rates from compensable factor scores, factors such as these may actually exhibit *negative* regression weights (i.e., jobs tend to receive lower pay to the extent that they involve working in unpleasant conditions). To the extent that the practitioner is concerned with developing a pay system that exhibits strong external equity, traditional point factor methods may prove to instead be biased toward maximizing internal equity when rational weighting is used.

Factor Comparison

Caruth and Handlogten (2001) characterized the factor comparison method of setting pay rates as being

> by far the most complex approach to job evaluation… [It is] a hybrid approach [that] contains aspects of job ranking as well as aspects of the point method [and] is similar to ranking in that jobs are compared with all other jobs, but it is also similar to point evaluation in that jobs are compared with a set of compensable factors. (p. 94)

This method will not be considered in detail here, given that it arguably manages to combine the subjectivity-based drawbacks noted above with respect to ranking procedures (by requiring the ranking of the key jobs on each compensable factor) with the negatives associated with traditional implementations of the point factor method (in particular, the measurement problems associated with accurately quantifying a small number of highly abstract compensable factors).

Policy Capturing Point Factor

Caruth and Handlogten (2001) considered factor comparison to represent the least-used method of job evaluation. However, that distinction probably should be reserved for the final method to be considered here, which represents a special case of the point factor method that incorporates both high-quality methods for quantifying the compensable factors, as well as a method for empirically deriving the factor weights that is desirable with respect to enhancing external equity.

One of the earliest descriptions of PCPF was published by McCormick, Jeanneret, and Mecham (1972). To quantify the compensable factors of jobs, instead of relying on holistic ratings of vague constructs as in traditional point factor methods, McCormick et al. used the work dimension scores produced via decomposed-judgment factor analytic means from item ratings on the Position Analysis Questionnaire (PAQ). Rather than relying on subjective judgments of the relative importance and predictive value of each factor, they used empirical policy capturing techniques (here, a multiple regression model in which market wage rates for each job are the criteria and the work dimension scores are the predictors). Once the policy capturing model has been derived in a sample of benchmark jobs, predictions of the point values for the remaining nonkey jobs can be produced by simply plugging the predictor (work dimension) scores into the multiple regression model that was derived using the key jobs.

The advantages of this approach are compelling. First, the concerns that were raised regarding the subjectivity, questionable psychometric properties, and general lack of demonstrable job-relatedness of data collected using traditional point factor and whole-job methods are reduced dramatically. Defending the quality of the job analysis database that produced the compensation system should be a very straightforward matter if one can successfully argue the following:

1. The items rated in the standardized job analysis questionnaire are sufficiently comprehensive and verifiable to describe the jobs in question.
2. Appropriate rating scales are used to judge the items (Harvey & Wilson, 2000, Chapter 29, this volume).
3. Appropriately job-knowledgeable and motivated raters provide the ratings.

Questions have been raised (e.g., Harvey, 1991a) regarding the high level of abstraction (and associated lower potential for independent verification of the ratings) that is seen for some of the items that are rated in the PAQ (e.g., a single-item rating is used to describe the overall decision-making responsibility of the job) and similar instruments (e.g., the Job Element Inventory; Harvey, Friedman, Hakel, & Cornelius, 1988). Fortunately, a number of standardized, common-metric job analysis questionnaires that describe work activities at a higher level of behavioral detail are available (e.g., Cunningham, Boese, Neeb, & Pass, 1983; Harvey, 1991b). When adequately specific items are rated, a very clear paper trail can be identified that leads directly from individual item ratings to the abstract work dimension scores that define the compensable factors. Should the need arise, literally every single job analysis item rating can be independently audited by job-knowledgeable individuals and their accuracy verified.

When using this approach, practitioners have the capacity to respond directly to potential criticisms that may arise regarding the quality or accuracy of the underlying job analysis data on which the compensation system was based. Based on the above discussions of the fundamental limitations of whole-job and traditional compensable factor methods in this regard, the fact that the PCPF method allows all of the data driving the compensation process to be independently reviewed and verified is unprecedented among job evaluation methods.

A second advantage of the PCPF method concerns the often troublesome task of slotting non-key jobs into the system that arises when using traditional point factor and whole-job methods; here, this task can be dealt with in a very straightforward fashion. That is, as long as one selects a large and representative sample of benchmark jobs for use when deriving the policy capturing regression model, the model should cross-validate well when applied to predict the wage rates for nonkey jobs. Hence, slotting nonkey jobs simply requires scoring them on the work dimensions and applying the policy capturing equation to predict their compensation levels.

A third advantage is the fact that actual market wage survey values are used as the criterion when deriving the policy capturing regression model, which provides considerable benefits with respect to both external equity and usability. The weighting system used in PCPF to combine factor scores to produce an overall point value is explicitly optimized with respect to producing pay predictions that parallel external labor market conditions as closely as possible in a least-squares sense (and hence, maximize external equity). The fact that the point values (regression model predictions) lie on an intrinsically meaningful scale (i.e., the scale of the actual compensation rates obtained from market surveys for the benchmark jobs) further simplifies the process of translating point values into an operational compensation system.

Finally, practical applications of this technique using standardized job analysis instruments as diverse as the PAQ (McCormick et al., 1972) and CMQ (Harvey, 1993; Harvey & Lozada-Larsen, 1993) have consistently demonstrated—at least by typical standards seen in applied psychology—levels of prediction of the market-pay criterion that have few parallels. For example, across five different organizations, Harvey (1993) reported shrunken (i.e., estimates of cross-validated) multiple R values ranging from .67 to .98 when predicting pay and from .55 to .94 when predicting the criterion of whether the job would be classified as exempt (e.g., professional, managerial, executive) under the Fair Labor Standards Act.

Consistent with the concerns noted above and in Harvey (Chapter 6, this volume) regarding the need to verify the accuracy of job analysis ratings that are collected for compensation purposes, the multiple R values reported in Harvey (1993) were considerably higher in the settings in which an independent review and verification of the item ratings had been conducted. When viewed in conjunction with earlier studies using the PAQ, such results indicate that market wage values are highly predictable from descriptions of the objective aspects of jobs, and they provide additional empirical justification for practitioners who seek a convincing method for documenting the job-relatedness and objectivity of their compensation systems.

Given the strong empirical results reported in the research literature to date, and the fact that the PCPF method has been in applied use since the 1970s, it remains surprising how little attention this market policy-capturing variant of the point factor method has received among compensation practitioners and applied researchers. Many standard texts on compensation ignore it entirely; if PCPF is mentioned, it is often only in passing.

Perhaps part of the problem involves the lack of a suitably catchy name for the procedure; unfortunately, the PCPF acronym offered here seems unlikely to help much in that regard. Hopefully, this chapter will contribute toward increasing the visibility of this method among compensation practitioners, especially those who are motivated by a need to be able to offer convincing evidence in support of both the quality and accuracy of the underlying data on which their compensation systems are based, as well as the strength of the linkage between that information and the external compensation criteria of interest.

One interesting aspect of the PCPF approach is that although it can be performed in a fashion that enhances the external equity of the pay predictions (i.e., when external labor market wage values serve as the criterion), by changing the pay criterion it can also be used in a fashion that instead enhances internal equity (or a mix thereof). As was described in Harvey (1993) and Harvey and Lozada-Larsen (1993), if instead of using external wage values as the criterion one uses compensation rates for selected benchmark jobs based on the existing rates *within* the target organization, the PCPF procedure captures and perpetuates the pay policies that determined the pay rates of those benchmark jobs within the specific organization in question.

The possibility of using a customized mix of benchmark pay criterion values based on internal (i.e., for jobs that are deemed fairly compensated by internal standards) pay rates for some titles, with external market-survey rates being used for others, allows practitioners essentially infinite flexibility with respect to balancing internal-equity versus external-equity concerns when deriving PCPF equations. Such flexibility is absent in traditional whole-job and compensable factor job evaluation methods, and depending on the circumstances of the specific organization and pay system in question, it may offer a compelling reason to favor PCPF over traditional methods.

A REAL-WORLD APPLICATION OF THE POLICY CAPTURING POINT FACTOR METHOD

This chapter concludes by providing a real-data illustration of the application of the PCPF method, using data collected with the CMQ on a diverse sample of occupations. The information used in this example was chosen to provide a realistic illustration of how the process can be conducted in a single organization that seeks to derive its own policy capturing equation. However, the same basic methods could also be used to apply the PCPF technique on a larger scale to develop pay-prediction equations that would be applicable across a range of organizations or industries.

Instruments and Data

A sample of 1,570 positions classified into 208 occupations from the standard occupational classification (SOC) taxonomy was drawn from the national CMQ database. These positions were analyzed using the web-based version of the CMQ (see http://cmqonline.com), which is fundamentally similar to the earlier paper-and-pencil and computer-based versions (e.g., Harvey, 1991a, 1993; Harvey & Lozada-Larsen, 1993) but adds some additional items and rating scales. Market wage survey values were obtained from the U.S. Department of Labor, Bureau of Labor Statistics (2008) using the Occupational Employment Statistics from May 2008, using the median value as the pay criterion for each SOC occupation.

Several different scoring systems for producing work dimension profiles from the CMQ item ratings were examined (i.e., scoring systems defining either 3, 23, or 71 work dimension factors; see Harvey, 2004, for further description of the 3-factor solution). To form the predictor profiles, the median rating on each of the CMQ work dimension scores (which were computed as factor score estimates based on the regression method) was computed across the multiple positions holding each SOC title. Appendix Table 25.1 lists a summary of the SOC occupational titles in the sample, as well as the median wage value for each.

Model Derivation

Multiple linear regression was used to derive a pay-prediction model for each of the three CMQ work dimension scoring systems. Although past studies of this type (e.g., Harvey, 1993; McCormick et al., 1972) have reported models that estimate only linear effects for the work dimension predictors, there is no necessary reason for assuming that the relationship between a given work activity and market compensation rates will always be linear. Indeed, especially for some of the most predictive work dimensions (e.g., the amount of human resource and financial decision responsibility), one might easily hypothesize that nonlinear effects (e.g., estimated using squared or cubed predictors in addition to the linear terms) could be appropriate.

For jobs scoring in the low levels of such dimensions, one might expect to find a modest increase in pay with a given increase in decision-making responsibility, yet a much stronger increase in pay with the same degree of increase in the predictor at the higher ranges of the scale (e.g., as might be seen for entry-level supervisors versus upper-level executives). Based on what is commonly seen in item response theory trace lines, a two-bend nonlinear model might also be expected in some cases, with the slope of the relationship flattening-out at the highest levels. Indeed, one might also wish to model interactive effects among the work dimension predictors (e.g., does the relationship between a dimension such as using keyboard devices and market pay change as a function of the degree of supervisory responsibility of the job?).

However, when considering the possibility of fitting more complex models of the types noted above, practitioners must identify what they find to represent the best tradeoff between stability of the model when applied to nonkey jobs versus the desire to obtain higher multiple correlations. Unless the samples are sufficiently large (recall that the unit of analysis is typically the job, not the position), practitioners may decide that the higher R values that are possible using more complicated models do not offset the increased stability of the simpler models.

A range of predictor granularity was chosen in order to illustrate the fact that one would typically expect to find higher levels of prediction of the pay criterion in models that have larger numbers of more detailed predictors. In the case of the most abstract scoring system (Harvey, 2004), this solution parallels Sidney Fine's data, people, and things worker-function constructs from functional job analysis (e.g., Fine, 1955; Fine & Cronshaw, 1999; Fine, Harvey, & Cronshaw, 2004; Chapter 15, this volume). Although one might not expect three highly abstract predictors to be able to account for a high proportion of the pay criterion variance, the results of this model are nevertheless of interest in terms of illustrating the kinds of pay policies for valuing the compensable factors that are operative in the national labor market.

Results of the model derivation analyses are presented in Appendices 25.2–25.4. As hypothesized (and consistent with prior research), a comparison of the results in these appendices indicates that strong levels of predictive power are seen when predicting market pay from work activity constructs (e.g., shrunken $R = .77$ for the 71-factor model and shrunken $R = .66$ for the more parsimonious 23-factor model). In addition, predictive power declines considerably when only a few highly abstract work-activity constructs are used as predictors (shrunken $R = .43$ for the 3-factor model).

The increased predictive power possible by using a larger number of more granular work dimensions as compensable factors is made graphically apparent in the scatterplots shown in Figures 25.1–25.3, which plot for each SOC occupation the actual wage-survey criterion medians (*y*-axis) by the predicted values produced by the 71-, 23-, and 3-factor PCPF policy-capturing models, respectively. Clearly, the increased detail with respect to defining general work activity dimensions offered by the higher-dimensionality solutions allows them to more effectively capture the policies governing the ways in which work activities are associated with market compensation rates.

In terms of the substantive interpretation of the market pay policies captured by these PCPF equations, the results in Appendix Table 25.2 for the most abstract predictor model underscore the observation made earlier regarding the limitations of rationally derived compensable factor weights. That is, as the Appendix Table 25.2 results indicate, although increases in both the data (decision-making) and people (interpersonal activities) dimensions are associated with increases in the amount of pay given to jobs in the external market, increases in the things dimension (which strongly reflects both gross physical activities and working in unpleasant and/or hazardous environments) are associated with decreased levels of pay.

Although given the sample size used here the number of predictor terms contained in the 23- and 71-factor models effectively precludes a search for the above-mentioned interaction effects among the work dimension predictors, the brevity of the 3-factor solution allows such a model to be tested. Unfortunately, adding the two- and three-way interaction terms to the model examined in Appendix Table 25.2 produced an increase in R of only approximately 1%, and none of the coefficients representing the cross-product terms approached the $p < .05$ level of significance. However, given the relatively low power seen here, and the possibility that such moderation might be more

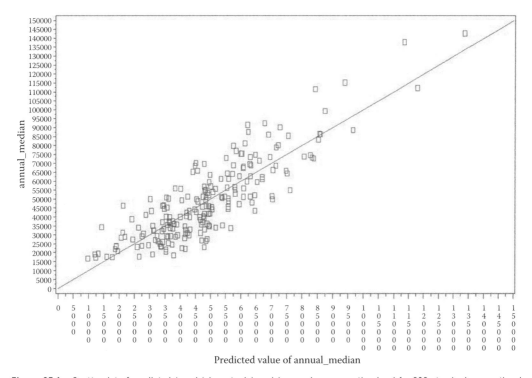

Figure 25.1   Scatterplot of predicted (*x*-axis) by actual (*y*-axis) annual compensation level for 208 standard occupational classifications based on a model predicting median May 2008 compensation levels from the Common-Metric Questionnaire (Harvey, 1991a) work dimension scores in the 71-factor solution ($R = .86$, shrunken $R = .77$).

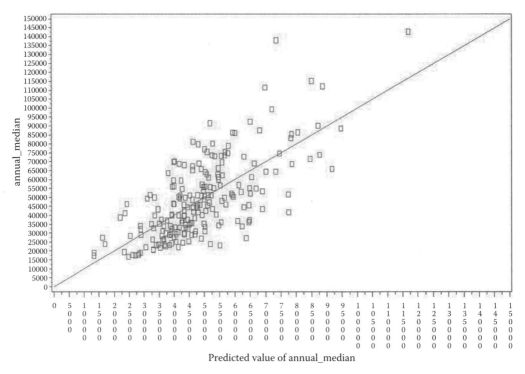

Figure 25.2   Scatterplot of predicted (*x*-axis) by actual (*y*-axis) annual compensation level for 208 standard occupational classifications based on a model predicting median May 2008 compensation levels from the Common-Metric Questionnaire (Harvey, 1991a) work dimension scores in the 23-factor solution (*R* = .70, shrunken *R* = .66).

likely to occur when more granular work dimensions are used as predictors, these null findings should not deter others from examining such effects in subsequent studies.

A similar situation is seen in the 23-factor model results in Appendix Table 25.3. Here, although increases in factors describing decision making and interpersonal responsibility dimensions (e.g., Factor 4, which describes internal contacts with professional/technical workers) are associated with increased market pay, increases in other work dimensions (e.g., Factor 20 describing sales-related contacts) are inversely related to pay. Likewise, in the Appendix Table 25.4 results for the 71-factor model, Factor 5 (gross physical activities) exhibits a significant negative partial regression coefficient. However, the factors showing the highest positive partial relationships predicting pay (e.g., Factors 55 and 64, both of which deal with relatively high-level interpersonal functions involved in external contacts with the press, regulators, and so forth) deal with activities in the managerial decision-making domains.

When comparing the levels of model fit seen in Figures 25.1–25.3, although there appears to be some support for the conclusion that the 71-factor model (Figure 25.1) does the best job in fitting the occupations that receive the highest levels of pay (presumably given the ability of the more fine-grained dimensions to capture more subtle aspects of pay policies), the more molar predictors used in the other two models seem to encounter difficulties in fitting both high- and low-paying occupations. For example, in the 23-factor solution in Figure 25.2, a sizable residual exists for concierges (SOC 39-6012), with the market wage average ($27,180) falling far below the level predicted from the work dimensions ($63,754). Conversely, one of the largest residuals in the other direction is seen for dentists–all other specialties (SOC 29-1029), with a predicted value of $73,541 falling far below the market average of $137,970. In both cases, the more fine-grained view of general work activities

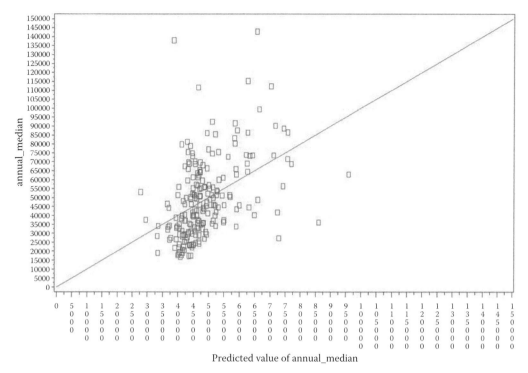

Figure 25.3 Scatterplot of predicted (x-axis) by actual (y-axis) annual compensation level for 208 standard occupational classifications based on a model predicting median May 2008 compensation levels from the Common-Metric Questionnaire (Harvey, 1991a) work dimension scores in the 3-factor solution ($R = .44$, shrunken $R = .43$).

provided by the 71-factor solution seems to be required to fully capture the market forces driving pay rates for such occupations.

Of course, the results in Appendices 25.2 and 25.3 also underscore the inherent tradeoff that exists between increasing the level of predictive power in policy-capturing models (in this case, by increasing the number and granularity of the predictors) versus obtaining statistically significant results for individual regression coefficients, as well as results that will show adequate stability in cross-validation. The sample size of titles used here is typical of the levels seen in many small- and moderate-sized organizations—that is, large enough to allow using fairly detailed job-side predictor general work activities, but hardly large enough to justify abundant confidence regarding the ability of the results to cross-validate (to other organizations, or additional samples of jobs in the same setting), or to suggest the use of other statistical techniques (e.g., stepwise selection of predictors) that may be even more prone to undue capitalization on chance variability.

Ultimately, the practitioner bears the responsibility for determining the best balance between increased variance-explained in the pay criterion versus stability of the PCPF model in cross-validation applications. In one respect, it could be argued that practitioners should focus on deriving PCPF equations in large samples of jobs and occupations obtained from nationally representative samples (i.e., a larger-scale version of the example shown here) in order to maximize the stability and generalizability of the prediction equation.

However, the ways in which various kinds of work activity are valued in the market may be moderated significantly by such factors as industry type, general occupation type, overall job complexity, geographic region, or similar characteristics. If so, locally derived models that are tailored to specific settings or combinations of such factors (and/or much more complex general models that incorporate the appropriate interaction terms) would be indicated. To date, very little empirical research exists to guide an informed decision in this regard.

Model Application to Form Grade Structure

The typical way in which point predictions are used to develop the categorical pay-grade structures seen in operational compensation systems is illustrated in Figure 25.4. As was noted earlier, rather than making compensation decisions based on the specific point-value predicted for each job, most organizations prefer to assign jobs to one of a relatively small number of ordered-category pay grades and to then treat all jobs within a given grade as being functionally interchangeable (at least, insofar as pay is concerned). When using point factor methods (including the PCPF technique illustrated here), the task of translating between a ranking of jobs based on their overall point value and a categorical pay-grade structure can be accomplished by simply plotting the actual versus predicted pay values and selecting the appropriate points on which to categorize the distribution of predicted values to form categorical pay grades.

Figure 25.4 illustrates one way in which these 208 titles can be grouped to form a 9-grade pay system. Although considerable thought can be invested in the various choices that are involved in developing an actual pay grade structure (e.g., regarding the number of grades, their height, the degree of overlap between successive grades), the basics of the process are quite simple.

In sum, the PCPF approach illustrated above offers the capability to dramatically reduce the degree of subjectivity that is present in the typical point factor-based compensation system, both with respect to the initial analysis of the jobs to produce compensable factor scores, as well as in

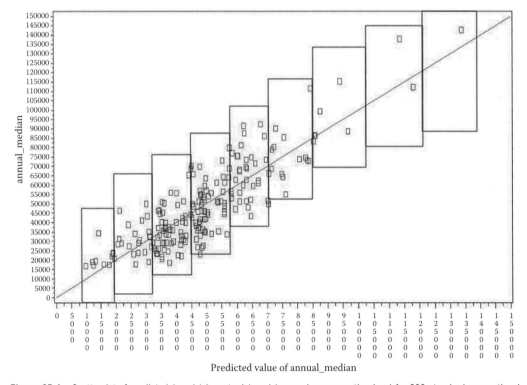

Figure 25.4 Scatterplot of predicted (*x*-axis) by actual (*y*-axis) annual compensation level for 208 standard occupational classifications based on a model predicting median May 2008 compensation levels from the Common-Metric Questionnaire (Harvey, 1991a) work dimension scores in the 3-factor solution.

terms of empirically weighting and linking the job analysis results to form overall point values for jobs and develop the pay grade structure. The fact that the PCPF method gives practitioners effectively infinite flexibility with respect to tailoring a compensation system's balance of internal versus external equity provides even more reason to prefer such an approach to either whole-job or traditional compensable factor methods. Hopefully, the next 40 years will see an increase in the use of this approach for linking job analysis results to compensation decisions, as well as increased research regarding the question of how variable pay policies tend to be across situations, and the types of situational moderators that most strongly influence the ways in which objective work activities are valued in the market.

APPENDIX

Table 25.1   National Average Wage Survey Values for 208 SOC Occupational Clusters

Observation	SOC Code	Annual Median	SOC Title
1	11-1021	91570	General and operations managers
2	11-3011	73520	Administrative services managers
3	11-3021	112210	Computer and information systems managers
4	11-3031	99330	Financial managers
5	11-3041	86500	Compensation and benefits managers
6	11-3042	87700	Training and development managers
7	11-3051	83290	Industrial production managers
8	11-3071	79000	Transportation, storage, and distribution managers
9	11-9012	33550	Farmers and ranchers
10	11-9021	79860	Construction managers
11	11-9031	39940	Education administrators, preschool and child care center/programs
12	11-9039	71630	Education administrators, all other
13	11-9041	115270	Engineering managers
14	11-9051	46320	Food service managers
15	11-9061	52210	Funeral directors
16	11-9111	80240	Medical and health services managers
17	11-9141	46130	Property, real estate, and community association managers
18	11-9151	55980	Social and community service managers
19	11-9199	90230	Managers, all other
20	13-1011	62940	Agents and business managers of artists, performers, and athletes
21	13-1022	48710	Wholesale and retail buyers, except farm products
22	13-1031	55760	Claims adjusters, examiners, and investigators
23	13-1041	48890	Compliance officers, except agriculture, construction, health and
24	13-1071	45470	Employment, recruitment, and placement specialists
25	13-1072	53860	Compensation, benefits, and job analysis specialists
26	13-1073	51450	Training and development specialists
27	13-1079	55710	Human resources, training, and labor relations specialists, all
28	13-1111	73570	Management analysts
29	13-1121	44260	Meeting and convention planners
30	13-1199	59920	Business operations specialists, all other
31	13-2011	59430	Accountants and auditors
32	13-2031	65320	Budget analysts

continued

Table 25.1 National Average Wage Survey Values for 208 SOC Occupational Clusters (Continued)

Observation	SOC Code	Annual Median	SOC Title
33	13-2051	73150	Financial analysts
34	13-2052	69050	Personal financial advisors
35	13-2072	54700	Loan officers
36	13-2099	57150	Financial specialists, all other
37	15-1021	69620	Computer programmers
38	15-1031	85430	Computer software engineers, applications
39	15-1032	92430	Computer software engineers, systems software
40	15-1041	43450	Computer support specialists
41	15-1051	75500	Computer systems analysts
42	15-1061	69740	Database administrators
43	15-1071	66310	Network and computer systems administrators
44	15-2031	69000	Operations research analysts
45	17-2051	74600	Civil engineers
46	17-2072	86370	Electronics engineers, except computer
47	17-2112	73820	Industrial engineers
48	17-2141	74920	Mechanical engineers
49	17-2199	88570	Engineers, all other
50	17-3011	44490	Architectural and civil drafters
51	17-3021	55040	Aerospace engineering and operations technicians
52	17-3026	47180	Industrial engineering technicians
53	17-3027	48130	Mechanical engineering technicians
54	17-3029	56850	Engineering technicians, except drafters, all other
55	19-1011	56030	Animal scientists
56	19-1012	59520	Food scientists and technologists
57	19-1022	64350	Microbiologists
58	19-1023	55290	Zoologists and wildlife biologists
59	19-1041	61360	Epidemiologists
60	19-3021	61070	Market research analysts
61	19-3022	36220	Survey researchers
62	19-3031	64140	Clinical, counseling, and school psychologists
63	19-3032	77010	Industrial-organizational psychologists
64	19-3039	86120	Psychologists, all other
65	19-3099	68720	Social scientists and related workers, all other
66	19-4011	33990	Agricultural and food science technicians
67	19-4021	38400	Biological technicians
68	19-4061	35650	Social science research assistants
69	19-4092	49860	Forensic science technicians
70	21-1011	37030	Substance abuse and behavioral disorder counselors
71	21-1012	51050	Educational, vocational, and school counselors
72	21-1013	44590	Marriage and family therapists
73	21-1014	36810	Mental health counselors
74	21-1019	39930	Counselors, all other
75	21-1021	39530	Child, family, and school social workers
76	21-1022	45650	Medical and public health social workers

Table 25.1   National Average Wage Survey Values for 208 SOC Occupational Clusters (Continued)

Observation	SOC Code	Annual Median	SOC Title
77	21-1023	37210	Mental health and substance abuse social workers
78	21-1092	45910	Probation officers and correctional treatment specialists
79	21-2011	41730	Clergy
80	21-2021	36100	Directors, religious activities and education
81	23-2011	46120	Paralegals and legal assistants
82	23-2092	37130	Law clerks
83	23-2099	50250	Legal support workers, all other
84	25-1066	63630	Psychology teachers, postsecondary
85	25-1081	56400	Education teachers, postsecondary
86	25-1191	29850	Graduate teaching assistants
87	25-1199	61360	Postsecondary teachers, all other
88	25-2011	23870	Preschool teachers, except special education
89	25-2021	49330	Elementary school teachers, except special education
90	25-2031	51180	Secondary school teachers, except special and vocational education
91	25-2041	50020	Special education teachers, preschool, kindergarten, and elementary
92	25-2042	50810	Special education teachers, middle school
93	25-3011	46310	Adult literacy, remedial education, and GED teachers and instructors
94	25-3099	31100	Teachers and instructors, all other
95	25-9011	43390	Audio-visual collections specialists
96	25-9031	56880	Instructional coordinators
97	25-9041	22200	Teacher assistants
98	27-1013	42650	Fine artists, including painters, sculptors, and illustrators
99	27-1019	51600	Artists and related workers, all other
100	27-1023	23230	Floral designers
101	27-1024	42400	Graphic designers
102	27-2012	64430	Producers and directors
103	27-2021	40480	Athletes and sports competitors
104	27-2022	28340	Coaches and scouts
105	27-2041	41270	Music directors and composers
106	27-3021	51260	Broadcast news analysts
107	27-3031	51280	Public relations specialists
108	29-1021	142870	Dentists, general
109	29-1029	137970	Dentists, all other specialists
110	29-1071	81230	Physician assistants
111	29-1111	62450	Registered nurses
112	29-1123	72790	Physical therapists
113	29-1127	62930	Speech-language pathologists
114	29-1129	50700	Therapists, all other
115	29-1199	65880	Health diagnosing and treating practitioners, all other
116	29-2011	53500	Medical and clinical laboratory technologists
117	29-2012	35380	Medical and clinical laboratory technicians
118	29-2034	52210	Radiologic technologists and technicians
119	29-2041	29330	Emergency medical technicians and paramedics
120	29-2052	27710	Pharmacy technicians

continued

Table 25.1 National Average Wage Survey Values for 208 SOC Occupational Clusters (Continued)

Observation	SOC Code	Annual Median	SOC Title
121	29-2053	29250	Psychiatric technicians
123	29-2081	32810	Opticians, dispensing
124	29-9012	45360	Occupational health and safety technicians
125	31-2022	23760	Physical therapist aides
126	31-9099	29350	Healthcare support workers, all other
127	33-1012	75490	First-line supervisors/managers of police and detectives
128	33-1021	67440	First-line supervisors/managers of fire fighting and prevention
129	33-1099	43570	First-line supervisors/managers, protective service workers, all
130	33-2011	44260	Fire fighters
131	33-2021	53030	Fire inspectors and investigators
132	33-3041	32390	Parking enforcement workers
133	33-3051	51410	Police and sheriff's patrol officers
134	33-9021	41760	Private detectives and investigators
135	33-9032	23460	Security guards
136	33-9092	18450	Lifeguards, ski patrol, and other recreational protective services
137	35-1011	38770	Chefs and head cooks
138	35-1012	28970	First-line supervisors/managers of food preparation and serving
139	35-2014	21990	Cooks, restaurant
140	35-3011	17770	Bartenders
141	35-3031	16660	Waiters and waitresses
142	35-3041	19380	Food servers, nonrestaurant
143	35-9031	17510	Hosts and hostesses, restaurant, lounge, and coffee shop
144	37-1011	33980	First-line supervisors/managers of housekeeping and janitorial workers
145	39-3031	17360	Ushers, lobby attendants, and ticket takers
146	39-5012	23140	Hairdressers, hairstylists, and cosmetologists
147	39-6012	27180	Concierges
148	39-6031	35930	Flight attendants
149	39-9011	18970	Child care workers
150	39-9041	23410	Residential advisors
151	41-1011	35310	First-line supervisors/managers of retail sales workers
152	41-1012	68100	First-line supervisors/managers of non-retail sales workers
153	41-2011	17660	Cashiers
154	41-2031	20510	Retail salespersons
155	41-3031	68680	Securities, commodities, and financial services sales agents
156	41-3099	49430	Sales representatives, services, all other
157	41-4011	70200	Sales representatives, wholesale and manufacturing, technical and
158	41-4012	51330	Sales representatives, wholesale and manufacturing, except technical
159	41-9022	40150	Real estate sales agents
160	43-1011	45790	First-line supervisors/managers of office and administrative support
161	43-2011	24220	Switchboard operators, including answering service
162	43-3011	30630	Bill and account collectors
163	43-3021	30950	Billing and posting clerks and machine operators
164	43-3031	32510	Bookkeeping, accounting, and auditing clerks

Table 25.1 National Average Wage Survey Values for 208 SOC Occupational Clusters (Continued)

Observation	SOC Code	Annual Median	SOC Title
165	43-3051	34810	Payroll and timekeeping clerks
166	43-3061	34780	Procurement clerks
167	43-3071	23610	Tellers
168	43-4031	33200	Court, municipal, and license clerks
169	43-4051	29860	Customer service representatives
170	43-4121	22630	Library assistants, clerical
171	43-4161	35750	Human resources assistants, except payroll and timekeeping
172	43-4171	24550	Receptionists and information clerks
173	43-5032	33850	Dispatchers, except police, fire, and ambulance
174	43-5061	40480	Production, planning, and expediting clerks
175	43-5081	20800	Stock clerks and order fillers
176	43-5111	26940	Weighers, measurers, checkers, and samplers, recordkeeping
177	43-6011	40030	Executive secretaries and administrative assistants
178	43-6012	39860	Legal secretaries
179	43-6014	29050	Secretaries, except legal, medical, and executive
180	43-9041	33100	Insurance claims and policy processing clerks
181	43-9051	25100	Mail clerks and mail machine operators, except postal service
182	43-9061	25320	Office clerks, general
183	43-9199	29320	Office and administrative support workers, all other
184	47-2051	35080	Cement masons and concrete finishers
185	47-2061	28520	Construction laborers
186	47-2081	37700	Drywall and ceiling tile installers
187	47-2111	46420	Electricians
188	47-2141	32960	Painters, construction and maintenance
189	47-2161	37470	Plasterers and stucco masons
190	47-3013	26390	Helpers—electricians
191	49-9042	33710	Maintenance and repair workers, general
192	49-9099	34240	Installation, maintenance, and repair workers, all other
193	51-1011	50440	First-line supervisors/managers of production and operating work
194	51-5011	27390	Bindery workers
195	51-5023	32170	Printing machine operators
196	51-7011	28980	Cabinetmakers and bench carpenters
197	51-8011	73320	Nuclear power reactor operators
198	51-8012	65890	Power distributors and dispatchers
199	51-8021	49790	Stationary engineers and boiler operators
200	51-9061	31240	Inspectors, testers, sorters, samplers, and weighers
201	51-9131	26010	Photographic process workers
202	51-9198	21790	Helpers—production workers
203	51-9199	26750	Production workers, all other
204	53-1021	41970	First-line supervisors/managers of helpers, laborers, and material
205	53-2011	111680	Airline pilots, copilots, and flight engineers
206	53-3032	37270	Truck drivers, heavy and tractor-trailer
207	53-6051	55250	Transportation inspectors
208	53-7064	19060	Packers and packagers, hand

Table 25.2 Pay Policy-Capturing Model Using 71 CMQ Factors

The REG Procedure
Model: MODEL1
Dependent Variable: annual_median
Number of Observations Used 208

Analysis of Variance

Source	DF	Sum of Squares	Mean Square	F Value	Pr > F
Model	71	7546355106	106285072	5.30	<.0001
Error	136	27259662925	200438698		
Corrected Total	207	1.02722E11			

Root MSE	14158	R-Square	0.7346	
Dependent Mean	48912	Adj R-Sq	0.5961	
Coeff Var	28.94517			

Parameter Estimates

Variable	Label	DF	Parameter Estimate	Standard Error	t Value	Pr > |t|	Standardized Estimate
Intercept	Intercept	1	50801	1817.24185	27.95	<.0001	0
factor1	Internal contracts: exchange information, consult, problem-solve -professional/technical employees	1	4901.78701	2096.39661	2.34	0.0208	0.19277
factor2	Internal contracts: exchange information, consult, problem-solve - senior, management	1	-2478.60495	2443.02587	-1.01	0.3121	-0.09273
factor3	Using senses to obtain information from the environment, related physical activities	1	2818.34390	2133.40066	1.32	0.1887	0.10650
factor4	Interpersonal contacts: exchange information, consult, problem-solve - non-supervisory employees outside own area	1	-2933.81751	2742.17529	-1.07	0.2866	-0.08939
factor5	Gross physical activities, related environmental conditions	1	-3711.73169	1407.69791	-2.64	0.0093	-0.18133
factor6	Interpersonal contacts: exchange information, consult, problem-solve - supervisory employees from other areas of orgnization	1	3077.31148	2687.27521	1.15	0.2542	0.09302
factor7	Provide treatment, therapy	1	524.17089	2349.89476	0.22	0.8238	0.02111

factor8	External contacts: exchange information, consult, problem-solve – professional/technical employees	1	4377.24636	1.60	0.1119	0.12166
factor9	Managerial decisions: making, impact of decisions re: establishing or changing lines of authorit, benefits, policies	1	7605.53821	2.35	0.0202	0.22607
factor10	Managerial decisions: implementing decisions re: operations effectiveness, performance goals, employee responsibilities, operations	1	-1815.40421	-1.90	0.0593	-0.13723
factor11	External contacts: solve problems, consult, resolve conflicts, coordinate, inform – customers	1	-2031.61093	-1.02	0.3113	-0.07626
factor12	External contacts: set policies, exchange information, consult, problem-solve - executives	1	1244.46868	0.90	0.3679	0.06125
factor13	Internal contacts: attend meetings to exchange information, consult, problem-solve - supervisory and nonsupervisory workers in own area	1	-4051.02886	-2.41	0.0174	-0.16323
factor14	External contacts: attend meetings to solve problems, coordinate, inform – supervisory and nonsupervisory employees of other organizations	1	4340.98688	2.43	0.0165	0.17744
factor15	Internal contacts: chair meetings to exchange information, consult, problem-solve - supervisory and nonsupervisory workers in own area	1	-334.72670	-0.21	0.8342	-0.01277
factor16	Language use: use written, spoken words in English, related office equipment	1	-4430.22126	-2.38	0.0189	-0.31836
factor17	Mechanical activities: operating stationary machines for grinding, milling, drilling, cutting, welding	1	617.97334	0.47	0.6426	0.02881
factor18	Interpersonal contacts: attending meetings to persuade or sell – employees of own, other organizations	1	4868.53991	2.43	0.0164	0.16538
factor19	Managerial decisions: making, impact of decisions re: discontinuing services, closing projects, phasing-out operations	1	332.46015	0.18	0.8573	0.01181
factor20	External contacts: solve problems, coordinate, inform – infants, children, juveniles, students	1	3687.82915	1.25	0.2119	0.11095
factor21	Managerial decisions: making, impact of decisions re: adding, discontinuing products or product lines	1	4869.63883	2.10	0.0376	0.22421

continued

Table 25.2   Pay Policy-Capturing Model Using 71 CMQ Factors (Continued)

			Parameter Estimates				
Variable	Label	DF	Parameter Estimate	Standard Error	t Value	Pr > ltl	Standardized Estimate
factor22	Internal contacts: exchange information, coordinate, supervise - managerial, professional/technical employees	1	-3890.72091	2457.74684	-1.58	0.1157	-0.15432
factor23	Interpersonal contacts: frequency of contacts with press, special interests, regulators	1	626.47133	1901.86973	0.33	0.7424	0.02300
factor24	External contacts: solve problems, coordinate, inform - governmental, regulatory employees	1	1470.68262	1701.96464	0.86	0.3890	0.05787
factor25	Mechanical activities: use water, air vehicles	1	740.35170	3095.60147	0.24	0.8113	0.03091
factor26	Mechanical activities: machines, vehicles, equipment, tools - test, assemble	1	-2044.49601	3320.28080	-0.62	0.5391	-0.06124
factor27	Language use: use written, spoken words in a language other than English	1	1460.53035	2414.05811	0.61	0.5462	0.04076
factor28	Interpersonal contacts: attend meetings to formally bargain or negotiate - professional/technical, supervisory employees	1	-2033.98694	1992.50824	-1.02	0.3092	-0.10200
factor29	Internal contacts: people who are in custody	1	-1283.93877	2205.39749	-0.58	0.5614	-0.04321
factor30	Interpersonal contacts: resolve problems, exchange information, bargain, coordinate — unions or special-interest groups	1	-2164.76594	1449.60168	-1.49	0.1377	-0.08569
factor31	External contacts: inform, consult, coordinate, delegate, problem-solve - managerial and non-managerial employees of other organizations	1	3577.83020	2208.29838	1.62	0.1075	0.08973
factor32	Mechanical activities: using weapons, providing protection	1	-3548.15703	1771.91688	-2.00	0.0472	-0.24023
factor33	Internal contacts: exchange information, coordinate, supervise, delegate - professional/technical, supervisors	1	-8519.80358	2091.84153	-4.07	<.0001	-0.24651
factor34	Managerial decisions: delegating implementation of decisions re: performance goals, operations, purchasing	1	4506.96036	1424.93623	3.16	0.0019	0.19838
factor35	External contacts: chair meetings to inform, coordinate, bargain - suppliers, contractors	1	676.52974	2510.42409	0.27	0.7880	0.02115
factor36	Internal contacts: exchange information, coordinate, supervise - personal services employee	1	2939.90756	2065.22426	1.42	0.1569	0.09978

factor37	External contacts: the public – chair meetings to formally exchange information, consult, resolve conflicts, train	1	1677.08757	1779.73621	0.94	0.3477	0.05914
factor38	Internal contacts: exchange information, coordinate, supervise – marketing or sales employees	1	-2548.75894	3233.00500	-0.79	0.4319	-0.07655
factor39	Language use: computer programming languages	1	1864.22293	1742.56212	1.07	0.2866	0.06939
factor40	Managerial decisions: making strategic decisions, plans	1	3840.26027	2020.03283	1.90	0.0594	0.14141
factor41	Managerial decisions: financial, investments, purchasing capital equipment	1	2133.59619	1993.41187	1.07	0.2864	0.07484
factor42	External contacts: exchange information, consult, problem-solve – regulators	1	-2843.33705	1596.15930	-1.78	0.0771	-0.23357
factor43	Managerial decisions: acquiring, selling existing businesses	1	2425.00485	1725.71618	1.41	0.1622	0.10491
factor44	Mechanical activities: cutting, welding, forming, grinding, milling, drilling machines, related equipment	1	2661.61368	1666.90785	1.60	0.1126	0.10323
factor45	Internal contacts: exchange information, coordinate, supervise – laborers	1	1996.17622	1781.32093	1.12	0.2644	0.07253
factor46	Mechanical activities: hand-held tools, mobile powered tools, measuring devices	1	-4369.68474	1752.52397	-2.49	0.0139	-0.17421
factor47	Mechanical activities: off-road/utility vehicles, machines that move materials, liquids, or gases	1	-2227.09475	1375.19816	-1.62	0.1077	-0.11927
factor48	Interpersonal contacts: chair meetings to formally bargain or negotiate - professional/technical, supervisory employees	1	-5336.84072	2504.13705	-2.13	0.0349	-0.16123
factor49	Interpersonal contacts: entertainment	1	529.15666	2399.69427	0.22	0.8258	0.01656
factor50	External contacts: the public, press – chair meetings to solve problems, make decisions, resolve conflicts	1	-983.64643	1662.28552	-0.59	0.5550	-0.03759
factor51	External contacts: inform, consult, coordinate - civic, community, or charitable organizations, press	1	-1147.95348	1443.68223	-0.80	0.4279	-0.05168
factor52	Mechanical activities: using computing equipment, office equipment	1	-5346.42295	2620.26485	-2.04	0.0432	-0.17116
factor53	Managerial decisions: starting up, selling new businesses or subsidiaries	1	-3412.83945	1553.15580	-2.20	0.0297	-0.13157
factor54	Mechanical activities: operate machines that move, process, or change materials, liquids, or gases	1	-3821.91205	2021.31066	-1.89	0.0608	-0.12553

continued

Table 25.2   Pay Policy-Capturing Model Using 71 CMQ Factors (Continued)

		Parameter Estimates				
Variable	Label	DF	Parameter Estimate	Standard Error	t Value	Pr > |t|	Standardized Estimate
factor55	External contacts: press, regulators, public - chair meetings to evaluate, coordinate, instruct, problem-solve	1	6827.11020	1485.27547	4.60	<.0001	0.39432
factor57	Managerial decisions: implementing decisions re: performance goals, evaluating operations, purchasing	1	-3929.27615	2558.44112	-1.54	0.1269	-0.09933
factor58	Internal contacts: protect, ensure safety of others	1	1160.67590	2720.66965	0.43	0.6703	0.03294
factor59	Internal contacts: Supervise, coach, coordinate - clerical or support staff	1	-2271.13076	1653.69358	-1.37	0.1719	-0.09905
factor60	Mechanical activities: printing presses or similar machines	1	-2628.86409	1940.97201	-1.35	C.1779	-0.10448
factor61	Mechanical activities: operate technical, scientific, or medical equipment	1	-2317.86928	1883.42933	-1.23	0.2206	-0.08187
factor62	External contacts: Resolve conflicts or disputes - professional/technical, supervisory employees	1	-1508.06829	1538.84022	-0.98	0.3288	-0.05807
factor63	External contacts: customers, clients - inform, consult, exchange information, problem-solve	1	-2487.71157	1759.21007	-1.41	0.1596	-0.08793
factor64	External contacts: regulators, press - coordinate, schedule, evaluate	1	8800.92207	2089.53037	4.21	<.0001	0.35556
factor65	External contacts: set policies, rules, or procedures - professional, technical, nonsupervisory employees	1	2266.77316	2233.70554	1.01	0.3120	0.08259
factor66	External contacts: exchange information, coordinate - students, public, job applicants	1	1758.03607	2471.20112	0.71	0.4780	0.07833
factor67	Mechanical activities: operate heavy highway vehicles	1	-3133.20449	2288.47175	-1.37	0.1732	-0.12626
factor68	Mechanical activities: canning, bottling, or packaging machines	1	-1669.73116	1147.57853	-1.46	0.1480	-0.08618
factor69	Managerial decisions: determining the kinds of equipment used in, or the process of, production	1	604.84242	1982.80226	0.31	0.7508	0.02200
factor70	Internal contacts: sell or persuade professional/technical, managerial, supervisory employees	1	3444.38639	2036.33630	1.69	0.0930	0.14195
factor71	External contacts: delegate activities to employees of other organizations, regulators, public, special interests	1	1901.72325	1378.31974	1.38	0.1699	0.13709

Adj R-Sq = adjusted R-squared; coeff var = coefficient of variation; DF = degrees of freedom; parameter estimate = raw-score regression coefficient; Root MSE = root mean square error; standardized estimate = z-score regression coefficient.

Table 25.3 23-Factor Model

The REG Procedure
Model: MODEL1
Dependent Variable: annual_median
Number of Observations Used 208

Analysis of Variance

Source	DF	Sum of Squares	Mean Square	F Value	Pr > F
Model	23	50674061373	2203220060	7.79	<.0001
Error	184	52047956658	282869330		
Corrected Total	207	1.02722E11			

Root MSE	16819	R-Square	0.4933
Dependent Mean	48912	Adj R-Sq	0.4300
Coeff Var	34.38573		

Parameter Estimates

Variable	Label	DF	Parameter Estimate	Standard Error	t Value	Pr > ltl	Standardized Estimate
Intercept	Intercept	1	48763	1403.30725	34.75	<.0001	0
factor1	Managerial decisions, strategic planning	1	3821.73657	1755.94895	2.18	0.0308	0.13950
factor2	Gross physical activities, environment	1	3771.86782	2364.51193	1.60	0.1124	0.11059
factor3	External contacts: supervisory, professional, technical - information exchange, problem solving	1	-2392.75664	1182.41847	-2.02	0.0445	-0.11824
factor4	Internal contacts: professional, technical - information exchange, problem solving	1	12968	1802.57587	7.19	<.0001	0.51168
factor5	Internal contacts: executive-level, problem solving, information exchange	1	-25.83619	2017.29121	-0.01	0.9898	-0.00093791
factor6	English language use: writing, editing, copying	1	-2112.26909	1612.56858	-1.31	0.1919	-0.08098
factor7	mechanical activities: drilling, cutting, welding, handling machines/tools/vehicles	1	150.16778	1783.73859	0.08	0.9330	0.00529
factor8	Interpersonal activities: formally bargain, negotiate, persuade	1	-4191.34576	2046.45702	-2.05	0.0420	-0.13708

continued

Table 25.3 23-Factor Model (Continued)

	Parameter Estimates					
Variable	Label	DF	Parameter Estimate	Standard Error	t Value	Pr > |t|	Standardized Estimate
factor9	External contacts: supervisory, executive, professional/technical - information exchange, consult	1	5042.03152	2051.31348	2.46	0.0149	0.19856
factor10	Internal contacts: low- and middle-level supervisors - resolve conflicts, coach, inform,	1	1732.08458	1819.35297	0.95	0.3423	0.05810
factor11	Supervision given: lower- and mid-level workers - supervise, coordinate, delegate	1	-2208.15660	2148.62969	-1.03	0.3054	-0.07637
factor12	Interpersonal contacts: information exchange, non-supervisory	1	465.51849	2033.08419	0.23	0.8191	0.01624
factor13	Internal contacts: supervisory employees in own area - make decisions, exchange information, problem solving	1	-2044.53477	1826.88512	-1.12	0.2645	-0.08617
factor14	Managerial decisions: add/delete products, services	1	-1713.55680	1350.34094	-1.27	0.2061	-0.09099
factor15	External contacts: infants, children, juveniles, students	1	2091.99721	934.55944	2.24	0.0264	0.14191
factor16	Providing treatment, therapy	1	-1732.32926	1780.73221	-0.97	0.3319	-0.08789
factor17	External contacts: customers, clients - exchange information, solve problems	1	2695.08452	2370.08106	1.14	0.2570	0.08010
factor18	Mechanical activities: guns, weapons, air/water vehicles	1	1129.24112	943.55307	1.20	0.2329	0.07731
factor19	External contacts: public, press - exchange information, persuade, solve problems	1	-1984.96109	2086.85188	-0.95	0.3428	-0.07751
factor20	Interpersonal contacts: entertainment, sales	1	-5058.35954	1401.11685	-3.61	0.0004	-0.22181
factor21	External contacts: governmental, regulatory	1	1846.23328	1805.86714	1.02	0.3080	0.06142
factor22	Managerial decisions: create, sell, acquire businesses, subsidiaries	1	-1854.71426	1447.83189	-1.28	0.2018	-0.08062
factor23	Foreign language use	1	2568.77881	1657.45217	1.55	0.1229	0.10686

Adj R-Sq = adjusted R-squared; coeff var = coefficient of variation; DF = degrees of freedom; parameter estimate = raw-score regression coefficient; Root MSE = root mean square error; standardized estimate = z-score regression coefficient.

Table 25.4 3-Factor Model

The REG Procedure
Model: MODEL1
Dependent Variable: annual_median
Number of Observations Used   208

Analysis of Variance

Source	DF	Sum of Squares	Mean Square	F Value	Pr > F
Model	3	19998233245	6666077748	16.44	<.0001
Error	204	82723784786	405508749		
Corrected Total	207	1.02722E11			
Root MSE	20137	R-Square	0.1947		
Dependent Mean	48912	Adj R-Sq	0.1828		
Coeff Var	41.17043				

Parameter Estimates

Variable	Label	DF	Parameter Estimate	Standard Error	t Value	Pr > |t|	Standardized Estimate
Intercept	Intercept	1	49712	1416.94121	35.08	<.0001	0
factor1	People	1	5906.78446	1692.63554	3.49	0.0006	0.22740
factor2	Data	1	8715.20850	1964.57073	4.44	<.0001	0.29051
factor3	Things	1	-2341.43790	1324.24122	-1.77	0.0785	-0.11199

Adj R-Sq = adjusted R-squared; coeff var = coefficient of variation; DF = degrees of freedom; parameter estimate = raw-score regression coefficient; Root MSE = root mean square error; standardized estimate = z-score regression coefficient.

REFERENCES

Age Discrimination in Employment Act, 29 U.S.C. § 621 (1967).

Americans With Disabilities Act, 42 U.S.C. § 12101 (1990).

Balkin, D. B., & Gomez-Mejia, L. R. (1984). Determinants of R&D compensation strategies in the high tech industry. *Personnel Psychology, 37,* 635–650.

Butler, S. K., & Harvey, R. J. (1988). A comparison of holistic versus decomposed rating of Position Analysis Questionnaire work dimensions. *Personnel Psychology, 41,* 761–771.

Caruth, D. L., & Handlogten, G. D. (2001). *Managing compensation (and understanding it too): A handbook for the perplexed.* Westport, CN: Quorum Books.

Civil Rights Act, 42 U.S.C. § 21 (1964).

Cunningham, J. W., Boese, R. R., Neeb, R. W., & Pass, J. J. (1983). Systematically derived work dimensions: Factor analyses of the Occupational Analysis Inventory. *Journal of Applied Psychology, 68,* 232–252.

Devers, C. E., Cannella, A. A., Reilly, G. P., & Yoder, M. E. (2007). Executive compensation: A multidisciplinary review of recent developments. *Journal of Management, 33,* 1016–1072.

Equal Pay Act, 29 U.S.C. § 206 (1963).

Fine, S. A. (1955). A structure of worker functions. *Personnel and Guidance Journal, 34,* 66–73.

Fine, S. A., & Cronshaw, S. F. (1999). *Functional job analysis: A foundation for human resources management.* Mahwah, NJ: Lawrence Erlbaum Associates.

Fine, S. A., Harvey, R. J., & Cronshaw, S. F. (2004, April). FJA strategies for addressing O*NET limitations in a post-DOT environment. In E. A. Fleishman (Chair), *Things, Data, and People: Fifty years of a seminal theory.* Symposium presented at the Annual Conference of the Society for Industrial and Organizational Psychology, Chicago.

Gibson, S. G., Harvey, R. J., & Harris, M. L. (2007). Holistic versus decomposed ratings of general dimensions of work activity. *Management Research News, 30,* 724–734.

Green, S. B., & Stutzman, T. (1986). An evaluation of methods to select respondents to structured job-analysis questionnaires. *Personnel Psychology, 39,* 543–564.

Harvey, R. J. (1986). Quantitative approaches to job classification: A review and critique. *Personnel Psychology, 39,* 267–289.

Harvey, R. J. (1991a). Job analysis. In M. D. Dunnette & L. Hough (Eds.), *Handbook of industrial and organization psychology* (2nd ed.). Palo Alto, CA: Consulting Psychologists Press.

Harvey, R. J. (1991b). *The common-metric questionnaire (CMQ): A job analysis system (first edition).* San Antonio, TX: The Psychological Corporation.

Harvey, R. J. (1993). *Research monograph: The development of the CMQ.* San Antonio, TX: The Psychological Corporation.

Harvey, R. J. (2004, April). Empirical foundations for the Things-Data-People taxonomy of work. In E. A. Fleishman (Chair), *Things, Data, and People: Fifty years of a seminal theory.* Symposium presented at the Annual Conference of the Society for Industrial and Organizational Psychology, Chicago.

Harvey, R. J. (2005, April). IRT strategies for identifying rater quality in job analysis ratings. In C. VanIddekinge (Chair), *Group differences in job analysis ratings.* Symposium presented at the Annual Conference of the Society for Industrial and Organizational Psychology, Los Angeles.

Harvey, R. J., Friedman, L., Hakel, M. D., & Cornelius, E. T. (1988). Dimensionality of the Job Element Inventory (JEI), a simplified worker-oriented job analysis questionnaire. *Journal of Applied Psychology, 73,* 639–646.

Harvey, R. J., & Lozada-Larsen, S. R. (1993). *The guide to using the CMQ for human resource applications.* San Antonio, TX: The Psychological Corporation.

Harvey, R. J., & Wilson, M. A. (2000). Yes Virginia, there is an objective reality in job analysis. *Journal of Organizational Behavior, 21,* 829–854.

Hazel, J. T., Madden, J. M., & Christal, R. E. (1964). Agreement between worker-supervisor descriptions of the worker's job. *Journal of Industrial Psychology, 2,* 71–79.

Henderson, R. (2005). *Compensation management in a knowledge-based world.* New York, NY: Prentice Hall.

Kilgour, J. G. (2008). Job evaluation revisited: The point factor method. *Compensation and Benefits Review, 40,* 37–46.

Lawler, E. E. III. (1987). Paying for performance: Future directions. In D. B. Balkin & L. R. Gomez-Mejia (Eds.), *New perspectives on compensation.* Englewood Cliffs, NJ: Prentice-Hall.

Ledbetter v. Goodyear Tire & Rubber Co. (2007). 421 F. 3d 1169, affirmed.

McCormick, E. J., Jeanneret, P. R., & Mecham, R. C. (1972). A study of job characteristics & job dimensions as based on the Position Analysis Questionnaire (PAQ). *Journal of Applied Psychology, 56,* 347–368.

Meyer, H. H. (1959). Comparison of foreman and general foreman conceptions of the foreman's job responsibility. *Personnel Psychology, 12,* 445–452.

Murthy, K. R. S. (1977). *Corporate strategy and top executive compensation.* Boston, MA: Harvard Press.

Rynes, S. L., & Milkovich, G. T. (1986). Salary surveys: Dispelling some myths about the "market wage." *Personnel Psychology, 39,* 71–89.

Sackett, P. R., Cornelius, E. T., & Carron, T. J. (1981). A comparison of global vs. task oriented approaches to job classification. *Personnel Psychology, 34,* 791–804.

Sanchez, J. I., & Levine, E. L. (2000). Accuracy or consequential validity: Which is the better standard for job analysis data? *Journal of Organizational Behavior, 21,* 809–818.

Smith, J. E., & Hakel, M. D. (1979). Convergence among data sources, response bias, and reliability and validity of a structured job analysis questionnaire. *Personnel Psychology, 32,* 677–692.

Stutzman, T. M. (1983). Within classification job differences. *Personnel Psychology, 36,* 503–516.

United States Department of Labor, Bureau of Labor Statistics. (2008). *May 2008 employment and wage estimates.* Retrieved from http://bls.gov/oes/oes_arch.htm

Wilson, M. A., Harvey, R. J., & Macy, B. A. (1990). Repeating items to estimate the test-retest reliability of task inventory ratings. *Journal of Applied Psychology, 75,* 158–163.

26

Career Planning
The Role of Work Analysis in the Work of Your Organization's Career Development Manager

Stephen G. Atkins

Otago Polytechnic of New Zealand

The word *career* has been defined as "the occupational positions a person has had over many years" (Dessler, 1997, p. 762). That is, a career is the sum of the particular jobs a person has had, viewed sequentially. The career management function in an organization is thus tied partially to the organization's understanding of its occupational positions and where its current and future workforce members fit (or could potentially fit) into those positions, based on their personal profiles of skills, abilities, interests, and career goals. Career management involves understanding the competing or worker-compatible alternatives for the workforce, both inside and outside one's current organization. The career manager looks at the employing organization and its competitors, partners, and business "neighbors" for multiple reasons, which are mainly related to recruiting potential, out-placement potential, and benchmarking. Career managers also want to be generally aware of their own employees' likeliest career alternatives.

An awareness of career incompatibilities requires an accurate and detailed description of job or occupational features, as well as worker requirements and preferences, which can only derive from work analysis (as detailed in Parts II and III, this volume). Rigorous work analysis is crucial for an effective career planning and management system.

The connection between careerwise thinking and the understanding of positions or jobs (within occupational fields) becomes more concrete in the context of fit theories. In this context, *fit* refers to the compatibility of job or occupational features with the qualifications, interests, and career goals of workers. A number of popular models for conceptualizing fit have been developed over the years in the career literature, such as the work adjustment theory (Dawis & Lofquist, 1984; Rounds, Dawis, & Lofquist, 1987), the Myers-Briggs Type Indicator (MBTI; Briggs-Myers, 1980), the job characteristic model (JCM; Hackman & Oldham, 1980), and the hexagonal vocational personality (realistic, investigative, artistic, social, enterprising, and/or conventional; i.e., RIASEC) model (Holland, 1997). These can, to varying degrees, be thought of as fit models because they posit various features of different occupations, and the compatibility or fit of these features to workers or candidates plays a crucial role in predicting worker commitment, success and tenure, and the career paths that workers seek. These fit theories provide alternative conceptual frameworks for strategically integrating work analysis with career planning.

These fit theories are reviewed here in order of increasing degrees of complexity in their application, with the intent of preparing the reader for engaging with the more complex models in work analysis-centered career thinking. It is perhaps worth noting that although the leading fit theories emerged decades ago, they remain central and crucial to the career development arena. In fact, their application is expanding via Web 2.0 technologies (e.g., current and future Occupational Information Network [O*NET] developments and career fit-related web sites). Regarding fit's criticality, Yost and Chang (2009) noted that person-job fit is one of the two crucial molar (i.e., omnibus) influences determining an employee's future potential. It is thus fitting to focus on it in this chapter.

WORK ADJUSTMENT THEORY

In the highly respected and oft-cited work adjustment theory (WAT) proposed by Dawis and Lofquist (1984), a variety of productive outcomes are thought to derive from greater degrees of fit or congruence (or correspondence) between work and workers. Figures 26.1 and 26.2 illustrate two examples of such congruence or fit—one relatively good and one comparatively bad. In Figure 26.1 (a good fit example), you see that Joe's interests, in each work dimension shown, match fairly closely to the values reinforced by the vocation under consideration. In WAT, the term *values* is used in a broad sense to mean what workers value in their work-life across 21 dimensions of evaluation (e.g., autonomy, authority, variety, job security, recognition, mentoring, creativity, ability utilization, moral values). Logically, a good fit between (a) the degree to which workers value such features in a job and (b) the degree to which their job reinforces or affords such features acts to evoke workers' satisfaction with said job. In Figure 26.2, where a mismatch is evident, one would predict low job satisfaction, among other negative outcomes.

Although there are numerous methods for quantifying such misfit, it is most straightforward to think of it as simply summing up the gaps between what workers value and what their jobs reinforce (or accommodate). Complementary to the assessment of fit between these interest-value profiles, Dawis and Lofquist (1984) also posited that simultaneous consideration be given to fit between a job's ability-requirements profile and a worker's actual ability profile. In other words, good things will come of a match between the requirements of a job (e.g., as assessed through work analysis) and the ability of a worker to meet those requirements (e.g., as assessed through employee

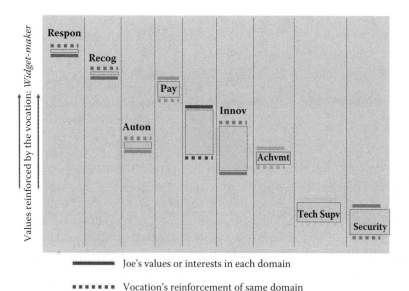

Figure 26.1 Visual example of reasonably good fit between a worker's values or interests and same as afforded or reinforced by the worker's occupation.

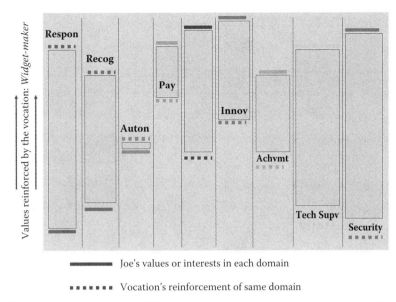

Joe's values or interests in each domain

Vocation's reinforcement of same domain

Figure 26.2   Visual example of a notably poor fit between a worker's values or interests and same as afforded or reinforced by the worker's occupation.

selection procedures). In this context, the evaluative dimensions read more as aptitudes or intelligences (e.g., verbal ability, numerical ability, spatial aptitude, form perception, clerical perception). However, the notion of fit or correspondence, in this case regarding ability profiles, works similarly; a greater degree of fit is expected to bring about more productive outcomes.

In the most immediate instance, what is predicted and/or evoked here (i.e., by increasing degrees of fit) is the degree to which a worker is satisfied with and satisfactory within a given role. In the bottom left of Figure 26.3, one sees that WAT focuses on fit or misfit between a worker's values and what values the job supports or reinforces. Thus (and quite logically), where values are concerned, increasingly good fit yields increasing degrees of job satisfaction. For introducing WAT to clients or staff, comparing Figure 26.3 to Figure 26.4 might be helpful. Then adding comparisons to

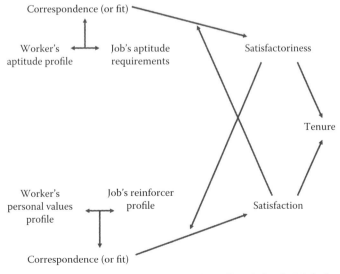

Figure 26.3   Directional flows as predicted by the work adjustment theory (Rounds, Dawis, & Lofquist, 1987).

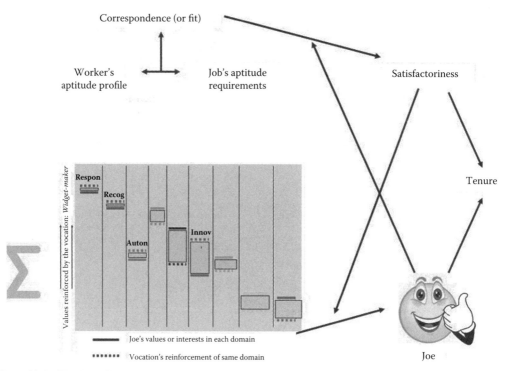

Figure 26.4 Directional flows as predicted by the work adjustment theory (Rounds, Dawis, & Lofquist, 1987) substituting visual depiction of reasonably good fit for what the worker values.

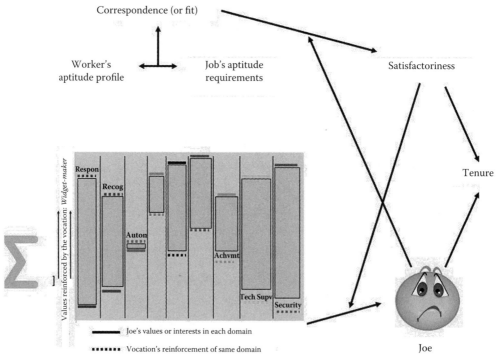

Figure 26.5 Directional flows as predicted by the work adjustment theory (Rounds, Dawis, & Lofquist, 1987) substituting visual depiction of notably poor fit for what the worker values.

Figure 26.5, the basic idea of fit theories should become very clear. The same sorts of figures could just as well be made for WAT's abilities domain, to which we now turn.

Where abilities are concerned (see the upper left of Figure 26.5), increasingly good fit should yield increasing degrees of what Dawis and Lofquist (1984) called *satisfactoriness.* Satisfactoriness is akin to job satisfaction, except that here it refers to how satisfactory the employee is viewed to be from the employer's (as opposed to the employee's) perspective. Of course, it is logical that supervisors will be more sensitive to misfit between the abilities required by the job (i.e., the job's abilities-profile) and their worker's ability profiles, while workers may be more sensitive to a misfit in the interest-value profiles. Nonetheless, WAT reflects the secondary impact of an abilities-profile mismatch via its proposed interaction with a worker's values-fit satisfaction (again see Figure 26.5 and the further explanations that follow).

Not entirely without controversy, the WAT suggests that aptitude-fit effects (being satisfactoriness) will interact with the values-fit effect (being job satisfaction) and vice versa. As Figure 26.5 indicates, the satisfactoriness outcome (the organization's satisfaction with the worker) modifies or moderates the connection between the workers' values-fit and job satisfaction. This is why the satisfaction outcome feeds an intersecting arrow or "causal path" that perturbs the causal flow from aptitude fit to satisfactoriness; likewise, satisfactoriness similarly influences how strongly values-fit yields satisfaction. From a personal perspective, an employee might reword this as "how satisfying I find my job to be is influenced by how satisfied my organization appears to be with me." Conversely, again as indicated in Figure 26.5, it indicates "how satisfactorily my organization views my employment with them to be is influenced by how satisfied I appear to be in my job."

For the abilities domain in the WAT context, the U.S. Department of Labor (DOL) initially applied the abilities taxonomy of the General Aptitude Test Battery (GATB). In similar fashion (e.g., continuing to use attributes like verbal ability, arithmetic reasoning, spatial ability, form perception), these notions live on within the most popular taxonomy for this domain: the DOL's vast O*NET. The O*NET technologies include work analysis questionnaires for assessing a job's ability profile and values. For career exploration or career development purposes, O*NET provides a compatible O*NET Abilities Profiler to measure and report on an individual's (i.e., a career explorer's) capability profile using these same sorts of attributes (e.g., verbal ability, mathematical reasoning).

By working through Figures 26.1 to 26.5 carefully and sequentially, clients or employees should be able imagine how varying levels of satisfaction and satisfactoriness might be predicted for a variety of occupations or positions under consideration by a given job seeker. Hopefully, they will see good sense in viewing job options in the light of these work analysis-driven predictions, so as to optimize their fit to a job or a career field. For example, the values-based work analysis afforded by O*NET's form of the Minnesota Importance Questionnaire (see http://www.psych.umn.edu/psylabs/vpr/miqinf.htm) allows career explorers to see what vocational values are likely to be reinforceable or affordable in a given occupation. Tinsley and Tinsley (1989) conducted such an analysis for the occupation "homemaker" (see Table 26.1). Their results reveal the sorts of insights that can be helpful for career exploration. Values such as recognition, supervisory relations, technical supervision, advancement, and coworker relations are largely absent in this occupation, whereas values such as authority, autonomy, creativity, and responsibility are reinforced in relative abundance. These matters are important considerations as one contemplates a particular career field, and the procedure used by Tinsley and Tinsley can be readily repeated for salaried or hourly-waged occupations more commonly contemplated in the context of career development.

The notion of contemplating a particular career field is possibly more often the context for applying other competing notions of career development, such as approaches by Super (1992), Gottfredson (1999), and especially Lent's social cognitive career theory (Lent & Brown, 2006; Lent & Hackett, 1987). All of these career theorists would strongly emphasize the importance

Table 26.1 Work Adjustment Theory Outcomes From a Study of Homemakers

Reinforcer Factor and Scale	Mean ASV	SD	Percentile Rank	Normative Interpretation	
Self-determination					
Ability utilization	1.00	0.41	41	Average	
Achievement	0.80	0.52	50	Average	
Autonomy	1.10	0.47	84	High	
Creativity	0.96	0.36	75	High	⬅
Responsibility	1.13	0.47	79	High	
Social status	−0.03	0.57	44	Average	
Variety	0.57	0.41	43	Average	
Supervision					
Company policies and practices	−0.15	0.52	1	Absent	
Recognition	0.38	0.52	5	Absent	⬅
Supervision–human relations	−0.30	0.57	1	Absent	
Supervision–technical	−0.58	0.62	1	Absent	
Service					
Compensation	−0.15	0.52	4	Absent	
Coworkers	0.14	0.47	1	Absent	⬅
Moral values	0.59	0.57	31	Absent	
Social service	1.12	0.47	66	High	
Working alone					
Advancement	−0.46	0.67	2	Absent	⬅
Authority	−0.12	0.47	71	High	⬅
Independence	0.92	0.72	87	High	
Comfort					
Security	0.98	0.67	28	Absent	
Working conditions	0.90	0.41	38	Average	
Loaded on no factor					
Activity	0.75	0.62	50	Average	

Source: From Tinsley, H. E. and Tinsley, D. J., *Journal of Counseling Psychology*, 36, 189–195, 1989. With permission.
N = 107. Normative interpretation of ASV is as follows: ≤33 = reinforcer is absent; 34–65 = reinforcer is average; ≥66 = reinforcer is high.
[a] This scale had a negative loading on this factor.
[b] This scale also loaded significantly (positively) on the comfort factor.
ASV = adjusted scale value.

of accurate vocational information on all relevant features of the world of work (Sharf, 2005), but the quantitative application of enumerated indices derived from work analysis is harder to operationalize or execute in their career models. Thus, I have chosen to provide examples of work analysis for career management via the work adjustment theory, Holland's (1997) RIASEC model, and Hackman and Oldham's (1976, 1980) JCM. Increasingly, career management has engaged the MBTI, and ground-breaking work was done by Brown and Harvey (1996) to tie the MBTI taxonomy to Harvey's (1991, 2004) Common Metric Questionnaire (CMQ). Because of the historical popularity of the MBTI and given that the CMQ is arguably the gold standard of its ilk, I also dedicate a section to the empirical connection between work analysis results and MBTI categories.

HOLLAND FIT: AIDING CAREER MANAGEMENT VIA WORK ANALYSIS-BASED INTERESTS CORRESPONDENCE

Holland's (1997) vocational personality theory posits that a person ranges from low to high on six interrelated dimensions of vocational personality. That is, individuals are, to differing degrees, typically realistic, investigative, artistic, social, enterprising, and/or conventional in their vocational desires, interests, and behaviors. Certain pairs of these dimensions are usually posited to act as opposites—artistic jobs contrast to conventional ones, the social dimension is contrasted to the realistic, the enterprising is contrasted to the investigative. Other pairs are posited to be positively correlated—the social dimension is expected to typically be at least moderately correlated with enterprising and artistic. That said, it is psychometrically possible, although rare psychologically, for some individuals or some jobs to truly score equally high on two dimensions thought to be opposites. Because of this oppositional nature, these dimensions can be described as defining the corners of a hexagon (see Figure 26.6), where the distance between two dimensions reveals the degree of typical consistency or inconsistency between them. This model is sometimes referred to as Holland's hexagon or the RIASEC hexagon (Inkson, 2007).

Some researchers have presented evidence that there are no truly preferred concentrations of interests around such a hexagonal model; therefore, a circle may be more appropriate than a hexagon, or possibly even a set of concentric circles (Tracey & Rounds, 1995). Fortunately, there is some evidence for the universal nature of this structure for vocational interest (Day & Rounds, 1998). In any case, in the vast majority of applications of job or career interests, Holland's proposed RIASEC hexagonal structure has maintained as valid. I treat it as broadly applicable, and essentially ubiquitous, in this chapter.

In addition to generating a profile of individuals' vocational personality dimensions, Holland's model involves profiling jobs along these same six dimensions. Holland originally did this by measuring the personality profiles of extremely large numbers of incumbents employed within each occupational field of noteworthy size (Holland, 1997; Inkson, 2007), believing that the typical profiles in large "in-vocation" samples would be prototypes of good fit for those vocations. Holland focused upon the three highest-ranked dimensions for both individual candidates and for jobs, with the highest of these three listed first. Figure 26.7 shows the RIASEC outcomes for several dozen occupational fields. In the simplest sense, good fit is indicated if an individual candidate's three highest codes (or *interests*) match those reported for his or her occupation, especially to the degree these three are in the same order.

Fortunately, formal job analysis-based research has also been conducted in the context of Holland's model (as opposed to just seeking typical incumbent profiles). Pioneering work in this regard was reported in Cunningham, Slonaker, and Riegel (1987); Gottfredson and Holland (1991);

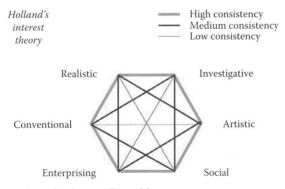

Figure 26.6   Holland's hexagonal vocational personality model.

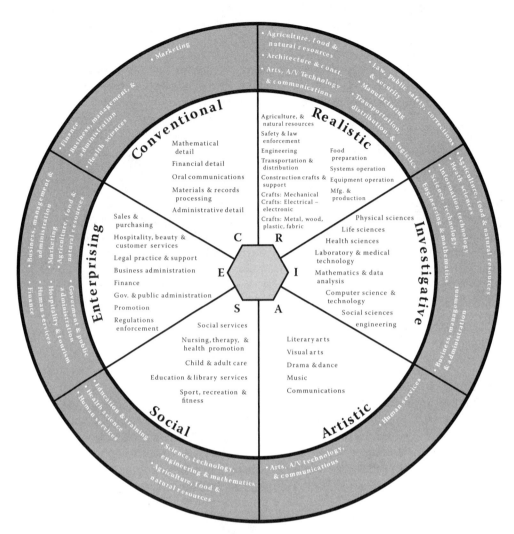

Figure 26.7 The Career Key map of Holland's types/work groups' model and the U.S. Department of Education's 16 career clusters. The Career Key map is based on a model from the Oklahoma Career Information System. Work groups are groups of occupations based on the traits of the workers—interests, aptitude, temperament, skills, and ability. They were originally developed by the U.S. Department of Labor. For more information, see http://www.careerkey.org. (Copyright © 2011 by The Career Key, Inc. All rights reserved.)

and Cunningham, Boese, Neeb, and Pass (1983). Today, work analysis-based measures for an occupation's Holland dimensions profile can be attained by using Gottfredson and Holland's (1991) Position Classification Inventory (PCI). The PCI uses an 84-item questionnaire comprised of six scales (one each for realistic, investigative, artistic, social, enterprising, and conventional interest domains). With a particular job as the referent target, it can be completed by incumbents, supervisors, or job analysts. The six scales each cover seven broad perspectives on interests (Vicente & Fernandez, 2003), each tied to a Holland RIASEC interest domain:

1. Typical on-the-job activities
2. Talents typically needed
3. Attitudes/perspectives reinforced
4. Values or work styles that can be expressed

5. Personal characteristics required or in demand
6. Needed skills or abilities
7. Frequency of activities

Of course, proceeding along the lines of the fit-or-misfit paradigm requires analogous or parallel data about potential employees or job seekers. Candidate or individual profiles (i.e., their affinity with each of the six vocational personality dimensions) can be attained via application of an instrument called the Self-Directed Search (SDS; see http://www.selfdirectedsearch.com). In addition, other vocational interest inventories, such as the Strong Interest Inventory and Career Assessment Inventory provide the test taker with their Holland codes. Competing services, tests, or surveys of this ilk usually provide codes that can be easily reclassified into Holland's dimensions.

The Dictionary of Holland Occupational Codes lists over 12,000 occupations with their three-letter RIASEC codes. Career management offices should be aware, however, that if applying the simplest notion of good career fit (i.e., hoping to see the same first three RIASEC codes when comparing individuals to jobs), due consideration should be given to the relative distinctiveness of individual preferences or interests, as well as their stability in the individual. For career exploration purposes, it would thus be reasonable for individuals to consider occupations manifesting a differing order, or where one or two RIASEC codes differ, but are from neighboring corners of the RIASEC hexagon to their own (Inkson, 2007). In other words, while Holland's approach to psychometric fit may have succeeded in demystifying matters for lay users, it may also oversimplify or overconstrain an individual's apparent career options.

O*NET (see Chapter 16, this volume) also uses Holland's model. In fact, within O*NET, you can search for occupations that match your Holland code or look up the codes for specific occupations. Although Holland's RIASEC hexagon is virtually always thought of as a theoretical structure for vocational interests, it is also (at least arguably) a legitimate framework for work analysis in its own right. In the context of O*NET, I have much more to say about fit theories like RIASEC and WAT later in this chapter. First, it is important to visit some alternative approaches to calculating fit (or its complement or opposite: misfit).

MORE SOPHISTICATED INDICES OF FIT BETWEEN CANDIDATE OR CAREER EXPLORER PROFILES AND JOB PROFILES FROM WORK ANALYSIS

Holland's approach to assessing fit between individuals and occupations can be fairly accused of oversimplifying such relationships or underutilizing the rich occupational information that can derive from properly-performed work analyses. Arguably, additional richness is retained when the fit between a work analysis-derived job profile and an individual's profile is based on correspondences amongst all assessed dimensions. One common example of this strategy is the WAT, where the Pearson product-moment correlation coefficient is used in assessing correspondences between fairly complex occupational and individual profiles. The idea is to move from a simplistic "typology" approach, such as a matching of broad categories of employee and job qualities, to a more detailed analysis of how well meshed the person and job profiles are.

Although application of the Pearson correlation is common, there has been substantial debate about its use to assess the goodness, strength, or quality of fit between individual and occupational profiles (whether or not the latter refers to job features or work environs; for discussion, see Drewes, Tarantino, Atkins, & Paige, 2000). It is tempting to first apply a simple correlation because even those with minimal spreadsheet (e.g., Microsoft Excel) skills will likely know how to compute the correlation between two columns of ratings (e.g., standardized ratings of an occupation's features in one column and likewise candidate or career explorer features in another column). Although all forms of quantitative fit assessment have limitations and have come under varying degrees of attack (see Hesketh, 2000; Hesketh & Myors, 1997), a comparison of the more common approaches leads one away from simple correlations (provided sufficient data analysis skills are available). Drewes et al. provided a concise and lay-friendly comparison of the popular alternatives, which is easily conveyed if one can visualize individual or career-explorer profiles and occupational profiles graphically (see Figures 26.1 and 26.2). Simple correlations suffer in the Drewes et al. comparison as being, for example, sensitive to differences in the two profile shapes compared but insensitive to differences in actual levels in those compared profiles.

This situation improves a bit for the most basic alternative, the square of the geometric distance between two profiles (which is referred to as the squared Euclidean distance). This simple geometric difference is sensitive to differences in profile levels and shapes but it suffers for failing to differentiate between a low frequency of large differences versus a very high frequency of very small differences. The latter situation is, intuitively, rather inconsequential in a relative sense, but the former often is not.

This flaw in assessing fit via simple squared geometric distance drives one to consider, instead, application of the so-called Minkowski distance. In this case, the main deficiency is that all attributes or dimensions in the two profiles to be compared influence fit outcomes equally (i.e., depending only upon the size of displacement in that attribute or dimension). Drewes et al. (2000) argued that a weighted Minkowski distance provides the best alternative amongst these competing notions of geometric distances as fit indices. They developed, for use within O*NET, a computer algorithm that allows some attribute profile gaps (or "misfits") to influence the profile comparison outcome substantially, while other gaps have minimal influence. Specifically, where some gaps are associated with especially crucial attributes, influence can be weighted highly; this is likewise the case where the direction of the gap is of much more consequence (e.g., moderate underqualification for a particular skill versus moderate overqualification).

Their system has been applied using O*NET work analysis data and is focused more on midcareer shifts or midcareer decision-making, but the underlying concepts in their weighted Minkowski algorithm can certainly be generalized to other career development contexts. A prudent recommendation here: Career development professionals, when evaluating the competing career management products on the market, should engage vendors in discussions of such alternatives for the metrics of vocational fit. In other words, while the exact details of a vendor's fit algorithm may be proprietary and thus hidden behind a user-friendly interface, it is obviously prudent to know its main features in the light of the Drewes et al. (2000) comparisons. This is especially so if a career management product is helping career managers to make decisions of great consequence.

Revisiting Figure 26.1, altered now as Figure 26.8, should be convincing here. The latter figure might be associated with the following columns (see Table 26.2) of vocational values scores. Note that this example could apply to many work analysis perspectives (e.g., aptitudes, interests, work styles).

If you use a simple correlation coefficient from Microsoft Excel to assess fit or misfit, you might think Joe is a perfect fit to the occupation in question. This is despite the apparent evidence that he values workplace responsibility, recognition, and autonomy far less than seen in the work analysis outcomes for this occupation. Additionally, you can say that all of these dimensions are influencing your summary outcome metric (the correlation coefficient) to perfectly equal degrees.

Alternatively, however, if applying a fit or distance statistic that squares (or more generally adds an exponential power to) the gaps or distances on these work-values dimensions, the substantial gaps seen in responsibility, recognition, and autonomy become far more influential. If you step up in sophistication to higher levels (e.g., weighted Minkowski distances for gap or misfit assessment), you could weight particular dimensions of greater litigiousness or health and safety consequence

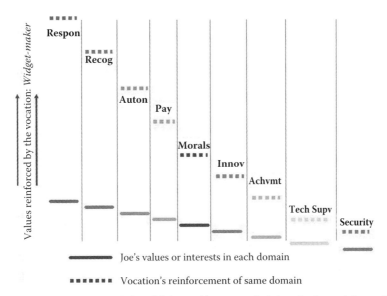

Figure 26.8   Visual example of a very poor "values fit" that would appear perfect via a simple correlation coefficient approach to calculating vocational fit.

(e.g., maybe Joe's substantially lower interest in having high morals feature in his targeted occupation). You could also weight gaps or deviations in a "bad" direction more heavily than deviations in a less or nonconsequential direction. These various refinements can yield notably different assessments of fit or misfit. Therefore, you should have at least these fundamental "visibilities" in the fit algorithms being applied in your organization (even if your consultant says they are proprietary "business secrets").

JOB FEATURES IN CAREER DEPARTURES: ORGANIZATIONAL COMMITMENT AND THE JOB CHARACTERISTICS MODEL

In the workplace-based example from the previous section, one can see how apparent misfits or incompatibilities between workers and their jobs might reasonably lead to major early or midstream career decisions. Although not thought of as a career theory per se, it should

Table 26.2   Hypothetical Data Table of Work Analysis-Based Misfit Outcomes Associated With the Visual Example Depicted in Figure 26.8

Dimension	Score of Occupation Targeted by Joe	Joe's Score
Responsibility	100	10
Recognition	90	9
Autonomy	80	8
Pay	70	7
Morals	60	6
Innovation	50	5
Achievement	40	4
Technical supervision	30	3
Vocational security	20	2

be noted here that characteristics of jobs, as illumined via Hackman and Oldham's (1980) JCM, are intuitively connected to career decision-making. In other words, because of rational linkages between job characteristics and organizational commitment (Zurriaga, Ramos, Gonzalez-Roma, Espejo, & Zornoza, 2000) and the latter's connection to intentions to leave one's work (Cohen, 1993), JCM surfaces as another potential lens to apply in this chapter's context. Partially, this is because work analysis outcomes will reflect prior job design actions (see Chapter 18, this volume), and these have often been undertaken to improve an incumbent's long-term growth, empowerment, and career enhancement via (at least implicitly) workplace applications of the JCM. For example, Pennington (1992) describes JCM (per Hackman & Oldham, 1976, 1980) as focusing on five core job characteristics (task identity, tasks significance, skill variety, autonomy, and job feedback) that play a role in job stimulation, and then subsequently in three psychological outcomes (experienced responsibility, experienced meaningfulness, and knowledge of results). These, in turn, are expected to increase individual work motivation, satisfaction, and performance.

Further to this, operating within the JCM, there are three moderators that will interact with or affect the JCM relationships just mentioned. These moderators (operating within the given employee) include knowledge and skills, growth need strength, and context satisfaction with respect to peers, compensation, job security, and supervisors. The only new term here is growth need strength—a term intended to reflect the degree to which an individual seeks and values personal growth or development, including a need to see increases in their knowledge and skills.

From a career development specialist's perspective, an important employee behaviour deriving from JCM influences is *job crafting* (i.e., where employees look for and act upon opportunities to make self-congruent or personally positive amendments within their existing job). High growth need strength is expected for employees especially interested in job crafting, if other opportunities for career shifts or advancement were unavailable.

Although you can expect intuitive relationships between workers' decisions for career shifts and relevant worker traits and job characteristics per the JCM, this model (and its typical instrumentation) fall far short of a comprehensive consideration of occupational features. For instance, the primary worker trait considered is growth need strength and the primary occupational feature is job scope level, which "reflects employees' perceptions of jobs in terms of variety, identity, significance, autonomy, and feedback" (Goris, Vaught, & Pettit, 2000, p. 4). Considerations and measurements of such job characteristics can broadly be viewed as a subset or narrow form of work analysis, but caution is conveyed here that many work analysts would take exception to that claim. That said, a career management chapter in a volume such as this would be remiss in not making reference to this classic model of employee career and vocational-developmental choice.

Within this classic model, growth need strength can be measured, somewhat subtly, via the Job Choice subscale of Hackman and Oldham's (1975, 1980) Job Diagnostic Survey (JDS). As described by Goris et al (2000, p. 4),

> [The JC subscale] provides an index of strength of higher order needs relative to lower order needs. It reflects employees' desire to obtain growth satisfactions from their work. This desire is determined by asking respondents to indicate their relative preference for pairs of hypothetical jobs, for example: "A job where you are often required to make important decisions vs. a job with many pleasant people to work with" (Hackman & Oldham, 1975, p. 161).

Somewhat in parallel to this, the JCM operationalizes the previously defined job scope level via the worker's perception of a job's Motivational Potential Score (MPS). The MPS derives from use of a standard seven-point job scope response scale (1 = low, 7 = high). This scale is applied against the job characteristics JCM focuses on (e.g., skill variety, tasks significance, autonomy).

Although the brevity and ease associated with workplace application of the JCM perspective on career development motivations is appealing, again caution is appropriate here. The JCM is dealing with a very narrow, albeit important, take on the world of job characteristics (despite the model's more ambitious title).

WORK ANALYSIS AND MYERS-BRIGGS TYPOLOGY IN CAREER MANAGEMENT

This chapter has focused on revisiting dominant career theories in the context of work analysis outcomes. In other words, it has looked at the work analysis edges engaged with the dominant career theories—at least those directly engaging work analysis data (or subsets of same; e.g., WAT's focus on values reinforcers data and aptitude requirements data, Holland's focus on interests, JCM's focus on motivational job scope). It is, however, very reasonable to argue that all career theories must engage with occupational information to make any sense, which would include the other works by leading career theorists, such as Super (1992, 1994, 2007), Gottfredson, (1999), Lent (Lent & Hackett, 1987; Lent & Brown, 2006), Hesketh (2000; see also Hesketh & Considine, 1998; Hesketh & Myors, 1997), and Inkson (2007).

However, where these leading theorists have directly engaged with job or work analysis data, their work has been connected to or derived from the leading quantitative data-driven career theories already revisited in this chapter. Beyond these, there has been interest (Sharf, 2005) in applying the popular Myers-Briggs typology to the context of career decision-making—specifically, in the context of assessing the compatibility of individual personality profiles to profiles of attributes required for success in various or particular occupations. The popularity of the Myers-Briggs approach within career management arenas is sufficient to justify some examination within this chapter. Like the JCM considered previously, the Myers-Briggs approach is also relevant only to a narrow subset of the fuller set of content domains ostensibly captured by comprehensive work analyses.

The pioneering work of connecting Myers-Briggs instrumentation to work analysis outcomes and, more generally, applying the latest psychometric technologies to both of these arenas, has largely been done by doctoral students under the supervision of R. J. Harvey (e.g., Bess & Harvey, 2002; Bess, Harvey, & Schwartz, 2003; Brown & Harvey, 1996; Harvey, Murry, & Stamoulis, 1995; Harvey & Thomas, 1996). Arguably most relevant to this chapter would be Brown and Harvey, in which job-component validity, a rigorous methodology derived from work analysis, was used to link MBTI dimensions to work analysis outcomes. Given the popularity of the MBTI in career counseling arenas (Sharf, 2005), it is valuable for career management specialists to have some appreciation for how the MBTI can connect to work analysis data.

Brown and Harvey (1996) sought to illuminate the MBTI-to-work analysis linkages via job-component validity (JCV). A detailed description of JCV theory, methods, and applications is presented in Chapter 6, this volume. Briefly, JCV was initially developed by McCormick, Jeanneret, and Mecham (1972) in the context of their work analysis instrument, the Position Analysis Questionnaire (PAQ; see Chapter 12, this volume) and the U.S. government's broadly applied GATB. JCV uses empirical and multiple regression-based methods to build up a set of expectations (as regards a profile of ability test scores, e.g., GATB) for abilities associated with successful tenure in a population of occupations (e.g., each such occupation then, via JCV, being associated with an expected GATB profile and suggested cut-scores guiding staffing selections). Its premise is the so-called *gravitational hypothesis*, whereby workers are expected to gravitate towards jobs at which they can succeed and also provide adequate challenge, esteem, and other rewards (e.g., such that these workers see themselves maximizing their vocational returns and are thus avoiding salient underemployment of their talents). Generally, this means that job complexity changes, in aggregate, will see workers who may have initially overreached (in terms of abilities or aptitudes) shift to less stressful vocational contexts (but ones in which they may perform better). Workers who initially underreached may choose to move up to more challenging industrial or economic sectors (or accept promotions within sector).

It was reassuring for commercial users of JCV to see context-relevant validation of the gravitational hypothesis provided in a pair of studies tracking thousands of workers longitudinally (e.g., Wilk, Desmarais, & Sackett, 1995; Wilk & Sackett, 1995). In fact, in their second longitudinal study, Wilk and Sackett (1995) replicated their earlier findings and also expanded upon them, such that they were able to conclude that "cognitive ability is not the sole determinant of job complexity change" (p. 22). Importantly, for this chapter's context, Brown and Harvey's (1996, p. 4) review yielded this summation:

> In short, the gravitational hypothesis should also apply to interests, values, and personality factors. To adapt the JCV procedure to non-ability tests, some changes may be required. In short, instead of focusing on selecting applicants with the highest scores above a predicted cutoff point on a given test, we might instead focus on selecting applicants whose personality or interest *profiles* match the profile that would be expected among successful incumbents in the job/occupation in question.

Thus, score profiles (rather than simple scores) on personality measures would be better used as predictors instead of expecting personality traits (e.g., one trait at a time) to globally predict success. It would be naïve to assume that monotonic increases in a given personality trait and in a generally favourable direction will be predictive of performance increases amongst hirees. For example, this assumption allows the critics of "personality testing in selection" to make straight comparisons of the predictive validity of agreeableness to the predictive validity of conscientiousness or IQ. Although agreeableness might be comparable (in that sense) across vast domains in the world of work, it might appear to be a very poor predictor in fields like sales, auditing, or safety inspection—or especially in validity studies within a corporation that typically merge data across jobs simply because all the jobs merged were thought to have personality-influenced performance outcomes. Thus, meta-analyses (e.g., Schmidt & Hunter, 2004) that simply merge validity evidence without consideration of personality fit are blurring crucial distinctions. For human attributes such as conscientiousness, generally more is better. But many aspects of personality do *not* work this way (Atkins, Carr, Fletcher, & McKay, 2006; Atkins & McKay, 2005); for these attributes, fit considerations are crucial.

A focus on personality profile fit or misfit makes the popular career-related use of the MBTI more palatable in modern times. This is because empirical and conceptual support arguably exists for seeking linkages between PAQ work analysis outcomes and MBTI outcomes, much the same as seen before between PAQ work analysis outcomes and ability profiles (e.g., GATB).

It is worth noting that MBTI personality profiles have sometimes been provided with PAQ work analysis results—and with multiple correlation indices similar to those seen in the more-traditional "abilities-domain" applications of the PAQ, or at least manifesting at reasonable levels (e.g., for MBTI Thinking-Feeling (TF) scale: median $R = .62$; Mecham, 1988, cited in McCormick, Mecham, & Jeanneret, 1989). This is not unexpected, given that Brown and Harvey (1996) found reliable statistical linkages between the MBTI's bipoled dimensions and the Big Five personality factors (extroversion, agreeableness, conscientiousness, etc., as used in a performance prediction context; see Barrick & Mount, 1991). This is also consistent with JCV linkages between the PAQ and the Big Five as found by Rashkovky (2006) when applying the commercially available Hogan Personality Inventory. Brown and Harvey (1996, p. 5) concluded that "the fact that one of the most popular worker-oriented job analysis instruments predicts the expected MBTI profile for each job may constitute some incentive for at least some PAQ users to base their employee selection decisions on these predicted MBTI profiles."

In the career management context of the present chapter, it seems reasonable to expand somewhat beyond "some" users of the MBTI, as long as sound work analysis connections are built into career path recommendations. Fortunately, work has been done to add rigour to the templates for such connections. Brown and Harvey (1996) began this work with the CMQ (likely this sector's most rigorous instrument). They did caution that their archival studies found very powerful gender effects (both main and moderator effects), which would be philosophically consistent with cautions made by the creators of the MBTI in its origins (e.g., Myers & McCauley, 1985, in which these founders argued strongly against the MBTI's use as a selection device). Thus, even in a somewhat softer careers context, the ethical and conscientious stance avoids MBTI guidance that becomes exclusionist or dissuading, regardless of the career managers now being armed with bridges between work analysis and MBTI. From a career development perspective, the MBTI may continue to be seen as a tool facilitating new insights within the employees—these then being for their self-directed application.

PROFILE MISMATCH AND CAREER-FIELD EXODUS: PRACTICAL EXAMPLE OF A SMALL WORKPLACE-BASED STUDY

Per the cautions noted previously, a comparison of complex Minkowski distance (or misfit) with simpler Euclidean distance (or misfit) was part of another effort that also serves to illustrate how simple work analysis studies can illuminate career decisions. A moderately small sample study ($N = 58$) of radio broadcast salespeople presents a simple methodology that most (and even small) corporate career development programs can readily replicate. Doing so can make clearer to career development managers just how misfit or discord between worker and job profiles may be influencing crucial career path decisions internal to their own companies. Specifically, a work analysis team can use a vocational personality-centered design that allows them to observe the effects of a career-relevant social psychological phenomenon—Schneider's (1987) Attraction-Selection-Attrition (ASA) process.

In this instance, broadcast salespersons' responses to a 100-item version of the popular Neuroticism-Extroversion-Openness Five-Factor Inventory (NEO-FFI)—a personality inventory based on a dominant personality model, the Five-Factor Model (Barrick & Mount, 1991)—had been used to assess personality profile dissimilarities (or misfit). Dissimilarity was initially calculated as the simple squared Euclidean distance from a work analysis-determined optimal profile (here using nine senior sales managers as work analysis raters). Poorer work performance outcomes were expected from employees with a poor profile fit to workplace optimums (Gustafson & Mumford, 1995), and indeed some clearly significant evidence supporting this was found (McKay & Atkins, 2002). In the present instance, optimal profile was calculated via a thoroughly decomprised (Gibson, Harvey, & Quintela, 2004) personality-focused work analysis instrument—the Personality-related Position Requirements Form (PPRF; Raymark, Schmit, & Guion, 1997)—a 107-item questionnaire focused on 12 lower-order personality-related work requirement factors (where all 12 lower-order factors are subsumed by one of the Five-Factor Model's higher-order factors now generally accepted globally). The PPRF was used, as it remains the primary source for personality-focused work analysis ratings and personality biases of same (Aguinis, Mazurkiewicz, & Heggestad, 2009).

In this example, workplace study (a workplace-based validation with additional analyses reported in Atkins, et al, 2006), a panel of nine managers performed reasonably using the PPRF (r_{wg}, or interrater agreement per James, Demaree, & Wolf [1984], ranging from .83 to .99 on the 12 subscales with mean = 0.898 and median = 0.885), yielding a reasonably robust optimum personality profile for the targeted career field (broadcast salesperson).

Not surprisingly, given the focus on personality profile misfit, the expected and significant negative correlation between magnitude of misfit and supervisor reports of worker performance was indeed found. But, much more importantly, from a career-path perspective, the results appeared most appropriately viewed in the context of Schneider's (1987) ASA theory. From this theory's perspective, organizations, and arguably career fields, are seen to be "functions of the kinds of people they contain and that these people are functions of an attraction-selection-attrition cycle" (p. 437). If this broadcast sales context is viewed from Schneider's ASA perspective, one would predict that broadcast salespeople not finding themselves to be similar in personality to their coworkers or manager's expectations would be more likely to leave this occupation.

Per the ASA theory's predictions, it was thus not surprising that squared Euclidean distance (from the broadcast sales manager-determined optimal personality profile) correlated negatively with years of sales experience. This correlation approached statistical significance when focusing entirely on broadcast sales experience ($r = -0.18, 0.10 > p > .05$). This effect became quite powerful when focusing on personality types sensitive to being misfits (Atkins et al., 2006). In that regard, it was interesting to note that focusing specifically on nonbroadcast sales experience dropped this to an apparently nil effect ($r = 0.001, p = .50$). Visual inspection of the data (see Figure 26.9) supports an interpretation consistent with ASA theory, as it clearly appears that salespeople lacking personality profiles similar to manager reported-optimums are exiting this population. This evidence supports recent findings and associated validity distortions (Atkins et al., 2006; Thomas, et al., 2000).

As an aside, subsequent analyses in Atkins et al. (2006) found further support for ASA by focusing upon workers high in misfit sensitivity or, alternatively, high in compensatory factors valuable in sales roles (e.g., extroversion). With elimination of outliers, the misfit sensitivity effect in Atkins et al. became quite powerful. For example, when comparing misfit-sensitive workers to

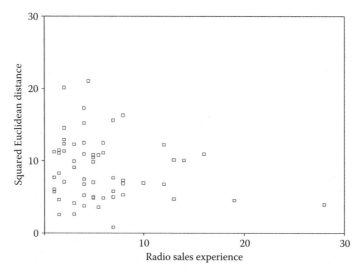

Figure 26.9 Scatterplot displaying relations between misfit and years of tenure from a validation study for broadcast sales (Atkins & McKay, 2005; reanalysis of data from McKay & Atkins, 2002).

misfit-insensitive workers, the former evinces a correlation of –0.74 (p = .001) between broadcast sales career longevity and personality misfit, suggesting that larger misfits are associated with minimal longevity. In the latter group, the strength of this relationship drops to –0.14 (p = .30). In other words, for misfit sensitive workers in this sample, over half of the variance in longevity (within this career field) is accounted for by personality profile misfit (i.e., operationalized by squared Euclidean distance, although noting that this effect likely has greater generalizability if applying more sophisticated calculations of misfit). For workers in this sample who were relatively insensitive to misfit, the variance accounted for by misfit drops to less than 2%.

Somewhat fortunately, comparisons regarding the strength of the career-path outcomes, as well as misfit (or distance) from the optimal work analysis-derived profile, did not vary via a switch to the much more complicated Minkowski distance algorithm. This is fortunate in that the simple Euclidean distance is easily calculated in spreadsheets (e.g., MS Excel) by lay users. This also lends some credence regarding use of this methodology (by virtually all career management practitioners) for relative small-sample "career-decision" field studies in real-world or corporate settings.

For example, because simple squared Euclidean distance can be calculated for profile mismatch (or "misfit") by summing squared differences in sets of paired scores, one can use MS Excel's SUMSQ command. If an individual's personality profile is recorded as a column of numbers in a spreadsheet—and likewise, an occupation's personality requirements profile (e.g., via Raymark, Guion, & Schmitt's PPRF) where both columns use a common metric—you can create a third column reflecting the simple arithmetic difference (via simple subtraction, assuming you have dealt successfully with scaling and standardization issues). Then, if you insert the Excel SUMSQ function (found in the Functions list) into any cell on the same worksheet, you can just follow the instructions in the dialogue box that appears. Upon striking the Enter key, the sum of the squared differences will appear.

Note that in some work analysis scenarios, simple squared Euclideans may serve as adequate expressions of mismatch or misfit. However, if you are concerned about the direction of misfit (e.g., far more concerned about candidates or employees well below a required level than those well above it) or if you wish to weight some trait dimensions more than others, then simple Euclideans will not do. O*NET's weighted Minkowski attempts to handle these situations. The interested reader should consult Drewes et al. (2000). This government document includes a text copy of the computer program that O*NET used to operationalize the weighted Minkowski algorithm. However, it must be customized substantially depending upon context, and such work would not likely be suitable for an amateur programmer.

FUTURE APPLICATIONS OF WORK ANALYSIS TO CAREER MANAGEMENT: THE PROMISE OF O*NET AND ITS KIN

For over a decade now, a substantial professional staff (and a small army of the world's leading industrial-organizational psychologists; e.g., see Peterson, Mumford, Borman, Jeanneret, & Fleishman, 1999), employed directly or indirectly by DoL, have been busy building the increasingly impressive and complex online shell or infrastructure called O*Net. O*Net's near-comprehensive myriad of hyperlinked web sites and web pages is hosting the envisioned future of data-supported career exploration and career management.

The latest O*NET offerings suggest much future potential for career management professionals, given adequate funding by DOL. Previously, it would have been very time consuming and expensive for most individuals to acquire a comprehensively multidimensional (indeed multiparadigm) perspective on their personal occupational compatibilities. O*NET's vision is to make such a grand multiparadigm perspective virtually free for everyone (although allowing for commercial providers to fine-tune these O*NET offerings and algorithms and subsequently charge clients, appropriately, for such value-added fine tunings). O*NET's online systems make freely available many career explorer and work analysis questionnaires. However, it must be noted that there has been considerable debate about the reliability, validity, and psychometric viability of these O*NET systems, materials, and rating samples (e.g., Harvey, 2007).

O*NET's power partially derives from its adroit use of hyperlinks, one of which connects to the U.S. government's Competency Model Clearinghouse, which features a tool that enables users to incorporate O*NET occupations and information within a customized "career ladder":

> Career ladders and lattices are devices that help people visualize and learn about the job options that are available as they progress through a career. Career ladders and lattices consist of a group of related jobs that comprise a career. They often include a pictorial representation of job progression in a career as well as detailed descriptions of the jobs and the experiences that facilitate movement between jobs. Career ladder/lattices are not necessarily organization-specific; they frequently span multiple organizations because movement within one organization may not be possible. Career ladders display only vertical movement between jobs. In contrast, career lattices contain both vertical and lateral movement between jobs and may reflect more closely the career paths of today's work environment. (U.S. Department of Labor, 2011, para. 1)

For the career management professional interested in tying work analysis insights to career planning or development, several possible uses are suggested. Such career ladders and lattices can help bring focus to workforce development plans. They also can help your workers see how various personal development efforts or career strategies can open up ascending opportunities within their own vocational futures. They can attract new recruits into your industry sector by illustrating what opportunities for positive progression such a move will afford them. Finally, they can make plain how a variety of positions or jobs can connect across organizations within an industry, or conceivably, across industrial sectors.

For both career management professionals and for individual employees, O*NET provides a variety of self-assessment features or tools:

> [These tools] are designed to assist a wide variety of individuals to gain personal insights that will help them identify occupations that they might find satisfying. These instruments will help individuals identify their work-related interests, [values] they consider important on the job, and their [relevant] abilities in order to explore those occupations that relate most closely to those attributes. The tools can help workers consider career options and plan career preparation and transitions more effectively. (U.S. Department of Labor, 2011)

As O*NET has always been about exploiting emerging Internet-based technologies in the interest of maximizing suitable vocational outcomes in the workforce, one can expect to see O*NET innovations manifesting on a regular basis. Hopefully, these innovations will include affordable ways within O*NET to recapture the detailed validity of more aggressively idiographic and microscopic (if now less affordable) taxonomies such as the *Dictionary of Occupations Titles*.

It does seem likely, given the broader data collection and data analytical affordances of modern social media circumscribed within the industrial-organizational psychology and human resource management professions, that meaningful advances will be seen in this arena. In an increasingly "wired" future, new empirical connectivities and subsequent expansions in vocational-theoretical perspectives should ensue. Collectively, these should yield enthusiasm for greater degrees of rigor in work analysis systems applied to career development practice. These new Web-supported connectivities will, no doubt, lead career managers to increasingly sophisticated, yet user-friendly, ways to validly collect incumbent worker inputs and increase job-seeker participation. Some of these may well be connected to new career theories. However, where work analysis data are concerned, the vast O*NET and the theories discussed in this chapter will likely be engaged and—at the very least— influential and foundational.

REFERENCES

Aguinis, H., Mazurkiewicz, E., & Heggestad, E. (2009). Using web-based frame of reference training to decrease biases in personality-based job analysis: An experimental field study. *Personnel Psychology, 62,* 405–438.

Atkins, S., Carr, S. C., Fletcher, R. B., & McKay, R. (2006, May). *Worker vocational fit from the perspective of personality-focused job analysis.* Symposium conducted at the Annual Conference of the APA Society of Industrial/Organisational Psychologists, Dallas, TX.

Atkins, S., & McKay, R. (2005, July). *Cross-sectional job analysis hints at a longitudinal process: Can misfit-driven attrition diminish some personality validities more than others?* Paper presented at 6th Australian Organisational Psychology Conference, Gold Coast, Australia.

Barrick, M. R., & Mount, M. K. (1991). The big five personality dimensions and job performance: a meta-analysis. *Personnel Psychology, 44,* 1–26.

Bess, T. L., & Harvey, R. J. (2002). Bimodal score distribution and the MBTI: Fact or artifact? *Journal of Personality Assessment, 78,* 176–186.

Bess, T., Harvey, R. J., & Schwartz, D. (2003, April). *Hierarchical confirmatory factor analysis of the Myers-Briggs Type Indicator.* Paper presented at the Annual Conference of the Society for Industrial and Organizational Psychology, Orlando, FL.

Briggs-Myers, I. (1980). *Gifts differing: Understanding personality type.* Mountain View, CA: Davies-Black Publishing.

Brown, R. D., & Harvey, R. J. (1996, April). *Job-component validation using the MBTI and the Common-Metric Questionnaire (CMQ).* Paper presented at the Annual Conference of the Society for Industrial and Organizational Psychology, San Diego, CA.

Cohen, A. (1993). Organizational commitment and turnover: A meta-analysis. *Academy of Management Journal, 36*(5), 1140–1157.

Cunningham, J. W., Boese, R. R., Neeb, R. W., & Pass, J. J. (1983). Systematically derived work dimensions: Factor analyses of the Occupation Analysis Inventory. *Journal of Applied Psychology, 68,* 232–252.

Cunningham, J. W., Slonaker, D. F., & Riegel, N. B. (1975). The development of activity preference scales based on systematically derived work dimensions: An ergometric approach to interest measurement. *JSAS Catalog of Selected Documents in Psychology, 5,* 355.

Cunningham, J. W., Slonaker, D., & Riegel, N. B. (1987). Interest factors derived from job analytically based activity preference scales. *Journal of Vocational Behavior, 30*(3), 270–279.

Dawis, R. V., & Lofquist, L. H. (1984). *A psychological theory of work adjustment: An individual differences model and its applications.* Minneapolis, MN: University of Minnesota Press.

Day, S. X., & Rounds, J. (1998). Universality of vocational interest structure among racial and ethnic minorities. *American Psychologist, 53*(7), 728–736.

Dessler, G. (1997). *Human resource management.* New York, NY: Prentice Hall.

Drewes, D., Tarantino, J., Atkins, S., & Paige, B. (2000). *Development of the O*NET Related Occupations Matrix.* Raleigh, NC: National O*NET Development Center.

Gibson, S. G., Harvey, R. J., & Quintela, Y. (2004, April). *Holistic versus decomposed ratings of general dimensions of work activity.* Paper presented at the Annual Conference of the Society for Industrial and Organizational Psychology, Chicago, IL.

Goris, J. R., Vaught, B. C., & Pettit, J. D. (2000). Effects of communication direction on job performance and satisfaction: A moderated regression analysis. *The Journal of Business Communication, 37,* 348–364.

Gottfredson, G. D., & Holland, J. L. (1991). *The Position Classification Inventory: Professional manual.* Odessa, FL: Psychological Assessment Resources.

Gottfredson, L. S. (1999). The nature and nurture of vocational interests. In M. L. Savickas & A.R. Spokane (Eds.), *Vocational interests: Meaning, measurement, and counseling use* (pp. 57–85). Palo Alto, CA: Davies-Black Publishing.

Gustafson, S., & Mumford, M. (1995). Personal style and person-environment fit: A pattern approach. *Journal of Vocational Behavior, 46,* 163–188.

Hackman, J. R., & Oldham, G. R. (1975). Development of the job diagnostics survey. *Journal of Applied Psychology, 60*, 159–170.

Hackman, J. R., & Oldham, G. R. (1976). Motivation through the design of work: Test of a theory. *Organizational Behavior and Human Performance, 16*(2): 250–279.

Hackman, J. R., & Oldham, G. R. (1980). *Work redesign*. Reading, MA: Addison-Wesley.

Harvey, R. J. (1991). Job analysis. In M. D. Dunnette & L. M. Hough (Eds.), *Handbook of industrial and organizational psychology, Vol. 2* (2nd ed., pp. 71–163). Palo Alto, CA: Consulting Psychologists Press.

Harvey, R. J. (1996). Reliability and validity. In A. I. Hammer (Ed.), *MBTI applications: A decade of research on the Myers-Briggs Type Indicator* (pp. 5–29). Palo Alto, CA: Consulting Psychologists Press.

Harvey, R. J. (2004). *Research monograph: Development of the common metric questionnaire*, Blacksburg, VA: PSTC.

Harvey, R. J. (2007, April). *Five things we need to know about job analysis*. Symposium presented at the Annual Conference of the Society for Industrial and Organizational Psychology, New York.

Harvey, R. J., & Murry, W. D. (1994). Scoring the Myers-Briggs Type Indicator: Empirical comparison of preference score versus latent-trait methods. *Journal of Personality Assessment, 62,* 116–129.

Harvey, R. J., Murry, W. D., & Stamoulis, D. (1995). Unresolved issues in the dimensionality of the Myers-Briggs Type Indicator. *Educational and Psychological Measurement, 55,* 535–544.

Harvey, R. J., & Thomas, L. (1996). Using item response theory to score the Myers-Briggs Type Indicator: Rationale and research findings. *Journal of Psychological Type, 37,* 16–60.

Hesketh, B. (2000). The next millennium of "Fit" research: Comments on "The congruence myth: An analysis of the efficacy of the person-environment fit model" by H. E. A. Tinsley. *Journal of Vocational Behavior, 56*(2), 190–196.

Hesketh, B., & Considine, G. (1998). Integrating individual and organizational perspectives for career development and change. *European Journal of Work and Organizational Psychology, 7*(3), 405–418.

Hesketh, B., & Myors, B. (1997). How should we measure fit in organisational psychology—Or should we? *Australian Psychologist, 32*(1), 71–76.

Holland, J. L. (1997). *Making vocational choices: A theory of vocational personalities and work environments* (3rd ed.). Odessa, FL: Psychological Assessment Resources.

Inkson, K. (2007). *Understanding careers: The metaphors of working lives*. Thousand Oaks, CA: Sage Publications.

James, L. R., Demaree, R. G., & Wolf, G. (1984). Estimating within-group interrater reliability with and without response bias. *Journal of Applied Psychology, 69*, 85–98.

Lent, R. W., & Brown, S. D. (2006). Integrating person and situation perspectives on work satisfaction: A social-cognitive view. *Journal of Vocational Behavior, 69*(2), 236–247.

Lent, R. W., & Hackett, G. (1987). Career self-efficacy: Empirical status and future directions. *Journal of Vocational Behavior, 30*, 347–382.

McCormick, E. J., Jeanneret, P. R., Mecham R. C. (1972). A study of job characteristics and job dimensions based on the Position Analysis Questionnaire (PAQ). *Journal of Applied Psychology, 56*, 347–368.

McCormick, E. J., Mecham, R. C., & Jeanneret, P. R. (1989). *Technical manual for the Position Analysis Questionnaire* (2nd ed.). Logan, UT: PAQ Services.

McKay, R., & Atkins, S. (2002, August). *Personality-based job analysis applied to New Zealand Broadcast Sales*. Paper presented at the Annual Conference of the New Zealand Psychological Society, Christchurch, New Zealand.

Myers, I. B., & McCauley, M. H. (1985). *Manual: A guide to the development and use of the Myers-Briggs Type Indicator*. Palo Alto, CA: Consulting Psychologists Press

Pennington, M. C. (1992). Motivating English language teachers through job enrichment. *Language, Culture and Curriculum, 5*(3), 199–218.

Peterson, N., Mumford, M., Borman, W., Jeanneret, P. R., & Fleishman, E. (Eds). (1999). *An occupational information system for the 21st century: The development of O*NET*. Washington, DC: American Psychological Association.

Rashkovky, B. (2006). Extending the job component validity (JCV) model to include personality predictors. *Dissertation Abstracts International: Section B: The Sciences and Engineering, 66*(7-B), 3986.

Raymark, P. H., Schmit, M. J., & Guion, R. M. (1997). Identifying potentially useful personality constructs for employee selection. *Personnel Psychology, 50*, 723–736.

Rounds, J. B., Dawis, R. V., & Lofquist, L. H. (1987). Measurement of person-environment fit and prediction of satisfaction in the theory of work adjustment. *Journal of Vocational Behavior, 31*(3), 297–318.

Schmidt, F., & Hunter, J. (2004) General mental ability in the world of work: Occupational attainment and job performance. *Journal of Personality & Social Psychology, 86*(1), 162–173.

Schneider, B. 1987. The people make the place. *Personnel Psychology, 40*, 437–453.

Sharf, R. (2005). *Applying career development theory to counseling* (4th ed.). Florence, KY: Cengage.

Super, D. (1992). Toward a comprehensive theory of career development. In D. H. Montross & C. J. Shinkman (Eds.), *Career development: Theory and practice* (pp. 35–64). Springfield, IL: Charles C. Thomas.

Super, D. (1994). A life span, life space perspective on convergence. In M. L. Savikas & R. W. Lent (Eds.), *Convergence in career development theories: Implications for science and practice* (pp. 63–74). Palo Alto, CA: CPP Books.

Super, D. (2007). Structure of work values in relation to status, achievement, interests, & adjustment. *Risorsa Uomo: Rivista di Psicologia del Lavoro e dell' Organizzazione, 13*(2), 163–175.

Tinsley, H. E., & Tinsley, D. J. (1989). Homemaker values. *Journal of Counseling Psychology, 36*(2), 89–195.

Tracey, T., & Rounds, J. (1995). The arbitrary nature of Holland's RIASEC types: A concentric-circles structure. *Journal of Counseling Psychology, 42*(4), 431–439.

U.S. Department of Labor. (2011). *O*NET resource center.* Retrieved from http://www.onetcenter.org/ladders.html

Vicente, J. M. M., & Fernandez, F. V. (2003). Study and analysis of the Position Classification Inventory of Gottfredson and Holland. *Electronic Journal of Research in Educational Psychology and Psychopedagogy, 1*(1), 121–136.

Wilk, S. L., Desmarais, L. B., & Sackett, P. R. (1995). Gravitation to jobs commensurate with ability: longitudinal and cross-sectional tests. *Journal of Applied Psychology, 80*, 79–85.

Wilk, S. L., & Sackett, P. R. (1995). *A longitudinal analysis of ability-job complexity fit and job change.* Paper presented at the conference of the Society for Industrial & Organizational Psychology, Orlando, FL.

Yost, P., & Chang, G. (2009). Everyone is equal, but some are more equal than others. *Industrial and Organizational Psychology, 2*(4), 442–445.

Zurriaga, R., Ramos, J., Gonzalez-Roma, V., Espejo, B., & Zornoza, A. (2000). Effects of job characteristics on job satisfaction, organizational commitment and absenteeism in health care organizations. *Revista de Psicologia Social Aplicada, 10*(3), 85–98.

27

Using Job Analysis Data to Perform Activity-Based Utility Analysis
Enhancement of a Technology

BRICE M. STONE

Metrica, Inc.

ROSALINDA VASQUEZ MAURY

Metrica, Inc.

By 1980, the U.S. Air Force determined training requirements by holding utilization and training workshops where trainers and training managers met with representatives from operational commands to consider issues and needs regarding training objectives, course content, and optional settings for accomplishing training (Mitchell, Sturdevant, Vaughan, & Rueter, 1987). These conferences evolved from earlier procedures where initial skills technical training was aligned with initial job requirements ("hasty grad" projects), while at the same time planning for training requirements deferred to field training detachments, mobile training teams, or on-the-job training (OJT; Ruck & Birdlebough, 1977; Vaughan, 1978). Only minimal data were available for determining appropriate training settings for Air Force specialty (AFS) tasks; thus, these decisions were, of necessity, based almost entirely upon conferees' personal experience or on known constraints at the resident training school. For these reasons, many decisions made in utilization and training workshops could not be consistently replicated. In addition, no formal evaluation or estimates were made of the impact of such decisions on personnel utilization, OJT costs, or mission performance (Ruck, 1982).

In the late 1980s, the Air Force Research Laboratory (originally called Armstrong Laboratory) began research and analysis into the development of a tool to analyze occupation specific training and utilization patterns and policies for its enlisted occupational specialties. The system that resulted from those efforts was called the Training Decision Support (TDS) system. In the mid-1990s, TDS was significantly modified and advanced into a system called the Training Impact Decision Support (TIDES) system. TIDES is a utility analysis tool that estimates the dollar value of benefits resulting from imposed changes in various aspects of the utilization and training of career field personnel over their entire tenure in the U.S. Air Force. The TIDES also provides managers with information they can use to evaluate the financial impact of policy, utilization, and training changes, including computing a return on their investment in implementing the changes.

To make good training decisions for an Air Force specialty or weapon system, decision makers must be able to visualize and understand the jobs and training programs of the specialty or weapon system under consideration, including its technical training and professional military education (PME) requirements, as well as the relative costs and payoffs of various training options. Such a model provides a concise summary of the current status of the specialty, creates a common language for discussion or negotiation, and forms the baseline against which various alternative proposals can be evaluated. Thus, a modeling capability was a very necessary and important element in any TDS. The Air Force Human Resources Laboratory initiated the TDS project in 1983 to develop a computer-based training decision support system to aid Air Force managers in making critical training decisions. The purpose of this research and development project was to explore the feasibility of such a system; develop technologies required to gather, estimate, or process information which could help Air Force managers make realistic training decisions for a specialty; and evaluate potential consequences of such decisions (Mitchell, Vaughan, & Knight, 1992). Based on successful demonstrations and use of the technology featured in the TDS, the Air Force decided to pursue development of a TDS-based system designed for a personal computer, and that employed current interface technologies. The system was redesigned as TIDES.

TIDES—A SINGLE AIR FORCE WORK ANALYSIS TOOL

TIDES is a entity-based career progression and training simulation model for analyzing utilization and cost implications of alternative career progressions, jobs, and training programs. The TIDES technology helps personnel and training managers balance an occupation/position's training needs versus requirements to optimize training management throughout the entire career of an individual or group of individuals. The TIDES methodology encompasses all training (formal and OJT), as well as jobs that an individual could perform throughout their career in an organization. Such specialized groups of individuals have different training needs, and substantial economies are possible through tailored job training. TIDES technology provides analysts and decision-makers with a tool to systematically analyze and integrate information about jobs/positions, tasks, career assignments, personnel flows, and training programs within an organization (or groups of related occupation/positions). TIDES forms the basis of a technology that can evaluate and compare the costs associated with reengineering of jobs/positions and associated training.

By dynamically modeling an occupation/position's career flow patterns, the TIDES technology provides a "what-if" capability to assess the long-term impact of current and future constraints stemming from changing training, personnel and resources. TIDES analyses also aid decision makers in determining what tasks associated with an occupation/position to train, when to provide that training (at what career points), and the method best suited for that type of training.

TIDES is a computer-based decision support technology. This technology was designed to generate information useful for decision-makers. This information (produced by the TIDES program) can be used as the basis for decisions to realign Air Force assignment, utilization, and training policies and practices. This is accomplished by defining current utilization and training patterns, enabling users of the technology to introduce scenarios involving changes to Air Force policies that modify those patterns, and generating data that reflect the impacts of introduced changes.

During the development of TIDES, several Air Force occupations were used to test the TIDES capabilities. They ranged from fairly homogeneous specialties, such as the B-1 Avionics Test Station (two jobs plus supervisors), to very structured specialties, such as Security and Law Enforcement (85 job variations), to complex electronics career fields, such as the Avionics Inertial Radar and Navigation Systems technicians (many distinct jobs driven by specialized equipment items, each with its own advanced skills training course). TIDES proves most useful when applied to occupations with high volumes of trainees and complex tasks. One occupation studied dealt with maintenance of sophisticated electronic computer and switching systems. The equipment was so complex that training and personnel assignments were specialized by the type of equipment they maintained. Problems were beginning to show up at a senior level; technicians were so specialized that they knew little about the entire occupation. Therefore, when decisions were being made, certain specialty areas may have been underemphasized due to the lack of the decision makers' experience with some equipment.

DATABASE DEVELOPMENT

The TIDES technology bases its analysis on the concept of task modules (TMs). TMs are groups of tasks related to one another (tasks that share required knowledge and skills, involve the use of the same tools or equipment, and distinguish among jobs and experience groups). TMs are often derived from task performance information gathered by the Air Force occupational analysis process. If no occupational analysis data is available, TMs can be constructed by analyzing Air Force personnel policy documents, training guidance, and operational guidance. Constructed TMs are validated by qualified subject matter experts (SMEs). The resulting TMs form the TIDES foundation for describing job assignment flows and patterns of training to model utilization and training patterns for the occupation. SMEs also validate other components of the model, including positions within the occupation (jobs), skills and experience required to perform jobs, and the duration a person is likely to hold a given job. Finally, SMEs identify locations considered representative of typical OJT programs. This information is used as a baseline for future comparisons in terms of training costs and resource requirements.

Cost estimates for conducting training are obtained by collecting information on travel to and from the training sites and per diem rates for students attend training courses. Information is also obtained on variable cost per student per formal training site, as well as the number of hours and wage rates of individuals (trainers and trainees) involved in formal training and OJT. All cost information is gathered for each TM by training setting (such as classroom, laboratory, self-study, and OJT). In addition to the detailed cost information, data are also collected on the number of hours required to train a typical individual to a specified proficiency (learning curves) by TM and training setting. All of these data are organized within a TIDES database to quantitatively model the current utilization and training pattern of a career field.

TIDES COMPONENTS AND FUNCTIONS

The TIDES process enables users to model the current (baseline) utilization and training pattern for an AFS. Once the baseline is established, users can then introduce changes to the utilization and training pattern, model the revised pattern, and contrast the differences between the baseline utilization and training pattern and the revised utilization and training pattern. To create a reliable and realistic baseline of an Air Force occupation and before running any simulation, a considerable amount of data must be collected and the database must be populated.

Once a simulation has been run, TIDES can generate reports within the following categories: training cost, personnel counts, personnel hours, resources, and summary. See Table 27.1 for a list of complete TIDES reports.

The TIDES capability produces baseline utilization and training patterns for the specialty, which enables the career field stakeholders to visualize how the members within specialty are currently being assigned and trained (see Figure 27.1). The TIDES capability also produces alternative utilization and training patterns based on proposed changes (e.g., decreases or increases in manpower, training, assignment lengths, maintenance procedures), which enables the stakeholders to visualize the impact of potential changes to utilization and training patterns.

When increasing the number of entries into the Air Force, the utilization and training pattern is altered by the increase of entrants into a job or training course, and thus increases the strain on

Table 27.1   TIDES-Generated Reports

Reports	Report Type	
Training cost	Cost summary	OJT cost by job
	Cost summary by year	OJT cost by job and task module
	Formal training cost by course	OJT cost by task module
	Formal training cost by job	
Personnel counts	Experience distribution	Training count by course and job
	OJT personnel counts by job	Training counts by course
	OJT counts by TM	Training counts by job
	Personnel job distribution by year	
Personnel hours	OJT personnel hours by job	OJT personnel by job and TM
Resources	Formal training resources requirements and availability	Formal training summary
Summary	Formal job summary	OJT job summary by group
	Formal job summary by group	OJT TM summary
	Formal training summary by group	OJT TM summary by group
	OJT job summary	

OJT = on-the-job training; TM = task module.

resources required for formal training, OJT, and unit qualification training (UQT). The TIDES application can produce data reflecting the consequences associated with each alternative. These include estimates of the following:

- Increases or decreases in job performance requirements
- Percentage of personnel within your specialty and jobs, which would require training
- Resources required to conducting training
- Capacities of training settings to conduct training based on resource availability

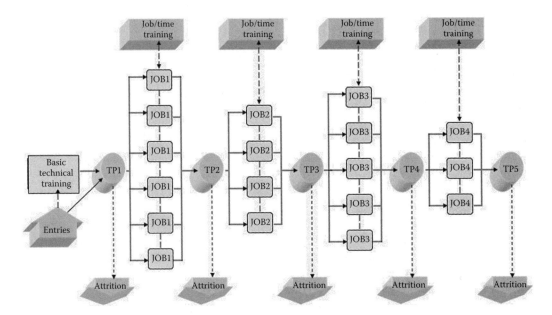

Figure 27.1   Utilization and training patterns.

- Cost for conducting training within specified training settings
- The most effective distribution of training hours for specified performance requirements across training settings to minimize training costs

METHODOLOGY

The functional requirements for the TIDES study involve gathering and analyzing job and training utilization patterns of the career field and its employment settings. The overall purpose of the TIDES data collection and analysis component is to gather all data needed for the TIDES to model current and alternative utilization and training patterns as well as the impacts of proposed or implemented decisions. The types of data gathered for the TIDES study includes the following:

- Job and training history from members assigned to AFS
- TMs applicable to the AFS and each job within the AFS
- Resources required to train each TM and the availability of those resources in each training settings
- Estimates of time required to train TMs to full proficiency
- Organizations and locations where AFS members are assigned
- Representative training sites and the organizations represented by those sites
- Salary, travel, and per diem costs
- Current AFS manning

The first step in the TIDES data collection effort is to review pertinent AF and Air Education and Training Command (AETC) publications and directives, as well as manning data received from the Air Force Career Field Manager (AFCFM). The AFCFM is the focal point for the designated career field within a functional Air Force community. He or she serves as the primary advocate for the career field, addressing issues and coordinating functional concerns across various staffs. He or she is responsible for the career field policy and guidance. If there are no current job inventory or occupational survey reports available, then the job inventory is constructed from basic sources. Beginning with the AFI 36-2108 specialty description, a list of task statements representing the responsibilities of the AFS is developed. That list is refined and expanded in consultation with the AFS Manager and the Command Functional Manager. When the process is completed, the task list is organized into TMs. The Command Functional Manager validates the TMs with the help of SMEs at several operational locations and ultimately approves the final set of TMs.

Questionnaire Development

To collect the majority of the required information, the following six questionnaires are developed as data collection instruments:

1. *Job and Training History Survey*: This questionnaire was designed to capture the personal history of job assignments, formal training courses, and PME throughout the careers of a large sample of personnel in the specialty. The objective is to capture a complete job history in a chronological order.
2. *Task Module-to-Jobs Map*: This questionnaire is designed to identify linkages between job titles and TMs. The Command Functional Manager and teams of knowledgeable SMEs at various headquarters and operational locations identify which TMs are associated with each of the job titles in the Job and Training History survey. The SMEs then rate the frequency with which members performed tasks associated with each TM for each job.

3. *Resident Course Training Times Questionnaire*: This questionnaire is designed to collect information about formal training courses that support the career field. Specifically, information is collected relevant to the amount of time dedicated within each course in terms of the TMs. Training times were specified by hours dedicated each TM in classroom, laboratory, and self-study as well as hours instructors spent preparing to teach each knowledge or performance requirement.

4. *Training Resource Requirements Questionnaire*: This questionnaire is designed to gather three types of information: (a) the identification of training resources required to deliver training in specified courses; (b) the maximum number of student each resource can support; and (c) the quantity of those resources currently available to the courses.

5. *Task Module Learning Curves Questionnaire*: This questionnaire is designed to collect information about the maximum proficiency that can be attained by an individual in training using specified training delivery methods (classroom, laboratory, self-study, and OJT or unit qualification training), and the maximum number of hours required to attain the Air Force standard "go/no-go" level of proficiency.

6. *On-the-Job Training Resource Availability Questionnaire*: This questionnaire is designed to estimate the capacity of an operational unit to conduct OJT. This is done by collecting the following information: (a) the amounts of time that personnel in specific grades are available to conduct or receive structured OJT; (b) the amounts of specific types of resources available for use by the unit when conducting OJT; and (c) the numbers of personnel who are performing specific jobs in the unit.

Data Aggregation

All of these types of data were organized into Microsoft Excel spreadsheets and imported into Microsoft Access files on which the TIDES simulation and report generation tools operate to quantitatively model the current utilization and training pattern of the specialty. The utilization and training simulation is created using STATA Statistical Software (version 8.0 for Windows) and reports generated on the total annual costs for the AFS and training capacity (including identifying critical constraints). Such summary data and reports became the baseline against which any proposed changes to specialty jobs and training programs could then be assessed.

MULTI-AFS ANALYSIS TOOL

Recently, several major enhancements were added to TIDES to allow it to analyze issues concerning not only specific Air Force career fields (occupations) but utilization and training issues relevant across multiple career fields (occupations), organizations (supported by multiple occupations), and processes (also supported by multiple occupations). This section describes the basis of the TIDES modeling system; the most recent advancements that have expanded its analysis capability beyond occupation specific jobs to agencies, organizations, and processes; and examples of the new TIDES analytical capabilities.

Initially, TIDES was developed to analyze and study single career fields (occupations). Often, organizational structure requires the analysis of jobs/agencies/organizations that use personnel from several occupational backgrounds. The new TIDES allows users to analyze multiple occupational groups in parallel, potentially focusing on common training or common jobs (jobs which are sufficiently generic that they can be performed by personnel from similar occupations or jobs in which significant formal training or OJT is provided to ensure proficiency in the performance of the job specific duties and responsibilities). Given the definition of the common job(s) based on TMs, the analyst can consider the affect of the job on training and utilization for each affected career field, as well as the training and utilization that are specific to the common job(s) of the organization or agency. Thus, the multicareer field TIDES provides all the information originally specific to a particular career field, as well as training and/or utilization common to multiple career fields.

For example, assume an agency or organization composed of three distinct jobs uses personnel from four different career fields. Personnel from any of the career fields are selected at some juncture in their tenure to become a part of the agency. The personnel are assigned to the agency for a tour of duty and then can return to their own career fields when the assignment is complete. The personnel assigned to the agency may receive formal training in terms of a course or OJT training to become proficient at the duties and responsibilities that they are assigned while a member of the agency staff. Personnel can also be assigned to the agency more than once at various junctures in their career, possible taking different jobs within the agency requiring additional training or expertise. Certain tenure or experience requirements may exist for each of the jobs in the agency that could affect the time type of personnel assigned to the agency from the AFSs. The enhanced versions of TIDES allows the user to track personnel from each of the four career fields and identify the necessary training, formal and OJT, required to perform the set of TMs relevant to each of the three specific jobs in the agency.

EXAMPLE

The TIDES has been applied to numerous Air Force enlisted, officer, and civilian career fields. Various training issues were studied from restructuring the jobs in the career field to transitioning from three level maintenance to two level maintenance of Air Force aircraft (aerospace mechanics) to reformulating the role of the school house (medical technicians). TIDES has been used to study privatization of military positions, reduction of temporary duty assignment (TDY) to school costs, identifying training cost centers for reengineering or restructuring, and evaluation of computer based training/computer based instruction (CBT/CBI) implementation (break-even analysis) across career fields of varying technical complexity and manning levels. The TIDES has been applied to large career fields such as aerospace mechanics and space system operators and small, complex career fields such as aerospace physiology and medical technicians.

The TIDES technology was used to examine alternatives to reorganizing seven separate tracks into a smaller set of subspecialties. The formal consensus among representatives of various constituencies (at a utilization and training workshop) was for a common (general) track plus three specialized tracks. The consolidation reduced overhead needed to manage the occupation and increased the experience base for future senior technicians. Most importantly, when combined with other Air Force personnel policy changes, including increasing the average assignment time from 32 to 48 months, a potential reduction or cost avoidance of $1.7 million in annual training costs was realized, even though each new trainee would receive more complete training focused on their job requirements than in the past. Several other successful TIDES studies included aircraft environment systems, aerospace propulsion, aerospace physiology, pavements, medical services, and electronic warfare systems.

Numerical Example for a Small Information Operations Career Field

For discussion purposes, a small information operations career field will be used without providing a specific name. This small information operations career field consists of approximately 304 assigned enlisted personnel. The reenlistment rate is defined as the ratio of the number of personnel that reenlist compared to the number of eligible to reenlist personnel that make a reenlistment/separation decision. The keep rate is defined as the ratio of the number of personnel that reenlist compared to the number of personnel that make a reenlistment/separation decision, regardless of eligibility to reenlist. The average reenlistment and keep rates for this small information operations career field over the 1994–2005 time period are 71.75% and 53.08%, respectively. The reenlistment rate will always be higher because the denominator for the keep rate is always larger (eligible to reenlist plus ineligible to reenlist). The average reenlistment rate for this small information operations career field is statistically different from zero (at the 95% level of confidence) and lower than the total average reenlistment rate for the Air Force as a whole: 77.32%. Conversely, the average of the keep rates for this small information operations career field is not statistically different from, though slightly higher than, the total keep rates for the Air Force as a whole: 52.05%. Thus, the small information operations career field has not exhibited statistically different and lower reenlistment rates over the last 12 years than the Air Force as a whole, although the keep rates for the small information operations career field are slightly higher than the Air Force as a whole.

Regardless of the characteristics of this small information operations career field, personnel flows and training flows produced by the TIDES' simulation provide a good representation of the baseline paradigm of the small information operations career field. The baseline indicates a total annual training cost, including formal and OJT training, of approximately $942,000 with OJT costs consisting of approximately 24.76%. Overall, manning resulting from the simulation averages approximately 300 personnel based on the established continuation rates from historical data and the accession flows of 41 airmen per year.

Assignment Length

On average, assignments for the personnel of the small information operations career field last approximately 24 months (±6 months based on the standard deviation), which is typical of most career fields from their job and training history survey data. If assignment lengths were increased approximately 50% across all jobs, the average assignment length across jobs would increase to 36 months. The annual training costs would drop approximately 11.63% to approximately $832,000 (see Table 27.2), with 23.12% of the decline coming from reduced OJT costs versus a 7.85% decline in formal training costs. A 100% increase in original assignment lengths across all jobs (increased to 48 months) results in a decline in annual training costs of approximately 13.11% to $818,000 with 32.04% of the decline coming from reduced OJT costs while formal training costs decreased 6.88%. The small changes on formal training costs are reflective of the significant amount of time driven training in this small information operations career field, which is not affected by assignment length. Table 27.2 provides a summary of these results.

Table 27.2 Annualized Training Costs Under Varying Assignments Lengths for the Small Information Operations Career Field

	Type of Costs			
Assignment Lengths	**Formal Training**	**OJT**	**OJT Percentage of Total**	**Total Training Costs**
Original assignment length baseline	$708,781	$233,216	24.76%	$941,997
50% increase in assignment length	$653,151	$179,305	21.54%	$832,456
Percentage change from original assignment length	−7.85%	−23.12%		−11.63%
100% increase in assignment length	$660,033	$158,499	19.36%	$818,532
Percentage change from original assignment length	−6.88%	−32.04%		−13.11%

OTJ = on-the-job training.

Entry Rates

Accession flows into the simulated small information operations career field were initially set at 41 airmen per year, which maintains an average annual inventory of approximately 300 person-nel, resulting in total annualized training costs of $942,000 (see Table 27.3). If accession flows are increased by 10%, the new accession flows will be approximately 45 per year with the inventory increasing to approximately 322. Total annualized training costs will increase by 5.12%, with OJT increasing 9.11%. If accession flows are increased by 20%, the new accession flows will be approxi-mately 49 per year, with the inventory increasing to approximately 335. Total annualized training costs will increase by 18.78% (compared to the baseline), with the increase in formal training costs markedly more than the increase in OJT costs, 19.88% versus 15.43% (Table 27.3).

Continuation Rates

Continuation rates for the TIDES simulation were calculated based on a 3-year average between 1999 and 2002. The continuation rates are specific to the small information operations career field and the manning levels for each year of the estimation time period. Selective reenlistment bonuses (SRB) are provided to enlisted personnel at reenlistment points (end of first term to reenlist for a second term, end of second term to reenlist for a career term, and during career reenlistment points) for selected career fields that are experiencing chronic shortfalls in reenlistment rates. SRB multiples are set at levels between 0 and 6 (at 0.5 increments) and represent the monetary incentive to reenlist for the eligible airman. Increases in the SRB multiple are expected to positively affect the reenlistment rate at the decision point to which the SRB is applied, thus increasing the continuation rates for the relevant year of service groups. For example, if an SRB multiple of four exists at the first-term reenlistment point, then any first term airman who reenlists will receive a SRB bonus of 4 times his or her monthly pay times the number of years for which the airman reenlists (usually between 4 to 6 years). SRB bonuses do not apply to end of term extensions (usually made for 2 or less years). For the TIDES example for this small information operations career field, a 5% increase in continuation rates will be assumed as a result of a SRB increase from multiple 2 to 3 at first- and second-term reenlistment points and a 10% increase will be assumed as a result of a SRB increase from multiple 3 to 4 at first and second term reenlistment points.

Table 27.4 presents the results of such a change in continuation rates at the first-term and second-term decision points while maintaining the personnel inventory at approximately 300. The 5% improvement in continuation rates (due to SRB increases) results in a 1.66% decrease in annual-ized training costs while maintaining the personnel inventory of the small information operations career field at approximately 300. The 10% increase in continuation rates (due to SRB increases)

Table 27.3 Annualized Training Costs Under Varying Accession Flows for the Small Information Operations Career Field

| Accession Flow Levels | Type of Costs | | | |
	Formal Training	OJT	OJT Percentage of Total	Total Training Costs
300 accessions baseline	$708,781	$233,216	24.76%	$941,997
322 accessions, 10%	$735,776	$254,467	25.70%	$990,243
Percentage change from baseline	3.81%	9.11%		5.12%
335 accessions, 20%	$849,682	$269,206	24.06%	$1,118,888
Percentage change from baseline	19.88%	15.43%		18.78%

OTJ = on-the-job training.

Table 27.4 Annualized Training Costs Under Increases in Selective Reenlistment Bonuses Multiples That Affect Continuation Rates (Maintaining the Personnel Inventory) for the Small Information Operations Career Field

| Continuation Rate Levels | Type of Costs | | | |
	Formal Training	OJT	OJT Percentage of Total	Total Training Costs
Baseline	$708,781	$233,216	24.76 %	$941,997
5% increase in continuation rates	$693,998	$232,330	25.08%	$926,327
Percentage change from baseline	−2.09%	−0.38%		−1.66%
10% increase in continuation rates	$688,959	$227,064	24.79%	$916,024
Percentage change from baseline	−2.80%	−2.64%		−2.76%

OTJ = on-the-job training.

exhibits a smaller reduction in annualized training costs of 2.76%, with formalized training costs exhibiting the largest reduction of 2.80%. The changes in continuation rates only affect those year of service groups between 3 years and 10 years, first-term and second-term decision makers.

Compensation

Another way of affecting continuation rates is through an overall increase in military compensation. Unfortunately, changes in overall compensation also affect training costs through trainer and trainee compensation. For this exercise, two levels of compensation increase will be assumed: 5% and 10%, along with their affect on continuation rates. The effect on continuation rates will be based on an elasticity of 1.1821 and an average rise in general wages of 2.5%. These changes will result in overall increase in continuation rates of 2.0% and 4.0%, respectively, in order to ensure enough change to be notable and not just random noise. The change in annualized training costs, resulting from the 2.0% and 4.0% changes in year of service continuation rates, were a slight increase of 0.63% and a decrease of 1.96%, respectively. The largest reductions occurred in formal training (Table 27.5) because improved continuation rates reduces costs associated with time-driven formal training. Maintaining the personnel inventory decreases the magnitude of the effect on the annualized cost of training for each incremental change/improvement in the continuation rates; that is, more people are staying in, thus less people need to be accessed to maintain the 300 yearly

Table 27.5 Annualized Training Costs Under Increases in Military Compensation for the Small Information Operations Career Field

| Continuation Rate Levels | Type of Costs | | | |
	Formal Training	OJT	OJT Percentage of Total	Total Training Costs
Baseline	$708,781	$233,216	24.76%	$941,997
2.0% overall increase in continuation rates	$713,038	$234,900	24.78%	$947,938
Percentage change from baseline	0.60%	0.72%		0.63%
4.0% overall increase in continuation rates	$697,650	$225,868	24.46%	$923,518
Percentage change from baseline	−1.57%	−3.15%		−1.96%
8.0% overall increase in continuation rates	$687,565	$234,616	25.44%	$922,181
Percentage change from baseline	−2.99%	0.60%		−2.10%

OTJ = on-the-job training.

personnel inventory. This tradeoff between accession flows and continuation rates as they affect annualized training costs is reflected even for an 8% change in continuation rates.

These are just a few of the types of changes which the TIDES technology can model. For comparison, the analysis of a large information operations career field will be provided.

Space Command Enlisted AFS TIDES Simulation Results

Space Command Enlisted AFS exhibits some nonstandard characteristics when compared to other enlisted career fields. First, approximately 50% of the new enlistees to the career field are retrainees (Stone, Tartell, Vasquez, & Borden, 2002). These retrainees predominately enter the career field near the beginning of their second term, while others tend to enter the career field with over 10 years total active federal military service.

With only 200 new accessions entering the career field each year, changes in the mix of new recruits versus retrainees can affect the cost of training through trainee costs, attrition rates, and/or reduced training. For example, if new accessions are increased to 166 and retrainees are reduced by 66 (to 33), total training costs will increase by approximately 6% in the steady state. The increase in training costs are driven by the fact that relatively more training will occur from initial qualification training (IQT) since new accessions will have more diversified assignments over their career requiring additional IQT. The large majority of new enlistees for Air Force enlisted career fields enter the career field at their first job, after basic and technical training. The significant retrainee flow translates into a large proportion of the space command enlisted AFS personnel entering their first job with 4 or more years of total active federal military service. This represents a more senior force in the career field, which was less involved in professional development training such as Airman Leadership School and Noncommissioned Officer Academy training because they had already attended those PME courses, which is different from the majority of other career fields.

Second, many "one-deep" jobs exist at bases using space command enlisted AFS personnel (Stone et al., 2002). In some cases, these one-deep jobs result in very low probabilities of assignment to these bases and the simulation may or may not always capture their job-specific contribution to training costs, although overall training costs remain representative. For example, of the 53 jobs identified as the first job assignment (Job and Training History Survey), 28 of the jobs were represented only once and four were represented only twice. Of the 40 bases identified in the first job assignment, only one job assignment was identified for 17 of the bases. This means that the simulation results will be representative of the career field as a whole but may not provide accurate information at base level of detail. Third, a large number of jobs were identified for the space command enlisted AFS (more than 150), which were validated by the Job and Training History Survey. Once again, the large number of jobs results in small probabilities of assignment to many of the jobs. Small probabilities of assignment will affect the ability of the TIDES simulation to mirror the baseline representation of the career field at the base level of detail.

Regardless of the unique characteristics of the space command enlisted AFS, personnel flows and training flows produced by the TIDES simulation provide a good representation of the baseline paradigm of the career field. Several modifications were made to the training probabilities to mimic the expected training flows provided by the career field manager for fiscal year 2002. The Enlisted Space Prerequisite Training Course was assessed at a probability of one in the first year of service to represent it as a required (mandatory) training course for all new enlistees (accessions and retrainees). The accession flow into the career field was set at 200, with 100 new accessions and 100 retrainees. Separation rates by years of service were estimated from the airmen master personnel files. The simulation always begins with an empty personnel pool and, based on the enlistment flows (accessions and retrainees) and loss rates, the TIDES simulation builds the personnel pool. The baseline simulation generates the annualized cost training based on the original parameter values, the baseline paradigm of the training and utilization patterns.

The TIDES technology is most useful when used to compare two utilization and training patterns. Generally, the user compares an alternative utilization and training pattern to the baseline. The baseline numbers generated by the simulation, costs and personnel counts, represent the steady state of the entity simulation. Any parameter of the simulation can be changed and retained as an alternative scenario to the baseline. For example, a run of the existing baseline scenario can produce annual training costs of over $3.86 million. The total annualized training costs are the sum of formal training and OJT (or UQT, in the case of Space Command).

The baseline scenario suggests that UQT costs comprise over 36% of total annualized training costs. UQT trainer costs comprise about 54% of the total annualized UQT costs, with UQT trainee costs comprising the remainder. UQT costs tend to be considered hidden costs to the career field versus the obvious costs of formal training where most cost reduction measures are directed. Student costs represent the largest share of the annualized formal training costs, more than 38%, followed by per diem. Travel and per diem costs represent approximately 28% of formal training costs and more than 18% of the total annual training costs for the career field. Table 27.6 presents the proportions of the annualized formal UQT training costs from a run of the simulation using the baseline parameters (Stone et al., 2002).

Because the simulation uses probabilities of utilization and training throughout the career of an airman, the annualized cost and personnel numbers will change slightly from one run (execution) of the simulation to another using the same specified parameters of the simulation. The steady-state solution will provide annualized cost and personnel numbers that are very close to the same when running the same scenario (parameters unchanged). The TIDES system is designed to automatically attain the steady-state solution for any scenario submitted to the software.

The baseline simulation generates a force size for the career field of about 1,390 annually, losing approximately 200 enlisted personnel per year. TIDES allows the steady state to determine the manning level for the career field, using changes to the accession flow and exit rates to alter manning levels. Of the approximately 1,390 enlisted personnel annually in the force, over 45% of the

Table 27.6   Components of Annualized Formal Training Costs From Baseline Simulation for the Space Command Enlisted AFS

Type of Cost	Annual Training Dollars	Percentage of Total	Percentage of Grand Total
Instructor cost	$264,294	10.74%	6.84%
Student cost	$1,498,190	60.88%	38.78%
Per diem cost	$584,715	23.76%	15.13%
Travel cost	$113,624	4.62%	2.94%
Total formal training costs	$2,460,823	100.00%	63.69%
UQT trainer costs	$758,766	54.08%	19.64%
UQT trainee costs	$644,203	45.92%	16.67%
Total UQT training costs	$1,402,969	100.00%	36.31%
Grand total	**$3,863,792**		**100.00%**

UQT = unit qualification training.

enlisted personnel are receiving some type of formal training (introductory, advanced, or professional development) during the year. Again, baseline figures vary from simulation run to simulation run, but the magnitude of the numbers are always close from one simulation to the next, given no change in the parameters of the system.

FUTURE DIRECTIONS OF TIDES

TIDES presently represents a highly advanced and tested utility analysis training evaluation technology in a Windows-based environment available to Air Force training and functional managers. It is a task-based technology whose use is only limited by the creativity of the user. The TIDES has the capability to respond to numerous questions and issues concerning training and utilization, as well as career field restructuring. The original code, which resided on a minicomputer, was transported to the personal computer and provided a user-friendly interface to allow access to the smallest bit of information supporting the technology. The TIDES is a proven technology that has been enhanced and extended with sound scientific research. Other agencies have considered the use of TIDES in their own organizations, such as the Federal Bureau of Investigation and the U.S. Marines Corps. TIDES applicability to the private sector is unlimited, but it is more appropriate for larger organizations where the training pipeline is larger and more measurable in percentage terms, avoiding the shortfalls associated with small number calculations.

REFERENCES

Mitchell, J. L., Sturdevant, W. A., Vaughan, D. S., & Rueter, F. H. (1987). *Training decisions system: Information gathering technical paper* (Technical Report, CDRL 23). Brooks AFB, TX: Training Systems Division, Air Force Human Resources Laboratory.

Mitchell, J. L., Vaughan, D. S., & Knight, J. R. (1992). *Training decisions technology analysis*_(Technical Paper, AL-TP-1992-0026). Brooks AFB, TX: Technical Training Research Division, Human Resources Directorate.

Ruck, H. W. (1982, February). Research and development of a training decisions system. In the *Proceedings of the Society for Applied Learning Technology.* Orlando, FL: Society for Applied Learning Technology.

Ruck, H. W., & Birdlebough, M. W. (1977). An innovation in identifying Air Force quantitative training requirements. In the *Proceedings of the 19th Annual Conference of the Military Testing Association.* San Antonio, TX: Air Force Human Resources Laboratory and the USAF Occupational Measurement Center.

Stone, B. M., Tartell, D., Vasquez, R., & Borden, K. (2002). *Space operations decision-making training and rehearsal* (Final Report for Contract F-41624-97-D-5000). Mesa, AZ: Air Force Research Laboratory.

Vaughan, D. S. (1978, October-November). Two applications of occupational survey data in making training decisions. In the *Proceedings of the 20th Annual Conference of the Military Testing Association* (vol. 1). Oklahoma City, OK: U.S. Coast Guard Institute.

28

A Comprehensive, Interactive, Web-Based Approach to Job Analysis
The SkillsNET Methodology

Darrel L. Sandall
Integra Management Associates

John Henderson
Personnel Science and Solution Architects

Roni Reiter-Palmon
University of Nebraska

Michael L. Brown
SkillsNET Corporation

Scott R. Homan
Purdue University

The use of the Internet for human capital practices has increased dramatically and has received significant coverage in the research literature (Crespin & Austin, 2002; Viswesvaran, 2003). Many of the empirical studies and descriptions of these applications have focused on using the Internet for sites that provide access to job postings or for advertising job positions via a company's web site (Chapman & Webster, 2003). Online employee screening and selection has become much more frequent via the Internet (Crespin & Austin, 2002; Konradt, 2003; Potosky & Bobko, 2004), with both test publishers and test distributers providing web-based testing services for virtually every type of personnel assessment available. The Internet is also being used for other personnel practices, including computer-based training and organizational surveys (Crespin & Austin, 2002; Sanchez, 1994) as well as for performance and learning management systems.

However, lagging behind some of the most innovative, web-based human capital developments is the practice of job analysis. Most organizations still identify job analytic data using traditional methods, including face-to-face interviews with individuals or panels (Sanchez, 2000). Despite the availability of online methods, the use of the Internet to generate job analytic information has not received widespread attention in research, practice, or theory. This is likely because online methodologies are perceived as less rigorous and defensible than traditional approaches, and there is a comfort level with the "tried and true." Although this perception of many web-based job analysis products is not necessarily inaccurate, there are certainly approaches and procedures that provide defensibility and ensure job analytic validity. The purpose of this chapter is to describe the development and implementation of a rigorous online job analysis system, already used globally, that relies upon the best practices from numerous approaches to enhance online job analysis data collection efforts and validity. The foundations of this system include taxonomic linkages, structured responses, standardized components, and embedded scientific principles as well as web-based facilitation practices.

GENERAL JOB ANALYTIC APPROACHES

Job analysis is a systematic procedure used to describe important aspects of work and the worker. This purpose has not substantially changed since 1922, when Morris Viteles first used his "job psychograph" questionnaire to help select employees (Landy & Conte, 2004). However, since then, several methods to carry out a job analysis have been developed, each with specific strengths and weaknesses, and each used with varying degrees of frequency and effectiveness (Table 28.1).

Although each method described above has utility in specific human resource management applications, no single approach is superior to all others across a number of diverse applications. Largely, this situation stems from the fact that different contexts often require different types of requirements, resources, or procedures. These different requirements often result in a need to approach job analysis projects with different philosophies (Table 28.2).

Irrespective of the selected approach or philosophy, the underlying processes remain relatively similar. Traditional job analyses procedures usually involve (a) gathering relevant job information from available documentation, (b) communicating with job incumbents and subject matter experts (SMEs) to define their perceptions of the job, (c) identifying important job dimensions, (d) observing or otherwise gathering information about the job, and (e) developing measures to assess various aspects of the job (Ash, Levine, & Bennett, 1980). Moreover, each end of the three approach continuums shown in Table 28.2 presents a number of advantages that should be considered when selecting a specific job analytic approach. In fact, because approaches described by differing ends of the continuums tend to share multiple process steps but differ generally by type of outcome, it is likely better practice to incorporate work and

Table 28.1 Job Analysis Methods

Documentation	Relying upon pre-existing documents, job descriptions, and internal or external occupational analyses for job data
Observation	Observing and recording the actions of job incumbents as they perform their duties
Interviews	Face-to-face discussions with individuals or groups of incumbents, supervisors, and subject matter experts that are typically facilitated by consultants or trained job analysts
Ability survey instruments	Easy-to-administer and low-cost checklists of preset abilities required for job performance that provide limited knowledge, skill, and task data (Fleishman & Mumford, 1989)
Structured behavioral questionnaires	Grouping of standardized, but also highly generalized, questions revolving around behaviors performed on the job
Critical incident technique	Incumbents and/or supervisors providing examples of highly effective and highly ineffective behaviors and actions executed on the job
Functional job analyses	Method producing standardized task statements with descriptions of job content and context
Task inventories	Incumbents and/or supervisors providing ratings (e.g., performance, criticality, frequency) of preset task lists with additional questions concerning incumbent background information

Table 28.2   Job Analysis Approaches

Work vs. worker orientation	Work-oriented approaches describe work in terms of tasks—the most specific level of job behavior reflecting performance of a meaningful job function. Each task typically refers to a specific action and object, must be observable, have a definite beginning and end, and result in a measurable product (Gael, 1990). In contrast, worker-oriented approaches describe general behaviors rather than tasks involved in job performance using a relatively small number of attributes (e.g., GWAs or KSAs) allowing dissimilar jobs to be compared.
Inductive vs. deductive	Inductive approaches rely on the collection of new, specific information about a job and are thus more costly and do not easily generalize to similar jobs in other organizations. Deductive approaches are less customized and based on the use of existing information such as previous job analysis data, job descriptions, training materials, and general lists of worker attributes that can be modified and surveyed to better fit a job (Peterson & Jeanneret, 1997).
Top-down vs. bottom-up	With top-down approaches, an analyst identifies important organizational outcomes and infers what attributes are required to accomplish results. Bottom-up approaches describe behavior driven by incoming information identifying work and worker job elements and making logical inferences about attributes needed for successful job performance.

worker, inductive and deductive, and top-down and bottom-up strategies when possible to ensure comprehensive coverage.

NEED FOR A COMPREHENSIVE WEB-BASED JOB ANALYSIS SYSTEM

Given the impetus of a dynamically and technologically changing, global workforce, two constants concerning job analysis can be definitively asserted. First, job analysis is necessary. As technological advances drive job differences, result in innovations to routine work activities, or lead to disparate geographic locations for personnel, job analysis presents the most effective and accurate way to update work and worker requirements for successful performance on the job. Second, current job analysis methodologies often do not meet organizational needs and do not take advantage of newer technologies. The contemporary business environment reflecting competition, globalization, technological change, and increased collaboration limits the usefulness of traditional job analysis methodologies (Sanchez, 1994). Certainly, all analysis methodologies carry with them specific strengths and benefits; otherwise, these methods would not have become popularized initially. However, traditional approaches can also be viewed as rigid and not easily adaptable to the rapid changes in work and organizations (Sanchez, 1994).

Although each traditional job analysis method may reflect particular advantages or strengths, there are nonetheless distinct disadvantages to how traditional job analytic procedures are implemented. For example, methodologies of job analysis that utilize face-to-face interviews and observations have been criticized because of the time and resource demands they place on organizations and job incumbents (Sanchez, 2000). Collecting data from documentation is not ideal in many instances, as documentation about the work may not exist or is frequently not valid or current. Observational data collection is very time intensive and only information on the work being performed during the observation period can be observed. Finally, interviews are extremely time consuming and have the significant potential for incumbent response bias because interviews sometimes carry with them the connotation of performance evaluation rather than simple data collection.

Moreover, traditional methodologies are not cost-effective with a global or even national workforce. Typical job analysis methodologies call for face-to-face interviews or workshops with representative samples of job incumbents, usually including top performers, and representing various ethnicities, genders, and geographic locations to ensure comprehensive coverage in the initial data collection phase. With large organizations and an increasingly global workforce, this requirement of face-to-face interviews may become much too cumbersome and expensive for organizations.

Often categorized as either work- or worker-oriented, most job analysis methodologies also focus efforts on collecting information related to either tasks or worker characteristics (Brannick & Levine, 2002). The type of approach selected is usually dictated by the intended use of the job analysis information (e.g., compensation versus training versus selection). This practice results in limited utility for other human capital efforts. As a solution, many practitioners use a combined approach that provides both task and knowledge, skills, abilities, and other characteristics (KSAO) information. However, the increased time and resource requirements lead many organizations to choose a more limited approach, which results in limited job data use and utility.

Finally, most data collection systems lack the structure required to compare job analytic data across jobs within an organization or across the same job in multiple organizations. Many traditional data collection methodologies do not provide data standardization or even a standardized structure to collect and relate the data. This greatly limits utility of the job analysis data within an organization, within industry groups, and across organizations and industries.

In the end, traditional job analysis methodologies demonstrate a number of drawbacks to successful implementation in current organizational landscapes (Reiter-Palmon, Brown, Sandall, Buboltz, & Nimps, 2006): (a) slow data collection, (b) difficulty updating job data, (c) difficulty collecting from representative samples, (d) time and resource demands, and (e) limited types of data collected. Considering some of the obstacles presented with traditional methods, SkillsNET began developing a new and integrated system incorporating dynamic and flexible data collection and updated techniques, collection of multiple types of data, increased efficiency, and more responsiveness to organizational needs. Because Internet applications were growing in use and provided a number of distinct advantages in reaching diverse geographic locations, a computerized, web-based system was determined to present the greatest opportunities for technological advancement. The Occupational Information Network (O*NET) content model provided yet another opportunity for advancement.

THE O*NET CONTENT MODEL

O*NET, developed by the U.S. Department of Labor, was created as a new, comprehensive system designed to provide a common language for describing jobs across organizations (Dye & Silver, 1999; Peterson et al., 2001). O*NET was chosen to serve as the base of SkillsNET's new system for four primary reasons. First, O*NET was developed to serve as a national framework for occupational data (U.S. Department of Labor, 1993) and thus was especially appropriate in the analysis of multiple jobs within or across organizations. Second, O*NET addressed the need for multiple descriptor domains (e.g., work- and worker-based) using a number of especially useful taxonomies. Third, O*NET addressed the need for a common language that could apply across a variety of jobs and organizations. Last, O*NET addressed the need for a hierarchical approach that allowed narrow and specific descriptors embedded within broad and general descriptors (Peterson et al., 2001).

The SkillsNET web-based job analysis systems uses various aspects of the O*NET taxonomies including the Enabling Skills, Enabling Abilities, and Generalized Work Activities. Additionally, all job data collected through the web-based system is mapped to O*NET's Standard Occupational Classification (SOC) code structure (U.S. Department of Labor, 2010). This is done by matching the job title of the job being analyzed to the most similar occupation in the O*NET framework and then designating the job with that occupation's O*NET-SOC code. This allows for industry-level data such as training, education and licensure, wage data, and job growth projection data to be obtained for the job.

THE SKILLSNET JOB ANALYSIS SYSTEM

Facilitating Without a Facilitator

One of the challenges in eliciting job analytic data has been ensuring coverage of all job areas, and this is especially noteworthy with online, job analytic practices. Historically, job analysis efforts have utilized a variety of methods to obtain information about tasks performed in jobs, most commonly using direct elicitation of information based on interviews with job incumbents and their supervisors. In this environment, the interviewer elicits job-related information such as tasks from the SMEs. Interviews may be unstructured or may start with questions such as, "Tell me what you did on the job yesterday" or "What do you do on your job?" However, broad questions provide very little structure (Hoffman, Shadbolt, Burton, & Klein, 1995), and lack of structure increases the importance and skill requirement of the interviewer (Brannick & Levine, 2002; Cooke, 1994). The interviewer is required to ensure that SMEs provide meaningful, job-relevant information, and that all aspects of the job are considered. To collect information in a distributed fashion, using a web-based methodology, it was necessary to find a way to elicit information without a facilitator. That is, the system had to provide SMEs all the structure that would otherwise be provided by a job analyst in a meeting.

Free recall is used when SMEs are asked no questions or only vague questions about their job to elicit job analysis information (Glass & Holyoak, 1986). Research in both laboratory and real-life settings suggests that cued recall is more effective and allows for more knowledge elicitation (Hudson & Austin, 1970; Koustall, Schacter, Johnson, & Gallucio, 1999; Wood, 1967). Cued recall guides information retrieval from memory (Glass & Holyoak, 1986). When information is elicited in meetings, facilitators provide additional cues by posing questions concerning more detailed information about the job.

In this context, instead of asking SMEs about their job as a whole, SMEs are asked to recall information about a specific subset or category of tasks on the job (e.g., financial and budgetary management tasks). In addition to providing structure to the recall process, presenting the SMEs with a specific category within which to recall job behaviors offers an additional benefit. Because information in memory is linked to similar information, the recall of one piece of information is likely to facilitate the recall of information that is similar or related (Glass & Holyoak, 1986). That is, similar or functionally related tasks will be more likely to be recalled at the same time. This is likely to facilitate better and more comprehensive knowledge elicitation within the category or job dimension. An additional benefit is that providing cues allows SMEs to not only focus on one aspect of the job at a time, but also facilitates the transfer to a different aspect, preventing interference when a new cue is introduced. Research supports the notion that providing a different cue, after recall for the first cue has been completed, results in improved recall (Wickens, Born, & Allen, 1963).

Mumford and his colleagues used the generalized work activities (GWAs) from O*NET to structure job analysis data collection meetings and provide cues (Clifton, Connelly, Reiter-Palmon, Gilbert, & Mumford, 1991; Connelly, Reiter-Palmon, Clifton & Mumford, 1991; Reiter-Palmon, Uhlman, Clifton, Connelly, & Mumford, 1990; Sager, Mumford, Baughman, & Childs, 1999). GWAs have been defined as "an aggregation of similar job activities that underlie the accomplishments of major work functions" (Jeanneret, Borman, Kubisiak, & Hanson, 1999, p. 106). GWAs were designed to be broad and general, as well as cover a wide range of job activities, making them applicable across occupations.

In Mumford's research, SMEs were asked to first select GWAs that were relevant to their job. Because the GWA list is intended to be applicable for a wide variety of jobs, not all GWAs are appropriate. SMEs were then asked to generate tasks within each GWA selected. The GWAs provided a structure to the job analysis interview, allowing SMEs to respond to more specific questions. Instead of "tell me everything about your job," the SMEs were asked, "tell me what kinds of things you do that relate to the GWA Inspecting Equipment." By using cued recall methodology to structure the session, tasks can be generated much more quickly and efficiently. For example, using cued recall, Mumford and his colleagues found that a 1-day panel meeting with 10 or fewer SMEs elicited 90–95% of the tasks for the job being analyzed as compared to traditional data collection sessions. In addition to a reduced number of meetings, the cued recall methodology has four additional advantages. First, because the data collection is structured based on GWAs, the resulting information is more organized because tasks are generated within the context of broader GWAs, resulting in reduced time demands on the job analysts after the meeting. Second, this process allows for recall within a specific category of the job, and then provides the additional cue (a new GWA) that facilitates further recall. The third advantage is that the cued recall methodology does not rely as much on the skill and training of the interviewer to elicit all tasks. Finally, because of the structure provided, this methodology can easily be transferred to a computer application. However, cued recall fails to provide all of the support and remote guidance required for successful online task generation.

Sager et al. (1999) suggested another way to structure the elicitation of tasks based on Prien's (1994) work. Common activity words (such as writing, supervising, installing) are identified to create an activity taxonomy. The taxonomy is then presented to a group of SMEs, and they select which activity words fit their job. A second group of SMEs is asked to list all the objects (e.g., documents, employees, wiring) of the activities selected by the first group. Sager et al. (1999) noted that this approach has features that may prove useful for online data generation. Specifically, although the generation of an activity list may be time consuming and difficult for SMEs, using a computer to generate an initial activity list and allowing SMEs to select from it is much more manageable.

The methodology developed for SkillsNET's web-based job analysis approach was an extension of the cued recall methodology. The challenge in allowing for individual, distributed job analytic work was to provide the user with enough information to understand the requirements of the task generation process and to navigate the system independently without assistance from an expert. The use of GWAs allowed for cued recall and breaking the work into smaller portions, enabling SMEs to focus on each GWA sequentially. For each GWA, a list of possible action words and object words was created to provide a starting point. For example, for the GWA *Interacting with Computers*, some common actions include type, program, write, connect, and edit. For the example of interacting with computers, common objects include program, software, hardware, spreadsheet, and database. Such lists were developed for each GWA and were included as part of the task generation process. Not only do these lists provide a queuing mechanism but they also allow development of appropriately worded task statements, such that each task includes an action and an object. Therefore, SMEs are able to generate better task statements with minimal introduction to the concept of a task statement.

Work Element Generation

Before each step of the web-based task generation process, a brief tutorial is provided to the participants that elaborates on the purpose of that specific phase in the entire process and explains how to use the system. The SMEs can return to each tutorial during the process to ensure understanding. Typically, 5–10 SMEs are used for each job being analyzed. The identification of SMEs is similar to that of traditional job analysis methods. SMEs should be above-average performers, job incumbents for the job they are analyzing, and have sufficient tenure in the position to be familiar with various aspects of the job (Cranny & Doherty, 1988). Written technical guidelines for use of the system specify that SMEs should typically be in the top one third of all performers in the job and have been in the job for at least 1 year. If there are anticipated differences in job performance based on location, shift, or other factors, then SMEs representing these aspects should be included to ensure coverage (Friedman, 1990). Once SMEs are identified by the client organization, their e-mail addresses are entered into the web-based system. An informational e-mail is automatically generated and sent, explaining the purpose of the job analysis effort and how and why the individual was selected for participation. The message also directs the SMEs to a uniform resource locator (URL) and provides a unique login and password needed to gain access to the system.

Legacy Data

The stages of content development in the SkillsNET system are shown in Figure 28.1. Once SMEs log into the system, a brief explanation of the process is given. The first step is a review of legacy task data. The system allows client-specific legacy data to be loaded for a job analysis. If no client-specific legacy data are loaded into the system, legacy data are pulled from a database with over 250,000 task statements from approximately 4,000 job analyses. Because legacy data specific to an organization

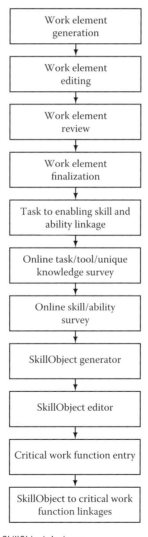

Figure 28.1   Stages of development within SkillObject designer.

can be used in the system, the previous efforts by the organization are not lost or ignored. Upon logging into the system, SMEs are presented the legacy task list and are asked to identify the tasks they perform in their job. In this deductively oriented approach, SMEs are required to review and make a simple "I do this/I do not do this" decision. Any task selected by any SME is kept for further review in later stages of the process.

Generalized Work Activities

In the next step, SMEs are instructed to review the full list of GWAs and associated definitions and select those that are applicable to their job. The SMEs are instructed to select 6–12 GWAs that represent work they do on their job. These GWAs will then serve as the starting point for generating tasks. An upper limit on the number of GWAs reduces potential overlap and repeat work, and also helps ensure that the task generation process can be completed in less than 8 hours. A lower limit on the number of GWAs selected ensures enough coverage by each SME. Each SME is presented with a different randomization of the GWAs to prevent order or response bias. In addition, because SMEs work independently, the selection of GWAs by one person is not influenced by the selections of another, which allows for the selection of the same or different GWAs by different SMEs. Once an SME has selected between 6 and 12 GWAs, he or she can move on to the next step. The system will not allow the person to progress if he or she selected fewer than 6 or more than 12 GWAs.

Task Generation

This step involves the use of action and object taxonomies, as suggested by Sager et al. (1999), created based on an analysis of over 200,000 task statements. Once the SME selects a specific GWA, a list of actions and a list of objects linked to the GWA become available. The GWA then serves as a cue, and the SME is instructed to consider all possible tasks or behaviors in which he or she engages that relate to that specific GWA. Then the SME is instructed to review the lists of actions and objects and select those that are reflective of their work. Moreover, because the lists of actions and objects are not meant to be exhaustive, the SMEs are provided a method of creating actions and objects that are job specific or utilize job-related terminology. Once the SME is satisfied with the lists of actions and objects, he or she advances to the next step.

The system then requires the SME to create action-object pairs. These two-word statements form the basic structure of a task statement. Each action may be paired with more than one object, and each object may be paired with multiple actions (e.g., evaluate work, evaluate subordinates, train subordinates). If the SME determines that actions or objects are missing, he or she can add the missing objects or actions. In addition, SMEs may choose to not use an action or object selected previously.

In most cases, the two-word statements are not descriptive enough to provide sufficient detail to fully understand the job. As a result, the system was designed to require further modification of the task statements. Detailed information is entered by the SME in the form of object and/or statement modifiers. Object modifiers provide more detail concerning the object of the task statement. Statement modifiers provide more detail concerning context, conditions, and purpose. For example, the modified task, "Write quarterly financial reports for managerial review," provides much more detail than simply "Write reports." SMEs are required by the system to provide at least one modifier per task and are told that at least 10 tasks are typically generated for each GWA. This information is based on prior experience and is provided to encourage SMEs to generate a sufficient number of tasks for each GWA to ensure coverage of the job. SMEs can move between these three steps (action and object selection, action and object pairing, elaboration) as often as they wish.

Once the SME determines he or she has generated all the tasks for the selected GWA, he or she is asked to select another GWA and repeat the process. The SME may also return to an already completed GWA and add additional tasks if necessary. SMEs may complete this inductively oriented task generation process in one session or may take breaks and complete the process over several days.

Tools, Unique Knowledge, and Resources

In addition to task information, other occupationally-specific information is collected from SMEs. Specifically, information about tools, equipment and machines, resources used, and occupationally specific knowledge are collected. Tools, equipment, and machines are physical objects used on the job that require training to be used. Unique knowledge is information that took time or training to learn. Resources are reference materials that are used to locate or house information. For example, IBM's *Statistical Package for the Social Sciences* (SPSS) is a tool used in conjunction with the unique knowledge of multiple regression, which may be supplemented by the statistical software manual as a resource.

After SMEs complete the task generation phase, they are asked to review lists of existing (legacy) tools and equipment, knowledge, and resources. These lists, similar to legacy task information, are available based upon previous job analyses for the current position, job analyses performed on similar occupations, or other sources available, and are designed to be a starting point in the generation of a comprehensive list of tools, knowledge, and resources. SMEs then can add to the list any tools, knowledge, or resources not listed and also modify the legacy items selected.

Work Element Editing

The result of the task generation process is the creation of multiple tasks generated by multiple SMEs. These tasks lists are combined in the software system with the SME-selected legacy tasks to form a single task list. This combined task list typically includes 300–1000 tasks depending on the number of participating SMEs and the complexity of the job. At this point, the task list contains duplications (either tasks that are identical or similar) or unnecessary information within individual task statements. Additionally, not all task statements generated by the SMEs are well written. The primary focus of the editing process is to fine-tune these task statements by eliminating redundancies, clarifying vague task statements, and eliminating unnecessary information. In addition, during the editing process, the job analyst can provide some uniformity to the content and structure of the task statements (e.g., using either "teach" or "instruct" but not both within the task list). The editing is done by a trained skills analyst familiar with the system as well as job analytic processes and an SME who answers questions.

The consolidation of information from multiple SMEs is conducted by scanning the list to identify similar task statements. This can become a time-consuming process. To ease this burden and to take advantage of a computerized platform, action and key word filters were built into the system to facilitate the editing process. The analyst simply navigates to the filter screen and either selects actions from a list of all the action verbs used in the task list or enters words or phrases into the key word filter box. Once a filter is applied, only the items containing the filter criteria are visible, allowing for an easy review of similarities and redundancies. For complex data sets, the system allows for multiple filters.

Once a group of similar or redundant tasks is identified, one representative task statement from the group is chosen as the primary task statement. If none of the original task statements represents the group of tasks well enough, the analyst writes a new task statement. The original task statements are all then removed from the task list; however, they are subsumed under the representative (primary) task statement and can be reviewed at a later time. This process leaves all tasks generated by the SMEs completely untouched as a historical record of the origin of the edited task. If during the editing process the analyst decides that a task statement was combined with others in error or inappropriately, should be combined with other task statements, or should stand alone, it can be removed from the group of subsumed tasks and placed more appropriately. This process of identifying similar or redundant tasks is repeated until all tasks have been combined with other similar tasks or designated as standalone tasks. In addition, all task statements are reviewed for clarity, typographical and grammatical errors, and are corrected if necessary. During the process, if there are any questions or tasks requiring clarification, the analyst can contact the designated SME for input. Finally, the analyst reviews the final edited task list and assigns all of the final tasks to a GWA. The editing of the tool, unique knowledge, and resource lists follows the same pattern as editing the task list. This editing process for the tasks, tools, unique knowledge, and resources is the most time-consuming phase of the job analysis but can be performed easily over the course of 1 week. The alacrity of the editing process compared to other methods is due in part to the computer system automatically removing redundant tasks selected from the legacy list by multiple SMEs, the use of the filters described above, specialized training provided by SkillsNET, and the common task structure utilized within the system. If the need to complete the job analysis quickly is critical, this editing process can usually be completed in 1–2 days depending on the exact number of tasks, tools, unique knowledge, and resources generated and with the assignment of larger jobs to more experienced personnel.

As an additional check and balance, a skills compliance officer (SCO) reviews the work performed by the analyst in the editing process to provide guidance, feedback, and to modify the edited work if necessary. The SCO is responsible for ensuring all job analysis work follows designated procedures and that the data quality is consistent with internally published quality control guidelines.

Work Element Review and Work Element Finalization

Once the task list has been edited and reduced to an appropriate number of clearly written task statements by the analyst, it is electronically presented to job stakeholders for review. Three to five supervisors are typically chosen for this role. However, any person that is knowledgeable about the job can be used as a reviewer if desired. Each reviewer works independently using the web-based process. The tasks are presented by listing each GWA, and then all the tasks assigned to it. In this way, all the tasks that relate to a similar job activity are grouped together, and redundancies and missing tasks are easier to identify than if the entire list of tasks were presented alphabetically. The reviewers are asked to review tasks for clarity and completeness and recommend any changes that are necessary. The reviewers can rewrite or modify a task, assign it to a different GWA, recommend it for deletion, and add new tasks that were not included in the task list. The reviewer can also add comments and explanations for clarification of his or her recommendations.

Once all of the reviewers have completed their review, the work element finalization process begins. The reviewers' recommendations and comments are presented to a trained skills analyst through the system for evaluation and final disposition. The analyst can incorporate the recommendation verbatim, incorporate it with wording revisions, or reject the recommendation because it would cause redundancy or violate quality guidelines. The analyst integrates the recommendations provided from the reviewers and chooses how to proceed. If further clarification is needed, the analyst can contact one or more reviewers for input and guidance.

The review and finalization of the tool, unique knowledge, and resource lists follows the same pattern as that used for the task list. As in the editing process, an SCO reviews the work performed by the analyst in the work element finalization stage to provide guidance, feedback, and to modify the finalizing work if necessary. Both the work element review and work element finalization processes usually take no more than a few hours.

Skill and Ability Linkages

The O*NET content model provides a comprehensive list of enabling skills and abilities that are applicable across all jobs in our economy (Fleishman, Costanza, & Marshall-Mies, 1999; Mumford, Peterson, & Childs, 1999). The ability section of O*NET is based on the prior extensive multiyear taxonomic research programs of Fleishman and his associates, which empirically identified and defined the abilities common to work tasks within the cognitive, psychomotor, physical, and sensory-perceptual domains of human performance (see, e.g., Fleishman, 1972a, 1975, 1982; Fleishman & Quaintance, 1984; Fleishman & Reilly, 1992). Abilities are general traits of individuals that have been identified from empirical relationships found among actual performances (see, e.g., Fleishman, 1964, 1972a, 1972b, 2003a, 2003b; Meyers, Gebhardt, Crump, & Fleishman, 1993). Skills are more dependent on learning and represent the product of training in particular tasks. Thus, skills tend to improve with practice, but the development of particular skills is dependent on the individual's possession of relevant underlying abilities (Fleishman & Mumford, 1989, 1991). The skills section of O*NET is based on the prior extensive research by Mumford and Peterson (1999). In identifying the skills taxonomy for O*NET, they differentiated skills differently than others had done before. The skills are divided into two main groups: basic and cross-functional skills. The basic skills are further subdivided into content skills, which are used for acquiring and conveying information, and process skills, which deal with knowledge acquisition and performance. The cross-functional skills are subdivided into five groupings: complex problem-solving skills, social skills, technical skills, systems skills, and resource management skills (Mumford et al., 1999).

To determine which skills and abilities are necessary for job performance, each task is linked to one primary skill and ability and one secondary skill and ability. A primary skill or ability is one that is critical and necessary to enable the successful performance of the task. A secondary skill or ability is one that is also necessary to enable successful performance of the task but may not be as important or critical as the primary skill or ability. Recent work on competencies has suggested that more accurate ability requirement descriptions are obtained when task level information is used (Lievens, Sanchez, & DeCorte, 2004). By linking at the task level, more accurate judgments about the importance of specific skills and abilities can be made. In addition, because each task is linked to skills and abilities independently, it is possible that a broader range of skills and abilities are selected than when the job as a whole is considered (Fleishman & Mumford, 1988).

Trained skills analysts complete the linkage of tasks to skills and abilities. The analyst is typically the same person who edited the task list and is therefore familiar with the job. The analyst reviews each task statement and a determination is made as to which skills and/or abilities the task should be linked. When linking the skills or abilities, the analyst makes use of two primary questions, "Can this task be performed without this skill/ability?" and "Is this skill/ability critical to performing the task?"

Previous research using the O*NET taxonomies suggested that analysts provide reliable and valid ratings for skills and abilities (Fleishman et al., 1999; Mumford et al., 1999). Additionally, Baranowski and Anderson (2005) found that a large number of incumbents or analysts is not required to obtain linkage reliability and that reliable linkages can be obtained regardless of whether the rater is an incumbent or an analyst. Moreover, although a perception may exist that a greater variety of skills and abilities are typically required to enable complex tasks, research has indicated that the mean number of skills linked to even high complexity tasks was 2.26 (James et al., 2007).

In the SkillsNET system, a skills analyst links the skills and abilities to tasks in an online tool. The analyst begins by reviewing the task list, selecting one or more tasks, and then selects a primary enabling skill for the task(s) from a list of O*NET skills. The definition for each skill is shown to assist the analyst in making appropriate linkages. Once a task has the primary skill assigned, a secondary skill may be assigned if appropriate. This process continues until each task has at least a primary skill linked to it. To assist the analyst, the online tool also provides reports showing the list of skills and all tasks grouped according to the skill to which they are linked. This report is a "reverse" view from when the linkages were originally created. Reviewing all the linkages in this fashion helps the analyst to determine if any of the linkages created require modification. The process for linking abilities to tasks is separate but identical to the process used to link skills to tasks. The time frame for enabling skill and ability linkages is one half to one day for each set of linkages. As an accuracy and reliability check, the SkillsNET methodology calls for an SCO or senior skills analyst to review the linkages created by the skills analyst.

Surveys

The final step in the job analysis process is to obtain data from a wide sample of the worker population using surveys. Surveys are conducted online using a survey tool with predetermined rating scales (e.g., frequency, criticality, time spent, difficulty to learn, or other scales based on how the job analysis data will be used) for tasks as well as those appropriate for skills, abilities, tools, resources, and knowledge. Additional scales may be added or specific scales may be modified if necessary based on the intended use of the data. The appropriate information (i.e., tasks, tools, skills) is automatically populated from the job analysis database to the survey tool. Invitations to participate in the survey are automatically generated and sent via e-mail with tailored information about the purpose of the survey as well as URL and login information. When an individual begins the survey process, they complete a series of demographic questions with answers used in statistical analysis of the data. Once an individual completes a survey, the data are automatically stored and are ready for statistical analysis.

All incumbent responses are stored in raw form for future use. Additionally, descriptive statistics are calculated by the computer system for each rating scale for each element. It is common to review the descriptive statistics for each element with the client organization to determine if any data require revision or does not meet an organizationally set threshold for inclusion in the data set.

SKILLOBJECT DEVELOPMENT

Occupationally Specific Skills

Traditional applications of job analysis produce data at varying levels of generality. Work-oriented methods usually rely upon tasks as the primary unit of analysis with jobs containing anywhere from 100 to 200 tasks. These types of analyses are especially appropriate with low- to mid-level jobs as well as with specific human resources applications requiring detailed aspects of the job (e.g., technical training). As such, tasks are typically considered the most specific level of meaningful job behavior. However, technological advances, an increasingly global workforce, and rapid work and workforce changes limit the value of traditional job analyses that focus only on static tasks and work behaviors (Sanchez, 1994). Tasks themselves run the risk of losing viability as technology and work evolve.

Worker-oriented methods, on the other hand, oftentimes find jobs comprising just a handful of broadly defined skills and/or abilities that are very useful in making comparisons across jobs, organizations, and even industries. In this respect, skills and abilities provide a more dynamic and flexible approach to job analysis with job requirements that are more stable and more easily transferable (Mumford et al., 1999).

Previous efforts to study and describe skills in the workplace have resulted in somewhat inconsistent levels of granularity. At one end of the continuum, SME meetings similar to those associated with task generation sessions are frequently used; these meetings often lead to information that tends to be extremely specific and narrow (e.g., ability to read and interpret job orders; skill to plan, organize, and schedule the activities of staff). At the same time, much of the research on worker requirements such as skills has been born from a focus on understanding broad and general worker characteristics required for job success (Brannick & Levine, 2002). In these instances, skill titles have ranged from critical thinking, team building, and problem solving to wide categories such as technical or interpersonal skills. O*NET defines skills as "procedures for acquiring and working with information" (Mumford et al., 1999, p. 50), and while the O*NET skill taxonomy incorporates constructs that fall between the two extremes noted previously, Mumford et al. suggest that these skills were intended to be both broad and general and provide commonality across all jobs to some extent.

It has been suggested that occupationally specific skills are ultimately dependent on incumbent experience and practice and should be defined in terms of the performance domains in which they are utilized (Reiter-Palmon et al., 2006). This thought process bolsters the suggestions by Peterson et al. (2001) that occupationally specific information is necessary for understanding jobs. The occupationally specific skills are broader and more general than the O*NET skills and involve the application to a specific performance domain (Mumford et al., 1999). For example, *Installation* is a commonly utilized enabling O*NET skill for technical occupations. However, there is a significant difference in the specific work activities (and thus how workers are selected, trained, and appraised) associated with *Computer Component Installation* and *Automotive Transmission Installation*. Occupationally specific skills provide an interpretable level of context unavailable with broad skill characterizations and obscured in narrow skill constructs. Occupationally specific skills were not designed to cut across all jobs or occupations without revision, but can be a demonstration of commonality within job families or jobs including similar occupationally specific skills.

Considering the results of previous job analytic efforts, SkillsNET determined that a different unit of analysis was needed for the rapidly changing human capital world. As a result, SkillsNET developed an occupationally specific skill architecture anchored in the broader, more

Figure 28.2   SkillObject components.

general, and theoretical O*NET content model with the occupationally-specific skills referred to as SkillObjects.

SkillObjects (see Figure 28.2) are measurable, detailed descriptions of occupational skills that people perform in accomplishing work. A SkillObject consists of logically clustered tasks that are performed, trained, or evaluated together along with the knowledge, skills, abilities, tools, and resources required for the successful performance of the task cluster. Defining SkillObjects in this manner draws from the best features of work- and worker-oriented approaches to job analysis. By clustering together job tasks that are *performed*, *trained*, or *evaluated together* with the tools and resources required to support those tasks, SkillObjects define the scope of work for the job. By grouping the unique knowledge, skills, abilities, and performance standards required to successfully perform those job tasks, SkillObjects cover the worker attributes required for successful job performance. Taken together, SkillObjects define the worker's required occupational skills for successful job performance as well as how those skills are applied in various job tasks (Reiter-Palmon et al., 2006). The SkillObject system ensures that information obtained through job analysis is viewed from a performance context as well as in context of other job elements. Thus, the SkillObject provides organizations with significant insight into jobs and what the jobs entail.

SkillObject Generation and Editing

Mumford et al. (1999) and Peterson et al. (2001) outlined a procedure for the development of occupationally specific skills. SkillsNET's web-based job analysis system generally follows this procedure in the SkillObject Generation process. The development of SkillObjects starts with the system presenting the tasks in groups that are formed using work dimensions such as GWAs or skills for initial presentation to the SMEs over the Internet. This initial grouping assists the SMEs in more easily recognizing tasks that should be grouped into the SkillObjects than if all of the job tasks are presented simultaneously. SMEs then review the tasks within the initial groupings and determine if any of the tasks within the group are related to one another. SMEs are encouraged to think about those tasks that are performed together, are trained together, or are evaluated in a similar fashion. Once several tasks have been identified and grouped into SkillObjects, SMEs provide a meaningful title for the group. Generating the title is an additional way to ensure that the tasks are grouped in a meaningful way, as experience shows that it is difficult to create a concise title if the tasks are not related or only loosely related to one another. The SkillObject titles can describe technical work or administrative work and are meaningful to people working in the job (e.g., database management, information reporting). Because the SkillObjects are occupationally specific skills versus job tasks or behaviors, the SkillObject names are formatted in a style more like that of a function than that of a task statement. Subsequently, the SkillObject titles do not begin with a verb, but rather with an object. Although the task to GWA linkages are used for the initial presentation of the tasks for SkillObject generation, the primary focus of additional analyses targets the grouping of tasks to SkillObjects. However, the GWA linkages to the tasks are maintained in the database for future analyses such as comparing GWAs across jobs, or using task survey results to calculate empirical GWA criticality values.

To further develop occupationally-specific skills, SMEs are asked to link each SkillObject to (a) the specific tools and equipment used when performing the group of tasks, (b) the unique knowledge required for performance of the group of tasks, and (c) the resources needed to complete the group of tasks. This additional information provides the context in which the tasks are performed and delineates further how the SkillObjects are applied in a specific performance domain. Moreover, each SkillObject carries with it the enabling O*NET skills and abilities associated with the tasks contained within each SkillObject. The result is a titled group of tasks that are similar, learned or performed or evaluated together, use similar skills, abilities, tools, knowledge, and resources, and which together describe the specific occupational skill requirements of a specific part of a job.

Once the SMEs have created the SkillObjects, a trained skills analyst reviews them to clarify occupationally specific skill titles and modifies the linked data as appropriate to remove redundant tool, knowledge, or resource linkages. As with previous phases, the SCO is responsible for ensuring all job analysis work follows the designated procedures and that the data quality is consistent with internally published guidelines. From experience, most jobs have 15–20 SkillObjects.

Because SMEs name the SkillObjects, they are named in ways meaningful to persons familiar with the job, following rules for properly organized names. Therefore, the content of two SkillObjects in different jobs can vary while having the same name. However, each SkillObject has a unique identification code in the database. The fact that different SkillObjects can consist of the same or similar elements also allows for SkillObjects to be compared across jobs. Figure 28.3 provides an example of an occupationally specific skill (SkillObject) including all of its elements. What are not shown in this example are the descriptive statistics for each surveyed element and the critical work functions (CWFs) to which the SkillObject is linked (e.g., mean and standard deviation for each rating scale surveyed, mean levels required for the enabling skills and abilities). Additionally,

---

SkillObject: Safety Administration

Task(s):
    Check Material Safety Data Sheet (MSDS) for chemical use and personal protective gear
    Climb structures such as scaffolds or small buildings safely
    Establish boundaries during radiographic operations
    Forecast problems to prevent injuries or rework
    Inspect facilities so that they are safe for workers
    Inspect manlifts and forklifts daily using a checklist to determine if in safe and working condition
    Provide job safety analysis
    Secure site with ropes and warning signs
    Set up environmental protection devices
    Set up safety lights
    Verify compliance with environmental protection procedures
    Verify regulations to make sure they are followed

Tool(s):	Knowledge(s):	O*NET Skills:
Come-along	Basic electricity	Reading Comprehension
Computer	Inspection procedures	Judgment and Decision
Crane	Layout and assembly	Making
Environmental protection devices	Non-Destructive Testing	Foresee Downstream
Forklift	(NDT) techniques	Consequences
Hand tools	Rigging techniques	Problem Identification
Hoist	Safety rules and procedures	Product Inspection
Hydraulic jacks	Ship repair techniques	Judgment and Decision
Jacks	Structural fabrication	Making
Joggle machines	techniques	Installation
Laser	Tying knots and lines	Monitoring
Manlift	Welding techniques	
Metalworking machinery shear		O*NET Abilities:
steel	Resource(s):	Written Comprehension
Personal Protective Equipment	Material Safety Data Sheets	Gross Body Coordination
(PPE)	(MSDS)	Deductive Reasoning
Scaffold	Safety manual & instructions	Inductive Reasoning
Test equipment	Technical manuals	Near Vision
	Training manuals	Problem Sensitivity
		Manual Dexterity

Figure 28.3 SkillObject example.

in the methodology described and utilized for this job analysis system, enabling skills and abilities are linked to each task. In the example provided, to save space, a nonduplicative list of skills and abilities linked to all the tasks of the SkillObject is provided. In reality, each task in the SkillObject would have one or more enabling skills and one or more enabling abilities linked in a subordinate fashion to each SkillObject task. Finally, the GWA to which each task is linked in a subordinate manner is not shown to save space.

Critical Work Function Generation and Critical Work Function–SkillObject Linkage

To provide greater understanding of work and to provide another cross-occupation manner of examining data, each SkillObject is linked to one or more CWFs. A CWF describes the major responsibilities that an individual must fulfill to achieve the work required for the job/role (Brown, Sandall, Osburn, Manning, & Dera, 2007). In the web-based job analysis system, one or more managers work to define the broadest and most essential ongoing responsibilities of the job. The managers are provided guidance on characteristics of quality CWFs and the typical number of CWFs per job, which for most jobs is three to six. Once the CWFs for the job are defined, the manager links each SkillObject in a subordinate fashion to one or more CWFs it helps to support. Because CWFs are typically orthogonal, it is rare to have overlap between CWFs. However, the work descriptors (SkillObjects) may be linked to more than one CWF as the work may support multiple functions of the job. Examples of CWFs include "Communicate company needs and perspectives to clients and contractors" and "Monitor and maintain equipment, tools, and workstations."

Updating Work Analytic Data

The SkillsNET system allows for relatively easy and efficient data collection and updates. Rather than completing a new job analysis whenever tasks change, organizations make simple modifications to one or more SkillObject elements. This efficiency and rapidity in updating the data is partially because all of the SkillObject data elements and relationships between the elements reside in a relational database that undergirds the web-based job analysis system. The data can then be modified through special interfaces for that purpose or can be loaded into the system as the starting data for an entirely new job analysis process. Additionally, the data can be loaded from the database directly to the work element review phase, skipping the work element generation and editing phases, if a complete processing of the work elements is not necessary and a simple review is all that is needed. Finally, data can be loaded from the database to the survey engine to resurvey data to determine changes in empirical ratings since the last survey. In any case, the process of updating the job analysis data is overseen by a skills analyst and follows a process of generation and review similar to that already described. However, because the data are being updated versus created initially, the process is much faster.

When determining what data should be reviewed and updated, the client's uses of the data and other factors such as the rapidity of job change are considered. If legal defensibility is required of the job analysis data, any data that are modified or added should be surveyed. Surveys may be warranted periodically to ensure that element statistics have not significantly changed since the last survey.

BENEFITS AND CONCERNS ASSOCIATED WITH THE SKILLSNET SYSTEM

Benefits

The SkillsNET web-based job analysis system uses the O*NET content model as a foundation, and therefore is based on solid, long established research on job and occupational analysis (Campion,

Morgeson, & Mayfield, 1999). Moreover, the system incorporates the strengths of numerous job analysis methodologies with specific scientific and technological advances to produce a fully integrated and comprehensive job data collection and classification system. The system itself relies upon a number of embedded attributes to ensure rigor, comprehensive data collection, legal defensibility, and validity (Table 28.3).

Table 28.3 SkillsNET Methodology Attributes

Attribute	Description
Data levels	The SkillsNET system captures tasks performed in the job, the skills and abilities that enable task performance, the tools, software, equipment, and devices that people use to perform work, the specific knowledge, processes, procedures, and guidelines that people need to know to perform the job, and the resources people refer to get information needed to do the job. Work elements are grouped into occupationally-specific skills and linked to higher-level Critical Work Functions (CWFs). The resulting data are both job-specific as well as portable and comparable across jobs, occupations, and industries.
Web-based	Participants can log into the system anywhere in the world at any time when an Internet connection is available, greatly enhancing the opportunities for data collection across diverse geographic locations and easing the cost and burden of scheduling face to face meetings with multiple participants in one location.
Inductive/deductive	While inductive methods are utilized when new task-oriented information is collected for each target job, the system also relies heavily on deductive methods (by using O*NET taxonomies and other standardized taxonomies).
System facilitation	The SkillsNET system resolved the challenge of how to elicit job related information with minimal intervention and guidance by breaking down job analytic steps into easy to follow processes and through specific text instruction. However, SkillsNET also incorporated cueing mechanisms and a task generation module that allows incumbents to build tasks directly to GWAs and presents lists of actions and objects that are commonly associated with each selected GWA as an initial step in task generation.
Legacy data	The system utilizes legacy data from previous job analyses, company documents, and a national job database as a starting point providing a quick start to the job analysis process and helping to ensure coverage through reuse and modification of data.
Format and structure	Within the SkillsNET system, work elements are required to adhere to specific structure rules to ensure consistent, quality data. For example, task statements all have an action verb and an object and include either an object modifier or statement modifier (or both) that adds context and further details about the task. By forcing tasks to follow stringent quality guidelines, even new tasks created by subject matter experts (SMEs) are consistently better than those created by the SMEs without the structure. Strict work element structure also benefits the input of job data into a database structure for easy use and retrieval.
Taxonomic reference	For nontask data such as skills, abilities, tools, knowledge, and resources, the new job analysis system incorporates an extensive use of taxonomies. By using taxonomies to group data elements, complete coverage of job data is enhanced, additional descriptors can more easily be associated with specific jobs and occupations, and comparisons across jobs is simplified.
Checks and balances	SkillsNET's system relies upon multiple personnel to ensure the valid flow of data. In the primary data collection phase, multiple SMEs working independently are utilized to ensure coverage of all aspects of the job. However, because of multiple SMEs, redundancy is often created in the data describing the job so trained skills analyst edit the data to remove redundancies and to clarify wording. The edited lists of data elements are then reviewed independently by multiple supervisory level personnel for the job being analyzed. The supervisory recommendations are then reviewed and incorporated by a skills analyst.

Knowledge elicitation and cognition principles provide a basis for the overarching framework and architecture (Cooke, 1994; Hoffman et al., 1995; Nisbett & Ross, 1980; Sauer et al., 2000), resulting in a structured, cued-recall methodology that allows for simple computer implementation with little need for external guidance or facilitation. The focus on the work, worker, and workplace descriptors combined with inductive and deductive data collection strategies and the use of standardized taxonomies also results in a common-language framework for describing work. All jobs and occupations generate specific, unique work element data but also use standardized taxonomies to describe various types of work data. As a result, the taxonomic information can be directly compared within and across organizations in an "apples-to-apples" manner.

Because of the variable nature of the types of comparisons desired, the comparisons are performed either through queries written to draw data from the database that holds the job analysis data, or the comparisons are performed in another tool such as Microsoft Excel, Microsoft Access, or IBM SPSS. Moreover, studies have revealed that the structured methodology resulted in more comprehensive tasks lists than traditional methodologies (Garcia, Gasch, & Wertheim, 2002; Sager, Mumford, Baughman, & Childs, 1999) with most tasks created by a single group of SMEs in less than 1 day.

This system also addresses some of the concerns presented by Morgeson and Campion (1997) regarding the social and cognitive sources of inaccuracy in job analysis. Social pressures such as conformity, impression management, and extremity shifts are often eliminated because SMEs generate work element data individually instead of within group settings. Similarly, cognitive sources of inaccuracy such as information overload and the use of heuristics should be greatly limited because of the structured nature of the recall and by forcing more controlled processing (Morgeson & Campion, 1997).

Of particular interest to most organizations are the flexibility and cost savings resulting from a distributive methodology that are not available in traditional forms of job analysis. Job incumbents from anywhere worldwide regardless of time or location can participate without incurring the travel costs associated with proctored sessions. In one effort, SMEs working on five continents participated with no travel being required and without any consideration for the time zone of the employees as the system is available 24 hours a day (Sandall, Reiter-Palmon, & Brown, 2000). The distributed system even allowed access to U.S. Navy personnel located in combat zones around the world. However, not only do organizations save direct travel costs, they also receive savings through reductions in indirect lost production opportunities because employees do not need to be away from their jobs for meetings or interviews. Further, because SMEs are able to participate in this process without leaving their job for an extended period of time, supervisors are more likely to nominate high performing SMEs. Finally, SMEs also can complete work at their own pace, which allows them to complete the job analytic work around normal job demands.

Because this system is web-based, there are many benefits that help to speed up the process of collecting and validating the job analytic data. First, because the system is web-based, data are collected, stored, manipulated, and presented to users very efficiently and quickly. Second, because of the cueing mechanisms implemented, SMEs spend less time thinking about information to provide. Third, the use of legacy data not only gives the SMEs a quick and easy starting point, but it also speeds the process because of the efficient inclusion of data from other sources in the job analysis process. Fourth, the standardized elements such as skills, abilities, GWAs, and so forth help to speed the process through the use of bounded taxonomies. Because of these and other efficiencies, clients are typically advised to allow 6–8 weeks for a complete job analysis, including validation surveys. The process is actually easily completed in less than 2 weeks, but most clients are not able to move quickly enough to complete the job analysis in that short of a time frame (e.g., they cannot identify and provide the needed SMEs in a timely enough manner to maintain the aggressive schedule). In one extreme situation with a highly motivated client organization, the entire job analysis, including validation surveys, was completed in 4 days.

One of the criticisms of traditional job analysis methodologies has been the difficulty in updating information. Because data collection in a traditional job analysis is typically so time consuming, it is possible that the data may be inaccurate by the time analysis is complete, especially for technology jobs or other rapidly changing jobs. Through the use of the web-based interface, the data can be revised and revalidated quickly ensuring its accuracy and timeliness. This process can entail simply resurveying the data, a supervisory review of the data, or new data generation to augment the data that currently exist.

The SkillsNET method can also be completely distributive, proctored, or a blend of the two approaches. Although typically more expensive than the distributed method, some of the travel-related cost of the proctored session can be mitigated by the fact that individuals from multiple occupations can generate tasks simultaneously in one session, with each SME working independently on a web-connected computer. The system itself still facilitates the effort with enforced work element structure, step-by-step instructions, and queuing mechanisms. Moreover, one analyst can monitor and help a large group of individuals from multiple occupations because the work for each SME is completed individually. In one situation, over 70 individuals from 20 different jobs completed the work element generation process using proctored sessions spanning a 3-day period.

It is important to note that the system provides for a transparent recording of the transaction history. The number of SMEs and incumbents who participate in each phase of the job analysis effort and basic demographic data for each is stored in the database along with the specific data generated, modified, or entered by each individual. These data can be used to generate reports for legal defensibility purposes showing the number and types of persons who were involved in the job analysis process, and the inputs each person contributed. As an example, the history of a specific task statement can be generated from these data to show edits made to the task in the review and finalization phases, which tasks were combined during the editing phase, and the source of the tasks that were combined.

The validity, reliability, and legal defensibility of the web-based job analysis data are established through the system's technology, structure, and checks and balances. The inclusion of job incumbents and managers throughout the job analysis process provides support for content validity. The process of work element generation, editing, and consolidation of the multiple task, tool, knowledge, and resource lists, and the subsequent work element review allows for input from multiple parties at multiple points of the job analysis process. Further, by reviewing the list of tools, resources, and unique knowledge at different stages with different personnel, it is more likely to identify possible gaps in task generation. Finally, the job analysis data are surveyed within the worker population to provide normative data and quantitative validation of the job analysis results through statistical analysis of the survey results as well as quantitative review of the empirical data for the work elements to determine usability of the work elements based on intended uses of the data.

Limitations of the SkillsNET System

No system works without limitations. It is not uncommon to have SMEs start the distributed process and not complete it by the deadline. In addition, it is sometimes challenging to get some SMEs to participate. Significant communication efforts must be maintained with the SMEs or organizational point of contact to ensure timely completion. Another potential issue, more prevalent with the fully distributed model compared to the proctored session model, is that the quality of the task statements generated can be quite diverse, with some task statements being vague or unclear. One solution for these problems is to enlist additional SMEs to ensure a large enough quantity of quality task statements after vague or poorly written tasks are taken into account. In addition to this strategy, providing help, either through e-mail or phone, significantly increases completion rates, as SMEs are able to get help with barriers that may have prevented them from completing their work. Another support mechanism that has been implemented is to remotely monitor the task statements being generated in real time. Feedback about the quality of task statements can then be provided to the SME immediately.

Although the use of the Internet for the job analysis framework is a strength, it can also be a limitation. In some situations, access to the web may not be available or reliable, requiring a consideration of alternatives. In the past, there have been occasions where the use of spreadsheets and paper/pencil versions were required. In the end, these sessions looked very much like traditional face-to-face facilitations used with most traditional methodologies but with the enhanced structure, architecture, and linkages embedded within the SkillsNET system. The lack of computer and Internet access may also be an issue for jobs where computer use is not required. When a job does not require computer use, the importance of assistance or facilitation, whether by proctoring or phone, increases.

FUTURE DIRECTIONS

The system described in this chapter provides promising evidence for the validity and utility of a web-based job analysis system that can generate both task and KSAO information in a cost and time effective manner. In addition, the system can provide both broad and general descriptors of work (GWAs, skills, and abilities) as well more occupationally-specific information (tasks, tools, knowledge, and resources). This system also provides a solution to some of the criticisms of traditional job analysis methodologies with regard to their flexibility, efficiency, cost effectiveness, and responsiveness to business needs (Sanchez, 1994, 2000). Moreover, this system may address some social and cognitive sources of inaccuracy of job analysis data generation (Morgeson & Campion, 1997). Of course, this system does not eliminate all sources of bias, particularly those related to other phases of the analysis such as judgment.

Preliminary results indicate that the task generation portion of the web-based system provides results equal or superior to traditional job analysis methodologies; however, more information is needed (James et al., 2008). Specifically, research should address the question of how many SMEs are required to generate the task data such that the data would be equivalent to traditional methods, and to determine at what point the addition of more SMEs becomes counterproductive. Further, it is possible that the number of SMEs may depend on the type of administration of the work element generation process (distributed versus facilitated session) and the type of job and job requirements.

In addition, research should address the question of the quality of the data generated using this methodology. Comparisons should be made not only to traditional job analysis methodologies, but also comparing distributed versus proctored models. For example, what is the rate of completion of the work element generation process in a distributed methodology, with or without phone or e-mail support compared with proctored group sessions? Are completion rates higher when support is provided in a distributed session compared to self-guided? Is the feedback provided by a skills analyst monitoring data generation remotely in real time via a web interface and providing feedback to SMEs via e-mail, telephone, or their computer screen as effective as feedback from a skills analyst in a proctored session?

ONGOING RESEARCH

As described previously, the content of two SkillObjects in different jobs can have different content and database identifiers, while having the same name. Work is currently being performed to create a standardized list of SkillObject names and definitions. The goal is to create a list of SkillObject names and a brief summary of the overall purpose and content of the SkillObject in a job. However, even though the SkillObject names would be standardized, the SkillObjects would still have varying content (tasks, tools, unique knowledge, resources, and skills and abilities) as relevant to the job. This standardization should maintain data fidelity and job specificity while also increasing standardization and comparability of SkillObjects across jobs.

Research is also ongoing by SkillsNET and the Texas Workforce Commission to update and validate the O*NET Detailed Work Activity (DWA) library, as well as to update and validate the DWA to Standard Occupation Classification (SOC) linkages. The DWAs are much more specific than the O*NET Generalized Work Activities, but less specific than job tasks. They are intended to be applicable to multiple occupations without modification or customization. While the format of the DWAs is very similar to the task structure in use in the SkillsNET system, the total number of unique DWAs across all SOC codes is expected to be less than 2,000 upon completion of the update and validation process. It is anticipated that the DWAs can be implemented into the SkillsNET system and will provide another level of job analytic data that can be used for comparisons across jobs and organizations. It is possible that for some intended uses, the DWAs could be substituted for job tasks in the SkillsNET system. Additionally, because there is a limited number of DWAs that relate to all jobs, the standardized nature of the DWAs could assist in developing standardizing SkillObjects.

Finally, research is currently ongoing into the use of network sensors to harvest content from job incumbents' e-mail, wikis, blogs, text messages, document preparation, and use of workforce-related applications. The content is analyzed using semantic web computational analysis to identity patterns and themes that can be utilized for job analysis data. Early findings suggest a significant amount of the work being performed in the job is contributed through informal processes and is often missed with traditional job analytic approaches. If the research is successful in determining how job analyses can be performed in whole or in part using network transactional data and Deep Packet Inspection (DPI) of content, it will further revolutionize the process of job analysis. This approach has significant potential implications to the future of job analysis.

REFERENCES

Ash, R. A., Levine, E. L, & Bennett, N. (1980). Exploratory comparative study of four job analysis methods. *Journal of Applied Psychology, 65*(5), 524–535.

Baranowski, L. E., & Anderson, L. E. (2005). Examining rating source variation in work behavior to KSA linkages. *Personnel Psychology, 58,* 1041–1054.

Brannick, M. T., & Levine, E. L. (2002). *Job analysis: Methods, research and applications for human resources management in the new millennium.* Thousand Oaks, CA: Sage Publications.

Brown, M., Sandall, D., Osburn, H., Manning R., & Dera, S. (2007). *Skills analyst certification trainers guide.* Waxahachie, TX: SkillsNET Corporation.

Campion, M. A., Morgeson, F. P., & Mayfield, M. S. (1999). O*NET's theoretical contributions to job analysis research. In N. G. Peterson, M. D. Mumford, W. C. Borman, P. R. Jeanneret, & E. A. Fleishman (Eds.), *An occupational information system for the 21st century: The development of O*NET* (pp. 297–304). Washington, DC: American Psychological Association.

Chapman, D. S., & Webster, J. (2003). The use of technologies in the recruiting, screening, and selection processes for job candidates. *International Journal of Selection & Assessment, 11,* 113–120.

Clifton, T. C., Connelly, M. S., Reiter-Palmon, R., Gilbert, J., & Mumford, M. D. (1991). *Development of selection methods for General Electric's lighting division sales representatives.* Cleveland, OH: General Electric Lighting Division.

Connelly, M. S., Reiter-Palmon, R., Clifton, T., & Mumford, M. D. (1991). *The C&I division regional manager position—summary of SME meetings.* Cleveland, OH: General Electric Lighting Division.

Cooke, N. J. (1994). Varieties of knowledge elicitation techniques. *International Journal of Human-Computer Studies, 41,* 801–849.

Cranny, C. J., & Doherty, M. E. (1988). Importance ratings in job analysis: A note on the misinterpretation of factor analysis. *Journal of Applied Psychology, 73,* 320–322.

Crespin, T. R., & Austin, J. T. (2002). Internet and the workplace—Computer technology application in industrial and organizational psychology. *Cyber Psychology & Behavior, 5,* 279–303.

Dye, D., & Silver, M. (1999) The origins of O*NET. In N. G. Peterson, M. D. Mumford, W. C. Borman, P. R. Jeanneret, & E. A. Fleishman (Eds.), *An occupational system for the 21st century: The development of O*NET* (pp. 9–19). Washington, DC: American Psychological Association.

Fleishman, E. A. (1964). *The structure and measurement of physical fitness.* Englewood Cliffs, NJ: Prentice Hall.

Fleishman, E. A. (1972a). On the relation between abilities, learning, and human performance. *American Psychologist, 27,* 1017–1032.

Fleishman, E. A. (1972b). Structure and measurement of psychomotor abilities. In R. N. Singer (Ed.), *The psychomotor domain: Movement behavior.* Philadelphia, PA: Lea and Febiger.

Fleishman, E. A. (1975). Toward a taxonomy of human performance. *American Psychologist, 30,* 1127–1149.

Fleishman, E. A. (1982). System for describing human tasks. *American Psychologist, 37,* 821–834.

Fleishman, E. A. (2003a). Cognitive/mental abilities in work and organizational settings. In R. Fernandez-Ballesteros (Ed.), *Encyclopedia of Psychological Assessments, Vol. 1.* London, UK: Sage Publications.

Fleishman, E. A. (2003b). Physical abilities in work settings. In R. Fernandez-Ballesteros (Ed.), *Encyclopedia of Psychological Assessments, Vol. 2.* London, UK: Sage Publications.

Fleishman, E. A., Costanza, D. P., & Marshall-Mies, J. (1999). Abilities. In N. G. Peterson, M. D. Mumford, W. C. Borman, P. R. Jeanneret, & E. A. Fleishman (Eds.), *An occupational information system for the 21st century: The development of O*NET* (pp. 175–195). Washington, DC: American Psychological Association.

Fleishman, E. A., & Mumford, M. D. (1988). The ability requirements scales. In S. Gael (Ed.), *The job analysis handbook for business, industry, and government* (pp. 917–935). New York, NY: John Wiley & Sons.

Fleishman, E. A., & Mumford, M. D. (1989). Individual attributes and training performance: Applications of abilities taxonomies in instructional systems design. In L. Goldstein (Ed.), *Frontiers of Industrial and Organizational Psychology* (pp. 183–255). San Francisco, CA: Jossey-Bass.

Fleishman, E. A., & Mumford, M. D. (1991). Evaluating classifications of job behaviour: A construct validation of the ability requirement scales. *Personnel Psychology, 44*(3), 523–575.

Fleishman, E. A., & Quaintance, M. (1984). *Taxonomies of human performance: The description of human tasks.* Potomac, MD: Management Research Institute.

Fleishman, E. A., & Reilly, M. E. (1992). *Handbook of human abilities: Definitions, measurements, and job task requirements.* Potomac, MD: Management Research Institute.

Friedman, L. (1990). Degree of redundancy between time, importance, and frequency task ratings. *Journal of Applied Psychology, 75,* 748–752.

Gael, S. J. (1990). Job analysis: A guide to assessing work activities. San Francisco, CA: Jossey-Bass.

Garcia, F. E., Gasch, J. L., & Wertheim, M. L. (2002). *Workforce assessment of information technology sailors.* Alexandria, VA: Center for Naval Assessment.

Glass, A. L., & Holyoak, K. J. (1986). *Cognition* (2nd ed.). New York: Random House.

Hoffman, R. R., Shadbolt, N. R., Burton, M. A., & Klein, G. (1995). Eliciting knowledge from experts: A methodological analysis. *Organizational Behavior & Human Decision Processes, 62,* 129–158.

Hudson, R. L., & Austin, J. B. (1970). Effect of context and category name on the recall of categorized word lists. *Journal of Experimental Psychology, 86,* 43–47.

James, J., Ashley, G., Gins, A., Hornberg, J., Yurkovich, J., & Reiter-Palmon, R. (2007). *Analysis of skill and ability linkage inter-rater reliability, Part 2.* Waxahachie, TX: SkillsNET Corporation.

James, J., Reiter-Palmon, R., Yurkovich, J., Gins, A., Ashley, G., & Hornberg, J. (2008, April). *Comparing two job analysis approaches: Web-based vs. focus groups.* Paper presented at the Society for Industrial/Organizational Psychology Meeting, San Francisco, CA.

Jeanneret, P. R., Borman, W. C., Kubisiak, U. C., & Hanson, M. (1999). Generalized work activities. In N. G. Peterson, M. D. Mumford, W. C. Borman, P. R. Jeanneret, & E. A. Fleishman (Eds.), *An occupational information system for the 21st century: The development of O*NET* (pp. 105–125). Washington, DC: American Psychological Association.

Konradt, U. (2003). Web-based assessment of call center agents: Development and validation of a computerized instrument. *International Journal of Selection and Assessment, 11,* 184–193.

Koustall, W., Schacter, D. L., Johnson, M. K., & Gallucio, L. (1999). Facilitation and impairment of event memory produced by photograph review. *Memory and Cognition, 27,* 478–493.

Landy, F. J., & Conte, J. M. (2004). *Work in the 21st century an intro to industrial & organizational psychology*. Columbus, OH: McGraw-Hill Higher Education.

Lievens, F., Sanchez, J. I., & De Corte, W. (2004). Easing the inferential leap in competency modeling: The effects of task-related information and subject matter expertise. *Personnel Psychology, 57,* 881–904.

Meyers, D. C., Gebhardt, D. L., Crump, C. E., & Fleishman, E. A. (1993). The dimensions of human physical performance: Factor analysis of strength, stamina, flexibility, and body composition measures. *Human Performance, 6*(1), 309–314.

Morgeson, F., & Campion, M. A. (1997). Social and cognitive sources of potential inaccuracy in job analysis. *Journal of Applied Psychology, 82,* 627–655.

Mumford, M. D., & Peterson, N. G. (1999). In N. G. Peterson, M. D. Mumford, W. C. Borman, P. R. Jeanneret, & E. A. Fleishman (Eds.), *An occupational information system for the 21st century: The Development of O*NET* (p. 21–30). Washington, DC: American Psychological Association.

Mumford, M. D., Peterson, N. G., & Childs, R. A. (1999). Basic and cross-functional skills. In N. G. Peterson, M. D. Mumford, W. C. Borman, P. R. Jeanneret, & E. A. Fleishman (Eds.), *An occupational information system for the 21st century: The development of O*NET* (pp. 46–69). Washington, DC: American Psychological Association.

Nisbett, R., & Ross, L. (1980). *Human inference: Strategies and shortcomings of social judgment*. Englewood Cliffs, NJ: Prentice Hall.

Peterson, N. G., Mumford, M. D., Borman, W. C., Jeanneret, P. R., Fleishman, E. A., Campion, M. A., … Dye, D. M. (2001). Understanding work using the occupational information network (O*NET): Implications for practice and research. *Personnel Psychology, 54,* 451–492.

Peterson, N. G. & Jeanneret, P. R. (1997). Job analysis: Overview and description of deductive methods. In D. L. Whetzel & G. R. Wheaton (Eds.), *Applied measurement methods in industrial psychology* (pp.13–50). Palo Alto, CA: Davies-Black Publishing.

Potosky, D., & Bobko, P. (2004). Selection testing via the internet: Practical considerations and exploratory empirical findings. *Personnel Psychology, 57,* 1003–1034.

Prien, E. (1994). *Job activities taxonomy*. Unpublished manuscript.

Reiter-Palmon, R., Brown, M., Sandall, D. L., Buboltz, C. & Nimps, T. (2006). Development of an O*NET web-based job analysis and its implementation in the U.S. Navy: Lessons learned. *Human Resources Management Review, 16,* 294–309.

Reiter-Palmon, R., Uhlman, C. E., Clifton, T. C., Connelly, M. S., & Mumford, M. D. (1990). *Describing sales position requirements: GE Lighting Division: SME meeting*. Cleveland, OH: General Electric Lighting Division.

Reiter-Palmon, R., Young, M., Strange, J., Manning, R., & James, J. (2006). Occupationally-specific skills: Using skills to define and understand jobs and their requirements. *Human Resources Management Review, 16,* 356–375.

Sager, C. E., Mumford, M. D., Baughman, W. A., & Childs, R. A. (1999). Occupation-specific descriptors: Approaches, procedure, and findings. In N. G. Peterson, M. D. Mumford, W. C. Borman, P. R. Jeanneret, & E. A. Fleishman (Eds.), *An occupational information system for the 21st century: The development of O*NET* (pp. 227–235). Washington, DC: American Psychological Association.

Sanchez, J. I. (1994). From documentation to innovation: Reshaping job analysis to meet emerging business needs. *Human Resource Management Review, 4,* 51–74.

Sanchez, J. I. (2000). Adapting job analysis to a fast paced and electronic business world.*International Journal of Selection and Assessment, 8,* 207–215.

Sandall, D. L., Reiter-Palmon, R., & Brown, M. (2000). *Cisco career certification task survey*. Waxahachie, TX: SkillsNET Corporation.

Sauer, J., Schramme, S., & Ruttinger, B. (2000). Knowledge acquisition in ecological product design: The effects of computer-mediated communication and elicitation method. *Behaviour & Information Technology, 19,* 315–327.

U.S. Department of Labor. (1993). *The new DOT: A database of occupational titles for the twenty-first century*. Washington, DC: U.S. Government Printing Office.

U.S. Department of Labor. (2010). *The Occupational Information Network*. Retrieved from http://www.onetcenter.org/overview.html

Visweswaran, C. (2003). Role of technology in shaping the future of staffing and assessment. *International Journal of Selection & Assessment, 11,* 107–112.

Wickens, D. D., Born, D. G., & Allen, C. K. (1963). Proactive inhibition and item similarity in short-term memory. *Journal of Verbal Learning and Verbal Behavior, 2,* 440–445.

Wood, G. (1967). Category names as cues for the recall of category instances. *Psychonomic Science, 9,* 323–324.

Part IV

WORK ANALYSIS RESEARCH AND INNOVATION

WINSTON BENNETT, JR.

United States Air Force Research Laboratory

SUZANNE TSACOUMIS

Human Resources Research Organization

Part IV covers a wide range of topics and advances in science and practice. The contributors represent an extensive and deep experience base that continues to advance the area of work design and job analytic related areas. Each chapter in Part IV is structured to accomplish several objectives: to review relevant literature, discuss the specific issue or topic through a review of the literature, provide a description of the approach undertaken, and finally to review their findings and results. The chapters also describe current limitations in the science and/or practice of relevance and identify key areas of additional research, further development, or activity needed to best apply and extend the results of the particular innovation or advance discussed.

Chapter 29 offers an evaluation of the evidence associated with determining the nature of the information that should be captured in a comprehensive job analysis study, as well as the best sources for collecting job analytic data. Robert J. Harvey and Mark A. Wilson compare job data that is collected by using broad, overall judgments (i.e., holistic judgment methods) with data collected by rating the specific elements of the job (i.e., decomposed judgment methods). They argue that it is too difficult to accurately rate job activity constructs; therefore, holistic ratings do not provide the same quality of information provided by decomposed judgments. In the second part of this chapter, the authors share the results of their research, which compares task ratings provided by incumbents with those provided by supervisors. Although researchers often believe that incumbents provide the most accurate information regarding job tasks, the results presented here highlight the importance of reviewing the resulting data with a critical eye and acknowledging that one cannot always assume that incumbents are the best source of task information.

In Chapter 30, Frederick P. Morgeson and Michael A. Campion highlight different factors that may lead to inaccurate job analysis data. The basic premise is that job analytic information is dependent on input from humans. Because human judgment is not perfect, it is reasonable to expect inaccuracy in the resulting data. These inaccuracies are categorized as either social or cognitive in nature, each of which is described in detail. It is important for practitioners and researchers to be aware of and monitor these likely sources of inaccuracies when collecting and interpreting job analysis data.

In Chapter 31, George M. Alliger and his colleagues describe the development of the Mission Essential Competency approach. It was developed as a way for the U.S. Air Force to improve the precision of specifications of work and training requirements. The approach has its heritage in industrial psychology job analysis and work design theory and practice from both behavioral and cognitive task analysis methods, and represents a creative and practical synthesis to define current and future needs. A variety of complex individual and team occupational areas and training systems have been impacted by this novel approach with data that annually influences over 20,000 job incumbents. Personnel in these areas include combat pilots, command and control decision makers, senior leadership, information operations, emergency first responders, disaster response watch command staffs, and intelligence, surveillance and reconnaissance analysts, and engineers. The chapter wraps up with a solid discussion of additional research needs and identifies a number of opportunities for expanding the approach to answer additional questions affecting military and civilian organizations and personnel.

In Chapter 32, Thomas R. Gordon and his colleagues demonstrate how cognitive task analysis can be integrated into a job model to yield a new classification system. By examining the job of Air Force Weapons Director (WD), this study discusses how cognitions and behaviors are linked in highly complex work environments. Relying on a meta-cognitive task analysis, the authors identified nine performance categories and then used verbal protocol analysis to capture the WDs' thoughts. This tool is designed to capture the cognitive processes associated with performing the job and shows how they link to job behaviors. The resulting information examines potential differences between experienced and inexperienced WDs. Although it is a very time-consuming tool, the results offer key insights into what the incumbents were thinking when performing the job. This study shows how verbal protocol analysis can be used to integrate cognitive task analysis into job models, which in turn yields information beyond the traditional task and knowledge, skills, abilities, and other data.

Winfred Arthur, Jr., and colleagues discuss some of their recent research on methods for team task analysis in Chapter 33. The chapter has an extensive review of the relevant literature and describes work on assessing team interdependence. One of the hallmarks of their work is their attempt to integrate team work flow and team relatedness metrics within existing work design methods being used in the Air Force. This is important as a mechanism for helping institutionalize innovations inside existing systems and processes. Lessons learned are also reviewed. The authors conclude with a discussion on implications of their work for research and practice with teams.

In Chapter 34, Charles E. Lance and his colleagues describe their work to develop a mechanism to examine and identify tasks and skills that have a high degree of transferability. The authors describe the dynamics of the military occupational environment that was a catalyst for the research and development of their taxonomy and method and they discuss the potential applications of their work to other aspects of military and civilian work. They argue that transferability of skills across jobs is an important aspect of work design that has not historically been looked at from an analytic perspective such as the one discussed. This lack of attention to transferability has created substantial duplication of work and training effort within and across jobs where transferability would save substantial personnel resources and reduce inefficiencies in the personnel and training system. The chapter makes several compelling arguments for changes in current work and training practice and it also identifies a number of opportunities for increasing both the efficiency and effectiveness of work and training systems and processes that are worthy of consideration and action.

Peter W. Foltz and colleagues describe some very interesting work to apply latent semantic analysis methods to work design and occupational analysis in Chapter 35. The chapter describes their approach to create definitions for new occupations and work based on highly accurate empirical clustering of common semantic indices across job content. The authors also describe needed data for the approach and for developing queries for data analyses. In addition, they underscore the importance of quality occupational content for analyses and for work design and decision making, a theme emphasized in several chapters in Part IV.

In Chapter 36, Rebecca Lyons and colleagues dive into the deep end of a discussion on work design and job analysis from a multinational perspective. As many local organizations become more global, it is important to ensure that methods for understanding people and people at work are appropriate for the task at hand. The authors examine current approaches and instruments used for multinational occupations and organizations and the need for researchers and practitioners to pay special attention to this as this will likely alter work design and analysis approaches that are undertaken in different multinational contexts.

In closing, we want to once again acknowledge the pioneering work accomplished by our contributors. We have had the pleasure of working with them in seeking the expansion of our understanding of work, how best to efficiently and effectively describe key aspects of the work, and how to integrate and institutionalize new approaches and methods within existing organizational processes and structures. We deeply appreciate their contributions to the advancement of our science and practice and their patience and commitment to this handbook. We further hope that some of the ideas, innovations, opportunities, and challenges discussed will excite and inspire a new generation of work designers and analysts to push advancements in both science and practice.

29

What and Who?
Research and Conclusions on Two of the Most Important Questions in Job Analysis

Robert J. Harvey

Virginia Tech

Mark A. Wilson

North Carolina State University

This chapter is organized into two major sections, each focusing on a critical big-picture question facing job analysts: *What* should be rated in job analysis, and *who* should do the ratings? When addressing these questions, we cover a range of issues involved in collecting, linking, assessing, verifying, and applying occupational information. Currently, the field of job and occupational analysis (JOA) stands at a crossroads, and its future direction will in large part be determined by the best-practices decisions that are adopted with respect to identifying the appropriate levels of analysis for describing work and selecting the best sources and methods for collecting data describing job characteristics.

WHAT SHOULD BE RATED?

Due in part to efforts by the U.S. Department of Labor to revise the *Dictionary of Occupational Titles* (DOT), considerable interest has recently been generated in the practice of using standardized profiles of general work behaviors (GWBs)—also termed generalized work activities (GWAs)—to describe jobs (e.g., Harvey, 1992; O'Leary, Rheinstein, & McCauley, 1989, 1990; Outerbridge, 1981; Rheinstein, McCauley, & O'Leary, 1989). The Department of Labor created the Advisory Panel for the Review of the DOT (APDOT) when it designed the DOT's replacement, the Occupational Information Network (O*NET; e.g., Peterson, Mumford, Borman, Jeanneret, & Fleishman, 1999). The interim report of the advisory panel identified GWBs as "work behaviors that do not include highly occupation-specific content, and [that] tend to occur across substantial numbers of different occupations" (APDOT, 1992, p. 10594).

As a practical matter, GWAs and GWBs can be thought of as work-descriptive items or categories that lie at a level of behavioral abstraction that is higher than that seen for detailed job tasks (e.g., Christal, 1974; Fine, 1955). It is important to stress that the GWA or GWB label does not uniquely define a single level of abstraction, but rather subsumes items that span a potentially wide range of levels of behavioral abstraction. For example, the most specific types of GWBs simply represent clusters of related task statements (e.g., a "using analog measuring devices" GWB might subsume a number of task-level items dealing with the use of micrometers, rulers, scales, and similar tools).

In contrast, GWAs/GWBs may also be defined at much higher levels of abstraction. For example, the items in the O*NET Generalized Work Activities survey that correspond to the relatively detailed "using analog measuring devices" GWB example include the far more abstract GWAs of *Getting Information*, as well as *Estimating the Quantifiable Characteristics of Products Events or Information* (although that one stresses the role of estimating as opposed to measuring), and *Controlling Machines and Processes* (although that focuses on taking actions to operate machines or processes, as opposed to using measuring devices as a source of required information).

Indeed, the overall *Data*, *People*, and *Things* dimensions of worker function identified by Sidney Fine's Functional Job Analysis theory (e.g., Fine, 1955; Fine & Cronshaw, 1999; Fine, Harvey, & Cronshaw, 2004; Harvey, 2004) can be thought of as defining an upper limit of abstraction for GWB-type elements. The fact that Fine's three rationally identified GWA constructs have been found via empirical factor analytic studies to underlie a wide range of job analysis instruments (e.g., Harvey, 1987, 2004) provides further support for their usefulness as a means for providing a big-picture view of work.

This first section of the chapter is organized in terms of seven aspects of the process of collecting GWB data. First, we examine how GWBs are used in job analysis and related personnel functions. Second, we address the decision processes that are involved in rating abstract work characteristics. Third, we examine research concerning direct versus indirect strategies for rating GWBs. Fourth, we review research concerning rational versus empirical identification of GWBs. Fifth, we report the results of an empirical study that compared holistic versus decomposed judgment strategies for rating GWBs. Sixth, we discuss the implications of that study for practitioners who seek to describe abstract GWB constructs. Finally, considering the fact that sharp disagreement exists with respect to whether holistic rating strategies represent best practices in JOA (e.g., Chapter 6, this volume), we present and rebut alternative views regarding the implications of the empirical findings and recommendations for practice presented previously.

Uses of Generalized Work Activities in Job Analysis and Related Personnel Functions

One of the main reasons for describing occupations in terms of GWBs is that such elements offer the potential for meaningful, quantitative, cross-occupational comparisons to be drawn. That is, if one relies on standardized, economy-wide databases such as the DOT or O*NET in order to draw meaningful quantitative comparisons between task-dissimilar occupations, one must rely on the common-metric profile of GWB (and/or worker-trait requirement) elements on which all occupations are described (e.g., see Geyer, Hice, Hawk, Boese, & Brannon, 1989; Harvey, 1992). For example, in the DOT, all occupations receive a rating on GWBs including *Data*, *People*, and *Things*; in O*NET, all titles are rated on the several dozen items included in its GWA survey (e.g., see Figure 29.1). Profile correlations, distance statistics, or other measures of cross-occupational similarity can then be derived from the ratings of these common characteristics and used to make decisions regarding occupational similarity.

Although the interest in GWBs that has been stimulated by the development of O*NET is a relatively recent phenomenon, it can be argued (e.g., Harvey, 1992, pp. 13–15) that the GWB concept has been around for many decades and that it forms the conceptual basis for the so-called worker-oriented approach to job analysis (e.g., McCormick, 1976). That is, instruments like the Common-Metric Questionnaire (CMQ; Harvey, 1991b), Occupational Analysis Inventory (OAI; Cunningham, Boese, Neeb, & Pass, 1983), Job Element Inventory (JEI; Harvey, Friedman, Hakel, & Cornelius, 1988), and Position Analysis Questionnaire (PAQ; McCormick, Jeanneret, & Mecham, 1972) are based on the concept that by rating jobs on a common profile of moderate-specificity activities (i.e., defined at a level more abstract than the task), practitioners can identify meaningful,

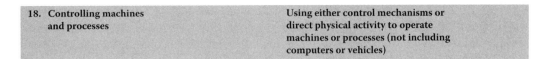

A. How <u>important</u> is CONTROLLING MACHINES AND PROCESSES to the performance of *your current job*?

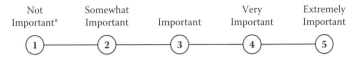

* If you marked Not Important, skip LEVEL below and go on to the next activity.

B. What <u>level</u> of CONTROLLING MACHINES AND PROCESSES is needed to perform *your current job*?

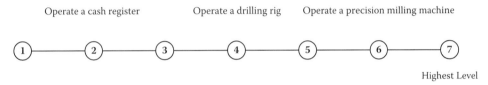

Figure 29.1   Example O*NET item from a generalized work activities survey.

more-abstract types of similarity between task-dissimilar positions, jobs, or occupations that would never be evident if described at the task-based level of analysis.

By combining multiple GWB item ratings via factor-analytic or other means to form work dimension scores, it is possible to estimate highly abstract GWB constructs. By having the option to use either the more behaviorally specific item-level GWB rating profiles, or the more abstract work-dimension profiles, practitioners gain considerable flexibility with respect to being able to meaningfully compare task-dissimilar jobs (e.g., for the purpose of developing job-title taxonomies; Harvey, 1986).

In sum, although GWB ratings (or derived work-dimension scores) for a given position, job, or occupation may be directly interpreted by practitioners and used to develop human resources applications, arguably their most important applied value lies in the fact that they provide a common-metric of work content that can be used to compare organizational entities that may be highly dissimilar at the more molecular task level. Without such a capability, when making job similarity decisions practitioners would be forced to rely on subjective, qualitative comparisons based on customized task-level narratives or, if using the task-inventory approach (e.g., Christal, 1974), to rely on quantitative comparisons of task overlap that are highly sensitive to molecular task-level differences between jobs that can conceal similarities that exist at a more behaviorally abstract level of analysis.

Decision Processes Involved in Rating Abstract Work Characteristics

Cornelius and Lyness (1980) offered a taxonomy of judgment strategies that is useful for classifying the various methods that exist for rating abstract characteristics of jobs (or workers). Two general decision strategies can be identified: (a) *holistic judgment* methods, "in which the incumbent is required to use his/her knowledge of the job to make an overall judgment about an underlying job characteristic" (pp. 156–157), and (b) *decomposed judgment* methods, "in which incumbents are required to make judgments about elements of the job … and an algorithm (either clinical or mechanical) is used to combine the information to derive an overall judgment about an underlying job characteristic" (p. 157).

Using this taxonomy, the practice of combining ratings of the moderate-specificity GWB elements contained in standardized, common-metric job analysis inventories (e.g., JEI, PAQ, CMQ, OAI) to form composites measuring more abstract GWB work-dimension constructs would be deemed a decomposed-judgment strategy, whereas methods that attempt to directly rate abstract, work-dimension GWB constructs would exemplify the holistic-judgment strategy. However, it must be kept in mind that the question of what makes a given decision process holistic versus decomposed is somewhat relative or context-specific. That is, some of the individual items contained in the previously noted standardized job analysis inventories are themselves relatively abstract, to the point that one might well label efforts to directly rate them as involving holistic judgment.

For example, although many of the items rated in the PAQ describe relatively specific aspects of work (e.g., "using long-handled tools"), it also requires single-item ratings of highly abstract characteristics, including *Decision Making, General Responsibility, Level of Physical Exertion,* and *Job Structure.* Obviously, one could consider each of these items as representing an attempt to directly rate an abstract, underlying construct, and it would be a straightforward matter to develop a decomposed-judgment rating process that could instead be used to measure each (e.g., for *Level of Physical Exertion,* by combining ratings of a number of more specific items describing the various possible weights of objects that must be lifted, carried, moved, pushed, pulled, or positioned in terms of the frequency of occurrence, duration of activity, required distance of movement, unilateral versus bilateral effort involved, and so forth).

The holistic versus decomposed judgment distinction is relevant to two different aspects of the process of describing highly abstract, work-dimension level GWBs: (a) the process of actually *rating* (or otherwise quantifying) positions, jobs, or occupations in terms of their standing on each GWB construct, and (b) the logically prior task of *identifying* the abstract dimensions of general work activity to be quantified. These two processes are considered separately below.

Holistic Versus Decomposed Rating of General Work Behaviors

With respect to the issue of rating GWBs, as a practical matter the choice of a holistic versus decomposed rating strategy has important implications, especially for applied human resources uses of JOA data that may be subjected to legal scrutiny in equal employment opportunity or related contexts (e.g., when setting employee selection requirements). That is, if a firm empirical basis existed to justify the inference that holistic versus decomposed judgment strategies for measuring GWBs would produce functionally interchangeable results, the holistic approach would offer obvious advantages regarding reduced time and cost.

Unfortunately, numerous conceptual and empirical reasons exist to question such a conclusion. At a conceptual level, in view of the high level of abstraction of the attributes being rated and the large amount of information that must be considered when making each holistic rating, one might conclude that the cognitive demands placed on raters by the holistic strategy are greater than those required when rating more behaviorally detailed, observable items. That is, given adequate knowledge of the job in question, it follows that it should be far easier to rate a behaviorally explicit item (e.g., "how frequently does the job require the use of handheld electric drills to bore holes in hardwood floors?"), as well as to independently review and verify the accuracy of such ratings, than it would be to directly rate an abstract work-dimension construct, such as the corresponding O*NET GWA of *Controlling Machines and Processes* (see Figure 29.1). This is particularly the case given that the rating scale for this GWA does not include anything even remotely similar to "handheld electric drills" among the behavioral anchors that define the scale's metric, a fact that considerably increases the subjectivity involved in making such a judgment (and the difficulty in later defending its accuracy).

In light of the fundamentally different information processing demands involved, one might expect holistic versus decomposed GWB rating strategies to diverge. Although the empirical base of research regarding the interchangeability of holistic and decomposed job rating methods is limited, it is quite consistent with the above conclusion. In one of the earlier studies in the JOA literature, Cornelius and Lyness (1980) examined interrater agreement levels for ratings of 13 worker trait requirements and job design constructs; holistic ratings were obtained by having incumbents read lists of tasks, then rate the 13 general traits. Decomposed ratings were obtained by (a) rating each task on the 13 traits, then holistically generating an overall rating (the "decomposed-clinical" condition), and (b) rating each task on the traits, then mechanically combining the ratings to form an overall score ("decomposed-algorithm"). Interrater agreement was generally poor for all rating strategies (mean $r = .40$, $.30$, and $.54$ for holistic, decomposed-clinical, and decomposed-algorithm); indeed, two jobs showed a *negative* average interrater agreement correlation!

Unfortunately, Cornelius and Lyness (1980) did not examine convergence between rating strategies. Additionally, the degree to which their decomposed rating methods reflect traditional detailed JOA methods (e.g., Christal, 1974) is open to debate. That is, although the decomposed conditions involved rating job tasks, the scales used to rate them required highly abstract judgments (e.g., rating the amount of *Reasoning*, *Autonomy*, and *Significance* associated with each). In effect, their detailed rating task was arguably comparable in degree of abstraction to their holistic rating task (i.e., the same highly abstract rating scale was used to rate individual tasks, as well as the job as a whole).

Accordingly, we suggest broadening the Cornelius and Lyness (1980) definition of *holistic* to include methods of both (a) using single-item scales to rate behaviorally abstract traits or characteristics of the job considered as a whole, and (b) rating specific aspects of the job with respect to one or more abstract traits or characteristics. Thus, a holistic rating process may result from rating job characteristics that are defined at a high level of abstraction, from rating any type of job element (even items with high specificity) using scales that require an abstract judgment, or both.

Viewed from this perspective, the Cornelius and Lyness (1980) decomposed tasks do not faithfully reflect the judgments required of raters in many detailed job analysis methods (e.g., task-inventory items rated using a nonrelativistic frequency scale; see Chapter 6, this volume). The fact that Cornelius and Lyness (1980) found poor interrater agreement in all of their rating conditions is therefore not surprising, given that all would be deemed holistic strategies using our definition. Thus, although the Cornelius and Lyness (1980) findings seriously question the ability of holistic methods to produce adequate crossrater agreement, they do not address the issue of ratings interchangeability.

In contrast, Butler and Harvey (1988) examined the convergence between holistic ratings of PAQ work dimensions (e.g., *Equipment/Vehicle Operation*, *Public-Related Contact*) versus the standard decomposed-judgment method for scoring the dimensions (i.e., weighted composites formed from the more detailed item ratings). Butler and Harvey found very poor convergence between holistic and decomposed ratings (mean r values were less than .10 in absolute value), despite the fact that professional job analysts who were highly familiar with the PAQ served as raters.

Gibson, Harvey, and Harris (2007) examined holistic versus decomposed judgment convergence with respect to ratings of the original 42 O*NET GWA constructs (e.g., Figure 29.1), as well as data collected using the CMQ. Because the GWA items rated in CMQ are far more numerous (over 1,200 items are combined to form its work-dimension scores) and behaviorally specific than the elements rated in O*NET, interrater agreement was examined by examining derived factor scores on the abstract *Data, People,* and *Things* constructs of FJA. Results indicated that much higher interrater agreement levels were produced for the CMQ scores, which were derived from much more detailed item ratings than the ones used to estimate the *Data, People,* and *Things* constructs from the O*NET ratings. For example, across the three work dimensions CMQ median r_{wg} values were .83 for incumbents and .81 for analysts, whereas for the same three dimensions derived from O*NET item ratings the medians were −0.61 and 0.10. Here, negative values for r_{wg} indicated that raters judging the same job produced higher levels of disagreement than would be expected from ratings of different, randomly selected jobs.

Comparisons between the abstract *Data, People,* and *Things* dimension scores derived from ratings of detailed (CMQ) versus abstract (O*NET) GWA items indicated considerable ratings divergence. For example, correlations of the *Data, People,* and *Things* scores across rating strategy were only $r = .14, .13,$ and $.30$ for incumbents, and $r = .71, .13,$ and $.43$ for analysts, respectively. Only the two larger correlations for the analyst group reached the .05 significance level, and of course such correlations are not sensitive to the critical question of *level-based* convergence (see Chapter 6, this volume). To address that question, visual examinations of the scatterplots of dimension scores computed from CMQ versus O*NET items revealed level-sensitive disagreement at magnitudes that flatly precluded a conclusion of ratings method interchangeability.

Although their study examined holistic versus decomposed judgment convergence in ratings of ability-traits (as opposed to GWAs), the DeNisi and Shaw (1977) results are highly relevant to the question of rating strategy convergence. DeNisi and Shaw asked people to self-rate their scores on a range of ability constructs that were quite similar to the traits rated in the O*NET *Abilities* survey (which is itself functionally identical to the Fleishman job analysis survey instrument; e.g., Fleishman, 1992; Fleishman & Mumford, 1991; Fleishman & Reilly, 1992; Fleishman, Wetrogan, Uhlman, & Marshall-Mies, 1995). Comparisons of direct holistic ratings to scores on the same traits obtained via decomposed judgment processes (i.e., standardized, multiple-item psychological tests) revealed convergence levels so poor (mean $r = .28$ across the 10 traits) that DeNisi and Shaw flatly concluded that they were "too small to have any practical significance" (p. 641).

Although they did not conduct direct comparative tests of holistic versus decomposed job ratings, other studies (e.g., Cain & Green, 1983; Geyer et al., 1989; Geyer & Hunter, 1992; Webb, Shavelson, Shea, & Morello, 1981) reported findings that raise further questions regarding holistic strategies for making job ratings. These studies examined the psychometric properties of single-item scales used to rate general work-activity and worker-trait requirements in the DOT. Results indicated that the holistic scales used to make the DOT ratings demonstrated highly variable (and often quite low) levels of average interrater agreement (e.g., several were <.50, and many were <.70).

Regarding the question of whether holistic versus decomposed methods of rating GWBs and required worker traits can be expected to converge at levels that would justify a conclusion of ratings interchangeability, the available research results clearly indicate that they do not. Although additional studies on the topic in larger samples of jobs and instruments would be desirable, the dramatic differences in the amounts and types of inferences required of raters when rating detailed versus abstract characteristics strongly suggest that these two methods of rating work activity will never be capable of providing functionally interchangeable results. The dramatically lower potential for holistic ratings of abstract traits to be independently verified further argues against their use for any human resources application in which the defensibility of the JOA ratings is at issue.

Rational Versus Empirical Identification of General Work Behaviors

With respect to the related question of whether rational versus empirical methods for identifying (as opposed to rating) GWBs can be expected to produce similar results, several studies (e.g., Cunningham et al., 1983; Harvey et al., 1988; McCormick et al., 1972) have provided comparisons of empirical (typically, factor analytic) versus rational methods for identifying the work-dimension level GWBs that underlie such instruments. Typically, standardized general-purpose JOA questionnaires are developed using some underlying conceptual model of work; however, when their items are factor analyzed, it is often the case that the empirically derived dimensions show little resemblance to the hypothesized rational structure (e.g., the factors combine items from separate logically derived divisions of the item pool).

We would not be surprised to find similar divergence between rational versus empirical methods for deriving GWB categories when task-based instruments are examined, as well as when more detailed common-metric instruments like the CMQ are analyzed. However, unlike the question of holistic versus decomposed methods for rating GWB work dimensions, the fact that rational versus empirical methods of identifying such dimensions may not converge strongly is not necessarily cause for alarm. That is, the primary question of interest with respect to evaluating a taxonomy of work-dimension constructs effectively reduces to one of utility; that is, are the GWB dimensions useful to practitioners in solving applied problems? In that regard, there is no reason to believe that either method is intrinsically likely to produce superior results.

Further Empirical Analysis of Holistic-Decomposed Convergence

In contrast, with respect to determining the future direction of the field of JOA and identifying sound best-practices recommendations, the question of whether holistic versus decomposed judgment methods for measuring work dimensions produce functionally interchangeable results is of critical importance. That is, if the results of the past studies reviewed above are valid and generalizable, this would fundamentally question the reliance on holistic judgment strategies that has been taken by large-scale JOA databases such as O*NET. At a minimum, it would dramatically limit the uses to which such information should be put (e.g., human resources applications for which demonstrable data quality and the capacity for independent verifiability are not important considerations).

In the study reported here, we examined the degree of convergence that exists between different methods for identifying, as well as rating, abstract GWBs. One approach, which we termed the *empirical/decomposed method*, involved constructing detailed task- and common-metric inventories for heterogeneous pools of jobs, rating each position on each item (i.e., a decomposed-judgment task), then using an empirical procedure (factor analysis of the item ratings, or a mechanical algorithm) to form the more abstract GWB scores. The alternative, which we termed the *rational/ holistic procedure*, involved using job content experts to rationally identify GWBs by sorting the job analysis items to form GWB clusters; once identified, the abstract GWB dimensions were then rated directly using single-item scales (i.e., a holistic-judgment task).

The comparisons of interest concerned (a) the qualitative convergence between the GWB categories identified by rational versus empirical means, and (b) the quantitative similarity between the holistic versus decomposed GWB ratings (i.e., cross-method convergent validity, ratings interchangeability). We hypothesized that significant divergence would occur with respect to both the identification and rating of GWBs: (a) based on the studies reviewed above, we expected to find low qualitative similarity in the rationally versus factor-analytically derived GWB categories; and (b) based on Butler and Harvey (1988) and Gibson et al. (2007), we predicted low quantitative convergence between holistic versus decomposed GWB ratings (even in cases in which the rational and empirical procedures produced qualitatively similar GWB categories).

We viewed this study to be necessary to provide a test of the generalizability of past studies, and especially because some authors (e.g., Cornelius, Schmidt, & Carron, 1984; Geyer & Hunter, 1992; Pearlman, 1980; Sackett, Cornelius, & Carron, 1981) have taken an aggressively positive view regarding the future of holistic rating methods for both job analysis and for inferring worker-trait requirements of jobs. Indeed, a common theme running through such studies is their conclusion that holistic ratings produce results that are functionally identical to—if not actually superior to—results obtained from job analysis methods that focus on rating observable, behaviorally detailed work activities. Given the poor levels of convergence reported in Butler and Harvey (1988), DeNisi and Shaw (1977), and Gibson et al. (2007), additional research is clearly necessary to determine which set of best-practice conclusions is most consistent with the empirical data.

Participants and Instruments

Four samples of incumbent ratings were examined:

1. 131 employees in a city government who rated an 886-item task inventory (28 duty-level GWBs were rated)
2. 3,581 employees in an insurance company who rated a 521-item task inventory (36 GWBs)
3. 119 employees in a city government who rated a 598-item task inventory (29 GWBs)
4. 4,552 raters from a variety of organizations who rated 189 CMQ frequency items (see Harvey, 1991b, for details) during the field test of the CMQ (26 GWBs)

The three task inventories were custom developed for each organization, and each consisted of a section in which tasks were rated (6-point relative time spent scales were used for both task and GWB ratings, with the zero point being *Does Not Apply* [DNA]) and a separate section in which the rationally derived GWBs were listed and rated. In the insurance company, the GWBs were rated first and the tasks were not organized by GWB category; in the city governments, the GWBs were rated after the tasks and the task statements were grouped into GWB clusters. The name of the GWB category was listed at the start of each section of tasks, making explicit the rationally derived linkages between tasks and GWB categories.

For the CMQ frequency ratings, the "row" items of the instrument were rated using a 6-point frequency scale (the zero point represented DNA); GWB ratings were collected after the item ratings. The standardization edition of the CMQ (Harvey, 1990) was used; this version of the CMQ is different in several respects from the first edition (Harvey, 1991b), including the fact that direct holistic ratings of the GWBs were collected only in the standardization edition, and several items used in this study were eliminated or combined when forming the first edition.

In each of the four inventories, the GWB categories that were rated holistically were developed via rational means. During the process of writing and editing the task statements for the three task inventories, the job analysis project coordinators developed task categories using a free-sort procedure. By repeatedly combining and splitting categories, the final GWB clusters were identified by consensus among the job analysts. The listings of tasks and GWB categories were then reviewed for completeness and accuracy (and additional tasks were added as needed) by subject matter experts in each organization at multiple points during the development of each instrument. For the CMQ, the rationally derived headings used to group the CMQ items in the rating booklet served as the GWB categories.

Two methods for identifying the empirical/decomposed GWBs were used, depending on the number of incumbents in each sample relative to the number of items rated. The insurance company had many more incumbents than task statements, and in that inventory a factor analysis of the task ratings was used to identify and score the empirical/ decomposed GWBs; the common factor model was used, with squared multiple correlations as communality estimates, the scree test to determine the number of factors, oblique Harris-Kaiser rotation, and regression-method factor scoring. The CMQ sample also had many more raters than items, allowing a factor analysis of the 189 frequency ratings that were the focus of this study. It should be noted that the CMQ collects over 2,000 item-level ratings for each position and that we used only a subset (i.e., the *Frequency* ratings). The reason that the 189 *Frequency* CMQ items were studied here (as opposed to including the much larger number of binary ratings that were made for each "row" item rated on the *Frequency* scale, as was done in Harvey, 2005) was that the *Frequency* ratings were the only multipoint ratings that could be matched directly to the 26 holistic GWB *Frequency* ratings.

In the city government organizations, there were many more tasks than raters; in these situations, we followed the strategy of Cornelius and Lyness (1980) and used mechanical algorithms to form the empirical/decomposed GWB scores for each position. Two methods for forming the decomposed GWB composites were used: (a) computing the mean rating given to the tasks in each rationally derived GWB category, and (b) taking the highest rating given in each GWB cluster as the GWB rating, using the Cornelius and Lyness (1980) rationale that based on "traditional" grounds, "the highest level required to perform the work" should be used as the decomposed rating (p. 157). For comparability across samples, these mechanical algorithms were also applied to the insurance company and CMQ samples (i.e., in addition to their factor analytically derived GWBs).

In the insurance company and CMQ samples, the qualitative convergence between rationally versus empirically derived GWB categories was assessed by comparing the rationally derived GWBs with the names assigned to the empirically derived factors. To assess the quantitative convergence between the holistic versus decomposed GWB ratings, the incumbents' holistic ratings of the rationally derived GWBs were correlated with their empirical/decomposed GWB scores. Because of the possibility that the names assigned to the empirically identified factors might not directly match the rationally developed GWB names and the possibility that the rational and empirical procedures would produce different numbers of GWBs, we examined all possible correlations between the factor scores and ratings of the rationally derived GWBs in the CMQ and insurance samples.

Finally, in the two city government samples, factor analyses were conducted on the holistic and decomposed GWB scores in an attempt to quantify the similarity between these ratings. These analyses were conducted in order to shed some light on the question of whether job analysis data collected using holistic versus decomposed methods would produce different results when used in a practical application: In this case, do holistic versus decomposed job ratings produce similar factor structures? Because the number and identity of the GWB categories rated using holistic versus decomposed methods were identical in the two city governments, any observed differences in the factor structures obtained by factoring the GWB ratings must solely reflect differences due to the rating strategies. Correlations between the factor scores produced by analyzing the holistic versus decomposed GWB data were computed to quantify their similarity.

It must be stressed that the correlational indices we examined here present a somewhat optimistic view of ratings interchangeability. That is, as was discussed in Chapter 6, this volume, such indices are primarily sensitive to relative similarity in profile shape and not to absolute level-based differences in the pairwise values. Thus, although high correlations between scores produced by different rating methods do not necessarily prove that the methods produce functionally interchangeable results, the *lack* of high correlations makes a decidedly negative statement regarding interchangeability (given that if level-sensitive differences were also considered, agreement levels could decrease even further).

Insurance Company Inventory Results

To obtain the factor analytically derived job dimensions, the 521-by-521 reduced task correlation matrix was factored; the scree plot indicated breaks at 11, 14, 17, 19, 21, 27, and 29 factors. Rotated solutions in each of these dimensionalities were computed and examined; these solutions were deemed quite similar, with solutions in the higher dimensionalities tending to add only very weak factors (i.e., ones with only one or two high item loadings). The 17-factor solution (which explains 76% of the total common variance) was selected as the best balance between general factors and solutions in which numerous weak factors were present; factor correlations in the rotated solution were quite low (only two correlations >.30). To conserve space, the factor loading matrices are not reported (these are available from the authors). Table 29.1 presents the names given to the empirically derived GWB factors, and Table 29.2 presents the convergent validity correlations between the GWB scores obtained by the factor analytic method versus direct holistic ratings of the rationally derived GWB categories.

With respect to the qualitative agreement between the rational and factor analytic methods of identifying GWB clusters, Tables 29.1 and 29.2 indicates that despite the fact that the factor analysis produced a different number of GWBs than the rational procedure, a modest degree of similarity is apparent in the GWB names; however, there are important points of difference (e.g., some empirically derived GWBs, such as *Cash Control, Ratefinding, Subrogation,* and *Arbitration,* have no analog in the rationally derived GWBs). Of course, the most important question concerns the degree of correlation that exists between the holistic versus decomposed ratings of these GWBs; that is, although different names may have been given to the empirically derived GWB categories, this would not preclude them from having high convergent validities with the rationally derived GWBs.

The convergent validities presented in Table 29.2 indicate that there is surprisingly poor numerical convergence between the rational/holistic versus empirical/decomposed GWB data. Using the highest cross-method convergent validity correlation for each GWB category, only 5 of the 36 rationally identified, holistically rated GWBs correlate ≥ .70 with the empirically derived GWB factor

Table 29.1 Names of Factor-Analytically Derived Generalized Work Behavior Categories in Insurance and Common Metric Questionnaire (CMQ) Samples

Factor	Insurance Company Task Inventory Factor Name	CMQ Frequency Factor Name
1	Human resource management	Meetings to decide/coordinate/schedule
2	General claims processing and decision making	Gross physical activities and related environmental conditions
3	Evaluating risk	Patrol activities
4	Subrogation and arbitration	Sensory input from work environment
5	Medical claims decision making	Stressful or demanding working conditions
6	Computer programming and related information systems activities	Production and human resource managerial decisions
7	Internal contacts, programs and operations management	Internal contacts: mid- and lower level
8	General claims management and decision making	Unpleasant and hazardous work environment characteristics
9	Payments, billing, and related financial activities	External contacts
10	Safety and hazard evaluation	Skilled/precise physical activity
11	Determining premium rates	Information processing/clerical activities
12	Policyholder and other external contacts	Strategic planning
13	Recordkeeping, clerical, and related office activities	Technical activities/higher level information processing
14	Computer operations	Higher level managerial activities
15	Inventory and resource management	Internal contacts/nonsupervisory professional employees
16	Ratefinding	Not applicable
17	Cash control	Not applicable

Table 29.2   Correlations Between Rationally and Empirically Derived Insurance Inventory Generalized Work Behaviors (GWBs)

Empirically Derived GWB Factor: Rationally Derived GWB	1	2	3	4	5	6	7	8	9	10	11	12	13	14	15	16	17	r max	r mean
1. Set premium levels	-0.04	-0.10	0.36	-0.11	-0.09	-0.07	0.03	-0.01	0.20	0.14	0.51	-0.04	0.07	-0.03	-0.07	0.23	-0.05	0.45	0.58
2. Make decisions about insurance policies	-0.01	0.05	0.49	0.09	0.14	-0.20	0.05	0.17	0.27	0.11	0.20	0.28	0.08	-0.12	-0.09	0.15	-0.08	0.52	0.56
3. Complete forms	-0.11	0.45	0.09	0.28	0.29	-0.16	-0.08	0.05	0.04	0.11	0.04	0.35	0.19	-0.10	0.02	0.10	-0.03	0.46	0.44
4. Communicate with customers	-0.14	0.46	0.02	0.43	0.36	-0.29	-0.09	0.12	0.19	0.13	-0.14	0.56	-0.01	-0.14	-0.02	0.10	-0.02	0.71	0.70
5. Debug computer programs	-0.08	-0.16	-0.15	-0.16	-0.13	0.69	-0.05	-0.08	-0.07	-0.06	-0.04	-0.21	-0.03	0.13	-0.03	-0.04	0.02	0.69	0.75
6. Attend meetings	0.46	-0.09	0.04	-0.08	-0.06	0.18	0.52	0.03	0.04	0.07	0.02	-0.01	0.05	-0.09	0.07	-0.12	0.03	0.66	0.65
7. Design, implement, monitor data systems	-0.01	-0.16	-0.15	-0.16	-0.15	0.67	0.21	-0.12	-0.11	-0.07	-0.05	-0.19	-0.03	0.16	0.02	-0.08	0.03	0.48	0.67
8. Maintain and keep records	0.29	0.16	-0.01	0.22	0.19	-0.08	0.17	0.03	0.03	0.04	-0.03	0.28	0.25	-0.03	0.10	-0.01	0.07	0.43	0.47
9. Operate computers	-0.09	-0.18	0.14	-0.08	-0.13	-0.03	-0.10	-0.07	0.14	-0.08	-0.09	-0.00	0.16	0.46	-0.00	0.12	-0.01	0.38	0.46
10. Engage in personal development	0.37	0.07	0.14	0.08	0.08	-0.02	0.27	0.12	0.03	0.15	0.07	0.12	0.12	-0.02	0.05	0	0.05	0.35	0.37
11. Make oral presentations	0.36	-0.04	0.08	-0.05	0.02	0.03	0.50	0.15	0.03	0.20	0.02	-0.02	0.05	-0.06	-0.03	-0.04	0.01	0.55	0.54
12. Code information	-0.13	-0.15	0.12	-0.14	-0.11	-0.01	-0.17	-0.07	0.34	-0.12	-0.11	0.02	0.39	-0.01	-0.00	0.20	0.03	0.62	0.62
13. Write reports	0.27	0.48	-0.10	0.22	0.34	-0.07	0.34	0.09	-0.09	0.21	-0.07	0.14	-0.01	-0.11	0.03	-0.09	-0.01	0.58	0.58
14. File/organize work materials	0.06	0.21	-0.02	0.22	0.22	-0.02	0.08	-0.01	-0.00	0.11	-0.00	0.25	0.29	0.02	0.06	0.02	0.04	0.37	0.38
15. Rewrite information	0.08	0.04	0.03	0.08	0.08	0.04	0.32	0.01	0.08	0.06	0.07	0.12	0.22	-0.04	0.04	-0.03	0.02	0.31	0.31
16. Write/document computer programs	-0.11	-0.15	-0.14	-0.15	-0.13	0.72	-0.07	-0.07	-0.08	-0.06	-0.03	-0.20	-0.04	0.09	-0.03	-0.05	0	0.76	0.81

continued

Table 29.2 Correlations Between Rationally and Empirically Derived Insurance Inventory Generalized Work Behaviors (GWBs) (Continued)

Empirically Derived GWB Factor: Rationally Derived GWB	1	2	3	4	5	6	7	8	9	10	11	12	13	14	15	16	17	r max	r mean
17. Communicate with company agents	−0.03	0.04	0.58	0.04	0.03	−0.30	0.05	0.08	0.42	0.16	0.14	0.37	0.10	−0.16	0.01	−0.01	0.01	0.79	0.76
18. Document that others have insurance coverage	−0.08	0.15	0.33	0.27	0.28	−0.15	0.01	0.15	0.21	0.10	0.09	0.36	0.14	−0.06	−0.05	0.14	−0.04	0.40	0.39
19. Evaluate company programs and work systems	0.38	−0.14	0.01	−0.13	−0.11	0.03	0.61	0.04	0.08	0.03	0.03	−0.05	0.06	−0.02	0.15	−0.04	0.03	0.46	0.59
20. Document/evaluate insurance applications	−0.10	−0.17	0.75	−0.18	−0.11	−0.08	0.02	−0.02	0.14	0.12	0.31	0.07	0.11	−0.07	−0.06	0.23	−0.01	0.75	0.77
21. Communicate with your work group	0.51	0.18	0.05	−0.12	−0.10	0.13	0.29	0.12	0.05	−0.00	0.06	0.05	0.18	0.02	0.04	−0.00	0.09	0.38	0.47
22. Evaluate another's performance	0.81	−0.18	−0.06	−0.15	−0.09	−0.02	0.35	0.25	0.01	−0.01	−0.02	−0.08	0.04	−0.01	0.09	−0.03	0.08	0.79	0.82
23. Document losses	−0.13	0.55	0.12	0.41	0.44	−0.17	−0.02	0.21	−0.08	0.10	0.03	0.28	−0.05	−0.08	−0.10	0.01	−0.06	0.61	0.63
24. Evaluate risk	−0.14	0.19	0.70	0.04	0.17	−0.18	0.02	0.10	0.04	0.38	0.25	0.15	−0.02	−0.11	−0.12	0.18	−0.05	0.61	0.75
25. Communicate with external people and organizations	−0.05	0.25	−0.01	0.36	0.33	−0.15	0.08	0.13	0.05	0.11	0.01	0.43	0.01	−0.09	−0.01	0.01	0.04	0.45	0.43
26. Plan and prepare for work	0.35	0.18	−0.04	0.07	0.13	0.07	0.27	0.06	−0.03	0.14	−0.01	0.14	0.18	−0.01	0.06	−0.03	0.08	0.36	0.32
27. Maintain, update insurance policies	−0.06	−0.17	0.51	−0.16	−0.15	−0.09	−0.01	−0.05	0.36	0.09	0.33	0.04	0.24	−0.04	−0.04	0.24	−0.06	0.44	0.52

28. Communicate with other organization members	0.24	−0.04	0.06	0.03	0.07	0.06	0.37	0.08	0.06	0.07	0.04	0.18	0.09	−0.03	0	−0.02	0.07	0.19	0.32
29. Verify information	−0.07	0.06	0.22	0.19	0.20	−0.07	0.06	0.01	0.22	0.08	0.05	0.34	0.32	−0.09	−0.04	0.05	0.01	0.22	0.19
30. Schedule work of subordinates	0.80	−0.16	−0.12	−0.14	−0.10	0.09	0.28	0.07	−0.01	−0.04	−0.03	−0.08	0.07	0.03	0.14	−0.01	0.10	0.76	0.80
31. Develop, evaluate, and change insurance policies	−0.08	−0.17	0.42	−0.16	−0.12	−0.08	0.05	−0.02	0.30	0.06	0.30	0.03	0.16	−0.05	−0.03	0.24	−0.05	0.46	0.45
32. Schedule own work	0.20	0.24	0.06	0.13	0.18	0.03	0.17	0.06	0.03	0.14	0.04	0.20	0.20	−0.02	0.02	−0.01	0.05	0.41	0.41
33. Evaluate extent of a loss	−0.14	0.66	0	0.51	0.49	−0.21	−0.03	0.29	−0.16	0.07	0.04	0.36	−0.10	−0.12	−0.12	−0.03	−0.09	0.64	0.77
34. Pay claims	−0.19	0.64	−0.20	0.59	0.53	−0.19	−0.14	0.14	−0.21	−0.06	−0.09	0.44	−0.06	−0.12	−0.08	−0.06	−0.07	0.79	0.77
35. Train others	0.50	−0.15	−0.01	−0.10	−0.06	0.03	0.24	0.26	0.05	0.02	0.01	−0.11	0.19	0.08	−0.04	0.05	0.04	0.74	0.62
36. Budget money	0.57	0.01	−0.07	−0.01	0.04	−0.05	0.48	0.27	0.02	0.06	−0.03	0.09	−0.14	−0.04	0.28	−0.08	0.10	0.58	0.66

Entries are *r* values between holistic (rows) and factor analytic decomposed (columns) GWB data; *r* max and *r* mean are the correlations involving the composites formed by taking the maximum and mean task rating in each rational GWB cluster, respectively.

scores (only 20 of 36 have *r* values ≥.50). Viewed from the opposite perspective, only 3 of 17 empirically derived, factor analytically scored GWBs have *r* values ≥.70 (9 of 17 have *r* values ≥.50) with the rationally derived GWBs. Although several of the names are virtually identical in the rationally versus empirically derived GWBs (e.g., *Operate Computers, Evaluate Risk*), even the most similar scales have only 50–60% of their variance in common. As was discussed in Chapter 6, this volume, far higher convergence *r* values than .70 would be desired before even beginning to argue that functionally interchangeable results were produced by the different methods.

The results involving the GWBs computed using the mechanical algorithms (the last two columns of Table 29.2) present a similar picture of poor cross-method convergence. However, because the identical profile of GWBs was scored using holistic versus decomposed methods, such findings arguably speak even more directly to the very poor convergence that exists between the two judgment strategies. Using the maximum task rating within each rationally derived GWB category as the decomposed score, only 8 of 36 holistic-decomposed convergent validity *r* values are ≥.70 (18 of 36 are ≥.50); across all GWBs, the median convergent validity is only *r* = .50. Similarly disconcerting results are seen when using the mean rating in each GWB cluster as the decomposed score; here, only 10 of 36 *r* values are ≥.70 (22 of 36 are ≥.50), and the median convergent validity is only *r* = .58.

Thus, the factor analytic and mechanical algorithms for forming GWB scores demonstrate very disappointing levels of convergence with the holistic GWB ratings, falling well short of the level (or consistency) of similarity that would be required to justify a conclusion of rating method interchangeability. Although some of the lack of convergence for the factor-analytically derived dimensions and the direct holistic ratings may potentially be attributed to differences in the content of the GWBs themselves, this alternative explanation lacks plausibility with respect to the comparisons of holistic versus mechanically derived scores for an identical profile of GWB constructs.

CMQ Results

To obtain the factor analytically derived GWBs from the CMQ frequency ratings, the 189-by-189 reduced item correlation matrix was analyzed; the scree plot indicated breaks at 4, 9, and 15 factors, and the 15-factor solution was chosen on the basis of providing the most detailed listing. As in the insurance company factor analysis, this solution (explaining 85% of the total common variance) exhibits desirably low factor correlations (only one *r* > .30); Table 29.1 summarizes the factors (listings of the loadings are available from the authors), and Table 29.3 lists the convergent validities.

With respect to the qualitative agreement between the rational and factor analytic methods of identifying the GWB clusters, Tables 29.1 and 29.3 indicate that some degree of similarity exists between the category names identified by the different methods; in only a few cases do empirically derived factors have no analog in the rationally derived categories (e.g., *Patrol Activities*). However, as in the insurance inventory, the convergent validities indicate poor convergence between holistic versus decomposed GWB scores (see Table 29.3): only 2 of the 26 rationally identified, holistically rated GWBs correlate ≥ .70 with the empirically derived GWB factor scores, and only 11 of 26 have *r* values ≥.50. Viewed from the opposite perspective, only 2 of 15 empirically derived, factor analytically scored GWBs have *r* values ≥.70, and only 6 of 15 have *r* values ≥.50.

The results involving the two mechanical algorithms also reveal unacceptably low cross-method convergence. Using the mean rating within each rationally derived GWB category as the decomposed score, only 3 of 26 *r* values are ≥.70 (14 of 26 are ≥.50), with a median of only .52. Using the maximum rating as the decomposed score, only 3 of 26 *r* values are ≥.70 (9 of 26 are ≥.50), with median of only .42.

Table 29.3   Correlations Between Rationally and Empirically Derived Generalized Work Behaviors (GWBs) in the Common Metric Questionnaire (CMQ)

Empirically Derived Factor: CMQ Rationally Identified GWB Category	1	2	3	4	5	6	7	8	9	10	11	12	13	14	15	r mean	r max
1. Work in demanding personal situations	0.18	0.11	0.25	0.23	0.45	0.11	0.07	0.17	0.19	0.18	0.08	0.11	0.03	0.05	0.05	0.46	0.20
2. Have responsibility for the safety of others	0.03	0.48	0.44	0.50	0.31	0.15	−0.08	0.28	0.03	0.07	−0.17	−0.07	0.05	0.01	−0.14	0.66	0.68
3. Supervise other employees	0.40	0.10	0.10	0.08	0.15	0.59	0.24	0.03	0.11	−0.02	0.02	0.12	−0.09	0.09	−0.04	0.64	0.76
4. Contact people in your organization who do not have supervisory job duties	0.18	−0.06	0.04	0.06	0.22	0.11	0.21	0.03	0.19	0.19	0.39	0.06	0.16	0	0.05	0.25	0.21
5. Contact people in your organization who do have supervisory job duties	0.20	−0.05	0.02	0.05	0.18	0.13	0.23	0.03	0.19	0.16	0.36	0.08	0.13	0.01	0.04	0.24	0.22
6. Contact people outside your organization	0.21	−0.08	0.21	0.11	0.33	0.08	0.17	0	0.43	0.07	0.28	0.15	0.07	0.03	0.03	0.48	0.53
7. Attend meetings initiated by other people	0.45	−0.11	−0.06	0	0.14	0.21	0.32	0	0.24	0.08	0.37	0.24	0.29	0.03	0.09	0.54	0.48
8. Chair or initiate meetings	0.70	−0.11	−0.00	−0.03	0.06	0.33	0.31	−0.01	0.26	−0.04	0.22	0.31	0.15	0.09	0.03	0.71	0.67
9. Use written or spoken information	0.13	−0.05	0.05	0.09	0.18	0.08	0.16	0.01	0.10	0.17	0.38	0.05	0.12	−0.01	0.04	0.35	0.34
10. Use mathematics	0.11	−0.01	−0.09	0.12	0.13	0.06	0.14	0.07	0.13	0.19	0.42	0.07	0.22	0.03	0.01	0.51	0.44
11. Use information from machines, displays, or pictures	0.10	−0.02	−0.04	0.12	0.16	0.05	0.14	0.09	0.08	0.27	0.39	0.06	0.25	0	0.03	0.20	0.18
12. Use your senses (sight, hearing, taste, smell, touch)	0.06	0.12	0.07	0.31	0.19	0.06	0.11	0.11	0.05	0.31	0.24	0.01	0.12	−0.03	−0.02	0.36	0.35
13. Make decisions about financial resources	0.38	−0.05	−0.01	0.01	0.05	0.33	0.21	−0.03	0.26	−0.04	0.19	0.35	−0.01	0.13	0	0.49	0.41
14. Make decisions about other employees	0.42	0.03	0.16	0.11	0.18	0.55	0.24	0	0.19	0	0.03	0.16	−0.10	0.09	0.03	0.61	0.58
15. Make decisions about production processes	0.28	0.05	−0.09	0.11	0.01	0.36	0.14	0.07	0.07	0.10	0.07	0.23	0.16	0.05	0	0.41	0.37
16. Made decisions about long-term business strategies for the organization	0.31	0	0.03	0.02	0.06	0.34	0.18	0.01	0.20	−0.03	0.06	0.42	−0.02	0.20	0.03	0.44	0.34
17. Make precise or steady hand, arm, or finger movements	0.02	0.15	−0.04	0.17	0.07	0	0.02	0.13	0	0.57	0.18	0	0.10	0	0.03	0.60	0.57
18. Perform work requiring physical coordination	0.06	0.40	0.19	0.41	0.17	0.02	−0.03	0.26	0.02	0.43	0.02	−0.02	0.09	−0.03	−0.01	0.54	0.44
19. Perform work requiring physical strength or endurance	0.09	0.64	0.33	0.44	0.20	0.01	−0.12	0.39	0.02	0.27	−0.15	−0.05	0.01	0	0	0.68	0.17

continued

Table 29.3 Correlations Between Rationally and Empirically Derived Generalized Work Behaviors (GWBs) in the Common Metric Questionnaire (CMQ) (Continued)

Empirically Derived Factor: CMQ Rationally Identified GWB Category	1	2	3	4	5	6	7	8	9	10	11	12	13	14	15	r mean	r max
20. Use stationary machines	0.04	0	−0.17	0.05	0.05	0.04	0.13	0.05	0.04	0.35	0.25	0.03	0.11	0	0.08	0.32	0.27
21. Use handheld tools	0.01	0.52	0	0.31	0	0.03	−0.04	0.31	0.03	0.20	0.01	−0.02	0.18	0.01	−0.12	0.55	0.32
22. Use mobile tools or equipment	0.05	0.62	0.06	0.33	0.04	0.03	−0.07	0.39	0.01	0.14	−0.08	−0.04	0.14	0.03	−0.10	0.48	0.48
23. Drive or operate vehicles	0.05	0.41	0.51	0.31	0.15	0.05	−0.06	0.29	0.15	0	−0.03	0	0.14	−0.01	−0.28	0.71	0.82
24. Carry or use firearms or weapons	0	0.04	0.84	0.22	0.30	0.06	−0.10	0.13	0.13	0.03	−0.05	−0.08	−0.12	0.01	0.10	0.83	0.88
25. Work in an unpleasant physical environment	0.03	0.26	0.24	0.19	0.21	0.03	−0.03	0.48	0.07	0.13	0	−0.03	0.08	0.03	0.02	0.52	0.34
26. Work in a hazardous environment, or work at risk of physical injury	0.06	0.49	0.51	0.39	0.26	0.03	−0.16	0.47	0	0.11	−0.13	−0.10	0.03	0	−0.03	0.59	0.61

The r max and r mean columns report the convergent r's between each holistically rated GWB category and the empirically derived GWB scores using the maximum rating algorithm and mean rating algorithms, respectively; the remaining columns report the convergent validities between the holistic GWB ratings (rows) and the factor analytically derived decomposed scores (columns; factor names are listed in Table 29.1).

Thus, across two very large, independent samples of task- and common-metric data collected from hundreds of different jobs, direct holistic ratings of GWBs show clearly unacceptable levels of convergence with GWB scores derived via factor analytic and mechanical algorithms (in the latter case, with a one-to-one match of GWB categories across method). Because our samples are far larger and more diverse than those used in past studies (e.g., Butler & Harvey, 1988; Cornelius & Lyness, 1980; Gibson et al., 2007), the unacceptably low convergence that is again seen between holistic versus decomposed judgment strategies underscores our conclusion that direct holistic ratings of abstract GWB categories cannot be viewed as a JOA best practice (at least to the extent that one is concerned with being able to replicate the results that would be obtained if traditional decomposed judgment measurement strategies were used).

City Government Results

Of course, defenders of the holistic judgment method may still argue that the poor holistic-decomposed convergence seen in the above two samples was due to the fact that the somewhat different results produced using rational versus factor-analytic procedures for identifying the GWB categories (see Table 29.1) "stacked the deck" against finding strong convergent validities. Although such an explanation is totally implausible with respect to explaining away the similarly poor convergence seen for the mechanical algorithms, one might still argue that when rating the more specific items that were combined in the decomposed judgment method, the raters did not share the same "cognitive schema" held by the instrument developers regarding the item-to-GWB category linkages underlying the mechanical algorithms (i.e., because the items were not explicitly grouped in the surveys under their rationally identified GWB cluster).

To address this concern, we repeated the comparisons using data collected from the two city government samples. Here, identical numbers and names of the GWB categories were used (as in the mechanical algorithms above). Significantly, the raters were explicitly made aware of what the instrument developers perceived the item-to-GWB linkages to be (i.e., when rated, the tasks were grouped into clusters labeled with the name of the GWB category). Thus, if there is any validity to the claim that holistic versus decomposed job analysis ratings are capable of produce interchangeable results, these two task inventories provided an ideal setting for such agreement to occur.

Table 29.4 presents the holistic-decomposed GWB *r* values for the first city government; Table 29.5 presents the results for the second city. These results indicate that, even when (a) the substantive content of the abstract GWB categories is kept constant, (b) the same number of GWBs are rated, and (c) raters are explicitly aware of the linkages between the tasks and GWB categories, holistic versus decomposed procedures still diverge. Using the task-mean algorithm, in the first city only 9 of 28 GWBs have *r* values ≥ .70 (25 are ≥.50) and median = .64; in the second city, 9 of 29 *r* values are ≥.70 (22 are ≥.50) and median = .56.

Even lower convergence is seen using the maximum-rating algorithm: only 4 of 28 *r* values are ≥.70 in the first city (median = .59), and only 5 of 29 are ≥.70 of in the second (median = .55). Although the number of GWBs with convergent *r* values ≥.50 is higher in the two city governments than in the insurance company and CMQ samples, the important fact is that less than one-third of these GWB scales have even 50% of their variance in common! When one considers the fact that such correlations are not sensitive to absolute level-based differences between the GWB rating profiles, these findings further underscore the point that convergence levels between holistic versus decomposed judgment strategies fall far short of the level needed to argue that they produce interchangeable results.

Finally, we conducted exploratory factor analyses of the GWB profiles produced using holistic versus the mean-rating decomposed algorithm (given that the mean-rating algorithm tended to

Table 29.4   Holistic Versus Decomposed Generalized Work Behaviors (GWBs) Ratings Results From First City Government Inventory

Dimension	Number	r max	r mean	Holistic Factors				Decomposed Factors				
				1	2	3	4	1	2	3	4	5
1. Office activities	13	.63	.67		71					78		
2. Writing, completing reports	32	.64	.70	29	48		28	32		48	44	
3. Recordkeeping	68	.52	.52		87				29	69		
4. Verifying accuracy	21	.75	.69	30	65				43	66		
5. Computing/compiling information	19	.54	.55	34	61					58		
6. Financial activities	25	.17	.42	27	43					72		
7. Exchanging information	24	.43	.45		60			25	28	34	39	27
8. Dealing with the public	64	.55	.53		48			40	30	37	27	45
9. Inventory, supply, purchasing	13	.59	.65	41	38				37	27		
10. Measuring, drafting, printing	12	.59	.56	51			25	59				
11. Coordinating	10	.53	.57	74				83				
12. Planning, scheduling	26	.74	.70	81				89				
13. Supervising, monitoring, directing	48	.61	.70	77				84				
14. Policy/budget development	24	.64	.70	74				87				
15. Evaluating, analyzing, deciding	62	.42	.62	61				67		35		
16. Training/instructing	15	.64	.63	64	32			66	37			
17. Maintaining/updating job knowledge/skill	24	.48	.56	41	26	32			73			
18. Inspecting	19	.52	.64	46				47	24		28	
19. Investigating	33	.65	.68	26		59				87		
20. Patrol activities	24	.55	.81			83				96		
21. Judicial activities	15	.72	.84	27		47				41	51	
22. Humane activities	9	.64	.77			56				39		
23. Fire fighting	41	.68	.85		77				90			
24. First aid	17	.76	.86		84				92			
25. Machine/tool/equipment use	108	.41	.33	29	64	33			83			27
26. Operating vehicles	15	.69	.54			32	68					80
27. Maintaining/cleaning	63	.54	.62	27	64				33			62
28. Repairing/constructing	41	.51	.59		52							89

"Number" denotes the number of items used to form the decomposed GWB score; r mean and r max are the correlations between the holistic (computed as the mean and maximum task rating, respectively) and decomposed GWB scores; the remaining entries are factor loadings (decimals omitted, values of .25 and up listed) obtained from factoring the holistic and decomposed GWB ratings.

produce higher convergence with the holistic ratings); the results are summarized in Tables 29.4 and 29.5. These analyses were not performed in the insurance and CMQ samples because their factor analytically derived GWB scores show very low levels of factor correlation and are thus poor candidates for a second-order factor analysis.

The results in Tables 29.4 and 29.5 indicate that the holistic versus decomposed methods for scoring GWBs produce factor structures that differ in terms of (a) the number of factors (sharp breaks are present in the eigenvalues for both the holistic and decomposed data, but they occur at different numbers of factors, with the decomposed methods consistently producing more factors); and (b) the patterns of factor loadings (although some similarities are seen, there are numerous points of difference). For example, in the first city, holistic Factor 3 has a somewhat similar pattern

Table 29.5   Holistic Versus Decomposed Generalized Work Behaviors (GWBs) Ratings Results From Second City Government Inventory

GWB Label	Holistic Factors								Decomposed Factors						
	Number	r max	r mean	1	2	3	4	5	1	2	3	4	5	6	7
1. Office activities	17	.61	.64	71									76		
2. Writing, completing reports	44	.45	.50	87									74		
3. Recordkeeping	26	.50	.45	73	35							55	38		
4. Verifying accuracy	19	.55	.51	76								69			
5. Computing, compiling information	13	.45	.44	70								81			
6. Financial activities	12	.58	.56	50								80			
7. Exchanging information	26	.23	.29	45	29	33			27		28		64		
8. Dealing with the public	22	.43	.43	36	47	25			33	60					
9. Information processing	11	.57	.54	59	42				25				41	51	
10. Supplies, purchasing	5	.50	.54		44		29		47				31		34
11. Measuring, drawing, drafting, printing	5	.34	.40		31	39							47		
12. Coordinating	8	.44	.57	79						58			26		
13. Planning, scheduling	17	.68	.59	75						86					
14. Supervising, monitoring, directing	19	.71	.80	77						83					
15. Policy, budget development	17	.61	.71	79						56			54		
16. Evaluating, analyzing, deciding	52	.44	.53	26	54	29			26	50	26		30		
17. Training, instructing	8	.57	.57		52				28	75					
18. Maintaining, updating job knowledge, skills	16	.54	.44	52	30					81					
19. External contacts	11	.57	.53	50	45					64					
20. Inspecting	19	.37	.57	1	36	32					29		57		
21. Investigating	25	.48	.76	3	73						87				
22. Patrol activities	18	.61	.81	11	85						93				
23. Judicial activities	11	.75	.82	13	48						61				
24. Humane activities	10	.48	.55	-3	46						26				
25. Firefighting	42	.84	.93	3				91	96						
26. First aid	9	.80	.91	1				89	97						
27. Using machines, tools, equipment, vehicles	45	.44	.26	20			73		59				25		35
28. Maintaining, cleaning	33	.60	.71	15			81		25	61					52
29. Repairing, constructing	38	.70	.81	14			78								83

"Number" denotes the number of items used to form the decomposed GWB score; r mean and r max are the correlations between the holistic (computed as the mean and maximum task rating, respectively) and decomposed GWB scores; the remaining entries are factor loadings (decimals omitted, values of .25 and up listed) obtained from factoring the holistic and decomposed GWB ratings.

of high-loading items to decomposed Factor 5; however, the substantive interpretation of these factors is different (in the holistic data, the factor is defined by firefighting and paramedic activities, whereas in the decomposed data, the factor is defined by machine-, tool-, and equipment-related activities).

To quantify this subjective comparison of factor structures, correlations between the factor score estimates computed for the holistic versus decomposed GWB factors are presented in Table 29.6. These results indicate that although some degree of similarity in the factors underlying the GWB scores exists for the holistic versus decomposed methods, the factors are by no means functionally interchangeable. Across both cities, only one comparison approaches the level at which one might begin to discuss interchangeability: in the second city, the firefighting factors (decomposed 1, holistic 5) correlate $r = .92$. However, many points of difference are still present: for example, in the first city, decomposed Factor 5 does not correlate appreciably with any of the holistic factors. Thus, although broad areas of similarity exist between the factors produced by analyzing the holistic versus decomposed GWB score profiles, the solutions are far from interchangeable.

Implications for Holistic Methods of Rating Job Characteristics

Across four separate instruments rated by over 8,000 incumbents holding hundreds of different jobs, the results presented above amply demonstrate that rational/holistic versus empirical/decomposed methods do *not* produce interchangeable results: (a) rational versus empirical procedures for deriving GWB clusters produced qualitatively divergent results in many instances; and (b) holistic ratings of abstract GWB clusters demonstrated poor convergent validity with ratings produced via decomposed methods (even when the linkage between items and GWB

Table 29.6   Correlations Between Factor Scores Computed From Holistic Versus Decomposed Generalized Work Behaviors (GWBs) Data

First City Government				
	1	2	3	4
1	79	24	09	05
2	17	15	83	04
3	49	60–	08	01
4	38	21	06	79
5–	15–	09	36	09

Second City Government				
	1	2	3	4	5
1	10	15	18	33	92
2	26	73	08	08	05
3	22	09	81	−14	−03
4	52	24	−09	−16	−14
5	68	35	22	08	17
6	35	61	26	02	07
7	−17	05	−10	75	32

Entries are the correlations between the factor scores computed by factoring the holistic (columns) versus decomposed (rows) GWB scores.

clusters was explicit). Clearly, JOA practitioners cannot simply skip the necessity of conducting a detailed job analysis based on the hope that holistic ratings will yield functionally interchangeable results.

The explanation we offer for the above findings is simple, and it has direct implications for our best practices recommendations: that is, the task of holistically rating abstract, hypothetical, job activity constructs (as well as the personal trait requirements of jobs) is far too complex for humans to perform well, regardless of their familiarity with the job or rating instrument. As Cornelius and Lyness (1980, p. 156) noted, "the limitations in human information processing ability have been well documented" by decades of basic research in decision making (e.g., Dawes & Corrigan, 1974; Miller, 1956). Our results significantly extend past JOA research (e.g., Butler & Harvey, 1988; DeNisi & Shaw, 1977; Gibson et al., 2007) by firmly establishing the generalizability of earlier findings and again demonstrating that the general laws that govern decision making apply equally to the special case of making job analysis judgments.

In particular, in light of the consistently poor convergence that has been seen in head-to-head comparisons of holistic versus decomposed JOA ratings, we conclude that calls from some applied psychologists (e.g., Cornelius et al., 1984; Sackett et al., 1981) to modify the regulatory guidelines and best practice recommendations to allow holistic ratings to substitute for detailed job analyses are fundamentally misguided. For example, Cornelius et al. (1984) offered several sweeping conclusions:

> Simple holistic job classification judgments perform as well as (if not better than) the elaborate statistical procedure. It is clear that direct job classification judgments from supervisors and incumbents are at least as accurate as the statistical procedure outlined above. This finding has potential legal and practical ramifications.... In truth, if it were not for today's legal climate, a study of this sort might not be necessary. However,... an analysis of court cases and government selection guidelines indicates that the type of holistic job classification judgment we used would most likely be considered by many to be indefensible legally. There is an apparent emphasis in the legal arena for detailed, task-oriented job analysis data when making personnel decisions (Thompson & Thompson, 1982).... Although this detailed job analysis information may be useful for other purposes, it is "quantitative overkill" if the purpose is to make a job classification decision for selection purposes.... Contrary to the evidence presented above, complex, task-based or behavior-based procedures may be required to satisfy government guidelines and/or judges in EEO cases.... Recent findings on the robustness of aptitude test validity, as well as the Sackett et al. (1981) finding regarding the utility of global judgments indicates such requirements are scientifically and professionally unnecessary.... This means that professional and legal criteria for conducting job analyses are at odds. (pp. 255–258)

We could not disagree more strongly. Indeed, serious questions can be raised regarding the adequacy, robustness, generalizability, relevance, and interpretation of the findings from the two studies that formed the basis for such conclusions. The Sackett et al. (1981) study examined eight foreman job titles in a chemical plant and compared the clusters of jobs to job families obtained by analyzing (a) detailed ratings of each job on 237 tasks versus (b) single-item holistic judgments of similarity between all possible pairs of titles by 15 foremen and 17 supervisors. Both methods suggested that the eight foreman titles be grouped into four clusters.

Cornelius et al. (1984) asked raters to judge 39 GWB task clusters and 26 worker ability traits, then make a single-item holistic judgment classifying the job in question into one of four possible clusters. The main comparison of interest involved the agreement between the cluster predicted from a discriminant analysis (predicting the raters' holistic job cluster judgment from the quantitative profiles of GWB and trait ratings) versus the holistic judgment made by a separate panel of "five people who were experts in all the jobs" (p. 251) classifying each job into a cluster. Results indicated that the classification predicted by the discriminant analysis agreed with the holistic "expert" classifications in 90% of jobs using GWB predictors and 72% using ability trait ratings.

Both of these studies arguably suffer from serious shortcomings. First, they examined only a small number of relatively distinct families (i.e., Maintenance, Security, Production, or General; Maintenance, Operations, Laboratory, or Miscellaneous), making the task of holistically sorting a job into one of these clusters relatively straightforward and raising obvious concerns regarding the generalizability of their results to other settings (especially ones with larger numbers of families or less obvious job-to-family relations).

Second, as Cornelius et al. (1984) acknowledged:

> Some readers of this paper may feel that [the above results] are trivial in nature. That is, it might appear to some that incumbents obviously should be able to classify job titles into one of four occupational categories with a high degree of accuracy (after all, shouldn't holistic judgments by incumbents predict holistic judgments by job experts?). (p. 256)

We agree, and we stress the inherent circularity and inadequacy of using the holistic judgments of one group of subject matter experts (SMEs) as the criterion by which to "validate" the holistic judgments of a second group. Although lack of agreement raises concerns (i.e., at least one group must be wrong), even perfect agreement has little or no probative value (i.e., both may be wrong) given the total absence of an independent criterion of cluster membership in the Cornelius et al. (1984) study.

Third, a closer inspection of the Cornelius et al. (1984) results serious questions regarding the quality of their holistic judgments. That is, in their Table 1, median cross-rater profile correlations (which are primarily sensitive only to profile shape, not elevation) when rating the abstract GWB clusters were disturbingly low (r = .56 to .69), and even lower for the ability traits (.48 to .53). Although Cornelius et al. considered these methods to represent "an elaborate quantitative procedure" (p. 247) for describing jobs, both the GWB-cluster and ability-trait rating tasks would be considered holistic judgment strategies under our definition.

Although such findings raise fundamental questions regarding ratings quality, the fact that such low levels of interrater agreement were obtained (which would likely have been even lower using level-sensitive agreement indices) hardly comes as a surprise, as they are quite consistent with the poor interrater agreement levels seen for holistic ratings of work- and worker-trait constructs in other settings (e.g., Butler & Harvey, 1988; DeNisi & Shaw, 1974; Harvey & Hollander, 2002). Thus, instead of offering convincing proof that best practice recommendations and legal regulations relevant to collecting and using JOA data must be revised to allow or promote the use of holistic judgment procedures, in our assessment the Cornelius et al. (1984) and Sackett et al. (1981) studies are primarily useful by providing further data documenting the disturbingly low cross-rater agreement (and by implication, ratings quality/accuracy) typically seen when abstract traits are rated directly using single-item judgments.

In sum, given the clearly demonstrated *lack* of convergence in head-to-head comparisons between holistic versus decomposed judgments (especially in the large, four-sample study reported above), we conclude that it is extremely unlikely that researchers will ever succeed in developing a holistic rating strategy that can produce data that are functionally interchangeable with those obtained via decomposed judgment methods rating observable, verifiable work characteristics. We recommend that researchers and practitioners accept this fact and instead focus on developing ways to achieve efficiencies when collecting ratings of detailed, verifiable work characteristics (e.g., via increased automation, adaptive item administration, and refinement of standardized job inventories).

Alternative Views Regarding the Future of Holistic Ratings: A Rebuttal

As was noted above, some authors (e.g., Cornelius et al., 1984; Pearlman, 1980; Sackett et al., 1981) have argued in favor of increased use of holistic ratings in job analysis. In response to the points made above, proponents of the holistic approach might well counter that the reason we found low convergence between holistic and decomposed ratings in the four-sample study reported above was that single-item scales suffer from reliability problems that restrict their ability to correlate with other scores, including the decomposed judgment based GWBs (e.g., Geyer & Hunter, 1992). That is, according to classical test theory, because multiple item ratings are typically combined to form the abstract composite score in decomposed judgment strategies (except in the maximum-rating mechanical algorithm case we examined), such composites will unavoidably be more reliable than a single-item holistic scale.

One strategy advanced by proponents of holistic ratings to improve their low inherent reliability involves the use of multiple raters, averaging the results to form the holistic estimate of an abstract trait. That is, using the same Spearman-Brown Prophecy Formula type of argument (but substituting raters for items), Geyer and Hunter (1992) claimed that "if we use enough raters, we can always reduce the error of measurement to any desired level" (p. 37). Thus, regardless of how poor quality the single-item holistic job ratings produced by a given rater may be, if a large number of them are averaged for each rated trait, holistic rating proponents contend that measurement errors will cancel out and the best estimate of "truth" will emerge. Thus, under this view, the holistic approach to rating jobs could be salvaged by simply using more raters (e.g., see Fleishman & Mumford, 1991; Fleishman & Reilly, 1992; Fleishman et al., 1995).

We reject this argument based on the tenuousness of its assumptions. That is, one must assume the following:

1. "Error varies randomly" (Geyer & Hunter, 1992, p. 33) across raters who make holistic job ratings.
2. Distributions of rating errors (i.e., all deviations between the holistic ratings and the "true" score for the rated position or job in question) are symmetric, normal, and mean deviation (i.e., so the average observed score would be an unbiased estimate of the "true" score and standard confidence interval formulas could be used).
3. The standard error of measurement (SEM) is constant across the range of scale values (i.e., so a single SEM can be used to set confidence intervals around any observed score average).
4. A "true" score actually exists for each holistically rated trait (many of which are in fact hypothetical constructs that are both unobserved and unobservable).
5. Every rater is capable of knowing—to at least to some degree—the "true" level of each underlying trait being rated (i.e., all raters have some "true" variance in addition to their random errors of measurement).

If any of these assumptions are violated—and there are numerous reasons for believing that they would be violated when raters serve as the multiple "items" of a test (see Harvey, 1992)—even if an infinite number of flawed ratings were averaged the resulting score would still not provide an unbiased estimate of the "true" score. Ironically, even if one is comfortable in making these questionable assumptions regarding the sources of variance in holistic job ratings, literally dozens—if not hundreds—of raters might be required before holistic GWB reliability estimates would reach appropriate levels. Thus, despite being highly questionable in terms of its required assumptions, the multiple-rater approach to improve the quality of holistic approach might not actually save any expense relative to judging multiple items in a decomposed rating task (i.e., due to the large numbers of job-knowledgeable raters required).

An alternative argument in favor of the utility of holistic ratings might instead cite the Geyer and Hunter (1992) claim that job analysis ratings need not be highly reliable to be useful. This argument was advanced to discount the poor reliability estimates seen for many of the holistic DOT worker-trait scales (e.g., Cain & Green, 1983; Geyer et al., 1989; Webb et al., 1981). That is, Geyer and Hunter claimed that holistic ratings are useful as long as they represent an improvement over having absolutely no information regarding the job (i.e., any reliability >0). As Geyer and Hunter (1992) put it, "even a reliability as low as .25 can mean a substantial improvement over guessing at the level of a job characteristic" (p. 31). Presumably, such reasoning could be cited to argue that GWB ratings need not converge strongly with more detailed methods, as long as they met the "better than guessing" standard.

We reject this argument as well, as it can easily be demonstrated (e.g., Harvey, 1992, pp. 32–35) that even when reliabilities are in the .70s, the confidence intervals around individual ratings can be so large that even 2- and 3-point differences (on a 5-point scale) between jobs cannot confidently be viewed as "real" differences. The advisory panel's interim report concluded that DOT ratings "must have a high degree of reliability and validity" and "identify major dimensions of occupations [using] scales that measure these dimensions following acceptable psychometric practices" (APDOT, p. 10591). We agree and suggest that this standard be applied to all methods of rating abstract job or worker characteristics.

Proponents of holistic ratings have also raised philosophical questions regarding the use of detailed job analysis methods as the standard against which holistic ratings are judged (e.g., Sanchez & Levine, 2000). That is, what proof exists that decomposed methods are any more valid than holistic ones, if it is effectively impossible to define a "gold standard" of accuracy to serve as a criterion?

In response (e.g., see Harvey & Wilson, 2000), we stress that decomposed-judgment methods rate jobs using items that possess an intrinsically high (i.e., tasks, specific GWB task clusters) or moderate (i.e., moderately abstract GWB task clusters) degree of behavioral specificity. By design, these methods describe observable, behavioral aspects of jobs that ought to be capable of being independently verified by SMEs. Thus, interrater agreement among independent SMEs provides evidence of the accuracy of individual decomposed job ratings (e.g., Harvey, 1991a; Schmitt, 1987). In contrast, holistic methods rate vague abstractions (i.e., constructs) that cannot be observed directly.

Accordingly, construct validity or similar strategies must be used to evaluate holistic ratings, and even demonstrations of high interrater agreement among SMEs offer only necessary—but not sufficient—evidence of their accuracy or validity (see Harvey & Wilson, 2000). Although scores on abstract GWBs produced via decomposed judgment methods cannot be guaranteed to be accurate, if done properly the underlying item ratings from which they are derived can be independently verified; such scores represent the only viable standard against which holistic ratings can be compared and evaluated. When judged against that standard, the results presented above are in complete agreement with those from past studies (e.g., Butler & Harvey, 1988; Gibson et al., 2007) in indicating that when a true head-to-head comparison is made, and direct holistic ratings are compared against scores for the same GWB traits produced via decomposed judgment from ratings of verifiable work content, the convergence levels do not even begin to approach the degree necessary to conclude that the methods produce interchangeable results.

Section Summary

The maxim that "there is no such thing as a free lunch" is clearly applicable to the question of holistic versus decomposed judgment. It reflects the fact that, in many cases, the only way to achieve dramatic reductions in cost is to sacrifice something else of value in the process. The results presented above show that the price that is paid for reducing JOA costs via holistic ratings is poor convergence with GWB scores produced by detailed rating methods and a near total inability to independently verify or document the accuracy and quality of the holistic ratings. Especially for HR applications that may be subjected to EEO scrutiny, we view this tradeoff to be fundamentally ill advised.

WHAT SOURCES OF INFORMATION AND DATA REVIEW/ VERIFICATION PROCEDURES SHOULD BE USED?

This section focuses on the second big-picture challenge facing job analysts—*Who* should you ask to provide JOA ratings and under what conditions should the information be collected? Obviously, lengthy chapters (e.g., Harvey, 1991a) or entire books could be written on just this question, so in the space we have available we will focus on providing a brief overview of the issues that arise when different rating sources produce divergent results and present the results of an empirical study that illustrates the significant degree to which such disagreements may be common in practice.

The Problem

Given that JOA ratings provide the foundation for many critical personnel decisions (e.g., performance appraisal, selection, training), the general lack of research attention or coverage in professional standards documents is surprising (e.g., Schmitt, 1987). In terms of the critical issue of who should provide job analysis data, the Society for Industrial and Organizational Psychology (1987) stated only that "sources of job information should be credible" and that "whatever job analysis method is used, it should be used carefully" (p. 5). The American Psychological Association standards and federal *Uniform Guidelines* are even less specific.

The general lack of concern that seems to exist regarding the question of which types of raters represent the best sources of JOA ratings is all the more surprising in view of the fact that the few research studies that examined this question show that job incumbents often disagree significantly among themselves (Stutzman, 1983), they rate as applicable items that we know are not part of the job (Green & Stutzman, 1986), they tend to give higher ratings than job analysts (Smith & Hakel, 1979), and they frequently disagree with their supervisors regarding both the tasks that are applicable and the ratings they should receive (e.g., Hazel, Madden, & Christal, 1964; Meyer, 1959).

Although some studies have concluded that incumbent characteristics do not exert an undue impact on JOA ratings (e.g., Conley & Sackett, 1987; Wexley & Silverman, 1978), the correctness and generalizability of such conclusions are open to debate. For example, other studies flatly contradict that conclusion (e.g., Mullins & Kimbrough, 1988), and the two studies cited above examined only a single job title. Additionally, in the case of Wexley and Silverman, the highly abstract JOA questionnaire examined in that study arguably bears little similarity to the standard task (e.g., Christal, 1974), GWB (e.g., Cunningham et al., 19882; Harvey, 1991b; McCormick et al., 1972), or ability-oriented (e.g., Fleishman, 1992) survey instruments commonly used in practice.

In sum, considerable evidence exists to indicate that the typical sources of JOA ratings (particularly job incumbents and their supervisors) may disagree substantially regarding the JOA results that they produce when rating the same target position or job. This begs several questions, including how should JOA practitioners decide which source(s) to use, and when rating sources disagree, what should be done? In an attempt to shed further light on these issues, we conducted a study to examine the degree of similarity that exists between incumbent versus supervisor ratings of task inventory items, using a much more diverse collection of titles than is typically studied.

AN EMPIRICAL DEMONSTRATION

First, in terms of hypotheses, because Smith and Hakel (1979) found consistent elevation differences only when comparing incumbents and supervisors versus job analysts, we expected that consistent over- or underrating effects (operationalized as a high percentage of agreed non-DNA tasks being rated higher by the incumbent or supervisor, respectively) would not occur when comparing incumbents versus supervisors. Although we of course cannot say per se which source is the more accurate one when incumbents and supervisors disagree, with respect to defining an arbitrary point of reference for determining the direction or sign of the rating differences, we chose the supervisor's rating as the reference point.

However, based on Hazel et al. (1964) and Meyer (1959), we expected to see some degree of disagreement involving both under- and overrating within each job (again, defining these using the supervisory rating as the reference point). We quantified over- and underrating by computing (a) the percentage of agreed-applicable tasks (i.e., ones for which both the incumbent and supervisor rated the task as being non-DNA) on which the incumbent and supervisor differed in the level-based rating given (as a way of quantifying the *extent* of ratings differences), and (b) mean differences in ratings given by the two sources for such disputed (but agreed-applicable) tasks (as a way of quantifying the *magnitude* of the differences).

Second, based on Hazel et al. (1964) and Meyer (1959), it was predicted that incumbents and supervisors would disagree regarding a job's task makeup at the DNA versus non-DNA level. This binary type of agreement was operationalized as the following:

- Percentage task overlap (termed *percent tasks-in-common* by Christal, 1974), a statistic that ranges from 0% (no agreement on which tasks are DNA versus non-DNA) to 100% (perfect agreement as to which tasks apply, ignoring the *degree* to which they apply)
- Percentage *false-present* tasks (tasks that supervisors rated DNA and incumbents rated non-DNA, using as denominator the number of incumbent non-DNA tasks)
- Percentage *false-DNA* (the opposite of false-present, using as denominator the number of supervisor non-DNA tasks)

Percentage false-present values operationalized contamination, whereas false-DNAs indexed deficiency; obviously, percentage task overlap is sensitive to both effects.

Third, mean ratings given false-present and false-DNA tasks were calculated to facilitate interpretation of the false-present and false-DNA percentages. That is, although some disagreement between incumbents and supervisors was considered to be likely, from a practitioner's standpoint it would clearly be preferable if such disagreements would be confined to relatively unimportant tasks (i.e., those receiving low time-spent ratings). In contrast, serious content-validity concerns would result to the extent that tasks receiving higher ratings (e.g., a score of at least 2 or 3 on a 1–5 scale) were falsely included or excluded.

Fourth, it was predicted that incumbent-supervisor disagreements would occur primarily on jobs that are relatively uncomplicated in nature and/or tend to have less verbally sophisticated incumbents (e.g., *Laborer, Custodian*). That is, on a long task inventory, less verbally skilled incumbents may produce incorrect ratings due to failure to understand directions or fully comprehend the meaning of individual task statements. For simpler jobs, incumbents may also be tempted to embellish their responsibilities to make their work appear more responsible; this tendency may be further exacerbated on long inventories, in which a high percentage of tasks are truly DNA (i.e., to enhance the apparent importance of the minority of tasks that apply).

Method

A total of 59 incumbent-supervisor dyads were used in the study; these represented all of the single-incumbent titles present in a larger sample of 131 positions that were studied as part of a job analysis project conducted in a small southwestern municipal government (i.e., the "first city government" sample used in the holistic versus decomposed study reported in the previous section). Single-incumbent titles were chosen in order to eliminate any potential ambiguities that might result when multiple incumbents in a job reported to a given supervisor. That is, when a supervisor has only one incumbent to supervise in a given job, there cannot be any ambiguity as to which position's activities are being described. JOA ratings were collected for the purpose of redesigning the city's performance appraisal and compensation systems; raters were aware of these purposes. A listing of the titles is presented in Table 29.7.

Instrument and Rating Process

The job analysis questionnaire consisted of three parts (only the first of which was used here) arranged in the following order: (a) an 886-item task inventory, organized into 28 GWB/duty areas, (b) a section in which the 28 duties were listed and rated holistically, and (c) the 153-item JEI (Harvey et al., 1988). A 6-point relative time spent (RTS) scale from McCormick (1976) was used: "Compared with other tasks I spend ___ on this task," with anchors of 0 = *no time*, 1 = *much less time*, 2 = *less time*, 3 = *about the same time*, 4 = *more time*, and 5 = *much more time*. Responses to the inventory were recorded on optical scanning forms.

The incumbent task inventory ratings were obtained by having raters read the questionnaire, check all tasks they performed, rate tasks that applied using the RTS scale, and record responses on the answer sheets. A 100% return rate was achieved; the inventory was completed on company time in approximately 2 hours. Supervisory ratings were obtained by presenting immediate supervisors with the following information, grouped by duty: (a) tasks rated as applicable, sorted in descending order of the incumbent ratings, followed by (b) DNA tasks.

Ratings considered by the supervisor to be incorrect were noted, and the supervisor made what he or she felt was the appropriate rating. This review process was done in a group setting and took 3 hours. Although this technique is obviously not the same as having supervisors independently complete the entire survey for each subordinate's position (and the possibility that the two procedures might lead to different ratings cannot be ruled out), this approach was taken because it most closely approximates the best practices procedure we recommend (see below) in actual practice (i.e., an accuracy review, as opposed to a blind re-rating process that could both take longer and be less well-received by the supervisors being asked to perform the verification function).

Results

Table 29.7 summarizes the comparisons computed between incumbent versus supervisor task ratings. In terms of the hypothesis that modest over- or underrating effects would occur on agreed-applicable tasks, the results in Table 29.7 are supportive. Inspection of the percentage of tasks rated higher (overrating) or lower (underrating) by incumbents (and the associated mean differences for these tasks) indicates that although the averages across jobs are not overwhelming in number (i.e., approximately 2% of tasks were over- or underrated), there is wide variation across jobs.

Although it is difficult to specify how many tasks must be involved before a significant practical problem can be said to exist, some jobs had many overrated tasks (e.g., *Captain/Police*, 33%, M difference = 1.8; *Crew Leader/Parks*, 11%, M = 1.0; *Equipment Operator/Limb Truck*, 21%, M = 1.3; *Equipment Operator/Streets*, 9%, M = 3.0) and underrated tasks (e.g., *City Secretary*, 10%, M = 1.9; *Director of Operations*, 23%, M = 1.6). Thus, at least for a nontrivial subset of job titles

Table 29.7   Summary Statistics for Task Agreement

| | | | | Over | | | False | | | |
| | N. Tasks | Lap | | High | | Low | | Present | | DNA |
Job Title	Inc.	Sup	%	%	M	%	M	%	M	%	M
Accountant/Jr Accts	116	116	93	3	1.5	0	0.0	3	3.0	3	2.5
Accountant/Jr EDP	98	102	94	1	1.0	0	0.0	1	3.0	5	2.6
Accountant/Jr Payroll	55	65	82	4	2.0	0	0.0	2	4.0	20	2.3
Assistant Mgr/Park	195	196	98	0	0.0	0	0.0	1	3.0	1	2.5
Capt/Police	253	209	76	33	1.8	0	0.0	21	2.3	4	1.2
Cashier/Head	99	107	93	1	1.0	0	0.0	0	0.0	8	1.5
Chief Building Ins	380	401	95	0	0.0	0	0.0	0	0.0	8	1.5
Chief/Fire	225	245	92	1	1.5	0	0.0	0	0.0	9	1.1
Chief/Police	151	185	82	0	0.0	0	0.0	0	0.0	23	1.4
City Manager	153	157	95	0	0.0	7	1.3	1	1.0	4	1.5
City Secretary	87	134	65	0	0.0	10	1.9	0	0.0	54	1.5
Code Compliance Off	135	166	80	1	2.0	3	2.5	1	2.0	24	2.5
Coord/Asst Sr/ Svc	98	102	94	1	1.0	3	1.0	1	2.0	5	1.0
Coord/Sr. Services	199	204	98	0	0.0	4	1.0	0	0.0	3	1.2
Court Clerk	162	174	90	0	0.0	0	0.0	2	1.0	9	1.2
Court Clerk/Asst	85	96	89	0	0.0	0	0.0	0	0.0	13	1.7
Crew Chief/Solid Waste	31	46	67	3	2.0	0	0.0	0	0.0	48	1.3
Crew Chief/Streets	58	81	70	0	0.0	0	0.0	2	1.0	41	1.8
Crew Chief/Waste Water	119	157	75	1	1.0	8	1.7	1	2.0	33	2.4
Crew Leader/Parks	36	66	55	11	1.0	3	1.0	0	0.0	83	1.4
Custodian/City Hall	31	36	63	0	0.0	0	0.0	16	3.0	32	3.2
Custodian/Park	133	115	85	2	2.0	0	0.0	14	2.2	1	2.0
Custodian/Comm Bldg	98	105	88	4	1.3	1	1.0	3	1.7	10	1.4
Detective	218	246	89	2	1.2	2	1.3	0	0.0	13	1.0
Detective Sgt	277	291	95	3	1.0	0	0.0	0	1.0	5	1.1
Director/Administer	175	191	92	0	0.0	0	0.0	0	0.0	9	1.1
Director/Operations	236	244	94	0	0.0	23	1.6	1	1.3	5	2.0
Equipment Op/Limb	14	24	52	21	1.3	0	0.0	7	2.0	79	1.2
Equipment Op/Sweeper	27	34	69	4	3.0	0	0.0	7	2.0	79	1.2
Equipment Op/Streets	47	63	64	9	3.0	0	0.0	7	3.0	33	2.1
Equipment Op/Waste W	60	101	59	0	0.0	0	0.0	0	0.0	68	2.9
Firefighter/2	218	206	91	5	2.3	0	0.0	7	2.1	2	1.0
Finance Director/Dpty	139	139	100	0	0.0	0	0.0	0	0.0	0	0.0
Foreman/Streets	219	232	94	2	1.8	3	1.5	0	4.0	6	1.4
Foreman/Waste Water	282	284	98	0	2.0	0	1.0	1	3.0	1	3.5
Foreman/Solid Waste	213	228	93	1	1.0	3	1.0	0	1.0	8	1.1
Game Room Attendant	40	29	35	3	2.0	0	0.0	55	2.6	28	1.4
Heavy Equipment Oper	16	59	27	0	0.0	0	0.0	0	0.0	269	2.1
Laborer/Waste Water	57	95	55	0	0.0	4	1.0	5	2.3	72	2.0
Laborer/Water	148	157	89	5	2.0	0	0.0	3	1.8	9	2.5
Lt/Inspection	215	225	82	1	1.3	0	0.0	8	2.6	13	2.0
Lt/Police	170	205	83	0	0.0	5	1.3	0	0.0	21	1.3

Table 29.7 Summary Statistics for Task Agreement (Continued)

Job Title	N. Tasks Inc.	Lap Sup	%	Over High %	M	Low %	M	False Present %	M	DNA %	M
Manager/Park	261	270	97	0	0.0	0	0.0	0	0.0	3	2.3
Manager/Community Bldg	191	231	82	0	0.0	0	0.0	1	2.0	21	1.4
Manager/Personnel	105	123	82	0	0.0	2	1.5	2	3.0	19	1.3
Mechanic	64	60	94	0	0.0	2	4.0	6	1.0	0	0.0
Meter Reader	5	23	22	0	0.0	0	0.0	0	0.0	360	3.5
Office Clerk	62	67	74	2	2.0	6	1.3	11	2.0	19	1.3
Office Manager Inspect	127	141	90	0	0.0	0	0.0	0	0.0	11	2.3
Operations Expeditor	56	72	75	4	1.5	2	1.0	2	2.0	30	1.5
Records Secretary	78	82	93	0	0.0	12	1.1	1	1.0	6	1.4
School Crossing Guard	109	58	52	0	0.0	1	4.0	48	1.0	1	3.0
Secretary/Admin	61	71	86	0	0.0	0	0.0	0	0.0	16	1.0
Secretary/Comm	70	115	61	0	0.0	11	1.6	0	0.0	64	1.2
Secretary/Personnel	104	112	86	13	1.7	1	1.0	4	2.3	12	1.2
Secretary/Receptionist	47	49	92	2	1.0	2	2.0	2	3.0	6	1.3
Supervisor/Utility	196	247	79	0	0.0	12	1.3	0	0.0	26	2.3
Superintendent/Pub Wk	238	249	91	1	1.5	2	1.5	3	1.8	7	2.6
Superintendent/Utility	186	287	65	0	0.0	5	1.2	0	0.0	54	2.6
Mean	131	145	80	2.4	0.8	2.3	0.7	4.3	1.3	30	1.7
Median	116	123	86	0.0	1.0	0.0	0.0	1.0	1.0	12	1.5
S	82	85	18	5.5	0.9	4.2	0.9	9.9	1.2	58	0.7
Q3–Q1	136	138	24	3.0	1.5	3.0	1.2	3.0	2.2	27	1.1

N. Tasks Inc. = number rated applicable by incumbent; N. Tasks Sup. = number rated applicable by supervisor; Overlap % = percentage task overlap between supervisor and incumbent profiles (computed as number of tasks rated applicable by both divided by (number rated by incumbent + number rated by supervisor − number in common); High % = percentage of agreed-performed tasks rated higher by incumbent; High M = mean incumbent-supervisor difference on tasks rated higher by incumbent; Low % = percentage of agreed-applicable tasks rated lower by incumbent; Low M = difference on tasks rated lower; False-present % = percentage of tasks falsely rated present by incumbent; False-present M = incumbent's mean rating of false-present tasks; DNA = does not apply; False DNA % = percentage of tasks falsely rated DNA by incumbent; False DNA M = supervisor's mean rating given to false DNA tasks; Q3–Q1 = interquartile range.

in this organization, the task-based job analysis results changed appreciably as a result of the supervisory review.

Our second hypothesis predicted that incumbents and supervisors would disagree when deciding which tasks are performed (as opposed to the level at which they are performed); the results in Table 29.7 support this prediction. Regarding contamination (i.e., falsely indicating that tasks are performed) incumbents made an average of 4.3% false-present ratings, giving an average rating of 1.3 to these tasks. At an overall level, these results might appear to suggest that contamination is not a serious problem, particularly because the disputed tasks received relatively low average ratings. However, an inspection of the results for individual jobs reveals high variability, with some titles exhibiting levels of false-present ratings that are unacceptable by any standard (e.g., *Police Captain*, 21%, $M = 2.3$; *Custodian/City Hall*, 16%, $M = 3.0$; *Game Room Attendant*, 55%, $M = 2.6$).

In terms of deficiency (i.e., giving DNA ratings to tasks that supervisors consider applicable), the results in Table 29.7 are even more disconcerting. At an overall level, incumbents gave DNA ratings to an average of 30% of tasks their supervisors considered to be part of the job (M supervisory rating = 1.7). Again, considerable variability was present, with many titles exhibiting false-DNA levels far in excess of the group averages (e.g., *Jr. Accountant/Payroll*, 20%, M = 2.3; *Crew Chief/Waste Water*, 33%, M = 2.4; *Equipment Operator/Waste Water*, 68%, M = 2.9; *Heavy Equipment Operator*, 269%, M = 2.1; *Meter Reader*, 360%, M = 3.5). Contrary to the third hypothesis (i.e., that DNA disagreements would tend to involve only tasks receiving very low ratings), these results indicate that contamination and deficiency are serious problems for many titles, affecting both low- and high-rated tasks.

Inspection of the task-overlap statistics leads to a similar conclusion regarding the disappointing degree of agreement between incumbents and supervisors regarding the tasks that constitute the job. At the overall level, task-overlap averaged 80%, ranging from 22% to 100%. The same titles that were identified as high false-present and/or false-DNA were found to also have low task-overlap values, which was expected due to the fact that the statistic is sensitive to both types of disagreement.

In terms of the fourth hypothesis (i.e., that incumbent-supervisor disagreements occur primarily in jobs that are relatively uncomplicated or that have less verbally sophisticated incumbents), the results in Table 29.7 are not supportive. That is, although some relatively uncomplicated titles were troublesome (e.g., *Meter Reader, Game Room Attendant, Custodian/City Hall, Laborer/ Waste Water*), many of the most responsible-sounding titles in the organization exhibited high disagreement (e.g., *Police Captain, City Secretary, Manager/Community Building, Superintendant of Utilities*). Additionally, several of the less complicated titles demonstrated good levels of incumbent-supervisor agreement (e.g., *Jr. Accountant/Accounts Payable, Laborer/Water*).

In an attempt to put the above results into perspective, as well as assess the validity of our use of supervisory ratings to define the reference point, we examined tasks on which supervisors and incumbents differed in order to qualitatively identify the types of task content on which disagreement occurred. Table 29.8 lists illustrative false-present and false-DNA tasks for a sample of jobs on which nontrivial disagreements were present.

Inspection of the results in Table 29.8 suggests several conclusions regarding the content and nature of incumbent-supervisor disagreements. In terms of false-present ratings, these tasks fall into two basic categories: (a) obviously incorrect items (e.g., a *Custodian* claiming to record payments of taxes and city council resolutions; a *Laborer* taking dictation), and (b) items that the incumbent may be qualified to perform, but which were not required by their present job (e.g., the *Fire Lieutenant* who claimed to perform building inspections was qualified to perform such activities, but did not have to do so in his present assignment). Although undoubtedly some of the disagreements observed between incumbents and supervisors may have involved tasks that the incumbents actually perform (in which case the incumbent's rating could be viewed as the correct standard), the false-present ratings overwhelmingly appear to represent contamination-type errors where incumbents embellish or overstate the requirements of their positions (or do not adequately understand what activity is actually described by the language used in the task statement).

In terms of the false-DNA ratings, which represent the largest problem in this sample, the results in Table 29.8 again support the use of supervisory ratings to assess accuracy in the review process. As was indicated by the mean ratings for false-DNA tasks, these disagreements clearly do not simply involve trivial tasks. Although some minor tasks were false-DNAs, a large number of highly rated tasks were omitted by incumbents. For example, a *Custodian* failed to indicate critical tools used (e.g., broom, vacuum cleaner) and activities actually performed (e.g., mowing grass); the *Fire Lieutenant/Inspection* omitted tasks dealing directly with the central focus of the job (e.g., "conduct building inspections"); the *Meter Reader* failed to include "read gauges" and "record water usage from dials and gauges," which are unarguably *the* critical core activities of the job; and the

Table 29.8   Examples of Incumbent-Supervisor Rating Disagreements

False-present tasks

Custodian/City Hall

    Record payment of taxes (3)

    Record miscellaneous expenses (3)

    Record city council actions, ordinances, resolutions (3)

    Establish fire lanes where necessary (3)

    Apply hose clamp before opening fire hydrant (3)

Lt/Inspection

    Write reports on ambulance usage (3)

    Record types of injuries suffered by victims (2)

    Provide ambulance transport to hospitals (5)

    Build and cross portable ladder bridges (1)

    Lower or hoist persons/equipment by lifeline/rope (2)

    Roll or fold hose after use (4)

    Wash city vehicles (4)

Laborer/Waste Water

    Keep magazine rack supplied (3)

    Take dictation (2)

    Use copy machine (2)

False-DNA tasks

City Secretary

    Send teletype/fax messages (1)

    Sort mail/correspondence/memos (1)

    Prepare reports for supervisor (2)

    Backup computer data (1)

    Generate bills, checks, or reports using computer (5)

    Obtain authorization signatures (3)

    Post notices of official meetings (4)

    Answer requests for service and other business from citizens (3)

    Print city forms and documents (4)

    Check records to ensure that information is in accordance with laws and ordinances (3)

    Gather information and evidence to present to attorneys (2)

Custodian/City Hall

    Deliver mail to post office (2)

    Post notices of official meetings (3)

    Use shovel (3)

    Use battery charger (2)

    Use broom (5)

    Use vacuum cleaner (4)

    Use hand-held tools (hammers, screwdrivers, wrenches, etc) (3)

    Mow grass (3)

    Wash city vehicles (2)

Laborer/Waste Water

    Note sighted water leaks (5)

continued

Table 29.8   Examples of Incumbent-Supervisor Rating Disagreements (Continued)

False-DNA tasks

    Record daily activities (5)

    Maintain daily contact sheet (5)

    Report unsafe conditions, malfunctions, and necessary repairs to supervisor (3)

    Report to supervisor on actions taken and decisions made (2)

    Get advice from others regarding policies and procedures (2)

    Obtain approval to perform work (2)

    Attend shift briefings (3)

    Receive work requests (1)

    Watch for children/others when operating city equipment (3)

    Look for conditions that may cause a future problem (1)

    Read gauges (1)

    Keep proficient in defensive driving techniques (3)

    Attend training classes (2)

    Investigate spills and point-of-discharge pollution (1)

    Work from ladder (3)

    Remove unwanted or excess water (2)

    Use blower (3)

    Use air chisel (3)

    Use power saw (2)

    Use exhaust fan (2)

    Use extension ladders (1)

    Wash and clean equipment, tools, and machinery (3)

    Check levels of water and sewage (2)

    Shore-up walls when repairing major water leaks (3)

    Install hydrants (1)

    Repair hydrants (2)

Lt/Inspection

    Review construction plans/maps (3)

    Suggest methods of construction that comply with regulations (3)

    Diagnose computer problems (1)

    Prepare training/continuing education courses (2)

    Educate city officials in fire safety practices (1)

    Instruct subordinates in policies/procedures/laws (2)

    Conduct field inspections (4)

    Conduct building inspections (4)

    Perform on-site inspections (4)

    Inspect and enforce adherence to city codes & specifications (4)

    Learn structural components of buildings (3)

    Research fire/electrical/other codes (3)

Meter Reader

    Record water usage from dials and gauges (5)

    Record daily activities (3)

    Record work, hours on time sheet (3)

    Report unsafe conditions, malfunctions, and necessary repairs to supervisor (3)

    Report to supervisor on action taken and decisions made (3)

Table 29.8 Examples of Incumbent-Supervisor Rating Disagreements (Continued)

False-DNA tasks

    Use radio properly during normal transmission (3)

    Attend shift briefings (3)

    Read gauges (5)

    Read meters (5)

    Ensure thorough completion of job activities (5)

    Use hook (2)

    Keep tools and equipment in good working order (5)

    Wash and clean equipment, tools, and machinery (3)

    Wash city vehicles (3)

Supervisor/Utilities

    Complete standard forms for city/state/federal authorities (3)

    Complete monthly activity report (3)

    Prepare list of bad/questionable meter readings, service disconnects, new service (3)

    Maintain records of attendance, time-off and sick/vacation leave (3)

    Maintain daily contact sheet (2)

    Maintain records of vehicle maintenance needs (2)

    Attend shift briefings (3)

    Give public talks (3)

    Conduct tours of city facilities (2)

    Monitor department-citizen relations (2)

    Assign cases to subordinates or refer to others (3)

    Setup meter book routes (2)

    Maintain and determine project schedules (3)

    Allocate personnel to adapt to changing needs (3)

    Supervise conduct of investigations (4)

    Suggest methods of construction that comply with regulations (3)

    Conduct performance evaluations of subordinates (3)

    Determine customer adjustment on utility/other accounts (3)

    Check water plant for sanitary conditions (2)

    Use pitot gauge (3)

Superintendant/Utilities

    Prepare list of bad or questionable meter readings, service disconnects and new service (3)

    Formulate list of possible problems in inspections of buildings, job sites, or fire sites (3)

    Complete request forms for service or termination of service (2)

    Prepare monthly, quarterly, or annual reports (3)

    Prepare statements to be sent to property owners and mortgage companies (3)

    Process requests for vehicle repair (2)

    Maintain records of equipment and materials used (3)

    Maintain records of maintenance needs on equipment (3)

    Maintain records of vehicle maintenance needs (3)

    Match purchase orders with invoices (3)

    Ensure accurate information release to public, press and employees (3)

    Attend shift briefings (2)

    Act as liaison with other agencies and news media (2)

continued

Table 29.8   Examples of Incumbent-Supervisor Rating Disagreements (Continued)

False-DNA tasks

Report problems to pertinent agencies or companies (3)
Attend applicant's oral interview (3)
Help calm emotionally distressed persons (2)
Maintain good community relations (3)
Take information regarding citizen complaints (3)
Interpret city ordinances for public (2)
Design forms (e.g., billing forms, police record forms) (3)
Produce brochures, forms, or posters (3)
Chart water fitness data (4)
Review, plan, or consider personnel assignments and shift changes (3)
Schedule meetings, programs, appointments, trials, inspections, or visitations (3)
Maintain and determine project schedules (4)
Schedule routine maintenance activities (3)
Schedule training schools and sessions (3)
Notify people of schedule changes (3)
Implement and enforce departmental rules, regulations, policies, and procedures (4)
Supervise gathering of evidence (3)
Supervise conduct of investigations (3)
Administer city bidding process, advertise bids and specs (2)
Authorize purchase orders (3)
Decide which cases require further investigation (3)
Instruct subordinates in policies, procedures, and laws (3)
Inspect and enforce adherence to city codes and specifications (4)
Gather, maintain resource information from public and private sectors (4)
Use emergency lights (4)
Use spot light (4)
Use flashlight (5)
Use pitot gauge (4)
Read and check dials, gauges, and meters (4)

Numbers in parentheses are the task ratings.

Superintendent of Utilities (a department-head level job) failed to rate a long list of supervisory and technical activities that were clearly central to the job.

Discussion

The results presented above cast considerable doubt on what appears to be a widespread belief in the area of job analysis: namely, that practitioners can confidently rely on job incumbents to provide high-quality task inventory ratings, and that such raters can effectively serve as the sole source of job analysis information (e.g., Archer & Fruchter, 1963; Cragun & McCormick, 1967; Morsh, 1964; Wexley & Silverman, 1978). In terms of over- or underrating tasks that are part of the job, as well as making false-present (contamination) and false-DNA (deficiency) judgments, these data indicate that incumbents and supervisors often disagree in important ways. Although some incumbents produced ratings that converged well with those of their supervisor, most jobs exhibited one or more of the four types of errors discussed above. These errors were not confined to low-complexity jobs or titles presumably dominated by less verbally sophisticated incumbents, and they involved both low- and high-rated tasks. Thus, there is no apparent way to predict which jobs would be rated accurately and which would not.

We conclude that it is simply incorrect to conclude that "all incumbents can represent a reliable source for obtaining job analysis information" (Wexley & Silverman, 1978, p. 649). When the present results are considered in conjunction with those of earlier studies (e.g., Green & Stutzman, 1986; Hazel et al., 1964; Laabs & Baker, 1989; Meyer, 1959; Mullins & Kimbrough, 1988; Stutzman, 1983), it is clear that practitioners should not uncritically accept the task ratings provided by job incumbents. Whether due to inattention, marking the wrong answer, wishful thinking, misunderstanding, deliberate distortion, or a difference of opinion, the results of this and previous studies indicate that a nontrivial proportion of task inventory responses are likely to contain potentially serious amounts of invalid information or (more likely, based on the present results) simply ignore critical aspects of the job.

Regarding best practices recommendations, we propose that a review of each job's data (e.g., using the supervisor, as in the present study, or another suitable SME with adequate knowledge of the way the job is performed in that organization) be made an integral part of all task analysis inventories. Additionally, the inclusion of scales or item-analysis techniques designed to assess the validity of job analysis response profiles and detect potential falsification or carelessness (e.g., Green & Stutzman, 1986; Harvey, 2005; Wilson, Harvey, & Macy, 1990) should be a standard practice when developing job inventories (including standardized common-metric GWB questionnaires). Such scales and techniques are commonplace in personality, clinical, and other settings in which self-report data are used, and the likelihood for falsification must be considered. In view of the potential for job analysis rating errors to have a cascading effect throughout an entire personnel system, it should be a matter of great concern that such little attention has been spent developing ways to ensure the quality of self-report job analysis data.

REFERENCES

Advisory Panel for the Review of the DOT. (1992). Interim report of the advisory panel for the Dictionary of Occupational Titles. *Federal Register, 57*, 10588–10599.

Archer, W. B., & Fruchter, D. A. (1963). *The construction, review, and administration of Air Force job inventories* (Report No. PRL-TDR-63- 21). Lackland AFB, TX: Occupational Research Division.

Butler, S. K., & Harvey, R. J. (1988). A comparison of holistic versus decomposed rating of Position Analysis Questionnaire work dimensions. *Personnel Psychology, 41,* 761–771.

Cain, P. S., & Green, B. F. (1983). Reliabilities of selected ratings available from the Dictionary of Occupational Titles. *Journal of Applied Psychology, 68,* 155–165.

Christal, R. (1974). *The United States Air Force occupational research project (AFHRL-TR-73-75).* Lackland AFB, TX: Air Force Human Resources Laboratory, Occupational Research Division.

Conley, P. R., & Sackett, P. R. (1987). Effects of using high- versus low-performing job incumbents as sources of job-analysis information. *Journal of Applied Psychology, 72, 434–437.*

Cornelius, E. T., & Lyness, K. S. (1980). A comparison of holistic and decomposed judgment strategies in job analyses by job incumbents. *Journal of Applied Psychology, 65,* 155–163.

Cornelius, E. T., Schmidt, F. L., & Carron, T. J. (1984). Job classification approaches and the implementation of validity generalization results. *Personnel Psychology, 37,* 247–260.

Cragun, J. R., & McCormick, E. J. (1967). *Job inventory information: Task and scale reliabilities and scale interrelationships* (Report No. PRL-TR-67-15). Lackland AFB, TX: Personnel Research Laboratory, Aerospace Medical Division.

Cunningham, J. W., Boese, R. R., Neeb, R. W., & Pass, J. J. (1983). Systematically derived work dimensions: Factor analyses of the Occupational Analysis Inventory. *Journal of Applied Psychology, 68,* 232–252.

Dawes, R. M., & Corrigan, B. (1974). Linear models in decision making. *Psychological Bulletin, 81,* 95–106.

DeNisi, A. S., & Shaw, J. B. (1977). Investigation of the uses of self-reports of abilities. *Journal of Applied Psychology, 62*(5), 641–644.

Fine, S. A. (1955). A structure of worker functions. *Personnel and Guidance Journal, 34,* 66–73.

Fine, S. A., & Cronshaw, S. F. (1999). *Functional job analysis: A foundation for human resources management.* Mahwah, NJ: Lawrence Erlbaum Associates.

Fine, S. A., Harvey, R. J, & Cronshaw, S. F. (2004, April). FJA strategies for addressing O*NET limitations in a post-DOT environment. In E. A. Fleishman (Chair), *Things, Data, and People: Fifty years of a seminal theory.* Symposium presented at the Annual Conference of the Society for Industrial and Organizational Psychology, Chicago.

Fleishman, E. A. (1992). *Rating scale booklet: F-JAS: Fleishman job analysis survey.* Palo Alto, CA: Consulting Psychologists Press.

Fleishman, E. A., & Mumford, M. (1991). Evaluating classifications of job behavior: A construct validation of the ability requirement scales. *Personnel Psychology, 44,* 253–575.

Fleishman, E. A., & Reilly, M. E. (1992). *Administrator's guide: F-JAS: Fleishman job analysis survey.* Palo Alto, CA: Consulting Psychologists Press.

Fleishman, E. A., Wetrogan, L. I., Uhlman, C. E., & Marshall-Mies, J. C. (1995). *Abilities. In Development of prototype occupational analysis network (O*NET) content model: Volume I: Report.* Salt Lake City, UT: Utah Department of Employment Security.

Geyer, P. D., Hice, J., Hawk, J., Boese, R., & Brannon, Y. (1989). Reliabilities of ratings available from the Dictionary of Occupational Titles. *Personnel Psychology, 42,* 547–560.

Geyer, P. D., & Hunter, J. E. (1992). *Issues of reliability and validity in ratings of occupational characteristics in the Dictionary of Occupational Titles.* Unpublished technical report.

Gibson, S. G., Harvey, R. J., & Harris, M. L. (2007). Holistic versus decomposed ratings of general dimensions of work activity. *Management Research News, 30,* 724–734.

Green, S. B., & Stutzman, T. (1986). An evaluation of methods to select respondents to structured job-analysis questionnaires. *Personnel Psychology, 39,* 543–564.

Harvey, R. J. (1986). Quantitative approaches to job classification: A review and critique. *Personnel Psychology, 39, 267–289.*

Harvey, R. J. (1987, April). *Alternative factor structures for the Position Analysis Questionnaire (PAQ).* In M. D. Hakel (Chair), *The dimensionality of work: Future directions, applications, and instrumentation.* Symposium presented at the Annual Conference of the Society for Industrial and Organizational Psychology, Atlanta.

Harvey, R. J. (1990). *The Common-Metric Questionnaire for the analysis and evaluation of jobs (Field Test Version 1.12).* San Antonio, TX: The Psychological Corporation.

Harvey, R. J. (1991a). Job analysis. In M. D. Dunnette & L. Hough (Eds.), *Handbook of industrial and organization psychology* (2nd ed.). Palo Alto, CA: Consulting Psychologists Press.

Harvey, R. J. (1991b). *The common-metric questionnaire (CMQ): A job analysis system.* San Antonio, TX: The Psychological Corporation.

Harvey, R. J. (1992). *Potential applications of generalized work behaviors (GWBs) for the Dictionary of Occupational Titles (DOT).* Technical report prepared under Department of Labor contract 92-451.

Harvey, R. J. (2004, April). *Empirical foundations for the Things-Data-People taxonomy of work.* In E. A. Fleishman (Chair), *Things, Data, and People: Fifty years of a seminal theory.* Symposium presented at the Annual Conference of the Society for Industrial and Organizational Psychology, Chicago.

Harvey, R. J. (2005, April). IRT strategies for identifying rater quality in job analysis ratings. In C. VanIddekinge (Chair), *Group differences in job analysis ratings.* Symposium presented at the Annual Conference of the Society for Industrial and Organizational Psychology, Los Angeles.

Harvey, R. J., Friedman, L., Hakel, M. D., & Cornelius, E. T. (1988). Dimensionality of the Job Element Inventory (JEI), a simplified worker-oriented job analysis questionnaire. *Journal of Applied Psychology, 73,* 639–646.

Harvey, R. J., & Hollander, E. (2002, April). Assessing interrater agreement in the O*NET. In M. A. Wilson (Chair), *The O*NET: Mend it, or end it?* Symposium presented at the Annual Conference of the Society for Industrial and Organizational Psychology, Toronto.

Harvey, R. J., & Wilson, M. A. (2000). Yes Virginia, there is an objective reality in job analysis. *Journal of Organizational Behavior, 21,* 829–854.

Hazel, J. T., Madden, J. M., & Christal, R. E. (1964). Agreement between worker-supervisor descriptions of the worker's job. *Journal of Industrial Psychology, 2,* 71–79.

Laabs, G. J., & Baker, H. G. (1989). Selection of critical tasks for Navy job performance measures. *Military Psychology, 1,* 3–16.

McCormick, E. J. (1976). *Job and task analysis.* In M. D. Dunnette (Ed.), *Handbook of industrial and organizational psychology.* Chicago, IL: Rand McNally.

McCormick, E. J., Jeanneret, P. R., & Mecham, R. C. (1972). A study of job characteristics & job dimensions as based on the Position Analysis Questionnaire (PAQ). *Journal of Applied Psychology, 56*, 347–368.

Meyer, H. H. (1959). Comparison of foreman and general foreman conceptions of the foreman's job responsibility. *Personnel Psychology, 12*, 445–452.

Miller, G. A. (1956). The magical number seven, plus or minus two: Some limits on our capacity for processing information. *Psychological Review, 63*, 81–97.

Morsh, J. E. (1964). Job analysis in the United States Air Force. *Personnel Psychology, 17*, 7–17.

Mullins, W. C., & Kimbrough, W. W. (1988). Group composition as a determinant of job analysis outcomes. *Journal of Applied Psychology, 73*, 657–664.

O'Leary, B. S., Rheinstein, J., & McCauley, D. E. (1989). Developing a taxonomy of generalized work behaviors. *Proceedings of the 31st annual conference of the International Military Testing Association* (pp. 221–226), San Antonio, TX.

O'Leary, B. S., Rheinstein, J., & McCauley, D. E. (1990). Developing job families using generalized work behaviors. *Proceeding of the annual conference of the International Military Testing Association* (pp. 58–63), Orange Beach, AL.

Outerbridge, A. N. (1981). *The development of generalizable work behavior categories for a synthetic validity model* (PRR-81-1). Washington, DC: U.S. Office of Personnel Management.

Pearlman, K. (1980). Job families: A review and discussion of their implications for personnel selection. *Psychological Bulletin, 87*, 1–28.

Peterson, N. G., Mumford, M. D., Borman, W. C., Jeanneret, P. R., & Fleishman, E. A. (1999). *An occupational information system for the 21st Century: The development of O*NET*. Washington, DC: APA Books.

Rheinstein, J., McCauley, D. E., & O'Leary, B. S. (1989). *Job analysis for examination development in professional and administrative occupations*. Paper presented at the annual conference of the American Psychological Association, New Orleans.

Sackett, P. R., Cornelius, E. T., & Carron, T. J. (1981). A comparison of global vs. task oriented approaches to job classification. *Personnel Psychology, 34*, 791–804.

Sanchez, J. I., & Levine, E. L. (2000). Accuracy or consequential validity: Which is the better standard for job analysis data? *Journal of Organizational Behavior, 21*, 809–818.

Schmitt, N. (1987, April). *Principles III: Research issues*. Paper presented at the second annual conference of the Society for Industrial and Organizational Psychology, Atlanta, GA.

Smith, J. E., & Hakel, M. D. (1979). Convergence among data sources, response bias, and reliability and validity of a structured job analysis questionnaire. *Personnel Psychology, 32*, 677–692.

Society for Industrial and Organizational Psychology (1987). *Principles for the validation and use of personnel selection procedures* (3rd ed.). College Park, MD: Author.

Stutzman, T. M. (1983). Within classification job differences. *Personnel Psychology, 36*, 503–516.

Thompson, D. E., & Thompson, T. A. (1982). Court standards for job analysis in test validation. *Personnel Psychology, 35*, 865–878.

Webb, N. M., Shavelson, R. J., Shea, J., & Morello, E. (1981). Generalizability of general education development ratings of jobs in the United States. *Journal of Applied Psychology, 66*, 186–192.

Wexley, K. N., & Silverman, S. B. (1978). An examination of differences between managerial effectiveness and response patterns on a structured job analysis questionnaire. *Journal of Applied Psychology, 63*, 646–649.

Wilson, M. A., Harvey, R. J., & Macy, B. A. (1990). Repeating items to estimate the test-retest reliability of task inventory ratings. *Journal of Applied Psychology, 75*, 158–163.

30

A Framework of Potential Sources of Inaccuracy in Job Analysis

FREDERICK P. MORGESON

Michigan State University

MICHAEL A. CAMPION

Purdue University

Job analysis forms the foundation upon which virtually all human resource management systems are built. Although the validity of job analysis information is rarely questioned (Harvey, 1991), job analyses are often based completely on human judgment (Goldstein, Zedeck, & Schneider, 1993). This is problematic because a considerable body of psychological research has demonstrated that human judgment is fallible and subject to considerable inaccuracy. The implications of this for job analysis are clear: Inaccuracies can have profound effects on job analyses and the subsequent human resource management systems arising from job analysis data.

The purpose of this chapter is to describe some situations that might occur when conducting a job analysis and highlight how the job analysis could be affected by systematic sources of inaccuracy. We then outline a framework of job analysis accuracy more fully described in Morgeson and Campion (1997). The framework is shown in Table 30.1. The two primary sources of inaccuracy are social and cognitive in nature. Social sources of inaccuracy reflect the fact that individuals exist in a social environment that produces pressures for certain kinds of behaviors. Cognitive sources, on the other hand, reflect the fact that individuals have distinct limitations when they process information.

These different sources of inaccuracy have six different effects on job analysis data, and these effects represent the domain of inaccuracy in the present framework. They are interrater reliability, interrater agreement, discriminability between jobs, dimensionality of factor structures, mean ratings, and completeness of job information. These effects reflect underlying issues of reliability (e.g., reliability and agreement; see also Dierdorff & Wilson, 2003) and validity (e.g., discriminability, dimensionality, mean ratings, and completeness) in job analysis data. The form of these effects will depend on the source of inaccuracy. Higher as well as lower levels of these effects could indicate inaccuracy. Thus, some presumed measures of job information quality, such as reliability and agreement, might be artificially inflated by certain sources of inaccuracy (e.g., conformity pressure).

QUALITATIVE REVIEW OF FRAMEWORK WITH JOB ANALYSIS EXPERTS

After an early version of this framework was completed, it was sent to 32 job analysis academics, consultants, and other experts to solicit feedback. Interviews, ranging from 15 to 60 minutes

Table 30.1   Social and Cognitive Sources of Inaccuracy on Job Analysis Data

Social sources of inaccuracy

A. *Social influence processes*
  1. Conformity pressures
  2. Extremity shifts
  3. Motivation loss
B. *Self-presentation processes*
  4. Impression management
  5. Social desirability
  6. Demand effects

Cognitive sources of inaccuracy

C. *Limitations in information processing*
  7. Information overload
  8. Heuristics
  9. Categorization
D. *Biases in information processing*
  10. Carelessness
  11. Extraneous information
  12. Inadequate information
  13. Primacy/recency and contrast effects
  14. Halo
  15. Leniency and severity
  16. Method effects

(approximately 35-minute average), were subsequently conducted with 26 individuals with respect to three broad issues: (a) their overall reaction to the framework, (b) examples that exemplify these errors, and (c) deficiency or contamination in the framework. The experts provided a wealth of information, with concrete feedback on the framework, examples that highlight many of the errors we had identified, and a number of additional considerations we had overlooked.

We undertook this extra "reality check" step to make certain that what we were developing was actually happening in job analysis practice. Fortunately, virtually all of the errors we had identified were recognized by the experts as relevant for job analysis, both from a theoretical and practical perspective. They see these errors in the course of conducting their job analyses, and many found our framework a useful way to describe and categorize the errors. Brief samples of some of the more general comments that relate to our framework are as follows.

With respect to impression management, one of the experts noted that he could never recall a time where he interviewed someone that they did not ask how the job evaluation would affect pay. Similarly, another expert noted that the efficiency experts have preceded the job analysts in terms of contact with organizational members. As a consequence, individuals are worried about losing their jobs and tend to inflate their job ratings. Both examples illustrate that individuals are often acutely aware of the use to which job analysis information is put and may systematically distort their responses. Another expert noted that in his experience, particularly in civil service/public sector positions, jobs become categorized according to an existing system that is known by the employees and this system drives job classification. That is, individuals are well aware of how jobs are classified in the organization and what is rewarded. This influences their information processing in terms of what they consider important and what they report when interviewed. This highlights how seemingly innocuous distal factors can affect the reporting of job tasks.

EXAMPLES OF HOW JOB ANALYSIS INACCURACY MAY MANIFEST ITSELF

As these examples suggest, job analysis inaccuracy can manifest itself in many different ways. To illustrate how inaccuracies might arise during job analysis data collection, we have developed the following three scenarios built on our own experience and the comments of the job analysis experts.

Job analyses are often conducted for the purpose of determining compensation levels (commonly referred to as job evaluations). Regardless of whether they are told the purpose of the job analysis, respondents are often aware that their responses have pay implications. As such, they may choose to exaggerate their responses. For example, the amount of supervision is often an important compensable factor. Although a given job analysis respondent might only supervise a secretary and student interns and others only on a project basis, they are likely to overestimate the amount of supervision they perform to positively impact the value of their job. If unchecked, this could upwardly bias the compensation level for the job, costing the organization additional money.

Job analysis information is often collected in group settings from subject matter experts (SMEs). The nature of these settings may produce some level of opinion conformity. For example, during a group meeting the discussion may turn to the importance of teamwork. One participant might know that teamwork is a major "buzzword" in the organization, although she has not really seen any increase in teamwork on her job. Nonetheless, she is likely to go along with the group with the conclusion that teamwork is important because she thinks it is the expected answer. If this occurs, some job aspects may be identified as important when they really are not.

Job analysis questionnaires are commonly used to collect information about job tasks. Unfortunately, these questionnaires are often long and tedious to complete, potentially affecting the accuracy of the data that is obtained. For example, at the end of the day a group of job incumbents might be required to come to a conference room and fill out some forms for "Personnel." The form turns out to be a 12-page, 300-item task survey that requires ratings on importance, time spent, and needed at entry. The purpose of the form may seem unclear and all the items might sound the same to the respondents. It basically seems like more busywork from Personnel. In addition, completing the questionnaire is all that stands in the way of "Miller Time." Consequently, the respondent circles answers as quickly as possible without really reading the items. If all respondents are responding similarly, the reliability and validity of the resulting information is likely to be low.

These hypothetical examples demonstrate how various aspects of job analysis may affect the accuracy of the data that is collected. Therefore, it is important to try to understand the social and cognitive influences on job analysis accuracy.

SOCIAL SOURCES OF INACCURACY

Social Influence Processes

Conformity Pressures

Considerable research suggests that groups exert considerable influence to reach judgment consensus (Deutsch & Gerard, 1955; Hackman, 1992). Conformity is likely to occur in SME committees if members adhere to a perceived group opinion. These committees often have implicit or explicit rules requiring the group to achieve unanimity, increasing the likelihood of conformity. This may reduce the accuracy of job analysis information by causing individuals to respond in a manner that differs from their own opinion.

Many factors could potentially influence conformity. For example, the status of various committee members may influence the level of conformity (Sackett & Wilson, 1982), with more conformity exhibited by lower status group members. In addition, the use of exchange tactics (e.g., suggesting that the sooner the group reaches agreement, the sooner they will get finished) is likely to result in members conforming or acquiescing. Finally, the evaluation of jobs is driven (in part) by conformity to organizational norms. For example, if the organization is focusing on teamwork-related competencies, these competencies may be overstated in terms of their relevance for the job.

Extremity Shifts

It has been observed that group member opinions sometimes become more extreme after group discussion (Meyers & Lamm, 1976). This seems to happen because individuals tend not to effectively discuss unique information in group settings (Gigone & Hastie, 1993; Stasser & Stewart, 1992; Stasser & Titus, 1985). This polarizes group judgments because shared information is discussed more frequently and is viewed as more representative of the job.

It appears that the initial level of opinion homogeneity (Williams & Taormina, 1993), coupled with the extremity of initial judgments (Sackett & Wilson, 1982), make extremity shifts more likely. Thus, if the information discussed by a group is generally shared by all members, and this information is modestly extreme, then individual opinions are likely to be reinforced (Moscovici & Zavalloni, 1969), making the discussed information appear more representative of the job than it actually is (Meyers & Lamm, 1976).

Motivation Loss

In many job analysis SME committees, some members participate less than other members. This failure to participate is often because of a lack of motivation (Shepperd, 1993). There are several reasons why motivation losses might occur. First, if individual member contributions cannot be evaluated, there is no contingency upon an individual's response and they cannot be held accountable (Tetlock, 1985). Second, if the job analysis task is not meaningful, the committee member has no intrinsic reason to contribute. Finally, if group members feel the information they hold is redundant (i.e., their job knowledge overlaps with others), they are not likely to contribute.

Self-Presentation Processes

Impression Management

Impression management involves behaviors individuals direct toward others to create and maintain certain perceptions of themselves (Gardner & Martinko, 1988). If a job incumbent engages in impression management behaviors, the resulting job information will not reflect what their job actually entails but will reflect what they want people to think their job entails. Morgeson, Delaney-Klinger, Mayfield, Ferrara, and Campion (2004) found that such impression management processes are more likely when job incumbents rate ability statements rather than task statements.

Several factors are likely to encourage impression management behaviors in job analysis situations. First, impression management is more likely when there is some level of ambiguity. Second, impression management is more likely when people are encouraged to examine their own behavior. Third, impression management is more likely when the audience is high status. Finally, impression management is more likely in situations that are particularly evaluative in nature or where it is in the incumbent's best interest to make a good impression.

Social Desirability

In job analysis situations, social desirability reflects a job incumbent's desire to gain social approval from job analysts, supervisors, or coworkers. In attempting to gain approval, incumbents may distort responses in such a way as to portray their job as having relatively more socially desirable or relatively fewer socially undesirable features.

For example, Smith and Hakel (1979) found that supervisors and incumbents tend to inflate their responses compared to analysts on socially desirable items in a job analysis questionnaire. Anderson, Warner, and Spencer (1984) found that job applicants extensively inflated (i.e., responded in a socially desirable manner) their ratings on a self-assessed task inventory. In addition, the degree to which job analysis information is a reflection of the individual providing the information, and his or her unique value to the organization, may moderate the level of socially desirable responding.

Demand Effects

Demand effects refer to the tendency of individuals to play the role of "good subject" and attempt to confirm a researcher's expectations (Orne, 1962). Demand effects in the job analysis context can occur in a number of different ways. For example, in choosing certain task and knowledge, skill, ability, and other characteristics (KSAOs), individuals are indirectly told what the organization thinks is important, thereby creating a demand effect. As another example, showing incumbents previous job analysis results is likely to foster demand effects, especially if the information is complex.

COGNITIVE SOURCES OF INACCURACY

Limitations in Information Processing System

Information Overload

Information overload is likely to occur in job analysis when the amount of information is very large. Because many job analysis questionnaires require respondents to rate large numbers of items on numerous dimensions (e.g., importance, time spent, difficulty) and these ratings may take hours to complete, individuals may be overloaded and seek to simplify the rating process.

Information overload can also occur when the information processing task is complex. For example, making judgments of an entire job (i.e., holistic judgments) are more complex than making judgments of specific tasks (i.e., decomposed judgments). Evidence suggests that that decomposed judgments yield more reliable and accurate data than holistic judgments (Butler & Harvey, 1988; Morgeson et al., 2004; Sanchez & Levine, 1989, 1994).

Heuristics

When individuals make judgments, they often use heuristics that imperfectly mirror reality (Kahneman, Slovic, & Tversky, 1982). The representativeness heuristic reflects the tendency of people to judge the degree of relationship between two things by assessing their similarity. Inaccuracies that result from the representativeness heuristic may be particularly likely for analysts who have evaluated similar jobs in the past and therefore have a number of implicit expectations concerning salaries, job titles, or the status accorded different jobs.

The availability heuristic reflects the fact that the frequency of events is based on the ease with which examples can be recalled. Thus, events more easily recalled will appear to be more frequently occurring. Inaccuracies resulting from the availability heuristic are more likely if a job requires some unusual tasks because they might be recalled and reported as more frequently occurring because of their unusual and memorable nature.

Categorization

Categorization helps minimize cognitive effort and maximize information intake (Rosch, 1978). It is likely that when rendering job-related judgments, job incumbents will recall the category instead of actual facts about the job. Job-related judgments are then made with respect to the recalled category, rather than the details of the job, thus yielding inaccurate job information.

Job categorization is especially likely when there are a large number of tasks to be performed (Kulik, 1989). If a job analyst completes an instrument that contains hundreds of items, he or she probably will not remember the specific KSAOs required to perform the job. If he or she had concluded that the job was complex, however, subsequent judgments may inflate importance ratings, thus reducing the accuracy of the job information.

Biases in Information Processing System

Carelessness

Carelessness reflects instances where incumbents intentionally respond inaccurately because of not reading each item closely enough or responding inappropriately given the wording of the question (Green & Stutzman, 1986). Carelessness is a particular threat for multiposition job analysis questionnaires that include many tasks not relevant for any given position. Although this saves time in terms of creating only one questionnaire for the entire sample, it may produce problems in terms of contamination due to careless responding. That is, individuals may carelessly indicate they perform certain tasks when they do not.

Extraneous Information

Research has demonstrated that biased information processing in job analysis can result from extraneous information not relevant to the analysis (Arvey, Davis, McGowen, & Dipboye, 1982; Mount & Ellis, 1987; Prien & Saleh, 1963; Rynes, Weber, & Milkovich, 1989; Schwab & Grams, 1985). Extraneous information can include such things as incumbent interest in the job, satisfaction, and compensation level (Conte, Dean, Ringenbach, Moran, & Landy, 2005). It is important to note, however, that extraneous information is not always a biasing force. That is, the extraneous information might provide relevant cues in many job analysis situations.

Inadequate Information

Possession of inadequate information can also lead to inaccuracies and usually occurs with analysts or "naïve" raters. Naïve analysts, or those with less information, tend to produce ratings that are less reliable and valid than expert raters (Cornelius, DeNisi, & Blencoe, 1984; DeNisi, Cornelius, & Blencoe, 1987; Friedman & Harvey, 1986; Hahn & Dipboye, 1988; Harvey & Lozada-Larsen, 1988; Richman & Quiñones, 1996).

Primacy/Recency and Contrast Effects

Primacy effects refer to the exaggerated influence of initial information, whereas recency effects refer to the influence recent information can have on judgments. It is possible that recently performed job tasks could overly influence incumbent judgments or recently conducted observations or interviews could overly influence analyst judgments because they are more available in memory. Contrast effects refer to distortions that are caused by the differences between stimuli. In job analysis, it is possible that after evaluating a number of lower-level jobs, an analyst will give excessively high ratings to an average-level job because of contrast effects.

Halo

Inaccuracy because of halo occurs when ratings are assigned on the basis of global impressions or highly salient features instead of distinguishing between dimensions (Borman, 1991). Any individual who provides job analysis information could potentially be affected by halo inaccuracies. For example, if job analysts fail to sample the incumbent's work behavior comprehensively enough, they are likely to rely on global impressions. In addition, if questionnaires have abstract or nonspecific descriptors overlapping dimensions are likely to result.

Leniency and Severity

Tendencies on the part of respondents to give consistently high ratings are termed leniency, and tendencies to give consistently low ratings are termed severity. Leniency is likely to occur in job analysis because respondents may be unwilling to be critical and downgrade the position. Severity is less likely to occur.

Method Effects

When job analysis data is collected through a single method (e.g., questionnaire), there may be problems with common method variance (Campbell & Fiske, 1959; Fiske, 1982). Job analyses are particularly susceptible to these problems because questionnaires are often completed by the same person, at the same time, using the same questionnaire, all conditions under which maximize the probability of method effects. Aside from the common source for the data, a number of other typical methodological practices in job analysis may further enhance method effects. For example, the use of a common response format, excessively long questionnaires, and fine or subtle distinctions between items may further enhance covariation among items.

CONCLUSION

As this chapter helps demonstrate, there is great potential for inaccuracy in job analysis. Job analysis researchers and practitioners should be aware of these potential sources of inaccuracy and seek to eliminate or minimize their potential negative effects. If unchecked, the quality of job analysis information is likely to suffer (Morgeson & Campion, 2000; Morgeson & Dierdorff, 2011).

REFERENCES

Anderson, C. D., Warner, J. L., & Spencer, C. C. (1984). Inflation bias in self-assessment examinations: Implications for valid employee selection. *Journal of Applied Psychology, 69,* 574–580.

Arvey, R. D., Davis, G. A., McGowen, S. L., & Dipboye, R. L. (1982). Potential sources of bias in job analytic processes. *Academy of Management Journal, 25,* 618–629.

Borman, W. C. (1991). Job behavior, performance, and effectiveness. In M. D. Dunnette & L. M. Hough (Eds.), *Handbook of industrial and organizational psychology* (Vol. 2, 2nd ed., pp. 271–326). Palo Alto, CA: Consulting Psychologists Press.

Butler, S. K., & Harvey, R. J. (1988). A comparison of holistic versus decomposed rating of position analysis questionnaire work dimensions. *Personnel Psychology, 41,* 761–771.

Campbell, D. T., & Fiske, D. W. (1959). Convergent and discriminant validation by the multitrait-multimethod matrix. *Psychological Bulletin, 56,* 81–105.

Conte, J. M., Dean, M. A., Ringenbach, K. L., Moran, S. K., & Landy, F. J. (2005). The relationship between work attitudes and job analysis ratings: Do rating scale type and task discretion matter? *Human Performance, 18,* 1–21.

Cornelius, E. T., DeNisi, A. S., & Blencoe, A. G. (1984). Expert and naive raters using the PAQ: Does it matter? *Personnel Psychology, 37,* 453–464.

DeNisi, A. S., Cornelius, E. T., & Blencoe, A. G. (1987). Further investigation of common knowledge effects on job analysis ratings. *Journal of Applied Psychology, 72,* 262–268.

Deutsch, M., & Gerard, H. B. (1955). A study of normative and informational social influences upon individual judgment. *Journal of Abnormal and Social Psychology, 51,* 629–636.

Dierdorff, E. C., & Wilson, M. A. (2003). A meta-analysis of job analysis reliability. *Journal of Applied Psychology, 88,* 635–646.

Fiske, D. W. (1982). Convergent-discriminant validation in measurements and research strategies. In D. Brinberg & L. H. Kidder (Eds.), *New directions for methodology of social and behavioral science: Forms of validity in research* (pp. 77–92). San Francisco, CA: Jossey-Bass.

Friedman, L., & Harvey, R. J. (1986). Can raters with reduced job descriptive information provide accurate position analysis questionnaire (PAQ) ratings? *Personnel Psychology, 39,* 779–789.

Gardner, W. L., & Martinko, M. J. (1988). Impression management in organizations. *Journal of Management, 14,* 321–338.

Gigone, D., & Hastie, R. (1993). The common knowledge effect: Information sharing and group judgment. *Journal of Personality and Social Psychology, 65,* 959–974.

Goldstein, I. L., Zedeck, S., & Schneider, B. (1993). An exploration of the job analysis-content validity process. In N. Schmitt, W. C. Borman, & Associates (Eds.), *Personnel selection in organizations* (pp. 3–34). San Francisco, CA: Jossey-Bass.

Green, S. B., & Stutzman, T. (1986). An evaluation of methods to select respondents to structured job-analysis questionnaires. *Personnel Psychology, 39,* 543–564.

Hackman, J. R. (1992). Group influences on individuals in organizations. In M. D. Dunnette & L. M. Hough (Eds.), *Handbook of industrial and organizational psychology* (2nd. ed., pp. 199–267). Palo Alto, CA: Consulting Psychologists Press.

Hahn, D. C., & Dipboye, R. L. (1988). Effects of training and information on the accuracy and reliability of job evaluations. *Journal of Applied Psychology, 73,* 146–153.

Harvey, R. J. (1991). Job analysis. In M. D. Dunnette & L. M. Hough (Eds.), *Handbook of industrial and organizational psychology* (Vol. 2, 2nd ed., pp. 71–163). Palo Alto, CA: Consulting Psychologists Press.

Harvey, R. J., & Lozada-Larsen, S. R. (1988). Influence of amount of job descriptive information on job analysis rating accuracy. *Journal of Applied Psychology, 73,* 457–461.

Kahneman, D., Slovic, P., & Tversky, A. (1982). *Judgment under uncertainty: Heuristics and biases.* London, England: Cambridge University Press.

Kulik, C. T. (1989). The effects of job categorization on judgments of the motivating potential of jobs. *Administrative Science Quarterly, 34,* 68–80.

Meyers, D. G., & Lamm, H. (1976). The group polarization phenomenon. *Psychological Bulletin, 83,* 602–627.

Mount, M. K., & Ellis, R. A. (1987). Investigation of bias in job evaluation ratings of comparable worth study participants. *Personnel Psychology, 40,* 85–96.

Morgeson, F. P., & Campion, M. A. (1997). Social and cognitive sources of potential inaccuracy in job analysis. *Journal of Applied Psychology, 82,* 627–655.

Morgeson, F. P., & Campion, M. A. (2000). Accuracy in job analysis: Toward an inference-based model. *Journal of Organizational Behavior, 21,* 819–827.

Morgeson, F. P., Delaney-Klinger, K. A., Mayfield, M. S., Ferrara, P., & Campion, M. A. (2004). Self-presentation processes in job analysis: A field experiment investigating inflation in abilities, tasks, and competencies. *Journal of Applied Psychology, 89,* 674–686.

Morgeson, F. P., & Dierdorff, E. C. (2011). Work analysis: From technique to theory. In S. Zedeck (Ed.), *APA handbook of industrial and organizational psychology* (Vol. 2, pp. 3–41). Washington, DC: APA.

Moscovici, S., & Zavalloni, M. (1969). The group as a polarizer of attitudes. *Journal of Personality and Social Psychology, 12,* 125–135.

Orne, M. T. (1962). On the social psychology of the psychological experiment: With particular reference to demand characteristics and their implications. *American Psychologist, 17,* 776–783.

Prien, E. P., & Saleh, S. D. (1963). A study of bias in job analysis and evaluation. *Journal of Industrial Psychology, 1,* 113–117.

Richman, W. L., & Quiñones, M. A. (1996). Task frequency rating accuracy: The effect of task engagement and experience. *Journal of Applied Psychology, 81,* 512–524.

Rosch, E. (1978). Principles of categorization. In E. Rosch & B. B. Lloyd (Eds.), *Cognition and categorization* (pp. 27–48). Hillsdale, NJ: Lawrence Erlbaum Associates.

Rynes, S. L., Weber, C. L., & Milkovich, G. T. (1989). Effects of market survey rates, job evaluation, and job gender on job pay. *Journal of Applied Psychology, 74,* 114–123.

Sackett, P. R., & Wilson, M. A. (1982). Factors affecting the consensus judgment process in managerial assessment centers. *Journal of Applied Psychology, 67,* 10–17.

Sanchez, J. I., & Levine, E. L. (1989). Determining important tasks within jobs: A policy-capturing approach. *Journal of Applied Psychology, 74,* 336–342.

Sanchez, J. I., & Levine, E. L. (1994). The impact of raters' cognition on judgment accuracy: An extension to the job analysis domain. *Journal of Business and Psychology, 9,* 47–57.

Schwab, D. P., & Grams, R. (1985). Sex-related errors in job evaluation: A "real-world" test. *Journal of Applied Psychology, 70,* 533–539.

Shepperd, J. A. (1993). Productivity loss in performance groups: A motivation analysis. *Psychological Bulletin, 113,* 67–81.

Smith, J. E., & Hakel, M. D. (1979). Convergence among data sources, response bias, and reliability and validity of a structured job analysis questionnaire. *Personnel Psychology, 32,* 677–692.

Stasser, G., & Stewart, D. (1992). Discovery of hidden profiles by decision-making groups: Solving a problem versus making a judgment. *Journal of Personality and Social Psychology, 63,* 426–434.

Stasser, G., & Titus, W. (1985). Pooling of unshared information in group decision making: Biased information sampling during discussion. *Journal of Personality and Social Psychology, 48,* 1467–1478.

Tetlock, P. E. (1985). Accountability: The neglected social context of judgment and choice. In L. L. Cummings & B. M. Staw (Eds.), *Research in organizational behavior* (Vol. 7, pp. 297–332). Greenwich, CT: JAI Press.

Williams, S., & Taormina, R. J. (1993). Unanimous versus majority influences on group polarization in business decision making. *The Journal of Social Psychology, 133,* 199–205.

31

Understanding Mission Essential Competencies as a Job Analysis Method

GEORGE M. ALLIGER

The Group for Organizational Effectiveness, Inc.

REBECCA BEARD

The Group for Organizational Effectiveness, Inc.

WINSTON BENNETT, JR.

United States Air Force Research Laboratory

CHARLES M. COLEGROVE

United States Air Force

The United States Air Force Research Laboratory (AFRL), Human Effectiveness Directorate, Warfighter Readiness Research Division, in conjunction with the United States Air Force Major Command, Air Combat Command (ACC), has for a number of years pursued a program of research whose focus is the rational integration of networked flying, flying-related, and command and control simulators into current training via Distributed Mission Operations (DMO). According to the Chief of Staff of the Air Force (2003, p. 15), "DMO is an initiative to enable full-spectrum battlespace dominance in Service, Joint, and Coalition operations through integration of real, virtual (man-in-the-loop), and constructive (computer generated) capabilities, systems, and environments."

The Mission Essential Competency (MEC) job analysis methodology was developed as one facet of this DMO initiative. The MEC approach addresses multiple AFRL/ACC DMO program needs. Among other purposes, MECs enable the determination of training requirements and the appropriate mix of live operation and virtual training media, allow ACC to identify the value of DMO, provide justification for funding, and directly enable the construction of air combat simulation scenarios for which validated measures can be developed.

Although much has already been written about the MECs, one particular unaddressed topic relates to the nature of this effort relative to other job analysis and competency methods. How are MECs different from other methods of work analysis? What outcomes does the MEC approach produce that are unique? Is the MEC process rigorous enough to be considered a job analysis method, as industrial/organizational psychologists understand the term?

To address these questions, we take a historical–comparative approach. First, we consider the origin and nature of the competency movement. Second, we review in some detail how MECs are developed and used. Third and finally, we discuss MECs as a job analytic technique, including some thoughts on the validity of the method.

WHAT ARE COMPETENCIES?

History and Definitions of Competencies

Compared to job analysis, competencies are a relatively recent development. They arose outside of the purview of job analysis in the sense that they did not originally represent an extension of any existing job analytic method. Rather, the term first appeared in one or more business books, after which it was increasingly adopted within organizations.

McClelland (1973) made the argument that intelligence tests and academic measures such as grades did not predict job performance and should be replaced by a measure of competence. One of his associates, Richard Boyatzis (1982) published *The Competent Manager: A Model for Effective Performance*. He defined a competency as an "underlying characteristic of a person which results in effective and/or superior performance in a job." Based on a large sample of managers from several organizations, Boyatzis suggested that there were a finite number of competencies that were related to job success. The reception to the concept of competencies in the business world was positive, and competencies seem to have increased in popularity since that point. It should be pointed out that not all authors attribute the beginnings of the popularity of competencies to Boyatzis. Brannick and Levine (2002), for example, suggested that it was the work of Prahalad and Hamel (1990) that was pivotal in this regard. However, the fact that Zemke (1982) was criticizing the concept of competencies and competency models as early as 1982 seems to suggest that 1990 is too late a date for the beginnings of the surge of popularity that we are discussing.

In any case, it can be said with certainty that competencies have been defined in many ways over the past 20 years (e.g., Blancero, Boroski, & Dyer, 1996; Spencer & Spencer, 1993; Ulrich, Brockbank, Yeung, & Lake, 1995). However, perhaps three discernible central or consistent characteristics of competencies emerge from these definitions (Catano, 1998). First, competencies underlie successful performance; second, they should in some way distinguish superior from average performers; and third, competencies ought to be measurable and observable in some way.

One way to understand competency modeling is to compare it to the units employed by job analysis. Competencies are the equivalent of what are sometimes called job specifications—they are statements of human attributes required for job performance. As such, they can be thought of as at the same level (although different than) job tasks or functions. That is, they are human attributes required for successful performance at one of two levels of complexity, either functions or tasks; this is illustrated in Figure 31.1.

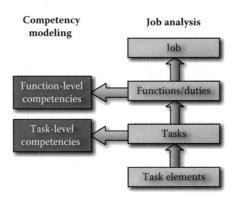

Figure 31.1 Levels of analysis in job analysis and competency modeling.

Criticisms of Competencies

Criticisms of competencies (e.g., Harvey, 1999) focus on their sometimes amorphous, broad character (e.g., Harvey, 1999), or a failure to include job analysis information in their development (Lievens, Sanchez, & De Corte,2004). It is true that general competency statements such as *Makes optimal decisions* or *Manages performance effectively* are insufficiently defined to serve much useful purpose. But in fact many competency models have behavioral descriptors that further elucidate the nature of the competencies. Good competency models are, just like job analysis, the result of systematic development (and may include job analysis as part of that development).

WHY IS COMPETENCY MODELING SO POPULAR?

Competency models have found great acceptance in modern organizations. Somehow, the worker-threatening characteristics of job analysis have been ameliorated in competency modeling. That is, competencies manage to objectify jobs in a more acceptable way than job analysis does. The reasons for this are presumably many; we discuss three. First, competency models tend to be used primarily for "white collar" working situations. It may be that such environments have a tendency to be less concerned about analytical approaches to jobs than more "blue collar," typically unionized, settings. There may simply be greater tolerance for management analysis of work in white collar settings because of their traditionally closer relationships between management. Unionized settings, on the other hand, often regard work analysis as being a tool of management. A second reason for the popularity of competencies is that they tend to be more obviously connected to the goals and strategies of the organization. Pearlman (1997) found that job analysis was superior to competencies in methods, descriptors, reliability, content revision, and documentation; it was not better, however, in linkage to business strategies and goals. This tighter linkage to organizational strategy may cause competency modeling to be seen by both management and employees as more important in a widespread, lasting sense than job analysis. Indeed, to the extent that competencies are seen as critical to the accomplishment of organizational strategy, it may be seen as a feature of the organization that should be carefully developed, nurtured, and vigorously employed.

A third reason for the popularity of competencies relates to the earlier discussion of subjective and objective descriptions of work. It was pointed out that although most people naturally use a subjective, personal narrative when talking about their jobs, job analysis is a highly (and intentionally) objective method for describing jobs. To the extent that people see their jobs described in naturalistic terms familiar to them, and close to the way that they themselves would discuss them, they should, it would be reasonable to assume, be more comfortable and satisfied. That is, if it can be argued that competency models use a more day-to-day language in describing work than job analysis does, then people should be happier and more inclined to credit the usefulness and validity of this approach. In fact, competency models do tend to be couched in the language of the job holder rather than that of the job analyst, in part because the outcome of competency modeling is often a tool, measure, or other organizational initiative that will be used by the employees themselves. For example, a 360-degree feedback initiative (where employees are rated by themselves, their peers and/or subordinates, and their managers) often uses competencies, and in fact may be one major reason for competency modeling. But employees, not analysts, are the end users of a 360-degree feedback system.

Thus, competencies appear to have accomplished, at least in some spheres, what job analysis has not: acceptance by employees. This fact has led to some perplexity among job analytic psychologists, given that job analysis (as illustrated in the results from Pearlman, 1997) is an exceedingly well-established, highly developed set of techniques. What, then, are job analytical psychologists to make of competencies? To their credit, psychologists seem to recognize the usefulness of competency modeling; moreover, its success is not to be denied. So there has been a tendency to accept the situation and to say that competency modeling is good but needs to be made better by applying the lessons of rigor derived from the history of job analysis. As Harvey (1999) put it, perhaps psychologists ought to declare victory and move ahead by ensuring that competency modeling is captured as one additional job analytic approach.

WHAT ARE MISSION ESSENTIAL COMPETENCIES?

A MEC is more than a simple competency. It reflects a set of outcomes developed via a fairly time-intensive and specific process. The outcomes (which can be called *elements*) comprise the full MEC model. This MEC model is both an end product and the input into a subsequent decision-making process (termed COMprehensive Mission Needs Analysis and Determination [COMMAND]). To be able to discuss the nature of MECs as a job analytic method, we discuss below (a) the elements of the MEC model, (b) the MEC development method, and (c) the COMMAND decision-making process.

Elements of the Mission Essential Competencies Model

The MEC process results in several outcomes: the MEC statements themselves—the MECs, supporting competencies (SCs), statements of knowledge and skills (KSs), and experiences. Depending on the system examined, there may be additional information (e.g., information about system-specific training programs) identified during the development process that is required to develop surveys capable of answering specific training needs questions.

Mission Essential Competencies

MECs are high-level functions that are job-contextualized and less general in most cases than competencies found in typical business environments. The term MEC has been formally defined as a "higher-order individual, team, and inter-team competency that a fully prepared pilot, crew, flight, operator, or team requires for successful mission completion under adverse conditions and in a non-permissive environment" (Colegrove & Alliger, 2002, p. 2). Note the conditions of performance specified in this definition. The United States Air Force (USAF) has not previously used combat conditions to define standards of warfighter performance. Interestingly, the high standard explicit in this definition is in accord with one of the central characteristics of competencies as originally conceived—specifically, standards of "success," and that in adverse conditions, are inherent in the nature of the MECs.

Each MEC is a brief statement, with clarifying text as appropriate. It also has a stipulated start, end, and purpose statement. Three example MECs are provided in the following lists—the first for Airborne Warning and Control System (AWACS), the second for Joint Terminal Attack Controller (JTAC), and the third from MCS/CRC (Modular Control System/Control and Reporting Center):

1. *Detects entities in area of interest*: Includes all air and surface tracks and emitters of interest.
   - Start: When systems operational.
   - Stop: When systems powered down.
   - Purpose: Assist in contributing entities to Single Integrated Operational Picture (SIOP) (e.g., using onboard and offboard sensors).

2. *Premission planning*: Receive mission; read, understand air tasking order/airspace control order/special instructions/operations order (ATO/ACO/SPINS/OPORD); extract information (e.g., command and control, intelligence, surveillance and reconnaissance, all lethal and nonlethal capabilities, communications plans, and priorities of fire) from all sources. Identify end state objective. Recognize and address problems (e.g., information that is absent or incorrect). Determine mission essential equipment and evaluate manpower requirements. Know supported unit's concept of operations.
   - Start: On receipt of warning order.
   - Stop: Begin execution.
   - Purpose: Prepare to support mission requirements.
3. *Mobilization/deployment/setup*: Site survey, pack equipment, deal with personnel readiness issues (e.g., weapons training, chemical warfare, self-aid and buddy care, cardiopulmonary resuscitation, radio frequency/radiation training, vehicle training, emergency action procedures [EAPs]); moving to site, airlift, convoy to permanent location and setup, unpack equipment and set up site: set up radar, set up satellite, data communications, housing, command post, medics tent, operations tent, complete equipment readiness checkout; notify higher headquarters that ready for operations; survive to operate.
   - Start: When mobilization order received.
   - Stop: When equipment ready for operation.
   - Purpose: To enable conducting of mission.

Often, the entire set of MECs that are defined by subject matter experts (SMEs) for a given weapon system reflect a broad chronological order, arising from the nature of the mission in question. For example, from an analysis of the tasks carried out by fighter pilots, MECs such as Detect, Target, Engage, as well as others usually emerge; the roughly sequential nature of these functions is mirrored in the MECs, so that one MEC may have as its start at the end of another. However, this is not always the case; some MECs may be temporally parallel, while others may be continuous or ongoing throughout the course of the performance of a job.

Not all MECs will necessarily apply to all positions in a multiperson system. For example, consider the Modular Control System (or, as it is also called, the Control and Reporting Center). This ground-based multiperson command and control center has a number of positions similar in function to

Table 31.1 Mapping of Mission Essential Competencies by Position for Modular Control System

Mission Essential Competency	AST	ST	ASO	DST	EPT	WD	SD	MCC	ICT	BC	BSC	OC
1. Mobilization/deployment/setup	P	P	P	P	P	P	P	P	P	P	P	P
2. Plans and prepares for theater mission	P	S	P	P	P	S	P	P	P	P	P	P
3. Crew mission planning	P	S	P	S	S	P	P	P	S			P
4. Establishes, maintains, and adjusts link and comm. Architecture	P	S	P	P	S	P	P	S	P			
5. Establishes, maintains, and adjusts radar picture	P	S	P	S	P		S	S				
6. Detects entities in Area of Interest	P	P	P		P	S	S	S				
7. Identifies entities in Area of Interest per ID matrix	P	P	P		S	S	S	S				
8. Updates/tracks entities in Area of Interest	P	P	P		P	S	S	S				
9. Conducts decentralized command and control	S	S	S			P	P	P		P	S	S

ASO = Air Surveillance Officer; AST = Air Surveillance Technician; BC = Battle Commander; BSC = Battle Staff Coordinator; DST = Data Systems Technician; EPT = Electronic Protection Technician; ICT = Interface Control Technician; MCC = Mission Crew Commander; OC = Operations Coordinator; P = primary duty; S = secondary duty; SD = Senior Director; ST = Surveillance Technician; WD = Weapons Director; blank = not applicable.

those of an AWACS. Table 31.1 provides a mapping of the MECs by MCS position, showing which MECs mapped onto which positions as primary duties, secondary duties, or not applicable.

Supporting Competencies

There are broad, high-level skills and knowledge that underlie the successful development and performance of the MECs. These SCs may include classic organizationally relevant competencies such as Decision Making or Adaptability, as well as more USAF-specific competencies such as Situation Awareness. SCs tend to have a similar nature to competencies typically developed in industry (that is, high-level and more or less context-free), as opposed to the MECs, which are highly contextualized job functions. Typical SCs include Situational Awareness, Leadership, Adaptability/Flexibility, and Information Management.

A review of example SCs (from the MCS/CRC) will give the reader their flavor:

- *Situational awareness*: Builds, maintains, and, when necessary, regains situational awareness throughout the mission; communicates as necessary; active listening
- *Multitasking*: Handles the requirements of multiple tasks simultaneously
- *Internal teamwork*: Establishes and executes contracts, requests assistance as needed, monitors indications of reduced performance in self and others, and provides timely assistance to others as needed
- *External teamwork*: Knows when, how, and to whom to handoff tasks and accepts handoff of tasks
- *Leadership/team management*: Establishes vision and objectives, sets tone and tempo, leads team by assigning tasks, delegates responsibilities, manages conflict, assesses performance, and models correct behaviors and performance levels

Knowledge and Skills

At a "lower" level of analysis than either MECs or SCs are KSs. These are deliberately elicited at the level of natural language—they are couched in terms and at an interpreted level of action clustering that is usual or common among job holders. This is intentional, both because it is deemed desirable to use the level of KS "chunking" that is common among warfighters because this facilitates data collection and ensures comprehension by the warfighter community, and because the USAF already has Training Task Lists (TTLs) that are written at a more basic level of analysis. Research linking existing TTLs to KS developed in the MEC project has begun.

Knowledge is defined as *information or facts that can be accessed quickly under stress*, and skill can be defined as *a compiled sequence of actions that can be carried out successfully under stress*. Because the emphasis is on performing under combat conditions, the use of the word *stress* in defining KS is highly important, and a baseline of initial training is assumed during the KS elicitation process. Below are some example knowledge statements (from Close Air Support [A-10]):

- *Environment effects*: Understands the effects of environmental factors on the mission (e.g., terrain, smoke, vegetation)
- *Systems/weapons capability*: Understands the capabilities of own and supporting aircraft and their weapons; knows penetration aids
- *Aircraft characteristics*: Understands aircraft flying characteristics in both medium- and low-altitude regimes
- *JTAC/forward air controller (airborne) operations*: Knows how the ground forces and tactical air control system typically operate

Some example skills (also from Close Air Support [A-10]) are as follows:

- *Identifies targets/threats*: Interprets the visual cues/system indicators that identify various targets/threats
- *Assesses risk*: Identifies and assesses risks related to mission accomplishment
- *Weaponeering*: Matches assets to targets; selects weapons to achieve desired goal; limits collateral damage; avoids fratricide
- *Positions assets/weapon systems*: Arranges assets for maximum impact and minimum threat exposure consistent with mission accomplishment

If MECs are being developed for a multiperson system or team, not every KS will apply to every position on that team. For example, the AWACS skill "AWACS employment: Positions AWACS to optimally meet mission tasking," actually applies only to the Mission Crew Commander and those other positions that have the responsibility for obtaining the best possible radar picture, given constraints and objectives. Thus, a position-by-KS matrix showing these dependencies is developed. Table 31.2 shows a partial example of such a matrix. In this table, a few KS are listed for the Air Operations Center Combat Plans Division. Note that there are four teams represented, each with a number of positions. The SME-stipulated required level of KS is shown for each position, such that a given position may be required to have a basic, intermediate, or advanced level for a given KS. In addition, some KS may be not applicable—that is, not required for that position.

Experiences

An element that is unique to the MEC model is experience. Experiences are captured during the MEC process as another measure related to the events in the life of warfighters that can be manipulated in training (either live or simulated). An experience can be defined as a developmental event that occurs during training and at various times across the career of a warfighter that facilitates learning a KS or practicing a MEC or SC under operational conditions.

There are essentially three types of experiences that are identified by SMEs: (a) an event that occurs to or situation encountered by, (b) an action that is performed by, or (c) an operation for a pilot, crew, team, or flight and that may be helpful in gaining the competencies required for successful mission completion under adverse conditions and in a nonpermissive environment. An experience is thus an identifiable event that is a facilitator of combat mission readiness. An experience can occur in any environment, training or actual combat operations. Examples of the first experience category—events that occur to or a situation encountered by the subject (i.e., the pilot, crew, team, or flight)—include the following (all examples from the MEC model for Air-to-Air [F-15C]):

- Flying where there are operating area restrictions (e.g., geographic, altitude, or political)
- Fatigue/time on task (e.g., long range force employment)
- Flying over mountainous terrain

Examples of the second category actions performed by the subject include the following:

- Using chaff/flare to deny/defeat enemy radar/weapons
- Live weapons employment (e.g., Weapon Systems Evaluation Program, combat)
- Employing cross-cue (off board) sources to locate and identify targets

Table 31.2 Example Stipulated Levels of Required Expertise by Position for Various Knowledge and Skills for the Air Operations Center Combat Plans Division

Knowledge or Skill	GAT					MAAP				ATO Production				C2 Planning				
	CCP	Chief	Planner	IW	ISR Element	Chief	Planner	IW Planner	ISR Planner	Chief	SPINS Officer	NCOIC	Tech Chief	Air Defense Planner	C2 Arch. Planner/	Air-space Planner	Air Support Planner	Comm/Freq Planner
Able to convert targets and threat situation to plan of action	I	A	A	A	A	A	A	A	A	B	B	B	NA	B	NA	NA	NA	NA
Understands the offensive and defensive capabilities, limitations, and effects of weapons systems	I	I		A	A	A	A	A	A	B	NA	B	NA	A	B	B	B	B
Understands package development process and procedures	I	B	B	B	B	A	A	A	A	B	NA	NA	NA	NA	NA	NA	NA	NA
Knows and understands current guidance (e.g., ROE, SPINS)	A	A	A	A	A	A	A	A	A	A	A	A	A	A	A	A	A	A
Able to lead team (e.g., communication, delegation, performance monitoring)	A	A	A	NA	NA	A	A	NA	NA	A	NA	A	NA	A*	A*	A*	A*	A*
Able to ensure quality of MAAP	A	NA	NA	NA	NA	I	I	I	I	NA	NA	NA	NA	NA	NA	NA	NA	NA
Able to develop briefing and brief effectively (ops)	A	A	I	A	A	I	I	A	A	—	NA	NA	A	A*	A*	A*	A*	A*

A = advanced; ATO = air tasking order; CCP = chief of combat plans; I = intermediate; ISR = intelligence, surveillance, and reconnaissance; IW = information warfare; MAAP = master air attack plan; NA = not applicable; NCOIC = noncommissioned officer in charge; SPINS = special instructions.

Examples of the third category of experiences (operations for a pilot, crew, team, or flight) include the following:

- Operations against air or ground adversary jamming
- Operations against a threat that uses chaff/flare
- Dynamic retasking/scramble operations

Experiences form the basis of most of the MEC surveys; they are crossed with MECs or training environments or mission types to answer particular questions (the surveys are discussed in more detail later).

THE MISSION ESSENTIAL COMPETENCY DEVELOPMENT PROCESS

As mentioned earlier, SME involvement is a critical factor in the development of the elements of the MEC models; it is basically a SME-centered process. Specifically, development involves (a) detailed facilitated workshops with SMEs identified by the operational customers according to stipulated criteria, (b) data gathered from the broader operational community via surveys, (c) a detailed analysis and organization of the survey results, and (d) facilitated workshops where SMEs view, interpret, and make recommendations based on the survey data. Thus, the initial set of draft MECs are developed following a workshop wherein SMEs provide information about the structure of their unit, missions and specific tasks performed, KSs, and SCs. All data gathered in the first workshop are compiled and organized and the MECs are developed prior to the second workshop. The second workshop provides a validation of the findings from the first workshop (the MECs and SCs) and allows the facilitators to delve deeper into the more detailed KSs and elicit experience components of the MEC model. Following the second workshop, an extensive database of expert knowledge about a career area exists. This information is organized into surveys that are presented to the broader operational community for that particular weapon system. After collecting and compiling the data, a comprehensive analysis of the weapon system and associated career field training status is performed, again via a facilitated, SME-centered workshop. As needed, other SME-centered work may occur (e.g., Symons, France, Bell, & Bennett, 2006).

MECs are developed for a given mission area, for example, Air-to-Air. There are several major weapon systems that perform the Air-to-Air mission; the MECs are the same for each. Conversely, multirole weapon systems have several sets of MECs, a set for each mission, that apply to that community. Different MEC efforts target different major weapon and command and control systems (e.g., AWACS, F-15C, Air Operations Center [AOC], Control and Reporting Center).

Identification of Subject Matter Experts

The MEC process is totally SME-centered; SMEs are involved in each step. SMEs are chosen based on their level of experience with the system under review. Generally, individuals with purely academic experience (e.g., course designers) are avoided in favor of operators (who may also have had instructional experience). The number of SMEs required for a workshop depends on the nature of the system. For example, a single-seat aircraft will require fewer SMEs than will a multiposition aircraft, for which each position should be represented by multiple individuals.

Mission Essential Competency Workshop 1: Mission Review, Task Identification, Knowledge, Skill, and Supporting Competency Generation

One of the weaknesses noted of competency modeling is that it is often not as thorough as traditional job analyses, and SMEs involved in competency development do not have job analysis information available to them (e.g., Lievens, Sanchez, & De Corte, 2004). The first MEC workshop is in part a task analysis; although the task listings are not a formal MEC product, the SMEs have a complete listing of tasks available to them. The way this is done is to review and identify the tasks involved in a number of missions: one of simple, one of intermediate, and one of high complexity. In most cases, the phases of the mission emerge, so that the tasks are elicited for each phase of each mission. For platforms with multiple positions, the tasks are identified by cycling through positions by phase by mission. In practice, because of the build from simple to complex missions, SMEs are often simply able to add additional tasks to the previously identified set of tasks as the mission difficulty increases. This is not always the case; sometimes equally difficult missions of rather different natures are identified. In this latter case, all relevant missions are reviewed and tasks identified. After tasks are identified, KS required to perform those tasks are nominated by SMEs. SMEs also generate a list of potential SCs.

It is important to point out that all of Workshop 1 is completed using flipcharts to record information. The facilitators write down verbal SME input onto flipchart paper, and the flip charts are posted in the room where the workshop is held. In this way, SMEs can at any time review any of the material previously generated and refer to it (e.g., by pointing to it and discussing it). This visual "memory" of the workshop is important to participants and is used by them extensively.

To clarify the nature of Workshop 1, the results are briefly reviewed for MEC Workshop 1 USAF Air-to-Ground.

Mission Review

As an example of this kind of Workshop 1 task analysis, we briefly review the results for USAF Air-to-Ground. SMEs in this workshop identified a number of missions that they felt reflected differences in both complexity and in character. A few of the missions discussed included Basic Interdiction, Strategic Attack, and Destruction of Enemy Air Defenses (DEAD). Basic Interdiction is relatively simple. The focus is on taking out lines of communication, supply lines, command, and control. The targets are operational and tactical (e.g., infrastructure, power, fielded forces); there is no immediate strategic goal specifically addressed. Strategic Attack, on the other hand, is a type of inherently complicated offensive mission. In this mission, pilots must consider factors such as the nature and context of the target and the type of weapons that are likely to be most useful. DEAD involves destruction of enemy air forces, surface-to-air missiles, and related communications and command and control systems. The phases common across missions that were identified included Planning, Administration, Ingress, Time Over Target, Administration 2, Checkout, and Debriefing.

Task Identification

After gathering this mission-level information, the missions, and phases within mission, were then cycled through to produce a complete task list. The level of tasks elicited in this manner is meant to be at a level at which it is natural for SMEs (pilots, in this case) to speak. For example, for the phase of the mission the SMEs called Planning, the task list for the Basic Interdiction mission included:

- *Risk analysis* (e.g., analyzing weather, nature of threat(s), assets available)
- *Game plan formulation* (e.g., making maps, weapons engineering, communications with scheduler and senior management official, obtaining all mission materials, determining timing, loading data transfer cartridge [DTC])
- *Develop contingencies* (e.g., consider strengths, weaknesses in game plan, what could cause mission and individuals within mission to succeed/fail, develop backup plans for situations where failure is possible, address failure to meet timing)

- *Brief plan* (e.g., communicate game plan to all assets available, review flow of mission and planned mission roles, use phone/presentations as needed, because not all personnel necessarily colocated)

Thus, the mission framework and the task list are only intermediate outcomes, but are nonetheless fairly complete and substantive. Their role during the workshop, however, is simply to serve as stimulus for generation of KS.

Knowledge Skill Generation

After identifying tasks, the SMEs have an outline of their missions (by phase, in most cases) and tasks within phase. With this in front of them, they are asked to generate the KSs that are required to carry out the missions. The goal is to obtain a list of KSs that is again (like the missions and the tasks) written at a level of language that is natural for the SMEs. In general, this results in KS that are of a moderate level of complexity (e.g., SMEs usually prefer to gather the various subskills for employing a particular weapons system, such as a bomb or rocket, under a single heading for that system). The SMEs are told that these are draft KS, which will be reviewed by them and/or similarly qualified individuals.

Developing Draft Mission Essential Competencies

After the first workshop, the facilitators review all the material gathered from the SMEs in that workshop. Taking into account the missions, mission phases, tasks, and the draft KS, MECs are drafted. Guidelines for constructing the MECs include: (a) they should be high-level, representing major functions or job responsibilities; (b) they should represent combat-level performance; (c) they should be in the SMEs' own language and reflect functions understandable and usable by them; and (d) they should not be abstract or general, but actual contextualized functions or responsibilities. Note that (a) effectively limits the number of MECs. Usually they range from 5 to 10 in number for a complete mission. We believe the reason for seeing this range of approximately 5–10 MECs in most cases reflects something about the interaction between what is designed to be accomplished by a team or platform (the mission) on the one hand and how people are most comfortable with describing that mission at a high level on the other. In other words, in the same way that any classification, taxonomy, or description must choose a level at which to speak and tends to gravitate to a level that makes sense to a majority of people, so the MECs tend to coalesce at a similar level across different jobs, platforms, or teams.

While the facilitators look closely at mission phases as identified by the SMEs developing the MECs, the MECs have never been synonymous with mission phases. For example, the first MEC effort, F-15C Air-to-Air, included such MECs as "Force Orientation" and "Recognition of Trigger Points"—functions that may occur throughout various mission phases. F-16 Air-to-Ground offers other examples of MECs that do not match mission phases. "Threat Mitigation during Ingress/Egress," for example, covers two phases; the similarity in the two phases suggested that they could reasonably be combined. "Employ Air-Ground Weapons," another MEC, was derived from the SMEs discussion of events very close in time. Thus, what for Air-to-Air appeared as separate MECs (e.g., Detect, Target, Engage) seemed to be combined in Air-to-Ground. The complete MEC reads

Employ air-ground weapons: Conduct airborne weaponeering; detect target(s); comply with rules of engagement (e.g., Positive Identification/Collateral Damage Estimation/deconfliction); position forces for optimum weapons effects; effectively deal with environmental/platform contingencies (e.g., weather, thermal blooming, secondary explosions, desired mean point of impact destroyed previously or missing); release weapons on target; apply countermeasures as required; assess weapons effects visually and/or with sensors when able; coordinate, deconflict, and execute reattack if able/required.

- Start: Approaching release conditions or arrival in target area.
- End: After weapons released, weapons impact, or effects assessed if able.
- Purpose: Optimize endgame execution to attain desired weapons effects.

Thus, the SMEs innate clustering of responsibilities gives rise in this instance to a single MEC.

Mission Essential Competency Workshop 2: Confirmation/Revision of Mission Essential Competencies and Workshop 1 Outcomes, Generation of Experiences

Workshop 2 further develops the MEC model by having SMEs review the MECs and KS and revise as needed. This is an important aspect of the content validation of the MEC model elements. In addition, it is during Workshop 2 that the Experiences are generated. Guidelines have been developed over time to facilitate the process of elicitation of developmental experiences. Specifically, it is important for experiences to be worded in a way that permits them to be easily understood, without confusion or misinterpretation. There are two main rules that will result in well-written experiences. First, in general, an experience should be single rather than compound. However, this is often an exercise in SME judgment because fusing two or more potentially separable features into a single experience may seem reasonable to them. For example, consider the experience "Operations against air or ground adversary jamming," which could be rewritten as two separate experiences: "Operations against air adversary jamming" and "Operations against ground adversary jamming." Ordinarily it would be recommended to break such a compound experience into its component parts. However, SMEs may determine that for training/educational purposes, it is reasonable to combine ground and air adversary jamming into a single statement. Second, experiences should be unambiguous and sufficiently clear to avoid misunderstanding. For example, the experience "Operations against a threat using chaff/flare" is ambiguous; it could be interpreted as meaning either that the threat is using chaff/flare or that the pilot is using chaff/flare to mitigate a threat. If the intended meaning is the former, it could be rewritten as "Operations against a threat which is using chaff/flare."

The Mission Essential Competency Surveys

For each MEC effort, custom surveys are developed, so that surveys for each system differ in MECs, KSs, SCs, and experiences. In addition, there are other system differences and the surveys are adapted accordingly. For example, different systems have different learning environments. Learning environments are defined as those locations or events where training and learning are accomplished. The learning environments form the basis of one of the surveys used in the MEC process and model. Beyond this, surveys may differ somewhat from system to system depending on the particular needs of the community, the missions that are performed, and the learning environments that are available. For example, The Ready Aircrew Program (RAP) is a training program to maintain readiness and proficiency among pilots. For systems that participate in RAP, there is a special survey that crosses experiences with major elements in RAP. However, there are typically several categories of surveys that are similar system to system. Each is described briefly below in Table 31.3 according to type of survey, primary question(s) addressed, rationale, type of respondents, primary analysis goal(s), and scale(s) employed. In multirole communities, surveys for each mission area are distributed according to the priority and frequency with which that community performs each mission.

Table 31.3   The Mission Essential Competency Surveys

Survey	Primary Question Addressed?	Rationale?	Respondents Experts or Nonexperts?	Primary Analysis Goals?	Scale
MEC Proficiency	How prepared are respondents to perform each MEC?	• Provide readiness assessment • Provide information about areas of MEC strength/weakness in current USAF	Both	• MECs rated by preparedness • MECs ranked by preparedness	**Rate each MEC:** 1 = I am not ready to perform this area in a nonpermissive environment. 2 = I am ready to go; however, I would like to get a substantial amount of additional experience in this area. 3 = I am ready to go; however, I would like to get a fair amount of additional experience in this area. 4 = I am ready to go; however, I would like to get a little additional experience in this area. 5 = I am ready to go, and I need no additional experience in this area **Rank each MEC:** Using numbers 1 to X, **rank** each of the X MECs in terms of your preparedness for performing each MEC in sustained combat operations. Use "1" for the MEC for which you have the highest level of preparedness, "2" for the MEC for which you have the next highest level of preparedness…
Experiences and MECs	How important is each experience for the development of each MEC?	• Identify relative and absolute importance of each experience for each MEC	Experts	• For each MEC, the most important experiences to develop that MEC	Indicate how important each experience is in developing each MEC. 0 = Not necessary/does not apply 1 = Slightly important 2 = Somewhat important 3 = Very important 4 = Mandatory
Experiences and Learning Environments – Ratings	To what extent is each learning environment reasonably appropriate for providing each Experience?	• Determine the extent to which experiences can be provided within various learning environments	Experts	• The most appropriate learning environment(s) under which to provide experiences	Rate to what extent it is reasonably possible to provide each experience in each environment. 0 = Not at all/does not apply 1 = To a slight extent 2 = To a moderate extent 3 = To a substantial extent 4 = To a great extent

continued

Table 31.3 The Mission Essential Competency Surveys (Continued)

Survey	Primary Question Addressed?	Rationale?	Respondents Experts or Nonexperts?	Primary Analysis Goals?	Scale
Experiences and Learning Environments – Frequencies	How often is each experience had in each learning environment?	• Identify the frequency of different experiences in different learning environments	Nonexperts	• Determine whether experiences are being provided at the right frequency in different learning environments	Indicate how often you have had each experience in each environment in the past X amount of time.
Experiences and Ready Aircrew Program (RAP)	How effective is each RAP mission in training pilots how to handle each experience?	• Analyze utility of RAP mission types in providing varying learning experiences	Experts	• The most effective RAP mission(s) for teaching pilots to handle each experience	Rate how effectively a pilot is taught to handle each experience in each type of RAP mission. 0 = Not at all effective 1 = Slightly effective 2 = Somewhat effective 3 = Quite effective 4 = Very effective N = Does not apply
Knowledge and Skills	What level of each knowledge or skill do respondents possess?	• Identify knowledge and skill levels compared to baseline	Both	• Identify opportunities to modify training (over- and undertraining)	Please indicate **your** current level of expertise in the following knowledge and skills by circling "B," "I," "A," or "NA." Basic (**B**): Understands primary concepts and fundamental methods; is able to perform activity at a foundational level. Intermediate (**I**): Understands main concepts and fundamental methods in some detail; performs activity above a basic level (e.g., could diagnose and solve some problems, could show someone with basic-level skill how to improve). Advanced (**A**): Understands concepts and methods in depth and detail; is able to perform activity at the expert level. Not Applicable (**NA**): The knowledge or skill is not applicable for your position.

Adapted and expanded from Colegrove, C. M. and Alliger, G. M., *Mission Essential Competencies: Defining Combat Mission Readiness in a Novel Way*, Brussels, Belgium, 2002. MEC = mission essential competency.

The Comprehensive Mission Needs Analysis and Determination Workshop:
Subject Matter Expert Interpretation of Survey Results

In the final workshop, the survey results are presented to a set of SMEs, who interpret the findings and identify training gaps. The data are formatted in a customized spreadsheet display, which is computer projected so that all SMEs can view it simultaneously.

Initial Subject Matter Expert Review of Results

First, the SMEs study the demographics to understand the nature of the survey sample. The demographics may show such breakouts as the number of survey responses by position or team (for a multiposition or multiteam system), the average number of years of service in the Air Force, the number of surveys collected per base, and so forth. Second, the SMEs review the results of the MEC proficiency survey to get a general sense of proficiency reported by survey respondents for each of the MECs. Again, this may be broken down by position or team as appropriate. Third, the SMEs review the results for each of the surveys; these are not studied in depth, but a general sense is gathered of the number and nature of the surveys and how data are displayed. For example, several unique conventions of the data display are highlighted, such as color coding of mean responses by the value range of the mean. The KS surveys are reviewed at this time as well as the other surveys but are a special case in that the results of these KS surveys are not used in the COMMAND process itself, but rather are presented as a takeaway for further study by the customer of the particular MEC project targeted by the COMMAND. Indeed, the entire set of COMMAND worksheets is delivered to the customer for further deliberation and study.

Comprehensive Mission Needs Analysis and Determination Process

After the review of all the results from each of the separate surveys, the SMEs are presented with the COMMAND worksheet. This worksheet is formatted to present the results from each survey (except the proficiency and KS surveys), experience by experience. Specifically, the SMEs see, for each experience, results that permit them to answer the questions:

1. How important is the experience in developing the MECs?
2. How effectively are pilots taught to handle the experience in current RAP training?
3. In what environments (e.g., Flag, MTC) can the experience be provided?
4. How often in the past year are pilots receiving the experience in each environment?
5. What conclusions/gaps can we identify based on this process?

If the system does not have a RAP program, the second question in the list is not included in the COMMAND worksheet. Using these results, the SMEs work through one experience at a time, considering what the results say about each experience as reflected in the responses to each survey. They answer the five questions and their responses (after discussion and consensus) are recorded real-time into the COMMAND worksheet. In this way, each experience is reviewed and conclusions about it are recorded. Typically, to run a COMMAND session for a given system requires 2 days. Figure 31.2 shows a screenshot of a portion of this worksheet.

Comprehensive Mission Needs Analysis and Determination Summary

A final worksheet in the COMMAND spreadsheet is a summary that transfers overall conclusions from the COMMAND worksheet and summarizes the data to show the number of gaps. It includes MEC proficiency data and permits the worksheet to be sorted by these data, by nature of the gap, and by experience. This COMMAND summary sheet, which brings the SME conclusions together in a single place, can be later used by decision makers. Figure 31.3 shows the format of this worksheet.

1 Operations in a robust low-tech IADS environment (e.g., Korean)

Step 1 - How important is the experience in developing the MECs? (0=Unnecessary, 1=Slightly Imp, 2=Somewhat Imp, 3/4=Very Imp/Mandatory)

Operations in a robust low-tech IADS environment (e.g., Korean)			Plan/ Prepare	Organize/ Optimize	Threat Mitigation	Oriented to Mission	Employ Air-Ground Weapons	Post Mission Analysis and Comm
		n	m	m	m	m	m	m
F-15E	22	- 23	3.3	2.8	3.4	3.2	3.3	2.6
Conclusion:								

Step 2a - How effectively is this experience taught in each type of mission? (0=Not at all, 1=Slightly, 2=Somewhat, 3/4=Quite/Very)

Operations in a robust low-tech IADS environment (e.g., Korean)			BFM	ACM	BSA	DCA	SAT	CAS
		n	m	m	m	m	m	m
F-15E	22	- 22	1.3	1.4	2.0	2.1	3.2	2.6
Conclusion:								

Step 2b - To what extent can this experience be provided in each environment? (0=Not at all, 1=Slight, 2=Moderate, 3/4=Substantial/Great)

Operations in a robust low-tech IADS environment (e.g., Korean)			Not Flag/CFTR	Flag	CFTR	MTC	UTD	WST	PCATD	MST	Post Combat Air Spt	Homeland Defense Ops	Sustained Combat Ops
		n	m	m	m	m	m	m	m	m	m	m	m
F-15E	1	- 22	2.4	3.5	3.0	2.0	2.0	2.1	0.7	1.0	1.4	0.1	2.7
Conclusion:													

Step 3 - How often have you had this experience in this environment in the past year?

Operations in a robust low-tech IADS environment (e.g., Korean)			Not Flag/CFTR	Flag	CFTR	MTC	UTD	WST	PCATD	MST	Post Combat Air Spt	Homeland Defense Ops	Sustained Combat Ops
		n	median	median	median	median	median	median	median	median	median	median	median
F-15E	0	- 45	2.0	3.0	2.0		5.0	3.0	0.0	1.0	0.0	0.0	0.0
Response Rate			100%	51%	56%	0%	2%	78%	2%	13%	16%	7%	24%
Conclusion:													

Step 4 - What overall conclusions/gaps can we identify based on these results?   Gaps? Yes (Y) Potential (P) No (N)

Overall Conclusions:

Figure 31.2   Part of a Comprehensive Mission Needs Analysis and Determination worksheet.

Return to Table of Contents — **F-15E Air-to-Air COMMAND SUMMARY** — Mean MEC Rankings: 1= mo

Instructions:
Use the buttons to sort this spreadsheet by different columns. You can reset to original order by clicking the left button.

0 Experiences with Gaps
0 Experiences with Potential Gaps
0 Experiences with No Gaps

#	Experience	GAP?	COMMAND Conclusions	Importance	Plan/prepare for mission	Force organization	Detection phase
1	Restricted weapons load (e.g., due to previous weapons employment, incompleted reload, or WRM limitations)			2.9	3.0	2.3	1.3
2	Limited fuel remaining (e.g., due to increased fuel consumption, low fuel remaining, lack of tanker support, or the inability to inflight refuel)			2.8	3.2	2.8	0.8
3	Operating area restrictions (e.g., geographic, altitude, or political)			3.0	3.5	2.5	3.0
4	Restrictions to visibility (e.g., haze)			2.3	2.7	1.5	2.2
5	Visual Illusions			1.7	2.2	1.0	2.0
6	Marginal/minimal cloud clearance			2.1	2.8	2.5	1.5
7	Daytime employment			2.3	2.7	2.2	2.2
8	Dusk employment			2.2	3.0	2.2	2.0
9	Night employment			2.4	3.5	2.5	2.2
10	Mountainous terrain			2.6	3.2	2.3	3.7
11	G-induced physical limitations			0.9	1.2	0.5	0.7
12	Degraded comm. (e.g., due to ownship systems malfunction, another aircraft's malfunction, or the inability to use HQ or secure voice by one or more aircraft)			2.8	2.7	3.5	2.8
13	Degraded nav.			2.3	2.3	2.5	2.2
14	Degraded weapons employment						

Ranks ⇓ Plan/prepare for mission — Force organization — Detection phase
Preparedness — Readiness

Figure 31.3   Part of a Comprehensive Mission Needs Analysis and Determination summary spreadsheet.

MISSION ESSENTIAL COMPETENCIES AS A JOB ANALYTIC METHOD

Mission Essential Competencies as a Type of Job Analysis

The first step in developing the MECs is task identification. Although those tasks are but a step in generating specific elements of the MEC model and not an end in themselves, nonetheless it can be stated that MECs are based on a task analysis. As such, the MEC approach can be categorized as a job analytic method. Almost certainly it can be said that the MEC approach is a hybrid of a task-based job analysis approach and a worker-oriented approach. Its task-based characteristics can be discerned from the fact that it incorporates a task analysis. It is also worker-oriented in that it attends to the demands that the job places on the operators. This blended nature allows the MECs to be compared to a broad range of job analysis methods. Table 31.4 shows such a comparison, including task analysis, worker-oriented analysis, functional job analysis (FJA), and cognitive task analysis (CTA).

Task analysis, as typified in the Management Position Description Questionnaire (Tornow & Pinto, 1976), focuses on identifying detailed tasks for a given position. In comparison, the MEC model does not focus on tasks as an outcome, but rather as a means to achieve other outcomes.

A comparison of the MECs can be made with worker-oriented analysis. An example is the Position Analysis Survey (PAQ); its development is considered an important milestone in job analysis (Harvey, 1991). One problem that has been noted about the PAQ is that it requires a high school or higher reading ability of job incumbents. Harvey, Friedman, Hakel, and Cornelius (1988) have developed a survey called the Job Element Inventory, which is similar to the PAQ but has a substantially lower reading level. Although the worker-oriented analysis focuses on only the human requirements of a job, it has a much narrower focus than the MECs.

A comparison can certainly also be drawn between MECs and FJA (Fine & Wiley, 1971). The MEC process is probably most similar to FJA than to other job analysis methods because of the wide range of outcomes. However, it is also different from FJA in that specific developmental experiences are identified, where FJA specifies only some training requirements. Further, FJA may specify tasks at a detailed level, while the MEC process does not. However, for U.S. Air Force jobs, the Training Task Lists (TTLs) fulfill that function.

In another type of job analysis, Cognitive Task Analysis (CTA), the focus is on mental representations or processes of the worker. The MEC process is different than CTA, in that detailed

Table 31.4 Comparison of Job Analysis Methods by Outcomes

	Outcomes							
			Human Requirements?				Cognitions?	
Job Analysis Method	Major Functions?	Detailed Tasks?	Knowledge/ Skill	General Abilities	Developmental Experiences?	Training Requirements?	Detailed Task or Decision Cognitions?	Overall Mental Model?
FJA	Y	Y	Y	Y	N	Y	N	N
CTA	N	N	N	N	N	N	Y	Y
Task Analysis	N	Y	N	N	N	N	N	N
WO Analysis	N	N	Y	Y	N	N	N	N
MEC Analysis	Y	N	Y	Y	Y	Y	N	Y

Source: Alliger, G. M., Colegrove, C., & Bennett, W. Jr., *Mission Essential Competencies: New Method for Defining Operational Readiness and Training Requirements,* Paper presented at the Thirteenth International Occupational Analyst Workshop, San Antonio, TX, 2003.

CTA = cognitive task analysis; FJA = functional job analysis; MEC, Mission Essential Competency; WO, worker-oriented.

understanding about decision factors and judgments, or the melding of perception level data to actions, is not addressed. However, to the degree that the MECs themselves somewhat capture the mental model commonly used by pilots (Find, Fix, Track, Target, Engage, Assess), MECs and CTA would appear to overlap in terms of philosophy and outcomes.

Mission Essential Competencies in the Context of Competency Modeling

MECs enjoy not only some of the advantages of job analysis, but also those of competency models. Like any good competency model, they employ the language and phrasing of the community for which they are developed; moreover, they are clearly linked to an organizational goal (in this case, strategic training realignment). Indeed, it may be said that the language and phrasing of the MECs are more intensely those of the user target group even than is true of most competency models. This is the case because they are not even slightly decontextualized, as many competency statements are. Another way to say this is that the MECs are not like worker-oriented job analysis statements, which are meant to be general and valid in a cross-job sense. Instead, MECs are high-level functions particularly appropriate to the mission and platform under consideration. MECs for Air-to-Ground will not be the same as MECs for Air-to-Air. Air-to-Ground MECs for the RAF Jaguar are not the same as those for the F-16 because of the differences in the capabilities and tactics of these two aircraft. Thus, the extreme contextualization of MECs means that operators immediately recognize the language and stated functions as their own. Other aspects of the MEC model, such as SCs, are general and decontextualized; SCs are more like competencies found in traditional models. Figure 31.4 maps some of the major elements of the MEC model to the levels of analysis in job analysis. Note that SCs are mapped at the duty/function level, KS at the tasks level; the thought here is that both are worker-oriented outcomes detailing human characteristics required for successful job performance. MECs are, like SCs, at the duty or function level (because they are, in fact, high-level functions), but also draw some of their character from specific tasks identified in the MEC process.

Evidence of the Validity of the Mission Essential Competency Process

The basis for the validity of job analysis is generally of two types: content and construct. Content validity is validity demonstrated on the basis of the methods employed; the domain of the job has been carefully depicted using rigorous techniques. Construct validity is validity demonstrated by the appropriate behavior of variables, such as raters agreeing with each other, or more experienced individuals scoring higher on job analytically derived measures. A third type of validity is the utility of the job analysis information: Do job analytic results prove useful to the organization? Are good decisions made on the basis of the job analysis? We briefly discuss the MECs regarding each of these approaches to validity.

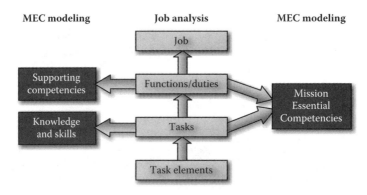

Figure 31.4 Levels of analysis in job analysis and Mission Essential Competency modeling.

Content Validity

As discussed previously, mission review and task identification are an initial and critical step in the MEC process; other parts of the MEC model, including the MECs, are based on it. The first workshop thus grounds the MEC model in the nature of the job; inferences such as those made in the KS are therefore clearly focused. Careful selection of SMEs and a time-tested process for Workshop 1 also support the content validity of its outcomes.

The careful development of the model continues during the generation of the MECs, where all sources (e.g., outcomes from Workshop 1) are constantly kept in view. Workshop 2 operates as a further check on SME understanding of, and agreement with, the elements of the model. The MEC surveys draw on these elements in their entirety; that is, there is no room for content selection bias to operate because every MEC, experience, and KS is to be found in the surveys. As a result of this careful development, the MEC model can be appropriately presented as having content validity.

Construct Validity

If a job construct is valid, it is reasonable to expect appropriate convergence (e.g., among ratings for similar platforms with the same mission or between years of service and proficiency) and also appropriate divergence (e.g., between experts and nonexperts).

Convergence

Alliger, Beard, Bennett, and Colegrove (in press) provided evidence that interrater agreement, as indexed by intraclass correlations, is high for each of the MEC surveys found in Table 31.3. Two striking displays of agreement on average are shown in Figures 31.5 and 31.6. In these figures, the average proficiency rankings are shown, comparing different platforms that perform the same mission (Air-to-Ground in Figure 31.5 and Air-to-Air in Figure 31.6). It is intriguing that the average rankings are in such close agreement. Although divergent average rankings might simply have reflected different levels of proficiency for each MEC, the convergent results should most likely be

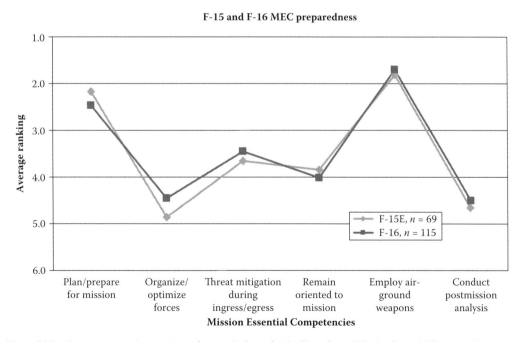

Figure 31.5 Average preparedness rankings for two platforms for the Air-to-Ground Mission Essential Competencies.

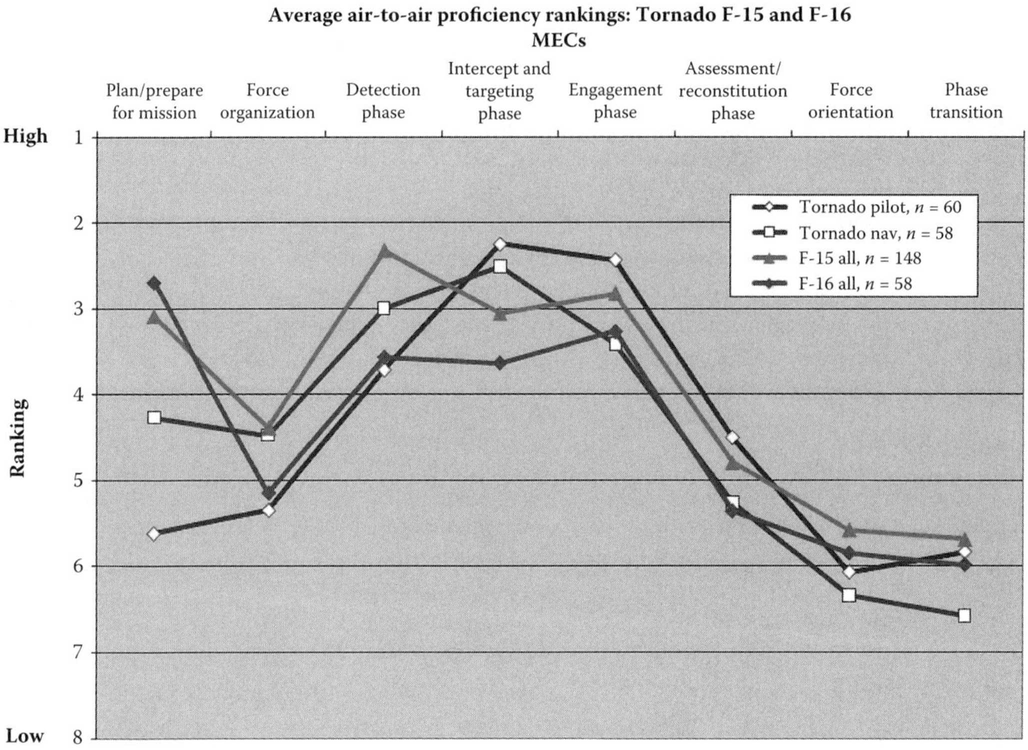

Average air-to-air proficiency rankings: Tornado F-15 and F-16 MECs

Figure 31.6   Average preparedness rankings for three platforms for the Air-to-Air Mission Essential Competencies.

accepted as evidence that there is not a "main effect" for platform, but only mission. Such convergence is not likely by chance.

Another example of convergence can be found in the virtually universally positive, nonzero correlations found between years of service and KS ratings, also as reported in detail in Alliger, Beard, Bennett, and Colegrove (in press).

Utility Validity

Finally, the MEC models developed for various platforms, and the results of various COMMAND sessions have proven useful to decision makers. As Colegrove (2005) outlined, the MECs have been used to drive decisions regarding training. For example, the training for the F-15C has been altered using MEC inputs:

> As part of the MEC process we identified the developmental experiences that were most important to exercising knowledge and developing proficiency in those skills necessary to build back up to the MECs. Pilots at five F-15C bases were then surveyed to provide direct warfighter input and the results subsequently analyzed by experienced F-15C pilots. Comparisons of the ability to provide important experiences were made between live training and virtual events in the MTC. Defensive Counter Air (DCA) and Offensive Counter Air (OCA) were found to be credibly trained in the MTC and three missions of each type were added to the annual simulation requirement for each pilot. The total live sortie requirement did not decrease but was remixed—removing three each DCA and OCA but adding six additional sorties to the Commander's Option category thereby allowing the unit commander a greater opportunity to direct and target training done in the aircraft. The new simulation requirements target specific experiences and the time spent in the MTC during those missions counts toward the pilots' total time required (500 hours) to become "Experienced"—a point at which the pilot flies fewer sorties per training cycle. (Colegrove, 2005, p. 9.4)

Another example of the application of the MECs is found within the extensive work completed on automatic simulation measurement development documented by Schreiber and his colleagues (e.g., Portrey, Keck, & Schreiber, 2005; Schreiber, Watz, & Bennett, 2003). Schreiber et al. detailed how the MECs both suggest what to measure and that they may in some cases be amenable to automatic measurement in a simulation environment.

FINAL COMMENTS

Although MECs can be seen, therefore, as a competency model that uses job analytic techniques, or perhaps as a job analytic method that generates competency-like outcomes, it is probably best seen in toto, as a unique approach to work in the military setting that serves its designated purpose, that of training analysis, particularly well. The MEC development process is both task- and worker-oriented, representing a blended job analysis approach. It is a rigorous approach, ultimately based in an understanding of the tasks of the job. Like other competency models, MECs are understood by their customers to address important strategic aspects of organizational needs—in this case, training in a DMO environment. MECs are highly contextualized, high-level functions, in part successful because they capture the warfighter's job in a way that is deemed practical and accurate. The MEC model is unique, in that it includes developmental or learning experiences, which in fact form the basis for many of the most influential aspects of the MECs (e.g., the COMMAND workshops and their outcomes). It is possible that the MECs retain a sufficient amount of the everyday, subjective descriptions of work that individuals are more comfortable with than they might be with more technical, lower-level job analytic results.

The MEC process and model show evidence of content, construct, and utility validity. MEC outcomes are being applied to different training-related situations, both applied settings (as in the determination of live-fly versus simulation training events) and more research based settings (as in the use of MECs to help guide development of simulator-based measures). In sum, it appears that the MEC model offers today's training researchers and training professionals a number of interesting points to consider. Whether and how MECs might generalize to a different, nonmilitary setting remains to be examined.

REFERENCES

Alliger, G. M., Beard, R. L., Bennett, W. Jr., & Colegrove, C. (in press). A psychometric examination of mission essential competency (MEC) measures used in air force distributed mission operations training needs analysis. *Military Psychology*.

Alliger, G. M., Colegrove, C., & Bennett, W. Jr. (2003, April). *Mission essential competencies: New method for defining operational readiness and training requirements*. Paper presented at the Thirteenth International Occupational Analyst Workshop, San Antonio, TX.

Blancero, D., Boroski, J., & Dyer, L. (1996). Key competencies for a transformed human resource organization: Results of a field study. *Human Resource Management, 35*, 383–403.

Boyatzis, R. E. (1982). *The competent manager: A model for effective performance*. New York, NY: John Wiley & Sons.

Brannick, M. T., & Levine, E. L. (2002). *Job analysis: Methods, research, and applications for human resource management in the new millennium*. Thousand Oaks, CA: Sage Publications.

Catano, V. M. (1998). *Competencies: A review of the literature and bibliography*. Halifax, Nova Scotia, Canada: Saint Mary's University.

Chief of Staff of the Air Force. (2003). *Distributed Mission Operations CONOPS*. Washington, DC: Author.

Colegrove, C. M. (2005). *Mission Essential Competencies: The operational application of today's training analysis for tomorrow's advanced distributed training*. Paper presented at the Royal Aeronautical Society Conference on "Multi Role and Networked Simulation," London, UK.

Colegrove, C. M., & Alliger, G. M. (2002). *Mission Essential Competencies:Defining combat mission readiness in a novel way*. Paper presented at the Analysis and Simulation Panel Symposium on Air Mission Training Through Distributed Simulation, Brussels, Belgium.

Fine, S.A., & Wiley, W.W. (1971). *An introduction to functional job analysis: A scaling of selected tasks from the social welfare field (Methods for Manpower Analysis No. 4.)*. Kalamazoo, MI: W.E. Upjohn Institute for Employment Research.

Harvey, R. J. (1991). Job analysis. In M. Dunnette & L. Hough (Eds.), *Handbook of industrial and organizational psychology* (2nd ed., pp. 71–163). Palo Alto, CA: Consulting Psychologists Press.

Harvey, R. J. (1999, March). *Dr. Competency love: or, How I learned to stop worrying and love "competencies."* Invited presentation for the North Carolina Industrial/Organizational Psychologists Association, Greensboro, NC.

Harvey, R. J., Friedman, L., Hakel, M. D., & Cornelius, E. T. (1988). Dimensionality of the Job Element Inventory, a simplified worker-oriented job analysis questionnaire. *Journal of Applied Psychology, 73,* 639–646.

Lievens, F., Sanchez, J. I., & De Corte, W. (2004). Easing the inferential leap in competency modeling: The effects of task-related information and subject matter expertise. *Personnel Psychology, 57,* 881–904.

McClelland, D. C. (1973). Testing for competence rather than intelligence. *American Psychologist, 28,* 1–14.

Pearlman, K. (1997, April). Competencies: Issues in their application. In R. C. Page (Chair), *Competency Models: What are they and do they work?* Practitioner forum conducted at the 12th Annual Conference of the Society for Industrial and Organizational Psychology, St. Louis, Missouri.

Portrey, A. M., Keck, L. M., & Schreiber, B. T. (2005).Challenges in developing a performance measurement system for the global virtual environment. In *Proceedings of the 2005 Spring Simulation Interoperability Workshop*. San Diego, CA: SISO, Inc.

Prahalad, C. K., & Hamel, G. (1990). The core competence of the corporation. *Harvard Business Review, 68,* 79–91.

Schreiber, B. T., Watz, E., & Bennett, W. Jr. (2003). Objective human performance measurement in a distributed environment: Tomorrow's needs. In *2003 Proceedings of the Interservice/Industry Training Systems and Education Conference (I/ITSEC)*. Orlando, FL: National Security Industrial Association.

Spencer, L., & Spencer, S. (1993). *Competence at work: Models for superior performance*. New York: John Wiley & Sons.

Symons, S., France, M., Bell, J., & Bennett, W. Jr. (2006). *Linking knowledge and skills to mission essential competency-based syllabus development for distributed mission operations*. Mesa, AZ: Air Force Research Laboratory, Warfighter Readiness Research Division.

Tornow, W., & Pinto, P. (1976). The development of a managerial job taxonomy: A system for describing, classifying, and evaluating executive positions. *Journal of Applied Psychology, 61,* 410–418.

Ulrich, D., Brockbank, W., Yeung, A., & Lake, D. (1995). Human resource competencies and empirical assessment. *Human Resources Management, 34,* 473–496.

Zemke, R. (1982) Job competencies: Can they help you design better training? *Training, 19,* 28–31.

32

Integrating Cognitive Task Analysis and Verbal Protocol Analysis
A Typology for Describing Jobs

THOMAS R. GORDON
University of South Florida

MICHAEL D. COOVERT
University of South Florida

LINDA R. ELLIOTT
Army Research Laboratory

Over the past decade there has been substantial growth in teams and team work, both in the world of research as well as in industry. This interest is due in part to the increasing complexity of the nature of work. That is, complex tasks lend themselves to using team structures (Sundstrom, De Meuse, & Futrell, 1990). Measuring and modeling team processes is important in understanding where and how teams can be employed in the accomplishment of tasks (Dickinson & McIntyre, 1997). It follows that modeling performance and establishing performance criteria in training environments are also important issues (Coovert & Craiger, 1997). Moreover, team competencies (knowledge, skills, and abilities [KSAs]) are vital to understanding and evaluating team performance in dynamic environments (Cannon-Bowers & Salas, 1998).

In addition to performing complex tasks, many teams work under stressful and sometimes dangerous conditions. Such team tasks are usually highly dynamic and require team members to think and act quickly to keep up with rapid situational changes. One such team is the Airborne Warning and Control System (AWACS)/Weapons Directors (WD) team. The AWACS is an aerial platform that serves as an airborne command post (Figure 32.1). It contains a number of suites with specialized missions in the areas of command, control, and communications (C3). Among these suites are the WDs (Figure 32.2), who control three aspects of the air battle: (a) high value airborne assets such as refueling tankers and the AWACS itself, (b) fighter aircraft that provide air cover and protection against enemy aircraft, sometimes referred to as CAP (combat air patrol) or DCA (defensive counter-air), and (c) fighter-bombers whose mission is to attack surface targets posing a threat to the overall mission of the command; the latter are called "strike" aircraft. The dynamic nature of the environment, the complexity and interdependence of team tasks, and the criticality of flawless performance combine to suggest the WD tasks ideal for the employment of teams. In this

Figure 32.1   E-3A, Airborne Warning, and Control Aircraft.

introduction, we first describe previous work to set the stage for reviewing initial and subsequent phases of a research effort that specifically addresses WD teams.

A number of team performance functions are important to effective team coordination (e.g., information exchanges among team members, monitoring, backup, and so forth) (Fleishman & Zaccaro, 1992; Hess, Freeman, & Coovert, 2008). Better anticipation of each other's actions and reduced, more efficient communication among team members can also result in better team performance (Klimoski & Mohammed, 1994). Cannon-Bowers, Salas, and Converse (1993) suggested that mental models encoded (and shared) by team members are particularly important to team performance. Thus, performance and cognitive processes have both been linked to team performance outcomes. In this chapter, we describe efforts to formulate an integrated cognitive-behavioral representation of performance in a dynamic and complex setting. Some of the task categories are specific to the operational performance per se; others are generalizable to other settings. The process of identifying these categories should be relevant to many other operations.

Figure 32.2   Weapons Directors, E-3A, Airborne Warning, and Control Aircraft.

Identifying the Weapons Director Performance Domain

A key change in decision theory has involved the increased use of naturalistic decision theory, whereby highly trained observers study complex human decision-making processes in naturalistic settings. Additionally, researchers in human-computer interaction (HCI) and other domains within cognitive science have been developing and utilizing a variety of cognitive task analyses (CTAs) to "analyze and model the cognitive processes that give rise to human task performance in specific domains" (Zachary, Ryder, & Hicinbothom, 1998, p. 315). Thus, the purpose of this chapter is show how CTA can be used to describe jobs in a way that goes beyond traditional job analysis.

Seamster, Redding, Cannon, Ryder, and Purcell (1993) describe a cognitive task analysis of en route air traffic controllers, whose functions are similar to those of WDs. For their study, CTA involved identifying key tasks and analyzing those tasks "from a cognitive perspective, identifying the task subgoals and the triggers that activate the individual task" (p. 260). The authors placed special emphasis on the relation of the tasks to the expert's mental model, while focusing on the planning processes and maintenance of situational awareness.

Miles et al. (1999) conducted research to analyze the functional team and the specific positions of WDs working within the AWACS aircraft. The goal of this research was to develop enough knowledge and understanding of the WDs' positions (and environment) to use as the basis for a model that would integrate both cognitive and behavioral task analyses. Although cognitive and behavioral analyses have been modeled separately, an integrative model, which links these two aspects, has eluded researchers. The difficulty in developing this type of model lies in the limitations of conventional methodologies. Specifically, task concurrencies and dynamic behavior pose a barrier to conventional tools, which can only handle static and synchronous properties. The problem with conventional tools has been exacerbated by cognitive task analyses/behavioral task analyses generally focusing on the individual rather than the team level. Therefore, Miles et al. conducted a qualitative "meta-analysis" using data gathered from previous cognitive task analyses to develop a working model of team performance within the dynamic AWACS environment. This effort resulted in a list of 230 tasks contained in the working model. Through a series of sorting exercises, the 230 WD tasks were reduced to a set of nine working categories. As noted, the meta-analysis leading to the 230 tasks was based on cognitive task analyses; accordingly the sorting emanated from an analysis of both empirical and theory-driven information. In other words, the categories are a combination of prior knowledge, critical thinking, and skill in different functions. Below is a list of the nine categories and brief descriptions:

1. *Directing*: This is viewed as the primary WD responsibility. The WD directing tasks are pre-prioritized according to Rules of Engagement, orders from higher authority, and Standing Operational Procedures, usually under the premise that the more critical the event, the greater the cognitive load on the WD. We further divided the directing category according to the extent to which the directing tasks impact operator cognitive load.

2. *A priori knowledge*: This category specifies the types of knowledge that WDs must bring to each mission. Much of this knowledge comes from experience and training, but it also includes mission-specific knowledge gathered from the pre-mission briefing.

3. *Individual internal cognitions*: This involves the broad types of cognitive activities that AWACS WDs engage in on the job. This category differs from some of the others (e.g., pre-mission planning and resource management) in that it is not usually tied to a specific function or goal. Rather, it addresses the requisite cognitive activities within and across many different aspects of job performance.

4. *Premission planning*: This category involves the various tasks that occur during the pre-mission planning process.

5. *Situational awareness*: This category involves maintaining an understanding of current and projected events involving aircraft in the area of responsibility (especially cognizance of the "big picture") to determine (or predict) events that will require WD activities.

6. *Resource management*: We view this category as a goal that WDs strive to achieve. Resource Management involves utilizing AWACS resources to an appropriate extent (i.e., maintaining enough resources while avoiding waste and overload).

7. *Dynamic operational planning and prioritizing*: This category includes the planning and prioritizing tasks that occur "on the fly," during the actual mission. This dimension involves reassessment of the situation, problem-solving, and reclassification.

8. *Team issues*: This category involves tasks and events that require or are otherwise related to teamwork, including member communication, coordination of tasks, and cooperation.

9. *Communication*: This category refers to the act of transmitting or exchanging information that occurs during premission planning; as part of dynamic operational planning and prioritizing; during directing; expressly for team issues; and to maintain situational awareness. It includes the specific protocols for communication.

These categories were developed as a useful aid in creating a model to examine the performance of WDs within an AWACS team. The nine categories are not exhaustive, nor are they mutually exclusive. Additionally, they are not hierarchical in nature. However, relationships can be and were ascertained among the categories. An example would be the relationships among cognitive categories (e.g., situation awareness) and behavioral categories (e.g., resource management). Once an accurate framework for performance was defined, then more fully specified models can be developed. For example, task categories can be further specified in functional areas (like objectives, goals, tasks, or subtasks) or cognitive areas (such as the specification of particular aspects of situation awareness). Further specification should be designed to encompass a purpose (e.g., development of training, assessment of performance, and so forth).

Weapons Director Model Development

The follow-on initiative was outlined by Gordon et al. (2000), in which a model of AWACS team performance was proposed and demonstrated. Models of team performance are generally consistent in considering three levels of analysis: individual performance, team performance, and organizational performance and support (Brannick & Prince, 1997). In this respect, team performance is considered in the traditional systems model, using input, throughput, and output as ways to judge important aspects of teams' operations, successes, and failures (Bertalanffy, 1968).

Gordon et al. (2000) examined team performance in the context of environmental complexity, using cognitive task analytic methodology to link cognitive and behavioral components of team performance (van der Schaff, 1993), then modeled this performance dynamically—that is, in a way that captured the complexity of team performance. Researchers were able to simulate linking explicitly the cognitive categories to operator behaviors, using Petri nets, a mathematical approach to modeling complex, multitask functions (Coovert, 1992, in press; Coovert & Dorsey, 2000; Yagoda & Coovert, in press). To date, access to a simulation or platform that allowed linking cognitions and behaviors temporally has not been available. With the future development of more event-based scenarios, we should be able to demonstrate rather easily the efficacy of modeling tools, such as Petri nets, for this purpose. Any scenario can be analyzed by applying the performance categories to "trigger" events; such events initiate a series of responsive actions by members of the AWACS team. These response actions can be modeled using our procedure.

Verbal Protocol Analysis

Described in considerable detail by Ericsson and Simon (1993), verbal protocol analysis (VPA) uses participants' verbal reports as data. The technique is used principally to explore cognitive processes. The authors made explicit the techniques to be used in the study and placed the methodology on firm ground by addressing the nature and reliability of the method. In its simplest form, verbal protocol involves recording orally communicated "thoughts," committing them to written form and comparing them with observed behavior. Reliability was addressed by evaluating consistency of agreement among observers.

The overarching objective of the studies described (Gordon et al., 2000; Miles et al., 2000) was to offer a method toward a better understanding of team performance in a dynamic environment through CTA and modeling (Coovert, Craiger, & Cannon-Bowers, 1995). These efforts were successful within the limitations posed by available tools and allowed for further study of the WD team. These studies also provided the foundation for development and testing of the hypotheses outlined below. The purpose of the latest phase of the WD study was to combine CTA and VPA to develop a better, more comprehensive picture of individual WD performance. In other words, we wanted to describe the WD job in a way that takes into consideration the dynamics of the job, thus going beyond traditional job analysis.

RESEARCH DESIGN

Participants

Participants consisted of WDs undergoing simulation training at an Air Force Base in the southwest United States. There were 17 "experienced" and 21 "inexperienced" WDs, for a total of 38. As explained below, experienced and inexperienced are relative terms. All had at least minimum qualifications achieved from basic WD training (approximately 1 year in length). There were four females and 34 males. The distinction between an experienced and inexperienced WD is important; WDs were categorized as experienced if they had more than 400 flight hours in the AWACS aircraft and at least 1 year designated as "combat mission ready." All others were categorized as inexperienced WDs. These distinctions were used because they are based on established policies of the 552nd Training Squadron for personnel assigned to WD positions and thus readily understood by Air Force members. Because of limitations with the platform and scenario, only six of the nine performance categories were considered (premission planning was not observed; communication and team issues were excluded because the scenario we used was set up as a single-operator task).

Procedure

Each participant underwent a 4-hour session on the simulation (see Schiflett, Elliott, Salas, & Coovert [2004] for a discussion of development, validation, and applications in scaled worlds). The first 2 hours were spent receiving instruction on the simulation and practicing to proficiency. After a break, participants performed two high-intensity scenarios (parallel forms) on which they received individual scores. Following these two graded sessions on the scenario platform, participants were trained on the "think aloud method" (Ericsson & Simon, 1993; van Someren, Barnard, & Sandberg, 1994). Participants then performed in three 30-minute simulation scenarios representing moderate to high workload. During the last scenario, audio recordings were made of WD comments for later analysis. Transcriptions were made and subsequently reduced to a series of single statements by a subject matter expert who had previously performed as a WD instructor. A checklist was compiled from Air Force documents to use in rating these statements (referred to as the Task Rating List) and was affirmed by a panel of subject matter experts previously involved in the meta-CTA described earlier.

The Task Rating List was used by a group who was trained in its use. The purpose was to rate each of the statements made by the WDs and classify them as primarily behavioral, cognitive, or a blend of cognitive and behavioral. Subsequent to rating the classes, they were asked to choose from among the tasks in the Task Rating List the three-digit code most nearly describing the activity or cognition (Figure 32.3 contains an extract from the Task Rating List for the "Directing" category of WD performance; the other eight categories were also listed). The three-digit code consists of the performance category (first digit), sub-category (second digit), and the specific task (third digit). Pairs

---

2 – Breakout of the "Directing" Category

Comment: Directing can be considered the primary responsibility of the WD. Fortunately, all WD directing tasks are preprioritized according to ROE, ATO, and SOP—usually under the premise that the more critical the event, the greater the cognitive load on the WD. Therefore, during routine events, WDs can coordinate several tasks at once; while less routine events require greater attention, significantly reducing the operator's multitasking capabilities. Consequently, WD directing tasks have been separated by their impact on operator cognitive load.

2.1   Routine Events (common operator actions that require little cognitive demand – multitasking optimum at this level):
 2.1.A   Command aircraft to stay at a point in 3-D space (orbit).
 2.1.B   Command aircraft to fly at a specific speed.
 2.1.C   Scramble a designated available aircraft.
 2.1.D   Command aircraft to fly together as a flight.
 2.1.E   Vector friendly aircraft to any point in 3D space.
 2.1.F   Patrol a quiet airspace.
 2.1.G   Command aircraft within a flight to split up.
 2.1.H   Send aircraft home (RTB).
 2.1.I   Direct friendly assets.
 2.1.J   Coordinate fighters to man CAP points.
 2.1.K   Direct additional aircraft in from another area

2.2   High-Demand Routine Events (routine operator actions which require significant cognitive functioning – some lesser responsibilities may be abandoned to perform these more difficult tasks):
 2.2.A   Direct aircraft toward each other, to orchestrate an aerial refueling.
 2.2.B   Direct fighters to intercept with tankers.
 2.2.C   Commit an aircraft to another aircraft (hostile).
 2.2.D   Direct friendly fighters to intercept targets.
 2.2.E   On-the-fly scheduling to refuel aircraft running low on fuel.
 2.2.F   Guide fighters to within range of their target.
 2.2.G   Send fighters to ID an unknown aircraft.
 2.2.H   Direct refueling of aircraft in the air.

2.3   Nonroutine Critical Events (events which isolate operator cognitive functioning WDs may abandon all other responsibilities to perform these tasks):
 2.3.A   Direct aircraft to shoot another aircraft.
 2.3.B   Directing reconnaissance
 2.3.C   Refueling in bad weather – tankers need to find clean air in which to work and requires considerable coordination with the HVA WD.
 2.3.D   Controlling an offensive strike package penetrating into enemy territory.
 2.3.E   Send fighters to investigate defector and escort it to base.
 2.3.F   Launch a defensive counter air strike in response to enemy attack.
 2.3.G   Conduct SAR missions.
 2.3.H   Use fighters to neutralize any threats in the way.

Figure 32.3   Extract from the Task Rating List (performance category relating to "Directing") for the Airborne Warning and Control Aircraft Weapons Director.

of raters rated the statements independently and then met to compare and achieve consensus. All consensus ratings were subsequently reviewed independently by two subject matter experts before they were ultimately recorded. Thus, each statement was rated four times, both as to selecting the class (primarily cognitive, primarily behavioral, or a blend of the two) and the three-digit task code.

The purpose of the ratings was to demonstrate the reliability and validity of the rating procedure, identify interrelationships, and test the hypotheses that predicted, primarily on the basis of experience level, how WDs were expected to express orally their behaviors and cognitions as they performed their duties in a simulated task environment. In general, we expected experienced WDs to be more expressive (i.e., talk more) about their activities as they proceeded through the scenario because they had performed these activities more often in the past than the inexperienced WDs.

Analysis

In Hypothesis 1, more experienced WDs will obtain higher individual scores than inexperienced WDs, as measured by the performance scoring algorithm contained in the computer simulation. It should be noted that the simulation platform provides total scores on individual, team, and mission tasks for each participant. Because the simulation was executed using only individual players, only individual scores were collected. Mean scores were calculated for experienced and inexperienced WDs on all three simulations on which scores were available and compared using a t-test for independent samples.

In Hypothesis 2 of verbal protocol analysis, experienced WDs will make more statements (from which cognitions can be inferred) in each of the six performance categories than will less experienced WDs, as measured by the frequency of hits on the task rating list.

Likewise, Hypothesis 3 is that experienced WDs will make more statements (from which behaviors can be inferred) in each of the six performance categories than will less experienced WDs, as measured by the frequency of hits on the task rating list.

Moreover, in Hypothesis 4, experienced WDs will make more statements (from which a blend of cognitions and behaviors can be inferred) in each of the six performance categories than will less experienced WDs, as measured by the frequency of hits on the task rating list.

Hypothesis 5 states that there will be statistically significant differences between experienced and inexperienced WDs, where total inferences of cognitions, behaviors, and a blend of the two, based on the total number of statements derived from verbal protocol analysis collapsed across the six cognitive categories.

The frequency data available to analyze Hypotheses 2–5 are nominal data. The appropriate method in this instance is the chi-square (χ^2) test of independence, generally used to test the relationship between two discrete variables. This procedure was used to test Hypotheses 2–5.

The Sample

Of the 38 WDs from whom data were gathered, a review of the verbal protocols showed that only 31 were usable (16 inexperienced WDs, 51.61% of the sample; and 15 experienced WDs, 43.39% of the sample). Those deemed unusable were primarily due to equipment malfunction (e.g., simulation crashed), although in four instances the WDs simply could not "get the hang of it" in terms of thinking aloud.

RESULTS

Scoring Performance

The platform on which the scenario was run has the capability of calculating scores for mission accomplishment and scores for team performance. For this study, the Air Force determined that WDs would play only as individuals (specifically as the Defensive Counter-Air WD, or DCA). Thus, the only performance scores obtained were for individuals.

Table 32.1 Individual Performance Scores as a Function of Experience Level

Experienced			Inexperienced			All Participants		
n	M	SD	n	M	SD	n	M	SD
21	140.67	6.68	17	138.99	5.78	38	139.92	6.28

M = mean; n = number; SD = standard deviation.

Hypothesis 1

Means, sample sizes, and standard deviations are shown in Table 32.1. These scores reflect all trials on the simulation (a total of three), not just the single trial where think aloud (verbal protocol) was employed.

An independent samples t-test was conducted; no significant differences were revealed between experienced and inexperienced WDs on individual performance scores ($t(36) = 0.828$, n.s.). Accordingly, Hypothesis 1 was not supported.

One of the interesting issues uncovered during this study was the lack of objective differences between those WDs classified as experienced vs. those classified as inexperienced. For example, in our study population, inexperienced WDs average 224 flight hours in the AWACS, with over 13 months of experience as a WD. This is compared with some 1,400 flight hours for the experienced WDs on average and over 7 years experience. Although the differences in flight hours and months of service are statistically significant, they may not be operationally significant. Training, simulation hours, check rides, and the like essentially blur the distinctions, particularly on a relatively simple simulation as this one. The mean scores were clearly not different between the experience levels; moreover, the maximum score that could be achieved on the scenario in use was 152 points; thus, it is highly likely that a ceiling effect was at work. We must look beyond individual scores to find meaningful differences between experienced and inexperienced WDs, as defined by the Air Force.

Hypothesis 2

Table 32.2 is the contingency table for a chi-square test of independence for statements classified as primarily cognitive in nature. Note there are a total of 3,467 statements so classified from among the 31 WDs considered in this analysis.

The critical value of χ^2 is 3.84, df = 1, $p < .05$. There was no statistically significant difference between the inexperienced and experienced WDs with regard to the frequency of their statements classified as principally cognitive in nature (i.e., experienced WDs did not make more such statements than did inexperienced WDs). Accordingly, Hypothesis 2 is not supported.

Hypotheses 3–5

Results are shown in Tables 32.3, 32.4, and 32.5, respectively. For Table 32.3, the critical value of χ^2 is 6.64, df = 1, $p < .01$. Hypothesis 3 was supported (i.e., experienced WDs make more

Table 32.2 Chi-Square Contingency Table for Cognitive Statements as a Function of Experience Level

Weapons Directors	Number of Statements (Observed Cell Values)	Expected Cell Values	χ^2
Inexperienced ($n = 16$)	1,768	1,789	
Experienced ($n = 15$)	1,699	1,678	
Column totals	3,467	3,467	0.51

Table 32.3 Chi-Square Contingency Table for Behavioral Statements as a Function of Experience Level

Weapons Directors	Number of Statements (Observed Cell Value)	Expected Cell Value	χ^2
Inexperienced ($n = 16$)	558	616	
Experienced ($n = 15$)	635	577	
Column totals	1,193	1,193	11.29

statements of a behavioral nature than do inexperienced WDs). For Table 32.4, the critical value of χ^2 is 3.84, df = 1, $p < .05$. Hypothesis 4 was not supported (i.e., there is no difference between experienced and inexperienced WDs). For Table 32.5, the critical value of χ^2 is 6.64, df = 1, $p < .01$. Hypothesis 5 was not supported (i.e., experienced WDs do not make more total statements than do inexperienced WDs). There is a significant difference at $p < .05$, although this appears to be a statistical artifact (there is a difference of only three total statements between experienced and inexperienced WDs).

Cognitive Statements

The ratio of cognitive statements to behavioral statements for experienced WDs was 2.68; for inexperienced WDs, the ratio was 3.17. A comparison of these ratios suggests that experienced WDs perform less cognitive work than their inexperienced colleagues. Further investigation was undertaken to determine if there were meaningful differences in the task codes used by experienced and inexperienced WDs within each class. Results are shown in Tables 32.6 and 32.7.

A comparison of Tables 32.6 and 32.7 confirms that experienced WDs talk about the same as inexperienced WDs as they go through the simulation (on average 113 cognitive statements for experienced WDs versus 110 cognitive statements for inexperienced WDs). They differ considerably, however, in their focus of attention. Experienced WDs attend first to maintaining situational awareness and do so substantially more than their less experienced colleagues (281 statements versus 205). Inexperienced WDs tend to talk more about individual internal cognitions (350 versus 209), suggesting that they are less apt to react quickly and automatically, likely due to a lack of experience with the situations they are facing in the simulation. From a qualitative perspective, experienced WDs focus on monitoring; inexperienced WDs focus more on tracking. It also appears that experienced WDs do a more efficient job of information fusion; that is, they do a better job of synthesizing the bits of information presented in the scenario into a cohesive whole.

Behavioral Statements

A comparison of Tables 32.8 and 32.9 shows that experienced WDs talk slightly more (on average 42 behavioral statements for experienced WDs versus 35 behavioral statements for inexperienced

Table 32.4 Chi-Square Contingency Table for a Blend of Cognitive and Behavioral Statements as a Function of Experience Level

Weapons Directors	Number of Statements (Observed Cell Value)	Expected Cell Value	χ^2
Inexperienced ($n = 16$)	525	539	
Experienced ($n = 15$)	520	506	
Column totals	1,045	1,045	0.75

Table 32.5 Chi-Square Contingency Table for Total Statements as a Function of Experience Level

Weapons Directors	Number of Statements (Observed Cell Value)	Expected Cell Value	χ^2
Inexperienced ($n = 16$)	2,851	2,944	
Experienced ($n = 15$)	2,854	2,761	
Column totals	5,705	5,705	6.12

Table 32.6 Top Five Cognitive Statements by Task Code for Experienced Weapons Directors

Number of Statements	Code	Definition	Example
175	32C	Situational Awareness: Monitor assets available for mission accomplishment.	Out of my 15 alpha, I've got almost 6,000 pounds of fuel. Fighters are due at 0530.
127	41G	Resource Management: Monitor resources available.	Check their states before I send them out.
112	63A	Individual Internal Cognitions: Interpret events in the environment.	Looks like it's doing something. Maybe it's launching Tomahawk cruise missiles.
106	32B	Situational Awareness: Make judgments about what to do with aircraft.	Let's see the Bs. We're going to drive the Bs all the way to the forward end of the island because they have enough fuel.
97	62A	Individual Internal Cognitions: Perceive events in the environment.	There are six targets coming out of the north.

Table 32.7 Top Seven Cognitive Statements by Task Code for Inexperienced Weapons Directors

Number of Statements	Code	Definition	Example
132	62C	Individual Internal Cognitions: Attend to relevant information.	J-Stars moved south. There are now four hostile tracks in the north.
125	41D	Resource Management: Track the headings of both friendly and hostile aircraft.	The tanker is still on his way northbound and I've got less than a minute before my next set of fighters comes up.
121	41G	Resource Management: Monitor resources available.	Checking fuel states on all my guys now at this time. Making sure I'm good to go.
114	63A	Individual Internal Cognitions: Interpret events in the environment.	Seems like a couple of bombers were destroyed— looking good.
105	32C	Situational Awareness: Monitor assets available for mission accomplishment.	Killed the westernmost bomber, so F15B is making sure he's committed on the current westernmost bomber.
104	64A	Individual Internal Cognitions: Evaluate formulated plan (or plans).	Everyone is committed at this time. The fight looks good.
100	32B	Situational Awareness: Make judgments about what to do with aircraft.	Let's see—there's another A-1 aircraft I can employ.

Table 32.8 Top Six Behavioral Statements by Task Code for Experienced Weapons Directors

Number of Statements	Code	Definition	Example
128	22C	Directing: Commit a friendly aircraft to a hostile aircraft (high demand, routine event).	Not good. Let's take 15B and commit him to that MiG-21.
79	21J	Directing: Coordinate fighters to man CAP (combat air patrol) points (routine event).	We have foxtrot up north with a weapon load out of five slammers each, so I'm having him set a CAP.
56	21I	Directing: Direct friendly assets (routine events).	15B—we're sending him up to the north right now.
46	22B	Directing: Direct fighters to intercept with tankers (high demand routine event).	I'm sending Delta to get some gas.
42	21E	Directing: Vector friendly aircraft to any point in 3D space (routine event).	Alright, send him over there to this point.
39	41I	Resource Management: Access information on an aircraft.	It's time to check the gas on F15D. F15D is down to 14,000 pounds—he's still very good.

WDs). The focus of attention for both is on directing and managing resources, major components of the WD task. Qualitatively, it is apparent that inexperienced WDs require more time and expend more effort on directing assets. Again, from a qualitative standpoint, experienced WDs appear more efficient at information fusion. There may also be a degree of automaticity in responses on the part of more experienced WDs.

Blended Statements

WDs talk about the same (on average, 35 blended statements for experienced WDs versus 33 blended statements for inexperienced WDs). Tables 32.10 and 32.11 show the top blended statements for experienced and inexperienced WDs, respectively. The focus of attention for both categories was on maintaining situational awareness, directing, and managing resources. In terms of frequencies, clearly the inexperienced WDs spent more time and effort on situational awareness. It appears to take more effort for inexperienced WDs to accomplish the same tasks that were accomplished in the same timeframe by their more experienced colleagues. Again, this argues for more efficient processing of information and the likelihood of a degree of automaticity of responses by experienced WDs.

Table 32.9 Top Five Behavioral Statements by Task Code for Inexperienced Weapons Directors

Number of Statements	Code	Definition	Example
151	22C	Directing: Commit a friendly aircraft to a hostile aircraft (high demand, routine event).	I just had two fighters heading out to the west. Engage the six group.
62	21J	Directing: Coordinate fighters to man CAP (combat air patrol) points (routine event).	Set Charlie up forward CAP.
55	21I	Directing: Direct friendly assets (routine events).	Moving my Cs to the north here.
42	22B	Directing: Direct fighters to intercept with tankers (high demand routine event).	F-15C is low on gas, so I'm committing him to the tanker.
36	41I	Resource Management: Access information on an aircraft.	F-15D—checking his status. See what kind of armaments he has.

Table 32.10 Top Four Blended Statements (Combination of Behavior and Cognition) by Task Code for Experienced Weapons Directors

Number of Statements	Code	Definition	Example
43	32B	Situational Awareness: Make judgments about what to do with an aircraft.	There are no (hostile) fighters at this point, so I'll go ahead and commit my fighters on the bombers that are up.
38	22C	Directing: Commit a friendly aircraft to a hostile aircraft (high demand, routine event).	F-15B is out in the east, now committed on the last couple of bombers. I will also commit him on some more bombers coming up.
35	41G	Resource Management: Monitor resources available.	Fighter Bravo has 18,000 pounds still. Fighter Alpha has 5,150.
35	41I	Resource Management: Access information on an aircraft.	F-15C's must be getting low on fuel, so I will check his fuel status—He's got about 5,300 pounds.

DISCUSSION

The goal of this study was to develop a methodology or process appropriate to model performance based on a meta-cognitive task analysis and to show how cognitions and behaviors are linked in highly complex environments through verbal protocol analysis. The methodology was developed by using the Air Force Weapons Director job as an exemplar of the type of position that is highly complex, contains elements of behaviors and cognitions, and would lend itself to examination as to whether the process had merit. Much was achieved and much has been learned on which to build.

Beginning with a meta-cognitive task analysis (Gordon et al., 2000; Miles et al., 2000), which resulted in a model containing nine performance categories, a major thrust of the study plan was to examine differences between experienced and inexperienced WDs on as many of the nine categories as feasible. It was hypothesized that experienced WDs would score higher than inexperienced WDs on a computer simulation exercise. This hypothesis was not supported (i.e., there were no differences between the groups in terms of their performance on the simulation). A partial explanation for these results likely lies in the degree of difficulty of the scenario. There was a substantial

Table 32.11 Top Five Blended Statements (Combination of Behavior and Cognition) by Task Code for Inexperienced Weapons Directors

Number of Statements	Code	Definition	Example
55	32B	Situational Awareness: Make judgments about what to do with aircraft.	Split them up because I've really only got F-15B on the west—correction, I mean on the northeast.
45	22C	Directing: Commit a friendly aircraft to a hostile aircraft (high demand routine event).	We've got a MiG-23, so I'm going to immediately commit F-15D on the MiG-23.
41	41G	Resource Management: Monitor resources available.	Checking Alpha's fuel—it should be fine.
29	32C	Situational Awareness: Monitor assets available for mission accomplishment.	There they are, they returned to base [referring to aircraft he lost track of].
27	21J	Directing: Coordinate fighters to man CAP (combat air patrol) points (routine event).	Now move the Alpha fighter to a more southern CAP to start off.

ceiling effect on the scores, with almost all WDs, regardless of their level of experience, achieving near maximum scores.

One area in which differences between experienced and inexperienced WDs were found was in the verbal protocol analysis. Originally intended to serve as a means to develop cognitions and to show links with behaviors observed in the simulation, the method proved highly informative for examining predicted differences between the experienced and inexperienced WDs. It was hypothesized that experienced WDs would render more statements through verbal protocol than would their less experienced colleagues in several classifications. Specifically, it was predicted that statements dealing principally with cognitions, and behaviors, and a combination or blend of the two, would be significantly greater in frequency for experienced WDs. These predictions were only partially supported.

Perhaps the most important finding is how the two groups differ on another aspect of the verbal protocol analysis. WDs tend to talk differently as a function of their experience level. With respect to statements principally of a cognitive nature (Tables 32.6 and 32.7), experienced WDs expend considerably more energy in maintaining situational awareness than do their less experienced peers; the inexperienced WDs appear to devote more energy to internal cognitions (getting their bearings, remembering to look around and see what needs to be done). Qualitatively, the experienced WDs appear to be more relaxed and comfortable with the simulation and the tasks to which they must attend than do the inexperienced WDs. As a practical matter, however, we could not identify and discuss these differences if we had not developed the three-part approach (cognitive, behavioral, blend) as a means to analyze precisely what the WDs were doing across the performance categories.

The differences are not quite so striking with the more behaviorally oriented statements. Both groups spend the bulk of their energy directing friendly assets and managing their resources, both functions that are taught early to new WDs in training. These are the "bread and butter" issues that all WDs must do to be successful, so it should come as no surprise that much time and effort are devoted to them. Perhaps a task-based approach would work here but would not be effective for cognitions or blends.

The blend classification proved very difficult for the task raters. It may be that there was something in the manner in which the WDs expressed themselves where a clear distinction could not be made between the cognitive and behavioral, making statements more difficult to interpret (i.e., more difficult to place in the cognitive or behavior classification). This situation might have forced the raters to resort to the blend classification. Investigating this would make an interesting study for someone so inclined, trained not only in verbal protocol analysis, but also in speech analysis.

Theoretical and Practical Implications

The application of verbal protocol analysis in this study was key to what has been learned. There was no other practical way to get at what the WDs were thinking. Using verbal protocol analysis is strongly recommended for future studies of this type. However, a word of caution is in order.

Verbal protocol analysis is manpower intensive and very time-consuming. In the present study, 14 people worked on the analysis in some fashion. Audio recording the participant, transcribing the audiotape, breaking down the transcriptions into single statements, analyzing them with four different judges (classifying the statements and assigning a task from the task rating list), and entering data into the computer takes an enormous amount of time and effort. For each of the WDs, it is estimated that 18 hours were spent on each audiotape from start to finish, meaning that some 558 hours were spent just on the 31 audiotapes. An effort of this magnitude should be carefully designed and executed to avoid wasting valuable resources, especially people's time. The research team discovered some automated programs advertised to conduct protocol analysis; however, these programs basically grouped like terms without considering the context that human judges could consider.

Application Beyond the Weapons Director Context

It appears that the methodology developed in the present study will have considerable utility in other sectors. Any complex job that has both cognitive and behavioral components can be subjected to the process. Demonstrating how to establish a model that is both descriptive and prescriptive through cognitive task analysis and verbal protocol analysis and then testing it, is a major contribution of this study. It would appear useful in a broad array of organizations well beyond the WD context.

For example, a manager charged with the responsibility of performing strategic planning in which he or she must undertake integrating a number of cognitively complex tasks would likely find this procedure useful. The model could be used in selecting new team members based on measuring varying amounts of expertise on the elements defined by a model similar to that developed for WDs. People could be trained to the standards specified by the model; it could also be used as a diagnostic tool and for providing specific types of feedback. In this regard, developing a model could provide the means for establishing meaningful criteria for performance appraisal.

Knowing the complexities of a series of multifaceted tasks which go to make up many jobs could assist in another way. In coming years it is reasonable to anticipate that a number of these complex tasks will lend themselves to performance, at least partially, by intelligent agents. Testing has already begun on providing an agent to assist in the performance of a WD's job (Hoffman, 2000). Knowing the cognitive complexities of the job, beyond that which could be provided by traditional job analysis, would greatly advance the development of these intelligent agents.

CONCLUSIONS

This study has provided a new classification system not previously discussed in the literature. Verbal protocol analysis has given us the opportunity to integrate cognitive task analyses into job models—in effect, we have a new typology for describing jobs that goes beyond the more traditional KSAs and other task-oriented tools. Job analysts have generally concentrated on behaviors associated with the job, while knowledge engineers basically ignored behaviors in favor of cognitions. With the present study, there is a good chance that members of the community can be persuaded to adopt the notion of looking at cognitive task analyses, integrating them with verbal protocols, and examining jobs in the context of the classifications described in this study (cognitions, behaviors, blends). These classifications are, of course, defined on the basis of a series of elements relevant to the job, such as our task rating list provides. A very important issue, which is fodder for future research, involves looking at tradeoffs among cognitions, behaviors, and blends. In other words, we need to improve the operational definitions describing what is contained in a cognitive, behavioral, and blended statement, and examine more fully the amount of overlap among them. It is also strongly suggested that more research be undertaken to validate the process we have begun here and to recommend additional strategies or approaches that would improve it. A good start in this regard is provided in work by Vicente (1999) in which cognitive work analysis is described. It appears that methodologies from our efforts can easily be integrated with many of the methodologies of cognitive work analysis.

REFERENCES

Bertalanffy, L. (1968). *General systems theory: Foundations, development, applications*. New York, NY: George Braziller.

Brannick, M. T., & Prince, C. (1997). An overview of team performance. In M. T. Brannick, E. Salas, & C. Prince (Eds.), *Team performance assessment and measurement: Theory, methods and applications* (pp. 3–18). Mahwah, NJ: Lawrence Erlbaum Associates.

Cannon-Bowers, J. A., Salas, E., & Converse, S. A. (1993). Shared mental models in expert team decision making. In N.J. Castellan, Jr. (Ed.), *Current issues in individual and group decision making* (pp. 221–246). Hillsdale, NJ: Lawrence Erlbaum Associates.

Cannon-Bowers, J. A., & Salas, E. (1998). Teamwork competencies: The interaction of team member knowledge, skills, and attitudes. In H. F. O'Neil (Ed.), *Workforce readiness: Competence and assessment* (pp. 151–174). Mahwah, NJ: Lawrence Erlbaum Associates.

Coovert, M. D. (1992). Team decision making and performance: A review and proposed modeling approach employing Petri nets. In R. W. Swezey & E. Salas (Eds.), *Teams: Their training and performance* (pp. 247–280). New York: Ablex.

Coovert, M. D. (in press). Petri nets. In R. Landis & J. Cortina (Eds.), *Frontiers of methodology in organizational research*. New York, NY: Routledge/Psychology Press.

Coovert, M. D., & Craiger, J. P. (1997). Modeling performance and establishing performance criteria in training systems. In J. K. Ford (Ed.), *Improving training effectiveness in work organizations*. Mahwah, NJ: Lawrence Erlbaum Associates.

Coovert, M. D., Craiger, J. P., & Cannon-Bowers, J. A. (1995). Innovations in modeling and simulating team performance: Implications for decision making. In R. A. Guzzo & E. Salas (Eds.), *Team effectiveness and decision making in organizations*. San Francisco, CA: Jossey-Bass.

Coovert, M. D., & Dorsey, D. W. (2000). Computational modeling with Petri nets: Solutions for individual and team systems. In C. Hulin & D. Ilgen, (Eds.), *The third discipline of scientific research in psychology: Computational modeling and computer simulation of behavior* (pp. 163–181). San Francisco, CA: Jossey-Bass.

Dickinson, T. L., & McIntyre, R. M. (1997). A conceptual framework for teamwork measurement. In M. T. Brannick, E. Salas, & C. Prince, (Eds.), *Team performance and measurement: Theory, methods, and applications* (pp. 19–43). Mahwah, NJ: Lawrence Erlbaum Associates.

Ericsson, K. A., & Simon, H. A. (1993). *Protocol analysis: Verbal reports as data*. Cambridge, MA: The MIT Press.

Fleishman, E. A., & Zaccaro, S. J. (1992). Toward a taxonomic classification of team performance functions: Initial considerations, subsequent evaluations and current formulations. In R. W. Sweezy & E. Salas (Eds.), *Teams: Their training and performance* (pp. 31–56). Norwood, NJ: Ablex.

Gordon, T. R., Riddle, D., Hoffman, K. A., Miles, D., King. T. S., Coovert, M. D., … Elliott, S. (2000). *Team performance: Integrative dynamic models linking cognitive and behavioral components*. Poster session presented at the annual meeting of the Society of Industrial and Organizational Psychology, New Orleans, LA.

Hess, K. P., Freeman, J., & Coovert, M. D. (2008). CENTER: Critical thinking in team decision-making. In M. P. Letsky, N. W. Warner, S. M. Fiore, & C. A. P. Smith (Eds.), *Macrocognition in teams: Theories and methodologies* (pp. 239–258). Burlington, VT: Ashgate.

Hoffman, K. A. (2000). *Trust and performance with intelligent agent technology: Implications for human-agent interaction* (Unpublished master's thesis). University of South Florida, Tampa, FL.

Klimoski, R., & Mohammed, S. (1994). Team mental model: Construct or metaphor? *Journal of Management, 20*, 403–437.

Miles, D. E., Hoffman, K. A., Foster, L. L., King, T. S., Gordon, T. R., Riddle, D., … Schiflett, S. (1999). *A qualitative methodology for integrating cognitive task analysis data* (unpublished manuscript). University of South Florida, Tampa, FL.

Seamster, T. L., Redding, R. E., Cannon, J. R., Ryder, J. M., & Purcell, J. A. (1993). Cognitive task analysis of expertise in air traffic control. *International Journal of Aviation Psychology, 3*, 257–283.

Schiflett, S., Elliott, L. R., Salas, E., & Coovert, M. D. (Eds.). (2004). *Scaled worlds: Development, validation and applications*. Hants, England: Ashgate Pub Ltd.

Sundstrom, E., DeMeuse, K. P., & Futrell, D. (1990). Work teams: Applications and effectiveness. *American Psychologist, 45*, 120–123.

van Someren, M. W., Barnard, Y. F., & Sandberg, J. A. C. (1994). *The think aloud method*. San Diego, CA: Academic Press.

van der Schaaf, T. W. (1993). Developing and using cognitive task typologies. *Ergonomics, 36*, 1439–1444.

Vicente, K. J. (1999). *Cognitive work analysis: Toward safe, productive, and healthy computer-based work.* Mahwah, NJ: Lawrence Erlbaum Associates.

Yagoda, R. E., & Coovert, M. D. (2009, October). *A Petri Net approach for modeling human-robot interaction.* Proceedings of the Human Factor Society, San Antonio, TX.

Yagoda, R. E., & Coovert, M. D. (in press). How to work and play with robots: An approach to modeling human-robot interaction. *Computers in Human Behavior.*

Zachary, W. W., Ryder, J. M., & Hicinbothom, J. H. (1998). Cognitive task analysis and modeling of decision making in complex environments. In J. Cannon-Bowers & E. Salas (Eds.), *Making decisions under stress: Implications for individual and team training* (pp. 315–344). Washington, DC: American Psychological Association.

33

Innovations in Team Task Analysis
Identifying Team-Based Task Elements, Tasks, and Jobs

WINFRED ARTHUR, JR.
Texas A&M University

ANTON J. VILLADO
Texas A&M University

WINSTON BENNETT, JR.
United States Air Force Research Laboratory

The two objectives of this chapter are to (a) present a review of the extant team task analysis literature, and (b) on the basis of this review, propose techniques and approaches on how current occupational and task analysis systems can be modified and revised to readily and effectively identify team-based tasks and their degree of team interdependency. In addition, for illustrative purposes, we present some empirical laboratory (Arthur, Edwards, Bell, Villado, & Bennett, 2005) and operational field data (Arthur et al., in press-b) on the use of three team task analysis metrics designed to quantify the extent to which tasks and jobs are team-based. These metrics resulted from the accomplishment of the second objective. The data provide initial support for the efficacy and viability of these team task analysis metrics. Finally, like traditional individual task or job analysis, information obtained from these metrics can be used for a variety of human resource functions and interventions such as training, selection, job design, and career exploration. They can also be used as diagnostic indicators and, of course, in research as well.

In the present chapter, team interdependence (or "teamness") is conceptualized and operationalized in terms of team-relatedness and team workflow. Team-relatedness represents the extent to which successful team performance requires the individual to work with members of the team to optimally perform the specified task or job. In this sense, team-relatedness can be conceptualized as representing the *amount* or *magnitude* of team interdependence or teamness. Conversely, team workflow represents the paths by which work and/or information flows through the team to optimally perform the specified tasks or job. Thus, in contrast to team-relatedness, team workflow is best conceptualized as representing or describing the *type*, *kind*, or *form* of team interdependence or teamness. A third metric, which we describe as the team-task-ratio, represents the ratio of the total number of tasks that constitute the job to the number of tasks that can be accomplished by one team member. This, like team-relatedness, also represents the amount or magnitude of team interdependence. These three metrics can be used to empirically and quantitatively represent the extent to which either a task or job is team-based (Arthur et al., 2005, in press-b). In this chapter, consistent with Baker and Salas (1997), our working definition of a team is two or more individuals who work interdependently, have specific role assignments, perform specific tasks, and interact and coordinate to achieve a common goal.

The Nature of Task Analysis

Task analysis entails the description of jobs in terms of identifiable units of activities. Although the level of specificity of analysis and description may vary, job and task analysis techniques are typically focused at the task level. Hence, job and task analysis is the process by which the major work behaviors and associated knowledge, skills, and abilities (KSAs) that are required for successful job or task performance are identified. A number of criteria for identifying tasks (McCormick, 1979) that are of relevance to the present chapter are as follows: (a) a task is a group of manual or cognitive activities directed toward a goal; (b) a task usually has a definite beginning and end; (c) a task involves individuals' interaction with equipment, other people, media, and/or data; and (d) a series of tasks constitute a duty and the totality of tasks define the job. It is recognized, from both a professional and legal perspective, that job analysis is the critical foundation for most, if not all human resource functions (Binning & Barrett, 1989; EEOC, 1978). In line with this, data obtained from task analyses can be used for a variety of purposes including the description of existing jobs, personnel selection, job redesign, the development of training programs, career exploration, and human resource planning. When it is used in the development of a new system, task analysis provides data for predicting the nature of the job activities required to operate and maintain the projected system.

The team task analysis approach presented in this chapter is based on the model presented in Figure 33.1. As indicated by this model, we posit that in a population of tasks that constitute a job, the percentage of tasks that are team-based can range from 0% to 100%. In addition, the percentage of team-based tasks proportionately covaries with the extent to which the job can be described as team-based. Two examples of jobs that might fall at opposite ends of this continuum are avionics trouble-shooting technician and a C5 (or C130) transport flight crew, with the former having few or no team-based tasks and the latter actually having distributed teams at two levels—the flight crew/operators (i.e., pilot, co-pilot, and navigator) and other air crew (e.g., load master, air medical technicians, pararescuers, and flight nurses). Still, other jobs such as medical technicians and crew chiefs may fall in the mid-range of this continuum. Specifically, medical technicians function autonomously and individually when performing intake tasks such as taking temperature and blood pressure readings; but they are members of triage or operating room teams when performing those specified tasks. The same is true for crew chiefs who may launch aircraft by themselves but lead teams in the processing of incoming and landing aircraft.

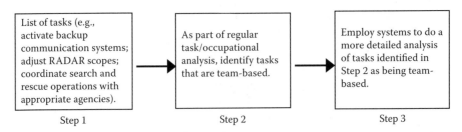

Figure 33.1 Sequence of steps involved in identifying team-based tasks and determining their degree and type of team interdependence (i.e., team-relatedness and team workflow).

The first objective of the present chapter entailed a review of the extant team task analysis literature. An extensive literature search was conducted to identify relevant team task analysis papers. The literature search encompassed studies published in journal articles, book chapters, and technical reports. The search process started with a search of *PsycINFO*. This electronic search was complemented with a manual search of the reference lists of identified papers. Finally, several researchers in the area were contacted in an effort to obtain additional papers.

REVIEW OF THE TEAM TASK ANALYSIS LITERATURE

We now present a review of the extant literature that both directly and indirectly addresses the topic of team task analysis. It was anticipated that this review would shed some light on how to readily and effectively identify team-based tasks and also provide a general framework for conducting a team task analysis. In reviewing the team task analysis literature, it quickly became apparent that there is substantial overlap between this topic and team performance—particularly, the *measurement* of team performance. Consequently, in some instances, it is difficult to distinguish between the two topics. Given this high degree of overlap, a review of the team performance measurement literature also seemed necessary to effectively accomplish the goal of presenting a detailed review of the team task analysis literature.

Although there has been an increased amount of attention paid to teams in recent years (e.g., Burke, Stagl, Salas, Pierce, & Kendall, 2006; Chen, 2005; Chen, Kirkman, Kanfer, & Rosen, 2007; De Drue, 2007; DeShon, Kozlowski, Schmidt, Milner, & Weichmann, 2004; Marks, DeChurch, Mathieu, & Alonso, 2005; Mathieu, Gilson, & Ruddy, 2006; Morgeson, Reider, & Campion, 2005; Mumford, Van Iddekinge, Morgeson, & Campion, 2008), team task analysis has received very little of this attention. For instance, a comprehensive search of the published literature identified only a small number of team task analysis papers such as Bowers, Baker, and Salas (1994), Bowers, Morgan, Salas, and Prince (1993), Dieterly (1988), and Swezey, Owens, Bergondy, and Salas (1998). This is consistent with what Baker, Salas, and Cannon-Bowers (1998) reported in their brief review of the extant literature in which they found only a handful of works that directly addressed team task analysis.

Team Task Analysis

We identified only five journal articles whose primary focus was the topic of team task analysis. Two of these articles were by Campion and his colleagues (Campion, Medsker, & Higgs, 1993; Campion, Papper, & Medsker, 1996). Campion et al. (1993) investigated the relationship between various work team characteristics and work team effectiveness. In developing measures of work team characteristics, they conducted an extensive literature review and subsequently derived five common clusters of work team characteristics based on the works of Gladstein (1984), Hackman (1987), Guzzo and Shea (1992), and Tannenbaum, Beard, and Salas (1992). These five clusters included job design, interdependence, composition, context, and process. To measure these characteristics, each cluster was broken down into more specific subscales and a 54-item questionnaire was constructed. Both employees (work team members) and managers completed the questionnaire. Results indicated that all three effectiveness criteria (productivity, satisfaction, and manager judgments) were predicted by the work team characteristics with the job design and process clusters being the most predictive. Finally, it is important to note that Campion et al.'s (1993) procedures were consistent with McGrath's (1986) recommendations for studying teams (groups) in that they (a) measured multiple constructs within both the team characteristics and effectiveness criteria domains, (b) reduced common method variance by using different data sources, and (c) analyzed data at the team level.

Campion et al. (1996) replicated their previous work by extending their procedures to include a different sample of work units, expanding the team effectiveness criteria, and including work teams that varied in the extent to which their members identified themselves as being part of a team. They also modified the team characteristics questionnaire by eliminating several items that showed few relationships in the previous study, adding items to several of the subscales, and expanding the response scale from a 5-point to a 7-point scale. The results supported the previous findings by showing that most of the criteria were related to most of the team characteristics. Moreover, work teams that were higher on team identity showed higher scores on a majority of the team characteristics.

The three other journal articles that we located were by Salas and colleagues (Baker & Salas, 1996; Bowers et al., 1993, 1994). In an attempt to enhance military aircrew coordination training, Bowers et al. (1993) developed a questionnaire to measure the coordination demands associated with cargo helicopter operations. Coordination demand was defined as "the extent to which a given flight task places a requirement (demand) for the crew to interact, cooperate, or coordinate their activities to accomplish the task" (p. 99). A coordination demands questionnaire was developed. First, 96 flight tasks and situations were selected from standard military flight manuals. Second, three subject-matter experts (SMEs, instructor pilots) reviewed the list of 96 tasks and identified those that they considered most important. Thirty-eight core tasks were identified. Respondents were then instructed to rate the extent to which each of these 38 tasks required coordination of the type defined by seven behavioral dimensions previously identified as the major components of aircrew coordination (Franz, Prince, Cannon-Bowers, & Salas, 1990; Morgan, Glickman, Woodward, Blaiwes, & Salas, 1986; Oser, McCallum, Salas, & Morgan, 1990; Prince & Salas, 1993). These dimensions were communication, situational awareness, decision making, mission analysis, leadership, adaptability, and assertiveness. An eighth dimension, total coordination, was also included. Bowers et al. (1993) based their procedures on those previously implemented for the purpose of measuring operator workload associated with flight tasks (Hart, Childress, & Bortolussi, 1981).

Bowers et al.'s (1993) initial results indicated that respondents used a considerable range when making their ratings. Cluster analysis, based on the seven dimensions, was then performed and three independent clusters of flight tasks were identified. In the final analysis, multiple regression was used to investigate the predictability of the total coordination ratings for each of the task clusters. For each of the three task clusters, total coordination ratings were regressed on each of the seven dimension ratings of coordination demand. The results indicated that different flight tasks were associated with different types of coordination. Bowers et al. concluded that subjective measurement procedures are appropriate for assessing coordination demands.

Bowers et al. (1994) noted that, although assessing the general dimension-level requirements related to flight tasks is useful, assessment tools designed to provide information pertaining to the task importance of specific coordination behaviors is needed. Although task importance indices have been utilized for individual tasks, Bowers et al. developed a technique for assessing the importance of team tasks based on a policy capturing approach used in more traditional job analysis contexts (Sanchez & Levine, 1989).

The team performance literature recognizes two distinct dimensions of performance. The first dimension, *taskwork*, consists of behaviors involved in the execution of team tasks and is typically task specific. The second dimension, *teamwork*, consists of behaviors required for cooperative functioning and focuses on team process variables such as communication, team cohesion (Barry & Stewart, 1997), cooperation, team spirit and morale, coordination, and adaptability (Glickman et al., 1987; Morgan et al., 1986). Furthermore, team process KSAs are generally generic instead of being task or job specific (Stevens & Campion, 1994, 1999). Teamwork was the focus of Bowers et al.'s (1994) team task inventory.

Bowers et al.'s (1994) team task inventory was constructed by identifying teamwork behaviors taken from the team performance and aircrew coordination literature and having SMEs review and modify the list of behaviors. Two task inventories were constructed—one for helicopters and the other for fixed-wing aircraft. Respondents were then asked to rate each task (behavior) along six dimensions. These were importance-to-train, task criticality, task frequency, task difficulty, difficulty-to-train, and overall task importance. Using these six dimensions, five indices of task importance were calculated similar to previous methods found in the literature (e.g., Sanchez and Levine's [1989] method of summing task criticality and difficulty-of-learning). Results indicated that (a) criticality and importance-to-train were the only dimensions that explained variance in overall importance ratings, (b) the five task importance indices showed similarly poor interrater-agreement, and (c) composite indices of task importance were more correlated with overall importance ratings than single indices, such as frequency and criticality. The authors concluded that traditional measurement techniques derived from individuals may not be adequate in assessing team tasks.

In light of previous research showing that differences in the importance ratings of individual tasks may be a function of the ratees themselves, particularly their tenure or job experience (Ford, Smith, Sego, & Quinones, 1992; Sanchez, 1990), Baker and Salas (1996) implemented procedures similar to those of Bowers et al. (1994) and found that more experienced team members had a tendency to emphasize time spent performing teamwork behaviors in their importance ratings. In contrast, less experienced members emphasized difficulty of performing teamwork behaviors. Baker and Salas (1996) subsequently suggested that like traditional task analysis, representative sampling should be utilized when conducting team task analysis. In addition, some inconsistencies with research results obtained for individual task analyses were indicated and subsequently, offered additional support for the notion that task analysis for individual jobs may not be completely transferable to team task analysis.

In addition to the five journal articles that we have just reviewed, we found one book chapter (i.e., Dieterly, 1988) devoted to the subject of team task analysis. Dieterly's chapter found in Gael's (1988) *Job Analysis Handbook for Business, Industry, and Government* briefly reviews the literature on team performance and then discusses the application of task and job analysis to understanding team performance requirements. At the outset of his discussion of task analysis and team performance, Dieterly (1988) states that traditional individual task analyses need to be reviewed and integrated with respect to team goals, and not simply to a set of individual tasks that may impact team performance. Dierterly identified eight dimensions along which tasks can be decomposed. Furthermore, each of the eight dimensions was subsumed under one of two categories. The first category concerns the aspects of tasks that are not team related, and the second category concerns task characteristics that *are* specifically related to teams. Although Dieterly's notion of dichotomizing team performance was not unique, his breakdown of the two dimensions differed substantially from the previously mentioned dichotomy of team performance (i.e., taskwork vs. teamwork; Glickman et al., 1987; Morgan et al., 1986).

Table 33.1 presents Dieterly's (1998) dimensions classified as either nonteam or team-based. The four dimensions that are pertinent to teams are best characterized in terms of the degree of task-required team interaction. Dieterly states that the variability associated with team performance may be a function of task design changes involving task interaction deemed necessary to adapt to changing situations (i.e., emergencies). Dieterly suggested that for a team to be effective, it must understand its task function design and have the control and capability to restructure the task function design should the situation and need arise to do so.

The crux of Dieterly's (1988) discussion of job analysis, in the context of team performance, is that the degree of task interaction is the major contributor to team performance. He also argues

Table 33.1   Dieterly's (1988) Eight Dimensions Along Which Tasks Can Be Decomposed

Nonteam-Related	Team-Related
1. If a task involves standard or emergency conditions.	1. The degree to which a task can be accomplished by only one member of a team.
2. If a task is sequential or nonsequential.	2. Whether the task is specifically designated to one team member.
3. If a task is necessary or unnecessary for goal attainment.	3. Whether a task is dependent on the completion of another task from another team member.
4. How critical a task is to the successful completion of the goal.	4. The ability to reallocate a task after a team begins to function.

that traditional job analysis techniques are acceptable within the context of teams only as long as the individual task analysis establishes a link across the job tasks. Dieterly went on to describe a method of graphically operationalizing task interaction and deriving an interaction ratio. He also described a method of operationalizing task interdependence, an approach that we describe as the team-task-ratio, which entails summing the total number of tasks and dividing the total by the maximum number that can be accomplished by one team member. Higher scores indicate more interdependence.

Team Performance

In the past several years, there have been several literature reviews pertaining to the measurement of team performance (e.g., Cannon-Bowers & Salas, 1997; Cannon-Bowers, Tannebaum, Salas, & Volpe, 1995; Tesluk, Mathieu, Zaccaro, & Marks, 1997). In their discussion of team performance, Tesluk et al. (1997) recommended that a combination of sources and techniques be used to provide a complete picture of team functioning and effectiveness. They cited a number of studies and showed that a diverse set of both sources and methods for measuring team performance has been utilized. Incumbents, subordinates, peers, external experts, and supervisors have been used as sources. Surveys, observations, interviews, and archival data are among the methods that have been employed. Although most investigations have relied on a single source and a single method, there have been a few studies where combinations of sources and methods have been used. For example, Dickinson and McIntyre (1997) provide a conceptual framework for teamwork measurement in which frequency measures and behaviorally anchored rating scales were developed from a combination of literature reviews, interviews, critical incidents, and expert judgment. In reviewing the literature, it appears that assessments of team performance have typically used some sort of observation-based frequency measures, behavioral checklists, and/or ratings of behavior. In developing these measures, some combination of literature reviews, interviews, archival data, critical incidents, and expert judgment has been employed (e.g., Brannick, Prince, Prince, & Salas, 1995; Dwyer, 1992; McIntyre & Salas, 1995; Oser et al., 1990).

In addition to their review of the team performance measurement literature, Tesluk et al. (1997) contributed to the extant literature by summarizing and highlighting four patterns of teamwork processes (i.e., work team arrangements or workflow; see also Thompson, 1967; and Van der Vegt, Emans, & Van de Vliert, 1998, 2000). These four patterns are pooled, sequential, reciprocal, and intensive interdependence. They also rank order, as listed, from the least to most, in terms of the integration and interdependence of team members. Table 33.2 presents a description of each of these workflow patterns. Tesluk et al. note that the assessment of team performance requires an analysis of not only individual-level characteristics, but also team-level characteristics. Their conception of work team arrangements is one such example of a team-level analysis. In fact, they refer

Table 33.2   Tesluk, Mathieu, Zaccaro, and Marks' (1997) Description of Four Team Workflow Patterns

Team Workflow Pattern	Description
1. Pooled/Additive Interdependence	Work and activities are performed separately by all team members and work does not flow between members of the team.
2. Sequential Interdependence	Work and activities flow from one member to another in the team, but mostly in one direction.
3. Reciprocal Interdependence	Work and activities flow between team members in a back-and-forth manner over a period of time.
4. Intensive Interdependence	Work and activities come into the team and members must work[a] as a team in order to accomplish the team's task.

[a] Tesluk et al. (1997) use the phrase "must diagnose, problem solve, and/or collaborate as a team" (p. 201). However, because this phrasing has more of a *teamwork* (versus) *taskwork* connotation to it, we instead use the term *work* in our conceptualization and operational measures as well.

to their framework of work team arrangements as a team task analysis and show how teams operating at each level differ in their selection, training, work design, motivation, and leadership needs.

Cannon-Bowers and associates (Cannon-Bowers et al., 1995; Cannon-Bowers & Salas, 1997; Prince & Salas, 1993) have provided a number of reviews of the team performance literature. These reviews have served as the basis for the development of strategies intended to enhance training for team performance. As a testimony to their thoroughness, Cannon-Bowers et al. (1995) identified 130 skill labels from the extant literature and extracted eight skill dimensions required for effective teamwork. In addition to these skill dimensions, Cannon-Bowers et al. (1995) and Cannon-Bowers and Salas (1997) identified 11 knowledge and 9 attitude requirements. Stevens and Campion's (1994) review, in which they identify the knowledge, skill, and attitude requirements for teamwork, appears to corroborate these findings.

Moreover, Cannon-Bowers et al. (1995) discussed team KSA competencies as being either specific or generic with respect to tasks and teams. In other words, each KSA can be thought of as being either *task* specific or generic. Likewise, they can be thought of as being either *team* specific or generic. This conceptualization of team competencies indicates the nature of each KSA. Cannon-Bowers et al. also identified five specific environmental factors that determine the extent to which *team* specific or generic and *task* specific or generic competencies are required. These factors were task interdependence, environmental stability, team member turnover, membership in multiple teams, and the variety of tasks performed by the team. In broad terms, Cannon-Bowers et al.'s (1995) framework of team competencies shows how the KSAs that are required for effective team performance vary across situations and organizations. In other words, although a set of team-based KSAs can be identified in the extant literature, the exact nature of the KSAs required for successful team performance is context-specific (Baker et al., 1998; Fleishman & Zaccaro, 1992; Foushee, 1984; McIntyre & Salas, 1995).

Building on their previous work, Cannon-Bowers and Salas (1997) developed a framework for measuring team performance. They conceptualized team performance measures as differing on two binary dimensions. The first is process versus outcome measures. The second is team versus individual measures. Next, they indicated where various teamwork criteria—based on the KSA requirements previously identified (Cannon-Bowers et al., 1995)—fall within these two dimensions. Finally, Cannon-Bowers and Salas (1997) go on to show that the appropriateness of techniques for measuring team performance vary according to where the criteria are aligned within the two dimensions. Among the techniques identified were observational scales, critical incidents, expert ratings, content analysis, archival records, protocol analysis, and policy capturing. To adequately interpret these measures, comprehensive team task analyses that delineate task and context demands are required. Cannon-Bowers and Salas further recommend the use of a variety of measures to ensure thorough assessment.

Summary of the Literature—A General Framework for Conducting Team Task Analysis

Based on the review of both the team task analysis and team performance literatures, a number of themes appear to be evident. Integrating these themes results in several emergent summary statements that serve as a foundation for a general framework for conducting team task analysis. First, similar to traditional job analysis, team task analysis can and should be the foundation for pertinent human resource functions such as team task design, team selection, team composition, and team training. In this regard, team task analysis is quite similar to traditional job analysis.

Second, there is a distinction between individual tasks and team tasks—that is *individual* taskwork and *team* taskwork. The former are performed by individuals and the latter require teams for their accomplishment. In addition, team tasks can vary in their degree of team-relatedness and team workflow. Team-relatedness represents the extent to which successful team performance requires the individual to work with members of the team to optimally perform the specified task or job, and team workflow on the other hand, represents the paths by which work and/or information flows through the team to optimally perform the specified tasks or job. Arthur et al. (2005, in press-b) have demonstrated that both of these metrics can be used to empirically and quantitatively represent the extent to which a task (or job) is team-based. An implication of the varying levels of task-level team interdependence is that in the context of team-based tasks or jobs, a distinction can be made between team performance (team taskwork) and individual performance (individual taskwork). Thus, it is important to distinguish between tasks and task elements that are dependent on more than one individual for their successful performance from those that are not. Both are essential to the success of a team and omitting either class will result in an incomplete and deficient analysis of the team. Information about the nature of team interdependence is important because as previously noted, the level of interdependence at which the team is operating has implications for its selection, training, work design, motivation, and leadership needs (Tesluk et al., 1997).

Third, the team performance literature (e.g., Glickman et al., 1987; Morgan et al., 1986) suggests a distinction between taskwork and teamwork. *Taskwork* consists of behaviors involved in the execution of team tasks. *Teamwork* consists of behaviors required for cooperative functioning and entails a focus on team process variables (Barry & Stewart, 1997; Glickman et al., 1987; Morgan et al., 1986). The task analysis approaches recommended later in this chapter focus on taskwork variables.

Fourth, as previously alluded to, there are some commonalities between team task analysis and the more traditional notion of job and task analysis. Thus, there are several methods that can be used when conducting *both* individual and team task analysis. These include the use of questionnaires, critical incident techniques, observation, interviews, expert judgments, and archival data. Similar to traditional job analysis, the use of multiple methods is strongly recommended in the implementation of team task analyses. In addition, like traditional job and task analysis, procedurally, at some point, task ratings on a number of dimensions can be obtained from SMEs. These dimensions or scales typically encompass but are not limited to importance, frequency, time spent, criticality, difficulty-of-performing, difficulty-of-learning, time-to-proficiency, and consequences-of-errors (Arthur, Doverspike, & Barrett, 1996). Although these scales have generally been studied in the context of tasks performed by individuals (e.g., Sanchez & Fraser, 1992; Sanchez & Levine, 1989), they are clearly applicable to tasks performed by teams and are recommended. These ratings should also be obtained from multiple sources, including incumbents and supervisors who should be selected to ensure a representative sample. However, because teams consist of two or more individuals who have specific role assignments, perform specific tasks, and must interact and coordinate to successfully achieve common goals or objectives, team tasks have an additional element of complexity that is not present in the analysis of individual tasks.

Finally, as just previously noted, there are some important differences between team task analysis and traditional job and task analysis that should be considered. Specifically, in the context of teams and team taskwork, individuals are indeed interdependent. The centrality of interdependence is highlighted by the fact that it is *the* feature that is used to distinguish teams from groups (e.g., Morgan et al., 1986). Describing the nature of this interdependence is central to what should constitute a team task analysis. Whether this is accomplished via behavioral dimensions of team taskwork that represent the underlying construct of interdependence or through some explicit measure (operationalization), the very nature of the interdependence must be assessed.

DETERMINING THE DEGREE OF TEAM INTERDEPENDENCE OR "TEAMNESS" OF TASKS AND JOBS

The second objective of this chapter is to make recommendations on how current occupational and task analysis systems can be modified and revised to readily and effectively identify team-based tasks and also their degree of team interdependence operationalized here as team-relatedness and team workflow (Arthur et al., 2005, in press-b). Again, it should be noted that unlike most foci on team task analysis, which are predicated on the assumption that the analyst is already cognizant of the fact that he/she is dealing with a team-based job, the focus of the following recommendations is predicated on the assumption that all the analyst has is a list of task statements with no information about their team-based or team interdependence status. Thus, the analyst's first goal is to identify which tasks and task elements are team-based. Subsequently, it is anticipated that after these tasks have been identified as such, systems will be employed to engage in a more detailed analysis of these tasks (see Figure 33.1).

Review of Active Verbs

One fairly simple means of obtaining *preliminary* information on the team interdependence of a task is to review the active verbs used to describe the task. Thus, active verbs such as assist, coordinate, forward, participate, provide, support, and other similar verbs should provide some initial insights as to whether the task is likely to be team-based. Additional probing by the job analyst should confirm or disconfirm whether the task in question is team-based.

Arthur et al.'s (2005) Team Task Analysis Approach

Another way to conduct a team task analysis is to use a task questionnaire-based approach. Arthur et al. (2005) present the development and initial validation of three team task analysis scales. Three main goals guided their questionnaire-based approach. First, the approach had to be sufficiently generic such that with only minor modification and revision, it could be readily applied to any set of tasks or job. Second, the team task analysis scales should lend themselves to being easily incorporated into existing occupational and task analysis systems to readily and effectively identify team-based tasks and also quantify their degree of team interdependence. Third, in addition to providing task-level information, the approach and its resultant scales should also permit a quantitative assessment of the extent to which *jobs* are team-based. To meet these criteria, Arthur et al. focused on the development of team task analysis scales that could be applied to any task or job. Based on reviews of the traditional job analysis, task analysis, and team task analysis literatures, their approach focused on ratings of team-relatedness and team workflow as metrics of team interdependence.

Structural Versus Perceived Interdependence

In discussions of team interdependence, it is important to acknowledge and draw the distinction between structural and behavioral interdependence in which the former (i.e., structural) pertains to what is designed or structured into the task and the latter (i.e., behavioral) pertains to how people actually behave (Wageman, 2001). In addition, perceived task interdependence is posited as a precursor to behavioral interdependence such that it can be conceptualized as mediating the relationship between structural and behavioral interdependence (Arthur et al., in press-b). Thus, perceived interdependence pertains to how people perceive the structure of tasks and jobs and subsequently, behave accordingly.

Structural task interdependence can be achieved by (a) how the task is defined to the team, (b) rules and instructions about process provided to the team, (c) the physical technology of the task, and (d) the distribution of task and work-related resources (e.g., skills, information, and material) among individuals (Wageman, 2001). Subsequently, perceived task interdependence refers to the extent to which individuals perceive the nature and form of the structural interdependencies of the task. Thus, structural interdependence influences team members' perceptions and awareness of the extent to which working with members of the team is required for optimal performance of the task or job. These perceptions are in turn instrumental in the manifestation of behavioral interdependence and ultimately, more effective task and job performance. Conceptually, the advantage of correctly perceiving the degree of structural interdependence is similar to that of teams who have similar and accurate mental models (Day, Arthur, & Gettman, 2001; Edwards, Day, Arthur, & Bell, 2006). That is, teams that recognize the structural interdependence inherent in specific tasks (and jobs) and, consequently, behave accordingly outperform teams that do not. This reasoning also serves as the basis for why interdependency ratings (perceptions) can also serve as both predictors of team performance and criteria in other team-related interventions such as team training (Arthur et al., 2005; Kyte, 2008).

Ratings of Team-Relatedness and Team Workflow

In our most current conceptualization of team-relatedness, it represents the extent to which successful team performance requires the individual to work with members of the team to optimally perform the specified task or job. Thus, team-relatedness can be conceptualized as representing the amount or magnitude of team interdependence or teamness. Earlier generations of the scale (Arthur et al., 2005) conceptualized it as the extent to which tasks could not be successfully performed alone. However, subsequent work (e.g., Arthur et al., in press-b) has found the current definition to be conceptually and operationally more sound. Information about the team-relatedness of tasks can be obtained by asking respondents (e.g., incumbents and supervisors) to rate the extent to which working with members of the team is required for optimal performance of an individual's specified tasks and activities for successful team performance. This allows us to identify, assess, and quantify the team-relatedness of tasks and ultimately, the job. Sample task analysis items and statements for assessing team-relatedness for general air traffic control are presented in Figure 33.2 for illustrative purposes. Importance and time-spent scales are also presented in this template.

In addition to team-relatedness, ratings of team work and/or information flow can also be obtained at the task level. Team workflow represents the paths by which work and/or information flows through the team to optimally perform the specified tasks or job and is best conceptualized as reflecting or describing the type, kind, or form of teamness or team interdependence. One model of workflow variation is Tesluk et al.'s (1997) dimensions of interdependence (see also Thompson, 1967; Van de Vegt et al., 2000), which posits that the degree of team interdependence for specified tasks (or jobs) can differ along four levels—pooled/additive interdependence, sequential

Team-relatedness represents the extent to which working with members of the team is required for optimal performance of your individual specified tasks for successful team performance.

Team workflow represents the way that work and/or information between team members flows for the optimal performance of specified tasks for successful team performance. The chart below presents the five TEAM WORKFLOW patterns as well as a description and illustration of each pattern. For each task/activity, please:

(a) Shade in the number corresponding to the importance of the task/activity in your position.
(b) Record the amount of time in hours and minutes that you spend performing the task/activity in your typical work period (e.g., shift or work day).
(c) Shade in the number corresponding to the team-relatedness of the task/activity.
(d) Shade in the number corresponding to the workflow pattern that best characterizes the way the work between members flows for the optimal performance of each task/activity for successful team performance.

		Importance		
①	②	③	④	⑤
Not at all important	Of little importance	Somewhat important	Very important	Of highest importance

Team-Relatedness

①	②	③	④	⑤
Not required to work with team members for optimal performance	Rarely required to work with team members for optimal performance	Somewhat required to work with team members for optimal performance	Often required to work with team members for optimal performance	Very much required to work with team members for optimal performance

Team workflow

①	②	③	④	⑤
Not a team task/activity	Pooled/additive interdependence	Sequential interdependence	Reciprocal interdependence	Intensive interdependence

Tasks/activities	Importance	Time spent	Team-relatedness	Team workflow pattern
1. Activates backup communication systems.	① ② ③ ④ ⑤	___ hrs.___ min.	① ② ③ ④ ⑤	① ② ③ ④ ⑤
2. Adjust radar scopes.	① ② ③ ④ ⑤	___ hrs.___ min.	① ② ③ ④ ⑤	① ② ③ ④ ⑤
3. Coordinate search and rescue operations with appropriate agencies.	① ② ③ ④ ⑤	___ hrs.___ min.	① ② ③ ④ ⑤	① ② ③ ④ ⑤
4. Coordinate use of airspace with other agencies or facilities.	① ② ③ ④ ⑤	___ hrs.___ min.	① ② ③ ④ ⑤	① ② ③ ④ ⑤
5. Coordinate or control aircraft surge launch and recovery (ASLAR) procedures.	① ② ③ ④ ⑤	___ hrs.___ min.	① ② ③ ④ ⑤	① ② ③ ④ ⑤

Figure 33.2   Example of a task analysis rating form incorporating team-relatedness and team workflow scales along with importance and time spent scales for a sample of general air traffic control activities.

interdependence, reciprocal interdependence, and intensive interdependence. These four levels of interdependence serve as the basis for the workflow scale presented by Arthur et al. (2005). Specifically, the four levels of team interdependence are used as response options to obtain ratings describing the level of interdependence. Arthur et al. added a fifth level to capture tasks that are performed by the individual *outside* the context of a team. Thus, these tasks would represent those performed by the individual alone and not in a team. An illustrative example of a holistic team workflow scale is presented in Figure 33.3.

Assessing the Degree of Team-Relatedness and Team Workflow of Jobs

As previously noted, the team task analysis approach presented in this chapter is based on the premise that in the population of tasks constituting a job, the proportion of tasks that are

Team workflow: The way that work and/or information between team members flows for the optimal performance of your job as a {_list job title here_}.

The chart below presents five *team workflow* patterns as well as a description and illustration of each pattern. Please indicate in the **Response** column (by shading in the appropriate response) the workflow pattern that *best* characterizes the way that work and/or information between team members flows for the optimal performance of your whole job as a {_list job title here_}.

Team workflow pattern	Description	Illustration	Response
1. Not a team job	Work and activities are ***not*** performed as a member of a team; they are performed alone outside the context of the team. Work and activities are performed by an individual working ***alone***, ***not*** in a team.	Work received by individual ○ Work leaves individual	①
2. Pooled/additive interdependence	Work and activities are performed separately by all team members, and work does not flow between members of the team.	Work enters team ○ ○ ○ ○ Work leaves team	②
3. Sequential interdependence	Work and activities flow from one member to another in the team but mostly in one direction.	Work enters team ○→○→○→○ Work leaves team	③
4. Reciprocal interdependence	Work and activities flow between team members in a back-and-forth manner over a period of time.	Work enters team ○⇄○⇄○⇄○ Work leaves team	④
5. Intensive interdependence	Work and activities come into the team, and members must work as a team in order to accomplish the team's task.	Work enters team ○ ○ ○ ○ Work leaves team	⑤

Figure 33.3 Example of a rating form to assess team workflow at the holistic (i.e., job) level. Note that ratees could alternatively be asked to *rank* the five patterns. Under certain conditions, ranking may be more informative because it allows ratees to indicate the existence of both individual and team tasks that are present in most jobs. If ranks are used, then the instruction set should read, "The chart below presents five team workflow patterns as well as a description and diagram for each pattern. Please rank order the five patterns (1 = high; 5 = low) in terms of the extent to which they are descriptive of the way that work and/or information between team members flows for the optimal performance of your whole job as a [list job title here]. That is, the pattern that *best* describes the work activities in your job would be ranked 1, and the pattern that is *least* descriptive of your work activities would be ranked 5."

team-based can range from 0% to 100%. This range represents the extent to which a job can be described as team-based. Therefore, at one extreme, if 0% of the tasks are team-based, then the job in question is not a team-based job. In its simplest form, assessing the extent to which a job is team-based can be accomplished by asking ratees to indicate the team workflow pattern or the level of team-relatedness that is required for the effective performance of the job as a whole. This, of course, represents a holistic rating. Figure 33.4 presents an example of a rating form that can be used to assess the overall team-relatedness of a job. Likewise, Figure 33.3 presents an example of a rating form that can be used to assess the overall workflow pattern of a job. Both of these indicators serve as metrics of the degree of team interdependence or the extent to which a job is team-based.

Alternatively, the extent to which a job is team-based can be determined by using aggregates of the task-level ratings. Thus, aggregates (mean or sum) of either the task-level team workflow or team-relatedness ratings (see Figure 33.2) could be used as indicators of the "teamness" of a job. In addition, the extent to which a job is team-based can also be operationalized by summing the total number of tasks that constitute the job and dividing the total by the number of tasks that can be accomplished by one team member (Dieterly, 1988), with higher scores indicating that the job is more team-based. However, due to the level of specificity, the number of ratings required, and the increased opportunity for information distortion (Pine, 1995), we do not advocate the use of item-level aggregates as operationalizations of the degree to which a job is team-based (Arthur et al., 2005). Related to this, based on the data we have to date, Table 33.3 presents a summary of our recommended approaches to determining the teamness of tasks and jobs. However, it should be noted that these recommendations should be considered as interim because we are in the process of collecting additional data on the efficacy of these approaches for the specified purposes.

In an initial assessment of the validity and efficacy of the team task analysis metrics, using 13 four-person teams training to perform a complex computer simulated combat mission consisting of both individual- and team-based tasks, Arthur et al. (2005) concluded the following:

1. The approach is effective at differentiating individual-based tasks from team-based tasks.
2. Ratings of team-relatedness and team workflow effectively quantified the extent to which tasks and jobs are team-based with the workflow operationalization appearing to be more effective.

Overall team-relatedness: The extent to which working with members of the team is required for the optimal performance of your overall job.

Using the scale below, please shade in the number the that corresponds to the level of team-relatedness that is required for **optimal** performance of your job as a whole.

> ① = Not required to work with team members for optimal performance
> ② = Rarely required to work with team members for optimal performance
> ③ = Somewhat required to work with team members for optimal performance
> ④ = Often required to work with team members for optimal performance
> ⑤ = Very much required to work with team members for optimal performance

Overall	Team-Relatedness
OVERALL job as a {_**job title goes here**_}	① ② ③ ④ ⑤

Figure 33.4 Example of a task analysis rating form for obtaining a holistic (i.e., overall) job team-relatedness rating.

Table 33.3   Recommended Approaches to Determining the Team Interdependence of Tasks and Jobs

Task Analysis Approach	Tasks and Task Elements	Job
Review of active verbs	Y	
Task ratings of team-relatedness	Y	
Task ratings of team workflow	Y	
Team-task ratio		Y
Job ratings of team-relatedness		Y
Job ratings of team workflow		Y

3. Acceptable levels of internal consistency were obtained for both team-relatedness (α = .80 and .92) and team workflow ratings (α =.92 and .96 for individual and team tasks, respectively) along with high levels of interrater agreement.

4. The correlation between task-level team-relatedness and team workflow ratings was only moderate (mean, r = .25; SD = 0.15, min = −0.11, max = 0.64). This is consistent with the position that they represent complementary but different facets of team interdependence or teamness and thus, should not be used interchangeably as measures of team interdependence. Specifically, team-relatedness represents the extent to which successful team performance requires the individual to work with members of the team to optimally perform the specified task or job and reflects the amount or magnitude of team interdependence. Conversely, team workflow represents the paths by which work and/or information flows through the team to optimally perform the specified tasks or job and reflects the type, kind, or form of team interdependence or teamness.

5. The team task ratings obtained from this approach can potentially serve as a criterion measure of team training effectiveness. Specifically, Arthur et al. obtained a strong correlation (r = .74) between the job-level (i.e., holistic) rating of team interdependence and team performance, suggesting that teams that recognized the team-based demands of the mission and subsequently performed the mission as such (as reflected in their task analysis ratings), had higher team performance scores than those that did not. In other words, better trained teams are those that recognize the interdependencies of their tasks with said recognition being reflected in their team task analysis ratings. The team mental models literature (e.g., Day et al., 2001; Edwards et al., 2006; Mathieu, Heffner, Goodwin, Salas, & Cannon-Bowers, 2000) provides the theoretical basis for this explanation. Kyte (2008) also provides additional evidence for the efficacy of these metrics as training evaluation criteria by using them to evaluate the effectiveness of a crew resource management training program in the railroad industry. Finally, the team task analysis scale ratings could also be used as predictors of team performance (see Arthur et al., 2011).

The efficacy of Arthur et al.'s (2005) team task analysis metrics and approach is reflected by their use in operational field settings. For instance, a team task analysis questionnaire based on the team-relatedness and workflow pattern scales is being used successfully in Air Force operational environments. One example involves efforts to identify the amount and type of interdependence associated with a set F-16 combat fighter pilot tasks and activities in an effort to provide researchers with an indicator of degree and form of "teamness," which is then subsequently used to identify the most logical opportunities for connecting distributed teams to achieve common training objectives. For example, if we know that a skill such as airspace

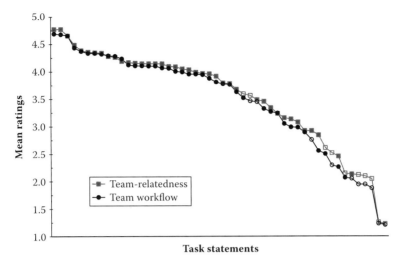

Figure 33.5 Mean team-relatedness and team workflow ratings highlighting rank-ordered position of predetermined team (closed markers) and individual (open markers) tasks.

management has high levels of interdependence because it requires a fighter pilot to interact with other aircraft and with an airborne air traffic controller, and we further know that other fighter pilots and the air traffic controllers need to develop the same skill, we can then develop a common training scenario that permits all of the constituent trainees to get training on the same skill at the same time. This provides significant economies of scale in terms of common training across multiple operators. It further provides an additional rationale for establishing connectivity amongst the training environments to achieve training success and realize the savings resulting from the economies of scale. Arthur et al.'s (in press-b) data from this operational use of the scales are summarized in Figure 33.5. These data were obtained from 182 F-16 combat fighter pilots (mean F-16 flight hours = 1051.00; SD = 756.41), who rated 50 task and activity statements in terms of their team-relatedness and team workflow. Ten of the tasks/activities have been predetermined by two instructor pilots to be individual-based tasks. As Figure 33.5 illustrates, 5 out of 10 predetermined individual-based tasks (i.e., low structural interdependence) were in the bottom five tasks for the team-relatedness and team workflow ratings. Likewise, for the team-based tasks, for both the team-relatedness and team workflow ratings, the top five tasks had been designated by the instructor pilots as being team-based tasks (i.e., high structural interdependence). Furthermore, additional aspects of Arthur et al.'s (in press-b) results also replicated those summarized above for Arthur et al. (2005; e.g., high levels of internal consistency and interrater agreement, and only moderate correlations between team-relatedness and team workflow ratings).

Differentiating Between Jobs

Data reported by Arthur et al. (2005, in press-b) clearly indicate that the team-relatedness and team workflow metrics can effectively differentiate between individual- and team-based tasks. In addition, in support of one of the major objectives that motivated their work, some lab and field data demonstrate that they can also differentiate between jobs that differ in their overall teamness. Data supporting this are presented in Table 33.4 for F-16 combat fighter pilots (Arthur et al., in press-b) and two combat lab tasks—Steel Beasts (Arthur et al., 2005) and Fleet Command (Arthur et al., in press-a). They show that the three "jobs" differ in their levels of team

Table 33.4 Differentiating Between Jobs in Terms of Their Level and Type of Team Interdependence

Job	Interdependence Metric	Scale Anchor Point *Below* Mean Rating	Mean Rating (*SD*)	Scale Anchor Point *Above* Mean Rating
Overall job as an F-16 combat fighter pilot[a]	Team-relatedness	④ Often required to work with team members for optimal performance	4.75 (0.52) N = 182	⑤ Very much required to work with team members for optimal performance
	Team workflow	Work enters team → Work leaves team ④	4.71 (0.48) N = 182	Work enters team → Work leaves team ⑤
Overall performance of steel beasts (DTS tank platoon trainer) combat missions[b]	Team workflow	Work enters team → Work leaves team ④	4.25 (0.54) N = 52	Work enters team → Work leaves team ⑤
Overall performance of fleet command (DTS command-and-control trainer)[c]	Team-relatedness	④ Often required to work with team members for optimal performance	4.11 (0.97) N = 203	⑤ Very much required to work with team members for optimal performance
	Team workflow	③ Work enters team → Work leaves team	3.84 (1.11) N = 203	④ Work enters team → Work leaves team

[a] Arthur et al. (in press-b).
[b] Arthur et al. (2005).
[c] Arthur et al. (in press-a).

interdependence as rank ordered. In addition, using sports as an analogue for jobs, Arthur et al. (2008) had 913 participants rate 25 sports in terms of the degree of team-relatedness and the type of team workflow. As Figure 33.6, which presents a summary of their results illustrates, and is further documented in Table 33.5, the ratings were very effective in differentiating team sports from individual sports.

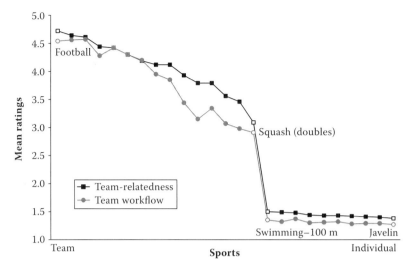

Figure 33.6 Arthur et al.'s (2008) mean team-relatedness and team workflow ratings for various sports. The 25 sports, listed from the highest to lowest team-relatedness ratings were (1) football, (2) basketball, (3) soccer, (4) volleyball, (5) ice hockey, (6) rugby, (7) lacrosse, (8) softball, (9) baseball, (10), tug-of-war, (11) polo, (12) tennis [doubles], (13) track relay, (14) swimming relay, (15) squash [doubles], (16) swimming 100m, (17) track 100m, (18) wrestling, (19) racquetball [singles], (20) fencing, (21) diving, (22) shot put, (23) tennis [singles], (24) golf, and (25) javelin.

SUMMARY AND CONCLUSIONS

The objectives of the present chapter were to review the team task analysis literature and to make recommendations on how current occupational and task analysis systems can be modified and revised to readily and effectively identify team-based tasks and also, their degree of team interdependence or "teamness." This was accomplished by first reviewing the team task analysis and team performance literatures. There is agreement in the extant literature that the study and conceptualization of teams can vary along a number of dimensions including taskwork versus teamwork

Table 33.5 Arthur et al.'s (2008) Team-Relatedness and Team Work Flow Ratings for the Top Five (Team) and Bottom Five (Individual) Sports

	Team-Relatedness			Team Workflow		
	N	Mean	*SD*	*N*	Mean	*SD*
Team						
Football	814	4.72	0.66	816	4.54	0.82
Basketball	852	4.64	0.67	858	4.56	0.74
Soccer	815	4.61	0.66	817	4.57	0.71
Volleyball	802	4.44	0.73	807	4.28	0.83
Ice Hockey	760	4.42	0.91	769	4.42	0.91
Individual						
Diving	771	1.43	0.84	781	1.32	0.62
Shot Put	751	1.42	0.93	760	1.28	0.73
Tennis (singles)	778	1.41	0.93	785	1.29	0.77
Golf	793	1.40	0.87	803	1.29	0.69
Javelin	746	1.38	0.84	755	1.27	0.71

and also the distinction between individual taskwork and team taskwork. Thus, the theoretical groundwork for delineating team- versus individual-based task behaviors has already been laid.

However, the utility of these distinctions to our understanding of teams is dependent on our ability to effectively analyze teams and the tasks they perform. Although Baker et al. (1998) represent the research literature on team task analysis as practically void, an extensive search of the literature identified a limited but sufficient relevant works to guide the development of a series of recommendations to not only identify whether tasks were team-based, but to also quantify the nature and degree of their "teamness." We believe that these recommendations can be readily and effectively incorporated into current occupational and task analysis systems and look forward to researchers taking the opportunity to empirically and operationally test their viability. Specifically, the flexibility and transportability of Arthur and colleague's questionnaire approach to various settings is a result of its "generic" nature such that its use in other settings requires only the insertion of the specified task statements into the questionnaire. This flexibility also means that this approach can be easily incorporated into existing occupational and task analysis systems.

To date, the empirical data for the team task analysis metrics presented by Arthur et al. (2005; see also Arthur et al., in press-b; Kyte, 2008) have shown that these metrics have enormous utility in both applied and research settings. Amongst others, they permit the use of teamness as both a criterion in team training and also as a predictor of team performance. Thus, they have the potential to be used for a variety of human resource functions and interventions such as training, selection, job design, and career exploration. They can also be used as diagnostic indicators and, of course, in research as well.

Team-relatedness and team workflow are also effective in distinguishing individual from team tasks in addition to quantifying the teamness of tasks and jobs. So, they are capable of quantifying teamness not only within but also between different types of teams. Thus, instead of describing specific teams as interdependent on the basis of self-proclamation, the degree and type of interdependence can be empirically determined using the metrics and scales presented here. We are also currently collecting data to investigate the relationship between teamness and other task characteristics such as importance. For instance, in team-based contexts, are team-based tasks (i.e., team taskwork) generally considered to be more important than individual-based tasks (i.e., individual taskwork)? Thus, in terms of team task analysis, future research investigating the relationship between team interdependence and other task characteristics including but not limited to important-to-train, criticality, time spent, difficulty-to-perform, importance, difficulty-to-train, time-to-proficiency, and consequence-of-error, is warranted.

REFERENCES

Arthur, W. Jr., Day, E. A., Villado, A. J., Glaze, R. M., Schuelke, M. J., Boatman, P. R., et al. (in press-a). Team skill acquisition and retention on a complex command-and-control simulation task. In W. Arthur, Jr., E. A. Day, W. Bennett, Jr., & A. Portrey (Eds.), *Individual and team skill decay: State of the science and implications for practice.*

Arthur, W. Jr., Doverspike, D., & Barrett, G. V. (1996). Development of a job analysis-based procedure for weighting and combining content-related tests into a single test battery score. *Personnel Psychology, 49,* 971–985.

Arthur, W. Jr., Edwards, B. D., Bell, S. T., Villado, A. J., & Bennett, W. Jr. (2005). Team task analysis: Identifying tasks and jobs that are team-based. *Human Factors, 47,* 654–669.

Arthur, W. Jr., Glaze, R. M., Bhupatkar, A., Villado, A. J., Bennett, W. Jr., & Rowe, L. (2008, April). *Team-relatedness and team workflow as metrics of task interdependence.* Paper presented at the 23rd Annual Conference of the Society for Industrial and Organizational Psychology, San Francisco, CA.

Arthur, W. Jr., Glaze, R. M., Bhupatkar, A., Villado, A. J., Bennett, W. Jr., & Rowe, L. (in press-b). Team task analysis: Differentiating between tasks using team-relatedness and team workflow as metrics of task interdependence. *Human Factors.*

Baker, D. P., & Salas, E. (1996). Analyzing team performance: In the eye of the beholder? *Military Psychology, 8,* 235–245.

Baker, D. P., & Salas, E. (1997). Principles for measuring teamwork: A summary and look toward the future. In M. T. Brannick, E. Salas, & C. Prince (Eds.), *Team performance assessment and measurement: Theory, methods, and applications* (pp. 331–355). Mahwah, NJ: Lawrence Erlbaum.

Baker, D. P., Salas, E., Campion, M. A., Cannon-Bowers, J., Higgs, C. A., & Levine, E. L. (1998, April). *Job analysis for teams: Fitting square pegs into round holes?* Panel discussion presented at the 13th annual meeting of the Society for Industrial and Organizational Psychology, Dallas, TX.

Baker, D. P., Salas, E., & Cannon-Bowers, J. (1998). Team task analysis: Lost but hopefully not forgotten. *The Industrial and Organizational Psychologist, 35,* 79–83.

Barry, B., & Stewart, G. L. (1997). Composition, process, and performance in self-managed groups: The role of personality. *Journal of Applied Psychology, 82,* 62–78.

Binning, J. F., & Barrett, G. V. (1989). Validity of personnel decisions: A conceptual analysis of the inferential and evidential bases. *Journal of Applied Psychology, 74,* 478–494.

Bowers, C. A., Baker, D. P., & Salas, E. (1994). Measuring the importance of teamwork: The reliability and validity of job/task analysis indices for team-training design. *Military Psychology, 6,* 205–214.

Bowers, C. A., Morgan, B. B., Salas, E., & Prince, C. (1993). Assessment of coordination demand for aircrew coordination training. *Military Psychology, 5,* 95–112.

Brannick, M. T., Prince, A., Prince, C., & Salas, E. (1995). The measurement of team process. *Human Factors, 37,* 641–651.

Burke, C. S., Stagl, K. C., Salas, E., Pierce, L., & Kendall, D. (2006). Understanding team adaptation. *Journal of Applied Psychology, 91,* 1189–1207.

Campion, M. A., Medsker, G. J., & Higgs, C. A. (1993). Relations between work group characteristics and effectiveness: Implications for designing effective work groups. *Personnel Psychology, 46,* 823–850.

Campion, M. A., Papper, E. M., & Medsker, G. J. (1996). Relations between work group characteristics and effectiveness: A replication and extension. *Personnel Psychology, 49,* 429–452.

Cannon-Bowers, J. A., & Salas, E. (1997). A framework for developing team performance measures in training. In M. T. Brannick, C. Prince, & E. Salas (Eds.), *Team performance assessment and measurement* (pp. 45–62). Mahweh, NJ: Lawrence Erlbaum.

Cannon-Bowers, J. A., Tannenbaum, S. I., Salas, E., & Volpe, C. E. (1995). Defining competencies and establishing team training requirements. In R. A. Guzzo & E. Salas (Eds.), *Team effectiveness and decision making in organizations* (pp. 333–381). San Francisco, CA: Jossey-Bass.

Chen, G. (2005). Newcomer adaptation in teams: Multilevel antecedents and outcomes. *Academy of Management, 48,* 101–116.

Chen, G., Kirkman, B. L., Kanfer, R., Allen, D., & Rosen, B. (2007). A multi-level study of leadership, empowerment, and performance in teams. *Journal of Applied Psychology, 92,* 337–346.

Day, E. A., Arthur, W. Jr., & Gettman, D. (2001). Knowledge structures and the acquisition of a complex skill. *Journal of Applied Psychology, 86,* 1022–1033.

De Dreu, C. (2007). Cooperative outcome interdependence, task reflexivity, and team effectiveness: A motivated information processing perspective. *Journal of Applied Psychology, 92,* 628–638.

DeShon, R. P., Kozlowski, S. W. J., Schmidt, A. M., Milner, K. R., & Wiechmann, D. (2004). A multiple-goal, multilevel model of feedback effects on the regulation of individual and team performance. *Journal of Applied Psychology, 89,* 1035–1056.

Dickinson, T. L., & McIntyre, R. M. (1997). A conceptual framework for teamwork measurement. In M. T. Brannick, C. Prince, & E. Salas (Eds.), *Team performance assessment and measurement* (pp. 15–43). Mahweh, NJ: Lawrence Erlbaum.

Dieterly, D. L. (1988). Team performance requirements. In S. Gael (Ed.), *The job analysis handbook for business, industry, and government* (pp. 766–777). New York, NY: John Wiley & Sons.

Dwyer, D. J. (1992). An index for measuring naval team performance. *Proceedings of the Human Factors Society 36th Annual Meeting* (pp. 1356–1360). Santa Monica, CA: Human Factors Society.

Edwards, B. D., Day, E. A., Arthur, W. Jr., & Bell, S. T. (2006). Relationships among team ability composition, team mental models, and team performance. *Journal of Applied Psychology, 91,* 727–736.

Equal Employment Opportunity Commission, Civil Service Commission, Department of Labor, Department of Justice (1978). Adoption by four agencies of uniform guidelines on employee selection procedures. *Federal Register, 43,* 38290–38315.

Fleishman, E. A., & Zaccaro, S. J. (1992). Toward a taxonomy of team performance functions. In R. W. Swezey & E. Salas (Eds.), *Teams: Their training and performance* (pp. 31–56). Norwood, NJ: Ablex.

Ford, J. K., Smith, E. M., Sego, D. J., & Quinones, M. A. (1992). *The impact of individual and task experience factors on training emphasis ratings*. Paper presented at the 7th annual meeting of the Society for Industrial and Organizational Psychology, Montreal, Canada.

Foushee, H. C. (1984). Dyads and triads at 35,000 feet. *American Psychologist, 39,* 885–893.

Franz, T. M., Prince, C., Cannon-Bowers, J. A., & Salas, E. (1990). The identification of aircrew coordination skills. *Proceedings of the 12th Annual Department of Defense Symposium* (pp. 97–101). Colorado Springs, CO: U.S. Air Force Academy.

Gael, S. (Ed.). (1988). *The job analysis handbook for business, industry, and government*. New York, NY: John Wiley & Sons.

Gladstein, D. L. (1984). Groups in context: A model of task group effectiveness. *Administrative Science Quarterly, 29,* 499–517.

Glickman, A. S., Zimmer, S., Montero, R. C., Guerette, P. J., Campbell, W. J., Morgan, B. B., & Salas, E. (1987). *The evolution of team skills: An empirical assessment with implications for training* (NTSC Tech. Report No. 87-016). Arlington, VA: Office of Naval Research.

Guzzo, R. A., & Shea, G. P. (1992). Group performance and intergroup relations in organizations. In M. D. Dunnette & L. H. Hough (Eds.), *Handbook of industrial and organizational psychology* (Vol. 3, 2nd ed., pp. 269–313). Palo Alto, CA: Consulting Psychologists.

Hackman, J. R. (1987). The design of work teams. In J. W. Lorsch (Ed.), *Handbook of organizational behavior* (pp. 315–342). Englewood Cliffs, NJ: Prentice-Hall.

Hart, S. G., Childress, M. E., & Bortolussi, M. R. (1981). Defining the subjective experience of workload. *Proceedings of the Human Factors Society 25th Annual Meeting* (pp. 527–531). Santa Monica, CA: Human Factors Society.

Kyte, T. B. (2008). *Crew resource management training's effect on railroad crews' perceptions of task interdependence and team work* (PhD dissertation). Texas A&M University, College Station, TX.

Marks, M. A., DeChurch, L. A., Mathieu, J. E., Panzer, F. J., & Alonso, A. (2005). Teamwork in multiteam systems. *Journal of Applied Psychology, 90,* 964–971.

Mathieu, J. E., Gilson, L. L., & Ruddy, T. M. (2006). Empowerment and team effectiveness: An empirical test of an integrated model. *Journal of Applied Psychology, 91,* 97–108.

Mathieu, J. E., Heffner, T. S., Goodwin, G. F., Salas, E., & Cannon-Bowers, J. A. (2000). The influence of shared mental models on team process and performance. *Journal of Applied Psychology, 85,* 273–283.

McCormick, E. L. (1979). *Job analysis: Methods and applications*. New York, NY: AMACOM.

McGrath, J. E. (1986). Studying groups at work: Ten critical needs. In P. S. Goodman (Ed.), *Designing effective work groups* (pp. 362–391). San Francisco, CA: Jossey-Bass.

McIntyre, R. M., & Salas, E. (1995). Measuring and managing for team performance: Emerging principles from complex environments. In R. A. Guzzo & E. Salas (Eds.), *Team effectiveness and decision making in organizations* (pp. 9–45). San Francisco, CA: Jossey-Bass.

Morgan, B. B., Glickman, A. S., Woodward, E. A. Blaiwes, A. S., & Salas, E. (1986). *Measurement of team behaviors in a Navy environment* (NTSC Tech. Report No. 86-014). Orlando, FL: Naval Training Systems Center.

Morgeson, F. P., Reider, M. H., & Campion, M. A. (2005). Selecting individuals in team settings: The importance of social skills, personality characteristics, and teamwork knowledge. *Personnel Psychology, 58,* 583–611.

Mumford, T. V., Van Iddekinge, C. H., Morgeson, F. P., & Campion, M. A. (2008). The team role test: Development and Validation of a team role knowledge situational judgment test. *Journal of Applied Psychology, 93,* 250–267.

Oser, R. L., McCallum, G. A., Salas, E., & Morgan, B. B. (1990). *Toward a definition of teamwork: An analysis of critical team behaviors* (NTSC Tech. Report No. 89-004). Orlando, FL: Naval Training Systems Center.

Pine, D. E. (1995). Assessing the validity of job ratings: An empirical study of false reporting in task inventories. *Public Personnel Management, 24,* 451–460.

Prince, C., & Salas, E. (1993). Training for teamwork in the military aircrew: Military CRM programs and research. In E. Weiner, B. Kanki, & R. Helmreich (Eds.), *Cockpit resource management*. New York, NY: Academic Press.

Sanchez, J. I. (1990). *The effects of job experience on judgments of task importance*. Paper presented at the 5th annual meeting of the Society for Industrial and Organizational Psychology, Miami, FL.

Sanchez, J. I., & Fraser, S. L. (1992). On the choice of scales for task analysis. *Journal of Applied Psychology, 77,* 545–553.

Sanchez, J. I., & Levine, E. L. (1989). Determining important tasks within jobs: A policy capturing approach. *Journal of Applied Psychology, 74,* 336–342.

Stevens, M. J., & Campion, M. A. (1994). The knowledge, skills, and ability requirements for teamwork: Implications for human resource management. *Journal of Management, 20,* 503–530.

Stevens, M. J., & Campion, M. A. (1999). Staffing teams: Development and validation of a selection test for teamwork settings. *Journal of Management, 25,* 207–228.

Swezey, R. W., Owens, J. M., Bergondy, M. L., & Salas, E. (1998). Task and training requirements analysis methodology (TTRAM): An analytic methodology for identifying potential training uses of simulator networks in teamwork-intensive task environments. *Ergonomics, 41,* 1678–1697.

Tannenbaum, S. I., Beard, R. L., & Salas, E. (1992). Team building and its influence on team effectiveness: An examination of conceptual and empirical developments. In K. Kelley (Ed.), *Issues, theory, and research in industrial/organizational psychology* (pp. 117–153). Amsterdam, Holland: Elsevier.

Tesluk, P., Mathieu, J. E., Zaccaro, S. J., & Marks, M. (1997). Task and aggregation issues in the analysis and assessment of team performance. In M. T. Brannick, C. Prince, & E. Salas (Eds.), *Team performance assessment and measurement* (pp. 197–224). Mahweh, NJ: Lawrence Erlbaum.

Thompson, J. D. (1967). *Organizations in action: Social science bases of administrative theory.* New York, NY: McGraw-Hill.

Van der Vegt, G., Emans, B., & Van de Vliert, E. (1998). Motivating effects of task and outcome interdependence in work teams. *Group and organization management, 23,* 124–143.

Van der Vegt, G., Emans, B., & Van de Vliert, E. (2000). Team member's affective responses to patterns of intragroup interdependence and job complexity. *Journal of Management, 26,* 633–655.

Wageman, R. (2001). The meaning of interdependence. In M. E. Turner (Ed.), *Groups at work: Advances in theory and research* (pp. 197–217). Hillsdale, NJ: Lawrence Erlbaum.

34

Development and Evaluation of a Task Taxonomy to Support Research on Cross-Job Transferability of Skills

CHARLES E. LANCE

University of Georgia

TRACY LAMBERT GRIGGS

Winthrop University

R. BRUCE GOULD

Damos Aviation Services

In the late 1980s, the United States Air Force (USAF) Armstrong Laboratory, Human Resources Directorate (AL/HR) undertook a large scale program of research and development (R&D) on cross-job transferability of skills that followed from previous research on the success of USAF retraining policies (Skinner, 1981, 1982, 1983; Skinner & Alley, 1980, 1984). Cross-job transferability of skills has been defined as "the continuous use of acquired knowledge and abilities when moving from one job to another" (Fine, 1957, p. 938) or "the ease with which individuals trained to proficiency on one job can apply acquired knowledge and skills in learning another job" (Lance, Kavanagh, & Gould, 1993, p. 68). There are large bodies of literature concerning topics that are related to cross-job transferability of skills such as job skills learning and retention (e.g., Arthur, Bennett, Stanush, & McNelly, 1998; Ginzburg & Dar-El, 2000; Lance et al., 1998; Taylor, Russ-Eft, & Chan, 2005), transfer of training to on-the-job performance (e.g., Arthur, Bennett, Edens, & Bell, 2003; Baldwin & Ford, 1988; Cheng & Ho, 2001; Richman-Hirsch, 2001; Yamnill & McLean, 2001), newcomer socialization following job transfer (e.g., Chao, O'Leary-Kelly, Wolf, Klein, & Gardner, 1994; Feji, Whitely, Peiro, & Taris, 1995; Fischer, 1986; Wanous, 1992), human resource planning for staffing and training needs (e.g., Jackson & Schuler, 1990; Niehaus & Price, 1991; Rousseau, 1988), and organizational learning and knowledge management (e.g., Chiva & Alegre, 2005; Huber, 1991; Thomas, Sussman, & Henderson, 2001). However, there is surprisingly little literature related to the relative ease or difficulty with which individuals can transition laterally across different jobs, taking advantage of whatever relevant knowledge, skills, and abilities they may have acquired in the previous job to learn and become proficient in a new assignment.

What research there is on cross-job transferability of skills indicates that old job–new job similarity is important in determining the extent of job skill transfer. For example, Gordon and Fitzgibbons (1982) and Gordon, Cofer, and McCullough (1986) found that interjob (i.e., old job–new job) similarity related positively to performance and negatively to retraining time required in the new job, but the range of jobs studied here was narrow (sewing machine operators) and the measurement of interjob similarity was coarse (whether the job was in the same or different department of a textile mill).

As part of AL/HR's R&D program, Lance, Kavanagh, and Gould (1993) proposed a much more sophisticated methodology for estimating cross-job transferability of skills whose foundation consisted of systematic analyses of relevant jobs' task contents and learning times. The rationale for Lance, Kavanagh, and Gould's methodology can be summarized as follows. First, it was assumed that a reasonably comprehensive and exhaustive specification of relevant jobs' task contents could be achieved. Given the military's (and especially the USAF's) long history and extensive experience with (especially task inventory) job analysis methods (Christal, 1974; Christal & Weissmuller, 1988; Morsh, Madden, & Christal, 1961), this assumption seemed reasonable. As will be explained shortly, however, this assumption implied the need for a common task taxonomy to which the very different tasks that comprise USAF enlisted jobs could be linked (the development of this taxonomy is the main topic of this chapter). It was also assumed that training times could be estimated for each of the task categories comprising the task taxonomy supporting Lance, Kavanagh, and Gould's methodology. Given the USAF's previous extensive R&D efforts on the measurement of task and occupational learning difficulty (Burtch, Lipscomb, & Wissman, 1982; Mead & Christal, 1970; Mumford, Weeks, Harding, & Fleishman, 1987; Ramage, 1987; Weeks, 1984), this assumption also seemed reasonable.

Thus assuming that learning/training times for relevant jobs' tasks, grouped according to categories in a comprehensive task taxonomy can be measured, Lance, Kavanagh, and Gould's (1993) methodology for estimating cross-job transferability of skills can be illustrated as in Figure 34.1. This figure shows five hypothetical task categories (A through E). The height of the

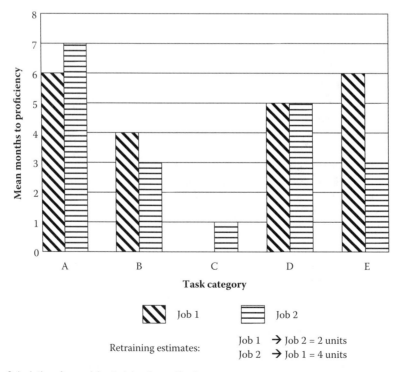

Figure 34.1 Calculation of cross-job retraining time estimate.

bars for each hypothetical task category show the estimated time that it would take a typical job incumbent to learn and become proficient on tasks included in each task category, separately for the two jobs being compared in this illustration. For example, Figure 34.1 shows that on average it takes Job 1 incumbents 6 months to learn to perform category A tasks proficiently, while it takes Job 2 incumbents 7 months, on average. The reverse pattern occurs for category B tasks: Job 1 incumbents take one month longer to learn these tasks on average (4 months) as compared to Job 2 incumbents (3 months), and category C illustrates a situation where Job 1 incumbents simply do not perform these tasks, whereas Job 2 incumbents require only 1 month to become proficient on them, on average. Task category "months-to-proficiency" (MTP) vectors, for example, the hypothetical MTP vectors shown for Jobs 1 and 2 in Figure 34.1, are then compared element-wise across all task categories to calculate two sums: (a) differences between Job 1's task category MTP values and Job 2's, but only those for which Job 1's are higher, and (b) differences between Job 1's MTP values and Job 2's, but only for those for which Job 2's are higher. The former quantity estimates additional job task content learning that would be required in retraining from Job 2 to Job 1 (4 months in Figure 34.1; i.e., 1 month associated with Category B tasks and 3 months associated with Category E tasks); the latter quantity estimates additional job task content learning that would be required in retraining from Job 1 to Job 2 (2 months in Figure 34.1; i.e., 1 month each associated with Categories A and C). As such, Lance et al.'s proposed methodology for estimating cross-job transferability of skills (a) actually estimates the relative *difficulty* of cross-job retraining because the resulting retraining time estimates represent additional job task skills that must be acquired in moving from one job to another (higher values indicate more difficult cross-job retraining transitions), (b) produces retraining time estimates that are *asymmetric* with respect to retraining between Job_i and Job_j (consider, for example, that it would likely be much more difficult to retrain from the job of nurse to surgeon, than vice versa), (c) generates retraining time estimates that represent the *relative* difficulty of cross-job retraining (i.e., no absolute metric of retraining times was assumed to have been established), and (d) supports the calculation of as many as $J(J-1)$ unique cross-job retraining time estimates for all possible transitions between any population of J jobs, leading to what can be thought of as a complete $J \times J$ skills transfer matrix.

A number of studies provided preliminary support for Lance, Kavanagh, and Gould's (1993) proposed methodology for estimating cross-job transferability of skills. For example, Kavanagh and Lance (1989) demonstrated that subject matter experts (SMEs; job incumbents and their first-level supervisors) provided the reliable and valid MTP judgments that are required for Lance, Kavanagh, and Gould's methodology. Lance, Kavanagh, and Gould themselves provided convergent validity evidence for cross-job transferability of skills estimates generated according to their methodology; as predicted, cross-job retraining times were estimated to be longer (a) *into* jobs that are generally more difficult to learn and (b) across jobs having different, rather than similar, aptitude requirements. Lance, Mayfield, Gould, and Lynskey (1991) demonstrated that cross-job retraining time estimates generated according Lance, Kavanagh, and Gould's methodology exhibited convergent validity with SMEs' global estimates of cross-job retraining times, and Lance, Mayfield, and Gould (1993) also demonstrated their criterion-related validity in a post-dictive study of actual retraining times across 43 different USAF-enlisted jobs. Finally, Lance, Mayfield, Foster, Stokes, and Mecham (1991) and Henderson (1993) demonstrated the transportability of Lance, Kavanagh, and Gould's methodology for estimating cross-job transferability of skills to the civilian sector.

Each of these studies provided some unique perspective and support for Lance, Kavanagh, and Gould's (1993) methodology, but it was also clear from each of these studies that the success of Lance, Kavanagh, and Gould's methodology ultimately depended on having first established a comprehensive, content-valid taxonomy to which comparisons of multiple jobs' task contents and learning times could be linked. To some extent, this was achieved in each of these studies. Lance and colleagues' work was based largely on a rationally defined taxonomy presented by Bell and Thomason (1984), but its limitations were recognized early on (this taxonomy is discussed in more detail later). Lance, Mayfield, Foster, Stokes, and Mecham's (1991) work was based on the taxonomy of work defined by the Position Analysis Questionnaire (McCormick & Jeanneret, 1988; McCormick, Jeanneret, & Mecham, 1972), a taxonomy that is broadly applicable to the world of work but which likely will be found too coarse to be useful for many particular organizational settings. Conversely, Henderson's (1993) taxonomy was developed on an ad hoc basis for a single organization in the telecommunications industry and so would not likely be readily transportable to other situations. This points to the need for the R&D effort described here, that is, to develop a comprehensive and content-valid task taxonomy to support USAF R&D on cross-job transferability of skills.

Considerations in the Development of a Task Taxonomy

A task taxonomy can be defined in terms of a scheme by which tasks and subtasks are classified into a logical framework (Companion & Corso, 1982) or a means of classifying tasks in such a way that useful relations among them are established (Miller, 1967). Dozens of work taxonomies have been proposed (e.g., Campion & Thayer, 1985; Companion & Corso, 1982; Cunningham, 1988; Cunningham, Boese, Neeb, & Pass, 1983; Dawis & Lofquist, 1975; Dunnette, 1976; Farina, 1973; Farina & Wheaton, 1973; Fleishman, 1972, 1982; Fleishman & Quaintance, 1984; Holland, 1973; McCormick, 1976; McKinlay, 1976; Peterson & Bownas, 1982; Ramsay-Klee, 1979, Ruck, 1986; Stolurow, 1964; Wheaton, 1973). Some of these have been intended to be broadly applicable to the world of work (e.g., Cummingham et al., 1983; McCormick & Jeanneret, 1988), while others were developed for more circumscribed work domains and/or classificatory purposes (e.g., Bennett, 1971; Dowell & Wexley, 1978; Ramsey-Klee, 1979). As alluded to earlier, general taxonomies often have limited usefulness in specific organizations, while more circumscribed ones usually lack generalizability beyond the specific purpose for which they are developed. For these reasons, our literature review failed to identify an existing taxonomy that was wholly appropriate for the purpose of conducting cross-job task content comparisons across Air Force Specialties (AFSs), pointing to the need for the research described here.

Literature on job classification suggests several steps in the development of an empirically validated taxonomic system, including (a) specification of the purpose for classification, (b) identification of the population of objects to be classified, (c) specification of the relevant characteristics of objects to be considered in classification, (d) development of some means for measuring these characteristics, (e) collection of data on a sample from the population of objects to be classified, (f) empirical identification of classificatory dimensions or categories, and (g) cross-validation of the classificatory scheme on additional samples (Aldenderfer & Blashfield, 1984; Milligan & Cooper, 1987; Sokal, 1974). In the present context, meeting each of these criteria optimally would have required the development of an USAF-wide job inventory, large-scale data collection on a large number of AFSs (i.e., jobs), empirical identification of task dimensions, and cross-validation of findings in a second sample of AFSs. However, time, budgetary, and manpower constraints precluded this large-scale effort. Furthermore, use of existing USAF Occupational Survey database (Christal, 1974) was not feasible. At the time the study described here was conducted, this database was probably the largest task-level job analysis database in the world (Christal, 1974), but its usefulness for assessing job content similarities *across* AFSs was extremely limited, because separate job inventories were developed individually for each particular career ladder or job family. Rather, we took an eclectic approach in developing the task taxonomy described here that integrated information from several sources, including (a) an existing set of rationally defined task categories developed by the USAF Occupational Measurement Center (Bell & Thomasson, 1984), (b) data collected expressly for the study described here from 675 SMEs on a questionnaire measuring the skills/knowledge requirements of 47 Air Force jobs, (c) an existing data set collected in 1982 from 2122 airmen in 180 AFSs on the General Work Inventory (Ballentine & Cunningham, 1981), (d) an existing set of data collected from 2494 airmen on an Electronics Principles Inventory (Ruck, 1977, 1987), (e) existing literature on task taxonomies (Fleishman & Quaintance, 1984), and (f) expert judgment. Finally, we evaluated the usefulness of the taxonomy developed here using additional data collected in July 1989 on a second survey of AFS skills and knowledge requirements. Each of these sources of information and its contribution to the development of the taxonomy is described in the following sections.

DEVELOPMENT OF THE TAXONOMY

USAF Occupational Measurement Center Job Categorization Project

The first source of information for this study was a set of task categories developed by the USAF Occupational Measurement Center (OMC). Today, as in the 1980s, the USAF uses four Armed Services Vocational Aptitude Battery (ASVAB) selector composites (Mechanical, Administrative, General, and Electronic [MAGE], Department of Defense, 1984; U.S. Air Force Enlisted Careers, n. d.; Zook, 1996) for classification purposes, and each AFS is classified according to one or more of these aptitude areas. The primary purpose of USAFOMC Job Categorization Project was to "determine the proper job category for each AFS based on the job/tasks actually performed" (Bell & Thomasson, 1984, p. 1). It was determined that four job categories (i.e., the MAGE areas) were "too broad to adequately describe the components or work characteristics of all jobs or specialties" (p. 1). Rather, USAFOMC scientists defined 26 subcategories that appeared to describe interjob similarities and differences in task content more meaningfully. The usefulness of these task subcategories was initially assessed using a modification of Smith and Kendall's (1963) retranslation technique in which, iteratively, task categories were defined, and tasks that comprised 50% of the total job time for 217 AFSs were categorized (Bell & Thomasson, 1984).

Subsequently, this task category list was revised to include Supervisory and Training categories and to reduce redundancy within one category (three *Mechanical* categories that differed only in terms of complexity were combined into one). Category names and definitions included in this revised taxonomy are shown in Table 34.1. Preliminary work with this taxonomy supported its usefulness for categorizing enlisted AFS tasks (Gould, Archer, Filer, Short, & Kavanagh, 1989) and for developing cross-AFS retraining time estimates (Lance, Kavanagh, & Gould, 1989).

Skills/Knowledge Questionnaire

The USAFOMC 26 task category taxonomy (Table 34.1) formed the basis for the second data source. A Skills/Knowledge Questionnaire (SKQ) was designed and administered for the present study to evaluate this taxonomy and to develop methods for estimating cross-AFS retraining time. The SKQ was designed to solicit three judgments from SMEs for each of the 26 task categories: (a) a binary "Part-of-Job" (POJ) rating (yes/no), (b) Relative Time Spent (RTS) performing tasks within categories endorsed as part of the job ("1 - Very small amount" to "9 - Very large amount"), and (c) average months to proficiency for a newly assigned airman on tasks included in each category ("1 - 0-1 Months" to "9 - 9 or more months"). Raters were instructed to consider a typical journeyman-level of proficiency for the job duties in completing the SKQ.

Table 34.1   USAF Occupational Measurement Center Task Categories and Definitions

CLERICAL—Performing secretarial type functions, such as filing, preparing forms, or answering phones. May involve understanding and application of rules, manuals, or regulations.

COMPUTATIONAL—Performing math computations, such as adding, multiplying, dividing, or computing simple averages. May involve understanding and applications of rules, manuals, or regulations. Also includes the operation of adding machines or calculators.

OFFICE EQUIPMENT OPERATION—Operating general office equipment such as typewriters, copy machines, or stenographs. Also includes minor maintenance such as changing fluid, changing ribbons, clearing jams, or replacing bulbs.

MECHANICAL—Tasks that involve manual manipulation of tools or equipment. Also involves those tasks that require an understanding of the mechanical principles and/or mechanical works of machinery or its components.

SIMPLE MECHANICAL EQUIPMENT/SYSTEMS OPERATION—Operation of simple equipment, machinery, or systems (other than office equipment) requiring only basic knowledge or understanding of the equipment.

COMPLEX MECHANICAL EQUIPMENT/SYSTEMS OPERATION—Operation of simple equipment, machinery, or systems (other than office equipment) requiring advanced or in-depth knowledge, complex skills, or significant manual coordination.

MECHANICAL-ELECTRICAL—Tasks involving *both* mechanical *and* electrical knowledge or skills but with the *primary* emphasis of the task being mechanical in nature. (Note: Tasks that appear to have approximately equal emphasis should be grouped according to the more important or critical aspect.)

MECHANICAL-ELECTRONIC—Tasks involving *both* mechanical *and* electronic knowledge or skills but with the *primary* emphasis of the task being mechanical in nature. (Note: Tasks that appear to have approximately equal emphasis should be grouped according to the more important or critical aspect.) These tasks may also involve some incidental electrical knowledge.

ELECTRICAL—Tasks that involve systems and equipment that produce or transmit electrical power, including transformers, generators, motors, and associated power lines and wiring. May involve small amounts of other components such as mechanical, electronic, or administrative, but the primary emphasis is electrical.

ELECTRONIC—Tasks that involve devices, circuits, or systems that conduct or transmit complex electrical signals, such as transistors, resistors, diodes, or printed circuit boards, including wiring, such as coaxial cables which carry coded signals. Requires and understanding of principles of electronics and/or the functioning of components. May involve small amounts of administrative components but the primary aspect is electronic.

ELECTRICAL-MECHANICAL—Tasks that involve *both* electrical and/or mechanical skills but the *primary* aspect is electrical.

ELECTRICAL-ELECTRONIC—Tasks that involve both electrical and electronic skills and knowledge. Does not involve significant mechanical skills.

ELECTRONIC-MECHANICAL—Tasks that involve *both* electronic and mechanical skills but the *primary* aspect is electronic.

SIMPLE PHYSICAL LABOR—Tasks involving manual labor, such as sweeping, lifting, carrying, or cleaning. Cleaning tasks would ordinarily be included in this category if no technical knowledge is involved or required.

MEDICAL–PATIENT CARE—Tasks whose predominant aspects involve physical or verbal interaction with patients.

MEDICAL–EQUIPMENT ORIENTED—The primary aspect of these tasks involves the use or operation of some type of *medical* equipment, instruments, or supplies. May involve some degree of patient interaction. Usually, medical X-ray or medical laboratory tasks would be grouped under this category.

MEDICAL PROCEDURES—The primary aspect of these tasks involves some procedure in a medical laboratory or operating room, and so forth. May involve some degree of patient interaction.

SIMPLE NONTECHNICAL PROCEDURES—These tasks are usually simple in nature, somewhat procedural and do not require a great deal of knowledge, training, or experience to perform; require only simple instructions or directions; may involve following a checklist.

COMMUNICATIVE–ORAL—Tasks whose *primary* aspect is communicative in nature; may involve the operation of communication devices, such as radios or telephones, when the primary emphasis of the task is to communicate something rather than strictly the operation of the device.

COMMUNICATIVE–WRITTEN—Tasks that involve communicating in a written manner; more than just a preparation of a standard form or a standard report requiring filling blanks.

GENERAL TASKS OR PROCEDURES—Any general task or technical procedure that does *not* involve *significant* amounts of mechanical, electrical, or electronic skills or knowledge and is not primarily administrative in nature, yet does require some detailed knowledge to perform. (Note: If a task involves some mechanical skill, or requires the individual to know electrical or electronic principles, it should be categorized under those categories.)

Table 34.1   USAF Occupational Measurement Center Task Categories and Definitions (Continued)

REASONING/PLANNING/ANALYZING—Tasks whose primary aspects involve reasoning or interpretive skills. May include coordinating when it involves reasoning problems or answering queries. (Note: Does not involve normal supervisory planning such as assigning work, evaluating performance, interpreting regulations, and so forth.)

SCIENTIFIC MATH REASONING OR CALCULATIONS—These tasks involve more than simple arithmetic computations; may involve using or applying formulas, using or preparing tables or charts; may require knowledge of physics, chemistry, geography, and so forth; may involve use of equipment such as gauges, slide rules, plotters, or calculators.

SPECIAL TALENTS—Tasks that involve skills which cannot be completely taught, such as playing musical instruments, drawing, or composing. Usually involves some elements of creativity.

SUPERVISORY—Tasks whose primary aspects involve supervision of others, including assigning individuals to workload, generating schedules, assessing performance, and so forth.

TRAINING—Tasks associated with the giving of job-oriented training.

Data Collection

In May 1988, SKQs, along with cover letters, detailed rating instructions, and rating category definitions, were mailed to 1356 supervisors in 47 AFSs. Because one purpose of the SKQ was to develop a prototype method for estimating cross-AFS training time, the 47 AFSs targeted for data collection were those that had the highest rates of retraining, either "out of"—into another AFS, or "into"—from another AFS over the previous 2 years. AFSs surveyed are listed in Table 34.2. Potential survey participants were identified by randomly selecting 30 supervisors' names for each AFS from personnel records. For AFSs in which there were fewer than 30 supervisors Air Force-wide, all were selected as potential respondents. Study participation was entirely voluntary.

Analyses and Results

Surveys were returned by mail in June 1988 from 675 respondents for a response rate of 50%. The typical SME was male (91%), had some college education (mean education, 13.49 years; SD = 1.46), supervised four persons (mean, 4.11; SD = 8.03), had been in the job over 3 years (mean, 38.09 months; SD = 33.22), and in the military services over 15 years (mean total active federal military service, 182.81 months; SD = 57.47 months).

Descriptive statistics for SKQ POJ and RTS ratings are shown in Table 34.3. As expected, there were large differences in the extent to which task categories were endorsed as being "part of" the job. This is consistent with the heterogeneity of 47 AFSs surveyed (see Table 34.2). Table 34.3 also shows Relative Time Spent (RTS) rating means and standard deviations. RTS responses that were "missing" because a task category was not part of the job were coded "0" to indicate "No time spent." Also as expected, mean RTS ratings varied considerably across task categories.

Interrater reliabilities (intraclass correlations, ICCs) for RTS ratings are also shown in Table 34.3. ICC (1,k) indexes the reliability of the mean of k judges' ratings (Lahey, Downey, & Saal, 1983; Shrout & Fleiss, 1979), and in the present study, there was a mean of 14.4 respondents from each of the 47 AFSs (i.e., k = 14.4). With the exceptions of Simple Nontechnical Procedures, General Tasks, Special Talents, Supervisory, and Training categories, most ICCs for the RTS ratings were high (>.75). Lower interrater reliabilities for the Simple Nontechnical Procedures and General Task categories indicate that they may not have been defined concretely. Conversely, lower reliabilities of the Supervisory and Training categories likely reflected restricted between-AFS variance on RTS ratings, because performance in most all AFSs involves some training and supervision of others. That is, because ICC is based on a comparison of between-job variance and within-job variance in ratings, lower between-job variance will lead to lower ICCs (James, Demaree, & Wolf, 1984).

Table 34.2   Air Force Specialties Surveyed With the Skills/Knowledge Questionnaire

Specialty Code	Specialty Title
113x0C	Flight Engineer
112x0	Aircrew Life Support
207x1	Morse Systems Operator
241x0	Safety Specialist
242x0	Disaster Preparedness
251x0	Weather Specialist
272x0	Air Traffic Control Operator
274x0	Command and Control Specialist
275x0	Tactical Command and Control Specialist
304x0	Wideband Communication Equipment Specialist
305x4	Electronic Component and Switching Systems Specialist
306x0	Electronic Communication and Cryptographic Equipment Systems Specialist
411x0c	Missile Systems Maintenance Specialist
411x1a	Missile Maintenance Specialist
426x2	Jet Engine Mechanic
431x1	Tactical Aircraft Maintenance Specialist
431x3	Airlift Aircraft Maintenance Specialist
451x4	F-15 Avionics Test Station and Components Specialist
451x5	F-16/A-10 Avionics Test Station and Components Specialist
451x6	F/FB-111 Avionics Test Station and Components Specialist
454x3	Fuel Systems Maintenance Specialist
456x1	Electronic Warfare Systems Specialist
472x4	Vehicle Maintenance and Analysis Technician
491x1	Communication-Computer Systems Operator
491x2	Communication-Computer Systems Programmer
492x1	Information Systems Radio Operator
493x0	Communication-Computer Systems Control
496x0	Communication-Computer Systems Program Management Specialist
603x0	Vehicle Operator/Dispatcher
645x1	Material Storage and Distribution Spec Specialist
645x2	Supply Systems Analysis Specialist
651x0	Contracting Specialist
661x0	Logistics Plans Specialist
702x0	Administration Specialist
705x0	Legal Services Specialist
732x0	Personnel Specialist
733x1	Manpower Management
751x1	Training Systems Specialist
811x0	Security Specialist
811x2	Law Enforcement Specialist
903x1	Nuclear Medicine Specialist

Table 34.3   Skills/Knowledge Questionnaire: Part-of-Job and Relative Time Spent Descriptive Statistics and Intraclass Correlations

Category	Part of Job	Relative Time Spent Mean	SD	ICC (1, k)
1. Clerical	84%	3.94	2.64	.852
2. Computational	73%	3.13	2.67	.817
3. Office Equipment Operation	73%	3.06	2.68	.848
4. Mechanical	51%	2.61	3.11	.885
5. Simple Mechanical	53%	2.54	2.87	.827
6. Complex Mechanical	39%	2.18	3.09	.792
7. Mechanical-Electrical	28%	1.29	2.35	.884
8. Mechanical-Electronic	27%	1.34	2.49	.772
9. Electrical	29%	1.32	2.40	.856
10. Electronic	35%	2.38	3.55	.978
11. Electrical-Mechanical	24%	1.23	2.46	.854
12. Electrical-Electronic	26%	1.50	2.80	.922
13. Electronic-Mechanical	29%	1.55	2.75	.934
14. Physical Labor	69%	2.98	2.74	.833
15. Medical-Patient Care	5%	1.09	1.11	.954
16. Medical-Equipment Oriented	4%	0.18	1.08	.971
17. Medical-Procedures	6%	0.26	1.21	.930
18. Simple Nontechnical Processes	68%	3.18	2.82	.478
19. Communications-Oral	76%	4.82	3.37	.882
20. Communications-Written	68%	4.01	3.33	.886
21. General Tasks	63%	3.58	3.21	.660
22. Reasoning/Planning	66%	4.15	3.41	.851
23. Science/Math	37%	1.92	2.87	.872
24. Special Talents	22%	1.27	2.63	.697
25. Supervisory	66%	3.46	2.88	.585
26. Training	91%	5.55	2.49	.600

ICC = intraclass correlations.

Intercorrelations among RTS ratings indicated some redundancy among rating categories, especially among Mechanical-, Electrical-, Medical-, and Clerical-oriented categories. This suggested that some of the task categories could be combined with little loss in discriminatory power. To explore this possibility, we conducted a principal components analysis (PCA) on the RTS intercorrelation matrix and, based on examination of the eigenvalue (scree) plot, retained a six-component solution. Significant varimax-rotated component loadings are shown in Table 34.4. The first two components were clearly interpretable as I: *Electrical/Electronic*, and II: *Mechanical/Maintenance*, although these overlapped somewhat. Component III represented *Medical* tasks, Component IV: *Technical* activities, Component V: *Clerical* functions, and Component VI: *Managing/Developing* others. As would be expected, General verbal and quantitative activities (i.e., Computational, Communicative–Oral, and Communicative–Written) had multiple loadings.

Overall, results in Tables 34.2 through 34.4 indicated that (a) SMEs generally provided reliable judgments of the Relative Time spent performing tasks described by the USAFOMC task categories, (b) SME judgments relating to this taxonomy differentiated among AFS task content, and

Table 34.4   Principal Components Analysis of the Skills/Knowledge Questionnaire Relative Time Spent Ratings

Task Category	Principal Component					
	I	II	III	IV	V	VI
1. Clerical					.800	
2. Computational				.523	.475	
3. Office Equipment Operation					.763	
4. Mechanical		.713				
5. Simple Mechanical		.780				
6. Complex Mechanical	.393	.571				
7. Mechanical-Electrical	.544	.626				
8. Mechanical-Electronic	.688	.411				
9. Electrical	.807					
10. Electronic	.826					
11. Electrical-Mechanical	.850					
12. Electricall-Electronic	.880					
13. Electronic-Mechanical	.880					
14. Physical Labor		.692				
15. Medical-Patient Care			.922			
16. Medical-Equipment Oriented			.870			
17. Medical-Procedures			.853			
18. Simple Nontechnical Processes		.469				
19. Commununications-Oral				.477	.419	.387
20. Communications-Written				.525	.499	
21. General Tasks				.409		
22. Reasoning/Planning				.651		
23. Science/Math				.687		
24. Special Talents				.653		
25. Supervisory						.744
26. Training						.741

(c) at least six broad taxonomic categories (Electrical, Mechanical, Medical, Technical, Clerical, and Managing Others) were descriptive of differences in AFS task contents.

General Work Inventory

The third source of information for this effort was a data set obtained from administration of the General Work Inventory (GWI) (Ballentine & Cummingham, 1982). The GWI was developed to meet needs for a shorter, more practical version of the Occupational Analysis Inventory (OAI; Cunningham, 1988). Both the GWI and the OAI were developed from an "ergometric" perspective, or "the application of psychometric principles and procedures to the study of human work" (Cunningham, 1988, p. 975). Unlike the Position Analysis Questionnaire (PAQ; McCormick, 1976; McCormick & Jeanneret, 1988), which was designed to describe general "worker-oriented" characteristics of jobs, the GWI attempts to capture more specific "job-oriented" contents of jobs and is designed to "achieve as much specificity in description as possible, while retaining applicability to the general population of jobs" (Cunningham et al., 1983, p. 233). GWI work elements are organized into eight sections:

A. Sensory Requirements
B. Information Elements

   C. General Mental Requirements
   D. General Physical Requirements
   E. Physical Activities
   F. Interpersonal Activities
   G. Work Conditions
   H. Job Benefits/Opportunities

GWI items are rated on 9-point "Part-of-Job" (Sections A–F) or "Extent-of-Occurrence" scales (Sections G and H; see Ballentine & Cunningham, 1981). Conceptually, these major divisions correspond to the components in the information processing paradigm presented by Cunningham et al. (1983).

Data Collection

The GWI, along with detailed rating instructions, was mailed to approximately 2500 experienced USAF enlisted personnel (technicians and supervisors) in 180 AFSs in the Fall 1982. Useable responses were obtained from 2122 respondents in 180 AFSs (see Ballentine & Cunningham, 1981 for details).

Analyses and Results

We conducted PCAs on GWI sections B through F items (217 items). Inspection of the eigenvalues for the first 100 components suggested the presence of 20 to 35 "significant" components. We subsequently conducted additional PCAs retaining 20-, 28-, 32-, and 35-component solutions based on breaks in the eigenvalue plot. Generally speaking, these analyses suggested the presence of (a) two broad "Mechanical" and "Electrical/Electronic" components, (b) several other specific, interpretable components, many of which were consistent across solutions, and (c) a small number of uninterpretable components.

To obtain finer distinctions between separate aspects of Mechanical and Electrical/Electronic activities, we conducted separate PCAs (a) on the items that loaded significantly on either of the first two broad Mechanical or Electrical/Electronic components and (b) on the remaining items (GWI items in sections B – F that did not load significantly on either the Mechanical or Electrical/Electronic components). A summary of findings from these separate PCAs is presented in Table 34.5, in which components identified from PCAs of the GWI are shown along with the revised USAFOMC task categories for comparison.

Table 34.5 shows that relative to the USAFOMC task categories, task categories derived from PCAs of the GWI (a) provided more detailed definitions of task content in certain areas (e.g., Clerical, Simple Physical Labor, and Special Talents), (b) combined certain other USAFOMC task categories (e.g., in the Mechanical, Electrical/Electronic, and other Medical areas), and (c) identified specific task categories that were not specified by the USAFOMC taxonomy (e.g., Manufacturing, Construction, and Engineering). However, these results did not identify meaningful subcategories of Electrical/Electronic tasks. The GWI, being a "general" work inventory, did not capture needed distinctions among electrical and electronic job activities, which are a significant part of a large number of AFSs, particularly in the weapons systems maintenance area. Consequently, additional data obtained on an Electronics Principles Inventory were analyzed to address this need.

Electronics Principles Inventory

The fourth source of data for this study came from administration to 2494 airmen of the Electronics Principles Inventory (EPI) developed at the USAFOMC for the purpose of training course validation. The EPI contains 1257 items covering the full scope of electronics principles or fundamentals

Table 34.5   Comparison between USAFOMC and General Work Inventory (GWI) Task Taxonomies

USAFOMC Task Categories	GWI Task Categories
1. Clerical	1. Clerical
	2. Personnel
	3. Maintaining Inventories
	4. Legal/Contractual
2. Computational	5. Computational
3. Office Equipment	
4. Mechanical	6. Mechanical–Maintenance
5. Simple Mechanical	
6. Complex Mechanical	
7. Mechanical–Electrical	
8. Mechanical–Electronic	
9. Electrical	7. Electrical/Electronic
10. Electronic	
11. Electrical–Mechanical	
12. Electrical–Electronic	
13. Electronic–Mechanical	
14. Simple Physical Labor	8. Physical/Manual Labor
	9. Semiskilled Labor
	10. Transporting/Shipping
	11. Manufacturing/Fabricating
	12. Building Construction
15. Medical-Patient Care	13. Construction: Other than Buildings
16. Medical-Equipment Oriented	14. Medical/Health
17. Medical-Procedures	
18. Simple Nontechnical Procedures	15. Apprenticing
19. Communication-Oral	
20. Communication-Written	16. Communication
21. General Tasks or Processes	
22. Reasoning/Planning/Organizing	17. Problem Solving
23. Scientific Math Reasoning or Calculations	18. Scientific/Technical
	19. Biological
	20. Physical Sciences
	21. Engineering
	22. Social Sciences/Services
24. Special Talents	23. Artistic/Visual
	24. Entertaining
	25. Vending/Merchandising
	26. Food Preparation
	27. Animal Care
	28. Fabric/Rope Work
	29. Operating Audio/Visual Equipment
	30. Operating Rail Vehicles
	31. Flying Vehicles
25. Supervisory	32. Managing/Developing/Influencing Others
26. Training	
	33. Policing/Surveillance

as defined for technical training courses and by instructors and supervisors of these courses. The EPI instructs respondents to indicate whether each principle is used on their present job (responses are in a binary yes/no format). The EPI has been used operationally by the Air Training Command to validate training courses for several years which, along with extensive validation studies, attests to the validity of the instrument (Ruck, 1986).

The 1257 EPI items are divided into 39 categories of electronics principles. Responses from 2494 respondents were averaged within categories to yield 39 scores indicating the percentage of electronics principles within each of the categories used. PCAs were computed on these category percentage scores, and four-, five-, and six-component solutions were retained based on breaks in the eigenvalue plot. The five-component solution was the most interpretable. These five components, along with significant varimax-rotated loadings, are show in Table 34.6.

Table 34.6   Electronics Principles Inventory Varimax-Rotated Five-Component Solution

Component	Significant Component Loading	Electronics Principle
I. Complex Electronic Circuit Maintenance	.7715	Electrontube Amplifier Circuits
	.7176	Tubes
	.6996	Limiter and Clamper Circuits
	.6849	Wave Shaping Circuits
	.6836	Multivibrators
	.6707	Oscillators
	.6682	Coupling Circuits
	.6514	Resistive Capacitive Inductive Circuits
	.6469	Frequency Sensitive Filters
	.6175	Resonant Cavities
	.5966	Power Supply Voltage Regulators
	.5679	Magnetic Amplifiers
II. Digital Systems Maintenance	.7481	Digital Logic Numbering Systems
	.7393	Digital Circuits
	.6974	Digital to Analog and Vice Versa
	.6962	Computers
	.5372	TV and Laser and Infrared Systems
III. Communication Systems Maintenance	.7727	Antennas
	.7509	Connections
	.7295	Radio Frequency Measurements
	.6314	Radio Frequency Calculations
	.5600	Signal Generators
	.5429	Oscilloscopes
	.5358	Microwave Oscillators and Amplifiers
	.4767	Transmitter and Receivers
IV. Basic Electrical/Electronic Repair	.8024	Multimeters
	.7845	Direct-Alternating Current
	.7539	Electro-Mechanical Devices
	.6787	Soldering and Solderless Connections
V. Electronic Peripherals Maintenance	.7919	Storage Type Display Tubes
	.5532	Microphones and Speakers
	.4978	Photosensitive Devices

Synthesis of Results

Although our analyses of SKQ, GWI, and EPI data succeeded in identifying potential redundancies among certain USAFOMC task categories, areas in which these categories should be expanded toward specificity and concreteness, and additional concrete task content categories that were descriptive of USAF enlisted job content, neither the SKQ, the GWI, nor the EPI were designed specifically for the taxonomic purposes of the present research. Consequently, we synthesized the empirical results presented here, existing literature of work taxonomies, and operational needs of the USAF, in developing an eclectic task taxonomy to support cross-AFS transferability of skills research.

Some of the GWI task categories in Table 34.5 were omitted in the development of this taxonomy because (a) their task content overlapped logically with others' (e.g., Transporting/Shipping activities were included in the categories *Maintaining Inventories, Mechanical Systems Operation,* and *Physical/Manual Labor*), (b) their task content had little or no operational implications for the USAF (e.g., *Vending/Merchandising*), or (c) they were too job-specific (e.g., *Flying Vehicles*). Other categories were expanded to be consistent with actual differences in task content in enlisted AFSs (e.g., *Mechanical Systems Operation* vs. *Mechanical Systems Maintenance* and *Medical–Patient Care* vs. *Medical–Technical*). Table 34.7 lists the names and definitions of the resulting revised task taxonomy.

Table 34.8 compares the USAFOMC task categories with those defined on the basis of an integration of the empirical results presented earlier, prior research on task taxonomies (Fleishman & Quaintance, 1984), and operational implications for the USAF. Although similar in some respects to the USAFOMC taxonomy, the taxonomy in Table 34.7 is supported by empirical evidence, defines task content areas in much more concrete terms (especially the electrical/electronic and mechanical areas), and redefines several of the USAFOMC task categories (e.g., *Simply Physical Labor, General Tasks or Procedures, Simple Nontechnical Procedures,* and *Special Talents*) into more concrete task categories (e.g., *Manufacturing/Fabricating, Construction, Artistic, Food Preparation,* and *Animal Care*).

EVALUATION OF THE REVISED TASK TAXONOMY

Desirable properties of a useful classification system (taxonomy) are that classification decisions are face valid to users of the system, characteristics of objects to be classified should be measured reliably, classification dimensions should be nonredundant, and classifications should result in meaningful groups of objects. In the following sections, we describe our evaluation of the taxonomy shown in Table 34.7 along these criteria using data collected using a revised version of the SKQ.

Development of Revised Skills/Knowledge Questionnaire

Although the basic format was similar, two changes were made to the earlier version of the SKQ in designing a Revised Skills/Knowledge Questionnaire (RSKQ) for the purpose of evaluating the taxonomy shown in Table 34.7. First, questionnaire instructions were rewritten toward brevity and clarity. Second, and more important, task rating items were changed from the USAFOMC task categories to those shown in Table 34.7. As with the earlier version of the SKQ, respondents were asked to make three judgments regarding each task category: (a) a binary (yes/no) Part-of-Job rating, (b) a 9-point Relative Time Spent rating, and (c) a 9-point Months to Proficiency (MTP) rating.

Table 34.7   Revised Task Taxonomy Category Definitions

CLERICAL—Tasks such as filing, preparing forms, answering telephones, typing reports, and proofreading. Operating office equipment such as computers, typewriters, calculators, and duplicating machines. Processing information related to military regulations, federal or state laws, contracts, and legal documents.

PERSONNEL—Processing data/information about individuals, such as employment applications, performance reviews, disciplinary reports, media releases, production records, personnel forecasts, training records, counseling information, and social services.

MAINTAINING INVENTORIES—Maintaining materials/merchandise/supplies/equipment records. Ordering, receiving, maintaining, routing, and accounting for inventory. Preparing, analyzing, and maintaining records of financial dealings, property, and assets.

COMPUTATIONAL—Performing numerical operations such as adding, subtracting, multiplying, and dividing. Computing statistics using formulas and equations. Locating statistics/data in graphs, tables, and charts. Using calculators or adding machines to solve math problems.

MECHANICAL SYSTEMS MAINTENANCE—Performing mechanical repair and maintenance activities, such as maintaining, repairing, assembling, installing, troubleshooting, and adjusting/tuning mechanical systems. Lubricating, bonding and sealing, and using tools (such as a hammer, screwdriver, or block and tackle) to repair/maintain mechanical systems.

MECHANICAL SYSTEMS OPERATION—Operating mechanical equipment such as a meat slicer, sewing machine, printing press, bulldozer, road grader, forklift, or tractor. Driving/operating/piloting vehicles. Using mechanical tools such as an electric drill, air wrench, chain saw, or jack hammer.

COMPLEX ELECTRONIC CIRCUIT MAINTENANCE—Maintaining and repairing equipment containing complex electronic circuitry such as electron tube amplifier circuits, tubes, limiter and clamper circuits, wave shaping circuits, multivibrators, oscillators, coupling circuits, power, supply filters, resonant cavities, and magnetic-amplifiers.

DIGITAL SYSTEMS MAINTENANCE—Maintaining and repairing digital systems such as digital logic numbering systems, computers, television, laser, and infrared systems. Maintaining and repairing equipment that contains digital circuits or processes digital to analog/analog to digital information.

COMMUNICATION SYSTEMS MAINTENANCE—Maintaining and repairing communication systems such as antennas, microwave oscillators and amplifiers, signal generators, and transmitters and receivers. Making radio frequency measurements and calculations. Using oscilloscopes.

BASIC ELECTRICAL/ELECTRONIC REPAIR—Maintaining and repairing basic electromechanical equipment with a working knowledge of multimeters, direct and alternating current, soldering, and solderless connections.

ELECTRONIC PERIPHERALS MAINTENANCE—Maintaining and repairing electronic peripheral devices such as storage type display tubes, microphones and speakers, and photosensitive devices.

PHYSICAL/MANUAL LABOR—Nontechnical manual and physical tasks such as sweeping, lifting, carrying, cleaning, sawing, lubricating, drilling, cutting, hoisting, chipping, and planing. Using basic tools such as a hammer, paint scraper, shovel, or wheelbarrow.

MANUFACTURING/FABRICATING—Making things from materials such as sheet metal, metal tubing, glass, brick, plastic, rubber, paper, or lumber. For example, pressing, mixing, forging, grinding, stitching, forming, melting, or chemically treating materials to manufacture things.

CONSTRUCTION—Using construction information such as materials lists, building designs, and so forth. Building/maintaining structures made of brick, stone, lumber, asphalt, or concrete, such as walls, floors, cabinets, houses, bridges, towers, roads, or runways. Laying/covering with roofing materials, floor coverings, and wallpaper.

MEDICAL–PATIENT CARE—Verbally or physically interacting with patients (e.g., bandaging, giving injections, applying medicines, drawing blood, performing physical therapy). Reading/interpreting medical charts, thermometer readings, and test results.

MEDICAL–TECHNICAL—Performing technical procedures in a medical, lab, or operating room (e.g., operating X-ray machine, microscope, electrocardiogram machine, respirator, ultrasound machine).

ORAL AND WRITTEN COMMUNICATION—Reading/speaking/writing, understanding words, and expressing ideas, including receiving/processing/initiating letters, books, reports, phone calls, orders, directions/instructions, lectures, contracts; attending/conducting meetings, and presentations.

continued

Table 34.7   Revised Task Taxonomy Category Definitions (Continued)

PLANNING/PROBLEM SOLVING—Using available information to anticipate/figure out/solve problems, and plan the steps and procedures required to reach a solution to the problem (e.g., identifying a traffic problem and formulating a plan for rerouting traffic).

SCIENCE AND ENGINEERING —Collecting/organizing/summarizing technical information, or information about people, events, places. Using systematic/scientific methods to test theories/ products/equipment. Writing reports of results/findings. Using technical information such as aerial photos, weather forecasts, maps, engineering plans, blueprints, circuit diagrams, and other designs/plans for equipment, manufacturing processes, and so forth.

ARTISTIC–AUDIO/VISUAL—Audio and visual art design/production, e.g., photography, movies, recordings, drawings, illustrations, layouts, musical compositions, interior decorations. Performing, e.g., playing musical instruments, singing, dancing, and acting. Operating equipment such as turntables, videotape players, slide projectors, film developing equipment, and so forth.

FOOD PREPARATION—Preparing/cooking food, using/producing menus, recipes, nutrition guides, food requests and estimates.

ANIMAL CARE—Caring for animals, including grooming, training, treating, exercising, or tending animals.

FABRIC/ROPE WORK—Sewing, stitching, threading, weaving, combining, or separating materials such as fabric, thread, rope, material, fiber, and string.

MANAGING OTHERS—Managing/administering/supervising/evaluating others (e.g., determining goals and coordinating others' activities, assigning work to others and supervising their work, evaluating others' performance, making staffing decisions, conducting group meetings, settling conflicts, and enforcing rules).

TRAINING—Explaining ideas/procedures to others, demonstrating how a task is done, monitoring learner progress, providing feedback on mistakes, preparing lesson plans, course outlines, and so forth.

SURVEILLANCE—Using codes/symbols (e.g., traffic control "lingo," flag, and hand signals), detecting, visualizing and recognizing objects that are difficult to see (e.g., ships and aircraft at a distance, criminal suspect in a crowd), tracking and pursuing moving targets or objects, using firearms or other handheld weapons, and enforcing rules or laws.

Data Collection

Using the same criteria as in the earlier SKQ survey, 43 AFSs were targeted for data collection. These are shown in Table 34.9. In July 1989, RSKQs, along with cover letters, detailed rating instructions, and task category definitions, were mailed to 1565 supervisors in the 43 AFSs shown in Table 34.9. Usable surveys were returned by 836 respondents for a response rate of 53%. The typical respondent was male (91%), had some college education (mean education = 13.26 years), supervised five others (mean = 4.86), had been in the job just under 3 years (mean = 32.72 months), and in the military services over 15 years (average = 183.63 months).

Results

The first criterion we used to evaluate the taxonomy in Table 34.7 was to determine its potential face validity to users. Some results bearing on this question are shown in Table 34.10. Here, the percentage of respondents making "Part-of-Job" endorsements varied widely across the task categories, indicating that tasks in some of the task categories are widely performed (e.g., *Clerical, Oral/Written Communication*, and *Training*), while others are relatively less often performed. More importantly, however, Table 34.10 also lists a representative job title for each task category in which a relatively high proportion of respondents endorsed as part of their job. These jobs are among those expected to have high Part-of-Job endorsements for the task categories.

A second criterion concerned the reliability with which the taxonomic categories are used in describing jobs. There are a number of ways in which rating reliability can be assessed (Jones, Johnson, Main, & Butler, 1983), but the reliability of job analysis data most often is assessed using

Table 34.8 Comparison Between USAFOMC and Candidate Task Taxonomies

USAFOMC Task Categories	Candidate Task Categories
1. Clerical	1. Clerical
	2. Personnel
	3. Maintaining Inventories
2. Computational	4. Computational
3. Office Equipment	
4. Mechanical	5. Mechanical Systems Maintenance
5. Simple Mechanical	
6. Complex Mechanical	6. Mechanical Systems Operation
7. Mechanical-Electrical	7. Complex Electronic Circuit Maintenance
8. Mechanical-Electronic	
9. Electrical	8. Digital Systems Maintenance
10. Electronic	9. Communication Systems Maintenance
11. Electrical-Mechanical	10. Basic Electrical/Electronics Repair
12. Electrical-Electronic	
13. Electronic-Mechanical	11. Electrical Peripherals Maintenance
14. Simple Physical Labor	12. Physical/Manual Labor
	13. Manufacturing/Fabricating
	14. Construction
15. Medical-Patient Care	15. Medical-Patient Care
16. Medical-Equip Oriented	
17. Medical-Procedures	16. Medical-Technical
18. Simple Nontechnical Procedures	
19. Communication-Oral	17. Oral & Written Communications
20. Communication-Written	
21. General Tasks or Processes	
22. Reasoning/Planning/Organizing	18. Planning and Problem Solving Science and Engineering
23. Scientific Math Reasoning	
24. Special Talents	19. Biological
	20. Artistic: Audio & Visual
	21. Food Preparation
	22. Animal Care
	23. Fabric/Rope Work
25. Supervisory	24. Managing Others
26. Training	25. Training
	26. Surveillance

either Pearson interrater reliability correlations or intraclass correlations (ICCs; Kavanagh & Lance, 1989). We assessed the reliability of RSKQ Relative Time Spent (RTS) ratings in both ways. The average Pearson correlation among different raters within the same AFS was $r = .57$. The Spearman-Brown correction for the reliability of the average number of respondents per AFS (19.44) was $r = .96$. ICCs are shown along with RTS means and standard deviations in Table 34.11. With the exception of *Managing Others* (ICC = .605), ICCs were uniformly high. Thus, both Pearson correlations and ICCs supported the reliability of RTS rating on the taxonomy in Table 34.7.

Table 34.9 Air Force Specialties Surveyed with the Revised Skills/Knowledge Questionnaire

AFSC	Specialty Title	MAGE Area
113x0c	Flight Engineer[a]	G
114x0	Aircraft Loadmaster	M
207x1	Morse Systems Operator[a]	A
241x0	Safety Specialist[a]	G
242x0	Disaster Preparedness[a]	G
251x0	Weather Specialist[a]	G
271x1	Airfield Management Specialist	A
272x0	Air Traffic Control Operator[a]	G
276x0	Aerospace Control and Warning Systems	G
303x2	Aircraft Control and Warning Radar	E
304x0	Wideband Communication Equipment Specialist	E
304x4	Ground Radio Communications Specialist	E
324x0	Precision Measurement Equipment Lab Specialist	E
423x0	Aircraft Electrical Systems Specialist	E
452x4	Tactical Aircraft Maintenance Specialist	M
454x1	Aerospace Group Equipment Mechanic	M&E
455x2	Avionic Communication Specialist	E
457x0	Strategic Aircraft Maintenance Specialist	M
461x0	Munitions Systems Specialist	M/E
462x0	Aircraft Armament Systems Specialist	M/E
472x1	Special Vehicle Mechanic	M
542x0	Electrician	E
545x0	Refrigeration and Air Conditioning Specialist	M/E
551x0	Pavements Maintenance Specialist	M
551x1	Constructions Equipment Operator	M
553x0	Engineering Assistant Specialist	G
571x0	Fire Protection Specialist	G
603x0	Vehicle Operator/Dispatcher[a]	M
631x0	Fuel Specialist	M&G
645x0	Inventory Management Specialist	A/G
645x1	Material Storage and Distribution[a]	G
645x2	Supply Systems Analysis Specialist[a]	A
651x0	Contracting Specialist[a]	A
661x0	Logistics Plans Specialist[a]	A
702x0	Administration Specialist[a]	A
732x0	Personnel Specialist[a]	A
741x1	Fitness and Recreation Specialist	A
791x0	Public Affairs Specialist	G
811x0	Security Specialist[a]	G
811x2	Law Enforcement Specialist[a]	G
902x0	Medical Administrative Specialist	G
981x0	Dental Assistant	G

[a] AFSCs also surveyed with the original Skills/Knowledge Questionnaire.
AFSC = Air Force Specialty Code; MAGE = administrative, electronic, general, mechanical.

Table 34.10   Revised Skills/Knowledge Questionnaire Descriptive Statistics: Part-of-Job Ratings

Task Category	Part of Job	Representative AFS With Percentage "Part-of-Job"
Clerical	73%	702x0 - Administration Specialist
Personnel	49%	732x0 - Personnel Specialist
Maintaining Inventories	58%	645x0 - Inventory Management
Computational	52%	113x0c - Flight Engineer
Mechanical Systems Maintenance	47%	454x1 - Aerospace Ground Equip Mechanic
Mechanical Systems Operation	52%	545x0 - Refrigeration and Air Conditioning Maintenance
Complex Electronic Circuit Maintenance	21%	324x0 - Precision Measurement Equipment
Digital Systems Maintenance	17%	304x0 - Wideband Communications Equipment Operator
Communications Systems Maintenance	18%	304x4 - Ground Radio Communications
Basic Electrical/Electronic Repair	32%	423x0 - Aircraft Electrical System
Electronic Peripherals Maintenance	13%	304x4 - Ground Radio Communications
Physical/Manual Labor	68%	551x1 - Construction Equip Operator
Manufacturing/Fabricating	16%	551x0 - Pavements Maintenance
Construction	16%	551x0 - Pavements Maintenance
Medical-Patient Care	8%	902x0 - Medical Service Specialist
Medical-Technical	5%	902x0 - Medical Service Specialist
Oral/Written Communication	83%	791x0 - Public Affairs Specialist
Planning/Problem Solving	70%	241x0 - Safety Specialist
Science/Engineering	22%	251x0 - Weather Specialist
Artistic–Audio/Visual	17%	242x0 - Disaster Preparedness
Food Preparation	3%	114x0 - Aircraft Loadmaster
Animal Care	2%	811x2 - Law Enforcement Specialist
Fabric/Rope Work	3%	571x0 - Fire Protection Specialist
Managing Others	68%	303x2 - Aircraft Control and Warning
Training	87%	242x0 - Disaster Preparedness Specialist
Surveillance	24%	811x2 - Law Enforcement Specialist

See Table 34.7 for detailed definitions of task categories. AFSs shown are representative of those having the highest proportion of respondents indicating that tasks within each category were part of their job. AFS = Air Force Specialties.

A third criterion concerns the distinctness of a taxonomy's categories. We examined this question in two ways. First, we calculated the average intercategory correlation in the 26×26 matrix of correlations among the RTS ratings, with $r = .09$. This indicated that, on the average, the task categories addressed distinct sets of job tasks. Second, we conducted a principal components analysis of the RTS intercorrelations. An eigenvalue plot suggested a four-component solution, which is shown in Table 34.12. These components accounted for 47% of the variables' variance, and were clearly interpretable as I: *Electronic*, II: *General and Administrative,* III: *Mechanical*, and IV: *Medical*. Together with the correlational results above, these results suggest that the taxonomic categories were distinct, but still could be related to a higher order categorization scheme.

Finally, perhaps the most important practical criterion for a classificatory system is whether it leads to meaningful classifications. We addressed this issue by determining whether RTS rating profiles clustered AFSs into meaningful job groupings. Specifically, we formed a 43×43 matrix of Euclidean distances among the AFSs in Table 34.9 based on their mean RTS profiles for input to Ward's (1963) hierarchical clustering algorithm. An inverse scree plot suggested either a three- or

Table 34.11 Descriptive Statistics and Intraclass Correlations: Revised Skills/Knowledge Questionnaire Relative Time Spent Ratings

Task Category	Mean	SD	ICC (1, *k*)
Clerical	3.47	2.95	.901
Personnel	1.97	2.47	.782
Maintaining Inventories	2.40	2.64	.866
Computational	2.36	2.80	.868
Mechanical Systems Maintenance	2.85	3.47	.972
Mechanical Systems Operation	2.96	3.39	.923
Complex Electronic Circuit Maintenance	1.92	2.79	.979
Digital Systems Maintenance	1.03	2.47	.979
Communications Systems Maintenance	1.16	2.68	.987
Basic Electrical/Electronic Repair	1.97	3.21	.987
Electronic Peripherals Maintenance	0.63	1.89	.926
Physical/Manual Labor	3.56	3.22	.910
Manufacturing/Fabricating	0.58	1.57	.779
Construction	0.72	2.01	.962
Medical–Patient Care	0.45	1.77	.982
Medical–Technical	0.29	1.45	.974
Oral/Written Communication	4.85	3.01	.868
Planning/Problem Solving	3.91	3.07	.748
Science/Engineering	1.17	2.48	.912
Artistic–Audio/Visual	0.74	1.92	.920
Food Preparation	0.07	0.47	.923
Animal Care	0.06	0.50	.754
Fabric/Rope Work	0.11	0.73	.714
Managing Others	3.44	2.87	.605
Training	5.14	2.71	.763
Surveillance	1.34	2.74	.926

ICC = intraclass correlations.

nine-cluster solution. These two solutions are shown in Table 34.13, where Roman numerals denote the three-cluster solution and uppercase letters designate subgroups within the nine-cluster solution.

The three-cluster solution was clearly interpretable as: I–*Mechanical*, II–*Electronic*, and III–*General and Administrative*. The nine-cluster solution also identified meaningful subgroups. Within the *Mechanical* cluster, three subclusters of AFSs were identified: IA–*Mechanical/ Construction*, containing AFSs involved in manufacturing and construction; IB–*Mechanical*, containing AFSs in which mechanical systems maintenance and operation were core activities; and IC–*Mechanical/ Electrical*, containing AFSs in which incumbents perform both mechanically- and electrically-oriented tasks. Conversely, five relatively homogeneous subclusters were identified within the broader *General and Administrative (G&A)* cluster: IIIA–*G&A: Medical*, IIIB–*G&A: Surveillance*, IIIC–*G&A: Clerical*, IIID–*G&A: Technical*, and IIIE–*G&A: Logistics*.

Summary

In summary, results in Tables 34.10 through 34.13 support the usefulness of the taxonomy in Table 34.7 in terms of (a) its face validity, (b) the reliability with which SMEs used it in describing their

Table 34.12   Varimax-Rotated Principal Components Results for Revised Skills/Knowledge Questionnaire Relative Time Spent Ratings: Four-Component Solution

Task Category	Principal Component			
	I	II	III	IV
Clerical		0.583	−0.330	
Personnel		0.634		
Maintaining Inventories		0.333	0.338	
Mechanical Systems Maintenance			0.788	
Mechanical Systems Operation			0.828	
Complex Electronic Circuit Maintenance	0.924			
Digital Systems Maintenance	0.926			
Communications Systems Maintenance	0.915			
Basic Electrical/Electronic Repair	0.794			
Electronic Peripherals Maintenance	0.792			
Physical/Manual Labor			0.788	
Manufacturing/Fabricating			0.549	
Construction			0.384	
Medical–Patient Care				0.910
Medical–Technical				0.900
Oral/Written Communication		0.683		
Planning/Problem Solving		0.679		
Science/Engineering		0.497		
Artistic–Audio/Visual		0.536		
Food Preparation				
Animal Care				
Fabric/Rope Work				
Managing Others		0.611		
Training		0.545		
Surveillance		0.327		

See Table 34.7 for detailed definitions of task categories. Only factor loadings >0.300 are shown.

jobs, (c) the distinctness of its categories, and, perhaps most importantly, (d) its ability to support the formation of meaningful subgroups of jobs.

CONCLUSION

The taxonomy shown in Table 34.7 was designed to support research on cross-job transferability of skills in the USAF. Compared to other taxonomies such as represented by the Position Analysis Questionnaire (PAQ), containing 187 job elements (McCormick, 1976), or the OAI with 617 work elements (Cunningham, 1988), the present taxonomy's categories are more macro. Conversely, it permits finer-grained analyses of interjob similarity than, for example, comparisons in Functional Job Analysis terms of people, data, and things (Fine, 1988). It was developed with the goals of presenting a reasonable number of nonoverlapping task categories that would support a comprehensive description of job tasks performed by USAF enlisted personnel in the late 1980s and early 1990s. At the time the taxonomy was developed, it was envisioned that it could possibly serve many purposes, including supporting research on forecasting the task content and skill requirements for projected USAF jobs, anticipating training needs for new USAF jobs, setting aptitude standards,

Table 34.13   Air Force Specialties Clusters Based on Mean Revised Skills/ Knowledge Questionnaire Relative Time Spent Profiles

Cluster IA: Mechanical/Construction

551x0 (M) – Pavements Maintenance Specialist

551x1 (M) – Construction Equipment Operator

Cluster IB: Mechanical

452x4 (M) – Tactical Aircraft Maintenance Specialist

457x0 (M) – Strategic Aircraft Maintenance Specialist

461x0 (M/E) – Munitions Systems Specialist

571x0 (G) – Fire Protection Specialist

631x0 (M&G) – Fuel Specialist

Cluster IC: Mechanical/Electrical

423x0 (E) – Aircraft Electrical Systems Specialist

454x1 (M&E) – Aerospace Ground Equipment Mechanic

462x0 (M/E) – Aircraft Armament Systems Specialist

472x0 (M) – Special Vehicle Mechanic

542x0 (E) – Electrician

545x0 (M/E) – Refrigeration and Air Conditioning Specialist

Cluster II: Electronics

303x2 (E) – Aircraft Control and Warning Radar Specialist

304x0/x4 (E) – Wideband and Ground Radio Communications Specialists

324x0 (E) – Precision Measurement Equipment Laboratory Specialist

455x2 (E) – Avionic Communication Specialist

Cluster IIIA: General & Administrative – Medical

902x0 (G) – Medical Service Specialist

981x0 (G) – Dental Assistant

Cluster IIIB: General & Administrative – Surveillance

207x1 (A) – Morse Systems Operator

272x0 (G) – Air Traffic Control Operator

276x0 (G) – Aerospace Control and Warning Systems Operator

811x0 (G) – Security Specialist

811x2 (G) – Law Enforcement Specialist

Cluster IIIC: General & Administrative – Clerical

651x0 (A) – Contracting Specialist

661x0 (A) – Logistics Plans Specialist

702x0 (A) – Administration Specialist

732x0 (A) – Personnel Specialist

791x0 (G) – Public Affairs Specialist

906x0 (G) – Medical Administrative Specialist

Cluster IIID: General & Administrative – Technical

241x0 (G) – Safety Specialist

242x0 (G) – Disaster Preparedness Specialist

251x0 (G) – Weather Specialist

553x0 (G) – Engineering Assistant

Cluster IIIE: General & Administrative – Logistics

113x0c (G) – Flight Engineer

114x0 (M) – Aircraft Loadmaster

Table 34.13   Air Force Specialties Clusters Based on Mean Revised Skills/ Knowledge Questionnaire Relative Time Spent Profiles (Continued)

271x1 (A) – Airfield Management Specialist
603x0 (M) – Vehicle Operator/Dispatcher
645x0 (A/G) – Inventory Management Specialist
645x1 (G) – Material Storage and Distribution Specialist
645x2 (A) – Supply Systems Analysis
741x1 (A) – Fitness and Recreation Specialist

MAGE = administrative, electronic, general, mechanical.

determining optimal strategies for internal (cross-AFS) retraining assignments, and designing alternative organizational structures for the operation and maintenance of emerging technologies. However, the taxonomy's primary intended purpose was to support research relating to cross-job transferability of skills.

Toward that end it proved useful. Kavanagh et al. (1997) used a modified version of the taxonomy in Table 34.7 to support data collection in a large-scale validation of cross-job transferability of skills estimates using an adaptation of Lance, Kavanagh, and Gould's (1993) methodology. The most comprehensive of its kind to date, the Kavanagh et al. (1997) study presented a wide range of validation evidence for cross-job retraining time estimates, including convergent, postdictive, and concurrent validity evidence. Lance, Kavanagh, and Brink (2002) also used a modified version of the taxonomy in Table 34.7 to investigate the effects of postretraining climate on the relationship between retraining time estimates and time to proficiency in the new assignment. They found that situational constraints in the posttraining environment had a moderating effect on this relationship. In particular, they found that cross-job retraining time estimates were significant predictors of time to achieve proficiency in the new assignment but only for situations that were low in situational constraints; in more constraining postretraining environments, achieving proficiency in the new job was uniformly difficult regardless of the similarity between the retrainee's old and new jobs.

Even though research on cross-job transferability of skills has ebbed in recent years, there have been occasional and isolated applications of methodologies similar to Lance, Kavanagh, and Gould's (1993) in other areas. For example, the "related occupations" module of O*NET (Peterson, Mumford, Borman, Jeanneret, & Fleishman, 1999; Peterson et al., 2001) uses a complex computational algorithm based on a modified Minkowski distance metric to identify other jobs in O*NET's database that are similar to the job being researched by the O*NET user that in some key respects is very similar to Lance, Kavanagh, and Gould's (1993) methodology. As a second example, Kubisiak, Hanson, and Buck (1999) and Hanson et al. (1998) used similar approaches to identify clusters of similar jobs for the purpose of delivering career information to career counseling clients. These are just a couple of examples of the many areas in the psychology of work behavior that could potentially benefit from systematic approaches to job classification such as discussed here.

REFERENCES

Aldenderfer, M. S., & Blashfield, R. K. (1984). *Cluster analysis.* Beverly Hills, CA: Sage Publications.

Arthur, W. Jr., Bennett, W. Jr., Edens, P. S., & Bell, S. T. (2003). Effectiveness of training in organizations: A meta-analysis of design and evaluation features. *Journal of Applied Psychology, 88,* 234–245.

Arthur, W. Jr., Bennett, W. Jr., Stanush, P. L., & NcNelly, T. L. (1998). Factors that influence skill decay and retention: A quantitative review and analysis. *Human Performance, 11,* 57–101.

Baldwin, T. T., & Ford, J. K. (1988). Transfer of training: A review and directions for future research. *Personnel Psychology, 41,* 63–105.

Ballentine, R. D., & Cunningham, J. W. (1981). Development of the General Work Inventory. *Proceedings of the Annual Conference of the Military Testing Association, 1,* 125–133.

Bell, J., & Thomasson, M. (1984). *Job categorization project.* Randolph AFB, TX: Occupational Analysis Program, United States Air Force Occupational Measurement Center.

Bennett, C. A. (1971). Toward an empirical, practicable, comprehensive task taxonomy. *Human Factors, 13,* 229–235.

Burtch, L. D., Lipscomb, M. S., & Wissman, D. J. (1982). *Aptitude requirements based on task difficulty: Methodology for evaluation* (AFHRL-TR-81-34). Brooks AFB, TX: Air Force Human Resources Laboratory, Manpower and Personnel Division.

Campion, M. A., & Thayer, P. W. (1985). Development and field evaluation of an interdisciplinary measure of job design. *Journal of Applied Psychology, 70,* 29–43.

Chao, G. T., O'Leary-Kelly, A. M., Wolf, S., Klein, H. J., & Gardner, P. D. (1994). Organizational socialization: Its content and consequences. *Journal of Applied Psychology, 79,* 730–743.

Cheng, E. W. L., & Ho, D. C. K. (2001). A review of transfer of training studies in the past decade. *Personnel Review, 30,* 102–118.

Chiva, R., & Alegre, J. (2005). Organizational learning and organizational knowledge: Towards the integration of two approaches. *Management Learning, 36,* 49–68.

Christal, R. E. (1974). *The United States Air Force occupational research project* (AFHRL-TR-73-75). Lackland AFB, TX: Air Force Human Resources Laboratory, Occupational Research Division.

Christal, R. E., & Weissmuller, J. J. (1988). Job-task inventory analysis. In S. Gael (Ed.), *The job analysis handbook for business, industry, and government* (Vol. 2, pp. 1036–1050). New York, NY: John Wiley & Sons.

Companion, M. A., & Corso, G. M. (1982). Task taxonomies: A general review and evaluation. *International Journal of Man-Machine Studies, 17,* 459–472.

Cunningham, J. W. (1988). Occupational analysis inventory. In S. Gael (Ed.), *The job analysis handbook for business, industry, and government* (Vol. 2, pp. 975–990). New York: John Wiley & Sons.

Cunningham, J. W., Boese, R. R., Neeb, R. W., & Pass, J. J. (1983). Systematically derived work dimensions: Factor analysis of the occupational analysis inventory. *Journal of Applied Psychology, 68,* 232–252.

Dawis, R. V., & Lofquist, L. H. (1975). Toward a psychological taxonomy of work. *Journal of Vocational Behavior, 7,* 165–171.

Department of Defense. (1984). *Test manual for the armed services vocational aptitude battery.* North Chicago, IL: United States Military Entrance Processing Command.

Dowell, B. E., & Wexley, K. N. (1978). Development of a work behavior taxonomy for first-line supervisors. *Journal of Applied Psychology, 63,* 563–572.

Dunnette, M. D. (1976). Aptitudes, abilities, and skills. In M. D. Dunnette (Ed.), *Handbook of industrial and organizational psychology* (pp. 473–520). Chicago: Rand McNally.

Farina, A. J. (1973). Development of a taxonomy of human performance: A review of descriptive schemes for human task behavior. *JSAS Catalog of Selected Documents in Psychology, 3,* 23.

Farina, A. J., & Wheaton, G. R. (1973). Development of a taxonomy of human performance: The task characteristics approach to performance prediction. *JSAS Catalog of Selected Documents in Psychology, 3,* 2627.

Feji, J., Whitely, W., Peiro, J., & Taris, T. (1995). The development of career-enhancing strategies and content innovation: A longitudinal study of new workers. *Journal of Vocational Behavior, 46,* 231–256.

Fine, S. A. (1957). A reexamination of "transferability of skills" - Part II. *Monthly Labor Review, 80,* 938–948.

Fine, S. A. (1988). Functional job analysis. In S. Gael (Ed.), *The job analysis handbook for business, industry, and government* (Vol. 2, pp. 1019–1035). New York, NY: John Wiley & Sons.

Fischer, C. D. (1986). Organizational socialization: An integrative review. In G. R. Ferris & K. M. Rowland (Eds.), *Research in personnel and human resource management* (Vol. 4, pp. 101–145). Greenwich, CT: Jai Press.

Fleishman, E. A. (1972). On the relation between abilities, learning, and human performance. *American Psychologist, 30,* 1127–1149.

Fleishman, E. A. (1982). Systems for describing human tasks. *American Psychologist, 37,* 821–834.

Fleishman, E. A., & Quaintance, M. K. (1984). *Taxonomies of human performance.* Orlando, FL: Academic Press.

Ginzburg, S., & Dar-El., E. M. (2000). Skill retention and relearning: A proposed cyclical model. *Journal of Workplace Learning, 12,* 327–332.

Gordon, M. E., Cofer, J. L., & McCullough, P. M. (1986). Relationships among seniority, past performance, interjob similarity, and trainability. *Journal of Applied Psychology, 71,* 518–521.

Gordon, M. E., & Fitzgibbons, W. J. (1982). Empirical test of the validity of seniority as a factor in staffing decisions. *Journal of Applied Psychology, 67,* 311–319.

Gould, R. B., Archer, W., Filer, J., Short, L. O., & Kavanagh, M. J. (1989). *Development of a methodology to esti-mate common task overlap*. Paper presented at the meeting of the Society for Industrial and Organizational Psychology, Boston, MA.

Hanson, M. A., Kubisiak, U. C., Horgen, K., Buck, D. E., Bunch, L. B., Foster, L., & Borman, W. C. (1998). *Basic research to support development of a career guidance system for displaced Air Force workers* (Institute Report #304). Minneapolis, MN: Personnel Decisions Research Institute.

Henderson, R. K. (1993). *A criterion-related validation of time estimates of cross-job retraining times within and across job sub-families* (PhD dissertation). University of Georgia, Athens, GA.

Holland, J. L. (1973). *Making vocational choices: A theory of careers.* Englewood Cliffs, NJ: Prentice-Hall.

Huber, G. P. (1991). Organizational learning: The contributing processes and literatures. *Organization Science, 2,* 88–115.

Jackson, S. E., & Schuler, R. S. (1990). Human resource planning: Challenges for industrial/organizational psy-chologists. *American Psychologist, 45,* 223–239.

James, L. R., Demaree, R. G., & Wolf, G. (1984). Estimating within-group interrater reliability with and without response bias. *Journal of Applied Psychology, 69,* 85–98.

Jones, A. P., Johnson, L. A., Butler, M. C., & Main, D. S. (1983). Apples and oranges: An empirical comparison of commonly used indices of interrater agreement. *Academy of Management Journal, 26,* 507–519.

Kavanagh, M. J., & Lance, C. E. (1989). *Transferability of skills methodology: Reliability of ease-of-movement judg-ments.* San Antonio, TX: Metrica, Inc.

Kavanagh, M. J., Lance, C. E., O'Brien, L., Stennett, R. B., McMillen, R., Solomonson, A. L., & Black, D. E. (1997). *Transferability of skills: Convergent, postdictive, criterion-related, and construct validation of cross-job retraining time estimates.* Brooks AFB, TX: United States Air Force Armstrong Laboratory, Human Resources Directorate.

Kubisiak, U. C., Hanson, M. A., & Buck, D. (1999, April). *Person-job matching in the context of computerized career information delivery.* Paper presented at the meeting of the Society for Industrial and Organizational Psychology, Atlanta, GA.

Lahey, M. A., Downey, R. G., & Saal, F. E. (1983). Intraclass correlations: There's more there than meets the eye. *Psychological Bulletin, 93,* 586–595.

Lance, C. E., Kavanagh, M. J., & Brink, K. (2002). Retraining climate as a predictor of retraining success and as a moderator of the relationship between cross-job retraining time estimates and time to proficiency in the new assignment. *Group and Organization Management, 27,* 294–318.

Lance, C. E., Kavanagh, M. J., & Gould, R. B. (1989, August). *Measurement and convergent validation of cross-job ease-of-movement.* Paper presented at the meeting of the American Psychological Association, New Orleans, LA.

Lance, C. E., Kavanagh, M. J., & Gould, R. B. (1993). Development and convergent validation of a methodology for estimating cross-job retraining times. *Journal of Business and Psychology, 8,* 67–90.

Lance, C. E., Mayfield, D. L., Foster, M. R., Stokes, G. S., & Mecham, R. C. (1991, April). *Cross-job retraining time estimates based on the Position Analysis Questionnaire.* Paper presented at the meeting of the Society for Industrial and Organizational Psychology, St Louis, MO.

Lance, C. E., Mayfield, D. L., & Gould, R. B. (1993). A postdictive validation of cross-job retraining time esti-mates for 43 U.S. Air Force enlisted specialties. *Military Psychology, 5,* 173–186.

Lance, C. E., Mayfield, D. L., Gould, R. B., & Lynskey, M. C. (1991). Global versus decomposed estimates of cross-job retraining time. *Human Performance, 4,* 71–88.

Lance, C. E., Parisi, A. G., Bennett, W. R., Teachout, M. S., Bewley, M. L., & Harville, D. L. (1998). Moderators of skill nonuse—performance decrement relationships in eight U.S. Air Force enlisted specialties. *Human Performance, 11,* 103–123.

McCormick, E. J. (1976). Job and task analysis. In M. D. Dunnette (Ed.), *Handbook of industrial and organiza-tional psychology* (pp. 651–696). Chicago, IL: Rand McNally.

McCormick, E. J., & Jeanneret, P. R. (1988). Position Analysis Questionnaire (PAQ). In S. Gael (Ed.), *The job analy-sis handbook for business, industry, and government* (Vol. 2, pp. 825–842). New York, NY: John Wiley & Sons.

McCormick, E. J., Jeanneret, P. R., & Mecham, R. C. (1972). A study of job characteristics and job dimensions as based on the Position Analysis Questionnaire (PAQ). *Journal of Applied Psychology, 56,* 347–368.

McKinlay, B. (1976). *Characteristics of jobs that are considered common: Review of literature and research* (Information Series No. 102). Columbus: The Ohio State University, The Center for Vocational Education.

Mead, D. F., & Christal, R. E. (1970). *Development of a constant standard weight equation for evaluating job difficulty* (AFHRL-TR-81-34). Lackland AFB, TX: Air Force Human Resources Laboratory, Personnel Division.

Miller, R. B. (1967). Task taxonomy: Science or technology? In W. T. Singleton, R. S. Easterby, & D. C. Whitfield (Eds.), *The human operator in complex systems* (pp. 67–76). London, England: Taylor & Francis.

Milligan, G. W., & Cooper, M.. C. (1987). Methodology review: Clustering methods. *Applied Psvchological Measurement, 11,* 329–354.

Morsh, J. E., Madden, J. M., & Christal, R. E. (1961). *Job analysis in the United States Air Force* (WADD-TR-61-113). Lackland AFB, TX: Wright Air Development Division.

Mumford, M. D., Weeks, J. L., Harding, F. D., & Fleishman, E. A. (1987). Measuring occupational difficulty: A construct validation against training criteria. *Journal of Applied Psychology, 72,* 578–587.

Niehaus, R. J., & Price, K. F. (1991). *Bottom line results from strategic human resource planning.* New York, NY: Plenum.

Peterson, N. G., & Bownas, D. A. (1982). Skill, task structure, and performance acquisition. In M. D. Dunnette & E. A. Fleishman (Eds.), *Human performance and productivity: Human capability assessment* (pp. 49–105). Hillsdale, NJ: Erlbaum.

Peterson, N. G., Mumford, M. D., Borman, W. C., Jeanneret, P. R., & Fleishman, E. A. (Eds.). (1999). *An occupational information system for the 21st century: The development of O*NET.* Washington, DC: American Psychological Association.

Peterson, N. G., Mumford, M. D., Borman, W. C., Jeanneret, P. R., & Fleishman, E. A., Levin, K. Y., … Dye, D. M. (2001). Understanding work using the occupational information network (O*NET): Implications for practice and research. *Personnel Psychology, 54,* 451–492.

Ramage, J. A. (1987). *Task learning difficulty: Interrelationships among aptitude-specific benchmarked rating scales* (AFHRL-TP-86-56). Brooks AFB, TX: Air Force Human Resources Laboratory, Manpower and Personnel Division.

Ramsey-Klee, D. M. (1979). *Taxonomic approaches to enlisted occupational classification: Volume I* (NPRDC-TR-80-7). San Diego, CA: Navy Personnel Research and Development Center.

Richman-Hirsch, W. L. (2001). Posttraining interventions to enhance transfer: The moderating effects of work environments. *Human Resource Development Quarterly, 12,* 105–119.

Rousseau, D. M. (1988). Human resource planning for the future. In J. Hage (Ed.), *Futures of organizations: Innovating to adapt strategy and human resources to rapid technological change* (pp. 245–266). New York, NY: Lexington.

Ruck, H. W. (Ed.). (1977). *The development and application of the electronics principles inventory.* Lackland AFB, TX: USAF Occupational Measurement Center, Air Training Command.

Ruck, H. W. (1986). *Skill/knowledge commonalities in selected electronics specialties* (AFHRL-TP-86-20). Brooks AFB, TX: Air Force Human Resources Laboratory, Manpower and Personnel Division.

Shrout, P. E., & Fleiss, J. L. (1979). Intraclass correlations: Uses in assessing interrater reliability. *Psychological Bulletin, 86,* 420–428.

Skinner, M. J. (1981). An evaluation of the Air Force airman retraining program. *Proceedings of the 23rd International Military Testing Association* (pp. 1109–1120), Arlington, VA.

Skinner, M. J. (1982). Retrained airmen: Volunteers versus non-volunteers. *Proceedings of the 24th International Military Testing Association* (pp. 645–651), San Antonio, TX.

Skinner, M. J. (1983). *Retraining program for Air Force enlisted personnel: An evaluation* (AFHRL-SR-83-31). Brooks AFB, TX: Air Force Human Resources Laboratory, Manpower and Personnel Division.

Skinner, M. J., & Alley, W. E. (1980). *Performance of retrained airmen in Air Force technical schools* (AFHRL-TR-80-7). Brooks AFB, TX: Air Force Human Resources Laboratory, Manpower and Personnel Division.

Skinner, M. J., & Alley, W. E. (1984). *Job aptitude requirement waivers for retrained airmen* (AFHRL-TR-83-42). Brooks AFB, TX: Air Force Human Resources Laboratory, Manpower and Personnel Division.

Smith, P. C., & Kendall, L. M. (1963). Retranslation of expectations: An approach to the construction of unambiguous anchors for rating scales. *Journal of Applied Psychology, 47,* 149–155.

Sokal, R. R. (1974). Classification: Purposes, principles, progress, prospects. *Science, 185,* 1115–1123.

Stolurow, L. M. (1964). *A taxonomy of learning task characteristics* (TDR Report No. AMRL-TDR-64-2; NTIS No. AD 433 199). Urbana, IL: University of Illinois.

Taylor, P. J., Russ-Eft, D. F., & Chan, D. W. L. (2005). A meta-analytic review of behavior modeling training. *Journal of Applied Psychology, 90,* 692–709.

Thomas, J. B., Sussman, S. W., & Henderson, J. C. (2001). Understanding "strategic learning": Linking organizational learning, knowledge management, and sensemaking. *Organization Science, 12,* 331–345.

U.S. Air Force. (n.d.). *U.S. Air Force enlisted opportunities.* Retrieved from http://www.airforce.com/opportunities/enlisted/careers/

Wanous J. P. (1992). *Organizational entry: Recruitment, selection, orientation, and socialization* (2nd ed.). Reading, MA: Addison-Wesley.

Ward, J. H. (1963). Hierarchical grouping to optimize an objective function. *Journal of the American Statistical Association, 58,* 236–244.

Weeks, J. (1984). *Occupational learning difficulty: A standard for determining the order of aptitude requirement minimums* (AFHRL-SR-84-26). Brooks AFB, TX: Air Force Human Resources Laboratory, Manpower and Personnel Division.

Wheaton, G. R. (1973). Development of a taxonomy of human performance: A review of classificatory systems relating to tasks and performance. *JSAS Catalog of Selected Documents in Psychology, 3,* 22.

Yamnill, S., & McLean, G. N. (2001). Theories supporting transfer of training. *Human Resource Development Quarterly, 12,* 195–208.

Zook, L. M. (1996). *Soldier selection: Past, present and future* (Special Report S-28; A608123). Alexandria, VA: United States Army Research Institute for the Behavioral and Social Sciences.

35

Analyzing Job and Occupational Content Using Latent Semantic Analysis

PETER W. FOLTZ

Pearson Knowledge Technologies

ROBERT J. OBERBRECKLING

Perceptive Research, Inc.

R. DARRELL LAHAM

Center for ReSource Conservation

Military, civilian, governmental, and corporate organizations currently face rapid changes in information technology, high-tech products, and organizational structure, which create the need for constantly changing mixes of personnel competencies and skills as well as for rapid training of new skills. Assembling just the right people with just the right knowledge and skills is increasingly critical for the successful conduct of complex tasks, such as military missions. Doing so is most important, and most difficult, when missions respond to novel challenges, such as needed for heterogeneous knowledge widely dispersed in the organization, involve systems or procedures for which there are few experts, and when there is little time to prepare. These are all situations to be expected in future warfighting scenarios. For example, warfighters have had to become more specialized in skills working with information technology, while still maintaining additional specialized skills in such areas as languages, leadership, communication, and diplomacy.

Nevertheless, for any novel complex task, a key problem is the ability to locate those people who have the appropriate skills as well as finding those who can most rapidly be trained to perform that task. Ideally, one would like the ability to design special training that will optimally build on each person's prior training and experience rather than spending time teaching things already known. Current solution methods for such problems require large investments of expert labor who can match appropriate personnel to tasks but are often either unacceptably slow or insufficiently effective. Thus, more effective methods are desired for characterizing, locating, and training personnel who can optimally perform the set of duties required by any new mission. This calls for information technologies that can (a) represent knowledge and skills, (b) identify personnel with all or parts of the knowledge and task experience required by a mission—wherever and in whatever occupation they are currently, (c) determine what, if any, retraining each person needs to perform which new duties, (d) reduce the effort required to create new training programs, and (e) effectively track performance during training.

This chapter reviews two research efforts that are aimed at improving matching of personnel and measuring performance of personnel during complex interacting team tasks. These efforts in career field analysis and training performance evaluation both make use of a technology called Latent Semantic Analysis (LSA) to model information about tools for career field analysis and training performance evaluation.

The first effort, called CareerMap, is developing new LSA-based agent software that helps decision makers to identify required job knowledge, determine which members of the workforce have the knowledge, pinpoint needed retraining content, and maximize training and retraining efficiency. Assembling personnel with the right knowledge and experience for a task is especially difficult when there are few experts, unfamiliar devices, redefined goals, and short lead-times for training and deployment. LSA is being used to analyze course content and materials from current training pipelines and to identify appropriate places in alternative structures where that content can be reused. This saves time for training developers because the preexisting content has already been validated as a part of its earlier application. Moreover, gaps in the content for the new training structure become readily apparent with this type of analysis.

The second research effort involves development and demonstration of a combined speech-to-text and LSA-based software agent for embedding automatic, continuous, and cumulative analysis of verbal interactions in individual and team operational environments. The agent can systematically parse and evaluate verbal communication to identify critical information and content required of many typical military teams. This approach is applied to assisting training through doing automated analyses of team communication and converting the results into performance metrics. This chapter focuses on one application of this technology for tracking and scoring the tactical communications that occur between the members of a four-ship air combat flight and their weapons director to identify areas of training need and as an additional tool for assessing the efficacy of Distributed Mission Operations (DMO) training scenarios and missions.

LATENT SEMANTIC ANALYSIS

To describe how these research efforts are being conducted, it is first necessary to describe the underlying technology being used. One of the critical difficulties in analyzing career information and team communications is the large amount of information contained in natural language form (e.g., résumés, course material, performance information, communication). The ability to analyze this information can permit better characterizations of personnel competencies and skills. Thus, what is needed is technology that can "understand" the information within the appropriate context that it is used.

LSA is a fully automatic corpus-based statistical method for extracting and inferring relations of expected contextual usage of words in discourse (Landauer, Foltz, & Laham, 1998). It has been used for a wide range of applications and for simulating knowledge representation, discourse, and psycholinguistic phenomena. Word and passage meaning representations derived by LSA have been found capable of simulating a variety of human cognitive phenomena, ranging from developmental acquisition of recognition vocabulary to word-categorization, sentence-word semantic priming, and discourse comprehension. Applications have included information retrieval (Deerwester et al., 1990), automated essay scoring (Landauer et al., 2001), and automated text analysis (Foltz, 1996), and monitoring online mission planning and training discussions (Lochbaum, Psotka, & Streeter, 2002; LaVoie et al., 2007).

In LSA, a training text is represented as a matrix, where there is a row for each unique word in the text and the columns represent a text passage or other context. The entries in this matrix are the frequency of the word in the context. A singular value decomposition (SVD) of the matrix results in a 100- to 500-dimensional "semantic space," where the original words and passages are represented as vectors. The meaning of any passage of text is the average of the vector of the words in the passage (Landauer et al., 1997). Words, utterances, and whole documents can then be compared against each other by computing the cosine between the vectors representing any two texts. This provides a measure of the semantic similarity of those two texts, even if they do not contain words in common.

The initial version of LSA used SVD and dimensionality reduction to convert the co-occurrence matrix into a form that expressed the latent, or underlying, meaning of the terms rather than just the surface characteristic of the actual word used. It was shown that after the mathematical treatment, synonyms, which rarely occur together in natural text, would have highly similar representations. In information retrieval this enabled searches to go beyond simple keyword matching. A search for "automobile" would now bring up documents that contained the word "car." This improved text retrieval results as much as 30% over the SMART methods (Dumais, 1994).

Modern instantiations of LSA are closely related to unsupervised neural net models, but are based on various "one-shot" learning techniques rather than iterative learning. This allows for derived solutions to be achieved with reasonable computational capacity on enormous text corpora meeting or surpassing the volume of relevant language experienced by people. Methods used currently for LSA and related approaches include SVD, semi-discrete decomposition (SDD), independent components analysis (ICA), and various probabilistic techniques (e.g., PLSA, Hoffman, 1999). The specific details of the LSA methods used in the research described here are proprietary and will not be disclosed in this book. For detailed information on LSA techniques as applied to information retrieval, we recommend Berry, Dumais, and O'Brien (1995).

CareerMap

The Problem

Modern organizations are increasingly faced with rapid changes in technology and missions and need constantly changing mixes of competencies and skill. Assembling personnel with the right knowledge and experience for a task is especially difficult when there are few experts, unfamiliar devices, redefined goals, and short lead times for training and deployment. When too few adequately trained personnel are available for suddenly critical tasks, organizations need the ability (a) to identify existing personnel who could perform the task with the least training, and (b) to create new training courses quickly by assembling components of old ones.

Current solution methods for such problems require large investments of expert labor and are often either unacceptably slow or insufficiently effective. For example, determining whether a particular person's background for a particular assignment requires some time-consuming training component, or allows it to be omitted, would probably necessitate intensive general training research as well as extensive individual questioning. Creating an efficiently individualized training course would be just as difficult. While a well-developed engineering art, in the best case, course design takes many months of specialized analysis and trial.

Thus, more effective methods are desired for characterizing, locating, and training personnel who can optimally perform the set of duties required by any new mission.

This calls for information technologies that can do the following:

- Represent knowledge and skills.
- Identify people with all or parts of the knowledge and task experience required by a mission—wherever and in whatever occupation they are currently.
- Determine precisely what, if any, retraining each person needs to perform which new duties.

- Reduce the effort required to create new training programs.
- Minimize the time required for training and retraining.

The objective of this research was to develop and test the practical capability of LSA in application to these problems. The new personnel data mining application of LSA exploits the explicit and implicit knowledge that already exists in extensive textual computer files of systems documentation, training and test materials, task analyses, and service records (Laham, Bennett, & Landauer, 2000).

Description of Latent Semantic Analysis Representations

The biggest advantage of LSA knowledge representation for the present purpose is that different types of data objects (e.g., occupations, job tasks, personnel, training materials) can all exist as vectors within the same semantic space and can therefore be directly compared to each other in meaningful ways. People can easily make holistic judgments of similarity between a task to be performed and a set of people who might be called upon to perform the task. However, the structure in which this information is usually stored in computer files (i.e., in relational databases) has precluded the possibility of automated judgments of this sort.

Traditional database structures are very brittle in that search and retrieval are overly dependent on specific data field choices (e.g., ZIP code field, job title field) and on exact keyword matching. While in many cases exact matching on highly structured data is desirable (e.g., find the names of all people in ZIP code 30405), in many other cases the choices can be overly restrictive and/or ambiguous (find all the people who list their job title as *doctor*). In the latter example, those people who listed their title as medical doctor, physician, surgeon, general practice doctor, and other medical specialties would not match the query and would be inappropriately excluded.

The Latent Semantic Analysis Solution

Figure 35.1 shows a two-dimensional representation of two LSA objects, a Job and a Candidate. In actual LSA representations, it requires 100–500 orthogonal dimensions to characterize an object—this two-dimensional representation is for illustrative purposes only. Unlike traditional factor analysis, where the dimensions have been interpreted and named, LSA dimensions are not *in and of themselves* meaningful. Both objects are seen as points in the Semantic Space having some score on the X dimension and an independent score on the Y dimension. In most of the work reported in this chapter, each of the objects has scores for 300 orthogonal dimensions; thus, each object is represented as a vector of 300 numbers, rather than a vector of 2 numbers. In actual LSA, the meaning of an object is determined when the full set of dimension scores is used in the comparison of the object to other objects. In most cases, LSA uses the cosine of the angle between objects as the measure of similarity.

In Figure 35.2, the capacity to make similarity comparisons between different data objects is illustrated. To determine which of two candidates is best suited for a job, the LSA system would use the smaller of the two angles 1 and 2. Cosines range between 1 and –1 for all possible angles—an angle of 0 degrees has a cosine of 1 (the vectors lay on top of each other), an angle of 90 degrees has a cosine of 0, and an angle of 180 degrees has a cosine of –1. The smaller the angle, the higher the cosine, and the more similar the two objects are considered. In the Figure 35.2 case, Candidate 1 is a better choice for the job.

The CareerMap Application

CareerMap (available online at http://www.careermap.org) is a demonstration of the Intelligent Search Agent that can aid in the performance of mission critical training management tasks.

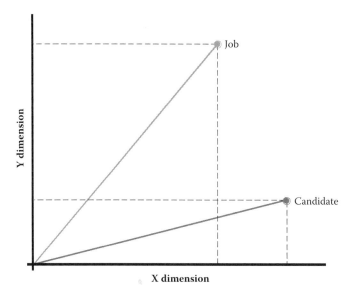

Figure 35.1   A two-dimensional representation of two Latent Semantic Analysis objects.

It is Internet-based, so it works with any browser. The demonstration system is populated with sample data from the Air Force, Department of Labor Occupational Network (O*Net), job listings from the Office of Personnel Management, and résumés from Yahoo! and other sources. In the demonstration system, one can create a text query to retrieve and rank any type of data object known to the system (e.g., Air Force Specialty Code [AFSC] descriptions or training records; see Figure 35.3).

The query will return the most similar objects in the system. The user can review the results and, if desired, expand the query using retrieved data (Figure 35.4).

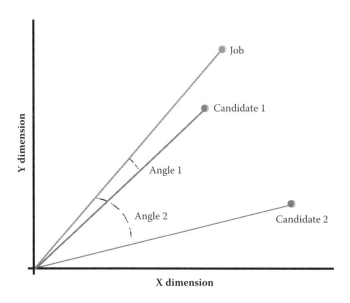

Figure 35.2   Two candidates for a job.

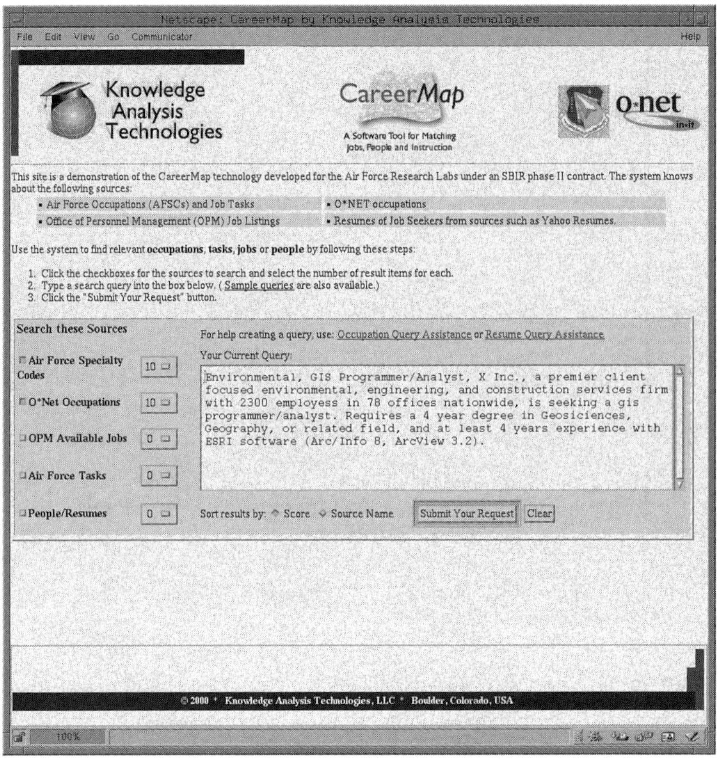

Figure 35.3   The CareerMap application.

An interesting data analysis feature of CareerMap employs visualization tools to help the user discover the relationships between the objects returned by the search (see Figure 35.5). The return list of objects is those that are nearest the query in semantic space. The visualization tools allow the interrelationships between the objects to be seen.

Potential Applications of the Method

Job Placement or Occupation Assignment

Practical applications to job assignment were most directly illustrated by the research just reported. The simplest case is direct replacement of one airman with another. For this, a query takes the form of the to-be-replaced airman's identification number, and the k most similar airmen known to the system (potentially all those in the Air Force plus others where relevant) are returned and listed in terms of their overall task-experience pattern—the closeness of their points in the joint semantic space representing tasks, occupations, and airmen. Their complete service records can then be displayed and compared. If it is desired to add a new member to a work group, the descriptions of those tasks that are most in need of additional help can be entered as the query and the system will list in order those airmen whose total experience is most like the new job requirements. Note that in performing this match, LSA goes beyond simply counting the number of tasks in common between the wanted list and the service record, instead factoring in previous experience (and, later, training) in occupations and tasks that are similar but not identical to those in need of performance. Thus, it would be quite possible, in the absence of any airman who had done any of the prescribed tasks, to nevertheless find one or more candidates who had done similar work, the

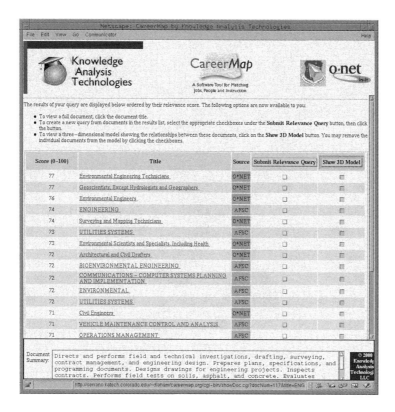

Figure 35.4   CareerMap object return list.

estimate of similarity having been automatically induced by LSA from the entire corpus of data without human intervention.

The technique could be used to add people to perform new jobs, by adding a freeform description of the tasks involved to the query. Because LSA captures semantic and conceptual similarity of verbal expressions, it will correctly match ad hoc task descriptions with official task definitions and job descriptions. The system can also form a representation of the overall mix of tasks required by a group by combining representations of the knowledge possessed by all its present members. In the case of having to remove personnel from a group (e.g., downsizing), the system would make it possible to find a set of personnel to transfer out of a group that would either leave it most like its previous composition, or desirably modified, again without relying on a crude counting operation or intuition.

The opportunity and manner of application for selecting airmen for missions—for example, expeditionary war-fighting missions with unique challenges—is relatively straightforward. The system can be given a careful verbal description of the mission, including all the tasks to be performed, the equipment, weapons, devices, procedures, numbers of airmen needed in each role, and perhaps even factors such as locale, terrain, and likely weather and other challenges. Then, the LSA matching technique would rank airmen for suitability to each task on the basis of the totality of their previous task and occupational experience, along with, if available, relevant (as determined by LSA) test scores and performance ratings.

Curriculum Overlap Analyses

The Air Force (like other military and civilian organizations) offers hundreds of specialty training courses, many of which overlap substantially in content, may contain content no longer relevant to

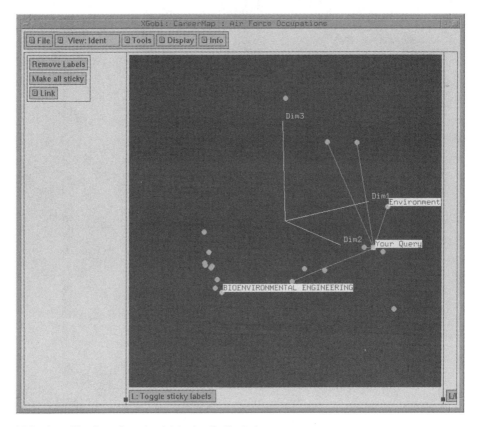

Figure 35.5   CareerMap three-dimensional data visualization tools.

tasks currently in demand, and some that are missing content made desirable by changes in technology, missions, or staffing. In many cases, it would be desirable to combine, condense, or modify courses. Teaching unnecessary numbers of courses or redundant components in multiple courses is expensive in instructional staff and facilities and even more expensive in wasted student time and resources. Teaching material that is suboptimally matched to work requirements, either by being superfluous, redundant, or by failing to equip airmen with the best skill sets to perform desired tasks, is likely even more expensive in the long run.

To rationalize the content and organization of content for multiple training programs, a method is needed by which the overlap in course content can be easily assessed. Presently such analyses are performed, if at all, by highly labor intensive efforts by subject matter experts (SMEs) and training specialists. We have already demonstrated that LSA can do this kind of analysis automatically to a quite useful degree. Our studies were based on analysis only of course examination items but appeared to give a great deal of useful information about course overlap.

LSA can also measure the overlap between course content and the full range of tasks performed in many different occupations. Information from such analyses will suggest where the training needed for different occupations overlaps and might be combined, where training is lacking, will point to components that may not actually be needed at all, and, in some instances, will suggest ways in which occupations might be restructured to increase training efficiency. LSA methods will not solve these problems completely, but we believe they can offer highly useful information for planners that is currently unobtainable or prohibitively expensive.

Just-in-Time Training Materials

In brief, the way we envision that LSA would be employed to help rapidly create new targeted training programs might be as follows. The component knowledge needed and tasks to be performed for a new device, system, or procedure would be carefully described by designers and relevant SMEs. LSA would determine the degree of match of each component to a wide range of tasks performed and to every paragraph in every possibly relevant training or operations manual. Tasks and paragraphs would be ranked by estimated relevance to the new system and the LSA similarity of each paragraph to each task determined. A custom retraining document for each candidate could initially be compiled from paragraphs highly relevant to the new system that are not highly similar to tasks the candidate has previously performed. In the case of urgent need for a small number of trainees, a subject matter or training expert could then edit each version. In case of need for large numbers and more available time, the collection of paragraphs could be crafted into a simple computer-based training program with branching to permit trainees to skip parts they already know.

MISSION COMMUNICATIONS ANALYSIS

In the second application, LSA is being used to assess communication among team members in Distributed Mission Training. This effort involves a speech-to-text combined with an LSA-based intelligent software agent for embedding automatic, continuous, and cumulative analysis of verbal interactions in individual and team operational environments. The goal here is to develop and implement an LSA-based "Automated Communications Analysis" pipeline for performance assessment of mission communications applicable to both simulated and live Distributed Mission Training. The analysis of communications will be used to inform instructors and students for feedback both during mission performance and in related After Action Briefings (Figure 35.6).

As a proof of concept, LSA was successfully able to predict team performance in a simulated unmanned air vehicle (UAV) task environment (Foltz, 2005; Kiekel, Cooke, Foltz, Gorman, & Martin, 2002) based only on communications transcripts. Using human transcriptions of 67 team missions in the UAV environment, LSA predicts objective team performance scores at a very high level of reliability (LSA alone, $r = .74$; LSA combined with additional text analysis measures, $r = .85$). Additional work (Foltz, 2005) has shown that this approach is generalizable reliable to performance measurement in teams across a range of domains. The Team Performance Score used as the criterion measure is a composite of objective measures including the amount of fuel and film used, the number and type of photographic errors, route deviations, time spent in warning and alarm states, unvisited waypoints, and violations in route rules. In this analysis, LSA compares the content of a mission transcript of unknown performance quality to those of known performance quality to generate the LSA Performance scores. A weighted average of the objective scores of the most semantically similar transcripts is calculated as the LSA score. The approach has further shown to be successful in a range of other domains including analysis of teams in Navy Tactical Decision-Making Under Stress (TADMUS) tasks, teams performing planning for stability and support operations, and teams in virtual and live convoy training maneuvers (Foltz, Lavoie, Oberbreckling, & Rosenstein, 2007; Foltz, Martin, Abdelali, Rosenstein, & Oberbreckling, 2006).

The application explored in this chapter tracks and scores the tactical communications that occur between the members of a four-ship F-16 air-to-air combat flight team and their airborne

Team mission communications →
Speech recognition speech-to-text →
LSA analyses and performance scores →
After action briefings & performance feedback

Figure 35.6 Automated communications analysis pipeline.

warning and control system (AWACS) operator. This application relies on a computer-based monitor that listens to the verbal interactions of teams while they conduct simulated missions. The monitoring system uses automatic speech recognition to capture what the team says. Then LSA techniques automatically analyze and correlate the communications semantic content with team performance ratings after a mission.

Teams of four F-16 pilots and an AWACS operator supporting the Air Force Research Laboratory distributed mission operations (AFRL DMO) training research program, flew simulated tactical combat missions over a week-long research trial. The teams flew two missions each day except Fridays, in which they flew one mission. Each team mission was assigned a mission number. This started at 1 for Monday morning, 2 for Monday afternoon, 3 for Tuesday morning, and so forth. Within each mission, there was one or more engagements depending on the scenario, and within each engagement, there may be one or more enemy encounters of type visual identification (VID) or beyond visual range (BVR). The unit of analysis in this work was the engagement. Our goal was to automatically analyze the engagement-level communication transcripts as well as to automatically predict each team's performance from them.

The structure of this work is as follows. We first describe the team performance measures we are automatically modeling along with the method used to automatically record the engagement transcripts. We then describe the properties of the transcribed communications text. We conclude with our modeling results and some analysis and conclusions.

Data Acquisition and Modeling Pipeline

At a high level, training the predictive models required two inputs. The first is a set of communications transcripts recorded during teams' task performances. The second is a set of corresponding indicators rating the teams' task performances. A set of these transcript/score pairs was used as a training set to construct any number of our predictive models (Figure 35.7):

In this particular effort, the training texts are transcripts from an automated speech-to-text system. The scores are human/SME scores.

Team Performance Measures

The teams' performance was assessed subjectively using the Scenario-based Performance Observation Tool for Learning in Team Environments (SPOTLITE). SMEs use a tablet personal computer to subjectively answer a standard set of evaluation questions during the teams' performances. The ratings are on a discrete scale of one through five. A second data gathering system recorded objective individual and team performance data. This is the Performance Evaluation Tracking System (PETS), a robust embedded performance measurement tool developed as a part of the AFRL DMO training research program. It records engagement summaries, shot logs, and more granular, time-based, variable snapshots.

Automatic Transcript Recording

The team communication transcripts were collected through a Nuance-based automatic speech recognition (ASR) system. This system receives each discrete radio audio transmission from each team member and transcribes them to text. Each text is concatenated onto a continuing transcript file.

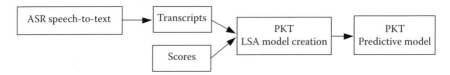

Figure 35.7 The model creation sequence.

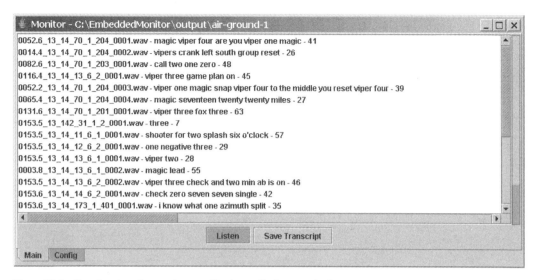

Figure 35.8 Sample automatic speech recognition transcribed communication.

As seen in Figure 35.8, each radio transmission is accompanied with additional data. At each mission start, a clock starts counting from zero. The leftmost number is a timestamp from this clock. The subsequent numbers help identify the speaker and radio. The rightmost number (at record end) is the confidence level of the text produced from the speech recognition (scale 0–100).

As the team communicates while performing their task, the ASR application converts each radio transmission to a line of text that is appended onto a monolithic transcript. From this monolithic transcript, we first split out the separate mission transcripts and then from those mission transcripts, we then needed to split the individual engagement transcripts. This produced a dataset of ~240 engagement-level transcripts with associated SPOTLITE engagement-level grades as previously discussed.

Properties of the Team Communication Transcripts

Vocabulary Frequency Properties

We performed word frequency analyses to better determine the nature of the corpus. As "F-16 brevity comm" suggests, the vocabulary within the transcripts is remarkably small when compared to everyday human spoken or written language. After looking at over 70,000 lines of transcript text, the number of unique words was 894. This indicates the team uses a restricted vocabulary that is task-specific, showing little extraneous language used during missions.

Vocabulary Distribution Properties

Because the communication vocabulary here is small compared to everyday spoken language, and knowing that LSA is aware of how words are distributed, we wanted to see if the reduced vocabulary's overall frequency distribution was similar to "regular" human language.

As a benchmark for a "regular" language's word frequency distribution, we used Zipf's law, which states that the frequency of occurrence of some event (P), is a function of the rank (i) when the rank is determined by the above frequency of occurrence, is a power-law function $P_i \sim 1/i^a$ with the exponent a close to unity (1). In other words, the first word appears most frequently, the second word appears approximately one half of that frequency, the third with one third of the frequency, the fourth with one fourth, and so forth. The following plot shows the transcripts' word frequencies

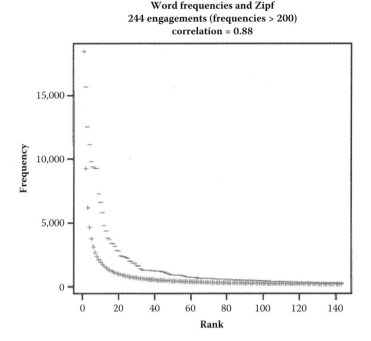

Figure 35.9 Frequency distribution of words in communication.

(the minuses) compared to Zipf's law (the plusses) (Figure 35.9). Words with frequencies below 200 are not shown to better display the curve.

Even though the transcripts' vocabulary are small, it is still reasonable to conclude here that the words are still distributed (in frequency) similarly to other natural languages. This model functioned as a cursory "natural language recognizer" suggesting our statistical knowledge experience in other natural languages could be reliably applied here. Zipf's law is not the only measure by any means. Further information can be found in Manning and Schutze (1999) as well as Jurafsky and Martin (2000).

The Speech Recognition Problem

For use in the Communication Analysis Pipeline, either in near-real time or in an After Action Briefing, human-typed transcription of the speech to text is not possible; therefore, the speech-to-text transcription must be produced automatically. Output produced by commercial Speech Recognition (SR) systems is known to contain errors, even under the best of conditions. The question we want to answer is how robust is LSA in the presence of such noise? In particular, how well does LSA correlate with human assessment of performance as errors are introduced into mission communications transcripts?

In prior work, LSA has been tested for the analysis of ASR input for a limited portion of a dataset of verbal communication (see Foltz, Laham, & Derr, 2003; Laham, Bennett, & Derr, 2003). The results indicated that even with typical ASR systems degrading word recognition by 40%, LSA's prediction performance degraded less than 10%. Thus, combining an ASR system with LSA shows that one can potentially still have robust performance with fairly high ASR rates.

In the present research, all of the text within the transcripts was processed automatically through the Nuance ASR system. Each transcript utterance (line) was accompanied by an ASR confidence value (0–100). We evaluated these confidence values to see the overall average, the standard deviation, and to see if these values varied significantly across missions and engagements. The average recognition confidence value from the ASR system was 42. The distribution indicated that our transcript text was likely not perfect; the transcripts would contain speech recognition errors. Visual transcript inspections during analysis confirmed this. One concrete example witnessed was "that's good tanks" instead of "that's good, thanks."

All of these observations suggested the ASR system added transcription errors. If the ASR system's errors are deterministic (misrecognizes the same words the same predictable ways), it is less of an issue than if the errors are random. This is because LSA is agnostic about which "words" are learned overall. LSA is more concerned with which words appear in which contexts with the other words (whatever those words may be). So if the ASR system deterministically misrecognizes a particular word in the same manner, the LSA learning is essentially unaffected. This relative symbol indifference is one of the main reasons why LSA can perform well with other languages with little a priori linguistic knowledge.

Speaker Frequency Properties

In the communication transcripts, along with confidence values and utterance text, radio identifications indicate which radio produced the utterance. Here we plot the relative pilot speaker frequencies per engagement (Figure 35.10). While frequency analysis is not new, it provides useful information. Note that speaker frequencies alone indicate the relative role the speaker plays within the team.

The x-axis is the percentage of the utterances spoken within the engagements. For example, Viper 1 typically speaks about 28% of the total engagement utterances. This plot is important

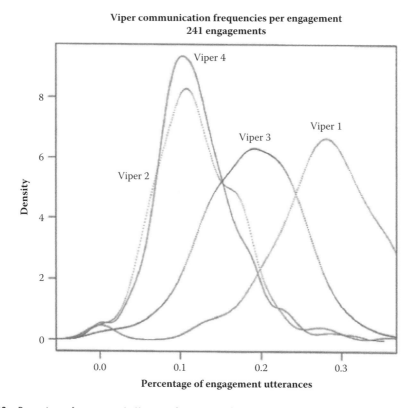

Figure 35.10   Percentage of engagement utterances by team member.

because it demonstrates identifying team roles based on speaker frequency alone. If one has voice identification ability, one can identify Vipers 1 and 3 (the flight leads) based on the frequencies of their transmissions. Vipers 2 and 4, which are typically in supporting roles, communicate less (and a similar amount). The difference between Vipers 1 and 3 is because in four-ship operations, Viper 1 is the flight lead while Viper 3 plays a subordinate role.

Speaker frequencies can help predict team performance. In a two-ship, if Viper 3 is killed, Viper 4's speaker frequency will often show this by going up. Certainly Viper 3's frequency would cease to increase. In these cases and others, it is useful to look at the ratios of the speakers to each other to distill additional team dynamics.

Team Performance Prediction Results

Separate models were created to predict each indicator using 230 engagement transcripts suitable for analysis. All subjective indicators were on a 1 through 5 discrete scale. The individual encounter scores were averaged to create engagement-level scores. AFRL also provided a subset of objective indicators for team performance.

Each predictive model for each indicator used the same LSA semantic space derived from information relevant to the domain. The model used an LSA k-nearest measure with a series of other natural language measures that have been used in characterizing essay quality and that account for effects of word order (see Landauer, Laham, & Foltz, 2001). Using a stepwise regression model, the system built a model that incorporated the best measures. Using these models, we computed predicted scores for both the subjective and objective indicators. The following tables show the correlation of the final models' predicted versus observed scores (Tables 35.1 and 35.2). All results are positive and significant, showing that our models are capable of accurately predicting team performance from ASR-based transcripts of communication.

Discussion on Team Communication Results

Overall, the results show that the LSA-based approach is able to provide accurate predictions of objective and subjective performance measures from speech-recognized transcripts. Related work has been done on the intergrader reliability within the grade sheets that preceded our subjective dataset. In Krusmark, Schrieber, and Bennett, (2004), intergrader reliability on grade sheets was studied on four of seven SMEs: "Intergrader reliability (alpha) of graded performance varied greatly across indicators. For most indicators, the reliability coefficient was small, suggesting that

Table 35.1   Subjective Indicator Prediction Results (Human-Rated SPOTLITE indicators)

Indicator	r ($p < .0001$)
Rate the communication about the detection	.40
Position, picture, and planning	.58
Do the fighters recognize and react to bandit maneuver?	.42
Does the flight shoot in accordance with shot doctrine?	.44
Rate the communications on targeting, sorting, and shot(s)	.50
Does the team effectively manage the engagement zone?	.35
Aggregate overall semantic analysis grade	.54
Aggregate overall communications grade	.42
Aggregate overall engagement grade	.44

SPOTLITE = Scenario-Based Performance Observation Tool for Learning in Team Environments.

Table 35.2   Objective Indicator Prediction Results (Human-Rated Performance Evaluation Tracking System Indicators)

Indicator	r ($p < .0001$)
Participant group number	.80
Mission essential competency (focused/based/unknown)	.74
Data link (yes/no)	.68
Mission number	.67
Day of week for engagement	.63
Mission engagement number	.53

the estimated reliability of graded performance on these indicators is questionable. The average alpha across indicators was .42 (SD = .13)." Thus, we believe within the subjective human-rated tasks, the predictive technology approaches the rating reliability of the humans/SMEs. Without explicit intergrader reliability correlations over the current subjective data subset, however, this is difficult to know with certainty.

The training of our models is sensitive to the accuracy, consistency, and agreement between the human raters. An ideal training set is where all raters agree and rate accurately and similarly. Conversely, a detrimentally noisy training set is where the human raters score inaccurately and concurrently always disagree. If our subjective interrater reliability is similar to the grade sheet interrater reliability, our models would be approaching the agreement limits of the human raters. This is one explanation for the upper values of our model correlations for subjective indicators.

Also supporting this is that our models consistently predict more accurately when training on and predicting the objective indicators (the participant group, data link, day of the week, and so forth). Because the humans are not present to disagree on these indicators, the interrater agreement "noise" limit is effectively removed. Additionally, there was evidence that the objective models not only predicted better, but they may also generalize better.

It is possible that some of the objective indicators may be "easier" to recognize within the transcripts. Certainly different types of scenarios are consistently run on specific days of the week. (This could also make day of the week and mission number more colinear.) Also, the scenario difficulty is known to be designed to increase during the week. The use of a data link will also certainly affect features appearing within transcripts (length being one of them).

However, these alternate explanations do not clearly account for the favorable performance when predicting the individual participant groups. When presented with an unidentified engagement transcript, our model is able to predict which team (participant group) actually performed that transcript. This indicator is likely independent of the day of week and the increasing scenario difficulty during the course of a week. By this reasoning, it is still consistent to suspect the original theory that the interrater agreement within our SPOTLITE subset may be near the grade sheet agreement level. This is also a more parsimonious explanation for why the majority of the objective indicators show higher correlations.

Aside from undetermined interrater reliability, there were some uncertainties during the process of joining the indicator data to the transcript data. It was not necessarily possible to know if all the corresponding scores were assigned to the right transcripts. This was because within our process, some SPOTLITE / PETS squadron numbers did not always match those assigned in the DMO test bed schedule spreadsheets.

In terms of being able to determine how well the model is able to predict relevant components of team member, the most useful indicator we employed was the increased predictive performance of the communications-intensive indicators. When predicting based on transcript data alone, one would expect to see stronger predictive performance on communications-intensive indicators. Within SPOTLITE, the three top performers were as follows:

.58 – Position, picture, and planning
.54 – Aggregate overall SA grade
.50 – Rate the communications on targeting, sorting, and shot(s)

All of these involve planning operations. They are more communications intensive. During these planning periods within an engagement, there is a comparatively large amount of communications between not only the team members, but also with the AWACS. We theorize that the models perform best on these SA and communications-related indicators because planning is where the majority of the engagement transcript is produced. This has the largest influence on what our LSA approach learns and it affects the models accordingly.

Conversely, at the bottom of the performance list were as follows:

.35 – Does the team effectively manage the engagement zone?
.40 – Rate the communication about the detection
.42 – Do the fighters recognize and react to bandit maneuver?
.42 – Aggregate overall communications grade

Regarding engagement zone management, this certainly involves many more skills than just communicating on the radio. This also holds for recognizing and reacting to an enemy threat. These other skills leave less of a communications trace in a transcript. Because of this, these two indicators are likely more difficult to predict from communications transcripts alone. Nevertheless, despite not having a major communication focus, they are still significantly predicted through communication analysis.

CONCLUSIONS

This chapter has shown two different approaches to career and performance evaluation. Nevertheless, both use the same underlying technology, a computational approach that can model domain knowledge and perform effective analyses of the similarity of information within the domain. The work shows that such technology can cover a wide range of applications for assigning, monitoring, assessing, and training personnel throughout their careers. Ideally, the modeling of the career, task, and activity information from CareerMap can be combined within models of the Team Communication Analysis to automatically monitor the progress of personnel within training and operational tasks. Through the Communication Analysis monitor, an individual can be tracked as he or she acquires skills in complex tasks. As the individual acquires additional skills, this information can be automatically updated within CareerMap, indicating which tasks, jobs, and teams might be most relevant for an individual at a particular time.

CareerMap

CareerMap software represents an initial demonstration of a usable World Wide Web-based Intelligent Agent for matching personnel to tasks. It demonstrates the necessary capabilities to match mission and job requirement statements with military personnel and training data. By measuring semantic similarity of training materials and tests, it facilitates combining occupations based on core competencies and similar work activities. It also helps to identify individuals qualified for work activities for which no current occupation exists.

An organization that has acquired a new or revised system can develop detailed descriptions of the activities required to operate or to maintain the system, based on system requirements documents, operations manuals, or provided by SMEs. Given such descriptions, and assuming an increase in its knowledge, CareerMap could automatically identify current jobs on fielded systems that are similar in component work activities and in their requirements for training. It could also identify similar paragraphs in existing course materials and rank them by probable relevance to work with the new system.

New occupations could be structured around these activities and new sets of training materials assembled, at least in major part, from subsets of existing material. In addition, individuals who work in jobs that use subsets of the competencies and experience required can be identified. This may permit the immediate employment of appropriate personnel or their more rapid and effective retraining for work in support of new systems. In this way, CareerMap could help the military to exploit Internet and other training resources to achieve information and training superiority.

The increasingly rapid rate of change in technology and in organizational structures means that employees, especially those in high-tech companies and organizations, are frequently transferred into new positions. Organizations are faced with frequent need to assemble new groups or departments, or even whole new branches or businesses. This effort may ultimately produce a cost-effective capability to systematically mine occupational personnel and training databases to develop new job and training structures to support a variety of requirements. This capability will help employers identify critical characteristics and competencies associated with work activities and then to identify individuals who have the requisite experience and competencies to perform the identified work activities.

Automated Mission Communications Analysis

The automated communication analysis work suggests that individuals and teams can be effectively monitored as they perform tasks without requiring full use of SMEs. The capabilities suggested by the work described—to automatically and in real-time predict levels of team performance based on their communications and to identify and diagnose common error patterns—should provide DMT systems with an enormous instructional advantage over current systems. The success of LSA-based tools are indicators of continuing improvement in simulator systems that will ultimately lead to better and more cost-effective training for personnel in realistic complex environments.

The results outlined in this chapter show the success in using our approach to record voice communication, automatically convert it to text with ASR, and then provide accurate LSA-based predictive models of team performance. These models appear to have reliability close to those of the human SME raters. Thus, the development of automated applications for monitoring and assessing performance of teams during distributed missions appears feasible and useful. The technology can be developed into a more complete toolset of techniques to analyze individual and team performance. Such a toolset has the potential for providing near-real-time assessment (within seconds) of individual and team performance including measures of situation awareness, knowledge gaps, workload, team errors, and group dynamics as well as predictions of future performance based on analyses of the current context.

The integration of such a toolset into personnel performance monitoring systems can be used to develop systems that can adapt interfaces to provide optimal team performance. By performing real-time monitoring, assessing, diagnosing, and adjusting feedback for teams, a host of products can be developed for improving training in simulators as well as monitoring live-real time communication. These products can include systems for generating automated After Action Reports, training systems to provide instant automated feedback to teams not functioning properly in Distributed Mission Training, and monitoring systems that can notify commanders of teams that need help.

There remain a number of opportunities and augmentations that can be done to enhance performance as well as to provide demonstrations of further integration of the technology described in this chapter. These augmentations include refinements to both CareerMap and the Team Communication Analysis tools, as well as work to integrate the two into a complete system for tracking, training, and assigning personnel throughout their career.

REFERENCES

Berry, M. W., Dumais, S. T., & O'Brien, G. W. (1995). Using linear algebra for intelligent information retrieval. *SIAM Review, 37,* 573–595.

Deerwester, S., Dumais, S. T., Furnas, G. W., Landauer, T. K., & Harshman, R. (1990). Indexing by latent semantic analysis. *Journal of the American Society for Information Science, 41,* 391–407.

Dumais, S. T. (1994). Latent Semantic Indexing (LSI) and TREC-2. In D. Harman (Ed.), *The Second Text REtrieval Conference (TREC2)* (pp. 105–116). Washington, DC: National Institute of Standards and Technology.

Foltz, P. W. (1996) Latent Semantic Analysis for text-based research. *Behavior Research Methods, Instruments and Computers, 28,* 197–202.

Foltz, P. W. (2005). *Tools for enhancing team performance through automated modeling of the content of team discourse.* Presented at HCI International 2005, Las Vegas, NV.

Foltz, P. W., Lavoie, N., Oberbreckling, R., & Rosenstein, M. (2007). Tools for automated analysis of networked verbal communication. *Network Science Report, 1,* 19–24.

Foltz, P. W., Laham, R. D., & Derr, M. (2003). *Automated speech recognition for modeling team performance.* Presented at the 47th Annual Human Factors and Ergonomic Society Meeting, Denver, CO.

Foltz, P. W., Martin, M. A., Abdelali, A., Rosenstein, M. B., & Oberbreckling, R. J. (2006). *Automated team discourse modeling: Test of performance and generalization.* Presented at the 28th Annual Cognitive Science Conference, Vancouver, BC, Canada

Hoffman, T. (1999). *Probabilistic latent semantic analysis.* Presented at the 15th Conference on Uncertainty in Artificial Intelligence, Stockholm, Sweden.

Jurafsky, D., & Martin, J. H. (2000). *Speech and language processing: An introduction to natural language processing, computational linguistics, and speech recognition.* Upper Saddle River, NJ: Prentice Hall.

Kiekel, P. A., Cooke, N. J., Foltz, P. W., Gorman, J., & Martin, M. M. (2002). *Some promising results of communication-based automatic measures of team cognition.* Presented at the Human Factors and Ergonomics Society 46th Annual Meeting, Baltimore, MD.

Krusmark, M., Schreiber, B. T., & Bennett, W. Jr. (2004). *The effectiveness of a traditional gradesheet for measuring air combat team performance in simulated distributed mission operations* (AFRL-HE-AZ-TR-2004-0090). Air Force Research Laboratory, Warfighter Readiness Research Division.

Laham, D., Bennett, W. Jr., & Landauer, T. K. (2000). An LSA-based software tool for matching jobs, people, and instruction. *Interactive Learning Environments, 9,* 1–15.

Laham, D., Bennett, W. Jr., & Derr, M. (2002, December). *Latent semantic analysis for career field analysis and information operations.* Presented at the Interservice/Industry Training, Simulation and Education Conference (I/ITSEC). Orlando, FL.

Landauer, T. K., & Dumais, S. T. (1997). A solution to Plato's problem: The Latent Semantic Analysis theory of the acquisition, induction, and representation of knowledge. *Psychological Review, 104,* 211–240.

Landauer, T. K., Foltz, P. W., & Laham, D. (1998). Introduction to latent semantic analysis. *Discourse Processes, 25,* 259–284.

Landauer, T. K., Laham, D., & Foltz, P. W. (2000). The debate on automated essay grading: The intelligent essay assessor. *IEEE Intelligent Systems, 15,* 22–37.

LaVoie, N., Streeter, L., Lochbaum, K., Wroblewski, D., Boyce, L. A., Krupnick, C. & Psotka, J. (2007). Automating expertise in collaborative learning environments. *Journal of Asynchronous Learning Networks, 11*(1), 2327.

Lochbaum, K., Psotka, J., & Streeter, L. (2002, December). *Harnessing the power of peers.* Presented at the Interservice/Industry, Simulation and Education Conference (I/ITSEC), Orlando, FL.

Lochbaum, K., Psotka, J., & Streeter, J. (2002, December). *Exploiting technology to harness the power of peers.* Presented at the Proceedings of Interservice/Industry Training, Simulation and Education Conference (I/ITSEC), Orlando, FL.

Manning, C., & Schutze, H. (1999). *Foundations of statistical natural language processing.* Cambridge, MA: The MIT Press.

36

The Science and Practice of Job Analysis Abroad

REBECCA LYONS
University of Central Florida

PETER MUSAEUS
Aarhus University

EDUARDO SALAS
University of Central Florida

KATHERINE A. WILSON
University of Central Florida

Job analysis is a fundamental organizational practice all over the world. Within the United States, the nascency of scientific job analysis as a systematic discipline can be attributed to early efforts in the industrial age to improve the process of work. Most recognized are Frederick W. Taylor (1911) and Frank and Lillian Gilbreth's (1919) time and motion studies at the beginning of the 20th century. Building upon the success of such work, literature over the last century bears witness to the continued study and utilization of job analysis within the United States (e.g., Algera & Greuter, 1998; Brannick & Levine, 2002; Cronshaw, 1998; Gael, 1988; Landau & Rohmert, 1989); yet, less has been published (in English) about how these processes are studied and applied internationally. This is despite the fact that the analysis of jobs spans different cultures, societies, and historical epochs—for example, ancient China around 1115 B.C. (Mitchell, 1988), ancient Greece around the 5th century B.C., and France around the 17th century (Primoff & Fine, 1988). To our knowledge, there is no up-to-date and comprehensive literature review of empirical job analysis as addressed outside of the United States. Because of the globalization of business and expatriation of workers, theorists and practitioners can no longer limit themselves to the practices of their home country. To help optimize the relationships and productivity between U.S. organizations and their counterparts abroad, it is necessary to understand the respective job analysis practices used in these countries.

The primary purpose of this chapter is to review the literature on job analysis research and practice abroad (i.e., conducted outside the United States and with non-U.S. subject populations); the terms *non-U.S.*, *abroad*, and *international* are used interchangeably throughout the chapter. In our discussion of this literature, we identify both (a) methods of job analysis, and (b) trends or themes in the applications of job analysis abroad. As a secondary objective, we briefly discuss three distinctions perceived by non-U.S. authors in the respective theoretical backgrounds that have informed job analysis in continental Europe compared the United States. To ensure a comprehensive review, we include literature that is conceptually similar to job analysis, namely content from the areas of task analysis and competency modeling. The decision to include literature from these areas was based on input from researchers and practitioners abroad, who naturally integrate these analysis approaches into their discussions of job analysis. As such, our discussion will integrate the literature from these topics within the larger discussion of job analysis.

THE REVIEW PROCESS

To obtain an understanding of job analysis work abroad, a comprehensive literature review was conducted to identify publications addressing methods of job analysis and their applications. Our literature review took a three-prong approach. First, we conducted an online search of the most common academic databases (e.g., PsycINFO, Academic Search Premier, EBSCOhost) using keywords common to this domain. Keywords included, but were not limited to, *job analysis, ergonomic job analysis, Arbeitswissenschaftliches Erhebungsverfahren zur Tätigkeitsanalyse (AET), Instrument for Stress-Oriented Task Analysis (ISTA),* and *Job Components Inventory (JCI).* Studies were included only if they focused on populations and processes outside of the United States. Second, the ancestry approach (i.e., a process in which the reference lists of all identified relevant literature are reviewed to identify additional relevant works) was used on all obtained and relevant empirical articles to identify studies that had been overlooked in the initial search. For the third and final step, attempts were made to contact prominent academics within the United Kingdom, Germany, the Netherlands, Israel, Hong Kong, and Canada (as these locations had authors who previously published on job analysis for which e-mail addresses were available) to see if they had knowledge of any current manuscripts or in-press publications in the area of job analysis. From these communications, it was determined that both task analysis and competency modeling were considered within the boundaries of job analysis. Thus, the online search and ancestry approaches were expanded using terms such as *task analysis, hierarchical task analysis (HTA), competency approach,* and *competence modeling.*

Due to language barriers caused by the international component of this review, only articles published in English or for which translations were available are included in this review. However, to provide sufficient background information on the various measures described in the review, we consulted various non-English sources when necessary (most notably Dunckel, 1999; http://www.baua.de; http://www.assessment-info.de). We acknowledge that the articles identified represent only a portion of the existing literature in various national languages. Our investigation identified several popular job analysis methods and purposes towards which job analysis has been applied. We discuss these next.

JOB ANALYSIS

Job analysis is a means of increasing clarity about job requirements and can be functionally defined as "the systematic process of discovery of the nature of a job by dividing it into smaller units, where the process results in one or more written products" (Brannick & Levine, 2002, p. 9). More specifically, the analysis process is used to identify either the specific tasks required for a given job and/or the specific knowledge, skills, abilities, and other attributes (KSAOs) an individual would need to successfully perform a job. Due to the ample discussion of the specifics of job analysis throughout this handbook, we do not further describe the general concept of job analysis within this chapter. However, to be consistent with distinctions commonly made in the U.S. literature (e.g., Brannick & Levine, 2002; McCormick & Jeanneret, 1988), our discussion is based around two primary categorizations of analyses: job-oriented analysis and worker-oriented analysis. In each of these categories, we first provide a review of the relevant analysis methods and then summarize the primary purposes for which the analysis methods were used. Although the job- and worker-oriented distinctions have been made for the benefit of the reader, it should be noted that authors outside the United States have less commonly categorized job analysis procedures in this fashion. Further, as many analysis methods contain elements of both job- and worker-oriented approaches, categorization decisions were based on the aspects of the measure most commonly emphasized within literature, as well as the stated aims of the procedure.

Job-Oriented Analysis

Job-oriented methods of analysis focus primarily on understanding the tasks a worker performs on the job and how the work is done. The information provided by job-oriented measures is used to help organizations, for example, identify the tasks of highest importance for a given position, the tasks which take the most time, or the tasks that are of the greatest difficulty to perform. Through our review of the literature, seven measurement methods were identified, which we discuss as job-oriented. We describe these next. An overview of these methods is available in Table 36.1.

Job-Oriented Measures

Analysis of Job Structures and Design in Automated Processes

The Analysis of Job Structures and Design in Automated Processes (ATAA; *Verfahren zur Analyse von Tätigkeitsstrukturen und prospektive Arbeitsgestaltung bei Automatisierung;* Wächter, Modrow-Thiel, & Schmitz, 1989), translated as "procedure for the analysis of activity structures and prospective work design by automation," is a job-oriented method of analysis that originated in Germany. According to Wächter, Modrow-Thiel, and Rossmann (1994), this instrument was developed to anticipate, evaluate, and redesign work forms under automation in the metal-working industry. The ATAA is aimed at objective task analysis and investigates the range of a worker's actual or possible actions while performing a task.

Task/Activity Analysis Inventory

Also from Germany, the Task/Activity Analysis Inventory (TAI, *Tätigkeits-Analyse-Inventar* in German; Frieling, Facauaru, Bendix, Pfaus, & Sonntag, 1993) is considered to be one of the most comprehensive job-oriented analytic instruments. It investigates safety, or potential exposure to danger, by analyzing the stressors and risk factors caused by technical and organizational conditions (Brauchler & Landau, 1998). The TAI also assesses the design of workplaces, physical and information demands, and qualification requirements. The TAI builds on activity theory (Leont'ev & Hall, 1978), action regulation theory (Hacker, 2003; Volpert, 1982), behavioral job analysis (McCormick & Jeanneret, 1988), and strain and demand analysis (Rohmert & Rutenfranz, 1975).

Safety Diagnosis Questionnaire

The Safety Diagnosis Questionnaire (SDQ, *Fragebogen zur Sicherheits-diagnose;* Hoyos & Bernhardt, 1987) is a standardized measure for assessing safety in the workplace. At the time of its development, the SDQ was progressive in that it considered the human behaviors related to safety versus a pure engineering approach. In the measurement process, the SDQ is similar to standard format job inventories such as the Position Analysis Questionnaire (PAQ; Hoyos & Ruppert, 1995). Both observation and inventory methods are used in gathering safety information. Through this procedure, potential physical hazards within the work environment and work tasks are identified, and also the behavioral requirements of safe performance.

Table 36.1 Job-Oriented Methods Abroad

Method	Investigative Purpose	Country of Origin	Description	Reference
Analysis of Job Structures and Design in Automated Processes	Analyze work content, disequilibria, and divergences in the hierarchical and sequential organization of tasks	Germany	105-item questionnaire with five dimensions: (a) orientation, (b) planning, (c) doing, (d) monitoring, and (e) interaction	Wächter, Modrow-Thiel, & Rossmann (1994)
Task/Activity Analysis Inventory	Assess workplace design; analyze stress and risk	Germany	2,055 items divided across 7 topics: (a) organization, (b) location and production area, (c) work conditions, (d) work content—sensor motor, (e) work content—information processing, (f) work content—information and tool use, and (g) personal data	Stahl, Muetze, & Luczak (2000)
Safety Diagnosis Questionnaire	Assess the degree of safety within the workplace and identify potential hazards	Germany	149 items addressing seven categories: (a) the workplace, (b) hazards and danger, (c) perceiving and attending hazard signals, (d) judging and foreseeing hazards, (e) planning and preventing, (f) acting, and (g) cooperating and communicating	Hoyos & Ruppert (1995)
Hierarchical Task Analysis	Analyze tasks in terms of goal hierarchies	United Kingdom	A seven-step process that hierarchically decomposes tasks in terms of goals and subgoals and identifies the operations (inputs, actions, feedback) that lead to goal attainment	Annett (2004), Annett & Stanton (2006)
Hand Tool Work Analysis Method	Analyze hand-operated nonpowered tool use	Germany	62-item questionnaire with five dimensions: (a) tasks, (b) work object, (c) work equipment, (d) work environment, and (e) work demands	Peterson, Wakula, & Landau (1999)
Workplace Design Checklist	Identify deficits in workplace design by assessing job requirements and the working conditions	Germany	138 items from the *Arbeitswissenschaftliches Erhebungsverfahren zur Tätigkeitsanalyse* (completed by a job analysis rater) related to body postures, physical support, work space, tools and controls, visual conditions, motion sequence, work surfaces, and environmental influences	Landau & Peters (2006)
Mensch-Technik-Organisations-Analyse	Analyze and evaluate the organization at the system level and down	Germany	An eight-step processes that analyses the organization from the top down, starting at the level of the enterprise and completing with the level of the individual; incorporates expert interviews, document analysis, company tours, group interviews, observational interviews, and written questionnaires	Strohm & Ulich (1998)

Hierarchical Task Analysis

Hierarchical Task Analysis (HTA) is a method of task analysis, developed in the United Kingdom in the 1960s (Annett & Duncan, 1967). As with other task analysis methods, HTA serves to obtain a better understanding of the intricacies of a task by breaking it down into break down into smaller components. Traditional task analysis methods are most suited for the analysis of standard, routine tasks; however, technological advancements have gradually changed the nature of many tasks by automating the physical demands of many tasks, increasing the cognitive demands on the worker. HTA was intended to help overcome the shortcomings of traditional task analysis for analyzing modern work tasks.

A primary distinction of HTA is that it emphasizes functional analysis over behavioral. Specifically, HTA seeks to hierarchically decompose work by defining tasks in terms of a hierarchy of goals and subgoals, and then identifying the operations required to achieve these goals. This approach has since been applied for multiple purposes including training development, system design, error analysis, and others (Annett, 2003, 2004). Although commended for is versatility across contexts and purposes (Shepherd, 2001), some have commented (e.g., Kieras & Meyer, 2000) that in the prime of its hype in Continental Europe, HTA received surprising little attention in the United States.

Hand Tool Work Analysis Method

The Hand Tool Work Analysis Method (HTWAM; Peterson, Wakula, & Landau, 1999) was derived from a German job analysis measure, the *Arbeitswissenschaftliches Erhebungsverfahren zur Tätigkeitsanalyse* (AET). The AET is an ergonomic job analysis approach addressed in detail later; however, the AET includes dimensions consistent with both work- and worker-oriented job analysis approaches, and the HTWAM aligns with components focusing on the analysis of the task and work system. The HTWAM contains a subset of 62 of the 216 AET items. Specifically, the HTWAM asks about the task, work object, equipment, work environment, and work demands required for a task. This content is applied to analyze the use of hand-operated nonpower tools.

Peterson and colleagues designed the HTWAM for use in viticulture (the science and production of grapes), where it was found to be effective in identifying shortcomings in system design and for informing the development of guidelines for the ergonomic design of hand tools, including safety precautions and the avoidance of health risks. Although designed for use in the viticulture industry, the HTWAM has been effectively applied in other occupations.

Workplace Design Checklist

Like the HTWAM, the Workplace Design Checklist (WDC; Landau & Bokranz, 1986) also derives from the AET. The WDC acts as a short version of the AET, drawing 138 of its 216 items. This item subset was selected for its capacity to assess the requirements and working conditions for a given position. More specifically, items relate to body postures, motion sequences, physical support, workspace, tools and controls, visual conditions, work surfaces, and other environmental influences. This measure is intended to be completed by a job analysis rater.

Mensch-Technik-Organisations-Analyse

Taking a multilevel approach to analysis, the *Mensch-Technik-Organisations-Analyse* (MTO; i.e., human-technology-organization-analysis) focuses on understanding work from the top down (Strohm & Ulich, 1998). To do this, the analysis procedure first considers the enterprise (e.g., strategies, product and production requirements), then organizational units (e.g., division of labor, units' functional separation or integration), groups (e.g., collective regulation of work), and finally the individual (e.g., employee's perceptions of the work conditions). Each level of analysis depends on the previous. This measure was developed from the sociotechnical system theory (Trist & Bamforth, 1951) and action regulation theory. Items were borrowed from tools like the SALSA (*Salutogenetische Subjektive Arbeitsanalyse*, discussed under worker-oriented measures) and *Verfahren zur Ermittlung von Regulationserfordernissen* (VERA), discussed in detail later in the chapter.

Applications of Job-Oriented Analyses

The preceding section provided background information on seven job analysis measures that we consider to focus on the job itself. In examining literature relevant to these methodologies, several trends emerge related to their application. More specifically, the job-oriented methods addressed in the previous section were predominantly applied towards two primary areas: system design/assessment and the analysis of team skills. Select research relevant to each of these applications is reviewed next. Table 36.2 presents additional literature relevant to each theme.

System Design and Assessment

Much research using a job-oriented analysis has focused on system design and assessment. One line of research in the area of system design stemmed from the HTA literature. Although our literature review only revealed three publications directly addressing task analysis related to system design, it would appear that task analysis for the purpose of system design and assessment is a method more commonly applied than written about. This assumption is based on the report of Ainsworth and Marshall (1998), who discussed the results of two surveys examining nearly 100 task analysis studies in the United Kingdom's defense and nuclear industries. Their report indicated system development and assessment as key objectives for the defense field. Furthermore, all of the task analysis applications in the nuclear industry were conducted either to aid in design decisions for new systems or to help validate existing systems. Although the use of task analysis within system design and development appears to be widely used, at least within the United Kingdom, Ainsworth and Marshall noted that measure inconsistencies (e.g., data sources, method, level of detail) influence the success of task analysis for system design and evaluation. The authors called for further study of task analysis techniques to help determine which approaches provide the most valuable output for various organizational needs.

Umbers and Reiersen (1995) described another incident in which task analysis was applied toward the goal of system design. Specifically, HTA was used as an aid in the design and development of five U.K. nuclear power plant safety systems. The purpose of HTA within this study was to help determine if the proposed designs were feasible both for the workers' and the organization's time constraints. More specifically, HTA was performed to provide information about the operations required, the information/equipment required for each operation, the number of staff involved, and the amount of time each action required. Task networks presenting the most logical sequence of tasks for each job position were determined to be a suitable means for predicting design feasibility.

In a third study, O'Hare, Wiggins, Williams, and Wong (1998) evaluated the usefulness of cognitive task analysis (CTA; i.e., a method for evaluating the knowledge required to perform a task; Schraagen, Chipman, & Shalin, 2000) for the purpose of system design. The authors described a case study of emergency ambulance dispatchers in Sydney, Australia, in which CTA was used to help in the redesign of ambulance dispatch display systems. More specifically, CTA was applied to determine what information dispatchers require to make appropriate dispatch decisions. In theory, CTA thus aids in the design of new systems by helping system developers to understand the information which is most critical to performance.

Table 36.2   Selected Job-Oriented Citations by Purpose

General Purpose	Method	Specific Use	Description of Use	Location	Reference
Systems design and assessment					
	Analysis of Job Structures and Design in Automated Processes	Information source	Used in the assessment of prospective work design in 131 workplaces	Germany	Wächter, Modrow-Thiel, & Roßmann (1994)
	Generic job analysis	Information source	Used to help produce a job description of occupational welfare officers working in Israeli civil services	Israel	Bargal & Shamir (1984)
	Hierarchical Task Analysis	System evaluation	Served as a tool to determine the feasibility of a system design based on the physical time and workers required.	United Kingdom	Umbers & Reirsen (1995)
	Hand Tool Work Analysis Method	Method evaluation	Analyzed hand work in the following occupations: viticulture, electrician, forestry worker, building laborer, bricklayer and tiler	Germany	Peterson, Wakula, & Landau (1999)
	Komplementäre Analyse und Gestaltung von Produktionsaufgaben in soziotechnischen Systemen (KOMPASS)	System design	Used to evaluate the human-machine system, work tasks of the human operator versus the work system	Switzerland	Grote et al. (2000)
	Items from Position Analysis Questionnaire, *Arbeitswissenschaftliches Erhebungsverfahren zur Tätigkeitsanalyse*	Job design	Used in an evaluation using job analysis and object-oriented modeling tools to develop a novel modeling method to analyze poorly defined information.	Germany	Stahl, Muteze, & Luczak (2000)
	Mensch-Technik-Organisations-Analyse	Information source	Analyzing the Australian documentary film industry	Australia	Jones & Kirsch (2004)
	Rechnergestütztes Dialogverfahren zur psychologischen Bewertung von Arbeitsinhalten (REBA)	Information source	Created job profiles by analyzing tasks, workflow, and the time associated with each task for 40 different jobs.	Sweden	Lantz & Brav (2007)
	Task Analysis	Method evaluation	Evaluated for effectiveness in contributing to system design and assessment.	United Kingdom	Ainsworth & Marshall (1998)
	Job Evaluation System/Task Diagnosis Survey	Information source	Used for the classification of jobs in terms of high strain versus low strain, personal development and psychophysiological outcomes	Germany	Rau (2004)
	Workplace Design Checklist	System evaluation	Assessed ergonomic factors and sequences of movement to identify design deficiencies	Germany	Landau & Peters (2006)

continued

Table 36.2   Selected Job-Oriented Citations by Purpose   (Continued)

General Purpose	Method	Specific Use	Description of Use	Location	Reference
Analyzing team skills					
	Team Hierarchical Task Analysis	Team skill measurement	Served as a means for identifying objective measures of team process outcomes	United Kingdom	Annett & Cunningham (2000)
	Team Hierarchical Task Analysis	Team skill measurement	Served to help validate the teamwork model proposed by Annett (1997)	United Kingdom	Annett, Cunningham, & Mathias-Jones (2000)
Other					
	Conventional, competency-focused	Predictor	Evaluated job analysis as a predictor of performance	United Arab Emirates	Siddique (2004)

Apart from task analysis, there are other lines of job-oriented analysis within ergonomics that focus on job redesign. In fact, many of the methods (especially European methods) listed in Table 36.1 focus on activity and task redesign. For example, Wächter et al. (1994) described a consulting project conducted for an automobile manufacturer in which the ATAA was used by consultants as a tool to evaluate the effectiveness of a work design plan developed by management and a works council. More precisely, the objective was to ascertain whether the automobile manufacturer's design had accomplished the declared aims to improve the training of personnel and utilization of personnel qualifications, and to facilitate autonomous planning and decision making by workers. The study reported that the ATAA not only served as an effective evaluation tool, but that the consultants reported that they were able to more intricately evaluate the work process to identify details in the work process that would otherwise have been missed. This tool was also effective in that it formed the basis for a dialogue between management and workers concerning workers' further education and designing work content towards this purpose.

Landau and Peters (2006) used the WDC in a study of 59 workplaces to assess ergonomic factors and movement sequences. The study found the following design deficiencies: unfavorable worker postures, failure to take into account variances in workers' body dimensions, level of applied forces, and load carrying. Furthermore, findings indicate that problems in the system design might lead to increased incidence of errors. The authors concluded that the WDC was sufficiently useful in revealing design deficiencies and pointing towards areas of redesign.

Team Skills Analysis

Another relevant and important application of job-oriented analysis is the application of task analysis for analyzing team skills. Annett (1997) provided a discussion of the potential for HTA as a means of understanding team skills (also see Annett & Stanton, 2006). More specifically, Annett proposed that HTA should emphasize the goals of a team, as it does the goal of individuals. As with individual goals, it is suggested that team goals could equally be decomposed to help understand team behavior. As a basis for understanding team goals, a teamwork model was proposed. This suggestion to apply HTA to teamwork was novel in that HTA had previously only been applied to the study of individuals.

To our knowledge, the first technical application of HTA to team analysis was performed by Annett and Cunningham (2000) for the purpose of analyzing naval command team skills. A goal of this analysis was that a set of objective measures could be developed to supplement or replace the subjective written assessments previously used to assess command teams. Furthermore, objective measures of performance would allow for better evaluation of team training procedures. In this study, teams were evaluated during a training program and analysis information was collected using a 30-item questionnaire related to attitudinal factors. From this analysis, eight factors (e.g., team familiarity, technical familiarity, communication) were identified, which accounted for 66% of the variance for predicting team outcomes. Team familiarity was the greatest individual contributor, accounting for 18.6% of the variance. Unfortunately, of the eight factors, only technical familiarity was predictive of performance as rated by experts. Thus, the authors indicated a necessary goal for future studies should be the use of more detailed HTA results, in hopes that this would allow for the identification of team process measures that more directly relate to team outcomes. In an effort to address this issue, Annett, Cunningham, and Mathias-Jones (2000) conducted a follow-up study in which HTA was used to analyze the team skills required by antisubmarine warfare teams. Based on the HTA output and the teamwork model proposed by Annett (1997), a scoring method was developed, which required a comparison between the number of occurrences of prespecified behavioral responses to preplanned trigger events. It was suggested that this scoring method could be used in future work to help validate the proposed by Annett (1997).

Worker-Oriented Analysis

Worker-oriented approaches to job analysis supplement the job-oriented approaches reviewed above by analyzing information about the specific KSAOs required of an individual worker to successfully perform a job. This category includes methods that directly measure KSAOs, as well as methods that indirectly inform on the required KSAOs by providing information about the work context. The results of such analyses can then be applied, for example, to assist organizations in selecting individuals who will be the most qualified or best suited for a given job. We selected 14 measures that were primarily worker oriented to discuss next (see Table 36.3). Several additional methods were also identified (e.g., *Fragebogen zur Arbeitsanalyse* [FAA]—the German version of the Position Analysis Questionnaire [PAQ]: Frieling & Hoyos, 1978; the KOMPASS from Switzerland: Grote, Ryser, Waler, Windischer, & Weik, 2000). However, due to a limited availability of information (in English), these methods will not be addressed within the present review.

Worker-Oriented Measures

Position Analysis Questionnaire

The Position Analysis Questionnaire (PAQ) is a worker-oriented analysis measure developed in the United States by McCormick and colleagues in the 1960s at Purdue (Brannick & Levine, 2002). It was later translated and validated into German in 1974 by Frieling, Kannheiser, and Lindberg. The measure was designed to draw upon the behavioral stimulus–organism–response model, addressing the interplay between individuals' work behavior and the environment. Information is gathered about the job using a combination of observations and interviews. Because a number of items require a high level of reading comprehension, it has been recommended that the measure be completed by an analyst. Because this measure is commonly addressed in the U.S. literature, we refer the reader to McCormick and Jeanneret (1988) for addition details on this approach.

Ergonomic Job Analysis Procedure

According to our review, among the most commonly cited job analysis techniques is the Ergonomic Job Analysis Procedure (AET; *Arbeitswissenschaftliches Erhebungsverfahren zur Tätigkeitsanalyse*) measure, translated as "ergonomic task (or activity) data analysis collection procedure." Originating

Table 36.3 Selected Worker-Oriented Methods Abroad

Method	Investigative Purpose	Country of Origin	Description	Reference
Position Analysis Questionnaire	Identify the person requirements of a job	United States	194 items relating to (a) Information input, (b) mediation (mental) processes, (c) work output, (d) interpersonal activities, (e) work situation and job context, (f) miscellaneous (e.g., compensation)	McCormick et al. (1969); McCormick & Jeanneret (1988)
Arbeitswissenschaftliches Erhebungsverfahren zur Tätigkeitsanalyse (AET)	Measure the degree of fit between the worker and required work in terms of the degree of strain caused by a given workload	Germany	216-item questionnaire capturing information related to (a) work system analysis, (b) task analysis (related to material work objects), and (c) job demand analysis (assessing both physical and mental demand)	Rohmert & Landau (1983); Rohmert (1988)
Instrument for Stress-Oriented Task Analysis	Assess stress-related problem areas within the workplace that need attention	Germany/ Switzerland	Developed in two versions, a questionnaire to be completed by job incumbents and a rating version to be completed by an observer; addresses three scales: (a) regulation requirements, (b) regulation possibilities, and (c) regulation obstacles	Semmer, Zapf, & Dunckel (1995, 1999)
Ergonomic Workplace Activity	Describe work activity, context, everyday life, work constraints and demands, and worker's strategies to protect health	France	A qualitative, ethnographic procedure with three stages: (a) general description, (b) preliminary observations, (c) detailed observations	De Keyser (1991); Messing, Chatigny, & Courville (1998)
Rechnergestütztes Dialogverfahren zur psychologischen Bewertung von Arbeitsinhalten (REBA)	Analysis the complete job	Germany	22 variables addressing five dimensions: (a) organizational prerequisites for sequential completeness, (b) demand on cooperation, (c) demand on responsibility, (d) cognitive demand, and (e) learning opportunities	Richter, Hemman, & Pohland (1999); Pohlandt et al. (2007)
Job Evaluation System	Analysis of the organizational tasks, decisions and work demands	Germany	Modular (52 scales) assessing 5 areas: (a) technological and organizational work requirements, (b) work-related cooperation and communication, (c) cognitive requirements, (d) responsibility, and (e) qualification and learning potential	Rau (2004)
Verfahren zur Ermittlung von Regulationserfordernissen (VERA)	Analysis of the regulation requirements of work tasks by analyzing the mental and planning processes induced by the task	Germany	Observation and interview methods are used to identify the regulation needs of a specific work task; the job acts as the unit of analysis	Volpert, Kötter, Gohde, & Weber (1989); Brauchler & Landau (1998)
Job Content Questionnaire	Analysis of the psychosocial demands of a job	United States	22 core items addressing five topic areas: (a) decision latitude, (b) psychological job demands, (c) social support, (d) coworker support, and (e) physical demands	Karasek (1989); Karasek et al. (1998)

Name	Purpose	Country	Description	Reference
Job Components Inventory	Analysis of the psychological and physical requirements of a job	Britain	Approximately 400-item questionnaire covering six topics: (a) tools and equipment use, (b) perceptual and physical requirements, (c) mathematical requirements, (d) communication requirements, (e) decision-making and responsibility requirements, and (f) job conditions	Banks (1988)
Develop a curriculum	Analysis of the knowledge, skills, abilities, and other attributes of a position and/or the broader competencies	Canada	A facilitated, workshop format information gathering session	Norton (1993)
Subjective job analysis	Analysis of work characteristics and work stress	Germany	50-item questionnaire with six dimensions: (a) scope of action, (b) transparency, (c) responsibility, (d) qualification, (e) social structure, (f) workload	Udris & Nibel (1989)
Salutogenic Subjective Work	Analysis of the work characteristics and work stress	Germany	60-item questionnaire with five dimensions: (a) work characteristics and qualification required, (b) work demands, (c) strains due to outer factors (e.g. noise), (d) organizational resources, and (e) social resources at work	Schnorpfeil et al (2002)
Work Profiling System	Analyze and calculate the most important tasks for a given job and identify the individual attributes associated with those tasks	England	Multisection questionnaire capturing information about the relevance of (a) general task categories, and then (b) individual task-items within selected categories; items vary based on occupational group (e.g., administrative/service)	Saville & Holdsworth Ltd. (1989, 1995)
Cognitive task analysis	Analyze the mental processes and skills required for performing cognitively complex, dynamic tasks	Europe and North America[a]	A process involving assessment of individual abilities and changes in knowledge, identifying task components, identifying conceptual and procedural knowledge of similar components, identifying what distinguishes novices from experts, identifying indicators distinguishing knowledge levels	Redding (1989); Kirwan & Ainsworth (1992)
Komplementäre Analyse und Gestaltung von Produktionsaufgaben in soziotechnischen Systemen (KOMPASS)	The human–machine system and the associated distribution of work between these two systems	Switzerland	Three dimensions: (a) the human–machine system, (b) work tasks of the human operator, and (c) the work system; topics such as tasks, autonomy, thinking and planning demands, learning possibilities, communication, authority, flexibility, and avoidance of strains are addressed	Grote, Waler, Windischer, & Weik (2000)

[a] CTA developed progressively through the merger or research and practice across Europe and North America.

in Germany, the AET was developed in response to a government investigation regarding wage discrimination between genders (Rohmert, 1988). An analysis technique was solicited that allowed for measurement of the degree of physical strain required for a given workload and which complied with new legal standards for industrial safety and quality of work life. Items on the AET were (at least in part) modeled after those in the well-established PAQ. Following suit of the PAQ, the AET is completed by an analyst and gathers information about the job using a combination of observations and interviews; however, diverging from the PAQ, the AET takes a broader, more ergonomics-based focus and is noted for placing a greater emphasis on equipment use than most job analysis measures (Brannick & Levine, 2002; Brannick, Levine, & Morgeson, 2007).

It can be disputed whether the AET is more appropriately considered a worker-oriented or job-oriented measure. This dispute arises largely due to the diversity of the three sections that comprise this measure: (a) work system analysis, (b) task analysis, and (c) job demand analysis. As noted, the job demands analysis section shares many content similarities to the PAQ (generally considered a worker-oriented analysis measure), and thus may be discussed as a worker-oriented measure (Brannick et al., 2007). However, the work system analysis and task analysis sections emphasize an understanding of the work conducted and more strongly align with work-oriented approaches. We chose to discuss the AET along with the worker-oriented approaches based on its primary application in the analysis of work-stress demands; however, we recognize the hybrid nature of this measure.

As evidence of the AETs prominence, it can be mentioned that universities in Darmstadt and Hohnheim, Germany, maintain AET databanks containing the results of more than 5,000 AET analyses (Ilmarinen, Suurnäkki, Nygård, & Landau, 1991). Additionally, the Institute of Occupational Health in Helsinki, Finland, has a databank of over 1,000 analyses. The AET has been used for a range of purposes. The three most frequently noted in this review include measuring a worker's physical and mental workloads (e.g., Seeber, Schmidt, Kiesswetter, & Rutenfranz, 1989), clustering jobs based on their physical demand level (e.g., Ilmarinen et al., 1991), and validating new instruments (e.g., Kemmlert, 1995).

Instrument for Stress-Oriented Task Analysis

Similar to the AET described above, another worker-oriented measure centered around the measurement of work stress is the Instrument for Stress-oriented Task Analysis (ISTA; *Instrument zur Stressbezogenen Tätigkeitsanalyse* in German). It has also been referenced as the Instrument for Stress-Related Job Analysis (e.g., Kinzl, Traweger, Trefalt, Riccabona, & Lederer, 2007). Proposed by Semmer (1982), the ISTA is a survey-based screening instrument designed to serve as a quick and easy means of analyzing the quality of task demands, control over work, and task related stressors. Problem areas in the work environment can be identified by estimating the stress associated with various tasks. Hence, it provides a general assessment of the work characteristics (e.g., How often are you pressed for time?) rather than highly specific information. Additionally, results are intended to inform on the characteristics of the job, independent of individual performance or experience level (Semmer & Zapf, 1989).

The measure is inspired both by action regulation theory (Hacker, 2003; Volpert, 1982) and transactional stress theory (Lazarus & Folkmann, 1984). Furthermore, the ISTA is distinguished from other stress-measurement techniques in that it focuses on chronic aspects of the job rather than single incidents (Semmer, Zapf, & Greif, 1996). Several versions of the ISTA are available, including short forms (e.g., Semmer, Zapf, & Dunckel, 1998, 1999); however, the 1999 version by Semmer and colleagues (Version 6) is commonly cited.

Several validation efforts have informed the present use of the ISTA. Early validation efforts explored multiple-versions of ISTA, as well as various rating measures, to evaluate how the measure should most appropriately be utilized. For example, Semmer and Zapf (1989) investigated the discriminant validity of three methods for rating stress. Incumbents' self-reports on the standard questionnaire version, ratings by trained observers on a rating version, as well as group estimates (i.e., the median questionnaire scores of 3 or more persons performing the same task) were compared for the dimensions of time pressure, organizational problems, uncertainty, and danger. Based on a sample of blue-collar workers, results indicated that all three measures were susceptible to strong method bias; however, group estimates appeared to provide the most valid and bias-free measure. Additionally, in comparing self-reports and observers, it appeared that observers had a greater degree of difficulty in differentiating between stressors. In a separate validation effort, the ISTA was also indicated as a valid instrument for assessing shared job strain (i.e., the mutual strain experienced by workers holding the same position). Two-thirds of the variance in shared job strain accounted for by the job stressors examined by the ISTA (Semmer et al., 1996).

Ergonomic Workplace Activity

Ergonomic Workplace Activity (EWA), sometimes simply referred to as analysis of activity, stems from the ergonomic work analysis of French ergonomists (for a discussion, see Daniellou, 2005; DeKeyser, 1991). The EWA is not a single method but rather an approach developed in Paris, France, under the influence of activity theory and phenomenology. Activity theory is based on historical materialism, which includes work such as studying people's actions in terms of the material societal activities and their production of work motives (Leont'ev & Hall, 1978). But the French EWA also has a phenomenological vein, with a focus on the everyday life of the worker (DeKeyser, 1991). Essentially the focus is both on the objective demands of the work and its impact on the worker's health as well as the worker's perspective on his or her social and material life. EWA later developed its own foundation, incorporating several other currents of thought (e.g., ethnographic and cognitive task analytic).

REBA: An Action-Oriented Software Tool

Another worker-oriented model based on the action regulation theory is the REBA (*Rechnergestütztes Dialogverfahren zur psychologischen Bewertung von Arbeitsinhalten* in German; Richter, Hemman, & Pohland, 1999). The REBA is an observation-based instrument that assesses a job in terms of five dimensions: organizational prerequisites for sequential completeness (e.g., number of different subtasks), demand on cooperation (e.g., contents of communication), demand on responsibility (e.g., group responsibility), cognitive demand (e.g., degree of participation in operational planning), and learning opportunities (e.g., use of qualifications). As a composite, these dimensions are intended to capture the complete job.

Job Evaluation System

The Job Evaluation System (TBS; *Tätigkeitsbewertungssystem* in German; Hacker, Iwanowa, & Richter, 1983), sometimes translated as Task Diagnosis Survey (TDS; Rudolph, Schönfelder, & Hacker, 1987), is a worker-oriented method aimed at analyzing and assessing the objective conditions of work activity. Theoretically, the procedure builds on action regulation theory. It analyzes the personality requirements of specific work activities and the causes of adverse work related effects such as stress and monotonous work. It exists in a long (TBS or TBS-L) and short form (TBS-K), as well as industry specific variants such as analyzing the building and construction industry, trading industry or office activities.

VERA: Procedure for Identifying Regulation Requirements in Jobs

Another worker-oriented method from Germany is the VERA (*Verfahren zur Ermittlung von Regulationserfordernissen*), literally translated as "Instrument to Identify Regulation Requirements in Industrial Work" (Volpert, Oesterreich, Gablenz-Kolakovic, Krogoll, & Resch, 1983). It is a psychological instrument for evaluating "the mental and planning processes of the worker that result from the specific action demands of the work task" (Volpert, Kötter, Gohde, & Weber, 1989, p. 882). Drawing on action theories, VERA was developed to assess the employee's opportunity to regulate his or her actions in fulfilling work tasks and can guide in the redesign of work. The instrument consists of a handbook and a manual with answer sheets. The manual is designed to be completed by a trained observer who assesses job incumbents as they work (Volpert et al., 1989; Webber & Oesterreich, 1989). Several versions of the VERA exist, which are designed for different occupational setting such as offices and hospitals.

Job Content Questionnaire

The Job Content Questionnaire (JCQ) is a self-administered instrument for assessing the social and psychosocial structure of a job. The measure was introduced by U.S. researcher Robert Karasek (1979) in the late 1970s and is well known for its basis on the demand-control model. In alignment with this model, the instrument includes items designed to assess the physical and psychological work demands, decision latitude, social support, and job insecurity (Karasek et al., 1998).

The JCQ is somewhat unique in that it was developed to support the cross-national comparison of jobs in terms of their psychosocial characteristics (Karasek, 1985; Karasek et al., 1998) and has been extremely successful towards this end. Our review identified literature incorporating JCQ versions in a minimum of eight versions distinct validated versions, including Japanese (Kawakami, Kobayashi, Araki, Haratani, & Furui, 1995; Kawakami & Fujigaki, 1996; Noborisaka, Ishizaki, & Yamada, 1995), Chinese for Taiwanese workers (C-JCQ; Cheng, Luh, & Guo, 2003), Chinese mainland (Li, Yang, Liu, Xu, & Cho, 2004), Korean (K-JCQ; Eum et al., 2007), Malay (Edimansyah, Rusli, Naing, & Mazalisah, 2006), Portugese (Araújo & Karasek, 2008), French (Brisson et al., 1998; Niedhammer, 2002), Dutch (Storms, Casaer, De Wit, Van Den Bergh, & Moens, 2001), and English (e.g., Seago & Faucett, 1997). Validation policies requiring the translation and back-translation of any translated versions of this survey have helped to ensure the integrity of the JCQ is maintained across versions. Additionally, validation studies have largely reported results that are generally comparable to those from the English version (Brisson et al., 1998; Karasek et al., 1998). However, where differences have been reported, reported deviations are most consistent surrounding the dimension of psychological demands. Specifically, both the Chinese mainland and C-JCQ versions, as well as the Malay and Dutch versions, reported internal consistency to be the lowest for this dimension (Cheng et al., 2003; Choi et al., 2008; Edimansyah et al., 2006; Karasek et al., 1998; Li et al., 2004; Storms et al., 2001). The cross-national nature of this measure provides a means of comparing jobs and worker experiences across cultures (Karasek et al., 1998). For example, based on research applying the JCQ as a measure of job stress, it is suggested that Japanese and U.S. workers differ in the psychological stress experienced by jobs requiring suppression of affective feelings (Kawakami & Haratani, 1999).

Job Components Inventory

In the early 1970s, the British Manpower Services Commission argued that there was a need to improve the preparation and training of youth for the workplace (Banks, 1988; Banks, Jackson, Stafford, & Warr, 1983). The idea was that vocation selection, along with later job mobility, would be enhanced if individuals were able to compare their current skills with the skills required for positions of interest; however, to do this, analysis of a wide variety of jobs was required because existing job analysis methods were not appropriate for analyzing KSAOs of the youth population. The JCI was developed to meet the project needs.

The JCI is a worker-oriented, fixed questionnaire consisting of approximately 400 items that shares the AET's emphasis on equipment. Specifically, the JCI covers a number of topics—the use of tools and equipment (e.g., the ability to operate a forklift), perceptual and physical requirements (e.g., the ability to climb a ladder), mathematical requirements (e.g., the ability to complete basic arithmetic), communication requirements (e.g., the ability to prepare memos), and decision-making and responsibility requirements (e.g., the ability to manage time efficiently). Additional information is also requested pertaining to job conditions (e.g., willingness and ability to work in extreme cold). Furthermore, at the time of its development, the JCI was unique in the following ways:

1. It used language that was accessible and appropriate for young adults in the British population who were preparing for entry-level, low-skill jobs.
2. It was designed so that professional analysts could be replaced by trained interviewers.
3. It was designed to be brief, making it easier to administer.
4. It provided greater flexibility by focusing on skills applicable to a wide range of occupations vice those necessary for a specific job (Banks, 1988).

Literature on the JCI as a job analysis tool is extremely limited.

DACUM: Develop a Curriculum

Originating in Canada in the early 1980s, Develop a Curriculum (DACUM) serves as a means to develop job profiles, training programs, performance tests, and needs-assessment analysis (Glendining, 1995; Norton, 1993). Like the JCI, the DACUM does not require an expert job analyst to complete it. However, unlike the JCI which involves an interview process, the DACUM analysis is performed directly by a group of experts who work together in a workshop format with the assistance of a facilitator (Peiser & Yaakov, 2004). Furthermore, the DACUM has been discussed by Rochow (n.d.), a Canadian Practitioner for CAPRA International, as capable of gathering data at both the level of general competences (i.e., broader areas of functioning) and/or at the element level (i.e., focusing on the specific tasks and skills required). In short, the DACUM likely serves as a measure for both analyzing of the KSAOs of a position and also the broader competencies. Our review indicated that the DACUM measure has proven successful at developing a competency model at the Virginia School of Nursing (Kosidlak, 1987). Though limited published literature was available on DACUM, our search indicated that it has also been applied at several locations in Europe, Asia, and Africa (Training Resource Center, 2007).

Subjective Job Analysis and Salutogenic Subjective Work

The Subjective Job Analysis (SAA, *Subjektive ArbeitsAnalyse*) and its derivative Salutogenic Subjective Work (SALSA, *Salutogenetische Subjektive Arbeitsanalyse*) are questionnaires for subjective work analysis (Udris & Nibel, 1989). SAA measures the subjective evaluation of work in terms of (a) alienation from work, specifically the degree of self-determination, social engagement and action potency; and (b) work stress, specifically the degree of qualitative and quantitative stimulation and under- and over-stimulation. The SALSA investigates person, work, private life and free time, personal attitude and most importantly health and disease with a focus on the factors that support human health (so-called salutogenic factors) in connection with work.

Work Profiling System

The Work Profiling System (WPS), developed in England by Saville and Holdsworth (1989, 1995), consists of three questionnaires, each applied for the analysis of a specific type of job:

(a) management and staff, (b) service and administration personnel, and (c) skilled and technical workers (Algera & Greuter, 1998). Each questionnaire consists of several sections related to different task categories, and individuals complete only those categories they perceive as most relevant to their job. Additionally, in the development of the WPS, individual attributes (e.g., personality) were identified relevant to each task included in the questionnaires. Thus, by identifying key tasks required by a job, the WPS can assist organizations in areas such as employee selection by suggesting the individual characteristics best suited to the job requirements. A unique feature of the WPS is that it can be completed and analyzed via computer.

Cognitive Task Analysis

As a modern variation on task analysis, Cognitive Task Analysis (CTA) emerged from the fields of cognitive psychology and the cognitive sciences, which emphasize the blending of computer science, engineering, and philosophy to describe the internal cognitive factors related to work (Hollnagel, 2003; O'Hare, 1998). The objective of CTA approaches is to analyze the mental processes required in the proficient performance of high complexity, dynamic tasks. Specially, CTA seeks to capture the knowledge, thought processes, and goal structures that underlie an individual's task performance (Schraagen et al., 2000).The information obtained through CTA offers particular value in system design and the development of training (Clark & Estes, 1996). A detailed description of this method can be found elsewhere in this volume.

Applications of Worker-Oriented Analyses

Further examining the literature, which has included the 16 worker-oriented measures previously addressed, several popular areas of application were identified (see Table 36.4). Key themes from this perspective include work-stress analysis, workforce preparation, selection, work-stress analysis, managerial performance, and training design. Select research relevant to each of these five applications is reviewed next.

Work-Stress Analysis

Commonly found in the international literature are applications of work-analytic measures for purposes of identifying and evaluating the mental and/or physical stress related to a task's characteristics. Of the previously introduced worker-oriented measures of job analysis, the AET, EWA, ISTA, JCQ, and TBS have all been used to inform on work stress. In looking across the literature, the underlying purposes for incorporating such analyses were to identify ergonomics-related issues in the work process, identify workload considerations related to the equality of jobs, or estimate the impact of workload on the job incumbent. Such workload considerations continue to be of great importance, as organizational practice and policy evolve to accommodate an ever-aging workforce.

One particularly notable effort in this area is the work launched by the Finnish Institute of Occupational Health, which spanned nearly two decades. The Finnish Institute of Occupation Health conducted a longitudinal study from 1981 to 1997 of aging municipal employees to better understand the impact of various occupations on work, lifestyle, health, functional capacity, and stress symptoms (Tuomi et al., 1997). Contributing to this research stream, Nygård and colleagues (1987) addressed the usefulness of AET for evaluating the degree of musculoskeletal load of various municipal occupations, with the ultimate goal of redefining retirement age criteria. As anticipated, AET results distinguished between occupational groups in the degree of musculoskeletal stress experienced. For example, workers in installation, auxiliary, home care, and transport groups experienced higher musculoskeletal loads, in comparison to positions such as teachers and administrative groups that experienced lower musculoskeletal loads. The authors inferred from these results that retirement ages should differ between occupational groups, at least related to

Table 36.4 Selected Worker-Oriented Citations by Purpose

General Purpose	Method of Analysis	Specific Use	Description of Use	Location	Reference
Work-stress analysis					
	Arbeitswissenschaftliches Erhebungsverfahren zur Tätigkeitsanalyse (AET)	Physical stress load measurement, clustering	Acted as a tool for clustering municipal jobs based on physical job demands to allow for the future study of relationship between work stress and health	Finland	Ilmarinen, Suurnäkki, Nygård, & Landau (1991)
	AET	Instrument validation	Served as a source of comparison to validate the PLIBEL, a new instrument for assessing musculoskeletal risk	Sweden	Kemmlert (1992)
	AET	Physical stress load measurement	Used to analyze musculoskeletal stress load of aging municipal employees in different occupation groups	Finland	Nygård, Suurnäkki, Landau, & Ilmarinen (1987)
	AET	Physical and mental load measurement	Tested as a tool for analyzing the physical and mental work demands of repetitive short cycle tasks	Germany	Seeber, Schmidt, Kiesswetter, & Rutenfranz (1989)
	AET	Information source, clustering	Applied as a tool for clustering 133 different occupational titles into 13 occupational groups	Finland	Seitsamo, Tuomi, & Martikainen (2006)
	Ergonomic Workplace Activity	Physical stress load measurement	Used to evaluation the physical stress demanded of various work tasks	Canada	Messing, Chatigny, & Courville (1998)
	Instrument for Stress-Oriented Task Analysis (ISTA)	Work stress measurement	Acted as a standard format by which self-report, observer, and group estimates of work stress could be compared	Germany	Seemer & Zapf (1989)
	ISTA	Shared stress measurement	Validated as a measurement tool for evaluating shared job strain across workers of the same job	Germany	Seemer, Zapf, & Greif (1996)
	ISTA	Work stress measurement	Used to analyze the stress impact of new technologies based on work content, environmental stressors, and resources	Germany	Zapf (1993)
	Job Content Questionnaire (JCQ)	Psychosocial job strain	Assessed the psychosocial job strain with experienced and inexperienced raters	British Columbia	Ostry et al. (2001)
	JCQ	Psychosocial job strain	Assessed job demands related to decision latitude, psychological demand, supervisor support, and coworker support	Japan	Kawakami et al. (1995)

continued

Table 36.4   Selected Worker-Oriented Citations by Purpose   (Continued)

General Purpose	Method of Analysis	Specific Use	Description of Use	Location	Reference
	Mento–Factor System	Mental work load measurement	Measured mental work load in flexible manufacturing systems (conceptually similar to AET)	Taiwan	Lin & Hwang (1998)
	Salutogenetische Subjektive Arbeitsanalyse	Information source	Assessed pathogenic and salutogenic work characteristics	Switzerland	Schnorpfeil et al. (2002)
	Safety Diagnosis Questionnaire	Instrument validation	Used in the identification of workplace hazards		Hoyos & Ruppert (1995)
	Verfahren zur Ermittlung von Regulationserfordernissen (VERA)	Mental and planning process measurement	Provided input for estimation of task regulation requirements in two case studies	Germany	Volpert, Kötter, Gohde, & Weber (1989)
Workforce preparation					
	Job Components Inventory (JCI)	Information source, clustering	Served as a tool for identifying job skills, which allowed for the clustering of occupations by job requirements	England	Stafford, Jackson, & Banks (1984)
Selection					
	Work Profiling System (WPS)	Information source	Served to identify the competencies required of an online facilitator by analyzing	South Africa	Cronjé, Adendorff, Meyer, & van Ryneveld (2006)
	Position Analysis Questionnaire (PAQ)	Information source	Served to identify job requirements of dentists for inclusion in selection instruments	South Africa	Ebersöhn & Maree (2003)
	WPS	Information source	Served as a tool for identifying task and personality requirements for food service providers	United Kingdom	Papadopoulou, Ineson, & Wilkie (2001)
	PAQ	Information source	Incorporated as one of many methods for developing a performance questionnaire	South Africa	Schepers (2008)
	Personality-oriented job analysis	Information source	Served to identify desirable personality traits for the position of Turkish Armed Forces officer	Turkey	Sümer, Sümer, Demirutku, & Çifci (2001)
	PAQ	Information source	Served to identify distinct occupations so jobs could be linked to Holland occupational codes	South Africa	Van der Merwe et al. (1990)

Managerial analysis

Method	Type	Description	Country	Reference
Multidimensional competences analysis	Method evaluation	Combined job, person, and role focused competencies to evaluate managerial performance	United Kingdom	Cheng, Dainty, & Moore (2005)
Competences analysis from previous study	Method evaluation	Served to evaluate the effectiveness, ability and importance of elements of competence elements for construction site managers	Australia	Fraser (1999)
Competences analysis	Information source	Provided a checklist of competences which could be used to evaluate training programs	England	North (1993)
Develop a curriculum	Information source	Used to identify the job competences required for a managerial position in an employment office	Israel	Peiser & Yaakov (2004)
Interviews, Hierarchical Task Analysis	Information source	Served to identify key managerial competencies for the development of a managerial model	China	Wang (2003)

Training design

Method	Type	Description	Country	Reference
Generic job analysis	Information source	Used to evaluate training of biotech-engineers (e.g., comprehension, communication, and teamwork skills) in connection with organizational and training factors in a manufacturing system	Israel	Doron & Marco (1999)
Cognitive Task Analysis (CTA)	Information source	Used to identify key cognitive areas related to performance on which training should focus	New Zealand	O'Hare, Wiggins, Williams, & Wong (1998)
CTA	Information source	Used to identify information utilized in emergency dispatch decision making for incorporation into system design	Australia	O'Hare, Wiggins, Williams, & Wong (1998)
VERA	Information source	Analyzed the work design to inform technical, organizational and training factors in a manufacturing system	Germany	Volpert et al. (1989)

Other

Method	Type	Description	Country	Reference
JCI (abbreviated)	Rater evaluation	Compared nurse-rated job characteristics versus job characteristic ratings of nursing–management	Netherlands	Boumans & Landeweerd (1992)
JCQ	Rater evaluation	Examined inter-rater reliability of expert job evaluators ratings of psychosocial job conditions	British Columbia	Ostry et al. (2001)
Work Profiling System	Rater evaluation	Compared managers, supervisors, and general employees ratings of task importance	England	Papadopoulou, Ineson, & Wilkie (1995)

musculoskeletal strain. However, a subsequent longitudinal study of the stability of physical and mental demands of Finnish municipal occupations over a four-year span suggested variation in work-stress demands over time, as well as by gender (Huuhtanen, Nygård, Tuomi, Eskelinen, & Toikkanen, 1991).

Work-stress has also been considered in terms of the role that stress-related job characteristics may play in the musculoskeletal and physiological health of a worker. For example, a study of fish industry workers in Sweden reported that female workers were more susceptible to negative musculoskeletal health issues due to the conditions of their work environment (i.e., posture, physical movements required) than were men (Nordander et al., 1999). The TBS and JCQ have also been applied towards understanding the physical effects of stress. In France, Rau (2004) elected to examine the physiological consequences of work-stress characteristics at a more microlevel. Specifically, self-reports about job characteristics, collected through the TBS analysis measure, were analyzed to evaluate the influence of task requirements and work strains on psychophysiological outcomes, including blood pressure, heart rate, and mood. In comparison, the JCQ has been utilized to consider the longer term health consequences of work-stress characteristics. The JCQ has been extremely well accepted within healthcare research, where it has been used to examine the influence of psychosocial work environment factors on individual health and the development of psychosomatic disorders (e.g., cardiovascular disease; Brisson et al., 1998).

Additional research has specifically emphasized the mental workload caused by a particular task. For example, Lin and Hwang (1998) described what they called the Mento-Facto System, a measure conceptually similar to the AET, but which focuses on mental over physical tasks. They used this Mento-Facto System to develop an index of mental workload within supervisory tasks (i.e., the degree to which mental processes such as visual perception, discrimination, and decision making, are required). Though the authors suggest that the Mento-Facto System may serve as a supplement to the AET, unfortunately, no additional studies could be located addressing this measure. Despite this shortcoming, studies from Austria, Germany, France, Switzerland, and Canada inform on of psychological-demands and consequences of work-stress characteristics on the psychological health of a worker.

From the healthcare domain, several studies in Austria have used the ISTA to analyze the work of anesthesiology staff in order to better understand how working conditions influence the experience of chronic stress, burnout, and job satisfaction in this population (Kinzl et al., 2005, 2007; Lederer, Kinzl, Trefalt, Traweger, & Benzer, 2006). Similarly, Sonnentag, Kuttler, and Fritz (2010) used the ISTA scales to survey the job stressors experienced by protestant pastors in Switzerland and how various job feature influence psychological detachment from the job while at home, as well as emotional exhaustion and need for recovery.

Workforce Preparation

One application of worker-oriented approaches to job analysis is worker preparation for the workforce. As worker-oriented approaches are generally geared towards identifying the KSAOs required for various jobs, results from these measures can act as a checklist for evaluating an individual's preparedness or fit for a specific job. From a counseling perspective, results may be used to help individuals identify the careers for which they are currently the best prepared. Those pursuing in a specific career path can plan ahead to ensure they develop the appropriate KSAOs they will need to be employable in the future.

Our review identified only one study that directly applied job analysis to inform a career guidance tool; however, we felt its purpose was novel and should be recognized. Specifically, Stafford, Jackson, and Banks (1984) attempted to identify occupational clusters within the youth labor market by using the JCI item responses as inputs for a cluster analysis. Results of the analysis indicated six main occupational clusters (i.e., clerical work, skilled interpersonal work, operative work, unskilled manual work, intermediate skilled technical work, and skilled technical work). Based on these results, Stafford and colleagues suggested that such information could be applied to help students focus their skill development and to help train students in their interest areas.

Selection

Another theme within the international literature is the application of worker-oriented job analysis for selection purposes. As in the United States, job analysis is being applied internationally to assist in determining selection criteria and to identify worker attributes. Several studies demonstrating this application will be discussed next.

First, Sümer, Sümer, Demirutku, and Çifci (2001) used a personality-oriented measure of job analysis in an attempt to identify desirable personality features for the selection of Turkish Armed Forces officers. Two consecutive studies were used to identify potentially relevant personality constructs. In the first study, semistructured interviews of current and formerly employed officers were completed to provide initial personality variable identification. The interviews resulted in a list of 72 attributes, with "conscientiousness, respect for chain of command, honesty, orderliness, adaptability, military discipline, and planning" (p. 135) most consistently emphasized. In a second study, the attributes were each evaluate in terms of their relevance and importance to the role of officer. Through these efforts, five personality factors were identified as being important for selection— conscientiousness/self-discipline, military factor, self-confidence, agreeableness/extraversion, and leadership. These outcomes provide support for personality as a potential selection measure.

Ebersöhn and Maree (2003) applied job analysis as a means to determine selection criteria for dentistry students. Specifically, the PAQ (as described above) was used to identify job requirements for dentists which could be used in selection. Criteria that appeared most relevant to future success included the individual's physical potential (e.g., finger dexterity), cognitive potential (e.g., aptitude in science), interpersonal potential (e.g., clear communication), and personality. Based on these results, it was determined that the current selection procedure lacked appropriate consideration of the life skills students would need after program completion (e.g., strong communication, realistic work schedule expectations).

Finally, in South Africa, Cronjé, Adendorff, Meyer, and van Ryneveld (2006) explored the factors that contribute to the success of online students (given that dropout rates in online courses are very high). As another component of this investigation, WPS was used as a basis for identifying cognitive, affective, and psychomotor competencies associated with observable facilitator actions. The authors proposed that the competencies identified through this analysis could be applied to help identify traditional classroom instructors that would be most likely to successfully transfer to online teaching.

Management Analysis

Also apparent within the worker-oriented techniques was an applied focus on identifying competences for the purpose of management development. Although few publications indicated a specific procedure for identifying competences, the DACUM was recognized as one measure used to identify necessary managerial competences. For example, Peiser and Yaakov (2004) discussed the successful application of DACUM in an Israeli company with the purpose of analyzing a management position at an employment office. They felt the use of a skilled and experienced moderator was critical to the success of the DACUM approach. Although the measure was praised for its requirement of group consensus and elimination of variance between raters, it was noted that this feature could equally be viewed as a negative aspect in that it prevents the expression of individual differences between experts. Furthermore, it is unlikely that all experts would have the same perspective.

Extending beyond the DACUM, a number of articles were identified that focused on the use of competences in management development, and have been extensively addressed (though not exclusively) by those in the United Kingdom, Canada, and China. For example, Robotham and Jubb (1996) discussed the appropriateness of using a competence approach for measuring the performance of managers. While noting the widespread use of competences as a means of measuring managerial performance, the authors expressed concern over the current ambiguity associated with these applications. It is argued that practitioners tend to assume that managerial competences can be applied across industries; however, the wide array of functions which mangers perform suggests otherwise (see Currie & Darby, 1995 and Jubb & Robotham, 1997, for a further discussion).

Additional discussion of management analysis was provided by North (1993), who applied a competence-based approach to the review of management training. Specifically, the British Employment Service surveyed over 1,000 managers using a competence checklist and identified several strengths associated with its use. For example, the method can be framed as a generic checklist and used by a large number of people at once, allowing for its use companywide. In addition, it provides a useful means of comparing the views of various management levels as to what is important in each job. A problem identified with such approaches, however, was that the complexity of many managerial positions may require a list that is excessively long. Further, concern was expressed about the ability of managerial competences to apply across organizations.

In China, Wang (2003) used a combination of interviews and hierarchical job analysis to develop a model of managerial competence. The model proposes three dimensions: (a) a leadership competence strategy, (b) a leadership networking strategy, and (c) a leadership commitment strategy. Further research is required to test the appropriateness of this model; although additional literature has been published on this topic (e.g., Wang & Chen, 2002), Wang (2003) was the only article available in English. This is not surprising when considering that the use of Westernized human resource practices is relatively new in China. Wang notes that it is only within the last 20 years that economic reform and social changes have allowed for the application of Western human resource practices.

Training Design Analysis

Task analysis approaches have been highly applied as tools in the development of training programs. Specific to this purpose, Annett and Duncan (1967) provided suggestions for the application of task analysis to training design. HTA contributes to the training design process by systematically identifying the content of a job, and then assisting in the prioritization of specific content areas for training based on difficulty. This information, along with consideration of task importance, can be applied to helps ensure that training programs address the most relevant and critical skills. Shepherd (1985) presents a similar discussion, proposing HTA as a basis for training decisions.

Application of task analysis for training purposes is demonstrated by two New Zealand case studies that applied CTA toward the understanding of the positions of whitewater rafting guide and general aviation pilot (O'Hare et al., 1998). In both cases, CTA outcomes were used as an information source for identifying the key cognitive processes to be addressed in training. Specifically, CTA outcomes for the whitewater rafting guide position revealed a key need for rapid decision making. A tool was suggested to train perception and judgment training by providing videos requiring guides to make judgments based on visual cues. Similar to guide outcomes, results from the CTA of aviation pilots indicated that novices should be trained to visually discern environmental cues in order to make the correct responses. Thus, a multimedia weather-related decision making tutorial system was designed to help pilots learn to differentiate between weather-related visual cues.

DISTINCTIONS IN THE THEORETICAL BACKGROUNDS THAT INFORM JOB ANALYSIS

Thus far in our review, we have excluded any discussion of job analysis as conducted in the United States, focusing strictly on developing an awareness of the job analysis measures and practices beyond the United States as portrayed through the literature. We now shift our discussion to a comparison of the predominant theoretical backgrounds upon which job analysis methods have traditionally been developed in continental Europe versus the United States. To inform this discussion, we draw upon several publications by authors outside of the United States that provide comment on job analysis theories and practices across countries (e.g., Krause & Gebert, 2003). We further make inferences based on the trends observed in our review, as to the extent to which these respective theoretical backgrounds remain evident in the current research and practice of job analysis. The objective in this section is not to make a systematic international comparison of all job analysis approaches, applications, and practices. Rather, we will consider general differences in the theoretical backgrounds underlying job analysis, and how these backgrounds have influenced the methods and practice of job analysis in various locations. As the majority of the non-U.S. literature represents work from European countries, we will restrict our comparison to our continental European counterparts.

Key strands of job analysis, most notably in continental Europe, have relied upon fundamentally different theoretical grounds than the United States. For example, organizational research in much of continental Europe has been heavily inspired by the Marxist theory of historical materialism (e.g. Daniellou, 2005; Hacker, 2003), which was previously introduced in our discussion of the EWA approach under worker-oriented measures. As a reminder, the theory of historical materialism emphasizes the embeddedness of acts in motive-directed societal, as well as institutional, activities. Conducting organizational research consistent with this approach necessitates looking beyond an analysis of the features and characteristics of a job and the physical work environment to consider the individual experience in performing activities, and the impact on broader social existence.

In contrast, the United States, from early on, was recognized by countries abroad as placing place great emphasis on qualitative empirical approaches to the study of industrial-organizational psychology. Early emphasis on job analysis as a tool for enhancing organizational productivity and managerial issues, without an equal emphasis on broader societal responsibilities, acted as a deterrent to the adoption of similar practices by foreign counterparts. For example, in the 1960s academic researchers in Holland expressed interest in the U.S. approaches, but were eventually dissuaded by strong social beliefs that such methods prioritized managerial interests of productivity and efficiency (Zickar & Gibby, 2007) and failed to equally support and protect workers and broader societal well-being (Warr, 2007).

The impact of these historical differences in terms of research and practice can be broadly inferred by the trends in the literature. Overall, the United States and continental European countries have applied job analysis for a host of similar purposes; however, differences are highly evident in terms of the prominence of these applications. In reviews of the U.S. literature, applications of job analysis generally address the development of job descriptions and selection procedures, the design of job evaluation and performance appraisal systems, the identification of training needs, and job design and redesign (e.g., Ash, 1988; Brannick & Levine, 2002). Ultimately, these applications support the productivity of the organization, but offer less to the overall well being of the individual. Although the same applications were noted in the non-U.S. literature, our review of job analysis beyond the United States was dominated by methods centering on the measurement of physical and mental demands placed on a worker by various tasks, in terms of the consequences of these work demands on the immediate and long-term mental and physical health of an individual. The U.S. literature also includes work-stress studies such as those abroad, but to a much lesser extent.

A second theoretical distinction between U.S. and European job analysis was suggested by Leplat (2004), who argued that the job analysis or psychological analysis of work as practiced in France is different from the taxonomic types of analysis more common in Anglo-Saxon countries. Aligning with previously addressed Marxist theory, and as mentioned previously in this chapter, there is a phenomenological inspiration in French ergonomics, which expands beyond a worker's experience in the immediate work environment to encompass the worker's life as a whole. In contrast, the traditional job analysis measures related to the Anglo-Saxon taxonomies, as common to early U.S. practice, break down the working environment into posited subcomponents, without consideration for or assessment of the individual's environment beyond their work.

According to DeKeyser (1991), the phenomenological focus of French ergonomics has separated supporters of this taxonomy from the traditional, Anglo-Saxon taxonomies of task and work analysis because traditional job analysis measures are not equipped to sufficiently represent the full spectrum of life factors considered by the phenomenological approach. This distinction helps to explain the near absence of common U.S. job-analysis approaches and the imbalance high ratio of worker- to work-oriented methods.

Another perspective from which to consider the historical backgrounds of job analysis in the United States and abroad is through the disciplines through which it has been examined. Warr (2007) has argued that compared to the United States, occupational psychology in the United Kingdom has borrowed more from allied disciplines, such as ergonomics. This theoretical blending is evident in that for many of the job analysis measures reviewed in this chapter, in that there is a blurred line between job analysis and ergonomics. Contemporary job analysis measures (both abroad and in the United States), such as CTA, ergonomic work system analysis (Carayon, Alvarado, & Hundt, 2007), and competence approaches, have evolved from cross-disciplinary fields. One area in the international literature in which this merge is evident is in the strong emphasis placed on job analysis as redesign, compared to traditional procedures. The focus on redesign is characteristic of theories such as activity theory and action regulation theory (e.g., see Hacker, 2003). Although the United States has been suggested as somewhat slower to adapt (e.g., Kieras & Meyers, 2000), recent years have demonstrated an increased acceptance for such contemporary approaches, particularly in terms of increased interest in the understanding the worker and the cognitive processes involved in task performance.

FUTURE DIRECTIONS

Although much knowledge was gained through this review, several constraints were encountered in reviewing this literature. We use these factors to highlight three areas for future research. First, the most notable challenge faced in this review was the inability to access the full range of job analysis literature abroad due to language barriers. This limited our knowledge regarding any specific area of job analysis by the extent to which the topic has been addressed within literature published in English. Although it is clear through our review (particularly through a historiometric review of article references) that a large body of international literature exists, a significant portion of this literature was not accessible in English. Thus language restriction might give a misrepresentation of job analysis measures and applications since a large body of literature (in Chinese, French, and German, for instance) was excluded. To effectively understand the literature abroad, greater efforts are required to translate, compare, and conduct research across national boundaries. Publications in English were significantly less available from continental Asia versus continental Europe. Collaboration efforts are needed to identify and translate this literature.

Still another area for future works is reevaluating the boundaries of job analysis as a construct. A second complication emerges in identifying the specific names for job analysis. Beyond the language barriers noted, an additional range restriction within our review could have occurred due to the fact that there are countless different names for specific job analysis measures. Also, relevant measures are not necessarily explicitly stated as measures of job (or work) analysis, increasing the probability of overlooking such measures if not previously aware of their specific titles.

The process of identifying a comprehensive inventory of job analysis methods is further confounded by the ill-defined and evolving boundaries (in the United States and abroad) regarding how job analysis should be conceived in the modern work environment and the methodologies that may constitute job analysis (Wilson, 2007). Traditional analysis measures were generally designed for the analysis of fairly stable tasks, or for identifying the behaviors and behavioral sequences of individuals performing such tasks. Although such measures have been highly effective in providing comprehensive, detailed analyses of behavioral tasks, traditional analysis measures have come under attack in recent years due primarily to changes in the structure of the work environment (Sanchez & Levine, 2000; Van Wart, 2000). As addressed previously, modern technological advancements have changed the nature of many tasks to increase cognitive demands on the worker. Thus, measures accessing the cognitive nature of the task (e.g., cognitive task analysis) are of growing necessity, often replacing more traditional behavioral job analysis instruments. Furthermore, the dynamic nature of jobs in 21st century can make maintaining accurate job information based on traditional job analysis measures impractical. Competency modeling is proposed as one potential solution to this issue, identifying characteristics required by an individual for a specific task; yet, competencies have the benefit of being transferable (Klemp, 1980). Jobs in the future will call for analysis measures that provide greater sensitivity to cognitive, contextual, and interactional descriptions (Carson & Stewart, 1996; Sanchez & Levine, 2000). There is a shared global need to critically assess contemporary approaches to job analysis.

A third important element for consideration in future work is the physical practice of job analysis abroad (i.e., how job analysis measures are used in international organizations). Although some indications are gleaned from our review of the empirical literature, the general trends in this literature may contribute to false assumptions about the actual procedures applied in business practice. Therefore, communication and research with organizations abroad is required to determine which measures are used and how they are applied. It should not be blindly assumed that business practices commonly applied and deemed successful in the United States will be equally relevant and successful within other cultures. A better understanding of the measures and practices used abroad may enhance inferences of the intercultural transferability of various measures by allowing for comparisons between specific procedural, as well as contextual, and content similarities between various measures of analysis. Additionally, following the example of the JCQ which has established guidelines (involving validation of translations) for its use, efforts to validate other existing job analysis measures in cultures beyond that for which the measure was initially validated will contribute to the understanding of the intercultural appropriateness of job analysis measures and practice.

CONCLUSION

Job analysis is indisputably a recognized and integrated organizational practice in countries around the globe, yet the discussions of job analysis measures and applications as used beyond the United States have been relatively limited in reviews by U.S. authors. Furthermore, despite sufficient evidence of the study and application of job analysis abroad, organizations continue struggling to merge local and national practices (Aycan, 2005). Due to globalization, the future success of organizations in this expanding market depends, at least in part, on their ability to understand the business practices of the countries they work with. Thus, our primary objective within this chapter was to broaden awareness of job analysis measures and practices outside the United States. Towards this goal, this review provided an introductory look at job analysis from an international perspective.

In our review of the literature, 21 measures were described (in English) in sufficient detail for inclusion in this review. Applications of these measures were noted in one or more of 18 countries and across five continents. Across the non-U.S. literature, a strong bias towards measures emphasizing worker-oriented approaches was noted. Theoretical backgrounds from which job analysis has evolved, particularly within continental Europe, can help us understand these trends. Furthermore, in addition to a presentation of the measures discussed by non-U.S. populations, this chapter has also summarized seven key areas of interest related to the application of job analysis measures. Specifically, we focused on job analysis applied to work-stress analysis, system design and assessment, training design, the measurement of team skills, workforce preparation, selection, and managerial analysis. The most widespread of these application areas, and also the most distinct from the U.S. literature, was the European emphasis on the use of work-stress analysis to better anticipate and plan for the growing population of elderly workers. Recent literature increasingly suggests similarities in the practice of job analysis, as the globalization of work and technological advancements generate common organizational challenges.

We hope this review will stimulate additional efforts towards understanding job analysis across the globe. This could lead to both practical benefits (e.g., competitive advantage) and greater cross-fertilization, where international approaches might inform studies and practices in the United States and vice versa. Just as organizations are merging efforts across national boundaries towards increased business productivity, researchers and practitioners must also work together in furthering the field of job analysis. There is clearly not a single or easy way to make job analysis universally more sensitive to context and cultural differences; however, studying internationally developed job analysis procedures and practices represents a vital first step in approaching this problem.

REFERENCES

Ainsworth, L., & Marshall, E. (1998). Issues of quality and practicability in task analysis: Preliminary results from two surveys. *Ergonomics, 41*(11), 1607–1617.

Algera, J. A., & Greuter, M. A. M. (1998). Job analysis. In J. D. P. Drenth, H. Thierry, & C. J. Wolff (Eds.), *Handbook of work and organizational psychology* (pp. 141–164). East Sussex, UK: Psychology Press.

Annett, J. (1997). Analysing team skills. In R. Flin, E. Salas, M. Strub, & L. Martin (Eds.), *Decision making under stress: Emerging themes and applications* (pp. 315–325). Aldershot, UK: Ashgate.

Annett, J. (2003). Hierarchical task analysis. In E. Hollnagel (Ed.), *Handbook of cognitive task design* (pp.17–35). Mahwah, NJ: Lawrence Erlbaum Associates.

Annett, J. (2004). Hierarchical task analysis. In D. Diaper, & N. A. Stanton (Eds.), *The handbook of task analysis for human-computer interaction* (pp. 67–82). Mahwah, NJ: Lawrence Erlbaum Associates.

Annett, J., & Cunningham, D. (2000). Analyzing command team skills. In J. M. Schraagen, S. F. Chipman, & V. L. Shalin (Eds.), *Cognitive task analysis* (pp. 401–415). Mahwah, NJ: Lawrence Erlbaum Associates.

Annett, J., & Cunningham, D., & Mathias-Jones, P. (2000). A method for measuring team skills. *Ergonomics, 43*(8), 1076–1094.

Annett, J., & Duncan, K. D. (1967). Task analysis and training design. *Occupational Psychology, 41*, 211–221.

Annett, J., & Stanton, N. (2006). Task analysis. In G. P. Hodgkinson & J. K. Ford (Eds.), *International review of industrial and organizational psychology* (Vol. 21, pp. 45–78). New York, NY: John Wiley & Sons.

Araújo, T. M., & Karasek, R. (2008). Validity and reliability of the job content questionnaire in formal and informal jobs in Brazil. *Scandinavian Journal of Work, Environment & Health, 34*, 52–59.

Ash, R. A. (1988). Job analysis in the world of work. In S. Gale (Ed.), *The job analysis handbook for business, industry, and government* (Vol. 1, pp. 3–13). New York, NY: John Wiley.

Aycan, A. (2005). The interplay between cultural and institutional/structural contingencies in human resource management practices. *International Journal of Human Resource Management*, 16(7), 1083–1119.

Banks, M. H. (1988). Job components inventory. In S. Gale (Ed.), *The job analysis handbook for business, industry, and government* (Vol. 2, pp. 960–990). New York, NY: John Wiley.

Banks, M. H., Jackson, P. R., Stafford, E. M., & Warr, P. B. (1983). The job components inventory and the analysis of jobs requiring limited skill. *Personnel Psychology*, 36, 57–66.

Bargal, D., & Shamir, B. (1984). Job description of occupational welfare: A tool in role development. *Administration in Social Work*, 8(1), 59–71.

Boumans, N. P. G., & Landeweerd, J. A. (1992). Some problems concerning the assessment of job characteristics in nursing work. *European Work and Organizational Psychologist*, 2, 303–317.

Brannick, M. T., & Levine, E. L. (2002). *Job analysis: Methods, research, and applications for human resource management in the new millennium*. Thousand Oaks, CA: Sage Publications.

Brannick, M. T., Levine, E. L., & Morgeson (2007). *Job and work analysis: Methods, research, and applications for human resource management* (2nd ed.). Thousand Oaks, CA: Sage Publications.

Brauchler, R., & Landau, K. (1998). Task analysis: Part II – the scientific basis (knowledge base) for the guide. *International Journal of Industrial Ergonomics*, 22, 13–35.

Brisson, C., Blanchette, C., Guimont, C., Dion, G., Moisan, J., Vézina, M., et al. (1998). Reliability and validity of the French version of the 18-item Karasek Job Content Questionnaire. *Work & Stress*, 12, 322–336.

Carayon, P., Alvarado, C. J., & Hundt, A. S. (2007). Work design and patient safety. *Theoretical Issues in Ergonomics Science*, 8(5), 395–428.

Carson, K. P., & Stewart, G. L. (1996). Job analysis and the sociotechnical approach to quality: A critical examination. *Journal of Quality Management*, 1(1), 49–65.

Cheng, M. I., Dainty, A. R., & Moore, D. R. (2005). Towards a multidimensional competency-based managerial performance framework: A hybrid approach. *Journal of Managerial Psychology*, 20(5), 380–396.

Cheng, Y., Luh, W. M., & Guo, Y. L. (2003). Reliability and validity of the Chinese version of the job content questionnaire in Taiwanese workers. *International Journal of Behavioral Medicine*, 10, 15–30.

Choi, B. K., Kawakami, N., Chang, S. J., Koh, S. B., Bjorner, J., Punnett, L., et al. (2008). A cross-national study on the multidimensional characteristics of the five-item psychological demands scale of the job content questionnaire. *International Journal of Behavioral Medicine*, 15, 120–132.

Clark, R. E., & Estes, F. (1996). Cognitive task analysis for training. *International Journal of Educational Research*, 25(5), 403–417.

Cronjé, J. C., Adendorff, D. E., Meyer, S. M., & van Ryneveld, L. (2006). Surviving the shipwreck: What makes online students stay online and learn? *Journal of Educational Technology & Society*, 9(4), 185–193.

Cronshaw, S. (1998). Job analysis: Changing nature of work. *Canadian Psychology/Psychologie Canadienne*, 39(1), 5–13.

Currie, G., & Darby, R. (1995). Competence-based management development: Rhetoric and reality. *Journal of European Industrial Training*, 19(5), 11–18.

Daniellou, F. (2005). The French-speaking ergonomists' approach to work activity: Cross-influences of field intervention and conceptual models. *Theoretical Issues in Ergonomics Science*, 6, 409–427.

DeKeyser, V. (1991). Work analysis in French language ergonomics: Origins and current research trends. *Ergonomics*, 34, 653–669.

Doron, R., & Marco, S. (1999). Syllabus evaluation by the job-analysis technique. *European Journal of Engineering Education*, 24(2), 163–172.

Dunckel, H. (Ed.) (1999). *Handbuch psychologischer Arbeitsanalyseverfahren*. Zürich: vdf Hochschulverlag AG.

Ebersöhn, L., & Maree, J. (2003). Determining selection criteria for South Africa dentistry students. *South African Journal of Psychology*, 33(1), 61–65.

Edimansyah, B. A., Rusli, B. N., Naing, L., & Mazalisah, M. (2006). Reliability and construct validity of the Malay version of the job content questionnaire (JCQ). *The Southeast Asian Journal of Tropical Medicine and Public Health*, 37, 412–416.

Eum, K. D., Li, J., Jhun, H. J., Park, J. T., Tak, S. W., Karasek, R., et al. (2007). Psychometric properties of the Korean version of the job content questionnaire: Data from health care workers. *International Archives of Occupational and Environmental Health*, 80, 497–504.

Fraser, C. (1999). A non-results-based effectiveness index for construction site managers. *Construction Management and Ergonomics*, 17, 789–798.

Frieling, E., Facauaru, C., Bendix, J., Pfaus, H., & Sonntag, K. (1993). Tätigkeits-Analyse-Inventar, Handbuch und Verfahren. Landsberg: Ecomed.

Frieling, E., & Hoyos, C. G. (1978). *Fragebogen zur Arbeitsanalyse (FAA)*. Bern: Huber.

Frieling, E., Kannheiser, W., & Lindberg, R. (1974). Some results with the German form of the Position Analysis Questionnaire (PAQ). *Journal of Applied Psychology, 59,* 741–747.

Gael, S. (1988). *The jobs analysis handbook for business, industry and government.* New York, NY: Wiley.

Gilbreth, F. B., & Gilbreth, L. M. (1919). *Applied motion study.* New York, NY: The Macmillan Company.

Glendining, D. (1995). *DACUM Roots* (CVA Occasional Paper, Number 7). Ottawa: Canadian Vocational Association.

Grote, G., Ryser, C., Waler, T., Windischer, A., & Weik, S. (2000). KOMPASS: A method for complementary function allocation in automated work systems. *International Journal of Human-Computer Studies, 52*(2), 267–287.

Hacker, W. (2003). Action regulation theory: A practical tool for the design of modern work processes? *European Journal of Work & Organizational Psychology, 12*(2), 105–130.

Hacker, W., Iwanowa, A., & Richter, P. (1983). *Tätigkeitsbewertungssystem.* Berlin: Psychodiagnostisches Zentrum.

Harvey, R. J. (1991). Job analysis. In M. D. Dunnette & L. M. Hough (Eds.), *Handbook of industrial & organizational psychology* (2nd ed., Vol. 2, pp. 71–163). Palo Alto, CA: Consulting Psychologists Press.

Hollnagel, E. (Ed.) (2003). *Handbook of cognitive task analysis.* Mahwah, NJ: Lawrence Erlbaum Associates.

Hough, L. M., & Oswald, F. L. (2000). Personnel selection: Looking toward the future—remembering the past. *Annual Review of Psychology, 51,* 631–664.

Hoyos, G. C., & Bernhardt, U. (1987). *Fragebogen zur Sicherheitsdiagnose (FDS)—Konzeption, Erprobung und Anwendungsmöglichkeiten eines verhaltensorientierten Instruments zur Sicherheitsanalyse von Arbeitssystemen.* In K. Sonntag (Ed.), *Arbeitsanalyse und Technikentwicklung.* Wirtschaftsverlag Bachem: Köln.

Hoyos, C. G., & Ruppert, F. (1995). Safety diagnosis in industrial work settings: The safety diagnosis questionnaire. *Journal of Safety Research, 26*(2), 107–117.

Huuhtanen, P., Nygård, C.-H., Tuomi, K., Eskelinen, L., & Toikkanen, J. (1991). Changes in the content of Finnish municipal occupations over a four-year period. *Scandinavian Journal of Work, Environment, & Health, 17,* 48–57.

Ilmarinen, J., Suurnäkki, T., Nygård, C-H., & Landau, K. (1991). Classification of municipal occupations. *Scandinavian Journal of Environmental Health, 17,* 12–29.

Jones, M., & Kirsch, C. (2004). *The road of trials: Management concepts in documentary film production in Australia.* Retrieved from http://ro.uow.edu.au/commpapers/49/

Jubb, R., & Robotham, D. (1997). Competences in management development: Challenging the myths. *Journal of European Industrial Training, 21*(5), 171–175.

Karasek, R. A. (1979). Job demands, job decision latitude, and mental strain: Implications for job redesign. *Administrative Science Quarterly, 24,* 285–308.

Karasek, R. A. (1985). *Job Content Questionnaire and user's guide* (Revision 1.1). Lowell, MA: University of Massachusetts.

Karasek, R. A., Brisson, C., Kawakami, N., Houtman, I., Bongers, P., & Amick, B. (1998). The Job Content Questionnaire (JCQ): An instrument for internationally comparative assessment of psychosocial job characteristics. *Journal of Occupational Health Psychology, 3,* 322–355.

Kawakami, N., & Fujigaki, Y. (1996). Reliability and validity of the Japanese version of job content questionnaire (JCQ): Replication and extension in computer company employees. *Industrial Health, 34,* 295–306.

Kawakami, N., & Haratani, T. (1999). Epidemiology of job stress and health in Japan: Review of current evidence and future direction. *Industrial Health, 37,* 174–186.

Kawakami, N., Kobayashi, F., Araki, S., Haratani, T., & Furui, H. (1995). Assessment of job stress dimensions based on the job demands-control model of employees of telecommunication and electric power companies in Japan: Reliability and validity of Japanese version of the job content questionnaire. *International Journal of Behavioral Medicine, 2,* 358–375.Kemmlert, K. (1995). A method assigned for the identification of ergonomic hazards—PLIBEL. *Applied Ergonomics, 26,* 199–211.

Kemmlert, K. (1997). *On the identification and prevention of ergonomic risk factors: With special regard to reported occupational injuries of the musculo-skeletal system.* Doctoral thesis, Luleå University of Technology, Luleå.

Kieras, D., & Meyer, D. (2000). The role of cognitive task analysis in the application of predictive models of human performance. In J.-M. Schraagen, S. F. Chipman, & V. L. Shalin (Eds.), *Cognitive task analysis* (pp. 237–260). Mahwah, NJ: Lawrence Erlbaum.

Kinzl, J. F., Knotzer, H., Traweger, C., Lederer, W., Heidegger, T., & Benzer, A. (2005). Influence of working conditions on job satisfaction in anesthetists. *British Journal of Anaesthesia, 94,* 211–215.

Kinzl, J. F., Traweger, C., Trefalt, E., Riccabona, U., & Lederer, W. (2007). Work stress and gender-dependent coping strategies in anesthesiologists at a university hospital. *Journal of Clinical Anesthesia, 19*, 334–338.

Klemp, G. O. (1980). *The assessment of occupational competence.* Washington, DC: National Institute of Education.

Kosidlak, J. G. (1987). DACUM: An alternative job analysis tool. *Personnel, 64*(3), 14–21.

Krause, D. E., & Gebert, D. (2003). A comparison of assessment center practices in organizations in German-speaking regions and the United States. *International Journal of Selection & Assessment, 11*(4), 297–312.

Landau, K., & Bokranz, R. (1986). Istzustands-Analyse in Arbeitssystemen, *Zeitschrift für Betriebswirtschaft, 56*, 728–754.

Landau, K., Imhof-Gildein, B., & Mücke, S. (1996). On the analysis of sector-related and gender-related stress at the workplace–An analysis of the AET data bank. *International Journal of Industrial Ergonomics, 17*, 175–186.

Landau, K., & Peters, H. (2006). Ergonomic demands in automotive component inspection tasks. *Occupational Ergonomics, 6*, 95–105.

Landau, K., & Rohmert, W. (Eds.). (1989). *Recent developments in job analysis.* London: Taylor & Francis.

Lantz, A., & Brav, A. (2007). Job design for learning in work groups. *Journal of Workplace Learning, 19*(5), 269–285

Lazarus, R. S., & Folkman, S. (1984). *Stress, appraisal and coping.* New York, NY: Springer.

Lederer, W., Kinzl, J. F., Trefalt, E., Traweger, C., & Benzer, A. (2006). Significance of working conditions on burnout in anesthetists. *Acta Anaesthesiologica Scandinavica, 50*, 58–63.

Leont'ev, A. N., & Hall, M. J. (1978). *Activity, consciousness, and personality.* Hillsdale: Prentice-Hall.

Leplat, J. (2004). L'analyse psychologique du travail. *Revue Européenne de Psychologie Appliquée, 54*(2), 101–108.

Li, J., Yang, W., Liu, P., Xu, Z., & Cho, S. I. (2004). Psychometric evaluation of the Chinese (mainland) version of the job content questionnaire: A study in university hospitals. *Industrial Health, 42*, 260–267.

Lin, D., & Hwang, S. (1998). The development of mental workload measurement in flexible manufacturing systems. *Human Factors and Ergonomics in Manufacturing, 8*(1), 41–62.

Mattila, M., & Klviniltty, J. (1993). Job characteristics and occupational safety of manufacturing jobs at different levels of automation. *International Journal of Human Factors in Manufacturing, 3*, 243–252.

McCormick, E. J., & Jeanneret, P. R. (1988). Position analysis questionnaire (PAQ). In S. Gale (Ed.), *The job analysis handbook for business, industry, and government* (Vol. 2, pp. 825–842). New York, NY: John Wiley.

McCormick, E. J., Jeanneret, P. R., & Mecham, R. C. (1969). *The development and background of the position analysis questionnaire (PAQ).* West Lafayette, IN: Purdue University, Occupational Research Center.

Messing, K., Chatigny, C., & Courville, J. (1998). Light and heavy work in the housekeeping service of a hospital. *Applied Ergonomics, 29*, 451–459.

Mitchell, J. L. (1988). History of job analysis in military organizations. In S. Gael (Ed.), *The job analysis handbook for business, industry, and government* (pp. 30–36). New York, NY: Wiley.

Niedhammer, I. (2002). Psychometric properties of the French version of the Karasek Job Content Questionnaire: A study of the scales of decision latitude, psychological demands, social support, and physical demands in the GAZEL cohort. *International Archives of Occupational and Environmental Health, 75*, 129–144.

Niedhammer, I., Goldberg, M., Leclerc, A., Bugel, I., & David, S. (1998). Psychosocial factors at work and subsequent depressive symptoms in the Gazel cohort. *Scandinavian Journal of Work and Environmental Health, 24*, 197–205.

Noborisaka, Y., Ishizaki, M., & Yamada, Y. (1995). The relationship between job status, gender and work-related stress amongst middle-aged employees in a computer manufacturing company, *Journal of Occupational Health, 37*, 167–168.

Nordander, C., Ohlsson, K., Balogh, I., Rylander, L., Pålsson, B., & Skerfving, S. (1999). Fish processing work: The impact of two sex dependent exposure profiles on musculoskeletal health. *Occupational and Environmental Medicine, 56*, 256–264.

North, D. (1993). Applying the competences approach to management: The employment service's experience. *Revue européenne de Psychologie, Appliquée, 43*, 49–52.

Norton, R. E. (1993, June 9–11). *DACUM and Tech Prep: Dynamic duo.* Paper presented at the Mid-America Competency-Based Education Conference, Bloomington, MN.

Nygård, C-H., Suurnäkki, T., Landau, K., & Ilmarinen, J. (1987). Musculoskeletal load of municipal employees aged 44 to 58 years in different occupational groups. *International Archives of Occupational and Environmental Health, 59*, 251–261.

O'Hare, D., Wiggins, M., Williams, A., & Wong, W. (1998). Cognitive task analysis for decision centered design and training. *Ergonomics, 41*, 1698–1718.

Ostry, A. S., Marion, S. A., Demers, P. A., Hershler, R., Kelly, S., Teschke, K., et al. (2001). Measuring psychosocial job strain with the job content questionnaire using experienced job evaluators. *American Journal of Industrial Medicine, 39*, 397–401.

Papadopoulou, A., Ineson, E. M., & Wilkie, D. T. (1995). Convergence between sources of service job analysis data. *International Journal of Contemporary Hospitality Management, 7*(2/3), 42–47.

Papadopoulou, A., Ineson, E. M., & Wilkie, D. T. (2001). Control and role conflict in food service providers. *Hospitality Management, 20*, 187–199.

Peiser, C., & Yaakov, M. (2004). Job analysis by consensus: A case study. *Man and Work, 13*, 26–43.

Peterson, P., Wakula, J., & Landau, K. (1999). Development of a hand tool work analysis method (HTWAM). *Occupational Ergonomics, 2*(3), 137–150.

Pohlandt, A., Schultze, F., Debitz, U., Hänsgen, C., Lüdecke, S., McClelland, C., et al. (2007). *Instruction manual with software computer assisted evaluation and design of job tasks for health and safety protection.* Bochum, Germany: InfoMediaVerlag.

Primoff, E. S., & Fine, S. A. (1988). A history of job analysis. In S. Gale (Ed.), *The job analysis handbook for business, industry, and government* (Vol. 1, pp. 14–29). New York, NY: John Wiley.

Rau, R. (2004). Job strain or healthy work: A question of task design. *Journal of Occupational Health Psychology, 9*(4), 322–338.

Resch, M. (2003). Work and off-the-job-activities: An important new field of work analysis. In D. Harris, V. Duffy, M. Smith, & C. Stephanidis (Ed.), *Human centred computing: Cognitive, social and ergonomic aspects* (pp. 1111–1115). London: Lawrence Erlbaum Associates.

Richter, P., Debitz, U., & Pohlandt, A. (2009). Evaluation of the quality of job design with the action-oriented software tool REBA – recent developments and applications. In C. M. Schlick (Ed.), *Industrial engineering and ergonomics: Visions, concepts, methods and tools* (pp. 321–333). Berlin: Springer.

Richter, P., Hemman, E., & Pohlandt, A. (1999). Objective task analysis and the prediction of mental workload: Results of the application of an action-oriented software tool (REBA). In M. Wiethoff & F. R. H. Zijlstra (Eds.), *New approaches for modern problems in work psychology* (pp. 67–76). Tilburg, Germany: University Press.

Robotham, D., & Jubb, R. (1996). Competences: measuring the unmeasurable. *Management Development Review, 9*, 25–29.

Rochow, G. (n.d.). The DACUM method of occupational analysis: The Canadian experience. Retrieved from http://www.capra.net/downloads/publications/occasional/OccasionalPaper4Dacum.pdf

Rohmert, R. (1988). AET. In S. Gale (Ed.), *The job analysis handbook for business, industry, and government* (Vol. 2, pp. 843–859). New York, NY: John Wiley.

Rohmert, R., & Landau, K. (1983). *A new technique for job analysis.* London: Taylor & Francis.

Rohmert, W., & Rutenfranz, J. (1975). *Arbeitswissenschaftliche Beurteilung der Belastung und Beanspruchung an unterschiedlichen industriellen Arbeitsplätzen; Forschungsbericht für den Bundesminister für Arbeit und Sozialordnung.* Bonn, Germany: Der Bundesminister für Arbeit und Sozialordnung.

Rudolph, E., Schönfelder, E., & Hacker, W. (1987). *Tätigkeitsbewertungssystem für geistige Arbeit mit/ohneRechnerunterstützung (TBS-GA)* [Task diagnosis survey for mental workload]. Berlin: Psychodiagnostisches Zentrum an der Humboldt Universität.

Sanchez, J. I., & Levine, E. L. (2000). Accuracy or consequential validity: Which is the better standard for job analysis data? *Journal of Organizational Behavior, 21*, 809–818.

Saville & Holdsworth Ltd. (1989). *Work Profiling System (WPS).* London: SHL.

Saville & Holdsworth Ltd. (1995). *Work Profiling System (WPS, updated version).* London: SHL.

Schepers, J. M. (2008). The construction and evaluation of a generic work performance questionnaire for use with administrative and operational staff. *SA Journal of Industrial Psychology, 34*(1), 10–22.

Schnorpfeil, P., Noll, A., Wirtz, P., Schulze, R., Ehlert, U., Frey, K., & Fischer, J. (2002). Assessment of exhaustion and related risk factors in employees in the manufacturing industry—a cross-sectional study. *International Archives of Occupational and Environmental Health, 75*, 535–540.

Schraagen, J. M., Chipman, S., & Shalin, V. (Eds.). (2000). *Cognitive task analysis.* Mahwah, NJ: Erlbaum.

Seago, J. A., & Faucett, J. (1997). Job strain among registered nurses and other hospital workers. *The Journal of Nursing Administration, 27*(5), 19–25.

Seeber, A., Schmidt, K.-H., Kiesswetter, E., & Rutenfranz, J. (1989). On the application of AET, TBS, and VERA to discriminate between work demands at repetitive short cycle work. In K. Landau & W. Rohmert (Eds.), *Recent developments in job analysis: Proceedings of the international symposium on job analysis* (pp. 53–77). New York, NY: John Wiley.

Seitsamo, J., Tuomi, K., & Martikainen, R. (2006). Activity, functional capacity and well-being in ageing Finnish workers. *Occupational Medicine, 57*, 85–91.

Semmer, N. (1982). Stress at work, stress in private life, and psychological well being. In W. Bachmann & I. Udris (Eds.), *Mental load and stress in activity* (pp. 42–55). Amsterdam: North Holland.

Semmer, N., & Zapf, D. (1989). Validity of various methods of measurement in job analysis. In K. Landau & W. Rohmert (Eds.), *Recent developments in job analysis* (pp. 67–78). London: Taylor & Francis.

Semmer, N. K., Zapf, D., & Dunckel, H. (1995). Assessing stress at work: A framework and an instrument. In O. Svane & C. Johansen (Eds.), *Work and health—scientific basis of progress in the working environment* (pp. 105–113). Luxembourg: Office for Official Publications of the European Communities.

Semmer, N. K., Zapf, D., & Dunckel, H. (1998). Instrument for stress-related job analysis (Version 6.0). Bern, Switzerland: Flensburg.

Semmer, N. K., Zapf, D., & Dunckel, H. (1999). *Instrument zur Stressbezogenen Tätigkeitsanalyse ISTA* [Instrument for stress-related job analysis]. In H. Dunckel (Ed.), *Handbuch psychologischer Arbeitsanalyseverfahren* [Handbook of psychological job analysis instruments] (pp. 179–204). Zürich, Switzerland: vdf Hochschulverlag.

Semmer, N. K., Zapf, D., & Greif, S. (1996). Shared job strain: A new approach for assessing the validity of job stress measurements. *Journal of Occupational and Organizational Psychology, 69*, 293–310.

Shepherd, A. (1985). Hierarchical task analysis and training decisions. *Programmed Learning and Educational Technology, 22*, 162–176.

Shepherd, A. (2001). *Hierarchical task analysis.* London: Taylor & Francis.

Siddique, C. M. (2004). Job analysis: A strategic human resource management practice. *International Journal of Human Resource Management, 15*, 219–244.

Sonnentag, S., Kuttler, I., & Fritz, C. (2010). Job stressors, emotional exhaustion, and need for recovery: A multi-source study on the benefits of psychological detachment. *Journal of Vocational Behavior, 76*, 355–365.

Stafford, E. M, Jackson, P. R., & Banks, M. H. (1984). An empirical study of occupational families in the youth labour market. *Journal of Occupational Psychology, 57*, 141–155.

Stahl, J. S, Muetze, M., & Luczak, H. (2000). A method for job design in concurrent engineering. *Human Factors and Ergonomics in Manufacturing, 10*, 291–307.

Storms, G., Casaer, S., De Wit, R., Van Den Bergh, O., & Moens, G. (2001). A psychometric evaluation of a Dutch version of the Job Content Questionnaire and of a short direct questioning procedure. *Work & Stress, 15*, 131–143.

Strohm, O., & Ulich, E. (1998). Integral analysis and evaluation of enterprises: A multi-level approach in terms of people, technology, and organization. *Human Factors and Ergonomics in Manufacturing, 8*(3), 233–250.

Sümer, H. C., Sümer, N., Demirutku, K., & Çifci, O. S. (2001). Using a personality-oriented job analysis to identify attributes to be assessed in officer selection. *Military Psychology, 13*(3), 129–146.

Taylor, F. W. (1911). *The principles of scientific management.* New York, NY: Harper.

Teiger, C., & Bernier, C. (1992). Ergonomic analysis of work activity of data entry clerks in the computerized service sector can reveal unrecognized skills. *Women and Health, 18*, 67–78.

Training Resource Center. (n.d.). *World Map Search.* Retrieved from http://dacum.eku.edu/WorldMapSearch.asp

Trist, E. L., & Bamforth, K. W. (1951). Some social and psychological consequences of the longwall method of coal-getting. *Human Relations, 4*, 1–38.

Tuomi, K., Ilmarinen, J., Klockars, M., Nygård, C-H, Seitsamo, J., Huuhtanen, P., et al. (1997). Finnish research project on aging workers in 1981–1992. *Scandinavian Journal of Work, Environment, and Health, 23*(Suppl 1), 7–11.

Udris, I., & Nibel, H. (1989). Situational diagnosis vs. social construction of jobs—Meta-analysis of the questionnaire Subjective Job Analysis. In K. Landau & W. Rohmert (Eds.), *Recent developments in job analysis* (pp. 79–80). London: Taylor & Francis.

Umbers, I. G., & Reiersen, C. S. (1995). Task analysis in support of the design and development of a nuclear power plant safety system. *Ergonomics, 38*(3), 443–454.

Van der Merwe, R. P., Le Roux, J. A., Meyer, J. C., & Van Niekerk, H. G. (1990). Predicting Holland occupational codes by means of PAQ job dimension scores. *Journal of Industrial Psychology, 16*, 27–31.

Van Wart, M. (2000). The return to simpler strategies in job analysis: The case of municipal clerks. *Review of Public Personnel Administration, 20*(3), 5–27.

Volpert, W. (1982). The model of the hierarchicalsequential organization of action. In W. Hacker, W. Volpert, & M. V. Cranach (Eds.), *Cognitive and motivational aspects of action* (pp. 35–51). Amsterdam: North Holland Publishing Company.

Volpert, W., Kötter, W., Gohde, H.-E., & Weber, W. G. (1989). Psychological evaluation and design of work tasks: Two examples. *Ergonomics, 32*, 881–890.

Volpert, W., Oesterreich, R., Gablenz-Kolakovic, S., Krogoll, T., & Resch, M. (1983). *Verfahren zur Ermittlung von Regulationserfordernissen in der Arbeitstatigkeit (VERA). Analyse oon Planungs- und Denkprozessen in der industriellen Produktion. Handbuch und Manual.* Koln: TUV Rheinland.

Wächter, H., Modrow-Thiel, B., & Rossmann, G. (1994). Work design and computer controlled systems: Job analysis under automation—ATAA. *Integrated Manufacturing Systems, 4*(2), 44–52.

Wächter, H., Modrow-Thiel, B., & Schmitz, G. (1989). *Entwicklung eines Verfahrens zur Analyse von Tätigkeitsstrukturen und zur vorausschauenden Arbeitsgestaltung bei Automatisierung (ATAA).* Trier: Eericht des HdA-Projektes.

Wang, Z. M. (2003). Managerial competency modeling and the development of organizational psychology: A Chinese approach. *International Journal of Psychology, 38*(5), 323–334.

Wang, Z. M., & Chen, M. (2002). Managerial competency modeling: A structural equation testing. *Psychological Science (China), 25*(5), 513–516.

Warr, P. (2007). Some historical developments in I-O psychology outside the United States. In L. L. Koppes (Ed.), *Historical perspectives in industrial and organizational psychology* (pp. 81–107). Mahwah, NJ: Lawrence Erlbaum Associates.

Weber, W.-G., & Oesterreich, R. (1989). Vera microanalysis: Applied to a flexible manufacturing system. In K. Landau & W. Rohmert. (Eds.), *Recent developments in job analysis* (pp. 91–100). London: Taylor & Francis.

Wilson, M. A. (2007). A history of job analysis. In L. L. Koppes (Ed.), *Historical perspectives in industrial and organizational psychology* (pp. 219–241). Mahwah, NJ: Lawrence Erlbaum Associates.

Zapf, D. (1993). Stress-oriented analysis of computerized office work. *European Work & Organizational Psychologist, 3*(2), 85–100.

Zickar , M. J., & Gibby, R. E. (2007). Four persistent themes throughout the history of I-O psychology in the United States. In L. L. Koppes (Ed.), *Historical perspectives in industrial and organizational psychology* (pp. 61–80). Mahwah, NJ: Lawrence Erlbaum Associates.

37

Concluding Thoughts
Challenges and Opportunities in Work Analysis

Winston Bennett, Jr.

United States Air Force Research Laboratory

George M. Alliger

The Group for Organizational Effectiveness, Inc.

Mark A. Wilson

North Carolina State University

Shanan Gwaltney Gibson

East Carolina University

In this handbook, we have tried to accomplish a number of key activities in the area of work analysis and design. First, we crafted the new handbook to be the most complete and comprehensive treatise of the practice, science, and innovation in the field since the original *Handbook of Job Analysis*. Second, we gave this text a strong practice and "how to do it" focus, but also maintained and embraced the tension between practice and the theoretical and scientific underpinnings for each approach or method. With this in mind, we organized the sections to make it easier for you to get where you want to go in the handbook quickly. Third, we identified and detailed research and practical innovation that has implications for the field both today and in the future. And finally, with this closing chapter we want to leave the reader with points to ponder related to a number of key challenges, issues, and opportunities facing the field.

In this final chapter, we would like to not so much to reflect back across the entirety of the handbook itself, but rather reflect on where work analysis and design as a discipline are today and where they need to go in the future. Accordingly, we describe a set of cases that represent from our perspective key challenges, new demands, or unique aspects of 21st century work that should promote discussion, identify targets of research opportunity, and hopefully help establish an agenda for research and practice.

As we started to think about these cases, we wanted each one to encapsulate a unique challenge, issue, or area of curiosity or need that would get you as readers, practitioners, and researchers in the field thinking about how we might address the case, what the assumptions might be, and what comparable experience or solutions each of you might have run across or developed that helped you address the issue you were facing. We expect that the cases point to things that you may have encountered or will encounter in your work analysis and design efforts.

"DYNAMIC" WORK ANALYSIS AND DESIGN FOR GLOBALLY DISTRIBUTED COLLABORATIVE ENVIRONMENTS

Creating Ad Hoc Occupations

We need to develop a way to define new work requirements or define ad hoc work requirements and then use those requirements to look across existing occupational and work data. As an example, an organization has identified the need for a team to accomplish a specific activity, such as deployed trauma care for humanitarian operations. One way to define work of the team is to conduct a detailed task analysis of the work activity to be done as a team member. This analysis, while proper, might not be prudent for the timeframe and urgency of the specific team requirements. An alternate approach might be to develop a global description of the job to be done by the team and then to have an analytic method to permit sorting through and matching specific work data to the description. This analytic sorting and mapping from specific occupations to the overall description and the degree of mapping could be used to identify the team membership, the key relevant work and personnel expertise and experience, and could potentially identify individuals who are incumbents in the occupations of relevance. The challenge today is that there is considerable variability in the actual work data; the analytic tools also vary considerably, and there are no current definitional standards or data warehousing methods that would facilitate the definition of new or virtual work domains for rapidly responding to changing global workplace dynamics.

We would submit that many of the methods identified and discussed in the handbook provide clear pathways to reducing the variety of data, help drive and define work design and analysis standards, and identify a number of analytic tools that can be applied within and across data and methodology.

A JOB-LEVEL NATIONAL DATABASE OF WORK INFORMATION

With the loss of the *Dictionary of Occupational Titles* (DOT) along with the professional infrastructure and resources that supported it, the nation does not have a job-level database of work analysis information to describe all work in the U.S. economy. Even though the DOT was not perfect by today's standards (Miller, Treiman, Cain, & Roos, 1980), it had detailed information on over 12,000 work titles that described most, if not all, of the work in the economy of the time. By comparison, the Occupational Information Network (O*NET), the Department of Labor DOT replacement, has a little over 900 entries (Tippins & Hilton, 2010). The reduction in specificity reflected in the fewer number of entries in O*NET is, in part, due to the enormous costs of keeping a detailed and up-to-date job level database of work information. Given modern technology, there is no reason that our professional organizations could not create and maintain a common work information database. Development and maintenance of a complete taxonomic structure that allows for the identification and description of all work is a practical and research necessity if we aspire to make work analysis a credible science. Indeed, such a database may be an additional source of funds for the participating professional organizations that control access to it.

SYNERGY ACROSS DISCIPLINES

Contrary to what some of us might think, industrial/organizational psychologists do not hold a monopoly on work analysis, and it is quite likely that this is a good thing. Although we frequently believe ourselves to be the better trained, more methodologically rigorous scholars of work analysis, many other fields also conduct and use work analysis. The need to identify the tasks, activities, knowledge, skills, and context involved in the performance of work is of interest to those who focus

CONCLUDING THOUGHTS   **743**

on vocational rehabilitation/counseling, disability determination, and/or management, ergonomics, occupational health, and vocational counseling (just to name a few). And while each of these groups has its own modus operandi relating to work analysis, there is the potential for our efforts to be complementary; however, we will never know if we do not consider the possibilities.

The sad truth is that the number of students choosing to study work analysis is extremely low. As of this writing, a search of ProQuest's Dissertation Abstracts International yielded only eight master's or doctoral theses with the words "job analysis" in their titles and three additional with the phrase "work analysis" in their titles from 2000–2010; if the search is expanded to include abstracts, just 48 additional documents are returned (ProQuest, 2011). Given the number of unanswered questions this very handbook has identified, efforts to encourage work analysis as a viable research realm must be intensified. Reaching out and collaborating across disciplines is one way to encourage this.

Is it possible that the time has come for academics and practitioners sharing a common interest in "studying work" to come together, regardless of discipline? Whether the focus is ergometric or econometric, theoretical or applied, psychometric or forensic, all share a common need for work analysis that is reliable, valid, legally defensible, and high in utility. If we are willing to consider the heresy of identifying and pursuing complementary goals, instead of retreating into the silos of our specialties, we may be able to further the aspirations of all.

RESOLVING THE "MILE-WIDE AND INCH-DEEP" AND "INCH-WIDE AND MILE-DEEP" TENSION

Considerable debate across several disciplines within psychology has focused on the issue of grain size in work analysis data and product. One side of the debate argues that the grain size should be large and the specifications broad of focus, ostensibly helping to make cross-job explorations more efficient. A further argument is that broader definitions of work and less detail allow for more rapid and responsive task and work analyses to support urgent requirements. However, the level of analysis is only as accurate as the level of definition obtained. Therefore, deeper decomposition of the analysis is not possible. If finer grain-sized analyses are needed, a different approach will have to be used and a new analysis accomplished. The other side of the debate argues that a more time-consuming and deeper exploration of specific incumbents typically referred to as "experts" leads to a definition that is context specific. Therefore, broader generalizations from those context-specific instances are not possible or are less accurate because the level of detail and grain size is so specific to a given set of data sources and work content.

What we do not have today is a single taxonomy that seeks to explicate different work analysis approaches both in terms of the depth of analysis and in terms of the potential for linking analytic results from different methods together—or more importantly, can determine which among several different approaches have the best likelihood of being combined together or are more complementary in terms of broader analysis needs and outcomes.

GENERALIZABLE WORK DESIGN SPECIFICATIONS AND INDICES OF JOB SIMILARITY AND PROXIMITY

Several of us have experience with military occupational analysis, and one of the most perplexing things we see even today is the use of different terminology for similar work activities or tasks. For example, it is not unusual for two occupations dealing with aircraft engine maintenance to use completely different terminology for exactly the same work. In one occupation, the term for checking a part on an engine may be defined variously as troubleshooting, removing and replacement, or ops checking. In each instance, if an analyst were to observe the tasks being performed, he or she might detect the same kind of work using similar tools and requiring access to the same kind of technical documentation and knowledge. However, when crosswalking from one occupation to another, trying to match occupations on similar or identical tasks and work activities, the analyst could not be accurate or successful because a nonstandard set of terms was used to define the work. What is needed is a taxonomy of activity terms and their requisite underlying task work and technical information that would facilitate a content crosswalk to identify common work and potentially gain economies of scale leveraging expertise, training content, and work experience for people who might come from a different occupational area, but who could potentially support needed work. Critics will argue that an all-for-one type of taxonomy is really an all-for-none approach because the specificity of work definition and occupational specialization precision are lost in the interest of creating cross work efficiencies. However, we see it as critical to the future of our discipline to empirically examine this issue and the potential for creating the efficiencies we need to realize.

Although a number of methodologies and tools have been described in this handbook, we see this continuing lack of a common taxonomy as a limitation to ultimately developing common and generalizable terminology for more rapid design and redesign of work in response to dynamic environmental demands.

EMERGENT WORK ANALYSIS VIA AUTOMATED TASK AND MOTION TRACKING

The thought of time-and-motion studies may evoke late 19th-century and early 20th-century images of steely-eyed men and women in white lab coats armed with clipboards and stopwatches. And indeed, one of the undertold stories in work analysis is the contribution of these people to the discipline, their vision and dedication, and the tension between their goals and the goals of the labor movement. They accomplished much, and Frederick Taylor and the Gilbreths will always be among the foundation stones of industrial/organizational psychology in general and work analysis in particular.

Those clipboards and stopwatches, pencils and charts were absolutely crucial to the study of time and motion (Pigage& Tucker, 1954). Laborious calculations and experiments were required to discover efficient techniques. One overarching question for us—more than a century later—is, given our technological advances, what is the extent to which this kind of work analysis can be automated (Alliger, 2006)? We can measure many things more easily now: motion via sensors attached at various points to the human body (e.g., Aggarwal & Cai, 1999; Yen & Radwin, 2000), various measures of exertion (oxygen consumption, oxygen level, stress hormones), eye-tracks, decisions, and cue response. Along with computerized data analysis, the opportunities in this area appear to be great.

However, there are several specific unanswered questions here. Just how can these technologies be best employed? How do we ensure the validity and reliability of the data they provide? Which among the many technologies and measures available provide the most useful time-and-motion information for feasible cost? Will this kind of research require a laboratory setting, or can we go onto the "shop floor," like Taylor, to conduct work analysis, or is that (a) infeasible and/or (b) too intrusive? Finally, how will such analyses be viewed by the worker and organized labor?

It is interesting to note that there may be an emerging third study domain in addition to laboratory and field. We can now create virtual work spaces and easily manipulate them (e.g., the placement of tools, distances among stations) and, in conjunction with motion analysis, assess work (Ma, Zhang, Fu, Guo, Chablat, & Bennis, 2010).

In any case, opportunities in the automation of work analysis appear to abound. Frederick Taylor would be very interested.

WORK ANALYSIS CURRENCY AND RELEVANCE: HOW OFTEN AND WHAT TYPE OF REFRESH?

A lot has been made of the changing or "dynamic" nature of jobs (e.g., Burke & Ng, 2006; Schabracq & Cooper, 2000), but little systematic thinking has been done on the implications of this for work analysis. It is a characteristic of many job analyses to capture important contextual information, such as equipment used, which is clearly subject to rapid and probably unpredictable change. Similarly, for any given job, its processes, the nature and number of task interdependencies, knowledge, skills, abilities, and other characteristics (KSAOs)—in short, everything captured by a job analysis—may change, slowly or quickly. Therefore, we need to know when a work analysis should be redone (let us call it a "refresh") to reflect the latest version of the work performed.

There are two potential categories that could help us think about this topic. One is triggering events; the other is the passage of some length of time. Some potential events that would trigger the need for a refresh are major system (equipment) changes, to include changes in system capabilities; changes in organizational structure (such as new dependencies among personnel); critical failures or events that have led to altered work processes/outcomes; and changes in jobs other than the target job (e.g., competitors) that have affected the purpose/processes of the target job.

The other category is time. Time would really just be a proxy for assumed actual changes in work. Thus, one might say "Our job analyses have a currency of about three years—after that, we lose confidence in their accuracy." This is equivalent to the concept of shelf life for food.

There will certainly be an interaction between the type of documented outputs of job analyses and when they would need to be refreshed. So, Position Analysis Questionnaire (PAQ) results might change more slowly and need a refresh less often than those of a Functional Job Analysis. Or the reverse—this is, after all, a "challenge and opportunity."

A slight variation on this question is, "If a refresh is needed, what kind?" That is, is it automatically the case that we perform the same kind of job analysis as the first time? Can we do the same kind, but in a limited fashion, targeting evident pieces/parts of the job that have changed?

It will help us to answer this question because work analyses do in fact become outdated (witness the DOT). If we know what causes a refresh to be needed, whether event or passage of time, we will be in the position to plan for these in advance. We will have an answer, or know how to obtain the answer, to the question, "Is this job analysis still relevant?"

TIME FOR USABILITY ANALYSIS IN THE DESIGN OF WORK ANALYSIS TOOLS AND REPORTS

Wilson (2007) has argued that work analysis has a perception problem. One important factor that may improve the problem and potentially improve performance is greater emphasis on the usability of work analysis instruments and reports (Bias & Mayhew, 1994). The more seriously we take usability, the more likely we will improve not only the experience of the end user but also the perception of the effort itself. Very little about modern work analysis is intuitive, visual, and uncomplicated; to suggest otherwise would bring snickers from most modern practitioners. At several points in this handbook, a systems perspective has been advanced as the best conceptual framework to adopt when considering work analysis. Organizations spend enormous sums on the usability of their products and services because they understand how important usability is to success. We should lead the way in bringing the concepts of usability to business systems.

THINKING SMALL—CONSIDERATION OF WORK ANALYSIS IN SMALL BUSINESS

Not only does work analysis have a "perception problem" (Wilson, 2007), it also suffers from the very practical problem of being unheard of by many in small business. Obviously you, as a reader of this book, do not suffer from this malady, and some may wonder why this is problematic; as researchers we are taught to focus on large sample sizes and generalizability. However, small businesses employ roughly one half the private sector, and since 1995 small firms have accounted for approximately 65% of private sector job creation (Head, 2010). That is a lot of jobs to be potentially analyzed. Unfortunately, most small business owners are not familiar with the field of industrial psychology; nevertheless, their need to effectively match the talents of prospective employees with company's needs, to develop effective training programs, and to implement equitable performance management all point to them as appropriate job analysis "customers." However, if we are to have an effect on these businesses (where even basic training in human resources is typically scarce), it is imperative that we begin to better understand the needs of small business owners, succinctly explain the ins and outs of job analysis in language that does not intimidate, and convey the utility of this process to a demographic that cares more about day-to-day outcomes than the best practices of large organizations and psychometric jargon. As a practitioner, if you intend to use your specialized knowledge and consult with small business owners, you must be prepared to teach your clients about job analysis and in return you may even find fertile soil for research at a micro level.

PERCEPTIONS OF WORK ANALYSIS INFORMATION BY DECISION MAKERS

For a number of reasons the field has focused on the development and application of work analysis procedures with very little attention to how they are perceived by those outside the field (Levine, Ash, & Bennett, 1980; Levine, Ash, Hall, & Sistrunk, 1983). As the workplace continues to adapt to unprecedented levels of competition and regulation, the "trust us" approach to the marketing and presentation of work analysis techniques and information seems flawed. What about work analysis makes it attractive to managers? Does the display of the information matter (Tufte, 1983)? Is it important to focus on the consequence, that is, how the information is used to solve specific workplace problems (Levine & Sanchez, 2007)? Do different types of workplace decision makers (e.g., lawyers versus managers) see the same work information differently? With the exception of some earlier work by Levine and his colleagues, we know next to nothing about how various types of work information are perceived by decision makers. At this point in the discussion, we are not even sure about all the variables that need to be included in the investigation of work analysis perceptions. In the first chapter, the importance of context analysis was stressed; is this the methodological key to improving work analysis perceptions? Does the purpose for which the information is gathered alter the view of the information that is collected? For example, is the work information that is collected for work process redesign viewed differently than the same information when gathered to respond to an external legal challenge? The more we know about the perception of work information and the process used to collect it, the sooner we will be able justify the enormous costs associated with these efforts.

CONCLUSION

As you finish reading this chapter, we sincerely hope that it does not mark the conclusion of your time and interaction with the handbook. The study and practice of work analysis are complex, dynamic, and challenging—and that is on a good day. We hope that this book has increased your appreciation for the myriad issues that confront the work analysis enthusiast; there is no one-size-fits-all answer for to how to conduct, how to analyze, how to utilize, or where to go next in the research realm. As the cases presented above demonstrate, every work analyst has his or her own unique ideas regarding what should be studied going forth and why. By now, you certainly have your own ideas, too. The prospects for practice, science, and innovation within the 21st century work analysis field are limitless; what exist today are opportunities.

REFERENCES

Aggarwal, J. K., & Cai, Q. (1999). Human motion analysis: A review. *Computer Vision and Image Understanding, 73,* 428–440.

Alliger, G. M. (2006). Leveraging distributed systems to enable job redesign: Performance criteria in the electronic age. In W. Bennett, D. Woehr, & C. Lance (Eds)., *Performance measurement: Current perspectives and future challenges* (pp. 273–295). Mahwah, NJ: Lawrence Erlbaum Associates.

Bias, R. G., & Mayhew, D. J. (1994). *Cost-justifying usability*. San Diego, CA: Academic Press.

Burke, R. J., & Ng, E. (2006). The changing nature of work and organizations: Implications for human resource management. *Human Resource Management Review, 16,* 86–94.

Head, B. (2010). *An analysis of small business and jobs*. Retrieved from http://www.sba.gov/sites/default/files/files/an%20analysis%20of%20small%20business%20and%20jobs(1).pdf

Levine, E., Ash, R., & Bennett, N. (1980). Exploratory comparative study of four job analysis methods. *Journal of Applied Psychology, 65,* 524–535.

Levine, E., Ash, R., Hall, H., & Sistrunk, F. (1983). Evaluation of job analysis methods by experienced job analysts. *Academy of Management Journal, 26,* 339–348.

Levine, E. L., & Sanchez, J. I. (2007). Evaluating work analysis in the 21st century. *Ergometrika, 4,* 1–11.

Ma, L., Zhang, W., Fu, H., Guo, Y., Chablat, D., & Bennis, F. (2010). A framework for interactive work design based on digital work analysis and simulation, *Human Factors and Ergonomics in Manufacturing, 20,* 339–352.

Miller, A. R., Treiman, D. J., Cain, P. S., & Roos, P. A. (1980). *Work, jobs, and occupations: A critical review of the Dictionary of Occupational Titles*. Washington, DC: National Academies Press.

Morgeson, F., & Campion, M. (2000). Accuracy in job analysis: toward an inference-based model. *Journal of Organizational Psychology, 21,* 819–827.

Pigage, L., & Tucker, J. (1954). *Motion and time study*. Urbana, IL: University of Illinois.

ProQuest. (2011). *ProQuest Dissertation Abstracts International*. Retrieved June 21, 2011, from http://search.proquest.com/pqdtft?accountid=10639

Schabracq, M. J., & Cooper, C. (2000). The changing nature of work and stress. *Journal of Managerial Psychology, 15,* 227–241.

Tippins, N. T., & Hilton, M. L. (2010). *A database for a changing economy: Review of the Occupational Information Network (O*NET)*. Washington, DC: National Academies Press.

Tufte, E. R. (1983). *The visual display of quantitative information*. Cheshire, CT: Graphics Press.

Wilson, M. A. (2007). A history of job analysis. In L. L. Koppes & P. W. Thayer (Eds.), *Historical perspectives in industrial and organizational psychology* (pp. 219–241). Mahwah, NJ: Erlbaum.

Yen, T. Y., & Radwin, R. G. (2000). Automated job analysis using upper extremity biomechanical data and template matching. *International Journal of Industrial Ergonomics, 25,* 19–28.

Author Index

Subject Index

Note: Locators followed by *t* denote tables, *f* denote figures, and A denote appendixes.